Life-Span Development

Life-Span

Development

John W. Santrock
University of Texas at Dallas

Wm. C. Brown Company Publishers
Dubuque, Iowa

wcb
group

Wm. C. Brown
Chairman of the Board

Mark C. Falb
President and Chief Executive Officer

wcb

Wm. C. Brown Company Publishers, College Division

Lawrence E. Cremer
President

Marcia H. Stout
Marketing Manager

James L. Romig
*Vice-President,
Product Development*

William A. Moss
*Production Editorial
Manager*

David Wm. Smith
Vice-President, Marketing

Marilyn A. Phelps
Manager of Design

E. F. Jogerst
*Vice-President, Cost
Analyst*

Mary M. Heller
Visual Research Manager

David A. Corona
*Vice-President,
Production and Design*

Cover illustration by Michael Meyer

*Cover photos, from left to right—© Donald Yeager,
Camera MD Studio; Phoebe Dunn, DPI; Phoebe Dunn,
DPI; © Ursula Kreis.*

Second Printing, 1984

2-06556-02

To my parents, Ruth and John Santrock

Brief Contents

Contents

Section II
Foundations of Development in Infancy

Section III
Early Childhood

Section IV
Middle and Late Childhood

Section V

Adolescence

14 Social, Emotional, and Personality Development 394

Section VI
Early and Middle Adulthood

15 Perspectives on Adult Development and Physical Development 428

Section VII
Late Adulthood

Preface

This text is about you and it is about me. It is about the life of every human being. It tells the story of human development from conception to death—from the point in time when life begins until the point in time when it ends, at least life as we know it. The awesome, complex, and exciting story of how we develop, of how we become who we are, is written and presented in a manner that I believe you will find is both informative and enjoyable.

You will see yourself as an infant, as a child, and as an adolescent and be stimulated to think about how those years influenced the type of person you are today. And, what about your adult years? Isn't what has happened, or will happen, to you as an adult also important? You will be motivated to think about how marriage, the birth of a child, divorce, the time when children leave, the change of a career, and the death of a spouse are critical events that influence adult development.

To the Instructor

When many authors write college textbooks that are intended to be enjoyable they sacrifice scientific rigor by providing a more casual description of development, rarely relying on scientific data for explanations. In *Life-Span Development,* scientific theory and research have not been compromised—in this sense, the text you are about to read is serious. But at the same time, scientific data are presented in an easy-to-read style and are freely applied to the real world of infants, children, adolescents, and adults.

For many years, we assumed that development was something that occurred between conception and the end of adolescence. But the next five or six decades are just as complex and important as the first two decades, not just to those adults who are passing through them but to their children as well, who must live with and understand parents and grandparents. The majority of textbooks on life-span development do not give adequate attention to adult development. In *Life-Span Development,* you will find six chapters (15–20) devoted exclusively to adult development and two other chapters (1 and 2) in which adult development is extensively discussed.

Audience

This book should be appropriate for students enrolled in an introductory course in life-span development. Depending upon the college or university, the course is likely to be titled life-span development, life-span developmental psychology, human development, or developmental psychology. The typical student in such a course is likely to be a sophomore, junior, or senior undergraduate student who has had a general introduction to psychology. However, *Life-Span Development* requires no previous knowledge of psychology and is written at a level that permits students to build a conceptual framework of the field from the ground up.

Instructor's Manual

Michael Walraven has prepared an instructor's manual for use with *Life-Span Development* that will save you time in preparing for this course. Included in the manual for each chapter is an overview, a list of learning objectives, suggested lecture outlines and classroom activities, questions for review and discussion, multiple-choice questions (with answers provided), and essay questions, in addition to an essay on how to use task groups in the classroom and a list of audiovisual aids.

To the Student

I believe that words can only go so far in my effort to give you a sense and a feel for what life-span development is about. This text is not only informative and enjoyable, it is attractive as well. The text is done in color, with carefully selected photographs pieced together in sequences to provide an image of how development unfolds. The humorous writings of Erma Bombeck and Phyllis Diller, as well as the Ziggy and Herman cartoons of Tom Wilson and Gary Unger, let you laugh at many aspects of life-span development. My hope is that after your course ends you will find this text to be very special, one that you may even want to keep (rather than kick) and refer to as you go through the remainder of your life.

Life-Span Development contains twenty chapters, which in turn are organized into seven sections. Section I introduces you to the concept of life-span development. Philosophical and scientific views of child development and the life cycle are described. You will read quotes from William Shakespeare and Carl Sandburg, both of whom wrote about the human life cycle. Erma Bombeck comments about what it is like to be forty years old, while life-span expert Bernice Neugarten describes how age is becoming a less predictable marker of what people are like. The graying of America also is described, as much more of our population lives to an older age. In chapter 2 you will read about psychoanalytic, cognitive-developmental, social learning, humanistic, ethological evolutionary, and sociological anthropological views of development.

Section II focuses on the foundations of development and infancy. Chapters 3 through 6 emphasize biological, cognitive, and social, emotional, and personality themes of development. There is continuing intellectual interest in understanding the origins and foundations of development. You will discover that we are making progress in unraveling some of the mystery between conception and birth, particularly in determining the point in prenatal development at which harmful agents, such as drugs, are most likely to do their greatest damage. Stunning photographs take you inside the mother's womb to see the world of the fetus. The interaction of heredity and environment is described as an important theme of human development. Two chapters are devoted to cognitive and language foundations and development in infancy. We explore what scientists know about sensory and perceptual development, cognitive development, and learning in infancy. You will learn that language is a remarkable phenomena and that in the last twenty-five years we have changed the way we view the nature of language development. The new developments focus on biological heritage of infants, regularities in the environment, and the processing activities of the infant or child himself. In chapter 6, we evaluate the role of early experience in development. You will discover how infants socialize their parents just as their parents socialize them, that it is important for parents to develop a synchronous relationship with their infants, and that the family is best studied as a system of interacting individuals. You also will learn that peer relations and play may serve important functions in development. Attachment, independence, and the development of the self also are given considerable attention.

Section III emphasizes development in early childhood and consists of two chapters—"Physical and Cognitive Development," and "Social, Emotional, and Personality Development." Information processing is presented as an important view of the young child's cognitive activity in addition to Piaget's theory. Changes in language, including prereading skills are included. How changes in family structure, particularly divorce and working mothers, influence young children is presented. Parenting techniques, child abuse, play and changes in the self, sex roles, and moral development are highlighted.

Section IV focuses on development in middle and late childhood—the elementary school years. Four chapters emphasize physical development and intelligence, cognitive development, social and emotional development, and personality development. Different views on the concept of intelligence and IQ are presented and you will gain an understanding of gifted and mentally retarded children. Piaget's ideas about mental development in childhood are emphasized but are discussed in the context of recent information collected by neo-Piagetians. You will read about how perception, memory, and problem-solving skills continue to develop during middle and late childhood. And while the child's family continues to be an important socializing influence, peers and schools take on even more important roles than in early childhood. Changes in personality development continue to focus on the self, sex roles, and moral development.

Section V chronicles development during adolescence and consists of two chapters—"Physical and Cognitive Development" and "Social, Emotional, and Personality Development." Physical development undergoes dramatic changes in adolescence—the section starts with a fascinating piece, "Can Puberty Come any Earlier?" Sexuality, early and late maturation, the role of work, and formal operational thought are discussed in interesting ways. The development of identity and independence, parent and peer conformity and conflict, and delinquency and drugs are other timely topics discussed.

The remaining two sections and six chapters focus on adult development. Section VI, "Early and Middle Adulthood" unveils the story of life from approximately eighteen to twenty-one years of age to fifty-five to sixty-five years. Three chapters are included, "Perspectives on Adult Development and Physical Development," "Cognitive Development," and "Social, Emotional, and Personality Development." Popular stage-crisis theories are critically evaluated, and how we adapt to life events, such as marriage, divorce, career change, and death of a spouse, is described as a viable way to study adult development. Changes in cognition during the early and middle adulthood years have not been studied extensively; nonetheless you will find in chapter 16 a thorough presentation of what some of those possible cognitive changes are. And, you will read about career development and the role of work in the lives of adults. In the final chapter of section VI, we explore the development of marital and family relationships, the lives of single and divorced adults, and the nature of adult relationships. We also ask, Is personality development stable in adulthood? You will discover that this important issue eludes an easy definition. And, the development of the self, sex roles, and morality continue to be highlighted.

The final section of the book—"Late Adulthood"—includes three chapters, "Physical and Cognitive Development," "Social, Emotional, and Personality Development," and "Aging and Death." We will find that the age and swiftness of biological decline varies extensively from one individual to the next. Our discussion of cognitive development continues the format of the preceding section by emphasizing psychometric, cognitive-developmental, and information processing views. Work and retirement also are given full attention. We explore the final stage of the marital process (the aging couple), further evaluate intergenerational relations, vividly portray the living environment of the elderly, and take you into the minds of elderly people as we explore how they engage in a review and summing up of their lives. You will answer questions that will give you a general sense of whether you have a chance to live to be 100. And, you will read about why scientists think we age. Finally, we close our portrayal of the life cycle with an investigation of many facets of death and the dying process—cultural comparisons, views of death at different ages, phases in the dying process, adjustment to the death of a spouse, and whether there is life after death.

Textual Learning Aids

Extensive learning aids are included in *Life-Span Development* to help you retain concepts, preview and review major ideas, and become self-motivated to progress competently from chapter to chapter. Each chapter begins with a topic outline followed by a prologue—an easy-to-read, interesting set piece designed to encourage and motivate the student to read further into the chapter. Terms with special meanings are boldfaced in the text and can be found in the glossary at the end of the text. Boxes appear often and provide additional information about other points of view, applications, or research. Photographs, illustrations, and cartoons give visual emphasis to important concepts, events, and people in the field of life-span development. And, each chapter ends with a summary, a list of key terms, review questions, and an annotated reading list.

Student Study Guide

A student study guide is available for use with *Life-Span Development*. For each chapter, the study guide includes a chapter preview, a list of learning objectives, a programmed review, a multiple-choice self-test, and a list of learning activities. Also included is an essay entitled, "How to Be a Better Student."

Acknowledgments

I continue to be impressed by the competence and effort shown by my publisher, William C. Brown. James Romig, my editor, is a special person. He has provided support beyond what any author could ask for in developing a textbook. I am indebted to him for sharing this text with me, and in removing any obstacles to making it the kind of text I wanted. I also owe special thanks to Laura Beaudoin, senior production editor, who has toiled long hours in making my writing more sensible and in overseeing the production of the text. Anthony Saizon, the designer, has made *Life-Span Development* a text that is simply beautiful to look at. Mavis Oeth also deserves credit for her expedient work in obtaining permissions.

I benefited considerably from the reviews of the text at different points during its development. The following individuals provided valuable feedback that forced me to temper my views: James A. Blackburn, Montana State University; Donald Bowers, Community College of Philadelphia; Shirley Feldman, Stanford University; David Goldstein, Temple University; Martin D. Murphy, The University of Akron; and Lyn W. Wickelgren, Metropolitan State College.

With 1,500 or more typed pages in the original manuscript and several revisions, typing was not an easy task. I owe special thanks to Laurie Bura, who not only typed the entire manuscript but served as a cheerful friend as well. Thanks also go to Mary Shattles, who prepared the glossary for this text.

Steven Yussen has allowed me to borrow liberally from various portions of *Child Development*. In particular, the information on children's cognition and language represent the wisdom and writing of Steven Yussen, and I am deeply grateful that he has allowed me to include this material in *Life-Span Development*. The ideas on information processing in the chapters on adult development are those of my colleague at the University of Texas at Dallas, James Bartlett. Dr. Bartlett's efforts go beyond a mere reporting of research, representing a synthesis of what we know about the development of adult cognition.

Michael Walraven deserves special thanks as well. He has prepared an instructor's manual and student study guide that will greatly enhance the use of this text.

Finally, thanks go to my family—my wife Mary Jo, and my two daughters Tracy and Jennifer. They have been a source of great pleasure and have been very understanding when I have had to spend long hours away from them while writing this text.

Life-Span Development

Section I

Introduction to
Life-Span Development

1

History, Description, and Methods

Prologue: Age-Related Changes in Development

> All the world's a stage,
> And all the men and women merely players;
> They have their exits and their entrances,
> And one man in his time plays many parts,
> His acts being seven ages. At first the infant, . . .
> Then the whining school-boy, . . .
> creeping like a snail
> Unwillingly to school. And then the lover,
> Sighing like a furnace, . . .
> Then a soldier,
> Full of strange oaths and bearded like the pard,
> Jealous in honor, sudden and quick in quarrel,
> Seeking the bubble reputation
> Even in the cannon's mouth. And then the justice, . . .
> With eyes severe and beard of formal cut,
> Full of wise saws and modern instances; . . .
> The sixth age shifts
> Into the lean and slippered pantaloon,
> With spectacles on nose and pouch on side;
> His youthful hose, well saved, a world too wide
> For his shrunk shank, and his big manly voice,
> Turning again toward childish treble, pipes
> And whistles in his sound. Last scene of all,
> That ends this strange eventful history,
> Is second childishness and mere oblivion,
> Sans teeth, sans eyes, sans taste, sans
> everything.

In this excerpt from Shakespeare, he was interested in the social roles individuals adopt, their life styles, and their phases of life. Carl Sandburg (1956), the famous American poet, also vividly describes some of the phases of life.

The first cry of a newborn baby in Chicago or Zamboango, in Amsterdam or Rangoon, has the same pitch and key, each saying, "I am! I have come through! I belong! I am a member of the Family." . . . babies arriving, suckling, growing into youths restless and questioning. Then as grownups they seek and hope. They mate, toil, fish, quarrel, sing, fight, pray. (From the Prologue by Carl Sandburg to *The Family of Man*.)

Many of the age-related changes in our **life cycles** are reflected in the comments of Robert Havighurst (1972), who described a number of developmental tasks to be accomplished.

Infancy and Early Childhood

Learning to take solid foods
Learning to walk
Learning to talk
Learning to control the elimination of body wastes
Learning sex differences and sexual modesty
Getting ready to read
Learning to distinguish right and wrong and beginning to develop a conscience

Middle and Late Childhood

Learning physical skills necessary for ordinary games
Building a wholesome attitude towards oneself as a growing organism
Learning to get along with age-mates
Beginning to develop appropriate masculine or feminine social roles
Developing fundamental skills in reading, writing, and calculating
Developing concepts necessary for everyday living
Developing a conscience, a sense of morality, and a scale of values
Developing attitudes toward social groups and institutions
Achieving personal independence

Adolescence

Achieving new and more mature relations with age-mates of both sexes
Achieving a masculine or feminine social role
Accepting one's physique and using one's body effectively
Desiring, accepting, and achieving socially responsible behavior
Achieving emotional independence from parents and other adults
Preparing for an economic career
Preparing for marriage and family life
Acquiring a set of values and an ethical system as a guide to behavior—developing an ideology

Early Adulthood

Getting started in an occupation
Selecting a mate
Learning to live with a marriage partner
Starting a family
Rearing children
Managing a home
Taking on civic responsibility
Finding a congenial social group

Middle Adulthood

Achieving adult civic and social responsibility
Assisting teenage children to become responsible and happy adults
Developing adult leisure-time activities
Relating oneself to one's spouse as a person
Accepting and adjusting to the physiological changes of middle age
Reaching and maintaining satisfactory performance in one's occupational career
Adjusting to aging parents

Late Adulthood

Adjusting to decreasing physical strength and health
Adjusting to retirement and reduced income
Adjusting to death of spouse
Establishing an explicit affiliation with members of one's age group
Establishing satisfactory physical living arrangements
Adapting to social roles in a flexible way

One age has been particularly imbued with psychological themes in recent years. In an article called "40 Anonymous," Erma Bombeck (1973) describes this point in development.

This country is extremely age-conscious. That is why a new group has been formed called "40 Anonymous" to help people overcome the problem. Here's how it works. Several months before reaching age forty, birthdayees are invited to a group-therapy program.

There is a ten-minute film where Doris Day wrinkles her nose, moistens her lips, and smiles, "I'm over forty and I still have all my own freckles," just to get the audience in a receptive mood. Then a testimonial is given. The one I heard was from Sylvia X.

"I'm over forty," she said in a faltering voice. (Applause) "A few months ago I was depressed and morose and thought life was not worth living. I got a chill when the furnace blower went on. I refused to eat apples even though I had my own teeth. I nipped at Geritol in the mornings after the kids went to school. I sent sympathy cards to myself and refused to start any long novels. A friend suggested I come to a 40 Anonymous meeting. That night I heard Senator Thurmond speak. He was wonderful.

"I went home and practiced saying 'forty' in front of the mirror. I thought I was cured. Then one night I went to a party. Everyone there was under thirty. It was terrible. No one knew the verse to 'Shine on Harvest Moon.' They had never heard of Lyle Talbot or Maria Montez. When I said Okey Dokey, they laughed.

"I went berserk that night and drew a mustache on an advertisement for 'Mod Squad.' A member of 40 Anonymous found me throwing rocks at a rock festival. 'Get hold of yourself,' he said. 'Just say out loud, "I am forty." '

" 'I am fooooofffffffooooorrrr . . . I can't do it,' " I cried.

" 'You can!' " he challenged.

" 'It's no use,' I said, 'this world is for the youth. Everyone around me is younger than I am. My doctor carries his stethoscope in a gym bag. My attorney has to shave only once a week. My son's math teacher is still wearing braces. I rode a plane the other day with training wheels on it. Good Lord, man, don't you understand, I am older than Mickey Mouse!' "

Sylvia's voice broke. "Today I am proud to say I have learned to live with my problem one day at a time." (Applause)

That night I stood in front of my mirror and said, "My name is Erma X and I'm fffff. . . . I don't look it, but I'm ffff . . . some days I look . . . ffffffoooo . . . last year I was. . . ." It was no use. I called 40 Anonymous. Sylvia came over and had a drink with me.

Actually, forty or any other age wouldn't be so hard to face were it not for the current trend of restaurants making a fuss over birthdays. This ranges anywhere from a drum roll and house lights to a group of waitresses in headbands and adenoids charging at you with a cupcake and a sparkler on top.

I have warned my family if they ever inflict a public birthday on me, I will impale myself on a flaming skewer. After age twelve, birthdays should be as private as hernia surgery. After all, they're as personal.

Philosophers and poets may be as cute as they like about middle age but the question remains, "*What* begins at forty?"

Your laugh lines turn to wrinkles, the dimples in your knees and elbows fill in, you need glasses to read billboards, you find yourself listening to every word of the commercials on motel management and when you at last figure your teenagers are old enough to be told about sex, you've forgotten what it is you weren't supposed to tell them until they were old enough to be told. (pp. 105–7)

Before you go on to the introductory section of chapter 1, think about yourself for a moment—is there a particular theme in your life now that has never surfaced before and is likely not to appear again as long as you live? If you are in your late teens or early twenties, perhaps the major theme in your life focuses on career decision making or career orientation. Or maybe it involves an intimate relationship with another individual. If you are in your late thirties or early forties, is the theme that of getting old and being conscious of younger individuals as Bombeck has suggested?

Introduction

In this first chapter, we introduce you to the field of life-span developmental psychology. It is a lively and exciting enterprise, and we hope to infect you with enthusiasm for it. In this chapter we will consider further the topic introduced in the prologue, age-related changes in development, as well as what we mean by **development.** As we study how our concepts of development have changed with history we will find that the history of interest in child development dates back much farther than is the case for life-span development. Finally, we will look at how the study of development has emerged as a scientific enterprise.

Life-Span Development: Today and Yesterday

Why study life-span development at all? Perhaps you are a parent or teacher and face children each day. The more you learn about them, the better you can deal with them. Perhaps you are preparing for some other career where you will serve future generations of children. Or you hope to gain some insight into your own recent history—the nature of your own childhood, adolescence, or early adulthood and how it shaped your present makeup. Possibly you want to know more about what your life will be like as you go through the later phases of the life cycle. Or, maybe you just stumbled into this course thinking that it sounded intriguing and that the topic of development would raise some provocative issues about the nature of our common human experiences. Whatever your reasons, you will surely find that human growth and development *is* a provocative field of inquiry.

The Contemporary Perspective

Everywhere a person turns in contemporary society, the development and well-being of children and adults capture public attention, the interest of scientists, and the concerns of policy makers. Consider some of the social topics you read about in newspapers and magazines everyday—genetic research, child abuse, homosexuality, mental retardation, parenting, intelligence, career changes, divorce, retirement, and aging. What the experts are discovering in each of these areas has direct and significant consequences for our understanding of children and adults and our societal decisions about how they are to be treated.

Genetic researchers are discovering new techniques to diagnose potential problems both prior to and after conception. They are learning how to predict genetic disturbances in development, various forms of deformities and retardation, and the child's sex. In addition, some remarkable breakthroughs have occurred in the ability to fertilize a human egg in the laboratory and to sustain growth of the fetus outside of its natural mother. All of these techniques and capabilities have profound consequences on genetic counseling for parents, arguments about when life really begins, debates about the legal right of women to have abortions, and ethical dilemmas about tampering in the laboratory with the genetic makeup of unborn children.

One contemporary social issue whose widespread occurrence has just become understood during the past decade is child abuse. Although there is no sure data on how many cases of abuse occur each year, we do know something about the profile of the people who abuse children, the emotional consequences of the children being abused, and short-term remedies for both the abused and the abusers. Medical professionals and social service practitioners have formed child abuse teams throughout the country to spot cases of abuse in their early stages and to offer help for the victims. Some progress is being made, but there are difficult hurdles to overcome. Chief among these is the complex historical and legal tradition in our country that places families in the driver's seat in any conflict over a child's welfare.

Divorce is another social issue in our culture for both new and old marriages. Those who divorce often remarry, with the result being a mixture of family structures. What effects do such family structures have on children? How do the family members cope with the stress involved? And, what effect does divorce have on an adult's self-esteem and relationships with the opposite sex? As you will see in later chapters, answers to such questions are beginning to formulate.

Yet another major change in our culture is the increasing age of our population. People are living longer and, in addition, are breaking the close link to their families. Because of this, the elderly no longer maintain such a strong socializing role in the young child's life. Who is to care for many of the elderly in our culture, who unlike fifty years ago, do not live with or close to their own children and grandchildren? What kinds of social services are needed for the elderly, and how can they be implemented? Should we reconsider the retirement age for workers because of the increased longevity of their lives? Are there alternate work patterns in late adulthood that need to be explored? We will address these and many other questions throughout this exciting field of study of life-span development.

The Historical Perspective

Remarkably, there was no explicit developmental psychology that focused on themes of life-span development before the middle of the twentieth century (Havighurst, 1973). That is, there was no systematic set of information that covered even half of an individual's lifetime, and there were no theories or models of psychological development that focused on this much of the life cycle. By contrast, there is a much longer and richer history pertaining to the section of the life cycle known as childhood.

Our present concept of childhood is a recent one. In the past, children were viewed as miniature adults.

Childhood

Our conception of childhood has changed dramatically from what it was in the not too distant past or in medieval and ancient societies. This historical change can be traced along several distinct lines. First is the concept of childhood itself. What is it? How long does it last? And, what is its purpose? Next, we ask how knowledge about childhood came into being. Why did adults study childhood and what were their conclusions?

The Concept of Childhood

Philip Aries' book *Centuries of Childhood* (1962) has become a classic source on the concept of childhood. He makes it clear that our present concept is a very recent one. We have only to look at representative samples of art across the ages to convince ourselves of this. Notice the way children of all ages are pictured in the accompanying photographs. They are dressed much like adults; their body proportions are the same as adults; they are in the company of adults; they are engaged in adultlike activities. It is hard to escape the impression that they *are* miniature adults. We have to go back very far—virtually to infancy—before seeing any signs of demarcation between young people and adults. It is not a simplification to state that writings about children—whether they were theological, pedagogical, or philosophical—also showed this impoverished view of development. Basically, there were two stages—*infancy* (lasting from birth to anywhere from three to six years) and *adulthood* (beyond infancy). We might generously add a third period—*preadulthood*—a time in which children (as we call them today) learned the ways of the world of grown-ups and acquired the skills for a livelihood. For females, puberty, and the subsequent ability to bear children, probably marked the end of preadulthood.

Absent from most of history was a clear vision of childhood that admitted the presence of many distinct stages with attendant differences in physical skills, intellectual capabilities, and personality characteristics. Instead, life periods were defined according to whether work and the business of life could be handled (adulthood) or not (infancy or preadulthood). According to this viewpoint, the years from infancy to adulthood served simply to ready the person for work, reproduction, and adult responsibilities. Absent was any consistent theme that childhood was a special period, with unique needs and purposes, unique opportunities for such things as fantasy and play, and unique contributions to make to the life cycle.

Acquiring Knowledge about Children

Scholars in the past tended to focus either on philosophical debates about children that were difficult to settle on empirical terms (i.e., on the facts of the matter), or they used the subject of childhood as a forum for offering theological pronouncements (Senn, 1975; White, 1980). They did not develop techniques for examining the actual lives of children or the forces that impinged upon them. Two classic philosophical debates, for example, concerned the *origin of knowledge* and the child's *moral status*.

Philosophers debated two extreme alternatives about the origin of knowledge. According to the position of innate knowledge, the child is born with both knowledge about the world and strong propensities to learn. Plato argued that knowledge is innate. He wrote in *The Republic,* Book VII, "But then, if I am right, certain professors of education must be wrong when they say that they can put a knowledge into the soul which was not then there before, like sight into blind eyes. . . . Whereas our argument shows that the power and capacity of learning exists in the soul already." By contrast, seventeen-century British philosopher John Locke suggested that at birth the child's mind is a blank slate, a **tabula rasa.** According to this position, all knowledge results from learned experiences, and the principal means of learning is through the association of ideas.

The second subject for philosophical debate concerned the moral goodness of the child and the need for moral training. This is translated today into a concern for the child's social awareness and the need to teach the child acceptable social skills. Two early perspectives on the child's moral status were that (1) the child is inherently bad, or sinful, at birth and must be led along the high road to piety in life and (2) the child is inherently good at birth, and this good start must be supported and reinforced by society to help the child stay clear of corrupting evils.

The "sinful" view of the child was espoused by the Catholic church through most of the period in history that has come to be called the Dark Ages, from about the fifth to the fourteenth centuries (Aries, 1962). It has persisted beyond that time as well in all theological preaching that actively applies the belief of **original sin** to everyday life. It can be seen today in a variety of mainstream Christian religions, for example the moral majority movement. According to this view, the child's development must be carefully guided, with social instruction provided to correct antisocial tendencies.

Child Development in Contemporary Times

In the past century and a half, our view of children has changed dramatically. We now conceive of childhood as a highly eventful and unique period of life that lays an important foundation for adult years and is highly differentiated from them. In most social science approaches to childhood, a large number of distinct periods are identified in which special skills are mastered and new life tasks are confronted. Childhood is no longer seen as an inconvenient "waiting" period during which adults must suffer the incompetencies of the young. We now value it as a special time for growth and change, and we invest great resources in caring for and educating our children. We protect them from the excesses of the adult work world through tough child labor laws; we treat their crimes against society under a special system of juvenile justice; and we have governmental provisions for helping children when ordinary family support systems fail or when families seriously interfere with the children's well-being.

Life-Span Development

Scholars sometime disagree as to whether change occurs throughout the life cycle. Traditional approaches to human development have emphasized extreme change from birth to adolescence, stability in adulthood, and decline in old age (Baltes, 1973; Baltes, Reese, & Lipsitt, 1980). See figure 1.1 for a look at how the traditional view of development contrasts with the life-span perspective. Note the powerful role allotted to infancy and early childhood and the absence of change in early and middle adulthood in the traditional view. In the life-cycle perspective, the emphasis is on

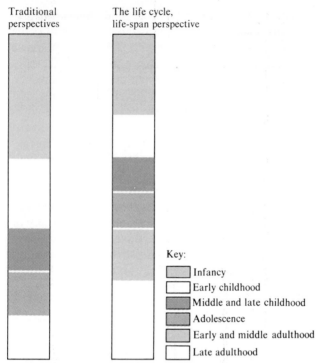

Traditional perspectives

The life cycle, life-span perspective

Key:

- [ ] Infancy
- [ ] Early childhood
- [ ] Middle and late childhood
- [ ] Adolescence
- [ ] Early and middle adulthood
- [ ] Late adulthood

Figure 1.1 Perspectives on life-span development reflecting points in the life cycle where change and development are thought to occur.

Robert Havighurst.

change in adulthood, while still recognizing the importance of infancy as the building block of life-span development. While some perceptive individuals like William Shakespeare saw that age-related changes occurred throughout the lifespan, the scientific study of life-span changes in development has occurred only in recent years. Paul Baltes (1979), in reviewing the historical roots of life-span developmental psychology, described the works of Tetens (1777), Carus (1808), and Quetelet (1835). The latter work, *A Treatise on Man and the Development of His Faculties,* provides the most logical connection to present-day perspectives of life-span development, emphasizing the concept of change over the entire life cycle.

By 1940, developmental investigations of infancy, childhood, and adolescence were commonplace, yet studies of age-related changes in adulthood were just beginning. Robert Havighurst (1973), in chronicling the history of life-span developmental psychology, indicated that some well-known psychologists who focused on the initial phases of development early in their careers (infancy, childhood, and adolescence) and later became interested in adulthood changes, rarely did serious research related to age changes in adulthood. For instance, G. Stanley Hall, known as the father of adolescent psychology because of the publication of the

G. Stanley Hall.

two-volume set, *Adolescence* (1904), wrote *Senescence: The Last Half of Life* in 1922 after his formal retirement. In introducing the latter book, Hall (1922) speculated:

Our life, bounded by birth and death, has five chief stages, each of which, while it may be divided into substages, also passes into the next so gradually that we cannot date, save roughly and approximately, the transition from one period to that which succeeds it. These more marked nodes in the unity of man's individual existence are: (1) childhood, (2) adolescence from puberty to full nubility, (3) middle life or the prime, when we are at the apex of our aggregate of powers, ranging from twenty-five or thirty to forty or forty-five and comprising thus the fifteen or twenty years now commonly called our best, (4) senescence, which begins in the early forties, or before in woman, and (5) senectitude, the post-climacteric or old age proper. My own life work, such as it is, as a genetic psychologist was devoted for years to the study of infancy and childhood, then to the phenomena of youth, later to adulthood and the stage of sex maturity. To complete a long-cherished program I have now finally tried, aided by the first-hand knowledge that advancing years have brought, to understand better the two last and closing stages of human life. (p. vii)

Hall was not the only famous psychologist who was initially interested in the earlier years of development and then later turned his attention to development in adulthood. Well-known psychoanalyst Erik Erikson focused mainly on the first twenty years of life in his earlier writings (e.g., *Childhood and Society,* 1952), only later showing strong curiosity about age-related changes in adulthood (e.g., *Gandhi's Truth,* 1969). Erikson's ideas about the eight stages of development throughout the life cycle represent one of the most widely discussed views of life-span development. In the next chapter we will discuss those eight stages.

Charlotte Buhler (1933, 1968) is yet another individual whose initial interest in childhood later changed to focus on life-span development. She divided the life span into the following five periods: (1) childhood—birth to fourteen; (2) youth—fourteen to twenty-five; (3) adult I—twenty-five to between forty-five and fifty; (4) adult II—between forty-five and fifty to between sixty-five and seventy; (5) aging—seventy and up. Buhler believes that self-fulfillment is the key to successful development and says that individuals are motivated to attain personal goals throughout the life cycle. Her five goal-related phases to self-fulfillment are described here:

Childhood—children have not yet set their life goals, but they may think about them in somewhat vague ways.

Youth—at this point in development, individuals first discover the concept that their lives are their own, and they begin to think about their potential.

Adult I—individuals develop more specific goals at this time.

Adult II—individuals look back on their past, evaluating their lives in the process, and revise their planning for the future.

Aging—individuals relax their concentration on achieving goals.

Buhler relied extensively on biographies as a source of data for her work in Vienna. In describing her interests and methods, she wrote to Robert Havighurst (1973):

My interest was in the whole of human life, . . . I studied infancy, to get an idea of life's earliest trends. But after some years, I decided that life as a whole could be better understood from its end than from its beginning. Thus my students and I studied biographies, which were well enough documented to know them in great detail. We chose biographies, because these lives were closed and one could study their actual end, not only late periods. (p. 22)

For too long, then, we believed that development was something that happened only to children. To be sure, growth and change are dramatic in the first two decades of life, but as Robert Sears and Shirley Feldman (1973) argue, there is a great deal of change that goes on in the next five or six decades of life as well.

But the next five or six decades are every bit as important, not only to those adults who are passing through them but to their children, who must live with and understand parents and grandparents. The changes in body, personality and abilities through these later decades are very great. There are severe developmental tasks imposed by marriage and parenthood, by the waxing and waning of physical prowess and of some (but not all) intellectual capacities, by the children's flight from the nest, by the achievement of an occupational plateau, and by the facing of retirement and the prospect of final extinction. By and large, people accomplish these tasks. Some do it more gracefully and effectively than others, and there is no denying the uniqueness of every personality. But the very nature of human growth, coupled with the commonality of human experience in a given culture, is reflected in the considerable similarity among age-mates in the adjustment problems they suffer and the particular personality qualities they develop at various ages. Parents have always been fascinated by their children's development, but it is high time adults began to look objectively at themselves, to examine the systematic changes in their own physical, mental, and emotional qualities, as they pass through the life cycle, and to get acquainted with the limitations and assets they share with so many others of their own age. (pp. v–vi)

When we study development from a life-span perspective, we can clearly see the importance of intergenerational relations. In box 1.1, David Hultsch and

Box 1.1
Intergenerational Relations

A major concern of social theorists is how the generations interact. What is the role of generational succession in the aging process? Two general approaches to the generational concept have been used by investigators. Those using the cohort perspective emphasize the characteristics of different birth cohorts or age strata. Those using the lineage perspective emphasize continuities and discontinuities in socialization resulting from intergenerational transmission processes (Bengtson & Cutler, 1976).

Cohort Perspective

The various generations differ from one another in many ways, for example, in kind and degree of social and political alienation. Three basic hypotheses have been proposed to account for generational differences in social and political alienation: (1) maturation, (2) generation, and (3) period effects.

Maturational interpretations propose that alienation is related to life-cycle stage. Alienation among youth (e.g., Seeman, 1959) has been found to relate to perceived powerlessness. Alienation among the elderly (e.g., Martin, Bengtson, & Acock, 1973) has been found to relate to losses in status, abilities, and resources. Thus, although alienation occurs among both young people and the elderly in our society, the reasons for that alienation seem to be different for different age groups. (Miller, Brown, & Raine, 1973).

A generational interpretation of alienation is based on evidence showing substantial discontinuities between birth cohorts. Certain labels (e.g., "lost generation" or "beat generation") are used to represent members of a cohort throughout their lives, not just during an age period. For instance, Kenniston (1968) portrayed student activists of the sixties as an alienated *generation* rather than as alienated *youth* per se. These feelings of alienation were said to persist among the members of the cohort over their life span. In contrast, Bengtson (1970) reviewed several "generational gap" studies and found that the supposed gap between the young and the old reflects differences in maturational level and life-stage responsibilities rather than cohort differences. Others (e.g., Friedenberg, 1969; Slater, 1970), still maintain that there is a considerable gap between parents and youth, but they feel that the youth will mature with the passage of time.

Finally, a period interpretation maintains that societal events (e.g., political assassinations, the Vietnam war, Watergate) account for alienation. For example, an analysis of the period from 1952 to 1968 showed that similar trends in political alienation existed for the population as a whole, regardless of age, sex, income, or educational level (House & Mason, 1975).

Which of the various explanations of alienation— maturational, generational, or historical—is most viable? Cutler and Bengtson (1974) used a cohort analysis to analyze three measures of political alienation during the period 1952 to 1968. They examined maturational, generational, and period effects. Their data showed that fluctuations in political alienation affected most people in a similar manner. All groups, except those people born between 1916 and 1923, felt that political alienation between 1952 and 1960 decreased and that there was a significant increase in alienation between 1960 and 1968. However, all groups reported that political alienation was higher in 1968 than in 1952. Cutler and Bengtson concluded that the period effect, that is, the impact of history, is the most viable means of accounting for these alienation data.

Lineage Perspective

A lineage perspective focuses on what is transmitted among the generations. Specifically, it focuses on what is exchanged between the young and the old in terms of knowledge and skills, power and responsibility, and caregiving of dependent members. According to Bengtson and Cutler (1976), three questions stand out in lineage generational analysis.

> What perceptions do older people have of cross-generational relationships—both within the family and the broader society? What is the nature and extent of interaction between aged individuals and their families—patterns of help or exchange, contact, and affection? How much consensus—and how much conflict—exists between older parents and their middle aged children or grandchildren. (p. 144)

Bengtson and Cutler (1976) identify five key points concerning socialization and lineage. First, the nature of intergenerational family relations alters over time. Interactional patterns and patterns of affection also change, as do patterns involving power, responsibility, and concern over one another's welfare (Bengtson & Black, 1973). Second, American families perceive high solidarity among members. Third, elders feel they receive slightly more affection than other family members, while younger family members feel they receive more goods and services than older members. Fourth, although the study of attitudes and values is complex, it is doubtful that the generation gap, whether assessed in terms of cohorts or lineage, exists. There appears to be more consensus among and between generations than differences. Fifth, many elements of the historical period need to be included in investigations of intergenerational relations. Thus, the socialization process in adulthood can be studied as one of transmission and interaction between family members, and between families and society.

Source: Hultsch & Deutsch, 1981, pp. 191–93.

Francine Deutsch (1981) describe two different perspectives we can use to study intergenerational relations—the **cohort** and **lineage perspectives.** More about the cohort perspective will appear later in this chapter when we discuss the various methods used to study life-span development.

In our overview of children and life-span development we have seen that philosophers and psychologists have different views on how the phases of childhood and the life cycle should be divided. Next we look at how the phases of the life cycle will be presented in this text and describe the nature of development.

Phases of Life-Span Development, the Changing Age Structure, and the Nature of Development

In the contemporary study of life-span development there is by no means agreement on what the phases of the life cycle actually are and when they occur. Further, you will soon see that during the twentieth century the age structure of our society has changed dramatically. This means that the number of people at a particular phase in the life cycle has changed dramatically. And, there also is a great deal of disagreement about the nature of the processes that lead to change from one phase to the next. For the purposes of organization and understanding, the life cycle can be divided into the following phases of development: infancy, early childhood, middle and late childhood, adolescence, early and middle adulthood, and late adulthood. Approximate age bands are placed on the periods to provide a general idea of the time in development when a period first appears and when it ends.

Phases of Life-Span Development

Infancy is usually recognized as extending from birth to eighteen or twenty-four months. (For the first few days after birth, an infant is referred to as a **neonate.**) Infancy is a time of extreme dependence upon adults, with many physiological and psychological activities just beginning (language, symbolic thought, sensorimotor coordination, social learning). This period usually ends when the child talks in short phrases and finds it easy to walk great distances from the caretaker.

Early childhood, which extends from the end of infancy to about five or six years, roughly corresponds to the period in which the child prepares for formal schooling. Sometimes this period of development is referred to as the preschool years. Among the tasks mastered are the ability to care for oneself (e.g., personal hygiene, dressing oneself), self-sufficiency (e.g., self-initiated play), and development of school-readiness skills (e.g., following instructions; using writing implements; identifying letters, numbers, and sounds). And, peer relations and play become more pronounced. First grade usually marks the end of this period.

Middle and **late childhood** extends from about six to eleven years of age, roughly corresponding to the elementary school years. Sometimes this period of development is called the elementary school years. Such fundamental skills as reading, writing, and arithmetic are mastered, and there is formal exposure to the larger world and its culture through the study of history, civics, business and government, art and music, and contemporary social problems. Thought processes usually are very concrete and less abstract than in the next period.

"I just can't believe I'm gonna look like you when I'm 35."

Adolescence is the period of transition from childhood to early adulthood, entered approximately at eleven to thirteen years of age and ending at eighteen to twenty-one years of age. Adolescence begins with the onset of rapid physical change—dramatic gains in height and weight, change in body contour, and development of secondary sex characteristics (e.g., enlargement of the breasts, development of pubic hair and facial hair, deepening of the voice). It is a time for readying the developing mind and body for an independent, productive life in the adult world. The development of identity and abstract, logical thought also characterize adolescence. More and more time is spent outside the family during this period.

Early adulthood usually begins in the late teens or early twenties and lasts through the thirties. It is a time of establishing personal and economic independence. Career development takes on an even more important role than in late adolescence. For many young adults, selecting a mate, learning to live with someone else in an intimate way, and starting a family and rearing children take up a great deal of time.

Middle adulthood characterizes the phase of the life cycle from approximately thirty-five to forty-five years to fifty-five to sixty-five years. It is a time of expanding personal and social involvement and responsibility; for assisting teenagers to become responsible and happy adults; for adjusting to the physiological changes of middle age; and for reaching and maintaining satisfaction in one's career.

Late adulthood lasts from approximately sixty to seventy years of age until death. It is a time of adjustment to decreasing strength and health and to retirement and reduced income. Establishing affiliations with members of one's age group and adapting to social roles are involved.

In the prologue you read about a number of age-related themes in development—some suggested by William Shakespeare and Carl Sandburg, others by Robert Havighurst, and even some by Erma Bombeck. In our historical account of life-span development, we again described characteristics of different phases of the life cycle. And, you have just finished reading about how the phases of the life cycle will be presented in this text. However, one expert on the life cycle, Bernice Neugarten, believes that we are becoming an age-irrelevant society (see box 1.2).

The Changing Age Structure

At the same time that it has become difficult to cluster people into age brackets that are characterized by particular conflicts, psychological characteristics, and social themes, the actual age structure in America has changed dramatically as well. One characteristic of contemporary life cycles that is very different from the pattern that occurred several generations ago is that we are no longer a youthful society (see fig. 1.2 for United States census data from 1900 through 1980). As more and more people have lived to older ages, the proportion of people at different age levels has become increasingly similar. In the 1980 census, the number of persons sixty-five and older climbed by 28 percent in the 1970s to 25.5 million. Population projections by the United States Bureau of the Census (1977) suggest that by the year 2030, the number of Americans in different periods of the life cycle indeed will be approximately equal (see fig. 1.3). Two of the major reasons for these age changes in the population are that fewer children are being born now than in past years, possibly due to improved contraceptive methods, and that improved health care has increased the life span of many older individuals (Hurlock, 1980).

In addition to the changing age structure of society, other data from the United States Census suggest some other important characteristics of the population. Note in figure 1.2 that beginning at the age of twenty-five (in the 1980 data), females begin to outnumber males, a gap that widens through the remainder of the adult years, such that by the time individuals reach the age of seventy-five, slightly more than 61 percent of the population is female, and for the eighty-five and over age segment, our population is almost 70 percent female.

Box 1.2
Are Many Age-Related Themes of Development Stereotypes?

Bernice Neugarten (1980) says that "we are already familiar with the twenty-eight-year-old mayor, the thirty-year-old college president, the thirty-five-year-old grandmother, the fifty-year-old-retiree, the sixty-five-year-old father of a preschooler, the fifty-five-year-old widow who starts a business, and the seventy-year-old student. 'Act your age' is an admonition that has little meaning for adults these days." Yet there are an increasing number of popular books that suggest very common patterns for our complex lives, such as the "Trying Twenties" and "Passage to the Thirties" in Gail Sheehy's (1976) widely read *Passages*. People who read such books worry about their midlife crises, apologize if they don't seem to be coping with them properly, and seem dismayed if they aren't having one. Such transformations, or crises, though, may not define what is normal or off-the-track. It is not that adults are changeless, but rather that adults change far more, and far less predictably, than many oversimplified stage theories suggest. Neugarten indicates that "my students and I have studied what happens to people over the life cycle. . . . We have found great trouble clustering people into age brackets that are characterized by particular conflicts; the conflicts won't stay put, and neither will the people. Choices and dilemmas do not sprout forth at ten-year intervals, and decisions are not made and then left behind as if they were merely beads on a chain."

Neugarten believes that it is no longer reasonable to describe the life cycle as a set of discrete stages. This is because our biological clocks have changed: puberty comes earlier than a generation ago; menopause comes later; and people are living longer. In addition, our social time clocks have changed: there are new trends in work, family size, health, and education; and people are starting new jobs and families at forty, fifty, and even sixty years of age.

Certainly there are some psychological preoccupations that are more powerful at one age than at another. A study of reminiscence, for example, found that middle-aged people consciously select elements from their past to help them solve current problems; the very old put their store of memories in order, dramatizing some and rearranging others for consistency—creating a coherent life history. But more intrapsychic changes evolve very slowly, and they may or may not be linked with specific events. Divorce may provoke painful soul-searching for one woman, while another sails through the experience with a minimum of stress.

Neugarten states that most adulthood themes appear and reappear throughout the life cycle. For example, the issues of intimacy and freedom may haunt couples throughout a relationship. Similarly, feeling the pressure of time, reformulating goals, and coping with success and failure are not the exclusive property of adults of any age.

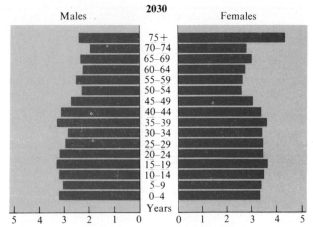

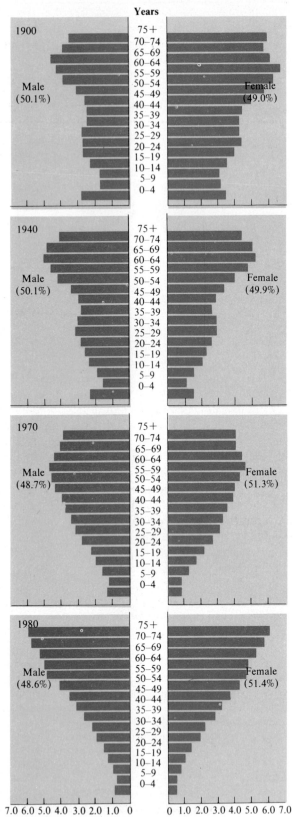

Figure 1.3 Percent of total population projected at each age group in the year 2030.

Figure 1.2 The age structure of America from 1900–1980.

Another major change in the 1980 census data compared to 1970 is the number of single-person households, now estimated at about 18 million. This is a stunning 65 percent leap since 1970, when single adults accounted for less than one-fifth of the total. Among households headed by a single parent, 8.7 million are headed by an adult woman and 1.7 million by an adult man. In 1970, 5.5 million were headed by women and 1.3 million by men.

The Nature of Life-Span Development

You are a fascinating creature. There is no one else in the world quite like you. Your thoughts, feelings, and behaviors are unique, yet you are a lot like other people your age. In school you have learned many of the same skills that other students have learned, and as a part of society you have learned to care about many of the same things that others care about.

How have you become simultaneously unique and yet similar to others of your generation? What processes and events have contributed to this outcome? These are the questions addressed by developmental psychologists, who attempt to understand the processes and events that contribute to change throughout life. Some of that change contributes to your uniqueness, while some of it moves you along a common pathway with others. Some of the processes and events recur throughout childhood and adulthood, making the task of seeing continuity in development easy. Others occur only during isolated periods of time; these help in gaining an understanding of the nature of age-related differences among people (Block, 1981; Brim & Kagan, 1980; Yarrow, 1981).

The central concept of this text is development. What do we mean when we say that a child or an adult has "developed" in some respect? Psychologists use the term to refer to a *pattern of movement or change* that begins at conception and continues through the entire life span. The pattern of change involves growth (as in infancy) and decay (as in death). The pattern of movement is complex because it is often the product of several processes—**maturation** and **experiences,** for example.

Maturation involves changes dictated by the genetic blueprint we each have. Our brain and central nervous system grow and become differentiated; our anatomy changes; and there are changes in our chemical and hormonal makeup as we move toward maturity. One example of maturation is the gradual specialization of the brain, in which each of the hemispheres directs different psychological activities (such as spatial processing in the right hemisphere and language in the left hemisphere). Prior to adolescence, these functions within the brain are flexible. So for example, an injury to a specific part of the brain during early childhood may temporarily disrupt one of these activities, but in some cases other parts of the brain will gradually take over, functioning as backup systems. As we approach adolescence and beyond, however, accidents are more likely to produce permanent damage, since the specialized functions acquired have become more rigidly locked into specific locations in the brain.

Experiences constitute the broadest and, in some sense, vaguest ingredient in the mix of development. Experiences run the gamut from the individual's **biological environment**—nutrition, medical care and drugs, and physical accidents—to the **social environment**—family, school, community, peers, and the media. Experiences can be understood in microscopic terms when we look at our specific vitamin intake or chart the specific interactions between a mother and child; alternatively, experiences can be reckoned macroscopically when we examine the overall medical care given a family or the mental health dynamics operating in a family (e.g., how the members generally get along with one another, the degree of family stress present, and the degree of family adaptation to the larger society). The level at which experiences are defined and studied very much depends upon the theoretical perspective of the expert involved. Learning is often defined in very precise, detailed terms. Thus a learning psychologist might choose to examine the specific behaviors an individual has learned through imitation or reinforcement in stressful situations at home, or try to understand how the individual handles stress and conflict with peers. By contrast, a sociologist would be more likely to study on a broader scale the social experiences in which an individual is involved by measuring changes in the social composition of the family's neighborhood or the family's socioeconomic status over a period of time to see what impact this has on the individual's opportunities and activities.

Whatever approach is taken, experiences are a key to development. Without them, maturation would not occur. As an extreme example, consider that children must have nourishment to grow and that they must have some stimulation of the five senses to function. The absence of human contact has had the dramatic and documented effect of producing children who are mentally retarded and lack a spoken language. Less dramatically, contemporary students of development seek to understand what kinds of experiences shape maturation and growth and the processes by which this interaction takes place. For example, what kinds of interactions promote adaptive attachments between young children and their caregivers? What early experiences promote the rapid and advanced acquisition of spoken language? How does experience influence the development of thinking and moral reasoning skills? One type of answer given is that environments rich in stimulation generally produce the most favorable results. If you interact with a baby boy frequently and show him love, you will produce a healthy attachment. If you spend time talking to a little girl, she will learn language quickly. Prod the child to think and exercise moral judgment and she will achieve intellectually and develop strong moral character. This type of answer would make life simple, but unfortunately it frequently does not prove to be right. As we probe the mysteries of change, we find that subtlety is necessary. More important than the amount of interaction, we find that timing is central in the development of healthy attachment; the caregiver must respond in synchrony with the infant's needs. More important than the amount of talk directed at the young child is the level at which the talk is structured; short phrases, clear pauses, and clear patterns of intonation are necessary.

Briefly, the contemporary study of development is concerned with the pattern of movement and change in the individual's life. Contemporary psychologists attempt to describe and predict this change and explain how maturation is shaped by the individual's experiences. You will see these themes appear repeatedly throughout the text. The insights gained about them will frequently be surprising.

Strands of Development
As you read about the different phases of the life cycle, you will soon see that the chapters have been organized around different strands of development. The five strands of development that will be emphasized in this

book are physical development, cognitive development, emotional development, social development, and personality development. As we describe each of the phases of the life cycle, we will discuss at length each of these strands of development.

Physical development refers to the simple changes in size and weight and the gradual, quantitative changes that can be charted for other physical and anatomical features. Weight gain, overall height changes, growth of head and limbs, and the changing size of the brain, heart, and lungs are all part of this process. Patterns of growth are important; we have learned much about them and can use them as clinical instruments to determine whether a child or an adult is healthy and developing normally. For example, the weight of the average newborn baby doubles from birth to six months. If a child deviates substantially from this average, a pediatrician may want to examine the baby's diet and check for other growth anomalies. Conversely, we can use growth patterns to predict when a child is making normal transitions from period to period. As we will see in chapters 3 and 11, there are two periods of very rapid growth spurts before adulthood—the first two years of life and the one- to two-year period that marks the early portion of adolescence. A careful record of the child's and adolescent's growth serves as a particularly useful tool to determine when late childhood has ended and adolescence has begun.

Cognitive development refers to the age-related series of changes that occur in mental activity—thought, memory, perception, attention, and language. As part of our study of cognitive development, you will probably be surprised to find out how precise we have become in discovering what infants know at different points in the first two years of their lives. You will learn how the child's memory development occurs, and whether there really is a decay in intelligence during late adulthood. You also will learn how the infant develops perceptions of depth and space, as well as the remarkable feats of attention a baby displays in the first month of life. How children's language develops and whether it is a good idea to push the child into learning to read in the infant years will also be discussed.

Social development and **emotional development** are broad labels that encompass many different aspects of the individual's world, aspects that often overlap. The word *social* refers to the individual's interactions with other individuals in the environment. Two elderly people consoling each other, a mother hugging her daughter for a good report card, a father spanking his son for being sassy, siblings arguing with each other, and a teacher warmly greeting a boy at the door of her classroom are all aspects of the social world. Social development focuses on how these many different aspects unfold as the individual grows.

Weight gain, overall height changes, growth of head and limbs, and the changing size of the brain, heart, and lungs are all part of physical development.

Researchers have become very precise in discovering what infants know at different points in the first two years of their lives.

Infant attachment is an important aspect of social and emotional development.

It is impossible to meaningfully present the aspects of personality development without frequently referring to the individual's interactions with and thoughts about the world.

Discussions of emotional development often contain many of the same components as social development. However, emotional development places more emphasis on the individual's feelings and affective responses (the words *affect, emotion,* and *feeling* can be used interchangeably). The attachment of an infant to the mother is an important topic discussed in chapter 6, as is the development of the self, which will be discussed throughout the text. The infant's cries and smiles are emotional responses that are important aspects of the attachment process. And, the individual's tendency to evaluate himself or herself positively or negatively is an important part of the development of the self. Other emotions that will be discussed over the course of the life cycle are anxiety, anger, and guilt.

As we discuss **personality development** through the life cycle, three aspects of personality development, in particular, will be emphasized: The self and self-perception, sex-typed behavior and sex-role development, and moral development. As a rule, the label *personality* has referred more to a property of the individual than to social development. Yet, you will see that it is impossible to meaningfully present the aspects of personality without frequently referring to the individual's interactions with and thoughts about the social world. And, when we discuss moral development, an important aspect of personality, you will discover that a prominent aspect of moral development is the individual's feelings or affective reactions to moral situations.

While it is helpful to study the different stands of life-span development in separate sections and chapters, keep in mind while reading this text that you are an integrated human being—you have only one mind and one body. Physical, cognitive, social, emotional and personality development are inextricably woven together. In many chapters, you will read how social experiences shape cognitive development, how cognitive development restricts or promotes social development, and how cognitive development is tied to physical development.

The study of life-span development now has become a full-fledged scientific enterprise. No longer is it merely a secondary interest for many psychologists. We do not rely only on notions from other fields, such as Shakespeare's notions about the seven stages of man, and we do not let ideas about age-related changes over the life span remain speculative and undocumented. Future policies and decisions about children and adults can be based upon an accumulating body of knowledge of what children and adults are like, which in turn is based on scientific evidence rather than philosophical speculation.

Life-Span Developmental Psychology As a Scientific Enterprise

Urie Bronfenbrenner (1970), an expert on social development, has observed child-rearing techniques in several different cultures. In the excerpt that follows, he describes how Soviet youth discipline themselves for violating accepted rules of behavior.

Ivanov is a fifth-grade leader of his school's youth group, the Pioneers. He went swimming with some friends without adult supervision and after a reprimand from the school authorities, he must now face a disciplinary council composed of his own peers. Ivanov is asked to stand and tell the group what he has done. The answer is barely audible, "I went swimming."

As his answers are written down by the secretary, a girl asks, "You and who else?" He names seven others. Another girl comments, "Fine thing; you're the commander leading your men." A boy asks, "Do you realize that last year a child drowned in that very pond?"

The questions and accusations continued. The major effort is two-sided: first, to impress Ivanov with the fact that, in violating the rule, he had jeopardized the lives of his classmates as well as his own; second, that his act constituted a betrayal of the faith invested in him as a Pioneer commander. Ivanov is speechless, and trembles slightly and struggles to hold back the tears.

This vignette illustrates one of the ways that people have investigated processes of development—through scientific observation. Thousands of professionals are actively involved in scientific inquiry into the nature of development and how the individual develops across the life span. Well over one hundred new doctorates in developmental psychology are awarded each year by the nation's universities. Millions of dollars are spent each year by federal, state, and local governments to support basic research. By conservative estimates there are more than a dozen highly respected technical journals in this country that publish annually over a thousand reports of original research dealing with developmental psychology. In short, developmental psychology is an active scientific field.

But what exactly do we mean when we say that life-span developmental psychology is a science? How are current efforts to understand children and adults any different from those of the philosophers and historians already mentioned? Scientific inquiry differs from philosophical speculation and the casual observations of historians in a number of ways. For one, scientists propose formal theories that are subjected to rigorous tests with actual individuals. For another, there are specific methods for conducting these tests and for uncovering additional facts about children and adults. Together, the theories and methods ensure that we do

Trained observers focus their attention on specific behaviors.

not delude ourselves with fanciful ideas or whimsy in describing individuals, for a bad idea or theory can be quickly dismissed with several well-chosen empirical tests. In the next chapter we will highlight the major theories of development, but first, we will describe a number of different scientific methods.

Scientific Methods

Of the many scientific methods employed in the study of children and adults we will focus here on *observation, experiment,* and *correlation.*

Observation

Perhaps the most basic tool of any science is systematic **observation.** If you want to examine some characteristic of human behavior, try to observe it in people themselves. In **naturalistic observation** you would do this in a real-life or natural context. Not just any type of observation qualifies as scientific inquiry; systematic observation has several requirements. First of all, the observer must be trained to look only for certain behaviors during an observation. For example, if the purpose of the investigation is to see how adults respond to aggressive behavior in young children, the observer must concentrate only on the children's aggressive responses and the adults' actions that follow.

A second requirement is that during observation, everything else becomes secondary. This may seem like a simple point, but it is surprising how many college students become sidetracked by endless irrelevancies

in a child's behavior during an observation. It is difficult to observe an individual continuously even if the behavior of interest is narrowly defined; fatigue and the need to record observations often make this impossible. As a result, most observational studies use **time samples,** a procedure in which the individual is observed only a portion of the time. For example, if you want to observe aggression during ten-minute recess periods at school, you can observe the child in alternating two-minute observe-record (on-off) cycles.

An ambitious exception to these two qualifications is **ecological psychology,** a specialized technique of naturalistic observation developed by Roger Barker (1968). With this technique, a person's behavior is monitored by teams of observers as the individual goes about a typical day's activities. This technique differs from other observational techniques in the exhaustiveness with which the individual's life is explored.

Finally, an essential factor in the observation is **reliability.** If one person is asked to observe the same event that another witnessed, the same observations should be reported by both. The observational records are reliable to the extent that independent observers have strong agreement on what occurred. If substantial agreement cannot be reached by the two observers, then the observational procedure is unreliable and, as a result, worthless.

The observational method is not only valuable when the goal of a study is to examine individuals in a natural context, but it is also useful for studying facets of

behavior that have gone largely unexplored. The use of videotaped records has greatly expanded the precision of observational techniques. A videotape can provide a complete record of an individual's behavior, allowing the investigator the luxury of poring over the record of behavior long after it has occurred.

Experimentation

An observation fails to control all of the forces operating on the individual as information is being collected. It is not possible, therefore, to discover precisely which factors are causing certain behaviors in the individual; observation can only provide clues. In an **experiment** an attempt is made to exercise just such control. The factors that are thought to influence or cause a certain behavior are referred to as **independent variables;** these are specified by the experimenter. Factors that are being influenced are referred to as **dependent variables;** these are measured in the study. By taking several precautions, the experimenter can ensure that no extraneous factors (independent variables other than those that have been defined) are systematically influencing the individual.

A concrete example may help to clarify what constitutes an experiment. Suppose it is believed that individuals learn to solve problems simply by observing other people solve them. This belief could be subjected to experimental test by means of the following procedure. Each person in one group is individually exposed to another person who repeatedly assembles a jigsaw puzzle that has thirty-five pieces. Each person in a second group is individually exposed to the same person and the same jigsaw puzzle but does not see that person assemble it. Each person in both groups is then asked individually to assemble the jigsaw puzzle, and a record is made of the time taken to do so.

The independent variable in this experiment would be the amount of exposure the individual has to the person solving the problem. There are two degrees of this—some exposure to the person assembling the puzzle, and no exposure. The dependent variable is the amount of time a person takes to assemble the puzzle.

If the group of individuals who had some exposure assembled the puzzle more rapidly than the group who had no exposure, the initial hypothesis would be confirmed: the persons learned something—rapid puzzle assembly—following an experience in which they saw someone else perform that action.

Other factors might explain the superior performance of the one group. Perhaps they were brighter or had more experience with jigsaw puzzles or had more experience watching people solve problems. How do we know that the independent variable selected was the influential one? One way is by matching the two experimental groups so that they are identical with respect to all other such potential factors. Another way would be the technique known as **randomization.** With randomization, only some individuals are selected from a much larger group for the experiment. They are then assigned randomly to one or the other exposure condition. If the assignment is truly random, then there is only a slim chance that the two groups will differ from one another on some particular characteristic since any extraneous factor will have been randomly distributed in the groups.

Experiments are useful when carefully controlled information about people is desired because this technique permits the experimenter to make inferences about **cause-and-effect** relations.

Correlation
Often it is of interest to know how one measured characteristic is associated with another—height with weight, intelligence with learning ability, parental discipline with child morality. One measure of association is the **correlation** coefficient. Correlations are referred to in discussions of heritability (chapter 3).

The correlation coefficient ranges from −1.00 to +1.00. A negative number indicates an inverse relation. For example, in a recent experiment a student found that children relatively high in ability to adopt the social perspective of other people were relatively low in impulsive behavior. A positive number indicates a positive relation. A frequent finding, for example, is that children with relatively high IQ scores are also relatively rapid learners. The higher the coefficient

(whether positive or negative), the stronger the association between the variables. A coefficient of zero indicates that there is no relation between the variables.

A correlation alone cannot be used to prove that one event causes another. We can't argue, for example, that because height and weight are positively correlated we grow tall because we gain weight (or vice versa). It is always possible that some unnoticed third factor is the causal agent, linking these two events with one another. However, correlations are useful because they suggest likely places to look for causal connections. If a correlation of a particular kind and value is repeatedly found when two characteristics are measured, then this is strong reason to test out a causal hypothesis by conducting a formal experiment.

Other Methods
Often a technique can be employed that resembles the experiment in all important respects except one—the degree of prior control exercised over the independent variable. In such a pseudoexperiment, sometimes called **quasi-experiment,** we accept a practically imposed definition of the independent variable, acknowledging that it may be important and partially confounded with others. For example, we might study the impact of day-care center care versus home care on children's social development by studying a group of children selected from each type of setting. Since families themselves determine where their child will be assigned, we do not know what other factors may be involved that could be confused with the one of interest here; parental education, work experience, child-rearing philosophies, and other background characteristics could also be different in the two groups. Quasi-experiments are useful in getting information about social phenomena that create tricky problems for exercising tight experimental control.

Another technique, known as the **interview,** is to question individuals directly about some facet of their lives or behavior. An interview can be especially valuable if the goal is to obtain a lot of information about an individual in a short period of time. If a standard set of questions is available, the interviewer can compare one individual's responses with those of others. A limitation is that individuals of different ages and abilities have different verbal skills, which may obscure actual differences in what they know and believe.

A final technique to consider is **standardized testing.** A standardized test is an instrument that has been administered to hundreds or thousands of children and adults to establish performance levels used in comparisons. Performance levels are specified in percentiles, so that any individual's score can be stated as a numerical percentile in which the number indicates what percentage of the standardization group scored lower than the individual (e.g., thirty-third percentile, fifty-fifth, ninetieth, etc.). These scores can be used to compare individual children and adults with others their

own age, to match children and adults at the same level on a characteristic, or to assess an individual's progress. Among the standardized tests widely used with children and adults are those used to assess infant development (e.g., Bayley, Denver Developmental tests), intelligence (Stanford-Binet, WISC, WAIS), self concept (Piers-Harris), personality (MMPI), and a variety of school achievement measures (e.g., Iowa Tests of Basic Ability, California Achievement Tests, etc.).

Developmental Comparisons

Suppose you have identified a significant question about development you wish to answer. Suppose the inquiry is to focus on changes in how children between four and eight years of age learn. The first decision to make is which method will be employed to study the question, that is, an experiment, an observational study, an interview, etc. Once this has been decided, there is a second decision of equal importance: how will the age change be measured? What comparisons should be made to determine whether an age-related change occurs?

There are several alternatives from which to choose when you attempt to measure age changes in development: the *longitudinal method,* the *cross-sectional method,* and the *combined longitudinal, cross-sectional method.*

Longitudinal Method

Repeated testing of an individual or many individuals over a significant developmental span of time is referred to as the **longitudinal method.** In the example of a study to investigate changes in learning, the repeated

testing would occur over the four-year period as children grow from four to eight years of age. It would be up to the investigator to determine just how many tests would be performed during this interval and over what periods of time. You might test each child once a year at the same time each year, for example. The longitudinal method is valued because it permits the observer to watch change unfold in an individual child or adult.

If you wanted to observe the stability of specific characteristics such as attachment or aggression over an extended period of time, you could do it only by the longitudinal method. In actual practice, however, this method has many drawbacks and is often impractical. It is difficult, for one thing, to complete a study adequately over a long period of time—like the four years of our hypothetical example. Children will drop out of a study as a result of school and residence changes, testing personnel may change, and the cost of the study in time and money may be excessive. Repeated testing is also a problem. The child's performance may improve at test sessions because of familiarity with the test rather than because of increased maturity. The shorter the span of time to be covered and the fewer the number of test repetitions planned, the easier a longitudinal study becomes.

Cross-sectional Method

Longitudinal studies have been important in life-span development, but considerations of cost and efficiency have limited the number of large-scale, long-term longitudinal projects. By contrast, a greater number of

Box 1.3
Studying the Effects of "Sesame Street" on Children

The following hypothetical example illustrates the value of the combined longitudinal, cross-sectional method. Suppose it is believed that children's prereading skills improve as children advance from three to five years of age. One of the indicators of this improvement is the number of letters of the alphabet that can be identified on sight. A study was conducted to test this idea. In 1968, three groups of children were tested: three-year-olds, four-year-olds, and five-year-olds. Each group was referred to as a *cohort,* which we will call cohorts A, B, and C. Individual children were presented with flash cards to see how many letters of the alphabet they could identify.

The results showed an apparent increase in letter identification with age. Children in the respective groups correctly identified an average of five, twelve, and nineteen letters. A longitudinal component was then added to the study, retesting cohort A (the original three-year-olds) in 1969 and 1970 and retesting cohort B (the original four-year-olds) in 1969. (The table illustrates the results.) Cohort A improved dramatically from 1968 to 1969—the children in this group advanced from five to twenty-four correct identifications. The children in cohort B also improved, advancing from twelve to twenty-four correct identifications. But notice what else happened. Cohort A, at four years of age, did as well as cohort B at five years of age. Both got twenty-four items correct. And both did better than cohort C, who at five years of age got only nineteen items correct. So although the original cross-sectional comparison (row 1—cohorts A, B, and C tested in 1968) yielded changes from ages three to four and from ages four to five, the longitudinal sequences did not. The changes for cohort A occurred between three and four years of age, but not between four and five years of age.

cross-sectional investigations have occurred. The **cross-sectional method** refers to a comparison in which groups of children or adults of different ages are studied at about the same time and age that changes are inferred from differences among the groups. In our hypothetical example, changes in learning can be studied by testing separate groups of four-, six-, and eight-year-olds. You might observe that most of the four-year-olds learn a problem best under one set of conditions, the six-year-olds under a second set, and the eight-year-olds under a third.

A cross-sectional study is valued because it permits the detection of a developmental change in a fairly short period of time. However, it has its drawbacks. For one, it is difficult to be sure that the group differences reflect individual change. For another, we don't know,

strictly speaking, that the difference in learning between the group of four-year-olds and the group of eight-year-olds is due to age. Maybe the eight-year-olds are different because they grew up under different circumstances, such as different educational environments, childrearing practices, and so forth.

The cross-sectional approach is valuable for obtaining answers to questions in which a quick, first estimate about some change is required and resources are limited. This condition often exists in research on how children learn and remember, attend and perceive, and interact with peers.

Combined Longitudinal, Cross-sectional Method
The cross-sectional comparison is suspect because it is not known whether apparent age changes of a group really reflect individual changes. The longitudinal

Test Date	Cohort A (Born: 1965)		Cohort B (Born: 1964)		Cohort C (Born: 1963)	
	Age	*Mean number of letters identified*	*Age*	*Mean number of letters identified*	*Age*	*Mean number of letters identified*
1968	3	5	4	12	5	19
1969	4	24	5	24		
1970	5	24				

For cohort B, change occurred between four and five years of age. And, the level of performance of the oldest children in the original cross-sectional comparison did not match the performance of the children retested in the longitudinal sequences.

What might account for these differences? It appears that something might have happened between 1968 and 1969 to produce a dramatic change in alphabet identification skills. Well, that was the first season of the popular children's television program, "Sesame Street." One of the major programming goals of "Sesame Street" is to teach young children to identify letters of the alphabet. The results of our hypothetical example seem to suggest that the producers of "Sesame Street" have accomplished their goal.

Obviously, our hypothetical example was a loaded one. Cohorts and test dates were chosen so that an apparent age change turned out not to be an age change at all, but the result of special educational experiences. But the phenomenon is real. For example, Hayne Reese (1974) observed cohort changes in young children's abilities to use mental imagery in a learning problem. The change occurred during 1969. Again, the nationwide broadcasting of "Sesame Street" may have been the cause. There are other documented cases of cohort effects. John Nesselroade and Paul Baltes (1974), for example, found changes in adolescent personality during the 1970 to 1972 period. As measured by several personality tests, adolescents became more extroverted and independent over this period of time. Although the causes of this change have not been precisely determined, the investigators speculate that an increase in student activism and a decline in respect for public and educational leadership noted during this period may have been responsible.

And, in one laboratory, cohort differences in the moral reasoning of adults drawn from different generations (those born in the 1920s, 1940s, and 1960s) have been uncovered (Yussen, Hiebert, & Enright, 1981). The effects seem to be linked to different amounts of exposure to formal education.

comparison also has another potential flaw—how can it be known whether change experienced by an individual over a period of time is due to a general age change? This individual change could as well be due to some unique experiences common to children or adults growing up at this particular time. For instance, children may have been exposed to an educational program on television or to a new curriculum in school. Would this age change be observed in another individual who was born at a different time and did not have this unique experience? The **combined longitudinal, cross-sectional method** allows us to see whether both techniques yield the same pattern of developmental change. It can also be seen whether special experiences occurring in one period of time, rather than through maturation and generalized experience, are accounting for longitudinal change. If the longitudinal and cross-sectional comparisons yield different patterns, the cause of the discrepancy can sometimes be identified. This is illustrated in box 1.3, "Studying the Effects of 'Sesame Street' on Children."

Now that you are familiar with the historical background, phases, nature, and methods of research of life-span developmental psychology, you are ready to read about the perspectives and theories that have been crafted to explain life-span development. The science of life-span developmental psychology not only includes methods of research but is characterized by a systematic body of theories that can be verified or proved false. These theories are described in the next chapter.

Summary

Historically, the last two centuries are significant in child development in that childhood has been understood for the first time as differentiated and unique; children are treated well; and philosophical debates have been replaced by scientific study. The point that change occurs throughout the life span and should be studied in a scientific manner is of more recent vintage. For many years, traditional views of human development stressed stability rather than change in adulthood. Increasingly, though, the field of developmental psychology is assuming a life-span orientation rather than focusing exclusively on children.

In the contemporary study of life-span development there still is by no means agreement on what the phases of the life cycle are and when they occur. In this text, the life cycle is divided into the following phases: infancy, early childhood, middle and late childhood, adolescence, young and middle adulthood, and late adulthood. Life-span development is defined as a pattern of movement or change that begins at conception and continues throughout the life cycle. The pattern of change involves growth (as in infancy) and decay (as in death). The pattern of movement is complex because it often involves different processes—maturation and experiences, for example. Five strands of development that are emphasized throughout the life cycle in this book are physical, cognitive, social, emotional, and personality development.

As a science, the study of life-span developmental psychology principally employs the methods of observation, experimentation, and correlation. In trying to identify age-related changes, three kinds of comparisons are used: the longitudinal method, the cross-sectional method, and the combined longitudinal, cross-sectional method.

Key Terms

adolescence
biological environment
cause and effect
cognitive development
cohort
cohort perspective
combined longitudinal, cross-sectional method
correlation
cross-sectional method
dependent variables
development
early adulthood
early childhood
ecological psychology
emotional development
experiences
experiment
independent variables
infancy
interview
late adulthood
late childhood
life cycle
lineage
lineage perspective
longitudinal method
maturation
middle adulthood
middle childhood
naturalistic observation
neonate
original sin
personality development
physical development
quasi-experiment
randomization
reliability
social development
social environment
standardized testing
tabula rasa
time samples

Review Questions

1. Describe some age-related themes in development. How sure are you that they are specific to a particular period of development?
2. Define what is meant by life-span development. Describe the nature of this development and its various strands.
3. Prior to the contemporary scientific era, how were children thought of and treated? How has this changed during the modern era?
4. Describe the historical background of life-span developmental psychology.
5. What are the basic methods for collecting information scientifically? Describe each and indicate when it is likely to be most useful.
6. How can we strike an age comparison? What are the advantages and disadvantages of each approach?

Further Readings

Achenbach, T. *Research in developmental psychology: concepts, strategies, methods.* New York: Free Press, 1978.
An easy-to-read introduction to how research is done in the field of development, with examples of different techniques and approaches.

Aries, P. *Centuries of childhood* (R. Baldick, trans.). New York: Knopf, 1962.
A fascinating, easy-to-read history of childrearing practices, beliefs about childhood, and the circumstances of children throughout history.

Brim, O. G., & Kagan, J. (eds.). *Constancy and change in human development.* Cambridge, Mass.: Harvard University Press, 1980.
This scholarly treatment of the issue of age-related change in development is written by a number of experts in the social and biological sciences. Reading level is medium to difficult.

Rand McNally atlas of the body and mind. Chicago: Rand McNally, 1976.
A beautifully illustrated, easy-to-read book that includes intelligently written sections on the evolution of humans and the life cycle.

Sears, R. R., & Feldman, S. S. (eds.). *The seven ages of man.* San Francisco: Kaufman, 1973.
An excellent, easy-to-read introduction to different phases of the life cycle written by a variety of authors.

2

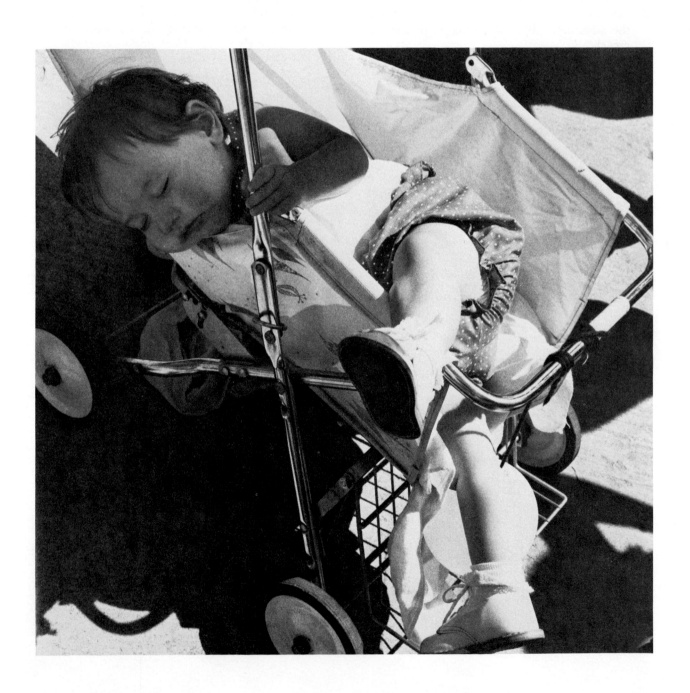

Theories and Perspectives

Prologue: Theories and Perspectives Reflected in the Comments of Youth

To introduce the six theories and perspectives on the nature of development, we have briefly described their main points and shown how they are reflected in the comments of young people.

Psychoanalytic theory stresses that emotions are at the core of development; in particular, the psychoanalytic theory of Sigmund Freud holds that these emotions are sexual in nature. The following comments of Gloria, age twelve, suggest that Freud was wise to think that sexual matters and emotions are important in development:

I could never enjoy a porno movie with my father. There was one movie I went to where there was sex in it, and my father was staring to see what's going on, thinking, "Oh, my god, I made a mistake with this movie." I mean I could hear him thinking it and, you know, he'd try to act like it wasn't happening. He'd turn around and say, "You don't like this, do you?" and he'd say, "Do you want some popcorn?" He was just trying to get me out of there. I mean, I knew what the hell was going on and I felt like going, "Daddy, I know what's going on, so don't worry about it."

I wish that my parents would talk to me about sex. I know it already, but I could act like I didn't. They're waiting too long, they're waiting too long. And that's why most kids, when they have sex, the parents go, "What? You don't know about sex." And the kids go, "Yes, I do." And they say, "How can you? I haven't told you." Parents think that if they don't tell you, you don't know. (Kavanaugh, 1978, pp. 147–48)

Jean Piaget was a famous psychologist who understood development from a **cognitive-structural perspective.** This view stresses that as children develop they change the way they see themselves and their world,

and that this change involves thinking processes. Consider the images and thoughts of Ann, age seventeen:

Women have been discriminated against long enough. I, for one, plan to do something about it. Next year when I go to college, I am going to work in campus groups that promote greater rights for women, and during the summer I am going to Washington to protest the fact that the Equal Rights Amendment has not passed the legislatures of enough states to be considered a law by the federal government.

The **behavioral social learning perspective** emphasizes that the actions of individuals are shaped through encounters with rewarding and punishing circumstances. The following comments of Jason, age sixteen, portray the importance of rewards and punishments in development:

If I don't flunk anything, my parents are happy. Last semester, when I got an A in one class, they gave me an extra ten dollars. If I do flunk a class, they really get on me. Two years ago, when I was in junior high school, my old man took me down in the basement, removed his belt, and left stripes on me. I felt a lot of hatred toward him for that—but I'll tell you this, I sure don't want to get beat like that again. . . . Sometimes my father gets out of hand, though, and punishes me for things I don't think he should. Like the other day, I accidentally drove the car over his chain saw. I couldn't help it. But, brother, did he get mad. He started yelling and cursing at me, and took the car away from me for two weeks. . . . He tells me that if I go to college he will buy me a new car. It's something worth thinking about.

Abraham Maslow was a well-known psychologist who helped develop the perspective in psychology known as **humanism.** Humanistic theorists believe that each individual has a unique core of being, or personality. Sometimes this being, or personality, is simply referred to by humanists as the self. The following comments of Robert, age eighteen, portray the importance of self-perceptions in development:

I think a lot about myself. "Who am I? Where am I going? Am I doing the right thing?" There are a lot of parts to me— I am a complex person. During the last few years I've been getting the feeling that I am not putting the pieces to myself together as neatly as they should be. There are so many things I don't like about myself. I am not very handsome—girls have told me so in so many words. And, I'm about ready to quit college—it's so boring. I just don't know what I am going to do with myself. I just feel like my life is falling apart, and I'm not going to be able to hold myself together. . . . As a last hope, two weeks ago I decided to go to see the school's counselor. She asked me to tell her about some of the things that were bothering me. She was a very nice person who genuinely listened to what I had to say. I felt very good about the hour with her. Maybe she can help me, but I just don't know.

The **ethological, evolutionary perspective** emphasizes the individual's biological heritage and adaptation to the environment. The following comments of Marty, age nineteen, suggest that we would be wise to not ignore this perspective:

I think a lot about why I am the way I am. While I don't have all of the answers, I know that my make-up is not entirely due to the way my parents have socialized me. Yet people tell me I'm a lot like my father and my mother's father. Some people also tell me I'm a lot like my Uncle Bob. He was a real character—quit school when he was fifteen, sired three children but never got married, and traveled around the world on a series of tankers. I even look a lot like him and my mother's father—brown eyes, curly hair, tall, muscular, and handsome, of course.

The **anthropological, sociological perspective** emphasizes that life-span development can be understood by analyzing the social structures of a society and the roles individuals adopt in a particular society. The importance of this perspective can be detected in the comments of Gretchen, age seventeen:

Money is very important to me, particularly since I don't have a whole lot of it right now. My parents never have been very well off financially and my parents did not go to college. There are a lot of different roles I fill now, and there are a lot I would like to try out that I have not yet experienced. I'm not doing too well in my role as a student, but I think I would do better as a wife.

Now that we have some preliminary ideas about theories of development, let's look at some of the formal requirements of these theories.

Introduction

A **scientific theory** is an organized and logical set of statements, laws, and axioms. One of its functions is to describe carefully some observable event. Suppose it is of interest to study how a mother's style of interaction with her child affects the child's style of interaction with other children. The best way to begin is with a theory that describes different styles of interaction. The theory provides a framework for defining the study.

Another function of a theory is to explain some observable event. Consider the example just given. Suppose it was observed that a mother punished and abused her child, who then responded in kind to peers. A common sense theory might explain this with the cliché, like mother, like child. This form of explanation is not very satisfying because it fails to indicate why children are like their mothers or how this likeness occurs. Answers to such questions as why and how children become what they are are part of a theory's explanatory function.

A third function of a theory is to predict observable events. Suppose the interactions of many groups of mothers and children were observed. Suppose further that three or four distinct styles of mother-child interaction were identified. A theory should predict how each group of children will behave with peers; this prediction should follow naturally from the network of statements, laws, and axioms that constitute the theory; and the prediction should be correct a large percentage of the time.

The value of a scientific theory lies in how well it fulfills each of these three functions. A good theory should be *complete* and *terse,* yet it is important for the theory to describe and explain as much as possible. A theory is not complete or terse if it must be changed to handle every new observation that is encountered. A good theory should also be *precise,* making specific predictions about what can be expected in different situations so that the theory can be clearly proved wrong. If a theory is to survive, the number of times its predictions are confirmed should greatly exceed the number of times its predictions are disconfirmed.

Developmental psychologists propose new theories and revise old ones as significant new observations appear. A good theory offers a formal and public statement about matters that may have been unclear or unknown previously. It is important to understand facts in formal, logical ways, and since there is probably no such thing as an isolated fact—all facts have prior assumptions, whether we are conscious of them or not—a good theory helps us to understand the formal assumptions that underlie these facts.

In their concern for explaining age-related sequential themes of development, psychologists have debated whether it is appropriate to describe different phases of development as **stages.** For example, does the child's biological, cognitive, and social functioning undergo dramatic transformation at the onset of adolescence and does something similar occur between adolescence and young adulthood? Or, by contrast, is the child's progress void of abrupt transition. In this chapter we look at four psychological perspectives of life-span development and two from outside of psychology. The first two perspectives described—psychoanalytic and cognitive-structural—argue for the existence of stages in development. The next two perspectives presented—behavioral social learning, and humanistic—are nonstage theories. Age-related themes of development are not to be found in the behavioral and humanistic views, rather development over the life cycle is seen as continuous and void of any abrupt transitions. While the final perspectives discussed—ethological, evolutionary and anthropological, sociological—are from outside the discipline of psychology, they have strongly influenced our views of life-span development.

As you read about the different perspectives on development, you will detect that most of the perspectives do not deal in very precise ways with change in the adult years. Theoretical development that focuses on changes over the entire life cycle is still in an embryonic stage. Two perspectives described in this chapter, however, are noteworthy because of their emphasis on possible changes throughout the life cycle—Erik Erikson's psychoanalytic theory and Bernice Neugarten's sociological theory. In the later chapters of this text, you will read about a number of perspectives that focus on changes in adulthood.

Stage Theories

The two dominant stage theories in developmental psychology are the psychoanalytic and cognitive-structural perspectives. This section reveals the psychoanalytic views of Sigmund Freud and Erik Erikson and the cognitive-structural approach of Jean Piaget.

The Psychoanalytic Perspective

The *psychoanalytic perspective* refers to the set of assumptions shared by Sigmund Freud and many followers of his psychoanalytic theory of development (Erikson, 1968; Freud, 1949; Horney, 1950). Among the contemporary psychologists whose works draw heavily upon Freud's ideas and assumptions is Erik Erikson. There are many others whose basic framework is psychoanalytic, but Freud and Erikson have had the greatest impact on the contemporary science of developmental psychology.

Sigmund Freud

The psychoanalytic theory of Freud stresses the biological forces that shape human destiny, one of which is **instinct**. Freud believed that the human infant is born with a collection of unconscious instinctive drives that supply energy and direction for behavior. All of development may be seen as the result of changes in the way instinctual energy is channeled and organized. Instinctual energy often changes direction and intensity to maintain a balance in the child. Even when balance is reached, however, instinctual energy continues to fluctuate. Thus, instinctual energy is dynamically organized—it is not static, but always changing.

Freud's theory is a structural one. It claims that the life of an individual can be divided into three different structures, or parts—the *id,* the *ego,* and the *superego.* The ego and the superego grow out of the id as the infant develops. As the different structures develop, the organization of instinctual energy shifts from a loose and uninhibited state to a structured and controlled one.

At birth the infant is dominated by instinctual impulses, the **id.** These impulses operate unconsciously and irrationally. The infant has both physical needs, such as hunger, and psychological needs, such as sensory stimulation. The instincts continually force the infant to find an object that will satisfy these needs as rapidly as possible. Since the infant is primitive in the way he or she perceives and thinks, he or she cannot evaluate between similar objects to satisfy a need. Thus an image of a bottle and an actual bottle of milk are both objects that the infant may actively seek out to satisfy thirst. This search for any object to satisfy a need, without regard for its reality or need-reducing value, is referred to as the **pleasure principle,** or primary process thinking.

The infant gradually learns to distinguish between objects that are truly satisfying and those that only appear to be satisfying. This learning constitutes the beginning of the development of the **ego.** The ego consists of rational thoughts, perceptions, and plans to help cope with reality. Much of its functioning is conscious and rational, and it attempts to channel instinctual energy toward objects that will realistically satisfy needs. This orientation toward reality and need-reducing value is referred to as the **reality principle,** or secondary process thinking.

The final mental system to develop is the **superego,** which consists of moral rules to guide the child's actions. The rules are internalized directives that develop from the various dos and don'ts the child learns while growing up.

All three mental systems, when fully developed, press for their demands to be met simultaneously. The id perpetually seeks to discharge instinctual energy immediately, the ego seeks to hold off acting until a realistic course of action can be found, and the superego

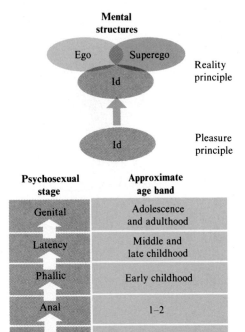

Figure 2.1 Development of mental structures and stages of personality, according to Freud.

continually directs the child to act in a good way or to refrain from acting in a bad way.

As the three mental systems evolve, the child experiences five clearly distinguishable developmental stages. Each one can be defined in terms of an overriding problem that guides the child's actions, thoughts, and feelings. The first three are closely tied to the satisfaction that is felt as the child stimulates or exercises particular parts of the body, the so-called **erogenous zones.** (See figure 2.1 for a representation of the mental structures and stages of personality from Freud's perspective.)

The first stage, known as the **oral stage,** centers on the child's pleasure from stimulation of the oral area—mouth, lips, tongue, gums. This stage lasts from birth to around one year. The activities of sucking, chewing, and biting provide the chief sources of pleasure. When the oral area is stimulated some instinctual energy is freed and tension is reduced.

The period called the **anal stage,** lasting from two to three years of age, centers on the child's pleasure with eliminative activity. The shift to the anal stage is brought about by maturation of the sphincter muscles and the child's ability to hold back or expel waste material at will. It is assumed that exercise of the anal muscles results in the freeing of instinctual energy and

The Oedipus complex
emerges during the phallic
stage.

The Oedipus complex emerges during the phallic stage.

the reduction of tension. This period is not easily forgotten by parents, who typically experience great concern over their initially unsuccessful efforts to toilet train their child. When toilet training has been accomplished, the anal stage has reached its peak—the child has achieved well-regulated control over anal activity. Many debates have arisen about the proper method and time for toilet training (e.g., Anthony, 1957), however, few of the premises offered have much to do with the specific theoretical claims of Freud (e.g., Beloff, 1962).

During the **phallic stage,** which lasts from about four to five or six years of age, instinctual energy is focused on the genital area. Physical changes in the child cause this area to be a pleasurable one when stimulated. It is during this period, Freud thought, that boys and girls become acutely aware of their sexual anatomy and the anatomical differences between sexes. This awareness sets up a number of complex psychological events referred to as the **Oedipus complex** in boys and the **Electra complex** in girls. Each complex consists of the child's alternating feelings of love and hate for each parent as the child competes with one parent for the love and attention of the other parent. Working through these complexes, which are actually highly stressful conflicts about sexual affiliation and identity, takes from eight to ten years and forms the basis for the mature adult's personal and sexual identity.

The troublesome feelings and thoughts experienced while attempting to work out these conflicts are often repressed, driven from consciousness and locked away in the unconscious id. This repression marks the onset of the **latency stage,** the long period of middle childhood from about six to twelve years of age. During the latency stage the child concentrates on exploring the environment and mastering the vast number of intellectual skills and tricks needed for getting along in society. This activity channels much of the child's psychological energy into "emotionally safe" areas that help the child forget the highly stressful problems of the previous stage.

The **genital stage,** the last of Freud's stages of development, occurs from about thirteen to nineteen years of age. During this period the repression of Oedipal and Electra conflicts is lifted and teenagers experience a sudden surge of interest in sexual matters. After a number of groping attempts, the adolescent forms a stable sense of personal and sexual identity. The period is brought on by, among other things, the rapid physiological changes occurring in the adolescent at about twelve or thirteen years of age.

Several processes and mechanisms in Freud's theory, when taken collectively, help to explain developmental changes in behavior. In addition to those already mentioned is **tension reduction.** Freud believed that the goal of all activity is the reduction of tension, the release of pent-up psychological energy in some sphere. Tension reduction is inherently pleasurable and is the principal motivating force behind all behavior. Tension can arise from physical growth, preoccupation with an erogenous zone, conflict between id, ego, and superego, or the environment.

Another mechanism for change is **identification.** Freud used this term to refer to several different phenomena, the most important of which is the incorporation of behavior and attitudes of another person into one's own structure of thought and action. Many different people serve as figures for identification as the child develops—peers, siblings, teachers, television heroes—and the child tries many on for size to suit different needs at different times. The most important figures, however, are parents, with whom most children form a stable identification by the time they are in their mid-teens. In general, the process of identification allows the child to take on similarity with an individual who seems powerful or who possesses other desirable characteristics.

When the child is overwhelmed by anxiety, the ego can reduce the anxiety in a number of ways. Among these ways are the so-called **defense mechanisms.** Defense mechanisms work unconsciously, that is, the child is not aware of them. They also tend to distort the child's perception of his or her own feelings, thoughts, and sensations. Several of the more prominent defense mechanisms are *repression, projection, reaction formation, fixation,* and *regression.* **Repression** has already been discussed in one specific context (the Oedipal conflict), however, it is actually quite general and can be defined as an anxiety-provoking thought or feeling being forced out of consciousness into the unconscious. With **projection,** an anxiety-provoking thought or feeling is shifted from its actual source (the child) to an external object or person. The child comes to believe that someone else has the troublesome feeling or thought, with the result that the anxiety becomes externally rooted and is thereby easier to deal with. **Reaction formation** is a defense that consists in changing a troublesome thought or feeling into its opposite. This defense alters the conscious source of anxiety but does not remove it from the unconscious.

Finally, there are the related defenses of **fixation** and **regression.** As the child moves from one stage to the next, there are times when movement is difficult. The difficulty may stem from the child's extraordinary satisfaction with the way he or she is satisfying excess tension. (For example, in the oral stage the child may really enjoy sucking a bottle.) Or the difficulty may stem from a reluctance to try out new ways. Whatever the reason, the child may become temporarily stuck, or *fixated,* in this stage. Regression refers to a backsliding in development. If a child experiences undue anxiety in a particular stage, he or she may temporarily shift back to an earlier one that provided a great deal of pleasure. It is not uncommon, for example, to see four- or five-year-olds emulate infants by crawling on the ground and using infantile speech to draw attention from a parent in a frustrating situation. Some occurrence of fixation and regression is a normal part of development. These defense mechanisms become abnormal when they occur frequently or persist for long periods of time.

Few psychologists today accept all of Freud's major theoretical concepts. Freud's belief that virtually all behavior is motivated by unconscious desires seems overdrawn; for example, many of the things that bother people and motivate their behavior are quite well known to them. Freud's belief that the major impetus for development lies in the resolution of psychosexual conflicts also seems a bit overdrawn; children's affections for each parent do grow hot and cold, but such fluctuations are not limited to any one period of time. And children do show plenty of interest in sexual matters during the so-called latency period.

How then should the concepts in Freud's theory be viewed? Each should be considered for the broad insight it provides and not for its literal accuracy. Certainly there is an unconscious level of functioning; people do many things without being aware of them. And certainly children learn sexual taboos that contribute to the formation of a sexual identity.

What caused Freud to develop such a theory? One possible cause is the tendency of most individuals to reflect on their own life experiences and try to impart some meaning to them. To obtain a glimpse of Freud's childhood and youth, look at box 2.1 and read an account by biographer Ernest Jones. Think about how such experiences in Freud's life might have led him to develop his psychosexual stage theory of development.

Erik Erikson

One serious misgiving of contemporary psychoanalytic thinkers arises from the fact that Freud shortchanged the importance of culture. He failed to see that each society handles children in very different ways. As a result, the stages of development only loosely describe the pattern of change for all children. That culture exerts a strong influence on the timing and dynamics of each stage is a theme reflected in the work of Erik Erikson, a German psychologist born in 1902.

Erikson accepts the basic outline of Freud's theory, however, he places more emphasis on the influence of culture and society as a shaper of the child's destiny. Much of his own professional work was with children and families in different cultures, which reflects his anthropological approach to the study of individual development. Erikson's theory is particularly important because it stresses rational, or *ego,* processes, and because it casts a life-span frame of reference on development.

Erikson postulates eight stages of development—sometimes called the **Eight Ages of Man.** Each one centers around a salient and distinct emotional concern stemming from biological pressures from within a sociocultural expectations from outside the person. These concerns, or conflicts, may be resolved in a positive and healthy manner or in a pessimistic and unhealthy way.

The Childhood and Youth of Sigmund Freud

Sigmund Freud was born in 1856 in Freiberg, Moravia, and died in London in 1939. Except for the first three years of his life in Moravia and his last year in London, Freud lived for all of his life in Vienna, Austria. His father, Jacob Freud, was a reasonably poor wool merchant, and his mother was Jacob Freud's second wife. Sigmund had seven siblings, all younger than he. The Freud family was Jewish.

Freud attributed his self-confidence to the love his young mother had for him: "A man who has been the indisputable favorite of his mother keeps for life the feeling of a conqueror, that confidence of success that often induces real success" (Puner, 1949). In contrast, his father's severe reprimands for events such as wetting the bed when he was two years of age probably influenced the role of denial, restraint, restriction, and authority Freud later attributed to fathers.

Freud apparently was a well-behaved child who rarely was unruly. He spent much of his time reading and studying when he was young. While his mother's favoritism likely promoted a sense of confidence and ambition in young Sigmund, for most of his adolescence the direction of this ambition remained uncertain. During his teenage years, Freud's room was filled with overflowing bookcases. The young Freud often substituted a snack in his room for an evening meal at the dinner table so he would not lose time from his studies.

Sports and athletics were not very popular in central Europe at that time, so young Sigmund's main exercise consisted of walking, and sometimes of hiking in the mountains. During his days as a student, Freud once remarked that going for walks alone was his greatest pleasure. At the age of seventeen he was graduated *magna cum laude* from the gymnasium (European high school).

What were Sigmund Freud's sexual interests during adolescence? It appears that he repressed many of his sexual desires while busily purusing intellectual matters.

Source: Jones, 1953, pp. 25–26.

Freud at sixteen with his mother.

Each conflict has a unique time period during which it ascends and overshadows all the others. In order for later stages of development to proceed smoothly, each earlier stage conflict must be resolved satisfactorily. These stages of development are represented in figure 2.2. In the left-hand column are the major phases of life-span development. The eight conflicts are listed diagonally, in order of their ascendancy.

Erik Erikson.

Phases of the life cycle	1	2	3	4	5	6	7	8
Late adulthood								Ego integrity vs. despair
Middle adulthood							Generativity vs. stagnation	
Young adulthood						Intimacy vs. isolation		
Adolescence					Identity vs. role confusion			
Middle and late childhood				Industry vs. inferiority				
Early childhood			Initiative vs. guilt					
Infancy		Autonomy vs. shame, doubt						
	Basic trust vs. mistrust							

Figure 2.2 Erikson's stages of development.

The first stage, **trust versus mistrust,** corresponds to the oral stage in Freudian theory. An infant is almost entirely dependent upon his or her mother for food, sustenance, and comfort. The mother is the primary representative of society to the child. If she discharges her infant-related duties with warmth, regularity, and affection, the infant will develop a feeling of trust toward the world. The infant's trust is a comfortable feeling that someone will always be around to care for his or her needs even though the mother occasionally disappears. Alternatively, a sense of mistrust or fearful uncertainty can develop if the mother fails to provide these needs in the caretaking setting. According to Erikson, she is setting up a distrusting attitude that will follow the child through life.

Autonomy versus shame and doubt is the second stage and corresponds to the anal stage in Freudian theory. The infant begins to gain control over the bowels and bladder. Parents begin imposing demands on the child to conform to socially acceptable forms and occasions for eliminating wastes. The child may develop the healthy attitude of being capable of independent or autonomous control of his or her own actions, or may develop the unhealthy attitude of shame or doubt because he or she is incapable of control.

Initiative versus guilt corresponds to the phallic period in Freudian theory. The child is caught in the midst of the Oedipal or Electra conflict, with its alternating love-hate feelings for the parent of the opposite sex and with fear of fulfilling the sexual fantasies that abound. The child may discover ways to overcome feelings of powerlessness by engaging in various activities. If this is done, then the basic healthy attitude of being the initiator of action will result. Alternatively, the child may fail to discover such outlets and feel guilt at being dominated by the environment.

Industry versus inferiority, coinciding with the Freudian period of latency, covers the years of middle childhood when the child is involved in expansive absorption of knowledge and the development of intellectual and physical skills. As the child is drawn into the social culture of peers, it is natural to evaluate accomplishments by comparing himself or herself with others. If the child views himself or herself as basically competent in these activities, feelings of productiveness and industriousness will result. On the other hand, if the child views himself or herself as incompetent, particularly in comparison with peers, then he or she will feel unproductive and inferior. This unhealthy attitude may negatively color the child's whole approach to life and learning, producing a tendency to withdraw from new and challenging situations rather than meet them with confidence and enthusiasm.

Identity versus role confusion is roughly associated with Freud's genital stage, centering on the establishment of a stable personal identity. Whereas for Freud the important part of identity formation resides in the adolescent's resolution of sexual conflicts, for Erikson the central ingredient is the establishment of a clear path toward a vocation—selection of a job or an occupational role to aspire to. This allows the adolescent an objective that he or she and other members of society simultaneously acknowledge. If the adolescent

comes through this period with a clearly selected role and the knowledge that others in society can clearly identify this role, feelings of confidence and purposefulness emerge. If not, the child may feel confused and troubled.

Erikson introduced the first of the post-Freudian stages, **intimacy versus isolation.** Early adulthood brings with it a job and the opportunity to form an intimate relationship with a member of the opposite sex. If the young adult forms friendships with others and a significant, intimate relationship with one individual in particular, then a basic feeling of closeness with others will result. A feeling of isolation may result from an inability to form friendships and an intimate relationship.

A chief concern of adults is to assist the younger generation in developing and leading useful lives. **Generativity versus stagnation** centers on successful rearing of children. Childless adults often need to find substitute young people through adoption, guardianship, or a close relationship with the children of friends and relatives. Generativity, or the feeling of helping to shape the next generation, is the positive outcome that may emerge. Stagnation, or the feeling of having done nothing for the next generation, is the unhealthy outcome.

In the later years we enter the period of **ego integrity versus despair,** a time for looking back at what we have done with our lives. Through many different routes, the older person may have developed a positive outlook in each of the preceding periods of emotional

In the later years we enter the period of ego integrity versus despair, a time for looking back at what we have done with our lives.

crises. If so, the retrospective glances will reveal a picture of life well spent, and the person will be satisfied (ego integrity). However, the older person may have resolved one or more of the crises in a negative way. If so, the retrospective glances will yield doubt, gloom, and despair over the worth of one's life.

It should be noted that Erikson does not believe the proper solution to a stage crisis is always completely positive in nature. Some exposure and/or commitment to the negative end of the individual's bipolar conflict often is inevitable (for example, the individual cannot trust all people under all circumstances and survive). However, in a healthy solution to a stage crisis, the positive resolution of the conflict is dominant.

Psychoanalytic theorists stress that individuals go through a number of different stages in their life cycle, and that these stages occur in a fixed sequence. They also believe that mental structures are an important

Jean Piaget was born August 9, 1896, in Neuchâtel, Switzerland. Jean's father was an intellectual who taught young Jean to think systematically. Jean's mother also was very bright and strongly religious as well. His father seemed to maintain an air of detachment from his mother, who has been described by Piaget as prone to frequent outbursts of neurotic behavior.

In his autobiography, Piaget (1952) detailed why he chose to pursue the study of cognitive development rather than emotional development.

> I started to forego playing for serious work very early. Indeed, I have always detested any departure from reality, an attitude which I relate to . . . my mother's poor mental health. It was this disturbing factor which at the beginning of my studies in psychology made me keenly interested in psychoanalytic and pathological psychology. Though this interest helped me to achieve independence and to widen my cultural background, I have never since felt any desire to involve myself deeper in that particular direction, always much preferring the study of normalcy and of the workings of the intellect to that of the tricks of the unconscious. (p. 238)

An amazing thing happened when Jean was only ten years old. He wrote an article about the rare albino sparrow, which was published in the *Journal of the Natural History of Neuchâtel*. The article was so brilliant that the curators of the Geneva Museum of Natural History, who had no idea that the article had been written by a ten-year-old, offered the preadolescent Piaget a job as curator of the museum. The heads of the museum quickly withdrew their offer when they discovered Piaget's age.

Piaget's interest in zoology continued through his adolescent years and culminated in his doctoral dissertation on the behavior of mollusks in 1918 at the University of Neuchâtel. During his adolescence, though, Piaget was not just interested in zoology. Philosophy and psychology books filled his room, and he spent much of his spare time reading Kant, Durkheim, and James (philosopher, sociologist, and psychologist, respectively).

While his studies had taken him in the direction of biology and other intellectual pursuits, the deteriorating health of Piaget's mother had an important impact on his first job after he completed his doctorate degree. In 1918, Piaget took a position at Bleuler's psychiatric clinic in Zurich, where he learned about clinical techniques for interviewing children. Then, still at the young age of twenty-two, he went to work in the psychology laboratory at the University of Zurich, where he was exposed to the insights of Alfred Binet, who developed the first intelligence test. By the time Piaget was twenty-five, his experience in varied disciplines had helped him see important links between philosophy, psychology, and biology.

part of development. From this perspective, psychoanalytic theory is no different than the next theory described, *cognitive-structural*. But the two theories differ radically in that cognitive-structural theory gives little or no attention to subconscious thought processes.

The Cognitive-Structural Perspective

The *cognitive-structural perspective* focuses on rational thinking processes in the child. In the psychoanalytic perspective, there is an interest in qualitative stages of change in children. These stages are seen as ordered in a uniform sequence for all children. The term cognitive in the cognitive-structural perspective underscores the interest in thought and rational mental process. The term *structural* highlights the concern with the way thought is organized at different stages. The leading contemporary figure who holds this point of view is Jean Piaget. (For a look at Piaget's youth see box 2.2.) Others include Lawrence Kohlberg, who has worked out an interesting theory of moral development that will be described in detail later in the text.

Jean Piaget

Piaget's ideas form one of the few complete theoretical statements about intelligence available in psychology. In common with others, Piaget believed that the core of intelligence was rationality—logical thinking—and that intelligence developed from the interplay of several hereditary and environmental forces. But there are many differences between Piaget's theory and other views of intelligence, particularly those with a psychometric (measurement) orientation. For one, Piaget was concerned with how children think rather than with what they thought or how many facts they knew. For

Jean Piaget.

example, it was important to Piaget whether a child could order the primary colors from lightest to darkest but quite unimportant whether the child knew the name of each color or could spell the names correctly. As a result, Piaget rarely looked at the content of thought but rather at its form.

For another, Piaget was interested in the general nature of children's thought rather than in how children at the same stage of thought differed. Finally, Piaget had a tendency to examine the ideal form of a child's thought, that is, the way the child could reason, given no distractions, good concentration, and high motivation. Ordinary reasoning exercised in everyday situations often fails to reflect a child's ideal potential. With most standard intelligence tests, by contrast, psychologists study the content of thought, individual differences in intelligence, and everyday thought.

A brief outline of Piaget's stages of thought follows. As is the case with all such theories, the time periods designated for various stages are only approximate. An individual child may move out of a stage sooner or remain in a stage longer than is indicated by the ages given. The more significant claim is that a child moves through the given stages in the established sequence and that no children violate this sequence.

The **sensorimotor stage** lasts from birth to about two years of age, corresponding to the period known as infancy. During this time the infant develops the ability to organize and coordinate sensations and perceptions with physical movements and actions. This coordination of sensation with action is the source of the term sensorimotor. The stage begins with the newborn, who has little more than reflexes to coordinate his or her senses with actions. The newborn sucks, turns his or her head, follows moving objects with his or her eyes, and performs other simple reflexes. The stage ends with the two-year-old, who has complex sensoriaction patterns and is beginning to operate with a primitive symbol system. For example, the two-year-old can imagine looking at a toy and manipulating it with his or her hands before actually doing so. The child can also use simple sentences—for example, "Mommy, jump!"—to represent a sensoriaction event that has just occurred.

The **preoperational stage** lasts from two to seven years of age, cutting across the preschool and early middle school years. During this time the child's symbolic system expands. The use of language and perceptual images moves well beyond the capabilities at the end of the sensorimotor period. Despite these advances, however, a number of limitations cause the child's thought to fall far short of what is seen in the later middle school years. Piaget perceives these limitations as "flaws" in the soon-to-develop "operational" structure of thought. Among the major flaws are the child's egocentrism, an inability to conserve, and a failure to order objects in a series and classify them. The child tends to see things from his or her own perspective and to confuse this perspective with that of others. He or she has difficulty manipulating the images and representations of events and is therefore likely to get stuck (centered) in static states and fail to reverse situations mentally. For example, if liquid is poured from a short, fat container into a tall, thin one, the child may notice only that the height of the water has changed (centering). If asked to imagine what would happen if the water were returned to the original container, the child would have a tough time visualizing the reversal (irreversibility).

The **concrete operational stage** lasts from seven to eleven years of age, cutting across the major portion of the middle school years. During this time the child's thinking crystallizes into more of a system, and the flaws of the preoperational stage completely disappear. The shift to a more perfect system of thinking is brought about by several changes. One of these is the shift from egocentrism to relativism. Relativism is the ability to think from different perspectives and to think simultaneously about two or more aspects of a problem. Another change is the child's ability to pose and operate on a series of actions mentally. Performing mental arithmetic, imagining a game of table tennis, and thinking about how to tie a knot are all examples of this change. Children in the sensorimotor and preoperational stages, by contrast, are unable to perform these mental operations.

One limitation of concrete thinking is that the child has to rely on concrete events in order to think in this way. The child needs to be able to perceive objects and events that he or she will think about. An interesting shortcoming of the child in this period is that he or she often fails to distinguish between representations of events and the events themselves, because the representations are closely tied to the concrete events. For example, a child may maintain a hypothesis about what a friend can be expected to do in a certain situation (e.g., Karen fights with people when she is angry) even if the friend seldom does what the child expects. The child treats the hypothesis as a fact rather than as the possibility of a fact.

The sensorimotor stage lasts from birth to about two years of age.

The concrete operational stage lasts from seven to eleven years of age.

The preoperational stage lasts from two to seven years of age.

The formal operational stage emerges between eleven and fourteen years of age.

The last stage of development is the **formal operational stage,** which emerges between eleven and fourteen years of age. By the time adolescence is reached, Piaget presumed that the child has reached this most advanced level of thinking. The most important single feature of this stage is the adolescent's ability to move beyond the world of actual, concrete experiences. He or she can think logically, using abstract propositions (e.g., suppose one country has as much democracy as another does tyranny; further suppose a third country. . .). He or she also can use make-believe events or statements that are contrary to reality (e.g., suppose you are looking at your hand, and it is invisible. What do you see in front of you?). Finally, the adolescent is able to conjure up many hypotheses to account for some

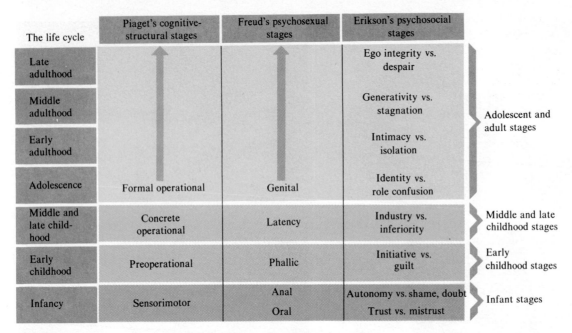

The life cycle	Piaget's cognitive-structural stages	Freud's psychosexual stages	Erikson's psychosocial stages	
Late adulthood			Ego integrity vs. despair	
Middle adulthood			Generativity vs. stagnation	Adolescent and adult stages
Early adulthood			Intimacy vs. isolation	
Adolescence	Formal operational	Genital	Identity vs. role confusion	
Middle and late childhood	Concrete operational	Latency	Industry vs. inferiority	Middle and late childhood stages
Early childhood	Preoperational	Phallic	Initiative vs. guilt	Early childhood stages
Infancy	Sensorimotor	Anal / Oral	Autonomy vs. shame, doubt / Trust vs. mistrust	Infant stages

Figure 2.3   Piaget's stages compared with Freud's and Erikson's stages.

event and then test these out in a deductive fashion, just as a scientist might. In figure 2.3 the Piagetian cognitive-structural stages are compared with the Freudian psychosexual and Eriksonian psychosocial stages. Note how both Piaget and Freud only presented one stage for adolescence and adulthood, while Erikson developed four.

Piaget used several interrelated processes to illustrate how change occurs in children's thought. Three are discussed here: adaptation, organization, and equilibration. If children are to develop normally, they have to interact effectively with the environment. Effective interaction is called **adaptation.** For Piaget the interaction is a cognitive one. It involves the child's use of sensorimotor, preoperational, or operational thinking skills. Adaptation is subdivided into **assimilation** and **accommodation,** which usually occur together. In assimilation, the child tries to incorporate features of the environment into already existing ways of thinking about them. In accommodation, the child tries to incorporate new features of the environment into thinking by slightly modifying existing modes of thought. An example may help to clarify these terms.

A young girl is presented with a hammer and nails to use in hanging a picture on her bedroom wall. She has never used a hammer before. From experience and observation, however, she realizes that a hammer is an object to be held, that it is swung by the handle to strike the nail, and that it is swung repeatedly. Realizing each of these things, she incorporates her behavior into a

conceptual framework that already exists (assimilation). But the hammer is heavy, so she must hold it near the top. As she swings too hard, the nail bends, so she must adjust the pressure of her taps. These adjustments show her sensitivity to the need to alter the concept slightly (accommodation).

A second mechanism of change is **organization.** Every level of thought, from sensorimotor to formal, is organized in some fashion. Continual refinement of this organization is an inherent part of development. The girl who has only a vague idea about how to use a hammer may also have a vague idea about how to use other tools. After learning how to use each one, she must interrelate these uses and organize her knowledge if she is to become skilled in using tools. In the same way, the child continually integrates and coordinates the many other branches of knowledge that often develop independently. Organization occurs within stages of development as well as across them.

Equilibration explains how a child shifts from one stage to the next. The goal of better organization is to reach a more lasting state of balance in thought. This goal is achieved as thought becomes more logical and abstract. But before a new stage of thought can be reached, the child must face the inadequacy of the current one. He or she must experience cognitive conflict, or uncertainty. If a child believes that the amount of liquid is changed simply because it was poured into a container with a different shape, he or she might be puzzled by such issues as where the extra liquid came from and whether there is actually more liquid to drink.

These puzzles will eventually be resolved as thought becomes concrete. In the everyday world the child is constantly faced with such counterexamples and inconsistencies.

Piaget's theory has guided European and North American scholars for over thirty years. It has offered a rich description of thought processes in children, a large number of hunches and hypotheses about how development takes place, and some dramatic claims about the structure of thought. As we move through the 1980s Piaget's influence will continue to remain strong. As John Flavell (1980) put it in a brief eulogy on Piaget's death in 1980, "We owe him nothing short of the whole field of cognitive development."

However, there are already signs that Piaget's style of theorizing has given way to a more modest approach, sometimes referred to as the information processing paradigm (e.g., Siegler, 1978; Flavell, 1980). The new wave of scholars remain skeptical about the validity of tightly knit stages of thought. As they persue the research evidence, it seems to them that children's thinking is more influenced by the specific form in which a problem is presented than in some monolithic stage capacities. And in place of Piaget's loose concepts about change (i.e., adaptation and organization), they offer mathematically precise processes that account for change, such as computer algorithms, models of attention and memory, and specification of concrete strategies. Significant advances have been made in understanding how children think in "real time" with this new approach, but the lasting contribution of Piaget's work is that he gave us a picture of where to look and some important phenomena to look at.

Nonstage Theories

The behavioral, social learning perspective and the humanistic perspective stress that human development is void of abrupt transitions. While the two perspectives share the belief that development does not occur in discrete phases, you will discover that they disagree about a number of other aspects of development.

The Behavioral Social Learning Perspective

Behaviorists and social learning theorists believe that overt, directly observable behavior is more important in understanding development than the covert feelings studied by psychoanalytic theorists or the private thoughts investigated by cognitive-structural theorists. Social learning theorists also emphasize the importance of environmental influences; they believe that the greatest changes in development come about through social experiences. Such changes in behavior are regulated by three basic laws and principles: reinforcement, punishment, and imitation, or modeling. These basic principles apply to all people in all cultures.

B. F. Skinner.

Two major variations of the behavioral social learning perspective will be discussed in this chapter: the stimulus-response, behaviorist approach of B. F. Skinner, and the cognitive social learning theory of Albert Bandura.

The Stimulus-Response Theory of B. F. Skinner

Few theories of human development have created as much controversy as the one proposed by B. F. Skinner. While much of his research work has involved rats and pigeons, Skinner has made numerous applications of his views to human development, as well (see, for example, *Walden Two*, 1948; and *About Behaviorism*, 1974). The book that has created the greatest controversy in recent years, however, is *Beyond Freedom and Dignity* (1971). The main theme of this book is that individuals are controlled by their external environments. Skinner argues that we are ruled and regulated by the consequences of our actions. He designs a futuristic culture that fosters individual dignity.

Skinner believes that if we are to understand the nature of development, we must examine the behavior—not the thoughts and feelings—of individuals. He believes that looking for internal determinants inhibits the search for the true determinants of behavior, which reside in the external environment. Some psychologists would argue that Skinner is saying that individuals are empty organisms, however, Skinner (1953) has stated that he objects to looking for internal determinants of behavior not because they do not exist, but because they are irrelevant to the relationships between **stimuli** and responses. (Stimuli may be defined as the observable characteristics of the environment that affect the individual and responses as the overt behaviors of the individual. A simple example: a child's mother tells her to clean her room [stimulus] and the child actually does clean the room [response].)

According to Skinner, one of the major ways stimuli and responses are linked together is through the principle of **operant conditioning** (sometimes referred to as **instrumental conditioning**). In this type of learning, the individual operates on the environment; that is, the individual does something, and, in turn, something happens to him or her. Another way of saying this is that the individual's behavior is instrumental in causing some effect in the environment. The lives of individuals are full of operant conditioning situations. For example, consider the following conversation:

John Hey, where did you get that new notebook?

Bob My mother bought it for me.

John Oh, yeah? Why?

Bob Because I got mad about something and started yelling at her.

John You mean if you get mad and throw a fit, your mom buys you a notebook?

Bob I guess that's the way it works!

At the heart of such occurrences is the principle, Behavior is determined by its consequences. According to this principle, behavior followed by a positive stimulus is likely to recur, while behavior followed by a negative stimulus is not as likely to recur. The positive experience is referred to as **reinforcement,** and the negative experience is labeled **punishment.**

Think for a moment about the last two weeks in your life, focusing on the positive and negative consequences of your actions. Perhaps a man frowned at you when you smiled at him, or a friend told you what a nice person you were for buying her a book. Perhaps a teacher wrote a note on the bottom of your term paper complimenting your writing skills, or your basketball coach made you run fifty extra laps around the gym for being late to practice. At any rate, the lives of infants, children, adolescents, and adults are full of situations in which behavior is followed by positive or negative consequences. These consequences have significant effects on the future behavior of the individuals involved.

One area of development in which the principle of operant conditioning has been applied liberally is **behavior modification.** This approach to changing behavior is widely practiced by clinicians, counselors, and teachers in an effort to resolve problems. Sometimes even parents are trained to more effectively manage problems by following the principles of operant conditioning (e.g., Patterson, in press). Basically, the procedure of behavior modification involves substituting acceptable patterns of behavior for unacceptable ones.

Albert Bandura.

Contingencies are established to ensure that acceptable responses will be acquired or learned; this learning is facilitated by reinforcement. Behavior modification experts argue that most emotional problems occur because their environment is arranged with the wrong set of contingencies—meaning that unacceptable behaviors are inadvertently reinforced. Hence, the adolescent who frequently engages in delinquent behavior may be doing so because he or she is rewarded for such behavior, either through the material rewards of the objects stolen or the social attention received from peers.

Skinner's ideas have been used extensively in restructuring the learning environments of individuals. Many psychologists, though, reject Skinner's notion that the cognitive determinants of behavior cannot be studied and are not important to understanding the linkage between stimuli and responses. Even some of Skinner's fellow behaviorists feel this way; while they give ball-park approval to Skinner's ideas about reinforcement contingencies, observable behavior, and careful experimental methodology, they nonetheless believe he is wrong to ignore the cognitive determinants of behavior.

The Cognitive Social Learning Theory
Cognitive social learning theory is a label that best describes the behavioral views of Albert Bandura (1977). From Bandura's perspective, the statement that behavior is determined by its consequences refers to the self-produced consequences of one's own actions as well as to consequences of the actions of others. In other words, self-reinforcement is often just as important as reinforcement from others.

Consider the achievement behavior of a woman who is required to perform certain duties on her job. Although she cannot ignore her desire for a salary increase, her own need for excellence will just as likely motivate her to improve and do a better job on her work assignment. Substandard performance, on the other

hand, might lead her to self-criticism. In this sense, the woman's achievement behavior is as much a function of her reaction to herself as to the reactions of others. This concept differs from Skinner's theory, since he argues that behavior is determined only by external consequences.

The existence of self-produced consequences and personal performance standards suggests that using reinforcement to control someone else's behavior will not always be successful. As Bandura (1977) has pointed out, if external reinforcement was always effective, we would behave like weather vanes—in the presence of a John Bircher we would act like a John Bircher, while in the presence of a Communist we would behave like a Communist. Instead, behavior develops through the process of reciprocal control. Consider the following conversation between a seventeen-year-old boy and girl:

Bob Oh, come on, Nancy, let's go to the drive-in tonight.

Nancy (looks away as if she doesn't hear him)

Bob Look, Nancy, I'm talking to you! Don't ignore me.

Nancy What, Bob?

Bob I said, let's go to the drive-in tonight.

Nancy Bob, I know what you want to do—you just want to make out.

Bob (Yelling) Don't make me look like a fool! You make me feel so stupid when you embarrass me like that.

Nancy Well, maybe we can go in a couple of weeks.

Bob Well, all right.

What has been learned in this interchange? Nancy has learned that she can control Bob's advances with vague promises. Bob has learned that if he gets upset and amplifies his feelings, he can at least get Nancy to make some kind of promise. This type of interchange occurs all the time in relationships throughout the life span. It is a coercive process in which two people attempt to control each other's behavior. Indeed, whenever one person is trying to control another, the second person is usually resisting control or attempting to control in return. In this sense, Bandura (1971) asserts that the manipulation and control of people suggested by Skinner in *Walden Two* could never evolve.

Bandura refers to this concept of behavior as **reciprocal determinism** (Bandura, 1977). The individual is not completely driven by inner forces or manipulated helplessly by environmental factors, rather, the person's psychological makeup is best understood by analyzing the continuous reciprocal interaction between behavior and its controlling conditions. In other words, behavior partly constructs the environment, and the resulting environment, in turn, affects behavior.

Bandura (1971, 1977) also believes that individuals learn extensively by example. Much of what we learn involves observing the behavior of parents, peers, teachers, and others. This form of social learning is called **imitation, modeling,** or **vicarious learning.** For example, the ten-year-old who watches the teacher smile at her friend for turning in her work on time may be motivated to do likewise.

Bandura believes that if learning proceeded in the trial-and-error fashion advocated by Skinner, it would be very laborious and even hazardous. For example, to put a fifteen-year-old girl in an automobile, have her drive down the road, and reward the positive responses she makes would be senseless. Instead, many of the complex educational and cultural practices of individuals are learned through their exposure to competent models who display appropriate ways to solve problems and cope with the world.

Sometimes it is said that social learning theorists take a mechanical view of development. Jonas Langer (1969), a cognitive-structuralist, has even labeled the social learning view as a **mechanical mirror theory.** The label suggests that individuals do not control their own destiny but instead are controlled and manipulated by environmental influences until they mirror their environments in mechanical fashion. On the other hand, the cognitive-structural and psychoanalytic views of development emphasize the internal forces that control the individual's growth. In the psychoanalytic view, the forces are the relationships of the three personality structures to each other, while in the cognitive-structural view they reside in the organization of rational thought.

Certainly it is valid to say that social learning adherents believe behavior is influenced by the individual's response to the environment. To this extent, the social learning model indicates that an individual's behavior is controlled by the external environment. However, as we have just seen, many social learning thinkers, such as Bandura, stress that the individual controls and even constructs his or her own environment. Recall the example of the boy trying to get his date to go to the drive-in movie. Not only was he controlling her behavior, but she was controlling his as well. Many contemporary social learning theorists stress just this type of bidirectional stimulus control (e.g., Bijou, 1976).

But probably the strongest criticism of behaviorism has come not from psychoanalytic and cognitive-structural theorists but from a group of psychologists referred to as humanists. The greatest area of controversy between humanistic and behavioristic theorists involves their views of the individual and his or her relationship to the environment. Specifically, humanists and behaviorists differ on whether the individual is an active creator of environment or a passive recipient of it, whether he or she is free to determine his or her own fate, and the nature of the construct referred to as the "self." Humanistic theorists believe that behaviorists like Skinner take the "person" out of personality and view the individual as a passive organism incapable of determining his or her own course of action. And while humanistic theorists see the self as a fundamental unity

of personality around which all aspects of the individual are organized, most behaviorists believe the construct of self as a mental structure is so global and broad in nature that it is meaningless as a predictor of an individual's behavior.

The Humanistic Perspective

The humanistic perspective includes a number of ideas to explain the nature of an individual's personality and techniques that can be used to change personality. Just as there is no single social learning theory, there is no single humanistic theory. However, humanistic theorists as a group all agree that human psychology should be studied with a human model, not an animal model, and that human psychology should not be viewed in a mechanical manner. What should be studied, say the humanists, are conscious feelings, ideals, and intentions.

This view of human development has produced an orientation that focuses on human growth, personal fulfillment, and self-actualization. Humanistic therapy attempts to enable the individual to reach his or her full potential through exploration of individual emotional dynamics (Poppen, Wandersman, & Wandersman, 1976). Humanistic theory is much farther away from the theory of development advocated by Skinner than from that proposed by Bandura. Remember that Skinner clearly does not believe that internal or cognitive processes control behavior; behavior is controlled by external, environmental events only. Most humanists are at the opposite end of the control continuum— they focus on the internal determinants of personality. Emphasis is placed on the subjective experience of the individual, or on how he or she interprets the world, rather than on actual behavior. And many humanists focus on uniquely human aspects of experience, such as creativity and intentionality, that do not exist in subhuman species.

From the perspective of the humanist, the individual has an internal, dynamic personality structure that organizes conduct, emotions, and thoughts. Although Freud also believed that individuals have an internal personality structure, he believed that subconscious forces controlled the person, while humanists believe that control is held by conscious mental processes.

The humanistic approach is less scientific than the other five approaches covered in this chapter. Many humanistic approaches represent a cluster of attitudes about how to view children, adolescents, and adults than a rigorous set of formal propositions and axioms. Nonetheless, despite the empirical insufficiency of many humanistic views, the theories themselves seem to have considerable clinical value and provide rich insight into the lives of individuals. One theorist, Carl Rogers, has been one of the dominant figures in the humanistic movement.

The Childhood and Youth of Carl Rogers

Carl Rogers was born in Oak Park, Illinois, a Chicago suburb, in 1902. He was the fourth born of six children, five of whom were boys. His parents had grown up on farms and were down-to-earth individuals who shared strong religious convictions (particularly his mother). They believed very strongly in the work ethic, and often expressed the value of hard work to Carl.

Rogers says that his parents devoted a considerable amount of energy to creating a family life that would "hold" the children and control the way their lives would go. He indicates that they were experts at the techniques of subtle and loving control. Carl never remembers being given a direct command, but he knew that he was never to dance, smoke, play cards, go to movies, or show any sexual interests. Swearing was not as great a taboo, probably because Carl's father often cursed to vent his anger.

Carl felt that his parents loved his next oldest brother more than him. This was such a preoccupation of Carl's that he once developed the notion that he had been adopted, feeling that this would explain why his parents didn't love him as much. Carl also remembers that he hero-worshipped his oldest brother.

Rogers mentions that he had virtually no social life outside of his family, although he doesn't remember this bothering him. When he was twelve, the family moved to a farm—apparently his parents, particularly his mother, wanted to shield her children from the evils of city life. Carl attended three different high schools and had to travel a long distance to get to them. When he returned home from school, chores awaited him, and he would begin work as early as 5:00 A.M. when he had to milk the cows. Even though he was saddled with so many duties at home, Carl managed to make straight A's in school. But there was little time for friendship; he points out that he never even had a real date in high school. Once he had to take a girl to a class dinner as a matter of custom. He remembers the anxiety of having to ask her out. She agreed to go, but Rogers says he doesn't know what he would have done if she had turned him down!

After high school, Rogers went to the University of Wisconsin to study scientific agriculture. Carl attended Sunday church services, and later became so interested in religion that he attended Union Theological Seminary. After several years of religious training there, he switched to clinical psychology at Columbia University.

Rogers talks also about an experience that helped him develop independence from his family. While in Wisconsin, Carl lived at the YMCA with his brother. During his junior year, he was selected as one of ten students to go to Peking, China, for a World Student Christian Federation conference. The trip took six months and had a great impact on Carl's life. He struggled with his religious identity while he was away and thought frequently about his world views compared to those of his parents. At the end of the China trip, Carl had developed confidence in his own views and his own future.

Source: Rogers, 1967.

Carl Rogers

Carl Rogers's theory defines the personality of the individual in terms of subjective experiences. (See box 2.3 for a sketch of Rogers's childhood and youth.) Rogers believes that subjective experience should be studied by focusing on the whole person rather than just parts of the person. He points out that every individual has a tremendous potential for self-understanding that usually is not brought out in everyday exchanges with people. Rogers feels that by providing the right psychological climate, this potential can emerge (Rogers, 1974).

Such thinking has implications for therapists who work with individuals as well as for people who need to communicate more effectively with each other. According to Rogers, the therapist must have an open mind to really hear what the individual is saying. Such careful listening benefits the individual and provides the therapist with the clearest possible perception of the workings of the individual's mind. The therapist must lay aside all preconceptions about the individual and strive to discover the true nature of the person's feelings and thoughts. And the therapist should role play often, trying to experience the world just as the individual does. Rogers's ideas about therapy have served as the basis for the widespread approach to dealing with problems called **Parent Effectiveness Training (P. E. T.).** This program was developed by Thomas Gordon (1970) to help parents communicate more effectively with their children. P. E. T. stresses open and honest two-way communication between the child and parents, problem-solving skills, positive ways to deal with conflict, and cooperative goal setting.

The **self** is an important construct in Rogers's theory. Calvin Hall and Gardner Lindzey (1978) describe the individual's need to find congruence between the self and real-world experiences. When the individual finds this congruence, he or she is considered well adjusted; but when there is a considerable degree of incongruence, the individual might be categorized as maladjusted. Congruence between the self and experience produces realistic thinking, whereas incongruence leads to anxiety, defensiveness, and distorted thinking.

In addition to emphasizing the relationship between the self and real-world experiences, Rogers (1959) also discusses the relationship between the individual's ideal self and real self. The real self, or self-structure, is the self as it really is, whereas the ideal self is the self the person would like to be. The greater the discrepancy between the ideal and real selves, the greater the likelihood that the individual will become maladjusted.

Unlike psychoanalytic and cognitive-structural theorists, but like social learning theorists, humanists do not view maturation of the self on a timetable or as a series of developmental stages. Rogers does, however, describe how childhood experiences with significant adults affect the individual's self-perception in later life. If the child's experiences with parents, siblings, peers, and teachers are characterized by what Rogers calls unconditional positive regard, significant adjustment problems are less likely to surface when the child reaches adulthood. However, if significant people often evaluate the individual in a negative way, the individual learns that many of his or her actions gain disapproval. The more negative feedback received, the more distorted the self-perception in an effort to be insulated from negative evaluations. The discrepancy between experiences and self-perception produces feelings of anxiety that can lead to maladjustment.

The gap between the perceived self and real experiences with others affects the individual's interaction with others. The anxiety and defensiveness that result from this type of discrepancy often lead the individual to act in hostile ways toward others. Rogers feels that these problems should be resolved through a nonthreatening relationship with a person who completely accepts everything the individual says. This unconditional positive regard encourages the individual to express true feelings and makes the person feel better about himself or herself.

Not everyone, however, agrees with Rogers's approach to helping children and adolescents mature into more competent adults. Calvin Hall and Gardner Lindzey (1978) provide a summary of problems that are inherent in Rogers's humanistic theory. One criticism of Rogers is that his theory is based on a naive

Carl Rogers.

view of individual perceptions. For instance, many factors unavailable to conscious experience motivate the individual to act in particular ways. Also, no concern for the biological basis of development is evident in the humanistic perspective.

Perspectives from Outside of Psychology: Ethological, Evolutionary and Anthropological, Sociological Theories

Trying to explain life-span development is an awesome, complex undertaking. While this text primarily is a psychological approach to life-span development, psychology, by no means, has exclusive rights to life-span development. Explanations of life-span development are housed in biology, anthropology, and sociology as well. In this section, we look at some of the most important perspectives of life-span development from outside of psychology—ethological, evolutionary and anthropological, sociological.

The Ethological, Evolutionary Perspective

Freud's and Piaget's theories are biologically oriented, but one biological perspective that has influenced the study of life-span development originated outside of psychology. Two European zoologists, Konrad Lorenz (1965) and Niko Tinbergen (1951, 1969), believed that behaviorism had led scientists to an unfortunate neglect of the innate nature of many behaviors. Their work formed the basis for a biological theory of behavior known as **ethology.** Some of their studies are now classic. Lorenz revealed the speed and totality with which young ducklings form rapid attachments to a variety of objects in their environment. He is also known for his work on the mating behavior of the stickleback fish. In these animal behaviors, we readily see stereotyped patterns of social behavior that are difficult to explain with traditional processes of learning, such as reinforcement.

Working mostly with graylag geese, Lorenz studied a behavior pattern that was considered to be programmed within the genes of the animals. A newly hatched gosling seemed to be born with an instinct for

Konrad Lorenz, a pioneering student of animal behavior, is followed through the water by three imprinted graylag geese.

following its mother. Observations showed that the gosling was capable of such behavior as soon as it hatched from the egg. Lorenz proved that it was incorrect to assume that such behavior was programmed in the animal.

In a remarkable series of experiments, Lorenz separated the eggs laid by one female goose into two groups. One group he returned to the female goose to be hatched by her; the other group was hatched in an incubator. The first group performed as predicted; they followed their mother as soon as they were hatched. But the second group, which saw Lorenz when they were first hatched, followed him everywhere, just as though he were their mother. Lorenz marked the goslings and then placed both groups under a box. Mother goose and "mother Lorenz" stood aside as the box was lifted. Without error, each group of goslings went directly to its adopted "mother."

Lorenz used the word **imprinting** to describe this early modification of behavior. A number of interesting facts have resulted from imprinting experiments. In every case in which imprinting is observed, there is a **critical period** of time when the individual will respond to an imprinting experience. For chicks and ducklings this critical period lasts from the time of hatching for about thirty-six hours. Peak sensitivity occurs at thirteen and sixteen hours. After the critical period for imprinting, young animals can still be taught to follow another object, but the nature of the learning

experience is distinctly different from the imprinting experience. Experiments with the young of rodents, dogs, and monkeys show that imprinting also takes place in mammals. In chapter 6 under the topic of early experiences, there will be extensive discussion of how biological predispositions may lead to a critical period, a time in the life cycle when development is most rapid and vulnerable to environmental experience.

Ethology is now receiving attention from many developmental psychologists who are searching for ways to understand how the individual's biological heritage influences the course of social development (Seay & Gottfried, 1978). The two areas of social development most influenced by ethological theory are attachment and aggression. As we will see in chapter 6, prominent theorists and researchers such as John Bowlby and Mary Ainsworth argue that newborn infants are biologically predisposed to orient toward people, an evolutionary fact that shapes the way we view the attachment process. The ethological perspective on attachment contrasts with the behavioral view that the infant learns through reinforcement to be dependent upon the mother. Ethologists also believe that aggression has evolutionary roots and that the child is preprogrammed with aggressive tendencies. Ethologists stress that there is continuity between the aggressive actions of lower animals and young children and that these aggressive actions can be unlearned (Suomi, 1977).

A basic point in the ethological approach to development that requires more attention than it can be given in this introductory chapter on perspectives of development is the belief that every individual carries a genetic code inherited from his or her parents. In chapter 3 you will read extensively about the basic ideas of behavior genetics, including the role of genetics in such characteristics as intelligence, physical traits, and mental retardation. To more fully understand the importance of the ethological approach to studying life-span development we focus now, in a more detailed way, on the ethologist's emphasis on evolution.

The Role of Evolution in Life-Span Development

The key to ethology is **evolution.** Ethologists believe that we can only fully appreciate the origin of behavior if we recognize that many patterns of behavior are transmitted through evolution. Biological evolution concerns the manner in which inherited genes predispose individuals to function in ways that are adaptively similar to their biological ancestors. Significant genetic change leading to an observable change in a characteristic (e.g., the disposition to be helpful) can typically take thousands of years. On the other hand, **cultural,** or **social, evolution** is much more rapid. It refers to the manner in which new behaviors are acquired and innate tendencies are modified through cultural transmission, for example, modeling, language, customs, and practices of a group. Thus, some ethologists believe that the tendency to be helpful and to empathize with others results from a biological predisposition, but the tendency to express these prosocial actions can be dramatically and rapidly shaped by a culture. Thus, history shows us that some societies teach individuals to be very helpful and humane, while other societies encourage callousness and inhumanity. What is unique about this perspective is the care taken to explain the subtle and intricate manner by which instinctual and environmental pressures combine to shape social destiny (Hinde, 1982; Hinde & Atkinson, 1970; Hinde & White, 1974; Von Cranach, Foppa, Lepenies, & Ploog, 1980).

In evolutionary terms, humans are relative newcomers to earth, but in a short time they have established themselves as the most successful and dominant species. As our earliest ancestors left the forests to feed in the savannas and finally to form hunting societies on the open plains, they changed physically, mentally, and socially. A basic point in the evolutionary theory is that the organism is closely adapted to the environment in which it lives because natural selection favors the survival and reproduction of those physical, mental, and behavioral characteristics that are advantageous. Over the course of many generations humans have modified

The better an animal is adapted to its environment, the more successful it becomes. Humans, more than any other mammal, are able to adapt to and control most types of environment. 1) Technological advances give greater freedom of movement and independence; 2) by becoming omnivorous, using fire, developing agriculture, and inventing methods of food storage, humans have been able to use a wider range of foods and to develop a sophisticated method of feeding; 3) greater intelligence has led to the use of complex objects that enhance existence; 4) because of longer parental care, humans learn more complex behavior patterns, which contribute to increasingly successful adaptation.

themselves to take advantage of the environment so they could survive. Regardless of the life cycle phase, whether it be infancy or late adulthood, the evolutionary perspective emphasizes this adaptiveness of the individual to the environment. And, while every human being is physically, mentally, emotionally, and socially unique there are communalities among all individuals because of their evolutionary heritage. For example, every living person is made up of cells, bones, muscle,

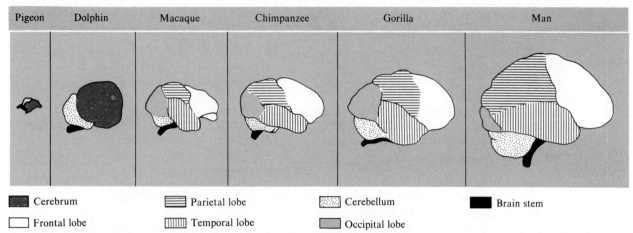

Pigeon	Dolphin	Macaque	Chimpanzee	Gorilla	Man

■ Cerebrum   ☰ Parietal lobe   ⠿ Cerebellum   ■ Brain stem

☐ Frontal lobe   ⦀ Temporal lobe   ▨ Occipital lobe

Figure 2.4 The evolution of the brain. As the brain has evolved, its more advanced functions have become centered in the forebrain. The higher up the evolutionary tree an animal is, the greater the size and complexity of the forebrain. In such mammals as the dolphin, folded outgrowths of the brain have become the dominating cerebral hemisphere, allowing greater thinking capacity. In primates like the macaque, chimpanzee, gorilla, and man, specified areas have evolved in the hemisphere.

blood vessels, and a brain (see fig. 2.4 for a view of the evolutionary development of the brain). Thus, the evolutionary perspective of the life cycle stresses not only the adaptiveness of the individual to the environment but communalities with all other members of humanity as well. An extended discussion of the role of evolution in language development will appear in chapter 5.

The evolutionary process proceeds in an undetectable, slow manner. The better we adapt to our environment from generation to generation, the better we will survive and the more successful we will become as human beings. In our description of the ethological perspective we indicated that attachment and aggression are two aspects of social development that likely can be traced to evolutionary beginnings. A third aspect of social development, dominance, also has an evolutionary history, as explained in box 2.4.

The Anthropological, Sociological Perspective

Anthropologists and sociologists look for explanations of behavior in cultural values, social structures, and roles. Ideas about the nature of development and the techniques used to raise children differ from culture to culture and within the same culture over time. The label **culture** refers to the existing cluster of behaviors, attitudes, values, and products of a particular group of people. We can refer to the culture of the United States, the culture of Russia, the culture of China, and so forth. Of course, the culture of any of these nations is made up of many different subcultures that have their own sets of behaviors and values. The way in which cultures and subcultures impart behaviors, attitudes, and values to their children is often referred to as **enculturation** (LeVine, 1973).

Ideas about the nature of development and the techniques used to raise children differ from culture to culture and within the same culture over time.

In every culture there are defined goals that reflect what individuals are expected to do and become and represent what the members of the culture value and feel is worth working for (e.g., Merton, 1957). For example, the United States is a culture that places a premium on work and achievement; it is also a culture that requires all children to go to an institution called school.

Dominance in Animals and Man

The question of man's evolution of social behavior is not simple. He does, however, show some features of social behavior which resemble those of other primates. One of the most important of these and something which is seen in nearly all primates, man included, is dominance behavior. Dominance is the name given to the phenomenon of status ranking in animal societies. High-status animals take precedence over those with low status and usually get preferential access to food, to females and to rights of decision making. Rather like its human counterpart, the high-status chimpanzee can be recognized by the relaxed indifference with which it moves about and the way in which it can usually get whatever it wants. The low-status chimpanzee is, by contrast, nervous, ever-watchful of what the dominants are doing and generally servile in its relations with them. Nevertheless, most primate societies, and especially that of the chimpanzee, are highly variable and often quite amorphous, since the membership of the groups is constantly changing.

If it is assumed that man's distant forest-dwelling, semibrachiating ancestors, who were so closely related to the chimpanzees, manifested a similar social behavior in conditions comparable to those of today's chimpanzees, then it can be concluded that at this stage man's ancestors lived in loosely structured societies where, as among the chimpanzees, sexual promiscuity was the rule and dominance, although present, was not strongly developed.

As man's ancestors moved out onto the savannas, it is likely that they became organized into societies similar to those of today's baboons which, like the early hominids (for example *Australopithecus*), are terrestrial. Because they live in a dangerous environment, they show a more rigid social structure and strongly developed dominance hierarchies. It is likely that ultimately man's ancestors may have formed societies such as those of today's gelada baboon, which man closely resembles in the matter of his teeth (which suggests that we have become adapted for a similar seed-eating way of life) and in the fact that the gelada female, too, has secondary sexual characteristics on the chest.

The gelada baboons live in rigidly demarcated groups centered around dominant males and consisting of one such male and his harem of females and immature young. Subdominant males live together in looser, all-male groups. It is possible that such "bachelor groups" of subdominant males began the first systematic big game hunting, because what is known of other hunting animals suggests that a quite different social structure to that of the gelada one-male group is required and that something like the gelada bachelor groups might be just right. If this is the case, then the appearance of Homo erectus as a big game hunter some eight hundred thousand years ago may signal the changeover from seed-eating, gelada-type structures to fraternal hunting bands of the type which we can still find among the Bushmen and Australian aborigines.

Whatever the final truth about man's social origins, there can be no doubt that such behavioral adaptations as have led to the development of structured societies and advanced material culture have been dependent upon the mental and physical adaptations which have given man the highly developed body and mind that he possesses today.

Source: *Rand McNally Atlas of the Body and Mind*, 1976, p. 19.

Achievement of these social tasks would reflect similar cultural expectations in many other cultures as well, but some behaviors may not be comparable for certain cultures. For example, sexual modesty is not expected in the Mangaian culture in the South Pacific, where sexual promiscuity is standard fare for youth (Hyde, 1979).

Cultures may vary considerably in the rate at which individuals achieve patterns of behavior, and individual development of a set of values is determined by the particular values of the culture. Masculinity and femininity often do not have the same referents from culture to culture; in one culture it may be considered masculine to wear plaid kilts while in another it may be thought masculine to play football. In box 2.5, the famous anthropologist, Margaret Mead, provides a revealing, perceptive look at what our American culture is like.

Cultures and subcultures can be described in terms of their **social structures.** The noted sociologist Alex Inkeles (1969) believes the following categorization of social structures provides a helpful system for understanding how culture influences development through the life cycle.

Ecological structure involves the size, density, physical distribution, and social composition of the population. These factors all determine the amount of control needed over individuals and groups.

Box 2.5
Margaret Mead's Perception of the American Culture

Margaret Mead.

Margaret Mead's famous investigations as an anthropologist have shown that the culture we experience in the United States is different from the cultures of the South Sea islands. Just before her death in 1978 she wrote about our culture.

Mead's main points focused on the American family. She indicates that in times of upheaval in a nation, such as war, famine, or mass emigration, family life has always suffered. However, the changes that are occurring in the American family today are the results of more subtle changes in the American way of life.

One change is the increased longevity of peoples' lives. Fifty years ago, the older people who survived were generally hearty and were still linked closely to the family, often helping to maintain its existence. The elderly no longer maintain such a strong socializing role in the family.

A second change in our culture, Mead points out, is the move away from farms and small towns to the cities and suburbs. In the small towns and farms, individuals were surrounded by lifelong neighbors, relatives, and friends. Today, neighborhood and extended-family support systems are rare. Moreover, the American family is much more mobile than in the past—families move all over the country, often uprooting the child from a school and peer groups he or she has known for a number of years. And for many families, this type of move occurs every year or two, as one or both parents are transferred from job to job.

Related to the migration from rural to urban life is the growth of suburbs. Suburbs developed rapidly after World War II. Essentially comprised of relatively young middle-class people, the growth of suburbs caused increasing numbers of young parents to be isolated from their own parents and families. The loneliness and boredom of many suburban housewives led them to make greater efforts to find employment outside of the home, not just as a means of economic support for the family, but as a means of self-development as well.

According to Mead, coinciding with the development of the affluent suburbs was the deterioration of the inner cities of our nation. Many people in the inner city, as a result, have grown up in families whose economic support is provided by the government. Inner city youth not only feel financial strains within their families but within their schools as well. Consequently, the inner city child generally receives an inferior education compared to that of the child who grows up in the suburbs.

Mead goes on to say that television has played a major role in the changing American way of life. Many children and adolescents who often watched television found that their parents were too busy working to share this experience with them. The youth increasingly experienced a world their parents were not a part of. Furthermore, instead of participating in neighborhood peer groups, many boys and girls came home after school and plopped down in front of the television set. Television also allowed different groups of people to see new ways of life. Lower-class individuals could look into the lives of other individuals more closely, particularly the lives of middle-class families.

Another change Mead points out is a general dissatisfaction and restlessness. Women have become increasingly dissatisfied with their way of life, placing a great strain on many marriages. With no elders to help and advise young people during the initial difficult years of marriage and childbearing, marriages begin to fracture at the first signs of disagreement. For those who marry, the cost of housing and other commodities places great strains on the marriage. Divorce has become an epidemic in this culture, for both middle-aged and young marriages. Many people who marry often divorce within a few years, and many children witness their own parents' divorce proceedings. Men become restless and look for stimulation and satisfaction outside of family life. The result of this restlessness and the tendency to divorce and remarry is a hodgepodge of family structures, with far greater numbers of single parent and stepparent families than ever before in history.

Mead believed that America is in great need of revised national policies regarding families. Who is responsible for the youth of divorced parents and the child whom nobody wants? Badly needed are better social services, revised welfare policies, and schools that are more responsive to the cultural diversity that now exists in the population. Mead also suggested that television became a positive force by portraying adult responsibility for youth, revealing the needs of inner cities, and suggesting ways for ruptured families to cope with the problems in their lives.

Economic structure entails the type and amount of material resources in a society. Patterns of occupational recruitment in industrialized societies have had strong influences on development. When farming and crafts were the primary occupations in our society, the child was socialized into an occupational role by serving an apprenticeship. This system has been replaced by instruction in specialized schools, a system that is more formalized and impersonal.

Political structure involves the importance of power structures and their subsystems in a society. Inkeles (1969) suggests that when youth are allowed to participate in politics and government—through their own efforts or through youth groups—the nature of socialization will be different than when adolescents are politically subordinate. The Little Red Soldiers and the Red Guard in China are examples of this type of socialization technique.

Value structure comes closest to the usual meaning of the label **culture.** Cultural ethics and morals, standards of right and wrong, and rules and regulations reflect the value structure of a culture. Moral education helps to transmit the value structure of a culture to the adolescent.

In addition to analyzing the social structures of a culture, sociologists stress that within those roles it is not the individual who should be studied but rather the *roles* of the individual (e.g., Neugarten & Datan, 1973). **A role** is both a range of actions and a set of functions. Thus, a child performs in roles such as student, son or daughter, peer, leader, athlete, musician, and so on. Development, for many sociologists, is defined in terms of the sum total of roles the individual plays and the changes that occur in the succession of these roles. Next we look at one particular perspective of life-span development that has a strong sociological flavor.

Bernice Neugarten's Multiple Time, Changing Life Cycle Perspective

Bernice Neugarten and Nancy Datan (1973) have described how studies of the life cycle have been more biological than social. They believe that it may be helpful to think of the life cycle in terms of three dimensions of time: life time, or chronological age; historical time; and social time, or the system of age grading and expectations that shape the life cycle.

Life time is based heavily on the biological timetable that governs the sequence of changes in the process of growing—Erikson's stages, described earlier in this chapter, are regulated strongly by this biological timetable. However, as Neugarten (1980) stated in

Bernice Neugarten.

chapter 1, chronological age is at best only a rough indicator of an individual's position on any one of numerous physical or psychological dimensions, because from early in infancy individual differences are a known fact of development. Neugarten and Datan (1973) also argue that age is often not a very good index of many forms of social and psychological behavior, unless there is accompanying knowledge of the particular society as a frame of reference. They give an obvious example of a girl in the United States who will be a schoolgirl, but the same-aged girl in a rural village in the Near East may be the mother of two children. It is argued that the significance of a given chronological age, or a given marker of life time, when viewed from a sociological or anthropological perspective, is directly a function of the social definition of age, or social time.

Social time refers to the dimension that underlies the age-grade system of a particular society. It has been characteristic of preliterate societies to have rites de passage marking the transition from one age status to the next, such as the passage from youth to maturity and to marriage (Van Gennep, 1960). According to Neugarten and Datan (1973), however, only a rough parallel exists between social time and life time in most societies. There are different sets of age expectations and age statuses in different societies.

Historical time controls the social system, and the social system, in turn, creates a changing set of age norms and a changing age-grade system that shapes the individual life cycle. For example, childhood as a distinct phase of life did not emerge until the seventeenth and eighteenth centuries, and the concept of adolescence did not emerge until the twentieth century. Similarly, middle age as a stage is a recent concept, resulting from our increased longevity. Changes in industrialization, urbanization, and our educational institutions account for these changing concepts. Scientists in this area also recognize the importance of the timing of major historical events in the life of an individual. Wars and depressions often act as historical watersheds, that is, major turning points in the social system. Significant historical events often affect levels of education, fertility patterns, sexual mores, labor participation patterns, and so forth.

"I found your birth certificate in the attic. You're not 54, you're 91."

The Life-Span Developmental Perspective: An Eclectic Approach

There is no single, indomitable theory in explaining life-span development. Each of the theories discussed in this chapter has made a contribution to our understanding, but none provides a complete description and explanation of life-span development. Cognitive-structural theory provides the best explanation of the individual's conscious mind and intellectual development, but it provides much less information on social development and the unconscious aspects of the mind. Psychoanalytic theory best describes how the subconscious mind affects development, but it tells us much less about the effects of the social environment on the individual. The behavioral social learning perspective provides the most detailed account of how the individual learns and the influence of environment on learning, but it does not give us much insight into the individual's thinking processes or emotions. Humanistic theory contains an abundance of information about the individual's self-structure and self-concept and suggests specific ways to work through problems, but it lacks a scientific base and provides little information about development through the life cycle. The ethological, evolutionary perspective has reawakened our interest in the biological underpinnings of life-span development, but it provides little information about different phases within a single life cycle. And, the anthropological, sociological perspective is the best view of the importance of social structures and roles in life-span development, but it has not been very beneficial in revealing knowledge about individual development. To help you remember the major organizing principles of each perspective, they are presented in table 2.1.

Life-span development is much too complex to be explained by a single theory. It is important to realize that although theories are often helpful guides in understanding development, relying on a single theory to explain development is probably a mistake. The two theories described in this chapter that come closest to

Table 2.1
Perspectives of Development

Theory	Organizing Principles
Psychoanalytic	Biological instincts, psychosexual stages, and family processes
Cognitive-Structural	Cognitive processes and stages
Behavioral Social Learning	Learning processes
Humanistic	The self and self-concept
Ethological, Evolutionary	Genes, evolution, and adaptation
Anthropological, Sociological	Culture, social structure, and roles

encompassing the entire life cycle are Erikson's and Neugarten's. Interestingly, both theorists have included both biological and social components in their perspectives, and both have been leaders in pointing out that change and development are not exclusive property of the early years of the life cycle.

An attempt was made in this chapter to present six major perspectives objectively. The same **eclectic orientation** will be found in the remainder of the text. In this way, you can view the study of development as it actually exists—with different theorists making different assumptions about development, stressing different empirical problems, and using different strategies to discover more about individuals. In the next section we begin our long and exciting journey through the life cycle, starting with the first phase, infancy.

Summary

Six perspectives of development have received prominent attention—psychoanalytic; cognitive-structural; behavioral social learning; humanistic; ethological, evolutionary; and anthropological, sociological. The first two perspectives—psychoanalytic and cognitive-structural—are stage theories; the second set of perspectives—behavioral social learning and humanistic—are nonstage theories; and the third set of views—ethological, evolutionary and anthropological, sociological—come from outside of psychology.

The psychoanalytic perspective is dominated by the theory of Sigmund Freud. Freud believed that individuals are driven by subconscious, instinctual forces. Conflict characterizes the life of the individual because the demands of reality (ego) and moral standards (superego) are never entirely freed from biological drives (id). Children pass through a series of psychosexual stages before they enter the genital stage, which begins with the onset of puberty and lasts throughout adulthood. The defense mechanisms of the ego help the individual conform to the pressures of reality and reduce tension. In Erikson's modification of Freud's theory, a greater emphasis is placed on conscious ego processes and on personality changes beyond adolescence. Erikson identified eight stages that cut across the entire life span. In each, the individual resolves a conflict between two emotional alternatives.

The cognitive-structural perspective, represented by the theory of Jean Piaget, holds that individuals are motivated by the intrinsic need to constantly adapt to their environments and reorganize their structures of thought. Piaget believed that children and adolescents progressed through stages of sensorimotor, preoperational, concrete operational, and formal operational thought.

The behavioral social learning perspective views development as the result of learning from environmental experiences. B. F. Skinner, the behaviorist, argues that the adolescent's behavior is determined solely by the external consequences of actions. The cognitive social learning theory of Albert Bandura still stresses the importance of studying behavior and the effects of the environment on it, however, Bandura believes that much of behavior is mediated by cognitive processes.

The humanistic perspective stresses that the core of development lies in conscious feelings, ideas, and intentions. Humanists focus on personal fulfillment and the sense of self-awareness. Humanistic therapy extends the humanistic perspective to help individuals reach their potential through the exploration of emotional dynamics. Carl Rogers has been one of the guiding forces behind the humanistic perspective, emphasizing a client-centered approach to understanding development.

From outside the discipline of psychology, ethological, evolutionary and anthropological, sociological perspectives provide additional valuable information about life-span development. The ethological, evolutionary perspective emphasizes the importance of individual biological heritage and adaptation to the environment. The role of evolution in shaping the life cycle over the course of many generations also is an important part of this perspective. The anthropological, sociological perspective stresses that life-span development can best be understood by analyzing the culture in which the individual lives. In particular, the way in which the culture transmits values, roles, and social structures to succeeding generations is important. One particular view of life-span development that includes many sociological referents is Bernice Neugarten's belief that life time, social time, and historical time interact to produce changing rhythms in the life cycle.

Finally, it must be stressed that no single theory can explain the rich and awesome complexity of life-span development. Each of the theories presented has made a different contribution, and it is probably wise to adopt an eclectic view as we continue to study life-span development.

Key Terms

accommodation
adaptation
anal stage
anthropological, sociological perspective
assimilation
autonomy versus shame and doubt
behavioral social learning perspective
behavior modification
cognitive social learning theory
cognitive-structural perspective
concrete operational stage
critical period
cultural, or social, evolution
culture
defense mechanisms
eclectic orientation
ecological structure
economic structure
ego
ego integrity versus despair
Eight Ages of Man
Electra complex
enculturation
equilibration
erogenous zones
ethological, evolutionary perspective
ethology
evolution
fixation
formal operational stage
generativity versus stagnation
genital stage
historical time
humanism
id
identification
identity versus role confusion

imitation
imprinting
industry versus inferiority
initiative versus guilt
instinct
instrumental conditioning
intimacy versus isolation
latency stage
life time
"mechanical mirror" theory
modeling
Oedipus complex
operant conditioning
oral stage
organization
Parent Effectiveness Training (P. E.T.)
phallic stage
pleasure principle
political structure
preoperational stage
projection
psychoanalytic theory
punishment
reaction formation
reality principle
reciprocal determinism
regression
reinforcement
repression
roles
scientific theory
self
sensorimotor stage
social structure
social time
stages
stimuli
superego
tension reduction
trust versus mistrust
value structure
vicarious learning

Review Questions

1. What are some of the formal requirements of a theory of life-span development?
2. What makes a theory of life-span development a stage theory? Give examples of stage theories and nonstage theories.
3. Describe the main points in the psychoanalytic perspective. Distinguish between the psychoanalytic perspective of Freud and Erikson.
4. Describe the main themes of the cognitive-structural perspective.
5. What are the most important aspects of the behavioral social learning perspective? What are some differences between Skinner's view and Bandura's view?
6. Outline the major ideas in the humanistic perspective.
7. Describe how evolutionary theory is important for the study of life-span development. What is ethological theory?
8. What are the main points of the anthropological, sociological perspective? Discuss Bernice Neugarten's multiple time, changing life cycle perspective.

Further Readings

Cowan, P. A. *Piaget with feeling: cognitive, social, and emotional, dimensions.* New York: Holt, Rinehart, & Winston, 1978.
Philip Cowan is head of the clinical psychology program at the University of California at Berkeley. He, like many clinicians, believe Piaget has more to tell us about social and emotional development than Piaget himself thought. Reading level is moderately difficult.

Erikson, E. H. *Identity: youth and crisis.* New York: Norton, 1968.
This book represents Erikson's most detailed work on adolescents and includes a full description of his eight stages of the life cycle. Exciting reading with many insights into the nature of lives, which you should be able to adapt to an understanding of your own life. Easy reading.

Havighurst, R. J. History of developmental psychology: socialization and personality development through the lifespan. In P. B. Baltes & K. W. Schaie (eds.), *Lifespan developmental psychology.* New York: Academic Press, 1973, pp. 4–25.
Havighurst, a leading figure in the study of life-span development, presents a number of theoretical ideas that focus on life-span development. Reasonably easy to read.

Neugarten, B. L., & Datan, N. Sociological perspectives on the life cycle. In P. B. Baltes & K. W. Schaie (eds.), *Life-span developmental psychology.* New York: Academic Press, pp. 53–71.
Neugarten, also a leading figure in the study of life-span development, describes her views of multiple time perspectives and the changing rhythm of the life cycle. This article stimulates thinking about the nature of life-span development and is reasonably easy to read.

Patterson, G. R. *Families.* Champaign, Ill: Research Press, 1971.
An extremely easy-to-read, intelligent discussion of behavioral ideas designed to help family members cope with conflict. Patterson is director of the Oregon Research Institute, one of the leading behavioral research and treatment centers in the United States.

Shostrum, E. V. *Man, the manipulator: the inner journey from manipulation to actualization.* New York: Bantam, 1972.
In a very easy-to-read style, Shostrum tells us how to grow from a manipulative to a self-actualized individual. Hundreds of examples are given that suggest specific ways to improve your communication with others so that psychologically healthier relationships can be developed. Shostrum is a former president of the division of humanistic psychology in the American Psychological Association.

Section II

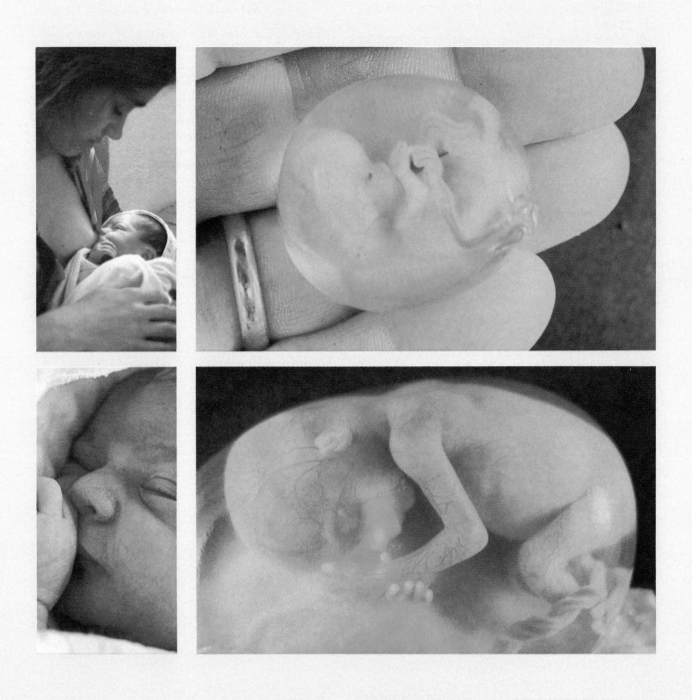

Foundations of Development in Infancy

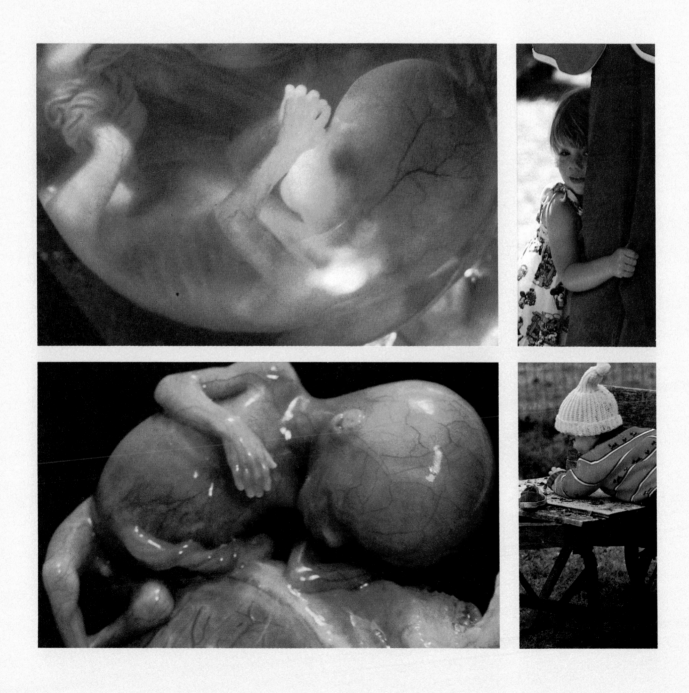

3

Biological Foundations
and Physical Development

Prologue: Test-Tube Babies

Perhaps the most dazzling occurrence in the past decade is the birth of several babies who were conceived outside of their mothers' bodies. The first documented case was of Louise Brown in England in 1978. Since then, a number of other births have occurred. The event signals the advances that have been made in genetics, the understanding of prenatal development, and the environment needed to sustain development after conception. It brings hope to millions of people worldwide who are infertile or would otherwise have little chance of bearing their own children. In each case, the procedure is to remove the mother's ovum surgically, fertilize it in a laboratory medium with live sperm cells obtained from a male donor, store the fertilized egg in a laboratory solution that substitutes for the uterine environment, and finally implant the egg in the mother's uterus.

Louise Brown and her parents.

Ruth Hubbard (1980), a professor of biology at Harvard University, has described this procedure in detail:

The woman who is a candidate for **in vitro fertilization** has her hormone levels monitored to determine when she is about to ovulate. She is then admitted to the hospital and the egg is collected in the following way: a small cut is made in her abdomen; a metal tube containing an optical arrangement that allows the surgeon to see the ovaries and a narrow-bore tube (called a micropipette) are inserted through the cut; and the egg is removed shortly before it would normally be shed from the ovary. The woman is ready to go home within a day, at most.

. . . After the egg has been isolated, it is put into a solution that keeps it alive and nourishes it, and is mixed with sperm. Once fertilized, it is allowed to go through a few cell divisions and so begin its embryonic development—the still mysterious process by which a fertilized egg becomes a baby. The embryo is then picked up with another fine tube, inserted through the woman's cervix, and flushed into the uterus. . . .

If the uterus is not at the proper stage to allow for implantation (approximately seventeen to twenty-three days after the onset of each menstruation) when the embryo is ready to be implanted, the embryo must be frozen and stored until the time is right in a subsequent menstrual cycle. (pp. 10–12)

As with other remarkable breakthroughs in modern biology and medicine, this one is not without its ethical dilemmas. Ruth Hubbard, for example, wonders whether it is better to focus on giving each woman the opportunity to have her own "biological child" or to attend to the many children already born in the world who need parents (e.g., foster care and adoption). Others have wondered about the criteria to be used in matching donor sperm with eggs and about the subsequent legal rights of the male donor. Finally, we don't yet have enough information to know what kinds of risks may be involved for the mothers and the children in these remarkable experiments. We won't really know until many years have passed and enough data have been collected.

Introduction

The story of human development begins at conception. Here a single male sperm cell fertilizes a female ovum and a biological process is begun that will lead to the development of a fully formed infant. The course of development during this prebirth span—called the **prenatal period**—is awesome. From a single fertilized egg a complex human develops, intact with an intricate anatomy, organs, nervous system, and response capabilities. And each human newborn is unique. A major task of this chapter will be to describe the manner in which this prenatal development takes place and to highlight the landmarks along its path. A second major task will be to describe the course of physical development during infancy. Before beginning, however, we must first understand some biological principles that are responsible for the process of prenatal development and for shaping the course of further human development—the principles of heredity.

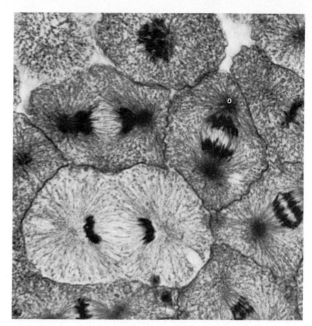

Cell division after fertilization of the ovum.

Heredity

Each of us has inherited a general biological code from our parents. Physically, this code is carried by biochemical agents referred to as **chromosomes** and **genes.** The chromosomes and genes guarantee that we are alike in one important respect: we are all human. A fertilized human egg cannot develop into a dog, a cat, or an aardvark. The general hereditary code that all humans share is important. Aside from the obvious physical similarities such as our anatomies, brain structures, and organs, this hereditary code accounts for many of the psychological sameness (universals) among us. The particular kind of brain we have inherited, for example, is largely responsible for how our thought processes develop (explored extensively in chapters 4, 7, 9, and 11), how we acquire language (chapter 4), and how we learn (chapters 4 and 7).

Most of us, however, think more about the *specific* hereditary code that we have. The particular way in which genes are organized in the chromosomes varies from person to person. This variation is why some people are tall and others are short. Some have blue eyes, others brown. Some are male, others female. Some have dazzling intellects, others are dull. Some are vivacious and outgoing, others quiet and introverted. These differences are caused by differences in our genetic makeup.

Basic Building Blocks

Conception occurs when a sperm cell from the male unites with the egg, or ovum, of the female. Once the fertilized egg begins to divide, the process of development is in motion. This process is directed by genetic material contained in the nucleus of each original cell—the sperm and the egg. The nucleus of each of these cells contains twenty-three chromosomes, each of which is a long and complex chainlike structure containing many thousands of genes. These two cells, sometimes called reproductive cells, or germ cells, are the only ones we possess that contain precisely twenty-three chromosomes. All other body cells contain forty-six chromosomes arranged in twenty-three complementary pairs—one in each pair contributed by each biological parent. In the fertilized egg, the two sets of chromosomes pair off physically, producing forty-six chromosomes. As the fertilized egg divides and redivides over the next several weeks—a process called **mitosis**—each new cell will have a replica of the same forty-six chromosomes arranged in the same way.

In each chromosome of a cell, there are thousands of smaller particles known as genes. A gene, once thought to be the smallest building block in the process of hereditary transmission, actually is a complex molecule. Watson and Crick (1953), two British scientists, astounded the world by describing the structure of this molecule, which is known as **DNA (deoxyribonucleic acid).** Their discovery is reported in *The Double Helix* (Watson, 1968), a book with all the fascination of a mystery story. The discovery was the result of years of patient and compulsive work—trying out a chemical model, rejecting it, trying out another, rejecting it, and so on.

In unraveling this mystery, it was discovered that the very structure of the DNA molecule suggested how the phenomenon of chromosomal splitting occurred. This splitting is perhaps the most important part of the hereditary cycle. It guarantees duplication and the

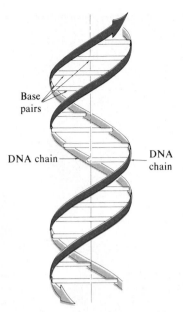

Figure 3.1 The double helix: the DNA molecule.

The relationship between genotype and phenotype is shown in this mother and daughter pair.

equal chromosomal partnership of the male and female parent cells. DNA consists of molecules arranged as if in a spiral staircase—the **double helix.** Two long strands (analogous to handrails or sides of a staircase) are connected by several short strands (analogous to steps on the staircase). The structure divides, or "unzips," with the two strands coming apart. (See fig. 3.1 for a diagram of the DNA molecule and its structure.)

Genetic Transmission

The arrangement and characteristics of the chromosomes and genes inherited make each person different. The total constellation of chromosomes and genes and their unique configuration in an individual is referred to as the person's **genotype.** All of the observed and measurable characteristics of an individual are referred to as the person's **phenotype.** Phenotypical characteristics may be physical, as in height, weight, eye color, and skin pigment, or they may be psychological, as in intelligence, creativity, memory, extroversion, self-identity, and moral character.

What is the relation between an individual's genotype and phenotype? How does heredity determine what each person becomes in life? The answer is complex; this complexity will be shown in our discussions of the different mechanisms and possibilities for hereditary transmission. By way of anticipation, however, consider the following assertions.

Identical phenotypical characteristics may be produced by different genotypes. For example, three unrelated individuals may each have a measured IQ of 110 but vastly different genes for intelligence. And the converse is also true; differences in a phenotypical characteristic may be produced by the same genotype.

For example, identical twins have been known to have different IQs (a not uncommon finding). So different IQs were produced by identical genetic makeups.

How are characteristics transmitted by the genes? How is it that one person develops blue eyes and another brown; one grows tall and another short? Many people believe that the child grows up to be the genetic average of the parents. According to this view, if one parent is tall and the other short, the child will attain a height that is intermediate between the two; if one parent is exceedingly bright and the other dull, the child will develop an average intellect. This view is patently false. Experience and careful observation indicate that children do not acquire the so-called average of their parents' characteristics.

It is true, however, that each parent contributes half of the chromosomes for the child. What does happen, then, when genes from the two parents are combined in their offspring? Some significant experimentation in the field of genetics, discussed in the next section, provides us with answers to this question. Increasingly, marital partners who want to have a child are turning to genetic counselors if they suspect some genetic problem may influence the health of the offspring—see box 3.1 for a description of what genetic counseling is like.

Mendel's Laws

Some human characteristics seem to be determined by the combination of one gene from the father with a corresponding gene from the mother. The color of the eyes

Genetic Counseling

Bob and Mary Sims have been married for several years. They would like to start a family, but they are frightened. The newspapers and popular magazines are full of stories about infants born prematurely who don't survive, infants with debilitating physical defects, and cases of congenital mental retardation. The Simses feel that to have such a child would create a social, economic, and psychological strain on them and on society in general.

Accordingly, the Simses turn to a genetic counselor for help. Genetic counselors are usually physicians or biologists who are well versed in the field of medical genetics. They are familiar with the kinds of problems that can be inherited, the odds for encountering them, and helpful measures for offsetting some effects. The Simses tell their counselor that there has been a history of mental retardation in Bob's family. Bob's younger sister was born with Down's syndrome, a form of mental retardation. Mary's older brother has hemophilia, a condition in which bleeding is difficult to stop. They wonder what the chances are that a child of theirs might also be retarded or have hemophilia and/or what measures they can take to reduce their chances of having a mentally or physically defective child.

The counselor probes more deeply, because she understands that these facts in isolation do not give her a complete picture of the possibilities. She learns that no other relatives in Bob's family are retarded and that Bob's mother was in her late forties when his younger sister was born. She concludes that the retardation was due to the age of Bob's mother and not to some general tendency for members of his family to inherit retardation. It is well known that women over forty have a much higher probability of giving birth to retarded children than younger women have. Apparently the ova (egg cells) are not as healthy in older women as in women under forty.

In Mary's case the counselor determines that there is a small but clear possibility that Mary may be a carrier of hemophilia and transmit that condition to a son. Otherwise, the counselor can find no evidence from the family history to indicate genetic problems.

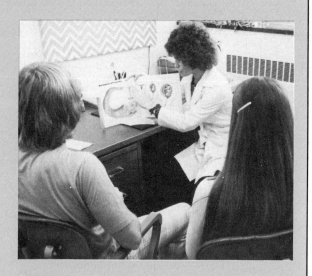

The decision is then up to the Simses. In this case the genetic problem will probably not occur, so the choice is fairly easy. But what should parents do if they face the strong probability of having a child with a major birth defect, as did pregnant women who were treated with the drug thalidomide? Ultimately, the decision depends upon the couple's ethical and religious beliefs. They must decide how to balance these against the quality of their child's life.

The moral dilemma is even more acute, of course, once a pregnancy has begun. **Amniocentesis,** a test that can detect Down's syndrome and more than one hundred other birth defects, can be performed about the fourteenth or fifteenth week of pregnancy. This test has been helpful to many older mothers. A long, thin needle is inserted into the abdomen to extract a sample of amniotic fluid, the liquid that cushions the fetus. Fetal cells in the fluid are then grown in a laboratory for two to four weeks and can then be studied for chromosomal and some metabolic disorders. The later amniocentesis is performed, the better the diagnostic potential. However, the earlier it is performed, the more useful it can be in deciding if the pregnancy will be terminated.

and straight hair or curly hair are determined in this way. Such abnormal conditions as lack of skin pigment (**albinism**), sickle-cell anemia, and **phenylketonuria,** sometimes called **PKU,** a form of mental retardation linked to an enzyme problem are also determined by the combination of one gene from the father and a corresponding gene from the mother.

In the nineteenth century, Gregor Mendel uncovered some basic principles, now known as Mendel's laws, that explain what happens when genes are combined. Mendel conducted experiments in cross-fertilization of different kinds of garden peas, and these experiments have significant application to humans.

For each human characteristic there are two genes (one from each parent), which may carry identical codes or different codes. A person may have two genes

Dominant genes produce curly dark hair when it is part of the specific hereditary code.

population, therefore, most individuals who carry them are not aware of it. It is only when two of the recessive genes come together that the undesirable trait appears.

Sex Linkage

Some characteristics depend on genes carried in the twenty-third chromosome pair—the pair that also determines the sex of the offspring—with the result that these characteristics are more or less likely to occur in members of one sex. Which way this sex linkage goes depends upon whether the gene is dominant or recessive and whether it occurs on the X (female) or the Y (male) chromosome.

A popular example of a sex linked characteristic is color blindness. Many people are unable to distinguish red from green, an inability caused by a recessive gene that appears only on the X chromosome in the pair. (Some X chromosomes have a dominant gene bearing a normal code for the trait.) The Y chromosome does not have a gene that influences the outcome in any way. The odds are much greater for a male offspring to inherit color blindness (50 percent) than for a female (25 percent). However, statistics show even more disproportion; something like seven or eight times as many cases of color blindness are observed in men than in women.

Other Genetic Mechanisms

Genetic determination is often more complicated than you might think from the preceding discussion. For one thing, dominance and recessiveness are not absolute; they are relative for some characteristics, resulting in qualitative mixtures. For example, some red and white parent flowers produce pinkish offspring rather than pure red and pure white flowers. For another, few characteristics are determined by the action of single gene pairs; most are actually determined by the interaction of many different genes in the chromosomes. These traits are described as **polygenically** determined. Most important, children develop very few psychological characteristics that are solely the result of a particular genetic code. Virtually all psychological characteristics are the result of an interaction between the child's inherited code and environmental influences. Neither heredity nor the environment acts alone.

Before continuing with the discussion of **genetic-environmental interaction,** read in box 3.2 how biologists are making monumental strides in their attempts to understand the intricate complex mysteries of genetic mechanisms.

The Heredity-Environment Interaction

We can be more precise about the nature of the interaction of genetic codes and environment than about genetic determination alone. Anne Anastasi (1958) developed the notion of a continuum of influence of heredity on development, which she referred to as the

carrying a code to signal the formation of brown eye pigmentation, or one gene bearing a code for brown and the other bearing a code for blue eye pigmentation, or two genes carrying the code for blue. Some gene codes are **dominant** and others **recessive.** If both combining genes have a dominant code, or if one has the dominant and the other the recessive code, the offspring will have the dominant feature. The recessive feature will appear only if two recessive genes—one from each parent—combine. In determining eye color, brown is dominant and blue is recessive. So a child who inherits a brown-brown or a brown-blue gene combination will have brown eyes. Blue eyes will appear only when a blue-blue combination is inherited.

Geneticists frequently attempt to trace the probability of transmitting a dominant or a recessive gene across several generations in a family, based upon knowledge of how the resulting characteristic has been distributed on the family tree. Such research is especially helpful for parents in cases where there is a history of a genetically linked disorder, such as PKU.

It is common practice for geneticists to refer to all the genes in a population as the population's gene pool. This idea is useful in studies to determine the number and kinds of **harmful genes** within a population. Examples are genes that cause certain kinds of muscular dystrophy, feeblemindedness, diabetes, heart disease, and nervous system disorders. Many of these are rare recessive genes that are distributed throughout the

You Are Different

Modern genetics has made it possible to distinguish one individual from another in a variety of ways. In addition to reinforcing our need to conceive of ourselves as unique—and we are—the techniques available do much more. Descriptions of two such techniques follow (Hutton & Harsany, 1980).

A technique in which all the pairs of chromosomes are stained and lined up to be examined under a high-power microscope is known as **karyotyping.** Chromosomes vary in size, so they may be numbered accordingly. In females, all chromosome pairs have members that match: in males, however, one pair, usually designated the twenty-third pair, does not. This is the pair that determines maleness. When physical and external anatomical features are atypical, chromosomal investigation often settles the question of the person's sex. (There are cases, however, where the chromosomes themselves are abnormal.) Some day karotype studies may be so accurate that we may be able to detect even minor differences in gene structure, perhaps analyzing one gene at a time.

A second technique can identify a person's blood type, which is transmitted genetically. Blood type refers to the presence or absence of certain substances (agglutinogens) in the red blood cells, and other substances (agglutinins) in the blood plasma. These can be identified through chemical tests that cause blood of different types to clump in different serum preparations. Blood types are most commonly divided into the following categories: O, A, B, and AB positive and negative. However, there are actually a couple of dozen blood groups that can be used to differentiate us.

Female   Male

How is knowledge of blood type useful? Knowledge of blood types is important for safe blood transfusions, for preventing hemolytic disease in the newborn, and for transplant surgery. It has also been used in conflicting claims of paternity, kidnapping, inheritance, and the inadvertent switching of infants in hospitals.

One of the most useful applications of blood typing is analyzing reproduction and childbirth. Couples with incompatible blood types, studies indicate, have a higher incidence of childlessness, since women of one blood type can produce antibodies against incompatible sperm cells.

continuum of indirectness. The most direct influence of heredity can be seen in inherited characteristics that cannot be changed by the environment. Various genetic forms of mental retardation, such as Tay-Sachs disease, fall in this category. No matter what educational or environmental intervention is tried, children born with Tay-Sachs will have progressive neurological deterioration, with the resulting impairment of mobility, sight, and speech.

A less direct influence of heredity can be seen in inherited characteristics that can be modified by society. For example, many congenital physical defects can be remedied through modern medicine; certain bone malformations or facial disfigurations can often be modified through surgery; and some forms of congenital blindness and deafness can also be corrected.

Anne Anastasi.

Table 3.1
Continuum of Indirectness of Genetic Influence

	Characteristics
Direct	Some forms of retardation (e.g., Tay-Sachs disease)
	↓
	Congenital defects
	↓
	Inherited susceptibility to disease
	↓
Indirect	Social stereotypes

The influence of heredity is less direct in cases in which a child inherits susceptibility to disease. There are some individuals, for example, whose blood develops no antibodies to fight ordinary colds, influenza, or bacterial infection. Life for these individuals must be maintained in a sterile environment, safe from germs. Others are born with weak lungs or hearts or with allergies to pollens or foods. Each of these can influence the patterns of children's lives—the amount of protectiveness in parents, the people with whom they associate, as well as the limits of their activities and achievements. But it is relatively easy to ameliorate these susceptibilities through fairly simple physical regimens and medical treatment. Children with weak lungs may limit their physical activity, children prone to infection can be treated with drugs, and children with allergies to pollens or to specific foods can simply avoid these irritants or be treated to develop immunity to them.

Perhaps the least direct effect of heredity is found in social stereotypes. Skin color, ethnic features, or other distinctive physical characteristics may make individuals vulnerable to stereotyping. This stereotyping can shape the way people respond to an individual. It may place the individual in a position of privilege; in the United States, for example, the white Anglo-Saxon male historically has held an economic and educational advantage over others. Or it may place the individual in a position of inferior status and ostracism; in the United States members of virtually every ethnic minority have had to struggle to overcome the disadvantages placed in their way because of stereotyping. See table 3.1 for an indication of the indirectness of genetic influences on various characteristics.

Strategies for Determining Hereditary Influence
There are several different ways to examine the influence of heredity in developmental processes. One way is to compare identical twins with nonidentical twins and make a determination about the degree of similarity of the two groups for a particular characteristic. This is related to a second type of study, referred to as a *consanguinity study.* Related pairs, such as fathers and sons, siblings, and cousins, are compared with randomly paired individuals who are unrelated. The closer

the blood relationship, the more similar the genetic makeup of the individuals. If some genetic mechanism influences the phenomenon under study, the scores of the related individuals should be more alike than those of unrelated individuals. In fact, it should be possible to specify several different degrees of relatedness in such a study. For example, parents and their offspring are more alike genetically than are grandparents and grandchildren, who in turn are more similar than third-generation cousins.

An assumption might be made in both kinds of inquiry that the environments are about the same for all the individuals being studied. But the assumption may clearly be unwarranted. Identical twins are genetically similar and are often treated alike because parents perceive them as similar. (This, of course, is a source of resentment and frustration for the twins themselves.) The same family might treat nonidentical twins very differently because the children are perceived to be different. Unrelated children grow up in different families with different economic, educational, religious, and cultural backgrounds—in environments as different as could be. Thus, there is likely to be a continuum of environmental sameness that ranges from the very similar to the very dissimilar. This continuum often coincides with the continuum of genetic sameness, so the two are confounded. A study that purports to examine genetic influence may in fact measure environmental influence.

Fortunately, there is a way out of this dilemma. It is possible to look at groups who are related genetically but whose environments vary. Twins and siblings, for example, are sometimes reared by different families as a result of the divorce or death of their parents. The environments of children reared apart would most likely be dissimilar. It is possible then to establish the similarity of some characteristic in, for example, twins reared together versus twins reared apart.

Of course, all research methods employed with humans are of a *correlational,* or *quasi-experimental,* nature. Generally speaking, it is not possible to manipulate genetics or the environment directly and to have complete control over the significant independent variables. Since many ethical questions are raised when anyone attempts to manipulate the genetic backgrounds of a group of humans, many students of genetics feel that humans are less than ideal subjects for study. They turn, instead, to lower animals with whom practical, ethical, and scientific considerations permit more tightly controlled research. It is possible to construct laboratory environments whose dimensions are well defined and well controlled and to breed many generations of animals over relatively short periods of time. Rats and mice are popular subjects because of the very short time they require to produce a new generation.

Research is of two types. In selective breeding experiments, animals are mated over successive generations on the basis of their similarities in a specific characteristic, like speed of running or performance in a maze. It is assumed that these characteristics have a strong hereditary component. Fast rats bred with other fast rats should produce a homogeneous strain of fast rats after several generations. Slow rats bred with other slow rats should produce a homogeneous strain of slow rats after several generations.

The second type of experiment is inbreeding. Male and female animals of the same parents (brothers and sisters) are mated with each other. Their children, their children's children, and succeeding generations of children are mated in turn. When different families of animals are kept distinct and inbred over several generations, a number of genetically determined characteristics should appear. Each family will have distinctive coloring, size, and weight. Each may also have a characteristic speed of running, level of activity, and performance in mazes.

What, then, is done with this evidence from experimentation with animal genetics? Of what value is it in understanding human development? It helps us to identify some characteristics that may be inherited by other animals, including humans; it suggests traits for us to look for in ourselves. It also improves our understanding of the mechanics of genetic transmission, helping us to refine our ideas about genetic dominance, sex linkage of characteristics, polygenic action, and so forth.

Genetic Influences on Development
What facets of development are influenced by inheritance? From our earlier discussion, one answer should pop out at you; namely, they all are. A better question is, What amount of variation in a charcteristic among different people is accounted for by genetic difference? For a summary of this discussion see figure 3.2. If we know the tested intelligence of a group of children and we know something about their genetic similarity or dissimilarity, we should be able to conclude something about the correlation between the two (i.e., intellectual similarity, genetic similarity). Unfortunately, most of the answers to this type of question are imprecise. Our ability to control other important variables, such as the similarity of the environments in which the children are reared, is often weak and we sometimes don't have precise enough measures of genetic similarity. Estimates often vary widely as to the **heritability** of a particular characteristic. Heritability is a mathematical estimate, often computed with a standard heritability quotient. For example, estimating how much more alike identical twins are than nonidentical twins would be expressed as a heritability quotient.

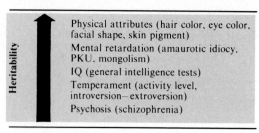

Figure 3.2 Comparative influence of heritability on aspects of development.

Although heritability quotient values may vary considerably from one study to the next, it is often possible to zero in on the average magnitude of the quotient for a particular characteristic. For some kinds of physical attributes and mental retardation, the heritability quotient approaches 1.00. That is, the environment makes virtually no contribution to variation in the characteristic. This is not the same as saying that the environment has *no* influence; the characteristic could not be expressed without it. For intelligence and temperament, evidence puts the heritability quotient in the neighborhood of .50 to .80 (e.g., Scarr-Salapatek, 1975). For some forms of psychosis—particularly for certain forms of schizophrenia—the heritability quotient is in the neighborhood of .30 to .50. Later in the text, we will consider the specific evidence for the heritability of such characteristics as intelligence and temperament. However one problem of development deserves special attention at this juncture—mental retardation.

Mental Retardation: A Genetic Anomaly
There are a number of genetic disorders that create the condition commonly called mental retardation. Retardation is easily assessed by extremely poor performance on any of several standardized intelligence tests. However, not every child who is diagnosed as retarded has inherited this problem. In cases where a hereditary link cannot be identified clearly it is difficult to pinpoint the precise cause or causes of retardation. Genetic transmission may easily be traced to the secondary features of retardation, such as the shape of the head or the appearance of the nose and mouth. In one form of retardation, amaurotic idiocy, blindness and physical paralysis result from impairments to the brain and nervous system. The syndrome seems to be due to the inheritance of a recessive gene from both the child's mother and father.

The PKU syndrome (phenylketonuria) is another type of retardation. Here the problem resides in a genetic code that fails to produce an enzyme necessary for metabolism. In the absence of this enzyme, the cells fail to break down an amino acid, phenylalanine, interfering with metabolic processes and generating a

Foundations of Development of Infancy

poisonous substance that enters the nervous system. Mental functioning deteriorates rapidly if the enzyme deficiency is not treated shortly after birth. Fortunately, the absence of this enzyme can be detected early and treated by diet to keep phenylalanine at a very low level so that normal metabolism can proceed and the poisonous substance will not be generated. Again, a recessive gene is responsible for this disorder.

Perhaps the most common genetically transmitted form of retardation is **Down's syndrome.** The Down's child has a flattened skull, an extra fold of skin over the eyelid, and a protruding tongue. Among other characteristics are a short, thin body frame and extreme retardation of motor abilities. The cause of Down's syndrome is an extra chromosome—Down's children have forty-seven chromosomes instead of the usual forty-six. It is not known why the extra chromosome occurs, but it may be related to the health of the female ovum or the male sperm. Women over forty years of age are many times more likely to produce a Down's child than younger women, ostensibly because the ovum is less healthy.

We have seen that heredity plays an important part in virtually every aspect of development through interaction with environmental experiences. And, while we know that such genetic-environmental interaction is so important in development, we still know very little about the precise nature of how this interaction works. We turn now to a consideration of the physical changes and patterns of maturation that are observable in infant development. We consider first the important changes prior to birth; second, we look at the birth process itself; and third, we provide a broad overview of the physical changes that follow during infancy.

Prenatal Development

Prenatal development can be divided into a number of discrete periods: *conception,* the *germinal period,* the *embryonic period,* and the *fetal period.*

Conception

The life processes begin when a single sperm cell from the male unites with the ovum (egg) in the female's fallopian tube in a process called fertilization, or **conception.** The ovum is produced in the ovaries at about midpoint in the female's menstrual cycle. Fertilization takes place within several days after the ovum begins its descent from the ovaries and through the fallopian tubes into the uterus. If the ovum travels to the uterus without being fertilized, it disintegrates within several days, rendering conception impossible until the next cycle.

Germinal Period

The **germinal period** lasts for two weeks after conception. Almost immediately, twenty-three chromosomes from the sperm cell and twenty-three from the ovum cell pair off, producing twenty-three pairs, or forty-six chromosomes. Within a day, chromosome pairs double and split, with half of them gravitating to each side of the cell. Then the fertilized ovum divides into two cells. Because the chromosome pairs in the original cell doubled, each new cell has exactly the same number of chromosomes as the original cell, that is, twenty-three pairs, or forty-six chromosomes.

During the next ten to fourteen days two major developments occur. One is continued cell division. Prior to each division the chromosome pairs first double, with

Fetus at eight weeks.

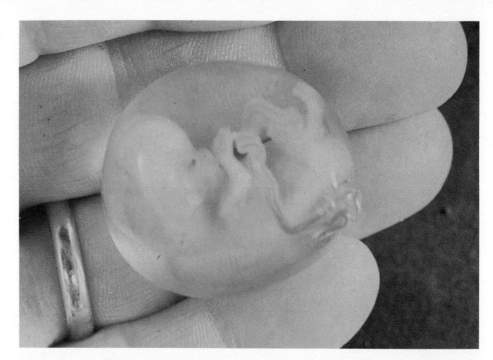

Fetus at nine weeks.

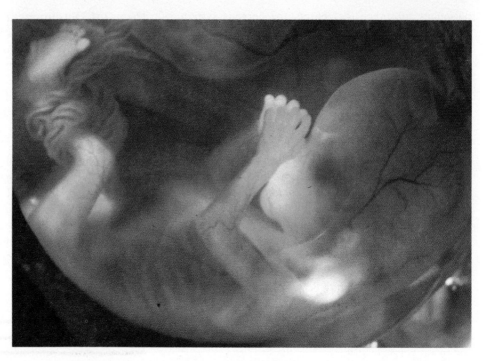

each new cell retaining a replica of the original twenty-three pairs of chromosomes. The second major development is the firm attachment of the ovum to the wall of the uterus within a week or ten days after fertilization. During this time the divided cells gradually form a spherical mass, which separates into an inner and outer part. The outer part becomes connected to the uterine wall and eventually forms part of the mother-fetus barrier that develops later. The inner mass becomes the fetus.

Embryonic Period

The **embryonic period** lasts from about two to eight weeks after conception. It is during this period that a primitive human form takes shape. The basic parts of the body—head, trunk, arms, legs—can be identified. Some finer features, such as eyes and ears, fingers and toes, are also discernible. Internal organs have begun to develop, some of which are functioning, at least to some degree. A primitive heartbeat, circulatory activity, liver and kidney function, and some nervous system action can be distinguished.

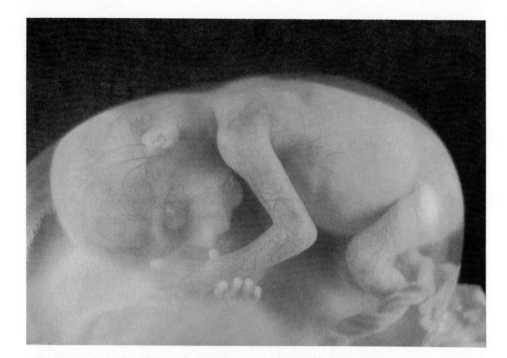

Fetus at twelve weeks.

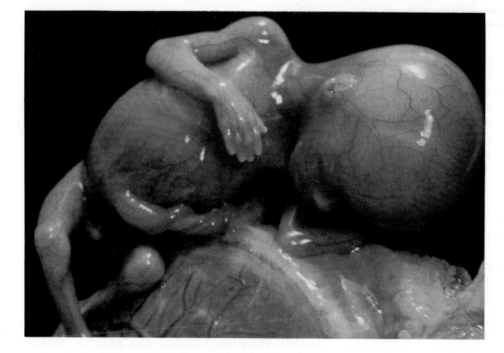

Fetus at sixteen weeks.

It is also during this period that the life-support system for the embryo is formed. The part of the embryo attached to the uterine wall becomes the placenta, the meeting ground for the circulatory system of both embryo and mother. Semipermeable membranes keep their bloodstreams separate but allow such substances as oxygen, drugs, vitamins, and some nutrients (sugar and protein) to pass through to nourish the embryo. The umbilical cord transports waste substances from the embryo to the placental barrier; the cord also has membranes that allow for the passage of only certain substances. Blood cells are too large to pass through the membranes of the placenta, so there is no direct link between the circulatory system of the mother and that of the embryo. By the end of this period the embryo is about one inch (2.5 cm) long and weighs about half an ounce (14 g).

WE HAVE THAT
OUTSIDE TOO

PROMISE
the baby it can go back where it came from. (They never do.)

Fetal Period

The **fetal period** lasts from about eight weeks until birth—a total of about seven months in full-term babies. By twelve weeks of age the fetus is about three inches (7.5 cm) long and weighs approximately one ounce (28 g). It has become active, moving its arms and legs vigorously, opening and closing its mouth, and moving its head. A number of physical and anatomical features become well differentiated. On the face, for example, forehead, eyelids, nose, and chin can be distinguished; the upper arms, lower arms, and hands are clearly distinguishable, as are the lower limbs. The genitals can be identified as male or female. Further progress is noted on a month-by-month basis.

By the end of the fourth month, the fetus is about six inches (15 cm) long and weighs about four ounces (110 g). Whereas a great deal of growth has already occurred in the head and facial structures, there is now an increased growth spurt in the lower parts of the body. A number of prenatal reflexes (automatic response involving one part of the body), such as arm and leg movements, become stronger and can be felt by the mother for the first time.

By the end of the fifth month, the fetus is about twelve inches (30 cm) long and weighs about a pound (450 g). Structures of the skin have formed; there are fingernails and toenails; and the fetus is more active, exhibiting a preference for a particular position in the womb.

By the end of the sixth month, the fetus is about fourteen inches (36 cm) long and weighs about two pounds (900 g). The eyes and eyelids are completely formed; there is a fine layer of hair on the head of the fetus; it exhibits a grasping reflex; and there is evidence of what appears to be irregular breathing movements.

By the end of the seventh month, the fetus is about sixteen inches (40 cm) long and weighs about three pounds (1.4 kg). It is at this time that the chances of survival are good if the child is born prematurely. For this reason it is sometimes called the "age of viability." If prematurely born, however, the infant is very sensitive to infection and must be cared for in a well-regulated environment provided by an incubator.

During the eighth and ninth months, the fetus grows longer and there is a substantial weight gain—about four pounds (1.8 kg). At birth, the average American baby is twenty inches (50 cm) long and weighs seven pounds (3.2 kg). During these months the fatty tissues develop and the functioning of various organ systems (e.g., heart and kidneys) is stepped up. See table 3.2 for a summary of these changes.

Environmental Influences on Prenatal Development

Some expectant mothers tiptoe about in the belief that everything they do and feel has a direct effect on their unborn child. Others behave more casually, assuming that their experiences have little impact on the unborn child. The truth lies somewhere between these extremes. Although living in a comfortable, well-protected environment, the fetus is not totally immune to the larger environment surrounding the mother. There are some well-documented ways in which this environment can affect the child. Thousands of babies every year are born deformed, mentally retarded, or suffer from other congenital defects as a result of events as early as two months prior to conception.

Geneticists and specialists in fetal life are finding that the mother's physical and mental health are critical factors in the development of a healthy infant. Some researchers believe that the months before a woman gets pregnant determine the health of the fetus and newborn infant (Witherspoon, 1980). Emotional upset and poor diet of a woman before pregnancy are implicated as possible problems that may alter the course of her infant's health. Environmental factors, such as the time of year the baby is born, also are associated with birth characteristics. For example, children conceived in the summer are about 20 percent heavier than those conceived in the winter, and about 10 percent heavier than those conceived in spring and fall. And, the rate of fetal malformations is one-third higher among children conceived in spring and fall than those conceived in the summer. Why this is so remains to be explained.

Hazards to Prenatal Development

For many years, scientists believed that almost all birth defects were genetically triggered. Now we know that many such abnormalities are also due to such factors as maternal diseases and blood disorders, diet, irradiation, drugs, temperature, and oxygen level. Maternal characteristics such as age and emotional well-being can influence the health of the newborn as well.

Table 3.2
Summary of Major Changes from Conception to Birth

Period	Age	Height	Weight	Notable Changes
Germinal	(0–2 weeks)			rapid cell division ovum attaches to uterine wall inner and outer mass formed
Embryonic	(2–8 weeks)	2.5 cm	14 g	human form takes shape internal organs begin to develop placenta and umbilical cord form
Fetal	(8–37 weeks)	50 cm	3.2 kg	growth and change to sustain independent life
Third Month	12 weeks	7.5 cm	28 g	activity, movement head growth, facial features
Fourth Month	16 weeks	15 cm	110 g	reflexes become brisker growth spurt in lower part of body mother feels movement
Fifth Month	21 weeks	30 cm	450 g	skin structures form fetus has characteristic life
Sixth Month	26 weeks	36 cm	900 g	eyes, eyelids formed fine layer of hair on head grasp reflex irregular breathing
Seventh Month	30 weeks	40 cm	1.4 kg	"age of viability"
Eighth–Ninth Months		50 cm	3.2 kg	rapid weight gain fatty tissues develop organ system activity (e.g., heart, kidneys, step up)

YOU MAY LISTEN
to Beethoven for 9 months hoping to have a musician, and still have a tone deaf baby boy who wants to be a cocktail waitress.

Scientists now label any agent that causes birth defects a **teratogen,** which comes from the Greek word *tera,* meaning monster, and the field of study that focuses on birth defects is called **teratology.** Some general conclusions from research in this embryonic field of research follow. Rarely is there a consistent link between specific teratogens (e.g., drugs) and specific birth defects (e.g., malformation of the legs). There are so many different teratogens that virtually every fetus is exposed to at least several of them. Consequently, it often is difficult to determine which teratogen causes a particular birth defect. And, sometimes it takes a long time for the effects of some teratogens to show up—only about half are present at birth.

Despite these uncertainties about teratology, scientists have been able to discover the identity of some teratogens and the particular point of fetal development at which they do their greatest damage. Figure 3.3 reveals the particular point in prenatal development that teratogens do the most harm. The most damaging effects occur in the first eight weeks of prenatal development, but damage to the brain can occur in the last months of pregnancy as well. Because the various organ systems begin and end their prenatal development at different times, their sensitivity to teratogens varies over time. Vulnerability to damage from teratogens for the brain is highest at fifteen to twenty-five days into prenatal development, for the eye from twenty-four to forty days, for the heart from twenty to forty days, and for the legs from twenty-four to thirty-six days (Tuchmann-Duplessis, 1975).

Now that you have been introduced to the general way in which problems may surface in prenatal development, let's look at three aspects of teratology that have been given particular attention in recent years—maternal diet, drugs and other chemicals, and the mother's emotional state.

Maternal Diet
Since the fetus receives all of its nutrients from its mother's blood, the mother must have a good diet if the fetus is to develop normally. Pregnant women whose diets do not provide adequate nutrients have more premature deliveries, more infants with low birth weights,

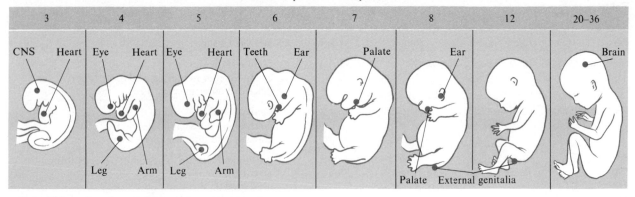

● Part of fetus where damage is greatest

Figure 3.3   The effects of teratogens at specific points in prenatal development.

more complications such as anemia and toxemia, and more prolonged labor (Drillien, 1964). Adequate protein seems to be particularly important for the development of the infant's nervous system (Rosenbaum, Churchill, Shakhashiri, & Moody, 1969).

Research also has revealed that too much of certain vitamins may cause problems for the developing fetus. Clinical studies have suggested that high doses of vitamin A during pregnancy produce growth retardation and birth defects. The mechanism is unknown but it seems to slow down the process by which cells are generated. High doses of vitamin D also have been implicated in dissolving calcium in the bone (Witherspoon, 1980).

Drugs and Other Chemicals
Many pregnant women take drugs, smoke, and drink alcohol without thinking about the possible effects on the fetus. Occasionally, a rash of deformed babies are born, bringing to light the damage certain drugs ingested by the mother may have on her offspring. This happened in 1961 when many pregnant women had been taking a popular mild tranquilizer, thalidomide. Thalidomide was a mild tranquilizer to the mother, but to a fetus, it was devastating. Not all infants were affected in the same way by the thalidomide. Each of the fetal organs or bodily parts appears at a particular point in development, often within a specified set of hours. Consider an arm—on the twenty-sixth day after conception, an arm is formed; and by the thirty-seventh day, the beginnings of hands appear. If the mother took thalidomide on day twenty-six (she probably didn't even know she was pregnant then), the arm probably wouldn't grow. If she took the drug two days later, the arm might not grow past the elbow. The thalidomide tragedy shocked the medical community and parents into the stark realization that a woman does not have to be a chronic drug abuser to damage the fetus—taking the wrong drug at the wrong time was enough to physically handicap the offspring for life.

Fetuses also are adversely affected when their mothers smoke or drink heavily. Infants who are born to alcoholic mothers, for example, tend to have more problems adapting to sights, sounds, temperature changes, and other demands of the environment than those born to mothers who drink moderately or not at all during pregnancy (Willemsen, 1979). And, women who smoke heavily during pregnancy have offspring who weigh less than normal for a number of months, which may make them more susceptible to a number of health problems. Further, infants whose mothers are heroin addicts are born addicted to heroin. These infants may suffer from withdrawal when they are born, a circumstance that may prove fatal.

There is no clear consensus on how much alcohol or cigarette smoking during pregnancy is safe. Some pediatricians suggest that several glasses of wine daily will not harm the fetus, while others recommend total abstention. Some women who smoke heavily switch to filtered cigarettes when they become pregnant to lessen tar and nicotine intake. But the smoke that comes through a filtered cigarette has more carbon monoxide than a nonfiltered one, and the resulting decrease in the oxygen in blood may impair fetal brain development.

The Mother's Emotional State
Eleanor Willemsen (1979) describes how emotional stress in the mother may influence fetal development. Since the nervous systems of the mother and the fetus are entirely separate, the reactions that occur in the mother's nervous system are not directly transmitted to the fetus. However, there are several ways her emotional state could influence the fetus. First, when the mother is under stress, gland secretions—adrenalin for example—increase. These secretions increase hormone levels in the blood stream. As the mother's blood circulates through the embryo, the same physical changes that have been stimulated in the mother could appear in the fetus—changes in heart rate, respiration, and blood pressure.

The mother's emotional state during pregnancy can influence the birth process. An emotionally distraught mother may have irregular contractions and a more difficult labor. This may produce irregularities in the baby's oxygen supply, or it may lead to irregularities after the birth. Babies born after extended labor may adjust more slowly to their world and show more irritability. One investigation revealed a clear connection between the mother's anxiety during pregnancy and the condition of the newborn infant (Ottinger & Simmons, 1964). Mothers answered a questionnaire about their anxiety every three months while they were pregnant. When their babies were born, their weights, activity, and crying were evaluated. The babies of the high anxious mothers cried more before feedings and were more active than the babies born to less anxious mothers.

Birth and the Importance of Infancy in Life-Span Development

The past twenty years have witnessed an explosion of knowledge about the period of development from the moment of birth to about two years old. Experts in many fields are rapidly producing information about the life of the newborn, physical growth and change, perceptual and intellectual capabilities, nutrition and health, and many other topics. The standard reference handbook in the field of child psychology, *Carmichael's Manual of Child Psychology,* has reflected the explosion as well (Mussen, 1970; 1982). In 1970, three of the book's two dozen research essays dealt explicitly with the period of infancy. The new handbook (in four volumes) devotes a whole volume (and a dozen essays) to infancy.

Many overlapping and complementary reasons explain this interest and explosion of knowledge. One is the continuing intellectual interest in the origins of psychological development. Psychologists want to know what the newborn is capable of doing, how advanced these early competencies are, and how they develop further during the next two years. Psychologists have provided some unique insights about what the newborn knows and about how the newborn processes information. Doubtless, philosophers will continue to debate the innate knowledge versus acquired knowledge controversy on logical grounds, but they must now incorporate new empirical insights into their arguments.

Second, new techniques are available to the experts. It is now possible to record an infant's eye movements with precise photographic records (e.g., Salapatek, 1975; Marsh, Hoffman, & Stitt, 1979); to measure brain activity while an infant is experiencing some event (e.g., Moskewitz-Cook, 1979; Molfese & Molfese, 1979); to measure rather precisely an infant's physiological state of arousal (Lipsitt, 1979); to measure changes in the infant's apprehension of events, as in studies of habituation (Cohen, DeLoache, & Strauss,

1979; Strauss, 1979; Miller et al., 1979); and to manage the detailed information spawned by these technical capabilities with widely available, high-speed computers.

Third, most classic theories of development (e.g., Freud, 1959; Piaget, 1952) make broad claims about the importance of events during infancy in laying a foundation for later development. If we believe Freud, then the parents' handling of the infant's oral and anal conflicts may fix later development. In his example, an individual's attachments to people, personal identity, gender attitudes, and emotional outlook all heavily depend upon how the parents interacted with the individual as an infant. And for intellectual development (e.g., Piaget, 1970), successful negotiation of the sensorimotor stages of thought is critical for mastering later stages of cognitive competency. If for some reason this early sequence is disrupted or retarded, later cognitive progress will be difficult. As these claims about the critical importance of early experiences have been taken more and more seriously, scholars have felt compelled to obtain evidence to test them. Some of the explosive growth in infant studies has been spawned by our newfound techniques for the very precise testing of such claims.

Fourth, there has been a renewed interest in clinical and medical diagnosis and in the prevention of birth and neonatal problems. Much has been learned about birth defects and their causes, and scientists can better identify serious problems in infants, for example, retardation and sensory and physical handicaps. The search for techniques and means of spotting such problems (and correcting them when possible) has increased our clinical knowledge as well as our knowledge about infants.

Let us turn our attention first, then, to the transition from fetus to newborn. This transition is an exciting one for parents as well as psychologists and the process by which it occurs is truly awesome. Prior to birth, the fetus is a completely dependent organism; afterwards, the child sustains many life-supporting activities independently. This section will consider both the birth process and the characteristics of the newborn baby.

The Birth Process

A few days or weeks before the child is born, the fetus becomes positioned head downward, with legs and feet extended upward. Labor, the activity by which the infant is pushed out of the mother's womb, is signaled by the onset of contractions in the uterus (see fig. 3.4). A contraction is an involuntary narrowing and lengthening of the uterine cavity, followed by a period of relaxation. At the beginning of labor, a contraction lasts for a few seconds; near the end of labor, it may last for

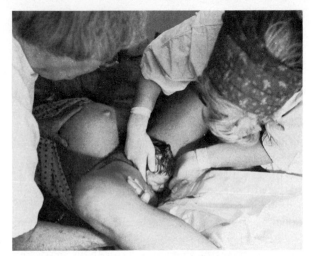

Birth marks a dramatic transition for the fetus.

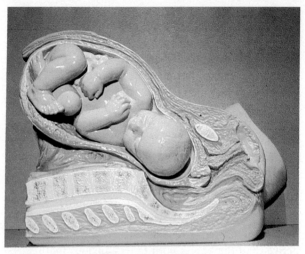

a. The uterus at term; cervix not dilated.
Figure 3.4　Six stages of childbirth.

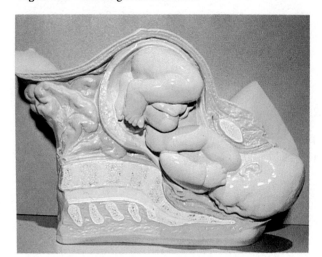

d. Emergence of the head as it rotates.

a few minutes. The mother's later-borns usually require a shorter delivery time than the first-born because the birth canal has usually been enlarged during the first delivery. It can take from four to twenty-four hours for the birth canal to widen sufficiently for delivery of the child, and delivery may be as difficult for the baby as for the mother. The new arrival to our world appears splattered with the mother's blood and a thick, oily material called vernix, which allows the child to slip through the birth canal.

In many births the attending physician may need to guide the infant through the birth canal with forceps. Sometimes a normal birth cannot take place because the fetus is positioned incorrectly or the mother's birth canal is too small or there is some medical complication. In these cases a caesarian birth takes place, which is a surgical procedure in which the baby is delivered through the mother's abdomen. (This procedure was named after Julius Caesar, who supposedly was delivered in this manner.)

Birth marks a dramatic transition for the fetus. In the womb the fetus was in a dark, free-floating, low-gravity environment with a relatively warm, constant temperature. At birth the newborn must quickly adjust to light, gravity, cold, and a buzzing array of changing stimuli. In addition, the very process of being pushed out of the womb is physically strenuous and exhausting. A French physician, Leboyer (1975), proposed an alternative to the conventional method of delivery employed in most modern hospitals. The **Leboyer method** seeks to minimize the birth shock for the newborn by offering a postdelivery environment that is calm and peaceful, like the womb. During the delivery itself everyone speaks in hushed tones, extraneous noise is kept to a minimum, and the room is dimly lit. Immediately after the birth the newborn is placed on the mother's abdomen, with the umbilical cord still intact.

The mother's body recreates the soft, warm feeling of the womb and the accustomed heartbeat. The baby is not spanked to start the breathing process, which begins by itself. The traditional practice of holding the baby upside down by its feet to straighten the spine is abandoned. Leboyer feels that this sudden straightening may be traumatic and prefers to let it occur more gradually. Thousands of newborns have been delivered in this fashion around the world. Their doctors and parents report that these infants seem to adjust calmly and happily to the world.

Birth Date and Weight
A full-term infant is one who has grown in the womb for the full thirty-seven to forty weeks from conception to delivery. Not all babies are born on schedule, however. Some are born *prematurely*. In a **premature birth** an infant is born after less than thirty-seven weeks in

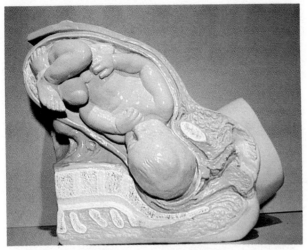

b. Cervix dilates as the uterus contracts.

c. Progress of the head to pelvic floor.

e. Further extension of the head.

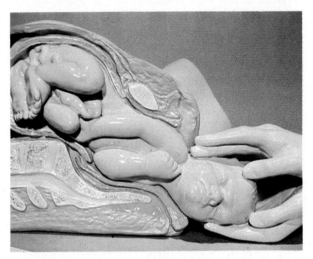

f. The shoulder begins to emerge.

the womb. Most premature infants are smaller and lighter in weight than full-term babies, but there are also small babies born after a full term. Generally speaking, a baby weighing five and one-half pounds (2.5 kg) or less is considered premature if born after less than thirty-seven weeks in the womb, or if born at four pounds or less at full term, is labelled **a high-risk infant.**

Premature and high-risk infants are placed in a protective environment until they have matured enough to brave the world on their own. The protective environment is an incubator, a small, transparent shell of plastic and metal that is a self-contained living space in which the atmosphere and temperature are carefully regulated, the infant's vital signs are closely monitored, and pleasant stimulation (e.g., soft music and rocking) is provided. Since premature and high-risk infants often have difficulty breathing, sleeping regularly, and warding off simple germs and infections, the

incubator environment is critical to their survival. Each year the intensive-care procedures for premature and high-risk newborns improve, and these infants have better odds for survival (Stewart & Reynolds, 1974; Kendall, 1977; Lipsitt, 1979).

There has been a great deal of interest in the development of premature babies stemming from the suspicion that they somehow grow up differently from normal children. The general finding is that children born at full-term and children born prematurely do differ somewhat in their development during infancy. For about six months after birth, premature infants sleep less regularly than full-term babies, cry more while awake, exhibit less interest in novel events, and develop social responses, such as smiling, more slowly (Parmalee, 1976; Sugar, 1977a, 1977b). But these differences generally disappear in later infancy. Nonetheless, some studies have shown differences between full-term and premature babies during early childhood and adolescence. Full-term children may display higher intelligence and school achievement (Drillien & Ellis, 1964; Wiener, 1968) than do the prematurely born, but the differences are usually exhibited by only the very smallest of the prematurely born children, those with birth weights as low as three pounds (.13 kg). It is likely that these children suffered from some neural or physical impairment that was not completely corrected. Premature birth itself, then, may not be the cause of later differences; a complication associated with the birth may be the culprit.

One dimension of prematurity often missed in the formal studies of development is the way in which the infant and caretaker interact. Susan Goldberg (e.g., 1977, 1980) has written extensively about this topic and suggests that there may be a number of important differences in the ways premature and full-term infants develop a pattern of interaction with their mothers. Preemies are small, fragile, less alert, less responsive to environmental events, and cry less intensely than their full-term counterparts. Parents cannot help but notice these differences, whether because of their experience with previous infants or because of the obvious contrast with other full-term babies in the nursery. Another factor is that parents cannot have close physical contact with their preemies for extended periods of time, as can the mothers of full-term babies, because the premature newborns must often be cared for in the protective neonatal care facility of the hospital (e.g., Rosenfield, 1980).

Goldberg postulates that mothers of preemies are likely to develop a sense of inadequacy because the close, postnatal bond is cut off (e.g., Klaus & Kennell, 1982). Several studies have shown that parents do interact differently with their preemies, perhaps because of this attitude Goldberg describes. Young preemies are not handled as much and are talked to and cuddled less (DiVitto & Goldberg, 1979). This difference tends to disappear in the older preemies, however, and there is some evidence that among parents of infants who are in the hospital for a long time, this pattern is reversed and the parent works harder at eliciting responses from and paying attention to the baby (e.g., Braun & Bakeman, 1978; Field, 1978).

The majority of infants, both full-term and premature, do not show serious impairments at birth—less than 10 percent have any abnormality, and most of these disappear during later development. One method that is frequently used to assess the health of the newborn is the **Apgar Scale,** shown in table 3.3. One minute and five minutes after birth the obstetrician or nurse

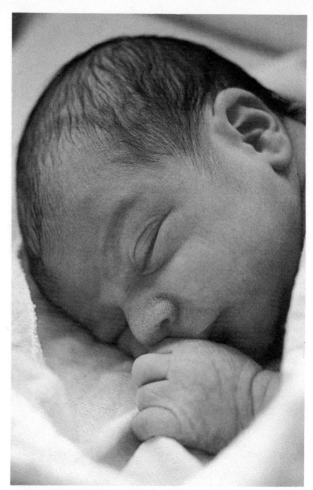

The majority of infants, both full-term and premature, do not show any serious impairments at birth.

gives the newborn a rating of zero, one, or two on each of five signs—heart rate, respiratory effort, muscle tone, body color, and reflex irritability. A high total score is favorable—seven to ten suggests the newborn's condition is good, five indicates there may be developmental difficulties, and three or below signals an emergency and that survival may be in doubt.

The Newborn's Capabilities

Because the newborn is capable of very few responses, for a long time, it was difficult to assess what the infant sensed, perceived, or learned. In the past two decades scientists have developed sophisticated techniques to make inferences about these matters. The prevailing view used to be that the newborn is a passive, empty-headed organism that perceives nothing, does nothing, and learns nothing. From the new evidence, however, this notion has been reversed. The neonate is now regarded as an active individual exploring the environment and picking up information through primitive, but

Table 3.3
The Apgar Scale

		Score		
		0	*1*	*2*
Neonate System	*Heart Rate*	Absent	Slow—less than 100 beats per minute	fast—100–140 beats per minute
	Respiratory Effort	No breathing for more than one minute	irregular and slow	good breathing with normal crying
	Muscle Tone	Limp and flaccid	weak, inactive, but some flexion of extremities	strong, active motion
	Body Color	Blue and pale	body pink, but extremities blue	entire body pink
	Reflex Irritability	No response	grimace	coughing, sneezing, and crying

Source: Adapted from Apgar, 1953, pp. 260–67.

nonetheless effective, perceptual apparatus, that is the eyes, ears, nose, mouth, and skin. In box 3.3 Frank Caplan (1981) provides an exciting account of the infant's body power at birth.

Infant Physical Development

The infant's pattern of physical development through the first year is exciting. Only twelve months ago the infant had a gigantic head (with dangerous soft spots) that flopped around in an uncontrollable fashion, reflexes were dominated by evolutionary movements, and the skin was wrinkled and blue. In a span of twelve months, however, the infant will be capable of sitting anywhere, standing, stooping, climbing, and probably walking.

The First Year

During the child's first year there are periods of relative quiet in growth and development and periods bursting with rapid change. One pattern of growth and development is particularly important for our discussion of the first year of the infant's life—the **cephalo-caudal pattern.** The cephalo-caudal pattern suggests that the greatest growth always occurs at the top of the person—the head—with physical growth in size, weight, and feature differentiation gradually working its way down from top to bottom (e.g., neck, shoulders, middle trunk, etc.). This same pattern is manifested within the head area, since the top parts of the head—the eyes and brain for example—grow faster than the lower portions—such as the jaw. An illustration of this type of growth pattern can be seen in figure 3.5, indicating the prominence of the head area. Notice that an extraordinary proportion of the total body is occupied by the head at birth, but that by the time the individual reaches maturity this bodily proportion is almost cut in

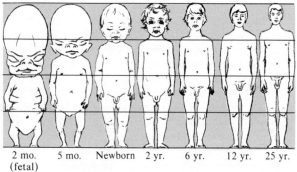

| 2 mo. (fetal) | 5 mo. | Newborn | 2 yr. | 6 yr. | 12 yr. | 25 yr. |

Figure 3.5 Changes in body form and proportion during prenatal and postnatal growth.
From *Human Embryology* by Patten. Copyright 1933. Used with the permission of McGraw-Hill Book Company.

half. Do you recall the artists' conceptions of children in ancient and medieval art (shown in chapter 1) with their childlike, but adult proportioned heads? The distortion of their perceptions of infants and children can now be seen.

What little motor maturity exists at birth is in the area of the head, reflecting the cephalo-caudal pattern. At birth, babies are able to move their heads a little from side to side—a performance that is easier when they are lying on their backs than on their stomachs. The adaptive nature of this ability becomes evident when we consider that infants would have trouble breathing if they could not turn their mouth and nose away in a face-down position. Breathing problems reflect one of the most puzzling issues in infant development. **Sudden infant death syndrome** (SIDS) refers to the unexplained death of a child during the first year

Box 3.3
Neonate Body Power

Newborns are just not as helpless as they look. First of all, the activities needed to sustain life function at birth. A newborn can breathe, suck, swallow, and get rid of wastes. He can look, hear, taste, smell, feel, turn his head, and signal for help from the first minute. Right from the start, a baby's attention can be captured by sharply contoured or circular shapes. This indicates your newborn's mental curiosity is not entirely swamped by his needs for food and comfort.

Physically, newborns are admittedly limited. A newborn is tiny. From head to heels, he may be about twenty-one inches long and weighs seven and one-half pounds. His head, about six inches long, is about one-third of his height and an inch bigger than his chest, so he is understandably awkward. Just try to image yourself in his shape. Even with your maturity and skill you would have a hard time getting around if your head were twice as big and your arms and legs half their size. He is bound by where you put him, and he is at the mercy of his bodily needs. His heart beats twice as fast as a grownup's, 120 beats a minute, and he breathes twice as fast as you do, about thirty-three times a minute. He may urinate as many as eighteen times and move his bowels from four to seven times in twenty-four hours. He sleeps fourteen to eighteen hours of his twenty-four-hour day. On the average, he is alert and comfortable for only thirty minutes in a four-hour period.

Reflexes govern his movements, which are automatic and beyond his control. For example, if you stroke the newborn's hand or foot on the back or top, the whole arm or leg withdraws slightly and the hand or foot flexes and then returns so that fingers or toes may grasp your finger. This withdrawal reflex only exists until the baby begins to use his limbs in a different way—legs for standing and stepping, arms for reaching.

There are many other reflexes the newborn will show you if you hold him in a standing position and gently press the sole of one foot and then the other to the bed, he will draw up each leg successively as if walking. Without helping it, the newborn can actually "walk" across a bed. Almost a year after the newborn's walk reflex vanishes, it reappears as the voluntary, complex art of walking.

One of the most frequent and dramatic reflexes of the newborn is the Moro reflex, a vestige from our ape ancestry. If the baby is handled roughly, hears a very loud noise, sees a bright light, or feels a sudden change in position, he startles, arches his back, and throws his head back. At the same time, he flings out his arms and legs, then rapidly closes them to the center of his body, and flexes it as if he were falling. As he cries, he startles, then cries because of the startle. This reflex, normal in all newborns, tends to disappear at three to four months of age. Steady pressure on any part of his body will calm him. If you hold his arm firmly flexed at his shoulder, he will quiet even though undressed and free of restraints.

Try stroking different parts of an infant's body. If you stroke the palm of his hand or the sole of his foot at the base of the toes, he will grasp your finger. The more premature he is, the more tenacious his grasp. By using his toe grasp, you can lift your baby's leg off a mattress. With his hand grasp, you can gently pull him to a sitting position or even suspend him in the air hanging onto your fingers for dear life, as if to a tree branch. (Better leave this one to the experts.) Stroking the outside of the infant's sole sets off an opposite reflex, called the Babinski. The toes spread and the big toe shoots up in the air.

As mothers learn as soon as they start feeding the baby, stroking his cheek or around his mouth makes him root or turn toward the stroking object. This rooting reflex helps him find the breast, and the sucking reflex follows. Touching the inside of his mouth, which is more sensitive than the surrounding area, stimulates this reflex most. A bottle is thus easier to suck than the breast because the bottle touches this area. [The following table is an overview of the newborn's reflexes.]

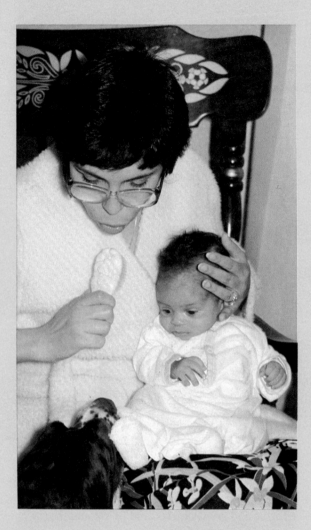

If you	Then the baby's
Stand infant; press foot to bed	Feet step.
Pull baby to sit	Eyes snap open, shoulders tense. Baby tries unsuccessfully to right head (China doll reflex).
Pull baby on tummy on flat surface	Head turns to side and lifts. Baby crawls, lifts self with arms.
Support chest on water surface	Arms and legs "swim."
Place on back and turn head to side	Body arches away from face side; arm on face side extends, leg draws up; other arm flexes (tonic neck reflex).
Stroke foot or hand on top	Limb withdraws, arches, returns to grasp.
Stroke palm or sole at base of digits	Limb grasps.
Stroke outside of sole	Toes spread, large toe sticks up.
Tap upper lips sharply	Lips protrude.
Stroke cheek or mouth	Mouth roots, head turns and tongue moves toward stroking object; mouth sucks.
Stroke cheek or palm	Mouth roots; arm flexes; hand goes to open mouth.
Place object over nose and mouth	Mouth works vigorously; head twists, arms fling across face.
Stroke leg, upper part of body	Opposite leg or hand crosses to push your hand away; withdraws.
Rotate baby to side	Head turns, eyes precede direction of rotation.
Suspend by legs	Body curls to upside-down ball, legs extend, arms drop into straight line; neck arches backwards.

If you	Then the baby's
Tap bridge of the nose, or shine a bright light suddenly into the eyes, clap hands about eighteen inches from infant's head, or touch white of eye with cotton	Eyes close tightly.
Make sudden contact or noise	Head drops backward, neck extends, arms and legs fling outward and back sharply (Moro reflex).
Extend forearms at elbow	Arms flex briskly.
Lightly prick soles of feet	Knee and foot flex.

Source: Caplan, 1981, pp. 7, 9, 21.

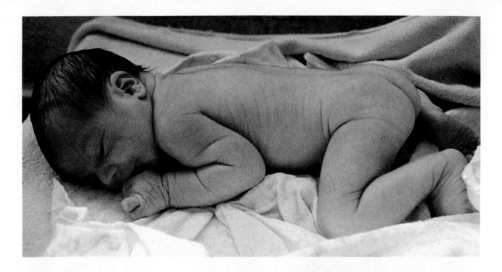

At birth, babies are able to move their heads a little from side to side.

It is not until eight or nine months that the infant learns to stand.

of life because of breathing failure. Autopsies and reviews of the infants' pediatric histories offer no explanation of why children simply quit breathing—usually at night. There are approximately two deaths of this kind—also referred to as crib death—for every one thousand births each year. After the first ten days of life, sudden infant death syndrome is responsible for more deaths in the first year of life than any other cause.

Control of Trunk and Arms

At birth, the infant has no appreciable coordination of the chest or arms. By three or four months, however, two striking accomplishments occur in turn. The first is the infant's ability to hold the chest up while in a face-down position. The other is the ability to reach for objects placed within the infant's direct line of vision, without, of course, making any consistent contact with the objects (since the two hands don't work together and the coordination of vision and grasping is not yet

possible). A little later, we see further progress in motor control; by five months the infant can sit up with some support and grasp objects, and by six months the child can roll over when lying in a prone position.

Use and Support of Legs

At birth, the neonate is capable of supporting some weight with the legs. This is proven by formal tests of muscular strength, which use a specially constructed apparatus to measure the infant's leg resistance as the foot is pulled with a calibrated spring device. This ability is also evidenced by the infant's partial support of its own weight when held upright by an adult. If the child is given enough support by the adult, some forward movement can actually be seen in a built-in stepping reflex, which disappears in a few months. Each leg is lifted, moved forward, and placed down, as if the infant were taking a series of steps. However, the sequence lasts only two or three steps and, of course, the infant does not have sufficient balance or strength to execute the movement independently.

Table 3.4
Milestones of Motor Development in Three Areas, Reflecting Cephalo-Caudal Sequence

Age in Months	Control of		
	Head	*Trunk and Arms*	*Legs*
Birth			
1	Side to side movement		Limited support stepping reflex
2	Hold head and chin up		
3		Hold chest up in face-down position	
4		Reach for objects in sight (without success)	
5	Head erect in sitting position		
6		Sit up with some support	
7		Roll over in prone position	
8			Walk with assistance
9			
10			Support self alone
11			Pull self up in standing position
12			
13			Walk alone
14			

It is not until eight or nine months that the infant can walk with limited help from an adult. Sometime later (perhaps ten or eleven months), the infant can support himself or herself standing alone, pull up into a standing position, and finally (perhaps by thirteen or fourteen months) walk. The actual month at which some milestone occurs may vary by as much as two to four months, particularly among older infants. What remains fairly uniform, however, is the sequence of accomplishments.

A summary of this cephalo-caudal sequence is presented in table 3.4. Note the lag in time from significant control of head and trunk with that of arms and legs.

Rhythmic Motor Behavior
During the first year of life rapid, repetitive movement of the limbs, torso, and head is common. Such **rhythmic motor behavior**—kicking, rocking, waving, bouncing, banging, rubbing, scratching, swaying—has intrigued scientists for many years. These infant motor behaviors stand out not only because they occur frequently, but because of the pleasure infants seem to derive from performing the acts as well.

Explanations of rhythmic motor behavior have been numerous. Arnold Gesell (1954) saw rocking as a specific stage in development, but warned (Gesell & Amatruda, 1941) that persistent rhythmic motor behavior was a sign of developmental delay or impoverished environment. Jean Piaget (1952) referred to kicking and waving as "secondary circular reactions," a stage of sensorimotor development when infants attempt to repeat a behavior that has an interesting effect on their environment. Psychoanalysts have interpreted rocking as the infant's attempt to establish relations with an "aloof" mother (Brody & Axelrad, 1970). And, pediatricians have suggested that head banging is due to a bad temper (Levy & Patrick, 1928). In one investigation (Kravitz & Boehm, 1971), mothers of 200 infants were questioned about their infants' rhythmic behavior. It was concluded that rhythmic behavior has no neurological explanation, a conclusion similar to that reached in a review of the functions of rhythmic behavior (Mitchell & Etches, 1977).

Esther Thelen (1981), however, believes that rhythmic behavior in infancy serves a more important developmental function than it has been ascribed in the past. She believes that rhythmic motor cycles serve an important adaptive function for infants in their first year of life, namely, they represent an important transition between uncoordinated activity and complex, coordinated motor behavior. She conducted extraordinarily detailed observations of twenty normal infants from the time they were four weeks old until they were one year old. More than 16,000 bouts of rhythmical behavior were observed. Infants generally spent about 5 percent of their time performing this type of behavior, but some infants at some ages performed rhythmic movements as much as 40 percent of the time they were being observed. The forty-seven distinct movements observed included variations of kicking, waving, bouncing scratching, banging, rubbing, thrusting, swaying, and twisting. When stereotyped movements were grouped by body part and posture, their frequencies showed characteristic developmental profiles over the first year, as shown in figure 3.6. Rhythmic leg behavior, for example, gradually increased at about one month, peaked at five to six months, and then declined.

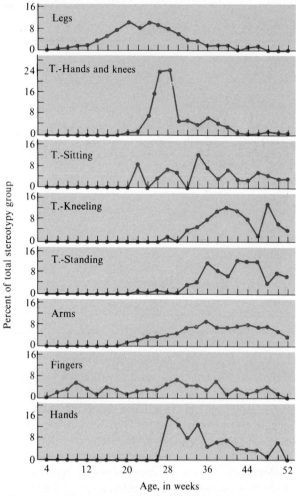

Figure 3.6 Frequency of rhythmic motor behavior in the first year of life. (Frequencies have been expressed at each age as a percentage of the total bouts of the stereotypy group seen at that age. Vertical scale indicated on the left is the same for each horizontal axis. Data have been pooled for the sample, N = 20, T = torso.)

Rhythmic arm movements also gradually increased but their first occurrence and peak frequency was later than for rhythmic leg movements. If all rhythmic cycles are summed, the age of peak frequency is six to seven months, with a small but real decline in the last few months of the year (Thelen, 1979).

Rhythmical stereotypies do seem to represent an important transition between uncoordinated activity and complex, coordinated, voluntary motor control. For example, kicking movements peaked just before the onset of locomotion and declined dramatically in the last third of the year. Rocking on hands and knees appeared just before crawling, and rhythmical hand and arm movements appeared before complex manual skills.

The neurological significance of rhythmic behavior also can be seen in studies of abnormal infants—see box 3.4 to understand how studies of abnormal infants point to the importance of rhythmic behavior.

Fine Motor Control and Coordination

In addition to the cephalo-caudal pattern of development, there is a second principle called the **proximo-distal** pattern of development. Simply put, this refers to the pattern of growth starting at the center of the body and moving toward the extremities. A concrete example is the early maturation of muscular control of the trunk and arms as compared with that of the hands and fingers.

The motor pathways to the brain mature sooner for areas in the center of the body than for areas at the extremities, however, coordination also progresses on the basis of sensorimotor linkages in the central nervous system. The sensory and motor control centers in the brain develop faster than the brain's ability to coordinate them. Environmental information picked up through the five senses (and registered in the **sensory cortex**) must be coordinated with an action stimulated by the **motor cortex.** When the infant reaches for an object, for example, the brain center that directs the movement must be in touch with the center that detects where the object is (perhaps the visual cortex). But that communication is governed by the **association areas of the cortex,** which develop later than the sensory and motor areas.

Some specific landmarks in the development of motor control and sensorimotor coordination follow. The focus on "eye and hand" is dictated by the importance placed on this system in many theories of development (e.g., Piaget, 1954; Bruner, 1973) and by our greater knowledge of this as opposed to other sensorimotor systems. Sensorimotor coordination will be considered again in the next chapter, where we explore Piaget's theory of cognitive development in greater detail.

From birth to one month, the infant shows little coordination of any sort but will briefly follow a slowly moving object, such as a hand or a light, until the object is out of the immediate perceptual field. In the next two or three months, visual pursuit becomes more intricate; the infant may follow the object in different directions and planes and will persist in viewing it for longer periods of time.

Manipulation of objects lags somewhat behind visual pursuit and exploration of objects. For example, depending upon the author consulted (e.g., Wood, 1974; Helms & Turner, 1981), the child does not systematically grasp and hold onto objects until four or five months. Prior to this, the child might make brief contact with objects, reach for them, or hold them briefly if they are placed in the hands by someone. Toward the end of the first year (nine to twelve months), the child becomes able to grasp, finger, and manipulate objects with more subtle use of the thumb, palm, and forefingers. The child may also hold an object in each hand, alternately inspect each, and bang the objects together.

If rhythmical stereotypies indeed span the stages between immature motor coordination and full voluntary behavior, infants with developmental delays should show not only retarded onset ages but also comparatively slower onsets of integrated behavior. Thus, once acquired, rhythmical stereotypies should tend to persist longer in these infants. Although systematic observations of the full developmental course, both onset and decline, of stereotypies in retarded infants have not been reported, stereotypies in general are common in retarded children, especially those in institutions. Stereotypies were observed to be the primary mode of expression of affect, social encounter, and object exploration in Down's syndrome infants (Wolff, 1968).

A dramatic confirmation of the developmental prediction of persistent stereotypy comes from Selma Fraiberg's (1977) studies of infants blind from birth. Motor development in blind infants was characteristically uneven. Blind infants attained postural milestones such as sitting alone, "bridging" on hands and knees, and standing at ages comparable to sighted infants. Their locomotor development was severely delayed, however, probably due to a lack of visual motivation to move forward. In normal infants, for example, crawling follows very soon after the infant assumes the hands and knees posture. In blind infants, there may be four or more months delay between these events. Nonetheless, all the infants rocked vigorously in sitting, hands and knees, and standing postures, and unlike in normal infants, this rocking did not disappear. In Selma Fraiberg's words,

> In the blind infant it (rhythmic activity) may be more prolonged because at each point along the gross motor sequence the self-initiated mobility that should follow upon the new posture is delayed. (p. 217)
>
> Thus, a child with good control of his trunk in a bridging posture, with "readiness" we would say for creeping, might be observed on all fours, rocking steadily, "ready to go" with "no place to go." The motor impetus, which normally leads to mobility, was exercised in a vacuum. Again, typically, when mobility was achieved, the stereotyped rocking was extinguished. (p. 278)

Source: Thelan, 1981, p. 246.

After one year, progress is often noted by the precision of physical movements and the concrete "products" a child is capable of making. Two favorite measures, for example, are the number of blocks a child can stack (Bayley, 1965; Cattell, 1947; Brazelton, 1974; Denver Developmental Assessment, 1973) or the strokes the child can make with a pencil (e.g., Wood, 1974). Thus, on the average, at eighteen months children can stack three blocks, and at twenty-four months they can stack five blocks. Not until about twenty-four months are children able to faithfully copy a horizontal or vertical line drawn on a piece of paper. Each activity, block stacking and writing, is viewed as an activity demanding precise coordinated use of the hands and eyes. Although adults take such coordination for granted, infants undergo a fairly lengthy course in mastering them. An outline of the milestones just listed is offered in table 3.5.

The Second Year
There is a deceleration in growth during the second year of the infant's life. The average infant gains approximately five inches in height and five to six pounds in weight. Somewhere around the last few months of the first year of life, and extending well into the second year, the infant begins to eat less. The plump infant gradually changes into a leaner, more muscular child during the second year. The brain also grows more slowly now. Head circumference, which increased by approximately four inches during the first year, increases only by about two inches this year. By the end of the first year, the brain has attained approximately two-thirds of its adult size, and by the end of the second year, about four-fifths of its adult size. During the second year, eight more teeth erupt to go along with the six to eight that appeared during the first year. By their first birthday, most infants have moved from an awkward, upright standing position to walking without support. Refinement of **gross motor skills,** such as walking, make significant strides during the second year.

Gross Motor Skills
Several months into the second year the infant may be able to run and can sit down on a chair unassisted if the chair is short (when the seat is about ten inches off

Table 3.5
Milestones in Selective Sensorimotor Coordinations

Age in Months	Coordinations		
	Visual Pursuit	*Use of Hands*	*Fine Hand-Eye Control*
1	Follow slowly moving object		
2			
3	Sustain viewing of objects		
4	Follow object in different	Systematically grasp and hold	
5	directions and planes	objects	
6			
7			
8			
9		Finger objects	
10			
11		Hold objects in each hand and	
12		inspect them	
13			
14			
15			Stack two blocks
16			
17			
18			Stack three blocks
.			
.			
.			
.			
24			Copy horizontal or vertical line. Stack five blocks.

the floor). At about eighteen months, the infant can climb stairs, by twenty months walk downstairs with one hand held, and by twenty-four months run efficiently without falling very often. Between eighteen to twenty-four months, the toddler (the name often given to the infant who is in the second year of life) enters the "runabout age"—scurrying from place to place, throwing caution to the wind, and evidencing no concern for the danger of his or her ventures.

The development of walking and running skills is important for the infant's emotional as well as physical development. They provide infants with a sense of mastery of their world. Initially, the infant performs very poorly at walking and running, but during the course of the second year will pick himself or herself up time and time again to face the world and test reality.

Fine Motor Skills
Frank and Theresa Caplan (1981) describe the development of fine motor skills during the second year of life.

The way she handles objects that go together is a good illustration of the halfway state the baby has reached. She puts her doll's sock next to its foot, for example, but cannot carry the operation further. She does the same thing with her own shoe, indicating that she knows where it belongs by holding it against her foot. She recognizes that her action is incomplete, gestures to any nearby adult for help, and gives a grunt of satisfaction when the task is performed for her. Her intentions clearly outrace her abilities at this point, a most frustrating state of affairs.

From the baby's point of view, unfamiliar objects are expressly made to be investigated, usually by being pulled apart. Doors that open and shut and drawers that pull out are much more interesting than his own small toys. If he can reach nothing else, his clothing will do. A period of silence in the playpen can often mean that he is busily pulling his garments off. Mothers who do not look on this particular activity with favor may come to tolerate it more easily if they regard it as an important prelude to their child's learning to dress himself. (p. 7)

Year-and-a-half-olds begin to show preference for one hand, either right or left. This tendency shows up in their play, holding of spoon or cup, handling of a crayon or pencil in scribbling. Fine-motor improvement is reflected, too, in the child's ability to dump raisins from a bottle (a test used by child psychologists to appraise the manual dexterity and thinking ability of very young children). (p. 219)

Infants as young as a year and a half begin to show a preference for right- or left-handedness.

By two years of age, the toddler has many of the physical skills we take for granted as adults.

The Two-year-old's Physical Capabilities

By two years of age, the toddler has many of the physical skills we take for granted as adults. But even though the two-year-old can climb and run actively, there still are some gross motor movements he or she cannot perform, hopping being one example. The two-year-old's vision is as sharp as it ever will be, and hearing is equally competent. A summary of the gross and fine motor developments during the second year are shown in table 3.6.

Table 3.6
Gross and Fine Motor Development
during the Second Year

Gross Motor

Visually monitors walking, watching placement of feet in
  order to be able to deal with obstacles in path by avoiding
  them
Runs, but generally lacks ability to start efficiently or stop
  quickly
Jumps crudely with two-foot takeoff
Walking rhythm stabilizes and becomes even
Goes up and down stairs alone without alternating feet
Can walk approximately on line
Likes to walk on low walls with one hand held
Can walk a few steps on tiptoe
Can be trusted alone on stairs
Can walk backwards ten feet
Can quickly alternate between sitting and standing
Tries to balance self on either foot, not yet successfully
Is sturdy on feet; less likely to fall
Still geared to gross-motor activity

Fine Motor

Turns pages of a book, one at a time
Manipulates more freely with one hand; alternates from
  one hand to the other
Has fully developed right- or left-handedness
Increased smoothness of coordination in fine-motor
  movements

Source: Caplan & Caplan, 1977.

In the next chapter we will discuss an important
aspect of physical development in infancy, that of *sensation*. Sensory development, reflected in seeing, hearing, touching, tasting, and smelling, is discussed in
conjunction with perception. We will see how sensorimotor development serves as a foundation for the infant's acquisition of knowledge about the world.

Summary

Human development begins at conception, when a single sperm cell from the male unites with the ovum from
the female to produce a fertilized egg. The hereditary
code transmitted by this fertilized ovum determines to
a large degree what the child becomes. The basic
building blocks that transmit this code are chromosomes and genes. There are twenty-three pairs of chromosomes formed in the original fertilized egg and

replicated in later cell divisions. One member of each
pair comes from each parent. The twenty-third pair of
chromosomes determines the sex of the infant. Within
a chromosome there are thousands of genes, which are
complex molecules composed of deoxyribonucleic acid
(DNA). Gregor Mendel established the principles of
dominant and recessive gene combination, sex linkage,
and polygenic action, which explain how characteristics can be transmitted. Every characteristic is determined jointly by the interaction of the environment and
hereditary background.

Conception takes place about midway through the
woman's menstrual cycle, with fertilization occurring
in the fallopian tubes. The fertilized egg becomes implanted in the uterus and undergoes a series of cell divisions (mitosis), forming a spherical mass (germinal
period) from which a human form and life-support system differentiate during the next six weeks (embryonic
period). During the final seven months (fetal period)
there is enormous physical growth, weight gain, and
completion of organ systems. During this prenatal period growth may be impeded by the poor health, diet,
and emotional temperament of the mother and by excessive use of any of several different drugs.

The birth process marks a dramatic transition for
the fetus from the dark, quiet chamber of the mother's
womb to the bright light and stimuli of our world. Procedures that have been used to deliver infants include
the caesarian method and the Leboyer method. Premature birth may lead to complications for the infant.
Because of such complications, many premature babies are exposed to protective environments that help
buffer their entry into the world. Some of the differences between premature and full-term babies, though,
are not due to prematurity but to the way parents interact with their infant.

The neonate (newborn) is an unusual sight with a
tiny body, large head, wrinkled skin, and mass of uncoordinated movement. Nonetheless, all senses operate
at birth and the newborn brings a wide array of reflexes
into the world. During the first year, patterns of physical development appear that do not change throughout the life cycle. One such pattern is labeled cephalo-
caudal, suggesting that the greatest growth always occurs at the top of the person. A second pattern is called
proximo-distal, which suggests that growth starts at the
center of the body and later moves to the extremities.

From the time of birth to the end of the first year,
dramatic physical transformations occur in the control
of the head, trunk and arms, use and support of legs,
and fine motor skills. However, there is a deceleration
of growth during the second year of the infant's life.
During the second year, the refinement of walking skills
matures and by the second birthday most toddlers can
run and climb efficiently.

Key Terms

albinism

amniocentesis

Apgar Scale

association areas of the cortex

cephalo-caudal pattern

chromosomes

conception

continuum of indirectness

DNA (deoxyribonucleic acid)

dominant gene

double helix

Down's syndrome (mongolism)

embryonic period

fetal period

fine motor skills

gene

genetic-environmental interaction

genotype

germinal period

gross motor skills

harmful genes

heritability

high-risk infant

in vitro fertilization

karyotype

Leboyer method

mitosis

motor cortex

phenotype

phenylketonuria (PKU)

polygenically

premature birth

prenatal period

proximo-distal development

recessive gene

reflexes

rhythmical stereotypies

rhythmic motor behavior

sensory cortex

Sudden Infant Death Syndrome

teratogen

teratology

Further Readings

Brazelton, T. B. *Infants and mothers: differences in development.* New York: Delacorte, 1969.
An easy-to-read description of several infants developing during the first two years of life, with special focus on individual differences in temperamental style and parental practices.

Caplan, F. *The first twelve months of life.* New York: Bantam, 1981.
An easy-to-read, well-written account of each of the first twelve months of life.

Falkner, F., & Macy, C. *Pregnancy and birth.* New York: Harper & Row, 1980.
An easy-to-read description of experiences during pregnancy and the nature of childbearing.

Leboyer, F. *Birth without violence.* New York: Alfred A. Knopf, 1975.
The French physician describes his highly influential practice of delivery and his opinions about its value. Written in easy-to-read language and accompanied by illustrative photographs.

Watson, J. D. *The double helix.* New York: New American Library, 1968.
A personalized account of the research leading up to one of the most important discoveries of the twentieth century—the discovery of the structure of the DNA molecule. Reading like a mystery story, it illustrates the exciting, serendipitous side of science.

Review Questions

1. Define and explain the terms *chromosome, gene,* and *DNA.*
2. Explain and give examples of: Mendel's law; dominant and recessive genes; sex linkage; polygenic action; the continuum of indirectness; and the heritability quotient.
3. What are the major developments during the germinal, embryonic, and fetal periods in prenatal development?
4. Describe the major events surrounding labor and delivery. What are the consequences of premature birth?
5. Why is infancy a popular topic today with scholars?
6. What does the newborn look like and what is he or she capable of doing?
7. Describe the milestones in infant motor development. Specifically consider control of the head, trunk and arms, leg support, and fine manipulation skills.

4

Cognitive Foundations and Development

Prologue: Can We Teach Math and Foreign Languages to Infants? Should We?

To date, Billie Rash has made somewhere between 8,000 and 10,000 eleven-inch square cards with pictures of shells, flowers, insects, flags, countries, words— you name it—on them. Billie has religiously followed the regimen recommended by Glenn Doman, the director of the Philadelphia Institute for the Achievement of Human Potential and author of the book *How to Teach Your Baby to Read*. Using his methods, learned through a $400 week-long "How to Multiply Your Baby's Intelligence" course she attended in Philadelphia, Billie has taught her children to read and is teaching them Japanese, geography, natural science, engineering, fine arts, and a little math. The children are now four and five years old and are enrolled in a language academy where they are taking courses in French and Spanish, while a private tutor coaches them in Persian. Both boys are learning violin at music school, and during the past summer they took swimming and tap dancing lessons.

Parents using the card approach print one word on each card using a bright red felt-tipped pen. The parent repeatedly shows the card to the infant while saying the word. The first word usually is "mommy," then comes "daddy," the baby's name, parts of the body, and all things the infant can touch. The infant is lavishly praised when he or she can recognize the word. The idea is to imprint the large red words in the infant's memory, so that in time he or she accumulates an impressive vocabulary and begins to read. Subsequently, the parent continues to feed the infant and young child with all manner of data in small, assimilable bits, just as Billie Rash has done with her two boys (Benson, 1981). With this method, the child will be reading by two years old, and by four or five, will have begun mastering some math and be able to play the violin, not to mention the vast knowledge of the world he or she will be able to display because of a monumental vocabulary. Maybe the SAT test you labored through on your way to college might have been knocked dead at six if your parents had only been enrolled in the "How to Multiply Your Baby's Intelligence" course and had made 10,000 flash cards for you.

It is too soon to tell whether programs like the Doman method will be successful or have a substantial impact on children's later development. Some developmental psychologists believe Doman's so-called "better baby" institute is a money-making scheme and is not based on sound scientific information. Before we invest such extensive effort in trying to teach such skills to infants, we must first determine what their basic capacities are. What evidence do we have, for example, that infants can work with numerical concepts?

A rather dramatic demonstration of one important competency has been offered by Mark Strauss (1982). He demonstrated that infants as young as ten to twelve months are able to discriminate between a complex stimulus containing three items and one containing either two or four items. One possible conclusion from this rather startling discovery is that one-year-old infants can count up to three or four items but no higher. Such a conclusion, however, is probably false. More likely, infants are able to notice in a single perceptual act up to five variations in the number of objects.

Not only is it important to ask the question of whether we can teach the concept of number to infants and conduct research that addresses this question, but it also is important to consider whether we should be trying to accelerate the child's development by trying to get him or her to a more advanced cognitive level during infancy. Jean Piaget, the famous Swiss psychologist whose cognitive-developmental theory was introduced in chapter 2, called the question, What should we do to foster cognitive development? the American question, because it was so frequently asked of him when he lectured to American audiences. Piaget, as well as other cognitive-structural psychologists, believe there is something fundamentally wrong with the intense tutorial practicing that characterizes such methods as Doman. As you read this chapter, you will see that Piaget stresses the importance of letting infants actively organize their experiences themselves and spontaneously explore their environment.

Introduction

We have just seen that there is controversy about how much an individual can learn at a particular point in development. Can we, by providing an infant with an optimally enriched environment, get him or her to reason at very advanced levels? In the last chapter this question was discussed under the topic of heredity. And, in this chapter we will devote an entire section to the topic of learning. We will see the issue appear, and reappear, throughout this text. For example, in chapter 6 it will reappear in our discussion of the role of early experience in life-span development. At the heart of the issue are the roles of heredity-maturation and environment-experience in the individual's development. In this chapter we will look at whether the infant's perceptual and cognitive development are influenced more by heredity and maturation or by environment and experience. What do you think? Before you jump to a conclusion, don't forget our discussion of hereditary-environmental interaction in the last chapter. As the chapter proceeds, you will be exposed to what developmental psychologists know about sensory and perceptual development, cognitive development, and learning in infancy.

Sensory and Perceptual Development

We make contact with the world around us though our five primary senses—hearing, touch, taste, smell, and sight. Psychologists distinguish between *sensation* and *perception.* **Sensation** is the pickup of information by our sensory receptors, for example, the ears, skin, tongue, nostrils, and eyes. The sensation of hearing occurs when waves of pulsating air are collected by the outer ear and transmitted through the bones of the middle ear to the cochlear nerve. The visual sensation occurs as rays of light are collected by the two eyes and focused on the retina. **Perception** is the interpretation of what is sensed. The physical events picked up by the ear may be interpreted as musical sounds, a human voice, noise, and so forth. The physical energy transmitted to the retina may be interpreted as a particular color, pattern, or shape.

What are the basic sensory capabilities of the newborn? How do these change during infancy and early childhood? In this section we will consider the development of sensory processes and in the next section we will discuss categories of visual perception, including how the infant perceives depth and size and recognizes patterns and forms.

Hearing

Are infants able to hear when they are born? Evidence suggests that they are (e.g., Bartoshuk, 1964; Steinschneider, Lipton, & Richmond, 1966; MacFarlane, 1978). One procedure proves that even the fetus responds to sound (MacFarlane, 1978). Just before the fetus is born and after the mother's membranes are broken, a very small microphone can be inserted in the uterus and placed near the fetus's ear. After a loud noise is made near the mother's abdomen (which can be recorded on the inside through an attachment to the microphone) the fetus's heart rate (recorded by fetal monitoring) speeds up, a sure sign that the sound has been detected. Just after birth babies tune in most notably to patterned, rhythmic sound (like a human voice), to high frequencies more than to low frequencies, and develop early preferences for one voice (e.g., the mother's). They are also able to localize sounds and can crudely distinguish sounds coming from left and right (Bower, 1974). Babies may make even finer disciminations; for example, they turn their heads more toward a sound coming from an eighty-degree angle from the midline than toward a sound coming from a fifteen-degree angle from the midline on the same side (MacFarlane, 1978).

One aspect of auditory perception that has interested modern students of infancy is **speech perception.** The human voice is an important stimulus for the infant (Parke & O'Leary, 1976; Rheingold & Adams, 1980). How much of it does the infant understand? Current evidence suggests that very young infants are able to perceive speech and distinguish speech sounds. For example, Cynthia Turnure (1969) showed that an infant as young as three months of age noticed when taped recordings of his or her mother's speech were distorted in various ways. By nine months of age infants were able to distinguish their mother's voices from those of strangers. Bernard Friedlander (1970) demonstrated that by twelve months of age children exhibit preferences for specific voice inflections and for speech redundancy in taped recordings.

Research with adults shows that the sounds of speech are perceived in discrete categories—vowel categories such as *a, e, i* and consonant categories such as *p, d,* and *t* (Liberman, 1970; Strange, Edman, & Jenkins, 1979). Are these categories learned, or are they largely present at birth? And are these categories narrowly defined in infancy as they are for adults, that is, with only narrow ranges of sound variation being permitted for a sound to be identified as being in a certain class? (Such a narrowness in speech sound perception is referred to as **categorical perception.**) Peter Eimas (1975) reviewed a number of studies on this question. Newborns distinguish various consonant sounds that differ only in small degrees from one another (e.g., the sounds represented by the letters *b, d, p, t, g*). Moreover, newborns make the distinctions in much the same way that adults do, using certain auditory features as cues for the category to which each sound belongs.

Touch

It is known that newborns are sensitive to touch. If they were not, then few of the reflexive responses mentioned in the last chapter (Babinski, Moro, rooting) would appear. It is also known that infants are responsive to mild electric shock (Lipsitt & Levy, 1959). Other reports suggest that females are more sensitive than males to gentle touch, although this observation has not been consistently supported (Bell & Costello, 1964). Contemporary theories of infant attachment have stressed the importance of tactile sensations for promoting social growth (e.g., Cairns, 1979).

Taste

The sense of taste is one of the more difficult senses to study because it is intimately involved with the sense of smell. However, a few observations can be made. Of the many different ways to categorize taste, the following is generally used as a basis for experimentation and discussion: sweet, sour, salty, or bitter.

The taste buds of infants are more widely distributed on the tongue than are those of older children or adults. Newborns are sensitive to strong tastes and can distinguish sugar, lemon, salt, and quinine (Pick, 1961, citing Neminova). Because newborns enjoy the taste of sugar, many experimenters have given them bottles of sugar water to reinforce a response or to orient them to a situation (e.g., Lipsitt, 1969).

Smell

Much of the information about the newborn's sense of smell (olfaction) comes from anecdotal reports and observations of experts. Newborns are sensitive to very strong odors, such as those produced by ammonia and onion, and quickly turn away from these pungent stimuli.

Lewis Lipsitt and his colleagues concluded that newborns undergo some sensory learning with odors because they seem to adapt to odors that are presented repeatedly. Much as they adapt to other kinds of stimuli, infants pay less attention to odors that have been presented several times (Engen, Lipsitt, & Kaye, 1963). Babies also learn the unique odor of their mothers breasts by six to ten days old (MacFarlane, 1978).

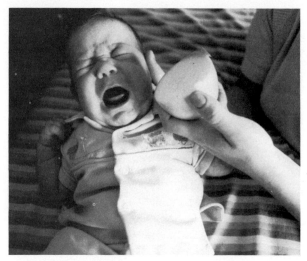

Newborns are sensitive to very strong odors.

Vision

What is the newborn able to see? How does this ability change? The infant can see a number of things; however, what the newborn sees is much more limited.

Visual acuity is a measure of the degree to which a person can see detail clearly. Normal vision for adults, according to the Snellen scale, is 20/20. For the newborn, visual acuity is poor, in the neighborhood of 20/150 or perhaps slightly better (Dayton, Jones, Aiu, Rossen, Steel, & Rose, 1964). Glen Dayton and his colleagues conducted experiments involving vertically striped patterns with alternating dark and white lines. By varying the width of the lines, they created striped displays with narrower and narrower vertical lines. The patterns were moved across the infant's visual field. Since infants follow movement with their eyes, eye movement indicates whether the pattern is perceived as moving. In order to see motion, the infant must be able to detect the stripes; otherwise, the array would appear to be a satisfactory visual field of one solid color. Results indicate that visual acuity seems to improve markedly during the first three or four months of life.

From studies of visual acuity it has also been established that young infants react to certain stimulus information. From the preceding work, for example, it is clear that infants respond to light-dark contrast. Other studies have shown that they respond to variations of movement, color, and brightness. Robert Fantz (Fantz, Fagan, & Miranda, 1975a) has developed a technique to study these abilities. He presents the infant with a pair of drawings in which the objects differ from one another in some important respect. He then observes whether the infant looks longer at one drawing that at the other. If so, it can be inferred that the infant has discriminated between the two objects.

Figure 4.1 Convergence and divergence.

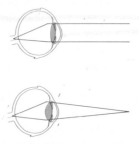

Figure 4.2 Accommodation; in focusing, the lens changes shape to adjust for the distance of the object.

In one study, for example, it was shown that two-week-old infants preferred to watch a moving point of light rather than a stationary form next to it (Fantz & Nevis, 1967). With a similar procedure Maurice Hershenson (1964) found that newborns preferred a brightly lit pattern to a dimly lit one. Patterns of intermediate intensity were preferred to intense or dim patterns.

In a classic study, newborn infants preferred blue to red and green (Stirnimann, 1944). Presented with a variety of colored cards, they looked longest at the blue card. Color preferences in infants may be related to other characteristics associated with color rather than to the color itself, however. Most investigators unwittingly vary brightness, saturation (the richness of the color), and other characteristics at the same time that they vary the hue.

The two eyes of a child are not well coordinated at birth (Salapatek, 1975; Banks, 1980). In children and adults both eyes work together to focus on objects and to perceive depth; in the newborn each eye functions as a semiindependent receptor of information. Hence, the neonate's perception of the world is very distorted as compared with the perception of older infants and children. Normally, in focusing on objects the two eyes may converge or diverge, as illustrated in figure 4.1. **Convergence** is the turning inward of the eyes to view an object close at hand. **Divergence** is the turning outward of the eyes to view an object far away. These **vergence** movements are important for depth perception, which we will discuss in a later section.

To focus on an object, the lens of each eye must also make adjustments for the distance between the eye and the object. It may foreshorten, creating a thick convex appearance, if an object is close to the eye. It will lengthen or stretch out, creating a flatter appearance, if an object is far away. These adjustments of the lens, illustrated in figure 4.2, are referred to as **accommodation.** (Piaget also uses the term accommodation but with a different meaning. Be sure to keep the two meanings straight.) The newborn's eyes do not accommodate. Each eye seems to have a fixed lens adjustment set for objects about eight to twelve inches away. Thus, objects that are very close or very far away are not in sharp focus.

Vergence movements and accommodation improve dramatically during the first three or four months of infancy (Salapatek, 1975; Banks, 1980). By this time the infant's focusing power is virtually as flexible as that of adults.

Visual Perception

A wealth of research enables us to examine the marked changes in visual perception in newborns in greater detail than is possible with any of the other senses. We will look at infant attention, perception of space, perception of pattern and form, and how infants perceptually learn about their world.

Attention

What do infants look at? What features of their environment draw their **attention?** And how do they scan their environments? One fascinating line of evidence has been provided by Philip Salapatek and his colleagues (Banks & Salapatek, 1981). Salapatek developed a technique whereby eye movements can be recorded photographically as the infant looks at simple geometric forms. This allows the experimenter to make inferences about how the infant scans the form. A number of interesting results have been obtained with this method. For example, even the newborn is interested in geometric forms, such as circles and triangles,

One-month-old Finish  Start

Two-month-old Start 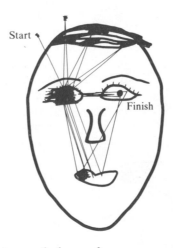 Finish

Figure 4.3 How one- and two-month-old infants scan the human face.

and will look at them for long periods of time. Additionally, the newborn selects a small portion of the figure for examination; there is very little broad scanning to inspect the whole figure. Salapatek suggests that the newborn is preoccupied with detecting individual features of an object rather than with the object as a whole. The older infant takes in more of the drawing and the contour is scanned more completely.

In another study, the way in which young infants scan more meaningful patterns was described (Maurer & Salapatek, 1976). Human faces were shown to one- and two-month-old infants. The faces were those of their mothers or of a stranger. By a special mirror arrangement, the faces were projected as images in front of the children's eyes so that the infant's eye movements could be photographed. Figure 4.3 reproduces the plotting of the eye fixations and movments of a one-month-old child and a two-month-old child. The human face is represented in a schematic fashion, but the plots are based on the infants' actual observations of real faces.

Notice that the one-month-old scanned only a few portions of the entire face, a narrow segment of the chin, and two spots on the head. The two-month-old scanned a wider area of the figure—the mouth, the eye, and a large portion of the head. The older infant spent more time examining the internal detail of the face, while the younger infant concentrated on areas on the outer contour of the face. It has been demonstrated, then, that the results obtained apply to the infant's scanning of simple forms as well as highly meaningful social figures.

Space Perception

To effectively navigate in our environment, we rely on a number of useful perceptions, many of which concern the space around us. It is helpful, for example, to perceive that certain objects are nearby and others are far away, that certain objects are in front of things and others behind. And it is also helpful to perceive the actual size of an object, even though it may be seen in a variety of different circumstances.

How are these perceptual feats accomplished? Do infants perceive depth and size? Are there important changes in these perceptions during childhood? Some of the sources of information for accurate perception of distance and the relative position of objects in space are discussed here. Several of these cues, called binocular cues, depend upon the use of both eyes. One such cue that has already been discussed is *vergence*, meaning that when both eyes focus on an object, the eyes converge or diverge. The greater the distance, the more the eyes diverge; the less the distance, the more the eyes converge. Another binocular cue is retinal disparity. When looking at a scene, each eye has a slightly different view of it. The greater the difference between the views (disparity), the closer the scene is to you.

There are also several cues to distance that are based on the use of only one eye. These are called monocular cues. One that has already been mentioned is accommodation, or the lengthening and foreshortening of the lens of the eye. Another monocular cue is perspective. Artists use perspective principles in their work. The farther away objects are in a drawing the smaller the portion of the visual field they occupy. As an object recedes into the distance, parallel lines in the object seem to converge; a popular example of this phenomenon is the apparent convergence of railroad tracks in the distance. Additionally, the farther away an object is in a drawing the higher it appears in the visual field.

The visual cliff technique.

Finally, some depth cues are provided by coloring and shading in the visual field. Objects farther away are colored in more faded, or "desaturated," tones than the colors used for objects at closer range. When a scene is viewed in natural sunlight, objects take on an increasingly bluish hue the farther away they are. This effect is created by an atmospheric scattering of sunlight; the further the object, the greater the scattering. Shadows indicate the position of an object in relation to known sources of light and to other objects.

One technique for investigating space perception is the **visual cliff technique,** first developed by Richard Walk and Eleanor Gibson (1961) and more recently utilized by a host of others (Sloane et al., 1978; Somervil & Nunez, 1978). Children and adults tend to draw back from a sharp precipice. Walk and Gibson created a visual situation that gave the impression of a sharp drop, or cliff, and hence the term visual cliff. The "cliff" consists of a clear glass surface with a runway across the middle. On one side of the runway, a pattern several feet below the glass simulates a steep cliff; the other side appears to be either solid or with a modest drop. When an infant is placed on the platform and someone attempts to coax the child to either side, the infant readily moves to the "shallow" side but hesitates to move to the "deep" side. This reaction is taken as evidence of depth perception, with the infant's hesitation resulting from fear of the apparent cliff.

In the original study Walk and Gibson observed this reaction in children as young as six months of age. In a later investigation Walk (1966) discovered that infants could be coaxed across the deep side under certain conditions. When the pattern used under the deep side was solidly gray, for example, the infants were more likely to cross than when the checkerboard design was used. And when the distance between the glass and the apparent supporting surface beneath the deep side was several inches rather than several feet, the infants were also more easily coaxed to venture out.

This work by Gibson is, of course, limited to infants who are able to crawl. Younger infants might also display a response to depth if there were some other way of measuring their reactions. In more recent work, in fact, other measures have been employed for this very purpose, including some that relied on changes in heart rate. One researcher, for example, found that infants as young as two months of age showed a change in heart rate when lowered face-down on the deep side and no change in heart rate when lowered onto the shallow side. We may conclude, then, that even young infants are sensitive to a steep drop.

For young infants incapable of moving about, another technique for gauging sensitivity to depth is the **looming** study. The experimenter creates the visual impression of an object being hurled at the infant by creating a rapidly expanding image of something (e.g. a colored circle) on a screen placed in front of the infant (e.g., Bower, 1972; Yonas, 1975). When something approaches us rapidly, it's visual size increases rapidly. Young infants show slight distress—their heart rate and breathing will change—indicating that they have interpreted this common visual information as evidence of something moving toward them.

Another major aspect of space perception is the perception of size and the **size constancy** of objects. How do you perceive a speck viewed from an airplane as a car that is actually fifteen feet long? How do you perceive a tiny person walking toward you from a distance as a person who is actually almost six feet tall? Objects are seen under many different circumstances, but you nonetheless manage, even at a distance, to perceive the object's actual size. One way of doing this is by recognizing the object from its basic shape and pattern. When the object is identified you have a fair sense of its size from everyday experience. But suppose that the object is unfamiliar or that the viewing conditions are poor, such as on a cloudy day or a dark, moonless night. Then how do you make this judgment? One answer turns on the availability of depth cues. Based on knowledge about how far away an object is and the apparent (retinal) size of the object, you can make a perceptual inference about the actual size of the object. This inference is made somewhat automatically; it is not a conscious process.

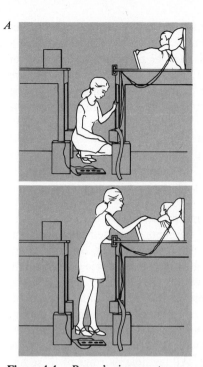

Conditioned stimulus	Test stimuli		
	1	2	3
True size *(cube)*	*(cube)*	*(cube)*	*(cube)*
True distance 1	3	1	3
Retinal size *(cube)*	*(small cube)*	*(large cube)*	*(cube)*
Retinal distance cues	Different	Same	Different
Average number of responses elicited 98	58	54	22

Figure 4.4 Bower's size-constancy experiment. A: The experimenter first hides and then reinforces the child for the desired response (head turning). B: The true size and retinal size of stimuli used in different test conditions.

A number of studies have examined how well children can identify the size of objects. In particular, the focus has been on judgment of size constancy. Size constancy is the perceptual recognition that an object is the same size in the face of different apparent (retinal) sizes (Piaget & Inhelder, 1969; Kling & Riggs, 1971). Evidence suggests that from the age of five or six a child's ability to judge size constancy undergoes very little change, although the judgments of younger children seem to be more influenced by such testing conditions as the method of comparison, the type of stimulus object, and instructions (Lambercier, 1946).

Are young infants also able to make accurate judgments about size constancy? Thomas Bower (1966, 1974) created an imaginative experiment to answer this question. He trained infants who were two and one-half to three months old to turn their heads to the left in the presence of a twelve-inch cube placed in front of them at a distance of three feet (see fig. 4.4). When this stimulus-response relationship was firmly established, Bower observed the infants' responses to three related test stimuli. After viewing the twelve-inch cube at a distance of three feet, the infants were shown (1) the twelve-inch cube at a distance of nine feet, (2) a thirty-six-inch cube at three feet, and (3) a thirty-six-inch cube at nine feet.

Only with the third test stimulus were the infants viewing a cube that had the same retinal-image size as that of the original cube; that is, both covered the same portion of the infants' visual field because, while larger, the test cube was placed farther away. The retinal-image size of the first test stimulus was smaller than that of the original cube because, although it was the same size, it was placed farther away. And the retinal-image size of the second test stimulus was larger than that of the original cube because the larger cube and the original cube were viewed at the same distance.

How would you expect the infants to respond? An infant who can make judgments about size constancy should perceive that the cube used for the first test stimulus is the same actual size as the original cube but at a different distance. On the other hand, if the child reacts only to the retinal-image size of an object, the larger cube at the greater distance (the third test stimulus) is perceived as most like the original cube in size. Based on the degree to which infants turned their heads to the left, it was found that the first test stimulus elicited the greatest response to perceived size constancy. The other two stimuli elicited weaker responses; the infants judged these stimuli as dissimilar. So we may conclude that infants are indeed able to perceive size constancy. They respond to the object of the same size under a different viewing condition in much the same way as they respond to the original stimulus.

A recent analysis of size constancy research (McKenzie, Tootell, & Day, 1980) casts some doubt on the specifics of Bower's findings. Although size constancy is achieved in infancy, retention changes dramatically from earlier to later infancy, and young

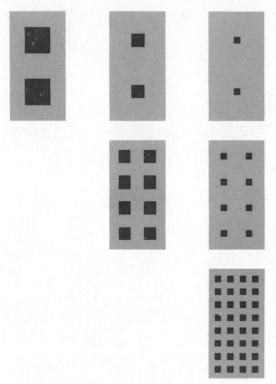

Figure 4.5 Stimuli used to measure young infants' preferences for size and number of elements.

infants show only spotty evidence of constancy. Infants up to four months old, for example (which would apply to Bower's sample), did not evidence any systematic constancy responses. Six- and eight-month-old children evidenced constancy with distances up to twenty-eight inches (70 cm) but not at three and six feet (100 and 200 cm).

Pattern and Form

At what age are infants able to perceive pattern and form? What evidence is there of pattern and form perception in young infants? Some of the classic work on this question has been done by Robert Fantz (1961). He showed children several different circular forms and recorded the amount of time they looked at each form. Among the forms used were a bull's-eye, solid-colored circles, a schematic face, and newsprint. It was found that children as young as two or three months of age exhibited clear preferences among these different, complex forms. They looked longer at the facelike figure than at the bull's-eye and longer at the bull's-eye than at the solid-colored circles. The bull's-eye has also been more attractive to young infants than different forms in other research (e.g., Ruff & Birch, 1974).

Since this early work, the focus has shifted to the specific properties of form that children prefer. The curvature or straightness of contour lines is one important property of form. Fantz has shown that infants

as young as seven days old prefer curved contour lines to straight lines (Fantz, Fagan, & Miranda, 1975b). To demonstrate this fact, he presented several pairs of objects to infants. Each pair included a curved figure and a straight-line figure, with the complexity of the two objects approximately the same. In each case the infant spent more time looking at the curved figure than at the straight-line figure. Interestingly, this preference for curvature disappears when the infant is about one month old and then reappears at about two months of age. So, there are changes in form perception even in early infancy.

Other significant properties of patterns are the number and size of elements contained in the pattern. A checkerboard pattern, for example, contains many elements, whereas a solid-colored circle contains only one; and elements within the pattern may be small or large. How do these characteristics influence an infant's perceptual preferences for such forms? Again, Fantz has presented evidence on this issue. He presented pairs of drawings that contained the elements shown in figure 4.5. All possible pairings of these figures were shown to each infant. Newborns just a few days old showed a strong preference for drawings with more and larger elements. Older infants also preferred larger patterns with more numerous elements. When the variable of size was pitted directly against number, however, older infants preferred the patterns with more elements (number), while the reverse was true for neonates.

Some investigators have turned to more macroscopic variables to explain infants' preferences for form. Jerome Kagan (1976), for example, has suggested that infants prefer forms that are both *meaningful* and *moderately discrepant* (different) from the familiar. Thus, an infant who has just learned to recognize his or her mother's face would find facial stimuli that mildly distort the features of a human face pleasurable. There is moderate support for this hypothesis among several studies that have provided facelike stimuli to infants (Lasky & Klein, 1980).

The human face is perhaps the most important visual pattern for the newborn to perceive. Eleanor Gibson (1969) reviewed several studies about infants' perceptions of the human face and concluded that the infant masters a sequence of steps in progressing toward full perceptual appreciation of the face. Gibson suggested that at about three and one-half weeks of age the child first becomes fascinated with the eyes in a face, perhaps because the child is capable of noticing simple perceptual features, such as dots, angles, and circles. At between one and two months of age, the child notices and perceives contour. At two months of age and older, the child begins to differentiate facial features: the eyes are distinguished from other parts of the face, the mouth is noticed, and movements of the mouth draw the infant's attention to it. By about five months

The human face is perhaps the most important visual pattern for the newborn to perceive.

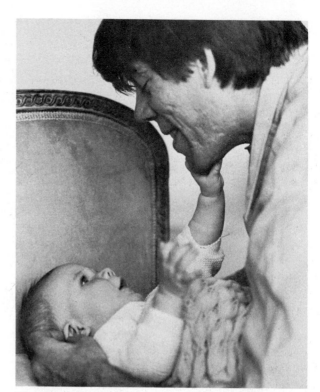

The older infant is able to distinguish familiar faces from unfamiliar ones.

of age, the infant has discriminated several other features of the face—its plasticity; its solid, three-dimensional surface; the oval shape of the head; the orientation of the eyes; and the mouth. Beyond six months of age, the infant is able to distinguish familiar faces from unfamiliar faces—mother from stranger, masks from real faces, and so on. This sequence of events is depicted in figure 4.6, where the drawings show the minimal facial features necessary to produce a smiling response from the infant, a significant social response of recognition and meaningful perception.

There has been a great deal of controversy about how perceptual learning in infancy occurs. Next we see that two schools of thought dominate this controversy—the *Gestalt view* and Eleanor Gibson's *distinctive features theory.*

Two Views of Perceptual Learning

Perceptual learning focuses upon changes in the way infants interpret and represent stimuli. Historically, there have been two broadly different theories about how perception changes during infancy and childhood. One is the **Gestalt view,** and the other is the **distinctive features theory** of Eleanor Gibson (1969, 1979).

The Gestalt view of perception dominated thinking in psychology from about 1925 to 1960. The work of three German psychologists—Kurt Koffka (1935), Wolfgang Kohler (1959 [1947]), and Max Wertheimer (1945)—formed this view. Most of the early work involved adults and lower animals, but not children. In

the 1960s and 1970s psychologists began to examine some aspects of the Gestalt view in their work with children.

The basic idea of the Gestalt approach is that perception is organized and dictated by several properties of the perceptual field. The perceptual field is the actual total sensory field, or scene, taken in at any moment by one of the senses (e.g., vision). A major property of the perceptual field is that perception of it is a holistic event. That is, the whole is something different from the sum of its parts—hence the term Gestalt.

A number of forces determine how the field is perceived. These are sometimes called the laws of organization, or good form. The German term for this is **Pragnanz.** One of these laws is the principle of similarity. For example, in looking at the patterns shown in figure 4.7 you would tend to see the direction of the surface as vertical in part *a* and as horizontal in part *b*. You would tend to group elements of the field that are similar.

A criticism of Gestalt theory (e.g., Hebb, 1949; Gibson & Levin, 1975) is that it is generally vague in describing how perceptual change comes about. What causes the sudden change, for example, as a person is examining a figure-ground display? The answer is not really clear in Gestalt writings. However, Gestalt ideas have been stimulating because they have led to the demonstration of unique perceptual phenomena such as the one presented in figure 4.7.

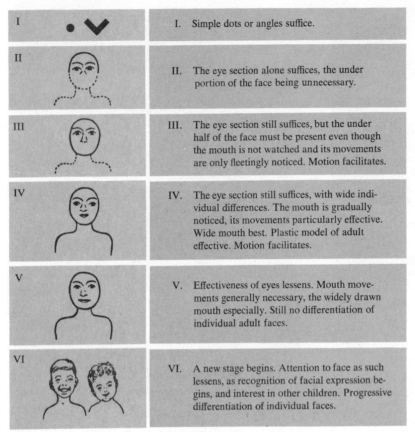

I	I. Simple dots or angles suffice.
II	II. The eye section alone suffices, the under portion of the face being unnecessary.
III	III. The eye section still suffices, but the under half of the face must be present even though the mouth is not watched and its movements are only fleetingly noticed. Motion facilitates.
IV	IV. The eye section still suffices, with wide individual differences. The mouth is gradually noticed, its movements particularly effective. Wide mouth best. Plastic model of adult effective. Motion facilitates.
V	V. Effectiveness of eyes lessens. Mouth movements generally necessary, the widely drawn mouth especially. Still no differentiation of individual adult faces.
VI	VI. A new stage begins. Attention to face as such lessens, as recognition of facial expression begins, and interest in other children. Progressive differentiation of individual faces.

Figure 4.6 Infants master a sequence of steps in progressing toward full perceptual appreciation of the face.

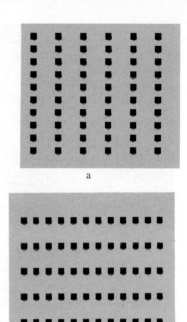

Figure 4.7 Similarity.

In contrast to the Gestalt perspective, Eleanor Gibson (1969, 1979) views perceptual change as a gradual process. The infant and child become aware of features of the environment that have gone unnoticed. Another difference is that, in Gibson's view, the infant takes an active part in perception. The infant constructs perceptions; the field does not pop out at him or her with its organizing forces. Here is Gibson's theory in her own words:

Perception is selective by nature. Selectivity can even be demonstrated at birth in some species, as studies of innate releasing stimuli have shown. But the extent of selectivity at birth varies with species. In man a rather gross selectivity at birth becomes progressively refined with development and experience.

Perceptual learning then refers to an increase in the ability to extract information from the environment as a result of experience and practice with stimulation coming from it. That the change should be in the direction of getting better information is a reasonable expectation, since man has evolved in the world and constantly interacts with it. Adaptive modification of perception should result in better correlation with the events and objects that are the sources of stimulation as well as an increase in the capacity to utilize potential stimulation. (pp. 3–4)

It's not a passive absorption but an active process, in the sense of exploring and searching for perception itself is active. . . . Perceptual learning is self-regulating, in the sense that modification occurs without the necessity of external reinforcement. It is stimulus-oriented, with the goal of extracting and reducing the information in stimulation. Discovery of distinctive features and structure in the world is fundamental in the achievement of this goal. (p. 14)

. . . The criterion of perceptual learning is thus an increase in specificity. What is learned can be described as detection of properties, patterns, and distinctive features. (p. 77)

But what is a distinctive feature? This concept is at the heart of Gibson's theory. She defines it as a simple dimension of difference between two forms. For example, look at the forms shown in figure 4.8 taken from a study by Anne Pick (1965). What is different about the triangle and the line on the left from the triangle and the line on the right? One has a curved line, the other a straight line; the two forms are otherwise the same. The figures differ from one another, then, on the basis of a single feature—call it line-to-curve. This feature is distinctive. Other features may be the number of lines present, orientation or slant, the degree of rotation, and so on. In distinctive feature learning, then, the infant and child gradually learn more and more basic dimensions of differences among objects and

Figure 4.8 These figures depict the distinctive feature line-to-curve.

events as they explore the world. Through repeated exploration of and exposure to the same stimuli, the infant and child perceive more and more differences and so have a richer basis for responding to and distinguishing events.

Keep in mind the information you have read in this section, for next, you will see that sensorimotor activities form the basis of the most important theory of infant cognitive development, that of Jean Piaget.

Cognitive Development

The contemporary study of cognitive development is dominated by the ideas and research of one man—Jean Piaget—and his colleagues. Because of the importance and dominance of his theory, the major portion of our material on cognitive development is devoted to it. You were introduced to Piaget and his theory in chapter 2; here we will focus on his ideas about the development of thought in infancy, and in later chapters describe his views of childhood (chapter 7), middle and late childhood (chapter 9), and adolescence (chapter 11). As an indication of how highly respected Piaget's view is, read box 4.1, a eulogy to Piaget. As part of our discussion of cognitive development in infancy, we also discuss further the nature-nurture controversy and describe the intelligence tests that have been developed for infants.

Piaget's Theory

Piaget believed that the child passed through a series of stages of thought from infancy to adolescence. Passage through the stages was the result of biological pressures to *adapt* to the environment (assimilation and accommodation) and to organize structures of thinking. These stages of thought are described as *qualitatively* different from one another, which means that the way a child reasons at one stage is very different from the way a child reasons at another. This contrasts with the *quantitative* assessments of intellect made in standard intelligence tests where the focus is on how much the child knows, or how many questions the child answers correctly. Thought development is landmarked by the following major stages: sensorimotor, preoperational, concrete operations, and formal operations (see table 4.1 for a brief account of each stage). In this chapter we will focus extensively on the stage of sensorimotor development, a stage that Piaget believed best described the cognitive development of infants.

Box 4.1
A Eulogy to Jean Piaget

Piaget's death was a shock to most of us in the field of child development. He was viewed as an immutable fixture, regularly churning out a new book every year or two, each of them remarkable in extending his theory and evidencing his brilliant scholarship. Shortly after he died, John Flavell (1980), a leading Piagetian scholar in the United States, wrote the following eulogy. It appeared in the newsletter of the Society for Research in Child Development.

Jean Piaget died in Geneva, Switzerland, on September 16, 1980. He was eighty-four years old. It is hard to think of anything important to say about this great scientist that is not already well known to readers of this Newsletter—so truly outstanding and widely recognized were his contributions to our field. A long and detailed obituary for such a figure would certainly be richly deserved, but it would hardly be needed in present company. So let us, instead, honor his memory by briefly reminding ourselves of some of the many things child developmentalists owe him.

First, we owe him a host of insightful concepts of enduring power and fascination—both mundane concepts that children acquire and theoretical concepts that illuminate their acquisition. My favorites include the childhood concepts of object permanence, perspective, conservation, and measurement, and the theoretical concepts of scheme, assimilation, accommodation, decentration, and invariance.

Second, we owe him a vast conceptual framework which has highlighted key issues and problems in human cognitive development and has informed and guided the efforts of nearly a generation of researchers in this area. This framework is now familiar vision of the developing child, who, through its own active and creative commerce with its environment, builds an orderly succession of cognitive structures enroute to intellectual maturity.

These two debts add up to a third, more general one: We owe him the present field of cognitive development—that is, we owe him a wide field of scientific inquiry. What would exist in its place today had Piaget never lived is anyone's guess, of course, but there are those of us who remember well what it was—and especially wasn't—before his influence was felt. Our task is now to extend and go beyond what he began so well.

Table 4.1
Piaget's Stages of Cognitive Development

Stage	General Description	Age Level
Sensorimotor Period	The child progresses from instinctual reflexive action at birth to symbolic activities, to the ability to separate self from object in the environment. He [or she] develops limited capabilities for anticipating the consequences of actions.	0 ½ 1 1 ½ 2
Preoperational Period	The child's ability to think becomes refined during this period. First, he [or she] develops what Piaget calls preconceptual thinking, in which he [or she] deals with each thing individually but is not able to group objects. The child is able to use symbols, such as words, to deal with problems. During the latter half of this period, the child develops better reasoning abilities but is still bound to the here-and-now.	2 ½ 3 3 ½ 4 4 ½ 5 5 ½ 6 6 ½ 7
Concrete Operations	At this stage, the child develops the ability to perform intellectual operations—such as reversibility, conservation, ordering of things by number, size, or class, etc. His [or her] ability to relate time and space is also matured during this period.	7 ½ 8 8 ½ 9 9 ½ 10 10 ½
Period of Formal Operations	This is the period in which the person learns hypothetical reasoning. He [or she] is able to function purely on a symbolic, abstract level. His [or her] conceptualization capacities are matured.	11 11 ½ 12 12 ½ 13 13 ½ 14 14 ½ 15

Source: Belkin & Gray, 1977.

The sensorimotor stage lasts from birth to about two years of age, corresponding to the period that most psychologists identify as infancy. During this time mental development consists of the infant's progressing ability to organize and coordinate sensations and perceptions with his physical movements and actions, hence the term sensorimotor (Piaget, 1970, 1975). This stage begins with the newborn, who has little more than reflexive patterns with which to work and ends with the two-year-old, who has complex sensoriaction patterns and is beginning to operate with a primitive symbolic system. Unlike other stages, the sensorimotor stage is subdivided into six substages, which demarcate qualitative changes in the nature of sensorimotor organization. The term scheme, or schema, is used to refer to the basic unit for an organized pattern of sensorimotor functioning. Within a given substage, there may be many different schemes—for example, sucking, rooting, and blinking in substage 1—but all have the same organization. In substage 1 they are basically reflexive in nature. From substage to substage, the schemes change in organization. This change in organization is at the heart of Piaget's descriptions of the substages.

Substage 1: Simple Reflexes (Birth to One Month of Age)

The basic means of coordinating sensation and action is through reflexive behaviors, such as sucking and rooting, that the newborn has brought into the world. During substage 1 the infant exercises these reflexes. More importantly, he or she develops an ability and penchant for producing behaviors that resemble reflexes in the absence of obvious reflex stimuli. For example, the newborn may suck when a bottle or nipple is only nearby. At birth, the bottle or nipple would have produced the sucking pattern only when placed directly in the newborn's mouth or touched to the newborn's lips. This reflexlike action in the absence of a triggering stimulus is evidence that the infant is initiating action and actively structuring experiences, even shortly after birth.

Substage 2: First Habits and Primary Circular Reactions (One to Four Months of Age)

The infant learns to coordinate sensation and types of schemes or structures during substage 2, that is, habits and primary circular reactions. A *habit* is a scheme based upon simple reflexes, such as sucking, which has become completely divorced from its eliciting stimulus. For example, an infant in the first substage might suck when orally stimulated by a bottle or when visually shown it, but an infant in the second substage may exercise the sucking scheme even when no bottle is present.

A **primary circular reaction** is a scheme based upon the infant's attempt to reproduce an interesting or pleasurable event that initially occured by chance. In

In substage 1, the infant practices the reflexive behavior of sucking.

In substage 2, the infant will practice the sucking reflex when no bottle is present.

a popular Piagetian example, a child accidentally sucks his fingers when they are placed near his mouth; later he searches for the fingers to suck them again, but the fingers do not cooperate in the search because he cannot coordinate visual and manual actions.

Habits and circular reactions are stereotyped, that is, the infant repeats them the same way each time. The infant's own body remains the center of attention; there is no outward pull by environmental events.

Substage 3: Secondary Circular Reactions
(Four to Eight Months of Age)
The infant becomes more object-oriented, or focused on the world, in substage 3 and moves beyond preoccupation with the self in sense-action interactions. The chance shaking of a rattle, for example, may produce a fascination in the child, and the child repeats this action for the sake of again experiencing fascination. The infant imitates some simple actions of others, such as the baby talk or burbling of adults, and some physical gestures. However, these imitations are limited to actions the infant is already able to produce. Although directed toward objects in the world, the infant's schemes lack an intentional, goal-directed quality.

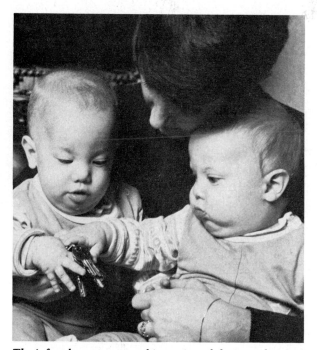

The infant becomes more object oriented during substage 3.

In substage 4, the infant begins to coordinate action.

The infant becomes intrigued by the variety of properties of an object in substage 5.

In substage 6, the child's functioning shifts to a symbolic plane.

Substage 4: Coordination of Secondary Reactions (Eight to Twelve Months of Age)

Several significant changes take place in substage 4. The infant readily combines and recombines previously learned schemes in a *coordinated* fashion. He or she may look at an object and grasp it simultaneously or visually inspect a toy, such as a rattle, and finger it simultaneously in obvious tactual exploration. Actions are even more outward-directed than before.

Related to this coordination is the second achievement—the presence of **intentionality,** the separation of means and goals in accomplishing simple feats. For example, the infant may manipulate a stick (the means) to bring a desired toy within reach (the goal). He or she may knock over one block to reach and play with another one.

As will be seen later, this substage has generated a great deal of interest on the part of investigators who wish to examine the logic and validity of the infant stages (e.g., Gratch, 1977; Fischer, 1980).

Substage 5: Tertiary Circular Reactions, Novelty, and Curiosity (Twelve to Eighteen Months of Age)

In substage 5, the infant becomes intrigued by the variety of properties that objects possess and by the multiplicity of things he or she can make happen to objects. A block can be made to fall, spin, hit another object, slide across the ground, and so on. **Tertiary circular reactions** are schemes in which the infant purposefully explores new possibilities with objects, continuously changing what is done to them and explore the results. Piaget speaks of this period as marking the developmental starting point for human curiosity and interest

in novelty. Previous circular reactions have been devoted exclusively to reproducing former events with the exception of imitation of novel acts, which occurs as early as substage 4. The tertiary reaction is the first to be concerned with novelty. As such, it is the mechanism par excellence for trial-and-error learning.

Substage 6: Internalization of Schemes (Eighteen Months to Two Years of Age)

The infant's mental functioning shifts from a purely sensorimotor plane to a symbolic plane in substage 6, and the infant develops the ability to use primitive symbols. For Piaget, a **symbol** is an internalized sensory image or word that represents an event. Primitive symbols permit the child to think about concrete events without directly acting or perceiving. Moreover, symbols allow the child to manipulate and transform the represented events in simple ways. In a favorite Piagetian example, Piaget's young daughter saw a matchbox being opened and closed and sometime later mimicked the event by opening and closing her mouth. This was an obvious expression of her image of the event. In another example, a child opened a door slowly to avoid disturbing a piece of paper lying on the floor on the other side. Clearly, the child had an image of the unseen paper and what would happen to it if the door were opened quickly. As we will later see, more recent scholars have debated whether two-year-olds really have such representations of action sequences at their command (Corrigan, 1981; Fischer & Jennings, 1981). An overview of the sensorimotor stages of infant mental development are shown in table 4.2.

Table 4.2
Multidimensional View of Development during the Sensorimotor Period

Stage	Developmental Unit	Intention and Means-End Relations	Meaning	Object Permanence	Space	Time
1	Exercising the ready-made sensorimotor schemes (0–1 mo.)					
2	Primary circular reactions (1–4 mo.)		Difference responses to different objects			
3	Secondary circular reactions (4–8 mo.)	Acts upon objects	"Motor meaning"	Brief single-modality search for absent object	All modalities focus on single object	Brief search for absent object
4	Coordination of secondary schemes (8–12 mo.)	Attacks barrier to reach goal	Symbolic meaning	Prolonged, multimodality search	Turns bottle to reach nipple	Prolonged search for absent object
5	Tertiary circular reactions (12–18 mo.)	"Experiments in order to see"; discovery of new means through "groping accommodation"	Elaboration through action and feedback	Follows sequential displacements if object in sight	Follows sequential displacements if object in sight	Follows sequential displacements if object in sight
6	Invention of new means through mental combinations (18–24 mo.)	Invention of new means through reciprocal assimilation of schemes	Further elaboration symbols increasingly covert	Follows sequential displacement with object hidden; symbolic representation of object, mostly internal	Solves detour problem: symbolic representation of spatial relationships, mostly internal	Both anticipation and memory

Source: From *The Origins of Intellect: Piaget's Theory,* second edition, by John L. Phillips, Jr. W. H. Freeman and Company. Copyright © 1975.

Object Permanence

One of the infant's most significant sensorimotor accomplishments is the understanding of **object permanence** (Bower, 1974; Flavell, 1977; Fischer, 1980). In order to think logically about themselves and the world around them, there are some simple ideas that children must grasp. One is that the self is physically separate, or distinct, from surrounding objects and events—a self-world differentiation. Another is that objects and events continue to exist even though the child is not in direct perceptual contact with them.

Imagine what thought would be like if people could not distinguish between themselves and other events in the world, or if events were believed to last only as long as the person has direct contact with them—highly chaotic, disorderly, and unpredictable, no doubt. This is what the mental life of the newborn infant is like; there is no self-world differentiation and no sense of object permanence (Piaget, 1952). By the end of the sensorimotor period, however, both are clearly understood. The transition between these extreme states is not abrupt; rather, it is marked by qualitative changes that reflect movement through each of the substages of sensorimotor thought.

Causality	Imitation	Play
	Pseudo imitation begins	Apparent functional autonomy of some acts
Acts, then waits for effect to occur	Psuedo imitation quicker, more precise. True imitation of acts already in repertoire and visible on own body	More acts done for their own sake
Attacks barrier to reach goal; waits for adults to serve him	True imitation of novel acts not visible on own body	Means often become ends; ritualization begins
Discovers new means; solicits help from adults	True imitation quicker, more precise	Quicker conversion of means to end; elaboration of ritualization
Infers causes from observing effects; predicts effects from observing causes	Imitates (1) complex, (2) non-human, (3) absent models	Treats inadequate stimuli as if adequate to imitate an enactment, i.e., symbolic ritualization or "pretending"

The principal way object permanency is studied is by watching the infant's reaction when an attractive object or event disappears. If the infant shows no reaction, it is assumed that he or she has no belief in its continued existence. On the other hand, if the infant is surprised at the disappearance and searches for the object, it is assumed that he or she has a belief in its continued existence. According to Piaget, the following distinct stages exist in the development of object permanence.

Sensorimotor 1: There is no apparent object permanence. When a spot of light moves across the visual field, the infant follows it but quickly ignores its disappearance.

Sensorimotor 2: A primitive form of object permanence develops. Given the same experience, the infant looks briefly at the spot where the light disappeared, with an expression of passive expectancy.

Sensorimotor 3: The infant's sense of object permanence undergoes further development. With the newfound ability to coordinate simple schemes, the infant shows clear patterns of searching for a missing object, with sustained visual and manual examination of the spot where the object apparently disappeared.

Sensorimotor 4: The infant actively searches for a missing object in the spot where it disappeared, with new actions to achieve the goal of searching effectively. For example, if an attractive toy has been hidden behind a screen, the child may look at the screen and try to push it away with a hand. If the screen is too heavy to move or is permanently fixed, the child readily substitutes a secondary scheme—for example, crawling around it or kicking it. These new actions signal that the infant's belief in the continued existence of the missing object is strengthening.

Sensorimotor 5: The infant now is able to track an object that disappears and reappears in several locations in rapid succession. For example, a toy may be hidden under different boxes in succession in front of the infant, who succeeds in finding it. The infant is apparently able to hold an image of the missing object in mind longer than before.

Sensorimotor 6: The infant can search for a missing object that disappeared and reappeared in several locations in succession, as before. In addition, the infant searches in the appropriate place even when the object has been hidden from view as it is being moved. This activity indicates that the infant is able to "imagine" the missing object and to follow the image from one location to the next.

Although Piaget's stage sequence is a neat summary of what might happen as the infant comes to fathom the *permanence* of things in the world, it cannot handle the weight of many contradictory findings—see box 4.2 for an overview of these contradictions.

To know the rabbit exists even though it is hidden from view signifies object permanence.

The Nature-Nurture Controversy and Infant Cognitive Development

The Piagetian perspective on infant cognitive development is a perspective with a strong heredity-maturation orientation. This section is based on a recent paper on the role of nature-nurture (heredity-environment) in mental development by Robert McCall (1981).

We have pointed out that the nature-nurture controversy is one of the most persistent issues in life-span development. McCall believes that the debates often fail to distinguish between what he calls developmental function and individual differences. **Developmental functions** are what scientists interested in the nature of the species study—for example, Piaget's attempt to describe in general the stages of mental development all members of the human species go through. By contrast, **individual differences** in the way infants proceed through the Piagetian stages do occur. The disagreement about Piaget's stages of object permanence reflects that there is a great deal of variation in the way one infant acquires and displays object permanence compared with how another goes through the process. Statements about developmental functions are general statements about the behavior, mental phenomena, or

developmental changes being discussed. The general statements summarize what is typical of the largest number of subjects or for the "average" members of the species—in our case here infants' mental development. However, we know that the results obtained for most infants may not apply to all infants—the concept of individual differences.

McCall offers a prime example of how developmental psychologists often have failed to distinguish between developmental function and individual differences. The study focused on the intelligence of adopted children and their biological and foster parents (Skodak & Skeels, 1949; Honzik, 1957). From the individual differences perspective, the IQ's of the adopted children correlated .38 with those of their biological parents but approximately zero with their rearing parents. *However,* the average IQ of the children was twenty-one points higher than the average of their biological parents and nearly identical with that of their rearing parents. Hereditarians tend to emphasize the individual difference result, and environmentalists focus on the mean difference (related to developmental function). Both observations are useful but distinct pieces of information, and while they are not contradictory, they rarely are seen as two pieces of the same puzzle.

Box 4.2
Other Views of Object Permanence

Piaget's stages broadly describe the interesting changes in object permanence fairly well, but the infant's life is not so neatly compartmentalized into six distinct organizations as Piaget supposed. As well, some of Piaget's explanations for the causes of change are simply wrong. In the spirit of constructive criticism, let us list the following major shortcomings of his account.

1. Ina Uzgiris and J. M. Hunt (1972, 1975, 1976) have offered convincing evidence that there are more than six landmarks in the general course of sensorimotor growth and in the development of object permanence in particular. These authors have identified a dozen or more behavioral accomplishments that the infant masters in a given developmental sequence. In their view infant change is more gradual and continuous than Piaget's description implies.

2. Piaget's account ignores the many psychological "performance variables" that influence what the child might do. The manner in which an object is hidden, the amount of time it is hidden, the way in which the adult alternates hiding places, as well as other variables all influence how the child performs (e.g., Bower, 1974; Harris, 1975; Corrigan, 1981).

3. Piaget claimed that certain processes are crucial in stage transitions. The data do not always support his explanations, however. For example, according to Piaget, the critical requirement for the infant to progress into sensorimotor substage 4 is the coordination of vision and the sense of touch, or hand-eye coordination. But several facts argue that the infant at substage 4 is oblivious to tactile experiences (e.g., Harris, 1975; Gratch, 1977). For example, if an object is covered while it is still in a six-month-old infant's hands, he or she does not look for it (Gratch, 1972).

According to Piaget, another important feature of progress into substage 4 is the infant's inclination to search for an object hidden in a familiar location rather than looking for the object in a new location. If new locations serve as hiding places, the infant progressing in substage 4 should make frequent mistakes, selecting the familiar hiding place (A), instead of the new location (B). This phenomenon is sometimes called the A-B error of substage 4, or perseveration. Unfortunately, perseveration does not occur consistently in an infant's behavior (Harris, 1975; Corrigan, 1981).

4. Sometimes Piaget described infant *competencies* incorrectly. According to him, for example, the infant in substage 6 is able to mentally conceive of a series of actions and operate with this mental conception over time. Thus, if an object is made invisible by placing it inside a covered container, and then the object is moved from one hiding place to another so the infant cannot see it directly, the infant should be able to follow the unseen object's movement, since he or she supposedly has the object in mind. A close look at such tasks (Corrigan, 1981) reveals that at sensorimotor stage 6 the infant may succeed at finding objects without using specific image or memory of the object. Instead, he or she may rely on understanding what the person hiding the objects is doing and simply look in those locations where that adult has been. Such performances, then, depend, on learning "how to search," not on where the invisible thing is. Some critics go so far as to argue that two-year-olds probably do not readily utilize mental images of absent events at all (Fischer & Jennings, 1981).

McCall argues that there may be a good evolutionary explanation for the possibility that one set of factors influences individual differences while another set operates on the species-general developmental function. If a given trait favors survival and reproduction, then such an attribute would tend to become characteristic of each member of the species. That is, this genetic trait would characterize the species-general developmental function. But genetic variability on this attribute would be reduced; consequently, individual differences in this attribute would be caused by environmental factors (McClearn & DeFries, 1973; Plomin & Rowe, 1979). It is not surprising then, that some anthropologists and geneticists (King & Wilson, 1975; Washburn, 1978) have indicated that 99 percent of our genetic material produces species-general characteristics, not individual differences.

This argument does not mean that genetic factors are unimportant in the study of individual differences. The point is that nearly the entire nature-nurture argument resides in the arena of individual differences and ignores the species-general developmental function. It is quite possible for the species-general developmental function to be almost completely under genetic control but for individual differences in that behavior to have no heritability and possibly no obvious relationships with environmental conditions. Such an occurrence seems to be the case for infant mental development (McCall, 1979a, 1979b).

Understanding the application to mental development requires an explanation of the concept of **canalization,** which implies a species-typical path. The species-typical path also has been called a **creod** by some—it is a path along which nearly all members of the species tend to develop (Waddington, 1957; Scarr-Salapatek, 1976). However, a characteristic follows the creod only as long as species-typical appropriate environments predominate. When such environments exist, development proceeds "normally;" when such circumstances deviate markedly, development can go awry.

A fundamental point made by McCall is that early mental development is highly canalized during the first eighteen to twenty-four months of life but thereafter becomes less canalized. That is, infants proceed along the species-typical path under a wide range of environments, and there is a strong self-righting tendency should extreme circumstances deflect an infant from this creod. However, beginning at approximately eighteen to twenty-four months, mental development becomes progressively less canalized with age, and it is after this point that the self-righting tendency is weaker.

Developmental Function in the First Eighteen Months

According to the concept of canalization, infants should follow a relatively common sequence of stages during the first eighteen months of life and those who deviate from this sequence should return to the norm once the deviating circumstance is removed. We have seen that Piaget (1954, 1966) proposed a stage sequence theory of early mental development that has received wide acceptance. We also have seen that although recent formulations have made slight changes in the Piagetian model, there is more agreement than disagreement. For example, several researchers agree that major stage boundaries occur at approximately two, seven to eight, thirteen, and twenty-one months of age (e.g., Fischer, 1980; McCall et al., 1977; Piaget 1954, 1966; Uzgiris 1976). Although individual investigators differ on what basic mental attribute underlies each stage, there is a

YOU'LL BE AMAZED
by baby's creativity. It's a sure sign of intelligence.

consensus about the timing and sequence of specific behavioral events (e.g., the exploration of objects and perceptual contingencies, object permanence, imitation, vocabulary, two-word sentences, symbolism).

Important from the standpoint of canalization is whether self-righting is possible for infants and children who differ markedly from the creod. Infants who have suffered major adversity—including nutritional deprivation, prematurity, anoxia, and other neonatal insults that produce depression in infant test scores—tend to recover and return to essentially normal development within three to six years if they are reared in adequate environments (Honzik, 1976; Hunt, 1976; Sameroff & Chandler, 1975; Scarr-Salapatek, 1976). However, if such infants are reared in markedly inferior environments, the effects of early injury can persist.

Next, we will discuss various mental tests and developmental scales that have been devised to access the individual differences among infants that Robert McCall describes.

Infant Intelligence Tests

It is advantageous to know whether an infant is advancing at a slow, normal, or fast rate of cognitive development. If the infant is advancing at a particularly slow rate of cognitive development, for example, environmental enrichment may be called for. And, if an infant is progressing at an advanced rate of cognitive development, parents may be advised to provide toys that are designed to stimulate cognitive development in slightly older infants. To assess cognitive development in infancy, intelligence tests, usually referred to as **developmental scales,** have been devised.

One of the most widely used developmental scales is the Bayley Mental and Motor Scales, consisting of

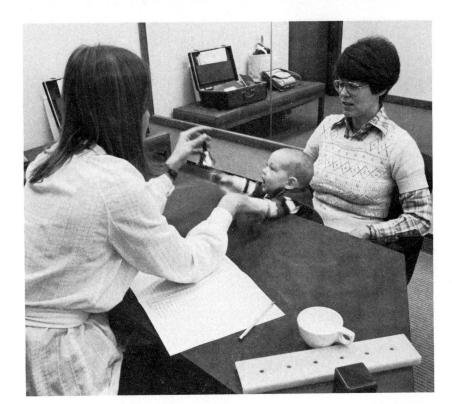

a series of items to measure mental skills and to evaluate motor skills. The components of the Bayley Mental Scale were designed to measure the infant's adaptive responses to the environment. They include attention to visual and auditory stimuli; grasping, manipulating, and combining objects; shaking a rattle; and ringing a bell. Items that measure the infant's social and cognitive skills also are included: smiling, cooing, babbling, imitating, and following directions. Showing memory and being aware of object constancy (looking for a hidden toy) are part of the Bayley Mental Scale, as is beginning to understand language. The language items include following directions that involve the use of object names, prepositions, and the concept of "one." The Bayley Motor Scale tests the infant's ability to hold up his or her head, turn over, sit, creep, stand, walk, and go up and down stairs. It also tests manual skills, such as grasping small objects and throwing a ball (Bayley, 1970). According to the Bayley Scales, at approximately six months of age the average baby should be able to (Kessen, Haith, & Salapatek, 1970)—

1. accept a second cube—baby holds first cube, while examiner takes second cube and places it within easy reach of the infant;
2. grasp the edge of a piece of paper when it is presented;
3. vocalize pleasure and displeasure;
4. persistently reach for objects placed just out of immediate reach;
5. turn his or her head after a spoon the experimenter suddenly drops on the floor; and

6. approach a mirror when the examiner places it in front of the infant.

At approximately twelve months of age, the average baby should be able to—

1. inhibit behavior when commanded to do so: for example, when the infant puts a block in his or her mouth and the examiner says, "no, no," then the infant should cease the activity;
2. repeat an action if he or she is laughed at;
3. imitate words the experimenter says, like "mama," and "dada;"
4. imitate actions of the experimenter: for example, if the experimenter rattles a spoon in a cup, then the infant should imitate this action;
5. respond to simple requests, such as "take a drink."

In chapter 7 we will look in greater detail at other approaches to assessing intelligence. Next, we will look at infant development from a learning perspective, and we will find that it is far less cognitive than any perspective we have described so far. Indeed, in Skinner's view of operant conditioning, cognitive development is given no importance. In Bandura's social learning perspective the cognitive representations of a model's actions, however, are important. As you read the section on the learning theory perspective of infant development, keep in mind how it stands in stark contrast to the cognitive structural perspective of Piaget.

Learning

The study of child development has been significantly influenced by principles and techniques drawn from the dominant American perspective in psychology for most of the twentieth century—the psychology of **learning.** In chapter 2 you were introduced to some of the basic concepts in the learning perspective, a perspective referred to as behavioral social learning. This section presents an overview of the concept of learning and an analysis of the major kinds of learning that occur in infancy.

Definition of Learning

What is meant by learning? When the term learning is used by psychologists, it refers to a change in behavior that occurs as a result of experience. From the discussion in chapter 2, recall that learning refers to behavior that can be observed. Private thoughts, feelings, and emotions are beyond the scope of study unless these can be translated into directly observable responses, however, these translations are often possible (e.g., Aronfreed, 1976; Mischel, 1977; Rosenthal & Zimmerman, 1978). A person who is angry, for example, may reveal this emotion in both facial expression and aggressive behavior. The thoughts of a child who is trying to solve a problem may be displayed in what the child says aloud or writes in a workbook. The behavior change should be relatively permanent, lasting for more than a few seconds or minutes. However, learning may last for several hours, days, or months; the particular time period is not important. **Practice** is the repetition of behavior that is being learned. Recall from the chapter prologue that practice is an important component of Doman's perspective.

Some responses are not the result of learning. For example, all babies blink when a light is shone in their eyes at birth; and all babies cry or make an abrupt, involuntary movement when they hear a sudden, loud noise. These are examples of **reflexes,** responses that are wired into a person's nervous system. They occur without any practice.

There are also responses that are influenced by experience but depend on physical maturation and growth processes. For example, virtually all normal children eventually walk regardless of the amount of practice at this activity. Practice may speed up the process a bit but not by more than a month or two. And regardless of how little experience children have had, virtually all will be walking by the time they are eighteen or nineteen months old. Such responses are *maturational* rather than *learned.*

Some behavior changes occur very slowly and have a profound impact on many areas of children's psychological life. The logical skills required to understand the laws of physics and principles of higher mathematics are good examples of such changes. Although some psychologists believe these skills are learned behaviors (e.g., Gagné, 1977; Staats, Brewer, & Gross, 1970), they are viewed here as structures of thought or cognition. These structures develop more slowly than learned behaviors, they are mental in nature, and they underlie a broad array of observed behavior.

Kinds of Learning

Psychologists attempt to simplify their explanation of behavioral change by describing several different kinds of learning. Three are presented here—classical conditioning, operant conditioning, and imitation. They are sometimes referred to as basic mechanisms, or laws of learning. They are very general; they apply equally to children of all ages and occur in diverse circumstances. A fourth form of learning, perceptual learning, described earlier in the chapter differs from the three being discussed here in that it does not involve an observable response.

Classical Conditioning

The theory of **classical conditioning,** first described by the Russian psychologist Ivan Pavlov (1927), was originally demonstrated by some simple behaviors of dogs. In classical conditioning it is assumed that learning occurs through a stimulus-response association. A stimulus (any event in the environment) initially causes some response to be made by the organism. For example, the presentation of food powder to a hungry dog causes the dog to salivate. The response occurs spontaneously without practice. The food powder is an **unconditioned stimulus (UCS);** the act of salivation is an **unconditioned response (UCR).**

Foundations of Development of Infancy

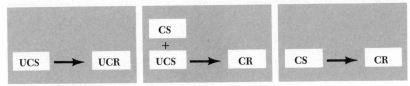

Figure 4.9 Steps in the classical conditioning of a response.
From *Introduction to Psychology* by Morgan and King. Used with the permission of McGraw-Hill Book Company.

Suppose another stimulus—a buzzer—is presented at the same time as the food (UCS). At the outset of the procedure, the buzzer does not cause the dog to salivate; it is a neutral stimulus. However, if the buzzer is repeatedly presented along with the food, the dog eventually salivates when the buzzer is presented alone. The buzzer is then referred to as a **conditioned stimulus (CS)**. When the dog salivates to the sound of the buzzer alone, the salivation is a **conditioned response (CR)**. Conditioning, or learning, has occurred as the result of the repeated association of a stimulus (buzzer) with a response (salivation)—hence, learning is based upon a stimulus-response association. See figure 4.9 for a simple diagram to help you remember classical conditioning.

John B. Watson (1924) was responsible for popularizing the concept of classical conditioning in the United States. In the 1920s he wrote extensively about its occurrence in everyday situations. Some of his writings were intended to give parents clues on how best to train their young children, and others to describe for educators how environments can be set up to ensure efficient learning. To contemporary psychologists some of Watson's statements seem fanatical. He claimed that a child can be manipulated to become virtually anything the adult desires. In a famous statement he said:

Give me a dozen healthy infants well formed and my own specified world to bring them up in and I'll guarantee to take any one at random and train him to become any kind of specialist I might select—doctor, lawyer, merchant, chief, yes, even beggerman and thief, regardless of his talents, penchants, tendencies, abilities, vocations, and race of his ancestors. (p. 10)

This statement indicates the degree to which Watson believed conditioning can shape a person's life. His most famous experimental work is his demonstration of conditioning in a one-year-old child named Albert (Watson & Rayner, 1920). Albert had no observable fears when Watson first began the experiment. However, it could be shown that when a loud sound was made next to his crib, Albert was startled and tried to escape from the situation. The loud sound served as an unconditioned stimulus, and Albert's startled response and attempt to escape were unconditioned responses of fear.

Watson demonstrated that Albert could learn to fear other objects through conditioning. He paired a neutral object (a little white rat) with the loud noise, and after several presentations of this object Albert showed a startle response and an avoidance pattern to the neutral object as well as to the loud noise. Albert had previously shown no fear of white rats. Watson later demonstrated that the fear become generalized to include other small, white objects resembling the rat. Fortunately for Albert, Watson had the good sense to undo the learned fear, so that no lasting harm was done to the infant.

Since Watson's time psychologists have demonstrated that many fears in young children may arise from just such a classical conditioning procedure (e.g., Jones, 1924). Some clinical psychologists today believe that the many fears adults harbor but cannot explain are due to early conditioning (e.g., Ringness, 1975; Pendery & Maltzman, 1979). Thus many smells, sounds, and sights elicit anxiety in older children and adults, even though the smells, sounds, and sights themselves seem harmless. These may be conditioned stimuli that have been associated with fearful events in childhood (Sameroff, 1972; Lamb & Sherrod, 1981).

Although there is some debate about classical conditioning, it seems that a number of responses are learned in this manner during infancy—for example, crying, head turning, sucking, and visual attention (Lipsitt, 1967). The younger the infant, the harder it is to demonstrate this phenomenon. One study offers perhaps the first clear demonstration of classical conditioning of young infants (Connolly & Stratton, 1969). Infants from two to four days old were studied in an attempt to show that the **Babkin reflex** could be conditioned. (In the Babkin reflex an infant opens his or her mouth when pressure is applied to the palms of the hands while lying on the back.) In the study a palm press (UCS) was paired with "white noise" (a neutral stimulus) for twenty-five trials. Then, for fifteen test trials, the white noise was presented alone. The infants made a number of mouthing responses to the white noise, demonstrating conditioning. And unlike other studies (e.g., Wickens & Wickens, 1940), infants who did not experience the pairing of a palm press with white

Classical Conditioning and Affective Behavior

Once upon a time a young psychologist wanted to train his small son to the potty. Since children don't ordinarily find the seat too comfortable or stimulating, he decided to change its image by introducing an element of pleasure. He obtained a circus poster of a clown—colorful, smiling, with a big nose. He then placed a red light bulb on the nose and switched it on while the child was on the potty. The child was entranced and often wanted to go to the bathroom. Later, it wasn't difficult to rig an electrical circuit so that when the child urinated, a connection was made, and there was the lighted red nose.

But conditioning processes often produce *stimulus generalization,* which means that stimuli like the original, specific stimulus can evoke a similar response.

As you might anticipate, father and son went for a car ride one day and were stopped by a big red traffic light. Guess what happened!

But some conditioning isn't funny. Most teachers have experienced one or more of the following:

Four-year-old Mary comes to nursery school with her mother, but when Mother leaves, Mary cries and carries on, with strong emotional behavior. Only when Mother promises to stay does Mary quiet down again. She continues to watch fearfully lest Mother show some signs of abandoning her.

Peter becomes slightly nauseated whenever a test is announced. Sometimes he becomes actively sick and has to go home.

And Monday depresses us—that's why it's "Blue Monday." But we enjoy Friday—it is T.G.I.F.(Thank God It's Friday).

Source: Ringness, 1975, pp. 41–42.

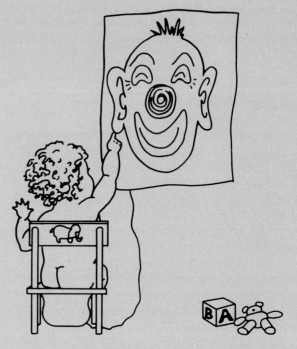

If you asked Mary, Peter, or yourself why these feelings occurred, you would probably get an answer, but it might well be a rationalization rather than the truth. That is because we frequently don't know enough about our real reasons for feeling as we do, although we can call upon our intellect for an explanation that may satisfy us. The behaviors described above can be considered examples of *classical conditioning,* in which form of learning we are frequently unaware that we are learning, and are certainly not motivated to try.

noise (the control group) showed a low level of response to the white noise.

Classical conditioning is also a well-established process in children and adults, accounting for the learning of such responses as conditioned fears (Wolpe, 1958), eye-blink conditioning (Lobb & Hardwick, 1976; Perry, Brown, & Perry, 1979), and verbal association (O'Donnell, 1974). See box 4.3 for more information about the importance of classical conditioning in emotional development.

Operant Conditioning

Operant conditioning is a form of learning made famous by B. F. Skinner (1971), an American psychologist. In classical conditioning the initial unconditioned response is reflexive, or spontaneous, to a specific stimulus at the outset of conditioning. In operant conditioning the response initially occurs freely—that is, not in reaction to a specific stimulus. For example, in Skinner's original experiments (Skinner, 1938) pigeons were used as subjects. A pigeon was placed in a small cage with a panel with several multicolored buttons and a sliding door on one wall. If the pigeon pecked a button, the sliding door opened to reveal a tray with a food pellet. The pigeon's pecking was a response that initially

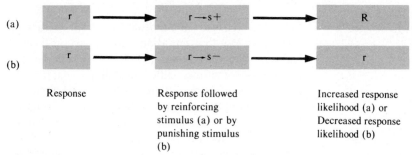

(a)

| r | r → s+ | R |

(b)

| r | r → s— | r |

Response   Response followed   Increased response
                            by reinforcing   likelihood (a) or
                            stimulus (a) or by   Decreased response
                            punishing stimulus   likelihood (b)
                            (b)

Figure 4.10   Steps in the operant conditioning of a response.

occurred randomly and freely. As a consequence of the response, the pigeon received food. Eventually the pigeon was conditioned to associate pecking the button with food.

Similarly, in everyday life many responses that begin with a random event later bear regularly associated consequences. For example, a young infant turns to look at her father, and he cradles her affectionately. In school a child raises her hand, and the teacher praises her initiative. An adolescent babysitter smiles at his young ward, and the child gives him a hug. In each example the behavior led to a consequence that increased the likelihood of that behavior occurring again. In Skinner's terminology, this effect on the response is called reinforcement. By contrast, many behaviors may result in consequences that decrease their likelihood of occurrence. A child may be scolded for seeking a parent's attention, or a bright student who raises her hand may be told not to ask so many questions. In Skinner's terminology, this effect is called punishment. Skinner is concerned with the functional value of an event rather than with whether that event is pleasant or unpleasant. Therefore, if an event follows a response and the response is repeated, the event is a *reinforcer,* whether pleasant or unpleasant. If an event follows a response and decreases the likelihood that the response will recur, the event is a *punisher.* See figure 4.10 for a representation of how the operant conditioning of a response works.

Most practitioners of operant conditioning emphasize the superiority of reinforcement over punishment for changing behavior (e.g., Bijou, 1976; Skinner, 1980). Punishment has some undesirable side effects in addition to reducing the likelihood that a behavior will recur. It may arouse the child unnecessarily, illustrate that aggression (by the punisher) is acceptable, and interfere with learning the acceptable behavior in the situation.

Punishment and **negative reinforcement** are frequently confused. In negative reinforcement the removal of a stimulus event causes a response to recur. This reinforcement is termed *negative* because the consequence of the child's response is that a particular event is removed from the situation rather than added

to it. Consider a simple example. A student has a teacher who constantly glares at her and scolds her because she is often looking around the room when she is supposed to be reading. The child buries her head in her reader, and the teacher stops berating her. If removal of the teacher's scolding occurs each time the child hides her head in a book, the child's response has been negatively reinforced.

As with classical conditioning, there is no lack of evidence that operant conditioning can alter a variety of behaviors during childhood, (Bijou, 1976; Bucher, Reykdal, & Albin, 1976). There are also many demonstrations that show how infant behavior changes as a result of operant processes (e.g., Papousek, 1967; Rheingold, Gewirtz, & Ross, 1959; Todd & Palmer, 1968; Lancioni, 1980; Kazdin, 1975; Lipsitt, 1979). A classical study was conducted by Harriet Rheingold and associates (1959) to demonstrate that vocalization in infants may be increased through simple contingencies of reinforcement. In the study three-month-old infants were tested with a now familiar operant-conditioning procedure. In a **baseline** period the investigators charted the frequency of vocalizations in children before reinforcement was introduced. In the **conditioning** trials that followed, all vocalizations were rewarded. Following the conditioning procedure, an **extinction** phase occurred. (Extinction is similar to baseline. The investigators simply observed the amount of vocalization without reinforcing it.) In each of the three phases of the experiment—baseline, conditioning, and extinction—infants were tested during two days. On each day, a woman visited the infant nine times, each time for about three minutes. During the sessions in the baseline and extinction phases the woman remained neutral. Standing passively in front of the child, she showed no expression on her face and did nothing when the child vocalized. During the conditioning phase the woman stood passively only until the infant vocalized. She followed the vocalizations with a series of socially pleasant events—smiles, soothing sounds, and gentle caresses.

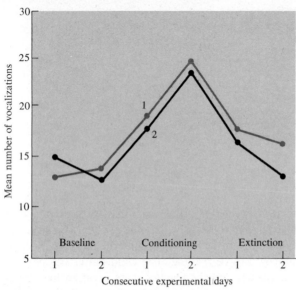

Figure 4.11 Changes in the level of infant vocalization through the phases of operant conditioning: 1) first group and 2) replication group.

The results of this study are shown in figure 4.11. Notice that during the baseline period, the infants produced about thirteen vocalizations on each day. The number of vocalizations increased to almost twenty-five by the second day of the conditioning phase. By the second day of the extinction phase, the response had decreased to its previously low baseline level.

A frequent criticism of operant learning is that it fails to give a very good account of how complex behavior (such as language, thought, and problem solving) is learned (e.g., Chomsky, 1965). Skinner himself (e.g., 1980) has acknowledged this criticism but thinks his critics are either wrong (e.g., Skinner's account of language, 1957) or prematurely demand too much from psychology, still in its youth as a science (Skinner, 1980). Despite these polemical arguments, however, there are good demonstrations of highly complex behaviors that are undeniably acquired under the well-described contingencies of reinforcement. For example, Donald Baer and his students at the University of Kansas have taught nursery school children to produce highly creative block constructions through reinforcement of "form diversity" (Baer et al., 1975); children have been taught to produce a number of language constructions (Sherman, 1975); and even young infants have been taught to discriminate abstract differences in the environment where they are reinforced (e.g., Fagan, 1980).

In chapter 2, as part of our discussion of social learning theory, we saw that imitation is an important form of learning. Albert Bandura (1977, 1969) believes that imitation—sometimes called modeling—requires the coordination of motor activity with a mental picture of the act that is being imitated. Because very young infants do not imitate others, it seems likely that they either cannot form a mental picture of the act of another individual or cannot coordinate their motor actions with that picture.

Earlier in this chapter, we saw that Piaget has studied imitation in infancy. According to Piaget, infants cannot imagine objects until approximately nine months of age. Before then, it is possible to get a baby to imitate such responses as opening and closing the hands, which babies master early in life and can see themselves doing, although Piaget calls this action pseudo-imitation.

Once the infant has reached the point in development when he or she can represent an action with a mental picture or words, Bandura believes that the processes involved in imitation are basically the same regardless of the age of the individual. In other words, the imitation process is no different for a two-year-old than a thirty-five-year-old.

Attention is the first cognitive process that must be activated before the observer can reproduce the model's actions. The child may not hear the teacher present an idea in class if his or her attention is on the person in the next chair. The child's attention to a model is influenced by characteristics of the models themselves. Warm, powerful, atypical individuals command more attention than cold, weak, typical individuals. The child pays closer attention when informed that he or she will be required to reproduce what the model does at a later time than when no such information is given.

Imitation also involves the child's **retention**. To reproduce a model's actions at a later time, the child must code and store the information in his or her memory to be recalled later. A vivid image of what the model did assists retention.

A third concept involved in modeling is **motoric reproduction**. The child may attend to the model and adequately code what was seen, but because of limitations in motor development the child may not be able to reproduce what the model has done. For example, catching a ball may involve motor coordination beyond that of a child, who is thus unable to reproduce the modeled behavior. Reproducing the letters a teacher has drawn may be difficult for some first-graders because their hand-eye coordination may not have developed adequately. Therefore, having first-graders spend long periods of time trying to print letters that exactly match

Imitation, or modeling, involves the coordination of motor activity with a mental picture of the act that is being imitated.

the teacher's is not a wise strategy. This is not to say that children should not engage in activities, such as printing, that call for hand-eye coordination, but they should not be expected to reproduce all written symbols exactly at such an early age. Failure to recognize the role of motor development in imitation may lead to emotional problems and difficulty in social interactions for the child.

A final consideration in Bandura's conception of modeling involves reinforcement, or **incentive conditions.** There are many situations in which a person can easily do what a model has done but may not be motivated to do so. A child who watches a teacher demonstrate lunchroom etiquette may not be motivated to imitate the teacher's actions unless appropriate incentives are provided—perhaps in the form of a special luncheon treat. The appropriateness of the incentives, of course, will vary for individual children.

In the next chapter, you will discover that concepts of learning, cognition, sensation, and perception are important in our effort to understand the foundations and development of language.

Summary

This chapter focused on several important aspects of infant development—sensation, perception, cognition, and learning. Sensation is the pickup of information by sensory receptors. Perception is the interpretation of what is sensed. At birth or shortly thereafter, each of the five senses is operating—hearing, touch, taste, smell, and vision. Except for vision, however, little is known about the senses. With vision, marked changes have been observed in acuity, accommodation, and vergence during the first few months of infancy. Infants attend to isolated features of objects and, as they grow older, scan them more completely.

Perception of space is necessary to negotiate effectively in the environment. Distance is perceived through several binocular and monocular cues. That infants can perceive depth has been demonstrated by Gibson's visual cliff procedure. Infants also display ability to perceive size constancy, although the precision of size-constancy judgments improve with the age of the child. Among the patterns and forms preferred by infants are those with facial features, curvature, large and numerous elements, and meaningful but moderately discrepant objects. Patterns of change were noted, particularly in the perception of facial features. Two-dimensional pictures pose special problems for three-dimensional perception. Young infants do not perceive pictured objects as objects; older infants recognize depicted objects without any previous experience with pictures, and children have difficulty only when identifying pictures with impoverished information.

In perceptual learning, there is a change in the way stimuli are perceived. There is either a radical change in the field organization (Gestalt view) or a change in the distinctive features of events that are noticed.

Piaget is the leading contemporary figure in cognitive development. He proposed a broad theory of development based upon his experiences with philosophy, biology, and psychology. His theory proposes a series of stages of development from infancy through adolescence. In the sensorimotor period the infant moves through a series of six substages. In the first substage the infant reacts to events with simple reflexes. Through the next several substages, simple sensoriaction patterns become increasingly differentiated and coordinated until by the last substage, the child can represent these patterns with mental images. A special acquisition during infancy is object permanence, the understanding that objects continue to exist beyond their immediately perceived presence. Another aspect of infant cognition is the measurement of infant intelligence—one such widely used instrument is the Bayley Development Scales.

Learning is a change in behavior that occurs as the result of practice. There are several different kinds of learning that are important in infancy: (1) in classical conditioning, a neutral stimulus is paired with an unconditioned stimulus (UCS) and, after several trials, becomes a conditioned stimulus (CS), which elicits a conditioned response (CR); (2) in operant conditioning, behavior may change through reinforcement or punishment. A stimulus that follows a response and increases the likelihood of its occurrence is reinforcing; one that decreases the likelihood of occurrence is punishing; (3) in imitation, responses are acquired through observing the behaviors of others.

Key Terms

accommodation

attention

Babkin reflex

baseline

canalization

categorical perception

classical conditioning

conditioned response (CR)

conditioned stimulus (CS)

conditioning

convergence

creod

developmental functions

developmental scales

distinctive features theory

divergence

extinction

Gestalt view

incentive conditions

individual differences

intentionality

learning

looming

motoric reproduction

negative reinforcement

object permanence

perception

practice

pragnanz

primary circular reactions

reflexes

retention

secondary circular reactions

sensation

size constancy

speech perception

symbol

tertiary circular reactions

unconditioned response (UCR)

unconditioned stimulus (UCS)

vergence

visual acuity

visual cliff technique

Review Questions

1. Distinguish between sensation and perception.
2. What are the newborn's basic hearing, feeling, tasting, and smelling capacities?
3. What are the newborn's basic capacities for vision at birth? How do these change?
4. What features of the environment attract the infant's attention? How does this change during infancy?
5. Describe the visual-cliff experiment, especially with regard to infants' reactions.
6. How does the infant's perception of the human face change during the first half-year of life?
7. What are the major changes during the period of sensorimotor development?
8. What is object permanence? What are the substages of object permanence during infancy?
9. Define learning.
10. Describe classical conditioning.
11. Describe operant conditioning.
12. Explain imitative learning.

Further Readings

Becker, W. C. *Parents are teachers.* Champaign, Ill.: Research Press, 1971.
An extremely easy-to-read paperback with step-by-step instructions of how to apply basic learning principles to everyday situations with infants and children.

Bower, T. G. R. *The perceptual world of the child.* Cambridge, Mass.: Harvard U. Press, 1977.
A scholarly introduction to the study of infant perception, including the topics of space perception, distance perception, and size constancy. Technical in places, but fascinating and easy to read.

Piaget, J. *The origins of intelligence in children.* New York: Norton, 1963.
This book focuses exclusively on Piaget's concept of the six stages of infant cognitive development. Examples of Piaget's theory reflected in his own three children should be focused on. Not easy to read, but worthwhile.

5

Language Foundations and Development

Prologue: Language Development in Bilingual Children

Octavio's Mexican parents moved to the United States one year before Octavio was born. They do not speak English fluently and have always spoken to Octavio in Spanish. At six years old, Octavio has just entered the first grade at an elementary school in San Antonio, Texas, and does not speak English.

What is the best way to reach Octavio? How much easier would elementary school be for Octavio if his parents would have been able to speak to him in Spanish and English when he was an infant?

According to the 1980 census, well over 6 million children in the United States come from homes where the primary language is not English. Often, like Octavio, they live in a community where this same non-English language is the major means of communication. These children face a more difficult task than most of us—they must master the native tongue of their family to be effective at home and in their own community, and they must also master English to make their way in and contribute to the larger society. The number of bilingual speaking children is expanding at such a rapid rate in our country (some experts, for example, predict a tripling in their numbers by early in the twenty-first century) that they constitute an important subgroup of language learners to be dealt with by society. Although the education of such children in the public schools has a long history, it has been only recently that a national policy has evolved to guarantee a quality language experience for them.

Widespread efforts in the early 1960s to incorporate bilingual education components into the American school curricula resulted in the enactment by Congress in 1967 of the Bilingual Education Act (as title VII of the Elementary and Secondary Education Act). The Educational Amendments Act of 1974 revised and strengthened the 1967 statute: in federal fiscal year (FY) 1975, congressional appropriations for bilingual education were 85 million. (Cordasco, 1976, p. 11)

This figure nearly doubled within three to four years.

Great debates have raged in the past several years concerning how best to conduct this bilingual education. Does one teach English as a foreign language, adopting the child's native tongue as the language of the classroom, or does one treat English as a second, equal language and strive for balance in usage of English and the native tongue? The answer to this has important consequences for the way school curricula and texts are written in cities with large concentrations of Spanish-speaking children (e.g., New York, Miami, San Antonio, and Los Angeles).

Before practical educational decisions can be made, however, it is important to understand the nature of how children acquire early competency in two separate languages. An excellent analysis of this issue has been provided by Virginia Volterra and Traute Taeschner (1978). They considered the language development of three children, each of whom acquired mastery of two languages from one to four years of age. The goal was to identify "stages" in the children's early usage and mastery. One child grew up in an English-speaking environment where her mother spoke to her mostly in English and her father spoke to her only in German. The other children were two sisters, living in Rome, who had been immersed in two languages since birth. Their father spoke Italian exclusively, while their mother spoke only German to them. The data used in the study consisted of extensive tape recordings of the two sisters and a detailed diary of the first girl made by her father (Leopold, 1970). Volterra and Taeschner (1978) believe there are three distinct stages in learning two languages.

In the first stage, the child seems to have one mixed vocabulary, or lexicon. Words from the two languages are often used together in short phrases, and for any single word in one language, there is not always a corresponding word in the other. The child seems to move freely among the two languages without clearly discriminating between them.

In the second stage, the child has separate vocabularies for the two languages and does not mix them. Phrases contain words from only one language, and for any single word in one language, there is a corresponding one in the other language. Generally, one child uses the same syntactic rules for both languages.

In the third stage, the child advances significantly in syntax. Different rules for producing utterances in the two languages emerge and there is a differentiation between the languages in all other ways. To help keep the languages distinct, the child only speaks the language associated with the person being addressed.

Noam Chomsky.

Introduction

Language is a remarkable phenomenon. It enables us to do a variety of things rapidly and efficiently. We use it to communicate with each other, with ourselves, and with others not present by way of the printed word. It is helpful in thinking, problem solving, remembering, learning, and perceiving the world. Without it today's modern civilization probably would not exist, for without language, how could society's complex social, technical, and political structures be maintained? Imagine maintaining friendships with people who live far away without being able to talk or write to them. Imagine constructing or operating a computer without verbal instructions to smooth the way. And imagine the members of a government body responding to their constituencies without the various language media.

No animal species other than humans can be credited with such an achievement as language. To be sure, other animals "talk" and even communicate with each other, but none do so with a language system quite like ours. Biological evolution and cultural evolution have conspired to make humans unique in this respect (Moskonite, 1978). Perhaps even more remarkable is the speed with which humans learn language. The newborn infant has a few distinguishable crying sounds; the twelve-month-old is uttering a few words; the four-year-old is producing adult sentences. What an incredible change in just a few short years!

The study of language development is one of the most exciting areas in child psychology today. Most of the insights into the nature of children's language development have come very recently—in the past twenty-five years or so—despite the interest taken in language by writers and philosophers for many centuries and by psychologists for as long as there has been a discipline of psychology. The insights stem from a basic change in the way language is defined, a change stimulated by developments in the field of linguistics, particularly the ideas of Noam Chomsky (1957, 1972). The study of language development is often referred to as developmental **psycholinguistics** to underscore how the two disciplines of psychology and linguistics now work hand in hand to further our understanding of language development.

The decade of the 1970s witnessed the impact of several other social science disciplines on the study of children's language acquisition—most notably sociology and anthropology (e.g., Nelson, 1978; Cherry-Wilkinson, Clevenger, & Dolloghan, 1981; Shuy & Griffin, 1981). From these disciplines has come the insight that the social structure of the setting (Keller-Cohen, 1978) in which children learn to talk has an important influence on what they say, the language rules they learn, and the language rules they apply. This perspective has been referred to as **sociolinguistics.** In this chapter, we will look at the basic building blocks of language development and describe its course of development through the infant years. In later chapters we will describe its developmental course in early childhood (chapter 7) and middle and late childhood (chapter 9).

Language: What Is It?

Language is a well-ordered system of rules that each adult member of the language community tacitly comprehends in speaking, listening, and writing. That is, the individual does not necessarily know these rules in the sense that he or she could state them, any more than a bicyclist needs to describe the regular (ruleful) motion of pedaling with the aid of differential calculus in order to be able to pedal. Both the speaker and the cyclist know the rules in the sense that they conform to them.

This system of rules is a precise way of describing language. To understand the nature of these rules, one must first understand the fundamental units employed to study language. Language is made up of basic sounds, or **phonemes.** English employs about thirty-six phonemes; other languages employ as few as twenty-five and as many as fifty.

The English alphabet was originally constructed so that a given letter of the alphabet might correspond to a given sound. In actual practice, however, many letters have several alternative phonemes associated with them. This is particularly true of the vowels. The multiple sounds associated with letters is one of the stumbling blocks in learning to read and write English. Some other languages, like Spanish, have a simpler system of correspondence between phonemes and letters.

The study of the sound system, **phonology,** is principally concerned with the rules used to combine sounds with each other. Phonological rules guarantee that certain sequences occur (e.g., *ax, kl, apo, br*) and that others do not (e.g., *mx, kz, pq, bc*). The phonological rules differ from one language to the next, but all languages employ such rules.

At the next level is the **morpheme,** a string of sounds that conveys meaning. Morphology is the study of the rules used to combine morphemes. All words in the language consist of one or more morphemes tied together. However, not all morphemes are words. Some morphemes are what we ordinarily think of as word fragments: prefixes (e.g., *pre-, re-, ex-, con-*), suffixes (e.g., *-tion, -est, -ic, -ly*), verb tense markers (e.g., *-ing, -ed*), and singular-plural markers (*-s, -es*). Some languages, such as Latin, Greek and Russian, use morphemes to mark the case for each noun in the sentence. As with phonology, morphological rules guarantee that certain sequences occur in the language (e.g., *caption, happiest, contrary*) and that others do not (e.g., *sadtion, princeest, conhappy*). Again, specific rules differ for different languages.

At another level is **syntax,** the rules for combining words to produce acceptable phrases and sentences. More work has been done in the area of syntax than in either phonology or morphology. In fact, the seminal work in psycholinguistics began with syntax (Brown & Fraser, 1964; Chomsky, 1957). It is perhaps most evident in the realm of syntax that the rules young children use as they first learn a language are radically different from those of older children and adults. As children move toward the linguistic productions typical of a four-year-old, they acquire several new stages of syntax. Roger Brown (1973) has described five such stages, which are discussed later in this and subsequent chapters.

A **grammar** is a formal description of a speaker's syntactic rules. In school most of us learned rules that were also referred to as grammar. These were principally rules of thumb that taught us how to construct acceptable sentences and how to avoid unacceptable ones. Some of us also learned how to diagram sentences, that is, how to identify the units and parts of speech. The rules we learned in school did not explain how a sentence is produced; they typically taught us what *not* to do in constructing a sentence (and some of today's educational critics claim that even this has been done poorly). Moreover, these grammatical rules did not explain some other important facts about sentences.

Some sentences have very different meanings and logical organization, yet are very similar in appearance. For example,

Robert is ready to come.
Robert is readied to come.

In the first sentence Robert is in a specific frame of mind. In the second sentence Robert is the implied object of an activity—someone got him ready.

Kinds of Language Rules
Phonology
Morphology
Syntax
Semantics
Pragmatics

Figure 5.1

Some sentences mean the same thing and have the same logical organization but are expressed in slightly different ways. For example,

The boy hit the dog.
The dog was hit by the boy.

In the first sentence the idea is expressed in an active form. In the second sentence the idea is expressed in a passive form.

These and other facts about the differences and similarities among sentences are captured in modern linguistic grammars that distinguish between the **deep structure** and the **surface structure** of sentences. The basic underlying idea and organization of a sentence is its deep structure. The deep structure may be expressed in alternative surface forms. What is actually spoken or heard is the surface structure. Since a sentence has one underlying structure and many possible surface structures, syntactic rules—called **transformations**—explain the different surface forms for a single sentence. Thus, there are transformations that explain passive and active forms of sentences, declarative and question forms, affirmative and negative statements and others.

At the same time, the distinction between deep structure and surface structure can be used to explain why some sentences seem alike even though they express different ideas and logical organization. They have similar surface structures but different deep structures. Different transformational rules were applied to the different deep structures and produced the similar surface forms. They can be likened to two children with different genetic backgrounds and different environmental experiences who grow up to have the same IQ.

In addition to phonology, morphology, and syntax, there are other kinds of rules that are integral to language (fig. 5.1). One concerns **semantics,** or the expressed meanings of words and sentences (e.g., Dale, 1976; Nelson, 1978; Chapman, 1981). Semantics has at least two components—the appropriate use of words in social contexts and the appropriate use of words in sentences. The child's appropriate use of words in social contexts develops partly as the result of expanding vocabulary. The more words in the child's vocabulary, the easier his or her task when asked to name an object or event. But knowledge also develops as the child gains a better understanding of the attributes that define the category to which a word refers. For example, a child may learn that "dog" refers to an animal that has four legs, barks, has a tail that wags, and so on.

The appropriate use of words in sentences is a more complex developmental process. It is one to which a growing number of language experts are turning their attention. They believe that a major mystery about language will be solved when semantic development is better understood (Bloom, 1975; Chapman, 1981).

Let's consider for a moment just what the problem is. Look at the following string of words: "The happy nose threw the river at the movie." Would you say that this collection of words forms a grammatical sentence? It certainly seems as though the right kinds of words appear at the right places. Would you say that it is meaningful? In our ordinary use of language, noses do not possess emotions and are not capable of throwing things. Rivers cannot be hurled at objects, but even if they could, it makes no sense to say that a movie is the target. In other words, this "sentence" violates the ordinary rules of semantic relations. The problem for the developmental psycholinguist is that children obviously produce many sentences they have never heard before. A sizable number of these are both grammatical and sensible. What are the rules they have learned that ensure the sensibility of the sentences? When and in what order does understanding of these rules appear in a child's development?

Finally, there are pragmatic rules in every language (e.g., Danks & Schwent, 1974; Nelson, 1978; Dale, 1980). **Pragmatics** concerns the appropriate use of language, with all of its social and physical requirements. Certain pragmatic rules guarantee that a specific sentence is uttered in one situation and not another. For example, it is appropriate to say "You look very nice" to someone who has obviously made an effort to present a pleasing appearance, but it is inappropriate to greet someone who is dirty and disheveled in this way. Other pragmatic rules specify that certain kinds of utterances are more appropriate in given situations than others. For example, it is more polite to request some milk with "May I have some milk please?" than with "Give me some milk." Pragmatic rules help us to get along smoothly in the world and assure that language is well integrated with other facets of psychological functioning.

One final distinction is in order. A child may know a linguistic rule but be unable to express it in actual speech. He may have *linguistic competence* but fail to evidence it with the appropriate *linguistic performance*. Adults often forget this and underestimate children's competence by relying on linguistic performance, with its qualities that seem different from adult language. Psychologists have had to find alternative ways to measure the child's language knowledge to avoid the trap of using any one performance measure as indicative of what the child knows.

How Is Language Learned?
For many years, some psychologists thought of language as just another collection of behaviors, much like walking, sitting, touching, eating, swimming, and laughing. And like other behaviors, its development was explained by the now-familiar principles of learning—stimulus-response, association, reinforcement, and imitation (e.g., Skinner, 1957, 1980). But learning theory leaves altogether too much unexplained. In this section we examine both old and new theories of how language is learned, including the roles of biology and the environment in language development.

The Old View
The father of American behaviorism, John B. Watson, in his classic work *Behaviorism* (1924), argued that language is complex behavior—complex because its most important representative, the fully formed sentence, consists of a series of stimulus-response associations. Each word itself is a series of stimuli and responses chained together, with the basic sounds being both responses and eliciting stimuli. (An eliciting stimulus is the sound that also activates the next response, another sound.) When a word becomes well learned, it becomes unitized, now serving as a single stimulus or response unit. The sentence in turn is a series of stimulus-response associations, with the word now serving as the basic unit (the stimulus and the response) in the chain. The means by which chaining occurs, according to Watson, is classical conditioning.

The stimulus-response view of language learning fails to explain the child's generativity satisfactorily. The child can utter hundreds and thousands of sentences; if Watson's intuition was correct, consider how many such chains the child would have to learn. Quite an extraordinary number. Some researchers have argued that the number actually exceeds the brain's capacity to store and retrieve information (e.g., Halwes & Jenkins, 1971).

This view of language as chains of stimuli and responses lasted a surprisingly long time in American psychology. A number of prominent behaviorists supported it. What changed were the mechanisms of

A child is not likely to produce a more grammatically complex sentence in describing an object as a result of parent modeling.

learning that were invoked to explain how a chain can be formed. Skinner (1957) and others (e.g., Staats, 1971) added *operant conditioning* and the concept of reinforcement to the picture. Bandura (1971) and others (e.g., Rosenthal & Zimmerman, 1978) added *imitation.*

Of the many sentences the child produces, a large percentage are novel. A novel utterance is one that the child neither heard nor spoke previously. How can the mechanisms of learning account for this novelty? Suppose a child learned the following sentence by being reinforced or by imitating what someone else said:

My truck fell into the wagon.

How would he or she then be able to produce the following sentence, which was never heard before?

The mirror dropped on the chair.

The mechanisms of learning cannot explain this.

There are still other problems for learning theory. Suppose the child produced only a small number of utterances, had a brain that could handle the processing requirements of numerous stimulus-response chains, and did not generate novel sentences. Is there any evidence that the mechanisms of learning can account for significant changes in children's language competence? Do imitation and reinforcement, for example,

change the child's manner of speaking? Is the child likely to produce a more grammatical complex sentence if such sentences are repeatedly modeled by a parent? Is a child more likely to utter sentences of a specific grammatical or semantic form if he or she has been previously reinforced for producing them?

The answers are all no. Several studies (e.g., Dale, 1976; Nelson, 1978) have demonstrated, for example, that a child is no more likely to utter a more complex sentence if the sentence is modeled repeatedly than if it is not. We sympathize with the mother who stubbornly tried to lengthen the form of her two-year-old child's two-word sentence, only to fail miserably.

Sandy Want milk!
Mother Oh, you mean "*I* want milk."
Sandy Want milk!
Mother Can you say "*I* want milk"?
Sandy Want milk!
Mother Sandy, please say "*I* want milk"!
Sandy Want milk!

Roger Brown (1973) has searched for evidence of naturalistic reinforcement in the language exchanges of mothers and their young children. There is evidence that parents do try to influence their children's speech with naturalistic rewards. They smile and praise their children for producing certain sentences that they like. But from the way parents choose to dispense rewards, it is amazing that children ever learn more mature speech. Some of the time parents reward children for uttering sentences that test grammatical limits without regard for their truth value or sensibleness. Thus, a toddler, picking up a bar of white soap, was praised for his statement "Mommy, soap black" because it was a three-word utterance while most of his speech was at the two-word stage. But what he said was actually incorrect.

Sometimes parents reward children for truthful or accurate statements that are phrased in a grammatically immature way. For example, the same toddler uttered the single word *white* and also was praised, this time for knowing the correct color. Brown's records indicate that parents are about equally likely to reward speech on each basis. If this is true, then children are being exposed to conflicting schedules of reinforcement. How do they ever learn anything? Perhaps a more compelling criticism is Brown's finding that the particular way a parent reinforces a child has little influence on the child's later speech.

A final criticism of learning theory is that it fails to explain the obvious orderliness, structure, and ever-present rules in children's speech. Strict learning theory predicts that there should be vast individual differences in the patterns of speech development for different children, since each child is exposed to a unique learning history. But a compelling fact is that there are certain sequences in each child's development that appear to be universal. For example, children emit cooing sounds before babbling sounds in infancy. They produce one-word utterances before two-word utterances. They master active forms of sentences before passive ones.

Children also struggle to uncover general rules for producing correct speech. We see them making similar "mistakes" ("The boy goed home." "The mouses runned.") at about the same time that they overgeneralize some of the early rules. Learning theory cannot account for these important facts about language development.

It seems obvious, then, that learning theory provides an inadequate explanation for language development. It cannot reasonably explain children's generativity or the novel statements they utter. Imitation and reinforcement do not seem to advance language rules. And the theory fails to explain the orderliness, structure, and ever-present rules in children's speech.

The New View

Psychologists now believe that learning takes a different form from that described by behaviorists. The exact nature of the learning remains elusive. Psycholinguists have not provided a precise account of the process in the way that behaviorists have precisely described how other behaviors are learned. There is general agreement, however, that language is learned as the result of the child's active attempts to induce rule systems from everyday speech. These systems are abstract from the very beginning of language learning, but the child is aided in several ways. First, the human brain seems especially sensitive to the structure and rules of language—the child has an innate propensity for learning language rules. Second, the everyday speech the child hears contains abundant information, redundancy, and feedback about language rules. And finally, the child has a strong, built-in motivation to learn language. He or she is continually exposed to people who have mastered it and cannot escape the need to communicate effectively with them (Brown, 1973).

We turn, now, to some specific components of the language learning process as it is conceived of in the new view.

The Role of Biology

It is clear that our biological heritage is a necessary foundation upon which language, more than other human acquisitions, is built. Without it, we would never have learned to talk.

Evolution Language is a skill that evolved in two phases. The first was physical evolution, which took quite a long time. The brain, nervous system, and vocal apparatus changed over hundreds of thousands of years as we evolved from *Homo erectus* (about a million years ago) to *Homo sapiens* (about one hundred thousand years ago). The change ensured the development of the requisite physical equipment for the natural form of language as we know it (speech) to develop. Prior to these changes, the physical equipment to produce speech was inadequate.

Then came the important second phase, social evolution, which occurred more rapidly. Humans, with their newly evolved language equipment, had to create a system for communicating. More important, they had to have a compelling social need to motivate its development. There is evidence about how long it took to develop a speech system that moved beyond the expressive grunts, groans, and cries of *Homo erectus* to the highly abstract speech of modern humans. Conservative estimates put this achievement in the neighborhood of tens of thousands of years ago. Another estimate is that a modern speech system was developed about 70,000 years ago. Language, then, is a relatively recent acquisition for humans in the evolutionary scheme of things.

There is also only speculation about the social forces that led to the creation of language. Some anthropologists believe that social changes forced humans to use abstract reasoning powers more and to

Our brain, nervous system, and vocal apparatus changed over hundreds of thousands of years as we evolved.

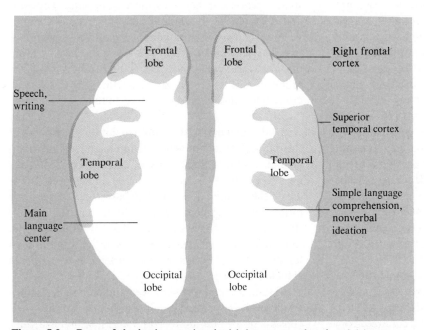

Figure 5.2   Parts of the brain associated with language-related activities.

develop an economical system for reflecting upon and communicating reasonings to others (Crick, 1977). Among the social changes credited to this are the development of complex plans and strategies to provide food, shelter, and physical comfort for the individual and the family. But there may very well have been an individual motivational pressure that was as important as the social one. Just as the young infant in modern times seeks to master and create new skills for the sheer pleasure of feeling competent, so the humans of so long ago may have felt the need to develop a new, abstract skill to gain a sense of competence.

The Brain and Physical Maturation   Of the physical equipment involved in language, the brain is the most important (Lenneberg, 1967, Nelson, 1978). Without a *Homo sapien's* brain, language as we know it would not have developed. In figure 5.2 you see a diagram of the areas of the brain and the principal psychological functions they govern. As you can see, the main language center is located in the left half of the brain, in the area of the superior temporal cortex. If the brain is damaged in this area, as in a lesion, language functioning is often disrupted. Aphasia is one of the frequent results. Aphasics have a variety of symptoms;

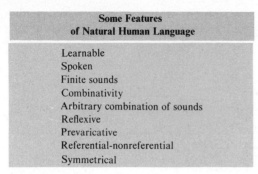

Some Features of Natural Human Language
Learnable
Spoken
Finite sounds
Combinativity
Arbitrary combination of sounds
Reflexive
Prevaricative
Referential-nonreferential
Symmetrical

Figure 5.3

they may be unable to name objects, to call forth words to produce a sentence, or to produce words at all. One of the first to notice these problems and the area of the brain associated with them was Pierre-Paul Broca (1861). Accordingly, the main language center is often referred to as Broca's area.

As figure 5.2 indicates, other areas of the brain are also implicated as centers for language activity. For example, the brain center for speech and writing is in the left frontal cortex. Simple language comprehension seems to be governed by an area in the right hemisphere that corresponds to the left hemisphere's main language center.

Scientists who study brain functions realize that these language centers do not tell the whole story of the brain's role in language activity. For one thing, not everyone who has a lesion in Broca's area suffers speech impairment. For another, language functioning may be disturbed if other areas of the brain are damaged, areas not specifically designated as language areas. The brain works as a system, and in any system each part plays some role in many activities (Pribram, 1971; Sagan, 1970).

As the child matures, two things happen to the brain that are significant for language. One is that identifiable language centers become localized. At birth each of the speech areas is not well differentiated from other areas of the brain in its functional operation, but by the end of the middle childhood there is marked localization of brain function and by adolescence localization is complete. A second change is that language activity becomes increasingly dominated by the left half of the brain. The earlier in life that a brain injury occurs, the more likely it is that the child will recover without language problems. Experts believe that the less localization and specialization, the greater the brain's adaptability after injury.

A study by Patricia Day (1979) is a representative example of this phenomenon. She analyzed the ability of two children who had undergone brain surgery to perform a number of perceptual motor, cognitive, and linguistic tasks. One twelve-year-old girl experienced damage to areas in the right hemisphere, while the second child, a six-year-old girl, experienced damage to areas in her left hemisphere. Language disruption was more pronounced for the second child than the first one.

There is also interest in the relation between the increasing dominance of language activity in the left hemisphere and reading ability (e.g., Dean, 1980; Sadick & Ginsberg, 1978). Ray Dean (1980), for example, believes that the degree of dominance (or asymmetry between the two halves of the brain) predicts reading comprehension ability. Sadick and Ginsberg (1978), by contrast, indicated that the association between dominance and reading ability will be different for children at different levels of reading ability. When children are just beginning to learn to read, (at five or six years) there ought to be little **laterality.** Children at this stage still must rely upon a great deal of visual-spatial processing and analysis of inputs. When visual-spatial processing becomes more automatic, however, and a generalized symbolic activity occupies center stage in reading, later dominance would be more adaptive (say by eight or nine years when many children have become skilled readers). In research with a large group of five to eleven-year-old children, this is precisely what Sadick and Ginsberg found.

Animal Language   Humans are not only members of the animal kingdom who communicate. Nonhuman primates gesture and shriek at each other, dogs bark and whine, bees have an elaborate dance ritual to indicate the location of nectar, and parrots and other birds mimic human speech. Do these communications qualify as language? Probably not. One list included more than one hundred characteristics of natural human language that no other communication system shares (Hockett, 1960).

Human language is *learned* and *learnable,* not instinctive. It is *spoken* (vocal) and *heard* (auditory). It consists of a finite number of sounds, which are combined in a multitude of complex ways. The sounds are perfectly *arbitrary;* that is, there is no obvious relation, a priori, between the sounds and the things they refer to. It is *reflexive;* that is, language can be used to discuss language. It is *prevaricative;* that is, it can assert things that are false. It includes both *referential* and *nonreferential* terms (in the sentence "It is a boy" the word *boy* refers to a discrete thing, while the word *it* has no referent). And finally, language is filled with dualistic *symmetry*—singular and plural forms, passive and active forms, positive and negative statements. A summary of some of the features of human language is provided in figure 5.3.

Several attempts have been made to teach primates an abstract language. In the 1930s the Kelloggs (1933) tried to raise a chimpanzee (Gua) with their infant son, talking and responding to the animal as they did to their own son. A similar experiment was tried in the 1950s by the Hayeses (1951). Both tries were failures in the sense that the chimpanzees learned very little language. They learned to produce a handful of single-word utterances and to communicate simple desires; in the latter case, they even produced some two-word utterances. Perhaps the problem is that animals do not have the vocal equipment to produce much human speech.

Because primates are adept at using their arms and hands in complex fashion, it seemed possible that they could be taught a kind of sign language. Allen and Beatrice Gardner (1971) taught a chimpanzee to produce manual signs adapted from the system of International Sign Language learned by the deaf. David Premack (1976) taught a chimpanzee to communicate by using physical forms as symbols for words. In both cases some remarkable results were obtained. The chimpanzees mastered a vocabulary of well over several hundred "words" and produced sentences of three and four words, and sometimes more. Some of their sentences were novel creations—that is, not first modeled by the experimenter. The chimpanzees engaged in play with their newly acquired languages; for example, they tried out new word sequences without any obvious intention to communicate, and they played jokes on the experimenter. This activity is similar to the word play of young children.

Have these animals, then, learned a language? The animals have learned to understand that signs represent specific objects and events, but there still is considerable controversy about whether these accomplishments qualify them for the distinction of being "language users." For example, language scientists argue that some chimps can produce sequences of three or four signs in order to get something they want (Premack, 1976), however, the skeptics suggest that the animals have only memorized specific sequences and are not applying general rules. Even pigeons can be trained to peck at four keys in a specific sequence in order to obtain food, but no one argues that they are using "language" to get the food. Thus, while researchers agree that the chimps can use signs, usually to get something they want, the skeptics do not believe the chimps can use language, a rule-governed system of symbols in which new sentences are generated (Terrace, 1979). So, the great ape language debate goes on.

The Role of the Environment
Just as the child's biological heritage is an important factor in language acquisition, so also is the environment. The child does not learn language in a social vacuum: he or she needs exposure to the speech of others. Speech complexity differs for children of different ages, so speech input must be geared to the child's level of development. It must be within a range of cognitive complexity that is not too far beyond the child's productive abilities but not too simple either.

A host of investigators have examined the way mothers address children at different stages of language maturity (Snow, 1972a; Broen, 1972; Cross, 1978; Snow & Ferguson, 1977; Furrow, Nelson, & Benedict, 1979) both in natural settings and in controlled laboratory situations. They found that mothers employed several simplifying devices when addressing infants and young children as compared with older children and adults. Sentences were shorter; vocabulary was simpler; grammatical structure was less complex; pauses between sentence boundaries were more definite and lasted longer; and key words and phrases were emphasized by volume and stress changes.

By contrast, mothers' speech addressed to older children and adults was complex and "messy." Sentences were very long. Often it was difficult to determine where one statement ended and another began because of elipses, sentence fragments, and lack of pauses. Grammatical structure was often incorrect or very complex. Complex forms included relative clauses, compound sentences, and embedded phrases.

Aside from selecting different levels of complexity of speech to address children, are there other means by which adults influence development? Courtney Cazden (1972), a well-known psycholinguist, believes there are. She has identified three strategies that adults use in verbal exchanges with young children. One strategy is **prompting.** In a typical exchange the adult asks a question, the child fails to respond, and the adult follows with a variation of the same question. For example:

Adult Where is your toy?
Child (Silence)
Adult Your toy is where?

Another strategy is **echoing.** The child says something that is only partially understood, and the adult repeats the understandable portion and calls for more information. For example:

Child The car is in . . . *(unintelligible speech)*
Adult The car is where?

A third strategy is **expansion.** The child utters a short phrase using a primitive language system, and the adult follows it with an expanded version designed to express a more complete thought. The adult seldom knows whether the expansion correctly captures what the child had in mind. For example:

Child Daddy car.
Adult Yes! Daddy has a car.

Each of these strategies can help the child to better understand the rules of grammar. More important, perhaps, they are valuable ways to provide feedback to

Picture Books and First Words

Young children are forever being asked to identify objects. This has been called the "great word game" and is motivated by adult pressure on children to identify the words associated with objects.

Recently, Anat Ninio and Jerome Bruner (1978) took a close look at the subtle interplay between a mother and her infant son as the two performed the great word game in its quintessential setting—reading picture books and playing with objects. The mother and child were part of a longitudinal study that covered the period from eight months to one year, six months in the child's life. The child was firstborn and his parents were white, English, and middle class. Labeling was part of the filmed play activity captured in the videotape records made every two to three weeks in the infant's home.

The investigators uncovered some remarkable findings. Chief among these was the ritualized nature of mother-child labeling activity. It seemed as though labeling of pictures was a highly structured activity that obeyed clear rules and had the texture of a dialogue. A number of scholars have described conversations as having fairly tight patterns in ascribing roles, turn-taking, imitating, and responding (e.g., Bruner, 1975; Snow, 1977; Cherry-Wilkinson et al., 1981). The labeling activity also had tight patterns. Each time mother and child interacted over a picture name, for example, they took about the same number of turns, lasting about the same length of time. And, the linguistic forms of the mother's utterances in book reading was very limited. She made repeated use of four key types of statements, (1) "Look!" (to get the child's

attention), (2) "What's that?", (3) "It's an X!" (labeling the picture for the child), and (4) "Yes!" (giving the child feedback on his utterance). These types of statements accounted for virtually all of the language the mother directed toward the child while reading books during the entire period of the study and obeyed some simple rules of occurrence. For example, the attention getter "Look!" always preceded the query, "What's that?" or the labeling phrase ,"It's an X!" Similarly, the query always preceded the labeling phrase.

At the outset of the study, few of the child's verbal responses to the mother's queries were distinguishable words, of course. At best, the child produced consistent bubble. By the end of the period, however, words were present. Associated with this change, the mother dropped reliance on one of her four statement types— "What's that?" Since the child now could produce a word for the picture, this part of the ritual could be dropped.

> To summarize the author's state that the book reading dialogue seems . . . to be a format well suited to the teaching of labeling. It has few elements and strict ordering rules between them. It is flexible in the sense of accepting a great variety of responses by the child. It is highly repetitive. Not only do the fixed elements ("Look," "What's that" and "It's a (label)") appear over and over again, with minimal changes in the wording, but the variable elements, the labels themselves, appear repeatedly as well. (Ninio and Bruner, 1978, p. 12)

Children are more likely to imitate their parents if the parents themselves imitate their children.

the child about the success of his or her communicative effort. There is some evidence to show that the parents of children who acquire language earlier may be engaging in these strategies more frequently than the parents of slower language learners (Brown, 1973). The parents who use these strategies, however, are probably doing other things differently with their children as well. Therefore, although the strategies are valuable, it is not clear just how valuable they are.

Recently, it was demonstrated that children are more likely to imitate parents' speech if the parents themselves imitate the children (Folger & Chapman, 1978). Six children between one and two years of age were studied and estimated to be in the Brown's stage 1 of language development. Parents' imitative expansions were not as frequently imitated by the child, but

they were imitated to some extent. At some point in the infant's development, parents usually begin showing and reading picture books to their offspring. The role of such picture books in language development is described in box 5.1.

In their work on the development of competence in infants, Burton White and Jean Watts (1973) conducted home observations of infants and mothers, finding that the amount of time most mothers spent directly teaching their infants was surprisingly small. Instead of plain instruction they tended to use various "low-keyed facilitative techniques" that generally were designed to encourage the child's activity. Indeed, the most effective mothers were those who excelled at performing the functions of "designer and consultant."

These mothers very rarely spend five, ten or twenty minutes teaching their one- or two-year-olds, but they get an enormous amount (in terms of frequency) of teaching in "on the fly," and usually at the child's instigation. Although they do volunteer comments opportunistically, they react mostly to overtures by the child.

According to Rudolph Schaeffer (1977), the mother

follows in order to lead: she lets her child in the first place indicate his interest at the moment and then proceeds, within the child's own context, to elaborate on that interest. In this way she lets him select his own topic and then begins to comment, demonstrate, and explain.

Children as young as four years of age can cater their language to the listener.

Children can also cater their speech to individual differences in children of about the same age.

It is no coincidence that these facilitative mothers are most effective in fostering competent language development. Katherine Nelson (1973), and expert on language development, emphasizes that a nondirecting parent who accepts a child's behavior—both verbal and nonverbal—facilitates the child's progress in language acquisition. But in those cases where the parent takes a highly active role and directs the child, the parent's behavior has an "interference effect" that delays the acquisition of new verbal skills.

Adults are not the only source of language stimulation for children. Children stimulate each other too. Recent evidence suggests that children as young as four years of age can cater their language to the speech maturity of the listener (Shatz & Gelman, 1973; Nahir & Yussen, 1977; Masur & Gleason, 1980; Dickson, 1981). It is not known how well children accomplish this, but a recent study by Elise Masur (1980) is illuminating. Testing a group of ten four-year-old boys, Masur asked each to explain how a toy worked to high-verbal and low-verbal two-year-olds. The two-year-old listeners were children identified as high or low on the basis of their average sentence (utterance) lengths. (The high-verbal children produced utterances between 1.8 and 4 words long, while the low-verbal children produced utterances between 1.0 and 1.5 words long.) When the four-year-olds addressed these younger children, they directed longer sentences with greater syntatic complexity toward the high-verbal listeners than to the low-verbal listeners. This study proves, then, that young children can fine tune their speech fairly well. Not only can they determine the speech appropriate for children of different age levels, they can also cater their speech to individual differences in children of about the same age.

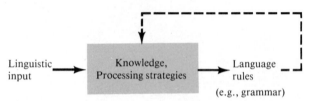

Figure 5.4   An imaginary language acquisition device.

The Child As a Language Processor

In addition to biological programming and environmental input, the child also contributes to his or her own learning of language. Psychologist David McNeill (1970) has offered an intriguing explanation of how this is done that has influenced the thinking of many experts. He draws an analogy of the child as an imaginary machine, a **Language Acquisition Device (LAD).** Figure 5.4 depicts how such a machine works. Linguistic input is fed into the machine. In analyzing the input, the machine is aided by some already existing information about language *(knowledge)* and by some built-in techniques for language analysis *(processing strategies).* The result of this analysis is a set of rules (the *output*) that describe how the input was generated. The rules are then incorporated into the knowledge component of the LAD. The output continually changes as additional information is fed into the device and as the device itself becomes reprogrammed *(new knowledge).* In this way new rule systems are continually learned. McNeill intended the model primarily as a description of how syntactic rules are learned, but it seems applicable to other domains of learning rules as well (e.g., phonology and semantics).

At birth all children bring the same *knowledge* and *processing strategies* to bear on the analysis of speech. Children begin life with the same capacity to process speech, regardless of which language their parents speak. This capacity, then, is universal and innate (inborn).

In box 5.2, Dan Slobin (1972) describes some of the basic ways all children around the world develop language.

Just what does the child know at birth about language? This question deals with a controversial issue. Some claim that so-called innate knowledge is no more than a tendency to learn language. Others, like McNeill, take a stronger position. They argue that there are several specific language categories that the brain is "prewired" to detect.

These **language universals** are phonological (consonants, vowels, syllables, distinctive features), syntactic (sentences, noun phrases, verb phrases, subject-object relations), and semantic (certain knowable concepts). A child can also detect the difference between deep structure and surface structure. This "prewiring" corresponds to the knowledge component of the child, or LAD.

But there are also processing strategies. Which of these are universal and innate? Again, this question touches on an area of controversy. Among those who represent the position of **nativism,** proposals have included innate analysis of (a) segments, the tendency to notice where words begin and end; (b) stress and pitch, the ability to distinguish stressed from unstressed syllables and high from low pitches; and (c) distribution frequency, the tendency to notice which speech units (words, sounds) occur in which contexts (Bever, 1970).

As the child develops language, the structure of the language processor (the LAD) also changes. More knowledge about the structure and nature of language is acquired, and processing strategies gain new efficiency and precision. A precise specification of these changes is difficult, because they are intimately bound up in the child's new output, that is, the rules that are learned.

Cognitive Prerequisites   A number of psychologists have long speculated that the child's ability to acquire language must also be related to general growth of cognitive skills. Language is, after all, a symbolic, abstract vehicle for capturing and communicating experiences. It is plausible that language-specific processing techniques, such as those mentioned in the last section, are wired into the brain's functioning. But cognition would be rather uneconomical if the child's language acquisition did not also build upon other cognitive abilities. There is evidence, in fact, of a relation between early Piagetian stages of thought and language acquisition.

A particularly intriguing proposition is that sensorimotor development is a prerequisite for some early landmarks in language. In sensorimotor stage 5, for example, the child begins to experiment with objects, noticing their different properties and noting the many

Parents bathe even the smallest of infants in language.

actions that can be performed on them. In sensorimotor stage 6, the child becomes adept at imagining and representing objects and events not in the immediate present. Both attainments advance the child's sense of object permanence. Perhaps we need the ability to examine objects purposefully and hold images of them in mind before being able to talk about them. A number of studies linking these Piagetian stage acquisitions to a variety of language acquisitions have been performed.

Roberta Corrigan (1978) did a longitudinal study following three children from about ten to twenty-eight months of age. She tested the children repeatedly on a modified version of a measure of object permanence (Uzgiris & Hunt, 1975) and measured growth and found a modest relation between the children's entrance into stage 6 and the onset of their *one-word* speech. As they moved just beyond stage 6 into the preoperational period, there was also a rapid increase in the children's total vocabulary output. A similar pattern of relationships has been found by other researchers (Dihoff & Chapman, 1977; Ingram, 1978) except that these investigators see the relationship as coming earlier—that is, stage 5 links up with one-word speech productions and stage 6 links up with rapid vocabulary growth.

Elizabeth Bates and her colleagues (1977) studied a group of nine to thirteen-month-olds and found a relation between other facets of sensorimotor growth and language. They found that level of sensorimotor imitation, means-ends behavior, and play with objects (all assessed by subscales of the object permanence instrument) were all predictions of the children's likelihood to communicate with gestures and produce a number of understandable words.

Box 5.2
Language Development around the World

Our research team at the University of California at Berkeley has been studying the way children learn languages in several countries and cultures. We have been aided by similar research at Harvard and at several other American universities, and by the work of foreign colleagues. We have gathered reasonably firm data on the acquisition of eighteen languages, and have suggestive findings on twelve others. Although the data are still scanty for many of these languages, a common picture of human-language development is beginning to emerge.

In all cultures the child's first word generally is a noun or proper name, identifying some object, animal, or person he sees every day. At about two years—give or take a few months—a child begins to put two words together to form rudimentary sentences. The two-word stage seems to be universal.

To get his meaning across, a child at the two-word stage relies heavily on gesture, tone and context. Lois Bloom, professor of speech, Teachers College, Columbia University, reported a little American girl who said *Mommy sock* on two distinct occasions: on finding her mother's sock and on being dressed by her mother. Thus the same phrase expressed possession in one context *(Mommy's sock)* and an agent-object relationship in another *(Mommy is putting on the sock).*

But even with a two-word horizon, children can get a wealth of meanings across.

Identification: See doggie.

Location: Book there.

Repetition: More milk.

Nonexistence: Allgone thing.

Negation: Not wolf.

Possession: My candy.

Attibution: Big car.

Agent-action: Mama walk.

Agent-object: Mama book (meaning, "Mama read book").

Action-location: Sit chair.

Action-direct object: Hit you.

Action-indirect object: Give papa.

Action-instrument: Cut knife.

Question: Where ball?

The striking thing about this list is its universality. The examples are drawn from child talk in English, German, Russian, Finnish, Turkish, Samoan and Luo, but the

Source: Slobin, 1972.

entire list could probably be made up of examples from two-year-old speech in any language.

Word A child easily figures out that the speech he hears around him contains discrete, meaningful elements, and that these elements can be combined. And children make the combinations themselves—many of their meaningful phrases would never be heard in adult speech. For example, Martin Braine studied a child who said things like *allgone outside* when he returned home and shut the door, *more page* when he didn't want a story to end, *other fix* when he wanted something repaired, and so on. These clearly are expressions created by the child, not mimicry of his parents. The matter is especially clear in the Russian language, in which noun endings vary with the role the noun plays in a sentence. As a rule, Russian children first use only the nominative ending in all combinations, even when it is grammatically incorrect. What is important to children is the *word,* not the ending; the *meaning,* not the grammar.

At first, the two-word limit is quite severe. A child may be able to say *daddy throw, throw ball,* and *daddy ball*—indicating that he understands the full proposition, *daddy throw ball*—yet be unable to produce all three words in one stretch. Again, though the data are limited, this seems to be a universal fact about children's speech.

Robin Chapman and her colleagues (1977, 1980) administered five tests of sensorimotor functioning to children from ten to twenty-one months of age and tested for their understanding that a word represented a particular relation (e.g., the presence of something, an action, the absence of something, action-object, or agent-action-object). Although a relation between cognitive stage and language comprehension was not always found, the two were linked for several of the language relations tested.

In a review of the literature on early linkages between cognition and language, Robin Chapman (1981) concluded that there are still problems in specifying the precise connections that exist due to the range of ways cognitive skills are assessed in infants and some of the inconsistent findings. Further discussion of the relation between thought and language will come later in the chapter.

The Course of Language Development

What is language like in infancy? What major changes can be observed? What are the major milestones—that is, when is the infant capable of various language feats?

For convenience, the discussion is divided into two parts dealing, respectively, with phonology and with syntax and semantics. Although it is easier to talk about these separately, the two are inseparable. Every speech act has a phonological, a syntactical, and a semantic component that exist simultaneously and interdependently. Meaning and grammatical structure cannot be conveyed without sounds.

Phonology

Phonology is the study of rules used to produce sounds. An understanding of language almost naturally begins with the basic sounds used to express linguistic ideas. In this section the basic sounds of the English language are described, along with some ideas about how infants and children learn to combine them to produce meaningful speech.

Basic Sounds

It has been estimated that an adult speaking standard English employs thirty-six basic sounds. Each of these basic sounds is called a *phoneme* and is perceived as identical by speakers of the language. A good example of an English phoneme is /k/, the sound represented by the letter *k* in the words key and ski and by the letter *c* in cat (Dale, 1976). Although the /k/ sound is somewhat different in each of these words, these variations are not distinguished and the /k/ sound is treated as a single phoneme. In the Arabic and Hindu languages, however, these variations would be distinguished and

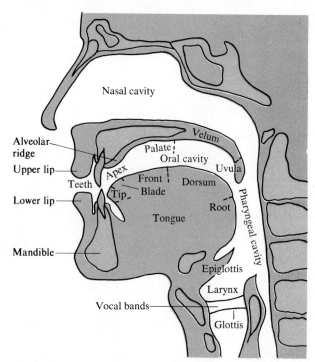

Figure 5.5 A cross-section of the head showing the principal speech organs.

treated as separate phonemes. Therefore, it is apparent that sounds recognized as a single phoneme in one language do not constitute the same phonemic class for all languages. A convenient way to describe a sound is to indicate how it is produced. What parts of the vocal system are employed, and how? The major phoneme classes in English are of two types, **vowels** and **consonants.** Basically, a vowel sound is produced by the vibration of the vocal cords (voicing) as air is passed over them. The air then flows through the mouth without being interrupted. Consonant sounds are produced by interrupting the flow of air somewhere in the mouth cavity and then releasing it. Some consonants are voiced, and some are not.

Further subdivisions in vowel sounds can be made, as Dale (1976) points out:

The tongue may be moved in an up-and-down direction and also a front-to-back direction. The difference between the sounds [i] and [u], as in "beat" and "cooed," is that in [i] the tongue is raised to a position near the ridge just behind the upper teeth, that is, the *alveolar ridge*. This position is quite far forward for a vowel. For [u] the back of the tongue is raised to a position near the rear of the roof of the mouth, the *palate*, which is quite far back. The [i] sound is said to be a *front vowel*, [u] a *back vowel*. To produce [a], as in "cod," the tongue is in its natural position, low and to the back of the mouth.

These three vowels are the extremes of the English vowels; all the other vowels fall between them along the front—back and low—high dimensions. There are twelve vowels in English. (pp. 197–98)

Table 5.1
Dale's Vowels of English

	Front				**Back**	
High	[i]	beat			[u]	cooed
	[I]	bit			[U]	could
	[e]	bait	[ə]	roses	[o]	code
	[ɛ]	bet			[ɔ]	cawed
Low	[æ]	bat	[ʌ]	but	[a]	cod

The twelve vowels that Dale describes are shown in table 5.1.

Subdivisions in the consonant sounds can be made by reference to the place where the stream of air is interrupted in the mouth. These are shown in figure 5.5. There are five major positions: (1) the lips, as in *pop* and *bath, father* and *vacuum* (/p/,/b/,/f/,/v/); (2) the tip of the tongue on the upper teeth, as in *thoroughly* and *therefore* (th/,/t͡h/); (3) the tip of the tongue on the point behind the upper teeth (alveola), as in *touch, dive, send, zoo* (t/,/d/,/s/,/z/); (4) the tongue on the front half of the palate, as in *splash* and *camouflage* (/sh/,/zh/); and finally, (5) the back of the tongue on the back half of the palate (the velum), as in *king* and *game* (k/,/g/). It may be helpful to examine figure 5.5 carefully to obtain a clear impression of these vocal positions.

Somewhat amazingly, four-week-old babies can discriminate between approximately forty consonant sounds that are used in various human languages. This phenomenon has been determined by scientists who monitor changes in babies' sucking and heartbeats when they hear different consonant sounds. These findings suggest that the ability to discriminate among different consonant sounds is innate because infants respond to more consonants than are used in their parents' language. Babies of English-speaking parents even react to the consonants present in the Japanese language. Children seem to lose this ability as they grow up.

Researchers now believe that the brain has detectors that recognize about one dozen consonant sounds. But these detectors need to be triggered by the environment—if not, they are likely to atrophy (Pines, 1981).

Early Speech Sounds

When an infant is born, the only sounds he or she utters that are related to speech are cries. (For an interesting discussion of whether parents can detect their own baby's cries from those of other infants see box 5.3.) For the next few months the infant also makes sounds we call **cooing**, which are vowellike sounds in which the /u/ phoneme appears frequently. Often this sound is preceded by a single consonant, as in *coo, moo, woo, roo, soo*. Other vowels are also heard, but the sounds are typically limited to a single syllable at a time.

At around six or seven months of age the infant begins babbling. Babbling is marked by strings of consonants and vowel phonemes put together. More phonemes are used, and there is a playful, experimental quality to their production.

Finally, near the child's first birthday, there are single-word utterances. Some are identifiable words in the language *(milk, want, see);* others are childish approximations to adult words *(mama, dada, dollie).* The child typically uses only a few phonemes in speech at this stage—fewer than during the babbling stage.

Syntax and Semantics

Syntax and semantics have been the most productive areas of language study in recent years. More is known about their development than about any other facet of language.

The place to begin is the child's first distinguishable utterances, his or her one-word statements, which appear at about one year of age. Up to this point, very little can reasonably be inferred about the child's knowledge of syntax and semantics.

A certain degree of caution must be exercised in assigning and interpreting stages of language development. Rachel Olney and Ellen Scholnick (1978), have shown that adults are highly influenced in the meaning and length they attribute even to single-word utterances produced by children, by their understanding of the context in which the speech occurs. The context, of course, may not always be read correctly.

One-Word Phrase

The child's first words appear one at a time—"Mommy," "sock," "haveit," "wanna," "byebye." The term *holophrase* was coined to indicate that the child's single word may actually be a whole phrase or sentence. Single words might seem poor substitutes for whole sentences, but those who keep frequent company with holophrastic speakers seem to divine the child's meaning quite well. This can be attributed to several factors. For one, these first words are often rich in informational value. The child has a knack for selecting the single word, from some longer adult speech form, that is the most important part of the thought (e.g., "Mommy" for "Mommy is here," "fell" for "the box fell," "hurt" for "I hurt").

In addition, the child uses variations in stress and pitch to distinguish between several possible meanings of the holophrase. Think how you might say "Mommy"

Box 5.3
Are Babies' Cries Distinctive?

Crying is one of the first ways babies communicate. It is a form of primitive language. Can parents distinguish the cries of their own baby from those of others? And, if parents can distinguish cries, can they interpret the meaning or cause of the crying?

Young infants don't tell us why they are crying, so it is hard to validate claims about differences in the origins of cries. However, it is possible to investigate parents' abilities to distinguish among the cries of different infants. Gisela Morsbach and Mary Murphy (1979) tape recorded the cries of five different babies between two and four days of age. Each of the babies was a healthy, full-term infant. Crying was elicited by an adult flicking the sole of the infant's foot with a finger, approximately three hours after the infant had eaten. By splicing fifteen-second taped segments of crying from different portions of their records, the experimenters were able to create a discrimination test with twenty pairs of crying segments. Some of the pairs contained crying segments for the same infants, while other pairs contained segments for different infants.

A total of 210 adult subjects were tested. The adults varied in their degree of experience with babies. For scientific purposes, each subject was considered to be responding knowledgeably to the test if he or she was able to identify at least fifteen of the twenty pairs correctly. The following table, adapted from the researchers' article, shows the percentage of people who were "correct." (pp. 175–79)

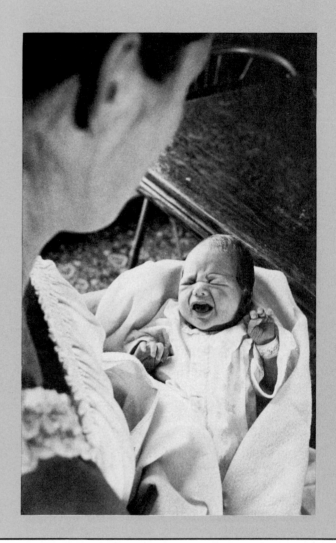

(a) to name a person who has just appeared in the room and (b) to implore a parent to help with a frustrating problem.

Finally, the child employs contextual cues to convey meaning with a single word. He or she may gesture at an object or mimic an action while producing the utterance or may depend upon the listener to understand the immediate events surrounding the statement so an appropriate inference can be drawn.

There seems to be some disagreement about what *syntactic* knowledge the child has. Some claim that it is absurd to speculate about whether the child grasps rules for combining words when the child never combines words. Others argue that the child must have an understanding of some rules, because he or she comprehends much of the complex speech that surrounds him or her. The argument is difficult to resolve because there is no direct means to test the child's sense of the grammatical content of a specific sentence or phrase.

Category	Percent
Midwives (twenty females)	57
Parents with children below one year (eleven female, eleven male)	27
Parents with children above one year (nineteen female, twelve male)	26
Nonparents who "sometimes" have contact (seventy-eight female, thirty-three males)	32
Nonparents who have "no contact" (fourteen females, twelve male)	34

A formal analysis of these results showed that the midwives, who, of course, had considerable experience with many newborns, did much better at discriminating the newborn cries than did all four of the other groups. However, the fact that from 25 to 35 percent of the remaining adults were able to perform the discrimination test correctly is a significant finding. Interestingly, it made little difference whether the remaining adults were parents or not (statistical comparisons among the four groups revealed no significant differences). And the male adults did about as well as the females, in a further breakdown of performances.

What *semantic* knowledge does the child have? Here a more satisfying answer can be offered. The semantic rules are the means by which the child separates the different functions that may be served by the same word. The single utterance "byebye" may be (a) a greeting (as in "good-bye"), (b) a description of an action ("She went away"), (c) a statement of location ("He is in the other room"), or (d) a depiction of a psychological state ("Brother is asleep").

Another component of semantics is how the child uses the words to refer to objects and events. There have been two contrasting explanations offered by investigators to explain how children initially attach meanings to words. One is called the **semantic feature hypothesis,** proposed by Eve Clark (1973). According to it, the meaning of a word is composed of semantic features attached to the word (e.g., four-legged, barks, tail, etc.). Initially, the child tends to notice features that are directly perceived through the senses and applies the word when one or more of these are present.

A contrasting view, sometimes called the **functional core hypothesis,** was proposed by Katherine Nelson (1974). According to this view, the child objects initially to concepts on the basis of their functional relation to the child's actions (e.g., a ball can be thrown, rolled, or bounced). This has led to debates about which types of words are acquired first and which attributes (perceptual or functional) appear first in word usage. There is no clear answer at this writing (Dodd, 1980; Barrett, 1978) and considerable contradictory evidence.

For words that are used as nouns, meanings are both overextended and underextended. Eve Clark (1973) has studied these early meanings and uncovered quite a large number of **overextensions.** For example, a child may first learn the word *papa* for his father. Then he applies this term to other people who are not his father—other men, boys, and strangers, perhaps. He has extended the term beyond the class of people for whom it is intended. Eventually, usage becomes more restricted, and the class of overextended referents becomes smaller and smaller until it disappears.

Overextensions may be noted more frequently than underextension, because underextensions are less obvious. When a child fails to use a noun to name a relevant event, we often view it as mere silence or as a hestitation to communicate and are likely to miss it as an instance of **underextension.** There are actually many cases of underextensions. For example, the child may learn the word *girl* to describe a four-year-old neighbor but not apply it to a female infant or a ten-year-old.

Early Language Stages
Beyond the one-word stage several important new developments occur in just a few short years. The changes are so rapid and so significant that psychologist Roger Brown (1973) has chosen to examine them at several arbitrary points in time to capture some of the landmark acquisitions. The result is a series of stages that describe different rule systems, but the stages are not tight systems of the Freudian or Piagetian variety.

In all, Brown has identified five early stages, two of which are described in detail here. A stage is identified by estimating the average number of words per sentence a child produces in a sample of from fifty to one hundred sentences recorded at about the same time. The average or **mean length of utterance** (MLU) for each stage is as follows:

Stage	MLU
1	$1+ \rightarrow 2.0$
2	2.5
3	3.0
4	3.5
5	4.0

The first stage begins when the child produces sentences that consist of more than one word. The 1 + indicates that the average number of words in each utterance is greater than 1 but not yet 2, since some utterances are still holophrases. It continues until the child averages two words per utterance. Successive stages 2 to 5 are marked by increments of 0.5 in the MLU. This scheme is valuable for at least two reasons. For one, Brown has found that children may vary by as much as one-half to three-quarters of a year in chronological age and yet have similar speech patterns. Children with a similar MLU index seem to have acquired very similar rule systems. So MLU is a better index of language development than chronological age would be. It is also a convenient way to group children who are at the same level of development.

Stage 1   At the beginning of stage 1, the child produces a few two-word utterances. For example, he or she may say "allgone truck," "Daddy byebye," "Mommy book," or "me soap." These are intermingled with single-word sentences. Later in this stage there are three-word utterances, for example, "I want book," "Mommy give candy," and "Dada went home." As MLU approaches 2.0, some children even produce four-word utterances; for example, "Mommy give toy here" and "I eat cookie kitchen." We can see that although MLU is 2.0, there is quite a spread in the complexity of speech, ranging from one to four words.

Children seem to be constructing abbreviated sentences, retaining the most infomative words and dropping less informative words. Brown dubbed the speech *telegraphic,* noting its similarity in brevity and information yield to a telegram. But children are also employing some unique rule systems to generate sentences. David McNeill (1970) and others attempted one such description of the child's two-word utterances. He claimed that the child has a grammar or rule system consisting of two kinds of word classes, the *pivot* class and *open* class, and rules restricting how the classes can be combined.

The pivot class (P) consists of a small number of words, each of which is frequently heard in everyday speech. Membership in the class grows slowly. The open class (O) consists of a large number of words, and its membership grows rapidly. Pivot words seem to be the focal point in the sentence; open words are attached to them—hence the term *pivot.*

Pivot words never occur alone; they always occur with an open word. Each pivot word has a fixed position; it occurs in the first or the second position, but not both. By contrast, open words can occur alone or with another word and in either the first or the second position. Table 5.2 shows some of the one- and two-word utterances of a child, a specification of the pivot (P) and open (O) classes present, and the rules that describe how the child produces a sentence.

The child's speech is more complicated, however, than the simple pivot-open system might suggest. Evidence has shown that this rule system does not describe all children's speech very well (e.g., Bowerman, 1973). The system does not easily explain the nature of the three- and four-word sentences that appear in the same stage. Three-word utterances seem to have either an agent-action-object form ("I want book") or an agent-action-location form ("Dada went home"). And four-word utterances seem to have an agent-action-object-location form ("Mommy give toy here"). These forms and the rules underlying them are not intuitively connected to the pivot-open system, but this system is presumably the forerunner of the more complex forms.

Equally important is a consideration of semantics. The pivot-open grammar ignores the many semantic relations present in two-word sentences (Nelson, 1978, Chapman, 1981). Many different functions are served by two-word utterances. Brown (1970) has provided a partial list of these (see table 5.3).

As the child moves from two-word speech to three- and four-word speech, no new semantic relations appear. Rather, the child seems to include several of the relations from table 5.3 in a single sentence.

Stage 2   In stage 2 the length of the child's sentences increases, and it is not unusual to observe sentences that include four or five words. The principal accomplishment, however, is the mastery of several inflections. The child learns how to pluralize nouns, specify verb tense, include prepositions like *in* and *on,* insert articles like *a* and *the* in appropriate places, include pronomial forms, and so on. In other words, the child masters a number of rules for morphemes in the language.

Brown has studied morphemes that are mastered in this period: the present-progressive verb form (e.g., *hitting*); the prepositions *in* or *on;* plural forms; past-irregular verb forms (e.g., *ran, bit, chose*); the possessive (e.g., *man's, sky's*); uncontractible copulas (e.g.,

Table 5.2
A Pivot-Open Grammar Inferred from a Child's Speech

Utterances		Word Classes		Rules (Grammar)
Mommy	Allgone milk	P1 →	on, down	1. O
sock	Byebye sock	P2 →	allgone, byebye	2. O + O
Daddy book	Daddy down	O →	mommy, sock, daddy,	3. O + P1
Sock Daddy	Byebye Mommy		book, table, dollie, milk	4. P2 + O
Table	Sock on			
Dollie on	Allgone Mommy			
Milk down	Dollie down			

Table 5.3
Semantic Relations in Two-Word Sentences

Semantic Relation	Form	Example
1. Nomination	that + N	that book
2. Notice	hi + N	hi belt
3. Recurrence	more + N, 'nother + N	more milk
4. Nonexistence	allgone + N, no more + N	allgone rattle
5. Attributive	Adj + N	big train
6. Possessive	N + N	mommy lunch
7. Locative	N + N	sweater chair
8. Locative	V + N	walk street
9. Agent-Action	N + V	Eve read
10. Agent-Object	N + N	mommy sock
11. Action-Object	V + N	put book

Source: Adapted from Brown, 1970, p. 220.

were, as in "they were going"); articles *(a, the);* the past-regular verb form (e.g., *walked, climbed*); the third-person singular in its regular form (e.g., "it smokes," "it bites") and in its irregular form (e.g., "she went," "he found"); and numerous uncontractible auxiliary verb forms (e.g., "had gone"); contractible copulas (e.g., "I am going" → "I'm going"); and contractible auxiliaries (e.g., "I have gone" → "I've gone").

Several interesting facts emerge about the development of these morphemes. One concerns their frequency of occurrence. Once the correct form begins to appear in the child's speech, he or she uses it in appropriate places virtually all the time; acquisition is very rapid, once begun. Another is that the order in which the morphemes are mastered is fairly uniform. The order of the list just given reflects the order. The present progressive is the first form mastered, the prepositions *in* and *on* appear next, and so forth, up to contractible copulas and auxiliaries, which are the last to be acquired. The order is constant, that is, for learning English; obviously, other languages that contain different rules for the use of morphemes cannot be directly compared.

One possibility for uniform order is that the forms mastered earlier are grammatically less complex than are the forms mastered later. This simply means that

mastery of earlier acquisitions require fewer rules than are required by later acquisitions. Another possibility is that the forms mastered earlier are semantically less complex, depending on concepts and ideas acquired earlier in cognitive development. For example, the use of the present progressive (hit + ing → hitting) requires that the child think about an act enduring over some period of time. But the use of the uncontractible auxiliary ("had gone") requires much more. The child must understand duration; the fact that two events can occur in the past, one before the other; and, in some cases, the difference between singular and plural.

More recent work on Brown's grammatical morphemes raises questions about the accuracy of all of Browns' claims (e.g., Kuczaj, 1978; Ingram, 1981; Bloom, Miller & Hood, 1975). As Robin Chapman (1981) suggested, not all of Brown's children mastered the morphemes at just the right stages, there is little evidence to show that each morpheme has separate unit of meaning from the others, and we are just beginning to acquire detailed knowledge of how the morphemes are acquired (e.g., Bloom, Liftler, & Hafitz, 1980).

*People from different
cultures have different
words to describe what they
see when looking at water,
and therefore may think
differently about water.*

The Functions of Language

Language is more than just an interesting phenomenon to examine and describe. It is also a system that is used for many purposes. No explanation of language would be complete without an account of the functions of language.

Perception

Language influences the way events are perceived. When a word or a sentence is uttered, the accompanying stimulus events are thereby made more distinctive. In sentences like "See the dent in the car's bumper" and "Look at the pinkish color the artist used to paint the man's foot," a responsive listener can perceive something about the event that would not have been perceived without language. Language helps to segment and call attention to certain facets of experience.

Each person acquires slightly different language habits. Each person uses different words, speaks and writes with different grammatical forms, and has favorite expressions and phrases. These differences in turn foster differences in perceptions of the world. Each person notices different things, segments experiences in different ways, and attaches unique meanings to events.

These differences are most pronounced in comparisons of people who speak different languages. Each language has unique connotative meanings associated with utterances; any translation will have a nuance different from that of the original. Such differences between languages lead native speakers to have very different perceptions of the world (Whorf, 1956; Sapir, 1958). In the realm of color perception, for example, the English language has many words to describe differences in hues (e.g., red, green, blue, orange, turquoise, magenta, and so on), while languages of some primitive societies have very few. In some Eskimo tongues there are about a dozen words to describe various colors, textures, and physical states of snow while English has just a few (e.g., snow, ice, sleet, hail). In each case the **Whorf/Sapir hypothesis** is that a language with more vocabulary, or lexical categories produces perceptions that are more differentiated. So the speaker of English actually sees more shadings of color than the speaker of some primitive language does. Likewise, the Eskimo perceives many more kinds of snow than the speaker of English does.

Other interpretations are possible, however. The speakers of the two languages may have the same perceptions but be less able to code or work with them (Cole & Scribner, 1974). Rosch (1973) suggests that color categories may actually be universal and independent of language. For these reasons few contemporary psychologists accept the Whorf/Sapir hypothesis in its original version.

Memory

Numerous studies have shown that memory for nonlinguistic events is enhanced when language is associated with them. For example, if we see a series of pictures, our recollection of them is better if we are also provided names for the pictures (Brown, 1975; Levin, 1981). The same is true for recollections of physical behaviors. Much of what is learned and remembered is the physical behavior of other people. If language is attached to these behaviors, they are more easily remembered (Coates & Hartup, 1969).

A number of explanations of why language has this effect on memory have been proposed. One is that events are processed through different levels as they are encountered (Craik & Lockhart, 1972, 1977)—this view is sometimes called the **depth-of-processing view.** The deeper the level of processing, the more memorable the event will be. A very deep level of processing usually involves analyzing the meaning of the event. Language creates highly meaningful associations for events and thus increases the likelihood that a deep level of processing will occur.

Another explanation is that language creates a simple code for an experience that can then be rehearsed or repeated. Many studies show that an experience is more easily recalled when it has been rehearsed (Brown, 1975). It is often easier to rehearse a description or a name of an experince than the experience itself.

Each of these views, however, must be tempered by developmental considerations. Clearly, language does not influence memory in exactly the same way throughout childhood. Preschoolers do not think to use linguistic devices to help themselves remember (e.g., Brown, 1975; Kail, 1978)—sometimes referred to as a linguistic production deficiency. Although elementary school children *do* think to use such linguistic devices, the language techniques they employ are very simple (e.g., naming an object). During the latter elementary school years and beyond, children's language techniques become more sophisticated in the service of memory. They generate words, sentences, and stories to recall events. They repeat or rehearse these. And as they progress, they monitor the effects of this language activity on their memory. Thus we see that language techniques become more useful.

Thinking

Language also helps us to think and to solve problems. It provides us with a tool to represent ideas and arguments and to deal with the representations. Language seems so important in the process of thinking that many people believe it is impossible to think without language. This belief has led to some of the most heated debates in developmental psychology. At the center of the arguments is the relationship between thought and language. Is one dependent on the other, is each dependent on the other, or is this a relationship of some other sort? There are almost as many answers to this question as there are people who have attempted to answer it. One writer (Jenkins, 1969) even suggested facetiously that the answer is "all of the above!" That is, language is dependent upon thought, thought is dependent upon language, each is dependent on the other, and (in some circumstances) the two are unrelated. It is instructive to understand some of the different points of view that have been expressed on the topic.

Some experts (e.g., Vygotsky, 1962; Bruner, 1964) believe that higher forms of human intelligence and thought are achieved because language is developed. Language is the vehicle that makes it possible to acquire concrete and formal operational thought, for example, because language develops early and becomes a rich and complete symbolic system soon after it is acquired. It provides remarkable power for representing an abstract experience. By contrast, other representational systems (e.g., imagery, operations) lag behind it in their development. For example, consider the abstract rules and classes the young child operates with by Brown's stage 2 of language development. Yet this same child is barely beyond the sensorimotor stage of thought in the nonlinguistic, cognitive realm. Language rules are clearly more sophisticated and abstract than early thought is.

As further evidence of the view that language leads to thought, some psychologists remind us of the importance of language in various cognitive tasks. There is evidence, for example, that children who solve concrete operational problems use more appropriate language than the children who fail to solve them do (Sinclair-DeZwart, 1969).

Jean Piaget (1968, 1970) has been the most prominent advocate of the position that thought is primarily independent of language. In his view, language is merely one symbolic vehicle for the expression of thought. There are also others, such as perception, imagery, and operations. Although language may become the best system humans possess for expressing thought, language is not the original vehicle for the development of thought; sensorimotor activity is.

As evidence for this position, psychologists point to a number of diverse facts about cognitive development. For one, children do not produce sentences—even two-word utterances—until they have progressed to sensorimotor stage 5 or 6. Perhaps some of the conceptual developments during this period actually serve as a foundation for language development, rather than the other way around. Some candidates are object permanence, the deferred internal image, and the tendency to experiment activity, all of which occur by sensorimotor stage 5 or 6. In order to use words in referring to things, the child must first be able to conceive of them as permanent and to image the ones that are not present. To form word classes or grammatical categories, the child continually juggles primitive, tentative rules, a process helped by a cognitive tendency to experiment actively (Bloom, 1970; Braine, 1976; Nelson, 1978, Chapman, 1981).

Another source of evidence is the cognitive development of deaf children. Furth (1971) has shown that on a variety of thinking and problem-solving tasks, these children perform at the same level as children of the same age who have no hearing problem. If by language we mean spoken language, then this evidence argues against the primacy of language for the development of thought. However, some of these children also had no command of written or sign language and performed at the same level as their hearing counterparts. So language, even in a broader sense, was not necessary for them to develop normal cognitive skills.

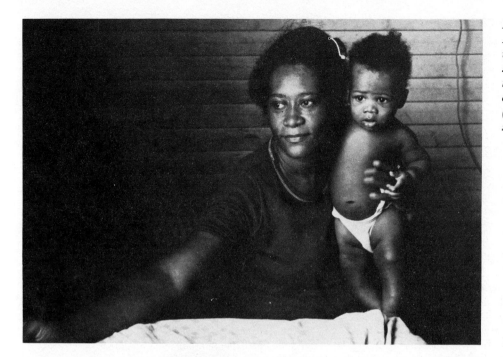

According to Mary Ainsworth, there is an underlying attachment system (e.g., bond between mother and infant) and overt attachment behaviors (e.g., crying or proximity system of infant).

mother in close contact and, functionally, the infant is the main actor. Signaling responses refer to smiling, crying, and calling. They also bring the infant and mother together, but in this case, the infant is attempting to elicit (reciprocal) behaviors from the mother.

The development of attachment as an integrated system of behaviors occurs in four phases during the first year of life. During the first phase, extending from birth to two or three months, the infant directs his or her attachment to human figures on the basis of an unlearned bias. Strangers, siblings, mothers, and fathers are equally likely to cause smiling or crying; the infant is not discriminating. In phase 2, from three to six months, attachment becomes focused on one figure—typically the primary caregiver (e.g., mother). Phase 3 extends from six to nine months and consists of an increase in the intensity of attachment to the mother. Because of increased locomotor skills, the infant now more readily seeks proximity to her. Finally, in the fourth phase (which extends from nine months to a year), the elements of attachment listed become integrated into a mutual system of attachment to which the infant and the mother both contribute.

Mary Ainsworth (1973, 1979) has contributed a number of ideas to the attachment field. Three stand out as salient. First, it is important to distinguish between an underlying attachment system (e.g., bond between mother and infant) and overt attachment behaviors (e.g., crying or proximity system of infant). The two will not always be mapped in a one to one relation. Second, there are vast individual differences in the patterning of caretaker-infant interactions that have profound consequences for the nature of the attachment

The Link between Attachment and Later Development

If, as the major theories claim, the first social bond(s) of attachment are critical for later development, it should be possible to establish a link between the degree or quality of attachment achieved in infancy and later social development. Such evidence is available.

In one recent investigation, Waters, Wippman, and Sroufe (1979) demonstrated two such important links. First, they showed that eighteen-month-old infants who were or were not securely attached displayed different types of *free play* behavior six months later. During a ten-minute free play period in which infants were placed in a room with their mothers and a number of toys, it was found that the secure infants showed and gave toys to their mothers—affectively *shared*—much more frequently than either avoidant or resistant children. Second, they showed that an independent group of fifteen-month-olds who were distinguished as securely or insecurely attached (employing a procedure similar to Ainsworth's) exhibited different levels of personal and interpersonal competence when

they were three and one-half years old. Competence was assessed by means of a Q-sort technique in which a series of "descriptors" were evaluated by judges who observed the children in preschool. Secure children received higher scores for "other children seek his or her company," "suggests activities," "peer leader," and "sympathetic to peer distress," while insecure children received higher scores for "basically withdrawn," "hesitates to engage," and "spectator (vs. participant) in social activities." This link between attachment and later social competence has been verified by other investigators as well (e.g., Main & Londerville, 1977; Lieberman, 1977).

Other research from Alan Sroufe's laboratory supports the link between attachment and other later behaviors. For example, in an investigation by Matas, Arend, and Sroufe (1978) a relation was shown wherein more securely attached infants at eighteen months were more capable in using specially designed tools and in solving simple problems six months later.

that develops. And third, the resulting attachment relations seem to fall into discrete categories that are relatively enduring in the child. More will be said about individual differences later in the chapter.

The approach taken by Bowlby and Ainsworth holds a great deal of promise. It offers the most general and subtle account of the development of attachment. One of the strongest pieces of support for the Bowlby-Ainsworth position is a longitudinal study conducted by Alan Sroufe and his colleagues (Waters, Wippman, & Sroufe, 1979). An overview of their project is described in box 6.2.

Course of Attachment

How does attachment develop? The theories reviewed earlier offer some suggestions. In this section, the empirical sources of evidence about attachment will be reviewed.

In perhaps the most widely cited longitudinal study of attachment, investigators followed sixty Scottish infants who were from five to twenty-three weeks old at the outset of the study until they were eighteen months old (Schaeffer & Emerson, 1964). They periodically interviewed the mothers about the infants' responses to separation episodes and observed the infants' responses

to several standardized situations in which the interviewer (a stranger) slowly approached the infant. As with the interviews, the observations were made repeatedly throughout the period of the study. Figure 6.2 depicts the course of the infants' attachment behavior over time. It indicates that the infants protested being separated from anyone (indiscriminate attachment) during the first months of life. Beginning at about six months (twenty-five to twenty-eight weeks) attachment to the mother became more focused and remained strong from ten months through the remaining portion of the eighteen-month period. Attachments to other specific caregivers were at about the same level of intensity as attachment to the mother. And there were some additional findings that are not shown in the figure: for example, from seven months until almost the end of the first year, the specific attachment to the mother became more intense and fear of strangers generally occurred at about eight months, approximately one to two months after the onset of attachment to the mother.

In another well-known study of infant attachment, Mary Ainsworth (1967) observed twenty-nine infant-mother pairs in Uganda, Africa, for a period of nine months. The children ranged in age from two to fourteen months during the investigation. Her observations

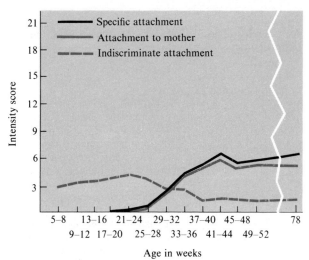

Figure 6.2 The course of infant attachment behavior.

included smiling, crying, vocalization, separation protest, following, touching, greeting gestures, and using the mother as a base of exploration as indicators of attachment. As in the Schaffer and Emerson study, the Ugandan infants began to show the most intense signs of attachment to their mothers around seven months. However, there was evidence that the specific attachments began to develop earlier than in the Schaffer and Emerson sample. For example, there were indications of attachment to the mother by four months in the Ugandan infants. And interestingly, there was also a difference in the time of onset for fear of strangers. This fear emerged later in the Ugandan infants, so the time lag between attachment and fear of strangers was much greater in this study.

There are reasons for differences across samples. The measures of attachment in the two studies just mentioned are not identical—that is, Ainsworth used a much larger number of measures, whereas much of Schaffer's and Emerson's data were derived from maternal interviews. Nonetheless, even with the wide range of individual differences and dissimilarity in measures, there is good evidence that most infants develop a focused attachment to significant adults at about seven months of age and this becomes intensified in the next few months. And, stranger anxiety seems to be positively correlated with the onset of attachment to the caretaker, usually following it by several weeks to several months.

A third major effort to study the attachment system of infants and mothers was conducted by Coates, Anderson, and Hartup (1972a, 1972b). They observed a group of infants at ten months and at fourteen months and another group at fourteen months and at eighteen months. Two observation periods were arranged, one in which the infant played on the floor for ten minutes while the mother sat quietly in a chair, and a second in which the mother and infant were in a neutral play

situation for several minutes, followed by the mother leaving the room for two minutes, and concluding with her reunion with the infant for several minutes. Observations were taken on proximity seeking, touching, vocalizing, crying, and orienting to the door when the mother left. Based upon evidence of how the different behaviors were correlated with one another, the investigator concluded that there was more evidence for an integrated attachment system (meaning that the system did not vary extensively across the different situations observed) at fourteen and eighteen months than at ten months. For example, crying after the mother left and approach behavior after the reunion were significantly related at fourteen and eighteen months, but not at ten months.

At the time Coates, Anderson, and Hartup conducted their research, there was little convincing evidence that differences in attachment-related behaviors persisted over time. Since then, a number of other investigators have amassed such evidence and have shown consistency over even longer periods of time (e.g., Lewis & Ban, 1971; Coates, 1978; Maccoby & Feldman, 1972). In addition both Waters (1978) and Connell (1976) have offered evidence that individual differences in attachment relations are very stable from twelve to eighteen months. And other investigators have shown clear relations between individual differences in attachment relations during the first year with other social behaviors during the second year, such as problem solving and tool using (Matas, Arend, & Sroufe, 1978), free play (Main & Londerville, 1977), and peer interaction (Waters, Wippman, & Sroufe, 1979).

Although the psychoanalytic view emphasizes the mother as the typical "singular" caregiver with whom the infant becomes "bonded," a consistent feeling in the literature is that attachment quite frequently is directed toward more than one caregiver. Note this finding in the classic studies by Schaeffer and Emerson (1964) and Ainsworth (1967). This point has also been emphasized by Michael Lamb, who has conducted extensive research on the influence of fathers in early socialization. As Lyle Joffe (1977) so ably summarized this issue:

Prior emphasis on the infant-mother relation has led . . . to the assumption that the infant experiences primarily a two person social world. The popularity of this assumption can probably be ascribed to the hypothesis that since mothers spend most time with infants, they must be the most affectively salient person in the infants' lives. From this, it seems, the inference was drawn that they must be solely and exclusively important. As Lamb (1977) points out, this presumption is discredited both by the fact that mothers and infants actually interact far less than most theories would have us believe (Clarke-Stewart, 1973), and by the increasing awareness that it is not the amount but the quality of interaction that is important in the formation of attachments (Bossard & Boll, 1966; Lamb, 1976; Pedersen & Robson, 1969; Schaffer, 1971).

Social, Emotional, and Personality Foundations and Development

Although it has been demonstrated that ten- to sixteen-month-old infants show a marked preference for their mothers over their fathers in a laboratory situation involving the disruption of the infant's activity every sixty seconds (Cohen & Campos, 1974), it is equally clear that when observed in a naturalistic setting infants of seven months of age and older show no preference for either parent in the display of attachment behaviors (Lamb, 1976, 1977). (pp. 2–3)

To briefly summarize, it appears that infants have an undifferentiated or nondiscriminating attachment during the first four to six months, followed by positive approach and proximity seeking in the next several months directed toward one or more caregivers including mothers and fathers. This primary attachment phenomenon may last for as long as a year to eighteen months. Fear of strangers usually appears one to four months after primary attachment and is evidenced by distress and crying when a strange adult appears. There is now modest, replicated support for the notion that individual differences in attachment persist over time for at least twelve to eighteen months.

Individual Differences in Attachment

To speak of attachment as a monolithic phenomenon experienced in the same way or in the same degree by all infant-caregiver pairs is, of course, a convenient fiction. There are striking individual differences among infants. For example, in the Schaeffer and Emerson (1964) investigation one-fourth of the infants showed fear of strangers before specific attachment to the mother. This is quite a striking and nontrivial variation in the normative pattern of development. And, in Mary Ainsworth's (1967) early inquiry, five of the twenty-eight infants never did evidence positive affiliation with their mothers (e.g., clinging, proximity seeking, visual contact). Other investigators have found similar patterns of individual variation (e.g., Waters, 1978, Main, 1978).

Perhaps the most widely cited and well-researched work on individual differences come from the laboratory of Mary Ainsworth, in conjunction with her Strange Situation methodology. Chiefly on the basis of infants' behaviors toward their mothers in reunion episodes, she makes a distinction between infants who seem to be securely attached versus those who are not. Among those who are designated as nonsecurely attached, a further distinction is made. One subgroup exhibits insecurity by avoiding the mother—ignoring her, averting her gaze, and failing to seek proximity. The other subgroup exhibits insecurity by resisting the mother—they may seek her proximity and cling to her, but at the same time fight against the closeness by, for example, kicking and pushing away. Finer subdivisions of these three categories are possible as shown in table 6.1. However, most investigators find that the major

Table 6.1
Ainsworth's Classification of Attachment: Individual Differences

	Characteristics
Securely Attached	
group 1	Seeks interaction on reunion but not proximity. Does not resist when held. Little or no distress during separation episodes.
group 2	Seeks interaction and more proximity on reunion. Does not resist when held. Little or no distress during separation episodes.
group 3	Approaches mother on reunion. May also cry. Clutches when held, resists release. May or may not be distressed. Very active in seeking contact and resisting release.
group 4	Greatest desire for proximity, interaction, and being held throughout. Distress evident in separation episodes.
Insecurely Attached—Avoidance	
group 1	Infant fails to greet mother upon return. Fails to approach mother or attempt is aborted if picked up; likely to squirm to get down and does not cling.
group 2	Infant greets mother with mixed response, both approaching and turning and looking away. If picked up, always shows mixed response, momentarily clinging, but also slipping away.
Insecurely Attached—Resistant	
group 1	May reach or approach mother upon reunion and seek contact. But great ambivalence shown, with hitting, kicking, and pushing.
group 2	Fails to even contact mother. If approached or held, ambivalence shown.

subdivisions are easier to work with and easier to score reliably. In most groups of infants, it is assumed that the majority will be securely attached (two-thirds of Ainsworth's first sample of twenty-three babies were). It is the minority who evidence some maladaptive attachment.

What Is the Source of Individual Differences?

Where do such individual differences come from? This question has been the source of widespread speculation and much research. Among those infants who eventually achieve some degree of attachment, one widely held hypothesis is that differences in the rate of achieving attachment reflect corresponding differences in the rate of cognitive development (e.g., Clarke-Stewart, 1973, 1978). In order to achieve a strong emotional bond with significant caretakers, goes the argument, the infant must first attain *object permanence* with respect to those people. That is, he or she must first divine that the people are permanent fixtures in the world who exist beyond the momentary time and place where they are experienced. Some research suggests that an infant's general level of cognitive development does correlate with the degrees of attachment (Clarke-Stewart, 1973; Stone & Chesney, 1978). An interesting side issue has also emerged. Since the time at which clear attachments first emerge in infants (about six to eight months) predates the time at which *object permanence* is usually observed with nonsocial objects (in conventional Piagetian testing, e.g., Uzgiris & Hunt, 1975), it has been speculated that the presence of attachment reflects a special, earlier-than-usual case of object permanence (e.g., Bell, 1970). However, clear experiments have not consistently confirmed some of the implications of this notion.

Individual differences in the temperament of mother and child may also contribute to differences in the way attachment develops. Infants may be born with relatively enduring and different styles of responding to the world around them, for example, easy, difficult, and slow to warm up (Chess & Thomas, 1977). If caregivers are unable to synchronize their own behavior toward the infant (de Chateau, 1977) due to a clash in temperaments or a simple inability to respond effectively to infant signals, attachment problems may arise. Although there is little hard evidence on the effects of such temperamental clashes on the development of attachment, there is evidence that temperamental differences do lead to clearly different caregiver-infant interactions.

For example, thirty-four infant-mother pairs were studied when the infants were two to three months old and two months later (Pantone, 1978).

At both time periods, seven dimensions of temperament (Activity Level, Rhythmicity, Adaptability, Approach/Withdrawal Tendency, Threshold of Response, Intensity of Mood) were assessed. Mother-infant interaction (including the quality and responsivity of each partner) was recorded during a naturalistic observation session. . . . The results suggested that the dimensions of Rhythmicity and Threshold of Response were particularly crucial to the pattern of mother-infant interaction during the two- to three-month age period. Stable, predictable functioning on the part of the infant was associated with all forms of stimulation and positive feeling expressed by the mother. The highly reactive, low threshold baby received more verbal stimulation. (11B, 5546)

Just as there are striking individual differences in the way infants express attachment, so are there powerful effects of the circumstances (situation) on the expression of attachment, as will be seen next.

Situational Variables

Recently, Alison Clarke-Stewart (1978) offered a penetrating analysis of the importance of **situational variability** when studying infant behavior. She focused on "fear of the stranger" and analyzed the factors that determine how much fear or wariness will surface in the stranger's presence. The motivation for the analysis was the controversy wherein some authors have doubted the reality of this fearful reaction in infants (e.g., Rheingold & Eckerman, 1970; Rheingold, 1973; Haith & Campos, 1977), suggesting it is largely the result of poorly conceived experiments in which infants are subjected to unnatural and atypical interactions with strangers. On the other hand, research that has corrected some of these problems continues to support the existence of some wariness in infants (e.g., Klein & Durfee, 1975; Ricciuti, 1974; Sroufe, Waters, & Matas, 1974), even if it is sometimes in the form of mild support. The title of her paper, "Recasting the Lone Stranger" reflects her opinion that we may have oversimplified the stranger and treated him or her as a static variable, when the stranger is actually much more complex.

Clarke-Stewart then proceeded to examine the influence of the stranger's *behavior* in a longitudinal investigation of fourteen middle-class infants over a one-and-a-half-year period (from one- to two-and-a-half years of age). A brief summary of her major findings follows.

In interactions lasting several minutes, strangers behaved in a hostile manner toward mothers by stomping into the room and launching into an angry and insulting dialogue with her, or in a happy manner by bouncing into the room full of joyous talk and animated conversation. Infants maintained less physical contact with their mothers during and after *hostile* interactions as compared with *happy* ones. Interestingly, the child's behavior toward the stranger was not influenced by the tone of the interaction between the stranger and the mother. By contrast, when strangers were either *nice* or *nasty* to the child directly, there were clear effects on the child's interaction with the stranger, but not with the mother. *Nice* strangers played with the child in a positive, pleasant, and friendly way with toys the child liked. *Nasty* strangers acted unpleasantly, unfriendly, and belligerently while playing with the child. The infants were more positive to the nice strangers (approaching, smiling, and touching) and more negative to the nasty ones (avoiding, crying, and aggressing).

In another series of manipulations, Clarke-Stewart tried to finely discriminate different modes of behavior that a stranger might exhibit to more precisely pinpoint which ones make a difference in the infant's interactions. Among the contrasts struck were ignoring versus looking at the child and exhibiting active versus passive behavior, and maintaining distant versus close interaction with the infant. The first manipulation produced the most interesting results. According to Clarke-Stewart:

When the stranger ignored the child—that is, did not look at him or her—children, although they watched her, uniformly initiated little or no interaction with her. . . . When the stranger merely "looked" at the children, however, this behavior opened the lines of communication between them. Then, children not only looked at the stranger, but also vocalized, smiled, and approached. The "eyes," it seems have it! (pp. 123–24)

Thus, it is fruitful to analyze a stimulus that at first looks simple—the presence or absence of a stranger—into its meaningful social components. Such an analysis reveals the powerful influence of situational variables on the expression of positive and negative responses toward a stranger.

Other situational variables have also been observed. For example, the one-year-old infant does not show as much distress to a stranger when sitting on the mother's lap as when sitting on a table (Morgan & Ricciuti, 1969). Infants fuss less and explore their environment more when a novel toy is present than when it is absent (Rheingold & Samuels, 1969). The readiness of infants to explore an unfamiliar object depends in part on how closely the mother is positioned to the infant (Schwartz, 1978). Eye contact may also be important. Adults who maintain visual attention to the infant may give him or her a sense of security. For example, five-month-old infants smiled and vocalized more and cried less when their mothers or a female stranger maintained eye contact with them as compared with visual orientation slightly farther away (Lasky & Klein, 1979).

In virtually every domain of social and emotional development, whether it be the study of attachment, self-concept, aggression, moral development, sex-role development, or achievement, we will find both individual differences and situational influences on the social and emotional characteristic being studied. In the next section, we consider the relation between attachment and the child's development of independence and exploratory tendencies.

Independence and the Development of the Self in Infancy

The initial discussion of the infant's development of independence focuses on how he or she performs the balancing act between attachment and independence. Two theories of how infants become independent will be discussed, developmental changes in independence will be described, and some fascinating ideas about how the

infant's sense of self emerges will be covered. When the infant can detect that he or she has a self that is distinct from other people and objects in the world will also be examined.

Attachment and Independence-Exploration

Infants are highly active explorers of their environments. Soon after birth, we see evidence of their systematic visual exploration (e.g., Cohen & Salapatek, 1975), of their object manipulation (e.g., Uzgiris & Hunt, 1975), and of their general interest in moderately novel experiences (e.g., Kagan, 1976). Exploration is one important source of learning about the properties of the environment.

In a classic study, Ainsworth, Bell, and Stayton (1971) examined individual differences in the way one-year-old infants exhibited exploration and attachment in a home setting. Based on the Strange Situation classification, those children judged as **securely attached** seemed to alternate between exploring their environments and seeking their mothers in a smooth, unstressed manner. However, infants in each of the **insecurely attached** groups had trouble exploring. Their activity was full of uncertainty and stress. The securely attached infants, for example, took pleasure in grasping and manipulating objects, while the others did not (Main, 1973).

To be securely attached to the mother, then, does not mean that the infant is less independent. Next, two theories about the development of independence, each of which emphasizes the symbiosis between the caretaker and the infant as an important part of the child's striving for independence, are discussed.

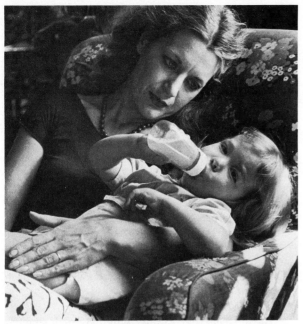

Securely attached children alternate between exploring their environments and seeking their mothers.

The child acquires a sense of separateness along with a sense of relatedness to the world through the process of separation-individuation.

Theories of Independence

Margaret Mahler and Erik Erikson have focused considerable attention on the child's push for independence from parents. First, Mahler's ideas about separation-individuation are described and, second, Erikson's comments about the stage of autonomy vs. shame and doubt are presented.

Separation-Individuation

Margaret Mahler (1965, 1979a, 1979b) is a well-known psychoanalytic theorist who has conducted very detailed clinical observations of infants and their mothers with the goal of finding out how infants and toddlers develop independence. Mahler believes that the child acquires a sense of separateness along with a sense of relatedness to the world through the process of **separation-individuation.** The process is characterized by the child's emergence from the symbiotic relationship with the mother (separation) and the child's acquisition of individual characteristics in the first three years of life. At the end of three years, the child has an independent, autonomous self. On the basis of these clinical observations, Mahler described subphases of the individuation process.

The newborn child is in an autistic stage, a time at which contact with the outside world is about to begin. The first change, called **differentiation,** begins at about four to five months and lasts for the next four to five months. There is a decrease in bodily dependence that coincides with significant increases in locomotor skills such as creeping, climbing, and standing up. The infant also begins to look beyond the immediate visual field, explores objects, and takes an active interest in the outside world. All of these activities emerge and are expressed in close proximity to the mother.

The next subphase of the development of individuation, referred to as **practicing,** lasts from about eight months to fifteen months. There is a steadily increasing interest in practicing motor skills and exploring and expanding the environment. The main characteristic of this subphase, though, is the infant's narcissistic interest in his or her own functions, body, and in the objects that are involved in reality testing. While the infant in this period may be absorbed in his or her own activities for long periods of time it may seem that he or she is oblivious to the mother. However, the infant returns to the mother periodically, as if he or she needs her physical proximity—a phenomenon referred to as emotional refueling.

The next subphase, called **rapprochement,** lasts approximately from fifteen to twenty-four months and roughly coincides with the period of development we sometimes refer to as toddlerhood. By the middle of the second year of life, the child has become more and more aware of his or her physical separateness. But as the child realizes his or her power and ability to move away from the mother physically, he or she now seems to have an increased need and a wish for the mother to share in every new acquisition of skill and experience. Thus, active approach behavior toward the mother and a seemingly constant concern for the mother's whereabouts characterize this period much more than was the case during the practicing subphase.

The final subphase of individuation is called **consolidation of individuality.** This subphase should occur at about twenty-four to thirty months of age and as the phase proceeds, the child is able gradually to accept once again separation from the mother (as during the practicing period). In fact, the child seems to prefer staying in a familiar playroom without the mother to going out of this room with her. During this phase, active resistance to the demands of adults and a strong desire for autonomy are apparent.

An example of how maternal-child interaction can interfere with the development of individuation was described by Mahler (1972). Anna's mother's marked emotional unavailability made Anna's practicing and exploratory period brief and subdued. Never certain of her mother's availability, and therefore always preoccupied with it, Anna found it difficult to explore her surroundings. After a brief spurt of practicing, she would return to her mother and try to interact with her in an intense manner. From such relatively direct expressions of need for her mother as bringing a book to read to her or hitting the mother's ever-present book in which she was engrossed, Anna turned to more desperate measures, such as falling or spilling cookies on the floor and stomping on them, always with an eye to gaining her mother's attention, if not involvement. Anna's mother was absorbed in her own interests, which were anything but child-centered. Along with her inability to let her mother out of her sight, Anna's activities were very low keyed: they lacked the vivacity and luster that characterized other children at her age.

Anna was observed during the preschool years at the nursery school she attended. When her mother would leave after dropping her off at school she often threw a temper tantrum and would cling to her teacher. But the clinging frequently turned to hitting and yelling. In Mahler's view, Anna wanted only one thing to happen: her mother to return through the door. But when the mother did return, Anna did not show even a flicker of radiance or happiness. Her very first words were, "What did you bring me?" and the whining and discontent started all over again. As can be seen in Anna's case, a very unsatisfactory mother-infant relationship led to problems in her development of independence. More information about problems in separation-individuation are given in box 6.3, along with a discussion of another severe psychological problem that develops in infancy—autism.

While Mahler's account of the separation-individuation process has stimulated thought about the development of independence in infancy and early childhood and given us a vivid picture of mother-infant interaction, it is not without problems. Susan Harter (1982) summarized some of the problems that surface in Mahler's perspective. Mahler's goal, at first glance, appears to be similar to that of cognitive-structural

theorists, who are interested in how the infant develops a sense of self as an active, independent individual. From the cognitive-structural perspective, we discover the infant is an inquisitive young scientist who is preoccupied with the serious business of locating objects and people in space and coordinating sensorimotor schemes. As Susan Harter (1982) evaluated Mahler's perspective:

The budding terrible two as described by Mahler is faced with different developmental hurdles, and tends to evoke more sympathy. The infant is wrenched from the blissful stage of need gratification, must endure separation distress, struggle to create a soothing image of mother, tolerate the fickleness of an environment which initially seemed to yield to the infant's every whim only to frustrate the infant in a subsequent developmental hour of need; and finally, to make matters worse, the toddler is greeted with social approbation for throwing him/herself, red-faced and screaming on the supermarket floor. (p. 23)

Harter feels that Mahler puts too much singular emphasis on the mother. Also, she feels that Mahler does not discuss individual differences in the rate of development through her subphases. Harter feels that many of Mahler's observations of mother-infant relationships have not been systematically documented.

Autonomy vs. Shame and Doubt
Another theorist, Erik Erikson (1963, 1968), also believes that the relationship between the mother and the infant is important in determining the extent to which the toddler will develop a sense of autonomy.

Autonomy vs. shame and doubt represents the second stage in Erikson's theory of development. It roughly coincides with the second year of life. The major significance of this stage in the life cycle lies in rapid gains in muscular maturation, verbalization, and the coordination of a number of conflicting action patterns characterized by tendencies to hold on and let go. Through such changes the highly dependent child begins to experience autonomous will. Mutual regulation between adult and child faces a severe test. This stage becomes decisive in whether the child will feel comfortable in self-expression or feel anxious and show extensive self-restraint. Erikson believes that if the child does not develop a sense of self-control and free will at this point in development, he or she may become saddled with a lasting propensity for doubt and shame.

For the toddler to develop independence, a firmly developed early trust is necessary. The sense of autonomy parents are able to grant their small children depends on the dignity and sense of personal independence they derive from their own lives. In other words, the toddler's sense of autonomy is a reflection of the parents' dignity as autonomous beings. Erikson believes that much of the lasting sense of doubt developed in the toddler is a consequence of the parents' frustrations in marriage, work, and citizenship.

Foundations of Development in Infancy

The child soon discovers that he has a self that is distinct from others.

Erikson goes on to describe how the struggles and triumphs of this stage of development contribute to the identity crisis all adolescents undergo, either by supporting the formation of a healthy identity or by contributing to estrangement and confusion. The most important contribution to the development of a sense of autonomy during the toddler years for the development of identity during adolescence is the courage to be an independent individual who can choose and guide his or her own future. The residue from successful resolutions of the autonomy-shame stage that influences the development of identity is reflected in one adolescent's statement, "I am what I can will freely."

Next, we review the research that has been conducted on the topic of independence in the infant and toddler years.

Independence in Young Children

Research on independence in infancy and childhood has received far less attention than attachment. Harriet Rheingold (1973) describes how, in reflecting on her earlier work on infants, it was only after a number of years she began to recognize how independent many of the youngsters' behaviors were.

Some eight years ago I began a series of studies designed to measure the effect of a strange environment on the behavior of infants at ten months of age. Only after the last sentence of the discussion of the study was written did I realize that it was not so much the strange environment that caused the distress of the children placed in it without their mothers, nor even the absence of their mothers, as it was being *placed* and

left alone (Rheingold, 1969). That this was so was demonstrated in a later study in which infants the same age were given the opportunity to leave their mothers and enter that same strange environment by themselves (Rheingold & Eckerman, 1969). All the children did enter on their own initiative, even when the environment contained no toy. Not only did they enter, but they crept to places in the room from which they could not see the mother. They returned to the mother's room, left again, and returned again—some infants many times—but on a third of the returns they did not contact the mother. (pp.182–83)

Rheingold (1973) indicated that in the process of investigating the influence of different environments, it was becoming clear that she was seeing infants move away from their mothers. A review of the nonhuman primate research on independence (Rheingold & Eckerman, 1970) provided support for the belief that the infant detaches himself or herself from the mother. As the nonhuman primate grows older, it leaves the mother more frequently, goes farther, and stays away longer. To find out how far from the mother a human child would stray, Rheingold & Eckerman (1970) placed a mother and her child in a backyard—the mother was seated and the child was left free. They found a positive relationship between the age of the children (from one to five years) and the distance they traveled from their mothers. However, the continuing relationship to the mother was evidenced in the observations by older children bringing small items to their mothers—pebbles and leaves for example. These observations are similar to the concept of emotional refueling described earlier by Mahler (1979b).

Slowly, a series of studies designed to explore in greater detail the young child's development of independence are beginning to appear. It has been found that the infant's exploration of the environment is affected by both physical (Bjorklid-Chu, 1977) and social characteristics (Menzel, 1974). The opportunity for infants to follow others has been shown to promote exploration (Hay, 1977, 1980). And, in one recent investigation infants were more likely to explore their environment when their older siblings was present (Samuels, 1980). Twenty-three-month-old infants were observed twice, once with and once without their older siblings, to determine the effect of the older child's presence on infant locomotor exploration. Observations were made, with the mother present, in the rear yard of a private home. When older siblings were present, infants went farther away from their mothers, traversed a larger area of the yard, left their mothers more quickly, and stayed away longer.

So far in this chapter we have described both the attachment process and the development of independence. In our discussion of independence in the infant

Box 6.3
Symbiotic Infantile Psychosis and Infantile Autism

A psychosis is a severe abnormality that involves personality disorganization and loss of contact with reality. Two types of psychosis that may appear are symbiotic infantile psychosis and infantile autism.

Symbiotic Infantile Psychosis

Barbara is a four-year-old child who clings desperately to her mother in a manner that forces her mother to attend to her needs on a moment-to-moment basis. When her mother leaves the house, Barbara reacts with paniclike screaming. Such children as Barbara have been described by Margaret Mahler (1979a) as having **symbiotic infantile psychosis.** Think again about our description of Mahler's separation-individuation process in which the child develops a sense of separateness and independence from the mother. In rare cases, this process goes completely awry and produces a child like Barbara, who has intense anxiety and panic about being separated from her mother. It usually is manifested between the ages of two and a half and five years of age and often is preceded by normal development. In contrast to the autistic child who wants to be alone, the symbiotic child cannot tolerate even a brief separation from the mother. If the psychosis persists, the child becomes withdrawn and seclusive, staying close to the mother most of his or her life.

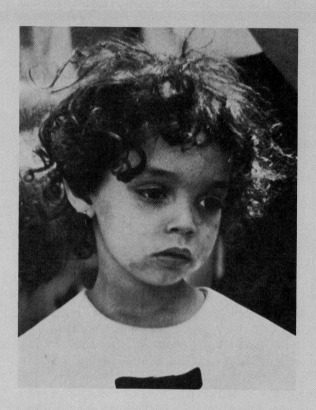

Infantile Autism

Infantile autism, often diagnosed during infancy, may persist well into childhood. Probably the most distinguishing characteristic of autistic children is their inability to relate to other people (Wing, 1977). As babies, they require very little from their parents; they do not demand much attention and they do not reach out (literally or figuratively) for their parents. They rarely smile. When someone attempts to hold them, they often try to withdraw by arching their backs and pushing away from the person. In their cribs or playpens they appear oblivious to what is going on *around* them, often sitting and staring into space for long periods of time.

In addition to deficits in attachment to others, autistic children often have speech problems. As many as one out of every two autistic children never learn to speak. Those who do learn to speak may engage in a type of speech called **echolalia**—the child echos rather than responds to

and toddler years, comments were made about the process of individuation proposed by Margaret Mahler. In the next section we see that some of the same ideas developed by Mahler are incorporated in developmental psychologists' description of the infant's sense of self, or sense of being, that is different from the mother or other humans in the environment.

The Development of the Self in Infancy

Individuals carry within them a sense of who they are and what makes them different from everyone else. They cling to this identity and begin to feel secure in the knowledge that this identity is becoming more stable. Real or imagined, the individual's developing sense of identity and uniqueness is a strong motivating force in life. But what about earlier in development—when does the individual begin to sense a separate existence from others?

what he or she hears. Thus, if you ask "How are you, Chuck?" Chuck will respond with "How are you, Chuck?" Autistic children also tend to confuse pronouns, inappropriately substituting *you* for *I,* for example.

A third major characteristic of autistic children is the degree to which they become upset over a change in their daily routine or their physical environment. Rearrangement of a sequence of events or even furniture in the course of their "normal" day causes them to become extremely upset. Thus, autistic children are not flexible in adapting to new routines and changes in their daily life.

The impact an autistic child can have on parents is decribed in the following excerpts from the popular book, *A Child Called Noah,* written in 1972 by Josh Greenfield about his autistic son Noah.

> 8–70: I also must note how very few people can actually understand our situation as a family, how they assume we are aloof when we tend not to accept or extend the usual social invitations. Nor have I mentioned the extra expenses a child like Noah entails—those expenses I keep in another book.

> 8–71: Even more heartbreaking has been the three-year period it has taken us to pierce the organized-medicine, institutionalized-mental-health gauze curtain. Most doctors, if they were unable to prescribe any form of curative aid, did their best to deter us from seeking it. Freudian-oriented psychiatrists and psychologists, if ill-equipped to deal with the problems of those not verbal, tried to inflict great feelings of guilt upon us as all-too-vulnerable parents. Neurologists and pediatricians, if not having the foggiest notions about the effects of diet and nutrition, vitamins and enzymes and their biochemical workings would always suggest such forms of therapy as practiced only by quacks. And county mental-health boards, we discovered, who have charge of the moneys that might be spent helping children like Noah, usually tossed their skimpy fundings away through existing channels that do not offer proper treatment for children like Noah.

> 4–16–67: We've decided to stop worrying about Noah. He isn't retarded, he's just pushing the clock hands about at his own slow speed. Yet . . .

> 8–16–67: We took Noah to a pediatrician in the next town, who specializes in neurology. He said that since Noah is talking now there was little cause to worry; that Noah seemed "Hypertonic," a floppy baby, a slow developer, but that time would be the maturing agent. We came away relieved. But I also have to admit that lately I haven't worried that much.

> 6–6–69: Noah is two. He still doesn't walk, but I do think he's trying to teach himself how to stand up. We're still concerned. And I guess we'll remain concerned until he stands up and walks like a boy.

> 7–14–69: Our fears about Noah continue to undergo dramatic ups and downs. Because of his increased opacity, the fact that he doesn't respond when we call his name and fails to relate completely to his immediate environment—pattern of retardation or autism—we took him to a nearby hospital. . . . I guess we both fear that what we dread is so, that Noah is not a normal child, that he is a freak, and his condition is getting worse.

> 2–19–70: I'm a lousy father. I anger too easily. I get hot with Karl and take on a four-year-old kid. I shout at Noah and further upset an already disturbed one. Perhaps I am responsible for Noah's problems. (pp. 91–92)

The specific cause of autistic behavior still is the focus of extensive speculation. Some experts stress the importance of underlying hereditary and biological mechanisms, while other experts believe social experiences are at fault.

Children begin the process of developing a sense of self by learning to distinguish themselves from others. To determine whether, in fact, infants are able to recognize themselves, psychologists have traditionally relied on mirrors. In the animal kingdom only the great apes can learn to recognize their reflection in a mirror, but human infants can accomplish this feat by approximately eighteen months of age. The ability of the toddler to recognize a mirrored reflection seems to be linked to the ability to form a mental image of his or her own face. This development of a sense of self does not occur in a single step but is rather the product of a complex understanding that develops very gradually.

Michael Lewis and Jeanne Brooks-Gunn (1979) have conducted a number of studies of the development of the infant's ability to recognize the self. Lewis and his colleagues (e.g., Lewis & Cherry, 1977) believe that the process of self-development parallels the development of the more traditional cognitive and

Real or imagined, the individual's developing sense of identity and uniqueness is a strong motivating force in life.

To determine if infants are able to recognize themselves, psychologists have traditionally relied on mirrors.

Table 6.2
Development of Self-Knowledge, Emotional Experience, and Cognitive Growth

Age	Self-Knowledge	Emotional Experience	Cognitive Growth
0–3	Interest in social objects; emergence of self-other distinction	Unconditioned responses to stimulus events (loud noise, hunger, etc.)	Reflexive period, primary circular reactions
3–8	Consolidation of self-other distinction, recognition of self through contingency	Conditioned responses (strangers, incongruity)	Primary and secondary circular reactions
8–12	Emergence of self-permanence and self categories; recognition of self through contingency and onset of feature recognition	Specific emotional experiences (fear, happiness, love, attachment)	Object permanence, means-ends, imitation
12–24	Consolidation of basic self categories (age, gender, emergence of efficacy); feature recognition without contingency	Development of empathy, guilt, embarrassment	Language growth; more complex means-ends; symbolic representations

emotional aspects of development. In table 6.2, the parallel development of self-knowledge, emotional experience, and cognitive growth is shown (Lewis & Brooks-Gunn, 1979).

The mirror technique, initially used with animals (e.g., Gallup, 1977), was modified for use with human infants (e.g., Bertenthal & Fischer, 1978; Lewis & Brooks-Gunn, 1979). The mother puts a dot of rouge on her child's nose. During a pretest, an observer watches to see how frequently the infant touches his or her nose. Next, the infant is placed in front of a mirror, and observers detect whether nose touching increases. In both sets of research, at about eighteen months of age children significantly increased their nose touching, suggesting that they recognized their own image and coordinated the image they saw in the mirror with the actions of touching their own body.

In the investigation of Bertenthal and Fischer (1978), the developmental aspects of a growing awareness of a sense of self were studied. They revealed that by six months of age, infants reached out and touched some part of their image in the mirror. And, by the time they were ten months of age, they had successfully passed what was called the hat test. In the hat test the mother dresses the infant in a special vest. Attached to the back of the vest is a wooden rod with a hat on top. When the infant moves, the hat moves. Without a mirror the infant cannot see the hat. With a mirror, ten-month-old infants usually look up at the real hat, suggesting that the infant understands that the movement of the hat is in some way connected to the movement of his or her own body and that he or she must use the mirror to locate the hat.

So, if the ten-month-old infant can locate the hat, why can't the child find the red dot of rouge? Bertenthal and Fischer (1978) argue that toddlers must build up an image, or a schema, of how their own face is likely to look in the mirror before they can detect the discrepancy created by the red dot. By eighteen months of age, then, toddlers do have a sense of self and the development of this self-concept is related to cognitive development.

Earlier in this chapter we described Mary Ainsworth's view of mother-infant interaction and attachment and Margaret Mahler's ideas about mother-infant interaction and separation-individuation. Next, we look at an impressive model of mother-infant interaction and the infant's emerging sense of self.

Louis Sander's Model of Mother-Infant Interaction and the Infant's Emerging Sense of Self
Louis Sander's model places considerably more emphasis on the infant's role in mother-infant interaction than Mahler's model. His data come from an extensive longitudinal study that included home observations, interviews with mothers, infant examinations, and play interviews over the course of the first three years of life. Susan Harter (1982) summarizes Sander's seven stages, each of which is defined by an issue associated to a particular behavior that must be coordinated by mother and infant.

Table 6.3
Summary of Stage Models Related to the Infant's Development of Self

Approximate Ages	Visual Recognition Studies	Mahler's Phases of Separation-Individuation	Ainsworth's Phases of Attachment	Sander's Stages of Mother-Infant Interaction
0–5	(1) No self-other differentiation	(1) Normal, autistic, and symbiotic phase	(1) Preattachment phase	(1) Initial regulation
5–10	(2) Awareness of bodily self as cause of movement	(1) Differentiation	(2) Attachment in the making	(2) Reciprocal exchange
				(3) Initiative
10–15	(3) Differentiation of self as active agent from others	(2) Practicing	(3) Clear-cut attachment	(4) Focalization
15–20	(4) Featural recognition of self	(3) Rapprochement		(5) Self-assertion
18+	(5) Verbal labeling of the self	(4) Resolution and consolidation	(4) Goal-corrected partnership	(6) Recognition
				(7) Self-constancy

Source: Harter, 1982, pp. 32–34.

During stage 1 (one to three months), the issue of **initial regulation** is manifest in the establishment of a predictable, comfortable pattern of sleeping, feeding, elimination, quieting, and arousal. The second stage of **reciprocal exchange** (four to six months) marks the first coordinated back and forth exchanges between mother and infant during feeding, dressing, and simple play. During the third stage of infant **initiative** (seven to nine months), the infant chooses or initiates activities in order to secure a reciprocal social exchange with the mother. **Focalization** defines the major issue of the fourth stage (ten to thirteen months) in that the infant now focuses his/her need-meeting demands on the mother. The infant's activities provide a basis for the infant to turn toward a wider mastery of the world beyond the mother.

In describing the latter stages, five through seven, Sander specifically highlights the implications for the developing sense of self. During the fifth stage of **self-assertion** (fourteen to twenty months), the infant, now able to explore and manipulate his/her world, begins to determine goals and activities independent of the mother, at times in opposition to the mother's wishes. Sander notes the convergence between his account of the infant's budding sense of autonomy and Spitz's (1957) description of the toddler's heightened awareness of his/her own intentionality, which may be thwarted by the constraints of socializing agents. For Spitz, this initiates the emergence of the "I" experience.

During the sixth stage of **recognition,** beginning at about eighteen months, new advances in representational skills and language allow the toddler to develop some appreciation for his/her "inner" intentions, fantasies, and wishes. For Sander, the coordination of verbal communication between mother and toddler constitutes "a first level in the experience of self-recognition, namely realization that another can be aware of what one is aware of oneself, i.e., a shared awareness" (1975, p. 142). Negotiations of this issue set the stage for the seventh and final step in this epigenetic sequence, the development of a sense continuity or **self constancy.** (pp. 30–32)

Harter notes the consistency between Mahler and Sander in describing directed aggressive behavior during this final stage. Sander believes that this aggressive behavior helps the child to view himself or herself as an active organizer or initiator.

Of utmost relevance in Sander's theory is his description of a sequence of interactions that provide the social context for the infant's emerging sense of self.

Summary of Information about the Development of the Self in Infancy

A summary of the four views of the development of the self are presented in table 6.3. They include the cognitive-structural, visual recognition studies; Margaret Mahler's phases of separation-individuation, Mary Ainsworth's phases of attachment, and Louis Sander's stages of mother-infant interaction.

Summary

The discussion of social, emotional, and personality development in infancy began with a description of the importance of early experience in development. Then the important roles of families and peers were evaluated. And, the last half of the chapter was devoted to a discussion of attachment, independence, and the development of the self in infancy.

How critical are early experiences in development? Experts do not all agree on the answer to this question, although the weight of theories and research suggests that early experience plays an important role. Empirically demonstrating that infancy is a critical period for later development is a difficult task. There is agreement, however, that the infant needs rich stimulation—recent research, for example, suggests that even moderately low caloric intake during infancy affects the social behavior and emotional characteristics of school-age children.

The infant's interaction and experiences with parents provide the beginnings of the life-long process of socialization. The birth of a child creates a disequilibrium in the family system that requires a great deal of adaptation on the part of the parents. The infant socializes parents just as they socialize the infant, a process called reciprocal socialization. As parents adapt to the presence of an infant in their lives, it is important that synchrony in parent-infant relationships develops. It has also been recognized that it is important to study the family as a system of interacting individuals.

Attachment is defined as a relation between an infant and one or more adult caregivers. Each individual has a strong emotional feeling toward the other, which may be exhibited by the infant in behaviors aimed at maintaining proximity, protesting separation from the caregiver, and being anxious in the presence of strangers.

The ethological view of attachment represented in the writings of John Bowlby and Mary Ainsworth was highlighted. These theorists stress the emergence of attachment as a natural biological result of certain instinctual response systems elicited by and directed toward the caregiver. The caregiver, in turn, may have some of his or her own biological needs met in the exchanges.

Several steps can be traced in the development of attachment. During the first four months, most infants have indiscriminate preferences for various adults. Between six and eight months, strong proximity-seeking behaviors are exhibited toward particular caregivers, and these may persist for as much as a year (attachment). Somewhat later infants protest and become anxious when separated from a caregiver (separation anxiety) and finally evidence anxiety when approached by strangers (stranger anxiety).

Individual differences in attachment were discussed, as were situational variables that may influence its expression. It was concluded that it is possible to observe moderately stable differences in attachment behaviors among infants over short periods of time (e.g., four to eight months), that a variety of situational variables can moderate its appearance, and that recent research evidence suggests some connection between the security of infant attachment and social and cognitive competence one to two years later.

Infants not only seek the company of their caregiver but they also spend a good deal of time out of the immediate reaches of the caregiver. An interesting question focuses on how infants perform the balancing act between attachment and independence. There is evidence that infants who are securely attached to their mothers show more exploratory tendencies than those who are anxiously attached. Two theories of independence—Mahler's individuation-separation and Erikson's autonomy versus shame and doubt—stress the importance of the symbiotic relationship between the infant and mother.

The push for independence seems to become most intense during the second year of life. There has not been nearly as much research on the early developmental aspects of independence as there has been in the area of attachment. Rheingold's work represents the most thorough attempt to study independence in infancy and young childhood. She found that from the ages of one to five children increasingly move away from their mothers to explore their environment. By eighteen months of age infants can recognize themselves, indicating the rudimentary beginning of the self-concept. Sander's model represents a promising attempt to combine information about the infant's cognitive, emotional, and social development to improve our knowledge of the infant's emerging sense of self.

Key Terms

asynchrony
attachment
comparative psychology
consolidation of
  individuality
differentiation
echolalia
executor responses
family system
focalization
infantile autism
initial regulation
initiative
insecurely attached—
  avoidance
insecurely attached—
  resistant
peer
practicing
psychosis

rapprochement
reciprocal exchange
reciprocal socialization
recognition
second-order effects
securely attached
self
self-assertion
"self" constancy
separation anxiety
separation-individuation
signaling reponses
situational variability
socialization
stranger anxiety
symbiotic infantile
  psychosis
synchrony
temperament
visually guided reaching

Review Questions

1. Discuss theory and research about the role of early experience in development.
2. How important is nutrition during infancy for the development of later social behavior and emotional characteristics?
3. What do we mean by the terms socialization, synchrony in parent-infant relationships, and family system? Give examples of each.
4. What is attachment and how does it develop?
5. Describe individual differences and contextual effects on attachment.
6. What are the effects of day care on attachment?
7. What is the relationship between attachment and independence?
8. Describe the theories of independence of Mahler and Erikson.
9. Discuss the development of the self in infancy.
10. Describe Louis Sander's view of how mother-infant interaction contributes to an understanding of the infant's sense of an emerging self.
11. Compare Ainsworth's, Mahler's, and Sander's approaches to understanding the development of the self in infancy.

Further Readings

Clarke, A. M., & Clarke, A. D. B. *Early experience: myth and evidence.* New York: The Free Press, 1976. *A controversial, scholarly book that challenges the notion that early experience is a critical period in development. Medium reading difficulty.*

Emde, R., & Harmon, R. (Eds.). *Attachment and affiliative systems: neurobiological and psychobiological aspects.* New York: Plenum, 1981. *A volume of papers by outstanding researchers in the field of attachment, including considerable information about the biological basis of attachment. Moderately difficult reading.*

Lewis, M., & Brooks-Gunn, J. *Social cognition and the acquisition of the self.* New York: Plenum, 1979. *An extensive overview of Lewis's work on the development of the self in infancy. Chapters explore the origin of the self, how to study the self in infancy, and ideas about a unified theory of the self. Medium reading difficulty.*

Mahler, M. S. *The selected papers of Margaret Mahler, vol. 2: separation-individuation.* New York: Jason Aronson, 1979. *A recent presentation of Margaret Mahler's insightful writings about the separation-individuation process in the first three years of life. Considerable information, including case studies, of aberrant mother-child relationships that restrict the development of independence. Medium reading difficulty.*

Parke, R. D. *Fathers.* Cambridge, Mass.: Harvard University Press, 1981, and Schaeffer, R. *Mothering.* Cambridge, Mass.: Harvard University Press, 1977. *These two books are part of the Harvard University Press series edited by Jerome Bruner, Michael Cole, and Barbara Lloyd on the developing child. Each of these books provides well-written accounts of the parent's role in infancy. Medium reading difficulty.*

Section III

Early Childhood

Physical and Cognitive Development

Prologue: Training the Senses

Maria Montessori was an Italian physician-turned-educator who developed a revolutionary approach to the education of young children at the beginning of the twentieth century. She began her work with a group of mentally retarded children in Rome. She was highly successful in teaching them to read, write, and pass exams meant for normal children. Some time later she turned her attention to poor children in the slums of Rome and had similar success in teaching them. Her approach has since been adopted extensively in private nursery schools, making its greatest impact on preschool education.

Montessori's approach is simultaneously a philosophy of education, a psychology of the child, and practical educational exercises that can be employed to teach children. Children are allowed a great deal of freedom and spontaneity to choose classwork, and they may move freely from one activity to another. Each child is encouraged to work independently, to complete tasks once they have been undertaken, and to put materials away in assigned places. The teacher serves as a facilitator rather than as the controller of learning, pointing out interesting ways to explore the various curriculum materials and offering help to any child who asks.

Montessori identifies four different sensitive periods, each concerning a different facet of development: the development of sensory abilities, the development of an awareness of order, the development of a sensitivity to language, and the development of a sensitivity toward movement.

A brief description is given of several different exercises used in the Montessori classroom to promote sensory and perceptual growth. The examples indicate the creative materials Montessori used to provide children with perceptual experiences as well as the unique way the Montessori program makes use of them.

Montessori (1967) here describes the materials to be used for teaching the young child tactile discrimination—that is, discrimination of different textures by touch:

a. a long rectangular plank divided into two equal rectangles, one covered with very smooth, the other with rough, paper
b. another board of the same shape as the first, but covered with alternating strips of smooth and rough paper
c. another board like the former, having strips of emery- and sandpaper in decreasing grades of coarseness
d. a board on which are placed pieces of paper of the same size, but of different grades of smoothness, varying from parchment to the very smooth paper of the first plank

These boards, which keep the various objects to be touched in a fixed position, serve to prepare a child's hand for touching things lightly, and they also teach him how to make a systematic distinction. (p. 121)

The child is encouraged to stroke different areas of the board, to name the textures that are felt, and gradually to learn to discriminate differences between rough and smooth surfaces and to arrange them in order from roughest to smoothest.

Montessori also describes the exercises employed to teach the child about taste and smell:

Our second attempt was . . . to organize games for the senses which the children could repeat by themselves. We had a child smell fresh violets and jasmine; or, late in May, we used

the roses gathered for the flower vases. We then blindfolded a child, saying to him: "Now we are going to give you something—some flowers." Another child would bring a bunch of violets close to his nose and he would have to recognize them. Then, as a test of the strength of an odor, he was offered a single flower, or a quantity of them.

Then we decided it would be easier to let the environment do much of this educational work. . . . We decided to sprinkle perfumes systematically about with the idea of making them progressively more delicate. . . .

The children become quite interested in distinguishing different tastes and coming to recognize the four basic flavors. Sweet and salt are both pleasant, but even bitter is tried as an experiment, and sour, especially in various fruits, is distinguished in various degrees.

Once interest has been aroused in tastes and their definite limitations, the world of fragrances is more clearly distinguished in its countless varieties of mixed sensations of taste and smell experienced in eating and drinking, as for example in milk, fresh or dried bread, soup, fruit, and so forth. And the tactile sensations of the tongue, which arise from contact with sticky, oily, and other types of substances, are distinguished from the sensations of taste and smell through an effort of the mind which is a real exploration of oneself and one's environment. (pp. 128–29)

Finally, Montessori describes exercises devoted to the perception of sound.

For the studying of noises, we have in our present system some rather simple and elementary material. This consists in boxes of wood (or cardboard). These boxes are made in pairs and are so constructed that a series of them will produce graduated noises. Just as with the other sense materials, the boxes are jumbled together and then paired off according to the noise they produce when struck. Then by judging the differences among the boxes in one series a child attempts to put them in a graduated order.

For the training of the musical sense, we have adopted a series of bells. . . . Each one of the bells is mounted on a separate stand. They constitute a group of objects which seem to be identical but which, when struck with a little hammer, reproduce [different] notes. Thus the only perceptible difference is one of sound.

The individual bells, which come in a double series, can be moved about. They can therefore be mixed up just as are the other objects used in the training of the senses. (p. 148)

These, then, are some of the exercises employed in the Montessori curriculum to teach children about the senses of touch, smell and taste, and hearing. They constitute a unique approach to the education of children's senses and perception. Many of these techniques have been employed in contemporary preschool education and continue to be used in present-day Montessori schools.

While the Montessori approach to preschool education is favored by some psychologists and educators, others believe that the social development of children is neglected. For example, Montessori attempts to foster independence and the development of cognitive skills, however, verbal interaction between the teacher and child and extensive peer interaction are deemphasized. The critics of Montessori also argue that imaginative play is restricted. Later in this chapter, various types of preschool programs other than Montessori's will be described. Keep the Montessori approach in mind so you can compare its focus with these programs.

Introduction

In this chapter we continue our discussion of the child's physical and cognitive development. Physical development in early childhood slows markedly compared to infancy, however, there is perceptible growth in gross motor skills and considerable growth in fine motor skills. As part of our description of fine motor skills we will look at the role of the child's scribbling and drawing—the artwork of early childhood—in development.

Our discussion of cognitive development begins with an overview of Piaget's ideas about the stage of cognitive development he calls preoperational thought. We also take our first look at a very important perspective of cognitive development that is getting increased attention from developmental psychologists—information processing. Attention, perception, memory, thinking, and problem solving are among the important cognitive processes involved in the information processing perspective. We will describe the main points of the information processing perspective and pay particular attention to how it can be used to explain cognitive development in early childhood.

We also continue our discussion of language development, looking further at the development of speech sounds, providing more information about Roger Brown's stages of language development, presenting more ideas about the role of cognition in language development, describing important aspects of prereading skills, and evaluating whether childhood is a critical period in language development.

We also explore early childhood education. We will discuss some of the forms of preschool education, focusing in particular on compensatory education programs.

Physical and Motor Development

Fortunately growth rate slows down in early childhood or we would be a species of giants. The average child grows two and one-half inches in height and gains between five and seven pounds a year during early childhood. It appears that growth rate is influenced by adequate nutrition as much as by genetic factors. And, bodily proportions change as the trunk, lower face, and legs grow more rapidly than the head. Some bodily systems show signs of maturing—for instance, the child's heart rate slows down and becomes more stable. The brain is more nearly complete in early childhood than the rest of the child's body, attaining approximately 75 percent of its adult weight by the age of three. And, by the age of four, most children are capable of fine control of many voluntary movements. Immaturity in many bodily systems, however, still exists—bones, joints, and muscles of children in this phase of the life cycle are still much more susceptible to injury than those of older children (Lundsteen & Tarrow, 1981).

By the age of four, most children are capable of fine control of many voluntary movements.

A summary of the manner in which a number of gross and fine motor skills change during the course of early childhood is outlined in table 7.1. One fine motor skill that is particularly important for children to practice is scribbling and drawing—the art of children—which is discussed in box 7.1.

While many aspects of physical and motor development are the result of maturational processes, it is important that children experience an environment that allows them to practice their physical and motor skills. Training programs designed to promote healthy physical development can be divided into three types: physical education, perceptual-motor, and movement. Until recently physical education programs have not begun until elementary school. For young children, most programs strive to balance free play with teacher-directed activities targeted at specific skills. In elementary school, children spend more time in competitive games, individual activities designed to promote bodily and motor development, and dance activities. Calisthentics and exercise routines are also common.

192   *Early Childhood*

For young children, most physical education programs strive to balance free play with teacher-directed activities targeted at specific skills.

Table 7.1
Some Landmarks in Motor Development During the Years from Two to Six, from Basic Normative Studies. The Item Is Placed at the Age Where 50 Percent or More of Children Perform the Act

Age Two	Age Three	Age Four	Age Five
Builds tower of six or seven blocks (GA)	Builds tower of nine blocks (GA)	Cuts on line with scissors (GI)	Folds paper into double triangle (TM)
Turns book pages singly (GA)	Makes bridge of three blocks (TM)	Makes designs and crude letters (GI)	Copies square (TM)
Spoon into mouth without turning (GA)	Catches ball, arms straight (MW)	Catches small ball, elbows in front of body (MW)	Catches small ball, elbows at sides (MW)
Holds glass in one hand (GA)	Spills little from spoon (GA)	Dresses self (GI)	Throws well (G)
Imitates circular stroke (GA)	Pours from pitcher (GA)		Fastens buttons he can see (GI)
Puts on simple garment (GA)	Unbuttons, puts shoes on (GA)		Copies designs, letters, numbers (GI)
	Copies circle (TM)		
	Draws straight line (TM)		

Locomotion			
Wide stance, runs well (GA)	Walks tiptoe (GA, B)	Gallops (G)	Narrow stance (GI)
Walks up and down stairs alone (GA)	Jumps from bottom stair (GA, B)	Descends small ladder, alternating feet easily (MW)	Skips (G, MW)
Kicks large ball (GA)	Stands on one foot (GA, B)	Stunts on tricycle (G)	Hops on one foot, ten or more steps (MW)
Descends large ladder, marking time (MW)	Hops on both feet (MW)	Descends short steps, alternating feet, unsupported (G)	Descends large ladder, alternating feet easily (MW)
Jumps twelve inches (MW)	Propels wagon, one foot (J)		Walks straight line (GI)
	Rides tricycle (GA)		
	Descends long steps; marking time, unsupported (MW)		
	Jumps eighteen inches (MW)		

B—Bayley, 1935.
GA—Gesell & Amatruda, 1951.
GI—Gesell & Ig, 1949.
G—Gutteridge, 1939.

J—Jones, 1939.
MW—McCaskill & Wellman, 1939, pp. 141–50.
TM—Terman & Merrill, 1960.

Source: Smart & Smart, 1972, p. 218.

Box 7.1

Scribbling and Drawing—The Art of Early Childhood

Children's art is a fascinating topic. There are dramatic changes in how children depict what they see. Art provides unique insights into children's perceptual worlds—what they are attending to, how space and distance are viewed, how they experience patterns and forms.

Rhoda Kellogg is a creative teacher who has been watching and guiding young children's artistic endeavors for over thirty years. She has assembled an impressive collection of tens of thousands of drawings produced by more than two thousand preschoolers ranging from two to five years of age.

Adults who are familiar with children's art often view the productions of this age group as meaningless scribbling. Kellogg (1970) has tried to destroy this idea by showing children's productions to be orderly, meaningful, and structured.

A number of different levels of organization are evident in children's drawings. At the earliest ages, children produce *scribbles*. These scribbles are anything but simple or meaningless. There are about twenty kinds of scribbles, and the scribbles tend to be located in specific positions on the page. This position is referred to as a *placement pattern*, and there are about seventeen of them.

At the next level of organization are *emergent diagrams*, followed at subsequent levels by *diagrams*, *combines*, and *aggregates*. Each adds a level of sophistication and organization superior to the previous one, so that a hierarchy of productions can be seen. Children's attempts to draw such commonplace objects as humans, buildings, trees, flowers, cars, and boats can be related to the hierarchical learning that occurs. Kellogg believes that this hierarchical organization may be universal—that is, observable in all cultures. And she illustrates that this organization of visual forms provides a good description of how art became transformed from its simplistic level to a more mature one in the history of adult art.

In Kellogg's view,

As each child proceeds in self-taught art, he gradually accumulates a visually logical system of line formations. The system is logical in the sense that one sort of line formation leads to another. Whenever he uses art materials without the constraint of adult direction, the child remembers and employs as much of the system as he has taught himself. (p. 51)

. . . What acccounts for the prevalence of shapes in spontaneous child art? Why do the various line formations tend to be made in a certain sequence? My analysis supports the belief that the human eye and brain are predisposed to see overall shapes, that this predispostion operates during the interplay of hand and eye in scribbling, that the child makes shapes with increasing purpose and clarity as he grows, and that he favors shapes that are balanced. In addition, the child's early pictorial work is strongly influenced by his previous scribbling, so that his drawings of Humans, Animals, Buildings, Vegetation, and Transportation items reflect the diagrams, combines, aggregates . . . that he has made before. (p. 248)

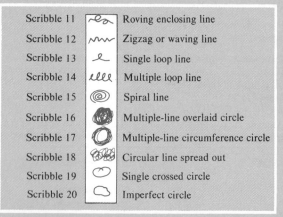

Scribble 1		Dot
Scribble 2		Single vertical line
Scribble 3		Single horizontal line
Scribble 4		Single diagonal line
Scribble 5		Single curved line
Scribble 6		Multiple vertical line
Scribble 7		Multiple horizontal line
Scribble 8		Multiple diagonal line
Scribble 9		Multiple curved line
Scribble 10		Roving open line
Scribble 11		Roving enclosing line
Scribble 12		Zigzag or waving line
Scribble 13		Single loop line
Scribble 14		Multiple loop line
Scribble 15		Spiral line
Scribble 16		Multiple-line overlaid circle
Scribble 17		Multiple-line circumference circle
Scribble 18		Circular line spread out
Scribble 19		Single crossed circle
Scribble 20		Imperfect circle

Twenty basic scribbles used by young children in drawing; an early stage of art.

. . . Children seem to thrive by making movements which to the adult appear to have no purpose other than pleasure. The movements of the child's body which produce an art work certainly are not made merely for the joy of movement. In fact, these movements aid in the coordination of moving and seeing. (p. 250)

. . . Perhaps scribbling gives the child a sense of body movement that he can enjoy fully because it is "safe" in comparison with the images that he must absorb to move with safety. That is, the child can scribble directional movement with a satisfying vigor far more safely than he can move his whole body. (p. 253)

 Vertical half. The scribblings are confined to one vertical half of the paper.

 Horizontal half. The scribblings are confined to one horizontal half of the paper.

 Two-sided balance. The scribblings are placed on one vertical or horizontal section of the paper to balance scribbles on the other side, with space between.

 Diagonal axis. The scribblings are evenly distributed on a diagonal axis so that two corners are filled and two are left empty.

 Quarter page. The scribblings are confined to a quarter of the paper.

 Two-corner pyramid. The scribblings cover one of the narrow edges of the paper and converge toward the center of the edge opposite, leaving two corners empty and making a pyramidal shape.

 Base-line fan. The scribblings flare up from one edge and move toward one or both of the adjoining edges.

Placement patterns representative of those produced by young children.

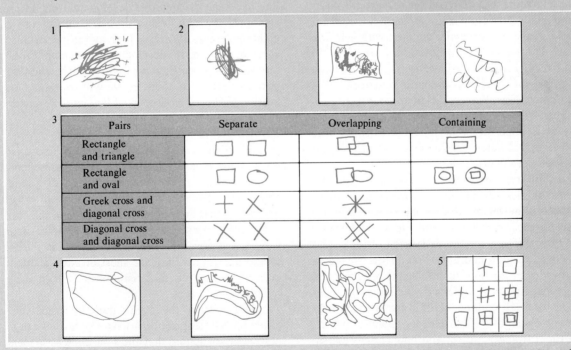

Later stages of children's art: 1) emergent diagram, 2) diagrams and scribbles, 3) combines, 4) aggregates, 5) combines.

Perceptual-motor training programs focus on input or reception, and how it influences the child's performance, in contrast to physical education programs, which emphasize performance alone. A majority of the perceptual-motor programs have been designed by experts in special education who hoped that such programs would remediate children's learning difficulties (e.g., Kephart, 1960; Cruikshank, 1963). Physical skills stressed in such programs include eye-hand and eye-foot coordination and locomotor skills. Activities designed to enhance eye-hand coordination include tossing, catching, rolling, and bouncing. Eye-foot coordination exercises include kicking, leaping, and climbing. Locomotor activities focus on walking, running, jumping, hopping, sliding, skipping, and leaping.

The educators who designed the perceptual-motor programs made grandiose claims that they would increase the academic success of children with learning problems. The available empirical data (Lahey, 1975) suggest that such claims are false. Most children, however, can benefit from the systematic practice of perceptual-motor skills. Perceptual-motor coordination is a significant aspect of development in itself—consequently, it is important that we be sensitive to any child's perceptual-motor development, not just a child with learning problems.

The third type of training program to promote children's physical development involves movement. Two aspects of movement that such programs attempt to improve are **expressive movement**—in which the body is seen as a medium for the expression of ideas and feelings (e.g., dance and drama)—and **objective movement**—in which the goal is to develop the body's power (e.g., gymnastics and athletics). Activities are designed to teach all children skillful use of their body through combinations of movements rooted in principles of time, strength, space, and flow (Lundsteen & Tarrow, 1981).

Next, we see that there are dramatic cognitive changes in early childhood. Among the cognitive feats of the four-year-old is that he or she has a vocabulary of approximately 1,500 words. By age five the vocabulary has grown to 2,200 words. Five-year-olds can remember a long sentence and repeat the plot of a simple story. And, by the end of early childhood, all the basic elements of grammar appear as well.

Cognitive Development

Recall that from Piaget's perspective infancy is characterized by *sensorimotor* thought. Piaget's cognitive-structural view has dominated discussion of cognitive development in early childhood as well. Next, we outline his stage of cognitive development called *preoperational* thought, which develops during the early childhood years. We also look at the important perspective of cognitive development that emphasizes the information processing capabilities of the child's computerlike mind. In addition, we will continue our discussion of the major aspects of language development.

Preoperational Thought

Piaget's preoperational stage lasts from about two to seven years of age, cutting across the preschool and early elementary school years. During this time the child's symbolic system expands and use of language and perceptual images moves well beyond the abilities at the end of the sensorimotor period. Despite these advances, however, a number of limitations in the child's thought cause it to fall far short of adult thought, or even of thought characteristic of a child in the late-middle school years.

At this stage the child's thought is not yet governed by full-fledged operations. **Operations** are internalized sets of actions that allow the child to do mentally what before was done physically. They are highly organized and conform to certain rules and principles of logic. The operations appear in one form in the concrete operations period and in a more advanced form in the formal-operations period.

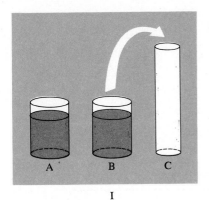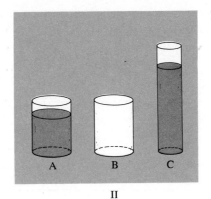

Figure 7.1 Liquid conservation.

The preoperational stage is sometimes divided into an earlier phase (two to four years of age) and later phase (five to seven years of age), with the limitations in operational thought appearing in full bloom during the earlier phase and withering away in the later phase. This development has prompted some people to call the later phase a transition period from the preoperational stage to the next stage of development, concrete operations (Flavell, 1972; Sigel & Hooper, 1968). Many children in the so-called transitional phase of the preoperational stage may give the appearance of concrete thinking in many situations, and progress toward concrete thinking about a problem may be speeded up with concentrated training efforts.

The most salient feature of preoperational thought is the child's **egocentrism,** that is, the inability to distinguish easily between his or her own perspective and that of someone else. The following telephone conversation between four-year-old Mary, who is at home, and her father, who is at work, is an example.

Father Mary, is Mommy there?

Mary (Silence; nods.)

Father Mary, may I speak to Mommy?

Mary (Again, silence; nods.)

Mary's response is egocentric in the sense that she fails to consider her father's perspective before formulating a reply. A nonegocentric thinker would have responded verbally. There are various other perspective deficits in the child's attempts to reconstruct how other people feel and think (Shantz, 1976) and to communicate with others (Glucksberg, Krauss, & Higgins, 1975).

Recently the idea of egocentrism has been attacked by a number of experts as being too broad and difficult to measure correctly in children (Dickson, 1981; Ford, 1978; Enright & Lapsley, 1980; Shantz, 1982). The child may show perspective confusion in one circumstance but not in another. And it is difficult to find any consistent difference in a child seen as more egocentric than another. However, such points of criticism do not necessitate abandoning the concept altogether (Yussen, 1981; Shantz, 1982) but rather refining it and applying it to very specific problems.

Another facet of preoperational thought is **animism,** the belief that inanimate objects have human qualities and are capable of human action. Remarks like "That tree pushed the leaf off and it fell down" or "The sidewalk was angry with me. It made me fall down" reveal this notion. Animism is a failure to distinguish the appropriate occasions for employing the human and the nonhuman perspectives.

Yet another characteristic of preoperational thought is the child's failure to *conserve* properties of objects in the face of superficial changes in their appearance. Consider the child confronted by two identical glass beakers, A and B, filled with milk to the same height. Beside them is an unfilled beaker, C. Beaker C is tall and narrow, beakers A and B are shorter and have a larger diameter (see fig. 7.1). The milk is poured from B into C, and the child is asked whether the amounts of milk in A and C are the same or different. The nonconserver will say the amounts are different, tending to judge sameness or difference in terms of the relative heights or widths of the two containers. The child fails to understand that both containers hold the same amount of milk, even though they look different.

The **conservation** concept is probably the most well-researched problem in Piaget's theory. In a recent year, for example, well over 100 articles appeared in scientific journals on this topic alone, and, cumulatively, there are probably more than 1,000 studies involving the conservation construct. Investigators have examined conservation of a dozen or more attributes of objects—for example, number, weight, volume, area, and discontinuous quantity (e.g., Brainerd, 1974; Flavell, 1976; Ginsburg & Opper, 1980). Experts have also related conservation ability to a host of other skills such as early reading ability, early arithmetic skills, reflection-impulsivity, gender concepts, and moral reasoning, to name just a few.

Figure 7.2 A random array of objects.

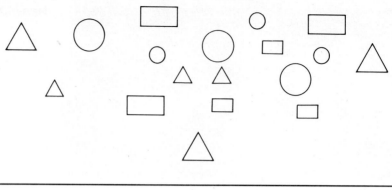

Figure 7.3 An ordered array of objects.

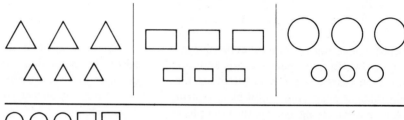

Figure 7.4 Class inclusion: more shapes or more circles?

Conservation also may be important in thinking about people as well. The child is often faced with physical changes in the appearance of significant social figures. For example, Mom has her hair cut in a new way, Dad grows a moustache, or the teacher comes to school with a broken arm. To what extent do these physical changes foster the child's belief that the adult has changed in some physical way or in some psychological way (the adult is happier, sadder, warmer, more hostile)? Perhaps, more important, to what extent do these physical changes foster a belief that the adult's attitude has changed toward the child? Unfortunately there is little evidence to show how extensive such beliefs might be for children in the preoperational stage. The one exception is the development of gender, or sex-role, conservation (Emmerich, Goldman, Kirsh, & Sharabany, in press; Kohlberg, 1969). The young child at this stage fails to realize "once a boy, always a boy; once a girl, always a girl." The child believes that the "sex" of a doll changes if such characteristics as hair, dress, and size are changed.

Another important limitation of the child's structure of thought in the preoperational stage is the inability to form and reason with hierarchical classification (Hooper, Sipple, Goldman, & Swinton, 1974). Faced with a random collection of objects that can be grouped on the basis of two or more properties, the child is seldom able to use these properties consistently to sort the objects into what an adult would refer to as a good classification.

For example, look at the collection of objects shown in figure 7.2. An adult would respond to the direction "Put the things together that you believe belong together" with a sorting based on the characteristics of size and shape taken together (e.g., Hooper & Sheehan, 1977). The adult's sorting might look something like that shown in figure 7.3. This kind of problem is often referred to as free classification.

The child's inability to reason with simple hierarchy is evident in a well-researched class inclusion problem (Brainerd, 1974; Piaget & Inhelder, 1969; Winer, 1980). Suppose a child is shown a picture of objects as in figure 7.4 and asked, Are there more shapes in front of you or more circles? The child in this stage would probably be puzzled by the question but in any event would answer that there are more circles. He or she has a hard time thinking about the whole set of forms taken collectively while simultaneously thinking about the subset, the three circles. The child tends to focus on the various subsets (in this case there are two, circles and squares) for purposes of the comparison, despite what the question calls for.

In a scholarly review of thirty-five studies of class inclusion reasoning, it was concluded that this ability emerges even later than Piaget had supposed (Winer, 1980). Whereas most recent work on Piagetian concepts generally finds that fairly young children are more accomplished than Piaget believed (e.g., Gelman, 1978; Flavell, 1981), this skill marks an exception. And, despite clever alterations in the usual format of the problem that make children solve it more easily, we don't really understand how the skill develops in children (Winer, 1980).

Figure 7.5 General stages of information processing.

S = Stimulus
R = Response
▨ = A particular step in processing information
▨→▨ = Consecutive steps in processing information

An important social consequence of these deficits in the young child's thinking with classes is that he or she fails to understand (a) the various ways people can be cross-classified with regard to social characteristics and (b) the different ways people can be compared with a group that includes them. Consider the cross-classification problem first. Suppose a little girl is given a list of her peers to divide into groups according to whether they are friends or enemies and whether they are boys or girls. She would rarely be able to arrive at a sorting arrangement with the following distinct clusters: friendly boys, unfriendly boys, friendly girls, unfriendly girls. Now consider class inclusion. Suppose a little boy lived on a street where five adults and six other children lived. The teacher asks: Are there more children or more people living on your block? The little boy would probably say that more children live there. The important point about these social classification and inclusion examples is that the child's thoughts about people are constrained in many important ways by preoperational limitations.

David Elkind (1978) illustrated one of these shortcomings in a series of studies to determine children's understanding of religious concepts such as God, denomination (Catholic, Protestant, or Jew), and religious rules. When asked the question, Can you be a Protestant and an American at the same time? the young six- and seven-year-olds frequently said no, whereas the older children (nine-, eleven-, and fourteen-year-olds) increasingly understood the possibility for simultaneous cross-classification.

Another feature of preoperational thought is that the child is incapable of serialization, that is, ordering a set of objects from least to greatest along some clearly quantifiable dimension. The approach to early childhood education described in the prologue of this chapter—the Montessori method—includes tasks that are likely to enhance the young child's ability to order objects in a serial fashion.

Two organizing forces in preoperational thought are **centration** and **irreversibility.** Many of the limitations of this stage are caused by these two forces. Centration is a narrow concentration on one feature of the situation to the exclusion of others (Piaget & Inhelder, 1969; Flavell, 1976). In the liquid conservation problem, for example, the child may focus on the liquid as being higher in its new container but not on the fact that it is simultaneously narrower than before.

Irreversibility can also be illustrated by reference to the conservation problem. One way for the child to see that the amount of liquid has remained unchanged is by mentally reversing the action—pouring the milk from beaker C into beaker B—and imagining the result. The child in the preoperational stage cannot do this (Piaget, 1977).

Piaget's theory focuses on how the child *thinks* and *represents* the world and how these capabilities change with development. There is another perspective, however, from which to view cognitive development. It is called the **information processing approach** (Klahr & Wallace, 1976; Yussen & Santrock, 1978; Siegler, 1982).

The Information Processing Perspective
The information processing perspective, in which mental activity is synonymous with the processing of information, is concerned with the nature of information children are capable of picking up from the flow of environmental stimulation around them. The various stages involved in this pickup—attention, perception, memory, thinking, and problem solving—are presented in figure 7.5. Cognitive psychologists who study how the child processes information also are interested in the mechanisms by which information is absorbed and transformed. The example give in figure 7.5 is a necessarily oversimplified one. For example, each hypothetical stage (e.g., perception) may overlap with other stages (e.g., memory) or be composed of several substages. Or, the child may generate an idea (thinking) that is placed back in memory for awhile for further reflection. The thoughts and memories may in this fashion flow back and forth.

The Roots of Information Processing Theory
In the context of recent history, information processing has three clear influential sources (Siegler, 1982). The first is the field of **communications.** Beginning over a quarter of a century ago, communication scientists sought to develop a general model of how someone sends a message over a particular **channel** of communication

to a specific **receiver** (e.g., Broadbent, 1958). In doing so, scientists developed ideas about how to define the information contained in a message, the capacity of different channels to transmit information, and the processes by which receivers pick up information. The theory was developed along physical science lines, drawing upon physics and electronics and treating radio and television transmissions as prototypical cases of communication phenomena to explain. However, the human was quickly added as a special case to explain the same phenomena, with the different human sensory systems treated as the sources for information pickup (e.g., seeing, hearing, feeling).

A second, closely related development was the growth of computer sciences and the interest in using the computer to model theories of artificial intelligence (e.g., Newell & Simon, 1972; Klahr & Wallace, 1975). Computers are essentially high-speed information systems that can be constructed and programmed. It was reasoned that computers offered a logical and concrete simplification of how information might be processed in the human mind. For example, both the computer and the mind employ *logic* and *rules* (Belmont, & Butterfield, 1971; Wallace, 1977). Both have *limits* imposed on their capabilities to handle information and on what types of information can be processed. Some of these limitations have to do with the physical **hardware**—for the computer, the physical machinery; for the human, the limits of the brain and sensory systems. Other limitations are imposed by the **software**—for the computer, the programming; for the human, presumably, learning and development. Many experts believe that as progress is made in understanding computers, we will gain an increased understanding of how the human mind works. Some go so far as to claim that unless we have working computer program that enumerates the steps needed to complete human cognitive activity, we really don't understand how the human mind might solve it (e.g., Simon, 1980). Thus, much (but not all) of contemporary work on information processing is devoted to using the computer to model the steps involved in solving a variety of logical problems confronted by people in the everyday contexts of school (e.g., reading and mathematics), work (e.g., decision making), and leisure activities (e.g., playing chess).

The third development that has influenced the information processing field focuses on advances in the field of modern linguistics (discussed earlier in chapter 5). From such scholars as Noam Chomsky (1965) have come brilliant models of how to describe the structure of language and the rules underlying linguistic productions. Since language is among the highest achievements of humans, it is a good candidate for building models of cognition. Information processing psychologists have used models of language to understand how rules are organized in people's minds, how natural events are structured, and how people use rules to interpret events (e.g., Schank & Abelson, 1977; Anderson, 1979; Stein & Glenn, 1979).

The Tools of Information Processing

The study of information processing has been aided by a number of formal techniques and procedures. Technology, task analysis and measuring processing time are described here.

Technology   The high-speed computer has been the creative inspiration for imagining how the human mind works. It also has been the most versatile tool for managing and evaluating the complex data collected about the workings of the mind. Among other feats, it allows us to make individualized decisions about what stimulus a child will be presented in an experimental procedure, record and evaluate a child's responses as they occur, present a variety of complex visual and auditory stimuli, time and store data on the amount of time taken for children to execute various steps of cognitive tasks, and perform very detailed and otherwise time-consuming statistical analyses of data. Without the computer, we would not have progressed very far in understanding such important phenomena as eye movements in reading, infant perception, short-term memory for sights and sounds, and speech perception, to name just a few important topics.

A second technology that has significantly advanced our knowledge is *high-speed movement* photography. In research on child development, one aspect of this is particularly important—eye-movement photography. Specialized equipment has permitted us to observe the discrete eye movements children make as they read, the visual scanning patterns of infants, and the manner in which children scan complex forms placed in front of them. This technology permits us to obtain a very detailed picture of how the eye takes in information in brief moments of time. As a person looks at something he or she will move the eyes rapidly in examining it. The rapid activity can be divided up into the movements themselves, called **saccadic,** and the place where eye stops following each movement. In reading, for example, this permits the investigator to study the way the eyes take in a line of print. How often do the eyes stop and fixate in a single line? How many words are taken in in a single fixation? What influence is exerted by grammatical structure, phrase boundaries, unfamiliar words and concepts, and so forth? It is not possible to observe and record these eye movements with the naked eye. However, with the availability of high-speed photography and computer assimilation of the results, it is possible to gain a very precise understanding of how the eye picks up information and how this information is interpreted.

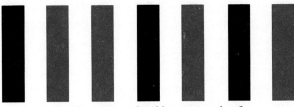

Are there more *colored bars* or more bars?

Figure 7.6 Class inclusion figure and question.

Task Analysis Another tool of the information processing approach is task analysis. Typically, the psychologist presents children with carefully defined tasks to solve that can be decomposed. By focusing on the smaller steps, the expert tries to describe the nature of the problems young children often have when they seem to "fail" the task from the perspective of the adult.

Piagetian theory will often explain a young child's inability to offer a "grownup" response to some task by indicating the child's early stage of development. The child does not yet have the cognitive skills and understanding to respond otherwise, in his view. By contrast, the information processing view focuses on the task requirements and considers the complexity of what the child is being asked to do. By understanding the components of the task, one may eventually discover how to simplify them, so that even young children may respond to the problem intelligently.

Class inclusion reasoning, discussed earlier in this chapter, can illustrate task analysis (see fig. 7.6). If you remember, class inclusion calls for the child to compare the relative number of objects in a subset with the number of objects in a larger set. If, as in figure 7.6, there are a set of rectangular bars—some colored and some black, can the child compare the number of red bars with the total number of bars present in the total set? The question posed for the child in its classic form is, Are there more colored bars or more bars? According to Piaget, the concrete thinker answers the question correctly, while the preoperational thinker does not. The difference between them is in some underlying ability to deal in part-whole comparisons.

The information processing (IP) psychologist takes a different view. In IP terms, we must understand the component steps required to solve the task. The information processing explanation might go something like this (Trabasso, 1976; Wilkenson, 1976). First, the child must encode the key elements of the question. Roughly speaking, this means that the child must attend to and store some critical information in its intended form. There are at least three key concepts in the question— 1) which of two sets has *more,* 2) the *colored bars,* or 3) all the *bars.*

Next, the child must formulate a *plan* to answer the question. One good plan is to take the first concept as a goal (that is, find the set with *more* items) and proceed with two *counting* steps—a) count the colored bars, and b) count all the bars. Finally, a *comparison* must be made between the outcome of counting step a (i.e., how many colored ones were there?) and counting step b (i.e., how many were there altogether?).

Notice, then, that in the information processing analysis, the child must do a number of things to solve the problem—he or she must encode the problem correctly, formulate a goal, engage in at least two counting steps, and compare the results of counting. There are a host of reasons, then, for the young child to fail the problem. Tom Trabasso (1976) has shown that young children often encode the problem incorrectly, perhaps because they find the form of the question unusual or unexpected. For example, usually when we are asked to compare sets of objects in the world, the sets do not overlap. And, if one set is described by reference to its color, perhaps the child assumes the other set also was meant to have a color in its description, even if the adult asking the question forgot to mention it.

Young children may have difficulty *counting,* because once they have counted an object, they have trouble counting it a second time to represent a place in its alternate set (Wilkenson, 1976). Many young children have just mastered a one-to-one correspondence rule in counting—that is, each counting number goes with one and only one object. To ask the child to disregard this rule and engage in double counting is to tamper with a fragile skill the child has just mastered.

Finally, we note that the information processing steps outlined in the model require the child to hold the problem in mind while it is being solved. Suppose the steps of planning, counting, and comparing, for example, require five to ten seconds to complete. Remembering the different parts of the problem may interfere with the counting operations, confuse the child over the next step to take, or make the child lose track of the overall goal of the task.

Information processing psychologists have subjected a number of other important cognitive problems to task analysis, including conservation (Brainerd, 1978; Siegler, 1981), arithmetic problems (e.g., Carpenter, 1980; Gelman, 1978; and Resnick, 1981), reading and ordering stories (Yussen, 1982), and logical problems such as transitive inference (Trabasso et al., 1970). They have come up with a number of suggestions of how to teach young children important skills and have shown that young children are capable of surprising competencies.

Measuring Processing Time Implicit in most theories of information processing is the idea that it takes some measurable time to complete each stage of solving a task. Actually, the idea that cognitive processes are time-dependent is not terribly novel. Even those psychologists who constructed intelligence tests forty to seventy years ago incorporated measures of time into the scores given for some task (more on the study of intelligence will appear in chapter 9). What is novel in the information processing approach, however, is the fairly detailed claims about what processes unfold over time, how long each is likely to take, and the precision in measuring cognitive events that occur in brief flashes of time (often ten to fifty milliseconds. A millisecond is 1/1000 of a second).

We turn to the first cognitive process described in the information processing paradigm displayed in figure 7.5—attention. Later, in chapter 10, we will look more closely at other cognitive processes in the information processing perspective—memory, thinking, and problem solving.

Attention

Simply described, attention consists of noticing an event (stimulus) in the environment. Our world consists of a bewildering array of stimuli and it is impossible to process all or even a significant portion of the stimuli at any one time. William James (1890) described this overwhelming environment as a "bloomin, buzzing," confusion over which the person must exercise some selectivity and choice. Remember that attention also is considered to be an important cognitive process in children's imitation (e.g., Bandura's view, chapters 2 and 4).

There seem to be great changes in a child's ability to pay attention during the early childhood years. The toddler, for example, wanders around a good deal, shifts attention from one activity to another, and generally seems to spend very little time focused on any one object or event. The preschooler, by comparison, is often seen playing a game or watching a television program for a half hour. The changes in ability to pay attention continue beyond the preschool years into the first or second year of school. In the classroom children are able to observe the teacher for extended periods of time, and they can pore over their books in long periods of independent study. These demands on attention exceed what was required of the preschooler, who is generally free to move about in various play activities (Yussen & Santrock, 1978). These apparent changes in attention, well documented in scientific studies, have a dramatic influence on the child's learning (Hagen & Hale, 1973; Pick, Frankel, & Hess, 1976; Stevenson, 1972; White, 1965; Wright, 1977; Zeaman & House, 1963).

Changes in a child's ability to pay attention continue beyond the preschool years into the first or second year of school.

The young preschool child who spends long periods of time at play or watching television does not have the same extended attention span for learning problems presented by psychologists, however. Researchers feel fortunate when they can sustain a three-year-old's attention for ten minutes and a two-year-old's for even two minutes (Wellman, Ritter, & Flavell, 1975; Perlmutter, 1980).

Because of this difficulty in working with very young children, there is little scientific information available about the changes in attention that occur in children from one to three years of age. However, a number of people researching the impact of educational television on young children have combined an interest in measuring the child's television viewing behavior with an interest in measuring the child's learning of television material.

In one study the attention of children from two to four years of age to an episode of "Sesame Street" was examined (Anderson & Levin, 1976). The children watched the program with their mothers in a setting

resembling a living room. The investigators found that the youngest children often got up to play with toys or turned and talked to other people in the room. These patterns of distraction declined among the older children.

A number of fairly clever techniques have been developed to help us understand more precisely the nature of children's attention (Day, 1975; Pick, Frankel, & Hess, 1976; Trabasso, 1968; Vlietstra, 1981; Zeaman & House, 1963; House, 1979).

Recall that recent advances in the field of modern linguistics served as one important base for the emergence of the information processing perspective. We turn our attention once again to the development of language. You may want to review some of the basic foundations of language development described in chapter 5 before going on to the next section.

Language Development

In chapter 5 we described the major aspects of language development during infancy, among them early speech sounds, Roger Brown's first two stages of language development, and the relation of cognition to language. In this section we explore later speech sounds, the final three stages of Brown's theory, and whether childhood is a critical period in language development, as well as the development of prereading skills.

Later Speech Sounds

Within a year or two after the first words appear, most of the basic sounds of standard English are heard in the child's speech, even though pronunciation quirks may be evident with some children for several more years. The /r/ and /l/ sounds may be confused, as in "rady," and "rightbulb." The /s/ and /sh/ sounds may be incorrectly substituted for one another, as in "shorry" "sore" (for *sure*), and "shertainly." And the /p/ and /t/ sounds may be juxtaposed, as in "tut" (for *put*), "tat" (for *pat*) and "perrible" (for *terrible*), to name but a few. Such quirks reflect the child's inability to discriminate phonemes that require very similar production (vocal) mechanics.

Perhaps the final hurdle the child must overcome, lasting well into the elementary school years, is the mastery of deep structure and surface structure properties of phonological rules. Learning these properties

converges with the learning of morphological and syntactic rules. A good example is the child's mastery of the sounds used to make singular nouns plural, described by Langacker (1973) and Dale (1976).

There are three sounds used to pluralize words in adult English: /s/ as in *cats,* /z/ as in *dogs,* and /ez/ as in *glasses.* One way to indicate when each form is to be used is to list the final consonants in words that take each form. But this method overlooks the deep structural relation present. The type of plural sound that is added is determined by the manner in which the final consonant is produced by the vocal apparatus. If the final consonant is **a voiced consonant** *(m, n, g),* then the plural form is voiced: /z/. If the final consonant is a *voiceless consonant (k, f, t, b),* then the plural form is also voiceless: /s/. However, whenever the final consonant and the plural sound are similar with respect to the location of articulation and the type of consonant, the schwa sound (/ə/) is inserted between them.

Children continue to make mistakes in plurals and tense markers into the early elementary school years because they have not mastered the rules that relate the underlying phonological structure to the surface sounds of speech.

The Later Stages of Roger Brown's Theory of Language Development

In stages 3, 4, and 5 of Brown's theory, the length of speech expands, but the major type of change that occurs involves the use of transformational rules. In chapter 5 these were described as rules that relate a common deep structure to many alternative surface structures in speech. The rules that are mastered include rules that produce negative forms of sentences ("The boy did not come"), questions ("Who came to the store?"), imperatives ("Come to the store"), relative clauses ("The boy who is here came home"), and compound phrases ("The boy came home and washed the dishes"). In each case the child must master several rules that transform a simple, structural sentence like "The boy came home" into one of the forms indicated.

Space limitations prohibit discussion of how each transformational system is learned, the topic of many scholarly articles (e.g., Bloom, 1970; Brown, 1973; McNeill, 1970). But there are some interesting parallels in the way each system is mastered.

At the earliest point in stage 3, children are able to add an element to a fixed location of the sentence to signal a transformational type. But they confuse word order, inflection changes, and verb-noun agreement. Here are some examples:

No eat cake.
What mommy read?
Do play?

In stage 4 inflections and some auxillary verbs appear, but word order is still a problem. Some examples are:

What mommy is reading?
No do eat the cake?
What want you to read?

In stage 5, most of the rules are mastered. Admittedly, this is a simplified account of what transpires in stages 3, 4, and 5, but it is essentially accurate.

In chapter 5 we saw that cognitive and language development can interact in different ways. Next, we explore the possibility that one aspect of cognitive development, *egocentrism,* may constrain or enhance communication.

Egocentrism and Communication

The problem of egocentrism has been central in the study of children's communication. We have all experienced situations in which children talk with total disregard for the listener. They babble on about some experience and show no interest in whether the listener *is* listening, much less comprehending.

A more commonplace problem is that children do not recognize how different the listener's perspective is from their own and fail to cater to it accordingly, even though they want to. The speaker may know something that the listener does not, and vice versa. The speaker may be privy to some experiences (e.g., perceptions, internal feelings) that the listener is not, and vice versa. To sustain an effective conversation, the speaker must bridge these two perspectives. He or she must be aware of the listener's perspective, discover how it is different from his or her own, and be sensitive to feedback from the listener as the conversation proceeds.

A widely used technique for demonstrating this problem is illustrated in figure 7.7 (Glucksberg & Krauss, 1967; Krauss & Glucksberg, 1977). Two children sit at opposite sides of a table facing each other. A solid, opaque screen across the table prevents the children from seeing each other. In front of each child is a row of six blocks, each with a unique line drawing of a nonsense figure that is difficult to name. Each child sees the same six line drawings, but they are arranged differently on each side of the screen.

The task is for one child (the sender) to select a block and describe it for the other child (the decoder) so that the second child is able to pick the one being described. This procedure is repeated for each of the blocks. Young children play this game poorly; the percentage of correct "picks" is very low. Performance improves gradually with age; seventh-graders get about half correct, and adults make virtually no errors. The problem for young senders is that they provide egocentric descriptions of the drawings—descriptions that capture the sender's experience of the drawing but are not general enough to make contact with the receiver's experience of it. The descriptions are not particularly informative for the decoder.

The speaker's task is made much easier by cues or feedback from the listener. Children as young as four years of age can effectively alter the messages they send in a problem like the one shown in figure 7.7 (Peterson, Danner, & Flavell, 1972) if they receive some feedback from the listener: "Huh? I don't get it! I can't figure out which one you mean! Can you tell me something else?" Children then altered their egocentric remarks and provided the listener with more information to help "pick" the correct picture.

Developmental psychologists (Krauss & Glucksberg, 1977; Dickson, 1981; Asher, 1981) have concluded that egocentrism itself may not be the sole reason for young children's poor performance in a problem of this kind. It may be that young children can take the other person's perspective but that the format of the problem makes the perspective-taking difficult.

It takes two to communicate—a listener as well as a speaker. Listening skills are a part of communication. Interestingly, very little is known about the development of children's abilities to be effective listeners (e.g., Dickson, 1981). What is an effective listener? For one, he or she is attentive to the speaker, maintains an expression of interest, and has frequent eye contact with the speaker. For another, an effective listener provides feedback to indicate whether the message is coming across; this may be in the form of facial expressions, nods, or verbal comments. It may be that the development of listening skills closely parallels the development of speaking skills, since each person is both speaker and listener in many communicative settings.

Self-Taught Reading and Prereading Skills Programs

If learning to read is like learning to talk, the contemporary view of psycholinguists would say that children do much of this on their own. Frank Smith (1976), a leading expert on language development and reading, demonstrated this. He observed a young child "on the threshold of learning to read" in a supermarket and a department store. He found the world of children to be full of meaningful print and that children not only know

FORM		CHILD				
		1	2	3	4	5
1		Man's legs	Airplane	Drapeholder	Zebra	Flying Saucer
2		Mother's hat	Ring	Keyhold	Lion	Snake
3		Somebody running	Eagle	Throwing sticks	Strip-stripe	Wire
4		Daddy's shirt	Milk jug	Shoe hold	Coffeepot	Dog
5		Another Daddy's shirt	Bird	Dress hold	Dress	Knife
6		Mother's dress	Ideal	Digger hold	Caterpillar	Ghost

how to learn words by their context, but that they will always turn to something new to learn if they have exhausted the possibilities of the situation they are in.

This is not to say, however, that reading instruction should be abandoned. Quite the contrary it should build on what the child already knows. Principles of individually guided instruction developed by educational experts at the University of Wisconsin are embedded in a program for teaching reading in early childhood. The program is referred to as the *Prereading Skills Program* (Venezky & Pittelman, 1977).

Three separate visual skills are central to the prereading skills program: attending to letter order, letter orientation, and word detail. A child must learn to recognize words by the left-to-right order in which the letters appear. Many kindergarten children, especially those who have not played with letters and words before entering school, have trouble attending to word order. The child must also pay attention to letter orientation. For example, to decide whether a letter is a *u* or an *n*, the child must pay attention to the relative

The contemporary view of psycholinguists is that children do a great deal of learning to read on their own.

positions of the line and the circle. A common mistake of children learning to read is to identify a written word by its first letter. This strategy may work with the limited vocabulary of a beginner, but as the reading vocabulary increases, the child must pay attention to all letters in a word to identify it.

In addition to exercises in the prereading skills program built around these visual skills, the program also concentrates on two basic sound skills, sound matching and sound blending. To associate sounds with letters a child must be able first to recognize individual speech sounds. Because isolating and matching individual sounds that occur in words is extremely difficult for many children, most children need special insruction to become familiar with speech sounds and to learn to identify them in words. Children who have learned to associate letters with sounds have acquired an important tool for beginning reading. Before they can make use of this tool, however, they must understand that sounds can be put together—blended—to form words. For some children the ability to blend sounds into words develops naturally. Other children require extensive practice before they acquire this skill.

"Genie" and Childhood
As a Critical Period in Language Development

Maya Pines (1981) vividly described the life of "Genie" and information about childhood as a critical period in language development. "Genie" is a pseudonym for a

thirteen-year-old girl who had been isolated in a small room and had not been spoken to by her parents since infancy. She was found in 1970 in California.

The case came to light when Genie's fifty-year-old mother took her and ran away from her seventy-year-old husband after a violent argument. The mother was partially blind and applied for public assistance. The social worker in the welfare office took one look at Genie and called her supervisor, who called the police. At the time, Genie could not stand erect. She was unable to speak and could only whimper.

Authorities sent the girl to the Los Angeles Children's Hospital for tests. Charges of willful abuse were filed against both parents. On the day Genie's father was due to appear in court, he committed suicide. Charges against the mother were dismissed after her lawyer argued that she "was, herself, the victim of the same psychotic individual." Nevertheless, for many years the court assigned a guardian for Genie.

The discovery of Genie aroused intense curiosity among professionals who study brain development. They were eager to know what Genie's mental level was at the time she was found and whether she would be capable of developing her faculties.

Genie now is twenty-four years old. During her years of rehabilitation and special training she was observed and repeatedly tested. Hundreds of videotapes recorded her progress and she has been the subject of several journal articles and a book. Although her case has failed to settle any scientific controversies, she has

provided fresh ammunition for arguments on both sides of a major issue: If language learning isn't stimulated during a critical period in a child's development, will language be impaired or not emerge at all?

Genie inspired Susan Curtiss, an assistant professor of linguistics at UCLA, to develop a controversial hypothesis about how language learning affects the two hemispheres of the brain. As described in Ms. Curtiss' book, *Genie: A Psycholinguistic Study of a Modern-Day "Wild Child,"* Genie is proof of human resilience. From the age of twenty months, and until she was thirteen and a half, Genie lived in almost total isolation. Naked and restrained by a harness that her father had fashioned, she was left to sit on her potty seat day after day. She could move only her hands and feet and had nothing to do. At night, when she was not forgotten, she was put into a sort of straightjacket and caged in a crib that had wiremesh sides and an overhead cover. She often was hungry. If she made any noise, her father beat her. "He never spoke to her," Ms. Curtiss wrote. "He made barking sounds (and) he growled at her."

When Genie arrived at Children's Hospital in November 1970, she was malformed, unsocialized, and severely malnourished. Although she was beginning to show signs of pubescence, she weighed only fifty-nine pounds. She could not straighten her arms or legs. She did not know how to chew and salivated a great deal and spent much of her time spitting. And she was eerily silent.

During those first months, various physicians, psychologists, and therapists examined her. Shortly after Genie was admitted as a patient, she was given the Vineland Social Maturity Scale and the Preschool Attainment Record; she scored as low as normal one-year-olds. At first, she seemed to recognize only her own name and the word "sorry."

Psychologists at the hospital eventually asked Victoria Fromkin, a UCLA psycholinguist, to study Genie's language abilities. Ms. Fromkin brought along Susan Curtiss. A graduate student at the time, Ms. Curtiss became so fascinated by Genie that she spent much of the next seven years researching the girls' linguistic development.

During her first seven months at Children's Hospital, Genie learned to walk with a jerky motion and became more or less toilet trained. She also learned to recognize many new words—probably hundreds by the time Ms. Curtiss started investigating her knowledge of language systematically in June 1971. And she had begun to speak. At first Genie spoke only in one-word utterances, as toddlers do when they start to talk. Then in July 1971, she began to string two words together on her own, not just while imitating what somebody else had said. She said "big teeth," "little marble," "two hand." A little later she produced some verbs. "Curtiss come," "want milk." In November of the same year she progressed to occasional three-word strings—"small two cup," "white clear box."

Genie inspired Susan Curtiss, an assistant professor of linguistics at UCLA, to develop an hypothesis about how language learning affects the hemispheres of the brain.

Unlike normal children, though, Genie never learned how to ask questions and didn't understand much grammar. A few weeks after normal children reach the two-word stage, their speech generally develops explosively. No such explosion occurred for Genie. Four years after she began to put words together, her speech remained like a somewhat garbled telegram.

Still, Genie's limited language development contradicted one aspect of a theory put forth in 1967 by Eric Lenneberg, a Harvard psychologist. Lenneberg asserted that language can be learned only between age two and puberty. The brain of a child before age two is not sufficiently mature for the acquisition of language, Lenneberg said, while after puberty, the brain has lost its flexibility and no longer can acquire a first language. Genie proved this wrong in one sense, Ms. Fromkin says, because the child "showed that a certain amount of language can be learned after the critical period."

On the other hand, Genie failed to learn the kind of grammatical principles that distinguish the language of human beings from that of animals. For example, she could not grasp the difference between various pronouns or between active and passive verbs. In that sense, she appeared to suffer from having passed the critical period.

Genie's language deficiencies could not be attributed to a lack of teachers. Within a few months after she arrived at Children's Hospital she began going to nursery classes for normal children. She soon transferred to a special elementary school for handicapped children. Next, she spent several years in a city high school for the mentally retarded. Outside school, speech therapists worked with her consistently. And one of the therapists and his wife took Genie into their own home to live with their three teenage children.

Genie's deficiencies never appeared to be inborn. Although Genie's mother has given contradictory accounts of her early history, Genie seems to have been a normal baby. During her first year of life, before she was isolated from the rest of her family, she may have been on the road to language. Her mother reported that she heard Genie saying words right after she was locked up.

Linguist Noam Chomsky believes human beings are born with a unique competence for language. But he says this competence must be activated by exposure to language at the proper time—before puberty, Chomsky speculates. Is this what had happened to Genie's brain? Ms. Curtiss raised that possibility. Genie is right-handed, but unlike 99 percent of right-handed people, she seemed to use the right hemisphere of her brain for language. That could account for some of the strange features of Genie's language development.

In her studies, Ms. Curtiss attempted to explain Genie's dependence on her right hemisphere. Possibly, language learning triggers the normal pattern of hemispheric specialization. So, if language is not acquired at the appropriate time, the tissues normally committed to language may atrophy. That would mean there are critical periods for the development of the left hemisphere. If such development fails, later learning may be limited to the right hemisphere.

Researchers who have studied deaf children report results that correlate with Ms. Curtiss' theory. In tests performed at the Salk Institute in La Jolla, California, right-handed children acquired either speech or sign language through the use of the left hemisphere. Researcher Helen Neville hypothesized that the nature of the language system learned determines, in part, what else goes to the same hemisphere. Together, these two hypotheses present a new view of the development of the brain's hemisphere.

In 1978, Genie's mother became her legal guardian. During all the years of Genie's rehabilitation, her mother also received help. An eye operation restored her sight, and a social worker tried to improve her behavior toward her daughter. Shortly after Genie's mother was named guardian, she astounded the therapists and researchers who had worked with Genie by filing a suit against Ms. Curtiss and the Children's Hospital among others—on behalf of herself and her daughter. She charged they had disclosed private and

Changes in cost and in attitudes about the importance of early childhood education have opened programs to children from a much broader range of backgrounds.

The Head Start Program provides children from low-income families an opportunity to experience an enriched early environment.

confidential information concerning Genie and her mother for "prestige and profit." She also accused them of subjecting Genie to "unreasonable and outrageous" tests to exploit the girl for personal and economic benefits. According to the *Los Angeles Times,* the lawyer representing Genie's mother estimated the actual damages at $500,000.

The case has not come to trial yet, but since 1978 Genie has been cut off from the professionals at Children's Hospital and UCLA. All research on Genie's language and intellectual development has come to an halt, however, the research that Genie stimulated continues. Much of it concerns the relationship between linguistic ability and brain development, a subject to which Genie has made a significant contribution.

In the prologue of this chapter some of the basic ideas involved in the Montessori approach to education were outlined. Next, some of the forms preschool education can take, particularly compensatory education programs, will be explored.

Early Childhood Education

Throughout the twentieth century the most popular form of education for children before the first grade has been the child-centered nursery school program. A typical program lasts for two or three hours a day and from three to five days a week. Until the last ten or twenty years, children who attended these schools were primarily from middle-class families. The number of such programs has multiplied dramatically in recent years; and with changes in cost and in attitudes about the importance of early childhood education, children from a much broader range of backgrounds now attend these programs.

The list of basic differences in these **child-centered** schools is almost endless. For example, some focus on enhancing the social development of the children, while others seek to accelerate cognitive growth. Some emphasize daily, structured activities, while others let the child do whatever he or she wants to do. Some stress group activities; others stress individual activities.

Many experts argue that some of the best educational environments have existed for many years in the child-centered nursery schools. With their emphasis on the individual child, providing that child with a variety of experiences outside the nursery school and making education a fun-filled adventure in exploration, they put many public schools to shame. It is not surprising, then, that many of the so-called liberal reforms of public education loudly called for in the 1960s (e.g., Silberman, 1970) looked remarkably like the programs already in operation in child-centered nursery schools. Free schools, open schools, and alternative education—educational proposals to remedy the problems of public schools—have existed for some time and work fairly well for the younger child.

Compensatory Education

For many years children from low-income families did not receive any education before they entered first grade. In the 1960s an effort was made to try to break the poverty/poor education cycle for young children in the United States through **compensatory education.** As part of this effort, **Project Head Start** was initiated in the summer of 1965, funded by the Economic Opportunity Act. The program was designed to provide children from low-income families an opportunity to experience an enriched early environment. It was hoped that early intervention might counteract the disadvantages these children had already experienced and place them on an equal level with other children when they entered the first grade.

Head Start Children in Young Adulthood

Robert Trotter (1981) described the following recent findings about Head Start children:

Project Head Start continues to yield impressive results and remains a favorite of lawmakers and money givers, so its future looks bright—except for two potential problems. One has to do with sex, the other with funding.

First the sex problem. It appears that boys and girls don't derive equal benefits from the types of intervention provided by preschool programs. All children who have had preschool training tend to do better in school than those who did not get a head start. But by the time they reach young adulthood, any advantage the females may have had seems to have disappeared, leaving them no better off than girls who did not attend a preschool program.

This is among the most recent findings to emerge from an ongoing study of a large group of poor, black children who took part in an experimental program in Harlem in the early 1960s. The research is being conducted by psychologists Cynthia Deutsch, Martin Deutsch, Theresa Jordan and Richard Grallo, all of the Institute for Developmental Studies at New York University. The researchers described the program (which was a forerunner of Project Head Start) and discussed their findings at the APA annual meeting in Los Angeles.

More than 150 young adults currently are involved in the study. Half of them entered an experimental preschool program when they were four years old. The others did not get this early training and are serving as a comparison group. All have been interviewed by the four psychologists every two or three years since the experiment started, and now, for the first time, sex differences are beginning to emerge.

In general, the males have been successful in school and in the job market: 32 percent are attending college, compared with 20 percent of those who did not get preschool training; 57 percent are employed full or part time, compared with 44 percent of the control group. The same positive benefits are not seen among the females. At this stage of their lives, they are no better off than those who started school at the usual age.

The researchers aren't quite sure why the young women aren't doing as well as the young men, but they suggest that the school system may have to take part of the blame. The preschool program emphasized verbal skills, inquisitiveness,

---

At first it seemed that Head Start was going to be successful; at the end of the preschool period, children who had been in the Head Start program demonstrated recognizable intellectual and social gains over comparable children who had not been in Head Start. However, as these children went through the first grade, no longer experiencing the enriched educational program they had in preschool, their gains began to diminish and ultimately disappeared. Congress established **Project Follow Through** in 1967 when it had become apparent that a program comparable to Head Start was needed for the early elementary school years.

Project Head Start consisted of many different types of preschool programs in different parts of the country. Little effort was made initially to find out whether some types of programs worked better than others; however, it soon became obvious that some programs and some centers were doing a better job with low-income children than others. A significant aspect of Project Follow Through, then, was *planned variation,* in which different kinds of educational programs

for children were devised to see whether specific programs are effective with all children or only with certain groups of children. For instance, one program may be more effective with the rural poor of Appalachia, and another may be more beneficial with ghetto children in New York City. By the 1972/1973 school year, twenty-two different Follow Through programs were being implemented in the United States, each in different areas. The results of these programs are still being evaluated, as indicated in box 7.2. Recent longitudinal data collected when the preschool children reached adulthood suggests that boys fare better than girls because of their Head Start experience.

In all of the Follow Through programs parents are included both in and out of the classroom. Parents work as paid teachers' aides, as volunteers in the classroom, and as social-service staff assistants. In many of the programs, educational workshops have been developed to inform parents about the Follow Through program in their area and to instruct them in the ways they can help their children. Thus, an important part of Project Follow Through is parent and community involvement.

and self-confidence. In elementary school, the boys were rewarded for displaying these qualities, but in many cases the girls were punished for the same behaviors. Some teachers, for instance, even complained that the girls were too assertive and asked too many questions.

These results, however, may not be the final word. The researchers are continuing to follow the progress of the young men and women, and already there are indications that the women may yet benefit from their early training. Many, for instance, had to leave school because they got pregnant, but there are preliminary indications that those who had been in the preschool program are more likely than the others to return to school and continue their education. If this proves to be the case, the girls, like the boys, may, as the researchers say, "have all of what it takes to make it."

And because many of them (at least the boys) are making it, Project Head Start will probably make it. The program, which provides a wide range of educational, nutritional, health and social services to economically disadvantaged children between three and five years of age, expired on September 30, but Congress is likely to vote to continue it for at least three and perhaps five years. In fact, Head Start is one of the few social programs that the Reagan administration stands

behind. A funding level of $950 million for the program has been proposed by the administration. This is the same as the Carter administration's request and $130 million above the fiscal 1981 level. The increase would be enough to maintain Head Start at its current level of participation (339,700 children) and upgrade some programs.

The bad news is that other proposed cutbacks in social services may harm Head Start—to the tune of $36 million. The expected reductions in Comprehensive Employment and Training Act (CETA) programs, for instance, are likely to adversely affect Head Start programs because approximately one-half of them use CETA workers for jobs such as bus drivers and clerical workers. The administration's proposed elimination of federal subsidies for snacks served to children through the child care food program would also affect Head Start. More than 10 percent of the funding for meals and snacks would be lost.

But despite these potential problems, it appears that Head Start, like many of its participants, is going to make it. (pp. 15, 37)

All Follow Through programs must be comprehensive; that is, they cannot focus on a narrow aspect of the child's learning or development. Thus, Follow Through programs include instruction, medical services, nutrition, psychological services, social services, and staff development.

Evaluation of Project Follow Through
Box 7.3 shows five of the ways Project Follow Through attempts to intervene in the education of the young child. In an effort to find out whether Project Follow Through is effective, a national evaluation is being conducted by Stanford Research Institute. Follow Through pupils are compared with pupils of similar social and intellectual backgrounds who have not participated in the project.

Means used to evaluate the success of Project Follow Through include observation to determine whether teachers are fulfilling their planned-variation goals, national standardized tests of achievement that measure children's math and reading skills, survey questionnaires and interviews with parents.

Because a new wave of children enters Project Follow Through each year, a large amount of information about Follow Through is accumulating. A recent national comparison of Follow Through and non-Follow Through programs supported the belief that educational intervention can have a positive effect on the child's social and intellectual development. Jane Stallings (1975) reviewed seven of the twenty-two variations in a national evaluation of Follow Through programs. In all, over two hundred first- and third grade classrooms were involved in the evaluation. In Stallings' own words, here are some of the major findings pertaining to Project Follow Through's social impact on children:

In our study, *independence* is defined as a child or children engaged in a task without an adult. This type of independent behavior is more likely to be found in classrooms where teachers allow children to select their own seating and groups part of the time, where a wide variety of activities is available, and where an assortment of audiovisual and exploratory materials is available. The adults provide individual attention

Five Follow Through Models

Project Follow Through reaches between ninety thousand and one hundred thousand children each year. It is the largest, most expensive attempt by the federal government to break the poverty cycle. The following brief descriptions of five of the twenty-two programs implemented in the United States suggest the scope and variety of Project Follow Through (U.S. Office of Education, 1973).

The University of Oregon Engelmann/Becker Model for Direct Instruction emphasizes that children fail in school because they have not been instructed properly. Disadvantaged children lag behind other children in developing appropriate skills. It is a highly structured program, with sequentially programmed lessons. Teachers systematically reward children for success and monitor them closely so that learning failures do not build up. This program is based on learning theory and behavior modification.

The *High/Scope: Cognitively Oriented Curriculum Model,* developed by Dave Weikart, is based on Piaget's theory of cognitive development. The child is seen as an active learner who discovers things about the world. He or she should not be "taught," in the sense of being told information; rather, should "learn" by planning, doing, experimenting, exploring, and talking about what he or she is doing. Communication and thinking skills are nurtured, and emphasis is placed on self-direction, not reliance on external reinforcement from others. Each child's level of development is continuously monitored so that appropriate materials can be used.

The *Florida Parent-Education Program* places more direct importance on the role of parents than the first two models mentioned. This program was developed by Ira Gordon to involve parents in the emotional and intellectual growth of their children. It assumes that the child's learning habits and personality are formed primarily through experiences in the early home environment; thus, parents are trained to supervise the child's learning at home. Parent educators work in the classroom and visit parents on a weekly basis.

---

and make friendly comments to the children. . . . children in the classrooms of EDC (a humanistic, child centered approach) and Far West Laboratory evidence more independence than do the children in non-Follow Through and other sponsor's classrooms. (p. 103)

For this study, *cooperation* is defined as two or more children working together on a joint task. This kind of cooperation is more likely to be found in classrooms where a wide variety of activities occurs throughout the day, where exploratory materials are available, and where children can choose their own groupings. If the adults interact with two children, asking questions and making comments about the task, the children seem to be encouraged to join each other in cooperative tasks.

The children in the Bank Street College, High/Scope Foundation, and EDC programs more often joined each other in a cooperative task than did children in other models and non–Follow Through children. (p. 104)

Thus, there is evidence that Project Follow Through enhances social development. The results even point to specific programs that have been the most effective in enhancing specific social behaviors. Not surprisingly, not all programs were shown to have facilitated all social behaviors equally.

Next, we find that education may be best when it is entertaining as we look at the impact the television show "Sesame Street" has on young children.

"Sesame Street": Education through Television

One of television's major programming attempts to educate children is "Sesame Street," which is designed to teach both cognitive and social skills. The program began in 1969 and is still going strong. Aimee Leifer (1973) showed that "Sesame Street" can influence the child's social development in such areas as cooperation. But the major evaluation of "Sesame Street" has focused on its impact on the child's cognitive development. A national study of "Sesame Street," conducted by Sam Ball and Gerry Bogatz (1970), evaluated such major cognitive outcomes as symbolic representation (e.g., letters, numbers, and geometric forms), problem solving, and reasoning. The results are impressive. Children who frequently watch "Sesame Street" scored higher on these measures of cognitive development than did children who watch infrequently. Children from both low-income and middle-income families who watched the show often made gains on the cognitive measures; children from low-income families who did not watch the show often did not make such gains.

The *Far West Laboratory Responsive Educational Program* emphasizes the development of a healthy self-concept in the child and the freedom to decide his or her own course of learning. Teachers try to build up the child's confidence in ability to succeed and provide many different alternatives in the classroom so he or she can choose and direct activities. This program has much in common with a humanistic view of child development.

The *Bank Street College of Education Approach* is an eclectic approach in which academic skills are seen as acquired within a broader context of planned activities. The program focuses on the child's interests at school, at home, and in the community, and views the child as an active learner seeking to become independent and to understand the world. To help the child in these efforts, he or she is encouraged to select from different alternatives, to make decisions, and to cope with the world. The individual nature of the child also is taken into account; learning experiences are constantly restructured to meet the needs of each child.

What are the educational goals of "Sesame Street?" The following discussion of these goals is based on an article in the *Harvard Educational Review* by Gerald Lesser (1972), who served as chairman of the National Board of Advisors to the Children's Television Workshop, which produces "Sesame Street." He discusses many different teaching techniques that are reflected in the actual production of "Sesame Street."

A fundamental message from "Sesame Street," Lesser asserts, is that education and entertainment can work well together. In the past, education and entertainment have been viewed as separate activities. Education is supposed to be work, not fun; with "Sesame Street," however, learning is exciting and entertaining.

A second point brought out in "Sesame Street" is that teaching can be done in both direct and indirect ways. Using the direct way, a teacher would tell the child exactly what it is he or she is going to be taught and then actually teach it. This method is often used on the program in teaching cognitive skills. But social skills are usually communicated in indirect ways. Thus, rather than merely telling children "You should cooperate with people," a sequence of events is shown so that the child can figure out what it means to be cooperative and what the advantages are.

"Sesame Street" is designed to teach both cognitive and social skills.

Should the world be shown to children as it is or as it ought to be? The advisory board of educators and psychologists decided that the real world should be shown, but with the emphasis on what the world would be like if everyone treated one another with decency and kindness. To show the world as it really is, the program might show an adult doing something unjustifiably inconsiderate to another adult, with alternative ways of coping with this stress then acted out. Finally, the program would portray the happy outcomes when people stop acting inconsiderately.

Gerald Lesser also offered several suggestions for implementing the production techniques of "Sesame Street" in classroom teaching situations. Most of these suggestions emphasize the important of attention in children's learning. For instance, in order to learn the social skills being shown in a "Sesame Street" episode on being a friendly person, the child has to attend to the television screen. If you, as a teacher or a parent, are trying to explain the value of cooperation, the child has to attend to what you are saying and doing in order for your commentary to be effective.

Few developments in society over the last twenty-five years have had greater impact on children than television. Many children spend more time in front of the television set than they do with their parents. Although only one of the vehicles of the mass media that affects children's behavior—books, comic books, movies, and newspapers also have some impact—television is the most influential.

In the next chapter, in the discussion of social, emotional, and personality development in early childhood, you will read further evaluations of the influence of television on children.

Summary

This chapter focused on physical and cognitive development in early childhood. Physical development in early childhood slows markedly compared to infancy. Gross and fine motor skills, however, noticably mature doing early childhood. Advances in height and weight, brain development, locomotion, and manipulative skills appear. One educational program used to advance sensory and perceptual skills in early childhood is Maria Montessori's approach. Programs designed to enhance children's physical development are of three types: physical education, perceptual-motor, and movement.

Our discussion of cognitive development focused on Piaget's stage of preoperational thought and the important emerging cognitive perspective referred to as information processing. The period of preoperational thought is marked by further advances in symbolic activity and the appearance of a number of differences between the child's thinking and full-fledged adult reasoning and logic. The child's thought is frequently *egocentric,* that is, lacking in self-other perspective discriminations, and is filled with *animism,* the belief that inanimate objects have human qualities. In addition, the child fails to *conserve* properties of objects, has limited ability to classify objects, and often does not serialize items correctly.

In the information processing view, cognition, or mental activity, is synonymous with the processing of information. The series of stages of processing include attention, perception, memory and retrieval, inferencing, and problem solving. Historically, the information processing tradition can be traced to interest in the development of communication theory, computer modeling—particularly of artificial intelligence—and advances in modern linguistics. The tools used in the contemporary study of information processing include high-speed computers, high-speed movement photography, task analysis, and the ability to measure processing time very precisely.

Attention is the *noticing* of specific features of the environment. There are striking changes in the ability of children to sustain interest in activities from the toddler years to middle childhood, and younger children take longer to notice relevant features of events for learning. Changes in attention can be explained in terms of *selectivity* and *completeness* in apportioning attention.

Our discussion of language development focused on later speech sounds, Roger Brown's stages of language development, the role of egocentrism in communication, the child's beginning reading skills, and the possibility of childhood as a critical period in language development. While the answer to the debate about whether childhood is a critical period in language development is still open, there is every reason to believe that in the development of language, early childhood is an important phase of the life cycle.

During early childhood the principal agencies for education are day-care centers, child-centered nursery schools, and special programs. Child centered nursery schools have been the major educational force for middle-class children, offering a form of progressive education since the turn of the century. Projects Head Start and Follow Through are two well-funded programs started by the federal government to provide an enriched educational experience for children from lower-class families during preschool and early elementary school years. In the 1960s Head Start programs had a positive effect on children's cognitive development, but gains were generally lost after a year or two of regular public school. A recent study of Follow Through, which tries to maintain the enriched environment through the early elementary school years, suggests that such gains can be maintained.

Key Terms

animism

centration

channel

child-centered

class inclusion

communications

compensatory education

conservation

egocentrism

expressive movement

hardware

information processing
approach

irreversibility

objective movement

operations

perceptual-motor
training program

Project Follow Through

Project Head Start

receiver

saccadic

software

voiced consonant

voiceless consonant

Further Readings

Curtiss, S. *Genie: A psycholinguistic study of a modern-
day 'wild child.'* New York: Academic Press, 1981.
*Susan Curtiss' vivid, exciting account of "Genie's"
language development, her abuse, and attempts at
rehabilitation. Easy reading.*

Montessori, M. *Discovery of the child.* (M. J. Costelloe,
S. J., Trans.). Notre Dame, Ind.: Fides, 1967.
*An exciting account of Maria Montessori's sensory
approach to early childhood education. Reasonably
easy reading.*

Siegler, R. S. Information-processing approaches to
development. W. Kessen (Volume editor).
Carmichael's manual of child psychology, vol. 1. New
York: John Wiley, 1982.
*A description of the information processing
perspective of development that includes many new
insights about this approach. Moderately difficult
reading level.*

Review Questions

1. Describe Maria Montessori's approach to early childhood education.
2. What are some important changes in gross and fine motor skills during early childhood?
3. Discuss Piaget's stage of preoperational thought.
4. What is the information processing view of development?
5. Historically, what events seem responsible for the evaluation of the information processing approach?
6. What are the major characteristics of attention? How does attention change as children get older?
7. Describe some of the important changes that take place in language in early childhood.
8. Describe the young child's role as an active participant in learning to read and how this fits in with prereading skills programs.
9. Outline the language development of "Genie," and evaluate whether the childhood years represent a critical period in language development.
10. Describe the results of the evaluation of Projects Head Start and Follow Through.

8

Social, Emotional, and Personality Development

Prologue: Changing the Sex-Typed Behavior of Children

In a recent review of children's **sex-typed behavior,** Aletha Huston (1982) concluded that efforts to change children's sex-typed behavior have taken two directions: *gender-deviant* children are trained to show more appropriate sex-typed behavior, and attempts are made to free normal children from rigidly sex-typed patterns. Both types of interventions create ethical concerns; yet both produce valuable information about sex typing, that is, the psychological aspects of being male or female.

Most studies of gender deviance have included only boys who are diagnosed as gender deviant when they play mostly with feminine sex-typed toys, dress up in female clothes, choose girls rather than boys as playmates, engage in female role playing, fantasize about being a girl, and express themselves with feminine gestures (Green, 1974; Rekers, 1979). These gender-deviant boys not only preferred feminine activities but also purposely avoided masculine activities. In particular they indicated that the rough-and-tumble play of other boys either disinterested or frightened them (Green, 1974).

Huston pointed out that gender deviance among girls has received less attention, possibly because our society allows girls more flexibility in their dress, play activities, and sex-typed interests than it does boys. The characteristics used to describe gender-deviant girls are similar to those used for boys—preferring masculine activities and boys as playmates, taking male roles in fantasy, fantasizing about being a boy, and dressing in male clothes. While masculine clothing and interests are commonplace among girls, the gender-deviant girls also are characterized by strong avoidance of feminine clothing, activities, and playmates.

Huston pointed out that while diagnosis and treatment of gender deviance has occurred, we have little knowledge of the origins of such patterns. One possibility is that many parents are indifferent to the occurrence of gender-deviant patterns of behavior in young children. Some parents think it is cute when little boys continue to dress up as females and play with dolls. Such children often are referred for treatment only after someone outside the family points out the child's effeminate characteristics. Other factors that show up in the case histories of some gender-deviant boys are maternal overprotection of boys and restrictions on rough-and-tumble play, absence of an adult male, weak father-son relationship, physical beauty on the part of the small boy that led to his being treated as a girl, absence of male playmates, and maternal dominance.

Both behavioral and psychoanalytic treatment procedures have been used in attempts to alter the sex-typed behavior of gender-deviant children. These treatment procedures have led to changes in children's play patterns but usually only in the situation where the treatment occurred. Consequently, clinical treatment has been augmented by direct interventions at home and at school.

Are such interventions ethical? Some experts believe that traditional sex roles should not be forced on children who deviate from expected societal patterns (Nordyke, Baer, Etzel, & LeBlanc, 1977). They point out that the individual behavior patterns of children should be respected and that it is the societal norm rather than the behavior that is wrong. The intervention advocates agree that efforts to change societal norms should be made, but they also add that gender-deviant males in particular often show extensive social isolation and unhappiness that lasts for many years. An additional argument for intervention is the belief that parental desires provide ethical grounds for intervening in children's lives. If parents believe their child's behavior is undesirable, then, it is argued, the psychologist should abide by those desires.

In addition to attempting to change the sex-typed behavior of gender-deviant children, another effort focused on teaching children about *androgyny*. Briefly, androgyny refers to the belief that positive, competent sex-typed behavior for both male and females includes a combination of feminine and masculine attributes. Many feminists have developed programs targeted to reduce traditional sex-typing in children. One such effort is the school program developed by Guttentag and Bray (1976). The curriculum lasted for one year and was implemented in the kindergarten, fifth-, and ninth-grade classes. It involved books, discussion materials, and classroom exercises. The program was most successful with the fifth-graders and was the least successful with the ninth-graders (who actually displayed a "boomerang effect" that produced even more rigid sex-typed behavior). The program's success varied from class to class, seeming to be most effective when the teacher produced sympathetic reaction in the peer group; however, students in some classes ridiculed and rejected the curriculum.

Ethical concerns are also aroused when the issue is one of teaching children to depart from socially approved behavior patterns, particularly when there is no evidence of extreme sex typing in the groups of children to whom the interventions are applied. The advocates of the androgyny programs believe that traditional sex typing is psychologically harmful for all children and that it has prevented many girls and women from experiencing equal opportunity. Huston concluded that while the research indicates that androgyny is more adaptive than either a traditional masculine or feminine pattern, it is not possible to ignore the imbalance within our culture, which values masculinity more than femininity.

Introduction

The development of sex-typed behavior is one of many aspects of social and emotional development to be discussed in this chapter. We continue our description of the development of the self, discussed earlier in chapters 2 and 6, and evaluate moral development in early childhood as well. However, we begin the chapter with information about the role of families, peers, and television in the young child's development.

Family

Developmental psychologists no longer rely exclusively upon socialization experiences within the family to explain children's social development. Biological and genetic factors, cognitive factors, peers, and other aspects of the culture in which the child grows up have received increased attention. However, it is important that we not go too far in the direction of thinking that the family is but one of many influences on the child's social and emotional development, because the family still is the most important influence.

Parenting Behavior, Maturation, and the Social Behavior of Children

For years heated debates have dominated the discussion of how parents ought to rear their children. Some child development authorities have argued that it is best to allow the child considerable freedom and not to interfere with his or her decision making. Other authorities believe that more control in parenting is warranted, particularly in combination with a nurturant orientation toward the child. Such control should not be punitive but should involve setting firm rules and regulations by the parent. These rules and regulations should follow discussion sessions with the child; but once the child and parents agree on the rules, the parents should consistently enforce them. Some parents believe a more authoritarian approach to rearing the child is called for; they believe that many parents are too "easy" on their children. These parents may interact in seemingly "cold" ways with their children and physically discipline them when they do something wrong.

There are many other parenting strategies in addition to the three just described. Many parents are inconsistent in the way they deal with their children; the mother might nurture and act permissively toward the child while the father acts in an authoritarian and distant manner. There is also inconsistency on the part of one parent; for example, the mother might spank the child one day for losing a book, and one month later reason with him or her about what happened.

One factor that should not be overlooked in considering the parent's behavior toward the child is the child's maturation. Mothers obviously do not treat a thirteen-year-old in the same way as a two-year-old.

Some child development authorities argue that it is best to allow the child considerable freedom.

The two-year-old and the thirteen-year-old have different needs and abilities, and the mother has different expectancies for the two children. According to Eleanor Maccoby (1980):

During the first year of a child's life, the parent-child interaction moves from a heavy focus on routine caretaking—feeding, changing, bathing, and soothing—and comes to include more noncaretaking activities like play and visual-vocal exchanges. During children's second and third years, parents often handle disciplinary issues by physical manipulation: They carry the child away from a mischievous activity to the place they want the child to go; they put fragile and dangerous objects out of reach; they sometimes spank. But as the child grows older, parents turn increasingly to reasoning, moral exhortation, and giving or withholding special privileges. As children move from infancy to middle childhood, parents show them less physical affection, become less protective, and spend less time with them (Baldwin, 1946; Lasko, 1954).

Eleanor Maccoby (1980) believes that these changes in parental behavior seem clearly linked to the child's physical and mental growth—to changes in motor skill, language, judgment, and perspective-taking ability. As the child grows larger and heavier, parents seem less likely to resort to physical manipulation. Parents seem unlikely to reason with a child who doesn't yet talk and who seems to have a limited understanding of other people's speech.

Maccoby (1980) goes on to discuss how children's understanding of the nature of authority can influence parent-child relationships. William Damon (1977) has shown that children progress through a series of stages in their ability to understand authority. Preschool children do not detect that authority is an issue. On occasion, they even express the wrong assumption that their wants and desires do not conflict with their parents' demands. Soon, though, children become aware of such conflicts, recognizing that parental authority means parental power. At this point, children think they have to obey their parents because of their parents' strength and size. However, they also believe that they can disobey, provided their parents do not catch them. As they enter elementary school, children begin to recognize the reciprocal nature of parent-child relationships—they think that they should be obedient because their parents have done so much for them. Parental authority is now legitimate, not because of power but because of kindness. During preadolescence, parental authority is viewed as more differentiated; that is, authority is more legitimate in areas where parents are competent and knowledgeable. Parental authority now becomes more of a mutual relationship between the parent and the child, with both having to agree upon the rules and regulations.

Another important factor that often goes unnoticed in parent-child relationships is that the child's parents are often maturing and changing at the same time their son or daughter is. Unfortunately, we have little information on how different levels of maturation in parents affect children. Parents may undergo significant maturational changes as they go from age twenty to thirty and forty. In his book *The Seasons of a Man's Life*, Daniel Levinson (1978) writes about these changes, distinguishing between the experiences of very young parents in their late teens and early twenties and those in midlife in their thirties and forties. The novice adult phase is a time of reasonably free experimentation and of testing one's dreams in the real world. Midlife brings an awareness of mortality and worrisome thoughts about gaps between parents' occupational aspirations and their actual accomplishments. Think about other families with children you know or have known; you probably can recall a number of situations where changes in adulthood affected parent-child relationships. Two such situations involve the divorce of parents and the increase in the number of working mothers, which will be discussed next.

Changes in Family Structure

The child's interactions and experiences with his or her mother, father, and siblings provide the beginnings of the lifelong process of socialization. However, fathers, siblings, other relatives, peers, and teachers generally have not been given the credit that mothers have for influencing the child's social development. Thus, if a son grows up to become a homosexual it is often argued that the mother was overprotective, robbing him of his virility. If he develops schizophrenia, she probably did not give him enough love. If he fails in school, it is because she did not provide him with enough achievement-oriented experiences. In particular, the attachment bond between the mother and the infant is viewed as the basis for the development of a healthy personality later in life. Jerome Kagan (1979) believes

this idea is one of the few sacred, transcendental themes in American ideology that remains unsullied.

Kagan predicts that the major result of an emotionally close parent-child bond is that it directs the child toward acceptance of the family's values. If these values coincide with those of the popular culture, all is well. If not, a close mother-infant bond may not be an advantage. As Kagan points out, the mother who establishes a deep mutual attachment with her infant daughter, but who promotes the once traditional female values of passivity, inhibition of intellectual curiosity, and anxiety over competence, may be preparing her daughter for serious conflict in adolescence and young adulthood.

Today more young children than ever before in the United States are spending less time with their mothers; more than one out of every three mothers with a child under the age of three is employed, and almost 42 percent of the mothers of preschoolers work outside the home (U.S. Department of Commerce, 1979). Is this change good for children? A recent opinion poll indicates that a majority of the public thinks it harms the family, but research evidence suggests a different conclusion. Discussion in the next section of the influence of maternal employment on the child's development is based on an overview by Lois Hoffman (1979).

Working Mothers

Because household operations have become more efficient and family size has decreased in America, it is not certain that children of working mothers actually receive less attention than children in the past whose mothers were not employed. Outside employment, at least for mothers with school-aged children, may simply be filling time previously taken up by added household burdens and more children. And it cannot be assumed that if the mother did not go to work, the child would benefit from the time freed up by streamlined household operations and smaller families. Mothering does not always have a positive effect on the child. In one longitudinal study (Moore, 1975), full-time mothering revealed some vulnerabilities. It was found that boys who experienced full-time mothering during preschool years were more competent intellectually but also more ready to conform, fearful, and inhibited as adolescents. And the educated nonworking mother may overinvest her energies in her children, fostering an excess of worry and discouraging independence. In such situations, the mother may inject more mothering into parent-child relationships than the child can profitably handle (Hoffman, 1974).

In the past, socialization experiences indicated that girls would spend most of their adult life as mothers while boys would spend it as breadwinners. But because there is greater availability of employment for women today, and there is a movement toward more

Contemporary American mothers are employed in a greater variety of jobs than at any other time in history.

equitable wages and opportunities, motherhood now takes up less of a woman's life and work outside the home takes up more. Although occupation is still a strong component of the male adult's identity, his role as the breadwinner is now more often shared with his partner, and he may be more active in childrearing than his father was.

Infant and Preschool Years   There is no compelling evidence that employment of the mother outside the home has negative effects on infants and preschoolers. In one investigation it was learned that employed mothers actually spend just as much time in one-to-one interaction with their preschool child as did mothers who are homemakers (Goldberg, 1977). In two other studies, no differences in the quality of the parenting

of women who work at home and those who work outside were found in the first year of the infant's life (Cohen, 1978; Hock, in press). However, one of these investigations did show that during the infant's second year of life, the infants of mothers who were at home did engage in more positive interactions, vocalized more, and performed better on developmental tests (Cohen, 1978). The results of this study are limited, however, because all of the babies were preterm, and the infants of the employed mothers weighed less at birth and were more likely to have absent fathers than the infants of the mothers at home. And in one investigation the four-year-old children of working mothers showed even better social adjustment than their counterparts whose mothers stayed at home (Gold, Andres, & Glorieux, 1979).

Father Absence and Family Structure
In previous eras, the majority of families consisted of a man and a woman who were married and who had one or more children living with them—known as a nuclear family. In most of these families the father was employed outside of the home and the mother was not. No longer is the majority of children exposed to this traditional family structure. Children are growing up in a greater variety of family structures than ever before in history (Eiduson & Zimmerman, 1978).

The increase in the number of children growing up in single-parent families is staggering. One estimate indicates that about 25 percent of the children born between 1910 and 1960 lived in a single-parent family sometime during their development. However, 40 to 50 percent of individuals born during the 1970s will spend some part of their childhood in a single-parent home (Bane, 1978). About 11 percent of all American households now are made up of so-called blended families, which include families with stepparents or cohabitating adults. Such families often expose the child to competing bonds of loyalty and changing authority roles.

Effects of Divorce on Children
Divorce is global in magnitude. Its effects on the child are mediated by a host of other factors, including the relationship of the child to the custodial parent; the availability of and reliance on family support systems, such as friends, relatives, and other adults; peer support; whether there is an ongoing, positive relationship with the noncustodial parent; and so forth. Many generalizations about the effects divorced parents have on children are stereotypical and do not take into account the uniqueness of many single-parent family structures.

One study (Santrock & Tracy, 1978) vividly showed that boys from divorced homes are often treated differently than boys from two-parent homes. Thirty teachers were shown a videotape that focused on the

The effects of divorce on children are mediated by a host of factors.

social interaction of a boy. Half the teachers were informed that he was from an "intact" home, while the other half were given a background information sheet that indicated the boy had parents who were divorced. The teachers were asked to view the videotape and then to rate the boy on eleven personality traits (e.g., anxiety, social deviance, and happiness) and to predict what his behavior would be like in five different school situations (e.g., ability to cope with stress, popularity). The teachers rated the "divorced" boy more negatively on three counts—in terms of happiness, emotional adjustment, and ability to cope with stress.

There are, of course, stress, conflict, and problems involved in family dynamics that predispose children from homes in which the father is absent to be less competent in social and cognitive development (e.g., Lamb, 1976; Lynn, 1974). Not all the blame, however, should fall on the family per se, as is indicated by the teachers' stereotyped responses toward homes in which the parents were divorced. Many people expect children from these homes to have problems, whether they actually do or not.

Family conflict, the child's relationship with both parents, and the availability of support systems are important aspects of divorce that influence the child's behavior (Hetherington, 1979). Many separations and divorces are highly charged emotional affairs that enmesh the child in conflict. Conflict is a critical aspect of family functioning, so critical that it appears to outweigh the influence of family structure on the child's behavior. Children in single-parent families function better than those in conflict-ridden nuclear families (Hetherington, Cox, & Cox, 1978; Rutter, in press; Santrock, Warshak, Lindbergh, & Meadows, in press). Escape from conflict may be a positive benefit of divorce for children, but unfortunately, in the year immediately following the divorce, conflict does not decline but rather increases (Hetherington et al., 1978).

At this time, children—particularly boys—in divorced families show more adjustment problems than in homes in which both parents are present.

The child's relationship with both parents after the divorce influences the ability to cope with stress (Hetherington et al., 1978; Kelly, 1978). During the first year after the divorce, the quality of parenting the child experiences is often very poor; parents seem to be preoccupied with their own needs and adjustment, experiencing anger, depression, confusion, and emotional instability that inhibit their ability to respond sensitively to the child's needs. During this period, parents tend to discipline the child inconsistently, be less affectionate, and be ineffective in controlling the child. But during the second year after the divorce, parents are more effective at these important childrearing duties (Hetherington et al., 1978).

The majority of information we have about divorced families emphasizes the absent father or the relationship between the custodial parent and the child, but child psychologists have become increasingly interested in the role of support systems available to the child and the family. Support systems for divorced families seem more important for low-income than middle-income families (Colletta, 1978; Spicer & Hampe, 1975). The extended family and community services played a more critical role in family functioning of low-income families in these two investigations. Competent support systems may be particularly important for divorced parents with infant and preschool children, since the majority of these parents must work full time to make ends meet.

A final issue involving children of divorce focuses on the age of the child at the time of the divorce. Preschool children are not as accurate as elementary school children and adolescents in evaluating the cause of divorce, their own role in the divorce, and possible outcomes. Consequently, young children may blame themselves more for the divorce and distort the feelings and behavior of their parents, including hopes for their reconciliation (Wallerstein & Kelly, 1975, 1980). Even adolescents experience a great deal of conflict and pain over their parents' divorce; but after the immediate impact of the divorce, they seem to be better than younger children at assigning responsibility for the divorce, resolving loyalty conflicts, and understanding the divorce process (Wallerstein & Kelly, 1974, 1975, 1980).

The relationship between parent and child is an important influence on the child's social behavior. In the next section we will look more closely at some different dimensions of parenting and discuss the reciprocal nature of parent-child relationships and how the family functions as a system.

Firm control in parenting occurs when the child is required to abide by rules and regulations.

Parent-Child Relationships

If I said it to them once I said it a million times. Is it my imagination or have I spent a lifetime shutting refrigerator doors, emptying nose tissue from pants pockets before washing, writing checks for milk, picking up wet towels and finding library books in the clothes hamper?

Mr. Matterling said, "Parenting is loving." (What did he know? He was an old Child Psychology teacher who didn't have any children. He only had twenty-two guppies and two catfish to clean the bowl.) How I wish that for one day I could teach Mr. Matterling's class. How I would like to tell him it's more than loving. More than clean gravel. More than eating the ones you don't like.

Parenting is frustration that you have to see to believe. Would I have ever imagined there would be whole days when I didn't have time to comb my hair? Mornings after a slumber party when I looked like Margaret Mead with a migraine? Could I have ever comprehended that something so simple, so beautiful and so uncomplicated as a child could drive you to shout, "We are a family and you're a part of this family and by God, you're going to spend a Friday night with us having a good time if we have to chain you to the bed!"

And a plaintive voice within me sighed, "Why don't you grow up!" (Bombeck & Keane, 1971, pp. 169–70)

Dimensions of Parenting

As this introduction by Erma Bombeck suggests, parents want their children to grow into socially mature individuals, and they often feel a great deal of frustration in their role as parents. Child psychologists have long searched for ingredients of parenting that will promote competent social development in their children. Recall John Watson's prescription in the 1930s

that most parents are too affectionate toward their children. In our discussion of divorce we found that parents often have a great deal of difficulty exercising control over their children in the year following divorce. The dimension of parenting referred to as *control* has been the focus of considerable debate in child psychology. When a wide variety of ways that parents can deal with children are surveyed, the dimensions of **control-autonomy** and **warmth-hostility** frequently appear.

Control-Autonomy The control-autonomy dimension of parenting refers to the parents' establishment and enforcement of rules and to the techniques used to promote or hinder the child's development of independence. Control-autonomy actually can be subdivided into **psychological control-psychological autonomy** and **firm control-lax control.** Psychological control consists of parental behavior that keeps the child closely tied to the parent, while psychological autonomy refers to parent behavior that allows the child to develop more independently. Firm control occurs when the parent sets rules and regulations and requires the child to abide by them, while lax control results when the parent establishes rules but does not enforce them or does not develop clear-cut standards for the child's behavior.

How do these parenting orientations influence the child's social behavior? A high degree of psychological control promotes dependent, regressive behavior—crying and thumb sucking, for example—and difficulty in establishing peer relationships (Armentrout & Burger, 1972; Schaefer, 1965). Also, extensive control of the child's activities and demands for obedience by

Box 8.1
Authoritarian, Authoritative, and Laissez-Faire Parenting

Diana Baumrind (1971) emphasizes three types of parenting that are associated with different aspects of the child's social behavior: authoritarian, authoritative, and laissez-faire (permissive).

Authoritarian parenting describes parents who are restrictive, have a punitive orientation, exhort the child to follow their directions, respect work and effort, and place limits and controls on the child, with little verbal give-and-take between parent and child. This type of parenting behavior is linked with the following social behaviors of the child: an anxiety about social comparison, failure to initiate activity, and ineffective social interaction.

Authoritative parenting encourages the child to be independent but still places limits, demands, and controls on actions. There is extensive verbal give-and-take, and parents demonstrate a high degree of warmth and nurturance toward the child. This type of parenting behavior is associated with social competency, particularly self-reliance and social responsibility.

Laissez-faire (permissive) parenting places relatively low demands, limits, and controls on the child's behavior.

The child is given considerable freedom to regulate his or her own behavior, with parents taking a nunpunitive stance. Parents are not very involved with their child. This type of parenting behavior is associated with the following social behaviors of the child: immature, regressive behavior, poor self-restraint, and inability to direct and assume leadership.

Perhaps the most significant distinction is between authoritarian and authoritative parenting. For many years arguments have been aired about the best way to rear children. Is an authoritarian style better than a permissive style? Or vice versa? Many parents were not completely satisfied with either approach. The same could be said for teachers. Many teachers were afraid they would be branded "punitive," "harsh," or "cold" if they tried to exert control over the children in their classrooms—particularly where child-centered, affective, and humanistic educational approaches are popular. However, many teachers and parents alike believe that a controlling but warm approach may be best.

parents may result in inhibited, shy behavior in children, while little or no parental control is often related to impulsive behavior in children (Armentrout & Burger, 1972; Baumrind, 1971; Kagan & Moss, 1962). Competent parenting is characterized, then, by behavior that is neither excessively high nor low in control. Diana Baumrind's (1971) research supports the belief that parents should be neither punitive toward their children nor aloof from them, but rather should develop rules and regulations for their children and enforce them. See box 8.1 for a description of Baumrind's parenting styles.

Warmth-Hostility   Note that one component of competent parenting in Baumrind's research is warmth and verbal give-and-take between the parent and child. Warmth-hostility (sometimes referred to as acceptance-rejection) in parenting is associated with predictable social behavior in children (Banister & Ravden, 1944; Goldfarb, 1945; McCord, McCord, & Howard, 1961). Overly hostile parents who show little affection toward their children have children who show patterns of hostile and aggressive behavior. Parents who show a high degree of warmth, nurturance, and acceptance toward their children have children who show

high self-esteem (Coopersmith, 1967) and altruism (Zahn-Waxler, Radke-Yarrow, & King, 1979). It also should be mentioned that parents who show warmth toward their children are more likely to use reasoning and explanation in dealing with their children's transgressions than parents who are aloof and cold toward their children. The use of reasoning during discipline helps children to internalize rules and regulations and to understand the circumstances in which they can act in particular ways. The parent's nurturant orientation toward the child makes that parent someone the child wants to approach rather than avoid, increasing the likelihood of interaction between them. And parental warmth, rather than hostility and punitiveness, helps to reduce anxiety and make the parent-child relationship less fearful and power-oriented for the child.

Child Abuse
Unfortunately, parental hostility toward children in some families reaches the point where one or both parents abuse the child. Child abuse is an increasing problem in the United States (Parke & Lewis, 1980, Starr,

1979). Estimates of its incidence vary, but some authorities say that as many as five-hundred-thousand children are physically abused in the United States each year. Laws in many states now require doctors and even teachers to report suspected cases of child abuse. Yet many cases go unreported, particularly those of "battered" infants.

The government, psychologists, and educators have shown more interest in child abuse in recent years. In 1974 the federal government gave $85 million to local communities for programs dealing with child abuse, and research efforts to understand the causes of child abuse and ways to help its offenders have increased.

For several years it was believed that parents who committed child abuse were severely disturbed, "sick" individuals. Recent research, however, reveals that parents who abuse their children are rarely psychotic (Blumberg, 1974). Ross Parke (Parke, 1976; Parke & Collmer, 1976; Parke & Lewis, 1980) has developed a model for understanding child abuse that shifts the focus from the personality traits of the parents to an analysis of three aspects of the social environment—cultural, familial, and community influences.

The extensive violence in the American culture is reflected in the occurrence of violence in the family. Violence occurs regularly on television, and parents frequently resort to power assertion as a disciplinary technique. Cross-cultural studies indicate that American television contains more violence than British television (Geis & Monahan, 1976) and that in China, where physical punishment is rarely used to discipline children, the incidence of child abuse is very low (Stevenson, 1974).

To understand child abuse in the family, the interaction of all family members should be considered, regardless of who actually performs the violent acts against the child. Even though the father, for example, may be the person who has physically abused the child, contributions of the mother, the father, and the child should be evaluated.

Many parents who abuse their children come from families in which physical punishment was used. They may view physical punishment as a legitimate way of controlling the child's behavior, and physical abuse may be a part of this sanctioning. Many aspects of the ongoing interaction among immediate family members also affect the incidence of child abuse. The child may have some effect—for example, an unattractive child experiences more physical punishment than an attractive child (Dion, 1974), and a child from an unwanted pregnancy may be especially vulnerable to abuse (Birrell & Birrell, 1968).

The interaction of the parents with each other may lead to child abuse as well. Dominant-submissive husband-wife pairs have been linked with child abuse (Terr, 1970). Husband-wife violence or such stressful family situations as those caused by financial problems, for example, may erupt in the form of aggression directed against the defenseless child. Such displaced aggression, whereby a person shifts an aggressive reaction from the original target person or situation to some other person or situation, is a common cause of child abuse.

Community-based support systems are extremely important in alleviating stressful family situations and thereby preventing child abuse. A study of the support systems in fifty-eight counties in New York state revealed a relationship between the incidence of child abuse and the presence of support systems available to the family. Both family resources—relatives and friends, for example,—and such formal support systems of the community as crisis centers and child-abuse counseling were associated with a reduction in child abuse (Garbarino, 1976). In sum, the family should not be viewed as an independent social unit, but as embedded in a broader social network of informal and formal community-based support systems (Parke, 1976).

Peers

Children show a heightened interest in peers during early childhood. Initially, the main functions of the peer group will be discussed, followed by an aspect of early childhood that dominates a great deal of many young children's lives—play. In the last section, the manner in which the family and peers interact is evaluated.

Functions of the Peer Group

Children spend a great deal of time with their peers; many of their greatest frustrations and happiest moments come when with their peers. The term *peers* usually refers to children who are about the same age, but children often interact with children who are three or four years older or younger. Peers also have been described as children who interact at about the same behavioral level (Lewis & Rosenblum, 1975). Defining peers in terms of behavioral level places more emphasis on the maturity of the children than on their age. For example, consider the precociously developed thirteen-year-old female adolescent who feels very funny around underdeveloped girls her own age. She may well find more satisfaction in time spent with adolescents of seventeen to eighteen years of age than with those her own age.

The influence of children who are the same age may be quite different from that of younger or older peers. For example, mixed-age groups often produce more dominant and altruistic behavior than do groups of

The term peers *usually refers to children who are about the same age.*

children of the same age (Murphy, 1937). Social contacts and aggression, though, are more characteristic of same-age peers (Hartup, 1979). Willard Hartup (1976), however, has emphasized that same-age peer interaction serves a unique role in our culture.

I am convinced that age grading would occur even if our schools were not age graded and children were left alone to determine the composition of their own societies. After all, one can only learn to be a good fighter among agemates: the bigger guys will kill you, and the littler ones are no challenge. (p. 10)

Perhaps one of the most important functions of the peer group is to provide a source of information and comparison about the world outside the family. From the peer group the child receives feedback about his or her abilities. The child evaluates what he or she does in terms of whether it is better than, as good as, or worse than what other children do. It is hard to do this at home because siblings are usually older or younger.

Studies about the necessity of peers for competent social development have been limited primarily to animals. For example, when peer monkeys who have been reared together are separated from each other, indications of depression and less advanced social development are observed (Suomi, Harlow, & Domek, 1970). Attempts to use peer monkeys to counteract the effects of social isolation prove more beneficial when

the deprived monkeys are placed with younger peers (Suomi & Harlow, 1972). Willard Hartup (Furman, Rahe, & Hartup, 1979) is trying out the younger-peer therapeutic technique with human peer isolates in a nursery school. Initial reports indicate that the technique is as effective with humans as it has been with monkeys.

In the human development literature there is a classic example of the importance of peers. Freud and Dann (1951) studied six children from different families who banded together after their parents were killed in World War II. Intensive peer attachment was observed; the children were a tightly knit group, dependent on one another and aloof with outsiders. Even though deprived of parental care, they became neither delinquent nor psychotic.

The frequency of peer interaction, both positive and negative, continues to increase throughout early childhood (Hartup, 1982). Although aggressive interaction and rough-and-tumble play increase, the *proportion* of aggressive exchanges to friendly interactions decreases, especially among middle-class boys. Children tend to abandon this immature and inefficient social interaction with age and acquire more mature methods of relating to peers.

Socialization cannot be described solely in terms of the quality of social activity, however. Evidence suggests that social differentiation is also a major achievement of the maturing child. They become more adept at using social skills, so that by the end of the preschool years, a rudimentary peer system has emerged.

Play

Perhaps the most elaborate attempt to examine developmental changes in children's social play was conducted many years ago by Mildred Parten (1932). Based on observations of children in free play at nursery schools, she developed the following categories of play.

Unoccupied The child is not engaging in play as it is commonly understood. He or she may stand in one spot, look around the room, or perform random movements that seem to have no goal. In most nursery schools unoccupied play is less frequent than other types of play.

Solitary The child plays independently. The child seems engrossed in what he or she is doing and does not care much about anything else that is going on. Parten found that two- and three-year-olds engage more frequently in solitary play than older preschoolers do.

The frequency of peer interactions, both positive and negative, increases throughout childhood.

Onlooker The child watches other children playing. He or she may talk with them or ask questions but does not enter into their play behavior. The child's active interest in other children's play distinguishes this type of play from unoccupied play.

Parallel The child plays alone but with toys like those that other children are using or in a manner that mimics the behavior of other playing children. The older the child, the less frequently he or she engages in this type of play; even older preschool children, however, engage in parallel play relatively often.

Associative Social interaction is involved in associative play, but with little or no organization. Children engage in play activities similar to those of other children; however, they appear to be more interested in being associated with each other than in the tasks they are involved with. Borrowing or lending toys and materials, and following or leading one another in a line, are examples of associative play. The child plays as he or she wishes; there is no effort at placing the group first and himself or herself last.

Cooperative Social interaction in a group characterizes cooperative play. A sense of group identity is present, and activity is organized. Children's formal games, competition aimed at winning something, and groups formed by the teacher for doing

things together usually are examples of this type of play. Cooperative play is the prototype for the games of middle childhood; little of it is seen in the preschool years.

Parten's categories are still a relevant and valuable method for observing children. You may want to plan a project of your own on the nature of children's play and use these categories as the basis of your study. Box 8.2 suggests a few projects involving observation of children's play.

To see whether Parten's findings were dated, Keith Barnes (1971) observed a group of preschoolers using Parten's categories of play. He watched the children's activities during an hour-long free-play period each schoolday for twelve weeks. He found that children in the 1970s did not engage in as much associative or cooperative play as they did in the 1930s. Several reasons were advanced to explain this difference: (1) children have become more passive because of television viewing; (2) toys today are more abundant and attractive than they were forty years ago, so solitary play may be more natural; and (3) parents today may encourage children to play by themselves more than parents did years ago.

During the preschool years peer interaction may involve highly ritualized social interchanges. A **ritual** is a form of spontaneous play that involves controlled repetition. These interchanges have been referred to as *turns* and *rounds* by Katherine Garvey (1977). The contribution of each child is called a turn, while the total sequence of alternating turns constitutes a round. Following is an example of a round between two five-year-olds.

Two- and three-year-olds engage more frequently in solitary play than do older preschoolers.

Boy	Girl
(1) Can you carry this?	(2) Yeah, if I weighed fifty pounds.
(3) You can't even carry it.	
Ritual	
(4) Can you carry it by the string?	(5) Yeah. Yes, I can (lifts toy fish overhead by string)
(6) Can you carry it by the eye?	(7) (carries it by eye)
(8) Can you carry it by the nose?	(9) Where's the nose?
(10) That yellow one.	(11) This (carries it by nose)
Ritual	
(12) Can you carry it by its tail?	(13) Yeah, (carries it by tail)
(14) Can you carry it by its fur?	(15) (carries it by fur)
(16) Can you carry it by its body?	(17) (carries it by body)
(18) Can you carry it like this? (shows how to carry it by fin)	(19) (carries it by fin)
(20) Right.	(21) I weigh fifty pounds almost, right? (pp. 118–19)

In this ritual between a five-year-old boy and girl, both language and motion were involved. The boy's turns were verbal; the girl's mainly variations of picking up and carrying the fish. In Garvey's (1977) work, there was a tendency for the five-year-old children to engage in more complex rituals than younger children, but three-year-old children were more likely to participate in longer rituals than their older counterparts. For

Box 8.2
Observing Children's Play

The best way to find out more about children is to spend some time observing them. If there is a preschool program at your college or university, try to spend some time there with the children. If not, you can observe children at playgrounds, at club meetings, on sport teams, in grocery stores, and in homes. As long as you ask for permission, most authorities are likely to let you observe children in natural settings. (It would not be a wise strategy simply to walk into a school and start taking notes!)

There are numerous projects that involve children's play. A simple one calls for observing same-sexed play groups and mixed-sex play groups. Develop a hypothesis about social interaction, whether it would be the same or different in all-boy, all-girl, and boy-girl play groups. Then find three groups of children that reflect these combinations. You can record your observations in the form of a running commentary about what you are seeing, or you can devise specific categories (e.g., Parten's classification or categories like aggression, dependency, and masculine-feminine interests) and check each incidence of the behaviors during your observation.

Other projects might focus on children of different ages, perhaps three-year-olds and five-year-olds, or children with same-aged peers and cross-aged peers.

example, a ritual among three-year-olds might involve the sequence "You're a girl," "No, I'm not," repeated for as long as several minutes. As children become older and enter the elementary school years, rituals may become more formal and can be found in games like red rover and London Bridge.

When children are asked what they enjoy most, they invariably say "playing." When children talk with each other, the word *play* is conspicuous: "What can we play?" "Let's play hide-and-seek." "No, let's play outside." "Why don't we play tag?" The major portion of many young children's days are spent in play. In the next section, we look at what could be called the typical play of children, pretend play, and discuss the various functions play can fulfill in the child's development.

Associative play is more characteristic of older children.

In pretend play, children try out many different roles.

Pretend Play

Greta Fein (1978) indicates that when children engage in **pretend play** they have transformed the physical environment into a symbol. Make-believe play appears rather abruptly at about eighteen months of age, continues to develop between ages three and four, peaks between five and six years, and then declines. In the early elementary school years children's interests begin to shift to games.

In pretend play, children try out many different roles—they may be the mother, the father, the teacher, the next-door neighbor, and so forth. Sometimes their pretend play reflects an adult role; at others it may make fun of it. An example of pretend play follows (Hartley, Frank, & Goldenson, 1952).

Harvey was playing with Karen, his twin sister. Karen began to push the carriage. Harvey said, "Let me be the baby, Karen," and started to talk like a baby. He got into the carriage. Karen pushed him around the room as he squinted his eyes and cried. She stopped the carriage, patted his shoulder, he squinted his eyes and cried. She stopped the carriage, patted his shoulder, saying, "Don't cry baby." He squirmed around, put his thumb in his mouth, and swayed his body.

Josie came to the carriage and wanted to push Harvey. He jumped out and hit her in the face. She walked away almost crying. He went to her, put his arm around her and said, in a sympathetic manner, "Come, you be the baby, I'll push you in the carriage." She climbed in. He ran and got the dog and gave it to her saying, "Here, baby." She smiled and began to play with the dog. He went to the housekeeping corner, got a cup and held it to her mouth. He smacked his lips, looking at her, smiling. He pushed her around in the carriage. Karen ran to him and said, "Harvey, let me push the carriage, I'll be the mamma, you be the daddy." Harvey said "O.K.," and reached his hand in his pocket and gave her money. He said, "Bye, baby," waving his hand. (pp. 70–72)

You probably can remember many episodes of pretend play from your own childhood—playing doctor, teacher, superman, and so on. One of the many functions of play is to maintain affiliation with peers. Play also allows the child to work out anxieties and conflicts, advances cognitive development, provides an opportunity to practice the roles he or she will assume later in life, and to explore the world.

Play is an elusive concept. It can range from an infant's simple exercise of a new-found sensorimotor talent to the preschool child's riding a tricycle to the older child's participation in organized games. One expert on play and games has observed that there is no universally accepted definition of play, probably because it can encompass so many different kinds of activities (Sutton-Smith, 1973).

Next we see that we can benefit by looking at the social worlds of peers and the family simultaneously.

Family and Peers

Peer relations are both similar to and different from parent-child relations. For example, infants touch, smile, and vocalize when they interact with both parents and other children (Eckerman, Whatley, & Kutz, 1975). However, rough-and-tumble play occurs mainly with other children and not with adults. Another difference in children's orientation toward peers and parents is that in times of stress, children usually move toward their parents rather than their peers (Maccoby & Masters, 1970). Willard Hartup (1979) described some of the most important ideas about the interrelation of the worlds of child-child and parent-child relations.

As children grow older, their interactions with adult associates and with child associates become more extensively differentiated: (a) Different actions are used to express affection to child associates and to adults, and (b) dominance and nurturance are directed from adults to children, but appeals and submissions are directed more frequently by children to adults than vice versa.

The evidence, then, suggests that children live in distinctive, albeit coordinate, social worlds. Family relations and peer relations constitute similar sociobehavioral contexts in some ways and different ones in others. Children may not conceive of separate normative worlds until early adolescence, because child associates are not used extensively as normative models before that time (Emmerich, Goldman, & Shore, 1971). But the family system and the peer system elicit distinctive socioemotional activity many years before these normative distinctions are made. The complex interrelations between the family and peer systems thus work themselves out over long periods of time (Hill, 1980). (pp. 947–48)

More specifically, it has been argued by ethologists that the role of the mother is to provide a "secure" base for the child's early attachment, which in turn reduces the child's fears and promotes exploration of the environment. The reduction in fear and increase in exploratory behavior could be expected to increase the likelihood that the child would seek out age-mates with whom to play. And, while parents are not usually as good at playing with their children as children are among themselves, parents, and particularly mothers, often take an active role in monitoring their children's choice of playmates and the form of their play.

Recent research supports the contention that a secure early attachment to the mother promotes positive peer relations (e.g., Easterbrooks & Lamb, 1979; Lieberman, 1977; Waters, Wippman, & Sroufe, in press). For example, in one investigation a group of fifteen-month-old infants were observed interacting with their mothers and classified by the observers as "securely" or "anxiously" attached. Later, when the children were three-and-one-half years old, they were observed during peer interaction for a period of five weeks. Compared with their "anxiously" attached age-mates, the "securely" attached children were more socially active, more often sought out by other children, more likely to serve as leaders, and more sympathetic to the distress of their peers.

Hartup (1979) cautions, however, that it is risky to conclude that healthy parent-child relations are a prerequisite for healthy peer relations. Nonetheless, the data are consistent with the theory that the child's relations with his or her parents serve as emotional bases for exploring and enjoying positive peer relations.

So far in this chapter we have seen that the social worlds of family and peers play primary roles in the child's social and emotional development. During early childhood, most children are extensively exposed to television—next we explore the effects of television on development.

The Role of Television

Television has been called a lot of things, not all of them good; depending on one's point of view, it may be a window on the world, the one-eyed monster, or the boob tube. Television has been attacked as one of the reasons that scores on national achievement tests in reading and mathematics are lower now than they have been in the past. Television, it is claimed, attracts children away from books and schoolwork. Furthermore, it is argued that television trains the child to become a passive learner; rarely, if ever, does television call for active responses from the observer.

Of particular concern has been the extent to which children are exposed to violence and aggression on television. Up to 80 percent of the prime-time shows include such violent acts as beatings, shootings, or stabbings. And there are usually about five of these violent acts per hour on prime-time shows. The frequency of violence is even greater on the Saturday morning cartoon shows, where there is an average of more than twenty-five violent episodes per hour (Friedrich & Stein, 1973).

Television also is said to deceive, that is, it teaches children that problems are easily resolved and that everything always comes out right in the end. For example, it usually takes only from thirty to ninety minutes for detectives to sort through a complex array of clues and discover the killer—and they always find the killer. Violence is pictured as a way of life in many shows. It is all right for police to use violence and to break moral codes in their fight against evildoers. And the lasting results of violence are rarely brought home to the viewer. A person who is injured appears to suffer for only a few seconds, even though in real life a person with such an injury may not recover for several weeks or months or perhaps not at all. Yet one out of every two first-grade children says that the adults on television are like adults in real life (Lyle & Hoffman, 1972).

"Don't worry over the African situation. Tarzan will turn up to straighten it out!"

Reprinted by permission of NEA.

Children watch a lot of television, and they seem to be watching more all the time. In the 1950s three-year-olds watched television for less than one hour a day, and five-year-olds watched for slightly over two hours a day (Schramm, Lyle, & Parker, 1961). But in the 1970s preschool children watched television for an average of four hours a day, and elementary school children watched for as long as six hours each day (Friedrich & Stein, 1973).

Aletha Stein (1972) has described some of the different patterns of children's exposure to the media. Other than television, the only medium reaching large numbers of children in this country is books. Children also read comic books, magazines, and some newspaper comic strips; they go to movies; and they listen to the radio and to their records and tapes. Television, comic books, movies, and comic strips can be thought of as pictorial media; the children who use one of these pictorial media regularly tend to use the others also. But children who frequently use pictorial media are not necessarily frequent consumers of the printed media, such as books and the written, nonpictorial parts of newspapers and magazines (e.g., Greenberg & Domonick, 1969). Their use of the pictorial media increases until they are about twelve, after which time it declines. Children from low-income backgrounds use pictorial media more than children from middle-income homes, and black children are exposed to pictorial media more than white children (Schramm et al., 1961).

Television As a Socialization Agent

George Comstock (1978) argues that television is such a strong socialization force on the child that it should be given status as a social agent, competing with parents, teachers, and other agents in providing models for emulation and information that influence the child's beliefs, values, and expectations. What social scientists are not sure of is whether television's influence is positive or negative.

Earlier, a number of negative comments were made about the effects of television on children. However, there are some possible positive aspects to its influences on children as well. For one, television presents the child with a world that is often different than the one he or she lives in. This means that through television the child is exposed to a wider variety of views and knowledge than may be the case from parents, teachers, or peers.

Television is also a medium through which the child can learn new behaviors. The modeling theory of Albert Bandura (e.g., Bandura, 1977) has served as a theoretical source for a number of inquiries about observational learning and the effects of television on children.

Television's Influences on Behavior

Television affects children's behavior as well as their values and attitudes. For instance, television violence contributes to antisocial behavior in children, particularly their aggression toward other children. Let's look at one example that demonstrates this fact clearly. One group of children was exposed to cartoons of the violent Saturday morning type; another group was shown the same cartoons with the violence removed. Children who saw the cartoons with the violence later kicked, choked, and pushed their friends more than the children who saw the same cartoons without the violent acts (Steuer, Applefield, & Smith, 1971).

When children watch television, they not only see cartoon shows and adult programs, but they also are exposed to commercials. The average television-viewing child, somewhat amazingly, sees over 20,000 commercials per year. A significant proportion of those commercials involve highly sugared food products (Barcus, 1978). To investigate the effects of television food commercials and pronutritional public service announcements on children's snack choices, Joann Galst (1980) exposed three- to six-year-old children to television cartoons over a four-week period. The advertising content of the shows consisted of either commercials for food products with added sugar content, for food products with no added sugar content, or pronutritional public service announcements. The children were allowed to select a snack each day after the television show. The no-sugar commercial and the pronutritional public service announcement were the most effective in reducing children's selection of sugar-added snacks.

Kohlberg's View of the Development of the Self

In Kohlberg's theory (1976) there are three major stages of the self that each individual moves through. The first stage is called the **concrete-individual perspective** and is usually attained during early and middle childhood. During infancy, the individual discovers that he or she is distinct from the objects of the world. During the early and middle childhood years, he or she becomes preoccupied with the distinctiveness of himself or herself and perceives the world as revolving around him or her. At this stage all social judgments and styles of interaction focus on the tangible feelings and needs of the self.

In late childhood and adolescence, a second stage of self-development appears, the **member-of-society perspective.** The individual at this stage sees himself or herself as a member of a larger social unit—a family, a school, a city, a culture, and so forth. Linked to such perceptions of self are judgments the individual makes to preserve the social order and fit each member of society into it.

The third and final level of self-development from Kohlberg's perspective is the **prior-to-society perspective.** At this stage, the self is perceived as a member of many different social units, each with an arbitrary membership determined by many uncontrollable factors. Social units are thought of as convenient and imperfect systems developed by people to assist them in getting along with each other. Consequently, the continued presence of these systems must be evaluated against the principles that all people share in common. Such universal principles are believed to be independent of a particular society or culture; instead, they rest in the mature structure of the individual's ego development.

Television can also teach children that it is better to behave in prosocial rather than in antisocial ways. Aimee Leifer (1973) has demonstrated how television can instill prosocial behaviors in young children. From the television show "Sesame Street" she selected a number of episodes that reflected positive social interchanges. She was particularly interested in situations that teach the child how to use social skills. For example, in one exchange two men were fighting over the amount of space available to them; they gradually began to cooperate and to share the space. Children who watched these episodes copied these behaviors and in later social situations applied the lessons they had learned.

Personality Development

In this section, we describe three of the most important aspects of personality development in early childhood—the self, sex-typed behavior, and moral development.

The Self

You saw in chapter 2 that the self is the fundamental unit in the humanistic perspective of development. The self also is an important part of the cognitive structural view of Lawrence Kohlberg. Kohlberg (1976) believes that personality develops within the framework of Piaget's stages of cognitive development. The concept of personality structure, then, is a part of rational thinking and the development of cognitive structures. The various strands of personality development (such as sex-role development, morality, identity, and so forth) are wired together by the child's developing sense of self and perceptions of the self in relation to other individuals (particularly in role-taking relationships). In box 8.3 Kohlberg's developmental view of the self is outlined.

Recently, investigators such as John Flavell (Flavell, Shipstead, & Croft, 1978) have found that children as young as three years of age have a basic idea that they have a private self to which others do not have access. Flavell reports the following exchange between an experimenter and a three-year-old:

(Can I see you thinking?) "No." (Even if I look in your eyes, do I see you thinking?) "No." (Why not?) "Cause I don't have any big holes." (You mean there would have to be a hole there for me to see you thinking?) Child nods. (p. 16)

Another child said that the experimenter could not see his thinking processes because he had skin over his head.

Young children also distinguish this inner self from their bodily self or outer self, a distinction that seems to emerge sometime between three and four years of age. After they have developed an understanding that they have a private self, children then set about the task of defining the characteristics of their private self.

A child's environment determines the degree of sex-typed behavior.

Eleanor Maccoby (1980) concluded that intially children's self-definition focuses on external characteristics, such as how they look, where they live, and what activities they are involved in, but later—after about the age of six or seven—they begin to describe themselves more in terms of psychological traits (e.g., how they feel, their personality characteristics, and their relationships with others). And with increasing age, group membership assumes a more important status in self-definition.

Sex-Typed Behavior

All of us, particularly young children, are curious about our gender. Do you remember the images you had when you were young of what girls and boys must be like? And the way your parents might have stumbled in trying to answer your questions about sexuality?

In this first section we will look in depth at a concept mentioned in the prologue, that of androgyny. As part of this discussion, definitions of a number of terms related to sex-role development will be given. The roles of biology, cognition, and the developmental course of sex roles will be discussed, followed by material on the role of the environment in sex-role development.

Androgyny and the Components of Sex-Role Development

The label **sex role** has been used to describe the different characteristics children display because of their sex. However, some experts (e.g., Spence & Helmreich, 1978) define sex role as the behaviors that are *expected* of children because they are either male or female.

Another important aspect of the child's sexual makeup is what is referred to as **sexual, or gender, identity.** We can define this as the extent to which individual children actually take on as part of their personalities the behaviors and attitudes associated with either the male or female role. In the United States and in most other countries, the well-adjusted child has traditionally been one who has developed a sex-appropriate sex role. That is, males are supposed to be "masculine" and females are supposed to be "feminine." In past years most research on children's sex roles has been conducted along this line; researchers have assessed the concept of sex roles as a bipolar construct, with masculinity and femininity considered as opposites. Recently, an alternative view of children's sex roles has been developed and is based on the concept of **androgyny.**

The belief that masculinity and femininity are opposites was refuted by psychologists in the mid-1970s when they began to suggest not only that masculinity and femininity are independent of one another but also that the healthiest way to conceive of sex roles may be to view all children as having both masculine and feminine characteristics.

Androgyny has become a byword in research on sex roles in the late 1970s and early 1980s. What does it mean if we say twelve-year-old Bob is androgynous? It means that his psychological makeup includes both masculine and feminine aspects of behavior; sometimes it is said that people like Bob have an androgynous sex-role orientation. Sandra Bem (1974, 1977) and Janet Spence (Spence & Helmreich, 1978; Spence, Helmreich, & Stapp, 1974) pioneered the notion that sex roles should not be looked at as bipolar sexual extremes but rather as dualistic dimensions within each sex. In other words every male child has and should have some feminine attributes, and every female child has and should have some masculine attributes. Furthermore, both Bem and Spence believe that androgyny is not only natural but allows the child to adapt more competently to a wide variety of situations (e.g., Spence, 1982).

Sandra Bem created the Bem Sex Role Inventory (BSRI) and Janet Spence developed the Personality Attributes Questionnaire (PAQ), both of which measure androgyny. Spence (Spence & Helmreich, 1978) recently developed the Child's Personal Attributes Questionnaire (Children's PAQ) to assess children's androgyny.

The Children's PAQ includes such positively valued "masculine" traits as independence, competitiveness, ability to make decisions easily, unwillingness to give up easily, self-confidence, and a sense of superiority; while positive "feminine" characteristics include gentleness, helpfulness, kindness, and awareness of others' feelings. While androgyny has been scored in different ways by researchers, Spence had her colleagues (Spence, Helmreich, & Stapp, 1975) advocate classifying those who score high on both the feminine and masculine scales as androgynous. Individuals who score low on both the masculine and feminine scales are labeled "undifferentiated"; and the sex role is categorized as "masculine" or "feminine" if the child scores high on one scale and low on the other.

Androgynous children are viewed positively for two reasons. First, the classification of a child as androgynous is based on the appearance of both masculine and feminine characteristics rather than the absence of both. Second, and more importantly, the attributes that comprise androgyny are those aspects of masculinity and femininity that are valued by our culture. The androgynous child is achievement oriented, shows high self-esteem, is a warm individual, and so on (Babladelis, 1979).

Not everyone agrees with Spence and Bem's belief that we ought to be developing androgynous individuals. For example, the culmination of Phyllis Katz's (1979) developmental view is conformity to socially prescribed sex roles. She believes that sex-role socialization is a lifelong process and that socialization agents outside of the family play more important roles than was previously thought. The first developmental period

in her theory is infancy-puberty, at which time children learn appropriate child sex roles. During adolescence, a second developmental period appears in the form of preparation for adult sex roles. Sexual maturation, heterosexual relationships, and career goals represent areas of sexual change in adolescence. The third developmental level refers to adult sex-role development, involving adjustment to changing family structure and occupational roles. And, Diana Baumrind (1982), whose parenting styles were discussed, earlier, agrees that the most competent parents, adults, and children are traditionally sex-typed.

Biological Forces and Cognitive Factors and Development

There has been increased interest in the developmental aspects of sex roles in recent years, as witnessed by the number of theoretical views on sex roles that contain developmental components. Most developmental views of sex roles rely heavily on biological and cognitive processes, as will be seen next.

Biological Forces   One of Freud's basic assumptions is that human behavior and history are directly related to reproductive processes. From this assumption arises the belief that sexuality is essentially unlearned and *instinctual*. Erik Erikson (1951, 1963, 1968, 1974), has extended this argument, claiming that psychological differences in males and females stem from anatomical differences between the two groups. Erikson argues that because of genital structure, males are more intrusive and aggressive, while females are more inclusive and passive. Erikson's belief is sometimes referred to as the "anatomy is destiny" doctrine.

One period during which sex hormones are produced extensively is before birth. Anna Ehrhardt has extensively studied the influence of prenatal hormonal changes on sex-role development (Ehrhardt & Baker, 1973). In the 1950s a number of expectant mothers were given doses of androgen (a male sex hormone); these women had a history of miscarriage, and the hormone is believed to ameliorate conditions that cause this problem. Six offspring of these mothers were studied, ranging from four to twenty-six years of age. They were compared with siblings of the same sex whose mothers had not been treated with androgen during the prenatal period.

Results indicate that hormones are an important factor in sex-role development. The girls whose mothers received androgen expended comparatively more energy in their play and seemed to prefer boys over girls as playmates. Instead of dolls they chose male sex-typed toys for play. They displayed little interest in future marriage and did not enjoy taking care of babies.They also preferred functional over attractive clothes and were generally unconcerned with their appearance. The boys whose mothers received androgen engaged in rough-and-tumble play and outdoor sports to a greater extent than their unaffected brothers did.

Ehrhardt's work has been criticized for a number of reasons. For one, the inflated androgen levels require that these individuals be treated with cortisone for the remainder of their lives. One of the side effects of cortisone is a high activity level. The high energy and activity levels of the girls and boys, then, may be due to the cortisone treatment rather than to high levels of androgen (Quadagno, Briscoe, & Quadagno, 1977). Second, "masculinized" girls may be perceived as deviant by their parents, siblings, and peers. Those around them may have thought of them as "boys" and treated them accordingly.

No one argues the existence of genetic, biochemical, and anatomical differences between the sexes. Even environmentally oriented psychologists ackowledge that boys and girls will be treated differently because of their physical differences and their different roles in reproduction. Consequently, the importance of biological factors is not at issue; what is at issue is the directness or indirectness of the effect of biological factors on social behavior.

According to Aletha Huston, if a high androgen level directly influences the central nervous system, which in turn produces a higher activity level, then the effect is reasonably direct. By contrast, if a high level of androgen produces strong muscle development, which in turn causes others to expect the child to be a good athlete and in turn leads her to participate in sports, then the biological effect is more indirect.

Cognitive Factors and Development   In addition to biology and culture, cognitive development is an important aspect of understanding children's sex roles. In order to have an idea of what is masculine or feminine, Kohlberg (1966) asserts, the child has to be able to categorize objects and behaviors into these two groups. According to Kohlberg, the categories become relatively stable for a child by the age of six; that is, by this age children have a fairly definite idea of which category they belong to. Furthermore, they understand what is entailed by the category and seldom fluctuate in their category judgments. This self-categorization provides the impetus for the unfolding of sex-role development.

Kohlberg reasons that sex-role development proceeds in this sequence: "I am a boy, I want to do boy things, therefore, the opportunity to do boy things is rewarding" (p. 89). The child, having acquired the ability to categorize, strives toward consistency between use of the categories and actual behavior. This striving for consistency forms the basis for the development of sex typing.

A second developmental theory that has received attention in recent years is Jeanne Block's view that sex-role development is a component of a more general personality structure called the ego. According to Block (1973), sex-role development proceeds in the following invariant manner:

Stage 1: Gender identity and self-enhancement

Stage 2: External sex-role standards

Stage 3: Internalized sex-role standards

Stage 4: Androgyny

This type of development follows closely the thinking of Kohlberg (1976), who argues that development proceeds from preconformity, through conformity, to postconformity levels. Block believes that very young children are mainly concerned with assertion, extending their self, and becoming independent of parental restrictions. The second stage is the point at which conformity to rules and roles becomes more apparent. An important sex difference occurs at this stage in that boys are rewarded for controlling and suppressing affect and nurturance, while girls are rewarded for repressing assertiveness and aggressiveness. Block's last two stages occur primarily in adulthood and involve the perception that masculine and feminine elements can be integrated in the form of an androgynous personality.

Environmental Influences
In our culture adults begin to discriminate between sexes shortly after the infant's birth. The "pink and blue treatment" is often applied to girls and boys even before they leave the hospital. Soon afterward the differences in hair styles, clothes, and toys become obvious. Adults and other children reinforce these differences throughout childhood, but boys and girls also learn appropriate role behavior by watching what other people say and do. For example, a seven-year-old boy who knows he is a boy readily labels appropriate objects as male or female, but he has parents who support the feminist movement and stress equality between the sexes. His behavior will be less stereotyped along masculine lines than that of boys reared in more traditional homes.

One considerable change in the role of environmental influences on sex-role development in recent years has resulted in a de-emphasis on parents as the critical socialization agents. There has been a corresponding increase in the belief that schools, peers, the media, and other family members should be given more attention when the child's sex-role development is at issue. Parents clearly are only one of many sources through which children learn about sex-role development. Yet it is important to guard against swinging too far in this direction, because particularly in the early years of life, parents do play a very important role in their child's sex-role development.

The Role of Parents   Father and mothers both are psychologically important for children even during infancy. Fathers seem to play a particularly important role in the sex typing of both boys and girls. Reviews of sex-typing research indicate that fathers are more likely to act differently toward sons and daughters than mothers are (e.g., Huston, 1982). And most reviews of the father-absence literature (e.g., Lamb, 1981) conclude that boys show a more feminine patterning of behavior in father-absent than in father-present homes; however, close inspection of those studies suggest that this conclusion is more appropriate for young children, while the findings for elementary and secondary school children are mixed. For example, Hetherington, Cox, and Cox (1978) found that children's sex-typed behavior reflected more than the unavailability of a consistent adult male model. While many single-parent mothers were overprotective and apprehensive about their son's independence, when single parents encouraged masculine and exploratory behavior and did not have a negative attitude toward the absent father, disruption in the son's sex-typed behavior did not occur.

Many parents encourage boys and girls to engage in different types of play activities even during infancy. In particular many parents emphasize that doll play is for girls only, while boys are more likely to be rewarded for engaging in gross motor activities. And often parents play more actively with male babies and respond more positively to physical activity by boys. There also is some evidence that parents encourage girls to be more dependent, show affection, and express tender emotions than boys; but there is no indication that parents show different reactions to aggression according to their child's sex. And with increasing age, boys are permitted more freedom by parents (Huston, 1982).

Thus, we can see that parents, by action and example, influence their child's sex-role development. In the psychoanalytic view this influence stems principally from the child's identification with the parent of the same sex. The child develops a sense of likeness to the parent of the same sex and strives to emulate that parent.

Parents provide the earliest discrimination of sex-typed behavior in the child's development, but before long peers and teachers have joined the societal process of providing substantial feedback about masculine and feminine roles.

Teachers and Peers   Children have acquired a preference for sex-typed toys and activities before most of them are exposed to school. During the preschool and elementary school years, teachers and peers usually maintain these preferences through feedback.

Actual observations of teacher behavior in both preschool and elementary school classes suggests that boys are given more disapproval, scolding, and other forms of negative attention than girls (e.g., Cherry, 1975; Serbin, O'Leary, Kent, & Tonick, 1973). However, the findings for positive teacher behavior are mixed; some investigators find that teachers give more positive attention to girls (Fagot, 1973) while others find that boys get more positive attention (e.g., Serbin et al., 1973). Similarly there is no consistent evidence that teachers reward sex-typed social behaviors differently for boys and girls (Huston, 1982). Sometimes, however, the fact that boys do not do as well as girls in school early in their development is attributed to the fact that either female teachers treat boys differently than girls or that boys have few male models as teachers.

Female teachers are more likely to reward "feminine" behavior than "masculine" behavior. Fagot (1975) reasoned that teachers would most probably support student behaviors that were a part of their own behavioral system. Since most preschool and elementary school teachers are females, they would be expected to reward behaviors consistent with the feminine, or "good girl," stereotype. As expected, she found that teachers reinforced both boys' and girls' feminine behaviors 83 percent of the time. In a similar study McCandless (1973) found that female teachers rewarded feminine behaviors 51 percent of the time and masculine behaviors 49 percent of the time. Perhaps if more male adults were involved in early education, there would be more support of masculine behavior and activity.

Moral Development

In one sense moral development has a longer history than virtually any aspect of development we will discuss in this text. As you may recall reading in chapter 1, in prescientific periods philosophers and theologians heatedly debated the child's moral status at birth, which they felt had important implications for how the child was to be reared. Today people are hardly neutral about moral development; most have very strong opinions about acceptable and unacceptable behavior, ethical and unethical conduct, and the ways that acceptable and ethical behaviors are to be fostered in children.

Moral development concerns rules and conventions about what people should do in their interactions with other people. In studying these rules, psychologists examine three different domains of moral development. First, how do children reason or think about rules for

Children at the stage of moral realism believe that rules are unchangeable and are handed down by all-powerful authorities.

ethical conduct? For example, cheating is generally considered unacceptable. The child can be presented with a story in which someone has a conflict about whether or not to cheat in a specific situation. The child is asked to decide what is appropriate for the character to do, and why. The focus is thereby placed on the rationale, the type of reasoning the child uses to justify his or her moral decision.

A second domain concerns how children actually behave in the face of rules for ethical conduct. Here, for example, the concern is whether the child actually cheats in different situations and what factors influence this behavior.

A third domain concerns how the child feels after making a moral decision. There has been more interest in a child's feelings after doing something wrong than after doing something right. Here the concern is whether a child feels guilty as the result of having cheated. In the remainder of this section, attention will be directed at these three facets of moral development—thought, action, and feeling.

Moral Reasoning: Piaget's View

Jean Piaget is best known for his general theory of cognitive development. His greatest contribution to understanding socialization has been his thoughts and observations about moral development. Piaget conducted extensive observations and interviews with children from four to twelve years of age. He watched them in natural play with marbles, trying to understand the

manner in which they used and thought about the rules of the game. Later he asked them several questions about ethical concepts (e.g., theft, lies, punishment, justice) in order to arrive at a similar understanding of how children think about ethical rules.

Piaget concluded that there are two different modes (or stages) of moral thought. The more primitive one, **moral realism** is associated with younger children (from four to seven years old); the more advanced one, **moral autonomy,** is associated with older children (ten years old and older). Children from seven to ten years old are in a transition period between the two stages, evidencing some features of each.

What are some of the characteristics of these two stages? The *moral realist* judges the rightness or goodness of behavior by considering the consequences of the behavior, not the intentions of the actor. For example, a realist would say that breaking twelve cups accidentally is worse than breaking one cup intentionally while trying to steal a cookie. For the *moral autonomist,* the reverse is true; the intention of the actor becomes more important.

The *moral realist* believes that all rules are unchangeable and are handed down by all-powerful authorities. When Piaget suggested that new rules be introduced into the game of marbles, the young children became troubled; they insisted that the rules had always existed as they were and could not be changed. The *moral autonomist,* by contrast, accepts change and recognizes that rules are merely convenient, socially agreed-upon conventions, subject to change by consensus.

A third characteristic is the *moral realist's* belief in imminent justice—if a rule is broken, punishment will be meted out immediately. The realist believes that the violation is connected in some mechanical or reflexlike way to the punishment. Thus, young children often look around worriedly after committing a transgression, expecting inevitable punishment. The *moral autonomist* recognizes that punishment is a socially mediated event that occurs only if a relevant person witnesses the wrongdoing and even then punishment is not inevitable.

Do all children go through the stage of moral realism before they reach moral autonomy? In general, the answer is yes. Children from different cultures and social classes and with varying levels of intelligence move from realism to autonomy; in only one of a dozen or more studies was this finding contradicted (Hoffman, 1970). In that study, in six out of ten groups of Hopi Indians moral realism increased with age (Havighurst & Neugarten, 1955). Further situational differences in the Indian's moral judgments were found when they stated that although the rules of Indian games cannot be changed, the rules of American games can.

A second question related to Piaget's stages of moral judgment concerns their association with IQ. Is the child's general reasoning a part of moral decisions? A large portion of moral thought *is* made up of the child's ability to reason about nonmoral situations and dilemmas (e.g., Johnson, 1962).

A final important question is: Can we speed up the change from realism to autonomy? Several studies have dealt with this question by investigating whether acceleration can be accomplished through imitation (e.g., Bandura & MacDonald, 1963). In all of these studies children individually observed an adult model being reinforced for judgment of moral realism or moral autonomy. The results were consistent: exposure to a model who espouses a specific stage of moral development leads to significant changes in the child's moral judgments. These changes were still apparent two weeks later for one group of children, and three months later for another group (Cowen, Langer, Heavenrich, & Nathanson, 1969; LeFurgy & Woloshin, 1969). It was also noted that children who were realistic in their moral outlook to begin with reasoned more autonomously after exposure to autonomous models.

In chapter 12, when we discuss personality development in middle and late childhood, we will introduce a second cognitive perspective on moral development—Lawrence Kohlberg's stage theory. We have seen that moral thought is a central aspect of the child's moral development, but understanding development would be bankrupt if something is not also known about how they actually behave.

Moral Behavior

The study of moral behavior has been influenced primarily by social learning theory. The familiar processes of reinforcement, punishment, and imitation have been invoked to explain how and why children learn certain responses and why their responses differ from one another, and the general conclusions to be drawn are the same as elsewhere. When children are reinforced for behavior that is consistent with laws and social conventions, they are likely to repeat these behaviors. When models are provided who behave "morally," children are likely to adopt their actions. Finally, when children are punished for "immoral" or unacceptable behaviors, these behaviors can be eliminated, but at the expense of sanctioning punishment by its very use and of causing emotional side effects for the child.

The effectiveness of reward and punishment, of course, depends on the consistency with which they are administered and the schedule (e.g., continuous, partial) that is adopted. The effectiveness of modeling depends on the characteristics of the model (e.g., esteem, power) and the presence of symbolic codes to enhance retention of the modeled behavior. More about moral behavior will appear in this section when we discuss altruistic behavior and in chapter 12, when we focus on cheating.

The third facet of moral development—feelings—has a direct link to early childhood. Next we see that some prominent psychoanalytic thinkers believe early childhood is the period when guilt feelings are formed.

Moral Feelings and Guilt

Moral feelings have traditionally been thought of in terms of guilt, but recently there has been a great deal of interest in the role of empathy. **Empathy** is the ability to understand the feelings or ideas of another person. Emphasizing empathic response stresses the positive side of moral development more than its negative side.

In psychoanalytic accounts the development of **guilt** occurs in the following way. Through identification with parents and their use of love-withdrawal for disciplinary purposes, the child turns his or her hostility inward and experiences guilt. This guilt is primarily unconscious and reflects the structure of the personality known as the *superego* (recall the discussion in chapter 2). It is assumed that guilt-prone individuals avoid transgressing in order to avoid *anxiety;* on the other hand, the person with little guilt has little reason to resist temptation. Thus, in this view, guilt is responsible for harnessing the evil drives of the *id* and for maintaining the world as a safe place in which to live. In the psychoanalytic perspective early childhood is a particularly important period for the child's moral development. Recall that Erik Erikson even refers to early childhood as the initiative versus guilt stage.

Guilt and Empathy Children as well as adults often try to make sense out of their world by attributing causes to their behavior and the events around them. For example, when someone is in distress it would be expected that the child would make inferences about the cause of the victim's distress. The child's ideas about the cause of the victim's distress likely combine with empathic feelings that are aroused because of the victim's suffering to produce a feeling of guilt.

Based on ideas such as these, Martin Hoffman (in press) has been constructing a developmental theory of guilt that highlights empathic distress and causal attribution. Summarizing his findings thus far, Hoffman (1979) concluded:

A full guilt response occurs in children as early as six years (Thompson & Hoffman, in press), and a rudimentary response of guilt as early as two years (Zahn-Waxler et al., 1979).

Discipline that involves pointing out the effects of the child's behavior on others contributes to the development of guilt.

Arousal of empathic distress seems to intensify guilt feelings (Thompson & Hoffman, in press).

The arousal of guilt usually is followed by some type of reparative act toward the victim or toward others (Regan, 1971), or if neither is possible, a prolongation of guilt.

Guilt sometimes sets off a process of self-examination and reordering of values, as well as a resolution not to act so selfishly in the future (Hoffman, 1975).

The positive side of moral development can be evaluated by examining a trait such as **altruism** (or the selfless concern for the welfare of others). Altruism has been given a phenomenal amount of attention in recent years—so much that the study of altruism is competing with Kohlberg's theory as the aspect of moral development receiving the greatest amount of research interest.

Altruism and empathy play important roles in moral development.

Altruism
Altruistic behaviors include sharing possessions, contributing to worthy causes, and helping people in distress. In the following sections we will explore a number of different aspects of altruism. First, the developmental course of altruism will be charted, followed by a discussion of the roles empathy and perspective-taking play in promoting altruism.

The Development of Altruism In general, altruism increases as children develop (e.g., Underwood & Moore, 1980): older children usually are more likely to be helpful or to share than are younger children, and older children show a greater variety of prosocial behaviors. However, as the following vivid episode suggests, very young children, even as young as the second year of life, may display altruistic behavior (Zahn-Waxler et al., 1979).

Today Jerry was kind of cranky; he just started completely bawling and he wouldn't stop. John kept coming over and handing Jerry toys, trying to cheer him up, so to speak. He'd say things like "Here, Jerry," and I said to John: "Jerry's sad; he doesn't feel good; he had a shot today." John would look at me with his eyebrows kind of wrinkled together like he really understood that Jerry was crying because he was unhappy, not that he was just being a crybaby. He went over and rubbed Jerry's arm and said "Nice Jerry" and continued to give him toys. (pp. 321–22)

Clearly, John was touched by his friend Jerry's disturbed state and acted in an altruistic manner toward him. Rather amazingly, John was not quite two years old when this incident occurred.

TELL ME GURU..
...WHAT IS THE DIFFERENCE
BETWEEN EMPATHY
AND APATHY?

i DON'T KNOW
AND i DON'T CARE!

Martin Hoffman (1975) agrees that toddlers less than two years of age show empathy toward individuals they perceive to be in distress. He believes that the initial stress the child senses involves his or her own primary discomforts—hunger, thirst, and pain. For example, the sight of an alarmed mother quickly becomes associated with feeling states in the infant that cause him or her primary discomfort. The infant cannot distinguish between "self" and "other" and so may produce a distress response when another person is distressed. And as we saw in the interaction between Jerry and John, children also recognize noxious events experienced by others that they themselves have felt and likewise react to them with distress.

It also has been speculated that internalized motives and self-rewards (intrinsic rewards such as increased self-esteem or feelings of satisfaction following an action) influence many prosocial actions. And it seems likely that, as children become older, motives for assisting others become less dependent on external rewards, punishment, and the approval of authority. In this sense the development of altruism becomes more internalized with increasing age (Mussen & Eisenberg-Berg, 1977). Next, we see that age differences also likely occur in empathic responding as well.

Altruism and Empathy Empathic responding is viewed as a critical building block in forming a basic motive to help others, hence its important role in moral development. For example, very young children, approximately two to four years old, typically show empathy toward a hurt child, even though they sometimes do nothing or act inappropriately (e.g., Zahn-Waxler

et al., 1979). In addition to empathy, another factor important in promoting altruistic tendencies in children is role taking or perspective taking.

Role Taking and Perspective-Taking Skills **Role-taking** and **perspective-taking skills** refer to the understanding that other people have feelings and perceptions different from one's own. By seven or eight years of age, the child has mastered complex role-taking skills (Flavell, Botkin, Fry, Wright, & Jarvis, 1968; Selman, 1971), but there are others mastered as early as the age of two or three (Flavell, 1977). The elementary schoolchild's empathy is directed toward helping the other person, but he or she seeks to find the true source of the other person's distress. The child is also likely to discover the tentative and hypothetical nature of inferences. Thus, motivation to relieve the other's distress is less egocentric and based to a greater degree on the accurate assessment of the other's needs, trial and error, and response to corrective feedback (Hoffman, 1975).

Research focused on the link between role taking and altruism suggests that children who have well-developed role-taking skills show more kindness and helping behaviors toward other children (e.g., Rubin & Schneider, 1973). One investigator has successfully trained six-year-old children in role-taking skills and found that they subsequently have more altruistic tendencies than a nontrained group (Iannotti, 1978).

In addition to empathy and role taking, researchers have focused on the role parents play in the development of altruism, paying particular attention to nurturance, modeling, and preaching.

Nurturance and Modeling The work of Marian Radke-Yarrow (e.g., Radke-Yarrow & Zahn-Waxler, 1975) suggests that family experiences play a critical part in the development of altruistic behavior in children. Parents who modeled altruistic behaviors had boys and girls who displayed an altruistic orientation. Parental nurturance, particularly in the context of parental modeling of altruism, also was an important factor in whether boys and girls developed altruistic motives. Assignment of responsibility, maturity demands, and inductive discipline are other parental practices that promote altruism in boys and girls. Paul Mussen and Nancy Eisenberg-Berg (1977) stress that cultural factors outside the family, peer relations, and cognitive factors also have to be taken into account when the child's altruistic orientation is evaluated.

Summary

Parents and peers are clearly two of the most important social agents who influence the child's development. Children are exposed to a greater variety of family structures than in any other era of history. The two most profound changes in family structure are the increase in single-parent families and the entrance into the work force of a large number of mothers. Divorce rates are increasing exponentially, often leaving the child with feelings of loss and deprivation. The fact that the child's mother works outside the home does not necessarily lead to incompetent parenting on her part; it likely benefits some aspects of her relationship with her child and harms others. Many complex factors mediate the effects of father absence and the mother's employment outside the home on the child's development.

Psychologists have applied many labels to the socialization techniques parents use to deal with their children. Two dimensions psychologists have used to categorize parenting techniques are control-autonomy and warmth-hostility. In a comparison of authoritarian, authoritative, and laissez-faire parenting styles, only authoritative parenting was associated with social competence in children. There has been an increase in child abuse in the United States—psychologists believe that by analyzing cultural, familial, and community influences rather than focusing solely on negative personality traits of parents, child abuse can be better understood.

The child's development is also extensively influenced by peers, or age-mates, as they sometimes are referred to. The peer group provides a unique opportunity for practicing roles and finding out information about the world outside of the family.

During the toddler years toys take on increased importance during peer interaction, and in the preschool years words begin to replace toys as the primary medium of peer interaction. During the early years of the child's life play takes up a large portion of the day. Perhaps the most prolific form of play is pretend play, which allows the child to practice many different roles.

Family relations and peer relations constitute similar social worlds in some ways and different ones in others. For example, infants touch, smile, and vocalize when they interact with both parents and age-mates. Yet rough-and-tumble play occurs mainly with other children, not with adults. Family experiences may serve as a basis for the development of peer relations, positively through the mother's role as a secure attachment for the infant and negatively through the stress of divorce.

Another aspect of our culture that has a pervasive influence on children's development is television. Children often spend more time watching television than they do interacting with peers or parents; for this reason alone television merits consideration as a socializing influence. Television can produce both aggressive and prosocial behaviors. Its programs project many stereotypes of different groups and distorts reality—and the child's perceptions of reality—in its portrayal of events in everyday life. Changes have been observed in children's ability to distinguish between reality and fantasy, to remember what was shown, and to comprehend complex character motivation and behavior on television.

Our discussion of personality focused on three important aspects of early childhood—the self, sex-typed behavior, and moral development. Lawrence Kohlberg believes that self-development is rooted in the development of rational thought—in early childhood Kohlberg argues that the child is in the concrete-individual stage, a time when he or she becomes preoccupied with the distinctiveness of himself or herself and perceives that the world revolves around him or her. At some point during the preschool years, the child does discover that he or she has a private self to which others do not have access.

Traditionally sex roles have been studied in terms of a bipolar construct of masculinity and femininity. More recently, the concept of androgyny has been introduced. This concept suggests that every child is to some degree androgynous, having both feminine and masculine attributes. Knowledge of sex roles begins very early in development and is influenced by both biology and culture. In the period from eighteen months to three years, children begin to show a great deal of interest in sex-typed play and activities, and from age three to seven, they begin to understand the concept of gender constancy and to enjoy being with same-sex peers. Environmental influences on the child's sex-role development include a host of social agents and other aspects of the culture in which the child grows up, among them, parental standards, teacher-child relations, peer relations, and the media.

Moral development can be analyzed in terms of thought, behavior, and feeling. According to Piaget, children pass through universal, sequential stages in the way they think about moral problems. Moral behavior is believed to be learned in much the same way that social learning takes place, with the same learning principles and processes involved. Specific behaviors investigated by psychologists to understand and evaluate moral development in children include resistance to temptation and altruism. Measures of guilt have been the principal focus in the study of moral feelings, although guilt is difficult to measure reliably and therefore its influence, if any, on behavior is undetermined.

Considerable attention has been directed at the development of altruism in recent years. In general, altruism increases with age as children develop. However, altruism does occur even among toddlers and is influenced by empathy and role-taking skills. Nurturance and modeling represent two socialization processes available to parents who wish to advance their children's altruistic tendencies.

Key Terms

altruism
androgyny
associative play
authoritarian parenting
authoritative parenting
concrete-individual
  perspective
control-automony
cooperative play
empathy
firm control-lax control
guilt
laissez-faire (permissive)
  parenting
member-of-society
  perspective
moral autonomy
moral development

moral realism
onlooker play
parallel play
perspective-taking skills
pretend play
prior-to-society
  perspective
psychological control-
  psychological autonomy
ritual
role taking
sex role
sex-typed behavior
sexual (gender) identity
solitary play
unoccupied play
warmth-hostility

Review Questions

1. Describe how parents should adapt to the developing child and how changes in parents can influence the child.
2. How is the structure of the family changing, and how have these changes influenced children?
3. What are some effective socialization techniques for dealing with children?
4. Discuss some of the positive and negative ways siblings can socialize each other.
5. Describe the development of peer relations in the first six years of life.
6. What function does play serve in the child's development?
7. Discuss the interrelation of the social world of the family and the social world of peers.
8. Describe some aspects of the child's life that are affected by television.
9. Describe some of the different components of sex typing.
10. How do cognitive developmental, social learning, and psychoanalytic theorists differ with regard to moral development?
11. Describe the development of altruism and processes that influence this development.

Further Readings

Becker, W. *Parents are teachers*. Champaign, Ill.: Research Press, 1971.
Wesley Becker has studied parental influences on children for many years. In his paperback he outlines some principles of behavior modification that can be taught to parents and includes a number of exercises for observing family interaction. Easy to read.

Garvey, C. *Play*. Cambridge, Mass.: Harvard University Press, 1977.
This short book is an excellent up-to-date overview of the most important aspects of children's play. Many examples reflecting the unique play experiences of children at different developmental levels are given. Medium reading level.

Huston, A. C. Sex-typing. In E. M. Hetherington (ed.), *Carmichael's manual of child psychology* (4th ed.). New York: Wiley, 1982.
A lengthy, up-to-date overview of what we know about the sex typing of children. Includes detailed information about androgyny and biological and cultural influences on sex role development. Moderately difficult reading level.

Journal of Social Issues, 1979, *35* (4). Children of divorce.
The entire issue is devoted to information about children from divorced families. Included is an excellent introduction that summarizes some of the most important issues involved in the study of the effects of divorce on children. Moderately difficult reading.

Lewis, M., & Rosenblum, L. A. (eds.). *The child and its family*. New York: Plenum, 1979.
This volume focuses on the immediate social world into which the child is born and subsequently develops. Various chapters deal with the social network of the family, including parent-infant and sibling relations and the early development of peer relations. Moderately difficult reading level.

Lewis, M., & Rosenblum, L. A. (eds.). *Friendship and peer relations* (vol. 4.). New York: Wiley, 1975.
Articles by experts on peer relations representing diverse ideas and including recent theoretical perspectives. Moderately difficult reading.

Lickona, T. (ed.). *Moral development and behavior*. New York: Holt, Rinehart & Winston, 1976.
Contemporary essays outlining the major theories, research findings, and educational implications of moral development. Included are essays by Kohlberg, Hoffman, Mischel, Aronfreed, Bronfenbrenner, and Rest. Moderately difficult reading.

Liebert. R. M., Neale, J. M., & Davidson, E. S. *The early window: effects of television on children and youth*. Elmsford, N.Y.: Pergamon Press, 1973.
Excellent overview of the effects of television on youth. Provides ideas about the psychological processes underlying the influence of television as well as critical analysis of whether television has a positive or negative influence on youth. Medium reading difficulty.

Section IV

Middle and Late Childhood

9

Physical Development and Intelligence

Prologue: Intelligence Tests and Educational Placement of Children

For many years heated debate in psychological and educational circles has focused on whether standard intelligence tests are culturally biased. This controversy has now entered the legal arena and has been the target of a major class action lawsuit challenging the use of standard IQ tests to place black elementary school students in classes for the educable mentally retarded (EMR).

The initial lawsuit, *Larry P. v. Riles,* was filed in a federal court in San Francisco. The intent of the suit was to test the plaintiff's claim that standard IQ tests are biased against blacks and that they systematically underestimate the learning ability of black children. The suit asked relief for all black elementary school children in California who have been inappropriately placed in EMR classes on the basis of results from individual IQ tests. The plaintiffs—children and their parents, represented by such groups as the National Association for the Advancement of Colored People, among others—asserted that IQ tests, such as the WISC-R and the Stanford-Binet, improperly evaluate blacks by unduly emphasizing verbal skills and by failing to account for the cultural background of black children. The result, they contended, is that thousands of black children have been incorrectly labeled mentally retarded and are forever saddled with the stigma of mental retardation.

The plaintiffs agree with the conclusions of sociologist Jane Mercer, who wrote in *Sociocultural Factors in Educational Labeling* that "present psychological assessment practices in the public schools violate five rights of children: Their right to be evaluated within a culturally appropriate normative framework; their right to be assessed as a multidimensional human

being; their right to be fully educated; their right to be free of stigmatizing labels; and their right to ethnic identity and respect."

In the California case it was ruled that IQ tests are biased and their use is racially discriminatory. The ruling continued the moratorium on the use of IQ tests in decisions about placement of a child in EMR classes. The litigation in California revealed a dramatic racial imbalance in EMR classes. At the onset of the case in 1971, 66 percent of elementary school students in EMR classes in San Francisco were black, while blacks comprised only 28.5 percent of the San Francisco school population. Statewide, the disparity was even greater. Although blacks comprised only 9.1 percent of the school children in California, more than 27 percent of children in programs for the mentally retarded were black. More recent figures reveal no drop in the statewide disproportion of blacks in EMR classes.

In the trial the plaintiff's argued that this marked imbalance in the composition of EMR classes results from culturally biased testing instruments, and furthermore that this test bias is not accidental but has been built into American IQ tests from the time of their formulation. They were able to convince the court that the perpetuation of racial imbalance as a result of state-required procedures constituted unconstitutional racial discrimination that violates federal laws.

Early in the history of the lengthy court battle, the plaintiffs produced graphic evidence that standard IQ tests do not properly assess the abilities of blacks and that they therefore should not be used to place black children in EMR classes. For example, six black EMR students were independently retested by members of the Bay Area Association of Black Psychologists who were fully qualified to administer such tests. These psychologists used techniques designed to take into account the cultural experiences of the black schoolchildren. The psychologists emphasized the establishment of good rapport with the children and made special efforts to overcome any defeatism or early distraction among the students. Certain items were rewarded in terms more consistent with the children's cultural background and language experience, and recognition was given to nonstandard answers that nevertheless showed an intelligent approach to problems in the context of that background. On retesting, each of the six children scored above the ceiling for placement in EMR classes. The scores ranged from 79 to 104, or 17 to 38 points higher than the scores the students received when tested by school psychologists.

During the long course of litigation, the state did little to explain the racial imbalance in EMR placements. At one point the state suggested that since black people tend to be poor and poor pregnant women tend to suffer from inadequate nutrition, it is possible that the brain development of many black children has been retarded by their mothers' poor diets during pregnancy. However, from the outset of the case, an undercurrent in the state's position was that blacks are genetically inferior to whites. In papers filed with the court, the state defendants suggested that the racial imbalance in EMR placements is caused by differences in the inherited intelligence of the races, presumably meaning that blacks are genetically not as intelligent as whites.

Ernest Brody and Nathan Brody (1976) have recently noted the "cooling out" function of IQ testing: the scores help educators to justify poor academic achievement. Brody and Brody say that the citation of intelligence test scores of black children essentially serves the purpose of absolving schools and teachers for poor academic achievement of blacks.

Their conclusion supports a central premise of the plaintiffs in the *Larry P.* case. California schools segregate pupils they believe are inferior into separate and unequal classes, and such segregation falls most heavily on blacks. Thus, the IQ test is used to give a seemingly scientific imprimatur to what is in effect institutional racial discrimination. When the asserted scientific basis for isolating black children (the IQ test) has been removed, the disproportion of blacks in EMR classes will be without a legitimate justification (Opton, 1977).

The decision in favor of Larry P. is currently being appealed, and in another court case, *Pase* v. *Hannon* in Illinois, it was ruled that IQ tests are not culturally biased (Armstrong, 1980). Many psychologists continue to take exception to the ruling in the *Larry P.* case, arguing that the required method for determining overrepresentation of minority children in special classes is not flawed, that the evidence does not suggest the tests are biased, and that informed consent procedures and regular review of children's progress in special education would protect rights to equal protection under the law, as well as rights to special education services when needed (Lambert, 1981).

Introduction

You have just read about two of the most important topics of this chapter—intelligence and mental retardation. In this chapter we will survey a number of different intelligence tests, focusing initially on the two most widely used individual tests, the Binet and the WISC. We will attempt to define the elusive concept of intelligence and compare the approach of those who measure intelligence to Piaget's ideas. The extent to which intelligence is stable from one period of development to another will be covered, and a discussion of the genetic basis of intelligence is included. The extremes of intelligence will be discussed toward the end of the chapter with topics on mental retardation and giftedness. The concluding section reveals that children may not only think intelligently, but that they may think creatively as well. To begin the chapter, however, we continue our description of physical development, focusing on the changes that occur during middle and late childhood.

Physical Development

The period of middle and late childhood involves slow, consistent growth—the calm before the rapid growth spurt that will appear in adolescence.

Basic Physical Attributes

During the elementary school years, children grow an average of two to three inches per year until at the age of eleven, the average girl is four feet, ten inches tall and the average boy is four feet, nine and one-half inches tall. Weight increases range from three to five pounds per year until at the age of eleven, the average girl weighs eighty-eight and one-half pounds while the average boy weighs eighty-five and one-half pounds (Krogman, 1970).

During middle and late childhood, children's legs become longer and their trunks slimmer, and they are steadier on their feet. Fat tissue tends to develop more rapidly than muscle tissue (which increases substantially in adolescence). Children who had a rounded, somewhat "chubby" body build (sometimes referred to as **endomorphic**) have noticibly more fat tissue than muscle tissue, while the reverse is true of children with **mesomorphic** body builds (athletic, muscular). **Ectomorphs** (skinny, thin body build) do not have a predominance of fat or muscle, which accounts for their tendency to appear somewhat scrawny (see fig. 9.1) (Hurlock, 1980).

During middle and late childhood, the motor development of children becomes much smoother and more coordinated than was the case in early childhood. For example, it is one child in a thousand who can even hit a tennis ball over the net at the age of four, yet by the age of eleven, most children can learn to play this sport. In the early elementary school years, children can become competent at running, climbing, throwing and catching a ball, skipping rope, swimming, bicycle riding, and skating, to name just some of the many physical skills that, when mastered, provide a considerable source of pleasure and accomplishment. Developing competence in these physical skills indicates increases in children's strength, speed, flexibility, and precision (including steadiness, balance, and aiming) (Lundsteen & Bernstein-Tarrow, 1981). Recall from our description of physical development in chapter 7 that there usually are marked sex differences in these gross motor skills, with boys outperforming girls rather handily. However, in fine motor skills, girls generally outperform boys.

By the time children reach middle and late childhood, they are predominantly right- or left-handed. Experts suggest that changing handedness, even in early childhood, is not easy and is generally not a wise strategy (Van Camp & Mixley, 1977).

During middle and late childhood, sensory mechanisms continue to mature. Early farsightedness is overcome, binocular vision becomes well-developed, and hearing acuity increases. Children of this age have fewer illnesses than younger children, particularly fewer respiratory and gastrointestinal problems. Widespread immunization has considerably reduced the incidence of disease, and many illnesses can be prevented by practicing habits of good health, safety, and nutrition (Lundsteen & Bernstein-Tarrow, 1981).

The Child in Competitive Sports

Competitive sports programs for boys and girls have increased in recent years, and parents often place their children in such programs at very young ages. Anywhere in the United States you are likely to find preschool and elementary school-aged children engaged in competitive sports—in Minnesota it might be hockey, in Texas football, in Florida soccer. While there is surprisingly little empirical information about the effects such competitive activities have on physical and emotional development, some researchers have investigated possible links between physical skills competition and the child's maturing bone structure, as well as the possible stress of early physical overload on the young child.

Bryant Cratty (1978) concluded that of all competitive sports, there is no team sport anywhere in the world in which the occurrence of injury is greater than in football. Soccer, baseball, and basketball, for example, appear to be far less frought with damage to the child's body. However, bone breaks, if properly set, are likely to heal and not cause growth retardation or malformation. Not every child can perform well in athletics. Some children are very awkward and clumsy—in box 9.1 we look at the awkward child.

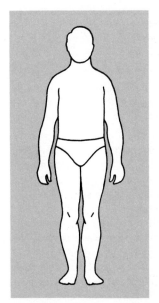
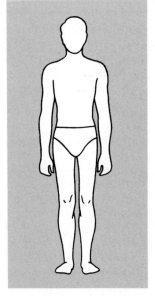
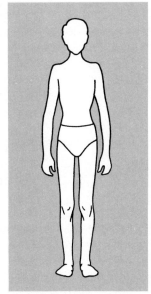

Figure 9.1 The endomorphic, mesomorphic, and ectomorphic body types.

Exercise provides children with a sound base for later superior endurance performance.

In addition to information about the effects of competitive sports on bone development, scientists have been interested in the exposure of young children's cardiovascular systems to moderate or severe stress. It appears that vigorous exercise in young children whose cardiovascular systems are sound (tested under exercise stress), if not carried to extremes (exercise that gives the child's system time to recover between "bouts" or sessions, rather than so severe as to produce chronic fatigue), is likely to be beneficial exercise and will probably provide a sound base for later superior endurance performance.

Intelligence

In everyday conversation we often equate **intelligence** with IQ. When asked what IQ and intelligence are, most children and adults respond, "That's how smart you are." Intelligence must be more than just IQ (an abbreviation for the intelligence quotient that is derived from performance on intelligence tests).

Although most of us have an idea of what intelligence is, not everybody defines it in the same way. Psychologists and educators have been trying to pin down a definition of intelligence for many years.

Definition and Measurement of Intelligence

One definition of intelligence emphasizes its global nature: intelligence is "the global capacity of the individual to act purposefully, to think rationally, and to deal effectively with the environment" (Wechsler, 1958, p. 7). Another definition stresses the global nature of intelligence as well as its genetic heritage: intelligence is "innate, general cognitive ability" (Burt, 1955, p. 162). Other definitions give specific abilities of the individual and learning more prominent roles. And, finally, the simplest—perhaps too simplistic—definition of intelligence has existed for many years: "Intelligence is what the tests measure" (Boring, 1923, p. 35).

The Awkward Child

In addition to bearing the brunt of playground hazing, the clumsy child has been a source of interest to child development experts around the world. As early as 1920, a Russian (Oseretzsky, 1948) devised a test for culling the physically less able child ("motor idiots" was the Russian's label) from the normal population. These tests, developed at the Neurological Institute of Moscow, are still being used in the United States and elsewhere to assess the development of motor skills.

Clumsy children make up approximately 8 to 15 percent of the school population in the United States. If carefully evaluated some of them may have neurological problems, while others may simply be late maturers. A majority (as many as 70 percent) of the children are boys (Rarick & Dobbins, 1975). They often have difficulty learning to print in the first grade, and by the second grade, their lack of coordination usually proves to be a social detriment. Clumsy children usually have difficulty in integrating various parts of their body and in seeing and executing a series of movements. However, ineptitude in one skill (e.g., printing) is often not associated with clumsiness in another skill (e.g., running, hopping).

The causes of minor to moderate motor problems in children is not easily discerned. Probable, rather than certain, causes include extremely low birthweight (below three and one-half pounds), anoxia (oxygen) problems at birth, falls, injuries from child abuse, and drugs. Yet the child may show motor problems without experiencing any of these factors—genetic inheritance, then, would seem to be a likely culprit in many such cases.

In the past twenty years Bryant Cratty (1978) has tested over 2,000 awkward children. Questions he invariably is asked by the parents of awkward children are, Can you make any changes? and How long will it take? Cratty concluded:

> A well-designed testing program, accompanied by a comprehensive program to cover a wide variety of problems, is likely to elicit positive changes in children. However, changes are more likely if the children are relatively young and if their problems are not great. Changes are also more likely in measures of fitness and the like than in motor control. (p. 270)

The origins of interest in intelligence testing can be traced to general psychology and its concern for measurement. In particular, the work of Sir Francis Galton in the latter part of the nineteenth century served as the background for the development of interest in intelligence and intelligence testing. Galton was intrigued by the possibility that intelligence might be genetically determined and could be measured empirically. His overall interest was in individual differences, and his work on intelligence was part of this interest.

Individual differences simply refer to the consistent, stable ways individuals differ from one another. The entire psychological testing movement was (and still is) concerned with how individuals think, act, and feel in a consistent manner and in relation to how other individuals think, act, and feel. Since measurement has played such a prominent role in the history of inquiry about intelligence, let's look more closely at the intelligence tests psychologists have devised.

The Binet Tests

Alfred Binet and Theodore Simon devised the first intelligence test in 1905 to determine which students in the schools of Paris would not benefit from regular classes and consequently should be placed in special classes. Binet and Simon did not work from a basic definition of intelligence but proceeded in a trial-and-error fashion, simply relying on the test's ability to discriminate between children who were successful in school from those who were not. On this basis they found that "higher" mental abilities (memory, attention, and comprehension) were better at making this distinction than "lower" mental abilities (reaction time, speed of hand movement in a specified amount of space, and the like). The latter measures had been used by the American psychologist James McKeen Cattell as indicators of intelligence, but Binet found that they were not very good at predicting which children would succeed in French schools.

Sir Francis Galton (1822–1911).

Alfred Binet (1857–1911).

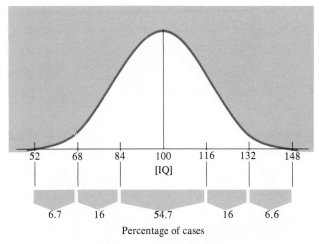

Figure 9.2 Normal distribution of IQ.

Although the Binet test was made up of items that tested several different mental capacities (including memory, comprehension, attention, moral judgment, and aesthetic appreciation), Binet was primarily concerned with the child's general intelligence, which he noted simply as the letter **g,** rather than the child's specific mental abilities.

Binet developed the concept of **mental age (MA)** to reflect the general level of the child's intellectual functioning. This term was devised to refer to the number of items an individual child answered correctly in relation to the number of items that the average child of a given age answered correctly. For example, if an eight-year-old child had only as many items correct as an average six-year-old, then that child would be said to have the MA of a six-year-old child even though he or she was eight years old chronologically. By comparing the child's general level of intellectual functioning with that of the average child at that age, Binet had a means of predicting how dull or how bright the child would probably be in the classroom.

Standardization of the Binet Over the years extensive effort has been expended to standardize the Binet test. The test has been given to many thousands of children and adults of different ages, selected at random from different parts of the United States. By administering the test to large numbers of people and recording the results, it has been found that intelligence, as measured by the Binet, has an almost **normal distribution** (see fig. 9.2).

The revisions of the Binet tests have resulted in what are now called the **Stanford-Binet** tests (*Stanford* for Stanford University, where the revisions were done). The Stanford-Binet has a mean of 100 and a standard deviation of 16. The mean is the average score, and the **standard deviation** tells how much the scores vary. As you can see by looking at figure 9.1, about 55 percent of the scores fall within what is called the average range: 88 to 112.

In the 1972 revision of the Stanford-Binet, preschool children scored an average of about 110 on the test, compared with a mean of 100. The 1972 sampling included more children from minority groups than was true of earlier samplings—the revision in the 1930s, for example, included only white children. What could explain the 1972 increase in IQ scores? Well, preschool children today are experiencing more visual and verbal stimulation from books, television, toys, and other educational materials than was true of earlier generations. And their parents average two or three more years of education than in earlier test standardizations.

Historically, labels have been used to reflect how far away from the mean a child scores on the IQ test. A child who scored 102 was labeled "average"; one who scored 60 was labeled "mentally retarded"; and one who

The Binet test includes verbal and nonverbal responses.

scored 156 was labeled "genius." The evaluation of intelligence is rapidly moving away from such categorization. Many experts believe than an intelligence quotient based on the results of a single intelligence test should not be the basis for classifying a child as mentally retarded or, for that matter, as a genius. Such a label has often remained with the child for many years even though circumstances of the testing may have led to inappropriate measurement of intelligence.

The Binet Today   The current Stanford-Binet test can be given to individuals from the age of two years through adulthood. It includes many different types of items, some requiring verbal responses and some calling for nonverbal performance. For example, items that characterize the six-year-old's performance on the test include the verbal ability to define at least six words, such as orange and envelope and the nonverbal ability to trace a path through a maze. Although it contains both verbal and nonverbal items and measures of attention, comprehension, memory, and so forth, these components of intelligence are not scored individually. The child is still given an overall score that indicates IQ, or general level of intellectual functioning, on the test.

While the Binet is still widely used as an individual measure of intelligence, another psychologist, David Wechsler, devised several different intelligence tests that are being used just as widely as the Binet.

The Wechsler Scales

The most widely used Wechsler scale for children is the Wechsler Intelligence Scale for Children (WISC), used for children from five to eighteen years of age. An updated and revised version of this test now being used is called the WISC-R. Another Wechsler scale, the Wechsler Preschool and Primary Intelligence Scale (WPPSI), was devised for children from four to six and one-half years of age.

Like the Binet, the Wechsler scales provide a score that reflects the child's general level of intellectual functioning. By providing a general score for intelligence, the test reflects Wechsler's belief that intelligence is a general capacity of the child. However, one of the main reasons many psychologists prefer the Wechsler Scales over the Binet is the division of the Wechsler Scales into a number of different subtests and into verbal and performance categories. The Binet is organized in terms of age levels rather than types of intellectual functioning. While retaining the idea of general intelligence, the Wechsler Scales also approach intelligence as clusters of many different abilities. In table 9.1 the various subtests of the WISC are listed, along with examples of items used to measure different types of intellectual functioning.

Because of its organization into various subtests, psychologists feel that the WISC provides a better opportunity than the Binet to analyze the strong and weak components of the child's thought processes. For example, a child may have a good vocabulary but have poor visual-motor coordination. The testing situation involves structured interaction between the psychologist and the child, thus the opportunity to develop inferences about the child is possible. The inferences are based on observation of the child's behavior as well as the responses to test items. Psychologists observe the ease with which rapport is established, the child's level of energy and enthusiasm, and the child's degree of frustration, tolerance, and persistence.

Wechsler is not the only psychologist who has devised tests to measure specific types of intelligence. Next we will see that many theorists believe that intelligence has several specific factors, or attributes, that can be analyzed and individually assessed as a means of determining intelligence.

The Factor-Analytic Approach

The **factor-analytic approach** is similar to that of Wechsler in its emphasis on specific components of intelligence. This approach differs from Wechsler's, however, in that it involves a mathematical analysis of large numbers of responses to test items in an attempt to determine the basic common factors in intelligence. Following are four different factor-analytic views on intelligence.

The most widely used scale for children is the Wechsler scale.

PEANUTS

WHAT'S THIS ABOUT YOU AND YOUR TEACHER AND SOME EGG SHELLS?

MISS OTHMAR WANTS US TO BRING SOME EGG SHELLS TO SCHOOL TO MAKE IGLOOS, BUT I KEEP FORGETTING...SHE'S VERY UPSET

IT'S JUST LIKE YOU... I'VE NEVER KNOWN ANYONE WHO COULD FORGET THINGS WITH SUCH CLOCKLIKE REGULARITY!

I GUESS I'M JUST MECHANICALLY MINDED!

© 1960 United Feature Syndicate, Inc.

Spearman The earliest proponent of viewing intelligence as a set of specific factors was C. E. Spearman (1927). His was called a **two-factor theory of intelligence;** he believed that intelligence consisted of a general factor (g) and a specific factor (s). Spearman believed that these two factors could account for an individual's performance on an intelligence test.

Thurstone An elaborate framework for understanding the idea that there are many specific types of intelligences was developed by L. L. Thurstone (1938). From time to time attempts have been made to distinguish between academic and nonacademic intelligence, social and nonsocial intelligence, mechanical and abstract intelligence, and so on. Many people who can do very well on a test in school may not be able to replace a fuse. Others can take one look at an automobile engine and tell what is wrong with it. Such observations led to the development of the multiple-factor theory of intelligence. This view generally stresses that a

number of specific factors, rather than one general factor, make up intelligence.

Before he became a psychologist, Leon Thurstone worked in the laboratory of Thomas Edison. He brought his engineering and mathematical background to psychology and applied it to the measurement of intelligence. He believed that a number of specific factors of intelligence could be extracted from the responses to test items on IQ scales. It was not expected that most people would do well on all of the factors; certain people would do better in some areas, other people in other areas.

An example of a test used to measure intelligence based on Thurstone's ideas is the SRA Primary Mental Abilities Test. The test consists of five different batteries, ranging from kindergarten to grade twelve.

Physical Development and Intelligence   255

Table 9.1
Subtests of the Wechsler Intelligence Scale for Children

Verbal

1. *Information:* The child is required to answer thirty general information questions that are supposed to sample experiences considered normal for children in our society. Example: "Who invented the telephone?"

2. *Comprehension:* This subtest is made up of fourteen questions designed to measure the child's judgment and common sense. Example: "What should you do when you get lost?"

3. *Arithmetic:* In this subtest sixteen problems measure ability to do arithmetic mentally. The child is required to add, subtract, multiply, and divide without using paper and pencil.

4. *Similarities:* The child must think abstractly and logically to answer sixteen questions. Example: "How are a skunk and a rabbit the same?"

5. *Vocabulary:* Forty words are used to test word knowledge. This subtest is thought to be an excellent indicator of general intelligence, measuring a variety of cognitive functions including concept formation, memory, and language development. Example: "Tell me what the word *cabinet* means."

6. *Digit Span:* This supplementary subtest may or may not be used by the examiner. It primarily measures attention and short-term memory. The child is required to repeat some numbers forward and backward.

Performance

1. *Picture Completion:* Twenty drawings are provided, each with a significant element missing. Within fifteen seconds the child has to differentiate essential from nonessential components of a picture to figure out which part is missing. Visual alertness and ability to organize visually are evaluated. Example: an elephant without its trunk.

2. *Picture Arrangement:* With each of eleven items the child is to rearrange parts of a figure or picture to make it complete or to tell a meaningful story. This test of nonverbal reasoning requires that the child understand how parts of a picture or a story go together. The pictures are shown to the child, who manually arranges the pieces in the right order.

3. *Block Design:* The child must put together a set of different-colored blocks ten times to match each of ten designs the examiner shows. Visual-motor coordination, perceptual organization, and an ability to visualize spatially are among the cognitive functions measured. This subtest is one of the best for measuring general intelligence.

4. *Object Assembly:* The child is to assemble four jigsaw puzzles: a mannequin, a horse, a face, and a car. This subtest measures visual-motor coordination and perceptual organization.

5. *Coding:* This subtest evaluates how quickly and accurately the child can link code symbols and digits. The child is shown paired symbols and digits—for example, a star and 1, a circle and 2, a straight line and 3. Then the child is shown a long list of numbers, each with a black space below it and is asked to transfer the appropriate code symbols to the blank spaces. The test evaluates visual-motor coordination and speed of thought.

6. *Mazes:* This supplementary subtest is made up of eight mazes. It is designed to evaluate the child's ability to plan and to organize perceptually.

Verbal reasoning

Choose the correct pair of words to fill the blanks. The first word of the pair goes in the blank space at the beginning of the sentence; the second word of the pair goes in the blank at the end of the sentence.

...... is to night as breakfast is to ......

    A. supper — corner
    B. gentle — morning
    C. door — corner
    D. flow — enjoy
    E. supper — morning

The correct answer is E.

Numerical ability

Choose the correct answer for each problem.

Add 13   A 14   Subtract 30   A 15
    12   B 25   20   B 26
        C 16   C 16
        D 59   D 8
        E none of these   E none of these

The correct answer for the first problem is B; for the second, E.

Abstract reasoning

The four "problem figures" in each row make a series. Find the one among the "answer figures" that would be next in the series.

Problem figures   Answer figures

The correct answer is D.

Clerical speed and accuracy

In each test item, one of the five combinations is underlined. Find the same combination on the answer sheet and mark it.

Scores are obtained separately on the following factors: verbal meaning, number facility, reasoning, perceptual speed, and spatial relations. Figure 9.3 provides examples of the types of items that are included in tests based on the factor-analytic approach.

Cattell-Horn   Thurstone's theory was not destined to remain unchanged for long. By 1940, Raymond Cattell proposed that two forms of intelligence acted to influence the primary mental abilities described by Thurstone. Cattell labeled the two forms *fluid* and *crystallized*. **Fluid intelligence** focuses on the child's adaptability and capacity to perceive things and integrate them mentally. It appears to be independent of formal education and experience. For instance, some children can intuitively think through problems with strategies that they have never been taught. By comparison, schooling and environment determined **crystallized intelligence,** which involves skills, abilities, and understanding gained through instruction and observation. For example, a child may learn how to play a particular game only after seeing someone else do it or being given instructions on how to proceed.

Cattell's theory of fluid and crystallized intelligence has served as the basis for a number of life-span developmental investigations of intelligence. Raymond Cattell's student, John Horn, has provided the impetus

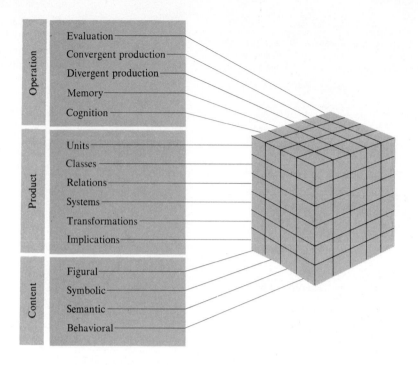

Figure 9.4 Three-dimensional model of the structure of the intellect. From *The Nature of Human Intelligence* by J. P. Guilford. Copyright 1967 by McGraw-Hill. Used with the permission of McGraw-Hill Book Company.

Operation
- Evaluation
- Convergent production
- Divergent production
- Memory
- Cognition

Product
- Units
- Classes
- Relations
- Systems
- Transformations
- Implications

Content
- Figural
- Symbolic
- Semantic
- Behavioral

for much of the life-span work. Cattell and Horn believe that crystallized intelligence increases throughout the life span because it is based on cumulative learning experiences. By contrast, they speculate that fluid intelligence increases from infancy through adolescence, levels off during young adulthood, and then steadily declines during middle and late adulthood. Keep the concept of crystallized and fluid intelligence in mind, because when we discuss the adulthood phases of the life cycle we will evaluate research that has focused on the Cattell-Horn factor-analytic perspective.

Guilford   J. P. Guilford (1967) developed what has been called the *structure of intellect* model of intelligence. As illustrated in figure 9.4, he conceives of intelligence as having three major dimensions, each with several subdimensions. The three major dimensions and their subdimensions are as follows. (1) *Operations* refers to what the child does; it includes thinking, memory, divergent production, and convergent production. (We discuss divergent production later in this chapter in connection with creativity.) (2) *Contents* indexes the information on which operations are performed; it includes letters and numbers (symbolic, in Guilford's terms), words (semantic), and behaviors. (3) *Products* describes the form in which information occurs; it includes units, classes, relations, systems, and transformations.

In all, there are five categories of operations, four of contents, and six of products. By multiplying these, we come up with 120 components in Guilford's model, each of which is supposed to represent a factor or trait.

Each factor is represented on all three dimensions. For example, a test to determine memory span for a set of unrelated letters would be classified as symbolic (content), memory (operations), and units (products) (Anastasi, 1976). While both Cattell and Horn and Guilford use factor analysis as a technique to describe intelligence, they differ markedly in the sense that Guilford believes intelligence is comprised of many factors (120) while Cattell and Horn believe two major aspects of intelligence predominate.

Why are the factors in the Guilford tests so different in number and type? The factors obtained from analyzing these items depend upon the types of items that are included in the tests. The factors are not magical; they are names the test constructor or theory constructor believes best describe the relations between the items on the test.

Evaluation of the Factor-Analytic Approach   During the 1950s the factor-analytic approach to intelligence reached its peak in the general field of psychology. Psychologists and educators believed that factor analysis would solve the problems of assessing intelligence accurately. Why is the factor-analytic model not received with as much acclaim today?

The factors are merely descriptive categories, labels that the theorist feels best reflect the content of items that are grouped when responses of several individuals are mathematically analyzed. As with other attempts to define and measure intelligence, responses can be influenced by different aspects of the testing situation and environmental changes in a person's life. In some cases, as in Guilford's model, there are almost as

..BOY, WHEN iT COMES TO A VOCABULARY... iT'S HARD TO TOP THAT GUY WEBSTER.. ..HE HAD A WORD FOR EVERYTHING !!

many factors as behaviors; there may not be much utility in devising 120 names to reflect the many different responses. The categories reveal nothing about how intelligence develops or how heredity and environment interact to produce intelligence.

Furthermore, as psychometric expert Jum Nunnally (1975, 1978) has pointed out, the factor-analytic theorists and test makers seem to be a group of about 200 persons in the United States who speak their own language, taken from computers and matrix algebra. They have not done a good job of translating their ideas into simple language.

Many experts accept the idea that intelligence is made up of a number of specific attributes, but they also believe that factor analysis has not added extensively to an understanding of intelligence. Many experts do believe, however, that the tester can gain valuable information about a person's intellectual functioning by piecing together and interpreting performance on different components and items of the test.

The factor-analytic approach has been involved in a number of life-span developmental studies of intelligence, as well as personality, as we will see in the sections of the text focusing on early, middle, and late adulthood. As a rule, it has been the life-span flavor of these investigations, rather than the tool of factor analysis, that has made those studies important aspects of life-span developmental psychology.

So far in our survey of intelligence tests we have described two widely used individual tests, the Binet and the Wechsler Scales, and have discussed the merits and demerits of the factor-analytic tests. Two other sets of tests, vocabulary and group IQ tests, have also been widely used with children.

Vocabulary Tests

The vocabulary part of intelligence tests is strongly related to **g** (overall intelligence). For example, Jerome Sattler (1974) reported that the vocabulary subtest of the Wechsler Intelligence Scale for Children predicts general intelligence more accurately than any other subtest. However, he warns that it is not wise to use the vocabulary subtest in isolation from the other subtests. Children's responses to the vocabulary items on the Stanford-Binet also are often good predictors of general intelligence and have been used as quick screening devices—not a good strategy according to Saddler and other experts, who believe that intelligence consists of much more than correct responses to vocabulary words.

One test of intelligence that is widely used is the Peabody Picture Vocabulary Test. This test, often referred to as the PPVT or the Peabody, was used as a measure in a national assessment of the effectiveness of Project Head Start. The Peabody was selected because it can be administered in about fifteen minutes and does not require the child to speak. The test is given individually, and the child merely points to indicate a response.

The experts who selected the Peabody for evaluating children's gains in Project Head Start felt that it would be less culturally biased in the assessment of children from low-income families than other intelligence tests. It was thought that since children do not have to respond verbally to the Peabody items, the language bias of traditional IQ tests like the Binet would be reduced. Ironically, subsequent research indicates that children from minority groups actually score lower on the Peabody than on other intelligence tests (Cundick, 1970). Verbal and experiential deficiencies have been given as reasons for these lower scores (Milgram & Ozer, 1967).

Prominent test authorities have pointed out that the Peabody measures the child's use of vocabulary (e.g., Anastasi, 1976). However, the Peabody measures only vocabulary the child has stored; it does not measure how he or she stores it or uses it. Therefore, when the Peabody is used as a quick screening device for intelligence, it should be used cautiously.

Most experts recommend that if intellectual functioning is to be evaluated, more than a vocabulary test is necessary, even though vocabulary is related to general intelligence in consistent ways. This recommendation underscores the fact that intelligence has many different facets and that measuring only one of them provides an incomplete picture.

Group Tests

The IQ scores on most permanent record files in schools come from intelligence tests administered in large group settings. Even more than the individual intelligence tests, group tests of intelligence have come under heavy criticism by opponents of the use of intelligence tests. While extensive training is required to administer the Binet and Wechsler tests competently, virtually any teacher can give group tests. There are certain uniform procedures the test administrator should go through, however, in order to standardize the conditions for different groups. Two group intelligence tests widely used with children are the Otis-Lennon Mental Ability Test and the California Test of Mental Maturity.

Although group tests have been heavily criticized, they can be used with very large numbers of people, and they are more objectively scored, easier to administer, and usually based on better established norms (standardized on large numbers of people). But the examiner cannot establish rapport with all of the people taking the test, and it is not easy to detect a child who is extremely nervous or sick in a large group testing situation. Furthermore, in group testing the examiner does not have the opportunity to observe what might be causing an individual child's good or bad performance on particular test items (Anastasi, 1976). A group test should not be used, then, as a substitute for an individual intelligence test.

In a fascinating article, "Brave New Worlds of Intelligence Testing," Berkeley Rice (1979) described a number of newly developed concepts and techniques that could change the way we think about intelligence. Read about Rice's conclusions and his description of two recently developed ideas about measuring intelligence—one focuses strongly on the physiology of the individual, the other heavily flavored by social characteristics—in box 9.2.

Regardless of the type of intelligence test given—whether it is a Binet or WISC, factor-analytic test, a vocabulary test, or a group test—cultural bias may be built into the test. In the next section we will take a closer look at attempts to eliminate or reduce cultural bias in intelligence tests.

Culture-Free and Culture-Fair Intelligence Tests
Cultural bias in intelligence tests has been identified as one of the reasons that children from minority groups and from low-income families do not perform as well on intelligence tests as children from white and higher-income families. In particular it has been emphasized that the language of most intelligence tests reflects a middle-class white society.

Accordingly, many nonverbal performance intelligence tests were constructed. It has been found, however, that subtle cultural biases often enter into performance tests as well (e.g., Vernon, 1965). For example, pictures and nonverbal items may be even more difficult to translate into a different culture than words are.

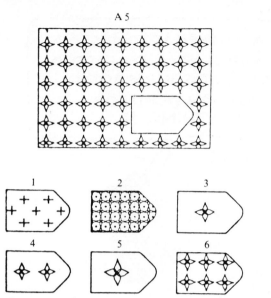

Figure 9.5 Sample item from the Raven Progressive Matrices Test.

One of the most widely used **culture-fair tests** is the Raven Progressive Matrices Test. The test consists of sixty designs, each requiring the person to select a missing part from alternatives presented. A sample item is shown in figure 9.5. Although this test was originally designed to be a culture-free test, there is evidence that it is actually not culture free. For example, in a review of research pertaining to the Raven test, Anne Anastasi (1976) concluded that individuals with more education do better on the test than individuals with less education.

Efforts to develop **culture-free tests** for blacks also have been attempted. The Dove Counterbalance General Intelligence Test, sometimes referred to as the Chitling Test, was developed by a black sociologist, Adrian Dove, as a sarcastic rejoinder to the middle-class bias of most intelligence tests. It should be mentioned that Dove's test was not presented as a serious effort to develop a culture-free test for blacks; it was designed to illustrate how the language used by many blacks differs from that of middle-class whites. The language black children experience as they are growing up is often not reflected in the intelligence tests they are given or in the language the tester uses in presenting test items to them. Some items from Dove's Chitling Test are presented in box 9.3. See how well you can do with this "intelligence test."

So far, test makers have not come up with culture-free or culture-fair tests that really are culture-free or culture-fair. Some experts believe that attempts to develop culture-fair tests sometimes focus too heavily on performance and not enough on competence—the Chitling Test is a good example. They point out that the underlying competence of the child's intelligence should always be kept in mind in developing culture-fair tests.

Cultural backgrounds do affect children's performance on tests of mental abilities.

So far, testmakers have not come up with tests that are truly culture-free or culture-fair.

What the experts believe is badly needed, then, are culture-fair tests that retain an evaluation of the child's underlying cognitive competence and effectively predict success in the academic and social world. They believe the Raven Progressive Matrices Test is probably the best effort in this direction so far, even though it too falls far short of what is needed.

Some experts believe it is virtually impossible to eliminate cultural bias in testing intelligence, even were it possible to develop a truly culture-free or culture-fair test.

Cultural Expectations in Intelligence Testing Knowing different facts about a child may influence the way a child is treated. For example, you are a teacher in the teacher's lounge the day after school has started in the fall. You mention a student, Johnny Jones, by name. A fellow teacher remarks that she had Johnny in class last year. She comments that he was a real dunce, that she saw his IQ test scores once—seventy-eight on one test and eighty-one on the other. You cannot help but remember this information, and it may lead to thoughts that children like Johnny Jones just do not have much on the ball and that it is useless to spend much time trying to help them.

Consider another conversation you (a teacher) might have with a well-to-do family in the community during the first PTA meeting of the year. Jimmy Smith's mother mentions to you that he spent the summer in Paris, where he studied French. At the end of the conversation, she points out that just before school started he was given a battery of tests by a professional testing service, and his IQ was measured at 136. How will this kind of information influence the way you interact with Jimmy in school? Will it lead you to provide him with more challenging work and spend more time with him because you know he is able to learn the material?

Questions like these led Robert Rosenthal and Lenore Jacobsen (1968) to study self-fulfilling prophecies in the classroom. According to the theory of **self-fulfilling prophecy,** once the teacher knows the child's IQ, he or she adjusts teaching to a level best suited to it and the child is thereby influenced to perform at that level, thus "fulfilling" his or her "prophecy."

Because of the effects of self-fulfilling prophecy, which stems from knowledge of a child's IQ, some states (e.g., New York, California, and Wisconsin) have stopped administering IQ tests to students. In these states tests are still given to individual students for special purposes, such as to determine whether or not a child should be placed in a learning disabilities program.

In addition to studying cultural bias in testing, psychologists also have been interested in charting cross-cultural similarities and differences in children's intelligence by comparing the intelligence of children from different countries and ethnic groups.

Box 9.2

Brave New Worlds of Intelligence Testing:
Neurometrics and Social Intelligence

In the current turmoil over intelligence testing, critics are calling for ways to measure mental ability that will be fairer, more precise, and more relevant to real life than those now in use. Fortunately, these demands come at a time when research into intelligence and its measurement has produced dozens of innovative approaches. What follows is a highly selective field report on some of the most interesting and promising new approaches to assessing intelligence. Some have already lead to actual tests; some remain in the experimental stages of research. Together, they promise to broaden and alter the way we think about the concept of intelligence.

Neurometrics

For many years, researchers have been measuring the electrical activity of the brain to test the extent of retardation or brain damage in children. But new techniques of measuring the brain's "evoked potential" now promise to develop a uniquely accurate test. Edward Beck, a psychologist who is one of the pioneers in evoked-potential research, describes the results of this test as "a fingerprint of the brain."

The basic technique consists of monitoring brain activity with an electroencephalograph, or EEG, to measure the brain's response to such sensory stimuli as sounds or flashes of light. Recent advances in computer technology have enabled neurophysiologists to sort out the minute changes that occur when a repeated stimulus suddenly stops or fails to continue in a predictable pattern. For example, a loud click normally followed by a soft one might suddenly be followed by another loud one, or by silence. The brain gradually disregards a regular sequence as it loses its novelty. The interruption, however, recaptures the brain's attention until the sequence returns to the normal pattern. The brain's response to such interruptions, or its evoked potential, gives a distinct measure that can be statistically compared with the response and IQ data of normal children (see "Brain Potentials: Signaling Our Inner Thoughts," by Richard Restak, *Psychology Today*, March 1979).

The Brain Research Laboratories at New York University Medical Center, under neuroscientist E. Roy John, recently developed a sophisticated "Quantitative Electrophysiological Battery," which includes not only EEG readings, but about thirty other measures of the brain's

Source: Rice, 1979.

electrical activity as well. The computerized brain diagnoses might someday be used for testing the intelligence potential of schoolchildren. It could be particularly useful for those too young to take written exams, or those whose poor command of English or late verbal development hinders their performance on written or oral tests.

The new brain-potential techniques have limits as measures of intelligence, however. They can only assess a modest range of mental abilities, like reaction speed. And their accuracy thus far has been confirmed largely by correlation with IQ scores, whose own validity is open to considerable debate. While some psychologists have hailed the measurement of evoked potential as a major breakthrough, others remain dubious. . . .

Social Intelligence

The adaptive-behavior inventory developed by Jane Mercer is typical of a growing number of attempts to measure what, for lack of a better phrase, can only be called **social intelligence** or social competence. However it is defined, social intelligence has attracted the attention of a growing number of researchers in recent years. One reason is that many psychologists, educators, and parents have begun to wonder about the relevance of most traditional measures of intelligence to the demands of everyday reality. Numerous studies, most recently Christopher Jencks's (see "Who Gets Ahead in America," *Psychology Today*, July 1979), have found only slight correlations between IQ scores in school and successful performance in later life. Since so much of life involves getting along with other people, interpersonal skills may be just as crucial for testing as spatial ability or analogical reasoning.

Researchers have identified a number of useful coping skills for children: getting attention from adults and peers; using other people as resources; expressing affection and hostility; recognizing these emotions in other people; being willing to accept substitutes for things they want; perceiving awkward or embarrassing situations; being sensitive to verbal and facial expressions.

As with more conventional forms of intelligence, defining such traits and skills is difficult. For instance, try distinguishing—intelligently—between "coping" and "adapting."

At Educational Testing Service (ETS) headquarters in Princeton, New Jersey, research psychologists Irving Sigel and Ann McGillicuddy-DeLisi have been asking three-and-a-half-year-olds what they would do during a game if there are three children and only two want to play.

The researchers ask groups of children how they would solve the problem, whether they think their initial strategy would work, and what their fallback strategy would be.

"I would play his game if he would play mine," said one child. "If he won't play," said another, "I'll have to hit him." Overall, the research has shown that girls are more optimistic than boys in predicting that their strategies will succeed. But if their first strategies fail, the girls tend to give up, rather than develop alternatives. When boys' civilized requests fail, they are more likely to adopt aggressive strategies like hitting.

In another pilot test of three-year-olds' interpersonal relationships, the researchers asked questions about friendship: "Are you still friends if your friend is playing with someone else?" "Are you still friends if your friend hits you?" In this test, girls are more willing to say they would end friendships than boys, particularly if the friend hits them. While their research is still tentative, Sigel and McGillicuddy-DeLisi have discovered that children's social behavior tends to reflect not only sex, but family structure and parental beliefs as well.

Further along the age spectrum, ETS researchers are working on tests of interpersonal skills that might become part of exams for professional schools. A prototypical test for medical school students measures "human dimensions" such as sensitivity using simulated patient interviews and medical history-taking. Another research group is exploring the use of a test for business school students in which the students would respond as "supervisors" to videotaped "employees" who present problems like requests for raises or promotions. The students' responses—spoken into a tape recorder—would test both their knowledge of what to do and their ability to do it.

The Chitling Intelligence Test

1. A "gas head" is a person who has a:
   - (a) fast-moving car
   - (b) stable of "lace"
   - (c) "process"
   - (d) habit of stealing cars
   - (e) long jail record for arson
2. "Bo Diddley" is a:
   - (a) game for children
   - (b) down-home cheap wine
   - (c) down-home singer
   - (d) new dance
   - (e) Moejoe call
3. If a pimp is uptight with a woman who gets state aid, what does he mean when he talks about "Mother's day"?
   - (a) second Sunday in May
   - (b) third Sunday in June
   - (c) first of every month
   - (d) none of these
   - (e) first and fifteenth of every month
4. A "handkerchief head" is:
   - (a) a cool cat
   - (b) a porter
   - (c) an Uncle Tom
   - (d) a hoddi
   - (e) a preacher
5. If a man is called a "blood," then he is a:
   - (a) fighter
   - (b) Mexican-American
   - (c) Negro
   - (d) hungry hemophile
   - (e) red man, or Indian
6. Cheap chitlings (not the kind you purchase at a frozen-food counter) will taste rubbery unless they are cooked long enough. How soon can you quit cooking them to eat and enjoy them?
   - (a) 45 minutes
   - (b) two hours
   - (c) 24 hours
   - (d) one week (on a low flame)
   - (e) one hour

Answers 1. c   2. c   3. e   4. c   5. c   6. c

Cross-Cultural Comparisons   Gerald Lesser and his colleagues (Lesser, Fifer, & Clark, 1965) revealed that a child's culture does influence mental abilities. They gave 320 Jewish, Chinese, black and Puerto Rican children from New York City four tests that measured different aspects of intelligence. The following patterns of mental abilities were found. (1) The Jewish children scored higher on the verbal part, lower on reasoning and number, and lower still on space. (2) The black children scored higher on the verbal and lower in reasoning, space, and number. (3) The Puerto Rican children scored lower on the verbal part but higher on number, space, and reasoning. (4) The Chinese children scored low on the verbal part but higher in number, space, and reasoning. In comparisons of the white and oriental children, the white children scored higher on the verbal part but lower on spatial orientation. We may conclude, then, that cultural and racial backgrounds do affect children's performance on tests of mental abilities.

One of the hottest controversies in the search for influences on intelligence is the extent to which black children and white children are intellectually different. Also controversial is the extent to which social class differences influence children's intelligence.

Race and Social Class   Do black children perform poorly on tests of intelligence in comparison with white children? Are the scores of children from lower-class homes lower than those from middle-class homes? The answer is yes to both questions. In a review of hundreds of studies, it was found that the mean IQ of blacks is ten to twenty points below that of whites (Shuey, 1966) (the average black child's IQ is eighty to eighty-five). Also, lower-class children and adults score lower on measures of intelligence than middle-class children and adults do (e.g., Havighurst, Bowman, Liddle, Matthews, & Pierce, 1962; McNemar, 1942).

In the cross-cultural study by Gerald Lesser (1965) comparisons of lower-class and middle-class children also were made. In all analyses the middle-class children scored higher on the IQ tests than the lower-class children. The children of laborers averaged about fifteen to twenty points lower than the children of professionals in these studies.

Arthur Jensen (1969, 1974) has made some provocative comments about the way children from lower- and middle-class society should be educated. He starts off with a basic idea that most would agree with: children should be taught according to their individual needs and abilities; educational programs should not be administered uniformly to all children. But he goes further, arguing that whites and blacks and middle-class and lower-class children should be taught differently. He believes this policy should be carried out because the children themselves are genetically different: Jensen stresses that middle-class children essentially learn in a cognitive manner, while lower-class children learn in an associative way (stimulus-response).

Harold Stevenson (1973) disagrees with Jensen's assertion that lower-class children should be taught associatively and that middle-class children should be taught cognitively. Cognitive tasks and associative tasks cannot always be separated; items that supposedly measure associative learning are often related to items that apparently measure cognitive learning. It may therefore be impossible to separate cognitive and associative learning. Many experts believe that all children, other than perhaps infants or children living in highly controlled or deprived environments, learn primarily in a cognitive manner.

Carl Bereiter (1975) has commented on Jensen's idea of fitting a specific educational curriculum to an individual child. Let's see how Jensen's idea of individualization might be applied to teaching children how to read. It could mean that some children should be given reading instruction at four years of age and that others should wait until they are ten or even older.

Consider the consequences if, as could easily happen, almost all the four-year-old starters in a school system were white and well-to-do and almost all the ten-year-old starters were black and poor. No matter how well-intended the policy, and no matter how serious the effort to apply it without bias, there would be no escaping the charge that the school system had given up on black kids and was consigning them to the status of second-class citizens. The use of an open classroom would conceal the segregation to some extent, but it would not take a very astute observer to notice that the children in the "reading corner" [are] predominantly . . . white while the children in the "block play" and similar corners tended to be predominantly otherwise. (p. 456)

Genetic and Environmental Influences on Intelligence

What is the influence of heredity and environment in the broad range of normal and superior intelligence? Arthur Jensen (1969) examined the research literature that addresses this question. The most compelling information concerns the similarity of IQ for individuals who vary on a dimension of genetic similarity. If hereditary variation among people contributes to differences in IQ, then individuals who have very similar genetic endowments should have very similar IQs, whereas individuals with very different endowments should have very different IQs. Identical twins have identical genetic endowments, so their IQs should be very similar. Nonidentical (fraternal) twins and ordinary siblings are less similar genetically and so should have less similar IQs. Children from different parents are the least similar genetically and should have the least similar IQs. If relevant groups existed in each of these categories, the correlation based on pairs of children should be high for identical twins, lower for fraternal twins and ordinary siblings, and lowest for unrelated children.

For each kind of group, Jensen was able to find some studies in which each member of the pair was reared in the same environment. He found that differences in correlation levels are generally greater for genetic differences than for environmental differences. For example, studies with identical twins produced an average correlation of about .82, if information on twins reared together and information on twins reared separately are combined. Studies about ordinary siblings revealed an average correlation of .50, again combining data about those reared together with data about those reared separately. The difference in correlations is .32. The environmental contrast with twins, however, yields a difference of about .11 (twins reared together; .89: separately; .78) and with ordinary siblings, a difference of about .10 (siblings reared together; .55: separately; .45).

So genetic differences seem to produce larger IQ variation than environmental differences do. Based on this kind of evidence and some complex calculations, Jensen places the heritability quotient at about .80 for intelligence. However, it must be noted that many scholars criticize Jensen's work, and few accept his estimate without qualification.

Perhaps most important is the very definition of intelligence. Standard IQ tests tap a very narrow range of intellectual functioning, most of it based on specific things learned at school and at home. There are many facets of mental life related to everyday problem solving, work performance, and social adaptability that are not covered in IQ tests; at best, the genetic arguments apply only to a limited part of mental life (Kamin, 1974).

Second, there are substantive disagreements on just how much variation can be fairly attributed to the environment. Some critics claim that most heritability studies have not included environments that differ from one another in radical ways so it is not surprising that results support the interpretation that environment contributes little to variation. If studies were to include environments that differ significantly from one another, then greater variation would be attributable to the environment (Bronfenbrenner, 1972; Scarr & Weinberg, 1976).

A third argument is a somewhat technical one. Leon Kamin (1974) claims that much of the original evidence reviewed by Jensen is itself flawed. There are apparent errors in the reporting of results in research reports, flaws in the designs of studies, and inappropriate statistical procedures. Also, it has been learned that a world-renowned British psychologist (C. Burt, now deceased) apparently fabricated the results that he reported in a classic study of IQ in twins (Burt, 1966).

Although there is indeed strong evidence for the heritability of IQ, there are also strong doubts that the actual figure is as high as Jensen claims. A more accurate estimate can be made only on the basis of future evidence that accepts a broader definition of intelligence, compares significantly dissimilar environments, and clarifies some of the technical problems with existing research literature.

Since heritability is an incomplete explanation of IQ, we have to look at environmental factors that can have an influence on intelligence. The important environmental influences on intelligence include experiences at home, the effects of being institutionalized, school experiences, culture, social class, and nutritional and biological factors. Is intelligence, then, due mainly to heredity or mainly to environment? The answer, of course, is that neither heredity nor environment acts alone; they interact to affect intelligence. The nature of this interaction is complex, and experts point out that unfortunately little is known about the specific input of genetics to intelligence (Scarr, 1981, Scarr-Salapatek, 1975). What is known however, does suggest that heredity cannot be ignored as an important influence on intelligence.

Next, we look at yet another aspect of intelligence that has interested psychologists—whether intelligence is stable over varying periods of time in development.

The Stability of Intelligence
Can you predict what a child's IQ will be when she is ten or eighteen years old from her scores on an IQ test administered when she is two, three, and four years old? IQ tests still do not provide very reliable predictions of this sort. Based on statistical techniques, IQ scores obtained at two and three years of age are related to the IQ scores of the same individuals even at ten and eighteen years, although they are not very strongly related.

IQ scores obtained at the age of four are much better at predicting IQ at the age of ten than at the age of eighteen (Honzik, MacFarlane, & Allen, 1948).

There is a strong relation between IQ scores obtained at the ages of six, eight, and nine and IQ scores obtained at the age of ten. For example, in one study the correlation between IQ at the age of eight and IQ at the age of ten was .88. The correlation between IQ at the age of nine and IQ at the age of ten was .90. These figures show a very high relation between IQ scores obtained in these years. The correlation of IQ in the preadolescent years and IQ at the age of eighteen is slightly less, but still statistically significant. For example, the correlation between IQ at the age of ten and IQ at the age of eighteen was .70 in one study (Honzik et al., 1948).

The figures on the stability of intelligence have been based on measures of groups of individuals. The stability of intelligence also can be evaluated through studies of individual persons. As will be seen next, there can be considerable variability in an individual's scores on IQ tests.

Patterns of Change in Intellectual Growth
Robert McCall and his associates (McCall, Applebaum, & Hogarty, 1973) studied 140 individuals and found that between two-and-one-half and seventeen years of age the average range of IQ scores was more than twenty-eight points. The scores of one out of three children changed by as much as thirty points, and one out of seven by as much as forty points. When individuals are assessed over long periods of time, their scores on intelligence tests often fluctuate considerably. Some experts also point out that while intelligence tests (and virtually all psychological tests) were designed to measure stable attributes of the individual, data like those collected by McCall indicate that intelligence is not as stable as the original theories of intelligence had predicted.

A Final Note about Intelligence Tests
Although intelligence tests have been widely criticized, they are still used pervasively in our society. At some point in your life you have had or may have some experience with intelligence tests, perhaps in elementary school or as part of a battery of tests for prospective employment. A child of yours may be given some type of intelligence test. If you become a teacher, you may receive reports from school psychologists telling you about your students' performances on the WISC or the Stanford-Binet. As a teacher or counselor, you may even administer intelligence tests.

Because intelligence tests are so widely used and misused, we have chosen to present extensive information about different kinds of intelligence tests. Many other developmental psychology texts prefer to rely almost exclusively on Piaget's theories and the cognitive-developmental emphasis on qualitative changes in intelligence. Indeed, many Piagetians are among the most vocal critics of the use of IQ tests to measure intelligence. In the next section we will explore the similarities and differences between Piaget's view and the psychometric view.

Comparison of Piagetian and Psychometric Approaches to Intelligence

By now you probably have guessed that Piaget's views about intelligence differ from the views of Binet, Wechsler, and Thurstone. The approach of the latter view is called the **psychometric approach,** referring to an emphasis on measurement-based tests. A professional who administers tests is sometimes referred to as a psychometrist, or psychometrician. David Elkind (1969) has described some of these similarities and differences, which are discussed briefly here.

Piaget began his career as a developmental psychologist by working in Binet's laboratory, but he was more intrigued by the errors children made on the tests than by their correct answers. Piaget and the psychometricians agree that intelligence has a genetic component and that the maturation of thought processes is critical to understanding intelligence. The two views also agree that the most important aspect of intelligence is reasoning.

The most obvious difference between Piaget and the psychometric theorists lies in their views on the course of mental growth. The psychometric theorists are interested in quantifying mental growth, which often produces a number to describe the person's general level of intellectual functioning and to predict intelligence from one age to other ages, since it is argued that IQ is reasonably stable. The psychometric approach, then, maximizes individual differences and seeks to measure them. The Piagetian approach essentially ignores individual differences. Piaget emphasizes the dynamic nature of intelligence and how it qualitatively changes. He is particularly concerned with how new cognitive structures emerge.

Another difference between the two approaches is evident in a comparison of their views on genetics. While both approaches stress the importance of genes in determining intelligence, the psychometric theorists are interested in differences across individuals—for example, they are very interested in how scores from a random sample of 5,000 children fall into place on a distribution of scores. Piaget, on the other hand, focuses more on changes within the individual that shape the organization of intelligence—for example, he is interested in how egocentrism constrains the way the child organizes information about the world.

Traditionally, IQ has been the primary criterion for identifying mental retardation.

Intelligence tests have been used to label children as either mentally retarded or gifted. In the next section we will explore in greater detail these extremes in intelligence.

Mental Retardation, Giftedness, and Creativity

In this section we not only will explore extremes in intelligence by evaluating the concepts of mental retardation and giftedness, but we also will explore what we mean by creativity and attempt to distinguish between intelligence and creativity.

Mental Retardation

What is mental retardation? How is it determined that one child is mentally retarded and another is not? Not everyone agrees on this important matter. In 1961 the American Association on Mental Deficiency defined **mental retardation** as "subaverage intellectual functioning which originates during the developmental period and is associated with impairment in adaptive behavior" (Heber, 1961, p. 3). Traditionally IQ has been the primary criterion for identifying a child as mentally retarded. Thus, on the Wechsler Intelligence Scale for Children the following ranges on IQ scores reflect different levels of mental retardation.

Mental retardation is a label that describes a child's position in relation to other children.

Level of Retardation	IQ-Score Range
Borderline	70–84
Mild	55–69
Moderate	40–54
Severe	25–39
Profound	Below 25

However, cultural and socioeconomic differences can influence performance on IQ tests. Such differences may result in the categorization of blacks, Mexican-Americans, and children from non–English-speaking backgrounds, for example, as mentally retarded even though they actually are not. Therefore, assessment for retardation should go beyond standardized IQ tests to include observations of children in everyday circumstances and environments—at home, in the community, in the classroom with an understanding teacher—to reveal whether or not they can follow instructions and handle problems successfully. Aspects of social competence should be considered in addition to intellectual competence.

Mental Retardation: A Label

Mental retardation is not some kind of disease; it is a label that describes the child's position in relation to other children, based on some standard (or standards) of performance. Thus, if a child scores below seventy on the WISC, he or she is demonstrating less efficient performance than that of a large majority of same-age children who have taken the test. The child is likely to be labeled "mentally retarded," generating a number of inferences (Ross, 1974).

For example, the term *trainable* has been applied to children whose scores are between twenty-five and fifty, and the term *educable* to those whose scores are between fifty and seventy-five. An educable mentally retarded child is supposed to be able to successfully perform academic work at the third- to the sixth-grade level by the time he or she is sixteen years old. A trainable mentally retarded child is supposed to be unable to perform academic work at all; he or she is generally taught personal care and how to cope with some basic, simple routines in life. These children are not taught to read and write. Thus, a child's score on an IQ test has important implications for the type of treatment program to which he or she is assigned.

It is important to remember that an IQ score reflects a child's *current* performance; it does not always indicate academic *potential*. Therefore, the use of diagnostic labels that suggest assumptions about a child's potential can be dangerous. Remarkable strides are sometimes made in teaching retarded children to perform academic tasks that were thought to be impossible. Many experts believe the terms *trainable* and *educable*, as well as *mental retardation*, should always be thought of as labels that index only current performance. Because a child's level of performance may well change later, it may be wise to discard the label.

A score in the mentally retarded range on an IQ test reveals nothing about why the child is retarded. Next, we will find that the most widely used classification of the causes of mental retardation distinguishes between organic and cultural-familial causes.

Causes of Retardation

Damage to the central nervous system, particularly to the brain, can produce mental retardation. This damage to the brain may occur during prenatal or postnatal development or as a result of an abnormal chromosome configuration. Down's syndrome is a well-known example of mental retardation that has an organic cause, the presence of an extra chromosome. Another type of organic disturbance that results in severe mental retardation is inadequate production of hormones, as in **cretinism.** Cretinism is caused by a hormone deficiency in the thyroid gland. When this deficiency is untreated, physical and mental development is stunted.

Many organic causes of mental retardation are linked to pregnancy and birth. For example, overdoses of radiation or the contraction of syphilis during pregnancy can cause retardation. Accidental injury to the brain of the fetus, as through a bad fall by the mother or the birth process itself, can cause mental retardation. Furthermore, although no clear link to mental retardation itself has been uncovered, inadequate protein intake on the part of the mother may be a contributing factor for mental retardation.

Most instances of mental retardation do not have a known organic cause. Such retardation is termed cultural-familial. For retardation to be considered cultural-familial, the following criteria must be met: there can be no detectable brain abnormality; the retardation must be mild; and at least one of the parents or one of the siblings must also be mentally retarded (Davison & Neale, 1975). It has been estimated that the number of people whose mental retardation is considered cultural-familial represents about 75 percent of the retarded population. Their intelligence test scores generally fall between fifty and seventy, whereas the scores of those with organic retardation are likely to be much lower.

Both genetic and environmental factors contribute to the occurrence of cultural-familial retardation. For instance, parents who have low IQs not only are more likely to transmit genes for a lower intelligence to their offspring but also tend to provide them with a less enriched environment (Ross, 1974).

Some experts believe that replacing the impoverished environment of the cultural-familial retarded child with a more enriched one may stimulate normal or even superior intellectual growth. Even though these children may make intellectual gains, however, the gains are usually limited. Of course, intensive effort at teaching mentally retarded children should not be abandoned—to the contrary, every effort should be made to encourage retarded children to learn and to achieve to the best of their abilities. However, the process of change is usually an arduous one that requires great patience and commitment on the part of the teacher.

Learning and Social Interaction
H. B. Robinson and N. M. Robinson (1970) have reviewed many different studies about the learning processes of retarded children. They believe it has been established beyond doubt that the laws of learning that apply to nonretarded children apply also to retarded children.

One aspect of learning by retarded children that has received considerable discussion is attention and distractibility. It is generally concluded that mentally retarded children are less efficient in focusing attention during a learning sequence and are more easily distracted than normal children. Thus, the learning process should be made as exciting as possible and the child's environment during the learning process should be simplified to minimize possible distractions.

In a review of specific facets of the learning process (e.g., stimulus generalization, memory, learning sets, and operant conditioning), comparing the performance of mentally retarded and normal children, the same conclusions are apparent: retarded children learn in the same way that normal children learn, although their level of performance is often lower.

There is evidence that parents do not interact in the same way with their retarded child as with normal children. The parents of a retarded child tend to be controlling, do not support the child's independent play, and use praise inconsistently and inappropriately (e.g., Buim, Rynders, & Turnure, 1974; Marshall, Hegrenes, & Goldstein, 1974).

Some parents' interactions with their retarded child seem to be based on the child's chronological age rather than mental age (Zigler, 1971). The child is probably frustrated because the demands placed on him or her exceed abilities. On the other hand, some people fail to challenge the mentally retarded child. They treat the child as incapable of any learning or independence. For example, in one class for the mentally retarded a child practiced a sequence of four steps to solve a difficult problem. Although the teacher had modeled the steps for over an hour to help the child, he continued to hesitate when asked to perform the task alone. The teacher finally finished her exhaustive modeling and left; afterward the boy unhesitatingly—and correctly—performed the four steps. Adults are often too ready to help retarded children do something they can do (or learn to do) for themselves.

At the other end of the intelligence spectrum are those children with well-above-average intelligence, often referred to as gifted children. In the next section, we will look at what it means for a child to be gifted and the educational programs that have been developed for such children.

Gifted Children
Many years ago the label "gifted" had a single meaning, namely high intelligence (White House Conference on Children, 1931). The **gifted child** still is described as an individual with well-above-average intellectual capacity (an IQ of 120 or more, for example), but he or she may also be a child with a superior talent for something (Owen, Froman, & Moscow,

1981). In their selection of children for gifted programs, most school systems still place the heaviest weight on intellectual superiority and academic aptitude and do not look as carefully at such areas of competence as the visual and performing arts, psychomotor abilities, and other specific aptitudes.

One classic study dominates our knowledge about gifted children, that of Lewis Terman (1925). He began to study approximately 1,500 children in the 1920s whose Stanford-Binet IQ scores averaged 150. Terman's research was designed to follow these children through their adulthood—it will not be complete until the year 2010.

The accomplishments of the 1,500 children in Terman's study are remarkable. Of the 800 males, 78 have obtained Ph.D.s, 48 have earned M.D.s, and 85 have been granted law degrees. Nearly all of these figures are ten to thirty times greater than would have been found among 800 men of the same age chosen randomly (Getzels & Dillon, 1973).

Scrutiny of the gifted 1,500 continues. The most recent investigation focused on whether the gifted individuals had been satisfied with their lives (Sears, 1977). When the average age of the Terman gifted population was sixty-two, four target factors were assessed: life-cycle satisfaction with occupation; satisfaction with family life; degree of work persistence into their sixties; and unbroken marriage vs. a history of divorce. The recorded events and expressions of feelings have been obtained at decade intervals since 1922. One of the most interesting findings of the study was that in spite of their autonomy and extensive success in their occupations, these men placed more importance on achieving satisfaction in their family life than in their work. And, furthermore, the gifted individuals felt that they had found such satisfaction. As Terman suggested, they were not only superior intellectually but physically, emotionally, morally, and socially more able as well.

Programs for gifted children usually follow one of three paths: **enrichment, grouping,** and **acceleration.** Enrichment focuses on special provisions for gifted children, including college-level courses in high school, advanced classes, independent study, and so forth. Grouping occurs when students with similar capacities are placed in a class together. Acceleration refers to any strategy that abbreviates the time required for a student to graduate, such as skipping a grade (Owen et al., 1981).

Do such programs work? Julian Stanley (1977), widely known for his study of gifted children, has pointed out that most gifted children enrichment programs are comprised of busywork, are irrelevant, and in many instances are just plain boring. Research directed at assessing the impact of acceleration provides a more favorable picture; a summary of the acceleration studies suggests that from first grade through college acceleration seems to have a positive intellectual and emotional effect on gifted children (Laycock, 1979).

In the Terman study, for example, the individuals who had been accelerated in school were more successful in their jobs, education, and marriage and maintained better physical health than those who had not been accelerated (Terman & Oden, 1959). Grouping has been much more controversial than enrichment or acceleration. Research on grouping children into tracks has produced mixed results (Esposito, 1973), and many critics point out that it is unfair to poor children and ethnic minority groups.

Closely related to the study of gifted children is creativity, an important aspect of mental functioning that is not measured by traditional IQ tests, a fact that has triggered considerable criticism of these intelligence tests. As will be seen in the next section, children not only think, they think *creatively.*

Creativity

Most of us would like to be creative, and parents and teachers would like to be able to develop situations that promote creative thinking in children. Why was Thomas Edison able to invent so many things? Was he simply more intelligent than most people? Did he spend long hours toiling away in private? Somewhat surprisingly, when Edison was a young boy his teacher told him he was too dumb to learn anything! And there are other examples of famous individuals whose creative genius went unnoticed when they were younger (Larson, 1973): Walt Disney was fired on a newspaper job because he did not have any good ideas; Enrico Caruso's music teacher informed him that he he could not sing and that he didn't have any voice at all; Albert Einstein was four years old before he could speak and seven before he could read; and Winston Churchill failed one year of secondary school. Among the reasons such individuals are overlooked as youngsters is the difficulty we have in defining and measuring creativity. In this section we also will look at development changes in creativity, the role of imagery in creative thinking, and educational programs developed to promote creativity.

Definition and Measurement

The prevailing belief of experts who study creativity is that intelligence and creativity are not the same (e.g., Getzels, 1975; Richards, 1976; Wallach, 1973). For example, scores on widely used tests of creativity developed by J. P. Guilford (1967) and by Michael Wallach and Nathan Kogan (1965) are only weakly related to intelligence scores (Richards, 1976). Yet is is as difficult to define creativity as it is to define intelligence. Just as intelligence consists of many disparate elements, so also creativity is a many-faceted phenomenon. An important question is whether measuring general creative functioning is appropriate or even possible.

David Ausubel (1968) emphasized that **creativity** is one of the most ambiguous and confusing terms in psychology and education. He believes that the term *creative* should not be applied to as many people as it is but should be reserved for describing people who make unique and original contributions to society.

The term creativity has been used in many ways. Following are the ways that some well-known figures define creativity and attempt to measure it in individuals.

Guilford's Concept of Divergent Thinking

Creative thinking is part of J. P. Guilford's model of intelligence (Guilford, 1967). The aspect of his theory of intelligence that is most closely related to creativity is what he calls **divergent thinking,** a type of thinking that produces many different answers to a single question. Divergent thinking is distinguished from **convergent thinking,** a type of thinking that goes toward one correct answer. For example, there is one correct answer to this intellectual problem-solving task: "How many quarters can you get from sixty dimes?" It calls for convergent thinking. But there are many possible answers to this question: "What are some unique things a coat hanger can be used for?" This question requires divergent thinking. Going off in different directions may sometimes lead to more productive answers. Examples of what Guilford means by divergent thinking (his term for creativity) and ways of measuring it follow:

1. *Word fluency:* How facile are you with words? For example, name as many words as possible and as fast as possible that contain the letter z.
2. *Ideational fluency:* Here you have to name words that belong to a particular class. For example, name as many objects as you can that weigh less than one pound.
3. *Associational fluency:* In this type of divergent thinking you have to name words that are associated with other words, such as similarity of meaning. For example, name as many words as possible that mean "easy."
4. *Expressional fluency:* Here you have to put words together to meet the requirements of sentence structure. For example, write as many sentences as you can that have four words, each word starting with these letters: *T, a, s, a. (One sentence using these letters might be: T*omorrow *a* salesman *ar*rives.)
5. *Spontaneous flexibility:* Even when you are not asked to give divergent answers, do you give unique answers as well as common answers? For example, if you are asked what a paper clip can be used for, do you spontaneously generate different categories of use for the paper clip?
6. *Adaptive flexibility:* In this type of divergent thinking you must be able to vary your ideas widely when this is called for. For example, if you are shown a series of matchsticks lined up on a table, you may be asked to put them together to form four triangles.
7. *Redefinition:* You might be asked to say how specific common objects can be used for new purposes.
8. *Originality:* This time you would be required to name some unique ways to use an object. For example, what are some unusual ways to use hairpins?

Torrance's Work

Torrance (1966) has defined creativity more broadly than Guilford. He talks about creativity in much the same way general intelligence has been described. That is, creativity is seen as problem solving that goes off in different directions. Creativity is the process of first identifying a problem and then carrying through until the results of the problem solving are communicated. In between, the person searches for answers, identifies difficulties, makes hunches, develops hypotheses, and then modifies and retests these.

Torrance has devised what are called the Torrance Tests of Creative Thinking. They were developed within an educational context as part of a research effort to define classroom experiences that promote creativity (e.g., Torrance, 1967). The scores a child receives on the tests, however, are related to Guilford's factors: fluency, flexibility, originality, and elaboration. The child is scored on each of these creativity factors, and then the scores are added to arrive at a total score for creativity. The Torrance tests are an attempt to measure specific aspects of creativity, but they also emphasize a belief that a general factor of creativity can be measured.

Because the Torrance tests are used widely with children of school age, several of the items are described here. The tests consist of both verbal and nonverbal items.

In the Ask-and-Guess test the child is shown a picture—one picture is that of a clown looking at a reflection of himself in the water—and is asked to list all the questions he can think of about the picture. Next, he is asked to name all the possible causes of the situation depicted. And last, he is asked to describe as many possible consequences of the situation as he can. He is given five minutes to do each of these tasks.

In the Just Suppose test the child is shown a picture of an unlikely situation; one that is used is a picture of clouds linked to the ground with strings. He is requested to tell all of the possible events that could happen in this unusual situation.

In one nonverbal Picture Construction test, the child is given an oval piece of green paper. Then he is given a larger, blank sheet of paper and is told that he can glue the green paper anywhere he wants to on the blank sheet. Then he is told to add lines to the picture in whatever way he desires. His work is scored for its originality and elaboration.

Some experts question whether the Torrance tests can appropriately be used as a general measure of creativity. The basic issue is whether some parts of the test are reflecting general intelligence rather than creativity. In a review of research involving the Torrance tests, Michael Wallach (1970) concluded that the parts of the tests most likely to evaluate creativity apart from intelligence are *ideational fluency and fluency-related forms of originality*. The items concerned with spontaneous flexibility and elaboration are not good measures of creativity. This comment can also be applied to items used by Guilford to measure divergent thinking.

Wallach's and Kogan's Work   Michael Wallach and Nathan Kogan (1965) attempted to refine the ability to separate creativity from intelligence. Their work has included efforts to specify how creative people in the arts and sciences think. People who are rated as highly creative individuals are asked to probe introspectively into what it is that enables them to produce creative pieces of work. Two major factors evolve from this self-analysis by creative people. (1) They have what is called **associative flow.** That is, they can generate large amounts of associative content in their effort to attain novel solutions to problems. (2) They have the freedom to entertain a wide range of possible solutions in a playful manner. These responses led Wallach and Kogan to remove time limits from tests of creativity and to make sure that the tests were given in very relaxed, nonthreatening, informal situations.

Wallach and Kogan sought the answers to these questions: How would a highly creative, highly intelligent child differ from a highly creative child with low intelligence? How would a child low in creativity but highly intelligent differ from a child low in creativity and with low intelligence? Their research (1965, 1967) revealed the following conclusions.

High creativity-high intelligence: These children often are described as superior children. They are popular, confident, able to concentrate well on what they are doing, and show great insight. Sometimes they show some uneasiness in the classroom, which may be a reflection of their disenchantment with traditional schooling.

High creativity-low intelligence: These children feel a lot of stress. They frequently disrupt the classroom and cause trouble for the teacher. They have low opinions of themselves and work best when there is no stress placed on them.

Low creativity-high intelligence: These children are oriented to conformity. They do well in school but have a strong fear of failure.

Low creativity-low intelligence: School is not a very enjoyable place for these children. They are often defensive about achievement in school, but they do frequently strive for success in social situations.

Most of the work on creativity—that of Guilford, Torrance, and Wallach and Kogan—has been conducted in the psychometric tradition; that is, extensive efforts have made to measure creativity. Creativity is conceptualized as a unitary attribute or ability of the individual, much in the way general intelligence is conceptualized. Recently, however, there has been new interest in developmental changes in creativity. This interest is discussed in the context of Piaget's theory of cognitive development.

Developmental Changes in Creativity

Some commonly held beliefs about developmental changes in creativity are: (1) it begins to weaken around the age of five because of the societal pressure to conform; (2) serious drops in creativity occur at the age of nine and at the age of twelve; (3) adults are less creative than children (Dudek, 1974).

These stereotypes are not supported by good research data. Actually, a drop in creativity probably does not occur at the age of nine; what happens instead is that the child's form of expression changes. At about eight or nine years of age the child begins to develop a more differentiated view of reality compared to an earlier, more global view. The child is freer from perceptual dominance and clearly into the concrete operations stage. Consider the child's art, for example. The child now paints as he or she sees, not feels. Feeling does not entirely disappear from art, but it now is less important to the child than realistic detail.

According to Steven Dudek (1974) this change represents increased subtlety in thought and increased imagination, not less. Others may interpret the art as less creative and less imaginative because surprise and vividness are missing. It has lost some of its spontaneity but not its complexity. At this point the child may require time to master the skills of the concrete operational period before he or she can use them spontaneously and freely.

The drop in creativity reported at about the age of twelve also occurs just after the child has entered a new stage in Piaget's theory. In the formal operations stage the child is learning how to develop hypotheses, how to combine ideas in complex ways, and how to think in more imaginative and abstract ways. Piaget has pointed out that when children begin to develop new cognitive skills, egocentrism often results and pressures to conform are very strong. An increase in creativity might be expected during adolescence as the child gradually masters the use of these newly acquired cognitive skills. Evidence suggests that if repressive forces are not too strong, creativity does seem to increase in adolescence (Greenacre, 1971). Hence, neither adolescents nor adults are necessarily less creative than young children.

In addition to interest in developmental changes in creativity, another area of considerable interest to psychologists who study children's creativity is the role imagery plays.

Imagery and Creativity

Most experts on creativity stress the importance of *flexibility,* a term referring to the replacement of a fixed set of ideas by a set of alternative views about a problem. The use of imagery does seem to be linked to flexible thinking and creative problem solving (Durio, 1975). For example, compared with verbalization, imagery seems to lead to a more playful shifting from one solution to the next (e.g., Walkup, 1965). Some writers believe that creative individuals are unusually competent in the use of imagery in their thought processes (Walkup, 1965).

Joe Khatena (1975, 1976) also believes imagery plays an important role in creativity. Khatena collaborated with Paul Torrance (1973) in an attempt to measure the link between imagery and creativity: their Onomatopoeia and Images Test assesses the break from sound and verbal stimuli to original verbal images. From responses to the test, the complexity of the person's images can also be scored. In one study Khatena and Torrance (1973) investigated the relation of children's originality to the types of analogies they produced. Children who showed more originality were more likely to engage in simple image analogies than in personal, symbolic, or fantasy analogies.

Encouraging Creativity

Brainstorming is one technique that has been effective in several programs developed to stimulate creativity in children. In brainstorming sessions a topic is presented for consideration and participants are encouraged to suggest ideas related to it. Criticism of ideas contributed must be withheld initially to prevent stopping the flow of ideas. The more freewheeling the ideas, the better. Participants are also encouraged to combine ideas that have already been suggested. Studies with children in regular classrooms (e.g., Torrance & Torrance, 1972) and in classrooms with educationally handicapped children (e.g., Sharpe, 1976) indicate that brainstorming can be an effective strategy for increasing creative thinking.

Another useful technique is called **playing with improbabilities.** This method forces children to think about the events that might follow an unlikely occurrence. Torrance gave the following examples of questions that can be used to foster classroom discussion:

What could happen if it always rained on Saturday? What could happen if it were against the law to sing? . . . Just suppose you could visit the prehistoric section of the museum and the animals could come alive? Just suppose you could enter into the life of a pond and become whatever you wanted to become? (pp. 436–37)

To answer these questions, the child must break out of conventional modes of thought and wander through fantasyland.

More important perhaps than any specific technique, however, is the need to foster a *creative atmosphere* in the classroom. Children need to feel that they can try out ideas, even if the ideas seem crazy or far-fetched, without being criticized by the teacher. The only way to produce a creative environment on a sustained basis is to *do* things creatively on a regular basis.

Creative thinking can be encouraged in any type of curriculum and in any kind of classroom situation; neither an open classroom nor progressive education is required. A word of caution, however: although experts believe that creative thinking exercises should be practiced in every classroom, they caution against spending too much time on creative activities at the expense of other equally important learning activities. Michael Wallach (1973), for one, has commented that many children do not need to read more creatively, they just need to learn how to read.

The discussion of creativity ends our discussion of physical development and intelligence. In the next chapter we continue our evaluation of cognitive development in middle and late childhood, focusing again on Piaget's cognitive-structural theory and the information processing perspective.

Summary

This chapter focused on physical development and intelligence. Physical growth slows during the middle and late childhood years. Most children become more proficient at athletic skills in middle and late childhood, and in most areas of motor development, movement is more coordinated and smoother than in early childhood.

The definition of intelligence is closely related to the way it is measured. One of the most widely used measures of intelligence, the Stanford-Binet test, was originally developed to determine which students would succeed in school. It focuses on measurement of general intelligence rather than specific mental abilities. The Wechsler Scales (WISC), also widely used, are designed to provide scores for overall intelligence as well as for the individual functions or abilities through which intelligence is revealed and by which it can be measured. The factor-analytic approach to intelligence and its assessment, advanced by Thurstone and Guilford, is generally regarded today as revealing little about the development of intelligence. Efforts to develop culture-free or culture-fair intelligence tests have been largely unsuccessful; the Raven Progressive Matrices Test is perhaps the best (though far from perfect) culture-fair test.

Piaget's views of intelligence differ substantially from those of the intelligence measurers, the psychometricians. Piaget is concerned with how new cognitive structures emerge and how intelligence changes qualitatively rather than quantitatively.

Is intelligence a stable attribute? While studies show it to be more stable than many other attributes, extensive fluctuations have been recorded for individuals tested at several different times in their lives, suggesting a degree of instability and susceptibility to influence from several factors. It also is important to remember that intelligence is influenced by the interaction of heredity and environment through the home, school, cultural and social environment, and even nutrition.

Two extremes of intellectual functioning are mental retardation and giftedness. Mental retardation refers to the lower-than-average intelligence of a child as measured by a standardized intelligence test. Some forms of retardation have an organic cause, such as Down's syndrome, while others, particularly the milder forms, stem from cultural-familial causes. The most successful techniques for educating the mentally retarded take into account the fact that the learning process itself is the same for both retarded and normal children but this process should be enhanced to address the specific problems of retarded children.

The term *gifted* applies to students of well-above-average intelligence. Despite the persistent popular belief that the highly intelligent are likely to be eccentric, longitudinal studies of such individuals suggest the opposite to be true. A group of 1,500 individuals whose IQs averaged 150 was followed by Lewis Terman from childhood through adulthood. The individuals were not only superior intellectually but emotionally and physically more able as well. Programs designed to help the gifted emphasize enrichment, acceleration, and grouping. Studies focused on the effectiveness of these programs indicate that acceleration may be the best strategy.

An important aspect of mental functioning not usually assessed by intelligence tests is creativity. Extensive efforts have been made to devise definitions and tests of creativity that are not measures of general intellectual functioning. Originality and flexibility are two factors that tests of creativity attempt to measure.

Developmental changes occur in creativity just as they do in general intelligence; these changes seem to coincide with the transitions in Piaget's stage of cognitive development. Although some have argued that creativity falls off as the child grows older, it seems more accurate to say that creativity merely changes form at different points in development. Imagery is viewed increasingly as a significant factor in creativity. Most experts believe that creativity exercises should be practiced in every classroom but not to the detriment of developing sound academic skills.

Key Terms

acceleration	grouping
associative flow	intelligence
brainstorming	mental age (MA)
convergent thinking	mental retardation
creativity	mesomorphic
cretinism	neurometrics
crystallized intelligence	normal distribution
culture-fair tests	playing with improbabilities
culture-free tests	psychometric approach
divergent thinking	self-fulfilling prophecy
ectomorphic	social intelligence
endomorphic	standard deviation
enrichment	Stanford-Binet
factor-analytic approach	two-factor theory of intelligence
fluid intelligence	
g	
gifted children	

Review Questions

1. What is the nature of physical growth during middle and late childhood?
2. How did Binet define intelligence? What kind of IQ test did he construct to measure it?
3. What is the Wechsler intelligence test? How is it like and unlike the Binet?
4. Describe the factor-analytic approach to intelligence.
5. What is the purpose of culture-free and culture-fair intelligence tests?
6. How does Piaget's approach to intelligence differ from that of the psychometricians?
7. How stable is intelligence during childhood?
8. Describe Terman's study of the gifted. What were the results of the study?
9. Name three types of programs developed to help gifted children. Describe them and discuss their effectiveness.
10. How does Guilford define and measure creativity?
11. How does Torrance view creativity? Describe the Torrance tests.
12. What has Wallach's and Kogan's research revealed about the relationship of creativity and intelligence?
13. What is the role of imagery in the development of creative thinking?
14. How can creativity be promoted in the classroom?

Further Readings

American Psychologist, vol. 36, no. 10, October, 1981.
Special issue testing: concepts, policy, practice, and research.
American Psychologist is the Journal of the American Psychological Association.
This entire issue is devoted to psychological testing and includes articles written by a number of experts. Reading level is moderately difficult.

Brody, E. G., & Brody, N. *Intelligence: nature, determinants, and consequences.* New York: Academic Press, 1976.
This book is an excellent source of information about the complex factors that affect intelligence. An up-to-date evaluation of the genetic-environmental controversy regarding intelligence.

Cratty, B. *Perceptual and motor development in infants and children,* 2d ed. Englewood Cliffs, N.J.: Prentice-Hall, 1979.
This book provides a detailed description of many different aspects of physical development in middle and late childhood. Extensive information is given about the awkward child and the child in competitive sport. Easy reading.

Davis, G. A., & Scott, J. A. (eds.). *Training creative thinking.* New York: Holt, Rinehart & Winston, 1971.
A collection of articles by several psychologists who study creativity, with practical suggestions on how to stimulate creativity in the classroom. Most of the articles are easy to read.

Gowan, J. C., Khatena, J., & Torrance, E. P. (eds.). *Educating the ablest,* 2d ed. Itasca, Ill.: F. E. Peacock, 1979.
A selected book of readings on a variety of topics that relate to gifted children and the process of creativity. Includes sections on programs and curriculum for gifted and creative children, the role of imagery, and developmental characteristics. Easy to read.

Sattler, J. *Assessment of children's intelligence,* 2d ed. Philadelphia: Saunders, 1980.
The author provides extensive information about the history of intelligence testing, with emphasis on the Binet and WISC tests. Extensive information is given about a variety of intelligence tests currently used with children.

Torrance, E. P., & Myers, R. E. *Creative learning and teaching.* New York: Dodd, 1970.
An easy-to-read introduction to ideas about what creativity is and how to foster it in the classroom. Torrance is one of the leaders in the field.

Cognitive Development

Prologue: Piaget, Education, and Thinking Games

Hardly a day passes without the appearance of a new article applying the principles of Piaget's theory of cognitive development to the education of American children. Frank Murray (1978) describes why Americans have moved so swiftly to embrace Piaget. Two social crises, the proliferation of behaviorism and the dominance of the psychometric approach to intelligence (IQ testing), have made the adoption of Piagetian theory inevitable, he says. The first social crisis was the post-Sputnik concern of a country preoccupied with its deteriorating position as the engineering and scientific leader in the world, and the second was the need for compensatory education for minority groups and the poor. Curriculum projects that soon came into being after these social crises include the "new math," Science Curriculum Improvement Study, Project Physics, "discovery learning," and Man: A Course of Study. All of these projects have been based upon Piaget's notion of cognitive developmental changes in thought structure. Piaget's theory contains a great deal of information about the young person's reasoning in the areas of math, science, and logic—material not found anywhere else in the literature of developmental psychology.

Piaget is not an educator, nor is he principally concerned with problems of education. However, he has provided a scientifically sound conceptual framework from which to view educational problems. Recall in chapter 7 our discussion of the similarity in the way Piaget and Maria Montessori believe children learn. In summarizing the general principles of education implicit in Piaget's image of the child, David Elkind (1976) concluded:

First of all . . . the foremost problem of education is *communication*. According to the Piaget image, the child's mind is not an empty slate. Quite the contrary, the child has a host of ideas about the physical and natural world, but these ideas differ from those of adults and are expressed in a different linguistic mode. . . . We must learn to comprehend what children are saying and to respond in the same mode of discourse.

A second implication is that the child is always unlearning and relearning as well as acquiring entirely new knowledge. The child comes to school with his own ideas about space, time, causality, quantity, and number. . . .

Still a third implication for educational philosophy . . . is that the child is by nature a knowing creature. If the child has ideas about the world which he has not been taught (because they are foreign to adults) and which he has not inherited (because they change with age) then he must have acquired these notions through his spontaneous interactions with the environment . . . education needs to insure that it does not dull this eagerness to know by overly rigid curricula that disrupt the child's own rhythm and pace of learning. (pp. 108–9)

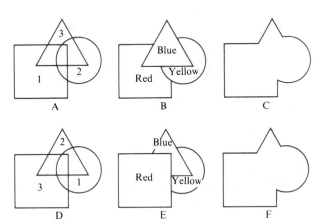

The game Overlaps.

This game demonstrates for children that an outline of overlapping forms does not always make clear which piece has been placed first. It emphasizes the importance of temporal ordering. A series of overlapping forms (triangles, circles, squares) is drawn on a card. Each form bears a number which indicates whether it was drawn first, second, third, and so on. The child is given similar forms cut out of cardboard or plastic. He follows the instruction of the model to discover that the pieces can be arranged in various orders of overlap to create entirely new patterns which retain the original outline.

In a variation, a concrete pattern constructed from the cutout forms becomes the model, and the child selects the proper card to match it. Later the child may construct and draw his own patterns. This can be considered as a permutation-combination task. The game can be varied by asking the child to transpose the parts of the pattern or attempt to think of how it would look from different positions. (p. 171)

An application of Piaget's ideas to education that is particularly creative and innovative is the elementary school program of Hans Furth and Harry Wachs (1975). They seemed to take the following comment by Piaget seriously:

Whenever anyone can succeed in transforming their first steps in reading, or arithmetic, or spelling into a *game* [emphasis added], you will see children become passionately absorbed in those occupations, which are ordinarily presented as dreary chores. (Piaget, 1970, p. 155)

Furth and Wachs developed 179 thinking games that were to be incorporated into the day-to-day learning of children in the primary grades. They tried out this method for two years in an experimental school in Charleston, West Virginia—the Tyler Thinking School.

One of the games they developed is called Overlaps. This game works on several different properties of thought at the same time—ordering things, seeing different perspectives, and working with combinations.

Some of the games were specifically directed toward such basic skills as reading and mathematics. Other games were directed to more general knowledge about the world—the typical preoccupation of Piagetians. This general knowledge is a foundation on which school learning builds.

Introduction

In this chapter we continue our discussion of cognitive development, focusing first on Piaget's stage of concrete operational thought. In the prologue you read how Piaget's ideas can be applied to education. In the discussion of concrete operational thought we will look further at how children in middle and late childhood use classification to organize their thoughts. In chapter 7 we introduced a paradigm that is competing with Piaget's cognitive-structural perspective to win the plaudits of developmental psychologists—the information processing approach. This approach analyzes the various steps involved in cognitive activity—in chapter 7 we described attention, the step that occurs first in many cognitive activities. In this chapter we explore in greater detail other steps involved in cognitive activity—perception, memory, and problem solving—paying particular attention to their role in children's cognition during middle and late childhood. And, we describe further the changes in language development that occur during middle and late childhood, emphasizing what comes after Roger Brown's first five stages and the development of reading skills.

Piaget's Stage of Concrete Operational Thought

In this section we not only will describe what Piaget means by concrete operational thought, but we will critically evaluate Piaget's theory and discuss several neo(modified)-Piagetian approaches to cognitive development.

The *concrete operational* stage lasts from about seven to eleven years of age, cutting across the major portion of the elementary school years. During this time the child's thinking crystallizes into more of a system, and the many flaws associated with the preoperational stage completely disappear. The actual system is described by Piaget in terms of relatively complex logic and treated in depth by John Flavell (1977) and by Herbert Ginsburg and Sylvia Opper (1980). By way of a simple comparison to the preceding stage, however, the concrete thinker has none of the limitations of the preoperational thinker and is capable of thought in all the respects that the preoperational thinker is not.

This shift to a more perfect system of thinking is brought about by several gradual changes. One of these is the shift from egocentrism to relativism. The child can now decenter, or operate with two or more aspects of a problem simultaneously. For example, Michael Chandler and David Greenspan (1972) told children stories about characters who experienced different emotions. In a story one character might feel sad because he lost a toy, and another might feel happy because she received a treat. The investigators asked children to repeat the stories. The seven-year-olds often confused the emotional perspectives of the characters in the stories. Ten- and eleven-year-olds rarely did.

During the concrete operational stage, the child's thinking crystallizes into more of a system.

Another change is reversibility. The child can now mentally pose and operate on a series of actions, for example, perform mental arithmetic, imagine a game of ping-pong, mentally pour liquids back and forth, and so on.

One limitation of concrete thinking is its reliance on clearly available perceptual and physical supports. The child needs to have objects and events on hand in order to think about them.

What is a concrete operation? A concrete operation is an idealized version of how a child's thought is structured. It can be described by reference to the different tasks that the child is able to solve, such as conservation or class inclusion, or more formally put in terms of certain properties of sets in modern algebra. That is, Piaget borrows some ideas from modern algebra to describe the logical properties of the child's thought processes, or the way the child is able to think and reason under ideal circumstances.

A Representative Concrete Operation: The Primary Addition of Classes

Many of the concrete operations identified by Piaget concern the manner in which children reason about properties of objects. As we have seen in the description of **classification** tasks and **class inclusion reasoning,** an important skill of middle and late childhood is to be able to divide things into different sets and subsets and to consider their interrelationships. By describing a simple hierarchy of classes below, we can see how one concrete operation is defined.

Box 10.1
Children's Classification of a Family Tree of Four Generations

Hans Furth and Harry Wachs (1975) conclude that many classifications occur on a horizontal level, that is, the different dimensions have no intrinsic relation to each other. Hair color, marital status, and education are unrelated characteristics by which people can be classified. However, this horizontal level is only the beginning of classification. Classification becomes more complex when we consider its vertical and hierarchical characteristics as well.

The family tree of four generations shown here suggests that the grandfather (A) has three children (B, C, D), each of whom has in turn two children (E to J), and finally one of these children (J) has three children (K, L, M). This is an excellent example of hierarchical classification in that all classes stand in necessary relation to each other. The class of sons at level II implies the presence of the class of father at level I and of the classes of children and grandchildren at levels III and IV. A child who comprehends the classification system can mentally move up or down a level (vertically) and across a given level (horizontally) or up and down and across (obliquely) within this system. He or she understands that a person J can be at the same time father, brother, son, and grandson. In addition, I and J are alike in that they are related children of the same parent (D), while H and J are alike in that they are related grandchildren of the same grandparent (A). These relations characterize the respective classes of siblings and cousins and show how the two classes are different, yet alike.

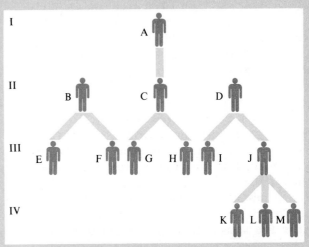

A family tree of four generations (I) to (V).

Let us suppose that a child is to deal with the following hierarchy:

A = class of spaniels

A = all other subclasses within the class of domestic dogs

B = class of domestic dogs

B = all other subclasses within the class of canines

C = class of canines

According to Piaget, the concrete thinker could add these classes together (for example, combining domestic dogs [b] with all spaniels [a]), subtract one from the next (for example, eliminating spaniels [a] from the larger class of domestic dogs [b]), and combine them in different ways. While doing so, the child's reasoning would obey the following principle.

1. The subclasses would be *associative;* the order in which they are combined does not matter.
2. The subclasses are a *composition;* if any two classes are combined, the resulting class is also part of the system.
3. There exists one or more *identity* operations. For example, a class could be spread out physically, but it is still the same class.
4. For every act in which the classes are combined in some way, it is possible to *reverse* the combination.

As we have seen, all classification involves a grouping or sorting of objects into classes according to some rule or principle. In box 10.1, an application of children's classification to different generations of families is provided.

Even as late as the mid 1970s, Piaget's theory was very much the central focus of attention in the field of cognitive development. While there were skeptics even then (e.g., Brainerd, 1972), the attitude seemed to be one of wait and see. Now in the 1980s, however, a new feeling has caught up with most contemporary scholars (e.g., Flavell, 1980; Kuhn, 1980; Gelman, 1978; Fischer, 1980, 1982). The last line in John Flavell's eulogy to Piaget (see chapter 7) states this new attitude well: "Our task is now to extend and go beyond what he began so well." Let us briefly consider what it is that Piaget began so well and what some of the current misgivings are with regard to his theory.

Evaluation of Piaget's Theory

Piaget was a brilliant observer of children. He collected thousands of firsthand observations of what children do and how they seem to think that have withstood the scrutiny of time (in some cases thirty to fifty years). There are many reasons for crediting Piaget with genius, but this accomplishment alone would be sufficient. Piaget's insights are easily and often surprisingly verified. The young infant really does fail to search for an object when it is hidden. The four-year-old who watches a liquid poured from one container into another differently shaped actually says that there is now "more" or "less" liquid than before. The nine-year-old really does get stuck in hypothetical-deductive problem solving. There are literally hundreds of such observations, first made by Piaget, that accurately describe how children generally reason in these situations.

A second contribution is that Piaget has given us many good ideas about what to look for in development. For example, he has shown us that infants are very complex and subtle creatures whose seemingly chaotic patterns of response are actually highly organized and structured. Contemporary experts on infancy have benefited to an extraordinary degree by his suggestions and descriptions of this organization. Or, as another example, he has shown us that the major change from childhood to adolescence involves a shift from the world of concrete and narrow logic to the plane of verbal reasoning and broad generalization. This insight has had a widely felt influence on educators and those who work with adolescents.

A third contribution is Piaget's focus on the qualitative nature of mental life. By always directing us to think of what the child's "mental environment looks like," he has served up a forceful argument for adults to learn how to deal with children on their own intellectual terms. This qualitative focus has also been a refreshing antidote to the behavioral psychologist's lack of concern for the subject's mental life and the psychometric expert's preoccupation with attaching numbers to intellectual performance.

A final contribution is the host of imaginative ideas that Piaget has offered about how the child changes. The concepts of *assimilation* and *accommodation*, for example, are now well-rehearsed terms in the vocabulary of most psychologists. The concepts remind us of the double-sided nature of each of our exchanges with the environment. We must make the experience fit our cognitive framework (schemas, operations), yet simultaneously adjust our cognitive framework to the experience. The concept of **equilibration** offers an elegant view of developmental pacing. According to this idea, significant cognitive change comes only when our cognitive frameworks are clearly shown to be inconsistent with each other and the environment. And the change will only be likely if the situation is structured to permit gradual movement to the next higher level of cognition.

But what are the major criticisms of the theory that have led to a mood for change? Perhaps the broadest criticism concerns Piaget's claim for stages of development (Brainerd, 1978; Brainerd and Pressley, in press; Flavell, 1981). To claim that a child is in a particular stage of development is to claim that he or she possesses a universally characteristic prototypical system by which he or she approaches many different tasks. It should be possible to detect many similarities in the quality of thinking in a variety of tasks, and there should be clear links between stages of development such that successful attainment of one conceptual understanding predicts successful attainment of another. For example, we might expect children to learn how to conserve at about the same time that they learn how to cross-classify or seriate items. All three capabilities are supposed to provide evidence of concrete operational thought. As several critics have noted, however, lack of similarity, lack of cross-linkages, and lack of predictability seem to be present everywhere (Brainerd and Pressley, in press; Flavell, 1981; Fischer, 1980; Kuhn, 1980). According to Fischer, unevenness seems to be the rule in cognitive development, rather than the exception.

Another problem is that the most interesting concepts in the theory—assimilation, accommodation, and equilibration—which are used to explain how progress is made in development, are tricky to pin down operationally, despite their theoretical glitter. That is, unlike concepts like reinforcement and imitation, these Piagetian concepts have very loose ties to experimental procedures and manipulations. Despite work over the years to flesh out these concepts and anchor them in concrete procedures, not much progress had been made.

A final problem to be considered here is the mounting evidence that very few of the cognitive phenomena discovered by Piaget behave in the precise way he claims or really depend upon the particular processes he invokes to explain them. It would take a whole book to list and describe all of this evidence. But a few examples might give you a sense of the difficulty. Helene Borke (1971, 1973) has shown, for example, that three- and four-year-old children can identify correctly the emotions experienced by characters in a story (e.g., happiness, sadness, anger, fearfulness); but to do so, children presumably need to understand an emotional point of view that is independent of their own. Marilyn Shatz and Rochel Gelman (1973) and others have shown four-year-olds to be capable of adapting their manner of speech to different listener's perspectives. Both the Borke and Shatz and Gelman findings fly in the face of *egocentrism*.

As another example, consider the phenomenon of *object permanence*. Piaget describes six major stages, but it is becoming increasingly clear that there are a dozen or more landmarks. And while Piaget describes certain competencies as necessary to attain stage 4 and stage 6 object permanence abilities, others have offered strong counterevidence to his account.

As a last example, consider *class inclusion* reasoning (e.g., "Are there more colored bars or bars"). According to Piaget, the preoperational child fails to reason with the different classes present in the problem because of an inability to consider the whole set (i.e., all bars) in opposition to one of its subsets (i.e., the colored bars). But Alex Wilkinson (1976) and Thomas Trabasso (1977) have offered at least two equally plausible counterexplanations. Wilkinson suggests that the child answers the question incorrectly because of a problem in keeping the two sets of objects distinct while having to count some of them twice. Trabasso lists a series of operations the child must perform in solving the task, among them correctly interpreting what each part of the statement refers to in the arrangement (encoding) and remembering this interpretation while searching for an answer (memory).

Each one of these examples poses no real threat to Piaget's theory. A theory could be wrong in a few respects but right in most others. But from the vantage point of the 1980s, we now have many "errors" or "exceptions" such as these, and they cannot be dismissed lightly. Taken together then, all of these concerns suggest a need for change in the theory. The stage concept is questionable, the concepts of change are hard to operationalize, and many of Piaget's explanations are simply wrong.

Neo-Piagetian Approaches

A number of influential scholars have tried to construct a new theory that preserves many of Piaget's better insights and observations. One of the more promising approaches will be described in detail here and others briefly mentioned.

Pascual-Leone

One influential neo-Piagetian approach is the model of Pascual-Leone (e.g., 1969, 1978, 1981). There are three critical ideas that serve as the foundation for their "revisionist" thinking and help to distinguish their ideas from those of Piaget.

The first is the notion that many Piagetian tasks actually require several cognitive strategies rather than a single strategy to solve them. Hence, it is important to identify each of the strategies involved in the task and to describe how the child executes them. The more strategies required to solve the problem, the more complex that problem is. Generally speaking, more complex strategies are also developmentally more advanced.

The second notion is that the child's ability to hold information in the short term, or "working," memory is the key to success in applying the strategies. For every strategy (or cognitive step) the child takes to solve a task, some space is required in working memory to preserve the results of the applied strategy as the next one is undertaken.

For example, suppose a problem required that we first add two numbers together (step 1: add 15 + 27) and next divide the sum (step 2: divide sum by 2). If we did this problem in our heads, we would need to preserve the result of step 1 (42) while we applied the next step (divide by 2). Some space in our short-term memory is necessary to preserve the results of step 1. In other tasks, the more steps we take before the final solution is reached, the more space is needed in working memory. Pascual-Leone assumes that the size of the working memory gradually increases during childhood, permitting more and more strategies to be applied. The size of working memory increases partly because the child's brain increases in memory capacity. Working memory also increases because of the child's increased automaticity in applying strategies.

Automaticity, then, is the third major part of the model. It is assumed that with practice and experience many cognitive strategies can be applied with little or no mental effort—we become automatic at them. For example, a second grader might have to work at the addition problem, 15 + 27, for a few seconds before solving it. He or she might add numbers first in the one's column, next carry a 1 to the ten's column, and finally add the numbers in the ten's column. By contrast an adolescent or adult might quickly add the whole number 15 to the whole number 27 in one rapid step. The adult performs the step more automatically; less time and effort are required. As children become more automatic in performing particular steps in a task, this frees up space in working memory to handle other steps. Development then, in the model of Pascual-Leone, is the process of acquiring new strategies, an ever increasing capacity for working memory, and increasing automaticity in applying strategies.

Other Neo-Piagetian Approaches

There are, of course, other neo-Piagetian approaches to cognitive development (e.g., Flavell, 1981; Fischer, 1980, 1982). Each shares the belief that Piaget is on the right tract but that his system needs to be considerably cut down in scale and focus on adequately describing specific intellectual capabilities and how they develop. Instead of focusing upon universal accomplishments of children alone, we should concern ourselves with individual differences as well.

John Flavell (1981), always one of the more balanced critics of Piaget, reminds us that it is still important to describe sequences of change in childhood. How does the child progress from point A to point B to point C? More important, what do each of these points in the sequence look like. Piaget has always been interested in sequences of change, if we only put aside his strong claims about how each of the sequences are interrelated.

As a final example, Kurt Fischer (1980, 1982) has emphasized that we need to describe individual skills that children acquire. Defined more narrowly than a Piagetian schema or an operation, skill always depends upon the context in which it occurs for its very definition. In object permanence research, for example, we would define the child's sensorimotor skill level by reference to the specific manner in which it was being tested. Hence, the child's skill in following the path of an object that is hidden differs from the child's skill in searching for it once it is hidden. Each skill identified by Fischer undergoes a series of transformations as the child matures, and it is possible to define a fairly universal sequence of changes for each skill. Unlike Piaget, however, Fischer believes that every skill will develop at a different rate and will not be part of any system of stages.

Next, we continue our discussion of another perspective on cognitive development—information processing—and see that it, like the neo-Piagetian models, strays from a strict Piagetian interpretation of children's cognitive development.

Information Processing

Piaget's theory focuses on how the child *thinks* and *represents* the world and how these capabilities change with development. There is another perspective, however, from which to view cognitive development. It is dubbed the *information processing approach* (e.g., Klahr & Wallace, 1975; Siegler, 1982; Yussen & Santrock, 1978). In this view, mental activity is synonymous with the processing of information. To make the exposition smoother, we will occasionally abbreviate the term information processing with the symbols *IP*.

Refer to figure 7.5 for an illustration of the general stages of information processing. And, to further help you understand the IP approach, we are going to describe a precocious eleven-year-old with an IQ of 170, who, unlike most others in late childhood, is capable of solving algebraic equations. Our eleven-year-old (called Allie) is taking an algebra class as part of his individualized instruction in the gifted program at his school. The mathematics teacher puts the following algebraic equation on the chalkboard with the accompanying instruction: "$2x + 10 = 34$; solve for x."

This event contains information that Allie can detect and understand. Success in detecting and making sense of the equation depends on how completely and efficiently Allie processes the information. One possible set of stages of information processing Allie may use in solving the algebraic equation includes attention, perception, memory, thinking, and problem solving. Once Allie's processing is complete, he produces an observable response (R). In this model, then, cognitive activity refers to the flow of information through the different stages of processing.

Consider how the computerlike, advanced mind of eleven-year-old Allie engages in cognition. Allie looks up and notes that something has been written on the board *(attention)*. This "something" is then determined to be a series of numbers, letters, and signs, and—at a higher level of identification—simply two statements: 1) "$2x + 10 = 34$" and 2) "Solve for x" *(perception)*. Allie must preserve the results of this perceptual analysis over a period of time *(memory)*, even if only for the brief interval needed to write the problem on a worksheet.

Many children fail at information processing by not paying attention.

Allie then begins to elaborate on the product of perception and memory *(thinking)*. This level of analysis can be described best with an imaginary mental soliloquy (do not take the soliloquy literally; in Allie's mind, the thoughts associated with the hypothetical words here may transpire in some nonverbal medium altogether): "Oh! It's an equation—x is the unknown, and I'm supposed to figure out the value of x. Let's see. How do I do that?" And the final level of analysis *(problem solving)* addresses this question: "How do I do that?" Problem solving then takes the following form: "Okay. $2x + 10 = 34$. First I have to collect the unknown on one side of the equation and the known values on the other side. To do this, I'll leave the $2x$ where it is—on the left. Then I'll subtract 10 from each side to remove the 10 from the left. This leaves $2x = 24$. Now I have to express the equation as '$x = $ something,' and it's solved. How do I do this? I know! Divide each side by 2 and that will leave $1x$, or x on the left side. Now I have $x = 12$. That's the answer!"

Most eleven-year-olds would get stuck in rendering a high-level analysis of this information for a variety of reasons. One child may fail at the first stage of information processing by not paying *attention*. A severely mentally retarded eleven-year-old may attend but be unable to decode the writing as letters, numbers, and symbols—a failure in *perception*. A "normal" eleven-year-old may attend, perceive, and remember, but fail to comprehend that he or she is examining a mathematical equation with an unknown (x) and an implicit goal to find the numerical equivalent of x. A thirteen-year-old just beginning the study of algebra

may attend, perceive, remember, and comprehend but not define the answer to the question, How do I do that?—a failure in *problem-solving*.

As we have suggested, it is useful to divide up complex information processing into its component parts. Next, we focus on three of these parts—perception, memory, and problem solving—that are important aspects of cognitive development in middle and late childhood.

Perception

The topic of perception was discussed extensively in chapter 4. We recap some of its major features and focus upon important dimensions of change in perception during childhood.

Whereas sensation is the pickup of information by our sensory receptors, perception is the interpretation of what is sensed. We know that all sensory systems operate at birth, though there is significant improvement in infancy—particularly in the coordination of different senses. Two particularly important perceptual accomplishments cue the ability to see and move around in three-dimensional space and to be able to identify and discriminate among many different patterns and forms. Chapter 4 emphasized some of the remarkable findings on these changes with infants and the clever techniques necessary for gathering evidence from this nonverbal group, as well as some of the mechanisms responsible for perceptual change that have been proposed over the years. Among these were the Gestalt principles of field organization and the Gibsonian view of distinctive features learning. A few additional points are offered here on the nature of perceptual change later in childhood.

Amount of Redundancy

One important way that perception changes in childhood is in the amount of information that must be present to perceive a variety of events. Often, young children need to have a lot of information presented under optimal sensory conditions to correctly identify an event. By contrast, older children and adults can recognize events with incomplete information under surprisingly poor sensory conditions. The amount of information present often can be roughly equated with the amount of redundancy, or duplicate information, present. Thus, in figure 10.1 panel *a* shows a human form, as does panel *b*. However, panel *b* offers us many visual features not present in panel *a*. We don't need the additional features in panel *b*, such as eyes, noses, etc., to identify it as a human form. For this identification task, these features are redundant; the overall form is sufficient for identifying the figure as a person. The additional features in panel *b* are extras.

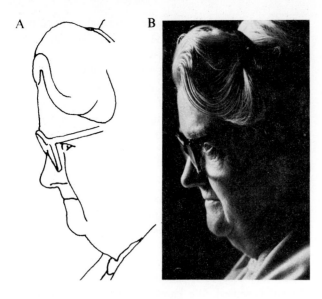

Figure 10.1 Two forms signaling a "human being" with different amounts of redundancy.

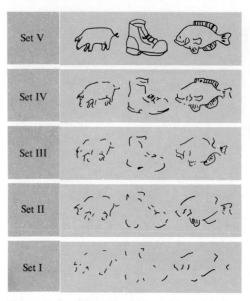

Figure 10.2 The more impoverished the picture, the less likely that the child can identify it.

Consider another example. In a classic investigation (Gollin, 1962), young children and adults were shown line drawings such as those in figure 10.2. Notice that some of the drawings are more incomplete or impoverished than others. Generally speaking, adults were able to identify more impoverished drawings than were children. The adults, in other words, required less information than the children.

Another classic example comes from the literature on the perception of depth and size constancy (e.g., Gibson, 1969; Yonas & Hagen, 1973). Children can be asked to judge an object's relative size or relative distance in comparison to some standard object. Under a variety of different testing formats, a very general pattern is that young children do worse than older children when the available visual information is sparse or when the viewing conditions are nonoptimal. Representative examples include scenes in which lighting and texture information is not available, where people cannot move their heads as they watch (e.g., looking through a peephole), or where a person can view the scene with only one eye (thus cutting off binocular information). In each case, the reduced viewing circumstances interfere with younger children's accurate perceptions more than they do with the perceptions of older children and adults.

Nature of Stimulus Dimensions

Another way perception changes in children is in how properties of objects and events are noticed. There are at least two different, well documented types of changes now widely cited. One type involves the **salience of dimensions.** As we look at an object, it is possible to identify many dimensions of it—its color, size, shape, density, and so forth. Which of these dimensions do we happen to notice? Richard Odom (1977; 1978) has shown that each child may have a different propensity for what he or she notices. One child may notice color, while another notices size, and yet a third notices shape. There are, then, individual differences in children's preferences for noticing different dimensions.

A second observation made by Odom is that these preferences seem to be organized into hierarchies for each child. As an illustration, consider the three-dimensional alternatives of color, size, and form present in a series of objects. One child may prefer color. When color variations are eliminated in objects (leaving only size and form differences), the child then notices size. Finally, form differences are the least noticed (i.e., preferred features of objects). We have, then, a salience hierarchy here: the child notices dimensions of objects in descending order of magnitude—color, size, form. Other children will have different hierarchies, such as size, color, form or form, size, color. Odom suggests that such hierarchies of salience are more prominent in the perception and learning of younger children than they are in older children and adults. The practical importance of such hierarchies is that for younger children especially, learning and solving problems will be easiest when their most preferred dimensions are accentuated in the learning environment and their least preferred dimensions are de-emphasized.

A second type of change is closely associated with the idea that younger children have relatively *undifferentiated* perceptions of objects, whereas older children's are more *differentiated*. Functionally, this idea has been reinterpreted by Deborah Kemler and Linda

Figure 10.3 Are these people fighting or dancing? Cultural differences tend to modify interpretations of the scene.

Smith (1978, 1979, 1982). They have shown that when younger children (kindergarteners) are forced to classify objects into groupings quickly, they tend to group objects based on an overall impression of similarity rather than an analysis of the underlying dimensions. The reverse is true for older children (older elementary grades).

As an example, consider that a young child might group objects that differ by size and shade of grey by overall impression (two large objects might go together, even though the shades of grey differed between them). Older children and adults would classify the objects by their separate dimensions (i.e., only large objects with the same shades of grey would go together). Kemler goes on to show that such a holistic response among young children is common across many combinations of stimulus dimensions, whereas it is much rarer in older children and adults. The young children are said to treat dimensions as *integral*, whereas older children treat dimensions as *separable*. There are, however, some combinations of stimuli that even adults have a hard time separating—e.g., forms that differ in their color saturation and brightness.

Meaningfulness and Organization
Yet a third way perception changes is in the importance of the meanings and organizations people attach to what they experience. It is perhaps trite to say that the unique experiences someone has had will significantly influence the way that person perceives events. Yet it is a profoundly important simplicity. From a developmental perspective, meaningfulness is likely to intrude upon perception the longer the child is exposed to the particular experience.

Consider, for example, the importance of culture in how we perceive drawings of familiar events. In Western society children are bombarded with experiences (e.g., photographs, television, movies) in which

two-dimensional objects represent three-dimensional events. Other societies can be identified in which children are not exposed to such representations of three-dimensionality. How do children from these societies perceive cues that portray depth in two-dimensional representations of three-dimensional objects?

A classic study was conducted by William Hudson (1960) to answer this question. He presented several different groups of children in South Africa with pictures such as in figure 10.3. Some of the subjects in his study attended school; some did not. Presumably those who attended school had more exposure to three-dimensional representations in the form of books and pictures. Hudson asked each of them questions to determine how they perceived each drawing. For the picture shown in figure 10.4, for example, children were asked such questions as "Which animal is closer to the hunter, the antelope or the elephant?" "Which animal is being hunted?" The younger children's answers revealed that they had difficulty perceiving the third dimension. With schooling, however, the older children became better at identifying the scene correctly. These results were true for some of the groups (e.g., white children) but not for all (black children), so the results were not due solely to the presence or absence of schooling.

Others have found different results. For example, one researcher (Mundy-Castle, 1966) tested a group of five- to ten-year-old Ghanian children. For those who had difficulty seeing depth perception, one of the difficulties was with the interpretation of some of the lines. As can be seen, the elephant is standing on a hill, the man is standing on level ground, and behind the antelope is another hill. These hills were not identified as such by children who had perspective difficulty. Some perceived them as holes or spears. Since the drawing is sketchy and interpretation relies on only a few lines, the problem may be one of inferring something from scant information.

Figure 10.4 Stimulus used to examine the perception of depth in two-dimensional pictures by people from different cultures.

There is no question that people from different cultures may interpret three-dimensional pictures in different ways. Hudson (1967) found that people in some African cultures interpreted the scene in figure 10.3 as a fight. Others, however, viewed the scene as depicting a dance ritual. Pictures of static scenes, of course, are often ambiguous in this way.

Perception, then, is indeed an important step in the processing of information. Next, we look at another aspect of the information processing approach—memory.

Memory

Memory is the retention of information over time. Three general topics are considered in this discussion of the manner in which children remember information. First, what are the different kinds of memory that play an important role in development? Second, what are the basic processes employed in remembering? And third, how do these basic processes change as the child matures?

Kinds of Memory

Although the word memory may conjure up an image of a singular, all-or-none process, it is clear that there are actually many kinds of memory, each of which may be somewhat independent of the others (e.g., Brown, 1975; Kail & Hagen, 1977; Perlmutter, 1980). One way to describe memory is by the different ways people are called upon to remember and the ways memory may be assessed—recall, recognition, and paired associates.

The most popularly studied kind of memory is **recall.** Recollection of a telephone number you have just heard, a list of items you are to purchase at the store, or a list of dates you learned in history class are all examples of recall.

A second type of memory is **recognition,** which is generally easier than recall. For example, someone lists three grocery items and you are to signal when one is mentioned that was on your last shopping list; or, your history instructor gives four dates and you are to choose the one that goes with a specific historical event. In recall, you try to repeat an experience; in recognition, you simply indicate which of several events was experienced.

People often underestimate just how powerful their recognition memory is (Levin, Yussen, DeRose, & Pressley, 1977). Roger Shepard (1967) showed hundreds of photographs of faces to adults and later presented them with a recognition problem: they were to identify which face in a pair they had previously seen in his collection. With literally hundreds of such test pairs, recognition accuracy was between 90 and 100 percent for most subjects. Such results have been repeated with children of all ages, using other materials (Brown, 1975). Recall improves substantially across the childhood years for reasons that will be considered later in this discussion (Levin et al., 1977), but for many kinds of recognition memory, there is little, if any, change across a wide span of childhood ages (e.g., Kagan, Klein, Haith, & Morrison, 1973; Perlmutter, 1980).

Another kind of memory, **paired associates,** has been studied extensively. Examples include remembering an article of clothing someone else was wearing, the color of a car, and the name of a person whose face is familiar. Since most models of learning and memory were based exclusively on the concept of association for the first fifty or sixty years of this century, paired-associates tasks were a natural means of testing the concept (e.g., Anderson & Bower, 1973).

Memory As the Flow of Information

One prominent view conceives of memory as the flow of information through the human mind. In a number of statements of this view (e.g., Atkinson & Shiffrin,

Children from different cultures interpret things in different ways.

1971; Siegler, 1982), three broad stages of information processing can be distinguished. First, there is a sensory register, that is, a very short-term sensory memory of the event. At the second level there is a short-term, or working, memory. At the third level there is a long-term memory, where information is held over a long period of time.

Roughly speaking, the *sensory register* concerns memories that last for no more than a second. If a line of print were flashed at you very rapidly—say, for one-tenth of a second—all the letters you can visualize for a brief moment after that presentation constitute the sensory register. This visualization disappears after one second. Recent evidence suggests that ability to retrieve information from the sensory register does not change much as children mature (Sheingold, 1973; Wickens, 1974; Siegler, 1982).

When you are trying to recall a telephone number that you heard a few seconds earlier, the name of a person who has just been introduced, or the substance of the remarks just made by a teacher in class, you are calling on **short-term memory,** or working memory. It lasts from a few seconds to a minute. You need this kind of memory for retaining ideas and thoughts as you work on problems. In writing a letter, for example, you must be able to keep the last sentence in mind as you compose the next. To solve an arithmetic problem like $(3 \times 3) + (4 \times 2)$ in your head, you need to keep the intermediate results in mind (i.e., $3 \times 3 = 9$) to be able to solve the entire problem. This working memory is therefore quite useful.

Operationally, the short-term memory of children may be studied by giving the child a list of items to recall and noting recall of the last few items on the list. These last few items are generally recalled better than the others—a phenomenon known as the recency effect. Several studies have shown that memory for these recent items is remarkably similar across a wide spectrum of ages in childhood (e.g., Cole, Frankel, & Sharpe, 1971), leading to the conclusion that short-term memory also changes very little throughout childhood.

Long-term memory lasts from a minute or so to weeks or even years. From long-term memory you can call up general information about the world that you learned on previous occasions, memory for specific past experiences, or specific rules previously learned. The most significant changes in memory development are presumed to occur in the long-term storage stage or in the phase of shifting information from short- to long-term storage.

Memory Processes

Among the processes assumed to be responsible for shifting information to long-term storage are rehearsal, elaboration, organization, and various constructive memory processes.

Rehearsal If a response to a stimulus is repeated, either aloud or only in the mind, it is more likely to be remembered than if it is not repeated. This repetition is one form of **rehearsal** (Flavell, 1970; Ornstein, 1978).

Repetition is just one way to rehearse a response. Another is to create an image for the response and rehearse the image "in one's head" (Paivio, 1971). A third is to employ gestures to repeat an observed response (Bandura & Jeffrey, 1973). And a fourth is to create a symbolic code for the response and then to rehearse the code (Zimmerman & Rosenthal, 1974).

There may also be differences in the manner of rehearsal. Given a list of items to remember, some children may rehearse each item in a list once and then stop, others may keep cycling through the list, and yet others may select a small subset of the list and rehearse only the items in the subset. Both the appropriateness of the kind of rehearsal as well as the manner in which it is used may influence memory (Ornstein, 1978; Naus, in press).

The nature of the task and the rehearsal technique employed may well influence whether or not the child spontaneously rehearses. There may actually be production deficiencies that are task-specific, with each undergoing its separate development. That is, a child may be deficient in one respect but not another; rehearse spontaneously in one situation but not another.

Elaboration   When you hear or see something, you may try to remember it by adding to it, or elaborating. By the memory process called **elaboration** you may associate the experience with something familiar to you, generate an image for it, or develop a sentence or short story about it in your mind. Many of these techniques improve retention of the experience (Rohwer & Levin, 1971; Pressley, Heisel, McCormick, & Nakamura, 1982).

In general, the study of elaboration has focused on the memory abilities of elementary and secondary schoolchildren, while the study of rehearsal has focused on the preschool and elementary school years. It has been suggested that elaboration skills are more advanced than rehearsal skills. However, there is probably a great deal of overlap between the two. And, as with rehearsal, there are different kinds of elaboration, each with its own history of development.

Organization   Yet another technique for extending the short-term life of experiences or for moving them into long-term storage is **organization.** George Miller, in a classic article, argued that most human memory is limited. Short-term, or working, memory cannot deal with more than about seven discrete experiences, or bits, of information. When we are confronted with more than this, we lose some of it, finding it difficult to move all the information into our permanent, long-term memory storage (Miller, 1956).

Unwieldy information may be retained by organizing it into smaller units, or **chunks,** as Miller calls them. If the number of chunks is seven or less and each one is well learned, there is a good possibility that all the information will be retained (Miller, 1956). Chunking is done frequently: we recall ten-digit telephone numbers by segmenting them into a three-digit area code, a three-digit exchange, and a four-digit final sequence. Similar chunking is done with social security numbers, bank numbers, and credit-card account numbers.

A more common way to organize information is to place items into meaningful categories (Mandler, 1967). If you are to remember fifteen things to be purchased at the grocery store, your task is made easier if you group them into such categories as meats, vegetables, and fruits. Many studies over the past two decades have shown that, within certain limits, individuals recall better when they categorize information in this fashion (Moely & Jeffrey, 1974; Kail, 1979). If there are too many categories, if the categories are abstract or not obvious, and if there are too many items within categories, categorization may be unable to benefit memory.

A typical finding with children from four to ten years of age is that the younger children engage in very little categorizing; there is a steady increase in categorizing as age increases. However, the pattern of change may not appear with children of this age group if the difficulty of the task is altered. The categories in a list may be made salient and thus easy to notice, or the list may be constructed with obscure or very abstract categories. Saliency markedly increases categorizing activity in the youngest children, while obscuring the categories may decrease it in the oldest.

In one demonstration, Erikson, Chase, and Faloon (1980) offered startling proof of the power of chunking joined together with meaningful categorization. An average college student was transformed into a virtual wizard at one memory task—recalling long strings of unrelated numbers (e.g., 3, 7, 9, 5, 8 . . .). Ordinarily, most of us can remember strings with only seven or eight digits in them. Over the course of a school year, the student practiced listening to and recalling longer and longer strings of numbers. The numbers were read at about one per second. Using a variety of tricks such as relating groups of numbers to running activities (e.g., imagined rare distances and times, training mileage) and historical events, eventually the student was able to recall number strings of over seventy digits.

A number of devices—called **mnemonics**—can be used to help us remember. Mnemonics are described in box 10.2, focusing in particular on the role imagery plays in helping us to remember.

Drawing Inferences

An **inference** is a relation noted between one event and another that is not directly stated. Thus far, we have considered three stages in information processing—attending to something, perceiving it, and remembering it. Our world would be a rather simple place, indeed, if our mental activity stopped there. It would consist of unconnected and unrelated events. So, what does it mean that the sun rises and soon after people wake up and get on with the day's business? What is the connection between a child falling off a bicycle one moment and an adult holding her the next moment while the youngster cries? Throughout our lives, we experience events that are logically or matter-of-factly related to one another. The study of inferencing helps us to understand how people construct these relations. Two topics, the major kinds of inferences people make and the processes that explain the growth of inferencing ability, will be considered.

Types of Inferences

Sometimes the connection between events is logical. We need not even experience the events directly to understand how they are related to one another. Thus, suppose we hear someone describe a situation as follows:

a.) There was an older man, a man, and a boy.
The older man said to the man, "I'm glad you're my son."
The man said to the boy, "And, I'm glad you're my son."
What is the relation between the older man and the boy?

The answer is based on our logical understanding of family relations and inference—the relationship is one of grandfather and grandson.

By contrast, sometimes the connection between events is *empirical*. That is, we need to have some specialized experiences with the type of circumstances being described to arrive at the correct inference. Suppose, for example, we heard someone describe the following situation:

b.) Bjorn Borg faced John Santrock in a tennis match.
Borg lost the first set 6–1.
The spectators got up and left the arena.

Why did the spectators leave? The answer is based on our specific knowledge about the relative talent of the two players in question and about the way fans might behave when a professional athlete performs poorly. Even then, any answer offered is only a probabilistic one, such as the fans were disgusted with the travesty.

Another distinction among types of inferences is that of literal vs. nonliteral. Sometimes, the task of seeing a relation between events is made simple because we have only to notice the temporal or spatial closeness of the two events. Thus, borrowing from a classic investigation by Paris and Lindauer (1976), consider the following paragraph:

c.) The bird flew over the lake.
The lake was in a city.
The city was Chicago.

The inference that "the bird flew over Chicago" is easily made by simply replacing the concept of "lake" with the concept of "city." And, since the two concepts are spatially contiguous, the replacement is easily done. This inference, readily made by young elementary schoolchildren in the Paris and Lindauer investigation is an example of a *literal* inference.

By contrast, the task of seeing a relation between events is often made arduous because we have to rely on substantial prior knowledge to interpret the experience. Thus, example b required substantial reliance on prior knowledge, as does interpretation of the following slightly edited version of a paragraph employed by Yussen, Mathews, Buss, & Kane (1980).

d.) Albert spotted a worm in the water.
He swam over to the worm and bit into him.

Albert was caught and pulled through the water. Who was Albert? Why did he bite the worm? Who caught him and how? The paragraph provides no clues to answer these questions, but our own experiences and prior knowledge offer some help. Albert is probably a fish who was hungry and was caught on the hook of a fisherman. These inferences are all *nonliteral*.

Imagery Helps Us to Remember

An ancient mnemonic attributed to the Greek poet Simonides (fifth century B.C.) is the method of places, or "loci." Simonides was able to use this method to identify all the guests who had been at a banquet with him and were then maimed beyond recognition when the building collapsed and crushed them. (Fortuitously, Simonides was not present when the building collapsed.) He was able to accomplish this great feat by generating vivid images of each individual and mentally picturing where they had sat at the banquet table.

This is a mnemonic device that you can apply to memory problems of your own. Suppose you have a list of chores to do. To make sure you remember them all, first associate a concrete object with each chore. A trip to the store becomes a dollar bill, a telephone call to a friend becomes a telephone, clean-up duty becomes a broom, and so on. Then create an image for each "object" so that you imagine it in a particular room or location in a familiar building, such as your house. You might imagine the dollar bill in the kitchen, the telephone in the dining room, and so forth. The vividness of the image and the unique placement of it virtually guarantee recollection. It helps to move mentally through the house in some logical way as the images are "placed."

Dual keyword illustration for learning the states and capitals.

The Process of Drawing Inferences
There is, of course, abundant evidence to show that children improve dramatically in their abilities to draw certain types of inferences as they mature. Nancy Stein and Thomas Trabasso (1981), for example, have shown that children's understanding of relations in narrative folktales improves across the elementary school years. Scott Paris has shown that children improve in making a variety of linguistic inferences. Robert Sternberg (Sternberg & Downing, in press) and others (e.g., Goldman, Pellegrino, Parseghian, & Sallis, in press) have documented improvements in analogical inferences (i.e., drawing analogies) across the elementary school years. And, in other laboratories, evidence has been amassed to show improvement in inferences on a host of traditional reading comprehension and cognitive assessment measures (e.g., WISC) (Yussen, 1982).

But the more interesting matter is the nature of the processes that underly successful inferential activity. What allows the person to draw inferences of the type mentioned?

Knowing When to Draw Inferences An important part of drawing inferences is knowing when to do so. Sometimes very little effort is involved in drawing an inference and no conscious decision is made to do so. Example c probably is of this type. Without concentrating very hard, we realize that "the bird flew over Chicago." Example b, however, is a different matter. We might not have an automatic interpretation of the reason for the spectators' behavior. More tellingly, we might not even think it necessary to interpret why the spectator's did what they did. Teachers are constantly

A very powerful imagery mnemonic first suggested by Richard Atkinson (1975) is the **keyword method.** It has been used to great practical advantage by Joel Levin (1980). Professor Levin and his associates have shown the technique to be an efficient procedure for teaching schoolchildren how to rapidly master new information such as foreign vocabulary words, the states and capitals in the United States, and the names of United States presidents.

Here, in Professor Levin's words, is an explanation of how it was applied to teach capitals:

> In one study, fourth and fifth graders learned the capital cities of the United States using what we called a *dual keyword approach.* . . . Let me illustrate using one of my favorites, Annapolis, Maryland. In the first of a three-stage process, students were taught keywords for the states, such that when a state was given *(Maryland)* they could supply the keyword *(marry).* Then, since the criterion task required that the student supply the capital in response to a state name, in the second stage we gave students the reverse type of keyword practice with the capitals. That is, they had to respond with the capital *(Annapolis)* when given a keyword *(apple).* Finally, in the third stage, an illustration . . . was provided. In comparison to a very liberal control condition that allowed unrestricted study and self-testing, keyword subjects were better at remembering the capitals. This was true on an immediate test, but especially so on a surprise retest three days later. (p. 20)

bewildered at the apparent lack of conscious inferential activity in young children and the children's frequent failures to analyze the implied meaning inherent in messages, instructions, and reading materials (Pearson & Johnson, 1978).

Although it is very much a mystery why young children and poor learners (e.g., Golinkoff, 1975–76; Kaufman, 1981) fail to draw inferences, recent research suggests two possibilities. One is that children don't monitor their own comprehension very well. They fail to take stock of what they are and so fail to analyze their experiences for further meaning (e.g., Markman, 1981; Yussen, Mathews, & Hiebert, 1982). Another reason is that children may not have the same cognitive purposes in mind as do adults. So, while the adult thinks to derive some inferential meaning from related events,

the child may be motivated to do something else entirely. For example, the adult may wish to understand the agent responsible in example d (Albert and the worm). That is, who or what caught Albert? Children, by contrast, may want to know what the worm looked like, how big it was, or how quickly Albert swam—answers not easily provided by any obvious inferential process. Whatever the reason, it is clear that there is developmental improvement in children's tendency to know when to draw inferences across the elementary and secondary school years.

Activating Relevant Prior Knowledge No topic, perhaps, has received greater attention in contemporary circles of information processing than the importance of what the individual already knows as an influence on what he or she will get out of some cognitive encounter (Schank & Abelson, 1977; Chi, 1978; Just & Carpenter, 1977; Kintsch, 1982). This prior knowledge has been described in a number of different ways, including **scripts** and **semantic networks.**

A script is a very general event sequence known to most people in a culture. The standard example of a script is our generalized understanding of what takes place when we "visit a restaurant." People have fairly consistent ideas about the major events that take place. These include entering the restaurant, being seated, ordering, eating, paying the bill, and leaving. An event that touches on a restaurant episode, then, would be expected to evoke the person's highly ritualized understanding of the activities mentioned. Consider this paragraph, for example:

The hungry man saw the sign for the steak house. An hour later he had wolfed down a delicious tenderloin and was on his way.

Since we all have common knowledge about restaurants, we can draw several inferences, such as that the man ordered a meal from a waitress and later paid for it. Research shows that we do draw such inferences spontaneously when we have scripts applicable to the situation, that young children tend to be rigid in their application of scripts (e.g., Wimmer, 1980), and that people have many different scripts (e.g., going to schools, going to the doctor's, playing baseball, taking a test).

A semantic network is a set of concepts that are related to one another in a variety of ways. For example, consider the hypothetical networks for the concept "university course" in someone not very knowledgeable about institutions of higher learning—perhaps an average seventh or eighth grader—and someone who is very knowledgeable—perhaps a university professor. Figure 10.5 shows, schematically,

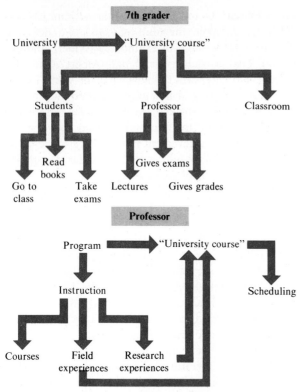

7th grader

University → "University course"

Students   Professor   Classroom

Read books   Gives exams

Go to class   Take exams   Lectures   Gives grades

Professor

Program → "University course"

Instruction   Scheduling

Courses   Field experiences   Research experiences

Figure 10.5 Hypothetical semantic networks for the concept of "university course" in a seventh grader and a professor.

what these networks look like. As you can see, the university professor has a very detailed, complicated, and rich network of interrelated ideas to draw upon, whereas the student does not. If either one were to hear or read something involving the concept "university," the professor would have the clear advantage in being able to draw a variety of inferences based on what he or she knows already about universities.

Thus, prior knowledge, in the form of scripts of semantic networks, helps the individual draw inferences. The more scripts available to interpret an event or the richer the semantic networks available, the more inferences will be drawn.

Calling up Information from Memory As stated earlier, the different steps in information processing are interrelated in important and intricate ways. It is clear that memory, for example, plays a key role in drawing inferences. Long-term memory, for example, is the repository of our ever growing permanent knowledge base. To call up a script or semantic network is to retrieve information from our long-term memory. Children may have equivalent knowledge bases but have different

abilities to quickly retrieve the information at the moment it is needed (e.g., Ford & Keating, 1981). So, one child might draw an appropriate inference, while another one does not, based on differences in the speeds with which they retrieve the necessary knowledge from long-term memory. Short-term, or working, memory is important as well. Often, as we are experiencing some event that unfolds over time (perhaps reading a story or an exposition), we can draw an appropriate inference only if we can remember something that occurred earlier. Two key ideas, for example, may be separated by a few sentences, as in this passage used by Nancy Kaufman (1981).

A baby kangaroo is only one inch long when it is born. It has no fur. It cannot see. As soon as it is born it crawls into the pocket. The baby kangaroo stays in the pocket for four months. The *pocket keeps it safe* and warm. The joey leaves the pocket after one month, because *it is so dangerous in there* [italics added]. (p. 48)

To draw the inference that something is *wrong* in the passage, the reader needs to remember the proposition that the "pocket keeps it safe" when he or she arrives at the point later in the passage stating "it is so dangerous in there."

Next, we look at yet another aspect of the information processing that has been given extensive attention—problem solving.

Problem Solving and Regulation of Information Processing (Metacognition)
The last stage of information processing to be considered here is problem solving. A helpful way to describe problem solving is: *processing information to fulfill a major goal.* Attention, perception, remembering, and drawing inferences may all occur rather quickly as the child examines information. And the child may devote little conscious effort or awareness to these former activities. By contrast, problem solving usually occurs over an extended period of time and mobilizes considerable cognitive resources of the child, that is, considerable effort and conscious awareness are involved.

Problem solving may also be construed as a *regulator of information processing.* It directs us to the particular information we will process and governs the manner in which the information is processed. In this sense, our decision to discuss problem solving as the last stage in information processing may be misleading. We just as easily could have conceptualized problem solving as the first stage. The best solution is to treat problem solving as a regulator or nonworking monitor for the flow of information. It helps decide what other information processing steps take place and in what order of occurrence. Reconceptualizing figure 7.5, then, we have the picture of information processing shown in figure 10.6.

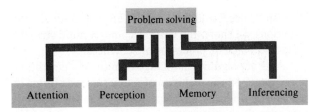

Figure 10.6 Information processing regulated by problem solving.

Another term for the regulation of information processing is **metacognition.** Metacognition is the knowledge individuals have about cognitive activity and problem solving and the strategic steps they take to regulate their ongoing information processing (e.g., Brown, 1975; Flavell, 1980; Borkowski, 1982).

Examples of Problem Solving The study of problem solving has a rich and diverse history in psychology. For example, Karl Duncker (1945), a famous Gestalt psychologist, posed the following question:

If a human being has an inoperable stomach tumor, how can the tumor be removed by rays that destroy organic tissue at sufficient intensity without destroying the healthy tissue surrounding it?

The question has been asked of many generations of college students to illustrate how they proceed to think through alternative solutions.

With children, a common tactic has been to formulate a problem that requires them to apply some newly learned academic skills in a practical contest. For example, Tom Carpenter and his colleagues at Wisconsin (Carpenter, 1980; Carpenter, Hiebert, & Moser, 1981; Carpenter, Moser, & Romberg, 1981) have studied young elementary schoolchildren's ability to solve "word problems" involving addition and subtraction. Following are four examples:

1. Wally has three pennies. His father gave him six more pennies. How many pennies does Wally have altogether?
2. Patrick has nine fish. His sister Jill has fourteen fish. How many more fish does Jill have than Patrick?
3. Fred has eight M&M's. How many more M&M's does he have to put with them so he has thirteen M&M's altogether?
4. There are five jars of paint. Three jars are red and the rest are blue. How many jars of blue paint are there?

As a final example, consider some of the exercises in creative problem solving suggested by psychologists such as J. P. Guilford (1967), Paul Torrance (1966), and Gary Davis (1981), described in chapter 9. At a conference for talented young writers (children from ages seven to twelve years) a developmental psychologist attended a session where children were asked to imagine *ice cream* and write out all of the different things it reminded them of. This is an example of an exercise in divergent thinking, discussed in some detail in chapter 9 under the topic of *creativity.*

Components of Problem Solving How do children and adults go about solving problems? What accounts for change, as children mature, in problem-solving ability? There are at least four important components of problem solving.

First, we have to figure out what the problem is, precisely, and set one or more goals. This has sometimes been referred to as *problem finding* and *goal setting* (e.g., Miller, Galanter, & Pribram, 1960; Schank & Abelson, 1977; Davis, 1981). The previous example problems are all pretty well defined. The creators of the problems have taken pains to set up the context and to tell us what they want us to find. In everyday problem solving, however, we often have to find out what the problem is and what, precisely, we have to do. For example, if a child is asked to clean up her room, she must first figure out what must be done. What must the room look like when she is completed and what currently is out of order?

Once the problem and goal have been defined, a second step is to *plan the approach* to solving the problem. Planning may involve isolating the correct pieces to the puzzle and working out the general pattern to solve the problem with these pieces. For example, in Duncker's "tumor-removal" problem, the student would have to isolate these crucial elements: a tumor is to be destroyed with an intense ray; the tumor is in the stomach; no tissue around the tumor can be destroyed. The problem then is to devise ways to make the ray intensely focused on the tumor, but not anywhere else. By brainstorming and calling upon popular knowledge about technology and physics, a number of ideas may be tried out and discarded as impractical, until a single elegant solution suggests itself. With Carpenter's arithmetic word problems, a similar phenomenon of planning may occur for younger children.

A third step is to *monitor the progress* of the problem-solving activity. Basically, this involves taking stock of how the solution process is faring—a kind of self-assessment in midstream. For example, as ideas for solving the tumor problem come forth, the student may stop to ponder whether a given idea is an improvement over the preceding one and whether he or she is still keeping the correct problem elements and goal in mind. As another example, younger children working out the arithmetic problem may wonder if they are proceeding smoothly. There are several common approaches taken by first and second graders to solve these problems.

Some count on their fingers; some rely on number facts "in their heads;" and some use counting props made available by the experimenter (Carpenter, 1980). The monitoring activity, then, may consist of children's self-assessments of the viability of the counting technique each has chosen.

Based on the results of monitoring activity, problem solvers may go in one of two directions. A sense of smooth progress will support continuation of the approach. By contrast, a sense that progress has been slow or impeded will direct them backwards to reconsider the problem definition or the solution plan. The problem may then become redefined or a new solution plan may be thought up. Negative progress and repeated monitoring efforts signal that the individual is faced with a challenging problem. Extensive discussions of cognitive monitoring have been offered (Flavell, 1981; Markman, 1981).

The fourth and final step is to *check solutions*. Whereas monitoring focuses on the progress of problem-solving efforts, this final step occurs when individuals feel they have completed their tasks. Simply put, it is to check the solution in whatever way possible. In the tumor problem the student may compare the final solution offered against the initial criteria that had to be met, against the solutions that other classmates have thought up, or against published accounts of its ideal solution. Children solving Carpenter's arithmetic problems may recheck their adding and subtracting.

Not only are there important changes in perception, memory, and problem solving during middle and late childhood, but some aspects of language development change as well. Next, we look beyond stage 5 of Roger Brown's theory of language development.

Language Development
It may be helpful for you to return to chapters 5 and 7 for a review of the five stages in Roger Brown's theory of language development. We describe what happens beyond stage 5 here and discuss one model of reading which is an important skill that most children develop during middle and late childhood.

Beyond Stage 5 in Brown's Theory
Beyond Roger Brown's stage 5 sentences become longer and, more important, the child juggles many types of transformations in a single sentence. For example, consider this sentence:

Did the boy come home and not tell his brother "Stop!"?

This sentence is *compound* and contains a *question*, a *negative*, and an *imperative* all rolled into one. There are fewer and fewer slips of the tongue, intrusions of

childish "rules," and instances of ungrammatical constructions. In short, the child becomes a more streamlined and efficient processor of sentences.

Another significant change is in the child's ability to comprehend the meaning of many sentence forms in which the underlying deep structure is not obvious. Consider these sentences:

The doll is eager to see.
The doll is easy to see.

These sentences appear to have a similar structure, but they are actually different. In the first one, "the doll" is the subject of the verb phrase "eager to see." In the second sentence, "the doll" is the implied object of the verb phrase "easy to see" (i.e., the doll is the object being seen). In English, it is common for sentences to have a surface structure in which the subject, or noun, phrase (NP) precedes the verb phrase (VP). Because of this frequency, young children tend to use this surface order to interpret the meaning of sentences. The first noun encountered is construed as the subject of the action, and the verb that follows indicates the action performed by the subject.

For the first sentence, this comprehension rule works fine. "Doll" is the subject and "eager to see" is the action performed by the doll. For the second sentence, however, this rule leads to trouble because there is no clearly stated subject of the action. In other words, the surface structure may convey the deep structural relation subject-action-object in a different order.

Carol Chomsky (1969) showed that children have difficulty understanding sentences where there is a mismatch between surface and deep structural order. In her experiment, she first posed the following question with a blindfolded doll on a table in front of the child: "Is this doll easy to see or hard to see?" The deep structure of this sentence is:

X [implied]	sees	doll
subject	*action*	*object*

The surface structure is:

Doll	easy to see	
object	*action*	*[no subject clearly stated]*

The children found the task easy and readily offered answers. However, many of their answers indicated that they did not understand the meaning of the question. This fact was made particularly clear when the following question was posed: "Would you make her easy/hard to see?" Here is a sample protocol of a child who misunderstood the sentence:

Eric H., 5.2 [5 years 2 months]
Is this doll easy to see or hard to see?
Hard to see
Will you make her easy to see.

Table 10.1
Children Who Comprehended Chomsky's Sentence

Age	Children Questioned	% Correct
5–6	16	31
7–8	15	80
9–10	9	100

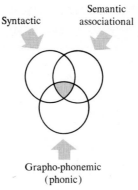

Figure 10.7 Sources of information used in reading.

OK (He removes blindfold)
Will you explain what you did.
Took off this (Pointing to blindfold)
And why did that make her easier to see?
So she can see (p. 28)

Mastery of this construction appeared with increasing frequency with children between five and ten years of age. The youngest children did very poorly, while the oldest made no mistakes. Table 10.1 indicates the percentage of children who correctly answered the first question.

Reading

Frank Smith (1976) has argued that at early stages children learn a great deal about the meaning of print by themselves. Very few people (including Smith himself), however, would seriously suggest that formal instruction in reading should therefore be abandoned. The concensus is that formal instruction does accelerate the process of learning to read and is therefore valuable. The problem, then, is to identify the best form of reading instruction.

David Pearson (1976) believes that just as language involves the acquisition of several different rule systems—phonological, syntactic, semantic, and so forth—so also does reading. In the natural course of events, children learn about different kinds of rules simultaneously. Pearson believes, therefore, that reading should similarly build upon the different kinds of rule learning in a simultaneous fashion. He identifies three kinds of rules, semantic-associational information, syntactic information, and symbol-sound information, and indicates which language-arts activities promote each kind of learning.

Semantic-associational information includes our knowledge of what words refer to in the real world and how words are hierarchically related to one another. But it also includes our knowlege of the fact that certain sets of words appearing in the same context "fit" together nicely, while other sets of words appearing in the same context are surprising to us. . . .

Syntactic information refers to the ordering relationships among words in sentences. . . .

Grapho-phonemic (phonic, symbol-sound, or in Smith's term, visual) **information** is what novice readers learn in the phonics component of their reading program. It includes the knowledge that "b" translates as "buh" or that "b" is the first sound you hear when you say "bird." It also includes the reader's knowledge, explicit or implicit, of phonics generalizations and silent letters.

Real reading occurs when all three kinds of information are utilized in concert [see figure 10.7]. Efficient readers maximize their reliance on syntactic and semantic information in order to minimize the amount of *print to speech* processing . . . they have to do. They literally predict what is coming and get enough grapho-phonemic information to verify their predictions. A single letter or a single syllable may be enough information to verify their predictions. For example, it doesn't take much visual or grapho-phonemic information to confirm the hypothesis that "telescope" fits into the sentence, "The astronomer looked through the _____ ." Readers must vary the amount of attention they pay to the graphic information according to their familiarity with the content. This helps to explain why one can read *Time* magazine much more rapidly than a philosophical treatise.

Novice or poor readers are so bound up in their search for phonic information that they have little chance to attend to meaning. Good readers, on the other hand, because they attend to meaning, may often make unimportant errors in decoding words accurately. (pp. 309–10)

The information in figure 10.8 indicates classroom language activities that emphasize each type of skill. This categorization is useful in identifying areas where children have difficulty and need more instruction and practice.

In addition to reading, language communication in the classroom becomes an important part of middle and late childhood. One of the problems faced by modern educators is how to teach children who come from a language background that is different from that of the majority culture. Recall our initial description of this problem in the prologue to chapter 5, which focused on bilingual children. In box 10.3, we discuss further the important problem of language in the classroom.

This concludes our discussion of cognitive development in middle and late childhood. In the next chapter we look at how children develop socially and emotionally during middle and late childhood.

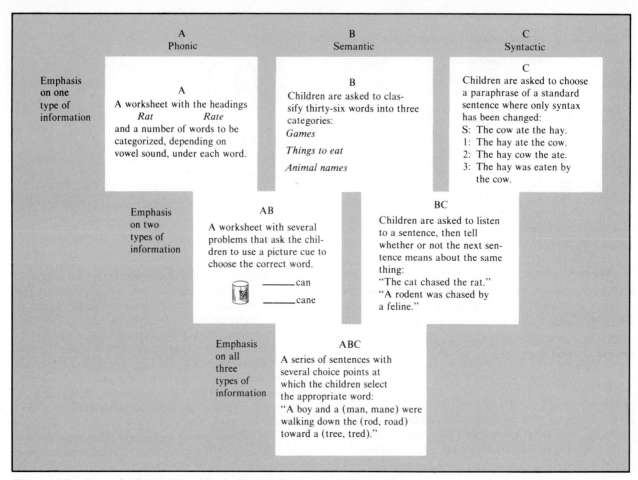

	A Phonic	B Semantic	C Syntactic
Emphasis on one type of information	**A** A worksheet with the headings *Rat Rate* and a number of words to be categorized, depending on vowel sound, under each word.	**B** Children are asked to classify thirty-six words into three categories: *Games* *Things to eat* *Animal names*	**C** Children are asked to choose a paraphrase of a standard sentence where only syntax has been changed: S: The cow ate the hay. 1: The hay ate the cow. 2: The hay cow the ate. 3: The hay was eaten by the cow.
Emphasis on two types of information		**AB** A worksheet with several problems that ask the children to use a picture cue to choose the correct word. _____can _____cane	**BC** Children are asked to listen to a sentence, then tell whether or not the next sentence means about the same thing: "The cat chased the rat." "A rodent was chased by a feline."
Emphasis on all three types of information		**ABC** A series of sentences with several choice points at which the children select the appropriate word: "A boy and a (man, mane) were walking down the (rod, road) toward a (tree, tred)."	

Figure 10.8   Type of information emphasized by various language-arts activities.

At early stages, children learn a great deal about print on their own.

Box 10.3
Language Communication in the Classroom

Children enter the classroom with one set of language skills and expectations, the teachers with another. During the last two decades several studies have been conducted by Hess and his colleagues (Hess & Shipman, 1965, 1968) to demonstrate that the language culture of poor blacks in the United States is different from the language culture of middle-class whites. Arguments rage about whether black dialect provides a good or a poor code for communication as compared with standard English (Bernstein, 1970; Labov, 1970, 1976).

There are also lively debates about whether black English is simply different from standard English or whether it is deficient in some respects (Engelmann, 1970; Williams, 1970). A complicating factor is that all children actually have different language codes and can switch from one to another (e.g., Gay & Tweney, 1976). Many teachers accept the point of view that the speech is deficient because black ghetto children do poorly on standardized tests of language comprehension and reading. One obvious reason for poor performance is that the tests are presented in standard English. However, there is another reason of equal importance. Children's language performance is often evaluated in the context of unnatural questioning and probing by teachers; teachers unknowingly set up barriers to good performance by the manner in which they ask questions. This is true both in language instruction and in formal testing for language achievement.

William Labov (1976) illustrated this point.

In our own research we have studied in some detail the general problem of how you get people to talk about what people are interested in talking about. . . . Many people assume that if you ask somebody a question, it's going to make them talk. It's not so. Questions are often very poor devices for getting people to talk. Commands such as "Tell me!" or "Talk to me" are even worse.

. . . If you press hard enough, the child has to give you some answer. Let me quote from another test case. The teacher puts a toy on the table and says, "Tell me everything you can about this" and there's a twelve-second silence. . . . If you say to a person, "What time is it" and if he doesn't answer, it's going to lead to some violent feelings on both sides. But here the children are defying the teacher. Do you realize how much effort it takes to sit there and not say anything? The teacher finally says, "What would you say it looks like?" Another eight seconds go by and he says "A space ship." Then there's a thirteen-second silence and he says, "Like a je-et." Now, he could have said a lot of things. He could have said, "Well, it's sittin' here on the table. And it's yours, and it ain't mine. And it's a block, and I know what it looks like, and I know what it's for funny look. It seems to be and it's kind of ugly." But instead of that, he says nothing (pp. 152–53).

Labov offers a number of ideas about how to get conversation started in the classroom. One way is to formulate the request so that it is more polite than a direct imperative. For example, the teacher might have posed the request in this form: "Please tell me what you can about this." Another way is to state the request with the implication that the child has the option not to answer: "Would you tell me what you can about this?" Finally, the teacher might abandon the questioning procedure altogether and generate conversation by taking the lead from children's spontaneous comments about objects and events that interest them.

Summary

During the period of concrete operations, the child moves beyond centrated thought to *relativism*, is able to mentally reverse and transform observed actions, and develops a network of thought structures called operations. Many of the operations are defined in terms of properties of an algebraic group.

Recently, Piaget's theory has come under increasing criticism. Despite the wealth of penetrating observations he offers, his sound ideas about the qualitative nature of thinking, and his imaginative concepts about cognitive change, critics worry that there is no good evidence for global stages, that his key concepts about changes are hard to operationalize, and that very few of the phenomena he describes behave precisely as he claims they do.

Several neo-Piagetian models have been proposed, most notably the theory of Pascual-Leone. In his view development consists of the acquisition of specific strategies made possible by experience, a growing "working" memory, and increased automaticity in using strategies.

A different starting point for analyzing the mind is the implicit framework of the information processing theory. With its roots in the early development of computers (e.g., Broadbent, 1958; Miller et al., 1960) and recent advances in the software of computing (e.g., Klahr & Wallace, 1975; Simon, 1980), this perspective assumes that for every event experienced in the environment, cognition involves a series of steps to process the event. Many information processing views of cognitive development recognize common, important steps: attending to the event; perceiving it; storing and retrieving representations of it over time (memory); and acting upon the memories of it in some abstract way—that is, drawing some inference about the experience or resolving a problem by virtue of it. Development can be equated with the individual's becoming a more complete and efficient information processing "mechanism."

Three parts in information processing were emphasized in this chapter—perception, memory, and problem solving. Perception is concerned with the interpretation of information through the five senses. The study of visual perception received the greatest attention in this text. Key changes underlying development include the *amount of redundancy* needed to interpret events, the nature of how *stimulus dimensions* are structured according to salience and integrality-separability, and the experiential *meanings* that organize what we see, such as depth in pictures.

Memory is the retention of information over time. Often it is studied by assessing *recall*, or *recognition*, of events or the ability to associate pairs of things—referred to as *paired associates*. Memory may be conceived of as the flow of information over time, captured in a fleeting moment in a *sensory register*, slightly longer in a *short-term* or working memory, or finally, in a relatively permanent, repository of knowledge called *long-term* memory. The processes that help explain how information is moved through the system include rehearsal, elaboration, and organization.

An inference is a relation noted between one event and another where the relation has not been revealed or identified directly. Some inferences are *logical*, based on our general understanding of how things go together in the world; other inferences are *empirical*, based on our specialized knowledge of persons, places, and things. Another distinction is that some inferences are *literal*, where a relation is seen by simply noticing the spatial or temporal juxtaposition of two events; other inferences are nonliteral. Successful inferential activity requires knowing when to draw inferences, activating relevant prior knowledge, and calling up information from memory.

Problem solving was defined as processing information to fulfill a major goal. It may also be viewed as a regulatory function of information processing involving metacognition. The important components of problem solving include problem finding and goal setting, planning, monitoring progress, and checking solutions.

Language development in the middle and late childhood years includes the mastery of more complex sentence structures and improving reading skills. Teachers can facilitate language development by establishing improved language communication in the classroom.

Key Terms

chunks

classification

class inclusion reasoning

elaboration

equilibration

grapho-phonemic
 information

inference

keyword method

long-term memory

metacognition

mnemonics

paired associates

recall

recognition

rehearsal

salience of dimensions

scripts

semantic-associational
 information

semantic networks

short-term memory

syntactic information

Review Questions

1. What is concrete operational thought?
2. Critically evaluate Piaget's theory.
3. Describe some neo-Piagetian approaches to cognitive development.
4. Discuss perception, including the major changes in it as children mature.
5. Discuss the different ways of assessing memory and the different memory storage systems.
6. Discuss the different processes underlying memory.
7. What is an inference? Describe the different types of inferences and the underlying improvement in inferencing ability.
8. What is problem solving? What are some key parts of regulating information processing?
9. Describe what comes after stage 5 in Roger Brown's theory of language development.
10. Outline Frank Smith's model of reading, and evaluate how we can improve language communication in the classroom.

Further Readings

Elkind, D. *Children and adolescents*, 2d ed. New York: Oxford, 1974.
An excellent, easy-to-read introduction to Piaget's ideas. Many practical examples are given to help you understand Piaget's theory.

Furth, H. G., & Wachs, H. *Thinking goes to school.* New York: Oxford, 1975.
An easy-to-read application of Piaget's view to education in the middle and late childhood years. Includes 179 thinking games that can be incorporated in the day-to-day teaching of children.

Gibson, E. J., & Levin, H. *The psychology of reading.* Cambridge, Mass.: MIT Press, 1975.
An authoritative text on the process of reading from a psychological perspective. Covers the perceptual, cognitive, and linguistic processes in reading, along with extensive ideas about how to teach reading. Reading level is moderately difficult.

Kail, Robert. *The development of memory in children.* Freeman, 1979.
An easy-to-read survey of ideas and research on children's memory.

Klahr, D., & Wallace, J. G. *Cognitive development: an information processing perspective.* Hillsdale, N.J.: Erlbaum, 1975.
A technical explanation of information processing theory by two leading experts. Moderate to difficult reading.

Social and Emotional Development

Prologue: Childhood in China

The first step after the Cultural Revolution was to shorten the period of school—primary to five years, middle to four or five (after experimentation, we have concluded that five is best), university to three years for the time being. Our second step was to change the system of education radically. In schools at all different levels, not only must the students study culture and intellectual knowledge, they must also learn from workers, peasants, and soldiers. To achieve this purpose, schools set up factories or move into the countryside. Camping is the chief way in which students learn from the people's Liberation Army.

Our aim is to criticize the bourgeois, to repudiate bourgeois thinking and the revisionism of Liu Shao-Ch'i and Lin Piao. There are two contradictions: between people and enemy and between people and people. Therefore, middle school graduates do not go directly to the universities; they must do physical labor in a factory or on a farm first. Most do farm work. Universities enroll students from communes and factories after the students have done at least two years of labor. Through this program we will change the system that divorces students from practice, politics, and physical labor. (Remarks of Hsiao Ching-Jo, Peking, November 22, 1973. Quoted in Kessen, 1975.)

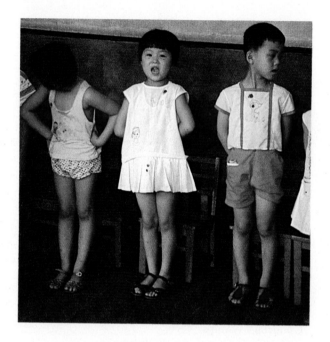

The following comments about childhood in China are based on the observations of a team of social scientists, including William Kessen, Harold Stevenson, Urie Bronfenbrenner, Eleanor Maccoby, Marian Radke-Yarrow, and Martin Whyte (Kessen, 1975).

Frequent communication between schools and parents occurs in Chinese education. These interchanges include formal meetings and notebooks with messages given to students to take home, referred to as "communication," or "connection," notebooks. Informal exchanges are also common when students are dropped off at school. The interface of schools and families appears to be much smoother and continuous than in the United States.

At home and at school, the child is exposed to standards that stress the importance of service and self-reliance. School assignments and out-of-school peer group sessions provide opportunities for the Chinese child to practice self-control and social control. Membership in groups like the Little Red Soldiers and the Red Guards serves the same purpose.

the nation. Parents and schools preach the same doctrine in China, and local committees, acting as arms of the national government, closely monitor how this doctrine is inculcated in Chinese children.

American observers indicate that they are surprised at the extent to which Chinese children are conforming, dutiful, well organized, and devoted to the values of adults. The students have no choice in the courses they take, and no free exploration of information sources (such as browsing in a library). Children in China clearly are exposed to a body of knowledge that is practical in nature. Compared to typical American schools, then, opportunities for student creativity and problem solving are low. For very talented students, there are opportunities to spend time inventing, creating musical productions, and so forth. But there is little or no creativity in the literature the average students read—most stories focus on the ideological message conveyed in revolutionary army practices.

However, close friendships actually may be more easily developed by Chinese children than American children since the Chinese often stay in the same class with the same students throughout the elementary and secondary school years. In the junior high years, there does seem to be easy, happy social interaction within peer groups, usually involving pairs of boys and girls.

Observers of Chinese children raise important questions about the way Chinese children are socialized—for example, what are the implications of a strong cultural indoctrination that is clearly laid out and closely monitored? What are the effects of the absence of independent decision making on a career? What are the effects of the absence of a distinction between the private and public life of the student and the parents? (Kessen, 1975)

Chinese extended family ties are strong. Even though children and family members often have had to spend large chunks of time away from home because of service to the country, the family system in China is a stable one. Grandparents and relatives interact with children more often than in most American families. And, if parents or grandparents fail to supervise their children, local committees look into the matter and provide support. Informal support systems of neighbors and retired workers are fairly common. The picture, then, with regard to the ties between schools, home, and community for Chinese children, is one of coherent support directed toward the development of

Introduction

In this chapter we explore many aspects of social and emotional development in middle and late childhood. Discussion of families and peers continues with further comments about the changing nature of families, the influence of siblings, and the powerful role peers play in middle and late childhood. And, the extensive role school plays in children's lives is discussed.

Families

During middle and late childhood, social agents outside the child's family take on more importance; peers, teachers, and other adults play increasingly important roles in the child's life. By the time children enter elementary school, they are capable of asking complex questions about themselves and their world. A parent needs to change from a model who knows everything to someone who doesn't know all the answers. Two frequent questions parents ask during the middle childhood years are How much do our children need us? and How much can they do without us?

The child entering elementary school can take care of himself or herself for a large part of the day and feels good about being able to do this. Competent parents need to adjust their behavior and let go of children at this time so that they can explore the world more independently. Eight-year-olds don't seek the attention of either parent to the extent that toddlers do; sometimes this can be disturbing to parents who see their children growing away from their control and influence. Children in the middle childhood years still are very much dependent on their parents and still require extensive guidance and monitoring, but parents need to operate more in the background at this time. Parents should recognize that while they still are the most important adults in the child's life, they are no longer the only significant adult figures.

Work and achievement are other themes of middle childhood that require adaptation and guidance on the part of parents. During the elementary school years, it is important that parents encourage children to develop a sense of industry and accomplishment, that is, being able to work and to make things work. In our American culture, parents sometimes push too hard and too early for achievement, shoving their children into tension-provoking comparisons with peers. The opposite extreme, that of lack of involvement and concern for the child's achievement and school success, can lead to difficulties as well. In the latter situation, children may feel that their parents do not value education and achievement and consequently will not be motivated to achieve.

The Changing Family

As indicated in chapter 8, children are growing up in a greater variety of family structures than ever before. Information on school-age children suggests that one reason employment of mothers may not have a negative effect is that many mothers compensate for their absence by increasing the amount of direct interaction with their children when they are at home. Such compensation does not always occur, however, and when it does it may be guilt induced and result in overindulgence (Hoffman, 1974).

When children enter elementary school, the problem of child care is reduced considerably since a greater number of socialization agents have an impact on the child—peer, teachers, and significant adults in the community. Children spend less time with their mothers, and even in traditional families, fathers are more often involved in the socialization process than during the child's earlier years.

Elementary school children whose mothers go to work are likely to be encouraged by their mothers to show independent behavior. It has been found that in lower-class and single-parent families employed mothers are more likely to have structured rules for their children (Hoffman, 1974). Both the independent behavior and the rule-governed households are logical adaptations to the working mother's role—they help the household to function more smoothly in her absence. In addition, there are some rather consistent findings in achievement of the daughters of working mothers; for example, compared to daughters whose mothers don't work outside the home, they admire their mothers more and hold the female role in higher esteem (Romer & Cherry, 1978).

In chapter 8 the effects of divorce on children were also explored. One aspect of divorce of growing interest is whether the custodial parent is the mother or the father. In studies of elementary school-age children in single-parent families it was found that the custodial parent has a strong influence on the child's behavior (Santrock & Warshak, 1979; Santrock, Warshak, & Eliot, 1982). The psychological well-being and child-rearing capabilities of the father or the mother are central to the child's ability to cope with the stress of divorce. It appears that divorced mothers have more difficulty with sons than they do with daughters. Mavis Hetherington (1979) believes that divorced mothers and their sons often get involved in what she calls a cycle of coercive interaction. But what about boys growing up in homes in which the father has custody—is there the same coercive cycle? Box 11.1 focuses on a comparison of children growing up in father- and mother-custody families.

Children in middle childhood still require guidance and monitoring, but parents need to operate more in the background at this time.

Stepparent Families

While research efforts have increased our knowledge about the effects of divorce on children (e.g., Hetherington, Cox, & Cox, 1978; Santrock & Warshak, 1979; Wallerstein & Kelly, 1980), much less is known about what happens to these children when their custodial parent remarries. Over six million children in the United States now live in stepparent homes. These "blended" families represented 11 percent of all American households in 1977 (Eiduson & Zimmerman, 1978). Current research explores the manner in which children are socialized in these stepparent families (Santrock, Warshak, Lindbergh, & Meadows, 1982).

The effects of remarriage on the parent's and the child's social behavior were studied by comparing twelve children whose mothers remarried, with twelve children whose mothers were divorced but had not remarried, and twelve children from intact, father-present families. Half of the children were boys and half were girls aged six to eleven years. The children had been living with their mother and stepfather for a minimum of eighteen months. The data consisted of videotaped observations of parent-child interaction, with the parent's and child's behavior coded separately. The most consistent findings suggested that boys in stepfather families showed more competent social behavior than boys in intact families, which corresponded with more competent parenting behavior in those stepfather families. By contrast, girls in stepfather families were observed to be more anxious than girls in intact families. Boys showed more warmth toward their stepfather than did girls, while there was a trend for girls

to show more anger toward their mother than boys in stepfather families. Divorced and stepfather children differed only in a trend for boys from stepfather families to show more mature behavior than boys from divorced homes. Mothers of boys in stepfather families did make more meaningful statements to them than the divorced mothers of boys. Few differences were found between divorced and intact families.

The same study also found that the fathers of boys in intact families were contemplating divorce more than the stepfathers of boys, and that the mothers of boys in intact families wished they had married someone else more often than the stepfathers and remarried mothers of boys. It appears, then, that the boys in stepfather families were experiencing not only more competent parenting, but also were living in families with less marital conflict than the intact family boys—two factors that help to explain differences in the social behavior of boys from the two family structures.

By contrast, girls in stepfather families showed more anxiety than girls in intact families, but there was no corresponding link with parenting behavior when the stepfather and intact families were compared. However, the stepfathers of girls said that they were contemplating divorce more than the mothers of intact family girls, suggesting the likelihood of greater marital conflict between the parents of the stepfather girls than the intact family girls. And, the possibilty that in some families stepparent-child disharmony may contribute to marital conflict also should be considered.

Box 11.1
Father Custody and Children's Social Behavior

In 1817 poet Percy Bysshe Shelley was denied custody of his children because of his "vicious and immoral" atheistic beliefs. This was a rare situation at the time because English law granted fathers nearly absolute right to custody of their children. This was a carry-over from Roman law, which protected the father's absolute life-and-death control over his children.

In the United States, the English common law tradition was perpetuated throughout the nineteenth century. Few women were permitted to own property, so few had adequate means to support children. Since the father was responsible for financially supporting the child, it was believed that he should be given custody.

The twentieth century brought forth a new interest in the child's welfare—the importance of maternal care was repeatedly emphasized, partly because of the sweeping impact of psychoanalytic theory. It was presumed that mothers are uniquely suited to care for their young. It became standard fare for judges to award custody to the mother because they thought it was in the best interest of the child, unless the mother was in a mental hospital or judged to have some severe physical handicap.

Until recently, many courts awarded custody of the children to the mother without considering the actual needs of the children and carefully evaluating the psychological climate in which the child would live. However, there is a growing movement toward a genuine commitment to the actual needs of the child involved without relying on generalizations that give an a priori claim to either parent. Mavis Hetherington (Hetherington, 1977) has argued that a coercive relationship develops between single mothers and their sons. The mother is overburdened with her responsibility as a single parent, thus reducing the quality of her interaction and increasing the use of coercion with her youth. Boys, because of their relatively greater tendency to engage in aggressive behavior, probably contribute to this coercive cycle.

In one study (Santrock & Warshak, 1979) boys showed more demanding behavior with their mothers in a mother-custody arrangement than with their fathers in a father-custody arrangement. While fathers with custody also have many responsibilities as a single parent, their sons may feel more comfortable with them and the fathers themselves may be more accepting or even encouraging toward traditional masculine behaviors, such as aggressive, rough-and-tumble play. A father is more likely than a mother to play football or other sports with his son, and often feels more comfortable in discussing sex-related issues with him. Conversely, because he lacks female role experiences, a father may be less sensitive to his daughter's needs and less capable of fulfilling those needs even if he senses them.

Sometimes, the opposite-sex child in a single-parent family serves as a substitute for the ex-spouse. In such cases, the relationship between the custodial parent and the opposite-sex child may become more intense than is psychologically healthy. Such a relationship may inhibit the child from engaging in peer interaction to the extent he or she normally would and keeps the child from developing independence. In keeping with this, boys in father-custody homes show more independence than girls, while in mother-custody homes girls show more independence than boys (Santrock & Warshak, 1979; Santrock, Warshak, & Eliot, 1982).

Divorced parents often enlist the aid of additional caretakers for their children, including the noncustodial parent, babysitters, relatives, day-care centers, and friends. Fathers with custody used these systems more than mothers with custody (about twenty-four hours per week versus about eleven hours per week). Father-custody children also had more frequent contact with the noncustodial parent than their counterparts in mother-custody homes (Santrock & Warshak, 1979).

It is clear that the effects of divorce on children are determined by a host of complex factors that include custody arrangement, sex of the child, aspects of the custodial parent-child relationship, and the availability and reliance on support systems.

It was concluded that the social behavior of children is not necessarily less competent in stepfather families than in intact or divorced families. The data suggested that such factors as parenting behavior, sex of child, and marital conflict in any type of family structure are implicated as possible explanations of the child's social behavior.

So far in our discussion of families we have paid attention to changing family structures, parent-child relationships, parenting techniques, and the maturation of the child and the parent. Next, we look at yet another important aspect of families—sibling relationships.

Siblings

Probably the least studied aspect of the family system is the nature of sibling interaction. Sibling interaction usually precedes peer interaction and, as such, may serve as a bridge between family relations and the social world of peers.

Competition among siblings—that is, brothers and/or sisters—along with concern about being treated fairly and equally by parents, are among the most pervasive characteristics of sibling relationships (Santrock, Smith, & Bourbeau, 1976).

More than 80 percent of American children have one or more siblings. Because there are so many possible sibling combinations in a family, it is difficult to generalize about sibling influence and conflict. Among a variety of important factors to be considered in studying sibling relationships are the number of siblings and the number of years separating the siblings in age. Despite the complexities of such studies, there has been considerable research on siblings. These studies usually compare firstborn children with their siblings (e.g., Koch, 1956). Most of the studies focus on two-child families since interpreting data on sibling experiences in larger families is difficult. In keeping with the text's approach to the family as a system of interacting individuals, let's look first at the mother's interaction with siblings.

The Mother's Interaction with Siblings

The influence of the mother's interaction with her children on sibling behavior usually has been studied indirectly; that is, children of a different birth order are compared with each other. As a result of such studies, it is speculated that mothers treat their children differently, presumably causing changes in their behavior and personality.

More than 80 percent of American children have one or more siblings.

For example, firstborn children are more achievement-oriented, affiliative (want to be around people), and compliant than children born later (Sutton-Smith & Rosenberg, 1970). It is usually believed that middle children tend to be somewhat neglected by parents. Mothers seem more anxious and solicitous with their firstborn than with children born later, perhaps causing differences in the children's behavior (Schacter, 1959).

In observations of mother-sibling interaction, mothers consistently gave more attention to their firstborn children than to children born later (Cushna, 1966; Gewirtz & Gewirtz, 1965; Rothbart, 1967). This is perhaps explained by the fact that many mothers anxiously await the birth of their first child and that both parents often have high expectations for the child. By the time the second child is born, much of the novelty and intrigue of rearing a child probably has worn off.

A newborn child can influence both the behavior of the mother and the behavior of the sibling. In one study working-class mothers were observed as they interacted with their firstborn children in a playroom situation, both before and shortly after the birth of a sibling. The mothers and the firstborn exchanged less open affection and were more neutral to each other after the sibling was born (Taylor & Kogan, 1973).

Siblings' Influences on One Another

A four-year-old child probably feels more threatened by the arrival of a brother or sister than does a child who is one or two years old or a child who is seven or eight. The cognitive development of the very young child is not advanced enough to understand much of what is happening. An older child probably has gained more independence, established stronger ties with peers, and has less fear of the parent's withdrawal of love. There are individual differences, however; an older child who is still tied to his or her mother and does not have many friends may feel just as threatened by the arrival of a younger brother or sister as the preschooler does.

Several studies have focused on the interaction of siblings. Helen Samuels (1977) observed the social interaction in a twenty-minute play situation of infants (mean age, nineteen months) with their older preschool siblings (mean age, four and one-half years). She predicted that infants would find the older siblings attractive and treat them as models. A comparison of the siblings' behavior supported her prediction. The infant tended to look at, imitate, and follow the older sibling about, whereas the older sibling tended to show comparatively little interest of this sort in the infant.

Interaction among older siblings also has been studied (Minnett, Santrock, & Vandell, 1981). In one study approximately seven thousand, twenty-second intervals of sibling interaction were coded as siblings engaged in cooperative, competitive, and unstructured tasks at their school. Sibling pairs were grouped according to the sex of the child (seven to eight years old), sex of his or her sibling, age spacing (zero to two or three to four years), and ordinal position of birth in relation to other siblings in the family (older or younger). Firstborn (older) siblings were more dominant than second-born siblings in all situations; however, the degree of their dominance was moderated by the age spacing of the siblings (wider age spacing produced more dominance) and sex of the sibling (the most dominant sibling was a girl aged three to four years apart). By the time both siblings have reached preschool age, those closer in age are more likely to share the same peer group and have more similar abilities than those farther apart in age, a situation likely to engender competition. Brothers close in age were found to have the least harmonious relationship of all sibling pairs. While sister pairs usually were more harmonious than brother pairs, sisters closer in age were less congenial with each other.

Many parents of siblings who took part in this study expressed concern about their children's constant bickering and fighting, hoping that participation in the study would shed some light on sibling rivalry. Indeed, the process of social comparison is intensified in any sibling relationship. The child has a built-in need to know

While competitive sibling interaction is a fact of life, so too is positive interaction.

where he or she stands vis-à-vis his or her brother or sister: is he or she as strong, as smart, as worthwhile a person? All children are concerned about where they stand in these regards, but a sibling provides a more concrete reminder to the child to question his or her status in the family. Competitive sibling interaction, then, is a fact of sibling life, but so, too, are positive and neutral interactions. However, parents may overlook many of the positive and neutral sibling exchanges, responding instead to negative behaviors that require parental intervention.

We know very little about how sibling pairs of different ages socialize each other. For example, is the social interaction of four- and eight-year-old sibling pairs the same as eight- and twelve-year-old siblings? Research focused on observations of sibling interaction suggests that one of the major differences between younger and older pairs of siblings involves the sex of the child (Santrock & Minnett, 1981). In comparing four- to eight- with eight- to twelve-, and six- to eight- with eight- to ten-year-old sibling pairs, more negative and less positive behavior was found among the older female sibling pairs than the younger female sibling pairs.

Is sibling interaction different from parent-child interaction? There is some evidence that it is. Linda Baskett (1974) observed the members of forty-seven families, each with two or three children. The siblings ranged from five to ten years of age. Observations were made for forty-five minutes on five different occasions. The children's observed behaviors included teasing, whining, yelling, commanding, talking, touching, nonverbal interacting, laughing, and complying. The interaction of the children with their parents was far more positive than their interaction with each other. Children and their parents had more varied and positive interchanges—they talked, laughed, and comforted one another more than siblings did. Children also tended to follow the dictates of their parents more than those of their siblings, and they behaved more negatively and punitively during interaction with their siblings than with their parents.

In some instances siblings are a stronger socializing influence on the child than parents are. Victor Cicirelli (1977) believes, in particular, that older siblings teach their younger siblings. Someone close in age to the child may understand his or her problems more readily and be able to communicate more effectively than parents can. In areas such as dealing with peers, coping with difficult teachers, and discussing taboo subjects, siblings often fare better than parents in the socialization process. Older siblings also may serve effectively in teaching younger siblings about identity problems, sexual behavior, and physical appearance—areas in which the parents may be unwilling or incapable of helping a child.

The potential benefits of using siblings as therapists has been demonstrated by Miller and Cantwell (1976). They found that in families where siblings are involved, therapy is more effective than in families where only the parents and the disturbed child are included. When siblings are not included, they may unknowingly encourage and perpetuate unwanted behaviors in the disturbed child. Instructing the sibling in ways he or she and the parents can more effectively manage the disturbed brother or sister produces more positive outcomes in family therapy.

As mentioned earlier, this sibling interaction may help the child to bridge life in the family with life with peers.

Peers

Peer interaction has been studied in almost as many ways as parent-child interaction. In this section we will see that peers are important models for their age-mates, that in some cases they can serve as effective tutors, and that they can be of great help to age-mates who have social problems. Popularity among peers, the nature of friendship patterns, and how children's groups are formed will also be discussed.

Peer Modeling, Tutoring, and Reinforcement

There has been little effort to use peer modeling in a formal way in our educational system. One technique that is gaining popularity in schools, however, is peer tutoring. Allen and Feldman (1976) found that when low-achieving fifth-graders were placed in the role of teacher, substantial gains in their reading scores resulted. The reading scores of the tutored third-graders, however, did not increase more than those of a comparable group of children who studied alone. The children may have felt embarrassed about being taught systematically by their own age-mates. Perhaps somewhat older peers should be used, as in the Allen and Feldman study, for tutoring in school subjects. It may be, however, that the greatest gains will be those made by the tutors themselves.

Other studies of the relationship between peer models and their observers indicate that a positive relationship with the model (Hartup & Coates, 1967) and a perceived similarity between the model and the observer (Rosenkrans, 1967) enhance modeling. In other words, if the tutor or model has a positive, warm relationship with the observer, or if the observer believes he or she has something in common with the model, modeling will be more effective. In keeping with the idea of perceived similarity, it seems that it would be best to have a middle-class student tutor a middle-class child and lower-class student counsel a lower-class child.

Peer relations are also affected by the extent to which the individuals dispense rewards to each other. The members of a peer group who give out the most reinforcements are the ones most likely to receive the most reinforcements in return (Charlesworth & Hartup, 1967). This indicates the reciprocal nature of peer interaction. In one investigation it was found that training peers to selectively use reinforcement reduced disruptive activity in the classroom (Solomon & Whalen, 1973).

In our educational system teachers and administrators sometimes deliberately have manipulated peer contact. For instance, at the beginning of the school year, students who are less advanced academically (and in some cases, socially) often are placed in classes for so-called slower students. This arrangement is designed to enable the teacher to teach at the cognitive level appropriate for the majority of students in the class (Hartup, 1976). While "tracking" (as it is referred to in educational circles) is usually designed for academic benefits, it may have a considerable effect on social development as well. For example, tracking may break down neighborhood friendships and supplant them with "tracking" friendships although such an influence on friendship patterns is regarded as incidental by school administrators.

As Bronfenbrenner (1970) points out, the educational system in the United States has not systematically called on the peer group to the extent that other countries have. Bronfenbrenner summarized some of the major aspects of socialization practices involving peer relations in the Soviet Union. There, the peer group is assigned important duties in assisting the teacher. Conformity to group norms is stressed through education, and the subordination of the individual to the group is an omnipresent goal. Group competition between grades, schools, rooms, and rows in rooms is emphasized. Although such practices are not foreign to American schools, they are not as systemized as they are in the Soviet Union. In the United States, the peer group may undermine the socialization practices of adults; in the Soviet Union peer-group norms support adult norms.

Probably no other cross-cultural work with children is more widely cited than the work of Beatrice and John Whiting. In 1954 the Whitings and their colleagues began reporting their observations of children in six different cultures. The most recent publication of their work is the book *Children of Six Cultures: A Psychocultural Analysis*. For these observations the Whitings placed six teams of anthropologists in six different cultures, five of which were primarily farming communities: northern India; the Philippines; Okinawa, Japan; Oaxaca, Mexico; and western Kenya. The sixth setting was a small, nonfarming town in New England. The teams interviewed the mothers and conducted standardized observations of the children in the six cultures.

Among the most intriguing findings of the project were the consistent differences in adult-child and peer interactions across the cultures. Dependency, nurturance, and intimacy were rarely observed in peer relations but were frequently observed in adult-child interaction. By contrast, aggressiveness, prosocial activity, and sociable behavior were the most frequently occurring behaviors in peer relations across the six cultures. Such findings support the belief that there may be universal differences between adult-child and peer interactions.

In this section we have seen that the relatively straightforward application of the principles of modeling and reinforcement often can be effective in influencing children's peer relations, and that there are similarities as well as differences when we study peer relations in different cultures. Next, we see that children are increasingly called upon to help their peers with problems.

Peer Sociotherapy

One **conglomerate strategy** (i.e., a series of coordinated strategies) used to help children get along better with their peers is called **coaching,** which combines demonstration (or modeling), rational discussion sessions, and shaping (the use of reinforcement). In one coaching study, students with few friends were selected for a coaching session that focused on how to have fun with your peers (Oden & Asher, 1975). The "unpopular" students were encouraged to participate fully, to show

interest in others, to cooperate, and to maintain communication. A control group of students (who also had few friends) were directed in play experiences but were not coached with specific strategies. Later, the coached group showed more sociability with peers than the uncoached group did.

Another example of effective conglomerate strategy in peer therapy is Robert Selman's (Selman, Newberger, & Jacquette, 1977) psychological and educational program, emphasizing the importance of peer relations in classroom settings, group activities, and sports. His work is described in box 11.2.

Popularity

Elementary and secondary schoolchildren often think, What can I do to have all of the kids at school like me? How can I be popular with both girls and guys? What's wrong with me? There must be something wrong, or I would be more popular. Sometimes children will go to great lengths to be popular; and in some cases parents go to even greater lengths to try to insulate their offspring from rejection and to increase the likelihood that they will be popular.

What makes a child popular with peers? In one study, for example, children who gave the most reinforcements were found to gain popularity among their peers (e.g., Hartup, 1970). In the coaching sessions discussed earlier (Oden & Asher, 1975) students were encouraged to overcome their difficulty in interacting

Certain physical and cultural factors also can affect a child's popularity. Some research has shown that children who are physically attractive are more popular than those who are not; and contrary to what some believe, brighter children are more popular than less intelligent ones. Children growing up in middle-class surroundings tend to be more popular than those growing up in lower-class surroundings, presumably in part because they are more in control of establishing standards for popularity (e.g., Hollingshead, 1975). But remember that findings such as these reflect group averages; there are many physically attractive children who are unpopular and physically unattractive children who are very well liked. And, with the increased concern for equal treatment of minority groups, lower-class and ethnic group children can be expected to gain more influence in establishing the standards of popularity.

Finally, popularity may fluctuate, and children sense the tenuous nature of popularity; even the child who is very popular with peers may have doubts about his or her ability to maintain popularity. Being popular with peers is an ongoing concern for almost every child. But not only do children want to be popular with their peers, they also want at least one or two best friends.

Friendship Patterns

Reading the following description of one girl's best friend may help you to remember some of your experiences with friendship during childhood and adolescence:

My best friend is nice. She's honest, and I can trust her. I tell her my innermost secrets and know that nobody else will find out about them. I have other friends, too, but she is my best friend. We consider each other's feelings and don't want to hurt each other. We help each other out when we have problems. We make up funny names for people and laugh ourselves silly. We make lists of which boys are the sexiest and which are the ugliest, which are the biggest jerks; and so on. Some of these things we share with other friends, but some we don't.

Unfortunately, many children do not have a best friend, or even a circle of friends in whom they can confide. One school psychologist always made a practice of asking children and adolescents about their friends. A twelve-year-old boy, when asked who his best friend was, replied, "My kite." Further discussion revealed that his parents had insulated him from the society of neighborhood peers. Similarly, in one investigation of college-age youth, as many as one out of every three students surveyed said that they had not found, or were not sure whether they had found a close, meaningful relationship with a same-sex peer (Katz, 1968).

Popularity is important to many youths and they will go to great lengths to achieve it.

with their peers by listening carefully to their peers' conversation and by maintaining open lines of communication with their peers. In another study (Hartup, 1970) it was found that being yourself, being happy, showing enthusiasm and concern for others, and showing self-confidence but not conceit are among the characteristics that lead to popularity. In many instances the opposites of these behaviors were found to invite rejection from peers (Hollingshead, 1975).

A Peer-Oriented Clinic for Children with Problems

Robert Selman's work has been conducted at the Manville School, a clinic in the Judge Baker Guidance Center in Boston for learning-disabled and emotionally disturbed seven- to fifteen-year-olds. Many of these students have great difficulty in interpersonal relationships, particularly with their peers. The staff at the Manville School has been trained to help peers provide support and encouragement to each other in group settings, a process referred to as **peer sociotherapy.**

Structured programs at the Manville School are designed to help the children assist each other in such areas as cooperation, trust, leadership, and conformity. Four school activities were developed to improve the student's social reasoning skills in these areas.

First, there is a weekly peer problem-solving session in the classroom in which the peers work cooperatively to plan activities and relate problems. At the end of each week the peers evaluate their effectiveness in making improvements in areas like cooperation, conflict resolution, and so forth.

Second, the members of a class, numbering from six to eight students, plan a series of weekly field trips, for example, going to the movies or visiting historical sites. While the counselor provides some assistance, peer decision making dominates. When each activity is completed, the students discuss how things went and what might have been done to improve social relations with each other on the outings.

Third, Selman recognizes that there are times when the student has to get away from a setting where intense frustration occurs. When the student finds himself or herself in a highly frustrating situation (e.g., angry enough to strike out at a classmate), he or she is allowed to leave the room and go to a private "time-out" area of the school to regain composure. In time-out, the student also is given the opportunity to discuss the problems with a counselor who has been trained to help the adolescent improve social reasoning skills.

Fourth, during social studies and current events discussion sessions, the student evaluate a number of moral and societal issues that incorporate the thinking of theorists such as Lawrence Kohlberg.

Many youths indicate that meaningful friendships are high on their lists of needs.

John Conger (1977) suggests several explanations for why many adolescents have difficulty establishing close friendships. While many youths indicate that meaningful friendships are high on their list of needs, they may lack the skills necessary to get and retain friends (for example, the ability consistently to demonstrate active listening and open communication styles). It also may be that adolescents have a more stringent definition of "meaningful" friendship than other age segments in the population. And, while many adolescents stress that they have a strong need for close friends, they may be suspicious of what such a commitment will mean.

John Gottman and Jennifer Parkhurst (1978) argue that young children's abilities to provide mutual support and to resolve conflict in imaginative fantasies is critical in establishing and maintaining intimacy among young friends. In coping with conflict young friends express considerable emotion, sympathy and support, and anguish about conflict.

Children's Groups

So far in our discussion of peer relations, little has been said about how the child functions in groups. In this section we will look at how children's groups are formed, compare children's groups with adolescent groups, and describe cultural variations in children's groups.

The most extensive work conducted on the formation of children's and adolescent's groups is that of Muzafer Sherif and his colleagues (Sherif, 1951; Sherif, 1966; Sherif, Harvey, Hoyt, Hood, & Sherif, 1961). The Sherif naturalistic experiments often proceed according to a particular format. Middle-class white Protestant boys are recruited and moved to a campsite during the summer. There they are exposed to an experiment in the natural setting of the camp. The observers are members of the camp staff.

In the first phase of the experiment, in-group formation is established by placing two groups of boys who don't know one another together for a few days. In the second phase the two groups are brought together for the intergroup conflict phase. This conflict includes win-lose competition and planned frustration that is expected to increase the tension between the groups. In the third phase, ways to reduce intergroup conflict are explored. The observers use strategies such as experiencing a common enemy, or constructing superordinate goals that the two groups can only achieve together, to reduce conflict.

Some of the important findings to come out of Sherif's naturalistic experiments are: (1) hierarchical structures invariably emerge within the groups. The top and bottom status positions are filled first, then the middle positions. (2) Norms develop in all groups. "We-they" talk is a frequent part of the groups' conversations. The groups often adopt nicknames, like the Bulldogs or the Sorcerers. (3) Frustration and competition contribute to hostility between the groups. (4) Intergroup hostility often can be reduced by setting up a superordinate goal that requires the mutual efforts of both groups. For example, Sherif's camp directors deliberately broke a water line so both groups of boys would have to pitch in together to help. Another time, the camp truck taking the boys to a movie in town was driven into a muddy ditch, requiring considerable team effort to get it out.

Children's Groups versus Adolescent Groups

Children's groups differ from adolescent groups in several important ways. The members of children's groups are often friends or neighborhood acquaintances. Their groups are usually not as formalized as many adolescent groups. During the adolescent years, groups tend to include a broader array of members—in other words, adolescents other than friends or neighborhood acquaintances are often members of the groups. Try to recall the student council, honor society, or football

The members of children's groups are often neighborhood acquaintances.

team at your junior high school. If you were a member of any of these junior high organizations, you likely recall that they were comprised of a number of individuals you had not met before, and that they were a more heterogeneous group than your childhood peer groups. Rules and regulations were probably well defined, and captains or leaders were formally elected or appointed. Formalized structure and definition of status positions probably did not characterize many of your childhood peer groups.

In addition to more formalized structure and greater heterogeneity of members, adolescent peer groups are also more often cross-sexed than children's peer groups (Dunphy, 1963). The increased frequency of formal groups in junior high, combined with the psychological changes of puberty, explain to some extent why adolescent groups have mixtures of boys and girls more often than children's groups do.

Cultural Variations in Childhood Peer Groups

Whether a child grows up as part of the peer culture in a ghetto or in a middle-class suburban area influences the nature of the groups he or she belongs to. For example, in a comparison of middle- and lower-class groups, lower-class children displayed more aggression toward the low-status member of the group but showed less aggression toward the president of the group than their middle-class counterparts did (Maas, 1954).

In many schools, peer groups are virtually segregated according to race and social class. Where middle- and lower-class students are both included, the middle-class students often assume the leadership roles in formal organizations such as the student council, the honor society, fraternity-sorority groups, and so forth. Athletic teams represent one type of group where blacks and lower-class students have been able to gain parity with or surpass middle-class students in achieving status.

Adolescent groups usually have a more formalized structure and greater heterogeneity of members.

Where a child grows up influences the nature of the group he or she belongs to.

Athletic teams represent one type of group where blacks and lower-class students have achieved status.

Black and white (and lower- and middle-class) students have spent more time with each other during the past two decades than in previous eras. But it has been in schools rather than in neighborhoods where the greatest mixture of different backgrounds has occurred. Even when schools are mixed in terms of ethnic and social-class background, it still appears that friendships, cliques, and crowds are more likely to follow social-class and ethnic group lines (Hartup, 1970). It is usually in formal groups, such as athletic teams and student councils, that the greatest mixture of social class and ethnicity occurs.

This means that family and cultural backgrounds play critical parts in the development of both informal and formal peer groups. As John Hill (1980) indicates, even though children often spend greater amounts of time with their peers than with their parents, isolation from parental values does not necessarily ensue.

Not only are there cultural differences in peer groups within the United States, but the role and function of the peer group may differ from country to country. In some cultures, children are placed in peer groups for much greater lengths of time at an earlier age than they are in the United States. For example, in the Murian culture of eastern India, both male and female children live in a dormitory from the age of six until they get married (Barnouw, 1975). The dormitory is seen as a religious haven where members are devoted to work and spiritual harmony. Children work for their parents, and the parents arrange the children's marriages. When the children wed, they must leave the dormitory.

The development of independence is even more extreme for children living in the Nyakyusan culture in East Africa (Barnouw, 1975). Children leave home with their peers when they are ten years old to develop a new village. They build huts, get married and have children, and cultivate fields. Many of the children, then, in the cultures of the Muria and Nyakyusa are given the chance to become autonomous and perform adult roles long before they actually reach adulthood.

In summarizing the major changes in peer relations from early childhood to middle and late childhood, Willard Hartup (1982) concluded:

Qualitative changes in child-child interaction continue beyond the preschool years. With school entrance, children increase their contacts with other children and begin to recognize that other individuals have ideas and points of view that are different from their own. Peer interaction undoubtedly profits from the decline in egocentrism as well as contributes to it. . . .

Reciprocity is necessary in many situations confronted by the older child—in playing games, participating in groups, and friendships. . . . The child's understanding of intentionality and the ability to cope with complex social messages increase in middle childhood and almost certainly underlie changes in social interaction. (pp. 46, 52)

Schools

Not all children attend preschool classes, but virtually every child in the United States does go to elementary school. For those who do not attend preschool classes, entering the first grade can be a shocking experience; the first grade is often the first time these children have been separated from their mothers for long periods of time.

Schools are one of the major institutions by which a culture transmits information and values to its children. By the time children have reached the age of five to six, most in America spend as many of their waking hours in school as at home.

Most children in American society spend twelve or more years in formal schooling. It is not atypical for many individuals to spend up to twenty-three years in school, including one or two years of nursery school, one year of kindergarten, twelve years of elementary and high school, four years of college, and four years of graduate or professional school. It would be surprising, then, if school were anything but a powerful force in the development of children. Indeed, it may be the most influential of society's many institutions.

We will look at the nature of children's schooling, including the different kinds of schools, the organization of schools, school and class size, and classroom structure and organization. And, we will focus on the teacher's role in children's social development.

The Nature of the Child's Schooling

Educators who stress the importance of humanistic and affective education believe that schools are often inhumane and fail to give adequate consideration to the child's feelings. They believe that educational institutions should be working toward developing the child's self-awareness and self-confidence as much or more than teaching how to write essays or do math problems. Advocates of humanistic and affective education feel that the child should receive more individual attention from the teacher, particularly in regard to problems, conflicts, and anxieties. Furthermore, they say, teachers should be less dictatorial and allow the child freedom to make decisions.

These types of schools are sometimes referred to as providing **progressive education.** Another view is that schools should be providing a **traditional education.** Traditional schools are preoccupied with transmitting basic academic skills to all children—skills that are seen as necessary for getting along in a complex society. In early elementary years this concern is seen in the familiar emphasis on reading, writing, and arithmetic.

Progressive schools take a broader view of education. They suppose that basic skills are important but that the child must also learn how to get along with other people, acquire an appreciation of aesthetics and

Traditional schools concentrate on transmitting basic academic skills to all children.

In progressive schools, the needs of the individual child are emphasized.

human values, and be exposed to activities that will be a source of pleasure in later life. In progressive education emphasis is on the needs and competencies of the individual child; no activity is so important that every child must be forced into it regardless of ability or motivation for participation

Open schools, free schools, and *alternative schools* are labels that have been applied to classroom settings and schools that differ from the structured, teacher-centered approach of traditional schools. These *progressive* schools became popular during the late 1960s and early 1970s at a time when educators were seeking new ways to stimulate students and allow for optimum growth. Humanistic and affective education may now be on the wane as advocates of traditional schools have become more vociferous. "Let's get back to the basics in our schools," they say. "Our schools are not teaching children how to write and read correctly." Advocates of the "back to the basics" movement cite declining achievement scores on standardized tests of verbal and mathematics skills as evidence that these basic skills are not being taught effectively (e.g., Forbes, 1976).

They want to do away with the new "frills" of moral education, innovative programs, and child-centered curricula and return to reading, writing, and mathematics, and science skills.

There is no easy answer to the question of which type of education, traditional or progressive, is better for children. It is very difficult to obtain empirical information about this matter; both traditional and progressive programs vary among themselves along many different dimensions. Also, different types of programs may have different outcomes for different children. Some education experts believe that the most important facet of education is variety; in other words, it is important to have several education modes to choose from in order to suit the specific needs and abilities of individual children.

One dimension of the traditional versus progressive education issue that has been quite thoroughly studied is control. This dimension is significant in many contexts—with school boards and principals, with reference to how much centralized control there is in a school system and within a school; in the classroom, with reference to how the teacher disciplines students; and in who controls the schools, with reference to how much influence parents have over what their children are taught.

John Hill (1978) suggests that how parents view the control issue depends upon their social class. A rather common prescription for junior high school education is *authoritarian control*, held by school administrators and teachers because it is believed that such power is necessary to repress the rebellious nature of young adolescents. Many lower-class parents agree with this strategy, since they themselves are more likely to use authoritarian discipline in dealing with their youth. But such a discipline strategy may be viewed skeptically by many middle-class parents who see authoritarian discipline as inhibiting and repressive.

The dimension of control also seems to be linked with the incidence of violence in schools. A recent report by the National Institute of Education (1978) suggests that violence is less likely to occur in schools where principals firmly enforce rules, where the rules and controls are considered reasonable by students, and where the students perceive that they have at least some control over their own lives. Also, vandalism occurs less frequently when rules are fairly and firmly administered than when teachers adopt hostile attitudes and discipline in an authoritarian fashion.

Organization of Schools

There are many ways the child's school years can be organized. Perhaps the most common is to divide the twelve years of schooling into six years at an elementary school, three years at a junior high school, and the final three years at a high school. However, there has been an increase in recent years in the number of school districts that have gone to a middle school organization. In this system, the child goes through first through fifth grades in an elementary school, sixth through eighth grades in a middle school and ninth through twelfth grades in a high school.

Very little is known about how different forms of school organization affect the child's development. In one review of the educational practices of middle schools compared with junior high schools, there were no differences between the two types of schools in teaching strategies, curricula, academic progress, student work load, or extracurricular activities (Gatewood, 1971). But what about the effects of the organization on students? It may be that the physical, social, and cognitive development of children is affected by such factors as whether they are the oldest, largest, and most competent in a group of 300 to 400 young people, or the youngest, smallest, and least competent among such a group. A sixth grader in a middle school is likely to have very different experiences than a sixth grader in an elementary school. This would apply as well to a ninth grader in a junior high school compared with a ninth grader in a senior high school.

In one of the few investigations that has compared sixth graders in a middle school with sixth graders in an elementary school, significant differences in the social development of the two groups were found (Shovlin, 1967). Girls in the middle school showed much greater interest in the opposite sex than girls in the elementary school, while there was little difference for sixth-grade boys in the two schooling structures. On the other hand, boys in the elementary school had higher levels of self-esteem than girls did, but the reverse occurred in middle school.

As John Hill (1978) indicates, these findings are likely due to the fact that more sixth-grade girls than boys have entered the pubertal cycle. The physical maturity of the sixth-grade girls fit better with the role expectations of the adolescents in middle school than with those of the boys and girls in grade school. By contrast, the sixth-grade boys are the biggest and strongest in the elementary school but are not as mature as most of the boys and girls in the middle school. Status in school, particularly for boys, is often influenced by physical size and athletic competence—hence, the low self-esteem of sixth-grade boys in middle schools.

In another investigation, when a transition to a new school was combined with the onset of puberty, the child's adjustment was difficult (Blyth, Simmons, & Bush, in press). In a longitudinal investigation, the effects of progressing from sixth to seventh grade in a kindergarten through eighth-grade school were compared with the effects of going from sixth grade in an elementary school to seventh grade in a junior high school. When both types of students were evaluated in the seventh grade, the following differences were found: students in the kindergarten through eighth-grade setting had more positive self-concepts, perceived themselves as better integrated into the school and various peer groups, and were involved in more activities and clubs than were the junior high students.

In sum, it appears that school organization is an important influence on the child's social development. But what about the size of the school and the size of the classroom? Do these factors also affect the child's development?

School and Class Size

School size does seem to have an effect on the child's social development. In a number of investigations, it has been found that students in small schools, while not necessarily participating in more extracurricular activities, do engage in a greater variety of activities than their counterparts in large schools (e.g., Barker & Gump, 1964; Schoo, 1970; Willems, 1967). It also appears that students in the smaller schools hold more leadership slots than students in larger schools (e.g., Barker & Gump, 1964).

There is little consistency, however, in how classroom size affects children's development. Traditional schools in the United States usually have about thirty students per class, give or take ten. Although most teachers insist that they do a better job with smaller groups, empirical evidence to support this belief has not yet been developed. The most comprehensive investigation of class size has been conducted with elementary school children in which 163 classrooms were evaluated (U.S. Office of Education, 1974). The results were contradictory; at some grade levels, small

The typical American classroom has seats fixed in rows facing the teacher.

Less structured physical arrangements have characterized schools in recent years.

Educational environment has some consistent effects on all children.

classes seemed to improve academic performance, while at others it did not. Thus, while there is every intuitive reason to argue for smaller classes, there is little empirical evidence to back up this argument.

Classroom Structure and Organization
Classroom environments also influence the child's development. Certain structures and organizations have dominated the classrooms of children in the United States.

The typical American schoolroom has seats fixed in rows facing the front of the room, where the teacher's desk is located. In recent years, however, many schools have developed less structured physical arrangements in the classroom. Some education experts have even commented that the most significant event in education in the last one-hundred years has been removing the bolts that attach seats to the floor, allowing children to move around the classroom (e.g., Smock, 1975).

An interesting study of the traditional seating arrangement indicates that in such an arrangement, the teacher interacts with some students more than others because of seat location (Adams & Biddle, 1970): Children who sit in the front and in the center are more likely to interact with the teacher than are students sitting on the fringes. This pattern of interaction occurred in both sixth- and eleventh-grade classrooms, with both male and female teachers, and in both social studies and mathematics classes. (It should be noted that the student's selection of a classroom seat may reflect his or her willingness to participate in classroom exchanges.)

There is a great deal of interest in educational circles on how classroom organization affects the child's development. One of the most controversial topics is the type of classroom setting that fosters the most effective teaching and learning—structured settings or flexible settings. As a rule, flexible classrooms provide a wide variety of materials, involve many different planned activities, and allow students the freedom to choose their own groups and seating arrangements.

Furthermore, in the flexible classroom setting teachers often interact with children on a one-to-one basis, open-ended questions are asked, and students tend to initiate verbal interaction. In structured classrooms specific sequences of tasks and similar formats are followed most of the time. An examination of the literature on the effects of classroom organization accumulated by educational psychologists during the past decade indicates mixed results (e.g., Good, Biddle, & Brophy, 1975). Structured classrooms are not always associated with better achievement, nor are flexible classrooms always associated with better social outcomes, although these effects have sometimes been reported. Studies show that sometimes the reverse is true, and sometimes there are simply no differences.

Part of the problem with studies of structured and flexible classrooms is that these terms are not always rigidly distinguished or adhered to in the classroom. As a result, in some classrooms defined as structured, the teachers may be using a teaching style more characteristic of flexible classrooms. An additional problem in these studies is the fact that too often in the past researchers have relied upon teachers or school officials (who may have varying definitions of what constitutes structured and flexible classrooms) to rate classroom organization.

In many instances the measures used to assess the effects of classroom organization have been standardized tests of intelligence and achievement. However, Rudolf Moos (e.g., Moos & Moos, 1978; Trickett & Moos, 1974) believes that it may be wise to assess educational effects in ways other than those evaluated by standardized tests. Cognitive preferences (Tamir, 1975), school satisfaction (Epstein & McPartland, 1976), and persistent motivation to learn (Maehr, 1976) are several additional factors on which students should be measured.

While it is now well documented that some educational programs are better for some students than for others, Pat Minuchin (1976) points out that an educational environment has some consistent effects on all children. She studied sixty, first-grade children in open classrooms, thirty of whom were cautious and reserved and thirty of whom showed strong exploratory tendencies. The basic purpose of the study was to show how very different kinds of children use an open-classroom environment. Many patterns of classroom behavior characterized both groups. For example, both groups of children interacted a great deal with other children, both in work and play; and both groups used the teacher as a resource but showed considerable autonomy in managing their own activities. In the next section we will explore the fact that some children more than others do seem to benefit from structure.

Aptitude × Treatment Interaction

Some children may benefit more from structure than others, and some teachers may be able to handle a flexible curriculum better than others. As a result, a whole field of educational research has sprung up, referred to as **Aptitude × Treatment Interaction,** or **(ATI).** The term *aptitude* refers to academic potential and personality dimensions in which students differ; *treatment* refers to the educational technique (e.g., structured class or flexible class) adopted in the classroom. Lee Cronbach and Richard Snow (1977), as well as other education experts, argue that ATI is the best way to study teaching effectiveness.

Recent research has shown that a child's achievement level (aptitude) may interact directly with classroom structure (treatment) to produce the best learning and the most enjoyable learning environment (Peterson, 1977; Porteus, 1976). That is, students with high-achievement orientation often do well in a flexible classroom and enjoy it; students with low-achievement orientation do not usually do as well and dislike the flexibility. The reverse is true in a structured classroom. There are many other ATI factors operating in the classroom. Education experts are just beginning to pin some of these down; further clarification of aptitude × treatment interaction should lead to useful information about how adolescents can be taught more effectively.

Richard Snow (1977) points out that individual aptitudes were virtually ignored for many years in the design of instruction and curriculum. Now, individual differences in student aptitudes, learning styles, cultural backgrounds, and so forth, are forcing curriculum teams to consider more specific instructional situations and more specific groups of people. The theories of instruction and curriculum that come out of ATI studies may, in fact, be very specific; one may apply, for example, to a course in economics in a private high school, or to a three-week social studies unit on racial relations in an urban junior high. Specifying the reference group such instruction is best suited for is called local description, a term coined by Lee Cronbach (1975).

While it may seem that what ATI would lead us to is a hopelessly complicated array of individual prescriptions for instructing children, Snow (1977) argues that this is not necessarily the case. He suggests that there are a number of common instructional objectives that should be considered in any aptitude × treatment investigation. These objectives can serve as a starting point for some limited generalizations.

To fully realize the importance of considering aptitude × treatment interaction, it is necessary only to look at information about teaching strategies. Two ways the teacher's orientation can be classified are as challenging and demanding, or as encouraging good performance. Jere Brophy (1979) reviewed several studies

The authoritative teacher encourages verbal give-and-take but still admires disciplined conformity.

The authoritarian teacher is dominant and controlling.

focused on these types of teacher orientation. Teachers who work with high-socioeconomic status/high-ability students usually are more successful if they move at a quick pace, frequently communicating high expectations and enforcing high standards. These teachers try to keep students challenged, will not accept inferior work, and occasionally criticize the students' work when it does not meet their standards.

Teachers who generally are successful with low-socioeconomic status/low-ability students also are interested in getting the most out of their students, but they usually do so by being warm and encouraging rather than demanding. They are friendly with their students, take more time out from academic subject matter to motivate the children, praise and encourage more often, rarely criticize poor work, and move the curriculum along at a slower pace. When they call on

individual students, they allow more time for the student to respond; they may provide hints to help the student get the correct answer (Brophy & Evertson, 1974, 1976). As can be readily seen in this example, successful teaching varies according to the type of student being taught—one teaching strategy is superior with lower-ability students, another with higher-ability students.

Personality Traits and Teaching Styles

For many years psychologists and educators have been trying to create a profile of the personality traits of a good teacher. Because of the complexity of the task, a definitive profile may never be produced; yet several studies suggest that some traits are better for teachers than others.

Figure 11.1 School achievement of compulsive children and anxious children in both structured and unstructured schools.

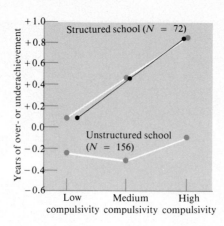
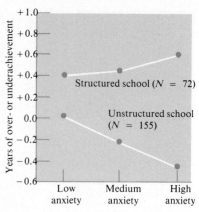

Teacher traits that relate positively to the student's intellectual development are enthusiasm, the ability to plan, poise, adaptability, and awareness of individual differences (Gage, 1965). Teachers who are impulsive tend to produce more impulsive students who are less reflective in solving school tasks (e.g., Yando & Kagan, 1968). And teachers who are warm and flexible and who encourage responsibility tend to produce students who respond constructively to failure and who usually engage willingly in class activities (Thompson, 1944).

Diana Baumrind (1972) indicates that the three styles of discipline she has discovered in parent-child interaction can be found in teacher-student interaction as well. The authoritarian teacher is dominant and controlling. The authoritative teacher is directive but rational, encourages verbal give-and-take, and values independence but still admires disciplined conformity. The laissez-faire teacher provides little or no direction and behaves passively. Baumrind argues that the authoritative teaching style fosters the development of competence in children.

In one study, the academic performance of two types of children learning to read was compared in two types of classroom organizations (Grimes & Allinsmith, 1961). One group of children was labeled "anxious," and the other was labeled "compulsive;" one classroom was highly structured and the other was relatively unstructured. Children who were neither very compulsive (e.g., upset by disorder) nor anxious (e.g., restless) were not influenced by the type of classroom organization. But the high-anxiety group of children did very poorly in the unstructured classroom and somewhat better than the low-anxiety group in the highly structured classroom. The highly compulsive group performed best in a highly structured classroom, while relatively uncompulsive children were not influenced by classroom organization.

These results (see fig. 11.1) clearly indicate that specific teaching styles are more effective with certain types of children in terms of their academic performance. Box 11.3 describes one technique that has been used to bring about a change in teacher behavior, thereby effecting a change in student behavior.

Next, we see that it often seems as though one of the major functions of schools in this country is to train children to function in and contribute to middle-class society, since politicians who vote on school funding are usually middle class, school-board members are predominantly middle class, and principals and teachers are often middle class. In fact, it has been stated many times that schools function in a middle-class society, and critics believe they have not done a good job in educating lower-class children to overcome the cultural barriers that make it difficult to enhance their social position.

Social Class and Schools

In *Dark Ghetto* Kenneth Clark (1965) described some of the ways lower- and middle-class children are treated differently in school. Teachers in the middle-class school spent more time in teaching their students and evaluated their work more than twice as often as teachers in the low-income school. And teachers in the low-income school made three times as many negative comments to students as teachers in the middle-class school; the latter made more positive than negative comments to their students.

Alexander Moore (1967) vividly describes an elementary class comprised of lower-class students in a large urban slum area.

The class is one that the principal himself warned visitors, with a kind of negative pride, to be one of the "wild" classes. He was not at all reluctant that visitors should witness the problems his school faced. The class is in ill repute throughout the school: several teachers commented on it, one calling it a "zoo." There are twenty-four students on the roll, fifteen boys and nine girls. They are all in the reading readiness stage (kindergarten level). On this day there are only eighteen present.

The song is over and the teacher, attempting to drill them on the days of the week, asks them, "What is today? What day will tomorrow be?" As the children call out the names of the various days, she stops to correct them: "Give me your answers in sentences!"

Meanwhile several children are noisily running around the room and hitting one another. Others sit in a stupor, apparently unaware of their surroundings. In the space of the first ten minutes, the teacher has used physical force and actually hurts the children in an attempt to control them. Yet she has not achieved control of the class, nor does she at any time during the morning. She frequently addresses her noisy, restless class, saying, "When I have everyone's attention and your hands are folded, then I will listen to what you're really trying to say." Since this never really happens, she never really listens to any of the children during the morning, yet many of them seem to want to say something to her. (p. 26)

School situations like these are described in Charles Silberman's *Crisis in the Classroom* (1970) and John Holt's *How Children Fail* (1964).

Educational Aspirations

Perhaps the most interesting information about children's educational aspirations is the relation between what they would like to do and what they expect to do. For instance, the discrepancy between job aspirations and job expectations is greater for lower-class adolescents than for middle-class adolescents (Gribbons & Lohnes, 1964). The aspirations of lower-class students are as high as those of middle-class students; however, when asked which occupation they actually expected to enter, lower-class adolescents mentioned occupations no more prestigious than those of their parents.

Parents can have a significant impact on their children's aspirations. Lower-class high-school boys whose parents encouraged them to advance their educational and occupational level revealed higher aspirations than boys whose parents did not (Kandel & Lesser, 1969).

Teachers' Attitudes

Teachers have lower expectations for children from low-income families than for children from middle-income families. A teacher who knows that a child comes from a lower-class background may spend less time trying to help him or her solve a problem and may anticipate that the child will frequently get into trouble. The teacher may also perceive a gap between his or her own middle-class position and the lower-class status of the child's parents; as a result the teacher may believe that the parents are not interested in helping the child and may make fewer efforts to communicate with them.

The maturational experiences of teachers with a middle-class background are quite different from those of children or teachers with a lower-class background. A teacher from the middle class has probably not gone hungry for weeks at a time or experienced the conditions of an overcrowded apartment, perhaps without electricity or plumbing, where several children may sleep with one or two adults in one small room.

There is evidence from at least one study that teachers with lower-class origins may have different attitudes toward lower-class students than middle-class teachers have (Gottlieb, 1966). Perhaps because they have experienced many inequities themselves, they tend to be empathetic to the problems that lower-class children encounter. In this study, for example, the teachers were asked to indicate the most outstanding characteristics of their lower-class students. The middle-class teachers checked adjectives like "lazy," "rebellious," and "fun-loving"; the lower-class teachers, however, checked such adjectives as "happy," "cooperative," "energetic," and "ambitious." The teachers with lower-class backgrounds perceived the behaviors of the lower-class children as adaptive, whereas the middle-class teachers viewed the same behaviors as falling short of middle-class standards.

School Textbooks

The books children read in school are usually oriented to the experiences and life settings of middle-class rather than lower-class children. The typical reader of the early elementary grades depicts children growing up in middle-class suburbia. The father is shown going off to work in a business suit, waving good-bye to his smiling family. The story characters experience few (if any) frustrations—life is easy and pleasant. Their world is not the world of the lower-class child (Blom, Waite, & Zimet, 1970).

Although there has been a healthy trend toward establishing a more realistic balance in the stories and pictures of school textbooks, the impression of the lower-class family presented in the readers is an idealized one (Waite, 1968). The family is shown as being integrated successfully into a middle-class white culture, with few accompanying frustrations. Middle-class standards predominate. A more realistic textbook would include more of the problems and frustrations of lower-class families and more of the frustrations of middle-class children as well. The stories would also demonstrate various coping mechanisms to help children deal with the frustrations of this imperfect world we live in. Such readers would present a world far more realistic than do those currently in use and might well serve to increase children's interest in reading and encourage them to think and reason more as they read.

In the next chapter, we look at personality development during middle and late childhood, focusing on the self, sex-role development, and moral development.

Box 11.3
The Use of Observations in Changing Teacher-Student Behavior

Trying to inform a teacher about ways to improve interactions with children in the classroom is a touchy subject. A supervisor may try to direct the teacher by saying something like this: "This is the way you are doing it, but you should be doing it this way instead." Teachers often reject feedback because they do not agree with the supervisor's criteria. In one study, teachers defiantly moved in the opposite direction of the feedback they received (Tuckman & Oliver, 1968).

Tom Good and Jere Brophy (1974) looked for nonthreatening ways to present feedback to teachers. Two techniques they devised involved using observational data that focused on the teacher's interaction with the child, emphasizing the teacher's interaction with an individual child rather than with an entire class. They observed eight first-grade classrooms for about forty hours and selected two types of situations they wanted the teachers to handle differently: (1) low participation—some children seldom volunteered to answer questions or initiated interaction;

(2) nonextension—some children generally were not given a second chance to answer a question; the teacher either selected another child to answer the question or gave the child the answer without extending the questioning. There were twenty-one "low participants" and twenty-eight "nonextension" students in the eight first-grade classrooms.

The treatment phase consisted in a short interview session with individual teachers. As part of the interview, the teachers were shown a list of students whom they were treating appropriately. These were included as contrasts to encourage the teachers to see their own behavior more clearly and to show them that they were actually doing a good job with some students.

When the teachers were told about their behavior, only about half of them realized that they had been interacting with the target students at a low level. Even fewer were conscious of the fact that they had not been extending their questioning with the selected target children; several expressed concern about embarrassing the shy

Summary

In middle and late childhood, the child's family continues to be an important socializing influence. To help children develop social competence parents need to adjust to the developmental changes that distinguish early childhood from middle and late childhood. Among the changes that parents need to adapt to are the child's increasing cognitive capabilities, heightened interest in peers, and schooling. In this chapter we continued our discussion of the changing family structure, which focused on custody decisions and stepparent families. While there is some evidence that boys seem to be better adjusted in father-custody families and girls better adjusted in mother-custody families, many factors mediate the effects of family structure and divorce on children—among those discussed were parenting behavior, marital conflict, and the availability of support systems.

The majority of children grow up in a family in which one or more siblings is present. Sibling relations often are characterized by competitiveness and the concern to be treated fairly by parents. In some instances, though, older siblings may be as effective, or more effective, than their parents in socializing the younger brothers and sisters. Competitiveness among siblings seems to be greatest when they are close in age.

With school entrance, children increase their contacts with other children and begin to recognize that other individuals have ideas and points of view that are different than their own. The child's development in middle and late childhood is extensively influenced by peers, or age-mates. The peer group provides a unique opportunity for practicing roles and finding out information about the world outside of the family. The socialization processes of reinforcement and modeling are important in peer relations as well as parent-child relations. In some instances these processes, as well as

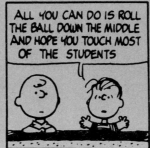

children. After this brief discussion and interview, the teachers were asked to increase their interaction with the low participants and to extend their attempts at seeking responses from nonextension students by repeating or rephrasing questions, or providing help in the form of a clue or a new question.

The treatment was very successful—more successful at changing the teacher's behavior than the children's, but significant improvement was found in the children's behavior as well. Also of interest was the finding that even though the teachers had improved their techniques in dealing with the target children, their positive treatment of the other children was not undermined.

others, have been combined to develop programs in peer sociotherapy. Other aspects of social relations in the peer group that are important to the child are popularity and friendships. Children participate in groups as well as peer relations. There are more formal groups in adolescence than childhood, and there is a greater mixture of males and females in adolescent than childhood groups. Status positions and norms develop in virtually all groups, but the nature of children's peer groups may vary from culture to culture.

Among the socializing institutions that directly or indirectly influence development are the schools. During middle and late childhood, education is usually provided by the public school system. Two characteristics of the traditional school are a standard class size and a standard, highly organized classroom structure. Although the seating arrangement in the structured classroom results in an uneven pattern of teacher-student interaction, the structured classroom generally

seems to be more effective than flexible classrooms in improving basic skills, whereas flexible classrooms tend to improve learning attitudes and social skills. However, classroom characteristics may prove less valuable to effective learning than an approach based on the interaction of aptitude and educational technique. The organization of schools may influence the child's social development and may affect boys and girls differently. Advocates of alternative educational movements share some of the concerns of progressive and humanistic education; one of the primary functions of school, they assert, should be to teach children skills for adjustment to life, not merely mastery of basic academic subjects.

Key Terms

Aptitude × Treatment
  Interaction (ATI)
coaching
conglomerate strategy

peer sociotherapy
progressive education
traditional education

Review Questions

1. Describe how parents should adapt to the developing child as he or she grows from early childhood into middle and late childhood.
2. What do we know about the effects of father custody on the child's social development? How is the child influenced by growing up in a stepparent family?
3. Discuss some of the positive and negative ways siblings can socialize each other.
4. Describe the development of peer relations during middle and late childhood.
5. What are some of the functions of the peer group in the socialization of the child?
6. How are children's groups in middle and late childhood different from adolescent groups?
7. How are children's schools organized, and what effects can organization have on their development?
8. What is meant by aptitude × treatment interaction? How can ATI be applied to teaching children?

Further Readings

Brophy, J., and Good, T. *Teacher-student relationship: causes and consequences*. New York: Holt, Rinehart & Winston, 1974.
An excellent book for understanding the social interaction of teachers with children. Includes many examples of teacher-student interaction and teaching strategies that can be used to modify student behavior. Level of reading is similar to that of this text.

Hartup, W. W. The peer system. In P. H. Mussen (ed. in-chief) and E. M. Hetherington (ed.), *Carmichael's manual of child psychology*, 4th ed. (vol. 4). New York: John Wiley, 1982.
Willard Hartup, a respected authority on peer relations, provides an up-to-date description of research and ideas about peer relations. Reading level is medium to difficult.

Harvard education review.
Go to the library and leaf through the issues of the last three to four years. You'll find a number of articles that address the issues raised in this chapter about schools. Moderately difficult reading.

Lewis, M., & Rosenblum, L. A. (eds.). *Friendship and peer relations*, vol. 4. New York: Wiley, 1975.
Articles by experts on peer relations representing diverse ideas and including recent theoretical perspectives. Moderately difficult reading.

Roman, M., & Haddad, W. *The disposable parent*. New York: Holt, Rinehart & Winston, 1978.
This book, by a prominent clinical psychologist, explores the case for joint custody. The stress of divorce and custody decisions on children are described. Easy to read.

Sutton-Smith, B., & Rosenberg, B. G. *The sibling*. New York: Holt, Rinehart & Winston, 1970.
Complete survey of theory and research pertaining to the sibling's role in the child's development. Extensive coverage of the impact of sibling order and age spacing. Easy to medium reading level.

12

Personality Development

Prologue: The Content of Moral Education

Cornel Hamm (1977) believes that Lawrence Kohlberg (1976) is incorrect in claiming that his theory is devoid of virtues. Hamm argues that Kohlberg's view emphasizes that moral education ought to include emphasis on virtues such as honesty, loyalty, courage, and fair play.

Hamm goes on to say that parents, teachers, and peers "teach" moral values by establishing rules and regulations and by rewarding and punishing behavior. Parents and teachers have not always effectively taught moral values to their children, but Hamm believes they are capable of doing so. There are some socialization techniques that are better than others for developing moral values in children. Sensible youth who have a feeling for fairness and respect for others usually come from social environments in which adult social agents show a warm acceptance towards them, combined with a firm and consistent enforcement of rules.

Hamm also believes that children need to be reminded consistently of why actions a and b and c are required, and why x and y and z are prohibited. This allows the child to call these rules and reasons to mind when moral decisions have to be made.

Furthermore, through social experiences with parents, teachers, peers, and other social agents, Hamm believes, moral virtues can be learned. But exactly what virtues should be taught? At a general level most people agree that we should teach children to be honest, fair, and impartial; to consider other people's rights and avoid interfering with their freedom; to refrain from killing or injuring others; to keep promises and abide by contracts; and to make no discriminations against others on the basis of irrelevant differences such as color, sex, or ethnic origin.

Some of Hamm's critics think that these moral virtues are too heavily laden with middle-class values, but Hamm (1977) insists that most people would agree that they are universal values rather than old-fashioned, middle-class standards.

Other educational theorists believe that, while it is difficult to specify the appropriate moral virtues to instill in children, it is possible to identify generally accepted moral virtues and to inform students about them (e.g., Hamm, 1977).

Yet other theorists believe that there are no universally agreed upon moral virtues and therefore that subjective "virtues" should not be taught to children. Led by Lawrence Kohlberg, this group of educational theorists stresses that it is the moral reasoning skills of children—not an adherence to any particular value system—that should be developed. In Kohlberg's view absolute rights and wrongs do not exist; what is important is to create settings that allow children to think about alternative, logical solutions to moral dilemmas. Many of the environmental experiences that Kohlberg feels are best suited to stimulate advanced moral thinking focus on democratic peer rule and discussion.

Not everyone agrees that Kohlberg's approach to moral development is the best one, but there has been an absence of alternative approaches to moral education (Aron, 1977). In most schools morality is approached either through a dogmatic statement of authority or by a complete avoidance of moral issues. Next to Kohlberg's theory, the two most widely practiced systematic programs of moral education are behavior modification and values clarification. Recall that behavior modification involves rewarding positive behavior and taking varied approaches toward negative behavior. **Values clarification** emphasizes that students need to have the opportunity to air their value judgments in group discussion. By being exposed to the value judgments of others, children may see the relative nature of values.

Introduction

In keeping with the theme that schools represent a very important socializing influence in middle and late childhood, the prologue describes some of the issues involved in moral education. In this chapter we will evaluate sex education, describe the development of sex differences and sex-role stereotypes, discuss Lawrence Kohlberg's cognitive structural theory and the social learning perspective of moral development, and outline some of the most common problems and disturbances in middle and late childhood. But, first, we begin with some introductory comments about how the self changes in middle and late childhood.

The Self

Eleanor Maccoby (1980) believes that an important part of the development of a self-concept is the child's increasing ability to understand how he or she is viewed by others. Very young children have difficulty in understanding others' perspective of them, and they often are not aware of the impressions their behavior makes on others. But gradually children begin to understand that their behavior will trigger reactions from others, and they begin to monitor their actions, acting differently depending on whom they are with and which aspect of their social-self they want to be seen. This represents a time at which children are more cautious about revealing themselves to others.

Boyd McCandless and Ellis Evans (1973) believe that developmental changes in self-concept occur as children go through early childhood, middle and late childhood, and adolescence. First, children develop a differentiated view of themselves as they grow older. As young children they may simply have perceived themselves as "good" or "bad." By late childhood and adolescence, they are likely to perceive themselves in more detailed ways, such as "I am a good person most of the time, except when my older sister bugs me, or when my father won't let me have the car, or when I have to study for an exam."

Second, older children develop a more individuated view of themselves than as young children. This indicates that older children have a more distinct view of themselves as unique persons and more readily differentiate themselves from others than young children. As young children, they may have labeled themselves in terms of how they were similar to their peers, but as they approach adolescence they tend to describe themselves more in terms of how they are different from their peers.

Third, the older child's self-concept is likely to be more stable than the young child's. But in an extreme form, stability can lead to rigidity and unrealistic self-appraisals. Even though we say that the self-concept of the child becomes more stable, this does not imply that self-concept does not change. It clearly does change, but as children and adolescents mature cognitively they become more capable of integrating incoming information into a stable sense of who they are and where they are going.

Another recent developmental approach to self-concept formation has been based on cognitive-developmental theory. Piaget's theory of cognitive development stress that the adolescent's cognitions are more abstract and less concrete than the child's. To test this hypothesis about the development of self-concepts, Raymond Montemayor and Marvin Eisen (1977) studied 136 males and 126 females in grades four, six, eight, ten, and twelve. The students were given the Twenty Statements Test (Bugental & Zelen, 1950) in which twenty spaces are available to write responses to the questions, "Who am I?" The responses were coded according to thirty different categories, such as sex, age, religion, occupational role, social status, intellectual interests, career, physical self- and body image, sense of unity, and situational references.

The result suggested that children do evaluate themselves in more concrete and less abstract ways than adolescents. The children were more likely to describe themselves in terms of their address, physical appearance, possessions, and play activities. By contrast, adolescents relied more on personal beliefs, motivations, and interpersonal characteristics to describe what they were like. Montemayor and Eisen (1977) provided the following quotations from a nine-year-old, an eleven and one-half-year-old, and a seventeen-year-old that reflect developmental changes in self-conception:

Nine-year-old boy: (concrete descriptions) My name is Bruce C. I have brown eyes. I have brown hair. I have brown eyebrows. I'm nine years old. I love! sports. I have seven people in my family. I have great! eye site. I have lots! of friends. I live on 1923 Pinecrest Drive. I'm going on ten in September. I'm a boy. I have an uncle that is almost seven feet tall. My school is Pinecrest. My teacher is Mrs. V. I play hockey! I'm almost the smartest boy in the class. I love food! I love fresh air. I love school.

Eleven and one-half-year-old girl: (increase in interpersonal descriptions) My name is A. I'm a human being. I'm a girl. I'm a truthful person. I'm not pretty. I do so-so in my studies. I'm a very good cellist. I'm a very good pianist. I'm a little bit tall for my age. I like several boys. I like several girls. I'm old fashioned. I play tennis. I am a very good musician. I try to be helpful. I'm always ready to be friends with anybody. Mostly I'm good, but I lose my temper. I'm not well liked by some girls and boys. I don't know if boys like me or not.

Some children believe their talents are true abilities, while others feel they are only a temporary state.

Seventeen-year-old girl: (increase in interpersonal descriptions, characteristic mood states, and ideological and belief statements) I am a human being. I am a girl. I am an individual. I don't know who I am. I am Pisces. I am a moody person. I am an indecisive person. I am an ambitious person. I am a big curious person. I am not an individual. I am lonely. I am an American (God help me). I am a Democrat. I am a liberal person. I am a radical. I am conservative. I am a pseudoliberal. I am an atheist. I am not a classifiable person (i.e., I don't want to be). (pp. 317–18)

Recently there has been considerable interest in a view of the self referred to as *attribution theory*. Next, we see how this perspective can be used to explain children's perceptions of their self and of others.

Children's Attributions about Their Self and Others

Borrowing largely from theory in adult social psychology, developmental psychologists explain social phenomena in childhood by referring to the attributions children make about others. In the simplest sense **attribution theory** encompasses how the child makes intellectual sense of the actions of others as well as of his or her own actions. The origins of the theory are often traced to the groundbreaking ideas of Fritz Heider and his common-sense theory. One of the elements of Heider's work has been particularly influential in attribution theory—the naive analysis of action.

In their everyday perceptions children try to simplify their understanding of people by pinpointing singular causes for behavior. A boy complains because a sport is too difficult for him, the athlete competes because he is motivated to achieve, the girl fails a math test because she was unlucky that day, the singer excels because she has extraordinary musical talent, and so on. Heider believes that these are naive analyses of action. Such analyses take one of two forms: the child attributes the action either to some personal force within the person or to some environmental force that impinges on the person from without. Within each category, two further subdivisions can be made. The child may presume that a personal force is a relatively permanent, long-lasting phenomenon; that is, he or she may believe some ability or predilection exists (for example, the singer's talent). Or, the child may view the personal force as a temporary state that fluctuates widely (for example, the athlete's motivation). Similarly, the child may perceive an environmental force as stable (such as the sport that is too difficult for a certain child) or unstable (such as the "bad luck" that caused a student to fail a test).

Personality descriptions children make in regard to themselves and others also follow patterns similar to those of their attributions. Of course, generalized personality descriptions can be very helpful when the child needs to describe broad, dominant personality characteristics of different persons. Such generalizations help children to organize and to make sense of human behavior. But such attributions do not tell us very much about variability in behavior and the specific conditions under which this variability occurs. It is in this sense, just as Heider argued, that children's attributions are often naive or simplistic. Not only may these attributions be ineffective predictors of behavior but they may actually be misleading at times.

Children who view themselves in positive ways could be expected to make attributions that are different from those of children who perceive themselves in negative ways. That is, differences in children's self-concepts should be reflected in the way they categorize incoming information and interpret their own or others' behavior. To investigate this idea, Carol Ames and Donald Felker (in press) studied 150 boys and girls by first rating them on the Piers-Harris self-concept scale. Those who either scored quite high or quite low were then given an achievement task on which they either succeeded or failed. Each child was asked to interpret his or her performance on the task, attributing success or failure to either skill or to luck (or the lack of them). Success was more often attributed to skill by the high self-concept boys and girls. Thus, the self-perceptions of children influence the way they interpret behavior.

One aspect of the child's self-evaluation that is closely linked with self-concept is self-esteem, which is discussed next.

Self-Esteem

Many theorists and researchers use the labels self-concept and self-esteem interchangeably. For example, one definition of self-esteem is the value children place on themselves and their behavior, which would be evaluated by finding out whether the children feel good or bad about themselves (McCandless & Evans, 1973). Other definitions of self-esteem embrace only the positive parts of self-concept, such as feeling proud of oneself or evaluating one's attributes highly (Wylie, 1974).

Stanley Coopersmith (1959, 1967) has developed a personality scale that attempts to measure boys' and girls' self-esteem. Like other measures of self-concept, Coopersmith's inventory (called the Self-Esteem Inventory, or SEI) asks the child to read a number of statements and check whether each of these is "like me" or "unlike me." The statements include the extent to which the youth worry about themselves, the degree to which they are proud of their school performances, how popular they are with peers, how happy they are, and so on.

In one investigation, the Self-Esteem Inventory was administered to a large group of elementary school-aged boys. In addition, the boys, their mothers, and the boys' teachers at school were interviewed about various matters relating to the social experiences and self-perceptions of the boys. The following parental attributes were linked with the development of high self-esteem in the boys:

1. Expression of affection
2. Concern about the youth's problems
3. Harmony in the home
4. Participation in friendly joint activities
5. Availability to give competent, organized help to the boys when they need it
6. Setting clear and fair rules
7. Abiding by these rules
8. Allowing the youth freedom within well-prescribed limits

Self-Esteem and School Performance

Many studies indicate a positive correlation between the child's self-concept and different measures of achievement and school performance (e.g., Taylor, Winne, & Marx, 1975). These studies seem to show that a student with a good self-concept excels in school. But what is the nature of this relationship? Does the child do well in school because of a positive self-concept? Or is a positive self-concept the result of doing well in school? There is evidence that the latter is closer to the truth. A teacher or counselor will apparently be more successful in changing a student's behavior (elevating achievement level), and thereby improving the student's self-image, than in changing the self-image and, as a result, improving achievement (Bandura, 1969).

It may even be hazardous to use techniques that give a child a falsely inflated view of his or her ability. Suppose, for example, that a child does not read well, and the teacher decides that the child's major problem is a negative self-concept. The teacher attempts to foster a positive self-image and some confidence in the child. After some progress, the teacher asks the child to read in front of the class. With newfound confidence the child begins to read, but as he or she stumbles and mumbles through several sentences and the other students begin to laugh, he or she is emotionally shattered. In this case it was not enough for the teacher to instill self-confidence in the child; working on the child's reading skills also was necessary.

Measuring Self-Concept and Self-Esteem

Although it is generally accepted that each child has a self-esteem and that self-evaluation is an important aspect of personality, psychologists, counselors, and educators have had a difficult time trying to measure self-esteem. One method that has been used frequently is the Piers-Harris Scale (Piers & Harris, 1964), which consists of eighty items designed to measure the child's overall self-esteem. School psychologists often use the scale with boys and girls who have been referred to them for evaluation. By responding yes or no to such items as "I have good ideas," children reveal how they view themselves. The Piers-Harris Scale requires about fifteen to twenty minutes for completion and can be administered to groups as well as to individuals.

Children's self-perception often changes according to the situation, although self-concept measures like the Piers-Harris Scale are designed to measure a stable, consistent aspect of personality. Also, with self-reporting, it is difficult to determine whether children are telling about the way they really are or the way they want someone else to think they are. Even though the instructions on the Piers-Harris Scale and other measures of self-concept direct youth to respond as they really are, there is no assurance that they will do so (Wylie, 1974).

A promising measure of self-concept recently has been developed by Susan Harter (1982). Her scale is called the perceived competence scale for children. Emphasis is placed on assessing the child's sense of competence across different domains rather than viewing perceived competence as a unitary concept. Three types of skills are assessed on separate subscales: cognitive (good at schoolwork: remembers things easily); social (have a lot of friends: most kids like me); and physical (do well at sports: first chosen for games). And, a fourth subscale, general self-worth (sure of myself: happy the way I am), independent of any particular skill domain, also is included. The importance of Harter's measure is that prior measures of self-concept, such

Many studies indicate a positive correlation between self-concept and school performance.

as the Piers-Harris, lumped together the child's perceptions of his or her competencies in a variety of domains in an effort to arrive at an overall measure of the child's self-concept. Harter's scale does an excellent job of separating the child's self-perceptions of his or her abilities in different skill areas: and when general self-worth is assessed, questions that focus on overall perceptions of the self are used rather than questions directed at specific skill domains.

Some assessment experts believe that a combination of several methods should be used in measuring self-concept and other personality traits. In addition to self-reporting, rating of a child's self-concept by others and careful observation of behavior in various settings could give a more complete, and hence more accurate, picture of self-concept. Peers, teachers, parents, and even others who do not know the child well should be asked for their perceptions. Peers are particularly good at rating each other, so it may be helpful to listen carefully to what children have to say about each other. The child's facial expressions and the extent to which he or she congratulates or condemns himself or herself are also good indicators of self-concept. When all of the indicators—peer perceptions of the child, observations and perceptions of parents and teachers, and the child's own judgments—are considered together, a reasonably accurate picture of a child's self-concept should emerge.

To conclude our discussion of the self in the middle and late childhood years, we present an overview of the developmental changes that occur in the self-system, as summarized by Susan Harter (1982).

Summary of Developmental Changes in the Self-System

In our discussion of the self we have seen that children's self-descriptions change from concrete, observable components, such as physical attributes and behaviors, to personality traits as they grow into middle and late childhood. And, in adolescence there is a further shift toward self-descriptions that are more abstract, such as thoughts, attitudes, and emotions. Susan Harter (1982), however, believes that this sequence confounds dimensions of the self based on content (e.g., particular behaviors or emotions) with structure (e.g., how these contents are organized into traits, abstractions, and networks).

Susan Harter's Developmental Model of Self-Perception

Susan Harter (1982) believes a clearer picture of developing self-conceptions might be possible if first we separated the content and structure of self-perceptions and then evaluated their interaction. The matrix shown in table 12.1 indicates such a strategy for understanding the development of the self. In the far left column are *content dimensions,* ordered to suggest one possible developmental sequence (e.g., physical attributes, behaviors, psychological dimensions). How these contents might become organized as the child develops, or the *structural changes,* is ordered along the top of the table (e.g., simple descriptions, trait labels, single abstractions, and higher-order abstractions). The first structural stage roughly corresponds to preoperational thought, the second to concrete operational thought, and the third to early formal operational thought. The fourth stage represents further change in adulthood.

Table 12.1
Hypothesized Dimensions of Developmental Change in the Self-Concept

		Structural Changes			
		Stage I: Simple Descriptions		**Stage II: Trait Labels**	
		Level 1	*Level 2*	*Level 1*	*Level 2*
Content Dimensions	**Observable Dimensions**	Global descriptions, all or none thinking	Differentiation, temporal shifts, vacillation	Descriptions integrated into *trait labels*, overgeneralized, all or none thinking	Trait labels differentiated, situation-specificity
	Physical Attributes (size, age, gender, race appearance possessions)				
	Behaviors (actions, skills, preferences)	Good at drawing, puzzles, climbing, singing, running, know numbers, alphabet, colors	Good at drawing, puzzles. Not good at knowing alphabet, numbers	All dumb because bad at math, science, social studies	Smart in creative writing, art, music. Dumb in math, science, social studies
	Psychological Dimensions				
	Emotions (feeling states, affects)				
	Motives (intentions, causes of behavior)				
	Cognitions (the thought process, attitudes)				

Source: Harter, 1982.

Based on Harter's research, how the developmentally oriented self-conception model might work can be illustrated with an example from the *behavioral* content domain. This domain can be traced across the stages and levels (i.e., structural dimension) with the focus on skills and competence.

Stage I: At the first level, the child who thinks he or she is good at one skill (drawing) will also think he or she is good at a variety of skills (puzzles, numbers, colors). At level 2, however, these judgments become more differentiated. A child will acknowledge that he or she is good at one skill but not so good at another.

Stage II: At the first level, there is an integration of behaviors and trait labels (for example, smart and dumb). Although these traits are opposites, the child can only control one trait label in the pair, and therefore thinks of himself or herself as all dumb or all smart based on one or two abilities or lack of abilities. At level 2, the traits become differentiated. The child realizes that he or she can be dumb at one thing (math) and smart at another (art).

Stage III: Single abstractions emerge in this third stage. If an adolescent is dumb at one thing (math) and smart at another (art), this person may conclude that he or she is only of average intelligence. This is a single abstraction based on an integration of the traits dumb and smart. At the second level, single abstractions become more differentiated. For example, an adolescent who is a skilled writer and also a skilled painter may combine the perception into a single perception of himself or herself as an artistic, creative person.

Stage IV: At the fourth stage, these single abstractions become further integrated so that there are no longer apparent contradictions and the self does not seem fragmented. For example, a young adult may view himself or herself as a Bohemian, that is, one who rejects conventional intellectual values of the society in favor of the pursuit of his or her artistic endeavors.

Structural Changes Stage III: Single Abstractions		Stage IV: Higher-Order Abstractions	
Level 1	*Level 2*	*Level 1*	*Level 2*
Trait labels integrated into *single abstractions,* overgeneralized, all or none thinking	Single abstractions differentiated, situation-specificity	Single abstractions integrated into *higher-order abstractions,* all or none thinking	Higher-order abstractions differentiated, situation-specificity
Average intelligence, smart at some things and dumb at others	Artistic, creative, poetry, stories, painting; modest conventional intelligence	Bohemian: artistic, creative and reject conventional values	Bohemian Political radical

This example is only of one content dimension, behavioral skills. At any given point in development, a child or adolescent may be at a particular structural stage and level for one content domain but at a different structural stage and level for another. For example, one may be at an advanced structural stage of self-description with regard to *behavior* but not *motives*. A child could view himself or herself as smart but not yet come to the conclusion, based on the intention to do well, that he or she is also hard-working.

In chapter 14 we will continue our discussion of the development of the self—we will discover that the governing theme of self-evaluation in adolescence is identity. Next, we look at one aspect of the self that takes on increasing importance in middle and late childhood, sex-role development.

Sex-Role Development

In the middle childhood years, two divergent trends in sex typing occur. Children increase their understanding of culturally defined expectations for males and females, and simultaneously the behavior and attitude of boys increasingly reflect masculine sex typing. However, during the middle years of childhood girls do not show an increased interest in feminine activities. Actually, many girls begin to show a stronger preference for masculine interests and activities, a finding that has appeared in research studies conducted from the 1920s to the present. But, on the other hand, boys and girls begin to show more flexibility in their understanding of sex-role stereotypes; they see that stereotypes are not absolute and that alternatives are feasible (Huston, 1982).

Sex-role stereotypes are rampant in our culture, not just on television but in the beliefs held by parents, teachers, and peers. In the United States, as in most industrialized countries in the world, stereotyped sex roles are gradually being eliminated, and women are engaging in activities previously viewed as available only to men. As a result, research data about sex differences in children is often dated. This further substantiates the role of cultural values and societal standards in determining sex-role behavior.

Sex Differences and Stereotypes

Walter Mischel (1970) defines sex-role stereotypes as broad categories that reflect our impressions about people, events, and ourselves. The world is extremely complex; every day we are confronted with thousands of different stimuli. The use of stereotypes is one way we simplify this complexity. If we simply assign a label (e.g., the quality of "softness" in women) to someone, we then have much less to consider when we think about the person. However, once these labels have been assigned, we find it remarkably difficult to abandon them, even in the face of contradictory evidence. Do you think you have a repertory of sex-role stereotypes? Box 12.1 provides a brief exercise in understanding sex-role behavior.

How Stereotypes Operate

Many stereotypes are extremely ambiguous. The stereotypes "masculine" and "feminine," for example, call up very diverse behaviors to support the stereotype. The stereotype, of course, may also be modified in the face of cultural change; whereas at one time muscular development might be thought masculine, at another time masculinity may be typified by a lithe, slender physique. Furthermore, the behaviors popularly agreed upon as reflecting the stereotype may fluctuate according to subculture.

Mischel (1970) comments that even though the behaviors that are supposed to fit the stereotype often do not, the label itself may have significant consequences for the individual. Labeling a person "homosexual," "queer," or "sissy" can produce dire social consequences in terms of status and acceptance in groups, even when the person is none of these. Regardless of their accuracy, stereotypes can cause tremendous emotional upheaval in an individual.

Sex Differences

How well did you do with the adjectives in box 12.1? According to Eleanor Maccoby and Carol Nagy Jacklin (1974), females are more verbal, males are more mathematical and aggressive, and all the other adjectives are really characteristic of neither.

With regard to verbal ability, girls tend to understand and produce language more competently than boys. Girls are superior to boys in higher-order verbal

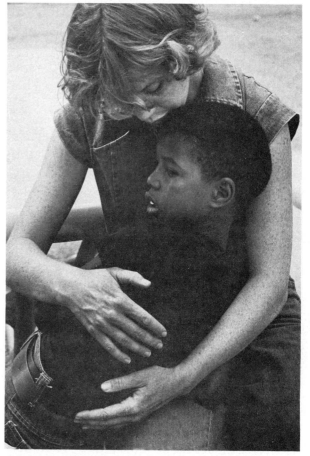

Once stereotyped labels are assigned it is difficult to abandon them.

tasks, such as making analogies, understanding difficult written material, and writing creatively, as well as on lower-order verbal tasks, such as spelling. Maccoby and Jacklin speculated that girls probably get an early start in the use of language, but studies indicate that differences in the verbal abilities of boys and girls are not consistent until about the age of eleven.

A similar developmental trend can be seen for mathematical skills, but this time in favor of boys. Boys' superiority in math skills does not usually appear until the age of twelve or thirteen and does not seem to be

Box 12.1
Knowing the Sexes

How well do you know the sexes? For each of the adjectives listed below, indicate whether you think it *best* describes women or men—or neither—in our society. Be honest with yourself, and follow your first impulse in responding.

a. verbal
b. sensitive
c. active
d. competitive
e. compliant
f. dominant

g. mathematical
h. suggestible
i. analytic
j. social
k. aggressive

After recording your answers, continue reading this chapter for an interpretation of your responses.

"Don't be too rough with Dolly! Remember—
she's just a little GIRL!"

entirely influenced by the fact that boys take more math courses. Likewise, male superiority on visual-spatial tasks does not consistently appear until adolescence. However, sex differences in aggression appear early, by the age of two or three, and continue through adolescence. The differences are not confined to physical aggression—boys also show more verbal aggression as well as more fantasy aggression (imagining harm to someone or to some object rather than actually performing an aggressive act).

Two of the myths about the sexes merit further examination: that girls are more social than boys, and that girls are more suggestible than boys. The measure of sociability was based upon diverse aspects of social interaction, whch included interest in social events (e.g., faces and voices), responsiveness to social reward, dependence on caregivers, time spent with playmates, and understanding of the emotional needs of others. There simply was no evidence to suggest that girls engaged in these practices more than boys did. In some cases the reverse was observed; for example, boys spent more time with playmates than girls did. Suggestibility was indexed by childrens' spontaneous imitation of models, susceptibility to persuasive communication, and social conformity to group norms. There are no consistent sex differences in a large number of studies measuring these characteristics.

Even though evidence shows that girls are not more social and not more suggestible than boys, do you believe it? If you do not, you have a firsthand example of how difficult it is to discard stereotypes.

In many of the studies reviewed by Maccoby and Jacklin (1974), the data were collected in a cross-sectional manner—that is, within a very limited time span. There have been very few longitudinal investigations of sex-role development. The most widely cited is that by Jerome Kagan and Howard Moss (1962), sometimes referred to as the Fels study. Details about this longitudinal study of sex-role behavior are discussed in box 12.2.

Stability of Sex-Typed Behaviors

The stability of a behavior is revealed by a study of that behavior and changes in it over an extended period of time—say, the incidence of aggression from preschool through adolescence. The basic point at issue is whether a behavior occurring at a given time has any relation to similar behavior at a later time. In other words, can behavior be predicted from knowledge of past behavior? Let's take a look at research into three aspects of sex-typed behavior and their stability over a number of years: masculine and feminine interests, aggression, and dependency.

Jerome Kagan and Howard Moss (1962) conducted a well-known longitudinal study of these behaviors in what is sometimes referred to as the Fels Institute study (named for the location in Ohio where they were working). Investigating ratings of behavior in age periods birth to three, three to six, six to ten, ten to fourteen, and adulthood, Kagan and Moss found that the stability of the behaviors is linked to cultural sex-role standards. Mastery of intel-

lectual tasks and sex-typed interests, which are reinforced for both boys and girls in our culture, were revealed by the Kagan and Moss study to be very consistent for both boys and girls from the six to ten age period through adult years. However, because in our culture boys are more frequently rewarded for being aggressive and girls for being dependent, the Kagan and Moss study revealed consistency across these time periods for boys' aggressive behavior and for girls' dependency behavior.

The Kagan and Moss study, completed in 1962, does not reflect our society's changing sex-role standards in the 1980s, when adolescence may lead to even more upheaval in commitment to sex-typed behaviors. Because distinctions in cultural standards for boys and girls are becoming blurred, it is now easier for the female at seventeen or eighteen years of age to choose a career once labeled "masculine" by society.

Not everyone agrees with all of the conclusions of Maccoby's and Jacklin's widely quoted work on sex differences. Jeanne Block (1976) acknowledges that Maccoby and Jacklin have made an important contribution to information about sex roles, but she also believes that some of their conclusions, and some of the data on which the conclusions are based, are shakier than Maccoby and Jacklin lead readers to believe. Block argues that Maccoby and Jacklin did not differentiate between those studies that were methodologically sound and those that were not. She further criticizes the decisions they made about what kinds of studies should go into a particular category. For example, Maccoby and Jacklin lumped together many measures of parental pressure on achievement motivation including the following: amount of praise or criticism for intellectual performance; parental standards for intellectual performance as expressed on a questionnaire item; expectations of household help from the youth; the ages at which parents feel it is appropriate to teach a boy or girl more mature behaviors; the number of anxious intrusions in the youth's task performance; and pressure for success on memory tasks. While many of the measures are clearly linked with the achievement dimension, others may be more peripheral.

Although Block does commend Maccoby and Jacklin for their completion of the long, difficult task of organizing a sprawling, unruly body of information, she also suggests that such data are open to error and reasonable argument at virtually every step of the analysis. In other words, anyone attempting to impose structure and meaning on some 1,600 disparate studies of sex role is bound to make a few questionable decisions. For those of you interested in reading more about sex differences in adolescence, both Maccoby's and Jacklin's book and Block's critique are highly recommended.

Another critic of Maccoby and Jacklin (Tieger, 1980) argues that sex differences in aggression are not biologically based but are instead learned. Tieger argues that consistent sex differences do not emerge until about the age of six and that there are ample conditions in the first six years of the child's life for aggression to be learned. In a rejoinder to Tieger, Maccoby and Jacklin (1980) reviewed their data and conducted some further analyses. The reassessment supported their earlier claim that greater aggression by boys occurs well before the age of six, is present in studies of nonhuman primates, and appears in cross-cultural studies of children.

Next, we look at a controversial aspect of sex differences in contemporary society—sex differences in achievement.

Achievement

Few topics have generated more controversy in the last decade than the belief that many women have been socialized to assume roles of incompetency rather than competency. Diana Baumrind (1972) has distinguished between **instrumental competence** and incompetence. Boys, she says, are trained to become instrumentally competent, while girls learn how to become instrumentally incompetent. By instrumental competence, Baumrind means behavior that is socially responsible and purposeful. Instrumental incompetence is generally aimless behavior.

The following evidence is offered by Baumrind in support of her argument: (1) few women obtain jobs in science, and of those who do, few achieve high positions; (2) being a female is devalued by society; (3) being independent and achieving intellectual status causes the female to lose her "femininity" in society's eyes—both men and women devalue such behaviors in women; (4) parents usually have lower achievement aspirations for girls than boys (for example, parents expect their sons to become doctors and their daughters to become nurses); and (5) girls and women are more oriented toward expressive behavior than boys and men are.

Aletha Huston-Stein and Ann Higgens-Trenk (1978) have discussed the developmental precursors of sex differences in achievement orientation. Women who as adults are career and achievement oriented usually show the signs of this orientation early in their childhood years. Adult women who are attracted to traditionally feminine activities were likely attracted to such activities during middle childhood and adolescence (Crandall & Battle, 1970; Kagan & Moss, 1962).

Achievement behavior was more consistent over the childhood, adolescent, and young adult years than any other personality attribute studied in these longitudinal investigations. Interest in "masculine" play activities in childhood (Crandall & Battle, 1970) and in "masculine" subject matter (Sears & Barbee, 1975) is linked with achievement orientation in females during adolescence and young adulthood. In sum, childhood socialization experiences seem to be critical in influencing the achievement orientation of females during adolescence and even into young adulthood.

A great deal of attention has been focused on expectancy for success, which seems to cross many areas of achievement. In general, girls tend to have lower expectancies for success, lower levels of aspiration, more anxiety about failing, a stronger tendency to avoid risking failure, and be more likely to accept failure than boys (Parsons, Ruble, Hodges, & Small, 1976; Stein & Bailey, 1973). And girls are more likely to attribute failure to their own inability and success to external causes, while boys are more likely to assign success to ability and failure to external causes.

Findings such as these have led researchers such as Carol Dweck (in press) to introduce the concept of **learned helplessness** as one explanation of the comparatively low achievement orientation of females. Basically, learned helplessness develops when the child believes that the reward he or she receives are beyond personal control (Seligman, 1975). While girls tend to show more learned helplessness than boys in achievement situations, box 12.3 suggests that there are many interesting, complex details in the development of learned helplessness in females.

When the total picture is considered, it does seem that girls have been socialized into roles of instrumental incompetence. There is reason to believe that differences in the achievement orientations of boys and girls are learned—not innately determined by sex.

Aletha Stein and Margaret Bailey (1973) have listed several parental characteristics or attributes that are associated with the development of achievement orientation in girls. For example, achievement orientation can be encouraged through the modeling of a mother who has a career. In some instances, particularly when the mother assumes a traditional female role, the social interaction of the father takes on greater importance. Stein and Bailey also point out that socialization practices fostering so-called femininity in girls often run counter to those practices producing achievement orientation. Moderate parental permissiveness, coupled with attempts to accelerate achievement, is related to achievement orientation in girls. This kind of parenting is not compatible with what is usually prescribed for rearing a young woman.

There is evidence that achievement settings entail many moral decisions. For example, in one investigation individuals were asked: "What might cause you to feel guilty?" A frequent response was "a failure to expend sufficient effort to accomplish one's aim" (Leedham, Signori, & Sampson, 1967, p. 918). And individuals seem inclined to be punitive toward others who are able but fail because of a lack of effort (Weiner & Kukla, 1970). Children, then, often feel guilty and are judged harshly for failing to use their capabilities.

The crime and violence that seem to increasingly characterize our society calls attention to moral development, which involves an understanding of how children come to handle the inevitable conflict between personal needs and social obligations (Hoffman, 1979).

Moral Development

In chapter 8 Piaget's cognitive-structural perspective of moral development was described. In this section, a cognitive-structural perspective of moral development that has received more attention than Piaget's in recent years—the stage theory of Lawrence Kohlberg—will

Box 12.3
Achievement Situations: The Learned Helplessness of Females

Two major systems of learned helplessness are a lack of motivation and negative affect. If the child in a failure situation sees her behavior as irrelevant to the outcome, she is displaying learned helplessness. Such perceptions lead to attributions that are seen as incontrollable or unchangeable, such as lack of ability, difficulty of the task, or presumably fixed attitudes of other people. In addition, attributions of failure to these factors are often linked with deterioration of performance in the face of failure. Individuals who attribute their failure to controllable or changeable factors, such as effort or luck, are more likely to show improvement in their performance (Dweck, 1975; Dweck & Reppucci, 1973; Weiner, 1974).

A number of investigations of achievement behavior suggest that girls are more likely to attribute failure to uncontrollable factors, like lack of ability, than boys (Dweck & Reppucci, 1973; Nicholls, 1975); to display disrupted performance or decreased effort under the pressure of impending failure or evaluation (Dweck & Gilliard, 1975); and to avoid situations in which failure is likely (Crandall & Rabson, 1960).

These sex differences in the effects of failure feedback on achievement behavior generally are attributed to girls' greater dependency on external social evaluation. However, some investigators believe that different evaluations of boys and girls by adults and peers may influence such sex differences. For example, Dweck and Bush (1976) found that when failure feedback for girls came from adults, little change in the girls' achievement behavior resulted; but when the feedback came from peers, the girls' achievement behavior increased substantially.

---

be outlined. We will also look at one aspect of the child's moral behavior that becomes more important in middle and late childhood than early childhood—cheating—and discuss further the social learning view of moral development.

Kohlberg

Lawrence Kohlberg elaborated upon Piaget's two stages and characterized moral thought as developing in six distinct stages. The stages are associated with changes in thought structures that begin around the age of six and may continue well into adulthood (the late twenties). Not everyone reaches Kohlberg's final stage of moral thought.

Kohlberg (1976) arrived at this view after some twenty years of interviewing children, adolescents, and adults, using a unique procedure. In the interview the individual is first presented with a series of stories in which characters face moral dilemmas. The following is one of the more popular Kohlberg dilemmas:

In Europe a woman was near death from a special kind of cancer. There was one drug that the doctors thought might save her. It was a form of radium that a druggist in the same town had recently discovered. The drug was expensive to make, but the druggist was charging ten times what the drug cost him to make. He paid $200 for the radium and charged $2,000 for a small dose of the drug. The sick woman's husband, Heinz, went to everyone he knew to borrow the money, but he could only get together $1,000 which is half of what it cost. He told the druggist that his wife was dying and asked him to sell it cheaper or let him pay later. But the druggist said, "No, I discovered the drug, and I am going to make money from it." So Heinz got desperate and broke into the man's store to steal the drug for his wife. (p. 379)

The interviewee is then asked a series of questions about each dilemma. For the Heinz dilemma, for example, Kohlberg asks such questions as these: Should Heinz have done that? Was it actually wrong or right? Why? Is it a husband's duty to steal the drug for his wife if he can get it no other way? Would a good husband do it? Did the druggist have the right to charge that much when there was no law actually setting a limit to the price? Why?

Based upon the types of reasons given to this and to other moral problems, Kohlberg arrived at the six stages of moral development described in table 12.2. Box 12.4 lists some specific responses to the Heinz and the druggist moral dilemma, placing each response at one of the six stages (Rest, in Kohlberg, 1969).

Table 12.2
Kohlberg's Six Moral Stages

Level and Stage	What Is Right	Reasons for Doing Right	Social Perspective of Stage
Level I: Preconventional Stage 1: Heteronomous morality	To avoid breaking rules backed by punishment, obedience for its own sake, and avoiding physical damage to persons and property.	Avoidance of punishment, and the superior power of authorities.	Egocentric point of view. Doesn't consider the interests of others or recognize that they differ from the actor's; doesn't relate two points of view. Actions are considered physically rather than in terms of psychological interests of others. Confusion of authority's perspective with one's own.
Stage 2: Individualism, instrumental purpose, and exchange	Following rules only when it is to someone's immediate interest; acting to meet one's own interests and needs and letting others do the same. Right is also what's fair, what's an equal exchange, a deal, an agreement.	To serve one's own needs or interests in a world where you have to recognize that other people have their interests, too.	Concrete individualistic perspective. Aware that everybody has his or her own interest to pursue and that these interests conflict, so that right is relative (in the concrete individualistic sense).
Level II: Conventional Stage 3: Mutual interpersonal expectations, relationships and interpersonal conformity	Living up to what is expected by people close to you or what people generally expect of your role as son, brother, friend, etc. "Being good" is important and means having good motives, showing concern about others. It also means keeping mutual relationships, such as trust, loyalty, respect, and gratitude.	The need to be a good person in your own eyes and those of others. Your caring for others. Belief in the Golden Rule. Desire to maintain rules and authority which support stereotypical good behavior.	Perspective of the individual in relationships with other individuals. Aware of shared feelings, agreements, and expectations, which take primacy over individual interests. Relates points of view through the concrete Golden Rule, putting oneself in the other guy's shoes. Does not yet consider generalized system perspective.
Stage 4: Social system and conscience	Fulfilling the actual duties to which you have agreed. Laws are to be upheld except in extreme cases where they conflict with other fixed social duties. Right is also contributing to society, the group, or institution.	To keep the institution going as a whole, to avoid the breakdown in the system "if everyone did it," or the imperative of conscience to meet one's defined obligations (easily confused with stage 3 belief in rules and authority).	Differentiates societal points of view from interpersonal agreement or motives. Takes the point of view of the system that defines roles and rules. Considers individual relations in terms of place in the system.

Table 12.2 (continued)
Kohlberg's Six Moral Stages

Level and Stage	What Is Right	Reasons for Doing Right	Social Perspective of Stage
Level III: *Postconventional, or* *Principled* Stage 5: Social contract or utility and individual rights	Being aware that people hold a variety of values and opinions, that most values and rules are relative to your group. These relative rules should usually be upheld, however, in the interest of impartiality and because they are the social contract. Some nonrelative values and rights like *life* and *liberty,* however, must be upheld in any society and regardless of majority opinion.	A sense of obligation to law because of one's social contract to make and abide by laws for the welfare of all and for the protection of all people's rights. A feeling of contractual commitment, freely entered upon, to family, friendship, trust, and work obligations. Concern that laws and duties be based on rational calculation of overall utility, "the greatest good for the greatest number."	Prior-to-society perspective. Perspective of a rational individual aware of values and rights prior to social attachments and contracts. Integrates perspectives by formal mechanisms of agreement, contract, objective impartiality, and due process. Considers moral and legal points of view; recognizes that they sometimes conflict and finds it difficult to integrate them.
Stage 6: Universal ethical principles	Following self-chosen ethical principles. Particular laws or social agreements are usually valid because they rest on such principles. When laws violate these principles, one acts in accordance with the principle. Principles are universal principles of justice: the equality of human rights and respect for the dignity of human beings as individual persons.	The belief as a rational person in the validity of universal moral principles, and a sense of personal commitment to them.	Perspective of a moral point of view from which social arrangements derive. Perspective is that of any rational individual recognizing the nature of morality or the fact that persons are ends in themselves and must be treated as such.

Source: Kohlberg, 1976, pp. 34–35.

Kohlberg (1976) believes that most children under age nine are at the **preconventional level of moral development** (stages 1 and 2). Interestingly, some adolescents, particularly those who are delinquent, also score at this level. From the late elementary school years on, most individuals think at the **conventional level** (stages 3 and 4) when they are faced with moral dilemmas. Only a small percentage of adolescents reach the **postconventional level** (stages 5 and 6), but usually this is not attained until after the age of twenty. Even then, only a minority of individuals reach the postconventional level.

The label *conventional* means that children conform to and uphold the laws and conventions of society simply because they are the laws and conventions of the society. The individual who reaches postconventional thinking understands, and for the most part accepts, the society's rules and regulations, but his or her reasoning goes deeper than that of the person who thinks in a conventional manner. For an individual at the postconventional level, the rules of the society have to mesh with underlying moral principles. In cases where the rules of the society come into conflict with the individual's principles, the individual will follow his or her own principles rather than the conventions of the society.

Similarities in Piaget's and Kohlberg's Views
For both Piaget (discussed in chapter 8) and Kohlberg, the child's moral orientation is an outgrowth of cognitive development that unfolds as a consequence of the interaction of genetic endowment and social experiences. The child is characterized as being at a particular moral stage of development and passes through the stages in an invariant sequence, from less to more

Box 12.4
Examples of Kohlberg's Six Stages of Moral Development

Following are examples of responses to the story "Heinz and the Druggist" that have been coded at the six different stages in Kohlberg's theory. There are no absolute, morally "correct" answers—as the pro and con answers to the moral dilemma might suggest.

Stage 1

Pro: He should steal the drug. It is not really bad to take it. It is not like he did not ask to pay for it first. The drug he would take is only worth $200, he is not really taking a $2,000 drug.

Con: He should not steal the drug; it is a big crime. He did not get permission; he used force and broke and entered. He did a lot of damage, stealing a very expensive drug and breaking up the store, too.

Stage 2

Pro: It is all right to steal the drug because she needs it, and he wants her to live. It is not that he wants to steal, but it is the way he has to use to get the drug to save her.

Con: He should not steal it. The druggist is not wrong or bad; he just wants to make a profit. That is what you are in business for, to make money.

Stage 3

Pro: He should steal the drug. He was only doing something that was natural for a good husband to do. You cannot blame him for doing something out of love for his wife, you would blame him if he did not love his wife enough to save her.

Con: He should not steal. If his wife dies, he cannot be blamed. It is not because he is heartless or that he does not love her enough to do everything that he legally can. The druggist is the selfish or heartless one.

Stage 4

Pro: Heinz should steal it. If he did nothing, he would be letting his wife die; it is his responsibility if she dies. He has to take it with the idea of paying the druggist.

Con: It is a natural thing for Heinz to want to save his wife but it is still always wrong to steal. He still knows he is stealing and taking a valuable drug from the man who made it.

Stage 5

Pro: The law was not set up for these circumstances. Taking the drug in this situation is not really right, but it is justified to do it.

Con: You cannot completely blame someone for stealing but extreme circumstances do not really justify taking the law in your own hands. You cannot have everyone stealing whenever they get desperate. The end may be good, but the ends do not justify the means.

Stage 6

Pro: This is a situation which forces him to choose between stealing and letting his wife die. In a situation where the choice must be made, it is morally right to steal. He has to act in terms of the principle of preserving and respecting life.

Con: Heinz is faced with the decision of whether to consider the other people who need the drug just as badly as his wife. Heinz ought to act not according to his particular feelings toward his wife but considering the value of all the lives involved.

Source: From J. Rest, quoted in Kohlberg, 1969, pp. 379–80.

---

advanced. The child is seen as acting on the world constructively while proceeding from one stage to the next, rather than accepting passively a cultural norm of morality.

Piaget and Kohlberg both believe that peer interaction is of major importance in the social stimulation that challenges the child to change moral orientation. Whereas adults characteristically impose rules and constraints on children, the mutual give-and-take in peer interaction provides the child with an opportunity to take the role of the other person and to generate rules democratically. Piaget (1932) did say that if parents and adults were to engage in more reciprocal discussion with children, acknowledge flaws in their own behavior, and impose fewer constraints whose reasons the child cannot grasp, they too would contribute more significantly to the child's moral development. Kohlberg stresses that role-taking opportunities fostered by peer relations can, in principle, be fostered by any group encounter.

Piaget and Kohlberg both believe that peer interaction is of major importance in moral development.

For Piaget and Kohlberg, however, it is the maturation of cognitive capacities that primarily determines moral thinking. The social environment merely provides the raw material on which cognitive processes actively operate. For Piaget, the cognitive processes most instrumental in advancing the child from moral realism to moral autonomy are egocentrism and realism. *Realism* refers to the child's inability to distinguish between objective and subjective aspects of experience; *egocentrism* involves failure to decenter and take the perspective of others. Kohlberg (1969) stresses that the development of information processing skills (attention, memory, inference making) are important in developing more advanced morality inasmuch as these help the child to piece together social experiences.

Evaluation of Kohlberg's Ideas about Moral Development

Questions about Kohlberg's theory that researchers have attempted to answer focus on such questions as: Are Kohlberg's six stages universal? Are they related to the age, IQ, social class, and social experiences of the child? And, How can children be encouraged to progress to more advanced stages? After we have reviewed evidence that bears on these questions, some criticisms of Kohlberg will be made and information about the relation of moral thought to moral action will be presented.

In his original work, Kohlberg (1958) found that as the age of the child increased, moral judgments become more advanced. He also reported that age changes in children's responses to moral judgment items have been found in most industrialized Western countries, such as the United States, France, and Great Britain. And these changes occur regardless of the child's sex or social class. The stages are also significantly related to intelligence (Kohlberg, 1969).

Kohlberg (1958) also found support for his belief that social participation in groups is one way to advance the moral judgment of children. Membership and leadership in groups may also be a factor. In one investigation, the moral judgments of fourth- and fifth-grade boys and girls who were leaders and members of extracurricular groups or activities such as Boy Scouts, Girl Scouts, athletic teams, and civic groups responded with more advanced moral judgments on the Kohlberg moral dilemma items than those who were not members or leaders of organized groups (Keasey, 1971). In other investigations, role-taking opportunities have been shown to precede advances in moral judgments (Selman, 1971a, 1971b; Walker, 1980; Walker & Richards, 1979). And in seventh graders the very early beginning of formal operations preceded movements from stage 2 to stage 3 in Kohlberg's theory (Walker, 1980).

As further support for his cognitive-developmental theory of morality, Kohlberg and his colleagues (Colby et al., 1980) reported data from a twenty-year longitudinal study of moral judgment. The subjects were fifty-three boys aged ten, thirteen, and sixteen at the first time of assessment. In addition to the original

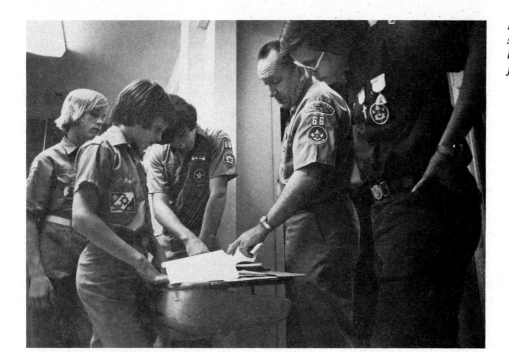

moral judgment interview, the boys were studied five more times at intervals of three to four years. The boys did proceed through the Kohlberg developmental stages in the predicted order, with no one skipping any stage and only 4 percent showing any backsliding within a stage from one testing time to the next. As with his earlier data, Kohlberg found that again moral judgment was significantly linked with age, sociometric status, IQ, and education.

Several investigators have attempted to advance the child's level of moral development in relation to Kohlberg's scales by providing arguments that are one stage above the child's established level. These studies are based on the cognitive-developmental concepts of equilibrium and conflict. By finding the correct environmental match slightly beyond the child's cognitive level, a disequilibrium is created that motivates the child to restructure moral thoughts. The resolution of the disequilibrium and conflict should be toward increased competence. The data are mixed on this question, however. In one of the pioneer studies on this topic, Eliot Turiel (1966) discovered that children preferred a response one stage above their current level over a response two stages above it. However, they actually chose a response one stage below their level more often than a response one stage above it. Apparently the children were motivated more by security needs than by the need to reorganize thought to a higher level. Other studies indicate that children do prefer a more advanced stage over a less advanced stage (e.g., Rest et al., 1969).

While stimulating a great deal of interest, Kohlberg's theory has not been without its share of criticism. Kohlberg has been attacked for his ideas about the cultural universality of morality, problems in the way he collects information about moral judgments, and his failure to incorporate the needs and feelings of the individual into his theory. Elizabeth Simpson (1974, 1976) and Urie Bronfenbrenner and James Garbarino (1976) believe that Kohlberg's theory is ethnocentric and culturally biased. In other words analysis of cross-cultural information about morality indicate that individuals around the world do not think as consistently at particular stages of morality as Kohlberg believes they do.

Bronfenbrenner (1970) argued that children in the American culture are taught to think in individualistic terms. To assess this belief, Soviet and American children were asked to respond to a situation in which they observed a classmate cheating on an exam. The Soviet children indicated that the cheating would be wrong because it violates a group rule, and they said that they felt it was their obligation to talk to the child who cheated and express the reasons why he or she should not cheat. The American children were much more concerned about getting caught and were three times as likely as the Soviet children to say that they would tell on the cheater by informing an adult about the deviation. Bronfenbrenner believes that the emphasis on individualism is largely responsible for the breakdown of moral responsibility in our culture.

Bronfenbrenner (Bronfenbrenner & Garbarino, 1976) points out that, except for the incest taboo which is virtually universal, the substance of moral prohibition varies greatly across cultures and is deeply embedded in the values of each individual culture. This view corresponds to the beliefs of many anthropologists and sociologists (e.g., Benedict, 1934, 1958; Murdock, 1949).

Bronfenbrenner also suggests that a child's moral development can be advanced by exposure to a variety of settings and social agents representing different expectations and moral sanctions. Such differences produce conflict in children and motivate them to reassess their own moral convictions; by contrast, a single setting exposes the child to only one set of rules. The pluralistic theory can be applied to families (two parents mean two moral systems instead of one), peers, schools, neighborhoods, communities, employment, and civic and political organizations.

Bronfenbrenner (1970) found support for this theory by further studying children in the Soviet Union. Soviet boarding school students were exposed to a single socialization setting, whereas day school students were exposed to multiple settings. The boarding school students made moral judgments that were more authority-oriented than those made by the day school students. Bronfenbrenner's interpretation is that students who lived at home were forced to develop a balance between competing social agents (school authorities, peers, and parents).

Kohlberg's detractors have also criticized the stories he uses to collect information about the moral judgment of children and adolescents, saying that these stories are not very representative of the actual moral problems of children and adolescents. For example, Steven Yussen (1977) studied 149 seventh-, ninth-, and twelfth-grade students, half boys and half girls. Each adolescent was requested to write a realistic moral dilemma in a thirty-minute session. In Kohlberg's moral dilemmas, the social relationships focus primarily on the family (e.g., father, brother, wife) and on authority relationships (e.g., boss-worker, principal-student). In Yussen's study the categories of social relationships described by the students emphasized family, friends, acquaintances, and authority figures; young adolescents wrote very few moral dilemmas about authority relationships, and their stories focused on friends as often as on family relationships. Curiously, not one of the Kohlberg stories centers on friendships.

James Rest, a former student of Kohlberg's, believes that more careful attention should be paid to the way moral judgment is assessed. Rest (1976) points out that alternative methods should be used to collect information about moral thinking rather than relying on a single method that requires individuals to reason about hypothetical moral dilemmas. Rest further points out that the Kohlberg stories are exceedingly difficult to score. To help remedy this problem, Rest (1976, 1977) has devised his own measure of moral development, called the Defining Issues Test, or the DIT.

In the DIT an attempt is made to determine which moral issues individuals feel are most crucial in a given situation by presenting them with a series of dilemmas and a list of definitions of the major issues involved (Kohlberg's procedure does not make use of such a list). In the dilemma of Heinz and the druggist, individuals might be asked whether a community's laws should be upheld or whether Heinz should be willing to risk being injured or caught as a burglar; they might also be asked to list the most important values that govern human interaction. They are given six stories and asked to rate the importance of each issue involved in deciding what ought to be done. Then the subjects are asked to list what they believe are the four most important issues. Rest believes that this method provides a more consistent and accurate measurement of moral thinking than Kohlberg's system.

Elizabeth Simpson (1976) also faults Kohlberg's idea that getting individuals to reason at a more advanced level will result in corresponding positive changes in their moral behavior.

Reasons can be a shelter, as we all know, especially when they are developed after the fact and are applied to our own behavior or to that of someone in whom we have an ego investment. In any case, reasons are inseparable from the personality of the reasoner, whether they apply to his own behavior or that of others. They are grounded not in the situation in which decisions are made, but in the reasoner's psychic definition of past experience, and that psychic definition frequently crosses all boundaries of rationality. Passionate irrationality in the name of impassioned reason occurs in the market, the classroom, and in science, as well as elsewhere, and often unconsciously. (pp. 162–63)

It is important to learn how individuals think when presented with a moral dilemma, but to fully understand development we must attempt to learn how they behave as well. Ultimately, it is behavior we seek to influence. No one wants a nation of minds reasoning at Kohlberg's stage 5 or 6, but when behavior is observed, cheating, lying, and stealing are prevalent.

Moral Behavior

In everyday life laws and conventions are compromised by people who allow themselves to act in accordance with a lax interpretation of them. A boy takes a test in school, with the understanding that his activity should be confined to his own work; instead, he decides to cheat and peeks at a classmate's answers. A woman files her federal tax return with the understanding that she can deduct only those business expenses for which she has

The actual moral behavior of children is influenced by the pressures of the situation.

a record or an accurate recollection; instead, she cheats by padding her deductions with fictitious expenses so that her tax bill will be smaller.

It has been found that students cheat more when they are informed that their scores will be posted outside the classroom, when they are told that other students have always scored just beyond what the student is capable of scoring, and when students are not monitored by adults (e.g., Hill, 1980). Such findings provide strong support for the view that the actual moral behavior of the child is heavily influenced by the pressures of the situation—rather than consistently showing honesty, children may cheat in one situation but not in others (e.g., Hartshorne & May, 1928–1930). In one investigation, lower-class boys cheated more on tests of physical strength than on vocabulary tests (Santrock, 1975).

Some Conclusions about the Behavioral Social Learning View of Morality

In the behavioral social learning view, each child has a unique learning history. Therefore, it is to be expected that his or her pattern of moral behavior will be different from that of every other child. There is no reason to expect, however, that a child will act in the same way in every realm of moral behavior. The socialization forces that contribute to one behavioral domain may have no effect on another. For this reason, a slightly different pattern of moral development emerges in each area, and any attempt to summarize findings must be approached cautiously. Still, there are some broad conclusions that seem applicable to the moral behavior of children and the social learning view.

First, there is little evidence of consistency in the moral behavior of an individual child. What children do in one behavioral realm is only weakly correlated with what they do in another. The evidence also suggests that this lack of moral unity may be reflected in

smaller behavioral patterns as well. For example, children do not seem to have a consistent trait for cheating (Hartshorne & May, 1928–1930), for behaving in an altruistic manner (Staub, 1974), or for resisting temptation (Toner, Holstein, & Hetherington, 1977). Although they will cheat in one situation, they may scrupulously avoid doing so in another. In other words, moral behavior is situation specific. The characteristics of the situation and the person's learning history (rather than some general trait) determine how the individual will behave.

A second conclusion is that social learning theory explains some of the results obtained from studies but leaves others unexplained. Some studies show that children who observe a model resisting temptation will themselves be more likely to resist temptation. But other studies have shown different findings, even in very similar situations (Toner, Parke, & Yussen, in press). Staub (1974) has found that although boys and girls donate gifts following a verbal lecture and modeling in one circumstance, they may not do so in another very similar situation. There are dozens of contradictions in developmental research, and they are not easily explained. The cognitive social learning theory may account for apparently contradictory findings that social learning theory alone is unable to explain.

Combining elements of the cognitive development process with elements of the behavioral learning process highlights the cognitive social learning view of Walter and Harriet Mischel (1975). They distinguish between the child's **moral competence,** or ability to produce moral behaviors, and **moral performance** of those behaviors in specific situations. In their view, competence depends primarily on cognitive-sensory processes; it is an outgrowth of these processes. The competencies include the child's abilities, knowledge, skills, awareness of moral rules and regulations, and cognitive ability to construct behaviors. Moral performance, or behavior, however, is determined by motivation and the rewards and incentives to act in a specific moral way.

In general, social learning theorists have been critical of Kohlberg's view. Among other reasons, they believe he places too little emphasis on moral behavior and the situational determinants of morality. However, while Kohlberg argues that moral judgment is an important determinant of moral behavior, he, like the Mischels, stresses that the individual's interpretation of both the moral and factual aspects of a situation lead to a moral decision (Kohlberg & Candee, 1979). For example, Kohlberg mentions that "extramoral" factors, like the desire to avoid embarrassment, may cause the child to avoid doing what he or she believes to be morally right. In sum, both the Mischels and Kohlberg believe that moral action is influenced by a complex number of factors.

Sometimes development does not proceed smoothly—in the next section we will look at the most common problems and disturbances that surface during middle and late childhood.

Problems and Disturbances

Entering school means conformity to routines for long hours and expectations of the child's productive performance. Children may develop *school phobia,* the inability to attend school because of the fears associated with being there. School phobia is but one of the many neurotic disturbances that may surface at this time. Neurotic disturbances refer to nonpsychotic disorders that involve a variety of symptoms such as anxiety, depression, obsessions, or compulsions. Considerable space will be devoted to anxiety. But first let's look at the range of problems elementary schoolchildren experience, as described by Thomas Achenbach (1978).

Frequent Problems Reported by Elementary Schoolchildren

Possibly because of the need for increased conformity to routines and the more noticeable comparisons of children's social and intellectual development, the rate of referrals to mental health clinics increases rapidly in the elementary school years. Referral rates for elementary schoolchildren are three times what they are for preschool children, and at all ages boys are referred more frequently than girls (Rosen, Bahn, & Kramer, 1964).

In table 12.3, the most common problems reported by parents who have taken their six- to eleven-year-old children to mental health clinics are numerically compared to similar problems reported by parents who did not refer their children to such clinics. (The latter group is labeled "normal" in the table.) The most noticeable difference between the two sets of boys is in the area of poor schoolwork, whereas for the girls the largest differences were unhappiness and nervousness. And, girls seem to show more internalized problems than boys, for example, showing off less, exhibiting fewer temper tantrums, and acting less impulsively. Achenbach (1978) concluded that the greatest increase in mental health referrals in the elementary school years is, indeed, school related.

Table 12.3
Percentage Comparison of Problem Frequency between Children Referred to Clinics and "Normal" Children

Problem	Boys Clinic	Boys Normal	Girls Clinic	Girls Normal
Acts too young for age	65	34	66	24
Argues a lot	88	64	83	58
Attention demanding	83	33	80	40
Bragging, boasting	67	57	42	40
Can't concentrate	87	44	72	29
Can't sit still, restless, hyperactive	84	38	61	32
Disobedient at home	83	40	75	37
Disobedient at school	73	20	43	10
Easily jealous	67	36	73	42
Feels that no one loves him/her	53	21	64	31
Gets teased a lot	72	36	62	32
Impulsive	78	38	63	28
Nervous, high-strung, tense	73	24	77	22
Poor schoolwork	71	17	55	7
Self-conscious	65	43	71	48
Showing off, clowning	80	57	54	44
Sudden changes of mood	62	20	65	21
Sullen, stubborn, irritable	79	45	76	37
Temper tantrums	69	31	57	21
Unhappy, sad, depressed	58	8	66	9

In a more recent analysis of behavioral problems and competencies, Achenbach and Edelbrock (1981) found that parents of lower-class children reported their children had more problems and fewer competencies than the parents of middle-class children. Most of the problems reported more frequently for lower-class children and for boys were undercontrolled, externalizing behaviors, while the problems reported more frequently for middle-class children and for girls tended to be either overcontrolled, internalizing behaviors or not clearly classifiable as undercontrolled or overcontrolled. Certain problems that have been the subject of a great deal of clinical literature did not distinguish between clinical and nonclinical children. These included fears of certain animals, situations, or places and bedwetting. Indications of unhappiness and poor schoolwork, however, clearly characterized the clinical group of children more than the nonclinical group.

Neurotic Disturbances

Anxieties, phobias, obsessions, compulsions, and depression are the most common neurotic disturbances experienced by children. **Anxiety** can have either a debilitating or a positive effect on the child's behavior. In this section we will look at situations in which anxiety produces problems and disturbances for the child. In its milder forms anxiety is experienced as a feeling of apprehension often accompanied by restlessness, fatigue, and some visceral reaction such as a headache, an empty feeling in the stomach, or a heaviness in the chest. During acute anxiety attacks, the child's apprehension is intensified. He or she may believe that something horrible is about to happen and may complain about an inability to breathe or a racing heart. An extremely anxious child may blame anxiety on others. He or she may be hostile and violent toward another one moment, and cling to the person as a source of security the next. Following the anxiety attack, the child may be as puzzled about the behavior as others.

Anxiety is one of the most difficult psychological terms to define; yet it is one of the most widely employed. Most people agree that anxiety is an unpleasant state, that it is linked to the physiological arousal of the child, and that it involves the anticipation of something uncomfortable or painful (e.g., Sarason & Spielberger, 1975). Anxiety is usually described as a diffuse state; that is, the child cannot pin down the specific reasons for nervousness. Fear also involves discomfort and pain, but the child knows what it is that is frightening. This is the most common distinction made between anxiety and fear.

A term closely related to fear is **phobia**—a strong, often unreasonable fear of certain people, objects, or situations. Children may develop many different types of phobias; one type of phobic reaction is fear of school. School phobia in childhood may be traced to worries about exams, peer problems, teacher problems, and real or imagined fear of parental desertion. In one investigation, it was reported that school phobia usually peaks around age eleven or twelve and occurs in as many as 2 to 8 percent of the children referred to child guidance clinics (Kahn & Nursten, 1962).

Chess and Hassibi (1978) paint the following clinical picture of a child suffering from school phobia. The child often begins to complain in a vague way at about breakfast time. He or she may feel nauseated, have a headache, or say his or her stomach feels funny. If forced to go to school, the child may not be willing to enter the classroom or may feel sick while in class. The child often worries about what is going on at home while at school and may even call home to see if everything is all right. At bedtime, he or she may begin to worry about the next morning.

Depression is one of the most common neurotic experiences of youths.

about orderliness, and very much a perfectionist. This problem rarely occurs in early childhood; it is most likely to appear at about six to ten years of age. The compulsive child may feel a great deal of anxiety if he or she doesn't carry out the compulsion. Such children often experience a great deal of anxiety, guilt, and fear of failure as well. Parental expectations of perfect behavior represent one likely cause of compulsive behavior.

The causes of anxiety reactions during childhood are varied. They may range from biological changes to shifting relationships with family, peers, and teachers. The majority of children are capable of handling everyday problems without developing acute anxiety reactions or phobias. The moderate degree of stress encountered by most children may even serve as a motivating force to energize efforts to cope with the world. Those children with consistently high levels of anxiety, however, may need professional help. In box 12.5 ways to help children with high anxiety levels are discussed.

We will conclude our discussion of problems and disturbances by presenting the work of Norman Garmezy (Garmezy, 1975; Garmezy & Rutter, in press), who for many years studied the abnormalities of children, but who recently discovered how some children who seem to be prime candidates for mental health problems cope amazingly well with their world.

The "Invulnerables"

Ten-year-old Alex has everything going against him; he comes from a broken home, his mother is on welfare, his father is in prison, his younger brother is dying of a chronic disease, and another brother is mentally retarded. However, his teachers say he is a delightful boy to be around; they like him, and so do his peers. His grades are good, and he is looked up to as a leader by others in his school.

Maya Pines (1975) has written an overview of Norman Garmezy's work with such youth, referred to as the "invulnerables." Garmezy says there is nothing in the psychological literature to explain such invulnerability or strength in the face of deprivation. Garmezy believes that we should focus more of our research efforts on how the invulnerables cope so well in such negative circumstances. In the past we have concerned ourselves only with how youth break down in such situations.

Too often we seem to work backwards in our efforts to pinpoint the answers to questions such as what causes schizophrenia? The past histories of adult schizophrenics are carefully searched for signs of what triggered the disturbance. Such retrospective studies have not proved very fruitful in providing answers to questions about the causes of psychological disturbances. Further, they tell us nothing about how some children seem to develop an immunity to serious disturbance in situations that appear hopeless.

In the majority of cases, the school-phobic child eventually refuses to go to school. The child may offer to study at home, however, if allowed to remain homebound, the child will isolate himself or herself more and more from the outside world. Parents may become angry about this behavior in such situations and openly display hostility. When such children appear at a guidance clinic or in a psychiatrist's office, they usually appear anxious, depressed, angry, and lacking in self-esteem.

Sometimes a high level of anxiety is associated with obsessive-compulsive behavior in childhood. **Obsessions** are usually unwanted ideas or fears that continue or intrude into the child's thoughts without any noticeable external cause. **Compulsions** refer to repetitive, stereotyped actions called into play to ward off some imaginary threat. When the child has an obsessive-compulsive personality problem, it means that he or she has a tendency to be rigid, excessively concerned

Box 12.5
Helping Children Cope with Anxiety

If children are experiencing a high level of anxiety, how can they best cope with it, or how can others help them cope? Lois Murphy (1962) has described the complex nature of the coping process.

> The child may attempt to reduce the threat, postpone it, bypass it, create distance between himself and the threat, divide his attention, and the like. He may attempt to control it by setting limits, or by changing or transforming the situation. He might even try to eliminate or destroy the threat. Or he may balance the threat with security measures, changing the relation of himself to the threat or to the environment which contains it, but which also includes sources of reassurance. Instead of dealing with the actual threat itself, he may deal primarily with the tension aroused by the threat: discharging tension by action, or by affect release displacement into fantasy, dramatizing activities or creative work. Or he may attempt to contain the tension via insight, conscious formulation of the nature of the threat, defense maneuvers such as being brave, reassuring himself that he would be able to deal with it. (p. 277)

Donald Meichenbaum (1975) believes that developing coping skills to help the child deal more effectively with achievement situations is a complex process. For example, a coping skill that works for one child may not work with another. Successful coping skills entail strategies that focus on challenging the child's interaction with his or her environment. These include cognitive plans for dealing with the anxiety in the world. Cognitive rehearsal is an important part of these cognitive plans. When children are being trained to reduce their anxiety in achievement situations, exposure to less threatening events may be helpful.

Cognitive rehearsal can be a valuable technique for decreasing anxiety. For instance, children who continue saying to themselves that they are afraid of college, that they cannot go to class anymore because it is too scary, or that they don't have enough talent to do well in school will probably not reduce their anxiety in such situations. The following examples of mind-set rehearsal statements (Meichenbaum, Turk, & Burstein, 1975) have been used successfully to reduce stress and anxiety at different times in anxiety-provoking achievement situations.

Preparing for anxiety or stress:

> What do I have to do?
>
> I'm going to map out a plan to deal with it.
>
> I'll just think about what I have to do.
>
> I won't worry; worry doesn't help anything.
>
> I have a lot of different strategies to call on.

Confronting and handling the pain:

> I can meet the challenge.
>
> I'll keep on taking just one step at a time; I can handle it.
>
> I'll just relax, breath deeply, and use one of the strategies.
>
> I won't think about the pain. I'll think about what I have to do.

Coping with feelings at critical moments:

> What is it I have to do?
>
> I was supposed to expect the pain to increase; I just have to keep myself in control.
>
> When the pain comes, I'll just pause and keep focusing on what I have to do.

Reinforcing statements:

> Good, I did it.
>
> I handled it well.
>
> I knew I could do it.
>
> Wait until I tell other people how I did it!

As can be seen, these statements focus on specific ways of coping with anxiety rather than on thinking general good thoughts about oneself. By following these guidelines and procedures, children can prepare more efficiently for anxiety and cope more effectively with it when it arrives.

Some children seem to develop an immunity to serious disturbances in situations that appear hopeless.

In studying the invulnerables, Garmezy says that he owes a considerable debt to Lois Murphy, who in 1962 wrote in the *Widening World of Childhood:*

It is something of a paradox that a nation which has exulted in rapid expansion and its scientific-technological achievements should have developed in its studies of childhood so vast a "Problem literature." A literature often expressing adjustment difficulties, social failures, blocked potentialities and defeat. . . . In applying clinical ways of thinking formulated out of experience with broken adults, we were slow to see how the language of adequacy to meet life's challenges could become the subject matter of psychological science. Thus there are thousands of studies of maladjustment for each that deals with the ways of managing life's problems with personal strength and adequacy. . . . We know that there are devices for correcting, bypassing, or overcoming threats, but for the most part these have not been directly studied. (p. 2)

Garmezy does not deny that such problems as unstable and fractured families, poor nutrition, and birth defects place an unnecessary burden on the lives of the poor. However, he believes that predispositions toward competence or incompetence are not always the result of the presence or lack of such problems. It remains to be discovered how competence grows out of disadvantage.

To study the invulnerables, Garmezy went to a number of schools and asked the teachers and principals to point out to him their invulnerables. In most schools, the principals and teachers had no difficulty giving Garmezy the names of several children. The most difficult factor to pin down was the amount of stress the youths were experiencing, since one person's stress may be another's challenge.

The most remarkable phenomenon about invulnerable youth is their recovery after stress; they seem to bounce back, often with a bite. Garmezy is continuing to study the invulnerable youth and hopes to follow them into adulthood. He evaluates these children both in school situations and through family interviews. Early findings suggest that attention is a critical factor in the invulnerable youth's competence. Garmezy believes that attentional deficiencies and difficulties are the substance out of which incompetence develops. In further research Garmezy wants to find out how modifiable attentional defects are, at what age can they be changed, and how can they be ameliorated.

Garmezy says that what we need is a science of developmental psychopathology. The field hardly exists now, but it will have to include aspects of both biological psychiatry and developmental psychology. Garmezy points out that Jean Piaget revitalized developmental psychology when he disproved the linear growth ("child as adult") model and demonstrated that children move through a sequence of cognitive stages. The same needs to be done in the field of developmental psychopathology. Otherwise, effective intervention will be nearly impossible. To help get the field of developmental psychopathology moving, Garmezy suggests that invulnerable youth need to be studied in much greater depth, variety, and frequency.

Summary

In this chapter we focused on three important aspects of personality development—the self, sex-role development, and moral development—and described the most common problems of middle and late childhood.

An important aspect of self-development involves the increasing ability with age to take the perspective of others—elementary schoolchildren are better at this than preschool children. Elementary school-aged children also are more likely to describe themselves in terms of traits, whereas preschoolers are more likely to refer to themselves in terms of physical attributes. And, compared to elementary schoolchildren, adolescents engage in more abstract self-perceptions. As children grow older their self-perceptions become more differentiated, individuated, and stable. Psychologists also have studied children's self-esteem, although self-esteem is described so broadly in terms of the child either having a positive or negative self-concept that it is difficult to measure.

A promising model for thinking about developmental changes in self-perception has been proposed by Susan Harter. She argues that we first have to distinguish between the content (physical attributes, behaviors, psychological dimensions) and structure (how these contents are organized as the child develops) of self-perceptions, and then evaluate their interaction. She believes there are four stages of structural self-development: simple descriptions, trait labels, simple abstractions, and higher-order abstractions. The first two roughly correspond to preoperational and concrete operational thought, and the third with early formal operational thought. The fourth stage emerges during adulthood.

Surprisingly, in the most extensive review of sex differences, it is indicated that many of the stereotypes for the sexes are unsupported by the facts. However, girls do have more verbal ability than boys, boys surpass girls in math and visual-spatial reasoning, and boys are more aggressive than girls. Some experts, though, believe there are many more psychological differences between the sexes than the four just mentioned. One possible sex difference that has stirred a great deal of controversy involves achievement. Ours is an achievement-oriented society; we rear children to be competitive, to be the best, to win. It appears, though, that females have traditionally been socialized differently than males in regard to achievement. It seems that girls, even as early as kindergarten, have been trained to become instrumentally incompetent, while males have been oriented toward instrumental competence.

Our discussion of moral development focused heavily on Kohlberg's cognitive structural stage theory. Most children in middle and late childhood are in stages 1, 2, 3, or 4 of Kohlberg's six-stage theory, suggesting they reason about moral dilemmas in either premoral or conventional ways. Our evaluation of Kohlberg's theory suggested that some experts believe there is more cultural variation in moral development than Kohlberg argues, there are problems in measuring the stages, and that reasons sometimes can be a shelter for immoral conduct. The behavioral social learning perspective of moral development emphasizes the importance of the child's moral actions. One of these moral actions—cheating—becomes more important during middle and late childhood as the child enters formal schooling. The behavioral social learning perspective emphasizes that morality often varies substantially from one situation to another, while the cognitive social learning view stresses a distinction between competence and performance. The content or moral education has been a value-laden issue for many years and still is comprised of many different approaches.

Entry into school brings with it problems related to demands for conformity to routines for long periods and increased expectations of the child's performance. There is an increase in referrals to mental health clinics during the elementary school years, and at all ages referrals for boys outnumber those for girls. Poor schoolwork is a major problem for boys in this age period, while girls tend to be characterized more by unhappiness and nervousness. Anxieties, phobias, obsessions, and compulsions are among the most common neurotic disturbances of children. All children experience anxiety and fear, but some encounter such high levels of anxiety that their competence is impaired. Anxiety is a diffuse state, whereas fear is related to a specific situation, person, or object. A phobia is viewed as an unreasonable fear, and one of the most common phobias among children is school phobia. However, some children, whose background suggests they have everything against them, turn out to be socially competent individuals—such children are called "invulnerables."

Key Terms

anxiety

attribution theory

compulsions

conventional level of
  moral development

instrumental competence

"invulnerables"

learned helplessness

moral competence

moral performance

obsessions

phobia

postconventional level of
  moral development

preconventional level of
  moral development

values clarification

Review Questions

1. Discuss the changes in self-perception that occur during middle and late childhood.
2. Evaluate the labels of self-esteem and self-concept and describe why they are so difficult to measure.
3. Discuss Susan Harter's developmental theory of self-perception.
4. What are some real and mythical differences between the sexes?
5. Discuss the role of learned helplessness in the development of achievement orientation in females.
6. Outline Kohlberg's theory of moral development. How has it been criticized?
7. Evaluate the behavioral social learning view of moral development.
8. Discuss the nature of moral education. Should moral education be a part of schooling?
9. What are some of the common problems and disturbances in the elementary school years?
10. Who are the invulnerables?

Further Readings

Achenbach, T. A. Developmental aspects of psychopathology in children and adolescents. In M. Lamb (ed.), *Social and personality development*. New York: Holt, Rinehart & Winston, 1978.
An excellent chapter on the developmental aspects of problems and disturbances in infancy, childhood, and adolescence. Includes information on hyperactivity and the treatment of children with problems and disturbances. Medium reading difficulty.

Coopersmith, S. *The antecedent of self-esteem.* San Francisco: Freeman, 1967.
A study of parental characteristics that are associated with children's low, medium, and high self-esteem in middle and late childhood. Includes a self-esteem measure that can be given to children, and an interview for parents. Easy to read.

Huston-Stein, A., & Higgens-Trenk, A. Development of females from childhood through adulthood: career and feminine orientations. In P. Baltes (ed.), *Life-span development and behavior (vol. 4)*. New York: Academic Press, 1978.
An excellent overview of achievement and career orientation in girls and women, with particular attention being given to the socializing influences that have led to different achievement and career paths for girls and boys. Reasonably easy reading.

Knopf, I. J. *Childhood psychopathology.* Englewood Cliffs, N.J.: Prentice-Hall, 1979.
A thorough overview of the major disturbances in children. Includes information on conceptual models of psychopathology, the nature of psychopathology, the assessment of children with problems, and treatment approaches. Reasonably easy reading.

Lickona, T. (ed.). *Moral development and behavior.* New York: Holt, Rinehart & Winston, 1976.
Contemporary essays outline the major theories, research findings, and educational implications of moral development. Included are essays by Kohlberg, Hoffman, Mischel, Bronfenbrenner, and Rest. Moderately difficult.

Section V

Adolescence

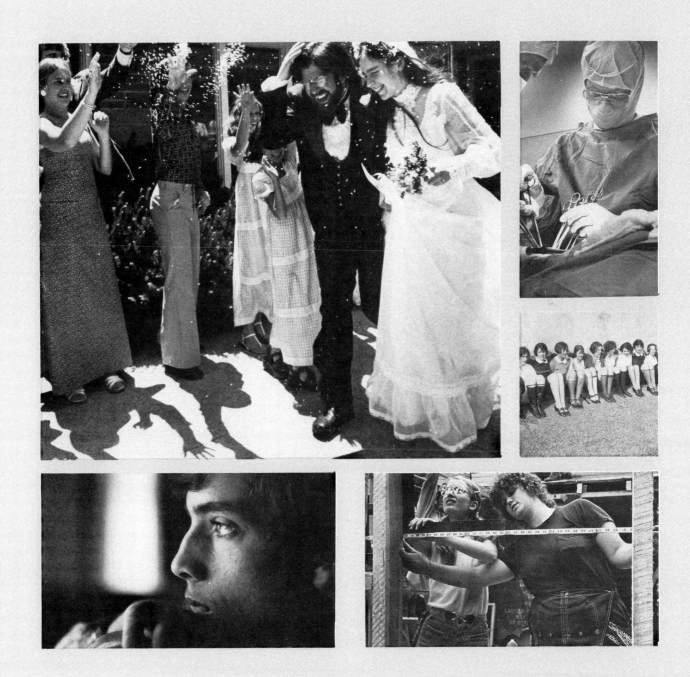

Physical and Cognitive Development

Prologue: Can Puberty Come Any Earlier?

Imagine a toddler displaying all the features of **puberty**—a three-year-old girl with fully developed breasts, or a boy just slightly older with a deep male voice. That is what we will see by the year 2250 if the age at which puberty arrives keeps getting younger at its current pace.

In Norway, the average girl begins to menstruate at just over 13 years of age, as opposed to 17 years in the 1840s. In the United States—where children mature up to a year earlier than in European countries—the average age at first menstruation has declined from 14.2 in 1900 to about 12.45 today. According to British pediatrician J. M. Tanner, who has compiled statistics on the subject, the age at menarche (first menstruation) has declined an average of four months per decade for the past century.

Fortunately, perhaps, we are unlikely to see pubescent toddlers, since what has happened during this century may be quite special. Tanner has noted that an extrapolation of the recent trend backward to medieval times would have the average woman beginning to menstruate in her early thirties, an age not much younger than the life expectancy in those times. Had this been the case, our species would have become extinct, or at least "endangered," because women's reproductive years would have been comparatively few. Writers from this period make references to menarche typically occurring somewhere between the fifteenth and twentieth year of life: the historian Quarinonium, writing in 1610, says that Austrian peasant girls seldom menstruate before their seventeenth, eighteenth, or even twentieth years.

If teenage puberty was a fact of life even in medieval times, something must have happened more recently to decrease the age of onset. The best guess is that that "something" is a higher level of nutrition and health. The available data show that the age of menarche began to get earlier at about the time of the Industrial Revolution, a period associated with an increasing standard of living and advances in medical science.

Cross-cultural data also suggest that better nutrition is related to earlier maturation. Girls growing up in countries or regions with adequate diets tend to begin menstruating earlier than those with less nutritious diets. Similarly, earlier menarche has been associated with higher social class, fewer children in the family, and living in urban rather than rural areas—all of which may reflect nutritional status.

If improved nutrition and the corresponding decrease in illness and disease are responsible for the trend toward earlier puberty in the past century, the trend should level off when people are nourished at an optimal level. There is some evidence that this is occurring in industrialized countries. The average age of menarche is becoming more similar from country to country. Where major variations exist, there also appear to be large differences in nutrition and the general level of health care. In New Guinea, for example, two highland tribes show ages at menarche of 17.6 and 18.1 years.

Does this mean that in the future all youth will begin puberty at the same age? It's unlikely. There are other sources of variation that appear to be unrelated to nutrition and health. For example, girls living at lower elevations menstruate earlier than those of similar socioeconomic status living at higher elevations.

Genetic factors also play a role. By comparing identical and fraternal twins, we see the impact of heredity when diet is presumably controlled. Identical twins typically differ in age at menarche by about two months (a minimal difference, attributable to slight differences in birth weight), while fraternal twins differ by about eight months. In addition, girls in countries with differing economic levels sometimes show the reverse of what we would expect if nutrition alone determined the age at menarche. One study found that Chinese girls, even those who were very poor, menstruated earlier than several different groups of much wealthier Europeans. Genetic factors currently account for only about 10 to 15 percent of the variation in age at menarche, a proportion that is increasing as growing uniformity of nutrition and health eliminates other variations.

What initiates the onset of puberty? Rose Frisch and Roger Revelle at Harvard have found that menarche occurs at a relatively constant weight in girls. Similarly, they have found that the adolescent growth spurt begins at relatively constant weights for boys and girls. Though the spurt occurs two years later in boys than in girls, and at a higher weight, it begins at a similar metabolic level for both groups. Frisch and Revelle speculate that attainment of a critical metabolic rate triggers the physiological processes of puberty. New data from Frisch suggest that for menarche to begin and to continue, fat must make up about 17 percent of body weight. Thus, both teenage anorexics (loss of appetite) whose weight drops precipitously and female athletes in certain sports may become **amenorrheic** (abnormal absence or suppression of menstrual discharge).

The Frisch and Revelle explanation is intriguing and does fit much of the existing information. Some researchers, however, remain skeptical; they note that causality has not been shown and that alternative explanations are possible.

Defining what puberty is has complicated the search for its "trigger." Puberty is not a single, sudden event, but part of a slowly unfolding process beginning at conception. We know when a young person is going through puberty, but pinpointing the onset and cessation of the process is more difficult. Except for menarche, which occurs relatively late in the process, there is no single event heralding puberty. In boys, the first

seminal emission ("wet dream") and the first whiskers are events that could be used to mark its arrival. Both may go unnoticed.

Pubertal changes, however, are well defined: there is a spurt in growth as well as clear changes in secondary sex characteristics, endocrine levels and processes, and other physiological factors. But these are all gradual processes. The gradual nature of puberty has made it difficult to study its causes.

Further complicating the study of what initiates puberty is that several different characteristics are changing and they do not all change together. For example, the development of reproductive capacities and the adolescent growth spurt have slightly different hormonal determinants, and may proceed at different rates, but are both components of the pubertal process.

Perhaps the most accurate way of thinking about puberty is that it is a phase in the maturational process over the life span from conception to death. It signals the beginning of reproductive capacity, a capacity that diminishes later in life. In general, reproduction requires a minimal level of nutritional adequacy and general health status; it is the first system to shut down when the body is poorly nourished or diseased.

Our improved health has led to a lengthening of the reproductive years; puberty is coming earlier, and, at the same time, the age when fertility ends is getting later and later. The longer period of reproduction has implications not only for biological processes, but also for social and psychological development.

Information on the social and psychological correlates of puberty is surprisingly meager. In our own research with adolescents, we have begun to examine the impact of pubertal development as a psychological experience, observing the way it affects relationships with peers and parents. When our research is completed, we may know what "growing up faster" really means."

Source: Petersen, 1979, pp. 45–56.

Introduction

In this chapter we will look at the historical background of the concept of adolescence and describe important physical changes in height, weight, and sexual characteristics. We will also review psychological changes that accompany physical development, as well as changes in temperament and interests that may be genetically influenced. The evaluation of cognitive development focuses on Piaget's stage of formal operational thought and the development of social cognition. We will also cover the role of work in adolescent development.

Historical Perspective

Ideas about adolescence were speculative before the nineteenth and twentieth centuries. G. Stanley Hall (1844–1924) was the first individual to write about adolescence from a scientific perspective.

G. Stanley Hall

Most historians label G. Stanley Hall the father of the scientific study of adolescence. Hall's ideas were published in the two-volume set, *Adolescence,* in 1904.

Charles Darwin, the famous evolutionary theorist, had a tremendous impact on Hall's thinking. Hall applied the scientific, biological aspects of Darwin's views to the study of adolescent development. He believed that all development is controlled by genetically determined physiological factors. Environmental influences on development were minimized, particularly in infancy and childhood. Hall did acknowledge that, during adolescence, the environment accounts for more change in development than in earlier age periods. Thus, Hall believed—as we do today—that at least during adolescence, heredity interacts with environmental influences to determine the individual's development.

Hall subscribed to a four-stage approach to development: infancy, childhood, youth, and adolescence. Adolescence is the period of time from about twelve to about twenty-three years of age, or when adulthood is achieved. Hall saw adolescence as the period of *sturm und drang,* which means storm and stress. This label was borrowed from the German writings of Goethe and Schiller, who wrote novels full of idealism, commitments to goals, revolution, passion, and feeling. Hall sensed there was a parallel between the themes of the German authors and the psychological development of adolescents.

According to Hall, the adolescent period of storm and stress is full of contradictions and wide swings in mood and emotion. Thoughts, feelings, and actions oscillate between conceit and humility, goodness and

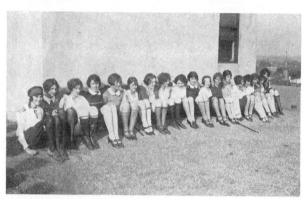

By 1950, the developmental period we refer to as adolescence had come of age.

temptation, and happiness and sadness. One moment the adolescent may be nasty to a peer, yet in the next moment be extremely nice. At one time the adolescent may want to be left alone, but shortly thereafter desire to cling to somebody. In sum, G. Stanley Hall views adolescence as a turbulent time charged with conflict (Ross, 1972).

Studies in different cultures indicate that stress and conflict are not inevitable during adolescent development. The famous anthropologist, Margaret Mead, found that in some societies adolescence is a pleasant period of development (Mead, 1930).

The Period of Adolescence: 1900 to the Present

Between 1890 and 1920 a cadre of psychologists, urban reformers, educators, youth workers, and counselors began to mold the concept of adolescence. At this time, young people, especially boys, no longer were viewed as decadent problem causers, but instead were seen as increasingly passive and vulnerable—qualities previously associated only with the adolescent female. When G. Stanley Hall's book on adolescence was published in 1904, it played a major role in restructuring thinking about adolescents. Hall was saying that while many adolescents appear to be passive, they are experiencing considerable turmoil within.

Norms of behavior for adolescents began to be developed by educators, counselors, and psychologists. The storm-and-stress conception that Hall had created influenced these norms considerably. As a result, adults attempted to impose conformity and passivity on adolescents in the 1900–1920 period. Examples of this conformity can be observed in the encouragement of school spirit and loyalty and hero worship on athletic teams.

During the three decades from 1920–1950, in which adolescents gained a more prominent status in society, they went through a number of complex changes. In the 1920s, the Roaring Twenties atmosphere rubbed off on the behavior of adolescents. Passivity and conformity to adult leadership was replaced by increased autonomy and conformity to peer values. Adults began to model the styles of youth, rather than vice versa. If a new dance came in vogue, the adolescent girl did it first, and her mother learned it from her. Prohibition was the law of the time, but many adolescents drank heavily. More permissive attitudes toward the opposite sex developed, and kissing parties were standard fare. Short skirts even led to a campaign by the YWCA against such abnormal behavior (Lee, 1970).

Just when adolescence was getting to be fun, the Great Depression arrived in the 1930s, followed by World War II in the 1940s. Economic and political concerns of a serious nature replaced the hedonistic adolescent values of the 1920s. Radical protest groups, critical of the government, increased in number during the 1930s, and World War II exposed adolescents to another serious, life-threatening event. Military service provided travel and exposure to other youth from different parts of the United States. This experience promoted a broader perspective on life and a greater sense of independence.

By 1950, the developmental period we refer to as adolescence had come of age—not only did it possess physical and social identity, but legal attention was paid to it as well. Every state by 1950 had developed special laws for youth between the ages of sixteen and eighteen or twenty. Adolescents in the 1950s have been described as the silent generation (Lee, 1970). Life was much better for adolescents in the 1950s than it had been in the 1930s and 1940s. The government was paying for many adolescents' college educations through the GI bill, and television was beginning to become a convenience in most homes. Getting a college degree, the key to a good job, was on the minds of many adolescents during the 1950s—so were getting married, having a family, and settling down to the life of luxury displayed in television commercials.

While the pursuit of higher education persisted among adolescents in the 1960s, it became painfully apparent that many black adolescents not only were being denied a college education, but were receiving an inferior secondary education as well. Racial conflicts in the form of riots and "sit-ins" were pervasive, with college-age adolescents among the most vocal participants.

The political protest of adolescents reached a peak in the late 1960s and early 1970s, when millions of adolescents violently reacted to what they saw as unreasonable American participation in the Vietnam war. As parents watched the 1968 Democratic presidential nominating committee, they not only saw political speeches in support of candidates but also their adolescents fighting with the police, yelling obscenities at adults, and staging sit-ins.

Parents became more concerned in the 1960s about teenage drug use and abuse than in past eras. Sexual permissiveness in the form of premarital sex, cohabituation, and endorsement of previously prohibited sexual conduct also increased.

By the middle 1970s much of the radical protest of adolescents had abated and was replaced by increased concern for an achievement-oriented, upwardly mobile career to be attained through hard work in high school, college, or a vocational training school. Material interests began to dominate adolescent motives again, while ideological challenges to social institutions seemed to become less central. The women's movement has involved the greatest amount of protest in the 1970s. If you carefully read the descriptions of adolescents in America in earlier years, you noticed that much of what was said pertained more to adolescent males than females. The family and career objectives of adolescent females in the 1970s would barely be recognized by the adolescent females of the 1890s and early 1900s. Later in the text much more will be said about the increased participation of females in the work force, including the impact this movement has had on the family and on the female's relationships with males.

Stereotypes of Adolescents

There is complexity and diversity in the thoughts, feelings, and actions of adolescents in any era. Unfortunately, many negative **stereotypes** of adolescents have developed, even in the face of contradictory evidence.

A study by Daniel Yankelovich (1974) indicates that many such stereotypes about youth are false. Yankelovich compared the attitudes of adolescents with those of their parents about different values, life styles, and codes of personal conduct. There was little or no difference in the attitudes of the adolescents and their parents toward self-control, hard work, saving money, competition, compromise, legal authority, and private property. There was a substantial difference between the adolescents and their parents when their attitudes

In any era, there is complexity and diversity in the thoughts, feelings, and actions of adolescents.

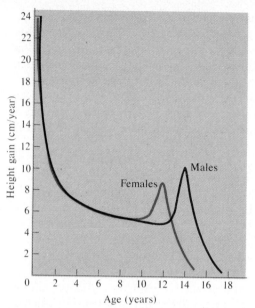

Figure 13.1 Typical individual growth curves for height in boys and girls. These curves represent the height of the typical boy and girl at any given age.

toward religion were sampled (89 percent of the parents said that religion was important to them, compared to only 66 percent of the adolescents). But note that even a majority of the adolescents subscribed to the belief that religion is important.

Joseph Adelson (1979) stresses that far too many stereotypes about adolescents exist—many of which, he says, are based on the visible, rebellious adolescents of the 1960s. Adelson points out that there is an adolescent "generalization gap" rather than a "generation gap," meaning that widespread generalizations have developed based on information about a limited set of adolescents. Adelson points out that one of the reasons such stereotypes have been accepted perhaps more readily than for other developmental periods is the weak research base from which we can make generalizations about adolescence. He mentions, for example, that in searching for information about the psychological impact of a young girl's first menstruation, he could find hardly any research information, even though clinicians and counselors report that such a developmental milestone seems to affect the psychological relationship between mother and daughter.

There has been a tendency to study the abnormalities and deviancies of adolescence more than the normalities. Consider the images and descriptions of adolescents that come to your mind when you think about this group—rebellious, in conflict, impulsive, faddish, and so forth. Adelson (1979) argues, just as Yankelovich (1974) does, that the majority of adolescents are not experiencing a generation gap any more than the adolescents of any other era. Most adolescents do not experience intense turmoil or deep emotional disturbances. Neither are they completely controlled by their immediate impulses; nor do they totally reject parental values.

Physical Development

There are many biological factors that distinguish the period of adolescence. Some of the most important physical changes that signal the beginning of the adolescence period were described in the prologue. Next, we will discuss further the onset of puberty by evaluating changes in height, weight, and sexual characteristics, early and late maturation, and the probable role of genetics in temperament and interests.

Height and Weight

As they undergo the adolescent growth spurt, both boys and girls make rapid gains in height and weight. But, as is indicated in figure 13.1, the growth spurt for girls occurs approximately two years earlier than for boys. The growth spurt in girls begins at approximately ten and one-half and lasts for about two years. During this time period, girls increase in height by about three and

"Why don't you grow up?"

one-half inches per year. The growth spurt for boys usually begins at about twelve and one-half years of age and also lasts for approximately two years. Boys usually grow about four inches per year in height during this growth spurt (Faust, 1977; Tanner, 1966, 1970). These averages do not reflect the fairly wide range of time within which the adolescent growth spurt begins. Girls may start the growth spurt as early as age seven and one-half or as late as age eleven and one-half, while boys may begin as early as age ten and one-half or as late as age sixteen (Faust, 1977; Tanner, 1970).

Boys and girls who are shorter or taller than their peers before adolescence are likely to remain so during adolescence (e.g., Tanner, 1970). In our society, there is a stigma attached to short boys and tall girls. At the beginning of the adolescent period, girls tend to be as tall or taller than boys their age, but by the end of the junior high years most boys have caught up or, in many cases, even surpassed girls in height. And even though height in the elementary school years is a good predictor of height later in adolescence, there is still room for the individual's height to change in relation to the height of his or her peers. As much as 30 percent of the height of late adolescents is unexplained by height in the elementary school years (Tanner, 1970).

The rate at which adolescents gain weight follows approximately the same developmental timetable as the rate at which they gain height. Marked weight gains coincide with the onset of puberty. During early adolescence, girls tend to outweigh boys, but by about age fourteen, just as with height, boys begin to surpass girls (e.g., Faust, 1977; Tanner, 1970).

It is important to remember that these growth curves represent averages. The wide age range during which the features of the adolescent growth spurt appear suggests the importance of considering both individual and cultural differences in physical development.

Obesity and Malnutrition
While weight gain in adolescence is associated with the skeletal change in height, many other factors also influence weight. An increase in weight can be due to an increase in the fat content of the adolescent's body. Only about 5 percent of all young adolescents are obese, but by the time they fully reach adolescence, the number increases to 15 percent (Nutrition National Canada Survey, 1973).

Obesity may be defined as weighing more than 20 percent over normal skeletal and physical requirements. For the most part, this is indicated by an excess of fat content in the body. Obesity is influenced by a number of factors, including diet, hormones, and exercise. As a rule, lean body weight increases between the ages of ten and twenty, but the extent to which lean body mass characterizes the adolescent is influenced extensively by energy input (nutrition) and energy output (physical activity and exercise) (Parizkova, 1970).

In one investigation of nutritional intake during adolescence (Maresh & Beal, 1970), data were collected from 100 youth in Denver, Colorado. The peak of nutritional intake during adolescence occurred in the thirteen-to-fifteen age range for girls and at about eighteen years of age for boys. Carbohydrates supplied about 47 to 48 percent of calories, fat about 38 to 39 percent, and protein about 14 percent. Again, remember that these figures are averages and that they can vary greatly when energy output is changed.

It is also important to note that the relationship between nutritional input and energy output is regulated to a great extent by the biological mechanism known as the **basal metabolism rate,** or **BMR.** The basal metabolism rate is defined as the minimum amount of energy a person uses in a state of rest. To a considerable extent, BMR is genetically determined (although it can be regulated, within limits, through exercise or drugs). Adolescents with a high basal metabolism rate can eat almost anything and not get fat, while adolescents with a low BMR must constantly monitor their food intake to keep from gaining weight.

As indicated in figure 13.2, an individual's BMR continuously drops from age eleven to age twenty (from then until old age, it begins to level out). Male adolescents generally have a slightly higher BMR than females. As a young adolescent grows older, then the basal metabolism rate drops but food intake does not usually decrease. This explains why there are fewer fat

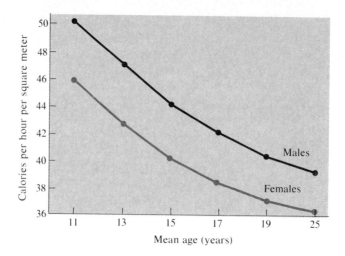

Figure 13.2 Basal metabolism rates in adolescent males and females.

young teenagers than fat older teenagers. But even though BMR exerts powerful control over weight gain and weight loss, energy intake and output still have strong influences on weight.

The adolescent's body fat develops through excess calories, regardless of whether the food source is carbohydrate, fat, or protein. Put simply, adolescents who eat less and exercise more are not as fat as those who eat more and exercise less. Many health experts point out that the average adolescent's high rate of food intake is mismatched with the sedentary life many adolescents lead (e.g., Mayer, 1968).

Information collected at a Massachusetts camp for adolescent girls indicated that the obese females were actually eating less than the girls of normal weight, but that when they exercised, the obese girls exerted less physical energy than the girls of normal weight, (Mayer, 1968) Activity charts computed on the girls suggested that the obese girls were just as likely to participate in sports and other physical activities at the camp. But a critical difference between the physical activity levels of the two groups of girls indicated that the obese girls did not exercise as vigorously as the normal-weight girls did. The fat adolescent girls played tennis, went swimming, and played volleyball, but they moved very little and very lethargically when they participated. When a special camera was set up to provide details about their movements, the films indicated that more than 50 percent of the time in all physical activities, the obese girls were essentially motionless.

It appears that just asking youth whether they engage in physical activities does not tell the whole picture of energy expenditure—the *intensity* of the physical activity seems to be most important in weight reduction. When intense physical activity is combined with reduced or even stable nutritional intake, adolescents lose weight.

While obesity is a major problem for many youth in the United States, malnutrition caused by starvation and/or infection is not. However, there are areas of the world where malnutrition is a major health problem. In the Bayambang area of the Philippines, for example, Keith Bailey (1970) reported that 19 percent of the ten- to-twelve-year-olds could be classified as malnourished. To determine which children suffered from malnutrition, Bailey used the Boston growth chart, which defines malnutrition as a state in which the individual weighs two-thirds of standard or average body weight. When malnutrition exists for prolonged periods of time, it retards physical growth and has even been linked with depression of cognitive growth.

The Development of Sexual Characteristics during Adolescence

The development of sexual characteristics is a dominant feature of adolescence. Sexual characteristics can be divided into two kinds: primary and secondary. **Primary sexual characteristics** are related to the external and internal sex organs. **Secondary sexual characteristics** include features that accentuate the anatomical distinction between girls and boys. These features are closely linked with male and female hormone systems. Both primary and secondary sexual characteristics are biologically determined.

Male Primary Sexual Characteristics

The penis, scrotum, and scrotal sac are the most noticeable parts of the adolescent male's sexual anatomy (see fig. 13.3). The adolescent male shows the greatest degree of curiosity about his penis. This organ serves several important functions involving reproduction, elimination of body wastes, and sexual pleasure.

Some penises are circumcised. Circumcision is a process in which the foreskin of the penis is surgically removed—this process is now practiced around the world and is done within the first few days of life on

Figure 13.3   Male sexual anatomy.

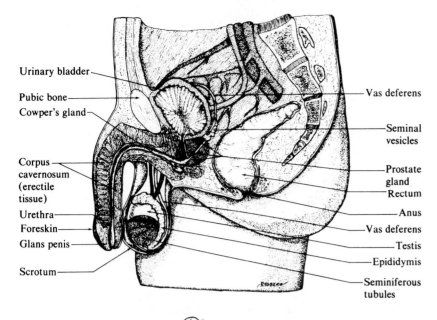

Urinary bladder

Pubic bone

Cowper's gland

Corpus cavernosum (erectile tissue)

Urethra

Foreskin

Glans penis

Scrotum

Vas deferens

Seminal vesicles

Prostate gland

Rectum

Anus

Vas deferens

Testis

Epididymis

Seminiferous tubules

Figure 13.4   Female sexual anatomy.

Ovary

Fallopian tube

Uterus

Cervix

Vagina

Clitoris

Inner labia

Outer labia

Urinary bladder

Urethra

Rectum

Anus

most male infants born in the United States. Circumcision is performed primarily for hygienic reasons in the United States, but in many other cultures the foreskin is removed as part of a ritual in the youth's development. In some cultures, circumcision is performed as evidence that the young boy has now become a man. Through such a rite de passage, the young adolescent shows he can withstand severe pain and is ready for the responsibilities of manhood.

The average size of the penis by the end of adolescence is between three and four inches when flaccid and between five and seven inches when erect. Contrary to common belief, the size of a penis is not linked with the adolescent's body build or skin color. Furthermore, some penises that are small, compared to other penises, when flaccid may be just as large as others when erect.

Female Primary Sexual Characteristics

The major external sex organs of the adolescent female consist of the mons veneris, or pubis, the inner lips, the outer lips, the clitoris, and the vaginal opening (see fig 13.4). During puberty, the mons veneris area becomes covered with pubic hair.

An important female sexual characteristic to be detailed here is the **menstrual cycle.** The function of the menstrual cycle, which is controlled by the hormonal system, is to prepare the lining of the uterus for the possible arrival of a fertilized egg. If no egg arrives, the lining breaks down and is discharged through the opening in the vagina. This emission process is known as menstrual bleeding or menstruation. When bleeding has stopped, the whole cycle repeats itself as the uterus again prepares for the arrival of a fertilized egg. Fertilization is possible only in the first twenty-four hours or so after ovulation. If the egg does not encounter any sperm during this brief time span, it dies.

The menstrual cycle usually repeats itself every twenty-eight to thirty-five days, although at the onset of puberty the cycle often occurs in irregular fashion. (The second menstruation, for example, may be much farther away from the first than a month.) Biologists, psychologists, and sociologists have divided the menstrual cycle into various phases. One such categorization is: *menstruation* (days one to five), *ovulation* (between days seven and twenty-one—the majority of ovulations occur between days nine and eighteen and peak from day twelve to day sixteen), and *premenstruation* (days twenty-two to the beginning of menstruation). Hormone secretions peak at about days twenty-two to twenty-four of the menstrual cycle in most females. The possibility that the menstrual cycle and its phases are linked with personality fluctuations in females is now being investigated. More details about the relation of such biological cycles to personality will be presented when we discuss physical development in adulthood.

Secondary Sexual Characteristics
Secondary sexual characteristics begin to appear during puberty as a result of hormonal changes in both boys and girls. By the time their physical growth is completed, adolescents undergo marked changes in appearance. There is great variation in the amount of time it takes these secondary sexual characteristics to develop. In some adolescents, the changes occur drastically and are completed within one or two years, while in others, the characteristics take as long as ten years to fully develop.

Researchers have found that male sexual characteristics develop in the following order: increase in size of testicles and penis, appearance of straight pubic hair, minor voice changes, first ejaculation (the first ejaculation usually occurs through masturbation or during sleep—the so-called "wet dream"), appearance of kinky pubic hair, onset of maximum growth, growth of axillary hair (in armpits), more detectable voice changes, and growth of facial hair (e.g., Faust, 1977; Garrison, 1968).

Adolescent females experience the following sequence of physical changes in puberty. First, either the breasts enlarge, or pubic hair appears. Later some hair will appear in the armpits. As these changes occur, the female grows in height, and her hips become wider than her shoulders. Fatty tissue in and encircling the breasts, shoulders, and hips creates a more rounded appearance in the adolescent female. Her first menstruation, referred to as menarche, indicates that sexual maturity

is near. Initially, her menstrual cycles may be very irregular, and even for the first several years she may not be ovulating in every cycle—in other words, it may be several years after her period begins that she becomes fertile. There is no exaggerated enlargement of the larynx in females during puberty and, hence, no voice change comparable to that occurring in adolescent males (e.g., Faust, 1977; Haeberle, 1978).

By the end of puberty, the female adolescent's breasts have become fully rounded and serve as the most obvious external female sexual characteristic. The breasts do not produce milk, though, until after pregnancy.

Sex Hormones
The development of sexual characteristics during puberty is regulated by a special set of glands. The functioning of these glands is often less noticeable than that of other glands in the adolescent's body. This is because the glands involved in the development of sexual anatomy are ductless glands that dispense their secretions directly into the bloodstream. They are called the **endocrine glands.** (The glands that are more obvious to us are called the **exocrine glands** because they send their secretions out through ducts. These secretions, which can easily be observed, include saliva, sweat, and breast milk.) The secretions of endocrine glands are referred to as **hormones.** Hormones often regulate organs that are far from where the secretions are first emitted.

The endocrine glands that are directly responsible for secreting sex hormones are the pituitary gland and the male and female gonads (or sex glands). The pituitary gland, located at the base of the brain, is sometimes called the master gland because it regulates a number of other glands. The sex glands—the ovaries in the female and the testicles in the male—produce gonadal hormones, which come in two distinct types: **androgens** (which mature primarily in males) and **estrogens** (which mature mainly in females). In addition, the female sex glands produce another hormone, known as **progesterone,** which is important in the adolescent female's reproductive capability. By the time boys and girls have completed the pubertal cycle their bodies contain both estrogens and androgens. However, estrogens dominate the hormonal production of the female sex glands while androgens dominate in males. Androgens and estrogens play critical roles in the sexual maturation of adolescents.

Early versus Late Maturation
John Money and his colleagues (e.g., Lewis, Money, & Bobrow, 1977) have used sex-hormone and sex-organ development as the major criteria for defining extended pubertal delay. For some of his subjects there was concomitant delay in skeletal growth, but in other instances skeletal growth was not stunted. Recall that

Early or late maturation has a significant influence on the personality and social behavior of adolescents.

both the pituitary and sex glands produce hormones that trigger the physical changes of puberty. In the complex interchange of the pituitary and sex glands, it is possible for skeletal growth to be normal while sex-organ development is slowed down. This appeared to be the case for some of Money's subjects.

The indicator that has been used to define early and late maturation in most studies is skeletal age. Many of the data used to support conclusions about the effects of early and late maturation during adolescence have been collected as part of a longitudinal growth study at the University of California (Jones, 1938; Jones, 1965, 1967; Jones & Bayley, 1950; Jones & Mussen, 1958; Mussen & Jones, 1957, 1958). One way in which skeletal age is measured in these investigations is to take X rays of hand and knee bones.

In most instances, early or late maturation has a significant influence on the personality and social behavior of adolescents (e.g., Jones & Bayley, 1950; Mussen & Jones, 1957, 1958). The upshot of the investigations concerning early and late maturation is that boys who mature early in adolescence (as measured by their skeletal growth) perceive themselves more positively and are more successful in peer relations than their late-maturing counterparts. Both peers and adults rated the early-maturing boys as physically more attractive, more composed, and more socially sophisticated than the late-maturing boys. Most of these investigations focused on the self-perceptions of boys in early and middle adolescence (about twelve to seventeen years of age).

In another investigation, late maturation has been implicated as an important factor in the personality of the college male (e.g., Weatherley, 1964). Also, the Berkeley longitudinal study found that some of the psychological characteristics associated with early maturation (such as dominance, independence, and self-control) were still apparent even when the individuals were in their thirties (Jones & Mussen, 1958).

Early maturation generally seems to have positive psychological benefits for adolescent girls as well (Jones & Mussen, 1958). But the results are not quite as clear-cut as they are for boys. For example, Margaret Faust (1960) has found that girls who are developmentally advanced in elementary school have less prestige among their age-mates, but in the junior high school years, early physical maturity is an advantage. However, even in the sixth grade, the more physically advanced girls have more prestige with adults and older friends than their less physically mature classmates have. Thus, it appears that at least in the junior high school years or later, early maturity benefits the social behavior of both girls and boys.

The possibility that early maturation may force premature identity formation has been investigated by Mary Cover Jones (1965) and Harvey Peskin (1967). Peskin found that adolescents who mature early tend to respond in an inhibitory and rigid manner. He, like Jones, believes that early maturers may be pushed into decisions about their identity too early. By contrast, those adolescents who mature late may have more time to handle their physical changes, and therefore may be more flexible in identity formation.

Jones (1965) reported that when late maturers were followed into their thirties, they were less likely to have familial, vocational, and marital commitments. However, an alternative interpretation of such findings is that delayed maturers also are having difficulty establishing an identity; while the early maturers may reach a "false" identity that comes too early in their development, the late maturers do not seem to attain an identity, even by the time they are thirty or thirty-five. Since comparisons with individuals who matured "on schedule" during adolescence were not made, a clear interpretation of these data is not possible. Researchers need to include a control group of adolescents who mature on schedule in future studies of early and late maturation.

It should be clear by now that the biological development of the adolescent cannot be ignored. Biological cycles apparently influence the development of various organs and glands; biology plays a critical role in the maturation of sexual characteristics; and biological changes have important implications for the psychological development of the adolescent.

Sexual Behavior and Attitudes

Parents are concerned about their adolescents' sexual behavior and often overreact and think their adolescents are much more sexually active than they really are. Sexual barriers in adolescence are being broken down, and adolescents in the United States today are not as inhibited about sexual behavior as they once were. In earlier eras in the United States, a young person's marital partner was often chosen by his or her parents, and adolescents were prohibited from spending time alone with each other prior to marriage. Still, sexual behavior among adolescents in the United States is far less permissive than in some cultures today.

Adolescence is a time when exploratory and experimental sex play turns into more purposeful sexual behavior. However, many adolescents, because of social and religious standards, stop short of sexual intercourse. Even when they find a partner they would sincerely like to have sexual intercourse with, they often restrict themselves to "petting." For the majority of adolescents, the main sexual outlet is masturbation. And as a rule, adolescent females are more sexually inhibited than adolescent males are. Most adolescent girls are not encouraged to acknowledge their sexual needs. While they are taught to make themselves attractive, their own sexual feelings often go undiscussed. Thus, the sexual drive of adolescent girls often tends toward fantasies about the future—becoming a bride, a lover, and so forth.

"That's not the way we learned it in Sex Ed, Dad. Mrs. Thompson said that ..."

By contrast, the sexual fantasies of adolescent boys focus more specifically on sexual activity itself. Erwin Haeberle (1978) concluded that it is only toward the end of adolescence that males begin to see sex as an important component of human communication and that females discover the robust potential of their bodies.

Self-Stimulation

The most extensive data collected about adolescent sexual behavior are those reported by Alfred Kinsey (Kinsey, Pomeroy, & Martin, 1948). According to Kinsey, there is a rapid increase in the incidence of masturbation for boys between the ages of thirteen and fifteen. By age fifteen, for example, 82 percent of all boys interviewed had masturbated. Girls tend to begin masturbating later, and do not do so as often as boys. For example, by the age of fifteen, only 25 percent of all girls have masturbated to orgasm while it is estimated that the figure is close to 100 percent for boys of the same age (Haeberle, 1978). There also is evidence that the frequency of masturbation among adolescent boys decreases during periods when they are having sexual intercourse, while it increases for girls under such circumstances (Sorensen, 1973).

The sexual fantasies of adolescent boys focus specifically on sexual activity.

Male adolescents today do not seem to feel as guilty about masturbating as they once did, although interview data collected in the 1970s suggest that they still feel embarrassed and defensive about it (Sorensen, 1973). Consider the following comments, though, taken from a popular handbook in 1913 entitled *What a Boy Should Know* (Schofield & Vaughan-Jackson, 1913). These comments reveal the stigma attached to masturbation in another era.

Whenever unnatural emissions are produced . . . he will be more easily tired. . . . He will probably look pale and pasty, and he is lucky if he escapes indigestion and getting his bowels confined, both of which will probably give him spots and pimples on his face. . . . The results on the mind are the more severe and more easily recognized. . . . His wits are not so sharp. . . . A boy like this is a poor thing to look at. . . .

. . . The effect of self-abuse on a boy's character always tends to weaken it, and in fact, to make him untrustworthy, unreliable, untruthful, and probably dishonest. (pp. 30–42)

As Janet Hyde (1979) points out, masturbation in past eras was thought to cause everything from warts to insanity. Today, as few as 15 percent of adolescents believe that masturbation is wrong.

Not only do adolescents (particularly males) masturbate, they also are prone to engage in frequent flights of sexual fantasy. As we said, the sexual fantasies of adolescent males usually involve actual sexual activity, while the sexual fantasies of adolescent females are more socially oriented. The adolescent boy may fantasize about having an orgy with a number of girls. He may daydream about having sex with a teacher. Such

daydreaming does not mean there is anything sick or wrong with the teenager—he also has flights of fantasy about being a millionaire, a sports hero, and so forth. David Elkind states that such daydreaming and egocentrism are typical of the adolescent, particularly the young adolescent.

Heterosexual Contact

From the middle to the end of the adolescent years, heterosexual behavior increases rapidly. Boys and girls, becoming young men and young women, are not as likely to be satisfied with "petting," as they were earlier. Instead, they are more inclined to engage in sexual intercourse.

The major sex surveys (e.g., Kinsey, et al., 1948; Hunt, 1974) have not included developmental data about the onset of sexual intercourse. However, it does appear that by the time they are twenty-five, almost all males have engaged in sexual intercourse at least once (e.g., Hyde, 1979). In contrast by the time they are nineteen, only about 46 percent of females have had sexual intercourse (Kantner & Zelnik, 1972).

One study indicated that an increase in premarital sexual intercourse among adolescents nineteen or younger had occurred between 1971 and 1976 (Zelnik & Kantner, 1977). Today, about 55 percent of adolescent females aged nineteen or younger have had premarital sexual intercourse. And according to Hunt's survey, approximately 70 to 80 percent of females aged eighteen to twenty-four have engaged in premarital sex. Clearly, it is no longer the norm in our culture for adolescents to remain virgins until they are married. More specific details about sex differences in sexual activity for thirteen- to fifteen- and sixteen- to nineteen-year-old adolescents are presented in table 13.1.

It is generally accepted that premarital sexual intercourse can be meaningful and educational for mature adolescents, usually those in late adolescence. However, because of the generally poor quality of sex education in the United States, many adolescents are ill equipped to handle the psychological ramifications of such experiences. Adolescents may attempt intercourse without knowing exactly what to do or how to satisfy their partners, leading to frustration and fears of sexual inadequacy. In addition, many adolescents are not well informed about contraceptives. Only about one out of five unmarried female adolescents who have sexual intercourse use birth control pills, and the majority of sexually active adolescents never use any contraceptives whatsoever (Jessor & Jessor, 1975). Even by late adolescence, only 60 percent of all females use any contraceptive method (Zelnik & Kantner, 1977). Perhaps

Table 13.1
The Heterosexual Activity of American Adolescents

Group	Total	Boys	Girls	Ages 13–15	Ages 16–19	White	Nonwhite
Virgins *(adolescents who have not had sexual intercourse)*	*48%*	*41%*	*55%*	*63%*	*36%*	*55%*	*49%*
Sexually inexperienced (virgins with no experience in any type of sexual activity)	22%	20%	25%	39%	9%	25%	23%
Sexual beginners (virgins who have actively or passively experienced some type of sexual activity)	17%	14%	19%	12%	21%	20%	9%
Unclassified virgins (virgins who could not be classified in the above groups)	9%	7%	11%	12%	6%	9%	17%
Nonvirgins *(adolescents who have had sexual intercourse one or more times)*	*52%*	*59%*	*45%*	*37%*	*64%*	*45%*	*51%*
Serial monogamists (nonvirgins having a sexual relationship with only one person)	21%	15%	28%	9%	31%	19%	14%
Sexual adventurers (nonvirgins freely moving from one sexual partner to another)	15%	24%	6%	10%	18%	11%	18%
Inactive nonvirgins (nonvirgins who have not had sexual intercourse for more than one year)	12%	13%	10%	15%	10%	11%	14%
Unclassified nonvirgins (nonvirgins who could not be classified in the above groups)	4%	7%	1%	3%	5%	4%	5%
Currently intercourse-experienced (nonvirgins who have had sexual intercourse during the preceding month)	31%	30%	33%	15%	45%	24%	31%
Noncurrent intercourse-experienced (nonvirgins who have not had sexual intercourse during the preceding month)	21%	29%	12%	22%	19%	21%	20%

more surprising, a majority of adolescent females reveal a complete misconception about when during the menstrual cycle they are most likely to become pregnant.

Even the careful use of contraceptives does not necessarily make sexual intercourse safe and harmless for adolescents. For example, they may encounter legal difficulties—most states require that an adolescent be at least sixteen to eighteen years of age to perform sexual intercourse; otherwise they are engaging in "fornication." If both adolescents are under age, they may be treated as delinquents. If only the girl is under age, a charge of statutory rape may be filed against the male. Admittedly, these laws are rarely invoked against teenagers, but sometimes law enforcement agencies use them as a means of confining so-called undesirables.

Contraction of a sexually transmitted disease is another danger involved in having sexual intercourse. Until recently, the two major sexually transmitted diseases are gonorrhea and syphilis. Of all age groups, the most affected individuals are those between fifteen to thirty (Carroll & Miller, 1982).

Another infectious disease common among adolescents is mononucleosis, or the "kissing disease." While mononucleosis remains somewhat of a mystery disease, it appears that the causative agent is a member of the herpes virus group that causes fever blisters. The disease is probably spread through the saliva. Mononucleosis is characterized by a sore throat, swollen lymph glands, and prolonged fatigue that may last for several weeks. There is no treatment available to cure it, although the body tends to develop immunity toward it after having it.

While at one time gonorrhea, syphilis, and mononucleosis were the most feared venereal diseases, in the 1980s an incurable virus, *herpes,* has threatened to undo the sexual revolution that has characterized the past two decades. The truth about life in the 1980s is that if you are going to have sex, you risk the chance of getting herpes. Approximately 20 million Americans have contracted genital herpes (including approximately one out of every thirty-five adolescents). Herpes causes general lesions and once it penetrates the skin it multiplies rapidly. First symptoms are usually a tingling or itching feeling. Blisters are likely to follow within two to fifteen days after infection. The first episode lasts for two to three weeks on the average, with subsequent bouts often less severe and not as long lasting. Ninety-five percent of the herpes victims are Caucasian and the majority are from middle-class backgrounds. The majority of victims are between twenty and thirty-nine years of age.

Usually when you get a virus your body produces antibodies that destroy the invading virus. The antibodies stay in your bloodstream for the rest of your life (such as with measles, mumps, and chicken pox) and spontaneously attack the virus when it appears . . . not so for herpes. The antibodies that combat help the individual recover but unfortunately they don't completely kill the virus. Rather, following the first attack, the virus retreats to the nerve cells at the base of the spine where it stays dormant for a few weeks to a lifetime. During new attacks, the virus travels down the nerve fibers to the genitalia and creates a new crop of painful blisters. Females need to be especially cautious since herpes has been linked to an increased incidence of cervical cancer—five to eight times more than females without herpes—and, herpes is extraordinarily dangerous—often fatal—to babies born when their mothers are having a herpes attack.

Some important questions will have to be answered before a cure for herpes is found. Why can the virus persist in our bodies? Why does it become dormant? Why does it get reactivated? And, how does our body attack the recurrances?

Genetic Influences on Temperament and Interests

Contemporary psychology often has left the impression that development is primarily the result of forces external to the adolescent. Parents have been blamed for rearing adolescents with obnoxious social behaviors; schools have been criticized for turning learning and exploration into dull activities; and society at large has been indicted for creating an empty value system, an unfair distribution of educational and work opportunities, and an arbitrary social hierarchy. Yet mounting evidence and theory suggest that the adolescent may have inherited predispositions toward certain types of behavior. One powerful illustration of this point involves individual temperament.

Temperament

At birth, children are psychologically different, despite their equal status under the law. Some children explore their environment eagerly and for great lengths of time; others do not. Some are extremely active, moving their arms, legs, and mouths ceaselessly; others are inactive. Some react to slight changes in the environment around them with concern and discomfort; others remain peaceful and calm. Some older infants respond warmly and openly to people; others fuss and fret. All of these characteristics are believed to be part of a child's inborn emotional temperament.

Differences in activity level seem to have a strong genetic component. Lee Willerman (1973) asked the mothers of several hundred twins ranging in age from one to thirteen years to rate each child's degree of activity (none, some, very much) in such everyday situations as eating, watching television, playing, sleeping, and studying. The families were drawn from several midwestern states, and ninety-three mothers responded. By classifying the twins as identical or fraternal and treating the results of the older children separately from the younger ones, a heritability quotient ranging from .62 to .77 was obtained.

Is a particular characteristic that is strongly influenced by heredity a stable trait? Does it appear continuously throughout childhood and adolescence? For example, are active, extroverted children always active and extroverted, or might they change during childhood and adolescence? An extensive longitudinal study (Thomas, Chess, & Birch, 1970) conducted with a group of boys and girls in New York City provided some answers to these questions. The study was begun in 1956, so the children are now adults. But because of the inevitable lag between research and the public reports on it, information is available only on their findings from birth to late adolescence.

Thomas and associates set out to describe temperament as broadly as possible and to obtain as much information as they could. To this end, they interviewed the parents of 138 youth from middle-class homes four times a year during the first year of life, twice a year for the next four years, and once a year after that. Interviews ranged over a wide variety of topics (eating, sleeping, playing, meeting new people, interacting with parents and siblings), with the goal of understanding the style of each individual's behavior across many situations.

The identification of temperament becomes more difficult as a child enters the adolescent period. Behavioral characteristics become increasingly influenced by the interaction of temperament, motivation, capability, and special events in life.

The only predictable aspect of the period from infancy through adolescence is that the individual will experience person-environment interaction. Consistency in development comes from continuity over time in both the youth and important aspects of the environment. Changes in development are produced by major changes in the adolescent or in the environment. In box 13.1, Stella Chess and Alexander Thomas (1977) describe three different individuals whose development clearly demonstrates how temperament and environment interact.

Interests

Harold Grotevant, Sandra Scarr, and Richard Weinberg (1977) have suggested that children may be born with certain predispositions toward some interests. This perspective contrasts with the belief of many behaviorists that any child can be trained to become a doctor, lawyer, or Indian chief. Most parents, as well, think that regardless of the abilities their child brings into the world, parental influence can provide their child with the opportunity to become whatever he or she desires.

Grotevant, Scarr, and Weinberg compared the interests of parents with those of their teenagers. In one group the teenagers were adopted, while in the other group the adolescents lived with their biological parents. The families did not differ greatly in terms of income or educational level.

Both the adolescents and their parents were questioned on such matters as whether they were oriented toward pursuits that were "rugged," "creative," or "scientific." There was extensive overlap in the interests of the teenagers and their biological parents, but in the adopted families there was virtually no correspondence between the interests of the adolescents and their parents.

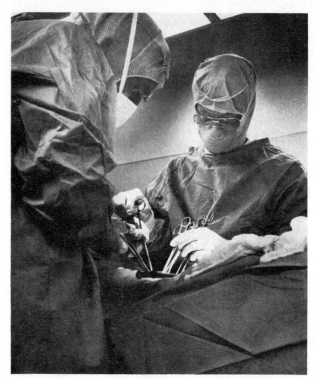

Many researchers have suggested that children may be born with certain predispositions, such as becoming a doctor.

In the biologically related group of adolescents and parents, it appears that the adolescents were drawing some interests from one parent and some from the other. Was this due to genetic transmission only? Not necessarily. It simply suggests that two people who are more alike biologically tend to have more similar interests. They not only share the same genetic pool, but the same environment as well.

Perhaps the most important point, though, is the implication that genes interact with environmental experiences to influence the adolescent's interests. The researchers suggest that no one is born with a gene to be a tennis pro, doctor, painter, or music composer. But one newborn may come into the world with more intelligence than another newborn, plus a predisposition to be more active, sociable, and able to withstand stress than another infant, and these predispositions may make him or her better suited for certain interests and occupations. The important thing for parents to do is to provide experiences that expose the adolescent to a variety of interests. In this way, the adolescent won't be pushed into something that does not fit with his or her skills, which, at least to some degree, are likely inherited.

Next, we see that not only are there dramatic physical changes in adolescence, but that significant cognitive changes take place as well.

Cognitive Development

In this section we will look at Piaget's stage of formal operational thought and see how his ideas have been applied to the education of adolescents. The important emerging field of cognitive development called social cognition and the nature of work and achievement will be described.

Formal Operational Thought

Piaget's formal operational stage of thought comes into play between the ages of eleven and fourteen. By the time the child reaches adolescence, he or she has reached the most advanced stage of thinking possible. Some may argue that reaching adulthood entails many significant cognitive changes. For Piaget, however, these changes are no more than window dressing. A nuclear physicist may engage in a kind of thinking that cannot be matched by the adolescent, but the adolescent and the nuclear physicist differ only in their familiarity with an academic field of inquiry—in the *content* of thought, not in the operations that are brought to bear upon that content (Piaget, 1970).

Most cognitive psychologists now recognize that the onset of adolescence does not necessarily mean that formal operational thought will appear. It even has been demonstrated that significant proportions of college- and middle-aged adults do not use formal operational thought when asked to solve problems (Keating, in press). One view that takes such findings into account is the branch model of adolescent cognitive development, discussed in box 13.2.

The style of problem solving the formal operational thinker uses has often been referred to as deductive-hypothesis testing. Jerome Bruner (1966) and his associates used a modification of the familiar game Twenty Questions in an extensive research project with children of varying ages. The subject is shown a set of forty-two colorful pictures displayed in a rectangular array (six rows of seven pictures each) and is asked to determine which picture the experimenter has in mind by asking only yes or no questions. The object of the game is to select the "correct" picture by asking as few questions as possible. The person who is a deductive-hypothesis tester formulates a plan to propose and test a series of hypotheses, each of which narrows the field of choices considerably. The most effective plan consists in a "halving" strategy; for example, the subject questions, "Is it in the right half of the array?" "Is it in the top half?" and so on. Used correctly, the halving strategy guarantees the questioner the correct solution in seven questions or less, no matter where the correct picture is located in the array. Even if he or she is using a less effective strategy, the deductive-hypothesis tester understands that when the experimenter answers no to one guess, several possibilities are immediately eliminated.

The concrete thinker, by contrast, may persist with questions that test some of the previously eliminated possibilities. For example, the child may have asked whether the correct picture was in row 1 and received the answer no, but later asks whether the correct picture is x, a picture that is in row 1.

The social implications of deductive-hypothesis testing are clear. When the adolescent meets people, abstract hypotheses about what they are like are more amenable to practical verification through the actions and attitudes the people convey. An adolescent boy's belief in the goodness of a friend may be quickly dispelled if he observes the friend being cruel to someone. A concrete thinker would be less open to disenchantment from practical experience.

Box 13.1
Temperament from Infancy through Adolescence

The following descriptions of three individuals traced from infancy through adolescence show how temperament-environment interaction can produce new behavioral patterns at different age periods.

Carl: He requested a discussion with Dr. Chess at the end of his first year in college because he felt depressed and was not coping very well with academic or social matters. He had few friends and said that he had difficulty studying, that he was unable to remember what he had read. By contrast, Carl had been a good student in high school, where he had had a number of friends and many interests. During his interview he did not appear depressed but expressed bewilderment at his situation, saying that it just wasn't like him to be doing so poorly socially and academically.

The background data indicated that during childhood Carl had been one of the most extreme "difficult child" types: he was intense, had negative reactions to new situations, and was slow to adapt to situations even after many exposures to them. This was true whether it was his first bath, his first day at elementary school, or his first shopping trip. Each of these experiences prompted Carl to stormy behavior, such as temper tantrums and shouting. The parents realized that Carl's reactions to his world were not due to their "bad parenting" but instead were part of his temperament. They were patient with him and often gave him considerable time and many opportunities to adapt to new situations that were frustrating to him. As a result, he did not become a behavior "problem," even though the "difficult group" has a higher risk for disturbed development (e.g., Thomas, Chess, & Birch, 1970).

Later on in his elementary and secondary school years, Carl met up with few new situations and in the process was able to develop a positive view of himself. College, however, meant a lot of changes in his life. He now was away from home in unfamiliar situations, with new teachers who placed more complex demands on him, with new peers who were harder to get to know, and with a girl with whom he started living. According to Chess and Thomas, the radically different college experiences reawakened the "difficult child" behavioral reactions and brought Carl in for help.

After only one session, Carl began to get back on a more positive track. He discussed his temperamental pattern with Dr. Chess, including coping mechanisms that he

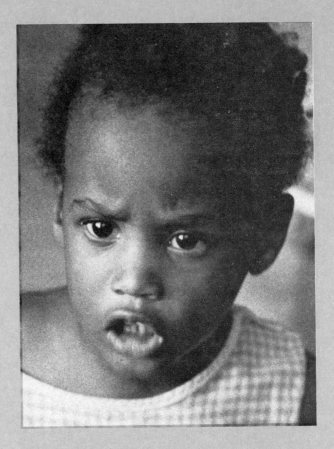

might employ to help him out in social and academic situations. By the end of the academic year, his grades had improved, he broke off the living arrangement with the girl, and he started forcing himself to get more involved in peer group activities.

David: While Carl's temperamental pattern was still apparent in late adolescence, David's temperament was expressed in a different pattern. In early childhood, David was one of the most active boys Chess and Thomas studied. He was always in motion and came across with a friendly and cheerful manner. Unfortunately, however, a considerable number of parental problems surfaced during David's childhood, including a growing sense of competitiveness in his parents. They continually bragged to others about what a superior child David was, although he did not have a superior IQ; any problems David has in school they attributed to poor teaching. As he developed in his elementary and secondary school years, his school

performance and interest in other activities went downhill. The parents totally blamed the school and its teachers. Picking up on his parents' cues that his failures were not his fault, David never developed a critical, evaluative approach to himself: when problems surfaced, he always put the blame—just as his parents did—on someone else. Apathy began to dominate his daily life, and, unfortunately, the attitudes of his parents as well as his own self-insulation and reluctance to take responsibility for his actions led to complete resistance to counseling that might have helped him out of his dilemma.

Nancy: When interviewed at age seventeen, Nancy was bright, alert, and happy. She was doing well in school, had many friends, and a positive relationship with her parents. Her parents did say she was "hot-headed" at times, but they did not believe this caused a great deal of trouble.

Just like Carl, Nancy displayed the "difficult child" syndrome during early childhood, but her parents responded differently to her than Carl's had. By contrast, Nancy's father was very critical of her. He punished her when she didn't adapt well and had rigid expectations for her academic performance. Since Nancy's father ruled the house, her mother went along with his demands, offering Nancy very little support. By the time she entered elementary school, Nancy reacted to the stress with outbursts of temper, hair pulling, and poor peer relations. Her behavioral patterning was severe enough to warrant the diagnosis of neurotic behavior disorder in the moderately severe range. In her early elementary school years she saw a psychotherapist, but something other than therapy triggered marked improvement in her late elementary school years. Nancy was quite talented in drama and music. She began to pursue these interests regularly and won increasingly favorable comments from both her parents and peers. Nancy's father began to reassess his earlier opinion of his daughter as a "bad child," now reading her temper outbursts and negative reactions as signs of a budding artist. Nancy was allowed more time to progress at her own pace, with accompanying positive effects on her self-image and confidence. During her adolescence, she had improved so greatly that there was no evidence of her earlier neurotic behavior.

A final property of formal thinking is the ability to appreciate metaphorical meaning. A metaphor is a figure of speech in which a word or phrase with one literal meaning is used to describe another object or event, suggesting a similarity between the two. A person's faith (like a piece of glass) can be shattered. A ship may *plow* the sea, and a *blanket* of snow may cover the ground. Concrete thinkers find it difficult to understand such metaphorical relations. Consequently, many elementary schoolchildren are puzzled by the meanings of parables and fables (Elkind, 1976).

Again, the social implications are obvious. Metaphor greatly extends the network of symbols that the adolescent can use in thinking about people. It makes possible a host of abstract comparisons between people and nonliving things, people and animals, and people and plants, among others. Coupled with the extended speculation about people and possibilities that comes with adolescents' formal thinking, there is a curious type of egocentrism that also lingers for awhile. Adolescent egocentrism is described next.

The Imaginary Audience of the Adolescent

Adolescents become trapped in the belief that other people who are nearby also share their own thoughts and behavioral perspectives. It is a sense that what is inside their own minds is transparent to anyone who observes them. This partially explains why young adolescents are hypersensitive about how they look and what they say to others. They don't want to offer too many overt clues about themselves because to do so is to reveal their inner selves and reduce their sense of being unique. David Elkind (1976, 1978; Elkind & Bowen, 1980) has dubbed this feeling of transparency to others the **imaginary audience,** and the sense of "fragile uniqueness" the **personal fable.**

Presumably, younger adolescents are more prone to play to an imaginary audience—that is, to be more self-conscious—than older ones because they are less experienced at using formal operational thinking. The egocentric self-consciousness should diminish during the adolescent years. A clever device has been developed to measure this characteristic—a self-inventory questionnaire called the Imaginary Audience Scale (IAS) (Simmons, Rosenberg, & Rosenberg, 1973). The

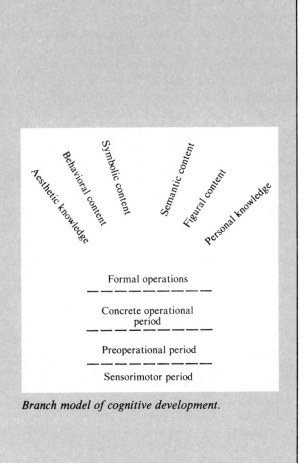

Branch model of cognitive development.

Table 13.2
The Imaginary Audience Scale (IAS)

Instructions: Please read the following stories carefully and assume that the events actually happened to you. Place a check next to the answer that best describes what you would do or feel in the real situation.

AS scale   Let's say some adult visitors came to your school and you were asked to tell them a little bit about yourself.
_____ I would like that.
_____ I would not like that.
_____ I wouldn't care.

AS scale   If you went to a party where you did not know most of the kids, would you wonder what they were thinking about you?
_____ I wouldn't think about it.
_____ I would wonder about that a lot.
_____ I would wonder about that a little.

TS scale   You are sitting in class and have discovered that your jeans have a small but noticeable split along the side seam. Your teacher has offered extra credit toward his/her course grade to anyone who can write the correct answer to a question on the blackboard. Would you get up in front of the class and go to the blackboard, or would you remain seated?
_____ Go to the blackboard as though nothing had happened.
_____ Go to the blackboard and try to hide the split.
_____ Remain seated.

TS scale   Your class is supposed to have their picture taken, but you fell the day before and scraped your face. You would like to be in the picture but your cheek is red and swollen. Would you have your picture taken anyway or stay out of the picture?
_____ Get your picture taken even though you'd be embarrassed.
_____ Stay out of the picture.
_____ Get your picture taken and not worry about it.

Source: Elkind & Bowen, 1980.

items pose situations about hypothetical teenagers who must perform in the presence of an audience and ask actual teenagers how willing they might be to do these things.

Several items like those in table 13.2 were used in the study. Working with children and adolescents ranging from eight to eighteen years of age, the authors found that the twelve-year-olds tested were the most likely to choose the more self-conscious alternatives.

David Elkind (Elkind & Bowen, 1980) distinguished between two facets of the imaginary audience. One centers on a subject's willingness to reveal characteristics of the self that are believed to be stable over time. For example, people probably view their levels of intelligence or features of personality as relatively constant over time. The other facet centers on the person's willingness to reveal characteristics of the self that are believed to vary considerably over time. For example, showing up dressed inappropriately, saying something inappropriate, or getting a bad haircut are all occasional occurrences, not permanent fixtures of the self. Elkind labeled the first phenomenon the **abiding self**

and the latter one the **transient self.** He predicted that adolescent self-consciousness would be more pronounced with items reflecting the concept of the abiding self than for those indicating the transient self. Correspondingly, he predicted that only the abiding self is related to the individual's self-esteem.

Elkind and Bowen constructed two scales (see table 13.2). The AS scale represents the abiding self, while the TS scale represents the transient self. Following pilot work, the authors tested 697 boys and girls in fourth, sixth, eighth, and twelfth grades in a large, middle-class suburban school district. Each child was asked to complete the two scales of imaginary audience along with other scales including a measure of self-esteem and self-concept.

There were two major findings of the study. The first was that both children and adolescents demonstrate relatively independent transient and abiding concepts of self. This independence was shown by the significant but low correlation between the TS and AS scales and by the fact that the AS scale was correlated more highly with measures of self-esteem than was the TS scale. This independence was also shown by the factor analysis, which gave evidence that the items on the two scales loaded on two different factors. It seems reasonable, therefore, to pursue this distinction between the transient and abiding components of self. When, for example, does it appear in the course of development? Our guess is that the two aspects of self do not become differentiated until children attain concrete operations. If this is true, it would suggest that measures of self-concept and self-esteem for preoperational children may have a different significance than they do for children who have attained concrete operations. This hypothesis should, of course, be tested.

The second major finding was that young adolescents were significantly less willing than children or older adolescents to reveal either the transient or the abiding self to an audience. This finding provides additional support for the hypothesis of heightened self-consciousness in early adolescence and for the construct of an imaginary audience during this age period. To the extent that the two subscales are comparable, the data also suggest that young adolescents are a little more self-conscious about their abiding than about their transient selves.

In recent years, psychologists have begun to recognize the appropriateness of separating formal operations into early and late phases. The nature of this dichotomy is discussed next.

Early versus Late Formal Operations

Philip Cowan (1978) has provided the following details to emphasize how important it is to distinguish between early and late formal operations. Early formal operational thought typically comes into play between the ages of twelve to fourteen, and late formal operational thought appears from about fifteen to eighteen years of age. Recall that Piaget's ideas about formal operational thought focus on the development of the adolescent's ability to consider all possible combinations of events and situations when given a problem to solve. In the early formal operational stage, the adolescent begins to see many of the possible combinations necessary to solve a problem, but he or she is not as likely as the late formal operational thinker to start with a plan and organize a search for a solution. In other words, early formal operational thinkers experiment with many different strategies, but they don't seem to have a systematic strategy from the start, as the late formal operational thinker does.

The changing relation between observations and hypotheses also reveals differences in the way the early formal operational thinker pursues a solution to a problem when compared with the late formal operational thinker. Piaget describes significant changes in the way adolescents deal with the relation between observations and hypotheses when tested with a pendulum problem. A weight is placed at the bottom of a string, which is fastened to the top of a rod. The boys and girls are asked to discover what causes the pendulum to move faster or slower. The subjects may change the length of the string, the weight of the object, the height from which they drop it, or the force with which they push it. Only the length of the string, however, influences the speed of oscillation.

The early formal operational thinker goes beyond providing a summary statement about observations; he or she looks for a general hypothesis that will explain what happened. For example, the early formal operational thinker might mention the idea that the length of the string may influence the speed of the pendulum after experimenting with it. But the early formal thinker is hardly ever concerned with trying out ideas that do not influence the pendulum. Consequently, the length of the string usually is not separated from the other variables when the causes of velocity are investigated, and the early formal thinker is left with uncertainty about the validity of the hypothesis. He or she is unable to systematically test ideas against observations.

By the late formal operational stage, the adolescent thinks differently about such matters. Hypotheses are not always derived from the data but are sometimes created at the beginning of the experiment to guide the adolescent's investigation. Also, the late formal operational thinker is not satisfied with just a general statement about cause and effect—he or she searches for something that tells what is *necessary* and what is *sufficient* to account for what has happened. In the pendulum problem, this leads to further separate the weight and length variables to ascertain what the necessary and sufficient causes of velocity are. Is the length of the string acting alone, or is it interacting to produce the effect? The formal operational thinker might design an experiment to test these speculations.

While there have been numerous efforts to apply Piaget's ideas to educational curricula for preschool and elementary schoolchildren, applications to the education of the adolescent have been meager. When Piaget's ideas have been applied to adolescent education, the focus has been on a single underlying theme: that many adolescents are still concrete thinkers and are not as yet formal operational thinkers.

Therefore, the curricula many adolescents are exposed to may be too complex and abstract for them to comprehend. Many adolescents are likely to benefit from instruction based on concrete explanation of different phenomena.

Piaget and Adolescent Education

Philip Cowan (1978) also reasons about why the application of Piaget's ideas to the education of the adolescent have been neglected:

First, those adolescents who do arrive at formal operations function at a level similar to their teachers and the authors of textbooks; it no longer seems necessary to pay attention to qualitative differences in intellectual structure. But the fact that the formal operations stage is divided into early and late substages indicates that there are noticeable differences.

Consider a curriculum area that virtually every adolescent is exposed to during the junior high and high school years—biology. Most biology courses (or at least the majority of the units taught in each of them) are taught in a reasonably formal, straight-lecture format. Classifications of animals and plants are memorized through exposure to the teacher's lectures and the text. Some educational experts believe that such a procedure is not a good approach to teaching the scientific method, or to promoting learning among many adolescents who have not yet reached the stage of formal operational thought. Instead, they believe that improved learning will occur if the adolescents observe and collect organisms from their natural habitats and then relate them to various subjects covered in the course. Through this method, often referrred to as **discovery learning,** the adolescent is forced to restructure his or her concrete way of thinking about the world and to logically categorize events and objects in more formal logical ways (Renner & Stafford, 1972).

Some researchers have compared biology students who learn about animals and plants in this manner with those who learn in the more traditional lecture-text format (e.g., Lawson & Wollman, 1975). By participating in laboratory experiments, collecting data, discussing ideas, and testing out hypotheses, the discovery-learning students far outdistanced their counterparts who learned in more traditional ways.

Recently, Piaget's theory has even provided the conceptual framework for a revision of curriculum at the university level. At the University of Nebraska at Lincoln, a Piagetian-based program labeled ADAPT has been developed for freshman students taking courses in economics, math, history physics, anthropology, and writing. The basic assumption underlying the program is that many student failures are due to the fact that many younger college students still function at the concrete level of thinking, while the curriculum they are exposed to is geared to formal operational thinking. The freshmen are introduced to a learning cycle in which basic information about the discipline is given to the students to whet their appetites for more information and increase their motivation to pursue solutions to problems. In this way, it is hoped that the students will develop, on their own, hypotheses and ideas about the subject matter—hypotheses and ideas that normally are presented by a lecturer.

The majority of theory and research about adolescent cognitive development has focused on how the adolescent thinks about impersonal objects and events, those that are inanimate and nonsocial. Piaget's ideas about adolescent cognitive development also downplay the role of social and environmental events in the development of cognitive structures. Recently, theory and research about adolescent cognitive development has begun to take into account the adolescent's reasoning about social matters as well.

Social Cognition

The field of **social cognition** recognizes that individuals reason about social as well as nonsocial matters. The study of social cognition has increased so rapidly in the last decade that it rightfully can be viewed as a subdiscipline of the cognitive structural perspective. According to cognitive developmentalist John Flavell (in press), social cognition, or "social cognitive enterprises," should be defined broadly to

include all intellectual endeavors in which the aim is to think or learn about social or psychological processes in the self, individual, others, or human groups of all sizes and kinds (including social organizations, nations, and "people in general"). Thus, what is thought about during a social-cognitive enterprise could be a perception, feelings, motive, ability, intention, purpose, interest, attitude, thought, belief, personality structure, or another such process or property of self or other(s). It could also be the social interactions and relationships that obtain among individuals, groups, nations, or other social entities. (pp. 1–2)

The ability to monitor social thoughts and make sense of them seems to increase during middle childhood and adolescence. An important aspect of social cognition is the child's development of conscious self-awareness. Statements such as "I think I am not easily fooled by others" or "I tend to give people the benefit of the doubt" evidence the development of such self- and social awareness.

Flavell (1979) also talks about the implications of children's and adolescents' ability to monitor their social cognitions as an indicator of their social maturity and competence.

In many real life situations, the monitoring problem is not to determine how well you understand what a message means but rather to determine how much you ought to believe it or do what it says to do. I am thinking of the persuasive appeals the young receive from all quarters to smoke, drink, commit aggressive or criminal acts, have casual sex without contraceptives, have or not have the casual babies that often result,

quit school, and become unthinking followers of this year's flaky cults, sects, and movements. (Feel free to revise this list in accordance with *your* values and prejudices.) Perhaps it is stretching the meanings of . . . cognitive monitoring too far to include the critical appraisal of message source, quality of appeal, and probably consequences needed to cope with these inputs sensibly, but I do not think so. It is at least conceivable that the ideas currently brewing in this area could some day be parlayed into a method of teaching children (and adults) to make wise and thoughtful life decisions as well as to comprehend and learn better in formal educational settings. (p. 910)

John Hill and Wendy Palmquist (1978) state that the majority of studies of social cognition have focused on moral development. In particular these investigations have stressed the importance of cognitive changes in the way the adolescent thinks about moral dilemmas. And it is argued that these changes in moral thinking filter down to affect the way the adolescent acts in different moral situations. For our purposes, however, other aspects of social cognition will be explored. These include impression formation and the development of role-taking skills. Keep in mind that these two aspects of social cognition join with the development of moral judgment to form the main body of material being studied in social cognition.

Impression Formation

The three aspects of **impression formation** that have received the most attention are *differentiation, inference,* and *organization*. Concept differentiation in regard to oneself and others seems to increase rapidly during the elementary school years and then continue at a slower rate during adolescence (e.g., Bigner, 1974; Fry, 1974; Peevers & Secord, 1973). In one investigation seventh-graders, twelfth-graders, and adults were asked about the different categories they used to describe themselves (Mullener & Laird, 1971). The older individuals tended to use a wider variety of categories to describe themselves. Thus, more differentiated and inferential cognitive strategies are used by adolescents than by elementary schoolchildren, but the changes in these strategies do not seem to be as rapid in adolescence as in the elementary school years.

The most distinct characteristic of impression formation during adolescence appears to be organization. Barenboim (in press-a, in press-b) suggests that the products of the concrete operational period are organized and coordinated into new, more abstract systems of thought during adolescence. Such changes have been investigated by focusing on how the adolescent develops impressions about himself or herself and others; the young adolescent appears to begin to develop a rudimentary but implicit personality theory.

The development of a personality theory during adolescence seems to consist of several elements that appear to be absent during the elementary school years.

Adolescents think deeply about the causes of each other's behaviors.

First, when the adolescent is given information about another person, he or she integrates this with previously acquired information rather than relying solely on the concrete information at hand. Second, rather than thinking that people always behave consistently, the adolescent is more likely than the elementary school child to detect the contextual or situational variability in his or her own and others' behavior. Third, rather than merely accepting surface traits as a valid description of another person or himself or herself, the adolescent begins to look for deeper, more complex—even hidden—causes of personality.

These factors are not merely considered in isolation but as interacting forces that determine personality. This complex way of thinking about oneself and others does not appear in most individuals until adolescence. As is the case with formal operational thought, though, these implicit personality theories are not always employed; whether the adolescent uses such a strategy to understand himself or herself and others may depend upon a number of specific factors. It is important to note, however, that it does not seem that the individual is even capable of such thought until the beginnings of adolescence (e.g., Barenboim, in press-a, in press-b; Livesley & Bromley, 1973; Stricker, Jacobs, & Kogan, 1974).

Role Taking
A second major aspect of the growing study of the social components of cognitive development in childhood and adolescence focuses on the ability to empathize with or understand the feelings of others. This ability is called role taking (e.g., Flavell, 1974; Flavell, Abrahams, Croft, & Flavell, in press; Shantz, 1976). In many investigations the intent is not only to understand cognitive changes in role-taking ability but also

to link these changes with empathy and moral judgment (e.g., Flavell, 1974; Rubin, 1973; Selman, 1976a; Selman & Byrne, 1974).

The most articulated view of the development of the children's role-taking abilities has been expressed by Robert Selman (e.g., 1976a, 1976b). From Selman's perspective, as a child approaches adolescence, he or she learns to reason in a complex manner in order to put together such complicated thoughts as "I think that you think that I think. . . ." Furthermore, the preadolescent discriminates more readily among alternative views of others than in the elementary years. Upon reaching early adolescence, he or she begins to be able to coordinate various thoughts about others into a cohesive perspective on people in general, termed by Selman the "societal perspective."

Another view of role taking in adolescence has been developed by David Elkind (1967, 1976). He believes that the onset of formal operations in adolescence brings with it a unique sort of egocentrism. In this type of egocentric thought, the adolescent acts as if others are as preoccupied with his or her behavior, feelings, and thoughts as he or she is (self-consciousness). Elkind believes that such adolescent egocentrism accounts for much of the boorishness and preoccupation with bodily parts that young adolescents seem to have.

Not only has there been increased interest in role taking in the elementary and adolescent years, but also a great deal of attention is being given to the early development of role-taking skills. The majority of this information focuses on how role-taking skills, or perspective taking as it sometimes is called, are related to the child's empathy and altruistic tendencies (e.g., Mussen & Eisenberg-Berg, 1977).

Yet another aspect of social cognition that has emerged is the individual's development of religious concepts. There is a close relationship between the development of moral values and religious concepts. In box 13.3 we explore adolescents' declining interest in church attendance, their strong concern about spiritual matters, and how they develop religious concepts.

There is increasing interest in the role of work in the adolescent's development. In particular, parents, as well as psychologists, want to know how work experiences influence achievement orientation and school performance. Next, we explore the positive and negative features of adolescent work.

The Church, Spiritual Interests, and the Development of Religious Concepts

While in other eras adolescents frequently accepted the doctrines of the church, many youth now question or even openly reject them. Some church leaders are attempting to create an atmosphere in which autonomous moral thinking is possible, but the specifics of how to accomplish this have not been mapped out and the efforts are few in number. The decline in church attendance indicates that an authoritarian approach by church leaders is not the best way to create more advanced moral thinking in adolescents. In one national poll (Gallup & Poling, 1981), only one in four adolescents admitted a "high degree" of confidence in organized religion.

Just as there has been a decline in church attendance among adolescents in recent years, there has been a corresponding downward trend in adolescents' concern with religious values. According to Daniel Yankelovich's national survey (1974), conducted in 1969, 64 percent of college youth felt that religion was a very important value. By 1973, this had declined to 42 percent; the figures for noncollege youth were 38 percent and 28 percent in 1969 and 1973 respectively.

However, it would be incorrect to say that adolescents are not at all interested in religious ideas and behavior—many feel confused about religious beliefs, worry about not going to church enough, don't quite know what to think about God, and are interested in beliefs other than those espoused by the churches they grew up in (e.g., Beit-Hallahmi, 1974). Teenagers show an abiding interest in spiritual questions. Gallup and Poling also found that nearly nine out of ten teenagers said they believed in God (or a universal spirit), and only one in one hundred adolescents said they did not have some kind of religious preference or affiliation. Some even leave home to live in religious sects such as the Hare Krishnas and the Moonies.

James Fowler (1976) stresses that late adolescence is a particularly important time in the development of religious identity. Beginning at about age eighteen, adolescents enter a state characterized by **individuating-reflexive faith.**

Fowler indicates that there is a close relationship between the adolescent's development of moral values and religious values, and that the individuating-reflexive faith stage is much like Kohlberg's self-principled level of moral

The Role of Work in Adolescent Development

In 1974, the government Panel on Youth, headed by James Coleman, concluded that work has a positive influence on adolescents. According to Coleman and his colleagues, a job during adolescence creates a positive attitude toward work, allows students to learn from adults other than teachers or parents, and may help keep them out of trouble. The Panel on Youth recommended that more youth should be included in the work force of our country. To accomplish this goal, the panel suggested that more work-study programs be developed, that the minimum wage be lowered, and that more flexible school-work schedules be allowed.

Over the past hundred years, the percentage of youth who work full-time as opposed to those who are in school has decreased dramatically. During the last half of the 1800s, less than one of every twenty high school-aged adolescents was in school, while more than

nine of every ten adolescents receive high school diplomas today. In the nineteenth century, many adolescents learned a trade from their father or some other adult member of the community. Now there is a much more prolonged period of educational training that has kept most adolescents out of the work force.

In a recent book, Sheila Cole (in press) analyzed the working lives of adolescents. More teenagers work today than at any time since 1940. For example, in 1940, only one out of twenty-five tenth-grade males attended school and simultaneously worked part-time, while in 1970, the number had increased to more than one out of every four. For tenth-grade females, only one out of every hundred combined school and part-time work in 1940, but in 1970, the figure had increased to one out of every six. Current estimates suggest that at some points during the school year, about one out of every two high school juniors and seniors and approximately one of every three ninth and tenth graders are combining school and work.

thinking. In both instances, for example, the adolescent makes the transition from a conventional perspective on values to an individualized perspective. And both of these theorists note that many adolescents and young adults never make the transition from conventional to individualized thinking about values.

As part of developing an individualized perspective on religious identity, Fowler believes that for the first time in their lives late adolescents have to take full responsibility for their beliefs and ideas about religion—as opposed to earlier in adolescence, when they could rely heavily on their parents' commitments. During late adolescence, individuals come face to face with personal decisions such as "Do I consider myself first, or should I act in the service of others?" and "Are the doctrines I have been taught absolute, or are they more relative than I have been led to believe?" Adolescents who have grown up in strongly religious families may go away to college and live with roommates who call into question their unwavering faith. Philosophy and religion classes expose the adolescent to varying points of view about religion, expanding the options the youth can follow.

Identity development is interwined with work.

Cole also reported research conducted by Ellen Greenberger and Lawrence Steinberg. Greenberger and Steinberg gave a questionnaire focusing on work experiences to students in four California high schools. Their findings disproved some common myths. For example, it generally is assumed that youth get extensive on-the-job training when they are hired for work—the reality is that they get little training at all, according to the researchers. Also, it is assumed that youth, through work experiences, learn to get along better with adults. However, adolescents reported that they rarely feel close to the adults they work with. The work experiences of the adolescents did help them understand how the business world works, how to get and keep a job, and how to manage money. Working also helped the youth to learn to budget their time, to take pride in their accomplishments, and to evaluate their goals. Working adolescents often have to give up sports, social affairs with peers, and sometimes sleep. And the youth have to balance the demands of work, school, and family.

In their investigation, Greenberger and Steinberg asked adolescents about their grade point averages, school attendance, satisfaction from school, and the number of hours spent studying and in extracurricular activities since they began working. The findings: working adolescents had lower grade point averages than nonworkers. More than one of every four students reported that their grades dropped when they began working, while only one of nine said their grades improved. But it wasn't just working that affected the adolescents' grades—more importantly, it was the number of hours worked. Tenth graders who worked more than fourteen hours a week suffered a drop in grades, while eleventh graders worked up to twenty hours a week before their grades began to drop.

In addition to the effect of work on grades, working adolescents also felt less involved in school, were absent more, and said they didn't enjoy school as much (compared to their nonworking peers). Adolescents who worked also spent less time with their families—but just as much time with their peers—as their nonworking counterparts.

In weighing the benefits and pitfalls of work during adolescence, Cole (1980) concluded, "Working is a part of growing up. Like other aspects of growing up, it brings young people independence and freedom. And, like growing up, it introduces teenagers to the limitations of their own lives."

In the next chapter we focus on social, emotional, and personality development in adolescence, where we will see that the exploration of vocational roles constitutes one of the most important ingredients of the adolescent's identity development.

Summary

While philosophers and educators discussed the period now known as adolescence for hundreds of years, it was not until the turn of the century that the scientific study of adolescence began. The nature of the developmentajl period of adolescence in America varied considerably from the eighteenth century to the present. The study of adolescents is concerned with the period of transition from childhood to adulthood, roughly eleven or thirteen to eighteen or twenty-one years of age.

Physical development during adolescence is distinct from physical development during other periods. Perhaps the most obvious physical changes in the adolescent are increased height and weight and the maturation of sexual characteristics. These facets of development are involved in the growth spurt at the onset of adolescence, which begins, on the average, at about ten to eleven years of age in girls and a few years later in boys.

Pubertal changes are occurring at younger ages every decade in our industrialized world, indicating the influence of nutrition and other environmental factors on physical development. Increases in weight accompany increased height and skeletal growth during adolescence, but other factors influence the weight of the adolescent as well. During early adolescence only about 5 percent of youth are obese, but by late adolescence about 15 percent are. Closely related to these figures is a significant drop in the basal metabolism rate (BMR).

The development of sexual characteristics in adolescence has received more attention (both by adolescents and the researchers who study them) than any other aspect of physical development. It is important to distinguish between primary sexual characteristics, or the external and internal sex organs, and secondary sexual characteristics, or the related aspects of physical development not directly tied to reproductive functions. In physical development research, increased attention is being directed at understanding the menstrual cycle and its relation to psychological changes in females. Sex hormones present the adolescent with a new sense of sexual awareness—the adolescent's body is literally flooded with hormones at the onset of the pubertal period. Sometimes the development of sexual characteristics in adolescence is delayed, a situation that may lead to psychological problems.

The most frequent approach to research on early and late maturation has been to study the adolescent's skeletal development. In several investigations, it has been found that early maturation gives boys a decided advantage over late-maturing peers. The picture for girls is not quite as clear, although after the elementary school years early maturation seems to have positive effects for them as well.

Heredity does not act in isolation to influence the adolescent's development. Every characteristic of the adolescent is determined by the interaction of the environment and genes. Heredity and environment interact to influence two adolescent characteristics—temperament and interests.

The ideas of Jean Piaget form the cornerstone for modern work in adolescent cognitive development. Through the processes of adaptation and organization, the concrete operational thinking of the child gives way to the formal operational thinking of the adolescent. Formal operational thought differs from concrete operational thought in that it is more abstract and more organized. However, most cognitive developmentalists believe that the onset of adolescence does not signal the appearance of full-blown formal operational thought. One alternative view, expressed in the branch model, holds that the dominant path of adolescent thought is formal operational in nature but that alternative routes are possible as well. It also may be helpful to think about formal operations as having two phases, one early and the other late in adolescence.

Piaget's theory has stimulated a great deal of current interest in extending formal operational thought to social as well as nonsocial matters—this part of cognitive development is called social cognition. Changes in social cognition during adolescence center on moral judgments, impression formation, and role taking. And work can have positive or negative effects on the adolescent's orientation toward school and achievement. The evidence suggests that adolescents who work more than twenty hours a week are likely to jeopardize their chances for getting good grades.

Key Terms

abiding self

amenorrheic

androgens

basal metabolism rate (BMR)

branch model of cognitive development

discovery learning

endocrine glands

estrogens

exocrine glands

hormones

imaginary audience

impression formation

individuating-reflexive faith

menstrual cycle

obesity

personal fable

primary sexual characteristics

progesterone

puberty

secondary sexual characteristics

social cognition

stereotype

transient self

Review Questions

1. Who is the father of the scientific study of adolescence? Describe his theory of adolescence.
2. Describe the components and sequencing of the adolescent growth spurt, first for boys and then for girls.
3. What factors contribute to the development of obesity in adolescence?
4. Describe the development of the sex organs and hormonal influences during adolescence.
5. Discuss the variety of sexual behaviors and attitudes of adolescents.
6. How do scientists study early versus late maturation during adolescence? What are the conclusions reached from research on this important topic?
7. How and to what extent do genes influence adolescent development? What is the influence of heredity on temperament and interests?
8. Outline and discuss Piaget's views about adolescent cognitive development.
9. What are some features of adolescent thought that Piaget may have overlooked in his attempt to describe how all adolescents think?
10. What is meant by social cognition? How are researchers investigating social cognition?
11. Describe the positive and negative features of work in adolescence.

Further Readings

Elkind, D. *Child development and education.* New York: Oxford University Press, 1976.
An excellent, easy-to-read introduction to the implications of Piaget's ideas for educators. Practical examples are given for approaching classroom teaching from the Piagetian perspective.

Hyde, J. S. *Understanding human sexuality.* New York: McGraw-Hill, 1979.
A scholarly but entertaining look at the physical aspects of sexual development, including much material focused on understanding our sexuality. Easy to read.

Kett, J. F. *Rites of passage.* New York: Basic Books, 1977.
Kett describes in great detail three major historical phases in the way the adolescent has been dealt with in the United States. The nature of adolescence from 1790 to the present is discussed. Easy to read.

Netter, F. H. *Reproductive system.* The Ciba Collection of Medical Illustrations (vol. 2). Summit, N.J.: Ciba, 1965.
A book filled with what are generally considered the best set of illustrations on sexual anatomy available.

Ross, D..G. *Stanley Hall: the psychologist as prophet.* Chicago: University of Chicago Press, 1972.
This is an intriguing biographical sketch of the father of adolescent psychology, G. Stanley Hall. Reasonably easy to read.

Thomas, A., & Chess, S. *Temperament and development.* New York: Brunner/Mazel, 1977.
A complete overview of the classic longitudinal study, still active, of Stella Chess and Alexander Thomas. Contains a number of insights into the lives of individual boys and girls as they move from infancy through childhood and adolescence that show how temperament and environment interact to influence individual behavior. Moderately difficult to read.

14

Social, Emotional, and Personality Development

Prologue: Parent-Adolescent Relationships and Adolescent Autonomy

Parenting is fearful, Mr. Matterling. You don't know how fearful until you sit next to your son on his maiden voyage behind the wheel of your car and hear him say, "My Driver's Ed teacher says I've got only one problem and that's every time I meet a car I pass over the center line."

And you worry. I worried when they stayed home. . . . I worried when they dated a lot. ("They're not meditating in the Christian Science reading room until 2 A.M., Ed.") I worried when they didn't date ("Maybe we should try a sixteenth of an inch padding.")

I worried when their grades were bad. ("He won't be able to get into karate school with those marks.") I worried when their grades were good. ("So swing a little. You wanta spend the rest of your life reading William F. Buckley and basting your acne?")

I worried when they got a job. ("She looks so tired, and besides it could bring back her asthma attacks.") I worried when they didn't get a job. ("Mark my word, he'll take after your brother, Wesley, who didn't get a paper route until he was thirty-three.")

And a tired voice within me persisted, "Why don't you grow up?". . .

This half-child, half-adult groping miserably to weigh life's inconsistencies, hypocrisy, instant independence, advice, rules, and responsibilities.

The blind date that never showed. The captaincy that went to the best friend. The college reject, the drill team have-nots, the class office also-rans, the honors that went to someone else. And they turned to me for an answer. . . .

"Gosh, Mom, nobody's PERFECT!"

And there were joys. Moments of closeness . . . an awkward hug; a look in the semidarkness as you turned off the test pattern as they slept. The pride of seeing them stand up when older people entered the room and saying, "Yes, sir," and "No, ma'am," without your holding a cue card in front of them. The strange, warm feeling of seeing them pick up a baby and seeing a wistfulness in their faces that I have never seen before. . . .

I shall never forgive Mr. Matterling for not warning me of the times of panic. It's not time yet. It can't be. I'm not finished. I had all the teaching and discipline and the socks to pick up and the buttons to sew on and those lousy meal worms to feed the lizard every day . . . there was no time for loving. That's what it's all about, isn't it? Did they ever know I smiled? Did they ever understand my tears? Did I talk too much? Did I say too little? Did I ever look at them and really see them? Do I know them at all? Or was it all a lifetime of "Why don't you grow up? . . . "
In my mind, I always dreamed of the day I would have teenagers.

Young boys would pinch me in the swimming pool and exclaim, "Gee, ma'am, I'm sorry, I thought you were your sensuous daughter, Dale."

The entire family would gather around the piano and sing songs from the King Family album. And on Friday nights, we'd have a family council meeting to decide what flavor of ice cream their father, Ozzie, would bring home from the ice cream parlor.

It never worked out that way. Our teenagers withdrew to their bedrooms on their thirteenth birthday and didn't show themselves to us again until it was time to get married. If we spoke to them in public, they threatened to self-destruct within three minutes. And only once a young boy grinned at me, then apologized quickly with "Gee, sir, I'm sorry. I thought you were Eric Sevareid."

Heaven knows we tried to make contact. One day when I knew our son Hal was in his bedroom, I pounded on the door and demanded, "Open up! I know you are in there, staring at your navel."

The door opened a crack and I charged into my son's bedroom shouting, "Look Hal, I'm your mother. I love you. So does your father. We care about you. We haven't seen you in months. All we get is a glimpse of the back of your head as you slam the door, and a blurred profile as the car whizzes by. We're supposed to be communicating. How do you think I feel when the TV set flashes on the message. 'IT'S ELEVEN O'CLOCK. DO YOU KNOW WHERE YOUR CHILDREN ARE?' I can't even remember *who* they are."

"I'm not Hal," said the kid, peeling a banana. "I'm Henny. Hal isn't home from school yet."

Another time I thought I saw Hal race for the bathroom and bolt the door.

"I know this isn't the place to talk," I shouted through the keyhole, "but I thought you should know we're moving next week. I'm sliding the new address under the door and certainly hope you can join us. I wouldn't have brought it up, but I thought you'd become anxious if you came home and the refrigerator and the hot water were gone."

A note came slowly under the door. It read, "I'll surely miss you. Yours very truly, Hartley."

Finally, my husband and I figured out the only way to see Hal was to watch him play football. As we shivered in the stands, our eyes eagerly searched the satin-covered backsides on the bench. Then, a pair of familiar shoulders turned and headed toward the showers.

"Hey, Hal," said his father, grabbing his arm, "Son of a gun. Remember me? I'm Father."

"Father who?" asked the boy.

"You're looking great, Hal. I remember the last time I saw you. You were wearing that little suit with the duck on the pocket. Your mother tells me you're going to be joining us when we move."

"You have me confused, sir," said the boy, "I'm not Hal, I'm Harry."

"Aren't you the guy I saw poking around our refrigerator the other night? And didn't you go with us on our vacation last year?"

"No sir, that was Harold. Incidentally, could you give me a lift to your house? I'm spending the night with Hal."

We thought we saw Hal a few times after that. Once when we were attending a movie and they announced a car bearing our license number had left its parking lights on, a rather thin boy raced up the aisle, but we were never sure.

Another time at a father-son banquet, someone noticed a resemblance between my husband and a boy who hung on the phone all night mumbling, "Aw c'mon, Wilma," but that was also indefinite.

One day in the mail, I received a package of graduation pictures and a bill for $76. It was worth it. "Look, dear," I said to my husband, "it's Hal." Our eyes misted as we looked at the clear-skinned boy with the angular jaw and the sideburns that grew down to his jugular vein. It made spotting him at graduation a snap.

"Son of a gun," said his father, punching him on the arm, "if you aren't a chip off the old block, Henny."

"Hartley," I corrected.

"Harry," interjected a mother at my elbow.

"Harold," interjected another voice.

"I'm Hal," said the boy graduate, straightening his shoulders and grimacing.

"Hal who?" we all asked in unison.

Source: Bombeck & Keane, 1971.

Introduction

The period of adolescence brings with it a number of important changes that require adaptation on the part of parents—we will look at what these changes are and the issue of parent-adolescent conflict. Peers truly become a powerful force in the lives of adolescents—we will evaluate peer versus adult-parent influences, peer conformity and pressure, the nature of adolescent groups, dating, and marriage. We will also discuss personality development during adolescence, focusing on the self and identity. The chapter concludes by outlining the most common problems and disturbances of adolescence—drugs, alcohol, delinquency, and suicide.

Family and Peers

In the prologue Erma Bombeck highlighted some of the confusions and strains that characterize parent-adolescent relationships. The nature of adolescent autonomy and how parent-adolescent relations contribute to autonomy will be evaluated in this section. We will also see how pervasive parent-adolescent conflict really is and look in detail at how extensive peer group influences are during adolescence.

Family

As we discussed in chapter 13, important maturational changes take place in adolescence. In addition to physical changes, adolescents move into the formal operational stage of thought as described by Piaget. According to John Hill (1980), the adolescent's concept of his or her family changes as well. These maturational changes need to be taken into account when studying adolescent-parent relationships. Hill emphasizes the importance of parental adaptation to the adolescent.

Parents are called upon to adapt to their sons' and daughters' changing physical stature and sexual capacity. And, perhaps at a less observable level, parents are called upon to adapt to their children's more sophisticated assessments of their fairness and their intentions, and to the alternatives that parents might adopt in relation to one another or their children—assessments that may be discussed increasingly as among near equals or dismissed as challenges unacceptable to parental authority.

While we know little about the typical developmental issues faced by parents while they are coping with pubertal change in their children, it is probable that transformations in parent-child relations during the period are influenced by the life circumstances that parents of this age themselves must face. During their children's early adolescence, most parents will be between thirty and forty-five years of age. Toward the end of that age bracket, current research (to be viewed in light of its limitation to middle-class samples) at least suggests an important, if ironic, complementarity between the

concerns of adolescents and their parents. The approach of midlife brings with it increased concern about body integrity, a change in time perspective such that time is considered in terms of what remains instead of how much has passed by, and worrisome concerns about gaps between parents' occupational aspirations and their actual achievements. There is evidence of greater marital dissatisfaction during midlife than in earlier or later periods. (pp. 1–3)

The study of adolescent-parent relationships, then, can benefit from a closer look at the developmental changes that occur in parents as well as in the adolescents. The increasing variety of adolescent-parent family structures further complicates the task of unraveling the forces in adolescent development. Read box 14.1 for a description of the differences in adolescent girls from homes where the father is missing due to divorce and due to death.

Parent-Adolescent Conflict

An unfortunate stereotype suggests that all parents and adolescents are in conflict with each other. However, as was discussed in chapter 13, in many instances adolescents and their parents have similar values and do not engage in battle with each other to the extent indicated in the popular media. Data collected by Albert Bandura and Richard Walters (1959) support this belief. Bandura and Walters found that by the time the boys in their study had reached adolescence, parents actually placed fewer restrictions on them than in childhood. Apparently, the boys had become reasonably capable of assuming responsibility by the time they reached adolescence.

In the Bandura and Walters study, the adolescents tended to select friends with value systems similar to their own, so membership in the peer group usually did not precipitate family conflict. Many of the parents were very pleased with their sons' peers. A similar picture was found in another investigation of adolescents (Elkin & Westley, 1955).

Family ties are close and the degree of basic family consistency is high. The parents are interested in all the activities of their children, and the adolescents, except for the area of sex, frankly discuss their own behavior and problems with them. In many areas of life, there is a joint participation between parents and children. . . . In independent discussions by parents and adolescents of the latters' marriage and occupational goals, there is a remarkable level of agreement. The adolescents also acknowledged the right of the parents to guide them, for example, accepting, at least manifestly, the prerogatives of the parents to set rules for the number of dates, hours of return from dates, and types of parenting. The parents express relatively little concern about the socialization problems or peer group activities of their children. (Bandura, 1964, p. 226)

Box 14.1
The Heterosexual Behavior of Adolescent Daughters of Divorced Parents

Mavis Hetherington (1972) has shown that the heterosexual behavior of adolescent girls from father-absent and father-present homes is different. The adolescent girls with absent fathers acted in one of two extreme ways. They were either very withdrawn, passive, and subdued around boys, or were overly active, aggressive, and flirtatious. The girls who were inhibited, rigid, and restrained around males were more likely to have come from widowed homes. Those who sought the attention of males, who showed early heterosexual behavior, and who seemed more open and uninhibited were more likely to have come from homes in which the parents were divorced. In addition, early separation from fathers usually was associated with more profound effects, and the mothers' attitudes toward themselves and marriage differed from that of widows and divorcees. Divorced women were more anxious, unhappy, hostile toward males, and more negative about marriage than were the widows. And perhaps not surprisingly, daughters of divorcees had more negative attitudes about men than did the daughters of widows.

Several examples of the actual behavior of the girls should provide a clearer picture of the study. One technique used to investigate the girls' behavior was to interview them sometimes with a male interviewer and sometimes with a female interviewer. Four chairs were placed in the room, including one for the interviewer. Daughters of widows most frequently chose the chair farthest from the male interviewer, while daughters of divorcees generally selected the chair closest to him. There were no differences when the interviewer was a female.

The interviewer also observed the girls at a dance and during activities at the recreational center. At the dance the daughters of widows often refused to dance when asked. One widow's daughter even spent the entire evening in the restroom. The daughters of the divorcees were more likely to accept the boys' invitations to dance. At school, the daughters of divorcees were more frequently observed outside the gym where boys were playing, while the daughters of the widows more often engaged in traditional "female" activities, like sewing and cooking.

Researchers have found conflict between parents and adolescents on certain issues and areas of conduct.

Hetherington (1977) is continuing to study these girls, following them into young adulthood to determine their sexual behavior, marital choices, and marital behavior. The daughters of divorcees tend to marry younger (eight of the daughters of widowed mothers still were not married at the time of the report), and tend to select marital partners who more frequently have drug problems and inconsistent work histories. In contrast, daughters of widows tend to marry men with a more puritanical makeup. In addition, both the daughters of the widows and the divorcees report more sexual adjustment problems than the daughters from intact homes; for example, the daughters from homes where the father is absent generally experienced fewer orgasms than daughters from intact homes. The daughters from intact homes also showed more variation in their sex-role behavior and marital adjustment. They seemed to be more relaxed and dealt more competently with their roles as wives, suggesting that they have worked through their relationships with their fathers and are more psychologically free to deal successfully in their relationships with other males. On the other hand, the daughters of the divorcees and widows appear to be marrying images of their fathers.

However, some researchers have found conflict between parents and adolescents on certain issues and areas of conduct. Drug use, dress, and sexual habits are areas where adolescent-parent conflict sometimes exists (Block & Langman, 1974). Parents and adolescents also may disagree on the number of hours of sleep the adolescent needs (Kelley, 1972).

Many parent-adolescent conflicts actually originate before adolescence is reached. Simply because the child was much smaller than the parents, the parents may have been able to suppress the oppositional behavior. But by adolescence, some individuals have grown as large or larger than their parents—and with increased size and strength may come an increase in indifference to parental dictates.

Nonetheless, for the majority of adolescents, there seems to be more compatibility than incompatibility in parent-adolescent relationships. Many adolescents and their parents agree on appropriate adult behavior and behavior in general (Chand, Crider, & Willets, 1975).

The Nature of Adolescent Autonomy

Trying to define adolescent autonomy is more complex and elusive than it might seem at first. Think about autonomy for a moment. For most people, the term connotes self-direction and independence. But what does it really mean? Is it an internal personality trait that consistently characterizes the adolescent's immunity from parental influence? Is it the ability to make responsible decisions for oneself? Does autonomy imply consistent behavior in all areas of life, including school, finances, dating, and peer relations? What are the relative contributions of peers and other adults to the development of the adolescent's autonomy?

It is clear that adolescent autonomy is *not* a consistent and regular feature of all adolescent thought and behavior. For example, in one investigation (Psathas, 1957) high school students were asked twenty-five questions about their independence from their families. Four distinct patterns of adolescent autonomy emerged from analyses of the students' responses.

One dimension, labeled "permissiveness in outside activities," was represented by questions such as, Do you have to account to parents for the way you spend your money? A second dimension, called "permissiveness in age-related activities," was reflected in questions such as, Do your parents help you to buy your clothes? A third independent aspect of adolescent autonomy was referred to as "parental regard for judgment," indicated by responses to items like, In family discussions, do your parents encourage you to give your opinion? And a fourth dimension was characterized as "activities with status implications" and was indexed by parental influence on choice of occupation. Adolescent autonomy, then, is not a unified phenomenon but a summary label for a variety of adolescent interests, behaviors, thoughts, and feelings.

Parent versus Peer Influence on Autonomy Adolescents do not simply move from parental influence into a decision-making process all their own. At the same time they are beginning to show signs of independence from parental influence, they rapidly come under more intense peer influence. But it is incorrect to think that adolescent autonomy from parents is synonymous with the adolescent's total conformity to peer culture. Instead, the adolescent's autonomy is influenced by a variety of social agents, the two most important agents being parents and peers.

In one investigation, the continuing influence of parents on adolescents was evident even when the adolescents were also influenced considerably by peers (Brittain, 1963). Adolescents were queried about

Adolescent autonomy is a summary label for a variety of adolescent interests, behaviors, thoughts, and feelings.

whether they are influenced more by their peers or their parents in a variety of contexts, such as taking different classes at school, selecting different styles of clothing, or choosing to decline or accept a part-time job offer. As you might anticipate, in some situations the adolescents chose to adhere to the wishes of their friends while in other contexts they chose to rely on their parents' advice. For example, when decisions involved basic values and vocation orientations they were more likely to listen to their parents; but when peer activities were involved, they were more likely to accede to the influence of their friends.

Parental Attitudes and Adolescent Autonomy   There have been a number of investigations focusing on the relationship between parental attitudes and the adolescent's development of autonomy. Parents who adopt authoritarian decision-making strategies in dealing with their adolescent sons and daughters have adolescents who show little autonomy. Whether the adolescent's

self-perceptions are sampled, whether confidence in decision making is evaluated, or whether initiative in joining parents in a mutual decision-making process is observed, the same conclusion about the relationship between adolescent autonomy and parenting strategies is evident (Hill & Steinberg, 1976).

While there is agreement that an authoritarian family structure restricts the adolescent's development of autonomy, there is not as much consistency in pinpointing the parenting practices that increase autonomy. Some investigations have found that a permissive parenting strategy allows the adolescent to become more independent (Elder, 1968). Others suggest that a democratic parenting strategy is best (Kandel & Lesser, 1969).

While investigators vary in how they define permissive and democratic parenting techniques, in most instances a permissive strategy entails little parental involvement and fewer parental standards. By contrast, a democratic strategy usually consists of equal involvement on the part of parents and adolescents, with

Adolescent autonomy is influenced mostly by parents and peers.

influenced by events during childhood and adolescence has been developed by David Ausubel—his theory is described in box 14.2.

Next, we look at the pervasive influence of the peer group in adolescence, evaluating first the contribution of peer versus parent-adult influence.

Peers

When children enter elementary school, they spend more and more time with peers, and by the seventh grade, boys and girls characteristically spend as much, or more, time interacting with peers as with their parents. In an investigation of 766 students in the sixth grade, it was found that children spent more than twice as much time over the course of a weekend with peers as with parents (Condry, Simon, & Bronfenbrenner, 1968). And in another investigation, by adolescence time spent with peers exceded time spent with other agents of socialization (Medrich, Rosen, Rubin, & Buckley, in press).

Because adolescents spend more time with peers, do they conform more to the ideas and behaviors of their peers than to those advocated by parents? There are several ways to look at peer conformity. First, the influences that are exerted by parents and peers may be contradictory, and adolescents may choose to conform to the perspectives of those they are with the most; or they may simply choose to rebel against parental authority. Second, adolescents may become more responsible for themselves, seeing themselves as more independent of their parents and capable of making their own decisions. A third possibility is that a combination of both these perspectives may come into play.

In an effort to explore the developmental patterns of parental and peer conformity, Thomas Berndt (1978) studied 273 third- through twelfth-grade students. Hypothetical dilemmas were presented to the students, requiring them to make choices about conformity with friends on prosocial and antisocial behavior and conformity with parents on neutral and prosocial behaviors. For example, one prosocial item questioned whether students relied on their parents' advice in such situations as deciding about helping at the library or instructing another child to swim. An antisocial question asked a boy what he would do if one of his peers wanted him to help steal some candy. A neutral question asked a girl if she would follow peer suggestions to engage in an activity she wasn't interested in—for example, going to a movie she didn't want to see.

Some interesting developmental patterns were found in this investigation. In the third grade, parent and peer influences often directly contradicted each other. Since parent conformity is much greater for third-grade children, children of this age are probably still closely tied to and dependent on their parents.

the parents having the final authority to set limits on their teenagers. When the overall competence and adjustment of the adolescent is evaluated (rather than just autonomy), an even more clear-cut advantage can be attributed to democratic over permissive strategies of parenting.

Adolescence is a period of development when the individual pushes for autonomy (or for the perception that he or she has control over behavior) and gradually develops the ability to take that control. This ability may be acquired through appropriate adult reactions to the adolescent's desire for control. At the onset of adolescence, the average person is not knowledgeable enough to make appropriate or mature decisions in all areas of life. As the adolescent pushes for autonomy, the wise adult will relinquish control in areas where the adolescent can make mature decisions and help the adolescent to make reasonable decisions in areas where his or her knowledge is more limited. Gradually, the adolescent will acquire the ability to make mature decisions. One theory of how autonomy in adolescence is

Box 14.2
Satellization and Desatellization

David Ausubel's theory of the development of autonomy (Ausubel, Sullivan, & Ives, 1980) begins with infancy, at which time, he says, parents cater to the infant's needs and demands. Later, parents expect children to begin to do things for themselves—for example, use the toilet, pick up their toys, control their tempers, and so forth. However, as they develop cognitively, children begin to realize that they are not completely autonomous from their parents. This perception creates some conflict for the child and may lead to a crisis wherein the child's self-esteem is threatened. One way the child can resolve this conflict is through what Ausubel calls **satellization.** This simply means that for the time being the child gives up his or her sense of autonomous power and notion of total self-reliance. The result is that the child accepts dependence on parents.

However, Ausubel believes that many parents are not capable of developing or maintaining a satellizing relationship with their children. For satellization to occur,

children must perceive that their parents love them unconditionally and entrust their care to their parents. Two parenting styles that do not produce satellization are *overvaluation* and *rejection*. When parents overvalue, they continually interact with their children as if the children are in control. An example is the parent who lives vicariously through the child and hopes that the child will accomplish things he or she didn't—such as becoming a baseball player or a doctor. When parents reject, they view the child as an unwanted part of their existence. The child's needs are served unwillingly and only if necessary. Love and acceptance are absent, or at least are perceived as being absent by the child.

As the child approaches adolescence, satellization is eventually replaced by **desatellization**—that is, breaking away and becoming independent from parents. Total self-rule is not achieved in desatellization. Instead, the adolescent achieves a preparatory phase wherein potential separation from parental rule begins to develop. When final desatellization is reached, an individual has secure feelings about himself or herself and does not demonstrate the

---

However by the sixth grade, parent and peer influences were found to be no longer in direct opposition. Peer conformity had increased, but parent and peer influences were operating in different situations—parents had more impact in some situations, while peers had more clout in others. For example, it has been found that parents are more influential in a discussion of political parties but peers seem to have more say when sexual behavior and attitudes are at issue (Hyman, 1959; Vandiver, 1972).

By the ninth grade, parent and peer influences were once again in strong opposition to one another, probably because the increased conformity of adolescents to the social behavior of peers is much stronger at this grade level than at any other. Figure 14.1 displays the increased conformity to antisocial peer standards in the ninth grade. At this time adolescent adoption of antisocial standards endorsed by the peer group inevitably leads to conflict between adolescents and parents. Researchers have also found that the adolescent's attempt to gain independence meets with more parental opposition around the ninth grade than at any other time

(Douvan & Adelson, 1966; Kandel & Lesser, 1969). As an indication of the importance of peers, consider the comments of one youth:

I feel a lot of pressure from my friends to smoke and steal and things like that. My parents do not allow me to smoke, but my best friends are really pushing me to do it. They call me a pansy and a momma's boy if I don't. I really don't like the idea of smoking, but my good friend Steve told me in front of some of our friends, "Kevin, you are an idiot and a chicken all wrapped up in one little body." I couldn't stand it any more, so I smoked with them. I was coughing and humped over, but I still said, "This is really fun—yeah, I like it." I felt like I was part of the group.

Youths engage in all sorts of negative conformity behavior. They may go places in cars with people they are afraid of, use vulgar language, steal, vandalize, and make fun of their parents and teachers. But many conformity behaviors are also positive. The majority of youth goes to school and does not cause trouble for teachers; they may belong to clubs or groups that have prosocial functions; and they may belong to cliques that engage in constructive rather than destructive behaviors.

need to prove anything. He or she shows strong exploratory tendencies and focuses energy on tasks and problem solving rather than self-aggrandizement. The desatellized individual also views failure as a learning situation rather than as a source of frustration.

Other desatellization mechanisms may occur during adolescence that do not represent the competent desatellization just described. In many instances, however, the other mechanisms may be preliminary steps in the adolescent's attainment of the final stage of desatellization. One of these preliminary stages is called **resatellization** by Ausubel. In resatellization, the individual's parents are replaced by other individuals or a group. Resatellized individuals subjugate their own identities to their spouse's identity, or to the identity of a fraternity, sorority, or other social group. As a permanent solution to self-other relationships, resatellization can be detrimental to the adolescent's development. But as a temporary solution, it can provide a testing ground for the development of a more complete, autonomous form of desatellization.

"*A SCARF? Nobody wears a SCARF!*"

"*Mom, have you seen my scarf?*"

A stereotypical view of parent-child relationships suggests that parent-peer opposition continues into the late high school and college-age years. But Berndt (1978) found that adolescent conformity to antisocial, peer-endorsed behavior decreases in the late high school years, and greater agreement between parents and peers begins to occur in some areas. In addition, by the eleventh and twelfth grades, students show signs of developing a decision-making style more independent of peer and parent influence.

The extent to which parents are involved with their children, particularly with adolescents, affects the extent of peer-group influence. The careful observations of Muzafer and Carolyn Sherif (1964) suggest that youth who show the greatest cohesiveness in and dependence on peer-group relations are almost invariably involved in unhappy family situations.

Adolescent Groups

So far in our discussion of peer relations, little has been said about how the adolescent functions in groups. Most peer group relationships in adolescence can be categorized in one of three ways: the **crowd,** the **clique,** or individual friendships (Mussen, Conger, & Kagan,

1974). The largest and least personal of these groups is the crowd. The members of the crowd meet because of their mutual interest in activities, not because they are mutually attracted to each other. By contrast, the members of cliques and friendships are attracted to each other on the basis of similar interests and social ideals. Cliques are smaller in size, involve greater intimacy among members, and have more group cohesion than crowds.

One of the most widely quoted studies of adolescent cliques and crowds is that of James Coleman (1961). Students in ten different high schools were asked to identify the leading crowds in their schools. They also were asked to name the students who were the most outstanding in athletics, popularity, and different activities in the school. Regardless of the school sampled, the leading crowds were likely to be composed of athletes and popular girls. Much less power in the leading crowd was attributed to the bright student. Coleman's finding that being an athlete contributes to popularity for boys was reconfirmed in an investigation by Eitzen (1975).

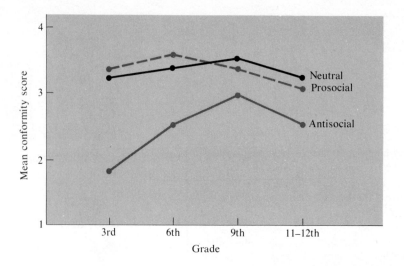

Figure 14.1 Mean scores for peer conformity on different types of behavior. Higher scores indicate greater conformity; the neutral point is 3.5.

Sociologists say that adolescents growing up in America usually must decide on which culture to go with—whether to be a "roper" or a "doper," an "intellectual" or a "going-steady type" (Hawkins, 1979). This decision often reflects some conflict that exists throughout society—in many instances, the students are making a political statement by siding with one clique or crowd rather than another. Political statements made during adolescence, though, may not be very strong; sometimes they boil down to nothing more than which radio station you listen to or which clothes you buy. The split is fairly easy to see in most high schools. In many instances, the two extreme groupings, such as the "ropers" and the "dopers," are not well integrated into the school system itself and are easily distinguished from students who are making good grades and who are social leaders.

Allegiance to cliques, clubs, organizations, and teams exerts powerful control over the lives of many adolescents. Group identity often overrides personal identity. The leader of a group may place a member in a position of considerable moral conflict asking, in effect, What's more important, our code or your parents'? or Are you looking out for yourself, or for the members of the group? Labels like "brother" and "sister" sometimes are adopted and used in group members' conversations with one another. These labels symbolize the intensity of the bond between the members and suggest the high status of membership in the group.

Cliques often provide a more intense camaraderie than membership in more formal adolescent organizations, such as an honor society, the student council, and so forth. However, intense feelings of group cohesion and brotherhood or sisterhood also may be felt by the members of athletic teams or political groups as well. For many adolescents, many hours of the day are spent performing the roles ascribed to them in these cliques and groups.

It isn't possible to gain a true feeling for what the adolescent culture in the United States is like without considering the material aspects of that culture. Money, cars, and clothes, to name a few, play a big part in the adolescent need system. They contribute to the adolescent's sense of self-esteem and identity. The adolescent with his or her own car or motorcycle achieves a status level in our culture beyond that of the adolescent who does not have these material goods.

Insights into the culture of the adolescent can be gained by looking closely at another aspect of behavior—language. Slang expressions characterize the communication patterns of many adolescent peer groups. The use of slang makes the adolescent feel that he or she is a part of a group. Sometimes it also serves as a time-saving method, so that longer, more elaborate explanations do not have to be given.

In addition to material possessions and slang, the telephone also serves as an important part of adolescent culture, particularly for the young adolescent not yet old enough to drive a car. Many young adolescents spend long hours talking with each other on the phone about school, members of the opposite sex, parents, clothes, and friends. And the telephone comes in handy when the moment comes to ask someone out for the first date—adolescents use the telephone as a "long-distance" communication system to avoid the anxiety of asking in person.

In some cultures, adolescents are placed in peer groups for much greater lengths of time and at an earlier age than in the United States. For example, in the Murian culture of eastern India, both male and female children live in a dormitory from the age of six until they get married (Barnouw, 1975). The dormitory is seen as a religious haven where members are devoted to work and spiritual harmony. Children work for their parents, and the parents arrange the children's marriages. When the children wed, they must leave the dormitory.

Cliques in high schools are fairly easy to see.

The most serious contact between adolescents of the opposite sexes occurs through dating.

The development of independence is even more extreme for children living in the Nyakyusan culture in East Africa (Barnouw, 1975). Children leave home with their peers when they are ten years old to develop a new village. They build huts, get married and have children, and cultivate fields. Many of the adolescents, then, in the cultures of the Muria and the Nyakyusa are given the chance to become autonomous and perform adult roles long before they reach adulthood.

Marriage and parenthood for adolescents is not nearly as rigidly defined in our present-day American culture as it is in the Murian and Nyakyusan cultures. Instead, most adolescents go through an extensive period of dating, and many individuals do not marry until well after adolescence.

Dating

While many adolescent boys and girls have social interchanges through formal and informal peer groups, it is through dating that more serious contacts between the sexes occur. Think about your junior high, high school, and early college years. You probably spent a lot of time thinking about how you were going to get a particular girl or boy to go out with you. And many of your weekend evenings were likely spent on dates or on envying others who had dates. Some of you went steady,

perhaps even during junior high school—others of you may have been engaged to be married by the end of high school.

Females seem much more likely to disclose themselves to males than vice versa and are much more prone to mutual self-exploration than males are in dating relationships (e.g., Douvan & Adelson, 1966). It also appears that girls bring the capacity for intimacy to courtship relations and train males to be intimate (e.g., Simon & Gagnon, 1969). In other words, girls are much more oriented toward revealing sensitive, intimate feelings and pursuing personality exploration than males are in the dating process.

As part of their social interaction, adolescents not only date but, in some instances, marry. In the next section, the effects of adolescent marriage are explored.

Adolescent Marriage

More than 20 percent of all females aged nineteen or younger are now married, or have been married, while less than 10 percent of the males in the same age group are married or have been married (U.S. Bureau of the Census, 1976). Many adolescent marriages fail—and the younger the adolescents are when they marry, the greater the likelihood that they will divorce (e.g., DeLissovoy, 1973). Many adolescents who do marry say later that it would have been better if they had waited.

The younger adolescents are when they marry, the greater the likelihood that they will divorce.

When adolescents do get married, what factors contribute to the likelihood that the marriage will be a good one? Lee Burchinal (1965) has summarized the major factors that contribute to whether adolescent marriages have a poor, intermediate, or good chance of being successful. These factors are displayed in table 14.1.

Why do adolescents marry early rather than waiting until they have finished their schooling and achieved a secure financial position? The main reason adolescents marry is pregnancy (e.g., DeLissovoy, 1973). Many adolescents do not foresee the problems an early marriage and childbearing may bring. They may cling to the idealized notion that love will conquer everything, wanting to show everyone that they can make it on their own.

A critical moral issue for the pregnant adolescent is whether she should get an abortion. Abortion counseling is now available through hot lines, clinics, and counselors in most communities, and the choice to have an abortion now carries less stigma than in past times.

Still, abortion is considered out of the question for many individuals, particularly those from certain religious backgrounds.

Many adolescents who marry drop out of school, although this is much more prevalent among females than males. Pregnant females are the most likely to quit school. At one time, schools barred married and pregnant students from attendance, and these students are still looked at with a jaundiced eye in many school systems. In 1972, a federal law was passed stating that all married students and pregnant adolescents are entitled to a full education in the public school system.

Even when they are encouraged to attend school, though, many pregnant adolescents feel uneasy and uncomfortable doing so, particularly as their pregnancy progresses. Some progressive school systems have instituted special programs that include counseling sessions for pregnant teenagers (e.g., Heller & Kiralry, 1973; Kappelman, 1974). These programs vary in the ways they try to help the pregnant teenager with her education. In some instances, special schools are set up in which pregnant females from an entire county come

Table 14.1
Hypothesized Relationship between Selected Characteristics and Outcomes of Young Marriages

Forecast of Marital Competence and Satisfaction

Characteristic	Poorest	Intermediate	Best
Ages at marriage	Both seventeen or younger	Female seventeen, male twenty or older	Female at least eighteen, male twenty or older
Educational attainment	Both school dropouts	Female dropout, male high school graduate	Both high school graduates; male, at least, with some post-high school education
Pregnancy	Premarital pregnancy	No premarital pregnancy; pregnancy immediately following marriage	Pregnancy delayed until at least one year following marriage
Acquaintance before marriage	Less than six months; no engagement period, formal or informal	One year, at least, with at least six months understanding or engagement to marry	Several years, with at least six months understanding or engagement to marry
Previous dating patterns	Limited number of dating partners; went steady immediately, or short period between first date and first date with fiancé	Some dating experience before dating fiancé	Numerous dates, played the field; some previous experience with going steady
Personality dynamics	Generally poor interpersonal skills; lacking maturity; limited interests; poor personal and social adjustment	Mixed	Generally competent in interpersonal relations; flexible, mature; maintaining healthy and pleasurable relations with others
Motivation for marrying	Drifted into marriage; because of pregnancy; seemed like the thing to do; just wanted to; other impulsive reasons with no strong emphasis on marital and parental roles	Mixed; marriage preferred to career, though had previous post-high school educational aspirations and, for females, perhaps tentative plans to work, etc.	No post-high school educational aspirations; and, for females, marriage, family, and homemaking preferred over working, living independently; positive emphasis upon role as wife and mother
Status of families	Both lower class	Mixed; lower and middle or upper class	Both middle or upper class
Parental attitudes before marriage	Strongly opposed	Mildly opposed or resigned acceptance	Supportive, once the decision was clear
Wedding	Elopement and civil ceremony		Conventional, hometown, church-sanctioned
Economic basis	Virtually completely dependent upon relatives	Low dependence upon relatives; mostly independent income, even if near hardship level	At least assured income above self-perceived hardship level
Residence	Always lived with in-laws or other relatives	Doubled up with relatives some of the time, independent other times	Always maintained own independent place of residence
Postmarriage parental views	Rejecting or punitive, assistance provided as a method of controlling the marriage	Cool	Psychologically supportive, sincerely want to help, assistance provided with no strings attached

Reprinted by permission from Burchinal, 1965, 251.

to a centralized location to attend classes; in others, more effort is made to mainstream the pregnant females into the regular classes at their high schools. The programs also vary in the extent and nature of the counseling they offer the girls. Most of the programs, though, attempt to help the adolescent deal not only with personal problems but with the prospect of handling the financial burden of caring for her infant after it is born.

This section on adolescent marriage concludes our discussion of families and peers. Next, we discuss personality development during adolescence.

Personality Development

We will continue the discussion of the self, focusing extensively on the development of identity in adolescence. First, let's examine the emergence of self-theory in adolescence and how the self functions as an information processing system during adolescence.

The Self

It is not until adolescence that individuals begin to develop formal theories about the self. At this time their self-theory begins to resemble a scientific search for the answer to a difficult question.

David Elkind (1971) pointed out the emerging characteristics of a self-theory.

During adolescence the young person develops a true sense of self. While children are aware of themselves, they are not able to put themselves in other people's shoes and to look at themselves from that perspective. Adolescents can do this and do engage in such self-watching to a considerable extent. Indeed, the characteristic "self-consciousness" of the adolescent results from the very fact that the young person is now very much concerned with how others react to him. This is a concern that is largely absent in childhood. (p. 111)

In early adolescence the individual's self-theory is somewhat tenuous. This is reflected in the self-consciousness and apprehension young adolescents express in regard to how others view them. Like a new scientific theory, the young adolescent's self-theory is particularly open to refuting data. However, adolescents are continually searching for new data that will generate support for their self-theory. Morris Okun and Joseph Sasfy (1977) point out that such adolescent events as getting a driver's license and going on a first date provide critical data for important components of this self-theory. After such events take place, an adolescent may think to herself, "I am competent," or "Boys like me."

It is true, however, that many adolescents have idealized images of themselves. The onset of formal operational thought allows them to step outside the concrete aspects of their experience and imagine what they might be like and what they are capable of becoming.

During adolescence the young person develops a true sense of self.

That is, adolescent self-theory begins to hinge more on idealized self-images than on actual concrete experiences. As teenagers mature into later adolescence, they accumulate experiences (often painful ones) that tell them whether their idealized self-images are accurate or not. Gradually, older adolescents begin to modify their self-theories to be less grandiose, more realistic, and more specific. Older adolescents place boundary lines on their self-theories so that they can function more competently and not be saddled with unnecessary disillusionments.

Psychologists are just beginning to understand how information processing and cognitive activities direct, regulate, and control behavior. In prior chapters we have emphasized the importance of the emerging field of social cognition (chapters 10 and 13) for understanding development. For the most part social cognition was discussed in chapters focusing on cognitive development. Here we will look at how various aspects of social cognition might be used to predict the social competence of the adolescent.

Rather than emphasizing a global, stable structure of self, such as self-concept, the social cognition perspective developed by Martin Ford (1982) stresses the information processing system of the adolescent's self. Two samples of ninth and twelfth graders participated in the research. Social competence was defined as "the attainment of relevant social goals in specified social contexts, using appropriate means and resulting in positive developmental outcomes. The social goal chosen for this study was being able to behave effectively in challenging social situations involving salient social objects." In summarizing the results of the investigation, Ford concluded:

Adolescents who are judged as able to behave effectively in challenging social situations involving salient social objects assign relatively high priorities to interpersonal goals such as helping others, getting socially involved, and getting along with parents and friends, and are likely to describe themselves as possessing the intrapersonal resources required to accomplish these goals. They also tend to be more goal-directed than their peers; that is, they like to set goals for themselves and control their own destiny rather than to just 'go with the flow' . . . [and during adolescence], empathy plays a crucial role in regulating behavior so as to promote social welfare and harmony (Clark 1980; Hogan 1973).

It is noteworthy that adolescents who are judged to be socially competent tend to perceive themselves as having a relatively large social support network surrounding them. One possibility is that they are superior in terms of both personal and environmental resources . . . socially competent adolescents are (also) more cognitively resourceful; that is, they are better able to think of ways to address interpersonal problem situations and to construct coherent plans or strategies for solving them. There is also some evidence that these individuals are more likely to consider the possible consequences of their actions for themselves and others. (pp. 335–36)

The governing theme of self-evaluation during adolescence is identity. Who am I? Where am I going? What kind of career will I pursue? How well do I relate to females, to males? Am I able to make it on my own? These are questions that clamor for solutions in the adolescent years and that are critical in the establishment of identity, as will be seen next.

Identity

A term that is virtually inseparable from the self is identity. Identity is an integrative concept that is used to capture the diverse, complex components of the adolescent's personality development. The description of identity development can be traced directly to the thinking and writing of psychoanalyst Erik Erikson (1963, 1968). As you may recall from chapter 2, identity development represents the fifth stage in Erikson's model of development, occurring at about the same time as adolescence. If postadolescents have not developed a positive sense of identity, they are described as having identity diffusion or confusion.

Certainly the idea of the identity crisis has permeated our society. The term is applied to practically anyone of any age who feels a loss of identification or self-image—teenagers who cannot "find" themselves; professionals who have lost their jobs; the newly divorced; business executives who are questioning their values. The term has even been applied to companies and institutions. For example, the federal government might have been undergoing an "identity crisis" when it was rocked by the Watergate scandal, or a school system may be having an identity crisis when it must choose between a traditional and an innovative curriculum. In fact, the use of the term identity crisis has become so pervasive that defining it is difficult.

These general applications have gone far beyond Erikson's original use of the term; for Erikson (1968), identity is primarily the property of an individual person, not a group or an institution. According to Erikson, although identity is important throughout a person's life, it is only in adolescence that identity development reaches crisis proportions. A positive or negative identity is being developed throughout childhood as a result of the way various crises have been handled. The positive resolution of earlier crises, such as trust versus mistrust and industry versus inferiority, helps the individual cope positively with the identity crisis that, Erikson believes, occurs in adolescence.

During adolescence, world views become important to an individual who enters what Erikson terms a "psychological moratorium"—a gap between the security of childhood and the new autonomy of approaching adulthood. Numerous identities can be drawn from the surrounding culture. Adolescents can experiment with different roles, trying them out and seeing which ones they like. The youth who successfully copes with these conflicting identities during adolescence emerges with a new sense of self that is both refreshing and acceptable. The adolescent who is not successful in resolving this identity crisis becomes confused, suffering from what Erikson refers to as *identity confusion.* This confusion may take one of two courses: the individual may withdraw, isolating himself or herself from peers and family or may lose his or her own identity in that of the crowd.

Box 14.3
Erik Erikson's Analysis of the Youths of Adolf Hitler, Martin Luther, and Mahatma Gandhi

In the following excerpts from Erikson's writings, the psychoanalytic method is used to analyze the youths of Adolf Hitler, Martin Luther, and Mahatma Gandhi. In one passage, Erikson (1962) describes the youth of Adolf Hitler:

> I will not go into the symbolism of Hitler's urge to build except to say that his shiftless and brutal father had consistently denied the mother a steady residence; one must read how Adolf took care of his mother when she wasted away from breast cancer to get an inkling of this young man's desperate urge to cure. But it would take a very extensive analysis, indeed, to indicate in what way a single boy can daydream his way into history and emerge a sinister genius, and how a whole nation becomes ready to accept the emotive power of that genius as a hope of fulfillment for its national aspirations and as a warrant for national criminality. . . .
>
> The memoirs of young Hitler's friend indicate an almost pitiful fear on the part of the future dictator that he might be nothing. He had to challenge this possibility by being deliberately and totally anonymous; and only out of this self-chosen nothingness could he become everything. (pp. 108–9)

But while the identity crisis of Adolf Hitler led him to turn toward politics in a pathological effort to create a world order, the identity crisis of Martin Luther in a different era led him to turn toward theology in an attempt to deal systematically with human nothingness or lack of identity.

> In confession, for example, he was so meticulous in the attempt to be truthful that he spelled out every intention as well as every deed; he splintered relatively acceptable purities into smaller and smaller impurities; he reported temptations in historical sequence, starting back in childhood; and after having confessed for hours, would ask for special appointments in order to correct previous statements. In doing this he was obviously both exceedingly compulsive and, at least unconsciously, rebellious.
>
> At this point we must note a characteristic of great youth rebels; their inner split between the temptation to surrender and the need to dominate. A great young rebel is torn between, on the one hand, tendencies to give in and fantasies of defeat (Luther used to resign himself to an early death at times of impending success); and the absolute need, on the other hand, to take the lead, not only over himself but over all the forces and people who impinge on him. (pp. 155–57)

Identity confusion may account for the large number of adolescents who run away from home, drop out of school, quit their jobs, stay out all night, or assume bizarre behavior. Before Erikson's ideas became popular, these adolescents were often labeled delinquents and looked at with a disapproving eye. As a result of Erikson's writings and analyses, the problems these youths encounter are now viewed in a more positive light. Not only do runaways, school dropouts, and those who quit jobs struggle with identity, virtually all adolescents go through an identity crisis, and some are simply able to resolve the crisis more easily than others.

Role Experimentation

Adolescents want to be able to decide freely for themselves such matters as what careers they will pursue, whether they will go to college or into military service, and whether or not they will marry. In other words, they want to free themselves from the shackles of their parents and other adults to make their own choices. At the same time, however, many adolescents have a deep fear of making the wrong decisions and of failing.

There are literally hundreds of roles for the adolescent to try out, and probably as many ways to pursue each role. Erikson believes that by late adolescence, occupational choices are central to the development of identity. Other important role choices involve sexuality (including decisions on dating, marriage, and sexual behavior), politics, religion, and moral values.

For example, many adolescents have been indoctrinated in the religious beliefs of their parents. By late adolescence, youth come to understand that they can make their own decisions about religion. The same can be said of political identity—most children report that they adopt their parents' political choices. But by late adolescence, youth make their own decisions. Unfortunately, some adolescents consistently and deliberately adopt choices that are opposite those of their parents as a means of attaining "independence." Such behavior does not meet the criteria for successful development of autonomy or identity but represents a negative identity.

Adolph Hitler.   *Martin Luther.*

And in his Pulitzer Prize-winning book on Mahatma Gandhi's life, Erikson (1969) describes the personality formation of Gandhi during his youth.

> Straight and yet not stiff; shy and yet not withdrawn; intelligent and yet not bookish; willful and yet not stubborn; sensual and yet not soft. . . . We must try to reflect on the relation of such a youth to his father, because the Mahatma places service to the father and the crushing guilt of failing in such service in the center of his adolescent turbulence. Some historians and political scientists seem to find it easy to interpret this account in psychoanalytic terms; I do not. For the question is not how a particular version of the Oedipal Complex "causes" a man to be both great and neurotic in a particular way, but rather how such a young person . . . manages the complexes which constrict other men. (p. 113)

In these passages, the workings of an insightful, sensitive mind is shown looking for a historical perspective on matters. Through analyses of the lives of famous individuals such as Hitler, Luther, and Gandhi, and through the thousands of youth he has talked with in person, Erikson has pieced together a descriptive picture of identity development.

Thus, the development of an integrated sense of identity is a complex and difficult task. Adolescents are expected to master many different roles in our culture. It is the rare, perhaps even nonexistent, adolescent who doesn't experience serious doubts about his or her capabilities in handling at least some of these roles competently.

Erik Erikson is a master at using the psychoanalytic method to uncover historical clues about identity formation. He has used the psychoanalytic method both with the youth he treats in psychotherapy sessions and in the analysis of the lives of famous individuals. Erikson (1963) believes that the psychoanalytic technique sheds light on human psychological evolution. He also believes that the history of the world is a composite of individual life cycles. In box 14.3, Erikson's analyses of identity development in Adolf Hitler, Martin Luther, and Mahatma Gandhi are provided.

Marcia's View on the Four Identity Statuses

James Marcia (1966) has analyzed Erikson's identity theory of adolescence and concluded that four identity statuses, or *modes of resolution,* can be applied to the theory—identity diffusion, foreclosure, moratorium, and identity achievement. The extent of an adolescent's commitment and crisis is used to classify him or her as having one of the four identity statuses. Marcia defines crisis as a period during which the adolescent is choosing among meaningful alternatives. He defines commitment as the extent to which an adolescent shows a personal investment in what he or she is doing or is going to do.

Adolescents classified as **identity diffused** (or **confused**) have not experienced any crisis (that is, they haven't explored meaningful alternatives) or made any commitments. Not only are they undecided upon occupational or ideological choices, they also are likely to show little or no interest in such matters.

The adolescent experiencing identity **foreclosure** has made a commitment but has not experienced a crisis. This occurs most often when parents simply hand

Adolescents in the moratorium status have commitments that are absent or only vaguely defined.

down commitments to their adolescents, more often than not in an authoritarian manner. In such circumstances, adolescents may not have had enough opportunities to explore different approaches, ideologies, and vocations on their own. Some experts on adolescence, such as Kenneth Kenniston (1971), believe that experiencing a crisis is necessary for the development of a mature and self-integrated identity.

Marcia states that adolescents in the **moratorium** status are in the midst of a crisis but that their commitments are either absent or only vaguely defined. Such adolescents are searching for commitments by actively questioning alternatives.

Adolescents who have undergone a crisis and made a commitment are referred to as **identity achieved.** In other words, to reach the identity-achievement status, it is necessary for the adolescent to first experience a psychological moratorium, then make an enduring commitment.

Some experts on adolescence argue that college experiences increase the likelihood that adolescents will enter a status of moratorium. The theory is that professors and peers stimulate older adolescents to rethink their vocational and ideological orientations (e.g., Waterman & Waterman, 1971). In one investigation, as many as four out of every five adolescents in a moratorium status switched their occupational orientation during their college years (Waterman & Waterman, 1972). As a rule, the incidence of successful resolution to the identity crisis and successful development of an identity commitment increases from the first year to the final year of college (Constantinople 1969).

Sex Differences in Identity Development
Is the identity development of the adolescent male the same as that of the adolescent female? An increasing number of researchers are finding sex differences in the development of identity during both the high school and college years (Dusek & Flaherty, 1981; Flaherty & Dusek, 1980).

For example, Joe LaVoie (1976) has found that vocational identity is central to the identity formation of mid-adolescent males, while affiliative needs are more important to their female counterparts. Similarly, in college-aged adolescents, ideological choices and vocational orientations provide the core for the identity development of males, while intimacy and interpersonal relationships play a more important role in the identity development of females (Constantinople, 1969; Toder & Marcia, 1973). Furthermore, it has been found that by the end of the college years, males have been able to resolve an identity crisis more readily than females (Constantinople, 1969).

Problems and Disturbances
Adolescence has traditionally been pictured as time of turmoil and conflict, although we have seen that a number of experts believe this picture has been exaggerated (Adelson, 1979; Hill & Steinberg, 1976; Yankelovich, 1974). These experts believe that the majority of adolescents are not experiencing intense turmoil or deep emotional disturbances. But some adolescents do have serious problems and disturbances. It is during adolescence that some disorders appear for the first time, including adult forms of schizophrenia, depression, and antisocial behavior.

Males are twice as likely as females to smoke marijuana.

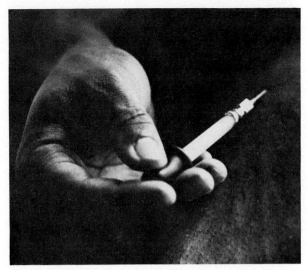

Drug use among adolescents is a primary concern of parents.

Thomas Achenbach (1978) described the developmental course of admissions to mental health clinics in the adolescent years. Following a drop of admissions during the ten- to twelve-year period, the rate of admission increases until it peaks at about fourteen years of age (Rosen, Bahn, & Kramer, 1964). Actually there is very little increase in admissions for boys from the age of nine to fourteen, but there is a substantial increase in the number of girls admitted.

In a survey of 2,303 fourteen- to fifteen-year-olds living in England, conflicts with parents were denied by most of the adolescents and their parents (Rutter, Graham, Chadwick, & Yule, 1976). Among those in the psychiatric sample, there was a greater incidence of parent-adolescent conflict than in the nonpsychiatric group. When the types of problems at ages ten and fourteen to fifteen were compared, there was a significant increase in depression and refusal to attend school at the later age; the refusal to attend school usually was part of a general anxiety pattern, however. Over half of all of the problems mentioned by the adolescents had appeared after the age of ten.

Now we will look more in depth at some of the major problems and disturbances of adolescence—drug abuse, delinquency, and suicide.

Drug Abuse

Probably no other aspect of teenage life is of greater concern to parents than the alarming rise in drug use and abuse, including adolescent consumption of alcohol. The most common drugs used by adolescents are listed in table 14.2. Notice that alcohol and tobacco, which contains the stimulant nicotine, are included on the list. Let's look more closely at two of the most predominant drugs listed, marijuana and alcohol.

Marijuana

Much of the controversy surrounding adolescent drug use has focused on marijuana. In 1972 the National Commission on Marijuana and Drug Use reported that more than one out of every two adolescents between the ages of eighteen and twenty-one had used marijuana. Furthermore, a White House paper on drug use prepared for the president indicated that slightly more than one of every four adolescents between the ages of twelve and seventeen had tried marijuana. Data from the Department of Health, Education, and Welfare (1978), collected between 1975 and 1977, suggest that more than one of every two high school students had tried marijuana. However, marijuana use among high school seniors may be leveling off; a 1979 national survey of reported daily use indicated that in 1978 10.7 percent of the students smoked marijuana, while in 1979 the figure had dropped to 10.3 percent (Johnson, Backman, & O'Malley, 1980).

It is now estimated that approximately one in twenty-five twelve- to thirteen-year-olds and about one in seven fourteen- to fifteen-year-olds smokes marijuana once a month. Interestingly, adolescent males are twice as likely as their female counterparts to smoke marijuana on a daily basis. While marijuana has been smoked for centuries around the world, scientific scrutiny of the drug is still in its infancy. Almost all of the studies of marijuana's immediate effects indicate that the drug interferes with short-term memory and intellectual performance, impairing thinking, reading comprehension, and verbal and arithmetic problem solving.

Table 14.2
Facts about Drugs

Name	Slang Name	Source	Classification	How Taken	Effects Sought
Heroin	H., Horse, Scat, Junk, Smack, Scag, Stuff, Dope	Semisynthetic (from morphine)	Narcotic	Injected or sniffed	Euphoria, prevent withdrawal discomfort
Morphine	White stuff, M.	Natural (from opium)	Narcotic	Swallowed or injected	Euphoria, prevent withdrawal discomfort
Methadone	Dolly	Synthetic	Narcotic	Swallowed or injected	Prevent withdrawal discomfort
Cocaine	Coke, Corrine, Gold dust, Bernice, Flake, Star dust, Snow	Natural (from coca, not cocoa)	Stimulant, local anesthesia	Sniffed, injected, or swallowed	Excitation, talkativeness
Marijuana	Pot, Grass, Hash, Tea, Dope, Joints, Reefers	Natural	Relaxant, euphoriant; in high doses, hallucinogen	Smoked, swallowed, or sniffed	Relaxation; increased euphoria, perceptions, sociability
Barbiturates	Barbs, Blue devils, Reds, Yellow jackets, Phennies, Downers, Blue heavens	Synthetic	Sedative-hypnotic	Swallowed or injected	Anxiety reduction, euphoraia
Amphetamines	Bennies, Dexies, Speed, Wake-ups, Hearts, Pep pills, Uppers	Synthetic	Sympathomimetic	Swallowed or injected	Alertness, activeness
LSD	Acid, Sugar, Big D, Cubes, Trips	Semisynthetic (from ergot alkaloids)	Hallucinogen	Swallowed	Insightful experiences, exhilaration, distortion of senses
Mescaline	Mesc.	Natural (from peyote)	Hallucinogen	Swallowed	Insightful experiences, exhilartion, distortion of senses
Psilocybin	Magic mushroom	Natural (from psilocybe)	Hallucinogen	Swallowed	Insightful experiences, exhilaration, distortion of senses
Alcohol	Booze, Juice, etc.	Natural (from grapes, grains via fermentation)	Sedative-hypnotic	Swallowed	Sense alteration, anxiety reduction, sociability
Tobacco	Cancer tube, Coffin nail, etc.	Natural	Stimulant-sedative	Smoked, sniffed, chewed	Calmness, sociability

*Persons who inject drugs under nonsterile conditions run a high risk of contracting hepatitis, abscesses, or circulatory disorders.
? Indicates conflict of opinion.
Adapted from Today's Education NEA Journal, Feb. 1971

Long-Term Symptoms	Physical Dependence Potential	Mental Dependence Potential	Organic Damage Potential
Addiction, constipation, loss of appetite	Yes	Yes	No*
Addiction, constipation, loss of appetite	Yes	Yes	No*
Addiction, constipation, loss of appetite	Yes	Yes	No
Depression, convulsions	No	Yes	Yes?
Usually none	No	Yes?	No
Addiction with severe withdrawal symptoms, possible convulsions, toxic psychosis	Yes	Yes	Yes
Loss of appetite, delusions, hallucinations, toxic psychosis	Yes?	Yes	Yes
May intensify existing psychosis, panic reactions	No	No?	No?
?	No	No?	No?
?	No	No?	No?
Cirrhosis, neurologic damage, addiction	Yes	Yes	Yes
Emphysema, lung cancer, mouth and throat cancer, cardiovascular damage, loss of appetite	Yes?	Yes	Yes

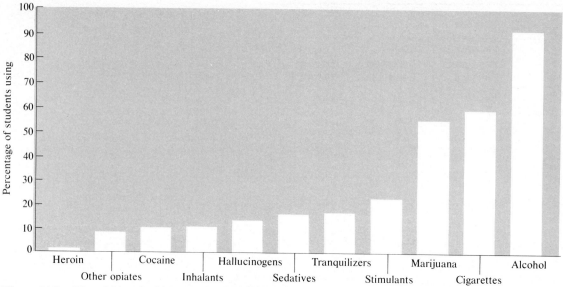

Figure 14.2 Use of drugs by high school-aged adolescents.

In addition marijuana reduces the ability to perform tasks that require concentration and coordination. According to the National Institute on Drug Abuse, frequent marijuana smoking could negatively affect school performance.

As long ago as 1893, the Indian Hemp Commission found a link between marijuana use and lung disease. Recent investigations involving both animals and humans suggest that marijuana can impair lung functioning. The National Institute on Drug Abuse reports that when marijuana is used daily in heavy amounts, it may impair the human reproductive system. A significant decline in sperm count may result from marijuana usage, as well as a greater incidence of abnormalities in the sperm produced. Women using marijuana daily run the risk of decreased fertility. And while there have been no human studies on the subject, animal studies link heavy marijuana use with an increase in birth defects.

Because of facts such as these, medical experts are initiating a campaign to discourage the use of marijuana on a regular basis. A 1980 health report by the National Institute on Drug Abuse emphasizes that individuals under the age of eighteen should not use marijuana. Occasional use of marijuana by healthy adults, however, appears to have negligible effects on physical health.

To what extent do parents and peers influence adolescents to use marijuana? A host of studies have indicated that there are positive correlations between parental drug use (such as tranquilizers, amphetamines, alcohol, and tobacco) and the use of marijuana by youth (e.g., Shafer et al., 1973). And adolescents whose peers smoke marijuana are also more likely to smoke than those whose friends do not (e.g., Tec, 1972).

In one investigation of parental and peer influences on marijuana use by adolescents, Denise Kandel (Kandel, 1974; Kandel & Faust, 1975) interviewed adolescents, their friends, and their parents about various factors associated with the use of marijuana. Kandel found that associating with friends who use marijuana is more likely to influence an adolescent than parental drug use. Kandel found that only 15 percent of the adolescents whose friends did not smoke marijuana smoked themselves. By contrast, 79 percent of the youth whose peers smoked also smoked themselves. The highest use occurred when an adolescent's friends smoked marijuana and his or her parents took drugs (barbiturates, alcohol, and so on).

Alcohol
Many parents and other adults do not consider alcohol to be a drug, although it is just that. Figure 14.2 indicates that adolescents are more likely to indulge in drinking alcohol than in smoking marijuana. Most surveys indicate that the great majority of youth have sampled alcohol, and that adolescent alcohol consumption increased throughout the 1960s and 1970s. In an ongoing national survey conducted by the Institute for Social Research in Ann Arbor, Michigan, 20 percent more high school seniors reported that they drank on three or more occasions in 1975 than did their counterparts in 1969 (Johnson, Backman, & O'Malley, 1978). However, alcohol consumption among high school seniors began to level off in the late 1970s. While there was a slight increase in the number of adolescents who drank from 1975 to 1977, the figures seem to reflect the increasing numbers of young females drinking rather than an overall trend.

Many factors interact to determine if an adolescent will become a problem drinker.

An adolescent's values and customs influence drinking behavior.

Alcohol, then, is the most commonly used and abused psychoactive substance among adolescents in the United States. Approximately 6.1 percent of all high school seniors consume alcohol on a daily basis (Office of Drug Abuse Policy, 1978). Too often this results in tragedy; approximately eight thousand youths die every year in alcohol-related car accidents.

Alcohol is a depressant that primarily affects the adolescent's central nervous system. It is popularly believed that alcohol increases arousal and excitement, but in reality it slows down or depresses many of the brain's activities. After a certain level of alcohol accumulates in the adolescent's bloodstream, the familiar pattern of drunkenness ensues, usually involving a loss of mental and physical alertness and coordination. After prolonged consumption, unconsciousness may result.

The use of alcohol in large quantities can have a variety of negative consequences for the physical development of the adolescent. For one, he or she may develop a chronic irritation of the stomach lining, leading to an ulcer. In addition, fat may accumulate in the liver and impair its functioning.

Family relationships, peer relations, the sociocultural context of the neighborhood, and the abilities and talents of the adolescent interact to influence the likelihood that the adolescent will become a problem drinker. Just as in other areas of psychosocial development, problem drinking in adolescence is determined by a complex set of factors. Certainly the family socialization process is one of the most important since adolescents initially learn how to communicate with others through interaction with their parents. The communication system of alcoholic parents often entails lies and mistrust. Families of alcoholics often become socially isolated from others (Sloboda, 1974). Quarreling and fighting may charactertize the social climates of such homes. None of these family conditions is conducive to the development of psychologically healthy adolescents.

Cultural factors, including the values and customs of the community, also influence the adolescent's drinking behavior. Rates of alcoholism vary considerably from one culture to the next—northern France, the United States, Italy, and northern Russia have high incidences of alcoholism, for example. But low rates of alcoholism are not necessarily due to abstinence. Moslems do not drink because of their religious beliefs, and their alcoholism rates are low; by contrast, a large percentage of Jews do drink, but their alcoholism rates are low also.

Customs, values, and sanctions in various cultures influence the degree to which alcoholism is a problem within those cultures.

The National Institute on Alcohol Abuse and Alcoholism (1974) concluded that among groups who use alcohol extensively, the lowest rate of alcoholism is linked with the following factors:

1. Youth are exposed to alcohol at an early point in their lives within a strong family or religious group. The alcohol is served in diluted form and in small quantities.
2. The beverage served is usually thought of as food and is taken with meals.
3. Parents show an example of moderate rather than excessive drinking.
4. No moral significance is placed on drinking—it is neither considered right nor wrong.
5. Drinking is not viewed as proof of adulthood or virility.
6. Abstinence is viewed as socially acceptable; it is no more inconsiderate to turn down a drink than to turn down a helping of green beans.
7. Excessive drinking or being intoxicated is not approved of; it is not stylish, vogue, or "cool" to drink heavily or get drunk.

In studies of delinquency, there is evidence that excessive drinking is fairly common among delinquents. Drinking to excess, even to the point of passing out, is common among approximately four out of ten delinquents but in less than one out of ten nondelinquents (e.g., MacKay, Phillips, & Bryce, 1967; Pearce & Garrett, 1970). According to the same investigations, approximately one out of every three delinquents had been arrested for drinking, while less than one out of twenty nondelinquents had been arrested for the same offense. And in one investigation of adolescent girls seen at the Massachusetts Youth Reception-Detention Center in Boston, more than one of every two girls drank on a weekly basis, and about four out of every ten girls had passed out while drinking (Widseth & Mayer, 1971).

Delinquents may drink for reasons different from those of nondelinquents. Grace Barnes (1977) points out that delinquents may drink more for the effect than nondelinquents, who are more likely to drink to help them socialize, celebrate, or simply to have fun.

Juvenile Delinquency

The label *juvenile delinquent* is applied to an adolescent who breaks the law or engages in behavior that is considered illegal. Like other categories of disturbance, juvenile delinquency is a broad concept; legal infractions may range from littering to murder. Because the youth technically becomes a juvenile delinquent only after judged guilty of a crime by a court of law, official records do not accurately reflect the number of illegal acts committed. Nevertheless, there is still every indication that in the last ten or fifteen years, juvenile delinquency has increased in relation to the number of crimes committed by adults.

Estimates regarding the number of juvenile delinquents in the United States are sketchy, although FBI statistics suggest that at least 2 percent of all youths are involved in juvenile court cases. The number of girls found guilty of juvenile delinquency has increased significantly in recent years. Delinquency rates among blacks, other minority groups, and the lower class are particularly high in relation to the overall populations of these groups. However, such groups have less influence than others over the judicial decision-making process in the United States and thus may be judged delinquent more readily than their white, middle-class counterparts.

The Nature of Delinquency

Alan Ross (1979) describes juvenile delinquency as the failure to develop sufficient behavioral control. Some children fail to develop the essential controls that others have acquired during the process of growing up. Most youths have learned the difference between socially acceptable and unacceptable behavior, but the juvenile delinquent has not. He or she may fail to distinguish between acceptable and unacceptable behavior or may have learned this distinction but failed to develop adequate control in using the distinction to guide behavior.

To understand the problem of delinquency, it is thus necessary to study different aspects of the development of self-control—for example, delay of gratification and self-imposed standards of conduct. Studies have found that failure to delay gratification is related to cheating and to a general lack of social responsibility often revealed in delinquent behavior (e.g., Mischel, 1961; Mischel & Gilligan, 1964).

Delinquents also may have developed inadequate standards of conduct. An adolescent about to commit an antisocial act must invoke self-critical thoughts to inhibit the tendency to commit the illegal action. These self-critical standards are strongly influenced by the models the youth experiences. Thus, adolescents whose parents, teachers, and peers exhibit self-critical standards can be expected to develop the self-control needed to refrain from an illegal or antisocial act. Others, however, may be exposed to models who praise antisocial acts. For example, an adolescent whose peers engage in antisocial deeds may follow their example, especially if he or she also lacks family models who are both strong and positive in terms of standards of conduct.

The expected consequences of negative actions also influence the youth's decision to engage in or refrain from delinquent behavior. When the youth expects

To understand delinquency it is necessary to study aspects of self-control.

some sort of reward for delinquent behavior, he or she is more likely to perform the antisocial act than if punishment is expected. The expected rewards can take many different forms—the acquisition of stolen goods, for example, or high status in the gang or in neighborhood peer groups.

Whether or not the adolescent engages in juvenile delinquency may also be affected by competence achieved in different aspects of life. Consider a youth who does well in academic subjects at school, who actively participates in socially desirable clubs, or who develops athletic skills. This youth is likely to develop a positive self-image and receive reinforcement from others for prosocial behavior. Most delinquents, however, have achieved few ego-enhancing competencies; antisocial behavior is one way they can demonstrate self-competence and receive reinforcement from the delinquent subculture.

Types of Delinquency

Alan Ross (1979) has described three types of delinquency: impulsive; unsocialized; and social. The **impulsive delinquent** knows that delinquent behavior is wrong and will probably be punished. For example, if he steals a pornographic magazine from a newsstand,

he knows he may be caught and taken to court for his action. But the magazine is a very attractive object to him, and his perception is the odds are against his being caught. These considerations override his restraint, and he steals the magazine. Since approximately 90 percent of all adolescents engage in some type of delinquent behavior at least once (Gold, 1966), most youth have probably committed this type of delinquent behavior. Whether this behavior continues to occur is often determined by complicated factors. For the adolescent with weak self-control, being caught or seeing someone else caught may be the event that puts an end to this type of behavior. For others, the guilt associated with having done something wrong may be sufficient to prevent future misdeeds.

The **unsocialized delinquent** has not developed appropriate internal controls to refrain from engaging in delinquent behavior. It is generally thought that the antisocial behavior is produced by deficient socialization on the part of the family (e.g., Glueck & Glueck, 1950). Although no specific parental behavior can be pinpointed as the cause of the adolescent's delinquent behavior, the unsocialized delinquent generally comes from what might be described as a "bad" family in which the parents fail to condemn antisocial actions and obscure the boundary between acceptable and unacceptable behavior. In one well-known study (Bandura & Walters, 1959), it was found that delinquent boys come from homes where the parents deal inconsistently with the children, the fathers reject the sons, and both parents use a great deal of physical force in disciplining their sons.

Although juvenile delinquency is less exclusively a lower-class problem than it was in the past, some forms of delinquency tend to be more prevalent among members of the lower class. The **social delinquent** develops control over his or her own behavior but gives in to the norms and delinquent standards of his or her gang or peer group. The norms of many lower-class peer groups and gangs are antisocial, or counterproductive to the goals and norms of society at large. In discussing the lower-class peer subculture, Miller (1958) indicated that getting into and staying out of trouble is a dominant feature of lower-class adolescent life. Since lower-class adolescents have less opportunity to develop skills that are socially desirable, they achieve attention and status by engaging in antisocial actions. Being "tough" and "masculine" are high-status traits for the lower-class boys, and these traits are often gauged by the adolescent's success in performing delinquent acts and getting away with them.

Both the community and the family may foster the development of delinquency. A community with a high crime rate allows the child to observe many models that engage in criminal activities. The child also may see these models rewarded for their criminal accomplishments. Such communities often are characterized by poverty, unemployment, and feelings of alienation toward the middle class.

Antagonistic relationships between parents often exist in families with antisocial children (e.g., McCord, McCord, & Gudeman, 1960; Rutter, 1971). For example, Michael Rutter (1971) studied a sample of London families in which one or both parents had undergone psychiatric treatment. When the families were divided into three groups according to the quality of the parents' marriage (i.e., in terms of affection, communication, and mutual enjoyment of each other's company), the percentage of boys showing antisocial behavior was strongly related to the lower groupings. No antisocial boys came from families where the marriage was "good," while 22 percent of the antisocial boys were in families where the marriage was "fair," and 39 percent came from homes where the marriage was "poor." In addition, when both the quality of the marriage and the quality of the boy's relationship with his parents were investigated, 90 percent of the antisocial boys came from homes where the quality of the marital relationship was very poor and the boy's relationship with his parents was also poor.

Similar findings have been reported in the United States (Johnson & Lobitz, 1974). Delinquents also are more likely to come from homes disrupted by desertion, divorce, death, or the absence of the father (Lamb, 1976). However, it is important to consider the type of family structure the adolescent grows up in and the quality of parenting. For example, the death of a father is associated less often with delinquency than divorce is, but the rate of antisocial behavior is higher for children from unbroken homes in which there is considerable marital discord than for those living in harmonious broken homes (Rutter, 1971).

Next, we look at a problem in adolescence that has increased in recent years—suicide.

Suicide

The incidence of suicide among adolescents is increasing at an alarming rate. Urie Bronfenbrenner (1975) cites statistics that show that adolescent suicide attempts have almost tripled since 1955. In the fifteen to nineteen age group, suicide ranks as the fifth major cause of death, outranked only by accidents, cancer, heart disease, and homicide. Some surveys indicate that as many as one in every twenty-five individuals attempts suicide at some point in their lives (e.g., Mintz, 1970). A conversation between a young boy and his therapist indicates how a suicide attempt may develop.

Therapist Tell me, what went wrong?

  Boy When?

Therapist I want to know why you have come to see me.

  Boy O.K. You might as well know. I tried to kill myself.

Therapist Why?

  Boy Things are horrible at home. My mother bitches at me all the time and my father is an alcoholic. I can't do anything right in their eyes. They never help me with anything, and they always are cutting me down. I don't have any friends either. I'm doing poorly in school, and my parents have gotten on me more and more about that. I just decided that the only way out was to kill myself.

In one investigation it was indicated that a broken home in itself is no more likely to appear in the backgrounds of adolescent suicide attempters than in those of adolescents who do not attempt suicide (Stanley & Barter, 1970). However, this same investigation did find that the parents of youth who attempted suicide talked about and threatened divorce more than the parents in the nonsuicidal group did.

Some of the youths in this study attempted suicide again after they had been hospitalized for their first suicide attempt. Those who attempted suicide again were more likely to have poor relations with peers than those who did not attempt it again. Thus, in some instances parental problems may be the main factor in the suicide attempt, while in others peer problems may be at the root of the disturbance. When the adolescent experiences few positive experiences in either of these spheres, depression and suicidal tendencies are likely to become even more pronounced.

Can we predict whether an adolescent will attempt to commit suicide? It isn't easy, but there are some signs that might serve as clues. For example, the adolescent who talks about committing suicide often is serious. And adolescents who attempt suicide once are likely to try it again. Severe family problems, the loss of a loved one, and other highly stressful events can signal a situation that may result in a suicide attempt.

Suicide hotlines have been established to help adolescents cope with severe depression.

As part of the effort to provide mental health services to those individuals in acute need of psychological help, a number of community mental health services have set up crisis intervention centers. Trained volunteers monitor incoming calls and try to comfort, reason with, and dissuade the callers from acting rashly. While such centers are a positive step in helping adolescents cope with severe depression, there is some indication that suicide prevention centers in their present form cannot always do the job. For example, in one investigation (Wilkins, 1970), it was estimated that 98 percent of the individuals who commit suicide never call such centers.

The increase in adolescent suicide during the last twenty-five years is a symptom of the stress that many adolescents now experience as they try to grow from dependent children to independent adults. But remember that while suicide attempts have increased, suicidal adolescents represent a very small minority of the adolescents in our culture. The large majority of adolescents learn to deal effectively with stress and tension and never become so immersed in depression that they would consider taking their own lives.

Summary

The adolescent's influence on parents and their influence on the adolescent are affected by maturational changes in both. Two aspects of adolescent development that require adaptation on the part of parents are autonomy and achievement. An unfortunate stereotype suggests that all parents and adolescents are in conflict with each other. In many instances adolescents and their parents have similar values and do not battle with each other to the extent the stereotype suggests. However, drug use, dress, and sexual habits are three areas where adolescent-parent conflict sometimes exists.

One common belief is that there is an almost complete change away from parent and toward peer conformity during adolescence. The evidence indicates that adolescent development is much more complex than this—in some situations, parents continue to exert greater influence over adolescents than peers do, even though peer group endorsement takes on greater significance for the adolescent than for the child. There seems to be a peak in conformity to the peer group's antisocial behavior around the end of the junior high years. By the end of the high school years, though, adolescents are engaging in more independent decision making, apart from both parent and peer influence.

Participation in cliques and crowds is important to many adolescents. And, while male and female adolescents mix with each other in school classes, organizations, and informal peer groups, the most serious encounters between them occur through a system called dating. While at one time dating served only as a form of courtship, it now provides a number of other socialization functions as well, including recreation, status sorting, and a testing ground for sexual behavior and social skills. In the dating relationship, it seems that females bring the capacity for intimacy and personality exploration to the relationship and train adolescent males in these behaviors.

Some adolescents not only date, but marry as well. One out of every five adolescent females is married, or has been married, by the time she is twenty. Many adolescent marriages fail, though, and the younger the adolescent is at the time of marriage, the less likely the marriage is going to be a success. The major reason adolescents get married is that the female is pregnant. This often leads to financial strain, coupled with the teenage parents' lack of maturity. Fortunately, more and more school systems are establishing special programs (including counseling and peer group discussion) for pregnant and married adolescents.

It is not until adolescence that individuals begin to develop formal theories about the self. We may be able to better understand the adolescent's self by focusing on how the adolescent processes information about his or her self and the world. Socially competent adolescents, compared to their socially incompetent counterparts, assign high priorities to interpersonal goals, tend to be goal directed, empathetic, and cognitively resourceful.

Erik Erikson's construct of identity is recognized by many psychologists as the most important integrative concept in the study of adolescence. Erikson believes that the onset of adolescence is associated with the beginning of his fifth stage of development, which he calls identity versus identity diffusion or confusion. Identity development requires adolescents to piece together information about themselves in a meaningful way.

Erikson has relied upon the methods of psychoanalysis to gain knowledge about identity development. As part of his attempt to understand the identity-formation process, he has analyzed the life histories of many famous individuals, including Adolf Hitler, Martin Luther, and Mahatma Gandhi. Other psychologists have developed questionnaires and interviews to assess the adolescent's development of identity.

Erikson believes that as part of identity development the adolescent must experiment with a variety of roles and personalities. In particular, exposure to vocational and ideological alternatives stimulates the achievement of a stable identity.

Following a drop in admissions to mental health clinics during the ten- to twelve-year period, the rate increases and then peaks at about the age of fourteen, with the increase due primarily to admissions of girls. Adolescents encounter a variety of problems as they grow from childhood to adulthood, but most teenagers are able to overcome these problems. Two areas where problems often surface involve the development of independence and identity.

Drug use and abuse have become paramount problems in recent years. Consumption of alcohol and smoking marijuana are the two most prevalent drug-related problems in adolescence. Juvenile delinquency is another problem in adolescence, a problem that appears to stem from inadequate behavioral control, the failure to delay gratification, and lack of conventional standards of conduct. Depression in its most severe form may lead to suicide, although most adolescents who commit suicide are emotionally upset but not psychotic.

Key Terms

clique	impulsive delinquent
crowd	moratorium
desatellization	resatellization
foreclosure	satellization
identity achieved	social delinquent
identity diffused (or confused)	unsocialized delinquent

Review Questions

1. Describe how maturational changes in both adolescents and parents affect parent-adolescent relationships.
2. How does divorce influence the behavior of adolescent girls?
3. Describe the nature of parent-adolescent conflict.
4. Describe the development of adolescent autonomy. Outline David Ausubel's theory of how autonomy develops.
5. Evaluate the adolescent's conformity to peers and parents.
6. What are adolescent groups like?
7. What factors contribute to whether adolescent marriages will succeed?
8. Outline the important aspects of Erikson's identity theory. What are Marcia's four statuses of identity?
9. Describe the pattern of alcohol and marijuana use by adolescents and some of the environmental correlates of this use.
10. What are some different types of delinquency?
11. What is the nature of adolescent suicide?

Further Readings

Engs, R. C. *Responsible drug and alcohol use*. New York: Macmillan, 1979.
Contains valuable information about intelligent, responsible choices related to drug and alcohol use. Includes many studies about the effects of various drugs on the human body, including possible harmful effects. Reasonably easy to read.

Erikson, E. H. (ed.). *The challenge of youth*. New York: Doubleday, 1965.
This excellent book of readings on youth includes articles by Erikson on the fidelity and diversity of youth, by Bruno Bettelheim on the problem of generations, and by Kenneth Kenniston on social change and youth in America. The focus of the articles is the adolescent's development of identity. Reasonably easy to read.

Hill, J. P. The family. In M. Johnson (ed.), *Toward adolescence: the middle school years. The seventy-ninth yearbook of the National Society for the Study of Education*. Chicago: University of Chicago Press, 1980.
An excellent overview of the role of the family in adolescence. Up-to-date research about parent-adolescent relationships by a top scholar in adolescent research. Reading level is moderately difficult.

Krain, M., Cannon, B., & Bagford, J. Rating-dating or simply prestige homogamy: data on dating in the Greek system on a midwestern campus. *Journal of Marriage and the Family*, 1977, 39 663–74.
This research article indicates that dating on a midwestern college campus is now relaxed compared to the pattern of competitiveness and materialism in dating relationships in the 1950s. There are a number of other articles on dating that have appeared in this journal from 1975 to the present. You may want to go to the library and leaf through those issues to find out if any of the articles on dating are of interest to you. Reading level is of medium difficulty.

Rice, F. P. *Marriage and parenthood*. Boston: Allyn & Bacon, 1979.
A number of references are made to adolescent marriages in this book on marriage and parenting. Reasonably easy to read.

Rutter, M. *Changing youth in a changing society: patterns of adolescent development and disorder*. Cambridge, Mass.: Harvard University Press, 1980.
An excellent discussion of problems and disturbances in adolescence—special emphasis is given to how problems and disturbances may be affected by adolescent development and the changing themes of a society. Reading difficulty is medium.

Sherif, M., & Sherif, C. W. *Reference groups*. New York: Harper & Row, 1964.
An entire book is devoted to the Sherifs' study of adolescent groups. It is an excellent source of information about everyday happenings in adolescent male cliques.

Weiner, I. B. *Psychological disturbance in adolescence*. New York: Wiley, 1970.
An excellent overview of the psychological disorders of adolescence. Medium reading difficulty.

Section VI

Early and Middle Adulthood

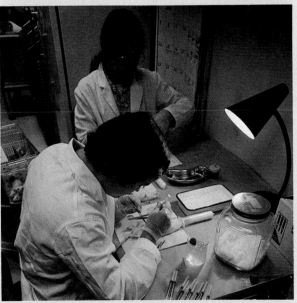

15

Perspectives on Adult Development and Physical Development

Prologue: Youth—the Transition from Adolescence to Early Adulthood

Many postteenagers spend an extended period of time in technical institutes, colleges, and postgraduate centers to acquire the specialized skills, educational experiences, and professional training needed to face the complex world of work. For many, this creates an extended period of economic and personal "temporariness." Earning levels are low and sporadic, residences may change frequently, and marriage and a family are shunned. Often, this period lasts from two to four years, although it is not unusual for it to last more than eight years.

This stage of development has been called **youth** by some social scientists. Kenneth Kenniston (1970) suggests that youth have not settled the questions whose answers once defined adulthood—questions about their relationship to the existing society, vocations, and social roles and life styles. Youth differs from adolescence in the sense that there is a struggle between developing an autonomous sense of self and becoming socially involved, whereas the struggle for self-definition represents the core conflict of adolescence. And, Kenniston also believes that adolescents are trying to develop toward an end point—an identity or self-definition, while youth already have such a sense of self and continually show an interest in change and development. Youth do not like being in a rut or getting nowhere in life, but rather see themselves as on the move.

Two criteria that may signal the end of youth and the beginning of early adulthood are economic independence and autonomous decision making. Probably the most widely recognized marker of entrance into adulthood is the occasion when the young individual

takes a more-or-less permanent full-time job. This usually happens after high school for some, college for others, and postcollege training for yet others.

For those who finish high school, move away from home, and assume a career, the transition to adulthood seems to have occurred. However, such a clear-cut pattern is the exception rather than the rule. One of every four adolescents does not complete high school, and many students who finish college cannot find a job. Furthermore, only a small percentage of graduates settle into jobs that will be permanent. Also, attaining economic independence from parents usually is a gradual rather than an abrupt process. It is not unusual to find many college graduates getting a job and continuing to live, or returning to live, with their parents, particularly in today's economic climate.

The ability to make decisions does not seem to be fully developed in youth. We refer broadly here to decision making about a career, values, family and relationships, and life style. During youth, the individual may still be trying out many different roles, exploring alternative careers, thinking about a variety of life styles, and considering the plurality of relationships available. While decisions about some or all of these alternatives may still not be made in early adulthood, and may reemerge in middle and late adulthood, the individual who enters early adulthood usually has made some of these decisions.

While there seems to be a great deal of change going on during late adolescence, youth, and the beginning of early adulthood, some researchers have found that some important patterns of behavior do not change very much from the tenth grade through five years after high school. In *Youth in Transition: Adolescence to Adulthood—Change and Stability in the Lives of Men*, Jerald Bachman, Patrick O'Malley, and Jerome Johnson (1978) reported longitudinal data collected on a national sample of more than 2,000 boys. They initially studied the boys when they were in the tenth grade in 1968, and then collected information on them for a period of eight years, following their movements along several paths—dropout or graduation, military service or civilian life, college or labor market, employment or unemployment. By individually interviewing the boys and having them respond to questionnaires over the eight years (measurement occurred five times—in the tenth grade, eleventh grade, twelfth grade, one year after the twelfth grade, and five years after the twelfth grade), the impact of various post–high school environments and experiences (educational, occupational, military, marital, and parental) on values, attitudes, and behaviors was determined.

The dominant picture of the individuals as they went through these eight years of their lives was stability rather than change. While there were a number of differences between the groups of young men studied—such as between high school dropouts and graduates, and between those who were delinquents and drug abusers and those who were not—these differences seemed to remain remarkably stable over the course of the eight years the young men were studied. For instance, the tenth graders who showed the highest self-esteem were most likely to show the highest self-esteem five years after high school. With some changes, a similar kind of patterning was found for achievement orientation. For example, data on illegal drug use suggested the effects of two different environments—marriage tended to reduce drug use, while unemployment tended to elevate it. Long-range occupational aspirations were influenced by post–high school experiences: individuals who were successful in school and in a career sustained their high achievement aspirations, whereas many of those with less educational and occupational success showed a decline in achievement orientation.

There is constancy as well as change during the transition from adolescence to early adulthood. The tendency on the part of many scholars has been to emphasize the tremendous upheaval and change that goes on during adolescence and youth—data such as those collected by Bachman, O'Malley, and Johnston (1978) remind us that there is continuity in the lives of individuals as they grow from adolescence to adulthood as well.

To end the prologue on youth on a light note, the *Harvard Lampoon Big Book of College Life* (1978) introduces the section, "Paradise Lost: Graduation and the Afterlife," with ten reasons not to get a job.

1. You have to work.
2. It's habit forming. Once you get a job, you'll want another, and then another. Many college graduates think, "Sure, I'll get a job. I might as well just try it and see what all the fuss is about. Everybody else is doing it. I can quit when I want." Well, they're wrong. They'll soon be caught in the vicious cycle of employment addiction. It's better not to start at all. Why do you think they call it work?
3. It's unbearably tedious. Not only that, but employees and their families are not eligible to win.
4. Once you stop being a student, you can never go back. Remember those pathetic people who came back to hang around your high school? You'll look even sillier showing up at mixers, pep rallies, and Sadie Hawkins dances after you've taken a position with some respectable accounting firm.
5. You will have to carpool with a sullen adolescent typist or a Hindu engineer/mathematician who "loves speaking my new language of English."
6. Taking a job means taking on new responsibilities. Before you know it, you'll be married to an overweight hypochondriac with four sickly brats with crooked teeth and a house in the 'burbs. And those remote-control garage openers aren't getting any cheaper. You'll have to take out insurance policies on everything from health care to rodent invasions. . . . Soon you'll be seriously considering buying a hairpiece and purchasing a condominium in Fort Lauderdale or the Rio Rancho Retirement Village. All this can be avoided by the simple decision not to take a job.
7. People will start calling you "mister" or "sir." Hippies will resent you and call you a "capitalist roader." People with better jobs will shake their heads and say, "What a waste of human talent." In minutes, you will lose the respect of everyone.
8. Fully employed people can never have sex.
9. You'll have to say nice things about the boss's new "flame-thrower red" polyester golf pants, laugh at the boss's jokes about people who mismanage their personal finances, and carry on endless conversations with your boss about "pennant rallies," "the primaries," and "resort areas." You'll have to nod your head with conviction when he refers to his employees as a "team" that works together to "bring home the bacon."
10. If you take a job, you'll be an adult. (pp. 170–71)

Introduction

In this chapter we will review some of the main ideas of life-span theories of development, focusing on the adult years. The popular stage-crisis theories of Gail Sheehy, Roger Gould, and Daniel Levinson are presented and critically evaluated. The roles of transition, life events, and individual differences in adult development are explored. And, physical development in early and middle adulthood are described. Physical peaks and declines are detailed, health status is outlined, the menstrual cycle, menopause, and the male climacteric are discussed, and various aspects of sexuality are evaluated.

Perspectives on Adult Development

It may be helpful for you to reacquaint yourself with the theoretical perspectives on life-span development at this time. Recall that some of the perspectives emphasize that stages of adult development exist while others do not. And, some of the perspectives focus on change, while others assume that development is more stable in the adult years. Briefly, some of the major points of the perspectives presented in chapter 2 will be recapped, emphasizing ideas about adult development. Then, some perspectives that focus more exclusively on adult development will be presented, and the section will conclude with a critical evaluation of the stage-crisis theories of adult development and a description of some alternatives to stage-crisis theories.

Review of Life-Span Developmental Perspectives— Emphasis on Adulthood

Recall that both psychoanalytic and cognitive-structural theories emphasize the importance of stages in development. The psychoanalytic perspective that has had the greatest impact on our study of life-span development is the theory of Erik Erikson, who has proposed that individuals go through eight different stages in the life cycle.

Erikson

Three of Erikson's eight stages focus on adulthood: early adulthood—intimacy versus isolation; middle adulthood—generativity versus stagnation; and late adulthood—integrity versus despair. Erikson (1968) emphasizes that the major developmental theme of early adulthood involves a mutually satisfying and intimate relationship with another individual. The danger in this stage is isolation—the avoidance of or lack of success at developing an intimate relationship with another person.

In middle adulthood, Erikson believes that individuals need to assist the younger generation in developing and leading useful lives. Generativity versus stagnation focuses on successful rearing of children.

Childless adults need to find substitute young people through adoption, guardianship, or a close relationship with the children of friends and relatives. The positive side of this stage—generativity—suggests a feeling of being able to positively shape the next generation. By contrast, stagnation, or the feeling of having done nothing for the next generation is the unhealthy outcome.

In late adulthood, Erikson believes that individuals enter the stage of development called integrity versus despair. Late adulthood is perceived as a time of reminiscence, or looking back at what we have done with our lives. Through many different routes the older person may have developed a positive outlook in preceding phases of the life cycle. If so, the retrospective glances will reveal a picture of life well spent, and the person will be satisfied (integrity). However, the older person may have resolved one or more of the preceding stages in a negative way. If so, the retrospective glances may produce doubt and gloom (despair) about the sum worth of one's life.

In chapter 1, we indicated that early in his career Erikson, like many other theorists who have become interested in life-span development, seemed to be more concerned with childhood and adolescence, but in his later years has written more extensively about the adult years. Erikson's latest book is coedited with Neil Smelser (1980) and is called *Themes of Work and Love in Adulthood*. This book builds on Freud's response to the question of what a healthy adult should be able to do, which is to love and work. As you read about the adult years in the remaining chapters of this book, you will find that love and work indeed are major themes of adult development.

Piaget

Remember that Jean Piaget's cognitive-structural theory of development has formed the foundation for the modern study of cognitive development. Yet Piaget had very little to say about cognitive-structural changes in development during the adult years. Piaget believed that, for the most part, formal operational thought characterizes the way adults think, just as it characterized the way most of those same individuals thought in late adolescence. As we discuss cognitive development in adulthood, you will see that while Piaget had little to say about adult changes in cognitive development his work has stimulated a search for a fifth cognitive stage, and that there is a great deal of interest in the variations of formal operational thought in adulthood.

Nonstage Theories—The Behavioral Social Learning and Humanistic Perspectives

Remember that traditional personality theories have emphasized change in childhood and adolescence and stability in adulthood. However, both the behavioral social learning and humanistic approaches stress that change in adulthood occurs, but that such change occurs in a continuous, nonstagelike manner. In the social learning perspective, change in adulthood comes about through the person's continuous interaction with other individuals in the environment, and in some cases, through the manner in which the adult processes information about the environment (cognitive social learning theory). By contrast, the humanistic perspective believes that change in adulthood comes about through the development of the self. In particular, the development of self-actualization and self-awareness are humanistic themes that have characterized adult development. These two perspectives have had a strong impact on how we view adults.

Havighurst and Neugarten

Two other perspectives on adult development that were described in chapters 1 and 2 are the views of Robert Havighurst and Bernice Neugarten. Both Havighurst and Neugarten have been pioneers in theory and research focused on adult development.

Havighurst Robert Havighurst (1952) described a number of developmental tasks that the individual must master during a specific phase of the life cycle in order to move on to the next phase. Havighurst stresses that there are seven stages in the life cycle, and like Erikson, emphasizes that three stages characterize adult development. *Early adulthood* ranges from eighteen to thirty years of age and consists of the following developmental tasks:

1. Selecting a mate
2. Learning to live with a marriage partner
3. Starting a family
4. Rearing children
5. Managing a home
6. Getting started in an occupation
7. Taking on civic responsibility
8. Finding a congenial social group

Early adulthood is perceived as a critical period in the life cycle because the individual has to make decisions and perform tasks that will have a strong influence in later adulthood. A major difficulty is that individuals have to make such decisions and perform the tasks with a minimum of help.

In *middle adulthood*, ranging from about thirty to fifty-five years of age, Havighurst feels that men and women reach their peak in productivity and have their greatest impact on society. Yet, it is during middle age that society places the greatest demands on the individual. According to Havighurst, the developmental tasks that must be mastered in middle adulthood are:

1. Achieving adult civic and social responsibility
2. Establishing and maintaining an economic standard of living
3. Assisting teen-age children to become responsible adults
4. Developing adult leisure-time activities
5. Relating oneself to one's spouse as a person
6. Accepting the physiological changes of middle age

Havighurst believes that the extent to which middle age precipitates stress and reaches a crisis level varies from culture to culture. And, in our American society, he feels that stress and crisis in middle age are more common in middle-class individuals than in lower-class individuals.

The seventh and last stage of Havighurst's developmental task theory is called *later adulthood*, ranging from approximately fifty-five years of age until death. It is important that individuals master six developmental tasks during later adulthood:

1. Adjusting to decreased physical strength and health
2. Adjustment to retirement and reduced income
3. Adjusting to the death of a spouse
4. Establishing an explicit affiliation with one's age group
5. Meeting social and civic obligations
6. Establishing satisfactory physical living arrangements

The developmental tasks of later adulthood differ from those of earlier stages in one important way—they represent more of a defensive strategy toward life.

Neugarten In chapter 2 we described Bernice Neugarten's multiple time, changing life cycle perspective. Recall that Neugarten believes too much attention has been given to the biological timetable of development and not enough to the social timetable. She stresses that we can more accurately understand adult development if we focus on how three dimensions of time interact: life time (or chronological age); historical time; and social time, or the system of age grading and expectations that shape the life cycle. And, in chapter 1, you read that Neugarten (1980) feels we are rapidly becoming an age-irrelevant society. She believes that choices and dilemmas do not sprout forth at ten-year intervals, and decisions are not made and then left behind like beads on a chain. She also argues that most of the themes of adulthood appear and reappear in new forms over many periods of time. Issues of intimacy and freedom, for example, which are supposed to concern young adults just starting out in marriage and careers, are never settled once and for all. They haunt many couples continuously; compromises are found for awhile, then renegotiated. Similarly, feeling the pressure of time, reformulating goals, and coming to grips with success (and failure) are not the exclusive property of middle-aged adults by any means, according to Neugarten.

This summary of perspectives presented earlier in the text reveals that there is agreement, as well as disagreement, about the most important themes of adult development. For example, theorists agree that work and love are important themes of adult development, but there is a great deal of disagreement about whether such themes become crises at particular points in the life cycle. Next, we look at several new perspectives on adult development. First, three well-known stage perspectives of adult development are presented, followed by an evaluation of the research on which the theories are based, a discusssion of the concept of transition versus crisis in adult development, information about the viability of a life events framework for understanding adult development, and a description of the extensive individual variation that exists in adult development.

Popular Stage-Crisis Perspectives on Adult Development

There has recently been a flourish of ideas about development in adulthood. Many of these ideas, particularly those that have been presented in the popular press and the media, have emphasized stages of adult development. A majority of the stage approaches also have stressed the importance of crises in adult development as well.

Gail Sheehy's Passages

Gail Sheehy's (1976) *Passages* has been so popular that it topped the *New York Times Book Review* best-seller list for twenty-seven weeks. Sheehy's goal in *Passages* is to describe adult development. She cites discussions with Daniel Levinson and Roger Gould, whose works are described later, and case study information based on 115 interviews with men and women as the main sources of her view.

Sheehy argues that we all go through developmental stages, roughly bound by chronological age. Each stage contains problems that must be solved before progression to the next stage is achieved. The periods between stages are *passages*. Sheehy uses catchy

phrases to describe each stage: the Trying Twenties, Catch 30, the Deadline Decade between thirty-five and forty-five, and finally the Age-40 Crucible. Sheehy's advice never wavers, no matter which stage is involved. The adult in transition may feel miserable, but those who face up to agonizing self-evaluation, who appraise their weaknesses as well as their strengths, who try to set goals for the future, and who try to become as independent as possible will be happier than those who do not fully experience and benefit from these trials.

Sheehy believes that through these passages individuals earn an *authentic identity*. This identity will not be based on the authority of one's parents or on cultural prescriptions. Instead, it will be constructed through the adult's own strenuous efforts. Sheehy says the adults who allow themselves to be halted and seized by issues, then shaken into reexamination, are the people who find their identity and thrive.

Roger Gould's Transformations: Growth and Change in Adult Life

Another well-known perspective on adult development that has linked stage and crisis with development is Roger Gould's view (1975, 1978, 1980). Gould emphasizes that mid-life is every bit as turbulent as adolescence, except that during middle adulthood striving

Table 15.1
Gould's Seven Stages of Adult Life

Stage	Approximate Age	Development(s)
1	16–18	Desire to escape parental control
2	18–22	Learning the family: peer group orientation
3	22–28	Developing independence: commitment to a career and to children
4	29–34	Questioning self: role confusion; marriage and career vulnerable to dissatisfaction
5	35–43	Period of urgency to attain life's goals: awareness of time limitation. Realignment of life's goals
6	43–53	Settling down: acceptance of one's life
7	53–60	More tolerance: acceptance of past; less negativism; general mellowing

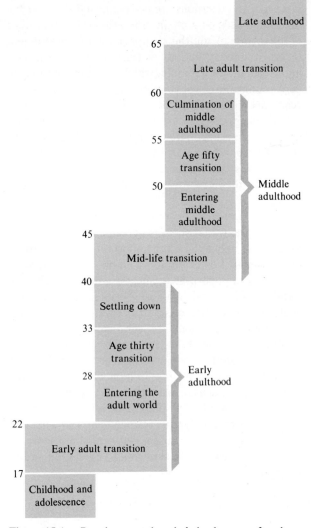

Figure 15.1 Developmental periods in the eras of early and middle adulthood.

to handle crisis is likely to lead to a healthier, happier life. Gould's study of 524 men and women lead him to propose the seven developmental stages of adult life shown in table 15.1.

Gould believes that in our twenties we assume new roles; in our thirties we begin to feel stuck with our responsibilities; and in our forties we begin to feel a sense of urgency when we realize our lives are speeding by. When we realize that each step is a natural one, Gould believes we are then on the path to adult maturity.

In *Transformations: Growth and Change in Adult Life,* Gould (1978) writes about growth as the obligation and opportunity of adulthood. Growth is necessary to cope with a predictable sequence of changing patterns and preoccupations during the adult years.

Adulthood is not a plateau; rather it is a dynamic and changing time for all of us. As we grow and change, we take steps *away* from childhood and *toward* adulthood—steps such as marriage, work, consciously developing a talent or buying a home. With each step, the unfinished business of childhood intrudes, disturbing our emotions and requiring psychological work. With this in mind, adults may now view their disturbed feelings at particular periods as a possible sign of progress, as part of their attempted movement toward a fuller adult life. (p. 14)

In addition, Gould saw the significance of specific events as milestones along the adult life course.

Certain key events—buying a first house, a first car, experiencing a first job, a first baby, the first loss of a parent, first physical injury or first clear sign of aging—force us to see ourselves more as the creators of our lives and less as living out the lives we thought were our destiny. (p. 13)

Daniel Levinson's Seasons of a Man's Life
Daniel Levinson's (1978, 1980) work on adult development has included his well-known book, *The Seasons of a Man's Life* (1978), which grew out of his research on the personality development of forty middle-aged men. Levinson uses biographical case material to illustrate the stages of personality. His interviews were conducted with hourly workers, business executives, academic biologists, and novelists. While Levinson's major interest has focused on mid-life transition, he has described a number of phases, stages, and transitions in the life cycle, as indicated in figure 15.1.

Like Robert Havighurst, Levinson emphasizes that developmental tasks must be mastered at each of these stages. In early adulthood, the two major tasks to be mastered are exploring the possibilities for adult living and developing a stable life structure. Levinson sees the twenties as a novice phase of adult personality development. At the end of the boy's teens, a transition from dependence to independence should occur. This transition is marked by the formation of a dream—an image of the kind of life the youth wants to have, particularly in relation to marriage and career development. The novice phase is a time of reasonably free experimentation and of testing the dream in the real world.

From about the ages of twenty-eight to thirty-three man goes through a transition period in which he must face the more serious question of determining his goals. During the thirties a man usually focuses and works toward family and career development. In the later years of this period, a man enters a phase of becoming his own man (or BOOM, becoming one's own man, as Levinson calls it). By age forty he has reached a stable location in his career, has outgrown his earlier, more tenuous attempts at learning to become an adult, and now must look forward to the kind of life he will lead as a middle-aged adult.

According to Levinson, the transition into middle adulthood lasts about five years and requires the adult to come to grips with four major conflicts that have existed in his life since adolescence. These four conflicts include: 1) being young versus being old; 2) being destructive versus being constructive; 3) being masculine versus being feminine; and 4) being attached to others or separated from them. The success of the midlife transition depends on how effectively the man is able to reduce these polarities and accept each of them as integral parts of his being.

The adult developmental perspectives of Sheehy, Gould, and Levinson emphasize the importance of stages of development in the life cycle. While information about phases and stages in the life cycle can be helpful in pointing out dominant themes that characterize many people at particular points in adult development, there are several important ideas to keep in mind when considering these theoretical perspectives as viable models of adult development. First, the research on which they are based has been neither as prolific nor as empirically based as in the case of some theories of child development (e.g., the literally hundreds of empirically based studies of Piaget's theory). Second, many of the perspectives tend to focus too extensively on stages as crises in development, particularly in the case of the midlife crisis. Third, there is an increasing tendency of theory and research on adult development to emphasize the importance of life events rather than stages or phases of development.

Fourth, there often is a great deal of individual and contextual variation in the manner in which the themes, stages, phases, or life events in adult development characterize any one particular individual. We will consider each of these points in turn.

Evaluation of the Stage-Crisis Theories of Adult Development

The popular stage theories of development just described, as well as the more theoretically robust stage approaches of scholars like Erik Erikson, have sensitized us to the fact that development does not end in childhood or adolescence, but rather that change is a life-long process. But, as we see next, the stage theories of development leave a number of issues unresolved, and in some cases these theories may be leading us to some erroneous conclusions about adult development.

The Data Base for the Theories Proposed by Sheehy, Gould, and Levinson

Gail Sheehy relied on interviews with 115 adults of different ages as the main source of data for her theory that passages are the key to understanding adult development. Roger Gould's theory that it is important to develop self-tolerance during our adulthood years is based on clinical observations and questionnaire data. And, Daniel Levinson's view that midlife represents a crisis in development relies on in-depth interviews with forty middle-aged men, conducted initially in 1968 with equally detailed follow-up in 1971.

These data bases are characterized by some well-known methodological problems that make those engaged in empirical research on adult development feel uneasy. In regard to Sheehy's case studies of 115 adults, there is no disclosure of such elementary information as the sex and racial composition of the sample, how the sample was selected, what questions were asked in the interview and by whom, and for what length of time the interviews lasted. When the cases are described they are used to buttress the concept of a developmental theme, with no indication of the representativeness of the incidents. And, no statistical analyses were conducted by Sheehy either.

Roger Gould used two different techniques to obtain information about adult development. First, eight medical school students listened to tape recordings of patient sessions. The medical students were asked to note the personal feelings of the individuals in the group sessions that stood out. And, second, a questionnaire was developed and given to a "normal, nonclinical" sample of 524 white, middle-class adults. While this approach is clearly more acceptable than the more casual approach of Sheehy, the clinical nature of ratings by medical students is a questionable strategy, the middle-class bias of both the clinical and the nonclinical sample leads to problems of generalization to a lower-class sample, and in neither the clinical observations nor the questionnaire was there any attempt to measure the reliability of the information obtained. In the clinical part of the study, we need to know if two individuals who listen to the same tapes agree that what they are hearing suggests a particular problem or not. And, in regard to the questionnaire, it is important to find out if the people consistently responded to the items in a particular way. As was the case with Sheehy, no statistical analysis was conducted in Gould's work.

In Levinson's interviews with middle-aged adult males, the data about middle adulthood can be considered more valid than the information about early adulthood. One reason for this is that when we ask people to remember information about earlier parts of their lives, they may distort and forget important things. And, the Levinson interview data included no females. *Seasons of a Man's Life,* like *Passages* and *Transformations,* is not a research report in any conventional sense. According to Robert Sears (1979), there are no statistics to speak of, and no quantified results. However, the data reported by Levinson are characteristic of the clinical tradition, and the quality and quantity of the biographies are outstanding.

In sum, the research base that could provide empirical support for the perspectives of Sheehy, Gould, and Levinson has not been adequately developed. Next, we will see that some experts on adult development believe that too much attention has been paid to the concept of crisis in theories of adult development.

Transition or Crisis in Adult Development?

David Hultsch and Francine Deutsch (1981) indicate that two major perspectives on middle adulthood exist—one emphasizing midlife as a period of **transition** and **crisis,** the other that midlife primarily is a period of transition rather than a crisis. Erik Erikson's perspective has contributed to the view that midlife is both a crisis and a transition period. And, the three popular stage perspectives just described are clearly in the crisis-transition category. George Vallient (1977), who has collected data on 300 Harvard graduates over a period of forty years (known as the Grant study), however, indicates that while change characterizes middle adulthood, the presence of a midlife crisis is an exception rather than a rule.

Just as pop psychologists have reveled in the not-so-common high drama of adolescent turmoil, just so the popular press, sensing good copy, had made all too much of the mid-life crisis. The term *mid-life crisis* brings to mind some variation of the renegade minister who leaves behind four children and the congregation that loved him in order to drive off in a magenta Porsche with a twenty-five-year-old striptease artiste. Like all tabloid fables, there is much to be learned from such stories, but such aberrations are rare, albeit memorable, caricatures of more mundane issues of development. As with adolescent turmoil, mid-life crises are much rarer in *community* samples than in *clinical* samples. The high drama in Gail Sheehy's best-selling *Passages* was rarely observed in the lives of the Grant Study men. (pp. 222–23)

Hultsch and Deutsch (1981), as well as other life-span experts (e.g., Neugarten, 1980; Riegel, 1975), believe that only a minority of individuals experience a crisis in midlife, and when it is experienced the cause is an unanticipated disruption in the rhythm of the life cycle. In summarizing their view of whether midlife represents a crisis or a transition, Hultsch and Deutsch (1981) concluded:

Perhaps the most valid conclusion that can be drawn about midlife is that this period, like other periods of the life cycle, is characterized by changes and transition. For some individuals this transition appears to precipitate a crisis; for others it does not. Thus, perhaps the question "Is midlife a crisis or not?" is not the right one to ask. Perhaps attention should be focused on how various events which tend to occur in the middle years affect the individual and on what role mediating variables play. To the extent that midlife is a transition with or without crisis, it is these events which are likely to trigger, mediate, or terminate it. (p. 293)

Life Events As a Framework for Understanding Adult Development

Many theorists and researchers have not been satisfied with the proposed stage-crisis approaches to adult development. To obtain a more integrated view of adult development, many experts believe that the study of life events adds valuable information to understanding adult development (Datan & Ginsburg, 1975; Hultsch & Deutsch, 1981; Neugarten, 1980; Riley, 1979; Riegel, 1975).

David Hultsch and Francine Deutsch (1981) believe that various life events define transitions. A representation of the distribution of such events and transitions is shown in table 15.2. When life events are seen as antecedents of behavior change a framework to explain this theory emerges.

Figure 15.2 includes four main elements of this framework: a set of antecedent life-event stressors; a set of mediating factors; a social-psychological adaptation process; and consequent adaptive or maladaptive responses. Within this framework, all life events,

Table 15.2
Levels and Events in Adult Life

	Gradual changes				
	Males		Females		
Level years	Psychosocial	Biophysical	Psychosocial	Biophysical	Sudden changes
I(20–25)	College/first job Marriage First child		First job/college Marriage First child		
II(25–30)	Second job Other children Children in preschool		Loss of job Other children Children in preschool		
III(30–35)	Move Promotion Children in school		Move Without job Children in school		
IV(35–50)	Second home Promotion Departure of children		Second home Second career Departure of children		
V(50–65)	Unemployment Isolation Grandfather Head of kin Incapacitation		Unemployment Grandmother Head of kin	Menopause	Loss of job Loss of parents Loss of friends Illness
VI(65+)	Deprivation	Sensory-motor deficiencies	Widowhood Incapacitation		Retirement Loss of partner Death

Source: Hultsch & Deutsch, 1981.

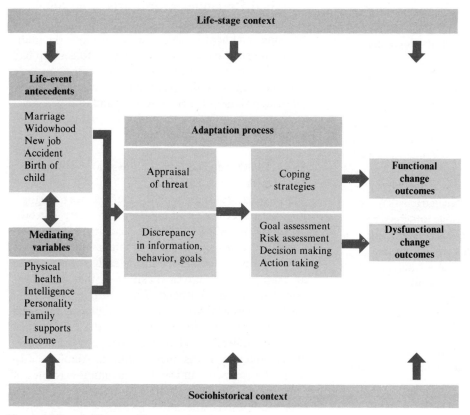

Figure 15.2   A life-event framework.

both positive and negative, are seen as potentially stressful. Mediating factors include both internal and external resources; social-psychological adaptation involves the application of coping strategies and resultant changes in behavior. According to Hultsch and Deutsch:

The stress or crisis of life events does not reside within the event or within the individual. Rather the crisis arises from an interaction between the individual and the situation—an **asynchrony** between change within the individual and change within the environment (Elder, 1974; Riegel, 1976). As illustrated in figure 15.2 both the life stage at which an event occurs and the sociohistorical context within which it occurs are crucial. Thus, two distinct time lines are involved in the life course—individual time and historical time. The same event occurring in a different context becomes, in many ways, a different event (e.g., becoming a widow at age thirty-two or at age seventy-three; bearing six children in the 1940s or in the 1980s). The occurrence of a life event at an "inappropriate" time in the life cycle or history is likely to create more asynchrony.

Thus, development may be characterized as adaptation to a series of crises, asynchronies, or transitions defined by life events. Such a perspective is useful since it forces us to focus on the interface between the individual and his or her world. (pp. 216–18)

Many things happen to adults—marriage, childbirth, parenthood, divorce, remarriage, promotion, retirement, economic prosperity, war, accident, or illness. A life-event framework allows us to examine these events as significant antecedents of development.

Individual Differences in Stages, Phases, Themes, and Life Events during Adulthood

Broadly speaking, there are two theoretical approaches to the study of personality development—one focuses on similarities, the other on differences. The stage theories of Sheehy, Gould, Levinson, Freud, and Erikson all attempt to describe the universals—not the individual variation—in development. It may be helpful to recall the comments of Bernice Neugarten: "We have found great trouble clustering people into age brackets that are characterized by particular conflicts; the conflicts won't stay put, and neither will the people."

In an extensive investigation of a random sample of 500 men at midlife, Michael Farrell and Stanley Rosenberg (1981) concluded that,

While some studies have found middle age to be the apex of satisfaction and effectiveness, others found it to be a period of identity crisis and discontent. . . . Both our research design and our findings suggest a more complex model (than

the universal stage model), one anchored in the idea that the individual is an active agent in interpreting, shaping, and altering his own reality. He not only experiences internal and external changes, he gives meaning to them. The meaning given shows a wide range of variation. (p. 2)

Think about yourself and other people you know. There are certain things you have in common with others, yet there are many ways in which you differ. Individual variation, then, is an important aspect of any viable model of adult development. Further information about the importance of individual variation, as well as contextual influences, in adult development is given in box 15.1.

Now that we have surveyed a number of different perspectives on adult development, we will turn our attention to the demarcation of adult development that has been most commonly used: early adulthood; middle adulthood; and late adulthood. The strands of development used to describe child development provide a fruitful framework for discussing adult development. Thus, the remaining portion of the discussion of adulthood will focus on different aspects of physical, cognitive, social, emotional, and personality development. In the remainder of this chapter, we will look at physical development in early and middle adulthood.

Physical Development in Early Adulthood

In this section we will see that the peak of physical performance and health usually is reached in early adulthood. Information about how it is easy to develop bad health habits in early adulthood is presented. And, we will see that at some point during adulthood some physical processes begin to decline, and that hormonal changes, particularly in women, are associated with personality change.

Early Adulthood: The Peak of Physical Performance and Health

The physical status of the individual reaches its highest level between the ages of eighteen and thirty. According to W. A. Marshall (1973), growth in stature is completed and men attain their highest skill at tasks involving speed and agility during early adulthood. As an example of the physical skill peak that can be attained in young adulthood, J. M. Tanner (1962), an expert on physical growth and development, reviewed the age strata of Olympic athletes. Of the 137 Olympic athletes Tanner studied, only 21 were over thirty years of age, and only 1 was under eighteen. All of the athletes who competed in events demanding extremes of speed or agility, such as the 100-meter dash and the broad jump, were under thirty years of age.

Physical status is at its peak between the ages of eighteen and thirty.

For most individuals, these peaks of physical performance actually occur between the ages of nineteen and twenty-six. For example, in one investigation it was found that reaction times improved from childhood until about the age of nineteen to twenty, remained constant until approximately the age of twenty-six, and then began a gradual decline (Hodgkins, 1962).

Individuals not only reach their peak physical performance during early adulthood, but it is during this phase of adulthood that they are the healthiest as well. According to data accumulated by the United States Department of Health, Education, and Welfare, more than nine out of ten people from the age of seventeen to forty-four view their health as good or excellent (1976). Few young adults have chronic health problems, and young adults have fewer colds and respiratory problems than during their childhood years. The most frequent reasons young adults have to be hospitalized are childbirth, accidents, and digestive and genitourinary system problems (U.S. Department of Health, Education, and Welfare, 1976).

It is from the ages of eighteen to thirty that individuals are their healthiest.

Not all people go through stages, phases, themes, or life events in exactly the same way. That is, there is a great deal of individual variation in the way people handle the transition from early adulthood to middle adulthood, and middle adulthood to late adulthood. At one level, there is evidence that men and women may experience stressful life events differently (Lowenthal, Thurnher, & Chiriboga, 1975). For example, the following table shows that the type of stress experienced by men and women differs.

In a discussion of life stress, an expert on anxiety and stress, Irwin Sarason (1980), has called attention to the wide array of individual differences in the frequency and preoccupying characteristics of stress-related cognitions.

Stress type	Men	Women	Total
Considerable Presumed Stress			
Challenged	23	14	19
Overwhelmed	28	34	31
Light Presumed Stress			
Lucky	32	26	29
Self-defeating	17	26	21
Total	*100*	*100*	*100*

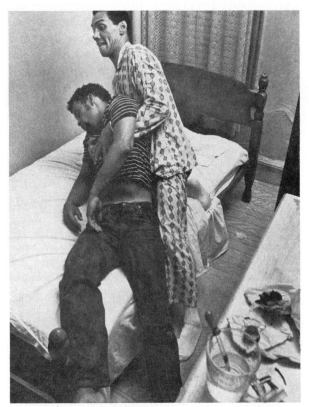

Many young adults push their bodies too far since they are able to bounce back so easily.

Physical Competence and Bad Health Habits
Young adults rarely recognize how much their bad eating habits, heavy drinking, and extensive smoking will influence their physical status when they reach middle adulthood. For example, despite the warnings on packages and in advertisements that cigarettes are likely to be hazardous to your health, there is evidence that as adolescents grow into early adulthood, there actually is an increase in cigarette usage. In the longitudinal study described earlier in the chapter conducted by Jerald Bachman, Patrick O'Malley, and Jerome Johnson (1978), as individuals went from their senior year of high school to the fifth year following high school, they increased their use of cigarettes. As suggested by table 15.3, they also increased their weekly use of alcohol, any use of marijuana, and any use of amphetamines, barbiturates, and hallucinogens as well.

Experts on health care suggest that during early adulthood it is important to begin preventive health care (Carroll & Miller, 1982). Recommended practices include proper nutrition, sleep, rest, and exercise. During early adulthood, few individuals take the time to think about how their personal life-styles will affect their health in middle and late adulthood. As young adults many of us develop a pattern of not eating breakfast, not eating regular meals and relying on snacks as our main food source during the day, eating excessively to

While the most adaptive response to stress is a task orientation that directs a person's attention to the task at hand rather than to emotional reactions, some individuals are task oriented while others are not. The adaptive value of being able to set aside temporary strong emotions in order to deal with a problematic situation is reflected in George Valliant's Grant study (1974, 1977). In reporting college students adjustments over a thirty-year period after leaving school, Valliant found that pervasive personal preoccupations are maladaptive in both work and marriage. Some individuals in the Grant study showed strong personal preoccupations, others did not.

Sarason (1980) emphasizes that the ability to set aside unproductive worries and preoccupations is crucial to functioning under stress. How stress is handled depends on both the individual and the situation, so an interactional approach is required that incorporates both individual differences and situational factors (Lazarus & Delongis, in press; Lazarus & Launier, 1978). Both of these are part of what is going on in an individual's life when stress appears. What is going on includes available social supports and what the person brings to the situation, and such tendencies as the ability to anticipate stress, to be obsessive, to feel secure, or to feel competent. At least five factors influence how an individual will respond to life stress, according to Sarason:

1. The nature of the task, or stress.
2. The skills available to perform the task or handle the stress.
3. Personality characteristics.
4. Social supports available to the person experiencing stress.
5. The person's history of stress-arousing experiences and events.

Table 15.3
Changes in Usage Rates for Cigarettes, Alcohol, Marijuana, and Other Drugs

	Percentage of Respondents Reporting Usage during the Period		
	1968–69	*1969–70*	*1973–74*
Daily use of cigarettes	35	40	44
Weekly use of alcohol	31	44	58
Any use of marijuana	21	35	52
Any use of amphetamines, barbiturates, hallucinogens	12	18	24

Source: Bachman, O'Malley, & Johnson, 1978.

the point that we exceed a normal weight for our age, smoking moderately or excessively, drinking moderately or excessively, failing to exercise, and getting by with only a few hours of sleep at night. Such poor personal life-styles were linked with poor health in one investigation of 7,000 individuals ranging in age from twenty to seventy (Belloc & Breslow, 1972).

There are some hidden dangers in the fact that physical performance and health are at their peaks in early adulthood. While young adults can draw on physical resources for a great deal of pleasure, the fact that they can bounce back so easily from physical stress, exertion, and abuse may lead young adults to push their bodies too far. While pushing your body too far physically in early adulthood may not show up in that time period, the negative effects are bound to appear in middle or late adulthood.

The Slowdown and Decline in Physical Development

W. A. Marshall (1973) concluded that only very slight changes can be detected in the brain and sensory organs of young adults. The weight of the brain does seem to decline slowly at about the rate of one gram per year beginning at the twentieth year of life, but the size of the brain is no indication of intelligence or wisdom. While sensory systems show little change in young adults, the lens of the eye loses some of its elasticity and become less able to change shape and focus on near objects. And, hearing is usually at a peak in adolescence, remains fairly constant in the first part of early adulthood, then begins to decline.

Muscle tone and strength often begin to show signs of decline around the age of thirty—sagging chins and protruding abdomens may appear. And, it is not unusual for a gray hair to signal aging in the latter part of early adulthood. For some individuals weight increases in early adulthood can become a serious problem. Basal metabolism rate (BMR) does not decline precipitously during early adulthood, but it does show a gradual dropping off so that an individual's body is burning up fewer calories in a resting state than was the case in adolescence. And, in the mid- to late twenties there is an increase in the body's fatty tissue. Early adulthood can be a particularly problematic time for individuals who exercised vigorously during adolescence and/or the first part of early adulthood, and then took sedentary jobs that require them to sit for long hours at a time. Individuals who were in athletic programs in high school or college are particularly prone to such problems if they do not get involved in vigorous exercise programs once they have ended their formal athletic competition.

The Menstrual Cycle and Hormones

From early adolescence until some point in middle adulthood, a woman's body usually undergoes marked changes in hormone levels that seem to be linked to the menstrual cycle. Recall that we described sex hormones and the various phases of the menstrual cycle in chapter 13—you may want to read that section again at this time. The possibility that biological cycles (such as menstruation) may influence the psychological orientation of an individual is one of the most underexplored areas of development. In the past, it was assumed that monthly biological cycles like menstruation occurred exclusively in the female. Males have no obvious physical signs such as a menstrual cycle to signal monthly or other periodic biological changes, however, some biologists now believe that both males and females are influenced by cyclic biological changes called circadian rhythms. The menstrual cycle is but one example of such a biological rhythm.

Researchers are gradually beginning to show more interest in how the menstrual cycle is related to personality fluctuations in the female. Judith Bardwick (1971) reports that the latter part of the menstrual cycle, from about day twenty-two on, is associated with a greater incidence of depression, anxiety, and irritability than is the middle of the menstrual cycle when ovulation is occurring. Bardwick reports that women show higher levels of self-esteem and confidence during ovulation in comparison to other parts of the cycle. Bardwick's study and most others have concentrated on females in young adulthood.

The weight of the research evidence shows that there are definite mood swings in the female associated with the middle of the menstrual cycle and the later premenstrual phase. However, it is not entirely clear whether the mood changes are due to a positive upswing of mood during the middle phase, a downward swing during the premenstrual phase, or a combination of both. Moreover, some studies point out that as many as 25 percent of all women report no mood shifts at all during these two phases (e.g., Hyde & Rosenberg, 1976).

Nevertheless, 75 percent of all women do experience mood shifts during different menstrual phases. What causes the changes in mood that occur in about three out of every four women? Hormonal changes are clearly one important factor. Female hormones reach peak levels at about day twenty-two to day twenty-four of the menstrual cycle, just at the time when depression and irritability seem to be at their peak, as well. On the other hand, the cause-effect relationship could be the direct opposite; in other words, it is possible that mood changes influence hormone levels. If this is true, intense feelings of irritability and depression may feed back to the endocrine system and produce more estrogen.

Sexual Activity in Early Adulthood

In this section three questions are evaluated. What are the sexual options available to adults? What is the biological nature of the sexual response? And, what is the nature of sexual activity in young adulthood?

Sexual Options for Adults

The importance of our body and our sexuality in establishing our identity as adults is reflected in the comment that whether we ignore it or not, our skins present us as male or female (Lerbinger, 1972). Our sexual identification and our human sexuality is, therefore, an important part of our personality and can influence interpersonal perceptions and relations. There are many different sexual options available to the adult. As can be seen in box 15.2, there often has been a tendency to document the sexual activities of bisexuals, transsexuals, homosexuals, and nonsexuals more than the sexual responses of the average person.

Many adults have a number of misconceptions about sexuality, and sexual myths are prevalent in our culture. We live in an era of fluctuating but contradictory attitudes about sexuality. For instance, many adults and parents believe that we, as a nation, should be better informed about the realities and myths of sexuality, yet large percentages of parents of high school students have never discussed sex with their offspring (McCary, 1971).

During the course of the life cycle, a person's sex drive fluctuates—a process that is independent of the amount of sexual activity the person engages in. Hormonal changes influence our sex drive as do cultural standards about sexual activity. There is evidence that some of the differences in sexual activity are due to the way we are socialized. William Van Hoose and Maureen Worth (1982) describe this socialization process.

Differences in sexual activity are often due to the way we are socialized.

Many adults have been socialized to believe that premarital sexual experiences are appropriate for males but not for females. These experiences then become the basis for the belief that males are more knowledgeable about sex than are females. Also through early sexual experiences, males are socialized to disassociate the erotic from a caring commitment to the other person. Thus armed supposedly with more experience and supposedly greater expertise, many males venture into long term sexual relationships and marriage believing that they are responsible for the couples' sex life. It is not surprising then that not all couples have been able to find sexual fulfillment.

Van Hoose and Worth believe that sexual satisfaction comes only through a thorough understanding of one's partner and one's own likes and dislikes. Each individual is responsible for expressing their sexual needs and desires.

The Biology of the Sexual Response
William Van Hoose and Maureen Worth (1982) also discuss the biology of the sexual response. They identify four basic phases of sexual response, which culminate in orgasm.

In terms of physical response males and females experience similar sensations in corresponding anatomical structures. William Masters and Virginia Johnson (1965, 1966, 1970) describe these four phases of the sexual response: first is the **excitement phase.** Through **vasocongestion** or swelling of the blood vessels the person feels sexual and physical arousal. Breathing increases, the heart rate increases and the skin becomes flushed. The second phase is the **plateau stage** which is marked by a varying length of intense sexual arousal. This stage may be prolonged by the male through various techniques so that the female is ready for the next stage which is orgasm. The **orgasm phase** is characterized by the body becoming rigid with experiences of intense pleasure and a sense of release. Women are capable of multiple orgasms. This ability increases with age and is especially frequent in middle adulthood. The final stage is the **resolution phase** when the throbbing sensations of orgasm diminish and the body continues to relax.

After achieving orgasm, males will experience a **refractory period** when arousal and orgasm are not possible. This period increases with age. Women however have no refractory period.

Type and Incidence of Sexual Activity
The data presented in the Kinsey reports, first described in chapter 13, suggest that most American males develop a pattern of orgasm and ejaculation during adolescence that continues into early adulthood, and is, to some degree, independent of marital status. By contrast, for most individuals the outlet for their sexual drive is different in early adulthood than it was during adolescence. Masturbation is the dominant form of male sexual behavior during adolescence, particularly during the early phases of adolescence, but sexual intercourse is more prevalent in early adulthood (Kinsey, Pomeroy, & Martin, 1948; Masters & Johnson, 1966).

Premarital Sex Our cultural standards for premarital sex have changed substantially during the course of this century. In recent years, a climate suggesting it is not morally wrong to engage in premarital sex has developed. For example, in a 1969 study of adults, 48 percent of the men surveyed under the age of thirty said that premarital sexual relations are not wrong, but even by 1972 this figure had reached 65 percent. For women, the figures increased from 27 percent to 42 percent (Udry, 1974). And, while earlier studies of premarital sex (e.g., Kinsey, 1948) indicated that males were more likely to have premarital sex than females, more recent data from a number of studies of the sex lives of college students suggest that women are as likely as men to have premarital sex (Luria & Rose, 1980).

In the United States, national surveys indicate that by the time they are twenty-five, 97 percent of males and 81 percent of females have engaged in premarital intercourse (Hunt, 1974). In West Germany, the incidence ranges from 44 percent of males and 33 percent of females among twenty- to twenty-one-year-old unmarried students, but among unmarried workers of the same age the figures rise dramatically to 81 percent of males and 83 percent of females (Sigusch & Schmidt, 1973). In France, the prevalence of premarital intercourse for the twenty to twenty-nine age bracket ranges from 75 percent for males to 55 percent for females (Gondonneau, Mironer, Dourlin-Rollier, & Simon, 1972). Yet there are other countries and cultures where premarital sex is unheard of.

While there is often variation in the precentages in different sex surveys, we usually find that as students go from the freshman to the senior year of college in the United States an increase in premarital sex occurs. The range of premarital sex for men is between 28 percent at the beginning of college to 82 percent during the senior year—for women the corresponding figures

Box 15.2

An Expert Discusses Information about Transsexuals, Transvestites, and Homosexuals

Dr. John Money is recognized as one of the leading authorities in the world on the biological basis of sex-role development. He is the cofounder of the Gender Identity Clinic at Johns Hopkins University and president of the Society for the Scientific Study of Sex. In the following interview Dr. Money talks about sexual aberrations.

What Is a Transsexual?

[A **transsexual**] is a person who wants to be a member of the opposite sex—whose sense of gender identity is at odds with the anatomic facts—and who may finally undergo surgery to change sex.

How Do Transvestites, Transsexuals, and Homosexuals Differ?

The **transvestite** is a person who throughout his or her life has a compulsive need occasionally to impersonate the other sex by dressing up. The transsexual, as far back as he or she can recall, has always had a feeling of belonging in the wrong sex and yearning to have the body of the other sex. The **homosexual** is a person who goes to bed with someone with the same sex organs. The common denominator in the three types is that they all have some degree of transposition of what we define as male versus female.

Do Transsexuals Lead "Closet" Lives?

Some who are born male are open and declared female impersonators. Then there are those who prefer not to be known as such, particularly at work. Thirdly, there are transvestite/transsexuals, who keep their cross-dressing secret until they can no longer resist the sex change. Male transsexuals often make an extraordinary effort to play a full stereotype macho role as a man. But once they reach that great moment of decision, they go public. It is a little like having an epileptic seizure creep up on someone, and there is nothing you can do about it.

What Are the Compelling Reasons for Going Public?

One is the desire to triumph over this lifelong problem. Second, it is really unbelievably difficult for a transsexual to stay private, to obliterate his footsteps in the snow. I advise my patients to change publicly without being stigmatized by it.

What Role Does the Transsexual Seek to Play after the Sex Change?

Each transsexual has an image of femininity or masculinity, and he or she draws it with a hard edge. In the male-to-female change, some want to play the harlot, others the midwestern farm wife, and still others the suburban matron. Only recently have some transsexuals identified with the feminists—this used to be out! A new role is the male-to-female who wants to live as a lesbian. In the female-to-male, most prefer the role of steady breadwinner, although I have seen one transsexual male who wanted to be a gangster.

Do Transsexuals Ever Marry?

One or two have married transvestites/transsexuals they knew before surgery. But usually they find a partner who does not initially know their medical history and upon discovering it does not panic.

How Could This Be?

By the time the partner finds out, he or she is already relating to the transsexual as a woman or man. An analogy is that a man does not get rid of a woman because she has had a mastectomy or a hysterectomy.

Estimates of the Number of Transsexuals Range from 10,000 to 20,000 in the United States. How Many Are There?

There are no statistics, and I prefer not to guess. Since the start of the clinic here in 1966 we have received more than 3,000 transsexual inquiries a year—and surgically completed a dozen or so sex reassignments annually for the past ten years. Most of the cases come from the United States.

What Makes a Person a Transsexual?

We are not sure. There is no clear evidence of a genetic factor. The nearest thing is men born with an additional X chromosome—instead of forty-six chromosomes, they have forty-seven. A dozen or so cases have been cited. The prenatal hormonal story in transsexuals is still unknown, although we do know from animal experiments that a prenatal hormonal factor influences brain pathways. After birth, parents, of course, have an extraordinarily large role in the development of any baby, but so far there is no consistent pattern that produces transsexuals.

Why, Before their Sex Change, Do Some Transsexuals Marry and Have Children?

Usually they are still in that transvestite/transsexual period with two vying personalities. They make a heroic effort to conform to their heredity and tune out the other personality. Another reason is that there is something magical about having children. Why do people about to divorce sometimes have one more baby? Somehow they figure this may resolve their divorce problem.

Why Are People Fascinated by Transsexuals?

They force the public to think of issues that were formerly taboo. Once past the sensationalist aspect, people, after thousands of years of maximizing differences between the sexes, are now looking for similarities. Transsexuals make us do this, and that is an extraordinary fascination.

Do You Foresee a Day When Transsexuality Will Be Acceptable?

I am reminded of a plains Indian tribe with the institution known as *berdache*, whereby a male would dress as a female and even marry. Somehow, I think this could happen in our society. But, with new scientific and medical discoveries, there might also be ways to prevent transsexuality.

Source: Money, 1976.

are 29 and 86 percent, not much different than for the men. The best current estimates indicate that between 33 and 75 percent of college women experience premarital sex before or during their college years (Luria & Rose, 1980).

Sexual Intercourse in Marriage   Evidence that sexual intercourse in marriage is a highly satisfying physical experience, particularly for women, comes from data reported by more than 2,000 middle-class American married women (Bell & Lobsenz, 1974). Married women in their twenties enjoyed the physical aspects of sexual intercourse more than their counterparts in their thirties, who were more inclined to enjoy its emotional aspects. Most of the women reported that they had orgasms, and those who had orgasms more frequently also were more likely to indicate that they were happy. And, married women in early adulthood were more likely than their adolescent or middle adulthood counterparts to experiment with love-making experiments. Married women in their twenties and thirties said that they practiced oral-genital sex more than the other two age segments of married women as well. The young married women also indicated that it was their husbands who were most likely to initiate love-making sessions rather than themselves. Since these data were collected in a cross-sectional manner, however, there may be cohort effects involved.

However, extramarital sex, while being considered appropriate by some individuals, still is not condoned as morally appropriate conduct by the majority of individuals in our society. Pollster Daniel Yankelovich (1981), writing in *New Rules in American Life,* found that 76 percent of adult Americans disapprove of men having extramarital affairs. And, while the popular press has given a great deal of attention to mate swapping by marital couples, a maximum of 2 percent of married pairs are involved (Bartell, 1971; Hunt, 1974).

Physical Development in Middle Adulthood

While decline appears in some aspects of physical development in the latter part of early adulthood, there is marked and gradual decline in many aspects of physical development during middle adulthood. In this section, we will look at how many different aspects of physical development change in middle adulthood, explore the health status of adults in midlife, discuss menopause and the male climacteric syndrome, and conclude with comments about sexuality.

"If this is gonna make me strong and handsome, I think you'd better eat it."

Physical Changes

A host of physical changes characterize middle adulthood—some have begun to appear in the thirties, but by the end of the forties, decline in physical development suggests the individual clearly has reached middle adulthood. As a rule, men in our culture show signs of aging earlier than women, and members of the lower class often show a physical decline earlier than those in the middle class.

Seeing and hearing involve two of the most noticeable and troublesome changes in middle adulthood. Accommodation of the eye (the ability to focus and maintain an image on the retina) experiences its sharpest decline between forty and fifty-nine years of age (Bruckner, 1967). In particular, it becomes difficult for individuals to view close objects. There also appears to be a reduced blood supply to the eye, although this usually does not occur until the fifties or sixties. The reduced blood supply may decrease the size of the visual field and account for an increase in the size of the blind spot. And, there is some evidence that the retina becomes less sensitive to low levels of illumination as an individual goes through middle and late adulthood. In one investigation, the effects of illumination level on the productivity of workers in early and middle adulthood was studied (Hughes, 1978). The workers were

Our personal life-style is one of the factors of health status.

asked to look for 10 target numbers printed on sheets that had a total of 420 numbers printed on them. Each of the workers performed the task under three different levels of illumination. While increased levels of illumination enhanced the efficiency of both the early and the middle adulthood workers, the performance of the middle adulthood workers was increased the most.

Hearing also may start to decline by the age of forty. Sensitivity to high pitches seems to decline first, while the ability to hear low pitched sounds appears not to decline very much in middle adulthood. And, men seem to lose their auditory acuity for high pitched sounds more than women (Farnsworth, McNemar, & McNemar, 1965). This sex difference may be due to the greater exposure of men to noise in occupations such as mining, automobile work, and so forth.

The heart and coronary arteries undergo change in middle adulthood. The heart of a forty-year-old can pump only twenty-three liters of blood per minute in times of stress, while the heart of a twenty-year-old can pump forty liters under comparable conditions. The coronary arteries that supply blood to the heart narrow during middle adulthood. And, blood pressure usually rises in the forties and fifties—at menopause, the blood pressure of women rises sharply and usually remains above that of men through the later years of life.

Our life styles seem to be associated with the incidence of cardiovascular disease in middle adulthood. One intriguing theory has been developed that classifies individuals as either having a high risk of heart disease (type A) or a low one (type B) based on behavioral patterns (Friedman & Rosenman, 1974). The **type A person** is excessively competitive, has an accelerated pace of ordinary activities, is impatient with the rate at which most events occur, often thinks about doing several things at the same time, shows hostility, and cannot hide the fact that time is a struggle in life. By contrast, the **type B person** is typified by the absence of these behavioral tendencies. About 10 percent of the subjects studied were clearly type A or type B.

The main investigation of the link between behavioral patterns and coronary risk consisted of data collected from more than 3,500 men between the ages of thirty-five and fifty-nine (Rosenman, Friedman, Straus, Jenkins, Zyzanski, Wurm, Kositcheck, Hah, & Werthessen, 1970). At the beginning of the study none of the men had any sign of coronary disease. At that time behavioral patterns were noted and physiological checks were made. Then, the men were assessed two and one-half, four and one-half, and eight and one-half years later. Coronary disease was much more likely to occur among the type A men than the type B men. For example, more than 70 percent of the thirty- to forty-nine-year-old men who developed coronary problems were type A while less than 30 percent were type B. The percentages for the older group were similar. Clearly, coronary disease is influenced by many other factors, such as diet, smoking, obesity, and genetic tendencies, however, these data suggest that our personal life-style is one of the factors associated with the incidence of coronary problems.

Muscular strength and the ability to maintain maximum muscular effort both decline steadily during middle adulthood. By the age of forty-five the strength of the back muscles in men has declined to approximately 96 percent of its maximum value, and by fifty it has declined to 92 percent. Men in their late fifties can only do physical work at about 60 percent of the rate achieved by men at the age of forty—much of this decline appears to be linked with such physiological changes as the thickening of the wall of the air sacs in the lungs, which hinders breathing, and the hardening of connective sheaths that surround muscles, which is linked with both a decrease in oxygen and blood supply (Marshall, 1973).

Box 15.3
Women and Weight Consciousness

Kim Chernin (1981) describes how we have become a nation acutely concerned about weight, suggests why women are more concerned about their weight than men, and discusses a number of other aspects of our weight conscious society.

A tall woman enters the locker room of the tennis club. She removes her towel, throws it across a bench, faces herself squarely in the mirror, climbs on the scale and looks down.

"I knew it," she mutters. "Two pounds. Two pounds!!"

Then she turns, grabs the towel and wings out at the mirror. The towel splatters water over the glass.

"Fat pig!" she shouts at her image in the mirror. "You fat, fat pig!"

Two facts make the current obsession with weight extraordinary. One is the scope of it. Throughout history, there have been dieters, including Roman matrons who were willing to starve themselves. But there never has been a period when such large numbers of people have spent so much time, money and emotional energy on their weight. Weight Watchers, for example, holds more than 12,000 individual classes every week and has enrolled 13 million members since it began in 1963.

The other extraordinary aspect of today's diet phenomenon is the degree to which it is focused on women. Of course, the nation has its share of fat men who want to lose weight. But interviews with physicians and psychologists make it clear that the truly obsessive dieter is almost inevitably female.

Representatives of diet organizations acknowledge that 95 percent of their members are women. According to Dr. Hilde Bruch, professor emeritus of psychiatry at Houston's Baylor College of Medicine and an expert on eating disorders, women make up more than 90 percent of the people suffering from anorexia nervosa, a personality disorder that leads to self-starvation. Bulimia, a condition in which periods of heavy eating are followed by self-induced vomiting, is almost entirely limited to women.

Why have so many millions of American women, in the last decade, become so concerned about their weight? The subject has not received much attention, except on a superficial level. It deserves better.

There is, for example, the medical explanation: Women diet because of the long-proclaimed correlation between obesity and ill health. Yet that fails to explain the intense upset many women experience because of two or three pounds of

"Small, medium or large?
Or need I ask?"

excess weight. And in any event, medical opinion has changed dramatically in recent years. Dr. Reubin Andres, clinical director of Baltimore's National Institute on Aging, has found, for example, that "there's something about being moderately overweight that's good for you." He bases his opinion on forty worldwide studies involving 6 million people.

Most Americans define their degree of "overweight" on the basis of the charts that hang on doctors' walls. Since 1969, when the Metropolitan Life Insurance Company began publishing one of the most widely used charts today, it has become routine for physicians to tell their patients to take off those ten or fifteen pounds that exceed the appropriate figure on the chart. "You'll look better," they say. "You'll feel better, and it's healthier."

Today, experts have their doubts. In fact, the insurance companies will be bringing out new charts within the next few months. The companies acknowledge that the weight guidelines will shift upward, but they won't say by how much.

This does not mean, however, that obesity is a desirable state, nor should it suggest that the medical world understands all the effects of being overweight.

But this much seems clear: By and large, an extra ten pounds beyond the figure on the old insurance-company chart is not harmful, and it may even be good for you. The weight obsession of the modern American woman cannot be dismissed as simply a medical issue.

The woman who lies in bed in the morning—counting the number of calories she ate the night before, wondering whether her body has added substance to itself at the expense of her will—actually is pursuing a line of philosophical inquiry.

In our culture we have strong, ambivalent feelings about the relationship between a woman's power and her size, and they are reflected in our dislike for large, fleshy women.

The male-dominated culture calls for slender women; unconsciously, society seeks to limit the symbolic physical expression of women's power. And women themselves accept this tyranny of slenderness not only in submission to the male but because of their own ambivalence about their bodies.

As long as this culture maintains its traditional, male-centered balance, there may be some limited variation in the acceptable weight of women. At the turn of the century, for example, the prevailing mood favored some excess weight, and the fashions in clothing were—as usual—a clear reflection of the psychological state of the culture. Women at the time were permitted to wear flowing clothes, cut on the bias, to complement their ample hips.

In the 1920s, a shift in fashion signified the arrival of a major cultural change. The suffragist movement was approaching the culmination of its efforts to obtain the vote for women. Suddenly, women were supposed to look like boys. They bound their breasts and bobbed their hair.

When women are clearly subordinate, when they don't seek to change their social status, men seem free to delight in them as physical beings. At such a time, voluptuous women may be welcome. But in an age when women assert their claim to power and autonomy, men have a different response. The culture calls for fashions that reflect a distinct male fear of a mature woman's power, particularly as it expresses itself through a woman's large body, with its capacity to remind men of a time when they depended upon a woman for their very survival.

In the last two decades, society's standards for the size of women have undergone an amazing change. In 1959, when Marilyn Monroe made the film *Some Like It Hot,* she was voluptuous, as large as a woman in a Renoir painting. For those of us who fell in love with her then and yearned as adolescent girls to look like her, that film today is a revelation. She was, by modern standards, fat.

Now, fashion model Kristine Oulman sets the standard for women's beauty. A recent television program showed Kristine behind the scenes. She is in a room filled with people who are combing her, making her up, preparing her to wear the latest in sophisticated clothing. When their labors are done, this is the result: a preadolescent girl, with slender arms and shoulders, undeveloped breasts and hips and thighs, whose body has been covered in sexy clothes, whose face has been painted with a false allure and whose eyes imitate a sexuality she has, by her own confession, never experienced. Kristine is thirteen years old.

This is the message that fashion conveys and society teaches. This is what a mature woman should attempt to look like. A woman who wishes to conform to her culture's ideal, in this age of feminist assertion, will not be large, mature, voluptuous, strong or powerful. She, who has the knowledge of life and birth, is to make herself look like an adolescent girl if she wishes to appease her culture's anxiety about female power.

During the last two decades, this society has witnessed the emergence of two significant movements among women. Because of the women's liberation movement and the weight-watcher's movement, the question of how large a woman is permitted to be has come to occupy Americans' lives in both a literal and a metaphorical form. Much has been said about the metaphorical side; now, serious attention must be given to the implications of society's very literal obsession with women's weight and size.

This social malaise, this tyranny of slenderness, is expressed in unhealthy dieting, in ever-more-widespread eating disorders, in the dictates of fashion. For millions of women it is a cause of unremitting pain and shame. And it cannot be obliterated unless we begin to address ourselves to resolving some of the most basic conflicts of this culture.

Source: Chernin, 1981.

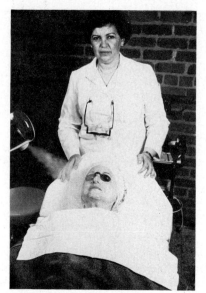

A youthful appearance is stressed in our culture. Many individuals go to great lengths to make themselves look younger.

Health Status

Health status becomes a major concern in middle adulthood, whereas among young adults it usually gets much less attention. Middle adulthood is characterized by a general decline in physical fitness and some deterioration in health is to be expected. The three health concerns that have received the greatest attention in middle adulthood are heart disease, cancer, and weight. Cardiovascular disease is the number one killer in the United States, followed by cancer (U.S. Department of Health, Education, and Welfare, 1979). Cancer caused by smoking often surfaces for the first time in middle adulthood.

The Harvard Medical School health letter indicates that about 20 million Americans are on a "serious" diet at any particular moment. Being overweight is a critical health problem in middle adulthood. For individuals who are 30 percent or more overweight, the probability of dying in middle adulthood increases by 40 percent. And, obesity increases the likelihood that the individual will suffer a number of other ailments, including hypertension and digestive disorders. In box 15.3 the interest of our nation in weight consciousness is explored further.

Women seem to show a much greater concern about dieting than men. And, since a youthful appearance is stressed in our culture, many individuals whose hairs are graying, whose skins are wrinkling, whose bodies are sagging, and whose teeth are yellowing strive to make themselves look younger. Undergoing cosmetic surgery, dying hair, purchasing a wig, trying out a cure for balding, getting in a weight reduction program, participating in an exercise regimen, and taking heavy doses of vitamins are frequent excursions of the middle-aged adult. In one investigation, it was found that middle-aged women focus more attention on their facial attractiveness than older or younger women and are more likely to perceive that the signs of aging have a negative effect on their physical appearance (Nowak, 1977). While some aspects of aging in middle adulthood actually are taken as signs of attractiveness in men in our culture, similar signs are looked at as a disaster in women. While facial wrinkles and gray hair symbolize strength and maturity for men, such signs of aging in women often are viewed as unattractive.

How we deal with physical change and decline varies greatly from one individual to another. One person may be able to function well in the world under rather severe physical problems or deteriorating health, while another person with the same problem may become hospitalized and bedridden. Some people call a doctor at the slightest indication that something is wrong and worry extraordinarily about their health. At the other extreme, an individual may ignore some serious signs of physical dangers that might indicate a heart attack is imminent or that cancer may be present.

Next, we see that another physical change in middle adulthood suggests a difference in the way women and men experience this phase of the life cycle.

Menopause and the Male Climacteric Syndrome

Most of us know something about **menopause.** But is what we know accurate? Stop for a moment and think about your knowledge of menopause. What is menopause? When does it occur? Can it be treated? In this section we will look at the nature of menopause, including myths and stereotypes that have been developed about it. And, we will explore the nature of the male climacteric syndrome, which involves the decline of the male's sexual and reproductive powers.

*There are both positive and
negative reactions to
menopause.*

Menopause

My first sign of menopause was the night sweat. Even though I knew why I was having the sweats, it was a little frightening to wake up in the middle of the night with my sheets all drenched. It was hard not to feel that something was very wrong with me. And I lost a lot of sleep changing sheets and wondering how long the sweats would go on. Sometimes I felt chilled after sweating and had trouble going back to sleep. It was a good thing I could absorb myself in a book at times like that.

I also had hot flashes several times a week for almost six months. I didn't get as embarrassed as some of my friends who also had hot flashes, but I found the "heat wave" sensation most uncomfortable.

I felt generally good around the time of menopause. My children were supportive and patient, particularly when I was irritable from lack of sleep. My husband, unfortunately, was quite insensitive and frequently accused me of "inventing" my "afflictions." Without the help of friends and children who *did* try to understand what I was going through, it might have been harder for me to be around him. . . .

I usually think of geriatric types: little old white-haired women in wheelchairs in nursing homes. It's such an ugly word and image. Dried-up womb—bloodless insides. I'll never forget a man's description of an elegant hotel in the Virgin Islands as "menopause manor"! It made me glad at that time that I was still menstruating and didn't qualify for his derogatory observation. Now, ten years (and Women's Liberation) later, I can see the folly of his remarks and his machismo. But the word by itself still gives me a chill. It seems so final—as if an important bodily function had ceased, and with it all the fun of youth—which, of course, isn't true. . . .

I am constantly amazed and delighted to discover new things about my body, something menstruation did not allow me to do. I have new responses, desires, sensations, freed and apart from the distraction of menses [periods]. . . .

I felt better and freer since menopause. I threw that diaphragm away. I *love* being free of possible pregnancy and birth control. It makes my sex life better. (*Our Bodies, Ourselves,* 1976, pp. 327, 328)

These comments suggest both negative and positive reactions to menopause. The popular stereotype of the menopausal woman has been negative—she is exhausted, irritable, unsexy, hard to live with, irrationally depressed, and unwillingly suffering a change that marks the end of her active reproductive life. However, many women handle menopause in very positive ways.

Biologically, menopause is defined as the end of menstruation, a marker that signals the cessation of childbearing capacity. A related term, climacteric, is often used synonomously with menopause. However, while menstruation refers to the onset of irregular menses (periods) and their eventual cessation as a result of ovarian degeneration and a decline of estrogen secretion, climacteric generally occurs over a more prolonged period of time, at least several years, and refers to the loss of the ability to reproduce. The term climacteric has been applied to such a loss in men as well as women.

The average age of menopause in the United States is fifty—it is considered to have occurred when twelve consecutive months have passed without a period (Block, Davidson, & Grambs, 1981). A number of symptoms accompany menopause, while only two, hot flashes and the atrophy of the vagina, are believed to be directly related to decreased estrogen levels. Recent estimates indicate that approximately 20 percent of women have no symptoms at all, while 15 percent have symptoms that are sufficiently severe to warrant treatment (Women's Medical Center, 1977). The majority of women (65 percent) experience mild symptoms and can cope with them without undergoing medical intervention.

The **hot flash,** a feeling of extreme heat usually confined to the upper part of the body and often accompanied by a drenching sweat, is the most commonly experienced symptom of menopause. Hot flashes gradually diminish in frequency and generally disappear completely within a year or two. A second symptom that often is associated with menopause is the atrophy of the vagina. The inner lining of the vagina becomes drier, thinner, and less flexible—conditions that can make intercourse painful for some women.

Depression also may be associated with menopause, but menopause does not cause depression. Menopause comes at a time when some women are losing their full-time jobs as mothers and as wives, when some middle-aged men are attracted by younger women, and when other aspects of the aging process—wrinkles, a bulging figure, and so forth—also are occurring.

Many women undergo a hysterectomy, a sort of artificial menopause. The uterus and cervix are removed in the case of a **simple hysterectomy,** while the ovaries and fallopian tubes are taken out as well in a **total hysterectomy.** Hysterectomy is the most common operation performed in the United States (Morgan, 1978). In recent years more women have had hysterectomies than in the past—by 1977, the figure had reached approximately 800,000 women per year. A hysterectomy is performed for various reasons, the most common of which involves the improper positioning and slippage of the uterus. This condition occurs most often in women who have had several children, since pregnancy stretches the ligaments that hold the uterus in place. A hysterectomy also may be performed to eliminate fibroid tumors, which as many as 25 percent of all women experience—such tumors are not cancerous, but they may cause abnormal bleeding. And, the third most common reason for a hysterectomy is cancer, which if detected early by a Pap test does not have to be life threatening (Block et al., 1981).

Estrogen Replacement Therapy   Perhaps one of the most controversial aspects of menopause focuses on the decrease in natural estrogen levels and the use of **estrogen replacement therapy (ERT).** Estrogen replacement therapy involves replacing the estrogen that a woman's body no longer produces and is usually prescribed for severe cases. Estrogen has been highly successful in relieving hot flashes and vaginal atrophy, and consequently, has been viewed as welcome relief by women. However, there are some negative, as well as some positive, aspects, to the use of estrogen therapy.

Marilyn Block, Janice Davidson, and Jean Grambs (1981) state that the use of ERT is highly controversial because of the unknown relationship between estrogen and cancer. Despite reports that contend that ERT does not cause uterine or breast cancer, the FDA warns that the chances for uterine cancer increase five to seven times with ERT. Much of the danger of ERT is that the medication is taken for long periods of time. The average amount of time spent on ERT by most women is ten years. According to Block, Davidson, and Grambs:

Even though ERT is effective in ameliorating hot flashes, women so affected must determine for themselves whether the condition is serious enough to warrant the use of a drug that causes cancer in animals and is associated with increased risk of cancer in women. (p. 28)

The Male Climacteric Syndrome
The **male climacteric syndrome** differs in two important ways from menopause—it comes later, usually in the sixties and seventies, and it progresses at a much slower rate. During their fifties and sixties most men do not lose their capacity to father children, but there usually is a decline in sexual potency at this time. Men do experience hormonal changes in their fifties and sixties, but not to the extent encountered by women. For example, testosterone production starts declining at about 1 percent a year during middle adulthood. Consequently, what has sometimes been referred to as "male menopause" has less to do with hormonal change than with the psychological adjustment men must make when they are faced with declining physical energy. Business, social, and family pressures may contribute to this fatigue. The fact that testosterone therapy does not relieve such symptoms suggests that they are not induced by hormonal change.

There are some common characteristics that indicate the beginning of a male climacteric in middle adulthood. But remember it occurs more slowly and usually begins later in men than in women. First, sexual functioning changes. For example, the older a man gets the longer it takes him to have an erection, but the longer he is able to maintain it (Wagenwoord & Bailey, 1978). But while sexual potency may decrease, sexual desire does not necessarily decline. There also are some changes in secondary sexual characteristics during the climacteric—the voice may become higher pitched, facial hair may grow more slowly, and muscular stature may give way to flabbiness.

Sexuality
While there is usually little biological decline in a man's or a woman's ability to function sexually in middle adulthood, sexual activity usually occurs less frequently than in early adulthood. Career interest, family matters, and energy level may contribute to the decline in sexuality.

Often sexual activity in middle adulthood declines because of career interests, family matters, and energy levels.

While there may be a decline of sexual interest and activity in middle adulthood compared with early adulthood, a large percentage of individuals in middle adulthood still show a moderate or strong sexual interest and still engage in sexual activity on a reasonably frequent basis. For example, in one national survey of 502 men and women from forty-six to seventy-one years of age, approximately 68 percent of the fifty-one- to fifty-five-year-old respondents said that they had a moderate or strong interest in sex (Pfeiffer, Verwoerdt, & Davis, 1974). And, approximately 52 percent of the fifty-one- to fifty-five-year old age group said that they had sexual intercourse once a week or more.

It is important to note that there typically are sex differences in surveys of sexual interest and activity in middle adulthood. Men consistently report greater interest in sex and indicate that they engage in sexual activity more than women. For example, in the fifty-one- to fifty-five-year age bracket of the study just mentioned, 81 percent of the men but only 56 percent of the women said they had a moderate or strong interest in sex, and 66 percent of the men but only 39 percent of the women said they had sexual intercourse one or more times per week (Pfeiffer et al., 1974).

The data for current levels of sexual interest on the part of the forty-six- to seventy-one-year-old age group is shown in table 15.4. In addition to the points already mentioned about these data, note that as individuals reach the end of middle adulthood and the beginning of late adulthood, sexual interest and activity does decline. One factor that seems to be particularly impor-

Table 15.4
Current Level of Sexual Interest (Percentage)

Age Group	Number	None	Mild	Moderate	Strong
Men					
46–50	43	0	9	63	28
51–55	41	0	19	71	10
56–60	61	5	26	57	12
61–65	54	11	37	48	4
66–71	62	10	32	48	10
Total	261	6	26	56	12
Women					
46–50	43	7	23	61	9
51–55	41	20	24	51	5
56–60	48	31	25	44	0
61–65	43	51	37	12	0
66–71	54	50	26	22	2
Total	229	33	27	37	3

Source: Pfeiffer, Verwoerdt, & Davis, 1974.

tant in the sexual activity of women in middle adulthood is the availability of a sexual partner. Thus, it is not surprising that women in middle adulthood who are married engage in sexual activity more frequently than those who are single.

Summary

This chapter focused on a number of perspectives of adult development and described physical development in early and middle adulthood. Initially the possibility that youth represents a transition between adolescence and adulthood was explored. Two markers that suggest that early adulthood has been reached are economic independence and autonomous decision making.

A number of perspectives of life-span development described in chapter 2 have implications for adult development. Erik Erikson's psychoanalytic perspective, Robert Havighurst's developmental task view, and Bernice Neugarten's changing time, changing rhythm of the life cycle theory merit special attention in our study of adult development.

There has been a flourish of popular stage-crisis views of adult development. Three of the most popular stage-crisis theories are those of Gail Sheehy, Roger Gould, and Daniel Levinson. Evidence was presented that indicate these three popular views do not have a very sound, empirical data base. And, most experts believe that transition rather than crisis characterizes change in adulthood. Many theorists and researchers in adult development also believe that a life-events framework represents a viable approach for understanding adult development. And, it is important to consider individual variations in themes, phases, or events in adult development.

We reach the peak of our physical performance and health in early adulthood, usually between the ages of nineteen to twenty-six. By the end of early adulthood, however, decline in some aspects of physical development has occurred. Because young adults can bounce back so readily from physical abuse of their bodies, it is easy for them to develop bad personal health habits.

The menstrual cycle is a biological rhythm in women that is linked with psychological change. Sexual activity usually occurs frequently in early adulthood, and there are many different sexual options available to young adults. One major change from adolescence to early adulthood is the replacement of masturbation with sexual intercourse as the main outlet for the sexual drive. Premarital sex is prevalent among young adults, and sexual activity seems to be a source of a great deal of physical pleasure among young married couples.

Physical development shows a marked, but gradual, decline in many different areas during middle adulthood. Seeing, hearing, the heart and coronary arteries, and muscular strength and ability show clear signs of decline in middle adulthood. Health status gets a great deal of attention from adults in midlife, much more than was the case when these individuals were young adults. Three major health concerns are heart disease, cancer, and weight. Heart disease is the number one killer in the United States and is influenced by many factors, including the personal life styles we follow. We have become a nation of overweight people, and a nation seriously concerned about weight gain and loss. Women, in particular, have flocked to diet reduction programs in attempts to maintain a slender, youthful appearance.

Menopause—the end of menstruation—is surrounded by many myths and stereotypes. The majority of women cope with menopause without having to undergo medical intervention, and for some women, menopause can be a positive event. Many women undergo estrogen replacement therapy to replace the estrogen they have lost at menopause, although controversy surrounds the use of this treatment. Many women undergo a hysterectomy—the most common operation performed in the United States—which is like an artificial menopause.

While males do not undergo hormonal changes that are nearly as drastic as those encountered by women in middle adulthood, they do experience a climacteric—which refers to the loss of reproduction and sexual functioning. This process starts later and is much more gradual than with females. While there is usually little biological decline in a man's or a woman's ability to function sexually in middle adulthood, sexual activity usually occurs less frequently than in early adulthood. Nonetheless, even by the age of fifty-five, a majority of men and women show a moderate or strong interest in sexual activity. By the end of middle adulthood such interest lessens, and women show less interest than men in sexual activity.

Key Terms

asynchrony	plateau stage
crisis	refractory period
estrogen replacement therapy	resolution phase
	simple hysterectomy
excitement phase	total hysterectomy
hot flash	transition
male climacteric syndrome	type A person
	type B person
menopause	vasocongestion
orgasm phase	youth

Review Questions

1. Decribe the main perspectives of life-span development from chapter 2 that have the most to say about adult development. Discuss their ideas about adult development.
2. Point out the main ideas in the popular stage-crisis theories of adult development.
3. What are the data bases for the theories of Sheehy, Gould, and Levinson? Evaluate the data from an empirical point of view.
4. Present an overview of the life-events framework for studying adult development.
5. To what extent are there individual variations in the way adults go through various phases or stages?
6. Discuss the major changes in physical development during early adulthood.
7. How are the menstrual cycle and personality fluctuations related?
8. Describe the sexual activity of young adults, including the incidence of premarital sex.
9. Describe the major physical changes that occur in middle adulthood.
10. What is the health status of individuals in middle adulthood?
11. What are menopause and the climacteric? Are there sex differences in the climacteric? How effective is estrogen replacement therapy for women and what is the controversy that is involved in its use?
12. Discuss sexuality in middle adulthood including trends in sexual interest and activity.

Further Readings

Block, M. R., Davidson, J. L., & Grambs, J. D. *Women over forty.* New York: Springer, 1981.
This book is an excellent source of recent information about the physical development of women in middle and late adulthood. Particular attention is given to presenting sound information that will help eliminate many of the myths involved about women that have developed in our culture. Reading level is reasonably easy.

Carroll, C., & Miller, D. *Health: the Science of human adaptation.* Dubuque, Iowa: Wm. C. Brown, 1982.
An excellent college level introduction to health. Includes a great deal of valuable information about health status in early and middle adulthood. Easy to read.

Hultsch, D. F., & Deutsch, F. *Adult development and aging.* New York: McGraw-Hill, 1981.
This is an excellent introduction to adult development. Included is extensive information about the life events view of adult development. Reading level is easy to medium.

Human Development
Human Development is an international journal that is devoted to interdisciplinary research on development throughout the life cycle. Go to your college or university library and look at several issues from the last five years. You will find many articles focused on adult development. Reading level is moderately difficult.

Levinson, D. *The seasons of a man's life.* New York: Ballantine Books, 1978.
This book presents extensive biographical material about the forty men in Levinson's study of early and middle adulthood. Interesting and easy reading.

16

Cognitive Development

Prologue: Memory at Midlife

Since age thirty-five, I haven't had an original thought, done anything significant and while others were making giant steps for mankind, I was making giant steps with the garbage.

To prove to you this is not an idle observation, I took the trouble to keep a diary for an entire week, during which time I scientifically dropped 700,000 brain cells.

Monday: Twelve-year-old working on an English assignment asked me who the Earl of Sandwich was. When I suggested he was the one who always carried his lunch to the castle, twelve-year-old shook his head and said, "I'll call up one of the guys."

Tuesday: Reached a high level of incompetence by absentmindedly pouring powdered milk in dishwasher dispenser. Daughter suggested a companion to sit with me all day until Daddy could relieve her in the evening.

Wednesday: Heard a suspicious rattle in the car. Drove it into the service station where they discovered an aerosol can of de-icer rolling around near my spare tire. I am permitted to drive now only if accompanied by a teen-ager.

Thursday: Was called upon to determine the sex of our hamster, which I did without hesitation, claiming no mating was possible. Male hamster is now in maternity tops.

Friday: Missed taking my discarded chicken innards from the freezer and putting them in garbage, thus bringing the total of chicken innards in my freezer to 320 pounds.

Saturday: Mental deterioration noted as someone mentioned having a paternity suit and I said I hoped they didn't catch on because I don't have the legs to wear them.

Sunday: Family found me laughing hysterically over Tom Jones singing, "I Who Have Nothing." Family saw no humor in it and concluded I should be sent to a church camp.

The scientist from California is on to something. He has already figured out the brain drain is caused by aging, impaired circulation, and other causes. He has not figured out why thirty-five is the magic year for deterioration.

Even in the prime of my senility, I figured that one out. At thirty-five most parents launch their first teen-ager. After that, professor, it's Bananasville all the way.

As far as my memory is concerned, as I was telling my husband, what's-his-name, "I've got to do something about my memory."

"Why?" he asked.

"Why what?"

"Why do you have to do something about your memory?"

"Oh, I don't know. Just little things have been getting by me lately. Like letting your insurance policy lapse . . . and forgetting Christmas the way I did and the humiliating thing that happened to me at the airport last week."

"What humiliating thing?" he asked, putting down his paper.

"Well, I was saying good-by to your sister when I saw this man smiling at me and he looked so familiar and I was sure I knew him, but I just couldn't put a name to him. So, just to be safe I ran over and grabbed his hand, pumped it and said, 'Gosh, it's good to have you home again. We've all missed you. As soon as you're settled, call and we'll get together for dinner.' "

"What's the matter with that?"

"In the car coming home I remembered who he is. It is Mr. Whitlock, the man who cleans our septic tank every year."

"It could happen to anyone," he said sympathetically.

"I suppose so. But ever since I took a memory quiz that appeared in the newspaper last week I've been real concerned."

"What quiz?"

"It's good to know someone else has a rotten memory. Don't you remember? It's the article I clipped out just before you got the paper. Here it is:

"1. When you cannot remember where you parked your car in town do you (a) have total recall of your make of car, serial number, and license plates, or (b) take a bus home and pretend it doesn't matter?

"2. At class reunions, do you (a) use the Association Method to remember names (i.e., he is hairy and paunchy; ergo, his name is Harry Paunchy), or (b) do you squint at name tags upside down and say, 'Nayr Mot, long time, no see'?

"3. Do you (a) have specific places for your sewing basket, office equipment, cleaning supplies, and cooking utensils, or (b) are you content to put in hems with Band-Aids and take down phone messages using a cuticle stick on wax paper?

"4. Do you (a) keep tabs on your grocery shopping cart by remembering its contents, or (b) do you have to 'mark it' by forcing your twelve-year-old to sit in the basket in a fetal position?

"5. Do you (a) always remember the ages, sex, names, and grades of your children, or (b) do you have to stop and count backward or forward the year the cat came to live with you?

"6. Do you (a) always repeat the name of the person you are introduced to, or (b) repeatedly look perplexed and say 'Abigail *Who?*'

"7. Do you (a) always make a note in your checkbook of the amount of the check and to whom it was made out at the time you are writing the check, or (b) do you tell yourself that you'll do it later when you're not in such a hurry?

"You know what I think the trouble is?" I asked, folding the paper. "I share my house with four disorganized people. It isn't easy trying to keep everything in a place with everyone going in separate directions. For example, the other day I opened the tea canister and some clown had put tea in it."

"That's wrong?" asked my husband.

"That's wrong!" I shouted. "So where's my rice now? And speaking of boots, do you know how long it took me to find the kids' boots the other morning?"

"I can't imagine."

"Three hours. And just because some ding dong took them out of the soft drink cooler in the garage and didn't put them back. I suppose I could be like Doris you-know-who."

"You mean my sister?"

"Yes. She's so organized she makes me sick. I was at her house the other day and she had a pad and pencil right next to the phone. Can you imagine that? And when she wants a needle she doesn't have to have kids run through the carpets in their bare feet. She keeps them in a package with her thread. (The needles, not the kids.) And here's the zinger. She keeps her car keys on a little hook in the utility room so she always knows where they are. Oh well, what can you expect from a woman who numbers her checks consecutively?"

"Don't you keep your car keys in the same spot?" he asked.

"Are you kidding? If it weren't for looking for my car keys I'd never know where anything is. Take the other day. I was looking for the keys in the trunk of the car where I always leave them and found my new sweeper bags.

"When I went to put the sweeper bags on the broomcloset shelf, I found my rain hat which I haven't seen in two years. And when I went to put the hat in the coat closet I discovered my checkbook, which had been missing.

"While returning the checkbook to the stove drawer where it belongs, guess what? There were the scissors I had been searching for during the last week. I returned the scissors to the bookcase where I hide them from the kids, and found my dental appointment, which I had been using for a bookmark. I always keep my dental appointment in my jewelry box, so when I dropped it in there, lo and behold, there was the freezer key."

"And where are the car keys?" asked my husband.

"Well, if you can't find yours either," I sighed, "maybe I'm not as bad off as I thought."

Minutes later the phone rang. As I replaced the receiver I said, "Hey, guess who's coming to dinner Saturday? Wilma and Leroy Whitlock. You wanta give me hint? Who are *they*?"

Source: Bombeck, 1973.

Introduction

The majority of the information we have about cognitive development in adulthood has come from comparisons of college students with adults in their sixties and seventies. More investigators now are recognizing that comparisons between young adults and middle-aged adults are important, and that some aspects of cognitive development seem to improve while others decline as individuals age from the early twenties through the late fifties.

In this chapter we will discuss some basic ideas about adult cognition and describe cognitive development in early and middle adulthood. We discuss the nature of formal operational thought in adulthood and whether there is a fifth stage of cognitive development. We will see what the psychometric approach has to say about adult intelligence and detail some important new ideas about cognitive development in adulthood from the information processing perspective. In particular, how memory develops in early and middle adulthood is described. We also discuss creativity, and productivity, as well as adult education in early and middle adulthood.

In the second half of the chapter we look at career development and work in early and middle adulthood. We survey theories of vocational choice, emphasize the importance of exploration, planning, and decision making in career development and describe sociocultural influences on career development, with particular emphasis on the changing role of women. The life contour of work in the adult years also is described, as is the reciprocal relation between work and intelligence.

Cognitive Development

In the discussion of theories and perspectives in chapter 2, infancy in chapter 4, early childhood in chapter 7, middle and late childhood in chapters 9 and 10, and adolescence in chapter 13, the basic foundations for cognitive development in adulthood have been layed down. It would be helpful if at this time you would go back through the parts of these chapters focused on cognitive development, or review in your mind the cognitive world of the individual that already exists when he or she reaches early adulthood. Many of you reading this text are at just this point in the life cycle. Think for a moment about what your cognitive capabilities are. Over the course of the next thirty to forty years, how do you think they will change? Will you become more intelligent as you go through early and middle adulthood? Or, will some of your cognitive capabilities become less efficient. These are some of the questions that will be answered in this chapter. During the course of our description of cognitive activity from infancy through adolescence, three main perspectives were described—cognitive-structural, psychometric, and information processing. Each of these will be considered in turn to see how they view cognitive activity in the adult years.

The Cognitive-Structural View

Recall that Jean Piaget believes there are four main stages of cognitive development—sensorimotor, preoperational, concrete operational, and formal operational—and that the last of these stages, formal operational thought, is reached during adolescence. For Piaget, then, the manner in which the adult thinks is basically no different than the way most adolescents think. However, many cognitive structuralists believe that it is not until adulthood that many of these individuals who reach formal operations actually consolidate their formal operational thinking. We also are certain that many adults do not think in formal operational ways. For example, only 17 to 67 percent of college students show this type of thinking (Elkind, 1961; Tomlinson-Keasey, 1972; Wheatley, 1971). And, some cognitive structuralists believe there may be a fifth stage of thought that is more advanced than formal operations.

Formal Operational Thought in Adulthood

Research on formal operational thought among adults is not as prolific as the work conducted with adolescents. In one investigation, Carolyn Tomlinson-Keasey (1972) administered several different formal operational tasks (pendulum, balance, and flexibility problems) to sixth-grade girls and young and middle-aged women. The young and middle-aged women were much better at the formal operational tasks than the sixth-grade girls, but there was little difference in the way the young adult women solved the tasks when compared with middle-aged women, although the latter did slightly worse.

In general, early reviews by scholars suggested that nothing very distinctive in cognitive development occurs from late adolescence and the beginning of early adulthood to middle adulthood (e.g., Hooper & Sheehan, 1977; Neimark, 1975). However, individuals at the beginning of early adulthood engage in formal operational thought more than adolescents do (Neimark, 1975). And, recent reviews of the adult Piagetian studies (e.g., Neimark, 1980) conclude that there is significant improvement during the college years in logical thinking and that there may well be improvement in logic later on in early adulthood, particularly for those individuals who pursue highly specialized and abstract educational disciplines (e.g., law, physics, medicine, or philosophy).

The likelihood of obtaining a fifth stage beyond formal operations generally depends on the level of education attained.

Is There a Fifth Stage beyond Formal Operations?

A number of writers have speculated about the nature of an additional "stage" of reasoning beyond formal operations (e.g., Riegel, 1973; Steinberg, 1981; Labouvie-Vief, 1980). Although the particular ideas about such a stage vary from one writer to the next, several common themes can be formulated about what these stages might be like.

One idea is that the thinker would be capable of abstractly analyzing the nature of formal operational thought itself, either in general terms or as it is applied to a specific domain of knowledge (e.g., physics or psychology). Piaget's own writings reflect this ability. Second, this particular stage would probably not be universal; that is, not all individuals would be expected to reach this level of thought. (Indeed, as we have seen, some writers have doubted that the formal operational stage itself is universal—e.g., Berzonsky, 1978.) Third, the likelihood of attaining this stage would generally depend upon the level of education attained by the person. And finally, the application of this post-formal operational reasoning skill might be limited to those aspects of life and experience where an advanced education is put to use. For example, a highly trained lawyer might exhibit this stage of reasoning when dealing with legal issues but not when reasoning about other things.

The Psychometric Approach

The psychometric approach (emphasis placed on measurement-based tests) that has received the greatest attention in our study of adult development is the Cattell-Horn view, described initially in chapter 8. Recall that Raymond Cattell believes that it is important to distinguish between fluid and crystallized intelligence. Remember that fluid intelligence involves the adaptability and capacity to perceive things and integrate them mentally. It appears to be independent of formal education and experience. By comparison, schooling and personal experiences determine crystallized intelligence, which involves skills, abilities, and understanding gained through instruction and observation.

Cattell's theory of fluid and crystallized intelligence has served as the basis for a number of psychometric studies of intelligence across the life span. Raymond Cattell's student, John Horn, has provided the impetus for much of the adult life-span work. Basically, as indicated in figure 16.1, Horn (e.g., Horn & Donaldson, 1980) believes that crystallized intelligence increases throughout the life span because it is based on cumulative learning experiences. By contrast, he states that fluid intelligence increases from infancy through adolescence, levels off during early adulthood, and then steadily declines in middle and late adulthood.

Prior to the work of Cattell and Horn, psychometric measures of intelligence in childhood and adulthood indicated that verbal abilities, such as scores on the Wechsler vocabulary and information subtests, tended to increase in adulthood, while perceptual-motor abilities, such as scores on the Weschler incomplete pictures and block design subtests, were more likely to decline in adulthood (Wechsler, 1958). However, distinguished psychologist D. O. Hebb (1978), in reflecting on his adult development, indicated that in his late forties he began to notice a loss in the effective use of vocabulary, and that by his sixties, he had to use a Thesaurus in his writing.

Horn and Cattell (e.g., 1966, 1967) believe that the increase in verbal abilities found by Wechsler reflect the development of crystallized intelligence, whereas the decline in perceptual-motor abilities is explained by the concept of fluid intelligence. In conducting their own research with 279 adolescents, young adults, and middle-aged adults, Cattell and Horn (1966, 1967) found that fluid intelligence performance declines and crystallized intelligence performance increases across the life span (see figure 16.2).

"Thanks for doing my homework last night. The teacher thinks I'm retarded!"

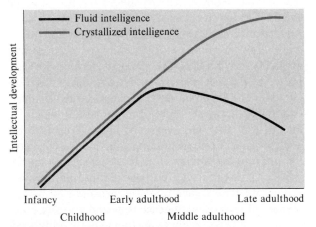

Figure 16.1 Fluid and crystallized intellectual development across the life span.

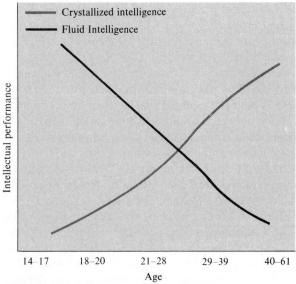

Figure 16.2 Fluid and crystallized intellectual performance across the life span.

Cohort and Context in the Study of Intelligence

We have seen that some aspects of intelligence seem to increase over the life span while others decline. One group of life-span developmental psychologists, however, believes that much of the data on intelligence is flawed because it has been collected in a cross-sectional rather than a longitudinal manner. K. Warner Schaie, Paul Baltes, and Gisela Labouvie (e.g., Baltes & Labouvie, 1973; Schaie, 1970, 1979) argue that the nature of cohort effects and historical change restrict data collected on intelligence (and personality) to the culture and generation(s) being studied.

This group of life-span developmentalists believes that many of the age-related changes we find in intelligence, such as those emphasized by John Horn, are cohort effects rather than actual age changes. You may want to again read the part of chapter 1 on research strategies where cohort studies in the context of a combined cross-sectional longitudinal method were discussed. In general, these researchers have conducted a number of large-scale studies in which they have shown that cross-sectional data support a number of age changes in intelligence, while longitudinal and combined cross-sectional-longitudinal data do not.

For example, in 1956, Schaie administered two intelligence tests, Thurstone's Primary Mental Abilities and Schaie's Test of Behavioral Rigidity, to 500 adults ranging in age from twenty-one to seventy. Seven years later, 301 of the adults were retested with the same tests. In analyzing the intelligence test data, four main aspects of intelligence were revealed: 1) *crystallized intelligence,* indicating formal reasoning and abstract thinking; 2) *cognitive flexibility,* described as the ability to shift from one way of thinking to another within a context of familiar intellectual operations; 3) *visuomotor flexibility,* the skill to shift from familiar to unfamiliar patterns in tasks requiring coordination between visual and motor abilities (e.g., when we have to copy words but interchange capitals with lower case letters); and 4) *visualization,* the ability to organize and process visual materials (e.g., finding a simple figure contained in a complex one or identifying a picture that is incomplete).

When their test data on adults were organized cross-sectionally, the traditional pattern of early decline in intellectual functioning appeared. However, when the data were analyzed longitudinally, a decline in only one of the four areas, visuo-motor flexibility, was noted.

The Baltes and Schaie study found no strong age-related change in cognitive flexibility. On the important dimensions of crystallized intelligence and visualization a systematic, steady increase in scores for the various age groups occurred through early and middle adulthood and into late adulthood.

John Horn (Horn & Donaldson, 1980), however, challenges the position of Baltes and Schaie, claiming it is oversimplified and overoptimistic. They believe that the longer a person lives the more likely it is that some important aspect of intellectual performance will decline. They admit the problematic nature of cross-sectional comparisons, but point out that longitudinal comparisons are not without shortcomings as well. For example, a longitudinal trend observed over time with one cohort may not be found with other cohorts. And, the practice of repeatedly testing the same individuals in a longitudinal study may cause problems. Past experience with a particular test might improve the person's performance when the person takes the test again. If so, true age declines might be masked. In addition, "selective drop-out" can plague longitudinal designs, since individuals who participated in the initial tests may not be available (perhaps due to illness or death) for later testing. The loss of these subjects can impair the generalizability of findings from longitudinal research.

While some of these problems can be solved by using sophisticated longitudinal designs, on balance, longitudinal methods may have as many problems as cross-sectional designs. Because of such concerns, the strategy of Horn and Donaldson has been to maintain the use of the cross-sectional approach, but to carefully control the nature of their samples from different age ranges. And, by concentrating only on individuals from the ages of twenty to fifty effects due to health or physical fitness are minimized. Horn and Donaldson also point out that results from cross-sectional and longitudinal studies seldom disagree, if analyzed carefully with important distinctions (like that between fluid and crystallized intelligence) in mind.

Baltes and Schaie (1976) have countered that Horn and Donaldson do not understand their theoretical position, misrepresent their data, and are guilty of selectively quoting from their writings. Schaie (1979) recently summarized what he has learned from his research on psychometric intelligence: First, reliable decline in intellectual abilities does not occur until very old age (e.g., the late eighties for most people) and does not occur for all abilities or all individuals. Second, for most individuals, there is a decline in abilities involving speed of response. Third, a decline in intelligence is likely to be found in those persons with severe cardiovascular disease at any age or for persons in socially deprived environments beginning with the late fifties and early sixties.

Of these three conclusions, the first is perhaps the most important; it is directly counter to that of Horn and Donaldson and is of considerable practical significance. Fortunately, some recent ideas developed by Nancy Denney (1981) may point the way to clarifying the nature of intellectual changes in midlife.

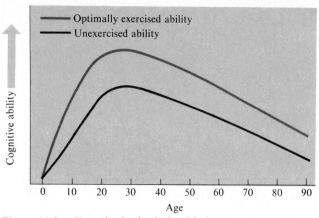

Figure 16.3 Hypothesized relationship between age and both unexercised ability and optimally exercised ability.

The Exercise of Mental Abilities

Nancy Denney (1981) believes that in order to better understand cognitive activity across the life span we should distinguish between **unexercised ability** (level of performance expected if the individual has had no exercise and/or training on the ability in question) and **optimally exercised ability** (level of performance expected if optimal exercise and/or training have occurred). The proposed developmental levels for these two ability levels are shown in figure 16.3, which indicates that both ability groups increase up to early adulthood and decrease gradually thereafter. The curve for unexercised ability level has been drawn to decrease starting in early adulthood because abilities that are not exercised, such as those measured by performance subtests of intelligence tests and abstract problem-solving tasks, begin to decline in early adulthood.

The curve for optimally-exercised ability also has been drawn to indicate a decrease starting early in adulthood because even in abilities that are the most resistant to age-change effects, such as verbal abilities and practical problem-solving abilities, there may be some decline. The region between the two types of abilities in the figure represents the degree to which exercise and/or training can affect abilities. Of course, exercise or training can accumulate over a long period of time, even years or decades. Thus, some types of ability might be essentially unexercised for many young adults, but optimally exercised for middle-aged adults. Such abilities should not decline from young adulthood to middle age. Indeed, they might even improve.

To illustrate the importance of distinguishing between unexercised and optimally exercised abilities, Nancy Denney (Denney & Palmer, in press; Denney & Pearce, 1981) conducted two investigations. In the first study adult performance on a traditional problem-solving task was compared with performance on a series of practical problems to determine whether different types of problem-solving abilities exhibit different developmental functions. Denney and Palmer found that adults between the ages of twenty and seventy-nine showed a linear decrease in performance on the traditional problem-solving task while there was an increase in performance on the practical problems up until the forties and fifties and a decline thereafter.

In the second study, adults of different ages were compared on three types of practical problems—problems that young adults would be most likely to have to deal with, problems that middle-aged adults would most likely have to deal with, and problems that elderly adults would most likely have to deal with in their everyday lives. Performance on the traditional problem-solving task decreased linearly with age during the adult years while performance on the practical problems increased from the twenties to the thirties and decreased thereafter. However, when the early adult, middle-aged adult, and elderly adult problems were analyzed separately, it was found that performance decreased linearly on the early adult problems, while performance increased up to the thirties, remained relatively stable through the fifties, and decreased thereafter on both the middle-aged adult problems and the elderly adult problems.

The results of these two studies are consistent with the proposed model of unexercised and optimally exercised cognitive abilities. The ability tested by the traditional problem-solving task is one that is not exercised very much during the adult years and, thus, it follows the unexercised ability curve rather closely. Practical problem-solving ability is exercised much more frequently by adults and, thus, is more likely to be maintained through the middle-adult years. The reason the twenty-year-olds' performance is lower than the thirty-, forty-, and fifty-year-olds' performance is, according to the model, that the twenty-year-olds have less frequently had to deal with the types of practical problems employed in the Denney and Palmer study and used for the middle-aged and elderly adult problems in the Denney and Pearce study. As a result they do not approach their optimally exercised ability level with these types of problems. Only the middle-aged adults who have had more experience with such problems and yet who have a relatively high optimally exercised ability level performs better.

According to the model, the elderly adults do not perform well even on problems designed specifically to be the types of problems they would most likely have to deal with in their own lives because during the later adult years the declining level of optimally exercised ability actually limits their performance.

Nancy Denney (1981) suggests that there are undoubtedly limitations to this model of adult cognitive development. For example, the effects of experience on performance are described only in the most general sense. And, the likelihood of sex and cohort differences would require further changes in the model. Contextual factors such as motivation, health, and the nature of the task used to study cognitive activity also need to be taken into account in the study of adult intelligence. Nonetheless, the idea that it is important to distinguish between unexercised and optimally exercised mental abilities is an intriguing addition to our conceptualization of adult intelligence.

In addition to information about cognitive-structural theory and lively debate about psychometric approaches to intelligence in adulthood, there is a long history of interest in adult cognition on the part of experimental psychologists, as we shall see next.

Experimental Psychology and Information Processing

Experimental psychologists have been studying adult cognition for over 100 years, originating with the work of Hermann Ebbinghaus (1885) on memory. The vast majority of this work has been carried out with young adults, usually college students, so that experimental psychology has added little to our knowledge of cognition in the midlife years. Recently, though, an increasing number of researchers have compared the cognitive activity of individuals in *early* and *late* adulthood (e.g., Craik, 1977). We will discuss this important work in chapter 18, which is concerned with cognitive activity in late adulthood. Here, the emerging ideas in experimentally oriented research that are beginning to provide some clues to possible cognitive changes in middle adulthood will be outlined.

There is little disagreement that the efficiency and quality of cognition declines at some point in adulthood. The critical question is, When does this decline begin, and how early might it create difficulties for an adult? Horn and Donaldson (1980) and Denney (1981) agree that the decline begins early, in the late thirties or before, though it may cause problems only on certain types of tasks (e.g., tasks involving fluid abilities or tasks that are unpracticed). Baltes and Schaie (1976) disagree, stressing that general intellectual declines, except those due to health-related or emotional problems, are restricted to very old age, that is, the seventies or eighties. Does research by experimental psychologists help to clarify this disagreement?

Experimental psychologists sometimes have compared the cognitive activity of individuals in young and middle adulthood using cross-sectional designs (generally a late adulthood group also is included in these studies). Most of these experiments focus on the cognitive activity of memory. These experiments indicate that several factors may be involved in whether there are differences between the early and middle adulthood groups: 1) whether the memory task relies mainly on short-term memory or long-term memory (see box 16.1); 2) the nature of the information processing activities that adults engage in during learning; 3) the nature of the memory test (e.g., recall versus recognition) used to assess learning; 4) the nature of the materials (familiar versus unfamiliar, verbal versus

How Short-Term and Long-Term Memory Work

Many years ago, the famous psychologist William James (1890) distinguished between **primary memory** and **secondary memory**. James identified primary memory with conscious awareness of recently perceived events and secondary memory with the recall of events that have left consciousness. James's distinction was based primarily on his own introspections, but today a similar distinction is supported by a great deal of experimental evidence. Further, we have today a host of *information processing models* that incorporate the distinction between primary, or short-term memory, and secondary, or long-term memory, assigning the two types of memory to separate memory "stores."

A generalized three-stage model of memory (Murdock, 1967) is presented here. Note that it includes a system of sensory stores in addition to a short-term store and a long-term store. (We consider age differences in sensory memory in chapter 18.) Note also that the model indicates processes that produce transfer of information from one store to another: transfer from sensory memory to short-term memory entails attention, and transfer from short-term memory to long-term memory requires rehearsal. Note finally that the model claims different laws of forgetting for the three memory stores. Forgetting from sensory stores is thought to result from an autonomous **decay** process; information is lost (within seconds or less)

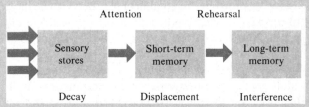

A generalized three-stage model of memory.

simply as a function of time. Forgetting from short-term memory generally results from **displacement;** new information "bumps out" old information. Forgetting from long-term memory is thought to result from **interference** between memory for a given piece of information and other information learned previously or subsequently. Interference in long-term memory is not equivalent to displacement. No one assumes that the learning of one fact causes a "bumping out" of another fact from long-term memory. Indeed, many investigators believe that interference does not destroy information *in* long-term memory, but simply impairs the *retrievability* of information *from* long-term memory. A popular notion is that older individuals suffer in memory tasks because of greater interference from their greater store of past learning. However, there is no convincing evidence for this idea (Craik, 1977).

Early models of short-term and long-term memory were deficient in their treatment of "transfer" from short-term to long-term memory. Today it is recognized that simple rote rehearsal is not the only path, or even a very

nonverbal) that adults are trying to learn; and 5) the nature of the learner, in particular, the repertoire of knowledge and skills accumulated by the adult. We will consider each of these factors in turn, and then present a conceptual framework developed by James Jenkins (1978) that seems to fit these findings.

Short-Term and Long-Term Memory
Tasks that rely primarily on short-term memory, or the conscious awareness of recently perceived events, generally show little or no differences when we compare the performance of young and middle-aged adults. Indeed, even elderly adults typically do well on such tasks (Craik, 1977). For example, memory span is a commonly used test that relies to some extent on short-term memory. A person's memory span is the number of

digits or letters he or she can repeat in order without error. The results of a representative study of memory span for letters (Botwinick & Storandt, 1974) are shown in table 16.1. Note that the fifty-year-olds performed just as well as the twenty-year-olds, though the sixty- and seventy-year-olds showed some decline.

In contrast to tests that rely on short-term memory, tests that require long-term memory, or the recall of events that have left consciousness, often show substantial age-related differences. A good measure of long-term memory can be derived from the task of **free recall.** In this task, a list of items (usually common words) is presented to adults, who then attempt to recall as many items as possible, in any order. A classic experiment (Schonfield & Robertson, 1966) examined free recall by adults in five age groups. The lower line in figure 16.4 shows the free recall for each age group.

efficient path, to learning. Processes of organization, semantic elaboration, and imagery can be highly effective for enhancing long-term memory. The importance of different *processes* in memory has led Fergus I. M. Craik and Robert S. Lockhart (1972) to question the view that separate "stores" exist for short-term and long-term memory. They prefer to describe short-term memory as a *process* that allows a person to hold material in conscious awareness for short periods of time. Craik and Lockhart argue that long-term retention also is based on processes. They claim that long-term retention is facilitated by "elaborate" semantic processing at the time of study (Craik & Tulving, 1975). Such retention also is facilitated by effective retrieval processes at the time of test (Lockhart, Craik, & Jacoby, 1976). A process view of memory has important implications for the psychology of aging because it suggests that age differences in memory can be understood (and perhaps removed) in terms of processing activities that people engage in when learning and remembering. Although Craik and his colleagues disagree with the notion of memory "stores," the distinction between some type of short-term memory (process or store) and some type of long-term memory (process or store) is widely accepted and well supported by evidence. Further, this distinction has proven invaluable for an understanding of age differences in human memory (Craik, 1977).

Generally, there is no difference between young and middle-aged adults when comparing short-term memory.

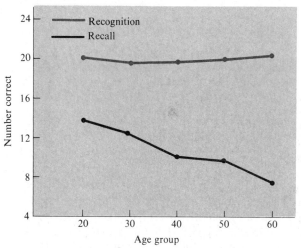

Figure 16.4 Recognition and recall scores as a function of age.

As can be seen, a clear age-related decline occurred for free recall. This trend clearly differs from the information about the memory span shown in table 16.1. Such comparisons have led some experts on adult cognition, such as Fergus I. M. Craik (1977), to conclude that the accuracy of short-term memory is unimpaired by aging, while the accuracy of long-term memory shows age-related decline.

However, there are some important exceptions to the rule that short-term memory shows no age-related decline. One exception is found when adults must *divide attention* during the presentation of items to be remembered. In what is called a "split-span" task, adults hear several items (usually six) simultaneously over two "channels." For example, imagine yourself wearing headphones—you might hear the digits 6, 4, 9 through your right ear, and, *at the same time*, the digits 5, 2, 8 through your left ear. Age-related deficits,

Table 16.1
Memory Span for Letters Presented Auditorily

	Age (Years)					
	20's	30's	40's	50's	60's	70's
Span	6.7	6.2	6.5	6.5	5.5	5.4

Source: Botwinick & Storandt, 1974.

with older adults performing more poorly, have been found with this task (Bann, 1980; Inglis & Caird, 1963).

Another exception concerns the speed with which an adult can "scan" or search through the contents of short-term memory. If you were exposed to the procedure developed by Saul Sternberg (1969), you would

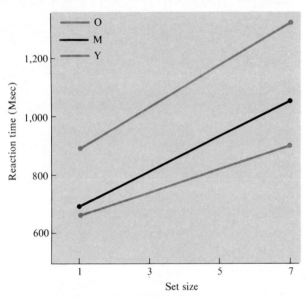

Figure 16.5 Mean response times as a function of age and set size.

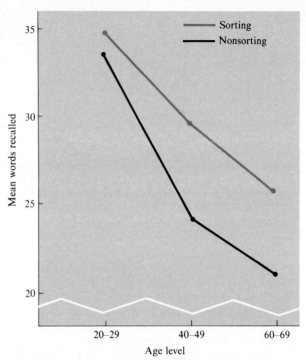

Figure 16.6 Mean number of words recalled as a function of age and experimental treatment.

be presented with a list of items (usually digits, such as 6, 3, 9) to hold in your memory. Then, you would be told another digit, and you would have to decide as quickly as possible whether it "matches" one of the digits in memory. Lists of varying lengths are examined, and, as you might expect, reaction times rise (answers are given more slowly) as the length of the list gets longer. Figure 16.5 shows the results from one study (Anderson, Fozard, & Lillyquist, 1972) that compared the memory scanning ability of individuals in early, middle, and late adulthood. Note that longer lists produced longer reaction times, which is a typical finding. Note also that the "slope" of the reaction-time curve is greater for individuals in middle and late adulthood than for those in early adulthood. This difference in slope indicates that the two older adult groups "scan" through lists of items in short-term memory in a slower manner.

In chapter 18, where we discuss cognitive activity in late adulthood in greater detail, additional evidence will be provided for age-related aspects of divided attention and speed of processing information. In spite of such effects as those presented here, though, the bulk of the evidence on memory at midlife suggests no detriment, relative to young adults, on the accuracy of short-term memory recall, even though there are clear detriments on the accuracy of long-term memory recall.

Information Processing Activities at Input

Another factor that determines the presence or absence of age-related differences in memory is the nature of the *processing activities* occurring at the time material is learned (see table 16.2). For example, free recall of verbal information is known to depend upon *"elaboration"* of the semantic or categorical aspects of the information (i.e., attention to the meaning they have for the subject, Craik & Lockhart, 1972; Craik & Tulving, 1975). Further recall is affected by *mental imagery* produced by the information at the time of study (Paivio, 1971). Recent research has suggested that all three processes—organization, semantic elaboration, and mental imagery—might be less efficient in middle adulthood than in early adulthood. However, this research also suggests that appropriate techniques can be used by middle-aged adults to overcome this deficiency.

Organization Evidence for the role of organization in recall comes from George Mandler's (1967) sorting task. To do Mandler's task, you would be asked to sort words into subjective groups or categories. Your subsequent recall of words would be heavily influenced by the number of categories you created, the more (up to about seven) the better. David Hultsch (1971) compared individuals in early, middle, and late adulthood on a sorting condition, and a nonsorting condition, in which individuals simply were told to study the words presented. The results are shown in figure 16.6. Young

Table 16.2
Information Processing Activities Involved in Memory

Process	Time of Occurrence in Memory Task	Description of Process	Importance for Recall vs. Recognition
Organization	Learning of to-be-remembered material	The learner actively groups input items together into higher-order "units" or "chunks." For example, in a long list of words, "raisin," "apple," and "pear" might be grouped together and treated as a single unit ("fruits") by the learner.	Definitely important for recall, can be important for recognition as well.
Semantic elaboration	Learning of to-be-remembered material	Involves contact between presented items and long-term memory representations, which give access to meaning. Is usually involved in organization as well as imagery, though it might occur without these processes.	Definitely important for both recall and recognition.
Imagery	Learning of to-be-remembered material	Involves generation of a representation experienced as a mental image or "picture in the head," "tape recording in the head," etc.	Important for both recall and recognition. Is also useful for organization, as when several items are placed together in a well-organized image.
Search or retrieval	Testing of previously learned material	Involves procedures for bringing long-term memory information into conscious awareness. Is thought to be facilitated if to-be-remembered information was well organized at input.	Widely agreed to be important for recall. Growing evidence that such processes can be important for recognition as well.

Note: While there are many different theories of how memory operates, the importance of these and other information processing activities is widely acknowledged. Thus, age-related differences in one or more of these processes would be expected to produce age-related differences in memory. By the same token, improving the utilization of these processes in individuals in middle or late adulthood may markedly improve the memory performance of these older people. We also note that these processes have been explored primarily in the domain of *verbal* memory; much less is known about their nature and importance for nonverbal memory (memory for faces, songs, etc.).

adults showed good recall regardless of whether they were told to sort or simply to learn the words. But, in contrast, recall by the two older-aged groups was improved by the sorting task. Thus, the difference between young and middle-aged subjects was reduced when the sorting task was used. The pattern suggests that middle-aged adults might be deficient at organizing material for recall. However, this deficiency can be reduced by the use of organizational strategies built into the sorting task.

Semantic or Categorical Elaboration　Related to effects of organization are those of **semantic or categorical elaboration** of to-be-remembered words. In one investigation (Smith, 1977), free recall of words under three study conditions was tested. If you were the adult in the no-cue condition, you would see each word presented by itself. If you were the adult in the structural-cue condition, you would see each word accompanied by its first letter (i.e., you might see "grape" accompanied by "G"). In the semantic-cue condition, you would see each word presented along with the name of a superordinate category into which it fit (i.e., you might

see "grape" accompanied by "fruit"). In the first two conditions, age-related differences appeared. The young group (aged twenty to thirty-nine) had the best recall, the late adulthood group (aged sixty to eighty) showed the poorest recall, while the middle-aged group (aged forty to fifty-nine) was intermediate. In the third condition, which involved semantic-category cues, recall was approximately equal in all age groups with no noticeable evidence for older adults to recall more poorly. These findings suggest that an age-related decline in recall memory exists, a decline that begins by middle age. Again, however, it is suggested that this decline can be eliminated by procedures that insure semantic elaboration of the words at the time of study.

Imagery　Another process relevant to recall is *imagery,* which is known to improve memory in many different situations (Paivio, 1971). One study (Mason & Smith, 1977) focused on the recall of individuals in early, middle and late adulthood. If you were in the

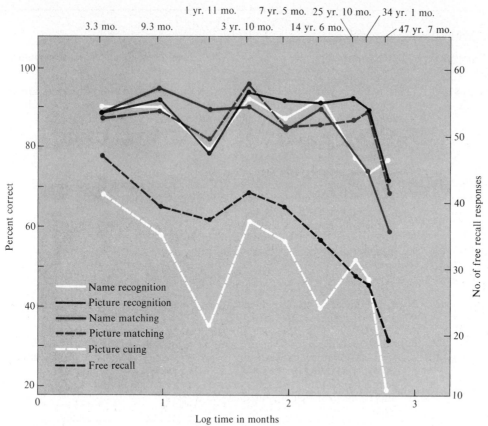

Figure 16.7 Recognition and recall of names and faces of high school colleagues.

"imagery" condition, you would be instructed to form mental images for each word, but if you were in the control condition you would have heard no mention of imagery. Imagery instructions did not affect recall in the early and late adulthood groups, but did improve recall in the middle adulthood groups. Indeed, middle-aged adults performed as well as young adults in the imagery condition, though they fell below young adults in the control condition. Again, the results suggest a deficiency in recall memory in middle age that can be overcome through appropriate task instructions.

Memory recall deficits in middle age, then, seem to exist but can be overcome through appropriate instructions and tasks during learning. In terms of Nancy Denney's framework, these findings suggest that recall abilities might often be *unexercised* in middle-aged individuals, so that training and experience, even the minimal training and experience introduced by appropriate study instructions, can have clear, facilitating effects. In contrast, individuals in early adulthood, college students in most studies, might exercise recall abilities quite frequently. Thus, their recall ability might approach that for optimally exercised abilities. This would give young adults a marked advantage over middle-aged individuals in recall tasks, an advantage that may vanish when there is training or practice on the relevant memory task.

The Nature of the Retention Test

A third factor determining memory deficits associated with middle age is the nature of the memory test. We previously discussed age-related differences in free recall (observed by Schonfield and Robertson (1966) and shown in fig. 16.4). This experiment also included a recognition test. The test included previously studied words along with "new" words, and adults attempted to recognize the former. Performance on this recognition test is shown by the top line in figure 16.4. As can be seen, there obviously was no hint of an age-related deficit.

A strikingly similar pattern was observed in another investigation (Bahrick, Bahrick, & Wittlinger, 1975), involving a more natural memory task of remembering one's high school classmates. Face recognition, name recognition, and name-face matching were assessed. And, free recall of names, as well as "cued" recall of names in response to faces, were evaluated. The individuals ranged from early (three months since high school graduation) to late (forty-seven years since graduation) adulthood. As indicated in figure 16.7, time since high school was directly related to age in this study; older adults have experienced a longer interval of time since high school. It is clear from figure 16.7 that recognition and matching performance remains virtually constant (and nearly perfect) up to a retention interval of thirty-four years, which means that adults who were over fifty years old were performing about as well as eighteen-year-olds. This finding occurred in spite of the disadvantage older adults might have faced due to the time lag since high school (indeed, the time lag might have produced the drop in recognition and matching that finally occurred at the forty-seven-year lag). In contrast, the recall measures, particularly free recall, showed clear evidence of age-related decline. Note especially the steady drop in free recall from the three-year interval (adults about twenty-one years old) to the forty-seven-year interval (adults about sixty-five years old). This decline could reflect forgetting, or it could reflect age-related changes in the efficiency of recall memory, or both. In any event, we again have a case where recall performance of middle-aged individuals fell below that of young adults, without a corresponding trend in recognition.

There currently is some controversy regarding just *why* recognition tests can remove age-related deficits. One possibility (Craik, 1977) is that recall tests place great demand upon effortful processes of "search" or "retrieval" from memory. Recognition tests might involve such processes to some degree but may also reflect what cognitive psychologists call less effortful "direct-access" mechanisms (Mandler, 1980). Note that in a recognition test previously presented items are actually presented to the adult; he or she only has to distinguish these items from "lures" that have not been previously presented. This procedure may lessen the need to "search" for items in memory. Students' often-stated preference for multiple-choice versus essay exams reflects in part our perception that the recall demanded by essay exams requires more work and effort than the recognition needed for multiple-choice tests. Thus, the recall findings may in part be due to an age-related decline in effortful search and retrieval.

Another interpretation of the recognition results emphasizes processes that occur during the initial study of information. For example, it is possible that the effort of organizing material during learning is not needed when testing is by recognition (Smith, 1980). Thus, age-related differences in organization may not be revealed with recognition testing.

Aside from distinguishing between recall and recognition, there are other aspects of memory testing that may determine the presence or absence of differences in the memory of young and middle-aged adults. One such factor is the *pacing* of the test (i.e., the time you are allowed to remember on the test). In one investigation (Monge & Hultsch, 1971), young and middle-aged adults were compared on a **paired-associates learning** task. If you took the paired-associates task you might study pairs of words (e.g., radio-paper, book-fence), and then be tested on your ability to recall one member of the pair when you are presented with the

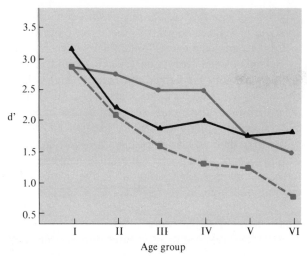

Figure 16.8   Average performances (d') of volunteers, divided on the basis of age decade (group I = twenty to twenty-nine years, etc.) into six groups, on the nonverbal recognition tests: visual (•), auditory (▲), and tactual (□) recurrent recognition.

second member (radio- _____ ; book- _____). The task is much like learning a foreign language vocabulary, or learning the names of people you meet at a party.

This task allowed the study of (a) the "inspection interval," during which pairs are studied, and (b) the "anticipation interval," during which adults try to recall one member of a pair given the other member as a cue. Young adults outperformed middle-aged adults, and both groups improved when the "inspection" (study) interval was lengthened. However, only middle-aged adults improved when the "anticipation" (recall) interval was lengthened. Indeed, with the longest anticipation interval (6.6 seconds for recall), the middle-aged adults performed as well as the young adults on the task. So, when middle-aged adults were given more time to recall, they performed as efficiently as young adults.

The Nature of the Materials or Information

A fourth factor to consider in understanding age-related differences is the nature of the materials that adults are trying to remember. The vast majority of research on memory has tested recall and recognition of familiar verbal materials, especially words. At present, our knowledge is limited concerning memory for other types of information. However, one study (Riege & Inman, 1981) suggests that differences between young and middle-aged adults may partly be due to the type of information adults are remembering. Recognition memory for three types of relatively unfamiliar, nonverbal information was examined: geometric art patterns (visual); bird songs (auditory); and wire shapes (tactual). As suggested by figure 16.8, clear age-related trends appeared, particularly with the tactually experienced wire shapes. The results with tactual stimuli stand in marked contrast to the absence of age effects in recognition memory for familiar words obtained by Schonfield and Robertson (fig. 16.4), and in recognition memory for names and faces of high school classmates obtained by Bahrick et al. (fig. 16.7). It is noteworthy that the tactual recognition task of Riege and Inman is perhaps even more unusual and unfamiliar than their visual and auditory recognition tasks. Possibly, then, memory for unfamiliar nonverbal information is especially susceptible to age-related deficits in middle age.

Characteristics of the Learner

A fifth factor relevant to age-related declines concerns the learner. Apart from age, many characteristics of the person can determine the level of performance in memory tasks. These characteristics include attitudes, interests, health-related factors, and, perhaps of greatest importance, previously acquired knowledge and skills. It now appears that individuals maintain their ability to use well-learned knowledge and skills throughout middle-age and into old age. Tests of common, factual knowledge (e.g., vocabulary, events in the news) typically show no decline from young adulthood up to old age (Perlmutter, 1980). This seems to be true even when factual knowledge is tested by recall (versus recognition).

Janet and Roy Lachman (1980) have developed a way to measure recall of previously learned facts while controlling for individual differences in the number of facts known. Using recognition tests to estimate the total amount of knowledge a person possesses, the Lachmans derived a formula for assessing the probability that a given piece of memory knowledge can be retrieved in a recall test. This retrieval measure showed no decline between early and middle adulthood, and, no decline between middle and late adulthood as well. Other recent evidence suggests that familiar words produce "spreading activation" of semantic knowledge in long-term memory (Collins & Loftus, 1975). Available research indicates that this "spreading activation" occurs in adults of all ages (Howard, Lasaga, & McAndrews, 1980).

In reviewing the complex evidence on age differences in memory, Marion Perlmutter (1980) suggests that a distinction between **memory processing** and **memory knowledge** may be useful. Aging may be associated with a decline in the efficiency of memory processes but not with the amount of memory knowledge that is available for use in many different tasks. Thus, age-related declines may be restricted to those tasks in which a person's prior knowledge is not useful. Memory tests for bird songs and abstract designs may be good examples of such tasks (see fig. 16.8). Other tasks, which capitalize upon previously learned information,

may show no age declines. Indeed, older subjects might outperform young adults. Perlmutter's distinction between memory processing and knowledge is similar to Horn's and Donaldson's distinction between fluid and crystalized components of intelligence, indicating at least some convergence of psychometric and information processing ideas.

The evidence from experimental psychology that we have reviewed thus far has focused solely on memory. Why have other important cognitive functions, such as problem solving and concept attainment been ignored? This is because our knowledge of such cognitive functions in midlife is still sparse (see Giambra & Arenberg, 1980). One recent study on problem solving in chess, however, points the way for future advances. Ned Charness (1980) has provided evidence that age differences in memory need not imply a decline in the ability to use well-learned knowledge for making intelligent decisions in chess.

Chessboard displays were presented to skilled players of the game. The quality of judgments in a "choose-a-move" task, as well as memory for the chess displays themselves were examined. Older adults showed poorer memory for previously presented chess displays. However, their "choose-a-move" judgments were equal in quality to those of young adult players. One very important implication of this finding is that memory, at least that measured in typical laboratory experiments, is not all there is to intelligent problem solving. These results converge with Nancy Denney's experiments, suggesting that practical problem solving apparently does not decline through the midlife years. They also are consistent with the Horn and Donaldson view that crystalized intelligence does not decline with age (up to sixty or so). The utilization of well-learned knowledge is exactly what crystalized intelligence measures are supposed to reflect. Clearly, then, the available evidence does *not* point to a decline in intelligent knowledge retrieval and problem solving from twenty up to sixty years of age. Yet, as we have seen there is good reason to suspect a decline in some types of memory during these years.

To summarize our discussion of factors that might influence memory decline, we present the "tetrahedral" model of James Jenkins (1978) in figure 16.9. The model emphasizes the importance for learning and memory of learning activities (e.g., organization, semantic elaboration), criterial tasks (e.g., recall and recognition), the to-be-learned materials (e.g., familiar words, unfamiliar bird songs), and the characteristics of the learner (e.g., knowledge and skills). The preceding discussion has touched on each of these factors, though we also have found it necessary to distinguish short-term memory (which generally shows no age-related decline in middle age) from long-term memory (which often does show decline, depending upon the other four factors). In general, the evidence reviewed

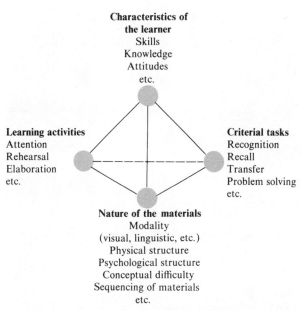

Characteristics of
the learner
Skills
Knowledge
Attitudes
etc.

Learning activities
Attention
Rehearsal
Elaboration
etc.

Criterial tasks
Recognition
Recall
Transfer
Problem solving
etc.

Nature of the materials
Modality
(visual, linguistic, etc.)
Physical structure
Psychological structure
Conceptual difficulty
Sequencing of materials
etc.

Figure 16.9 An organizational framework for exploring questions about learning, understanding, and remembering.

suggests that a memory deficit in middle age is most likely when (1) the task taps long-term memory, (2) effective learning strategies are not mentioned to the learner, (3) criterial tasks demand effortful "search" or "retrieval", (4) the materials are unfamiliar and difficult to verbalize, and/or (5) adults cannot perform well simply on the basis of previously acquired and well-learned knowledge and skills.

Recall from our discussion in chapter 9 that children not only think, but they think creatively as well. Next, we see that some of the most creative efforts of individuals come in early and middle adulthood, and that early and middle adulthood usually represent the most productive years of an individual's life.

Creativity and Productivity

For many years it was assumed that such attributes as creativity and scholarly productivity declined with age (e.g., Lehman, 1953). Scientists and artists often do produce more and better work during their thirties and forties than in the latter parts of middle adulthood and late adulthood. In one investigation of the creative achievements of adults, except for artists whose creative talents tend to peak earlier, the most productive years for most individuals were found to be in the thirties and forties (Dennis, 1966).

William Van Hoose and Maureen Worth (1982) offer several explanations for why creativity and productivity usually peak during the thirties and forties. It often takes time and experience to prepare for some occupations and crafts. For some, selecting a career, marriage, and parenting often are obstacles to the development of creative attributes. And, society expects more of the middle-aged.

This final explanation is unfortunate because the capacity to produce in the arts, the sciences, politics, and other fields extends well beyond middle age. Van Hoose and Worth offer the following examples:

Michelangelo (1475–1564) a High Renaissance architect, sculptor, painter, and poet, became chief architect of St. Peter's Church, Rome at age seventy-two. He is credited with completing some of his most important work both in painting and in poetry between age seventy and his death at age eighty-nine. Georgia O'Keefe, now past ninety, is not only a renouned artist but recently has mastered pottery skills. Picasso, one of the most renowned artists of the twentieth century, continued working until his death at ninety-one.

Examples from other fields abound. For example Zuckerman (1966) in her study of Nobel Laureates in science discovered that the first major paper of these eminent scholars was published at the average age of twenty-five. All laureates in this study who were past seventy continued to publish scholarly papers in professional journals. The antibiotic aureomycin was discovered by Benjamin Dugger when he was seventy-two. These facts support an earlier conclusion: people who are bright and productive during their early years maintain their ability and productivity into the later years of life.

Next, we look at adult education, paying particular attention to why adults do not initiate or continue learning and the reasons adults seek educational experiences. And, we note examples of transitions and triggers in adulthood that may lead to education.

Adult Education

In recent years, there has been a tremendous increase in adult learning—both formal and informal. Adults today constitute more than half of all full-time and part-time college students and will make up well over half the total in the years to come. Millions more are learning at their places of employment, through private lessons, in local school districts, in their churches, through their professional associations, and in voluntary community organizations. Even more are learning on their own through television, libraries, museums, correspondence courses, and other sources (Aslanian & Brickell, 1980).

Why Adults Initiate Learning or Continue Learning
Cyril Houle (1961) suggested that five factors lead adults to life-long learning: family background; teachers and schools; public libraries; occupation; and the exchange of friends. And in one investigation (Morstain & Smart, 1977) the following five distinct types of adult learners were identified: (1) nondirected learners with no specific goals; (2) social learners who want to improve their social interests and personal associations; (3) stimulation-seeking learners who want to escape boredom and routine; (4) career-oriented learners who learn because of occupational interests;

Individuals who continue to show an interest in education and learning are often already well educated.

and (5) life change learners who learn to improve multiple facets of their lives (e.g., career, intellectual, and social aspects).

Individuals who continue to show an interest in education and learning throughout adulthood are often already well educated. Individuals who are highly motivated, have had past success, have good information networks, and have adequate funds get more and better education, while those already dragging in the educational race when they reach early adulthood continue to fall farther and farther behind as they go through the adult years. For this latter group, the same things that led to relatively early exit from school contribute to a lack of interest in returning (Cross, 1978).

Why Adults Do Not Initiate Learning or Do Not Continue Learning

Patricia Cross (1978) examined the results of a number of surveys that have asked adults not oriented toward education to indicate the possible barriers that have kept them from learning. She concluded that three such barriers exist:

1. *Situational barriers*—those that arise for the individual in a particular situation, such as a lack of time due to home or job responsibilities, lack of transportation, geographical isolation, lack of child care, and so forth.
2. *Dispositional barriers*—those referring to attitudes about learning and perceptions of one's self as a learner—feeling too old to learn, showing a lack of confidence, or being bored with school.

3. *Institutional barriers*—those erected by learning institutions or agencies that exclude or discourage certain groups of learners—included are such factors as inconvenient schedules, full-time fees for part-time study, or restrictive locations.

However, in one recent investigation undertaken by the College Entrance Examination Board (Brickell, 1979), which for more than seventy-five years has worked toward improving access to higher education for the nation's youth, but for the last twenty years has been extending services to adults desiring further training, it was found that economic barriers are not always at the heart of why adults do not initiate or continue their education. Information was collected from 3,500 workers in a truck plant to find out why 99.5 percent did not use the tuition reimbursement plan that their own union leaders negotiated into their current contract with the manufacturer. The tuition reimbursement plan is a method designed to remove economic barriers to learning by having the company pay for any job-related training—training that can include earning college degrees. The economic barriers were removed, but the workers themselves never become motivated to go to school, to take television or correspondence courses, or even to undertake independent study. Apparently, the economic barriers were less real than rationalization.

We do not have good information about why some adults do not continue their learning. In one analysis of an extensive amount of data on the characteristics of adults who discontinued their learning, it was concluded that 90 percent of whatever it is that leads adults to participate in and drop out from adult education has

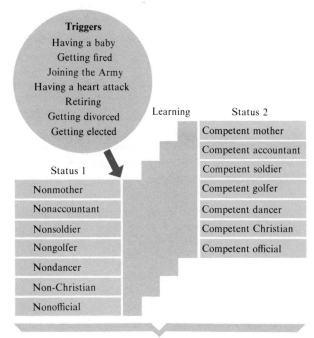

Triggers
Having a baby
Getting fired
Joining the Army
Having a heart attack
Retiring
Getting divorced
Getting elected

Learning

Status 1
Nonmother
Nonaccountant
Nonsoldier
Nongolfer
Nondancer
Non-Christian
Nonofficial

Status 2
Competent mother
Competent accountant
Competent soldier
Competent golfer
Competent dancer
Competent Christian
Competent official

Transitions

Figure 16.10 Examples of transitions and triggers. Reprinted with permission from *Americans in Transition* by Carol B. Aslanian and Henry M. Brickell, copyright © 1980 by College Entrance Examination Board, New York.

not been identified (Anderson & Darkenwald, 1979). The strongest relationships among a generally weak set suggested that younger adults are more likely to drop out of a learning situation than older adults, that those with fewer years of schooling are more likely to drop out than those with more education, and those who are black are more likely not to continue their education than others.

Transitions and Triggers As Instigators of Adult Education

In the book *Americans in Transition,* Carol Aslanian and Henry Brickell (1980) described a number of life changes as possible reasons for adult learning. They indicate that many transitions occur and that information available on current and prospective social and economic changes make it apparent that more adults will experience life transitions in the future. Changes in population, mobility, technology, occupations, housing, income, inflation, government, family life, politics, minority affairs, and leisure will mean an even faster rate of change in adult life than ever before.

In one investigation probing for reasons for career changes in adults, Aslanian and Brickell (1980) found significant transitions for many adults. Those transitions included entry, progression, and exit not only with respect to specific jobs, but even with respect to career fields. They concluded that some 40 million adults in the United States anticipated making a job or career change.

Life transitions may be a reason for learning and life events may trigger learning. Examples of these life transitions and triggers are presented in figure 16.10. Aslanian and Brickell (1980) end their important book

on adult education with a number of questions that indicate we need much more information about the nature of adult education.

Presumably a large number of adults experience important transitions in their lives. Why do some adults choose learning as a means to cope with these transitions, while others do not? Do other adults fail at their transitions? Or do they have alternative ways of coping that make it unnecessary for them to learn?

Why do the advantaged learn more often than the disadvantaged? Do the disadvantaged not have as many transitions, or do they not see school as useful in making those transitions?

Is there some optimum match between a given type of transition and a given provider of learning? Are employers the best providers for those in career transition?

Adult participation in learning is increasing, but at a slower rate than in earlier years. If social and economic changes are taking place at an ever increasing rate, why isn't adult participation in learning taking place at an ever-increasing rate?

Is there some maximum proportion of adults in the society who can be engaged in learning at the same time? Is there some maximum proportion of all adult time that can be constructively dedicated to learning rather than to other activities needed to maintain the society?

Cognitive Development   477

Careers and Work

In this second part of the chapter, we will look at various sociocultural influences to determine what influence they have on career orientations. Before doing so, let's look at several theories of vocational choice and see what they say about an individual's career orientation.

Contemporary Theories of Vocational Choice

When asked what they want to be when they grow up, young children may answer, "a doctor," "a superhero," "a teacher," "a movie star," or any of a number of other occupations. During the elementary school years, the future seems to contain almost unlimited opportunity. Eli Ginsberg's theory of vocational choice (1951, 1972) emphasizes that the fantasies children entertain about future occupations are an important aspect of career development. Ginsberg believes that until about age eleven, children are in the **fantasy stage** of occupational choice. At this stage, children imagine what they want to be with little or no concern for their abilities, training, or the demands of reality.

From the ages of eleven to seventeen, boys and girls are in what Ginsberg calls the **tentative stage** of vocational choice. It is during the adolescent years that a transition from the fantasy orientation of childhood to the realistic decision making of early adulthood occurs. Ginsberg believes that adolescents progress from evaluating their interests (ages eleven to twelve) to evaluating their capacities (thirteen to fourteen) and their values (fifteen to sixteen). At around the ages of seventeen and eighteen, thinking shifts from a less subjective to a more realistic orientation. The age period from seventeen or eighteen through the early twenties is called the **realistic stage** of vocational choice by Ginsberg. During this stage, the late adolescent or young adult conducts an extensive search of available occupations (called the period of exploration), zeros in on a particular occupation or a set of occupations (called crystallization), and then decides on a specific job within the occupation decided upon (such as family practitioner or orthopedic surgeon from the more general category of doctor).

Ginsberg's theory has been subjected to criticism on a number of grounds. For one, the initial data were collected from middle-class youth, who may well have had more career options open to them. Also, just as with other developmental theories (such as Piaget's and Freud's) some critics feel that the time frames are too rigid. Moreover, Ginsberg's theory does not adequately account for individual differences—some individuals make mature decisions about careers (and stick with them) at a much earlier age than Ginsberg suggests,

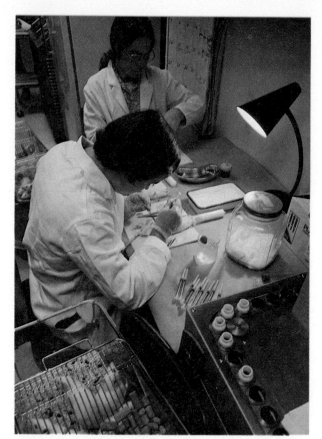

Children's fantasies about future occupations are an important part of career development.

and not all children engage in extensive fantasies about careers during childhood. In a revision of his view, Ginsberg (1972) has conceded that lower-class youth do not have as many options available to them as middle-class youth do when career decisions are at issue. Ginsberg's general point, though—that during adolescence boys and girls become more realistic in their appraisal of career matters—is probably correct.

While at one time Ginsberg's theory dominated thinking about career choice, in recent years the career choice theories of Donald Super and John Holland have been given considerably more attention.

Donald Super's Developmental Self-Concept Theory
Donald Super's theory of vocational choice (e.g., Super, 1967, 1976) emphasizes the importance of the individual's self-concept. Super believes that it is during adolescence that boys and girls first construct a vocational self-concept. Other aspects of the adolescent's self-concept undoubtedly appear earlier than adolescence (such as perception of the self as good or bad, perception of maleness and femaleness, and so on), but it is not until adolescence that vocational identity begins to appear.

Super argues that individuals go through five different phases of vocational development. First, at about fourteen to eighteen years of age, adolescents develop ideas about work that mesh with their already existing global self-concept—this phase is called crystallization. Next, between eighteen and twenty years of age, they narrow their vocational choices and initiate behavior that will enable them to engage in some type of career—this phase is referred to as specification. Between twenty-one and twenty-four years of age, young adults complete their education and/or training and enter the work world. Super calls this stage implementation. The decision on a specific, appropriate career is made between the ages of twenty-five and thirty-five—this phase is labeled stabilization. Finally, after the age of thirty-five, middle-aged adults seek to advance their careers and reach high-status positions. Super calls this consolidation.

The age ranges Super suggests should not be thought of as rigid, but rather as approximations of when a large portion of individuals pass through the different phases. Super believes that although some individuals are endowed with skills in certain areas, there usually are many vocations that individuals can succeed in that coordinate with their talents. Clearly, exposure to alternative careers is one aspect of the environment that promotes career development.

John Holland's Personality Type Theory

Another theory of occupational choice that also has received a great deal of attention during recent years is John Holland's. Holland (1973) emphasizes that individuals select careers that match their personalities. Once an individual finds an occupation that fits with his or her personality, he or she is more likely to enjoy that particular occupation and stay in the job for a longer period of time than an individual who works at a job that is not suitable for his or her personality. Holland believes there are six basic personality types to be considered when matching the individual's psychological makeup to an occupation.

Realistic. These individuals show characteristically "masculine" traits. They are physically strong, deal in practical ways with problems, and have very little social know-how. They are best oriented toward practical careers such as labor, farming, truck driving, and construction.

Intellectual. These adults are conceptually and theoretically oriented. They are thinkers rather than doers. Often they avoid interpersonal relations and are best suited to careers in math and science.

Social. These individuals often show characteristically "feminine" traits, particularly those associated with verbal skills and interpersonal relations. They are likely to be best equipped to enter "people" professions such as teaching, social work, counseling, and the like.

Conventional. These individuals show a distaste for unstructured activities. They are best suited for jobs as subordinates, such as bank tellers, secretaries, and file clerks.

Enterprising. These adults energize their verbal abilities toward leading others, dominating individuals, and selling people on issues or products. They are best counseled to enter careers such as sales, politics, and management.

Artistic. These adults prefer to interact with their world through artistic expression, avoiding conventional and interpersonal situations in many instances. They should be oriented toward careers such as art and writing.

If all individuals fell conveniently into Holland's personality types, vocational counselors would be obsolete. But people are more varied and complex than Holland suggests. Even Holland now admits that his categorization of individuals into six basic types probably is too simplistic and that most individuals are not "pure" types anyway. Still, the basic idea of matching the abilities and attitudes of the individual to a particular occupation that meshes with those abilities and attitudes is an important contribution to the vocational field.

Exploration, Planning, and Decision Making

At some point toward the end of adolescence or the beginning of early adulthood, most individuals enter some type of occupation. Most career choice theorists and counselors believe that before deciding upon a particular career, exploration of a wide number of occupational alternatives is a wise strategy. Again, Donald Super believes that exploration of alternative career paths is the most important aspect of career development.

Exploration

Donald Super and Douglas Hall (1978) believe that in countries where equal employment opportunities have developed—such as the United States, Great Britain, and France—exploration of various career paths is critical in career development. The role of the school is especially important in career exploration, since families and friends tend to be from the same social class and often know little about educational opportunities and occupations other than their own (e.g., Reynolds, & Shister, 1949).

Individuals often approach career exploration and decision making with a great deal of ambiguity, uncertainty, and stress (e.g., Jordaan, 1963; Jordaan & Heyde, 1978). In one investigation, Donald Super and his colleagues (Super, Kowalski, & Gotkin, 1967) studied young adults after they left high school. In their career pattern study, they found that over half the position changes (such as student to student, student to job, job to job) made between leaving school and the age of twenty-five involved floundering and unplanned changes. In other words, the young adults were neither systematic nor intentional in their exploration and decision making about careers.

Several recent efforts have been made to increase career exploration among high school students. In one investigation (Hamdani, 1974), a career education and guidance course was developed for disadvantaged inner-city high school students. A regular teacher, who was not especially motivated or competent, was the instructor, with Hamdani acting as a consultant. The semester-long course did produce an increase in the disadvantaged students' career planning, as well as their use of resources for exploration and decision making.

The nature of the career exploration is important in determining whether a positive effect on individuals will accrue. Some counseling programs that have been self-oriented (that is, students are left to their own devices more so than in the more directive environmental approach of Hamdani) do not show positive effects on students' career exploration and decision making (Corbin, 1974; Hammer, 1974). In many cases, these programs fail to involve the students in enough exploration for changes to occur. When self-directed student programs are instituted, some instruction, monitoring, and discussion with a counselor seems necessary for the student to benefit from the program. It is just not enough for the high school or college student to engage in career exploration without any guidance.

Most high school and college students have not explored the world of work adequately on their own and receive very little direction from high school and college counselors about how to do this. According to the National Assessment of Educational Progress report (1976), students not only do not know what information to seek about careers, they do not know how to seek it. Just as discouraging is the fact that, on the average, high school students spend less than three hours per year with the guidance counselors at their schools (Super & Hall, 1978).

Planning and Decision Making
The first step in making a decision about a career, according to Super and Hall (1978), is to recognize that a problem actually exists. After individuals become aware that a vocation problem exists, they can seek and weigh various pieces of information about the problem, make and test various plans, and then, if necessary, revise the plans.

In one study of career decision making developed by Super and Overstreet (1960), a large number of ninth-grade boys were asked about their career decision making. Vocational maturity was evident in terms of the boys' ability to engage in planning for short- and long-term career goals. The ability of vocationally mature adolescents to develop a structured time perspective about their future career emerged also in the work of Jepsen (1974a, 1974b) with high school juniors.

Exploration, planning, and decision making about careers then, are important cognitive activities that need to be encouraged in adolescents and young adults.

Sociocultural Influences
Not every individual born into the world can grow up to become a nuclear physicist or a doctor—there is a genetic limitation that keeps some young adults from performing at the very high intellectual levels necessary to enter such occupations. Similarly, there are genetic limitations that keep some young adults from becoming professional tennis players or golfers. But there is usually a wide range of vocations available to us that are compatible with the abilities we inherited from our parents. The sociocultural experiences of an individual exert a strong influence on career choice (Grotevant, 1979). Parents, peers, and schools are among the most important socializing influences in this respect. And the social class of the individual's family has important implications for his or her educational and career orientation. Further, there are profound cultural changes occurring in the standards used to gauge the woman's role in the world of work.

Parents, Peers, and Schools
Many individuals receive little or no push from their parents to obtain an education or to aspire to any career. From a very early age, boys and girls see and hear about what kinds of jobs their parents engage in. In some cases, parents even take their children to work with them on jobs. The influence of parental occupations on young adults is nowhere more profound than in the vocation of farming, where as many as nine out of every ten young adults whose parents were farmers become farmers themselves (Gottlieb & Ramsey, 1964).

Peer interaction represents another potential source of information about career development. However, since most peer groups tend to be organized according to social class, youth often do not receive any new information about career choices from peers. Peer group

"My counselor recommended Penn or Purdue, the coach's advice was Michigan, I won a scholarship to Syracuse, my best friend picked Southern Cal, and I like Arizona State.... But, I'm going to Ipswich College because that's where my father graduated from."

influences likely have the greatest impact on youth whose parents have not socialized them strongly in the direction of a particular career or set of careers. Peer discussions about what to do after high school, the role of vocational training in getting a job, and so forth take on added importance when parental influences on occupational aspirations are weak.

However, when lower-class youth associate frequently with middle-class youth, they are more likely to show interest in college and higher-status careers th n when they only associate with peers from similar lower-class backgrounds (Simpson, 1962). Interestingly, there appears to be a reverse trend as well for middle-class youth—when they have a number of lower-class friends, their educational and occupational aspirations are lowered.

Teachers, counselors, and coaches can have strong influences on an individual's career decision making. In addition, esteemed adult figures other than parents and school personnel sometimes can have a marked effect on an individual's career choice. O. J. Simpson recently commented that Willie Mays, the famous baseball player, had a striking effect on his decision to go to college and try to become a professional football player. Simpson had been introduced to Willie Mays by a high school counselor, who saw the tremendous potential in O. J. that was quickly going to waste. Simpson grew up in a broken home with little parental

supervision and spent much of his time with a delinquent group of peers. He had been in jail several times before he talked with Mays. Mays talked with Simpson about his future, his talent, and what he needed to do to get on the right track. Obviously, his influence had a remarkable effect on the young Simpson.

Different types of career education models have been given a great deal of attention by vocational experts in recent years. In the 1970s, the United States Office of Education funded four different career education models: the school-based model; the employer-based model; the home-based model; and the rural-residential model. Many experts believe that the school is a critical influence on career development. School is the primary setting where youth first encounter the world of work, and it provides an atmosphere for continuing self-development in relation to achievement and work. Further, it is the only institution in our society presently capable of providing the several delivery systems necessary for career education, such as instruction, guidance, placement, and community interaction. The elements of career education toward which the school-based model is directed, as well as the outcomes sought by the model, are detailed in table 16.3 (Herr, 1974).

Social Class

Most sociologists believe social class is a powerful force in career development (e.g., Little, 1969). They point out that the individual growing up in a New York ghetto family on welfare has much less chance of entering a middle-class occupation than the individual whose parents live in an affluent suburb. In one widely cited study of 4,000 male high school seniors (Little, 1969), students who aspired to higher-status occupations came from higher socioeconomic backgrounds, usually had a father who had gone to college and who held a white-collar job, were more likely to go to high school in an urban area, had above-average achievement test scores, and planned on going to college. By contrast, high school seniors who aspired to lower-status occupations more often came from a lower socioeconomic background, had a father who had not gone to high school and who worked as an unskilled laborer, had below-average achievement test scores, and planned on no education beyond high school.

Other research supports Little's conclusions. For example, in one investigation (Blau, 1965) over 40 percent of the sons of self-employed professionals entered a profession and 30 percent some other white-collar job. By contrast, only about 5 percent of the sons of laborers entered a profession and only 15 percent entered other white-collar jobs. The vast majority ended up in lower-class blue-collar or service jobs. The chances of attaining true economic security in an upper white-collar professional or business career appear to steadily decrease as socioeconomic background goes toward the lower classes.

Table 16.3
Some Elements and Outcomes of a School-Based
Career Education Model

Element	Outcome
Career awareness	Career identity
Self-awareness	Self-identity
Appreciation, attitudes	Self- and social fulfillment
Decision-making skills	Career decisions
Economic awareness	Economic understanding
Skill awareness and beginning competence	Employment skills
Employability skills	Career placement
Educational awareness	Educational identity

The channels of upward mobility open to lower-class youth today are largely educational in nature. The school hierarchy from grade school through high school, as well as through college and graduate school, is programmed to orient youth toward some sort of career.

Less than a hundred years ago, only eight years of education was believed to be necessary for vocational competence and anything beyond that qualified the individual for advanced placement in high-status occupations. By the middle of the twentieth century, the high school diploma had already lost ground as a ticket to occupational success. College rapidly became a prerequisite for entering a higher-status occupation. Employers simply reason that an individual with a college degree is a better risk than a high school graduate or a high school dropout. Hence, students keep entering college at reasonably high rates in hope that an education will ensure occupational success.

There is increasing evidence, though, that higher education does not do a very good job of training youth to think more critically or to hone their particular abilities and skills for the vocational world. The integration of work and education may be a more effective strategy of career development for adolescents and young adults.

The Changing Role of Women
No greater change has taken place in the working world than the increase in the number of females entering occupations that previously were thought to be appropriate only for males. More women than ever before are working outside the home. From 1900 until about 1940, about 20 percent of women fourteen years old and older worked. Since 1940, there has been a steady, marked increase in the number of women who work—by 1980, about 51 percent of all American women held jobs.

However, although some women are entering previously all-male occupations, the majority of women still have not achieved parity with men in the occupational marketplace. The difference between the average salaries for women and men is still huge—less than $10,000 per year for women and almost $17,000 per year for men in 1980. While women have entered the work force in greater numbers than ever before, many of the jobs they have taken have been low-paying, low-status positions such as clerical jobs (Wright, 1982).

Aletha Huston-Stein and Ann Higgens-Trenk (1978) have discussed some of the sociocultural factors that have affected the increasing numbers of women in colleges and jobs outside the home. The demand for female employees increased significantly after World War II because the number of job openings in traditionally female occupations (e.g., nurse, teacher, clerical worker) increased at a more rapid pace than job availability in male occupations. Many married women were induced to enter the labor market for the first time. More recently, the number of traditionally female professional jobs, particularly in teaching, has declined, so the greatest demand for female employment is in low-status positions (VanHusen & Sheldon, 1976).

Another factor affecting the increasing numbers of working women involves divorce. The divorce rate has been increasing expotentially in recent years; this might be viewed either as a *reason* more women are working or as a *consequence* of the economic independence women are gaining. The woman who works and knows she can support herself may be more likely to end an unhappy marriage. And on the other hand, divorce often forces a woman to work to support herself and her children.

There are still many barriers preventing women from entering occupations that are intellectually and financially rewarding. While discrimination in education and employment have been reduced, they have not been eliminated (e.g., Astin & Bayer, 1975; Harway & Astin, 1977).

Because of the structure and demands of many occupations, many women may not be able to enter them as easily as men can. Particular difficulties arise for the woman who feels committed to being a homemaker and mother. Many professional and managerial positions require extensive amounts of time and travel. Such jobs virtually require that the female have a "helpmate" to fulfill her home responsibilities (Papanek, 1973). Perhaps one reason so many women select teaching as a profession is that the time schedule permits them to be home reasonably early in the evening so they can cook dinner and take care of their children. Some social scientists (for example, Gronseth, 1972) suggest that as long as the male is viewed as the primary economic provider in a culture, the career plans and achievements of women will continue to be underdeveloped and subordinate.

Although some women are entering previously all-male occupations, the majority have still not achieved parity with men.

The Achievement Orientation and Career Development of Females in Early Adulthood

Although many of the factors influencing young women's decisions about careers and families occur in childhood, early adulthood is a critical period (Husten-Stein & Higgens-Trenk, 1978). The timing of marriage, childbearing, education, and work have long-term implications for the life patterns of women. Once a choice is made, particularly having a child, a women's range of options becomes more limited, or at least more difficult to pursue.

Although the majority of college women anticipate both a career and marriage, many are unrealistic about the difficulties of this combination (Shields, 1973). The dissatisfaction and conflict in combining a family and career seems to result more from role overload than role conflict. Women who cope with these time pressures and conflicts by redefining their own and their families' responsibilities are more satisfied than those who attempt to meet all demands alone.

Women who return to higher education or careers after marrying and having children show high levels of commitment. Women often search for avenues of self-fulfillment outside the home. Women who are employed have higher levels of life satisfaction and feelings of adequacy and self-esteem than full-time homemakers. However, the psychological benefits of employment are greater for the educated middle-class and the liabilities are greater for lower-class women.

These findings suggest that future research should focus on the developmental changes in women caused by home and work roles. Effective coping techniques could help women deal with these rapidly changing life patterns.

The Life Contour of Work in Adulthood

Research on work in adulthood suggests that there are four major stages in the occupational cycle: (1) selection and entry; (2) adjustment; (3) maintenance; and (4) retirement. These stages are readily identifiable in careers that entail an orderly progression; they may become obscure in work patterns that are disorderly or that change in ways that require readjustment of some sort.

Entering an occupation signals the beginning of new roles and responsibilities for the individual. The career role is somewhat different from the roles the individual may have had as a temporary or part-time worker during adolescence. Career role expectations for competence are high and the demands are real for the adult. When a person enters a job for the first time he or she may be confronted by unanticipated problems and conditions. Transitions will be required as the person attempts to adjust to the new role. Meeting the expectations of a career and adjusting to a new role are crucial for the individual, not only during this era, but during other periods of life as well.

Some career development experts suggest that the second stage in the occupational cycle should be labeled the *adjustment* stage. This is the period Daniel Levinson (1978) describes as "Age 30 Transition" in men. According to Levinson, once a person has entered an occupation, he must develop a distinct occupational identity and establish himself in the occupational world. Along the way, he may fail, drop out, or begin on a new path. He may stay narrowly on a single track or try several directions before settling firmly on one. This adjustment phase lasts several years. A professional may spend several years in academic study while an executive may spend his early years in lower- or middle-management jobs. Hourly workers typically need several years to explore the work world, become familiar with the industry and a labor union, and move beyond the apprentice status to a permanent occupational role.

The level of attainment a person reaches by the early thirties also varies. A professional may just be getting started or may have already become well established and widely known in his or her profession. One executive may be on the first rung of the corporate ladder or a few may be near the top. An hourly worker may be an unskilled laborer without job security or a highly skilled craftsman earning more than some executives or professionals.

The *midlife career experience* has been described as a major turning point in adulthood. We have described midlife or middle age as the twenty-year period extended from approximately between thirty-five and fifty to between fifty-five and sixty years of age. Robert Havighurst writes that a major developmental task of this era is *establishing* and *maintaining* an economic standard of living. One aspect of the midlife phase involves adjusting idealistic hopes to realistic possibilities in light of how much time is left in an occupation. Middle-aged adults often focus on how much time they have left before retirement and the speed with which they are reaching their occupational goals. If individuals are behind schedule, or if their goals are now viewed as unrealistic, reassessment and readjustment are necessary. Daniel Levinson (1978) commented that for many middle-aged men there is a sense of sadness over unfulfilled dreams. Levinson and his colleagues found that many middle-aged men feel constrained by their bosses, wives, and children. Such feelings may lead to rebellion, which can take several forms—extramarital affairs, divorce, alcoholism, suicide, or career change.

Van Hoose and Worth (1982) discuss the issues involved in a midlife career change. It is important to consider the deeper meanings of career change during the middle years. Midlife career changes are quite often linked to changes in attitudes, goals, and values (Thomas, 1977). Divorce can be used as an analogy in describing the relationship between changes in life style and career change. A change in career, in and of itself, provides only a rough indicator of what is going on with a person psychologically, just as divorce is a gross indicator of the quality of a marital relationship. Some marriages remain intact despite prolonged conflict, while others are terminated with only slight signs of deterioration. Likewise, some persons hang on to their jobs despite intense dislike for their work, while others change careers even when their jobs are still satisfactory.

Daniel Levinson notes that a person of middle age wants desperately to be affirmed in the roles that he or she values most. At about age forty Levinson's subjects fixed on some key event in their careers as carrying the ultimate message of their affirmation or devaluation by society. This might be a promotion or a new job or a symbolic form of success, like writing a bestseller. Levinson concludes that the inevitable result of changes and pressures in midlife is alteration. Even if nothing in the individual's external life changes, the individual does. The person simply does not remain in the earlier life structure. Even if the structure stays relatively intact externally, there are inevitable internal changes that give it a different meaning.

Two additional career-related changes in midlife must be noted. Midlife is often accompanied by fiscal events that influence career decisions. For example, in some families midlife is accompanied by a severe strain on financial resources caused by children in college. In other families there is a reorientation toward retirement and concerns begin to mount about financial resources for retirement (Heald, 1977).

Another problem of this era may result from role changes brought on by fiscal conditions. The wife may assume a working role, or resume such a role, to help with college expenses or to pursue her own vocational interests after children have left the house. In either case the husband must adapt to the competition for the "breadwinning" role. This adaptation may prove especially difficult if the wife's career outranks the husband's either in status or in salary (Heald, 1977).

We have discussed a number of aspects of careers and vocations, but as adults, we must not only learn how to work well, but we need to learn to relax as well. Recent data from the 1980 census suggest that compared to those in early and late adulthood, individuals in middle adulthood see themselves as the most hurried. In box 16.2, we look at the role of leisure in early and middle adulthood, as described by William Van Hoose and Maureen Worth (1982).

In this chapter we have seen that the years of early and middle adulthood mark the development and integration of cognitive capacities that enable individuals to attain a purposeful, organized mastery of their personal lives and their work world. We also have seen that society—especially in contemporary times—has constructed some of its major institutions to specialize in work. The spectacular development of the modern occupational-bureaucratic complex has provided the locus of most of the work activities of society. Our modern social organization, then, has developed in response to the central role work plays in our lives.

Box 16.2
Leisure

W̲e should be able not only to work well, but to use leisure well, for the first principle of all action is leisure. Both are required but leisure is better than work and is its end.

Aristotle

Leisure has generally been seen as a source of satisfaction and delight. In a society in which most people had to work for most of their lives, leisure was scarce and was regarded as a reward to be earned for hard work or a good thing conferred by inherited wealth or marriage to wealth.

With the coming of more leisure time in the lives of most people, not all the rosy promises have been realized. Some people have found themselves with more leisure than they want or know what to do with. The values of more leisure time have been questioned not only by social scientists but by people who have it. It is clear that modern leisure is not an unmixed blessing.

Studies of normal aging at Duke University have concluded that our society is a work-oriented, not a leisure-oriented society. In a study of middle-class adults, aged forty-six to seventy-one, the Duke researchers found that almost 90 percent of the men and 82 percent of the women would still work even if it was not necessary to work for a living. The majority of subjects in this study reported that they gained more satisfaction from work than from leisure and only a small percent wanted more leisure time.

While social class, sex, and occupation have some obvious effects on leisure, other factors also influence leisure time during the adult years. Leisure activities vary for people from one age to another, and one's views of leisure and how it should be used undoubtedly change with age. Likewise, some activities which may not be appropriate for young adults may be very appropriate during midlife. Further, the options that are available to a person at one stage of life may be dependent on what has been done before. What a person does in the past will help to determine what will be done in the future (McDaniel, 1977). Some understanding of this concept as it relates to midlife and the later years is vital.

Leisure and Midlife

When David turned forty-two he began to want some activity outside of work. He and a close friend bought and restored a vintage automobile, the first of several antique cars that David describes as a pleasant and profitable

hobby. At thirty-eight Helen sent her last child off to kindergarten and announced that she was going to spend the next three years reading the numerous books she had purchased but had found no time to read.

David and Helen have different views about leisure time, but whatever it is that people like to do, middle age appears to be a time when leisure takes on added significance. Roger Gould (1978) describes how the midlife era is a time of questioning how one's time should be spent and of reassessing priorities. This is an era when the person wants more freedom and more opportunity to express his/her individuality. As noted in an earlier discussion, midlife is a period when some people restructure the whole fabric of their lives.

Source: Van Hoose & Worth, 1982, pp. 174–75.

Leisure is particularly important in midlife because of the changes that most people are going through. These changes involve the self (i.e., physical changes, value changes), changes in relationships with spouse and children, career change, and others. By middle age, more money is generally available to most people, financial responsibilities begin to decline, and people who have worked steadily for years have some job security. There may also be more free time and more paid vacations. These midlife changes lead to expanded opportunities not only for leisure time activities but for new career experiences as well. For many people at midlife this may be the first time in their lives that they have had the opportunity to diversify—to develop themselves—to follow their own inclinations. Now a person may enjoy something without worrying about whether the product or skills developed are salable in the job market.

Changing life styles during the past three decades has also provided increased opportunity for new leisure time activities. Adults may now feel a greater sense of freedom to engage in a variety of activities which were previously unavailable (Corbin & Tait, 1973). By midlife people are aware of new opportunities and have the confidence and the freedom required to participate in leisure activities of their own choosing.

Constructive and fulfilling leisure activities in midlife are of considerable importance in preparing for retirement. The individual needs to begin preparing both financially and psychologically for retirement during midlife. If a person develops leisure time activities that can be continued into retirement, then there will be some continuity from full-time work to full-time leisure (McDaniel, 1977).

One perspective on work that recently has been proposed by Neil Smelser (1980) merits attention. He believes that to better understand the role of work in the life cycle, we need to study what he calls life contours. The life contour for the role of a professional in our society (doctor, engineer, academic) varies from that of a semiskilled blue-collar worker. After a long period of training, involvement in a professional role is expected to grow steadily throughout the adult years, level off in the late fifties or early sixties, and then cease abruptly upon retirement. By contrast, rewards and responsibilities come quickly for a blue-collar worker, the leveling-off period is much longer, but there is an equally abrupt termination upon retirement.

Contours vary, of course, as values, norms, and social structures vary. Contours also vary according to the degree to which life events and transitions give them shape. For example, the passage of time is inevitable in a contour. Advanced occupational training, marriage, and other events may also alter a contour. Sex and race also have an impact on the life contour of an individual. Smelser believes that taken together, these factors

spell out the relative degree of freedom or choice that is left to the individual. Insofar as a person's life has ingredients that are inevitable, irreversible, tightly scheduled, and normatively dictated, to that extent it is predetermined, leaving little room for choice. . . . not all contours possess all these restraining features, and each personal history is not determined entirely by biological and sociocultural agendas. Furthermore, we may expect individual differences in the ways people come to terms with the inevitable, irreversible, and binding features of the life course. For this reason it is important to leave room for the notion of personal career, characterized in its own right, above and beyond the influences which play upon it. The personal career always unfolds in relation to its environmental agendas but not solely according to their dictates.

Work and Intelligence
Psychologists have been interested in the extent to which we can predict job success through the use of IQ tests (see box 16.3 for how successful we have been in using IQ tests for this purpose and some possible alternatives to IQ testing). However, sociologists have been more interested in how work influences the cognitive characteristics of the individual (e.g., Simpson, 1980).

Sociologist Melvin Kohn (1980) has written extensively about the relations between work and intelligence and conducted extensive research on this topic. Kohn (1969, Kohn & Schooler, in press) argues that the nature of a person's work has a direct bearing on his or her cognitive structure. Kohn identifies a variable he calls occupational self-direction, which denotes the degree to which a job is self-directed, time-pressured, and intellectually demanding (i.e., involves work with data more than with people or things).

Box 16.3
IQ Tests, Adaptive Competence, and Job Success

Most textbooks on psychological testing report that scores on intelligence tests are reasonably good predictors of job success (e.g., Cronbach, 1970). And, there is evidence that IQ measured in adolescence is a good predictor of occupational prestige at the age of forty (McCall, 1977). Further, a measure of intellectual flexibility has been used to predict changes in occupational self-direction over a ten-year period (Kohn & Schooler, in press).

A discussion of the relation between IQ and job success by David McClelland (1973), however, suggests that it may be wise to think further about the use of IQ tests to predict job success. It has been found, for example, that intelligence test scores predict performance more reliably for jobs requiring abstract, symbolic thinking than for those that are less dependent on these skills (Ghiselli, 1966). For example, they are better at predicting job success as a stockbroker, an occupation that requires the ability to make financial analyses and projections, than success as a police officer, an occupation that calls for extensive person-to-person contact and routine reports. Even for jobs requiring abstract, symbolic thought, however, IQ tests are not as reliable in predicting success as they are in predicting performance in school. As an example, one study (Ghiselli, 1966) revealed a correlation of .45 between IQ and success as a stockbroker. Although the correlation does show that success in being a stockbroker is related to intelligence test scores, it also very clearly indicates that there is room for many other factors to contribute to this success as well.

In Ghiselli's study (1966) there was a correlation of .27 between scores on an intelligence test and efficiency as a police officer. This is a statistically significant relation but not a very strong one. McClelland (1973) discusses further the problems involved in using IQ tests to try to predict success as a police officer. In many cities it is necessary to take an intelligence test that requires understanding of such words as *quell, pyromaniac,* and *lexicon.* A person who does not perform well on this test does not qualify for the job. And that person probably wonders why city, state, and federal governments still use tests that include words like these as a basis for selecting police officers or firefighters or clerks.

Intelligence tests, by themselves, are not good predictors of occupational success. What should be done, then, when it is necessary to predict whether a person may expect to be successful at a particular job? McClelland (1973) makes some recommendations that should be considered when assessing potential job success.

The best type of testing is what is called criterion sampling. If you want to find out whether a senior graduating from high school can expect to be successful as a police officer, you would start by defining what a police officer does. Certainly one of the criteria would have to be communication skills and the type of vocabulary used by a police officer on the job (not the vocabulary previously mentioned). In criteria testing, then, the first step is this:

In a ten-year longitudinal study (Kohn & Schooler, in press), however, it was found that occupational self-direction did not have a long-term effect on intellectual flexibility. Instead, intellectual flexibility had a strong impact on occupational self-direction. Miles Simpson (1980) concluded that cognitive attributes may direct individuals into particular lines of work because (1) certain jobs suit persons with certain attributes, (2) certain cognitive attributes confer an advantage in the competition for a particular job, or (3) the cognitive attributes in question provide a competitive advantage in obtaining an education.

As part of their interest in the relation between work and intelligence, sociologists also have studied how rural occupation and life styles affect cognitive characteristics. When ethnic groups in America are classified by the recency of their emancipation from serfdom (Schooler, 1976), for example, group serfdom experience for 930 ethnics is related to intellectual flexibility and other personality variables. In another investigation, the personal functioning of rural individuals from different occupations were compared (Fromm & Maccoby, 1970). The personalities and cognitive characteristics of Mexican villagers differed radically according to their occupations. Peasants living on haciendas were passive-receptive, while farmers who

Define the criteria for success at what you are trying to predict. Testers must rely less on paper-and-pencil measures, like IQ tests and abstract word games, when it comes to predicting success in many areas of performance; instead, they should go out into the real world and watch what successful people do in specific occupations. For example, Jacob Kounin (1971) attempted to define the criteria for good teaching by going into classrooms and videotaping the performance of "good" and "bad" teachers.

The second recommendation McClelland makes is this: *Tests should be designed to reflect changes in what the individual has learned.* Intelligence tests have been designed to measure intellectual skills that were thought to be stable. In other words, if a person's scores on tests administered at different times and under approximately the same circumstances vary greatly, the tests are probably not doing a good job of measuring what they are supposed to measure. McClelland believes tests should be designed to measure the person's increased competence in skills related to the criteria of success on a job. Thus, instead of developing tests that measure stability, we should be attempting to measure criteria that reflect areas in which people can improve. For example, if it is found that teaching in elementary school requires a great deal of patience and highly developed communication skills, ways to measure these skills should be designed. It should be expected that individuals who initially do poorly in these criteria can improve and may perform better in later tests.

This leads to McClelland's third recommendation for improving assessment: *How to improve the characteristic tested should be made public and explicit.* How to do well on important tests has often been viewed as a deep, dark secret. McClelland stresses that we should be as open as possible about the criteria that are evaluated by a test and state in a simple way how to improve on the test. Thus, if an important test measures reading comprehension and arithmetic skills, the individual should be aware of exactly how he or she is going to be tested, how to best prepare for the test, and how the test will be scored. Some tests follow this procedure, but many do not.

Most experts find merit in McClelland's recommendations, but some do not agree that intelligence testing should be eliminated completely. Intelligence tests are often efficient in predicting such significant outcomes as success in school subjects, different aspects of reading ability, and some aspects of job success. Again, however, it is important to remember that intelligence tests are invariably used most effectively when used in conjunction with the types of criterion testing McClelland recommends. Their use in isolation from other measures of intellectual functioning, particularly observations of the individual in situations relevant to what is being predicted, can lead to inaccurate and even harmful predictions.

owned their own land but were living on a small margin were better organized and had more independent personalities. Men engaged in capitalistic enterprises were the most adaptive.

In a remarkable study that remained unpublished for forty-five years (Luria, 1976), the impact of little education, factory work, or collective agriculture on cognitive functioning among the Uzbekistan peoples of central Asia was examined. Subjects were selected to reflect the extremes of contact with the "modernizing influence" of Soviet society; they were examined on categorizing and grouping of objects, generalization and abstraction, deduction and inference, reasoning and problem solving, imagination, self-analysis, and self-awareness. In the absence of formal education or experience in a highly rationalized organization such as a collective farm or factory, no systematic intellectual development took place. These people regarded the logical procedures of categorization and generalization as irrelevant; they analyzed an object according to its rudimentary practical function.

In sum, there is every reason to believe that a reciprocal relation between intelligence and work exists—in some ways intelligence influences work, and in other ways work affects intelligence.

Summary

This chapter focused on the nature of adult cognition, cognitive development in early and middle adulthood, and the roles of careers and work in early and middle adulthood.

The three main perspectives that were relied upon to describe children's cognitive development also guide our study of adult cognition: cognitive-structural; psychometric; and information processing. From the cognitive-structural view, Piaget emphasizes that the manner in which adults think is no different than the way adolescents think. However, many cognitive structuralists now believe that formal operational thought increases during the early adult years. Nonetheless, they also believe that many adults do not systematically think in formal operational ways. Piaget's theory has stimulated the search for a fifth stage of structural thought—current ideas about the fifth stage focus on the individual's capability of abstractly analyzing the nature of formal thought itself.

The psychometric approach that has received the most attention in our study of adult development is the Cattell-Horn view, which emphasizes a distinction between crystallized and fluid intelligence. John Horn believes that crystallized intelligence increases throughout the life span because it is based on cumulative learning experiences. By contrast, fluid intelligence is thought to increase from infancy through adolescence, level off in early adulthood, and then steadily decline in middle and late adulthood. One group of life-span developmental psychologists, headed by Schaie, Baltes, and Labouvie-Vief, believe that much of the data on adult changes in intelligence are flawed because they have been collected in a cross-sectional manner, and therefore do not take into account cohort and contextual influences. A recent addition to the psychometric views of intelligence is that of Nancy Denney, who proposes that we should distinguish between unexercised and optimally exercised mental abilities.

The majority of our information about information processing in early and middle adulthood focuses on memory. Short-term memory generally shows no age-related decline in middle age while long-term memory often does show a decline. In general, if a memory deficit appears in middle adulthood it most likely occurs (1) on tasks that tap long-term memory, (2) when effective learning strategies are not mentioned to the adult, (3) when tasks demand effortful search or retrieval of information, (4) the materials or information are unfamiliar and difficult to verbalize, and/or (5) adults cannot perform well simply on the basis of previously acquired and well-learned knowledge and skills.

For many years it was assumed that such attributes as creativity and scholarly productivity invariably declined with age. Scientists and artists do usually produce more and better work during their thirties and forties, but there are many individuals in the latter part of middle adulthood and in late adulthood whose creativity and productivity have been exceptional. In recent years there has been a tremendous increase in adult learning—both formal and informal. We discussed reasons why adults initiate or continue learning, why they do not initiate or discontinue learning, and how life transitions and triggers can instigate adult education and learning.

While a greater variety of jobs are available to the female than ever before, sex bias against females still exists in many careers. Information about the achievement orientation and career development of females in young adulthood suggests this period is a crucial one. There are strong social class, as well as cultural, differences in career development. For example, the sons and daughters of lower-class parents are less likely to go to college or enter a white-collar profession than their middle-class counterparts. Three theories of vocational choice have dominated the career development field—Ginsberg's, Super's, and Holland's. Exploration, planning, and decision making are three cognitive activities that are important in any viable career development model.

Research on work in adulthood suggests four major steps in the occupational cycle: selection and entry; adjustment; maintenance; and retirement. The midlife career experience has been described as a major transition in adulthood. One aspect of the midlife phase involves adjusting idealistic hopes to realistic possibilities in light of how much time is left in an occupation. We are a work-oriented rather than a leisure-oriented society. However, many psychologists believe that constructive and fulfilling leisure activities in midlife are important in preparing for retirement. Work is one of the two most important themes of adulthood, according to Freud. One perspective on work in adulthood emphasizes the importance of developing more flexible life contours for work in different occupations. Another aspect of work that has interested psychologists and sociologists is its relation to intelligence—the relation appears to be reciprocal, namely, intelligence influences work and career development, and work affects intelligence and thinking styles.

Key Terms

decay

displacement

fantasy stage

free recall

interference

life contours

memory knowledge

memory processing

optimally exercised
ability

paired-associates
learning

primary memory

realistic stage

secondary memory

semantic or categorical
elaboration

tentative stage

transitions

triggers

unexercised ability

Review Questions

1. Describe the cognitive-structural view of adult cognition. Is there a fifth cognitive stage? If so, describe what it is like, or might be like.
2. Discuss John Horn's ideas about the development of adult intelligence. Discuss the psychometric view of Schaie, Baltes, and Labouvie. What is the nature of the argument between these two perspectives. Also, outline Nancy Denney's ideas about the exercise of mental ability.
3. Discuss the experimental psychological information processing approach to adult cognition.
4. Are there age declines in memory during middle adulthood? If so specify the nature of such decline and ways the decline can be removed.
5. Outline the developmental course of creativity and scholarly productivity in adulthood.
6. Evaluate why adults do and do not initiate or continue their learning, as well as transitions and triggers that may instigate learning.
7. Discuss the three most important theories of vocational choice.
8. List some of the most important social class influences on career development.
9. Outline the achievement orientation and career development of women in early adulthood.
10. What are the four main stages in the life cycle of work?
11. Discuss the concept of life contours of work.
12. Evaluate the relationship between work and intelligence.

Further Readings

Aslanian, C. B., & Brickell, H. M. *Americans in Transition: life changes as reasons for adult learning.* New York: College Entrance Examination Board, 1980.
This book is an excellent source of information about adult education. The authors incorporate current thinking about perspectives of adult development in their attempt to show how transition and triggers stimulate adult learning. Easy reading.

Farrell, M. P., & Rosenberg, S. D. *Men at midlife.* Boston: Auburn House, 1981.
An excellent source of information about midlife career change in men as well as vocational development in men. Reading level is of medium difficulty.

Hultsch, D. F., & Deutsch, F. Intellectual processes, chap. 4; Learning and memory processes, chap. 5. In *Adult and aging.* New York: McGraw-Hill, 1981.
These two chapters of the Hultsch and Deutsch adulthood text are excellent sources of the current state of our knowledge about the development of intelligence and cognition in adulthood. Reading level is reasonably easy.

Huston-Stein, A., & Higgens-Trenk, A. Development of females from childhood through adulthood: career and feminine role orientations. In P. Baltes (ed.), *Lifespan development and behavior* (vol. 1). New York: Academic Press, 1978.
An excellent overview of the achievement and career orientations of females, with particular concern for socializing influences that have led to different achievement and career paths for young adults. Reasonably easy reading.

Smelser, N. J., & Erikson, E. H. *Themes of work and love in adulthood.* Cambridge, Mass.: Harvard University Press, 1980.
An edited volume of essays all focused on the themes of work and love in adulthood, written by experts such as Erik Erikson, Neal Smelser, Robert LeVine, Melvin Kohn, Marjorie Fiske, Roger Gould, and Daniel Levinson. Easy to read.

17

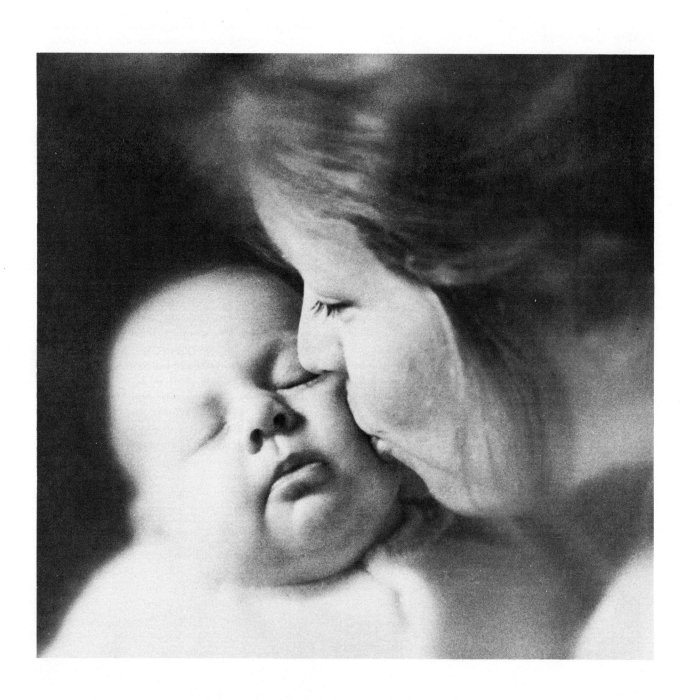

Social, Emotional, and Personality Development

Prologue: I Gave Him the Best Years of My Life

The other day I went into the Bureau of Motor Vehicles to have my driver's license renewed. The man behind the counter mechanically asked me my name, address, phone number and, finally, occupation.

"I am a housewife," I said.

He paused, his pencil lingering over the blank, looked at me intently, and said, "Is that what you want on your license, lady?"

"Would you believe, Love Goddess?" I asked dryly.

In my lifetime, I have had many identities.

I have been referred to as the "Tuesday pick-up with the hole in the muffler," the "10:30 A.M. standing in the beauty shop who wears Girl Scouts anklets," and "the woman who used to work in the same building with the sister-in-law of Jonathan Winters."

Who am I?

I'm the wife of the husband no one wants to swap with. . . . People are always asking couples whose marriage has endured at least a quarter of a century for their secret for success.

Actually, it is no secret at all. I am a forgiving woman. Long ago, I forgave my husband for not being Paul Newman. Those are the breaks. I realized, being mortal, he couldn't possibly understand my dry skin, boot puddles on my waxed floor, hips that hang like saddlebags, and a house that holds for me all the excitement of a disposal plant.

How could he appreciate that my life is like a treadmill with stops at tedium, boredom, monotony, and the laundry room. That is why he comes bounding in each evening with a smile and a report of his day. Last night, for example, he munched on a stalk of celery and said, "I've had quite a day. Worked like a son of a gun this morning with Fred. Then we got in the car and toured an installation north of town. Suddenly I remembered it was Sandy's birthday. You remember Sandy, don't you? (I remember Sandy. She was the one who burnt her bra and five engine companies showed up.) So, we treated Sandy to lunch. By the time I got back to the office, it was time to wrap up. I'm late because I stopped off at John's to see his new boat. What did you do today?"

"I fired my deodorant," I said. When he left the room I mumbled, "Paul wouldn't have been so unfeeling."

"Who's Paul?" asked my eleven-year-old.

Now, trying to explain Paul Newman's mystique to an eleven-year-old is as futile as explaining Dr. Wernher von Braun to Goldie Hawn.

"Paul Newman," I said patiently.

"The guy in *Butch Cassidy and the Sundance Kid?* He rode a neat horse in that picture."

"What horse?"

"How come you're smiling and looking funny?" he asked.

"Like what?"

"Like when you find a quarter in Daddy's chair."

"It's Paul Newman," I shrugged.

"Would you like to be married to him?"

"It has nothing to do with marriage," I said.

"You mean you'd like him to be your friend?"

"I wouldn't have phrased it quite that way."

"He's about as tall as Daddy, isn't he?"

"Daddy who?"

"Boy, ladies sure act silly over movie stars."

"I don't know if I can explain it or not," I said slowly, "but Paul Newman to a tired housewife is like finding a plate of bourbon cookies at a PTA open house. It's putting on a girdle and having it hang loose. It's having a car that you don't have to park on a hill for it to start. It's matched luggage, dishes that aren't plastic and evenings when there's something better to do than pick off your old nail polish. . . .

Naturally, I don't want any recognition or awards, but I've forgiven my husband for a lot of things during our twenty-three-year marriage.

1. I forgive him for not tanning. Actually, I have devoted my entire life to getting my husband tanned. I have basted him with oil, marinated him with lotions, tossed him on all sides, and broiled him to perfection. (Frankly, if I had spent as much time in the kitchen as I spent on him, I'd outdistance the Galloping Gourmet.)

It has all gone in vain. The other day I watched him inch his way out into the sunlight. He was swathed in six beach towels, a pair of dark glasses, and a pair of sandals that buckled to his knees. . . .

2. I forgive him for that performance he puts on every time he orders wine for dinner. Right away, he's Cesar Romero. First, he makes a circle with the glass under his nose. Then he tilts back his head like he is going to make Jeanne Dixon materialize. Finally, his tongue touches the wine.

The rest of us at the table sit there like idiots waiting for this man who doesn't know a vintage port from last week's Kool-Aid to decide whether or not the wine will meet with his favor or disfavor. . . .

3. I forgive him for flunking Campfire in the Boy Scouts. It's amazing how a careless camper will flip a match during a rainstorm and seconds later the entire forest will be in flames.

We will give a party and my husband will "lay a fire," using thirty pounds of paper, a mound of brittle kindling, and a seasoned log with a guarantee stapled on the side. Within minutes, an entire party will be driven into the streets by smoke.

He's the only man I know who had a fireplace with a gas lighter go out on him. . . .

My husband and I have produced three children, survived three wars, comforted one another at funerals, and dedicated ourselves to one another through sickness and in health. The other day, I backed out of the driveway, turned too sharply, and hit the side of his car. He was a perfect stranger.

"Where are you going?" I asked as he left his dented fender and bolted toward the house.

"Don't move your car," he said. "I'm going to call the police."

"The police!" I shouted. "For crying out loud, I'm your wife."

"This is no time for nepotism," he said stiffly.

I should have known better than to compete with a man and his car. For years, psychologists have been telling us that a man's relationship with his automobile supersedes even sex.

For you women who are skeptics, let me ask you a few questions.

Does your husband have an insurance policy on you that includes no-fault, comprehensive, and is fifty-dollar deductible? Or do you have the basic ninety-six-dollar burial policy that puts you on a public bus and takes you to the edge of town?

Do you have a guarantee for a complete oil change every six months and/or 1,000 miles, whichever comes first? Or do you only visit a doctor's office for major surgery?

Does your husband fly into a rage if he finds someone stuck a candy wrapper in your pocket or a piece of bubble gum on your instrument panel?

Has your husband ever patted you on your trunk and remarked what a beautiful trade-in you'd make?

Does he take you to a restaurant three times a week and instruct the waitress to "Fill her up"?

Does he care if the kids put their feet on your upholstery?

Does he object if your teen-agers drive you all over town?

Would he pay eight dollars to have you towed anywhere?

If you didn't start in the morning, would he stay home from work?

If you answered "No" to any or all of these questions then you have a four-wheel correspondent in your divorce suit.

As the policeman surveyed our situation, he turned to my husband and said, "Sir, you are illegally parked. Your car should be at least fifteen feet from the edge of the driveway. Are there any witnesses to this accident?"

"Just my wife," said my husband smiling at me.

"I never saw this bum before in my life," I said.

After the policeman had gone my husband mumbled, "Joanne wouldn't have been so unfeeling."

"Who's Joanne?" asked our eleven-year-old.

"Joanne Woodward," said my husband. "I don't know if you'll understand this or not, son, but Joanne Woodward is like shaving at twelve, she's like going to buy a car and having the salesman take you directly to the convertibles. She's like having your mother-in-law allergic to you, and not having to have a belt to hold your suitcase closed.

"Joanne isn't mortal. She never wears hair rollers, never has chenille marks on her face, and never cleans a fireplace without gloves. She doesn't have to stand up to lose her stomach or talk about worming the dog during dinner. Joanne is. . . ."

"Does she ride a horse good?" asked his son.

"I knew you were to young to understand," he said sadly. "But I forgive you and I forgive your mother."

Source: Bombeck, 1973, pp. 1, 22–23, 25, 26, 27, 28, 35–37.

Introduction

In this chapter we will look at many different aspects of social, emotional, and personality development in early and middle adulthood. As indicated in Erma Bombeck's comments in the prologue, marital relationships are an important part of the lives of many adults. We will explore the development of marital relationships and attempt to pin down the factors that contribute to marital satisfaction. We discuss many ideas about parenting relationships in adulthood, as well as sibling relationships. Information about the increasing number of single adults is given, with particular interest in the nature and variety of this life-style. Affiliation, attachment, intimacy, and love are important aspects of interpersonal relationships in adulthood—we will survey the nature of these relationships and how they may change over the course of the adult years.

In the final section of this chapter we will explore the development of personality in adulthood. Information is given about the development of maturity, the nature of life satisfaction, continuity and change, and various aspects of self and self-systems, such as sex roles and moral development.

Families

Throughout history the family has been an important institution of society. We begin our discussion of families with a look at marital relationships and move on to a discussion of parenting. We will also discuss a variety of family forms that have increased recently in number in America, including marriages with no children, divorced families, and step-parent families.

The Development of Marital Relationships

Marital roles are often renegotiated over and over as each member ages. For example, the traditional division of labor between husband and wife that place the wife in the childrearing role and the husband in the occupational career role requires many adjustments during the life cycle of a family. The idea that many adjustments have to be made during the life cycle of a marriage and family is shown in figure 17.1. From the time a couple marries, an average of two years goes by before they have their first child, and the next twenty-five to thirty-five years are devoted to childrearing and launching. While this represents a sizable segment of the life span, the typical married couple experiences more than one-half of their total years together after their last child leaves home. This extended period of shared time is a recent occurrence. Since the turn of the century, as people have married earlier and stayed married longer, an average of ten years has been added to married life, assuming that divorce has not occurred. In the average family of 1880 the last child left home about two years after the death of one parent.

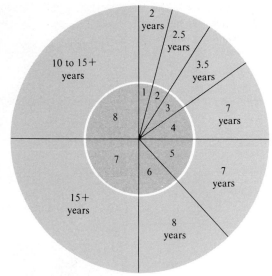

1. Married couples prior to the arrival of children.
2. Families bearing children (oldest child, two and a half or less).
3. Families with preschool children (oldest child six or less).
4. Families with schoolchildren (oldest child thirteen years or less).
5. Families with children in their teens (oldest thirteen to twenty years).
6. Families in launching-of-children stage (first child gone to last child leaving).
7. Parents in middle age (post-child rearing; empty nest to retirement).
8. Parents in old age (retirement to death of both spouses).

Figure 17.1   Eight stages of the family life cycle.
"The Family Life Cycle by Length of Time in Each of Eight Stages," page 121, from *Family Development,* fourth edition, by Evelyn Millis Duvall. (Fifth edition title: *Marriage and Family Development*) Copyright © 1957, 1962, 1967, 1971 by J. B. Lippincott Company. By permission of Harper & Row, Publishers, Inc.

Today both parents are usually alive when the youngest child departs. The husband will be working about fifteen more years, and often both marital partners now live long enough to go from a "young-old" (fifty-five to seventy-four) category to an "old-old" (seventy-five plus) category of the life cycle (Neugarten, 1975).

The developmental description of marriage and the family follows this sequence: courtship; the early years of a marriage; the childrearing years; and the post-childrearing years (Van Hoose & Worth, 1982). A final sequence, the aging couple, is described in chapter 19.

Courtship

What causes us to choose a marriage partner? Some psychologists believe that the choice of a mate entails a selection process based on mutual qualities and interests (Murstein, 1970). Initially physical appearance often is an important factor. If after becoming acquainted two individuals discover that they share similar values, attitudes towards life, ideas about the roles of men and women, politics and religion, sex, and the

Some psychologists believe that the choice of a mate is based on mutual qualities and interests.

role of men and women in society and marriage, then a closer relationship between the two is likely to develop. Once two people find that they have similar qualities and ideas about many areas of life the couple may explore the possibility of marriage and how each would perform certain vital tasks in the marriage.

However, some sociologists (e.g., Winch, 1958) have argued that complementary needs play an important part in the mate selection process. Complementary needs are defined as opposite qualities in a spouse that compensate for perceived inadequacies. For example, if one member tends to be introverted, a spouse who is socially outgoing might be chosen to "compensate" for this perceived inadequacy. Not all role choices, of course, are made on the basis of such complementarity. The individual likely will choose a mate who has some characteristics that are similar to his or her own and some that are not.

The Early Years of Marriage

The first few months of marriage are filled with exploration and evaluation. Gradually, a couple begins to adjust their expectations and fantasies about marriage with reality. For couples who have lived together before marriage, there may be fewer surprises, yet, undoubtedly, as the two people explore their new roles, they will both negotiate a life-style based on each person's past experiences and present expectations.

Economic situations, as well as educational aspirations, may influence initial role delegation in the newly formed marriage. Traditional roles may be reversed in instances where the husband is still in college and has to depend on his wife for financial support.

Birth control now permits a couple to delay children until a time when both feel emotionally and financially prepared for this expense and personal commitment. Since most marriages are begun when people are in their twenties, most couples are not only involved in the marriage role but also in becoming established in an occupation (Levinson, 1977). As more women become involved in meaningful careers, decisions must be made as to when and if her career will be interrupted to bear children.

Early communication patterns set the tone in a marital relationship. Research (e.g., Reedy, Birren, & Schaie, 1981) confirms that good communication is more characteristic of marital relationships in early adulthood than in middle or late adulthood. Passion and sexual intimacy also seem to be more important to young adults, while loyalty and sensitivity to feelings may be stressed more among middle-aged and older adults. During courtship and the early portion of a marriage an important issue to be resolved is the extent to which the relationship leads to intimacy rather than idealization or disillusionment (Rhodes, 1977). In building an intimate relationship, each partner needs to find ways of relating that are mutually rewarding. A constructive marital relationship also depends on each partner assuming responsibility in the relationship, as well as their ability to negotiate differences and conflicts. During the early part of a marriage each partner also needs to relinquish unrealistic fantasies and idealizations, since romantic ideas, sooner or later, clash with reality and produce disillusionment.

The beginning of the martial relationship involves the establishment of a family unit apart from the families of origin. A couple must independently re-examine their knowledge about roles involved in a marriage,

A constructive marital relationship depends on each partner assuming responsibility in the relationship.

much of which has been based on their experiences in their family of origin. Some previous family practices may be considered and accepted, others modified or rejected. The task at hand is to come to an agreement as to which roles each marriage partner will perform and how each can find a meaningful life-style within the institution of marriage.

The Childbearing and Childrearing Years

Of course, not all married couples plan to have children. However, for the majority who do choose to have children a number of concerns arise. Recall from our discussion of family history and the life cycle that early adulthood, the time when most women give birth to children, also is the time period when many adults are busy trying to establish a career. It is not surprising, then, that it is during the early years of a child's life when parents report the greatest degree of dissatisfaction with marriage (Rollins & Feldman, 1970), possibly because of role conflict or overload. When the peaking of demands in family coincides with the peaking of demands in the occupational world, conflict may result. The childbearing and early childrearing stages of the family are the times when such peaking generally occurs.

During these periods, married women tend to drop out of the labor market; three-fifths of women who have preschoolers are full-time homemakers. Costs go up with children and financial resources often go down. Conversations between husbands and wives change from general topics and couple interests to a focus on children, and there is less companionship between husbands and wives. Wives may feel less able to share their problems with their husbands. Power may become more husband-centered, and there is less sharing of tasks around the house. The demands on husband-fathers and wife-mothers to engage in child care, housework, and companion roles increase. And, while parental and spousal role demands are up, occupational demands are peaking at the same time.

Jo Ann Aldous (1978) goes on to discuss further ideas about the childrearing years and the adjustments adolescents require a family to make.

Another stage of family conflict is the intersection of the adolescent's educational career and his parents' work careers. The discrepancy between parental income and the societal event of longer economic dependency of adolescents obtaining advanced education creates "life squeeze" stress.

To pay a youth's college expenses, family expenditures must increase by between 10 and 25 percent with two or three children, and with more children, they go up even more. These financial demands peak at the same time in all families, but financial remuneration patterns from different occupations do not peak at the same time, and the amount of their increase also varies.

This financial squeeze in the family life cycle may lead many older women back into the working world.

Postchildrearing Years/The Empty Nest

A time comes in a couple's life when their children become independent and begin to provide for themselves and form friendships outside the family unit. Instead of a parent-child relationship at this time, the interaction gradually changes to that of one adult relating to another adult.

This period is a time of reorganization for the parents where the focus of family life again may be oriented toward relationships between marital partners.

The beginning of the marital relationship involves the establishment of a family unit apart from the families of origin.

During the childrearing years, most aspects of a couple's lives focus on the children.

For couples who have learned to relate to each other through their children, they no longer have their children as props for their relationship. They must now rely more on their relationship with each other (Rhodes, 1977).

When their adolescents or youth leave home, some parents experience what has been called the **empty nest syndrome.** The relationship between strict role division and the empty nest syndrome has been identified through lengthy interviews with middle-aged women who were suffering from acute depression after their children had left home (Bart, 1973). The greater a mother's involvement with her children, the greater was her difficulty in living without them. Those women who defined themselves primarily in terms of their mother roles, whose entire lives had been wrapped up in their children, felt as though they had nothing to live for when offspring left the nest. They had dedicated themselves to the cultural mandate of living a selfless, nurturing life on behalf of spouse and children and expected some reward for this self-denial at the end of their childrearing years. What they expected was to share their adult children's lives, and when children failed to comply with this expectation, the women felt lost and suffered from depression. As one postparental woman put it, "I don't feel like I'm going anywhere. I feel just like I'm standing still, not getting anywhere" (Bart,

1973). All of these "supermothers," when asked what they were most proud of said, "My children." None mentioned an accomplishment of their own.

Marital Satisfaction and Conflict

Family sociologists have been interested in documenting the factors that contribute to marital satisfaction for a number of years. Some years ago Blood and Wolfe (1960) interviewed 900 Detroit housewives to find out how the length of their marriage and birth of children in the marriage are related to marital satisfaction. In general, they found that marital satisfaction declines in a linear fashion from the beginning of a marriage through thirty years of marriage. They also found that it simply was not the addition of children that contributed to marital dissatisfaction, since women in childless marriages reported the same decline in marital satisfaction over time. The drop in satisfaction for the childless wives was less over time than was the case for

Sociologists have been documenting for years the factors that contribute to marital satisfaction and dissatisfaction.

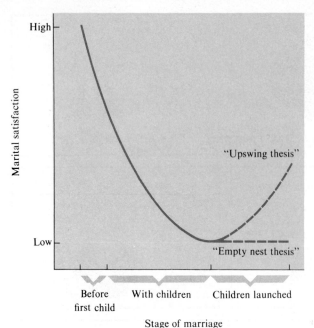

Figure 17.2 Relationship between marital satisfaction and stage of marriage.

"Do you recognize this pan as the one your wife used?"

women who had children, but it was a significant decline. The components of marital satisfaction in this investigation included love, companionship, children, understanding of mate, and standard of living. The decline in marital satisfaction over time was the same for all five components.

Other research suggests that marital satisfaction peaks in the first five years of marriage and then declines through the period when parents have adolescents (Pineo, 1961). In this investigation, after the youth left home marital satisfaction increased but never reached the level of the first five years. Support for this **upswing thesis** in marital satisfaction has been found in other studies as well (e.g., Glenn, 1975; Stinnett, Carter, & Montgomery, 1972). To a considerable degree, the issue of whether there is a continuing decline in marital dissatisfaction when adolescents leave home or whether there is an increase focuses on the concept of the empty nest syndrome described earlier. The two patterns of marital satisfaction suggested by the empty nest syndrome and the upswing thesis are shown in figure 17.2.

Several reasons for the upswing thesis have been offered by David Gutmann (1975, 1977). He suggests that since the divorce rate has increased, divorced couples who earlier in history were likely to be represented in the married group as maritally dissatisfied, are no longer in the middle-aged marital grouping. And, as men and women age from early adulthood to middle adulthood, aspects of their sex roles seem to reverse.

Women appear to be more assertive later in their married life, while men seem to show more affiliative and sensitive tendencies as they age. More about changes in sex roles in adulthood will appear later in this chapter.

There also is some evidence that if individuals do not assume marital and family roles according to the standard age-graded system in a culture, greater marital dissatisfaction may result. For instance, in one investigation (Nydegger, 1973) middle-class women indicated that when they married either at very young or old ages they were more dissatisfied with their marriage. In a similar fashion, men who married very young reported a low level of marital dissatisfaction. But, men who married when they were older, at age forty or beyond, indicated that they enjoyed their role as a parent and reported more marital satisfaction than men who married in their twenties and thirties. The increased marital satisfaction for the men who married later may have occurred because it allowed them to avoid the role conflict or overload created by the peaking of occupational and family demands in early adulthood. And, marital satisfaction is greater when a child is conceived after marriage than before (Russell, 1974).

One final note about marital satisfaction is important. Measuring marital satisfaction is not an easy task. Most of our information about marital satisfaction comes from self-reports by one or both marital partners—these self-reports may be contaminated by social desirability. That is, each of the partners may try to place themselves in a more positive light than is really

The family is a system of interacting individuals.

true and characterize their marriage as more satisfactory than it truly is. And, individuals vary in their willingness to disclose information about themselves, particularly on such sensitive issues as how satisfactory or conflicted one's marriage is. There has been an almost complete absence of observational approaches in the study of marital satisfaction and marital relationships. Some family sociologists also believe we should study marital adjustment more than satisfaction. In this case, marital adjustment is conceptualized in dyadic rather than individualistic terms (the strategy in much of the marital satisfaction literature).

Jay Belsky (1981) indicates that another strategy for assessing marital relationships would focus on marriage as a romance (emphasizing infatuation and sexuality) and as a friendship (emphasizing efficiency and mutuality). Belsky goes on to say that in the transition to parenthood, more stress may occur when the marriage is romance-oriented than when it is partnership-oriented.

For some years family sociologists have argued that marital satisfaction and family satisfaction are not the same thing (e.g., Reiss, 1971). In most cases, but not all, adults are not high on one of these factors and low on the other, but it often is the case that an adult is high on one of the factors and moderate on the other. For example, a husband may have a very enjoyable relationship with his wife that may include sexual satisfaction and companionship. By contrast, this same indivdual may not enjoy being around a noisy, intrusive child who wants his attention when he comes home from work, not to mention the likelihood that the child

also drains some of his wife's energy as well as attention. In such cases, the parenting role would be viewed with less satisfaction than the marital role by the husband, and in all likelihood, would lead this particular husband to report lower marital satisfaction than if the couple had not had children. Clearly, the link between marital and parenting roles is complex, and there are a myriad of combinations of events, attitudes, and situations that contribute to satisfaction in one or the other. In box 17.1, the link between marital relations and parenting is described in greater detail. Next, we look more closely at the parental role itself.

The Parental Role and Intergenerational Relationships

Earlier in this text we presented a great deal of information about parents, including ideas about reciprocal parent-child relationships, synchrony and asynchrony, the family as a system of interacting individuals, and the parenting strategies that seem to be most effective in rearing competent children. We also described the changing roles of parents during infancy, early childhood, middle and late childhood, and adolescence. At this time it would be helpful if you would either return to the sections of earlier chapters focused on the role of the family in infancy, childhood, and adolescence, or take several minutes and review in your head some of the most important things you remember from those earlier chapters about the role of parents in the child's development.

Social, Emotional, and Personality Development   503

Box 17.1
Marital Relations and Parenting

Jay Belsky's (1981) model of direct and indirect effects in the family system were described initially in chapter 6. His model is repeated here since the ideas have important implications for understanding the link between marital relations and parenting. Belsky's review of research on the link between marital relations and parenting follows.

One investigation of families in the infant's first month of life indicate that tension and conflict between marital partners are associated with problems in the mother's ability to competently feed the infant. In this same study, the husband's esteem for his wife as a mother, by contrast, was positively related to her feeding skills (Pedersen, Anderson, & Cain, 1977). Other information suggests that, on the basis of investigating changes in mother-infant reciprocity across the first month of the baby's life that the mother's ability to enjoy and affectionately interact with her infant, may, in part, be due to the quality of her relationship with her husband (Price, 1977).

The effects of marital relations on parenting, of course, are not all positive. In one investigation, the more husbands criticized and blamed their wives for various problems, the more these mothers showed negative orientations toward their five-month old offspring (Pedersen et al., 1977). And, when marital relationships are not satisfactory, parents, particularly mothers, may make compensatory (sometimes of an overprotective nature toward the child) investments in the parenting role (Vincent, Cook, & Messerly, in press).

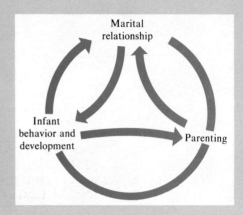

The possibility that the affect of the marital relationship on parenting may eventually touch the infant's development is indicated by recent research on child abuse and parental visiting patterns in neonatal intensive care nurseries. In one investigation, it was revealed that the quality of marriage predicted the frequency with which mothers visited their hospitalized premature infants (Minde, Marton, Manning, & Hines, 1980). And, in another study, infrequent visits to hospitalized infants was related to parenting disorders, such as child abuse (Faranoff, Kennell, & Klaus, 1972). It also has been discovered that divorce may be associated with prematurity and infant hospitalization—the possibility exists that this

---

In our culture it has been the standard to think that when you grow up you will get married and have children. Most parents still socialize their children in this manner, although in recent years, as divorce has become an epidemic, an increasing number of parents are adaptively socializing their offspring for more flexible adult roles, one of which may involve marriage and children, but instead might be that of an unmarried single adult or of marriage without children.

The Parental Role
In discussing the parental role, William Van Hoose and Maureen Worth (1982) point out some basic ideas about parenthood, as well as some of the myths that enshroud it. For many adults the parental role is well planned and coordinated with other roles in life and is

developed with an individual's economic situation in mind. For others the discovery that they are about to become a parent is a startling surprise. In either event, the prospective parents may have mixed emotions as well as romantic ideas and illusions about having a child. Parenting involves a number of interpersonal skills and emotional demands, yet there is often little formal education for this task. Most parents learn parenting practices from their own parents—some they accept, some they discard. And, husbands and wives may bring divergent viewpoints of parenting practices to the marriage. Unfortunately, when methods of parenting are passed from one generation to the next, both desirable as well as detrimental practices are perpetuated.

complex process could even be triggered by the infant who functions, inadvertently, as producer of his or her own development: infant development→marital relations→parenting→infant development (Belsky & Tolan, 1981).

Repeatedly, it has been argued by family sociologists that much of the difficulty that the birth of a first child creates is linked with the role strain experienced by spouses (e.g., Rollins & Galliger, 1979). With the arrival of the baby, husbands and wives must function not only as maintainers of a household, friends, and employees (at their places of work), but as parents as well (Nye & Berado, 1973). To the extent that the responsibilities of being a parent become a burden that overwhelms the mother and the father, it is likely that these other roles will be adversely affected. It has been frequently found that the degree of crisis experienced by a marital couple following the birth of the child is systematically tied to wives' physical exhaustion and lack of interest in sexual relations (Dyer, 1963; Hobbs, 1965; Hobbs & Wimbish, 1977; LeMasters, 1957).

And, while it is doubtful that successful parenting turns poor marriages into good ones, there is reason to believe that the shared activities the care of a child creates (like bathing, picture taking, and playing) can provide the opportunity for enjoyable marital interaction. One possible patterning of events in Belsky's model that this occurrence might produce is: parenting→marital relations→parenting→infant development→spousal relations.

The needs and expectations of parents have stimulated many myths about parenting (Okun & Rappaport, 1980): (1) the birth of a child will save a failing marriage; (2) as a possession or extension of the parent, the child will think, feel, and behave like the parents did in their childhood; (3) children will take care of parents in old age; (4) parents can expect respect and get obedience from their children; (5) having a child means that the parents will always have someone who loves them and be their best friend; (6) having a child gives the parents a "second chance" to achieve what they should have achieved; (7) if parents learn the right techniques they can mold their children to be what they want; (8) it's the parents fault when children fail; (9) mothers are naturally better parents than fathers; and (10) parenting is an instinct and requires no training.

In earlier times, women considered being a mother a full-time occupation. Currently, there is a tendency to have fewer children, and as birth control has become common practice, many people choose the time for children and the number of children they will raise. And, the number of one-child families is also increasing. Advances in medical practices also have decreased the risk of death and illness for both mother and child. Today, many women have never had to nurse their children through long bouts of serious illnesses wondering if their child would live or die. Instead of endurance, patience, fortitude and tenderness—the traditional virtues of women in all previous historical periods—we now have contraception and penicillin (Binstock, 1972).

Giving birth to fewer children and the reduced demands of child care free up a significant proportion of a woman's life span for other endeavors. Three such changes are: (1) as a result of the increase in working women there is less maternal investment; (2) men are more apt to invest a greater amount of time in fathering; and (3) parental care in the home is often supplemented by institutional care. As a result of these changes, questions of how to incorporate child care with other roles and responsibilies is frequently cited as an issue in the lives of many adults (Rossi, 1977).

The parenting role has other distinctions as well. Unlike most adult responsibilities the parenting role cannot be acceptably changed or discarded. We can quit one job and take another or we can go through retraining for an entirely different job. We also can divorce and remarry. However, once children are born, they require a commitment over a period of time; we cannot acceptably revert to nonparent status. Ideally, potential parents would realistically assess whether they are willing to make the extensive investment in time, physical energy, and emotional involvement required to rear competent children.

Intergenerational Relationships
In chapter 2, in discussing perspectives, we indicated that the concept of evolution has important implications for the study of life-span development. One line of research suggesting the need for an evolutionary perspective is intergenerational constancy and change (Baltes, Reese, & Lipsitt, 1980; Bengtson & Black, 1973; Clausen, 1972; Featherman, 1980; Riley, 1979). Examples of behavior systems involved in intergenerational relationships include fertility, parenting, and grandparenting (Baltes et al., 1980). And, in chapter 1, we described two different approaches that can be used to study intergenerational relations—cohort and lineage strategies.

While intergenerational relationships can be comprised of many different age segments in child and adult development, the age period of the life cycle that has received the most attention is middle adulthood—a time when adults often have adolescent-aged offspring and parents who have entered, or are beginning to enter, late adulthood. In discussing the role of middle-aged parents, Erik Erikson (1968) believes that it is important for parents at this point in the life cycle to assume some responsibility for the new generation of adults that are about to emerge. While Erikson does not argue that the transmission of values and attitudes to the next generation has to occur through parent-child or parent-adolescent rearing, his major focus clearly is on the important role parents play in the generativity process.

At the same time middle-aged parents may be working hard on trying to guide their adolescent offspring into mature youth or young adults capable of performing competently in a job and making autonomous decisions, they at the same time may have to deal increasingly with the aging of their own parents. A symposium at the 1981 annual meeting of the American Psychological Association called "The older generation: what is due, what is owed," focused on this latter set of intergenerational relationships. As part of this symposium, Louis Lowy (1981) described the nature of intergenerational relationships.

The adult at the chronological age of around forty or forty-five or fifty reaches what can be called **a filial crisis.** This is a time when parents can no longer be looked upon as a rock of support in times of emotional trouble or economic stress, but when they themselves may, and often do need, comfort, support and affection from their offspring. Or, to put it differently, when their offspring need to be depended upon in times of stress or trouble, or for advice, nurturance, or tangible financial or other type of assistance. In a filial crisis, adult sons or daughters do not take on a parental role vis á vis their aging parent, rather they take on a filial role (Lowy, 1977). In other words, they can be depended upon and therefore are dependable as far as the parent is concerned. A healthy resolution of this "filial crisis" leaves behind the rebellion against one's parents initiated during adolescence and quite often unresolved long after. One sees the parents now as more mature adults would see them, someone who has made peace with them. One sees them in a new perspective, as individuals with their own foibles, strengths and weaknesses, needs and rights, with a life history all of their own, that made them the persons they are now, and were before their own children were born. If the filial crisis is resolved successfully, the person has achieved filial maturity and the process of crisis resolution provides now an opportunity to adult children to prepare themselves eventually for their own aging, to cope with their own developmental tasks as they are getting older, and cope with the demands of their later years. Naturally, this is not a smooth process.

Lowy also discussed the issue of conflict between parents and their children.

It is my thesis that intergenerational conflict is essential for a healthy discharge of the normal tensions that exist among family members. It has been said that only in the cemetery is there absence of any conflict. But we want to engender a continuing sense of life and vitality among members of different generations, when grand- or great-grandchildren will be growing up with grand- or great-grandparents who will be in their eighties and nineties and can enjoy each others' company in a give-and-take relationship. Therefore, there must be opportunity for ventilation and expression and handling of conflict. When conflict becomes overwhelming, or when it ceases to be manageable by the families themselves and becomes destructive, a "third party" is needed to which families can turn in order to get help.

Lowy believes that the resolution of conflict is even more of an issue now that families span three and often four generations.

Another aspect of family relationships in adulthood that is receiving increased attention involves siblings, as we see next.

Sibling Relationships in Adulthood
While we have extensive information about siblings in childhood, we have very little knowledge about the nature of sibling relationships in adulthood (Lamb & Sutton-Smith, 1982). In one longitudinal study focused on stress and adaptation at different points in the adult life cycle, it was concluded that sibling perceptions change very little during the adult years (Lowenthal, Thurnher, & Chiriboga, 1975). There is support for the belief that same-sex adult sibling relationships are characterized by more rivalry and ambivalence than opposite-sex adult sibling relationships (Lowenthal et al., 1975; Croake & Hayden, 1980). There also is reason to believe that adult siblings who live in geographical proximity are more likely to be salient figures in the lives of adults than those who live far away (Sutton-Smith & Rosenberg, 1970).

One aspect of sibling relationships in adulthood that seems to have captured the attention of researchers is the sense of feeling affection or closeness toward a sibling (e.g., Allan, 1977; Cicirelli, 1980, 1981; Ross & Dalton, 1981). In one investigation of closeness in sibling relationships, sixty-five adults aged twenty-five to ninety-three were interviewed about their sibling relationships. Adults who felt "close" to their siblings placed emphasis on the family unit, revealed memories of shared experiences, and had frequent contact with their siblings (Ross & Dalton, 1981). Just as is true in childhood, there is evidence that siblings can be important socializing influences in adulthood, and that such influence involves both rivalry and affection.

Approximately 37 percent of all adult females are single.

The Diversity of Adult Life-Styles
A greater proportion of the adult population is now single than in the past. William Van Hoose and Maureen Worth (1982) describe the nature of single adulthood and some of the stereotypes about single adults.

Single Adults
In contrast to 4 to 5 percent of fifty-year-old adults who never marry, 8 to 9 percent of twenty-year-olds will never marry (Glick, 1979). For some being single is a preferred life-style. For others, however, being single did not occur because of their own choosing, but because of the death of a spouse, divorce, personal characteristics, or other circumstances that have hindered them in the selection of a mate. In fact at any given time about 30 percent of all adult males and 37 percent of adult females are unmarried (Macklin, 1980). One circumstance that has caused more women to remain single has been called the "marriage squeeze" (Glick & Carter, 1976). In the 1940s and 1950s a postwar baby boom occurred. Because of the custom of females marrying a male who is older, a shortage of males of desirable age developed in the 1970s. However, this discrepancy should slacken in the 1980s. Nonetheless, in the 1980s, there seems to be an increasing number of women who have difficulty finding a desirable mate. Some ideas about this dilemma are presented in box 17.2.

Common issues of single adults center around intimate relationships with other adults, confronting loneliness, and finding a place in society that is marriage-oriented. While some adults are legally single, they are involved in an intimate living arrangement with another person. The focus here, however, is on those adults who are not currently married or living with someone else.

There is a history of myths and stereotypes that encompass being single, ranging from "the swinging single" to the "desperately lonely, suicidal single" (Libby & Whitehurst, 1977). Most singles, of course, are somewhere in the middle of such extremes. Singles are often challenged by others to get married so they no longer will be selfish, irresponsible, impotent, frigid, and immature (Edwards, 1977). Clearly, though, there are advantages to being single—time to make decisions about the course of life you want to follow, time to develop the personal resources to meet goals, freedom to make autonomous decisions and pursue your own schedule and interests, opportunity to explore new places and try out new things, and availability of privacy (Edwards, 1977).

Today there is more flexibility to choose a particular life-style. This freedom partially explains why some adults choose to marry later in life and why the number of people aged thirty-five and under who are single is rapidly growing. One factor in this choice is the changing attitudes of many women toward careers and personal fulfillment. Some women choose to develop a career before assuming marriage responsibilities. Some men also use their early adult years for pursuits other than marriage. Birth control devices and changing attitudes about premarital sex make it possible for single adults to explore their sexuality outside the bounds of marriage.

Many single adults cite personal freedom as one of the major advantages of being single. One woman who never married commented "I enjoy knowing that I can satisfy my own whims without someone else's interferences. If I want to wash my hair at two o'clock in the morning, no one complains. I can eat when I'm hungry and watch my favorite television shows without contradictions from anyone. I enjoy these freedoms. I would feel very confined if I had to adjust to another person's schedule."

And, some adults never marry. Initially, they are perceived as living glamorous, exciting lives. However, once the young woman reaches her late twenties and the young man his early thirties there is increasing societal pressure on them to "settle down." If a woman

Looking for Mr. . . . Anybody

Don't look now, but there's a large gray elephant in the room and nobody's talking about it.

Well, not exactly nobody. Many unattached women seem to talk about it a lot—in some cases even obsessively—though rarely in mixed company.

"It" is the *Great Man Shortage,* which happens to be the title of a book by William Novak.

Novak is a gentle, gray-suited, bespectacled, thirty-three-year-old man who looks more like an accountant than a writer and who is also—he hastens to add—a happily married Boston suburbanite. Until about four years ago, though, he lived among the ranks of the single males, a fact which he believes lends credibility to his conclusions about the relatively greater frustrations of single women compared to single men.

He had barely announced the title of his book and lecture to an overflow audience recently when an attractive older woman in a lavender silk blouse fired off the first question to a gale of knowing laughter from the heavily female audience: "How many have you brought with you?"

Novak's view is that there is a lot of truth in the observation-fear-belief commonly held by more or less liberated women in their late twenties, thirties, and forties that all the good men around are either married or gay.

And it's true both quantitatively and qualitatively, says Novak.

The quantitative part, of course, doesn't raise too many hackles. According to 1980 United States Census figures, for every 100 men over fifteen who have never married or are widowed or divorced, there are 123 women; for blacks, the ratio is 100 men for every 133 women.

Even in midlife, well before the ages at which women's life expectancies outdistance men's, the ratios begin to get worse: for every 100 unattached men aged thirty-five to thirty-nine, there are 124 women; between forty and forty-four, there are 128 available women for every 100 men, and between the ages of forty-five and fifty-four, there are 159 available women for every 100 men.

According to census figures, this imbalance is compounded by the fact that men, on the average, marry women 2.3 years younger than themselves, which makes the odds especially tough for women born in the baby boom years. Furthermore, 83 percent of divorced men eventually marry, while only 75 percent of divorced women do.

But it's the "quality gap" that packs the wallop in Novak's message.

"This is a bit anxiety-provoking and depressing," begins Novak, who quickly adds, "and the best way to cope is to be funny." The quality gap, Novak believes stems from the fact that over the last thirteen years or so, the combination of the feminist movement and women's greater tendency to seek therapy when their personal relationships don't work out has made women, overall, outgrow the available men emotionally.

Beside the therapy gap, Novak adds, most single men still tend to treat women in terms of beliefs about feminism that are often as much as five or six years out of date.

Some men tell Novak there is a shortage of good women, too, and want to know, "Where can I meet the women you quote?" Men also tell him they believe women's talk and women's real feelings do not always line up, that women sometimes seem to sabotage their relationships, that they're ambivalent about settling down, that they have impossibly high standards for men, that they're afraid to fall in love because they get dependent and moody and that it is all very confusing, as one man asked Novak, "Do they want us to cry all the time now?"

To which attitude Novak responds, "You may not accept that if you're a woman, and I don't accept that, but that is reality for some men. Some men don't understand what women mean by a lack of intimacy."

wants to bear children, she may feel a sense of urgency to marry before her childbearing days diminish. This is the period when many single adults make a decision to marry or to remain single.

Formerly Married Adults

William Van Hoose and Maureen Worth (1982) continue their description of single adults by evaluating the lives of the formerly married—each year through divorce, separation, desertion, or the death of a spouse, many adults become single. In our discussion of child development in earlier chapters we focused on the stress

The Great Man Shortage idea took root in Novak's mind during an interview for his marijuana book, when a "terrific, attractive, intelligent" woman lit up and began rambling, mentioning that she hadn't met an interesting man in six months and hadn't had a date for a year. She added the same was true of her friends, too.

Novak couldn't figure it out. "Laura," aged thirty, had everything going for her. He looked at his wife's friends, one of whom told him, "I can't even meet a man I don't want to go out with." He looked around at parties, where there seemed always to be 50, 70, 90 percent more women than men.

Women were out there, he noticed, taking courses, going to restaurants, joining clubs and they all "seemed to be very aware there didn't seem to be many good men."

He is quick to add that not all single women find it difficult to connect with men, not all single women even want to meet men, and that he doesn't "mean to imply that it's terrific for single men. But when all is said and done," Novak says, "there are a lot of bright and talented women not meeting members of the opposite sex. When women say there's a shortage of good, available counterparts, I think they're right. And I think it's important that I, a man, say that."

Grateful nods from the women in the audience, who seem to have been dropped into their seats by careful, age-conscious demographers, and thoughtful-to-understanding nods from the sprinkling of men.

The whole thing does depress many women, Novak observes to more vigorous nodding, because society has conditioned women to assume their lack of a marriage partner is their own fault.

"A lot of women at these lectures come up to me afterward," says Novak, "and say 'You haven't told me anything new, but at least I can send this to my mother.' "

The feminist movement, says Novak, "has achieved a lot," and in many of the "outer modalities," has enabled women to catch up to men in terms of success, power, money and the like.

Simultaneously, Novak adds, "There were also a lot of inner resources—therapy, consciousness-raising, feminist literature—and these appealed to the gut issues; women built on these resources. It has turned out that (in external terms) there wasn't all that much to catch up to, while internally women were leaving men far behind."

Today, Novak says, "There is simply no comparison between what women have gone through and what men have gone through," and he notes that, except for a few, tiny clusters around the country, there has been no comparably intense men's movement.

The eligible men around today for women in their late twenties, their thirties, forties and beyond are often, Novak says, "disappointing as people. They might be successful in their careers but in terms of human relationships, they seem to be lacking something. They're often unable to tolerate intimacy and commitment," which women at least seem to find in female friendships.

"Women are really saying to men: 'You don't have to earn all the money anymore, and I don't want to have to do all the emotional work,' " Novak says.

"The surprising thing," he adds, "is that these comments by women are made with little or no anger. . . . It's not a man-hating ideology. The women's comments show disappointment, a wish that things were not this way; in fact, you more often see humor than anything else."

To wit, an anecdote that brings down the house: a thirty-seven-year-old woman told Novak, "I'm no longer waiting for a man on a white horse. Now I'd settle for the horse."

Source: Forman, 1981.

---

and adaptation such life events instigate. And, we emphasized the role parents and ex-spouses play in mediating stress for children in many of these circumstances. Here we focus primarily on the effects of such events on the adults themselves.

The transition from being married to being single is often marked by grieving focused on the former relationship. This is true even when the marriage ends in divorce. Holidays may be a particulary difficult time for those individuals who are separated from their children or for those who remember previous times when a spouse was present.

At present, one out of three families is affected by divorce.

The process of separation and divorce is usually complex and emotionally charged.

Divorced Adults In many respects divorced and widowed adults experience the same emotions. In both instances the individuals experience the death of a relationship and next to a death of a spouse, a divorce causes the most trauma in the lives of individuals (Krantzler, 1974). Whether an adult initiates the divorce or is divorced by a spouse seems to have little impact on the grieving process. However, factors related to emotional problems and poor adjustment include a sudden or unexpected separation and an unwanted divorce (Spanier & Castro, 1979; Weiss, 1975).

At present, divorce is increasing annually by 10 percent and one out of every three families is affected. And, since the median age for divorce is thirty-eight many divorced people must rear dependent children (Messinger, Walker, & Freeman, 1978). Although divorce has increased for all socioeconomic groups, those in disadvantaged groups have a higher incidence of divorce (Norton & Glick, 1976). Youthful marriage, low educational level, and low income are linked with an increased divorce rate. So too is premarital pregnancy. In one investigation, half of the women who were pregnant before marriage failed to live with their husband for more than five years (Sauber & Corrigan, 1970).

For those who do divorce the process of separation and divorce is usually complex and emotionally charged. Yet despite such emotional turmoil, Mavis Hetherington (Hetherington, Cox, & Cox, 1978) reported that of forty-eight divorced couples observed, six of these couples had sexual intercourse during the first two months after separation. Prior social scripts and patterns of interaction are hard to break. Robert Weiss (1975) suggests that although divorce is a marker event in the relationship between spouses, it often does not signal the end of the relationship. He believes that the attachment to each other endures regardless of whether the former couple respects, likes, or is satisfied with the present relationship.

Further information about the divorce/separation process suggests that former spouses often alternate between feelings of seductiveness and hostility (Hunt & Hunt, 1977). They also may have thoughts of reconciliation. And, while at times they may express love toward their former mate, the majority of feelings are negative and include anger and hate. Divorce, then, is a complex emotional process for adults, as well as children.

Sex Differences in Divorce Divorce may have a different effect on a woman than a man. For example, one investigation has found that divorce is more traumatic for women than for men, while the majority of both sexes indicate that the period before the decision to divorce is the most stressful (Albrecht, 1980). And, women who have gained much of their identity through the role of wife and mother are particularly vulnerable after divorce. Many divorced women need to work outside the home and may not be adequately prepared for managing a new job and home responsibility. Four out of five divorced women have school-aged children (Women's Bureau, U.S. Bureau of the Census, 1979). Women, more often than men, must also cope with less income (Santrock & Warshak, 1979).

The term **displaced homemaker** describes the dilemma of many divorced or widowed women. These women always assumed that their work would be in the home. Although their expertise at managing a home may be considerable, future employers do not recognize this experience as work experience. Donna is typical of this type of woman. She married young and at eighteen she had her first child. Her work experience consisted of a part-time job as a waitress while in high school. Now Donna is thirty-two and has three children ages fourteen, twelve, and six. Her husband divorced her and married again. The child support payments are enough for food, but little is left for rent, clothing, and other necessities. Without any marketable skills, Donna is working as a sales clerk in a local department store. She cannot afford a housekeeper and worries about the children being unsupervised while she works, particularly on Saturdays and summer vacations. Creating a positive single identity is essential for these divorced adults so that they can come to grips with their loneliness, lack of autonomy, and financial hardship (Carter, 1977; Hancock, 1980).

Men, however, do not go through a divorce unscathed. They usually have fewer rights to their children, experience a decline in income, and receive less emotional support. The separation/divorce process also may have negative effects on a man's career (Hetherington et al., 1978).

What accounts for the increased divorce rate in the United States? Aside from the social sanctioning of divorce, it appears that the major causes of divorce are intrinsically bound in what our American society expects of marriage, discussed earlier in this chapter. When such unrealistic demands fall short, adults assume that the solution is to divorce.

Remarriage and the Stepfamily   The number of remarriages in which children are involved has been steadily growing. Now about 10 to 15 percent of all households in the United States are comprised of stepfamilies (Espinoza & Newman 1979). Labels applied to remarried families include stepfamilies, blended families, and reconstituted families (Kompara, 1979).

Unfortunately, much of our stepparenting knowledge is not empirically based. Folklore has painted the stepmother as "wicked" and "a witch." Childhood stories of Cinderella and Hansel and Gretal both portray the stepmother in the role of wicked woman. While the stepfather has not been stereotyped as negatively in children's literature, he often is regarded, at best, as taking on the responsibility of stepchildren out of love for his new spouse.

The word stepparent itself is ambiguous; its plural definitions include "parent," "stepparent," and "nonparent" (Fast & Cain, 1966). In our American culture the stepparent is encouraged to accept the role of the parent; however, stepparents cannot totally assume the roles of mother or father; they also are nonparents. With regard to three important parental functions—biological-reproductive, financial, and socialization—a stepparent cannot assume the biological role, in the case of the stepfather financial obligations for a child often are shared with the natural father, and the socialization process often has to be shared with the natural parent as well.

Some researchers have found no differences between stepparent and intact families (e.g., Duberman, 1973), while others have found significant differences (Bowerman & Irish, 1962). While the literature on relationships in stepparent families is mixed, there are some difficulties with which members of a stepparent family have to cope. When a remarriage occurs, adjustment to the new family may be overwhelming. The mother who remarries not only has to adjust to having another father for her children but also has to adapt to being a wife again. There may not be time for the husband-wife relationship to develop in stepfamilies. The children are a part of this new family from the beginning, a situation that leaves little time for the couple to spend time alone and grow with each other (Visher & Visher, 1978).

As single parents, many women find their self-image improves because they discover that they can support themselves and their family. The divorced woman's independence and performance in both the maternal and paternal role may be difficult to relinquish when she remarries (Westoff, 1977).

The stepfather also has many stressful situations to deal with when he becomes a husband and father simultaneously. The stepfather must remember that he is following a preceding parent, who may still be around to see his children from time to time. The stepparent should be a supplement, then, rather than a replacement for the natural father. The stepfather may feel that the nuclear family still exists somehow, and the stepfamily, in which he is a major cog, is an appendage. Family sociologists point out that the relationship in a first marriage often does continue in some way when children are involved (e.g., Stinnett & Walters, 1977). The child often continues to see the natural father and when this happens regularly, the stepfather is confronted with his nonparent role. The stepfather needs time to develop rapport, trust, and love with his stepchildren and wife. During this developing phase, problems may arise. When the remarriage is in its infancy, the stepfather may encounter difficulty in disciplining his stepchildren. If the stepfather left his own children, he may feel guilty and resent caring for his stepchildren. The mother also may feel that punishment is dealt out in a seemingly undemocratic way to her own children by the stepfather. Blood ties run deep and favoritism may occur—whether it does or does not, the members of a stepparent family often think it exists.

In one investigation it was found that the relationship between stepchildren and stepfathers was more negative when the stepfather had been married previously (Duberman, 1973). These fathers may move too quickly into the prerogatives and authority of a parent without making allowance for their stepchildren's initial suspiciousness and resistance (Wallerstein & Kelly, 1980).

After a divorce and remarriage, the newly formed couple may begin to feel hemmed in; after all, the divorce was the result of failing to make a relationship work. This may create a distancing in the remarriage in order to protect oneself from getting hurt (Stinnett & Walters, 1977). Such fears do not create a harmonious marriage and may interact with any parent-child difficulties that may arise.

In a remarriage names can create difficulties. What does the stepchild call his or her stepfather, for example? There is somewhat of a double bind. What may make the stepfather pleased and feel accepted may be very disturbing to the natural father. The child's last name may also create problems. The fact that a child has a different last name than the other family members may be embarrassing for all members. However, the natural father may insist that the child retain his last name. Of course a stepfather sharing his name with a child may be an indication of his acceptance. Approximately one-third of the adoptions in this country include a stepchild and a stepfather—so, many stepfather families are making the name change.

Recurrent in the remarriage literature are references to money problems (Roosevelt & Lofas, 1977). Although the divorced mother may bring some financial support to the newly formed stepparent family, the stepfather usually is saddled with the major financial burden—not only does he have to support his new family, but he often has to pay alimony and child support to his ex-wife. The reality of child support either coming in or going out of the stepfamily can produce worry and resentment. It can be a burden that is next to impossible to carry. The current wife may resent the stepfather's payments to the former wife and the former wife may resent what he gives to his present wife. And, money may become a symbol of love, used as a weapon in a remarriage. For example, the child may be denied something until the natural father increases child support, even when in reality the stepfather could and would have been able to make the purchase—another instance when the stepfather encounters the reality of the nonparent role.

Remarriages may suffer from some of the same problems that a first marriage encountered, but often in more intense and extensive ways since more individuals are involved. One of the pluses the remarriage may have going for it is the maturity of the adults involved. The growth and the psychological changes that a person undergoes between twenty and thirty years of age may help the success of a remarriage. The mother who has been divorced once usually does not want to go through it again. She may still vividly remember the pain and the hurt of the first marriage and the ensuing divorce. Such bad visions and motivation for success may help cement the stepparent family together when strained circumstances occur.

Relationships

So far in this chapter we have talked primarily about relationships within families. But peer relations, like sibling relations, do not end when we enter adulthood. Initially we will describe the nature of peer relations and friendships in adulthood and then focus on some important aspect of relationships within and outside of families—attachment, love, and intimacy.

Peers and Friendships

During the course of adult development we come into contact with many adults other than our marital partners. For the most part, we meet acquaintances through our activities at school or college, at work, through other adults' children, or in community activities. In one investigation of friendships in early adulthood, the close acquaintances of 275 women, whose average age was twenty-nine years, were likely to be next-door neighbors. The friendships of their children increased the likelihood that the mothers would be friends. These women tended to affiliate with other women whose marital status was similar to their own, who were close to their own age, had about the same number of children, and were at about the same level of family income. When women lived farther away from each other, the fact that they were friends was more likely to be related to occupation and education than in the cases where the women lived close to each other.

One life-span developmental study of friendships found that the newly married have more friends than adolescents, middle-aged adults, or the elderly. During early adulthood friendships that were established earlier may dissipate, particularly in the case of young adults who get married. Decisions must be made about whether the couple will see such friends separately or as a couple. And, often friendships develop that are based on a four-party relationship (two couples) rather than a two-party relationship (one couple).

In middle adulthood, many friends are old friends. Still, new acquaintances may develop, often through formal organizations, which middle-aged adults participate in at a fairly high rate (Troll, 1975). During middle adulthood, closeness and convenience seem to be less salient in the nature of friendships than in early adulthood. In one investigation of 150 middle-aged adults who had moved within the last five years, a majority of the individuals named as their best friend someone from the locale where they had lived before (Hess, 1971).

Early and Middle Adulthood

Often, friendships between children determine friendships between adults.

Attachment and Love

The concept of attachment was extensively discussed in chapter 6, which focused on infant social, emotional, and personality development. Indeed, many researchers and theoreticians have emphasized that the concept of attachment should be used only during the period of infancy. One recent effort, however, suggests that the concept may be successfully used to study other aspects of the life cycle as well (Antonucci, 1981). Recall from our discussion of infant attachment that some stability and consistency in the patterns of both infant and mother interactive behaviors have been found (e.g., Waters, 1978). And different patterns of infant attachment have been able to predict with reasonable accuracy play and problem solving behavior in the preschool years (e.g., Matas, Arend, & Sroufe, 1978).

Toni Antonucci (1981) studied the social interactive/social supportive behaviors of adolescents and considered them in relation to the adolescents' own attitudes about future social interaction (specifically age at marriage) and their own actual behaviors (reported eleven years after high school graduation). The data used in this investigation came from Project Talent, an enormous effort to study the personal, educational, and experiential factors that promote or inhibit the development of human talent. Of the original sample of 400,000 ninth to twelfth graders in Project Talent, 4,000 subjects were selected for study by Antonucci. High school students were asked several questions that could be considered to reflect attachment to family and peers. The high school attachment measures included discussion of future plans with father and with mother; age at which marriage is intended; and activity level in affiliative high school activities, such as groups and clubs. The age at which the respondent first married was assessed. And, in adulthood, questions focused on such factors as marital satisfaction, parenting satisfaction, and happiness in social life.

Attachment is a concept that can be studied and observed throughout the life cycle.

What were labeled as attachment behaviors in adolescence were linked with social behavior and interaction in adulthood. Some of the findings indicate that what has been described as insecure attachment in infancy may have some applicability to later social interactions as well. For example, adolescents who date very early and often marry early may be showing a form of insecure attachment, according to Antonucci. Adolescents who engage in appropriate and varied sex-typed behaviors, such as affiliative behaviors for boys and achievement/vocational related behaviors for girls may be expressing a more secure attachment. Indeed, these latter adolescents were more likely to report high levels of marital satisfaction, life satisfaction, and a happier social life some eleven years after their high school graduation.

Love has been the domain of poets and novelists more than it has been the province of scientific psychology. While not easily defined and measured, love, nevertheless, is a pervasive aspect of interpersonal relationships in adulthood. And, many adults spend hour after hour thinking about love, anticipating a romantic love relationship, watching themes of love on soap operas, reading about such themes in magazines or books, and listening to music filled with references to love. One psychologist, Zick Rubin (1970, 1973) has attempted to measure one type of love, romantic love. He developed two scales, one for liking, and one for loving. Rubin believes that liking refers to the sense that someone is similar to us and involves our positive evaluation of that person; loving, on the other hand, indexes being close to someone and includes dependency, a more selfless orientation to help the other person, and qualities of exclusiveness and absorption. The last several qualities—those of exclusiveness and absorption—seem to differentiate liking and loving more than others. If you just like someone, that individual probably does not preoccupy your thoughts and you are not likely to be overly concerned that she likes someone else. By contrast, love stimulates a great deal of preoccupation with another person, including feelings of possessiveness.

Attachment and love seem to be important to our survival and well-being throughout life (e.g., Bowlby, 1969; Spitz, 1945; Reedy et al., 1981). Recall that the data on marital satisfaction suggest love does not increase as marriages age, but instead often decreases. We know little about what keeps love alive and well as lovers grow older, but there is increased interest in studying various dimensions of attachment across the life span (e.g., Antonucci, 1976, 1981; Hartup & Lempers, 1973; Troll & Smith, 1976; Weinraub, Brooks, & Lewis, 1977). Recently, Margaret Reedy, James Birren, and K. Warner Schaie (1981) examined the theoretical and research literature on the developmental nature of attachment in adult love relationships and found that two themes are suggested. The first theme indicates that relationships move toward deeper levels of intimacy over time and the passionate fires of youthful love are somehow transformed into the deeper, more serene and tender love of advanced age (e.g., Levinger, 1974). From this perspective, physical attraction, perceived similarity of the loved one, self-disclosure, romance, and passion are important in new relationships, while security, loyalty, and mutual emotional interest in the relationship sustain love relationships over long periods of time. According to George

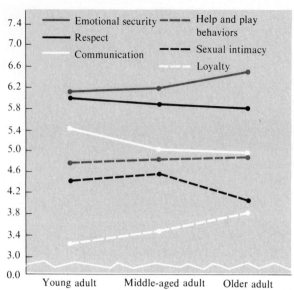

Figure 17.3 Changes in the components of satisfying love relationships across the life span.

Levinger (1974), "mutuality" supports love relationships over time and occurs when partners share knowledge with each other, assume responsibility for each other's satisfaction, and share private information that governs their relationship.

The second theme in the literature on the development of love relationships suggests two basic marital types, *institutional* and *companion* (Hicks & Platt, 1970). The **institutional relationship** is oriented toward tradition—loyalty and security are primary aspects of the relationship. And, normative rules for behavior are sex-differentiated along traditional lines. The husband's role is more instrumental, while the wife's role is more expressive. By contrast, the **companionship relationship** stresses the importance of the affective interaction, including passion, expressions of love, rapport, communication, and respect. Investigators have found that over time tradition may replace companionship as the primary bonding force in love relationships (e.g., Feldman, 1964; Pineo, 1961). For example, in a twenty-year longitudinal study, it was found that decline in marital satisfaction from youth to middle adulthood was associated with decline in companionship, demonstration of affection and passion, common interests, and communication (Pineo, 1961).

In order to further explore the nature of age and sex differences in the characteristics of satisfying love relationships, Reedy, Birren, and Schaie (1981) studied 102 happily married couples in early (average age was twenty-eight), middle (average age was forty-five), and late adulthood (average age was sixty-five). As can be seen in figure 17.3, age differences in the nature of satisfying love relationships resulted. The idea that passion and sexual intimacy are relatively more important in early adulthood, while tender feelings of affection and loyalty are relatively more important to later-life love relationships, was supported. And, it was indicated that young adult lovers rate communication as more characteristic of their love relationships than their counterparts in middle and late adulthood. This result, combined with the data about emotional security and loyalty being more important in later life, supports the second major theme on the development of love relationships—that of distinguishing between institutional and companionship aspects of love.

Aside from the age differences, however, there were some striking similarities in the nature of satisfying love relationships. At all ages, emotional security was ranked as the most important factor in love, followed by respect, communication, help and play behaviors, sexual intimacy, and loyalty. Clearly, then, there is a great deal more to love than sex. These results indicate that a new historical trend in the quality of relationships may be emerging. While in the past decade there was extensive interest in individual freedom and independence, these data suggest a historical shift toward security, fidelity, trust, and commitment in relationships. This historical trend mirrors the theme of Daniel Yankelovich's popular book, *New Rules in American Life: Searching for Self-Fulfillment in a World Turned Upside Down* (1981), in which he elaborates on the changing orientation of adults away from self-interest toward an ethic of commitment to others.

The findings of Reedy, Birren, and Schaie (1981) also suggest that the nature of love in satisfying relationships is different for men and women. Women rated emotional security as more important in love than men did. No sex differences were found for communication and sexual intimacy, and somewhat suprisingly, men, more than women, rated loyalty as more characteristic of their love relationship.

While the research just reported suggests that intimacy is a more central factor in a satisfying love relationship as marriages age, life-span theorist Erik Erikson believes that early adulthood is the period when the development of intimacy becomes a crisis.

Intimacy versus Isolation
Erik Erikson believes that intimacy should come after individuals are well on their way to achieving a stable and successful identity. The development of intimacy, in Erikson's view, is another life crisis—if intimacy is not developed in early adulthood, the person may be left with what Erikson refers to as isolation.

Erikson (1968) refers to intimacy in terms of both sexual relationships and friendships. He comments:

As the young individual seeks at least tentative forms of playful intimacy in friendship and competition, in sex play and love, in argument and gossip, he is apt to experience a peculiar strain, as if such tentative engagement might turn into an interpersonal fusion amounting to a loss of identity and requiring, therefore, a tense inner reservation, a caution in commitment. Where a youth does not resolve such a commitment, he may isolate himself and enter, at best, only stereotyped and formalized interpersonal relations; or he may, in repeated hectic attempts and dismal failures, seek intimacy with the most improbable of partners. For where an assured sense of identity is missing, even friendships and affairs become desperate attempts at delineating the fuzzy outlines of identity by mutual narcissistic mirroring; to fall in love means to fall in love with one's mirror image, hurting oneself and damaging the mirror.

An inability to develop meaningful relationships with others during young adulthood can be harmful to an individual's personality. It may lead him or her to repudiate, ignore, or attack those who appear frustrating. Erikson (1968) asserts that such situations can account for the shallow, almost pathetic attempts of youth to merge themselves with a "leader." Many youth want to be apprentices or disciples of the leaders and adults who will shelter them from the harm of an "outgroup" world. If this fails, and Erikson believes that it must, then sooner or later the individual will recoil into a self-search to discover where he or she went wrong. Such introspection sometimes leads to painful feelings of isolation and depression and may contribute to mistrust of others and restrict the individual's willingness to act on his or her own initiative.

One classification of intimacy suggests five styles of interaction: intimate, preintimate, stereotyped, pseudointimate, and isolated (Orlofsky, Marcia, & Lesser, 1973). The **intimate** individual forms and maintains one or more deep and long-lasting love relationships. The **preintimate** individual has mixed emotions about commitment—this ambivalence is reflected in the strategy of offering love without any obligations or long-lasting bonds. In most instances, the **stereotyped** individual has superficial relationships that tend to be dominated by friendship ties with same-sex rather than opposite-sex individuals. The **pseudointimate** individual appears to be maintaining a long-lasting heterosexual attachment, but the relationship has little or no depth or closeness. Finally, the **isolated** individual withdraws from social encounters and has little or no intimate attachment to same- or opposite-sex individuals. Occasionally the isolate shows signs of developing interpersonal relations, but usually such interactions are anxiety provoking. One investigation indicated that intimate and preintimate individuals are more sensitive to their partners' needs, as well as more open in their friendships, than individuals characterized by the other three intimacy statuses (Orlofsky, 1976).

Research with both college males and females has indicated that individuals who attain a stable sense of identity are more likely to attain intimacy than to remain at one of the other four intimacy stages. By contrast, students who are characterized by foreclosure, moratorium, and diffusion identities show more variable levels of intimacy (Kacerguis & Adams, 1978). This work supports Erikson's belief that identity development is closely linked (and perhaps even an important precursor) to intimacy.

How do researchers investigate intimacy? The strategy usually is the same as in the search for pinning down the adolescent's identity; often, a questionnaire is developed that focuses on various aspects of intimacy. One such instrument is the Yufit Intimacy-Isolation Questionnaire, which has twenty intimacy questions (for example, "Do you lead an active social life? Talk with people about their innermost problems? Are you consistent in giving affection?") and twenty isolation questions (for example, "Do you avoid excitement or emotional tension? Do you often feel unnoticed in a group?").

Personality Development

One elusive but important aspect of personality development in adulthood is the concept of maturity. Although defining maturity is difficult, we will attempt to describe some criteria that seem to characterize maturity in adulthood. An issue that crops up in any discussion of personality focuses on continuity and change—we will evaluate the extent to which there is continuity and change in personality as an individual grows from the beginning of early adulthood to the end of middle adulthood. In the last part of our discussion of personality we emphasize the self and aspects of the self-system in adulthood, stressing the importance of self-awareness and possible transitions in self-development. Also discussed are various themes of sex-role and moral development in adulthood.

Maturity

Maturity is not easy to define. Take just a minute and think about what the concept of maturity means to you. One way to define maturity is the individual's ability to competently cope with changing aspects of adult life. Thus, a mature person in early adulthood might have different characteristics than a mature person in middle adulthood. If we were to follow Erik Erikson's suggestions, then, a mature young adult would be characterized by the ability to be intimate and to give

and accept love, and he or she would have a stable sense of identity. He or she also would have a strong interest in productive work and be successful in an occupation. To the extent that such statements characterize a young adult, that person would be considered mature.

Clearly, though, it is difficult to get experts to agree on exactly what the criteria for maturity are. Many humanistic psychologists, for example, stress that maturity involves self-perception. For instance, James Birren and Margaret Reedy (1978) indicate that in the mature person there is a fairly close fit between self-image, ideal image, and the way other people see the individual, while descrepancies between these aspects of the self characterize the immature person.

Most social scientists recognize that a mature person is capable of adapting and coping with various life events and experiences. Such flexibility indicates that maturity is not a terminal state, but rather a process that develops throughout the life span. For example, as the individual enters middle adulthood, a common perception is that there is too much to do in life yet too little time to do it—recall our earlier statement that the 1980 census data suggest that middle-aged adults feel more hurried than any other adult age group. While in early adulthood the mature individual may go full steam ahead in work and career, he or she may have to learn to pull back so that he or she won't feel overburdened. By middle adulthood, mature individuals have usually developed a set of strategies that allow them to competently cope with the physical and emotional stresses that they will experience in the middle years of their life.

By combining some of the most important ideas in Erik Erikson's and Lawrence Kohlberg's theories, David McClelland (McClelland, Constanian, Regalado, & Stone, 1978) believes that the following four stages represent a developmental progression of maturity.

Stage I: **Receptivity.** The individual shows respect for authority or tradition. He or she behaves properly, decently, or obediently.

Stage II: **Autonomy.** The individual is self-reliant, can make up his or her own mind about things and is not always dependent on others. He or she shows willpower, determination, or courage.

Stage III: **Assertion.** The individual does well in a vocation, develops skills, speaks well, and is able to influence others.

Stage IV: **Mutuality.** The individual understands other points of view and is interested in serving others as part of the common good for both parties.

From McClelland's perspective, then, a person is more mature when he or she shows mutuality than when he or she displays assertion, autonomy, or receptivity. And he believes that mutuality is more characteristic of individuals at the end of early adulthood than when they were younger. McClelland's ideas conform to the data on satisfying love relationships collected by Reedy, Birren, and Schaie (1981) and Daniel Yankelovich's (1981) thesis that as we live through the 1980s we are becoming a society more concerned with commitment to others than commitment to self. And, McClelland's mutuality thesis supports both Erikson's and Kohlberg's belief that maturity in early adulthood is likely to involve more mature reciprocal relationships and reasoning about such relationships.

In sum, though, no one has come up with a set of criteria that everyone can agree on when the problem of defining maturity is raised. Next, we will see that social scientists also do not agree on the extent to which there is stability and continuity in adult development as opposed to change.

Change and Continuity

The question of whether adult personality development involves a great deal of change or whether it is more continuous and stable involves a number of complex issues, so complex that some prominent developmental psychologists, such as Leon Yarrow (1981), argue that whether or not individuals show constancy or change or whether certain characteristics show continuity over time are questions that not only are too simple, but may no longer have meaning. The findings with regard to continuity and change in personality, indeed, are complex when we take into account the social context in which indiviudals live and develop, the particular characteristics being measured, the measuring instruments being used, the developmental period at which assessments are made, the dynamic factors that influence transformation, and ultimately, the criteria used to define continuity.

There are many forms to the constancy-change issue, and the developmental discontinuity thesis has been set forth in various versions. In its mildest form, it seems to mean only that humans have the capacity for change across the entire life span, a statement that would cause no ripples among most social scientists. But in its stronger form, the emphasis on developmental discontinuity has been troublesome for many psychologists. The discontinuity contention, in its strong form, declares that early development has little implication for later development, that is, early personality and early experience have few connections with later personality characteristics and behavior. Another corollary put forth by some strong discontinuity proponents is that subsequently experienced environments are the primary shapers of personality, with earlier formed intra-individual psychological, or personality structures, having little subsequent influence on how the individual's personality turns out.

In an interesting article, "Does Personality Really Change after 20," Zick Rubin (1981) discusses continuity and change.

"In most of us," William James wrote in 1887, "by the age of thirty, the character has set like plaster, and will never soften again." Though our bodies may be bent by the years and our opinions changed by the times, there is a basic core of self—a personality—that remains basically unchanged.

This doctrine of personality stability has been accepted psychological dogma for most of the past century. The dogma holds that the plaster of character sets by one's early twenties, if not even sooner than that.

Within the past decade, however, this traditional view has come to have an almost archaic flavor. The rallying cry of the 1970s has been people's virtually limitless capacity for change—not only in childhood but through the span of life. Examples of apparent transformations are highly publicized: Jerry Rubin enters the 1970s as a screaming, war-painted Yippie and emerges as a sedate Wall Street analyst wearing a suit and tie. Richard Alpert, an ambitious assistant professor of psychology at Harvard, tunes into drugs, heads for India, and returns as Baba Ram Dass, a long-bearded mystic in a flowing white robe who teaches people to "be here now." And Richard Raskind, a successful opthalmologist, goes into the hospital and comes out as Renée Richards, a tall, well-muscled athlete on the women's tennis circuit.

Even for those of us who hold on to our original appearance (more or less) and gender, "change" and "growth" are now the bywords.

Studies defending personality stability and studies advancing the theory of constant change are numerous. Zick Rubin believes that all of these studies may have an impact on personality development by calling attention to what is "normal" and desirable. Researchers have established that there is considerable stability in adult personality. Rubin feels that further research may move on to a clearer understanding of how we can grow and change, even as we remain the same.

The Self and Self-Systems

You may recall from chapter 12 our discussion of Susan Harter's ideas about the self and the development of self-systems in childhood. If not, take several mintues to review her ideas discussed in chapter 12 that focus on the self. One important aspect of the self in adulthood is awareness. In chapter 14, we indicated that acute self-consciousness seems to characterize many adolescents.

Self-Awareness and Self-Actualization

Self-awareness likely dissipates as an individual establishes an identity and moves into early adulthood. Mark Snyder (1979) believes that an important aspect of self-awareness is the extent to which an adult engages in self-monitoring. His work has included attempts to classify individuals as either high or low on self-monitoring. An adult who is high on self-monitoring is particularly sensitive to the way others present themselves in various social situations and picks up on such information as cues for self-monitoring. By contrast, the adult who is low in self-monitoring is not nearly as vigilant about how others present themselves and is not adroit at using such information as cues for his or her own self-monitoring.

Our ability to observe ourselves and to be aware of ourselves is paraded by many clinicians as the avenue through which successful therapy can be achieved and by which we can gain insight about personality. However, one famous humanistic theorist, Abraham Maslow, believes that the highest attainment of identity or personality development is being able to transcend the self and lose your self-consciousness. Maslow's orientation converges with the central thesis of the Eastern philosophies that emphasize the need to destroy the illusion of the ego or self.

Maslow believes that the highest sense of self-accomplishment is self-actualization. In his hierarchical need view of development, Maslow suggested (1943) that we initially have to satisfy certain primary physiological needs, such as food, water, oxygen, then we move on to a higher level of safety and security needs that focus on such matters as avoiding pain, threats, fears, and dangers. Next, Maslow believes that we are motivated to satisfy love and belongingness needs, such as desiring to be wanted by family and friends. The fourth level of needs are called self-esteem needs and include self-respect, achievement, attention, and appreciation. The fifth and highest need, self-actualization, includes being able to do what you can, realizing your full potential, being creative, and being motivated to learn.

One research endeavor evaluated age changes in Maslow's system (Goebel & Brown, 1981). Individuals were asked to rank statements representing Maslow's five needs in eleven different aspects of life (e.g., friends, family, job, and money). Individuals from the ages of nine to ninety were included. The security need did not appear in the need system when Maslow thought it would, the order of love and esteem needs were reversed, and there was only partial affirmation of the importance of the self-actualization need. At all ages, love was viewed as the most important need. In sum,

At level 9 in Fischer's system, adults are able to understand their own identities in relation to others.

most of the needs Maslow suggests are important aspects of an adult's motivational makeup, but the extent to which they appear in the sequential fashion he suggests, and the extent to which self-actualization is the highest form of an individual's need system, are open for debate.

We have emphasized the importance of cognitive structural theory in this text, yet we have indicated that by far the majority of its applications have involved the child's development. Next, we look at the aspects of Kurt Fischer's theory of cognitive development that apply to adult cognition and suggest possible connections between Fisher's ideas and those of Erik Erikson (as described by Susan Harter, 1982).

Levels of Abstraction during Adulthood

Level 7 in Fischer's theory marks the first appearance of abstract thought. At level 7 an individual can construct a simple abstract set of ideas in which two representational ideas about the self can be coordinated. For example, the adolescent can develop a single abstraction about occupational identity. The limitation of this level is that he or she can only control one abstraction at a time. For example, the adolescent cannot relate this newly formed occupational identity concerning the self to another abstraction that involves the identity of someone else.

Table 17.1
The Possible Integration of Fischer's and Erikson's Theories of Identity

Age Period	Fischer's Levels of Abstractions	Erikson's Life Crises during Adulthood
Adolescence	Level 7. Identity defined in terms of single abstractions.	Identity vs. role confusion
Early Adulthood	Level 8. Abstract mapping of one's own identity onto that of another person.	Intimacy vs. isolation
Middle Adulthood	Level 9. Abstract System. Reciprocal coordination of one's own identities with those of significant others, and with societal expectations.	Generativity vs. stagnation
Late Adulthood	Level 10. System of abstract systems. Coordination of one's own identities over a lifetime, with those of others and with cultural values, so as to form a meaningful whole.	Ego integrity vs. despair

Source: Harter, 1982.

At level 8, he or she can begin to relate one abstract identity—his or her own—to that of another person, but only in a very rudimentary way. Fischer calls this an **abstract mapping.** For instance, a male adolescent may consider certain relationships between his own career identity and his concept of his potential spouse's career identity; he may indicate that his own career identity requires that his spouse be in a closely related career, or that his spouse be primarily a homemaker. However, there is a somewhat rigid, undirectional, and egocentric flavor to the cognitive mapping at this point in the sense that its focus is on what his career requires of someone else. While one abstract thought is mapped onto another, the relationship is not really reciprocal.

For the adult at level 9 of cognitive development in Fischer's system, there is considerably more reciprocity and differentiation in relating two identities. According to Fischer, the person can relate several aspects of both his and his spouse's identity, such as career and parental identities. In doing so, he also can develop a more differentiated, flexible, and sensitive picture of what his own identity requires of his spouse's identity, as well as what his spouse's identity requires of his identity. Such level 9 thinking is called an **abstract system.**

At level 10, the highest level of Fischer's system, the adult can relate two abstract systems to another in a reciprocal manner. In Fischer's example, the individual might relate his own and his spouse's career and parental identities now (one level 9 system) to their career and parental identities ten years ago when they were first married (a second level 9 system). As such, these identities are placed in temporal perspective, indicating a sense of continuity over time.

Susan Harter (1982), in reviewing developmental perspectives on the self-system, related Fisher's cognitive-developmental ideas to Erikson's psychosocial stages. Erikson's stage of intimacy versus isolation would seem to require Fisher's level 8 skills, at a minimum. It is at this level that the young adult can first begin to relate his or her own abstract identity to that of another individual. It is likely that the kind of mature mutuality required of true intimacy would presuppose Fisher's level 9 skills, wherein the identities of two individuals truly are reciprocal. Level 9 skills also would be required to cope successfully with Erikson's crisis of generativity versus stagnation, which might involve the meaningful coordination of an individual's own occupational and parental identities with those of his or her spouse. Finally, in successfully dealing with Erikson's last crisis, ego integrity versus despair, Fisher's level 10 cognitive skills would be needed. At this level, individuals can place their various identities into a larger perspective, not only coordinating these identities with those of others, but considering them within a temporal context, as individuals review their lives. While there remains much to be worked out in the integration of Fisher's cognitive-developmental ideas with Erikson's psychological states, the initial convergence suggested by Harter (1982) is interesting—the possible compatibility is shown in table 17.1. Such cross-fertilization of the fields of cognitive and social development supports this belief, initially described in chapter 1, and continued as a theme throughout this text, that the various strands of life-span development, such as social and cognitive development, are intricately interwoven.

Two important aspects of personality development that we have discussed throughout this text are sex-role and moral development. We consider each of these important strands of adult personality development in turn.

Sex-Role Development

In writing about sex-role development in adulthood, Sharon Nash and S. Shirley Feldman (1981) indicate that not only do we not have good empirical data about the nature of change in most of the grand theories of adult development (e.g., Erikson, Havighurst, Levinson, & Neugarten), but the same picture exists for most of the various strands of adult development, one in particular being sex-role development. To help provide some information about the development of sex roles across the life cycle, Nash and Feldman designed a study to systematically assess the development of sex-related aspects of self-concepts from adolescence through grandparenthood. They theorized that changes in the demand characteristics of family-related life circumstances would be related to fluctuations in sex-related self-perceptions during adulthood.

The Bem Sex-Role Inventory (BSRI) (Bem, 1974) was used to assess sex-related personality attributes in 804 individuals who were classified according to stage in the family life cycle. Eight groups were assessed, including one of adolescents, three of preparenting adults (singles, married-childless, and expectants), two active parenting groups (parents whose youngest child was less than ten years old, hereafter called young parents, and those whose youngest child was fourteen to seventeen years old, hereafter called mature parents), and two postparenting groups (empty nesters, whose grown children no longer lived at home, and grandparents). Four factors were derived from responses to the twenty "masculine" and twenty "feminine" items—leadership (acts as a leader, dominant, competitive, ambitious); autonomy (self-reliant, self-sufficient, independent, individualistic); compassion (understanding, sensitive, sympathetic); and tenderness (affectionate, warm, gentle, cheerful, loves children).

Since the researchers expected sex differences to wax and wane across the life cycle, they examined sex effects separately for each stage of life. The results indicated that men and women were similar in instrumental qualities in the young adult years, when, typically, both sexes are involved in salaried work. By contrast, expectancy and the early years of parenthood were marked by sex differences in both autonomy and leadership. By the height of the mature parenting years, only the sex difference in leadership remained, possibly because the roles of both father and mother require a

Researchers believe that women surpass men at most stages of life in the ability to show compassion and tenderness.

considerable amount of autonomy, although in different domains: men make career-related choices, and women resolve family-oriented issues. The sex difference in autonomy was ephemeral, emerging only during expectancy and young parenthood, a period of time marked by the woman's withdrawal from the role of wage earner and the presence of dependent children.

On the expressive factors, compassion and tenderness, women surpassed men at most stages of life. Sex differences in tenderness were absent at two stages as a result of men's elevated stress. The first was among married-childless adults, whose developmental task is to establish intimacy. The second was among grandparents. Without the responsibility and demands of daily interactions with children and with the reduction of both work pressures and the need to provide for an expanding family, grandfathers seemed more comfortable than younger men in being emotionally demonstrative or tender.

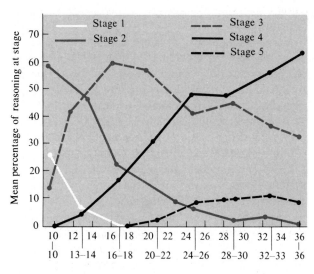

Figure 17.4 Mean percentage of reasoning at each stage for each age group.

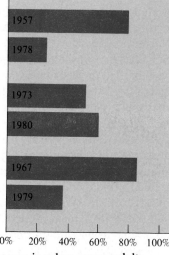

1. For a woman to remain unmarried she must be "sick," "neurotic," or "immoral."

2. Favor decision making abortion up to three months of pregnancy legal.

3. Condemn premarital sex as morally wrong.

Figure 17.5 Three changes in values among adults.

Nash and Feldman (1981) concluded:

By studying sex-role behaviors and related self-attributions across the life span, it becomes clear that sex roles do not merely define a catalogue of traits that consistently differentiate males and females. The psychological study of sex roles must include a consideration of social context, from the subtle to the more pervasive situational constraints. In particular, the performance of sex-role behaviors is affected by the presence of other people, and may vary as a function of the age or sex or role status of these people (Berman, Sloan, & Goodman, 1979; Feldman & Nash, 1979; Fullard & Reiling, 1976). (p. 31)

Moral Development

Lawrence Kohlberg's theory of moral development was presented in chapter 12. Recall that Kohlberg believes that there are six stages of moral development that unfold in a sequential fashion. Stages 1 and 2 represent a premoral orientation, in which the individual shows no internalization of morality but rather responds almost entirely on the basis of rewards and punishments in the environment—this level of morality is called either premoral or preconventional. The middle two stages, 3 and 4, indicate that an individual thinks about moral dilemmas as an intermediate level of internalization—the individual makes his or her own moral decisions, but those decisions are by-and-large those that are merely adopted from either parents or society. This level of moral thinking is called conventional. Stages 5 and 6 in Kohlberg's theory represent more advanced moral thought in the sense that the individual's morality is more fully internalized and has been developed through a consideration of alternative moral strategies that eventually leads to a level of moral thought that is truly his or her own. This level of thinking is referred to as postconventional and reflects self-principled morality.

Recently, Lawrence Kohlberg and his associates (Colby, Kohlberg, Gibbs, & Lieberman, 1980) have conducted a twenty-year longitudinal study of the subjects who were in Kohlberg's original sample in 1956. Thus, these data allow Kohlberg to chart the developmental course of moral judgments from early adolescence through the latter part of early adulthood. The mean percentage of reasoning about moral dilemmas at each of the first five stages in Kohlberg's theory across the twenty years of the individual's lives are shown in figure 17.4. The data show a clear relation between age and moral judgment stage. Over the twenty-year period, the use of stages 1 and 2 decreased, and stage 4, which did not appear at all in the moral reasoning of the ten-year-olds was reflected in 62 percent of the moral thinking of the thirty-six-year-olds. Stage 5 did not appear until the age of twenty to twenty-two, but never rose above 10 percent of the individuals interviewed. Thus, just as formal operational thought does not always emerge in adolescence, neither do the higher stages in Kohlberg's theory of moral development. Reasoning about moral dilemmas does seem to change in adulthood—adults in their thirties reason at more advanced levels than adolescents or children.

Concern about moral development in adulthood eventually leads to a discussion of values. Daniel Yankelovich (1981) summarized changes in a number of norms and values that characterize American life—three of these are shown in figure 17.5. Note that compared to 1957, when 80 percent of the adult population indicated that it is "sick," "neurotic," or "immoral" for woman to remain unmarried, only about 25 percent said this was the case in 1978. Also note that in 1967, 85 percent of adults regarded premarital sex as wrong, while the figure was less than 40 percent in 1979. And, recognize that in 1973 approximately 51 percent of the adults said that abortion up to three months of pregnancy was legal, while by 1980 the percentage had risen to 60 percent.

However, while there has been change in some values among adults in America, there are still some time-honored traditions as well. For example, 87 percent of the adult population today believe that the use of hard drugs is "morally wrong," 81 percent feel "mate swapping" is morally wrong, 79 percent disapprove of married women having affairs, and 76 percent disapprove of married men having affairs (Yankelovich, 1981).

There are, of course, many other areas of life in which adults have to make moral decisions. A recent poll by *Psychology Today* sampled over 24,000 Americans about their views on a wide variety of moral dilemmas that seem to be more ecologically valid than some of the moral dilemmas Kohlberg uses. While the readership of a magazine does not constitute a random sample of adults in the United States (the percent of its readers who are young, middle class, financially well-off, and white is greater than in the total United States population), the data support the belief on the part of many individuals that there is a great deal of variability in morality, and that for the most part we are not a very honest nation of people. For example, eight detailed scenarios of everyday ethical problems were developed to test moral decision making. Individuals were asked if they would knowingly buy a stolen color television set. More than one of five respondents said they would, even though 87 percent of the respondents said that such an act probably is morally wrong. And, approximately one out of three of the adults said that if they knew they would not get caught, they would be more likely to buy the stolen television. While moral thought clearly is an important aspect of morality, data such as these glaringly point out that what people say does not always reflect how they will act in a moral situation.

Summary

Social and emotional development in adulthood focuses on families, including marital and parent-child relationships, the diversity of adult life styles that individuals now follow, and the nature of relationships, including friendship, intimacy, attachment, and love. And, to understand personality development in adulthood we need to consider the criteria for maturity, the extent to which there is continuity and change in personality development, the nature of the self and self-systems, as well as various strands of personality such as sex role and moral development.

Experts who study families believe that by applying a life cycle perspective to families we can more readily see the interdependence of the life histories of its members. The development of marital relationships indicates that couples who have children go through five phases: courtship, the early years of marriage, the childbearing and childrearing years, the postchildrearing years/empty nest, and the aging couple. Two perspectives on marital satisfaction are the empty nest syndrome, which indicates that marital satisfaction peaks early in a marriage and continues to decline even after adolescents leave home, and the upswing thesis, which suggests the same early pattern of satisfaction in marriage, but that when adolescents leave home an increase in marital satisfaction results. There also is evidence that marital satisfaction is related to the timing of a marriage in the life cycle and whether a child is conceived after marriage or before. A key factor in marital satisfaction involves the ability of a couple to coordinate their careers and their family. The task demands of career and family often peak in early adulthood, which may account for the decrease in marital satisfaction that begins to occur at that time.

Marriages that involve children require a coordination of marital and parental roles. There is some evidence that marital relationships influence parenting competencies, and in some cases the reverse may be true as well. Many myths about marriage and parenting have developed in our culture, some of which may contribute to the dissatisfaction we find in many marriages. In particular, there has been a tendency in our culture to imprint our children with the message suggesting that when they grow up they will fall in love, get married, and have children. One aspect of parenting that is receiving increased attention by life-span developmentalists is intergenerational relations. Middle adulthood has been the focus of attention when parents not only may be working hard to guide their adolescent offspring, but also a time when their own aging parents may require more of their attention. Siblings relationships represent another aspect of adult family relationships—as in childhood, they may involve conflict and affection—and vary according to such factors as geographical location and frequency of interaction.

There is increasing diversity in adult life styles in our culture. In particular, a greater proportion of the adult population is single than in the past. Just as there have been myths in our culture about marriage, love, and parenting, so too are there some damaging myths about single adults, ranging from "swinging singles" to "isolated, depressed, lonely hearts." However, there are positive aspects to being a single adult as well, such as independence and time to meet goals and develop personal resources. An increasing number of single adults never become married, and an increasing percent of our population also are formerly married. Many divorced adults remarry to form stepfamilies, whose numbers are rapidly increasing as well. The divorce process has complex effects on the adults involved, usually instigating a great deal of stress and readjustment. Divorce may be particularly difficult for women who have been homemakers.

Relationships between people are an important aspect of social, emotional, and personality development in adulthood. Friendships continue to be important in adulthood and may change when individuals marry. Attachment and love are two important aspects of relationships in adulthood. Scholars are beginning to explore how the nature of attachments in adolescence is linked up with attachment and competence in adulthood. And, investigations of love across the life cycle suggest that "mutuality" supports love relationships over time—it occurs when partners share knowledge with each other and assume responsibility for each other's satisfaction. The concept of intimacy also has been an important theme in the study of relationships among adults—Erik Erikson believes that early adulthood is a critical time for developing an intimate relationship with another individual.

One elusive, yet important, aspect of personality development in adulthood is the concept of maturity. While experts do not always agree on the criteria for maturity, one promising approach suggests that maturity involves the individual's ability to competently cope with changing aspects of adult life. Some of the important ingredients of maturity in early adulthood likely include the development of intimacy, a stable sense of identity, and a strong interest in productive work and success in an occupation. Another issue that stimulates a great deal of controversy in adult personality development focuses on constancy and change. Experts agree that this issue is complex and takes many different forms, hence, there is no simple answer to the question of whether personality development is stable as the individual goes through adulthood or whether it changes a great deal. Most all psychologists do agree with the mild form of the discontinuity thesis, namely, that humans have the capacity for change across the entire life span. While for many years stability in adult personality was emphasized, recent views of adult development have stressed the change that goes on in adulthood. Some prominent developmental psychologists, such as Jack Block, suggest that the change proponents have gone too far and that there is more stability in adult personality development than the change theorists lead us to believe. The issue of continuity and change, then, has no simple solution, and the debate is likely to continue for many years to come.

Three important aspects of personality development during the infant, child, and adolescent years that continue to be important in adulthood are the self, sex roles, and moral development. One aspect of the self that likely declines in early adulthood from its peak in adolescence is self-preoccupation. Abraham Maslow has argued that the highest level of self-actualization occurs when we lose our self-awareness and transcend the self. A cognitive-structural view of the self developed by Kurt Fischer suggests how our developing cognitive capabilities influence the way we think about ourselves and others—his view seems to be compatible with Erikson's stage-structural view. Data about sex-role development across the adult years is sparse, although there is some evidence that during the early adult years both men and women show instrumental sex-role orientations. On expressive factors, such as compassion and tenderness, women surpass men at most stages of life. However, it is important to remember that sex roles do not merely reflect a catalogue of traits that consistently differentiate males and females. The performance of sex roles in adulthood is affected by the presence of other people, and may vary as a function of the age or sex or role status of these people.

With regard to moral development, there is evidence that individuals in early adulthood show more advanced moral judgments on Kohlberg's stages of moral thought than children and adolescents. Still, a small percentage of adults reach the highest level of moral thinking, that of self-principled morality. The study of moral development eventually leads to a concern about the nature of values in a culture and the extent to which those values change or remain constant. There is evidence that some values seem to remain reasonably stable over many years in our culture—such as attitudes about extramarital sex—while other values seem to change—such as attitudes about premarital sex. The current moral climate of our society reflects a wide gap between what adults say is moral and what they actually do. Moral development among adults, then, is strongly influenced by situational factors, and there is not good evidence for a trait of honesty in most adults.

Key Terms

abstract mapping

abstract system

assertion

autonomy

companionship
    relationship

displaced homemaker

empty nest syndrome

filial crisis

isolated

institutional relationship

intimate

mutuality

preintimate

pseudointimate

receptivity

stereotyped individual

upswing thesis

Review Questions

1. Describe how historical events and a life cycle perspective can influence our understanding of family development.
2. Discuss the development of marital relationships, as well as the factors that contribute to marital satisfaction.
3. Outline the role of parents in the family, the myths that have developed about the nature of marriage and the family, and the nature of parenting relationships across generations.
4. Discuss the diversity of adult life styles that now exist in our culture. Describe the lives of single adults who have never married, single adults who have been divorced, and adults who have been divorced and remarried.
5. Evaluate the nature of friendships, attachment, love, and intimacy in the adult years.
6. Define maturity. To what extent do you think you can get others to agree about your criteria for maturity? To what extent do the criteria for maturity vary according to the phase of the adult life cycle an individual is in?
7. Evaluate the debate on change and continuity in adult personality development. Is there an answer to the issue of whether adult personality development is stable rather than changing?
8. Discuss the most important aspects of the development of the self in adulthood.
9. Describe Kurt Fischer's cognitive developmental theory of self-development. And, show how his ideas may be compatible with Erikson's theory.
10. What is the nature of sex-role development in adulthood?
11. Outline the changes in Kohlberg's stages of moral development from adolescence through early adulthood, and discuss the nature of moral values in our culture.

Further Readings

Aldous, J. *Family careers over time*. South Bend, Ind.: Department of Sociology, Notre Dame, 1978.
Jo Ann Aldous is a family sociologist who is a recognized expert on family development. By reading this pamphlet you get a feel for how family sociologists view family development, in particular ideas about marital relationships, marital satisfaction, and the interface between family and work careers. Reading level is of medium difficulty.

Brim, O. G., & Kagan, J. (eds.), *Constancy and change in human development*. Cambridge, Mass.: Harvard University Press, 1980.
The latest in a long series of articles and books on the issue of whether development is stable, or whether it involves a great deal of change. Chapters have been written by such experts as John Horn, Howard Moss, and Kagan and Brim. The book is a scholarly treatment of the subject of constancy and change in personality development. Reading level is medium to difficult.

Huston, T. L. (ed.), *Foundations of interpersonal attraction*. New York: Academic Press, 1974.
A book of readings focused on what attracts people to each other, with extensive information about the formation, maintenance, and termination of relationships, as well as valuable ideas about what makes relationships enjoyable experiences for the parties involved. Includes an article by George Levinger, whose ideas about relationships were described in this chapter. Reading level is of medium difficulty.

Libby, R. W., & Whitehurst, R. N. *Marrriage and alternatives: exploring intimate relationships*. Glenview, Ill.: Scott Foresman, 1977.
A selected book of readings about the variety of adult life styles that exist in our contemporary society, including information about the many life-style options married adults have available to them. Easy and entertaining reading.

Weiss, R. *Marital separation*. New York: Basic Books, 1975.
Robert Weiss is one of the leading theorists and researchers in the area of separation and divorce. Extensive, knowledgeable information is given about the nature of relationships between spouses before separation, during separation, and after divorce. Reading level is reasonably easy.

Yankelovich, D. New rules in American life: searching for self-fulfillment in a world turned upside down. *Psychology Today*, April, 1981, pp. 35–91.
Yankelovich is a social scientist viewed as an expert at conducting national surveys of trends in American life. The material in Psychology Today *is adapted from his book,* New Rules, *a best seller, in which he attempts to show how we are becoming a nation concerned more with commitment to others in the 1980s. Easy and very interesting reading.*

Section VII

Late Adulthood

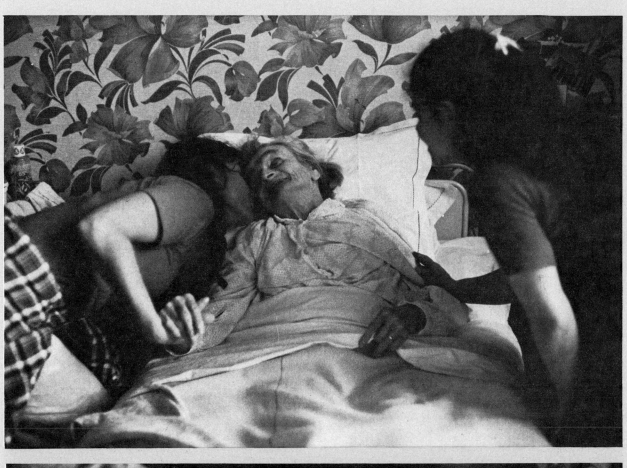

18

Physical and Cognitive Development

Prologue: Growing Old

Late adulthood, or old age as this phase of the life cycle is called by some, is often seen as a curse. For example, in a light, highly entertaining book, *The Joys of Aging and How to Avoid Them* (subtitled *Can Sex Keep You Young? and other Silly Questions Thoroughly Demolished*), Phyllis Diller (1981) describes her pervasive attempts to stay young.

This book is a primer on how to look and stay young. You may be asking yourself, "Why is Phyllis Diller writing a book giving advice on staying young?" That's like Don Rickles writing a book on "Common Courtesy."

The fact is I've dedicated my life to staying young. It may not look it, but I have. In fact, I've worked so hard at staying young it's beginning to age me.

I've done *everything*. . . . I've gone to spas in Switzerland, taken hormone shots, had plastic surgery, cellulite treatments, vitamins, miracle drugs, miracle moisture cream, Miracle Whip. I've stolen some cells from Dick Clark's body and transplanted them in mine. . . . Yes, even though I chug-a-lug Geritol, I will show you how to become part of the Pepsi Generation. If I can do it, you can do it. . . . Sure you may say there were some brilliant, vital old people. And there *were*. Albert Schweitzer was a great humanitarian, but could he get a date for New Year's Eve? Grandma Moses could paint the hell out of a landscape, but could she paint the town red? Let's face it—young is definitely better than old. Okay, now that that's settled, how do we stay young? How do we keep our youth? (I have one friend, Lenore, who keeps him in the guest closet.)

There are practical ways to stay young. . . . Things like spas, clinics, diet, exercise, sex (look through the book for the "well-thumbed" pages). We can have ourselves tucked, pinched, pulled, snipped, surgically adjusted. . . .

Dorian Gray is a man (in an old motion picture, *The Picture of Dorian Gray*) who sells his soul in exchange for eternal youth. He continues to stay young while his portrait keeps getting older and older. You may be saying to yourselves: would Phyllis Diller sell her soul to be younger? *Are you kidding?!!* Would Farrah Fawcett endorse shampoo? Would Dean Martin say yes to a martini? Would Ronald Reagan pop jelly beans? . . .

There have been a lot of changes in sexual attitudes and codes the last few years. . . . For those of you (like me) who may have forgotten what's what, take this quiz and see how much you can remember.

1. A man's sexual powers diminish rapidly after
   a. age seventy
   b. Johnny Carson's monologue
   c. you short sheet his bed
2. Vitality and lust are
   a. two prerequisites for sex
   b. a team of accountants on Fire Island
   c. the names of Cher's two youngest children
3. Foreplay is
   a. a new pong game
   b. a golf course
   c. a new TV series starring Ted Bessel

. . . Your life-style is the total image you project to those around you. Is it a young, exciting life-style or an old, doddering one? . . . Which is it? Do you read *Rolling Stone* or do you sit in bed at night with a glass of warm milk and browse through *The Dead Sea Scrolls?* Is whip and chill part of your food or sex budget? . . . Do you put on your "threads" and get into your "wheels," or do you slip into your nylon stockings with a seam and crank up the Tin Lizzie? . . .

Okay, there are no *highlights* (of old age). There are, however, certain advantages to old age:

You will not be asked to join the Coast Guard.
You will not have to worry about sexual harassment at the office water cooler.
Boy scouts will help you across the street.
People will start cutting your meat for you.
You are allowed to be eccentric. . . .

There are joys of aging! I've put down the aging process and falling faces and creaking bones only because I, like many of us, are going through it.

It's like jumping on a bicycle without a seat. It hurts as it's happening, but it's also . . . funny when you think about it.

Wrinkles, of course, are not the end of the world. They are "love lines" that we women have spent a lifetime earning. . . .

Once you've reached your senior years you can find lots of little things to be thankful for.

Be thankful for green grass, grandchildren and Gable movies on the "Late Show." . . .

And be thankful that your birthdays are like phonograph records. You were good at thirty-three . . . even better at forty-five . . . and still going around at seventy-eight. (pp. 9, 10, 14, 18, 134, 135, 166, 167)

Unfortunately much of the humor about old age does not involve people like Phyllis Diller poking fun at themselves, who in tongue-and-cheek fashion lets us know that she has done an excellent job of coping with the aging process. Too often our humor about old age involves poking fun at others—such as wickedness of sex in men (old goat, dirty old man) and ugliness in women (biddy, hag, crock).

A new word in our vocabulary is **ageism**. Like sexism, it is one of the uglier words in our society. It refers to prejudice against older people. Many individuals in late adulthood, unfortunately, face painful discrimination that they often are too polite and too timid to attack. Too often elderly individuals are not hired for new jobs, and are eased out of old ones, perhaps because they are perceived as too rigid or feebleminded. They are often shunned socially, sometimes being thought of as senile or boring. And, at times they are perceived as children, being described with such adjectives as "cute" and "adorable." Too often the elderly are edged out of their family life by children who see them as sick, ugly, and parasitic. In sum, the elderly often are perceived as incapable of thinking clearly, learning new things, enjoying sex, contributing to the community, and holding responsible jobs—inhumane perceptions to be sure, but often real perceptions.

In the course of the next several chapters, some of the myths about late adulthood will be dispelled. We will see that the needs of old people often are not that different from those of younger people. True, the elderly are more vulnerable to stress, have less resistance to disease, are more prone to loneliness, dependence, and loss of status, but they get along well in the world when they can enjoy friendships and social contacts, keep busy with work and leisure activities, and maintain reasonably good health.

Introduction

In this chapter physical and cognitive development in late adulthood will be described. The discussion of physical development focuses on the nature of physical decline in late adulthood—information about cerebral atrophy, including brain activity and sensory and motor systems, is provided. The role of exercise programs in preventing physical problems and maintaining good health is evaluated. We will also discuss the nature of health care and describe the role of sexuality in late adulthood.

Our overview of cognitive development begins with ideas about possible cognitive-structural changes in late adulthood. Contributions of the psychometric and information processing perspectives (including attention, perception, and memory) to our understanding of cognition in late adulthood are presented. The link between physical health and cognition is described, as are various cognitive interventions that attempt to improve the cognitive performance of the elderly. The chapter concludes with extensive information about work and retirement.

Physical Development

We will begin our discussion of physical development in late adulthood by describing some biological changes in the lives of Jim and Mary Johnson—changes that characterize many individuals in late adulthood.

The Decline in Physical Development

Meet Jim and Mary Johnson, American. Both are sixty-five years old, married to each other. . . . As a married couple of sixty-five, the Johnsons are typical in some ways and unusual in others. The marriage itself is unusual and important: married elders live on the average longer than unmarrieds. . . . Physically, Jim and Mary have aged in similar fashion. Both have slowed: their base metabolic rate has dropped about 20 percent since they were thirty. This means they need slightly less to eat and the effects of drugs and alcohol last longer (Dr. Robert Butler, director of the National Institute on Aging, recommends no more than one-and-a-half ounces of hard liquor a day or two six-ounce glasses of wine). Their body temperature has declined to as low as 90°F (the aging King David tried to prolong his life by lying against the bodies of warm young virgins).

Perhaps the most significant change is that the entire circulatory machinery is less efficient. There is less elastin, the molecules responsible for the elasticity of heart and blood vessels, and more **collagen,** the stiff protein that makes up about one-third of the body's protein. The heart rate does not rise as well in response to stress, the heart muscle cannot contract and relax as fast and the arteries are more resistant to the flow of blood. Heart output—about five quarts a minute at age fifty—has been dropping at about 1 percent a year. With the heart muscle less efficient and the vessels more resistant, heart rate and blood pressure both rise—and are both related to heart disease. Jim's blood pressure was 100/75 when he was twenty-five; now it is 160/90. His blood carries less oxygen to the brain and lungs. If he rises too suddenly from a chair he gets dizzy. Likewise, if Mary climbs the stairs too fast she must stop to catch her breath.

Both are slightly shorter than they used to be, and have a tendency to stoop. This is due both to muscle wastage (less skeletal muscle to hold the skeleton upright) and to loss of bone tissue. The individual vertebrae settle closer together as the discs that separate them flatten and collapse. Mary's bones began a steady loss when she was about forty; by the time she is eighty her skeleton will be 25 to 40 percent less. Jim's bone loss, unsuspected until two decades ago, began just a few years ago and will be less severe. Gerontologists do not understand the mechanism or cause of bone loss, though there is some evidence that a good diet (containing adequate calcium, in particular) and regular exercise can slow it.

Both Johnsons are in less direct communication with the world around them. Each is slightly nearsighted and slightly farsighted; to focus near or far the lens of the eye must flex, and their lenses are more rigid; the ciliary muscles that control the flexing are also weaker. But neither condition will get much worse and both can be corrected by bifocals. Eye pressure increases (which may lead to glaucoma) and the lens may become more opaque, leading to cataracts; the latter can now be corrected by surgery. The Johnsons cannot smell as well. Both optic and olfactory nerve fibers will eventually dwindle to about 25 percent of the number present at birth, and they are irreplaceable. Elsewhere in the body the sense of touch has begun to dull, faster in the feet than in the hands, and the pain threshold has risen, creating a greater danger from hot or sharp objects. The taste dims; the number of taste buds will have decreased by a third by age seventy-five.

The nerve cells people worry about most are those of the central nervous system—principally the spinal cord and the brain. Studies as early as the 1920s indicated that brain cells begin to die off around age thirty and in 1958 one researcher estimated the loss rate at 100,000 a day. Unlike skin, blood, liver and other regenerative cells, neurons cannot be produced after maturity. It is now known that the brain of an aged person weighs about 7 percent less than it did at maturity. But there is no direct correlation between brain size and intelligence, and there is still no evidence that loss of brain cells means loss of intelligence. [However, while some researchers have speculated that we lose brain cells as we age, there is no direct research evidence to support this claim.]

There are, of course, other changes in the brain more worrisome—changes that seem to impair mental function. These changes are all microscopic, and involve the proliferation of abnormal blobs, tangles and intracellular "garbage." The blobs are plaques containing an abnormal protein called amyloid. By now both Jim and Mary are almost certain to have some plaques, but their role in the aging process is unknown. The tangles—called neurofibrillary—are inside nerve cells (and others) and just as poorly understood. They resemble old, snarled fishing line. The "garbage" is a mysterious brown pigment called lipofuscin, or age pigment. The accumulation of lipofuscin among cells is thought always to accompany aging, but it is not known whether the pigment is simply a by-product of cellular activity or is harmful. Pellets of lipofuscin form an outer coat by the same process oil-based paints harden, and are resistant to normal "garbage-removal" enzymes.

These mysterious blobs, tangles and pigments are linked to one of the least understood and most abused terms in the lexicon of aging: senility. The word is frequently used to apply to any act or gesture by an "old" person—forgetfulness, selfishness, a desire for a nap and so on. Health care professionals now seldom use it except to indicate senile brain disease, sometimes called chronic brain syndrome. Even these terms are vague; Robert Butler calls them "wastebasket diagnoses." Their greatest weakness is that they fail to separate those who are "senile" from those who are "normal." One expert, Adrian Ostfeld of the Yale University School of Medicine, decides it this way: "If a person knows when to get out of bed, wash, dress, eat and pay his bills, he is not a case."

Nor is there any certainty about whether dementia (the commonest designation is Alzheimer's disease) is really a disease or simply a normal part of the aging process. One reason for this confusion is that the primary indicators of dementia (plaques, tangles, lipofuscin) are also present in "normal" older people like Jim and Mary. Most cases of Alzheimer's disease show no simple pattern of inheritance, and no evidence that they are contagious. What is certain is that they are rare—more so than commonly supposed. Because diagnosis is so uncertain, the true incidence is not known. But it is known that only about 5 percent of elders live in institutions, and only a very small percentage of them can truly be called senile. In one study of 3,141 low-income persons between sixty-five and seventy-four, only 12 could be identified as cases of senile brain disease. Most of the institutionalized elderly are victims of stroke, injury, arthritis, chronic respiratory diseases, alcoholism and other nonsenile conditions.

Physically, then, the elders have slowed somewhat, but they are by no means incapacitated. There is no physiological watershed at age sixty-five that should prevent people from working if they want to. Their strength is down slightly, their wind reduced; but neither condition is crippling and certainly not serious enough to disqualify them from most activities of "normal" life. (Anderson, 1980, pp. 291, 292, 293)

The Role of Exercise

In table 18.1, a summary of the major physiological changes that occur as a result of the aging process and which would most likely affect the individual's ability to perform physical exercise is presented; also included in the table is information about possible physiological benefits of regular exercise. Physical exercise here is defined as an activity that would require a relatively high percentage of maximal aerobic capacity over a prolonged period of time (Wiswell, 1980).

While such changes suggest a need for a decrease in exercise intensity as an individual ages, people often vary extensively in the degree to which such reduction is necessary. The body's capacity for exercise in late adulthood likely is influenced by the extent to which the individual has kept his or her body physically fit at earlier points in the life cycle. It is not uncommon to find individuals in late adulthood who participate in the Senior Olympics to have a greater capacity for exercise than some individuals in early adulthood.

The majority of individuals in late adulthood do not exercise regularly. Major reasons involve the negative attitude they, their relatives, and health professionals as well have shown about such exercise and its possible risks. Some of the misconceptions about exercise in late adulthood follow (Conrad, 1976).

1. The need for exercise decreases and eventually may even disappear at some point in late adulthood.
2. The risks involved in vigorous exercise after middle adulthood are grossly overexaggerated.
3. The benefits of light, sporadic exercise is overrated.
4. The abilities and capacities of individuals in late adulthood are underestimated.

Robert Wiswell (1980) discusses further such barriers to exercise in late adulthood. Many older people simply feel that they don't need to exercise, but many experts suggest that the single most effective method of accelerating the aging process is to do nothing. The perception of risks continues to be a major barrier. The news media has helped to promote such risks by dramatizing the occasional cardiac problem that occurs during exercise. In practical terms, we can expect that in an exercise class of fifty people meeting three times per week, a cardiac fatality will occur only once in six and a half years.

Jogging hogs have even become a part of scientist's attempts to determine whether an outpouring of sweat helps adults become healthier. At the University of California at San Diego, Colin Bloor and Frank White trained a group of hogs to run approximately 100 miles a week. Then, the scientists narrowed the arteries that supply blood to their hearts. The hearts of the jogging hogs developed extensive alternate pathways for blood supply, and 42 percent of the threatened heart tissue was salvaged (compared to only 17 percent in hogs that did not jog).

Other investigations (those with humans) have been designed to demonstrate the physical benefits of exercise to men (deVries, 1970) and another to women (Adams & deVries, 1973). By getting adults aged fifty to eighty-seven to do calisthenics, run, walk, and engage in stretching exercises or swim for forty-two weeks, dramatic changes in the oxygen transport capabilities of their bodies were observed. The improvements occurred regardless of the age of the individuals or their prior exercise history. Clearly, then, exercise and physical activity in late adulthood seem capable of slowing down the deterioration of an aging body.

While exercise does seem to have some demonstrable positive effects on our physical health status, we know much less about its possible effects on our mental health. While it is generally accepted that exercise is beneficial to emotional well-being, the existing scientific literature is at best contradictory and incomplete

Table 18.1
Physiological Decline Associated with Aging and the Possible Benefit
of Regular Strength and Endurance Exercise

Structural Change	Functional Effects	Effects of Exercise
Musculo-skeletal System		

1. Muscular atrophy with decrease in both number and size of muscle fibers
2. Neuro-muscular weakness
3. Demineralization of bones
4. Decline in joint function—loss of elasticity in ligaments and cartilage
5. Degeneration and calcification on articulating surface of joint
	1. Loss of muscle size
	2. Decline of strength
	3. Reduced range of motion
	4. Reduced speed of movement
	5. Joint stiffness
	6. Declining neuromotor performance
	7. Changes in posture
	8. Frequent cramping
	9. Gait characteristics affected:
	   a. Center of gravity
	   b. Span (height/arm length)
	   c. Stride length, speed
	   d. Width of stance
	10. Shrinkage in height
	11. Increased flexion at joints due to connective tissue change
		1. Increased strength of bone
		2. Increased thickness of articular cartilage
		3. Muscle hypertrophy
		4. Increased muscle strength
		5. Increased muscle capillary density
		6. Increased strength of ligaments and tendons

Respiratory System		
1. Hardening of airways and support tissue 2. Degeneration of bronchi 3. Reduced elasticity and mobility of the intercostal cartilage	1. Reduced vital capacity with increased residual volume 2. O_2 diffusing capacity is reduced 3. Spinal changes lead to increased rigidity of the chest wall 4. Declining functional reserve capacity	1. Exercise has no chronic effect on lung volumes but may improve maximal ventilation during exercise and breathing mechanics
Cardio-Vascular System		

1. Elastic changes in aorta and heart
2. Valvular degeneration and calcification
3. Changes in myocardium
   a. Delayed contractility and irritability
   b. Decline in oxygen consumption
   c. Increased fibrosis
   d. Appearance of lipofuscin
4. Increase in vagal control
	1. A diminished cardiac reserve
	2. Increased peripheral resistance
	3. Reduced exercise capacity
	4. Decrease in maximum coronary blood flow
	5. Elevated blood pressure
	6. Decreased maximal heart rate
		1. Increased heart volume and heart weight
		2. Increased blood volume
		3. Increase in maximal stroke volume and cardiac output
		4. Decreased arterial blood pressure
		5. Increase in maximal oxygen consumption
		6. Myocardial effects increased:
		   a. Mitochondrial size
		   b. Nuclei
		   c. Protein synthesis
		   d. Myosin synthesis
		   e. Capillary density
		7. Decreased resting heart rate

Source: Robert A. Wiswell, "Relaxation, Exercise, and Aging," in *Handbook of Mental Health and Aging,* ed., by Birren/Sloane, © 1980, p. 945. Adapted by permission of Prentice-Hall, Inc., Englewood Cliffs, N.J.

(Wiswell, 1980). Those who argue for the possible mental health benefits believe that exercise increases stamina, and thus the tolerance for work, builds confidence, and promotes group participation. However, there may be a more direct link. It has been suggested that exercise raises the level of a natural, morphinelike substance (called beta-endorphin) in the blood. And this chemical may elevate mood. Researchers argue over whether it is this chemical that produces the so-called runner's high.

Health Care
In the mid-1970s, the National Council on Aging commissioned a national survey to explore American attitudes toward aging and the elderly. Few of the people polled chose old age as the most desirable period of life; generally it was viewed as the least desirable (Harris, 1975). Regardless of whether the respondent was over or under the age of sixty-five, poor health and physical impairment were listed as the biggest problems of aging. But while the general public perceives that people over the age of sixty-five seem to have major health problems, a survey of noninstitutionalized people over the

The body's capacity for exercise in late adulthood likely is influenced by the extent to which the individual has kept his or her body physically fit at earlier points in the life cycle.

"You're what we call 'a reverse rejection case.'
I've got to find a suitable kidney that won't
reject YOU."

prevalent chronic conditions that impair the health of the elderly are arthritis (38 percent), hearing impairment (29 percent), vision impairment (20 percent), and heart condition (20 percent) (Harris, 1978). Sex differences in health indicate that elderly women are more likely to have higher incidences of arthritis and hypertension, are more likely to have visual problems, and have less difficulty with hearing than men (Harris, 1978).

Although adults over the age of sixty-five often have a physical impairment, many of them still can carry on their everyday activities or work. Chronic conditions linked with the greatest limitation of activity or work are heart condition (52 percent), diabetes (34 percent), asthma (27 percent), and arthritis (27 percent) (Harris, 1978).

Low income is strongly related to health problems in late adulthood (and at other points in the life cycle as well). Approximately three times as many poor as nonpoor people report that their activities are limited by chronic diseases. In the elderly population, the health gap between low and middle income seems to continue (Wilson & White, 1977).

Health Treatment

An important aspect of health is the interaction between people who seek health care and those who provide it. Unfortunately, it has been revealed that physicians and other health care personnel share our society's general stereotypes and negative attitudes toward the elderly. In a medical setting, such attitudes can take the form of avoidance, dislike, and pained tolerance rather than positive types of treatment. Slower, less spectacular preventive medicine and chronic care are often perceived as boring, tedious, uninteresting, and unproductive by health care personnel, who too frequently are more stimulated by acute cases and greater chances of successful treatment with younger individuals (Butler, 1975). It is not uncommon for physicians to diagnose an elderly person's problems with some catchall diagnosis—age, hardening of the arteries, and senility are three such catchall categories.

One of the most widely discussed issues in the medical treatment of the elderly focuses on drugs. While drugs often can relieve suffering and pain and delay death, there is increasing realization that many health care personnel do not exercise caution in dispensing drugs. Clearly, the elderly take a lot of drugs—while they make up approximately 10 percent of the United States population, they take 25 percent of the nation's prescription drugs (Basen, 1977). Tranquilizers and sedatives are used more frequently than any other drug in the late adulthood. While these particular drugs can help to reduce anxiety, depression, and insomnia, some health experts believe that their use is often excessive (Butler, 1975).

age of sixty-five suggested that two of every three respondents considered their health good or excellent (U.S. Department of Health, Education and Welfare, 1977). Are the elderly healthier than the public thinks? Are the conclusions of these studies based on the same definition or perception of health?

In order to define and recognize poor health we have to define the standards of good health. While physical criteria such as pulse rate and body temperature are clearly important in assessing an individual's health, such criteria are interpreted subjectively by each individual. One person who has a rapid pulse and wheezes often may see these as symptoms of poor health, whereas another individual may not. Assessing health status, then, is a complex task.

Illness and Impairment

Many of the chronic diseases of the elderly, such as cancer and heart disease, lead to long-term illness and impairment. Other chronic conditions, such as arthritis and hypertension, do not directly cause death, but usually leave the person with some kind of physical impairment, such as lameness or blindness. Almost two of every five persons between the ages of sixty-five and seventy-five have some impairment of physical functioning. After age seventy-five, the rate rises to three of five persons (Riley & Foner, 1968). The four most

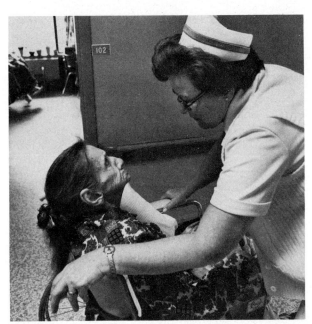
The interaction between patient and health care providers is important.

Medicaid and Medicare

The attitudes of policymakers affect the health of persons in late adulthood, just as do the attitudes and competencies of physicians and other health care personnel. By deciding on the type of publicly funded medical care that is to be made available to the elderly, policymakers can have a powerful impact on the health of the elderly in our society. Health care is the second largest expenditure in the national budget, outranking even defense. But public medical care is not adequate for all who need it—there are gross inequalities in treatment of the rich and poor and the young and old. While Medicare and Medicaid programs were implemented to help the quality of health of the aged and poor, such quality of care has not reached a satisfactory level (Williamson, Munley, & Evans, 1980).

We have seen that there are marked individual differences in the manner in which people in late adulthood show deterioration in different aspects of physical development. And, we have seen that the quality of medical care in late adulthood shows a great deal of variation as well. Next, we will see that there is a considerable variability in sexuality in late adulthood as well.

Sexuality

Alex Comfort (1976), a noted expert on the elderly, concludes that aging does induce some changes in human sexual performance, more often in the male than in the female. Orgasm becomes less frequent in males, occurring in every second or third act of intercourse rather than every time. More direct stimulation usually is needed to produce an erection. In the absence of

two disabilities—actual disease and the belief that "the old" are or should be asexual—sexual desire and capacity are lifelong. Even if and when actual intercourse is impaired by infirmity, other sexual needs persist, including closeness, sensuality, and being valued as a man or a woman.

Such a view, of course, is contrary to folklore, to the view of many individuals in our society, as well as to many physicians and health care personnel. Fortunately, many elderly people have gone on having sex without talking about it, unabashed by the accepted and destructive social image of the "dirty old man" and the asexual, undesirable old woman. Bear in mind that many individuals who are now in their eighties were reared when there was a Victorian attitude toward sex. In early surveys of sexual attitudes, older people were not asked about their sexuality possibly because everyone thought they didn't have sex, or because it was thought it would be embarrassing to ask them about sex.

Most all of the published work in the area of sexuality and aging suggests or concludes that there are no known age limits to sexual activity (e.g., Masters & Johnson, 1970; Kaplan, 1974). Healthy older persons who want sexual activity are likely to be sexually active in late adulthood (Pfeiffer & Davis, 1974; Comfort, 1976, 1980). Various therapies also have been shown to be effective for elderly people who report various sexual difficulties (e.g., White & Catania, 1981). For example, sex education led to increased sexual interest, knowledge, and activity in the elderly in one investigation (White & Catania, 1981).

In reviewing the existing literature on sexuality and aging, Charles White (1981) concluded the following:

1. Males are more active than females, except for very old age groups (e.g., eighty-five plus), where males and females do not significantly differ.
2. When sexual interest or activity ceases or declines in the aging female, it usually is due to declining interest or illness in her male partner.
3. Males do show a gradual decline in sexual activity with advancing age, though this decline may be a cohort difference since some males actually show an increased interest in sex with age. In the absence of longitudinal data, a cohort explanation cannot be ruled out.
4. Physiological changes in the sexual organs with advanced age, while presenting some difficulties for some individuals, do not adequately explain decreased or nonexistent sexual activity in either sex.
5. It is difficult to find research on aging and sexuality that does not suffer from sample bias and methodological problems.

In an investigation of sexual activity and interest, White (1981) evaluated a group of elderly people whose sexuality rarely has been studied—those who are institutionalized in nursing homes. Eighty-four males and 185 females in fifteen nursing homes in Texas, whose mean ages were eighty-one and eighty-three respectively, were asked about their sexuality. Attitudes and knowledge about sexuality were significantly related to sexual activity and to prior sexual habits earlier in adulthood. A substantial percentage (17 percent) of sexually inactive residents indicated a desire to be sexually active, which conforms to other data collected from noninstitutionalized individuals in late adulthood, suggesting that sexual interest exceeds sexual activity (e.g., Verwoerdt, Pfeiffer, & Wang, 1969).

In summarizing his ideas about sexuality in late adulthood, Alex Comfort (1980) made a number of suggestions about how health care personnel can help the elderly with their sexual needs. Sexual responsiveness should be fostered but not preached. The elderly need to be reassured against their own false expectations, the hostility of society, including children and potential heirs, and the interference of some health care personnel who do not understand such needs. Comfort suggests that where a partner is not available, masturbation should be viewed as an enjoyable release of sexual tension and not looked at with a jaundiced eye. He believes that explicit discussion of masturbation with the elderly may relieve anxiety caused by earlier prohibitions. And, group discussion among elderly couples can be a valuable means of ventilating sexual anxieties and needs, needs that may not be sanctioned in conversations with others. Comfort believes that sexual dysfunction usually is produced by culture-based anxiety, and that it is never too late to restructure sexual attitudes. He reports that many couples in their seventies have for the first time achieved communication and fulfillment that had been denied them earlier in their lives.

Next, we will look at many different aspects of cognitive development in late adulthood, including the roles of work and retirement.

Cognitive Development

In chapter 16, a number of ideas about cognitive development in adulthood were presented. The three main perspectives on cognitive development—cognitive-structural, psychometric, and information processing—were discussed. Before reading how such perspectives view cognitive activity in late adulthood, it would be helpful either to reread the sections of chapter 16 that pertain to these three perspectives, or review them in your head.

Some researchers believe that there are advances in cognitive-structural thought in late adulthood.

The greatest interest in the cognitive activity of individuals in late adulthood has been generated by the psychometric and information processing approaches. However, as we will see next, ideas about declines and advances in cognitive activity from a cognitive-structural perspective also have been developed.

Cognitive-Structural Theory

Several earlier investigations of cognitive-structural change in late adulthood (e.g., Papalia & Bielby, 1974; Storck, Looft, & Hooper, 1972) implied that regression from formal operational thought to lower cognitive stages occurred in the elderly. More recent data, however, suggest that such observations may be attributed to the fact that many of these older adults had never achieved formal operational thought even in their younger years. In an investigation of forty-two males aged sixty-five to ninety-two (Protinsky & Hughston, 1978), it was revealed that all of these individuals could conserve mass, better than seventy-five percent conserved surface, and more than 90 percent conserved volume, indicating that the majority of these individuals function at the concrete operational level of thought.

Also, when we present the elderly with intellectual problem-solving tasks, such as those used to assess Piaget's stages, it is important that the tasks are relevant to the interests of the elderly. One researcher (Sinnott, 1975) has found that individuals in late adulthood perform better on adult-relevant tasks that have more meaningful content for the elderly than on standard Piagetian tasks that were designed for use with children.

So far in our discussion of cognitive-structural change we have only been concerned with whether there is decay in the Piagetian stages as individuals age. Recall, however, that in chapter 16 we speculated about the possibility of a fifth structural stage that may exist in adulthood. The speculation is that the stage involves thinking about formal operational thought. The idea that advances in cognitive-structural thought, such as a fifth Piagetian stage, occur in adulthood are recent and are still not well understood. One individual, whose major research has involved a psychometric approach to the study of intelligence, even has speculated about the existence of three cognitive stages in adulthood, the most advanced coinciding with late adulthood.

K. Warner Schaie (1977) speculated about the possible existence of four cognitive stages of development: acquisitive; achieving; responsible; and reintegrative. The **acquisitive stage** refers to the childhood and adolescent years. During the acquisition stage, the individual functions in a protected environment. With the achievement of adult status, though, the individual is less protected from the consequences of failing at problem solving. At this stage, the goal no longer is the acquisition of knowledge, but rather the achievement of potential. Schaie calls young adulthood the **achieving stage.** The **responsible stage** corresponds with the middle adulthood years. It is a time when the individual has attained competence and independence and now has to assume responsibility for others. Schaie believes that this stage requires solutions to problems that focus on an individual's family and/or important other people in life.

The **reintegrative stage** corresponds with the late adulthood years. According to Schaie (1977), the three previous stages require the individual to integrate intellectual abilities at higher levels of role complexity. However, during this final stage of cognitive development, the focus is on simplification. This does not mean that the individual stops performing intellectually, but that attention becomes focused more on those aspects of life that are more meaningful. Schaie says that the reintegrative stage completes the transition from the "what should I know," through the "how should I use what I know," to the "why should I know" phase of life. Consequently, in late adulthood, Schaie believes that cognitive activity is influenced more by motivational factors than at any other stage. Clearly, the measures of adult intelligence we now use would have to be greatly modified if we believe Schaie's stages have merit as a viable approach to the study of cognitive-structural change in adulthood.

Measures of adult intelligence also would have to be altered significantly to evaluate the cognitive-structural view of Kurt Fischer (1980), whose ideas were presented in chapter 12 and again in chapter 16. Fischer's ideas were discussed in those chapters because they lend themselves so well to enhancing our knowledge about the development of the self. However, his theory merits attention as one of the most differentiated cognitive-structural theories of adult cognitive activity as well.

Recall that Fischer believes there are ten cognitive-structural stages of development, the last three of which have important implications for our study of cognitive development in adults. Level 8 of Fischer's view is called *abstract mapping,* which involves the abstract mapping of one's identity onto another individual. Level 9 is called *abstract system,* which entails the reciprocal coordination of one's own identities with those of significant others and with societal expectations. The most advanced level of the system, level 10, is called **system of abstract systems.** The coordination of one's identities over the life cycle into a meaningful whole is involved at this level of thinking. It is possible that levels 8 to 10 in Fischer's theory can be attained by the end of the early adulthood years, although no developmental data have been collected that would support or negate such an idea. A major point here, though, is that the kind of cognitive skills described by Fischer may be prerequisites for the psychosocial stages of development set forth by Erikson. Thus, if the individual can reason at level 10 of Fischer's cognitive skills, he or she is more likely to be able to put together a cohesive account of the complexities of his or her life that form some meaningful pattern.

Fischer (1980) believes that most adults probably master some of the cognitive skills at levels 8 to 10. Identity concepts are the most plausible area where cognitive skills are likely to involve some type of abstract mapping. Other skills that probably belong in these levels are advanced moral judgments, the managerial skills of a corporation or a school system, the skills required to write an effective essay or novel, and the skills involved in programming and operating a computer (Fischer & Lazerson, in press).

In both Schaie's and Fischer's perspectives, reasoning about social matters clearly comes into play in their attempts to develop levels or stages of adult thought. Both perspectives also go further than Piaget or the fifth-stage theorists in differentiating cognitive-structural thought in adulthood. A comparison of the main cognitive-structural perspectives of adult development are summarized in table 18.2.

Table 18.2
Cognitive-Structural Perspectives of Adult Cognitive Development

Developmental Period		Piaget's Theory	Fifth-Stage Theory	Schaie's Theory	Fischer's Theory
	Adolescence	Formal operations	Formal operations	The acquisitive stage (childhood and adolescence)	
	Early Adulthood		Thinking about formal operations	The achieving stage	Abstract mapping
	Middle Adulthood			The responsible stage	Abstract systems
	Late Adulthood			The reintegrative stage	System of abstract systems

Psychometric Approaches

In chapter 16, we described the lively debate between John Horn and the Schaie, Baltes, and LaBouvie-Vief group. Recall that Horn believes crystallized intelligence, based primarily on education and experience, increases in adulthood, while fluid intelligence, comprised more of cognitive abilities such as abstract thinking, declines with age. Also remember that the Schaie, Baltes, and Labouvie-Vief group disagree vehemently with Horn. This group believes that bias explains in part the lower scores of the elderly on measures of intelligence. After all, most all of our intelligence tests were designed for children and young adults, not the elderly. Furthermore, they argue that the environment of the elderly is not culturally and educationally enriched. And, they believe that because many younger people have a negative view of old age, the elderly face age discrimination.

Some researchers have speculated that when a drop in intelligence does occur, it happens just before death (Riegel & Riegel, 1972). They investigated the stability of IQ in old age in a unique way. IQ was plotted retrospectively as a function of the number of years prior to death instead of the number of years since birth. They found a sudden deterioration of intelligence in the five years preceding death. In other words a sudden decline in intelligence test scores seemed to signal approaching death. The decline in scores is probably due to neurophysiological decline, but it may be influenced by psychological factors as well (Baltes & Schaie, 1974).

In sum, the group of researchers headed by Schaie, Baltes, and LaBouvie-Vief argue that there is a great deal of plasticity in the cognitive functioning of elderly individuals. Rather than evaluating such plasticity, our standardized tests of intelligence have been designed to measure stability, and further, the majority of them have been developed for use with younger individuals. Later in this chapter we will follow their suggestion that studies of cognitive intervention are important in understanding the nature of intelligence in late adulthood.

The importance of plasticity in adult intelligence also supports the view of intellectual development proposed by Nancy Denney in chapter 16. Recall that Denney believes it is important that we distinguish between unexercised and optimally exercised mental abilities. Since some cognitive activities are unexercised in most individuals, using such abilities should improve performance on them. However, Denney has speculated that unexercised and exercised activities are closer together in childhood and old age and farther apart during the young and middle adult years because of the data on both the structural changes in cognitive abilities across the life span and the relative effectiveness of training on various age groups.

There seems to be a growing consensus that as the child develops, his or her cognitive abilities become more differentiated. That is, with increasing age during childhood there appears to be a larger number of factors that represent cognitive ability, with lower correlations between the factors, and a weak general factor (e.g., Garrett, 1946; Asch, 1936). While there has

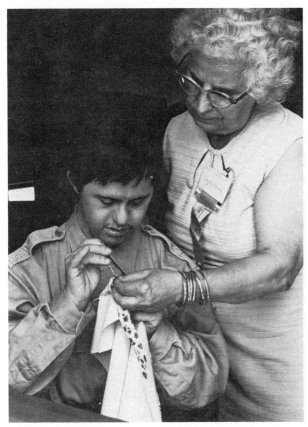

Exercising cognitive abilities improves performance of them.

Memory, perception, and attention are intricately interwoven.

been less research conducted on structural changes in adults, there is some evidence that there is reintegration of cognitive abilities during late adulthood—that is, there are fewer factors, higher correlations between the factors, and a much stronger general factor (e.g., Balinsky, 1941; Green & Berkowitz, 1964). While there are some methodological problems with the research conducted on this topic, the suggestion that cognitive abilities differentiate as the child develops and reintegrate in old age merits more attention. Denney (1981) points out that the training (cognitive intervention that attempts to improve cognitive functioning) research also indicates that there may be more room for experience to have an effect on cognitive ability in young and middle-aged adults than in either younger or older individuals.

Thus, while Nancy Denney (1981) agrees with Paul Baltes (1980) that we ought to be looking at unexercised mental abilities in late adulthood, and that we should study their plasticity, she does not believe there is as much room for change in late adulthood as in early and middle adulthood.

Psychometric theorists, then, disagree about the degree of plasticity in intellectual functioning during

late adulthood as well as the extent to which such functioning declines. Next, we turn our attention to the approach that has dominated experimental research on cognitive activity in late adulthood during the last decade, the information processing perspective.

Information Processing

In chapter 16, we considered the contribution of information processing to our understanding of cognition in middle adulthood. Due to the limited research available, we concentrated primarily on memory. Though central to the study of cognition, memory is only one of several cognitive activities that can be examined from an information processing perspective. Here, in our discussion of cognition in late adulthood, existing research allows us to consider not only memory, but also the important processes of perception and attention. We will see that the processes of perception, attention, and memory are not totally independent but are intricately interwoven. For example, aspects of attention, as well as of perception, in late adulthood have implications for our understanding of memory.

Perception

A. T. Welford (1980) recently reviewed ideas about the nature of perceptual change in late adulthood and described some of the most important experiments that have been conducted. Three aspects of perception that have received attention in late adulthood are masking, irrelevant material, and context. We will consider each of these in turn.

If a visual pattern is presented briefly and then, after a brief interval, another visual stimulus is given, the individual's perception of the first pattern may be impaired: the second stimulus has **masked** the first. Presumably it takes time for the data from the initial pattern to build up to a critical level at which they trigger a judgment and so become immune to interference by further stimulation. In the absence of a masking stimulus, data from the initial pattern can continue to be accumulated from some kind of **iconic** (sensory) image up to at least one-half of a second or so after the initial experience has stopped. It has been predicted that the time over which this can occur lengthens with age (e.g., Fozard, Wolf, Bell, McFarland, & Podolsky, 1977). It has been found that in order to see the pattern initially presented, individuals in their sixties required either a longer exposure or a longer interval before the masking stimulus than did individuals in their twenties (Kline & Szafran, 1975; Walsh, 1976).

A plausible interpretation of these results is that the rate of visual information processing becomes slower with age (Hoyer & Plude, 1980). This "perceptual slowing" might itself be due to stimulus-persistence; the visual system in elderly adults might be "slowed in rate of processing owing to the extended refractory period of aged neurons" (Hoyer & Plude, 1980, p. 231), a belief consistent with a large body of research (e.g., Botwinck, 1978). However, we still need to determine more precisely the mechanisms and locus of perceptual differences between young and elderly adults. Is age-related slowing due to changes in the photoreceptors of the retina (Pollack, 1978), a more peripheral explanation, or does slowing reflect changes in more central structures such as the visual cortex of the brain? Researchers are actively involved in attempting to answer such questions.

Investigators have found that individuals in late adulthood have more difficulty than young adults in detecting figures embedded in target designs (e.g., Crook, Alexander, Anderson, Coules, Hanson, & Jeffries, 1962). This difficulty might reflect age-related deficits in attention, which we will consider. In any event, this research suggests a need for careful design of displays to provide only essential information without confusing detail and clutter. Such obvious applications of these ideas can be made in the design of symbols on industrial and domestic machines, road signs, notices, and the layout of accommodations.

Hearing provides an excellent example of how *context* influences perception in late adulthood. For example, individuals comprehend more of what is said when a conversation continues on a line of previous discussion or thought than when there is a change in subject matter. Older people often request repetition of what has been said, especially if there has been a sudden change in topics being discussed. To some degree

this is understandable in light of a hearing deficit. In everyday life the first remark in a conversation often is to convey a meaning rather than to alert and orient the older listener to the speaker. One special technique for communicating with the elderly is to begin a conversation with an alerting remark, such as "I say," or "Listen to this." Any change of topic could be prefaced by a remark such as "Changing the subject, . . ."

Many individuals who deal effectively with the elderly adopt such techniques, but many of us do not. By becoming aware of the importance of such communication techniques we should be able to improve the elderly person's ability to perceive what is said. It is always important to remember that an individual does not perceive a piece of information in isolation from the context in which it is presented. In the case of hearing, the speaker's ability to use attention-focusing statements in everyday conversation suggests the importance of context in the elderly person's perception of information in their world.

Attention

According to current perspectives on attention, there are two main ways our attention can fail us. First, there are **divided attention** deficits that occur when we have problems processing all of the information that currently is present in a situation (try listening to two or more conversations simultaneously). Second, there are **selective attention** (or focused attention) deficits that occur when we have difficulty ignoring irrelevant information (try reading difficult material while ignoring a television playing full blast in the same room). Studies of aging and cognition have focused on both types of deficits in order to determine whether elderly adults have specific problems with attention.

William Hoyer (e.g., Hoyer, 1977, 1980; Farkas & Hoyer, 1980) has conducted a number of research projects that focus on information processing in late adulthood, and in particular on selective attention. One of his studies (Farkas & Hoyer, 1980) used a card-sorting task in which adults place cards into one of two different piles as fast as possible. The basis for sorting is the orientation of a single "target" stimulus on each card (the letter *T,* which can be presented in one of two orientations). In addition to the target stimulus, each card contains three background (irrelevant) stimuli (*I*'s). The perceptual similarity of the background stimuli to the target stimulus is varied as is the nature of the selective attention task that adults must perform. In the *selective search* task, the position of the target on each card is unpredictable, so adults presumably "search" through the irrelevant stimuli in order to find it. Age differences in this selective search task are found, but they may have more to do with *discriminating* targets from irrelevant information than with *ignoring* irrelevant information. Performance of adults in the *selective filtering* task is more relevant to the

In David Madden's experiments, the young subjects were college undergraduates and the older subjects were healthy, community-dwelling adults in their sixties and seventies. In the first two experiments, a visual search task was used in which the individuals held two target items (letters) in memory, and on each trial responded yes or no as to whether one of these targets was contained in a visually presented display of six letters. The display was composed of three red and three black letters. One-half of the trials were cued: before each display, subjects were shown either a black dot or a red dot, which meant that the target (if present) could only be one of the three black or red items, respectively. The presence of this cue effectively partitioned the display into three relevant and three irrelevant items. Half of the trials were noncued (e.g., preceded by a green dot that gave no information regarding the target item's potential color). On the noncued trials all six display items, therefore, were relevant.

In the first experiment, twenty-four young and twenty-four elderly subjects performed this visual search task. On each trial, the cue was presented for 100 msec, followed by a 900 msec delay, followed by the item display, which remained in view until the individual responded. Any presence of selective attention deficit in the elderly then would appear as greater age differences on the cued trials than on the noncued trials. Analysis of reaction times suggest no selective attention deficit in the elderly in this experiment. Other more complex experiments reported by Madden support this conclusion as well. Madden, therefore, believes that attentional deficits in the elderly are more likely to be of the divided attention variety than the selective attention type.

process of "ignoring." In this task, the position of the targets on the cards always is constant, so adults know in advance where to direct their attention in a display. Farkas and Hoyer found evidence that elderly adults did not do as well at this task, but *only* when the irrelevant information was highly similar perceptually to the targets.

Considering the mixed evidence of William Hoyer and others, David Madden and Robert Nebes (Madden & Nebes, 1981) conclude that difficulties of attention in late adulthood are due primarily to *divided attention* rather than selective attention. This conclusion is substantiated by their own research, which examines selective attention in a more complex and perhaps naturalistic manner than prior studies. One of their experiments (Madden & Nebes, 1981) involved a task that combines the demand to "filter" irrelevant information with that to "search" through a set of more than one target. This study is described in box 18.1.

Although age differences in selective attention are questionable, age differences in divided attention are not. Age-related deficits in divided attention often are observable in middle-aged individuals (see chapter 16) and they are readily apparent in most elderly adults. As Fergus I. M. Craik (1977) has stated, "One of the clearest results is the experimental psychology of aging is the finding that older subjects are more penalized when they must divide their attention, either between two input sources, input and holding [information in memory], or holding and responding" (p. 391). Craik describes several experiments that support this claim, including two by Donald Broadbent, a pioneer of information processing psychology. In one of these studies (Broadbent & Heron, 1962), adults performed a visual letter cancellation task while monitoring a series of auditory letters for a repeated letter. "Younger adults coped moderately well with both tasks while older adults tended to concentrate on one task while performance on the other task deteriorated markedly" (Craik, 1977, p. 391). In the other study (Broadbent & Gregory, 1965) adults were presented three visual and three auditory items simultaneously. When adults were asked to recall the visual items and then the auditory items, performance remained at a constant level with age up to forty-five, and then dropped significantly (Craik, 1977).

Given that elderly persons have a deficit in divided attention tasks, we need to ask why. One plausible explanation focuses on the concept of **limited attentional capacity** (Kahneman, 1973; Hasher & Zacks, 1979). Attentional capacity is thought of as a type of psychological energy needed to perform mental work. The amount of this capacity can vary depending upon a person's level of arousal and other factors. Nonetheless, at any one moment, capacity is thought to be limited. And, the limited supply of capacity is thought to be responsible for the difficulty of divided attention tasks. If the supply of capacity in elderly adults tends to be smaller than that in younger persons, it follows that elderly adults should have particular difficulty with divided attention tasks, which they do.

Evidence for a deficit in attentional capacity in late adulthood comes from other studies besides those that have examined divided attention specifically. Particularly relevant are investigations of controlled or **effortful information processing,** which presumably draws heavily on capacity, and **automatic information processing,** which presumably does not draw heavily on capacity. In one of William Hoyer's experiments (Plude & Hoyer, 1981), young and elderly women seached for two or four target letters in displays of one, four, or nine letters. Half of the women in each age group were in the *varied mapping* condition; they looked for different target letters on different trials. The remaining women were in the *constant mapping* condition; they looked for the same letters on all trails. There is good evidence (Schneider & Shiffrin, 1977) that practice on the constant-mapping procedure results in automatic processing, that is, processing that is independent of other demands on limited attentional capacity. Interestingly, Plude and Hoyer found only very small age differences in that condition. In contrast, the varied mapping condition produced a large deficit in the elderly group of women. The results support the contention that there are age differences in effortful processing (which does not draw on limited capacity). Age differences in processing, then, may result from limitations in capacity. These results have important practical implications: though elderly persons might suffer processing deficits, these can be overcome if opportunities for practice can bring about automatic processing. Shortly, we will discuss the possibility that the distinction between effortful and automatic processing is important in long-term memory tasks, as well as short-term memory and perceptual tasks such as those just described.

Memory
In chapter 16, we considered a wide variety of evidence on the question of age-related differences in memory functioning. This evidence indicated that the presence or absence of age-related differences depends upon at least five factors: the role of short-term versus long-term memory; the nature of the information processing activities engaged in at input; the nature of the retention test; the materials or information to be remembered; and the characteristics of learner, especially his or her

previously acquired knowledge and skills. In the prior chapter, we were concerned with comparisons of young and middle-aged adults. Here the focus is upon comparisons of young and elderly adults. Before reading further, it could be helpful to review the discussion of memory in chapter 16.

Short-Term Memory   We concluded in chapter 16 that young and middle-aged adults perform similarly on short-term memory tasks. Elderly persons also perform well on such tasks, as indicated, for example, by the Botwinck and Storandt (1974) study cited earlier. Though short-term memory may show deficits in old age, these deficits are generally small. Of course, such differences can become larger if divided attention requirements are added to the task of short-term recall. Further, there is evidence for age-related *slowing* of short-term memory processes.

Earlier, we considered evidence that the rate of "scanning" through short-term memory is slower in older persons (Anders, Fozard, and Lillyquist, 1972). There also is evidence that **spatial processing** in short-term memory is slower in older persons. Spatial processing tasks reveal the functions of mental imagery and are extremely important for that reason.

The *mental rotation* task (Shepard & Metzler, 1971) is one of the best techniques available for exploring spatial processes involved in mental imagery. In one version of this task, a capital letter is presented on a screen, sometimes normally, and sometimes "reflected," that is, reversed from left to right. As a subject in this task, you would decide, as quickly as possible, whether each letter presented was normal or reflected, and you would indicate your judgments by pressing one of two response keys in front of you. The latencies (how long it takes) of these responses are measured. All of this sounds simple enough, except that the letters are usually presented at a "tilt" rather than upright. The degree of tilt can range from 0° (upright) to 180° (upside down), with reference to the vertical. The key finding from such studies is that latencies get longer as the "tilt" gets greater. This effect of tilt on latency indicates that adults must "rotate" the tilted letters in their heads, making the letters mentally vertical, before making their "normal" versus "reflected" judgment (see fig. 18.1 for examples of the way the letters were presented).

One study of mental rotation (Cerella, Poon, & Fozard, 1981) was performed with young and elderly adults. The results are shown in figure 18.2. Note that the latencies grow longer with greater departures from vertical orientation—this is, the phenomenon that supports "mental rotation." But note also that the *slope* of the line relating orientation to latency is greater for older adults. This pattern suggests that mental rotation is slower in older adults than in younger adults.

Correct   Correct   Incorrect

Figure 18.1   Mental rotation.

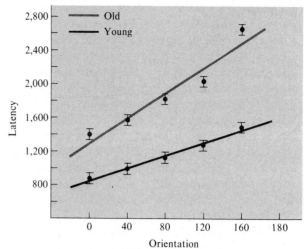

Figure 18.2   Mean decision latency for young and old subjects as a function of stimulus orientation.

The mental rotation results raise several interesting questions. One question is the relationship of these results to evidence for age-related slowing of short-term memory "scanning." Cerella et al. (1981) point out that the degree of age-related slowing in rotation was quite close to the degree of age-related slowing in scanning observed by Anders et al. (1972). This might be a coincidence, or it may suggest a common factor that produces age-related slowing in many different processes (Birren, 1974). Another important question concerns the implications of the rotation results for imagery abilities of the elderly (Winograd & Simon, 1980). Imagery helps our memory, our problem solving, and many other types of cognitive abilities. Do the rotation results imply a general imagery deficit, or simply a slowing in certain imagery processes with no loss in the effectiveness of imagery when time is not a factor? Still a third crucial question pertains to the role of life-style and educational factors in producing the results of Cerella et al. Another experiment (Jacewicz & Hartley, 1979) examined mental rotation in young and elderly adults currently enrolled in college. No age differences in rotation rate were observed. It is far too early for firm conclusions, but education and life-style may be critically important in whether age differences in rotation and other cognitive processes appear.

Long-Term Memory   The remainder of this section on memory focuses on long-term memory, where age-related differences are more common and pronounced. The discussion is organized in a way similar to chapter 16, but we will see certain differences between conclusions drawn for elderly persons and those drawn for middle-aged adults in our earlier discussion.

Information Processing Activities at Input   In chapter 16, we reviewed evidence that middle-aged persons often remember as well as young adults, *if* they are given appropriate instructions or tasks at the time input material is presented. Some experiments have indicated that this same principle holds for elderly persons, but other experiments have not. Consider first an experiment in which words were accompanied by no cues, by structural cues (first letters), or by semantic cues (category names) (Smith, 1977). In the first two conditions, clear age-related deficits in memory appeared,

with young adults remembering better than middle-aged adults, and middle-aged adults remembering better than their elderly counterparts. In the semantic cue condition, however, no age-related differences were observed; memory was virtually constant in learners ranging from twenty through eighty years old. Smith's study is a dramatic illustration of the fact that *in some memory situations* appropriate activities at input can remove age-related deficits.

In other memory situations, appropriate input activities can *reduce* age deficits, but not *eliminate* them. The experiment by David Hultsch (1971) on organization is a good case in point. Refer to figure 16.6 in chapter 16. The figure shows the recall of young, middle-aged, and elderly adults in a sorting condition, which insures good *organization* of material, and a nonsorting condition, which does not insure organization. The sorting condition produced substantially improved recall in the middle-aged and elderly groups. However, this condition did not *remove* the age-related differences between young and older adults. Rather, these differences were merely *reduced* to some extent.

Studies such as those by Smith (1977) and Hultsch (1971) suggest the optimistic view that age differences in memory can be removed, or at least attenuated, by appropriate information processing at input. Unfortunately, not all studies support this view. Consider another of the studies discussed in chapter 16, that by Mason and Smith (1977). Recall memory in three age groups of adults was examined under standard learning instructions and under instructions to use imagery during learning. We noted earlier that the young learners outperformed the middle-aged learners under standard instructions, but that imagery instructions improved memory in the middle-aged group, removing any age-related deficit. The elderly learners performed differently. Their performance was *not* improved by imagery instructions, and they showed poorer memory than young learners under *both* standard and imagery instructions. There is other evidence that imagery instructions fail to remove memory deficits shown by elderly persons. Indeed, Eysenck (1974) found that age differences were *greater* under imagery instructions than under other types of instruction. And, Fergus Craik (1980) has described studies in which semantic categorization tasks (similar to the semantic categorization task of Smith, 1977) failed to reduce, or even increased, age-related deficits in recall memory.

Why do appropriate processing instructions sometimes fail to help the memory of elderly persons? One idea is that of a **processing deficit** in old age (Eysenck, 1974); elderly persons might simply be *less capable* of engaging in the organizational, semantic, and imagery processes which are helpful in memory tasks. Processing deficits might be explained by age-related declines in attentional capacity (Hasher & Zacks, 1979). That is, elderly persons might show processing deficits because they have less of the capacity needed for processing. Another less pessimistic idea is that our manipulations of processing activity sometimes fail with the elderly learner. Due to low motivation, lack of practice on memory tasks, or other factors, simple instructions to use imagery, or semantic categorization, might be insufficient to influence what elderly persons actually do. That is, the same instructions might produce different information processing activity in elderly persons than in young adults. Still a third explanation calls attention to possible *retrieval* problems in the elderly. Even if input processing is equivalent in young and elderly adults, the latter might have difficulty finding information in memory during the memory test. The experiments cited here all used *recall* tests, which might exacerbate problems of retrieval. The next section considers how procedures of recognition testing can affect age-related differences in memory.

The Nature of the Retention Test   In our discussion of memory in middle adulthood, we called attention to the fact that recognition testing *sometimes* reduces age-related differences found in recall (Schonfield & Robertson, 1966, fig. 16.4). More recent research with elderly persons supports a similar conclusion, but also shows that the caveat, *sometimes,* is critical. Specifically, this research indicates that age-related deficits can be minimal or absent *if recognition testing (of familiar material) is combined with controls over information processing activities at input*. One investigation that precisely illustrates this point was conducted by

Sharon White (described in Craik, 1977). If you were a subject in Sharon White's experiment, you would be given a long list of words, some accompanied by questions for you to answer and some accompanied by the instruction, "learn." You would be told that the "learn" words should be memorized for subsequent recall. The question-words should simply be used to answer the questions. These questions were of three types; *capital* questions (you say whether the word is printed in capital or lower-case letters), *rhyme* questions (you say whether the word rhymes with another word presented), and category questions (you say whether the word fits into a certain semantic category, such as "fruits" or "vehicles"). White followed her list with a test of free recall and recognition for all of the words (note that these tests were unexpected for the question words).

The results of Sharon White's experiment are shown in figure 18.3. Note first that young adults outperformed elderly adults in free recall, particularly in the category-question and learn conditions. This study closely was a case where beneficial processing instructions (the category condition) did not remove age differences in recall. Note second that the capital-question, rhyme-question and category-question conditions produced no age differences in recognition. Thus, these conditions represent a case where recognition testing removes age-related differences. Finally, note recognition performance in the learn condition. Here, a very large age-related deficit was obtained. This clearly was a case where recognition testing does *not* remove age-related differences.

Studies such as White's (see also Craik, 1980; Perlmutter & Mitchell, 1982) suggest a complex interplay between the factors of age, processing activities at input, and type of test. When subjects are told to "learn" materials, age-related deficits often are found, *regardless of recall versus recognition testing*. Apparently, younger persons respond better to the learn instructions than elderly adults. This might be because young persons are frequently still in school and well-practiced at the tasks of memorizing. When adults are *not* told to memorize, but simply to process the materials in some way, age differences in input-processing are less likely to occur. And, age differences in memory under these conditions often are small, if not absent altogether. An absence of age differences is especially likely with recognition-testing procedures, perhaps because these minimize demands for effortful processes of "search" or "retrieval" at test. As Perlmutter and Mitchell (1982) concluded, "when retrieval support has been provided, and encoding operations directed, age differences seem to vanish." Their interpretation of this conclusion is provocative: apparently *encoding abilities* of younger and older adults do not differ, although their *spontaneous use of encoding operations do* (Perlmutter & Mitchell, 1982).

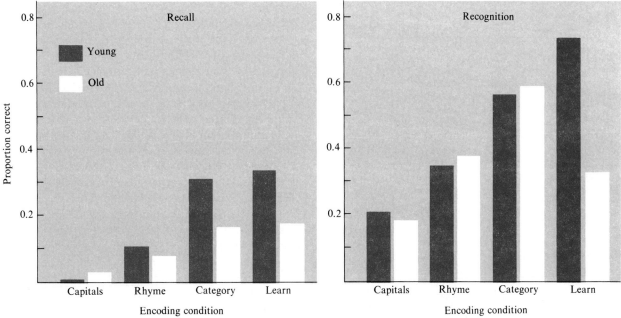

Figure 18.3 Age differences in recall and recognition as a function of depth of processing.

The Nature of the Materials or Information In our earlier discussion of memory in middle age, we raised the possibility that unfamiliar materials might pose particular problems for middle-aged adults compared to young adults. The role of familiarity probably is of equal importance among the elderly. Indeed, a recent study by Barrett and Wright (1981) has shown that manipulations of familiarity can eliminate and even reverse memory differences between young and elderly persons. Barrett and Wright examined recall memory for "young-familiar" words, such as bummer, narc, and pinball, and for "old-familiar" words, such as gooseberry, blotter, and bolster (see table 18.3 for a complete listing of these words). The former were more familiar to young adults than to elderly individuals, while the latter were more familiar to older persons. The results were clear-cut: young adults outperformed elderly adults on recall of "young-familiar" words, but elderly adults outperformed young adults on recall of "old-familiar" words. Clearly, then, any comparison of memory in different age groups must consider the factor of familiarity, and especially the possibility that to-be-remembered materials might be more familiar to one age group than to the other.

Familiarity is not the only important dimension of information to be remembered. Recent research supports a crucial distinction between information that is learned through *automatic processes,* and information that is learned through *controlled,* or *effortful, processes* (Hasher & Zacks, 1979). Earlier we distinguished between automatic and effortful processes in perceptual and attention tasks. The evidence supported large age differences in effortful processing, but not in automatic processing. A similar conclusion is supported in memory research.

Most learning seems difficult. Thus, it may sound silly to propose that some types of learning are automatic in that they do *not* require attentional capacity. However, research has supported automatic learning of certain aspects of a stimulus, such as how recently the stimulus occurred, how frequently it occurred, and where it occurred. Processing of such aspects of stimuli appears to occur without our intention or awareness, yet we are able to remember such aspects later. An example is our ability to remember where on a page we read certain information (on exams, it sometimes seems as if remembering *where* we read something can help us remember *what* we read). Recent experiments have compared young and elderly adults on memory for aspects of stimuli such as those just described (Attig & Hasher, 1980; McCormack, 1981, 1982). The result has been little or no difference between younger and older adults. This finding supports the conclusion of no age differences in memory for automatically learned information, and it is consistent with the view of age differences in information processing capacity that we considered earlier. If elderly adults do have a reduction in processing capacity, they should not do as well on effortful memory tasks, such as free recall. However, they should not be hampered on automatic memory tasks, such as memory for spatial location.

Table 18.3
The Young and Old Word Lists

Young List	Old List
afro	drugget
tweeter	poultice
bummer	gooseberry
ripoff	phaeton
gig	slate
spa	slacker
freon	crony
sunspot	counterpin
turntable	panteloons
terrarium	pompadour
denim	flitters
disco	settee
synthesizer	fedora
dude	petticoat
foreplay	blotter
cassette	parasol
communes	bungalow
narc	teacakes
readout	flivver
decoupage	gramophone
reefer	davenport
stereo	hollyhock
calculator	flapper
bellbottom	bolster
gauchos	bloomers
pinball	doiley
frisbee	victrola
orgy	vamp

Source: Barrett & Wright, 1981, pp. 194–99.

Characteristics of the Learner In chapter 16, we covered evidence that an adult's ability to retrieve and utilize previously acquired knowledge holds up quite well through middle age. Indeed, the same evidence suggests that **knowledge actualization** maintains itself in old age as well. For example, the research on *retrieval efficiency* by Roy and Janet Lachman indicates no age-related decline in retrieving facts from memory, through the early sixties at least. Such findings support Marian Perlmutter's (1980) generalization that while memory *processing* is susceptible to age-related deficits, memory *knowledge* is not.

It is encouraging, of course, that actualization of previously acquired knowledge is relatively invulnerable to age effects. But age-related deficits in new learning are distressing. Should we conclude that capacities for new learning decline with age, that you can't teach an old dog new tricks? An interesting study by Kathryn Waddell and Barbara Rogoff (1981) rules strongly against such a pessimistic claim. Middle-aged and elderly women were asked to remember the spatial locations of objects. In one condition, the objects were placed in a naturalistic "panorama," while, in the other condition, the objects were simply placed arbitrarily in cubicles. Performance in the two conditions was equivalent among middle-aged women, but elderly women performed more poorly than middle-aged women in the cubicle condition. The authors concluded that "age differences in adult memory performance may be limited to tasks that remove previously learned relationships between items (as in recall of lists of unrelated words), requiring subjects to invent an organizational structure to facilitate recall" (Waddell & Rogoff, 1981, p. 878). In other words, elderly persons are apparently quite good at new learning, as long as the material to be learned and the learning task itself are compatible with previously acquired knowledge and skills.

What can we conclude from this complex information about memory in late adulthood? Quite clearly, the factors of short-term versus long-term memory, processing activities at input, types of memory test, nature of information tested, and learner characteristics all emerged as critically important, just as they did in our discussion of middle adulthood in chapter 16. Again, we can conclude that age-related deficits are greatest when (1) the task taps long-term memory, (2) effective learning strategies are not enforced (3) criterial tasks demand effortful "search" or "retrieval," (4) the materials are unfamiliar, and (5) previously acquired knowledge and skills cannot be applied.

In addition, several new observations have emerged. First, while effective learning processes might be sufficient to improve memory in middle adulthood, they are *not* always sufficient to improve the performance of elderly persons. With elderly persons the use of appropriate tests (usually recognition) also may be required. Second, even recognition testing can produce large differences between young and elderly adults, *if* learning activities at input are not controlled (existing data do not tell us if this observation also is true when young and middle-aged adults are compared). Third, instructions to "learn" produce particularly large deficits in elderly groups, at least on tasks in which older adults are not highly skilled. Apparently, elderly persons are capable of using many learning strategies, but may fail to use them spontaneously when told to learn (unfortunately, existing research with middle-aged persons has not compared "learn" conditions with conditions designed to specifically direct processing at input). Fourth, elderly persons perform as well as young adults in tests of memory for aspects of stimuli such as recency, frequency, and location of presentation. Such aspects apparently are stored automatically in memory. Hence, we have evidence that automatic memory processes do not decline with age. Fifth, elderly persons can be very effective learners, *if* their considerable knowledge and skills are applicable to a task. Otherwise, their performance can be poor, even when compared to middle-aged individuals.

Conclusions about Information Processing in Late Adulthood

Having discussed age-related deficits in perception and attention, as well as age-related deficits in memory, the question arises, Do the former help explain the latter? The answer seems to be yes. Consider first the evidence from perceptual tasks, which support age-related slowing. Such slowing also is implicated in memory tasks. Age differences in memory are usually reduced, and sometimes eliminated, when more time is allowed for recall (Hultsch & Deutsch, 1981). Consider second the evidence from attentional tasks. This evidence points to strong age-related deficits in divided attention. These deficits have been interpreted with the notion of age declines in the amount of attentional capacity. A great deal of the memory research also can be explained with the notion of a decline in capacity. Indeed, some recent experiments suggest that young adults perform much like elderly adults when attentional capacity is "drained" during learning by performance of an interfering task (Rabinowitz, Craik, & Ackerman, 1982). Thus age-related slowing, and age-related declines in attentional capacity, both are implicated in memory deficits. However, it seems likely that other factors, such as failure to spontaneously use effective learning strategies, also are involved.

Our discussion of information processing has avoided the issue of "cohort" effects raised by Baltes and Schaie (1974) in reference to psychometric testing. The information processing research has relied almost invariably upon *cross-sectional* designs in which groups of young adults are compared to groups of elderly and/or middle-aged adults. Such designs are susceptible to the interpretation that the differences between age groups are not due to *age changes,* but rather to social, cultural and/or educational differences between the groups (perhaps older adults perform more poorly because their educational background is deficient). Fortunately, recent work on memory using *longitudinal* designs (Arenberg & Robertson-Tchabo, 1977; Arenberg, 1978) is beginning to appear. This work supports true age changes in memory, particularly in the years after sixty. However, we still do not know if these changes are *universal,* or if they are *irreversible.* There may be large individual differences in the "aging" of the information processing system. Further, it may be possible to reverse age declines through appropriate intervention techniques. These crucial possibilities are currently at the forefront of research attention in the study of developmental changes in the cognitive activity of adults.

This concludes our discussion of the three main perspectives on cognitive activity in late adulthood—cognitive-structural, psychometric, and information

Intellectual decline is likely in those individuals experiencing some pathology.

processing. Profitable ideas about the nature of cognition can be gained from all three perspectives. Next, we look at the link between physical health and cognition in late adulthood.

Physical Health and Cognition

Clearly, at some point in late adulthood biological processes begin to degenerate (as was discussed at the beginning of this chapter). The broad scope of biological degeneration supports John Horn's claims that the decline of fluid intellectual abilities is due to physiological deterioration involving the brain and nervous system. However, it is important to distinguish whether such declines are genetically-related or are due more to life stress and disease.

Intellectual decline is more likely to be observed in individuals who are experiencing some pathology, such as a cardiovascular disease. A well-known study linking health and cognition was conducted by James Birren and his associates (Birren, Butler, Greenhouse, Sokoloff, & Yarrow, 1963). On the basis of health status, the men studied were classified into two groups: group 1, those with only trivial incidences of diseases, such as partial deafness or varicose veins; and group 2, those who showed evidence of a potentially serious disease, such as arteriosclerosis. Even though the individuals in group 2 showed these characteristics, they were not seriously ill individuals at the time they were studied. The two groups of men performed differently on a number of cognitive measures. The scores of the "healthy men" on the verbal part of Wechsler Adult Intelligence Test were significantly lower than was the case for the "unhealthy" men. And, there were a number of other correlations between health and cognitive activity that appeared in the assessment of the group 2 men that did not emerge for the group 1 men.

Investigations that have focused on specific aspects of health also have shown that deteriorating health conditions influence cognitive activity. Individuals with various brain disorders, cardiovascular disease, and hypertension do not perform as well on measures of intellectual functioning as healthy individuals do (e.g., Wang, 1973; Spieth, 1965; Wilkie & Eisdorfer, 1971).

Until recently there has been little theoretical guidance that would help to explain the association of physical health and intellectual functioning. One possible strategy for explaining the link between health and cognition has been developed by Walter Cunningham (1981)—his views on the cascade model of intellectual functioning are presented in box 18.2. In capsulated form, the cascade model refers to the relationship between three types of health status or aging—primary (normal), secondary (individual has a disease that is serious but does not involve a death threatening state), and tertiary (death threatening, pathological disease state is present)—and various forms of intellectual functioning, such as speed of intellectual response, active thinking, and passive thinking.

Earlier in the chapter we indicated that many psychometric theorists believe there is substantial plasticity in the intellectual functioning of individuals in late adulthood. Others believe that while there is some plasticity, the capacity for intellectual improvement is less in late adulthood than at earlier points in adult development. Next, we look at the cognitive intervention strategies that have been used in attempts to improve the intellectual functioning of individuals in late adulthood.

Cognitive Intervention Strategies

Marian Perlmutter (in press) recently summarized the findings from investigations that have attempted to train complex skills in older adults. Studies have shown that such complex skills as fluid intelligence can be modified and can be shown to transfer to thinking on tasks other than the ones the older adults were trained on (e.g., Baltes, & Willis, 1978). Nonetheless, when these older adults were retested six months later the effects were not as clear.

Older adults also have been successfully trained to perform better at tasks that require them to learn an efficient strategy for solving reasonably simple identification problems (Sanders & Sanders, 1978), a finding that generalized to improved performance on more complex cognitive tasks given one year later. Older adults also have been trained to improve their performance on Piagetian-type conservation tasks (e.g., Hornblum & Overton, 1976) and on perspective-taking (e.g., Schultz & Hoyer, 1976) and role-taking tasks (Zaks & Labouvie-Vief, 1980). And, in one intriguing study that has direct application to helping individuals in late adulthood deal more effectively with their environment, the information processing skills necessary for effective driving were significantly improved through a training program, with the effects lasting for at least six months (Sterns & Sanders, 1980).

In conclusion, the fact that cognitive skills in late adulthood can be improved through training is encouraging. However, there clearly are limitations to how much improvement can be made. The future should provide more precise information about how elastic various cognitive skills are in late adulthood and how easily they can be modified.

Remember from our discussion in chapter 16 that intelligence and work likely are interrelated. Some types of work in late adulthood may not only promote cognitive skills, but work also seems to be related to life satisfaction as well. In the next section we explore the complex world of work and retirement in late adulthood.

Work and Retirement

One myth that needs to be eliminated (and fortunately does seem to be abandoned more every day) is that older persons are not proficient at work and should retire. There are many examples of individuals who refute this myth—two prominent ones are Winston Churchill, who did not hit his prime until well past middle age, and Margaret Mead, who was still writing, lecturing, and making fields trips well into her seventies. Ronald Reagan, in his seventies, seems to have found a healthy balance between work and leisure in adulthood. Let's look more in depth at work, the role of leisure activities, and the nature of retirement in late adulthood.

Work

Productivity in old age actually seems to be the rule rather than the exception. Persons who have worked hard throughout their life often continue to do so until their death. Some elderly keep a schedule that exhausts the young worker and some continue to demonstrate highly creative skills, often outperforming their early- and middle-adulthood counterparts. In business

Among individuals in their seventies, 4 percent of men work full-time and 12 percent work part-time.

and industry, there is a positive relationship between age and productivity that favors the older worker. And, older workers have a 20 percent better attendance record than younger workers. Somewhat surprisingly, they also have fewer disabling injuries and their frequency of accidents is lower than for young adults (Comfort, 1976). It appears, then, that the recent changes in federal laws allowing many people over sixty-five to continue productive work was a wise and humane decision.

Work that people enjoy doing may increase the likelihood that they will live longer. The evidence for the link between work and longevity is discussed in box 18.3.

The Characteristics of Seventy-year-old Workers in the United States John Flanagan (1981) recently reported the results of a national survey of individuals in late adulthood that focused on the characteristics of people who work. The age range of the people studied was sixty-eight to seventy-three, but for convenience, Flanagan refers to the sample as the "seventy-year-olds." Each of the 500 men and 500 women in the sample participated in an extensive four- to five-hour interview that included questions about their education,

family history, and employment. Each individual also reported on his or her overall quality of life. And, the elderly adults indicated whether they were currently employed, and if so, the importance to them of eighteen different aspects of a job.

The first question evaluated by Flanagan was, How many of these individuals are working and what are they doing? Only 4 percent of the men were working full-time, while an additional 12 percent were working part-time. The same percentage of women were working full-time but only 8 percent more were working part-time. Most of the men were in jobs that did not require professional training. About 41 percent were in general labor and service-type jobs requiring no special skills. Nearly 14 percent more were in mechanical, technical, or construction trades, while 33 percent were in sales and clerical positions. Only about 12 percent were in jobs requiring college training. However, more of the women (about 29 percent) were in jobs requiring college training, with teachers accounting for many of these jobs. Unskilled labor jobs accounted for about 31 percent of the women who worked, while sales and clerical jobs represented 39 percent of women who worked either full- or part-time.

Box 18.2
The Cascade Model
of Intellectual Functioning

Walter Cunningham (1981) emphasizes that in our study of cognitive development we should be studying three strands of aging: primary, secondary, and tertiary. A distinction between **primary** (or normal) **aging** and **secondary** (or disease-related) **aging** has been made. Primary aging involves gradual and modest declines in efficiency, speediness, and flexibility at both the physiological and behavioral levels. This gradual deterioration is believed to be the result of gradual cell loss and less efficient cell functioning in the central nervous system. Secondary aging involves a variety of chronic disease conditions that could affect the functioning of the brain. The most likely candidate to impede intellectual functioning is cardiovascular disease. A third type of aging referred to by Cunningham is **tertiary aging,** a term used to denote behavior resulting from very serious disease that has pronounced effects on the person's physical status and may lead to pathological breakdown. The phrase *terminal decline* is sometimes used to refer to this tertiary aging process.

To assess how different types of aging might be related to cognitive activity, Cunningham selected measures that would reflect three types of cognitive activity: intellectual speediness, active thinking, and passive thinking. Intellectual speediness is the ability to quickly carry out simple cognitive operations. Perceptual speed and reaction time are examples. There is good evidence that the speed of responsiveness in late adulthood is sensitive to primary aging (Cunningham, 1981). Active thinking refers to basically the same kind of cognitive operations described by Horn as fluid intelligence and Piaget as accommodation. Inductive reasoning is an example. There is good evidence that secondary and tertiary aging influence active thinking, while the relationship of primary aging to active thinking is still being debated. Passive thinking, reflected in behaviors that are redundantly recorded in the nervous system is close to what Horn and Cattell call crystallized intelligence and what some information processing researchers refer to as automatic processing (e.g., Hasher & Zacks, 1979). There is good evidence that passive thinking is relatively insensitive to primary and secondary aging but is probably influenced by tertiary aging.

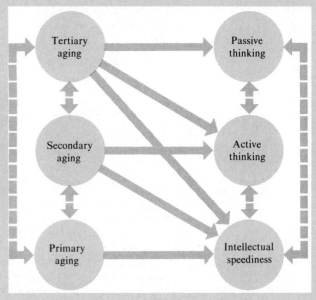

The Cascade model of intellectual functioning.

Cunningham's **cascade model** of intellectual functioning is shown in the figure. The straight arrows in the model represent causal relationships, while the curved, dotted lines represent reciprocal relationships. Variations in the model are possible in that there may be causal links between three types of aging and between the different forms of intellectual functioning as well.

To evaluate his cascade model, Cunningham (1981) analyzed physical health and intelligence test data for 300 males and 240 females ranging in age from seventy to seventy-nine years of age. Cunningham was able to classify these individuals into either primary or secondary aging categories, but no individuals experiencing tertiary aging were present in the sample. Based on the correlations between the two types of aging and a number of cognitive measures used to evaluate the three kinds of intellectual functioning described, Cunningham revised the cascade model to look like the second illustration shown. Note that

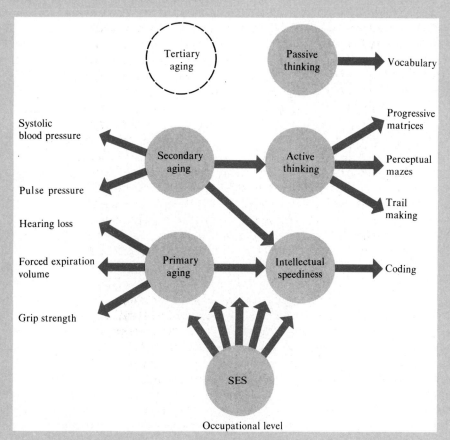

The Cascade model of aging and intelligence.

socioeconomic status is represented in the revised model, because it was found to be related not only to the cognitive measures but to the two types of aging as well.

Cunningham's model is an interesting attempt to explain links between different types of aging, defined according to health status, and different types of intellectual functioning. It will be intriguing to see if future data collected on the relationship between health and intellectual functioning fit this model.

Box 18.3
Work and Live Longer?

In one investigation the best predictor of how long a person would live was work satisfaction, outpacing even general happiness (Palmore & Jeffers, 1971). These two factors were even better predictors of longevity than a medical doctor's examination or genetic inheritance.

Other evidence that longevity and work are related comes from observations of the Abkhasian people in Soviet Russia (Benet, 1976). At the time of the observations, approximately 2.5 percent of the Abkhasians were ninety years or older while only .1 percent of all Russians and .4 percent of Americans reached this age. The Abkhasian society has a positive, active view of aging—old people have status and work in late adulthood is highly valued. One additional factor may be very important as well—these people have very healthy diets. But one distinguishing factor is the life-long, continuous work patterns in the Abkhasian society. Individuals who have reached or have passsed the 100-year mark still work as much as four hours per day on their farms. Both Russian doctors and the Abkhasian people themselves attribute their longevity primarily to their work habits. The Abkhasian medical philosophy is that work helps vital organs function properly, which produces a healthy person. The Abkhasians say that without rest they cannot work, but that without work, the rest does not lead to any benefits.

Clearly there are other factors that influence longevity, such as genetic inheritance, diet, and medical care, which we will discuss further in chapter 20, but it appears that a life-long pattern of enjoyable, productive work may help you to live a longer life.

The total group of seventy-year-old men and women who were working either full-time or part-time were asked to report what they saw as the most important aspects of a job. The seven characteristics of the seventy-year-old workers included—

1. work that I feel I do well (listed by almost everyone);
2. work that I feel is important or worthwhile;
3. friendly, likable coworkers;
4. work in pleasant surroundings;
5. interesting work;
6. work that is challenging and permits me to use my abilities fully; and
7. a supervisor who is pleasant and interested in my welfare.

In comparing the life satisfaction of the seventy-year-old workers with those who do not work it was found that the overall quality of life is much the same for seventy-year-olds who work and those who do not. These findings suggest that many elderly individuals can make valuable contributions in the world of work with no loss in the overall quality of life. Indeed, as was seen in the case of the Abkhasians, working in late adulthood may prove beneficial to many individuals, not just in terms of life satisfaction but in terms of longevity as well.

Throughout the history of our country many people believed Henry Ford, who emphasized that our salvation rested in our work. Few people were aware of

Mr. Ford's frequent trips to his mansion in Dearborn, Michigan, where he relaxed and participated extensively in leisure activities. And, as indicated earlier, Ronald Reagan seems to have found a better balance between work and leisure than most of us.

With the kind of work ethic on which our country is based, it is not surprising that many adults view leisure as boring and unnecessary. During the later years of life, when elderly individuals find it necessary to reduce their workload or to retire, they often find themselves with more free time than they know how to handle. Next, we look further at such aspects of late adulthood as we evaluate various dimensions of retirement.

Retirement

Until recently, many individuals did not have a choice between work and retirement. The social security system provided benefits at the age of sixty-five and most private pension plans mandated retirement at sixty-five. In 1978, however, Congress extended the mandatory retirement age from sixty-five to seventy in business and industry and removed the age limit completely for federal employees. A best guess is that the future will see even further reductions in regulation of mandatory retirement, and we can expect more individuals to be confronted with the decision of when to retire rather than being forced into retirement.

Financial security, health status, attitudes toward work, job satisfaction, and personal interests contribute to an individual's decision of whether to retire or

Many of our elderly have accomplished great things in their old age. Pictured here, clockwise, *are Pablo Picasso, Arturo Toscanini, Gloria Swanson, and Agatha Christie.*

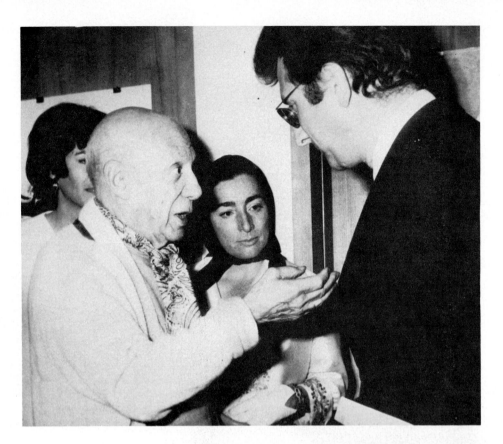

continue working. And, it is not uncommon for individuals to retire from one job, become restless, and then pursue another job. For example, Frank Baird, a seventy-two-year-old motel manager found that he could not tolerate the inactivity of retirement (Van Hoose & Worth, 1982).

"They gave me a gold watch—a beautiful thing—six months pay, a new car, and a fabulous pension," Baird explained. "We spent three months traveling, playing golf, fishing, and getting lazy. At first, I thought it was great. You know, for years you look forward to the freedom, the leisure time, the no hassles. But, let me tell you friend, it gets old. After six months I was bored stiff, and my wife, she was getting fed up too. You know, she had her friends and her activities and didn't need me under foot. Then, I found this job, and it's great. I love it! New people; people from all over and I am able to make their stay a little more pleasant. Don't ever retire friend, if you got a job, stick with it. Retirement is for the birds. Unless you're a lazy bird."

While disillusionment with retirement and financial problems seem to be the major reasons individuals continue to work after a conventional retirement age, in the case of Frank Baird the major factors in his decision to return to work seemed to be his feelings of

uselessness and isolation. And, some individuals have developed a second or third career during adulthood—at some point in middle or late adulthood they may retire from one of their jobs and work full-time at the other.

Still there are many individuals who look forward to retirement and relish the time when they will not have to work long hours. Van Hoose and Worth (1982) describe the feelings of Katy Adams, a retired teacher, who expresses this sentiment.

I don't feel any great loss at all. No, No. I taught math and science for thirty-one years and if I hadn't taken time out to raise two daughters, I would have made it forty. I loved every minute of it, but now it is time to take a rest. After all that time I have earned it, don't you think? Why would I want to go on teaching? I have my retirement, my insurance, and my health. Now I just want to enjoy it.

While more people now have the option of working until seventy and many of us will continue to work beyond the mandatory retirement age, there appears to be no major trend in that direction. In fact, the number of males aged sixty-five and older in the labor force is dropping. One of the reasons may be that the United States Civil Services Commission has encouraged earlier retirement through rules that allow employees to

"I'm 65 today! I guess I'm retired."

This retirement community is typical of many residences of our elderly.

retire after twenty-five years of service. And, some industrial firms and labor organizations have cooperated and developed programs that allow some individuals to retire in their mid-fifties.

In sum, in the United States there is considerable variability in the age at which individuals retire and the reasons they retire. In Japan, most companies force their workers to retire at the age of fifty-five. However, many of the fifty-five-year-old Japanese want to continue work—at least 25 percent of these individuals find other full-time employment after they have been released by their companies.

Phases of Retirement   Atchley (1977) suggests that many individuals go through seven phases of retirement: remote phase, near phase, honeymoon phase, disenchantment phase, reorientation phase, stability phase, and termination phase—the sequence of phases is shown in figure 18.4.

Most individuals begin work with the vague belief that they will not die on the job, and that they will enjoy the fruits of labor at some point in the distant future. In this **remote phase** of retirement, most individuals do virtually nothing to prepare themselves for retirement. As they age toward possible retirement they often deny the fact that the event eventually will happen.

Only when the **near phase** is reached do workers usually participate in preretirement programs. And, such preretirement programs, which could significantly help individuals make the transition to retirement, are not that pervasive. Preretirement programs, when they do exist, usually either help individuals to decide when they should retire by familiarizing them with the benefits and pensions they can expect to receive or involve discussion of more comprehensive issues, such as physical and mental health. Only about 10 percent of the labor force is involved in such preretirement programs, and most are of the first type mentioned. Such programs, however, do seem to be beneficial. In one investigation (Atchley, 1976), individuals who had been exposed to a retirement preparation program had higher retirement incomes, engaged in more activities after retirement, and held fewer stereotyped beliefs about retirement than their counterparts who were not exposed to the preretirement program.

As indicated in figure 18.4, after retirement, five remaining phases remain in this model of the retirement process. Of course, many individuals do not go through these phases, and many others do not go through them in the manner indicated in the figure. How significant each phase will be in the adjustment of the retired individual depends upon such factors as the individual's preretirement expectations and the reality of retirement in terms of money, available options, and the ability to make decisions (Williamson et al., 1980).

Remote phase	Near phase	Honeymoon phase	Disenchantment phase	Reorientation phase	Stability phase	Termination phase

Preretirement   Retirement event   Retirement   End of retirement

Figure 18.4 Seven phases of retirement.

It is not unusual for individuals to initially feel euphoric in the period of time just after their retirement. Individuals may be able to do all of the things they never had time to do before, and they may derive considerable pleasure from leisure activities. People who are forced to retire, or who retire because they are angry about their job, however, are less likely to experience the positive aspects of this early phase of retirement, called the **honeymoon phase.** This phase eventually gives way to a routine. If the routine is satisfying, adjustment to retirement is usually successful. Individuals whose life-styles did not entirely revolve around their jobs before retirement likely are able to make the retirement adjustment and develop a satisfying routine easier than those who did not develop leisure habits during their working years.

Even individuals who initially experience retirement as a honeymoon usually feel some form of letdown, or in some cases, even serious depression. Preretirement fantasies about the retirement years may be unrealistic in such cases. Atchley calls this the **disenchantment phase.**

At some point, though, individuals who are disenchanted with retirement come to grips with themselves and *reorient* themselves to the reality of their retirement and begin to reason about how to successfully cope with it. The major purpose of this **reorientation phase** is to explore, evaluate, and make some decisions about the type of life-style that will likely lead to life satisfaction during retirement.

The **stability phase** of retirement is attained when individuals have decided upon a set of criteria for evaluating choices in retirement and how they will perform once they have made these choices. For some individuals, this phase may occur after the honeymoon phase, yet for others the transition is slower and more difficult.

According to Atchley (1977), at some point the retirement role loses its significance and relevance in the eyes of the older individual. For some of these individuals, they go to work again, often accepting a job that was totally unrelated to what they had done before retirement. Full-time leisure may become boring to them or they may need money to support themselves. Sickness or disability, or course, can alter the retirement process as well. The autonomy and sufficiency that was

Many individuals cope well with retirement, even in the face of societal standards that seem to devalue the retired individual.

Physical and Cognitive Development   559

developed in the stable phase may begin to give way to dependency on others, both physically and economically. This final phase of retirement is called the **termination phase** by Atchley.

Clearly, because individuals retire at different ages and for a variety of reasons, there is no particular timing or sequencing to the seven phases of the retirement process described by Atchley. Nonetheless, the seven phases help us to understand what some of the most important adjustments to retirement are.

For individuals who retire in the 1980s two particular problems are likely to influence their adjustment. First, the individual who retires is automatically pushed into a more leisurely pace of life, whether he or she wants such a life or not, and at the same time, the individual will likely be deprived of financial resources. Second, the retired individual will have to live in a work-oriented world in which retired individuals often are perceived as outsiders. Such circumstances contribute to feelings of helplessness, low self-esteem, isolation, and not being wanted. But as we have seen in our discussion of retirement, many individuals seem to cope well with retirement, even in the face of societal standards that seem to devalue the retired individual.

Evidence that the issues involved in work and retirement are important in late adulthood can be found in the nature of debate that surfaced during the 1981 White House Conference on Aging, and in a 1980 colloquium at the Andrus Gerontology Center at the University of Southern California. At the White House Conference on Aging, delegates were sent from all fifty states. The four-day conference ended with a series of recommendations that were to be forwarded to the leaders of congress and the president as policy recommendations developed by senior citizens that would benefit senior citizens. Among the resolutions adopted that pertained to work and retirement were calls for no reduction in Social Security Benefits or Medicare and Medicaid spending, as well as the creation of a national health insurance program that would cover home health services for the elderly. From these recommendations, we can conclude that health and money are pervasive concerns of the elderly.

At the colloquium on work, aging, and retirement at the University of Southern California (Gonda, 1981), individuals from a variety of fields—academia, government, business, and industry—convened to address a number of key issues related to retirement and work. Claude Pepper, chairman of the United States House of Representatives Committee on Aging, described why older Americans should be allowed to continue to work: mandatory retirement wastes valuable talent, places a further burden on the public and private pension system, and devalues the dignity of the older person. Stephen McConnell and Malcolm Morrison discussed alternative work patterns for older workers, such as (1) alterations in time spent on job (e.g., phased retirement, part-time work, job sharing); (2) alterations in the design of the job itself (e.g., slower pace); and (3) alteration of roles within the organization (e.g., lateral transfers). Michael Batten called for a broader look at company policies and programs as they relate to age factors operating within personnel and retirement systems. He suggested examining age structures within organizations and occupations, with particular emphasis on hiring, promotion, training and development, performance appraisal, terminations, retirement policy, and employee benefit plans.

One theme that characterized a number of colloquia at the Southern California conference involved changing work patterns across the life span. Alternatives such as part-time work, job sharing, and phased retirement were suggested. Since much of our research on older people (whether the focus is on physical, cognitive, or social development) has been conducted with retired individuals, it will be interesting to see what effect, if any, these alternative patterns will have on our future studies of late adulthood (Gonda, 1981).

Summary

This chapter focused on physical and cognitive development in late adulthood. At some point in late adulthood, biological deterioration is inevitable. The age and swiftness of such decline varies extensively from one individual to another, influenced by such factors as heredity, diet, exercise, and psychological orientation. One of the most significant changes in the body's machinery is that the circulatory system becomes less efficient. While some scientists have speculated that the brain loses a large number of cells, as we age, there is no scientific evidence to support such a claim. The label *senility* has been used too often in categorizing individuals in late adulthood who may show some physical and mental decline.

There are many myths about the role of exercise in late adulthood. While the intensity of exercise likely should be lessened, evidence suggests that a regular exercise program promotes physical health. Surveys of the physical health status of the elderly indicate that almost 40 percent of sixty-five to seventy-five-year-olds have some impairment of physical functioning, and after seventy-five the rate rises to 60 percent. Arthritis, hearing and vision impairments, and heart conditions are the most prevalent impairments. But most adults, even those with a physical impairment, still carry on their everyday activities and work.

Information about the type of health care the elderly receive suggests that some health care personnel share society's negative stereotypes about the elderly, may not be as enthusiastic about treating them compared to younger individuals, and may too readily prescribe drugs when they may not be called for.

A final aspect of physical development we discussed focused on sexuality. Sexual activity can occur throughout late adulthood. While there is a decline in sexual activity in late adulthood, it appears that many individuals still show a strong interest in sexuality. Healthy older persons who want to be sexually active usually are.

Our discussion of cognitive development in late adulthood followed the pattern of earlier chapters. The three familiar perspectives—cognitive-structural, psychometric, and information processing—were described. Little has been written about cognitive-structural change in late adulthood. While it has been argued that formal operational thought may give way to less advanced stages of thought, the evidence does not support this claim. One theory, proposed by K. Warner Schaie, indicates that cognitive activity in late adulthood is characterized by the *reintegrative stage,* a time when the individual begins to focus on those aspects of his or her life that are meaningful. Another cognitive-structural view developed by Kurt Fischer indicates that in order to positively resolve Erikson's integrity versus despair crisis, the individual likely has to reach a level of thought called system of abstract systems.

A major issue in the psychometric approach to intelligence in late adulthood is plasticity. While virtually all theorists agree that there is some decline in mental ability at some point in late adulthood, the theorists disagree on the extent of the decline, the nature of the decline, and to what extent cognitive intervention programs can improve intellectual functioning in the elderly. Some theorists believe that in the absence of serious disease, intellectual decline in late adulthood is barely perceptible. Our discussion of physical health and intelligence suggests experts agree that our physical health status is related to our intellectual functioning. Others have argued that it is only when we approach death (particularly in the five years preceding death) that intellectual decline begins to occur.

The study of information processing in late adulthood has emphasized the appearance or absence of a decline in memory, and if there is a decline, whether there are ways the decline either can be reduced or eliminated. Attention and perception are other aspects of the information processing system that have been studied in late adulthood. Age-related deficits in information processing in late adulthood are greatest when (1) the task taps long-term memory; (2) effective learning strategies are not enforced; (3) tasks demand effortful search or retrieval; (4) the materials are unfamiliar; and (5) previously acquired knowledge and skills cannot be applied. Further, sometimes effective learning strategies that improve memory in middle adulthood do not do so in late adulthood. Also, while elderly persons are capable of using many learning strategies, they may fail to use them spontaneously when told to learn. And, while effortful memory processes seem to decline in late adulthood, automatic processes do not. Finally, elderly persons can be very effective learners if their knowledge and skills are applicable to the task. Attention and perception also influence memory—in this regard, age-related slowing, and age-related declines in attentional capability, may be implicated in memory deficits.

The final section of this chapter focused on work and retirement. It is a myth that older persons are inefficient at work and should retire. Evidence on workers in late adulthood suggests that they often are more efficient than individuals who are much younger. And, there is some evidence that a productive, enjoyable work schedule in late adulthood can increase longevity. However, many of the jobs individuals in late adulthood work at are not of the highly skilled, high-income variety. Only 4 percent of the men and women in the United States, aged sixty-eight to seventy-three, work full-time. For those who do work, there seems to be no decrease in their life satisfaction.

While most individuals now have the option of working until the age of seventy before they are forced to retire, it appears that the number of older workers in the United States actually is declining, possibly because of early retirement clauses in the contracts of many employees. Financial security, health status, attitude toward work, job satisfaction, and personal interests are factors that contribute to an individual's decision to work or retire. Among the phases an individual may go through before and during retirement are remote, near, honeymoon, disenchantment, reorientation, stability, and termination phases. This sequence does not characterize all individuals, but the phases describe many of the adjustments individuals must make when they retire. Two major problems of individuals who retire today are financial difficulties and living in a work-oriented society as a nonworker. Some experts believe that we need to restructure work patterns across the life span—part-time work, job sharing, and phased retirement are three possibilities that require more attention in late adulthood.

Key Terms

achieving stage	masking
acquisition stage	near phase
ageism	primary aging
automatic information processing	processing deficit
	reintegrative stage
cascade model	remote phase
collagen	reorientation phase
disenchantment phase	responsible stage
divided attention	secondary aging
effortful information processing	selective attention
	spatial processing
honeymoon phase	stability phase
iconic	system of abstract systems
knowledge actualization	termination phase
limited attentional capacity	tertiary aging

Review Questions

1. Describe the nature of physical decline in late adulthood. What role can exercise play in physical development in late adulthood?
2. Discuss the nature of health care in the United States. What are some ways health care for the elderly can be improved?
3. Evaluate sexual interest and activity in late adulthood.
4. Describe the cognitive-structural views of cognitive activity in late adulthood.
5. What do psychometric theorists say about the plasticity of intelligence in late adulthood?
6. What kinds of changes in attention and perception seem to occur in late adulthood?
7. Evaluate the complex issue of whether there is a decline in memory during late adulthood.
8. How do information processing theorists explain memory decline in late adulthood?
9. What is the relation between physical health and intelligence?
10. What are some of the cognitive intervention strategies that have been used to improve intellectual functioning in late adulthood? How successful are they?
11. Discuss the role of work in late adulthood. What are some of the main characteristics of workers in late adulthood? Make some suggestions for how we might restructure the work cycle in the United States to better accommodate individuals in late adulthood who want to work.
12. Describe the nature of the retirement process in the United States. What are some of the major adjustments those who retire must make?

Further Readings

Benet, S. *How to live to be 100*. New York: The Dial Press, 1976.

The book that describes the lives of the Abkhasian culture in Russia, where many of the inhabitants live to be 100. Description of the working habits of the Abkhasians provides some insight into their longevity. Fascinating and easy reading.

Kastenbaum, R. (ed.), *Old age on the new scene*. New York: Springer, 1981.

A series of articles on late adulthood that include ideas about many of the topics discussed in the chapter. Examples of interesting and informative chapters include the old man as a creative artist in India, formal educational opportunities for older adults, and motivation, capacity, learning and age. Reading level is of easy to medium difficulty.

Ragan, P. K. (ed.), *Work and retirement: policy issues*. Los Angeles: University of Southern California Press, 1980.

This edited volume contains a number of papers that were presented at the University of Southern California conference on aging, work, and retirement described in this chapter. Reading level is of medium difficulty.

Welford, A. T. Sensory, perceptual, and motor processes in older adults. In J. E. Birren & R. B. Sloane (eds.), *Handbook of mental health and aging*. Englewood Cliffs, N.J.: Prentice-Hall, 1980.

This article surveys what we know about changes in sensory, motor, perceptual systems in late adulthood. An up-to-date, authoritative overview. Reading level is moderately difficult.

Williamson, J. B., Munley, A., & Evans, L. *Aging and society: an introduction to social gerontology*. New York: Holt, Rinehart & Winston, 1980.

This introductory book on social gerontology has excellent essays on a number of topics described in this chapter. Topics included are work, retirement, and leisure; sexuality; and nursing homes. The reading level is easy.

Wiswell, R. A. Relaxation, exercise, and aging. In J. E. Birren & R. B. Sloane (eds.), *Handbook of mental health and aging*. Englewood Cliffs, N.J.: Prentice-Hall, 1980.

This article provides a thorough review of our knowledge about the role of exercise and relaxation in late adulthood. Implications for physical and mental health are given. Reading level is of medium difficulty.

19

Social, Emotional, and Personality Development

Prologue: Helplessness, Helping, and the Voice of the Elderly

It is not unusual to think of the elderly as helpless beings, incapable of contributing to their world. Indeed, some researchers have found that many elderly individuals often do feel helpless (e.g., Cohn, 1981). It is argued that the elderly often feel that they do not have control over their environment, a finding assessed most often through the use of a locus of control measure (e.g., Lawton, Nahemow, Yaffe, & Feldman, 1976). However, recent research on locus of control suggests that individuals in late adulthood do not necessarily show more external than internal control (e.g., Gatz & Siegler, 1981).

The fact that the elderly have generally been viewed as more helpless than helpful can be found in the literature on altruism. In the few investigations of altruism that have included elderly individuals, older people were studied as recipients rather than givers. However, elderly individuals are often competent people who provide help to others. Indeed, in one investigation of the service needs of urban people (Kahana & Felton, 1977), it was found that elderly people living in the community provided more services than they received.

Elizabeth Midlarksky and Eva Kahana (1981) summarized how altruism and helping can contribute to life satisfaction among the elderly. They indicate that being useful to the community is considerably more meaningful to those above the age of sixty-five than to younger individuals. The elderly also have been found to be useful service providers for one another (Ehrlich,

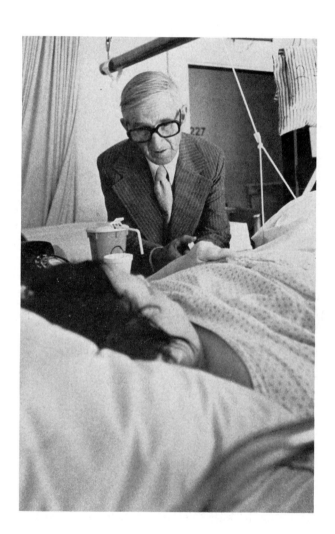

1979) through neighborhood support services, civic activities, group activities, and dyadic helping situations. Types of help given included telephone reassurance, performing chores, providing emergency assistance, and empathetic interactions. And, in another investigation of altruism among elderly individuals, helping behavior was positively related to self-esteem (Trimakas & Nicolay, 1974).

Whereas being a resource to others is likely to enhance self-esteem, being a recipient of help can decrease positive regard for the recipient in others' eyes. The reluctance of older persons to seek and accept assistance has been well documented (e.g., Butler & Lewis, 1977). It clearly is possible that such reluctance is motivated by the need to preserve one's self-esteem. Indeed, it has been suggested that the current attempts to raise the public's consciousness about the elderly should not lead to thoughtless "helping," (Rodin & Langer, 1980). Instead, we may benefit many elderly individuals by providing them with increased opportunities to be of help to others. Such opportunities are likely to increase the elderly person's self-worth, contribute to the belief that their life still has meaning, and enhance the likelihood that they will feel like they are contributing members of their family and community.

The fact that the elderly are not helpless beings is evident in the increased political voice they seem to have in our country. Led by Representative Claude Pepper, Chairman of the House of Representatives Committee on Aging, many older people are arguing vociferously for a greater say in determining the factors that have pronounced consequences for their lives—items such as the removal of mandatory retirement, improved health benefits, and better living conditions. As our population of older people increases, we can expect the elderly to have an even greater voice in determining the standards of our culture.

There are an increasing number of individuals in late adulthood who have joined forces to organize groups in their behalf. The California Legislative Council for Older Americans, and national groups such as the National Retired Teachers Association/American Association of Retired Persons, the National Council of Senior Citizens, and the National Association of Retired Federal Employees seem to include more assertive members than in the past. One example of the effectiveness such organized groups have had as lobbyists is the extension of the mandatory retirement age to seventy.

Many individuals who have reached late adulthood are outgrowths of the Victorian era—they believe strongly in working from dawn to dusk, in paying their own way, and feel embarrassed if they don't. They not only have been silent but have been reluctant to receive charity or welfare of any type. However, they are beginning to make demands on government agencies as it becomes clear that many who worked from dawn to dusk are not protected from the spirals of inflation. One elderly suburbanite said that "we old people may be an outgrowth of the Victorian Era, brought up to speak only when we are spoken to, but now we're getting mad. And we're going to yell real loud when somebody steps on our toes." (Williamson, Munley, & Evans, 1980)

Introduction

In the prologue we discovered that while many elderly individuals are perceived as helpless, they have a strong desire to be helpful. In this chapter we will explore many other aspects of social, emotional, and personality development in late adulthood. We continue our discussion of marriage and families, focusing on the aging couple, and we describe the lives of widows and widowers. The relationships between adult children and their aging parents is evaluated, with particular emphasis on coordinating family and community support systems to assist the elderly. The meaning of being a grandparent is discussed, and various styles of grandparenting are presented. The importance of social networks and friendships is emphasized.

Our discussion of the living environments of the elderly stresses the importance of analyzing the attributes of environments, such as accessibility and adaptability. The problems of the elderly poor are described, and cross-cultural comparisons with other industrialized countries and with primitive societies are presented. Our presentation of personality development emphasizes the eighth and last stage of Erikson's theory—integrity vs. despair—and the importance of the life review through reminiscence. We also evaluate what makes life satisfying for people in late adulthood, describe the mental health problems of older people, with particular emphasis on depression and senility, and conclude by discussing how older people can adapt and cope with the later years of their lives.

Marriage, Family, and Relationships

In the discussion of early and middle adulthood the earlier phases of the marital cycle were discussed—in this section we will look at the last phase, the aging couple. We will also explore the nature of relationships between adult children and their parents, and the importance of friendship in late adulthood.

Marital Relations—the Aging Couple

The time from retirement until the death of a spouse is the final stage of the marital couple. Retirement undoubtedly alters a couple's life-style and requires some adaptation in their relationship. The greatest changes may occur in the traditional family (in which the husband works and the wife is a homemaker). The husband may not know what to do with himself and the wife may feel uneasy having him around the home all of the time. In such families, both spouses may need to move toward more expressive roles. The husband has to adjust from being a good provider to helping around the house, while the wife has to change from functioning only as a good homemaker to being even more loving and understanding (Troll, 1971). And marital

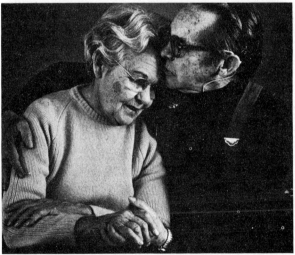

Retirement undoubtedly alters a couple's life-style and requires some adaptation in their relationship.

Grief work can lead to a new identity for the individual, an identity that can be healthy or unhealthy.

happiness in late adulthood may be influenced by each partner's ability to deal with personal conflicts—aging, illness, and eventual death, for example (Levinson, 1977).

Individuals who are married in late adulthood appear to be happier than those who are single (Lee, 1978). Such satisfaction appears to be greater for women than for men, possibly because women place more emphasis on attaining satisfaction through marriage than men do. However, as more women develop careers the relationship between satisfaction and marriage may not hold.

Of course, there are many different types of adult life-styles—not all individuals in late adulthood are married. At least 8 percent of persons who reach the age of sixty-five have never been married. Contrary to the popular stereotype, those old persons who have always been single seem to have the least difficulty coping with loneliness in old age. Many of these individuals found how to live autonomously and developed self-reliance long ago (Gubrium, 1975).

Eventually, for married couples, one spouse dies and the surviving spouse must adjust to being alone. As we will see next, there are a number of age and sex differences in widowhood, and individuals vary extensively in their ability to cope with the death of a spouse.

Widowhood

When a spouse dies, the surviving marital partner goes through a period of grieving. In one investigation, 83 percent indicated they still felt a great deal of distress over their spouse's death over the course of a year. Men seem to adjust better than women to the death of a spouse, and older individuals seem to adjust better than younger people (Carey, 1977).

Some researchers call the bereavement process of surviving spouses in the year after the death "grief work" (Parkes, 1972). The individual's working model of the world becomes disrupted because of the loss of a strong attachment (Bowlby, 1980). Grief work may lead to a new identity for the individual, an identity that can be healthy or unhealthy. Four stages that many individuals go through in the grief process are (1) numbness, (2) pining for the lost attachment figure, (3) depression, and (4) recovery. To successfully cope with the death of a spouse, many psychologists believe that it is important for the surviving spouse to go through these four stages (Rux, 1976).

The death of a husband may be particularly difficult for a wife who has not developed a separate identity of her own (e.g., through a career). When identity as a wife is stripped away, such women may feel that there is no meaning left in their life. Not having a husband in the provider role, she may have to live on public support or find a job. And, she may experience social problems, having become accustomed to socializing with other couples or relying heavily on social interaction with her husband. She also may be criticized if she develops a relationship with another man too soon after the death of her husband. But even for women who have many interests outside of their husband's identity, his death will be a traumatic experience. Feelings of loneliness and a range of emotions that include grief, hostility, and ambivalence are likely to appear. And, for many widows, sexual needs will go unmet.

Men are not isolated from the trauma of a spouse's death either. They may have come to rely heavily on their wife for emotional support, intimacy, and sexual satisfaction—her loss likely triggers a great deal of grief and stress. Support systems, such as a circle of friends, usually are more available to the wife whose husband dies than vice versa, particularly since there are many more older women in our society than older men. And, it appears that older individuals' children are more likely to allow a widow to move in with them than a widower. One advantage the widower in late adulthood has over the widow is that if he decides to date and/or remarry the available pool of women is large.

Even though loneliness is fairly common among widowed older persons, the marriage rate for individuals in late adulthood is not very high. Among some older individuals, remarriage may be viewed as a betrayal of the deceased spouse. Some elderly individuals are limited by mobility, energy, or budget constraints in their efforts to meet new people, including potential mates—such limitations suggest why the remarriages that do occur in late adulthood often are between people who have previously known each other.

Family relations in late adulthood involve not only marital relations, but parent-child relations as well. Next, we look further at the relationship between adult children and their aging parents.

Parents of Adult Children

Parent-child relationships do not end when the child leaves home at the end of adolescence. As the life span of individuals in late adulthood has lengthened, it is not unusual for the child in the parent-child relationship to be in the sixties and the parent to be in the eighties. An interesting reversal occurs in some parent-child relationships. During the early years of the child's life, the child is dependent upon the parents for money, care, food, and other necessities: but when the parent reaches late adulthood, the dependency may move from child to parent. The dependence of older adults on their children and the children's acceptance of this dependency has been called **filial maturity** (Blenkner, 1965).

Most parents do not expect their adult offspring to totally repay them for what they have done for them earlier in their lives. In our society, we do not have a standard that tells us adult children have to support their aging parents. However, filial maturity is the rule in many cultures—in Japan, for example, it is the children's responsibility to care for their aging parents. As a consequence, nursing and retirement homes are virtually nonexistent in Japan.

Family responsibility in the United States is **serial,** while in Japan it is **reciprocal.** What this means is that in the United States, each generation is seen as responsible for each succeeding generation—parents are supposed to care for their own offspring, and their first priority is to them, not to the parents who cared for them. In Japan, generational responsibility is reciprocal—adult children are responsible for both their own offspring and their aging parents.

In truth, the vast majority of older Americans are not completely disconnected from kin. Some social scientists have described the relationships between adult children and their aging parents as either a "modified, extended family type" or "intimacy at a distance" (Litwak, 1965; Rosenmayr & Koekeis, 1963). If we look at the frequency of interaction and association of adult children and their parents, the stereotype of the abandoned, lonely older person does not hold up. In one investigation, 84 percent of elderly parents lived within one hour of at least one child, and 85 percent had seen at least one child during the previous week (Shanas, 1968).

But the relationship between adult children and aging parents can become stressful. Stress may become acute when the elderly parent gets sick and needs to be cared for yet cannot afford to pay for medical expenses. The elderly parent's illness may coincide with increased financial demands on their children, whose offspring may be just entering college. Emotional feelings of guilt, anger, and resentment may surface on the part of the middle-aged adult who may vascillate between caring and not caring for their elderly parent. And, the aging parents may also feel guilty about becoming a burden on their children, both financially and emotionally.

In sum, relationships between adult children and their aging parents are varied and complex, sometimes positive, sometimes negative. In the majority of cases, individuals in late adulthood never become completely financially dependent on their adult children, and the majority of elderly individuals are not isolated from their adult children and have not been abandoned by them. Still, in other cases, intergenerational stress may result, particularly in the face of ill health and financial strain.

In order to ensure that the elderly will be dealt with in humanitarian ways, regardless of whether or not they have children to care for them, in the United States we

Box 19.1
Support Systems for the Elderly

In the last few years, greater attention has been paid to caring for the "frail older person" who is in need of special assistance. A reasonable array of services in each of the fifty states and territories of the United States has developed, funded to a large extent through the Older Americans Act and its subsidiary programs, the Mental Health Act and through the Social Security System. Most of these programs have been individual-oriented. Even our best counseling centers and mental health agencies have focused on the *individual* older person without including the older person as a part of the total family network. Grandchildren and their relationship to grandparents have hardly been noticed. Research has been sparse. We know little about the effects of interpersonal relationships of grandparents and grandchildren. Relatively little attention has been paid to what I call the "sandwich generation," the family in the middle that has to care for their own aging parents and come to terms with their demands, needs and pressures, who have to cope with their own feelings of guilt when they can no longer care for them and have to place them in nursing homes and, at the same time, raise their own offspring in times of many pressures.

In the past few years we have witnessed a growing interest in the role of the family in providing support to its older members—a result, in part, of humanitarian concerns for the well-being of the elderly as well as of economic concerns, as the costs of providing services for the long-term care of the dependent elderly have become apparent.

In many countries, families are providing the bulk of the assistance needed by the elderly so they can continue to remain in the community. At the same time evidence is becoming available on the many stresses that care of chronically sick older persons can place upon families, who themselves may be in need of supportive services to assist them in their caregiving role.

While help and services are more often provided by older persons to children and grandchildren than the other way around, this situation reverses during the later years of old age and its accompanying health problems. Services important to older people in this stage of life, such as physical care, shelter, escort, and help with household tasks, are commonly provided by children and other kin members.

The day-to-day responsibilities for care of an elderly relative usually fall on one person, generally a spouse, a daughter, or a daughter-in-law. Even if there are other family members in the household or nearby, pooling of responsibilities may not occur and in many cases, there are no other family members in the household to share the

---

have designed and implemented formal health and social support systems for the elderly in our communities during the last twenty years. These formal support systems are found in public and private social agencies, in health institutions, in nursing homes, in counseling centers, and in mental health agencies. The development of such support systems, and ways that they may be improved further, are described in box 19.1.

Grandparenting

Each of you probably has some ideas about what grandparents are like. Think for a moment about your ideas, images, and memories of grandparents. While the grandparent role is a prevalent one in our society, it still is not well understood. We generally think of grandparents as old people, but there are many middle-aged grandparents as well. And, there are styles that

some grandparents follow that others don't. In one investigation (Neugarten & Weinstein, 1964), seventy pairs of grandparents were interviewed about their relationships with their grandchildren. Emphasis was placed on the degree of comfort the grandparent felt in their role, the significance of the role, and the style in which the grandparent carried out the role. At least one-third of the grandparents said they had some difficulties with the grandparent role, both in terms of thinking of themselves as grandparents and how they should act and in terms of conflicts with their own children over how to rear the grandchildren.

Three prevalent meanings were given to the grandparent role. For some individuals being a grandparent was a source of *biological renewal and/or continuity*. In such cases, feelings of renewal (youth) or extensions

burden of care. Psychological stresses appear to play a paramount role in the feelings of burden. There is some evidence that the psychological burden on the caregiver is in almost all cases more difficult to bear than the physical burden. In addition, role conflicts are bound to occur. Filial responsibilities, for example, often impinge on the quality of a husband-wife relationship. Despite these problems, stresses and tensions that exist, family members are vital resources for older persons as they provide a great deal of care to them.

The Community Service Society of New York, for example, has been engaged in a research and demonstration project to provide services to families in order to strengthen the capacity to care for their aged members (1978). Preliminary data so far indicate that the extended family members' involvement is considerable, but that incentives need to be provided to insure that such care and support efforts are rewarded and continued. The existence of respite care programs that allow for agencies to take over the role of family members when they feel they cannot shoulder it both for the family members and the older person is an example of such community services. Our public policy has barely caught up with this issue in contrast to other countries where income tax rebates have been provided or when family members have been paid to ease the burden, particularly in low-income families. The informal support system can work in two ways: one, as a reward system for family members to meet their role obligations to the aging parents or grandparents; and two,

to insure a closer link between the family to stay together on an emotional level. To what extent intergenerational conflicts will be reduced or enhanced through formal and informal supports is still subject to speculation rather than verification by empirical research.

In 1980, I had testified in a Hearing in San Diego by the Select Committee on Aging of the United States House of Representatives on "Families: Aging and Changing" that public policies have to address family supports not only relative to caretaking functions, but also relative to growth and developmental functions of all generations, because we know that many older people give to their children and grandchildren time, money and affection. They also provide care and services in innumerable ways. We must assess these contributions and include them in the credit side of the ledger. Social policies can no longer ignore these contributions when the costs of caring are totalled up. Reciprocal exchanges between and among generations are an established fact. We need now the necessary continuity to insure that all families, but particularly those who are the victims of discrimination and poverty, can afford to support and nurture each other for mutual and societal benefit.

Source: Lowy, 1981, pp. 7–9.

of the self and family into the future (continuity) appeared. For others, being a grandparent was a source of *emotional self-fulfillment,* generating feelings of companionship and satisfaction from the development of a relationship between adult and child often missing in earlier parent-child relationships. For yet others, the grandparent role was seen as *remote,* indicating that the role of grandparent had little importance in their lives.

In addition to evaluating the meaning of the grandparent role, the styles of interaction exhibited by the grandparents were assessed. Three styles were dominant—formal, fun-seeking, and distant figure. The formal style involved performing what was considered to be a proper and prescribed role. While these grandparents showed a strong interest in their grandchildren, they left parenting to the parents and were careful

not to offer childrearing advice. The fun-seeker style was typified by informality and playfulness. Grandchildren were seen as a source of leisure activity, and mutual satisfaction was emphasized. And, a substantial portion of grandparents were distant figures. While this style of grandparenting is benevolent, it occurs on an infrequent basis. Grandparents who were over the age of sixty-five were more likely to display a formal style of interaction, while those under sixty-five were more often fun-seeking.

Grandparents often do play a significant role in the lives of their grandchildren. In one investigation (Robertson, 1976), young adult grandchildren showed highly favorable attitudes toward their grandparents. A full 92 percent indicated that children would miss some important things in life if there were no grandparents

For some, being a grandparent is a source of emotional self-fulfillment.

present when they were growing up; and 70 percent of the respondents said that teenagers do not see grandparents as boring. Such information suggests that the grandparent-grandchild relationship is reciprocal, often benefiting both grandchildren and grandparents.

The grandparent role may be particularly significant in the lives of older adults since it is one of the few social roles potentially available for them. And, participation can occur either as a biological or a foster grandparent, giving many older adults the sense that they have an important social function in our society.

Regardless of whether individuals in late adulthood are married or single, and whether they have children or grandchildren, social networks and friendships are important to them. Next, we will look at the role of such networks and friendships in the lives of individuals in late adulthood.

Social Networks and Friendships

Regardless of age, people seem to place a very high value on time spent with friends, often higher than time spent with relatives (Adams, 1967). The particular point in the life cycle and the life events an individual experiences influence friendships. During adolescence when the child-in-family role is being shed, friendships often increase in their frequency and intensity. And in

divorce or death when a marital partner is lost, friendships may represent an important support system. Further, some researchers have suggested that the cohesiveness found in many retirement communities may reflect a loosening of kin relationships (Lowenthal & Robinson, 1977).

John Williamson, Anne Munley, and Linda Evans (1980) found that women have an easier time making and sustaining friendships after the death of a spouse than men, probably because women have traditionally been encouraged to function as the initiators of social contacts. These researchers also found that friendship contacts are more frequent among persons of higher socioeconomic status, however, personality and life-style are important factors in friendships of all classes. The more frequent contacts among middle- and upper-class persons may be offset by lack of involvement and intensity in friendships. Because the life-style of those in the lower classes often involves less geographic mobility, these persons may have friendships in their later years that have extended from childhood.

Friendships among the elderly may become increasingly important in years to come. Because people are having fewer children, families on the whole are getting smaller. As people age in our society, they will have fewer people to depend on for emotional and financial assistance. Friendships with unrelated adults may serve as a replacement for the warmth, companionship, and nurturance traditionally provided by families.

Many elderly place a high value on friendships.

Questions and solutions about the role of the environment of the elderly come from many diverse fields.

Family and social relationships are not the only important aspects of the elderly person's life. Next, we look at another major concern of the elderly—housing.

Living Environment, Social Class and Poverty, and Cross-Cultural Comparisons

Within the last decade there has been an increasing interest in improving the living environment of the elderly. In this section we look at how the living environment of the elderly can be analyzed and changed for the better. We also explore the difficulties poverty brings in late adulthood, particularly in the form of substandard housing. And, in the last part of this section we compare the culture of the elderly in the United States with that of other cultures, such as Japan, China, and primitive cultures.

Living Environment

During the 1970s and early 1980s there has been a substantial increase in concern for the way various environmental factors affect the behavior of older persons. Some of this interest arose from a recognition that many behaviors considered to be less than optimal may be caused by specific environments rather than increasing age. Housing design, work arrangements, and social rehabilitation are three areas that have received special attention. Questions and possible solutions to the role of the environment in the life of the elderly have come from such diverse fields as architecture, ecological psychology, social gerontology, clinical psychology, and social work (Parr, 1980).

The environment in which we live is complex—how should we analyze it in our effort to improve the living conditions of the elderly? One framework for studying the impact of the environment on the elderly has been developed by Paul Windley and Rick Scheidt (1980).

They distinguish between taxonomies of attributes of environments and taxonomies of environments themselves. Taxonomies (or categories) of physical environments include schools, churches, commercial buildings, government buildings, neighborhoods, or on a smaller scale, kitchens, classrooms, and corridors. Attributes of environments include the potential for privacy or social interaction, level of sensory stimulation and comfort, or degree of accessibility. They believe that if we are to design better environments for the elderly we have to take into account the attributes of environments rather than focusing only on the environments themselves.

These researchers also argue that we need to keep in mind that environment-behavior interactions change over time, and that environmental attributes are more sensitive to change than are categories of environments. For instance, bedrooms often become studies or sewing rooms when children move away, shifts in function that usually occur slowly. Attributes such as lighting level, or potential for privacy, may fluctuate hourly.

Another important point to remember in designing environments for the elderly is the **scale of environment** involved. Taxonomies of environments are scale specific—that is, categories for the scale of housing are not the same as categories for neighborhoods, districts, or cities. For instance, when studying the mobility patterns of the elderly across different environmental scales, it is difficult to tie these patterns to categories of environment because of continually shifting frames of reference. Attributes, by contrast, cut across all scales and categories of environment. Degree of environmental accessibility may apply to architectural barriers for a dwelling unit as well as for the neighborhood of a city.

Windley and Scheidt (1980) developed a list of environmental attributes that they believe can profitably be studied to enhance the living conditions of the elderly. Eight of the most important attributes are sensory stimulation, legibility, comfort, privacy, control (territoriality), sociality, accessibility, and adaptability.

Sensory stimulation. What should be the quality and intensity of environmental stimuli? For example, the elderly often experience difficulty with ambiguous and intense stimuli, such as those encountered in large buildings or while driving. Redundant cueing (presenting information via more than one sense modality) has been used by designers to help the elderly—for example, allowing smells from the kitchen to penetrate the dwelling unit in addition to sounding a bell or buzzer announcing meal times.

Legibility. How can the organization and clarity of the environment be improved? **Legibility** refers to the extent to which a setting is perceptually understandable and facilitates orientation, predictability, and direction finding. Environments that do not have identifiable components, such as streets in a city or distinct hallways in a building, likely increase nonadaptive behavior. In one investigation, it was found that services perceived to be within a three to six block radius from the dwelling were used more often than those six blocks away (Regnier, 1975). The cognitive maps developed by the elderly are influenced by such factors as: the kind and number of barriers separating two points; the magnitude of distance separating the points; and the attractiveness of the connecting path between the two points (Thompson, 1965; Stea, 1969; Lee, 1970).

Comfort. What environmental conditions contribute to subjective feelings of comfort and ease in task performance? Temperature and lighting are two of the most important factors in comfort. While there is debate about the ability of the elderly to cope with extreme temperatures, some researchers believe that the elderly do not adapt well when temperatures change drastically. And, some researchers have found that elderly individuals require as much as three times as much illumination as individuals in their twenties to perform daily tasks (Pastalan, Mautz, & Merrill, 1973). Further, sensitivity to glare is twice that for eighty-year-olds as it is for twenty-year-olds (Wolf, 1960).

Privacy. To what extent do the features of a setting permit a person to control unwanted visual and acoustical stimuli from others? It is generally agreed that privacy is essential to maintaining positive self-perception and autonomy. Some researchers have argued that for maximum privacy, resident rooms should be located in a house-porch-street configuration, and that semiprivate areas (e.g., lounges) should be between residents' rooms and public areas (e.g., hallways) (Koncelik, 1976).

Control (territoriality). To what degree does an environment facilitate personalization and convey individual ownership of space? For example, it has been found that the fewer the tenants on a single floor, the more responsible they will be in questioning or reporting strangers (Newman, 1972). The consensus among researchers is that defensive behavior would probably decline with the provision of private space and room to display personal effects.

Sociality. To what extent do features of an environment encourage or discourage social contact among people? Social interaction among the elderly is related to building-centered social activities, proximity to resources in the larger community, and even the degree to which tenants leave their doors open (Lawton, 1979).

"One good thing -- I'll finally have a crowd who'll appreciate my Ben Turpin and Francis X. Bushman imitations!"

Reprinted by permission of NEA.

Accessibility. There are two interrelated concepts underlying the attribute of accessibility: the ease with which a person can go from point A to point B in a given setting, and the degree to which more stationary objects or products can be manipulated. Distance to services affects service utilization (Newcomer, 1973), and household features, such as kitchen cupboards and bathroom fixtures, which require extensive bending and reaching, decrease accessibility (Windley, 1977).

Adaptability. How easily can a setting be rearranged to accommodate new or different patterns of behavior? Older persons may require changes due to health. One investigation (Windley, 1977) focused on thirty case studies of elderly persons who were living in single-family dwellings that had many rooms doubling for activities not originally intended. Many adaptations were required to make living conditions acceptable.

In this section we have seen that the living conditions of the elderly are not usually optimal. Next, we look at living conditions among the elderly at the lowest end of the socioeconomic scale—those in poverty.

Table 19.1
Poverty Rates[a] among Aged Persons[b] by Race and Sex of Household Head, 1959 and 1977

	1977	1959
Male Head		
Whites	7%	28%
Blacks	28%	59%
Female Head		
Whites	21%	47%
Blacks	48%	70%

[a]Percent poor.

[b]Household Head age sixty-five or older.

Source: Williamson, Munley, & Evans, 1980, p. 183. U.S. Bureau of the Census, Current Population Reports, P60, No. 116.

Social Class and Poverty

We have indicated that one of the major concerns of individuals in late adulthood is the decrease in income they likely are to experience. A classic complaint of the aged and aggrieved parent is that a mother can care for five young children more readily than five adult children can care for one mother. In most families, though, children don't neglect an elderly relative out of heartlessness but out of helplessness. Aiding someone who is growing frail and infirm can be frustrating and difficult.

The elderly have a higher poverty rate than any other adult age category. For example, in 1977 of the 22 million people aged sixty-five and over, 3.2 million or 14 percent were classified as poor by the federal government. In 1977, the federal poverty line for a nonfarm family of four was $6,200. For an elderly couple it was $3,700 and for an elderly person living alone it was $2,900. The number of elderly poor probably would be much greater if the "hidden poor" were included, that is, those individuals who would be classified as poor on the basis of their own income, but who have been taken in by relatives who are not poor. Some estimates place the number of hidden poor at 5 million people (U.S. Senate, 1977).

While there are many elderly people who are poor, table 19.1 shows that there has been a marked improvement in the economic status of the elderly in recent years. It also is evident from the table that there is a higher rate of poverty for elderly women than men and a higher rate among elderly blacks than whites.

Housing

John Williamson, Anne Munley, and Linda Evans (1980) describe the housing problems many elderly individuals face.

Life in the Slum Hotel

An estimated 146,000 poor older persons reside in run-down hotels or rooming houses in the blighted sections of cities (Carp, 1976). Though SRO's house a very small percentage of all older persons, residents' life-styles reflect the same staunch desire for privacy, independence, and autonomy that is also manifested by elderly residing in "more desirable" homes.

An ethnography of a slum hotel in a "large Western city" (Stephens, 1976) shows how the elderly live who are near the bottom of the economic ladder. Approximately 30 percent of the occupants of this particular hotel were elderly. . . .

Isolation in one form or another was the hallmark of this social environment. For the most part, the ninety-seven elderly males avoided not only the eleven elderly females but each other as well. These people were virtually required to relinquish their needs for intimacy to survive in the hotel. The two principal reasons for developing or maintaining relationships were common economic interests or shared leisure activities. Relationships among residents seemed to require some justification; simple social interaction never seemed to be enough.

The prime source of income for many older residents involved "hustling"—scavenging, peddling, pushing drugs, or shoplifting. In some cases, two or more residents developed relationships which facilitated hustling schemes. It was also necessary for a "hustler" to let others know of hustling successes, since hustling was a key determinant of social status along three dimensions: its profitability, its dependability as a source of income, and the degree of autonomy it provided. Besides socializing over successful hustling feats, residents also related to one another through drinking or betting activities.

Only minimal social activity took place at the hotel, and it served as the focal point for little physical activity other than sleep. Most residents had to go outside the hotel for food and routine health needs. Some took meals at the least expensive places in the neighborhood where muggings were frequent. The rooms had no cooking or refrigeration facilities, but some residents cooked using a hot iron braced by two bibles as a hot plate. . . .

Locked into this situation by poverty, ill health, and a desire to maintain independence, many older residents of this hotel planned to die there.

Source: Williamson, Munley, & Evans, 1980, pp. 259–60.

In the motion picture *Harry and Tonto,* Harry is a retired teacher living with his cat, Tonto, in a condemned apartment building within one of New York City's deteriorating slum neighborhoods. Despite confrontations with muggers and the areas other undesirable characteristics, Harry insists on remaining and must be removed bodily by police when the wrecking crew arrives. Harry moves in with his son's family because they live sufficiently near his former neighborhood for Harry to visit his best friends frequently; and, as Harry tells Tonto, "When you have friends, that's home." In his new household, Harry puts up with constant bickering. As soon as his friend dies, Harry and Tonto leave the unhappy environment and embark on a series of adventures in search of a living situation they can tolerate.

Though presented in a humorous vein, Harry's quest for satisfying housing demonstrates that living situations can be an important concern for the aging person. Harry's need is not just for housing. He is seeking an environment which is suited to his physical, psychological, and social needs. . . .

Ironically the bulk of research concerned with the living environments of the elderly has focused on special situations such as nursing homes, public housing, mobile home parks, welfare hotels, or retirement communities. In reality, however, these living conditions account for less than 10 percent of this country's elderly population. Approximately 90 percent live in age-integrated settings, but relatively little is known about their environmental circumstances (Carp, 1976). Although the percentage of older persons who own their dwelling units is high, data concerned with housing quality are less optimistic. The United States Senate Special Committee on Aging (1977) estimates that 30 percent of the elderly occupy housing which is deteriorating or substandard . . . (and) one in five lives in a housing unit which lacks basic plumbing facilities (Carp, 1976). (pp. 256, 257, 259)

An example of the haphazard matching of life-style and environment is the mode of urban living referred to as SRO (Single Room Occupancy), described in box 19.2. Social isolation and lack of desirable social activity often characterize such settings.

Income plays an important role in the living conditions of the elderly. Only about 1 percent of aged families and .01 percent of unrelated elderly have incomes of $50,000 or more (U.S. Bureau of the Census, 1975). For such individuals, housing options are virtually unlimited. At the other extreme are individuals who live in places like the slum hotels described in box 19.2. Of course, most of the elderly fall between these two extremes, and typically their number one expense is housing. For individuals aged seventy-five and over, housing accounts for almost one-half of their budget (Harris, 1978).

Fortunately, more help than ever is available in the form of improving institutions and expanding in-home services. Candace Trunzo (1982) has found that more and more health-care workers are helping the elderly to live on their own by finding them roommates to share quarters, costs, and provide companionship. Trunzo found that the current trend is to help the elderly remain independent.

For example, a state-sponsored program in Florida called Community Care for the Elderly is helping more than 10,000 old people stay out of institutions. The agency delivers meals to elderly people in their homes or shuttles them to a community dining facility to nourish both body and spirit. Through the program the elderly also can hire helpers who will wash windows and rake lawns, and homemakers who can help with shopping and light housekeeping. A health maintenance staff attends the elderly in their homes, helping them bathe and shave, and administering physical therapy and some other medical treatments. In addition, the plan provides transportation to doctors' offices. Fees are based on ability to pay; a homemaker costs from nothing to $5.46 an hour. Community Care for the Elderly has benefited the state as well as its older citizens. Administrators of the program estimate that by providing these services in lieu of institutionalization, Florida saved itself $9.5 million in the past fiscal year. (pp. 71, 72)

So far in this section we have focused on the living conditions of the elderly in the United States, emphasizing how such conditions can be improved, and the role of income. Next, we compare the elderly who live in the United States with the elderly of other cultures.

Cross-Cultural Comparisons

In the United States many elderly people live an age-segregated life. And, we have seen that the United States is a youth oriented society, one that places a higher value on being young than being old. This perspective stands in contrast to the lofty status of the elderly in some cultures, particularly in certain peasant and primitive cultures. In such cultures, the elderly are rewarded for their experience, knowledge, and skill. They are seen as the most important figures in such cultures, as individuals who are best equipped to be the leaders in magic displays and rituals. And, in some societies, ancestor worship is practiced—a situation in which a son is obligated to show respect and to obey his father in all circumstances.

China and Japan are two major countries where the elderly also have been given a higher status than in the United States. In China and Japan, intergenerational relations are reciprocal rather than linear. Filial piety runs high in China—respect and homage to family and community elders is a way of life. In Japan, the elderly are more integrated into their families than the elderly in most industrialized countries. More than 75 percent live with their children, and very few single older adults live alone. Respect for the elderly in Japan is evidenced in a variety of everyday encounters—the best seats are usually given to the elderly, cooking caters to the tastes of the elderly, and people bow to the elderly. However, such respect appears to be more prevalent among rural than urban Japanese, and more frequent among middle-aged than young adult Japanese (Palmore, 1975). And, while retirees in Japan are often rehired, it typically involves lower status, lower pay, loss of fringe benefits, and loss of union membership as well.

Respect for the elders is pervasive among Muslim families as well. It is thought that the blessings of the elders, whether they are dead or alive, are necessary to avoid disaster and problems.

It is possible that the elderly attain high status in many primitive and peasant cultures because so few individuals live to be old. Since there are so few elderly in such cultures, the younger members may believe that the few surviving elders are imbued with special powers and wisdom. However, in most industrialized societies, like Japan and the United States, where the aged now constitute a sizeable proportion of the population, it is no longer a special feat to live to an old age.

In this section, we have seen that living environments of the elderly vary extensively in the United States. While there has been a decrease in the number of American elderly living in poverty, a substantial proportion still are poor and many of the elderly live in substandard housing. We also have seen that, compared to many cultures, the elderly in the United States are not accorded with a high status. Next, we focus more on individual development in late adulthood as we describe various aspects of personality development.

In some cultures it is thought that the blessings of elders are necessary to avoid disasters and problems.

Personality Development

Erik Erikson's ideas have been among the most widely discussed aspects of personality development in late adulthood—in this section we look at the last stage in Erikson's eight stages of development, integrity versus despair, as well as other major perspectives on personality development. We also explore the criteria that are most likely to contribute to a perception that life is happy and satisfactory in late adulthood. And, we will outline the most important aspects of mental health in late adulthood, focusing on the nature of mental health, stress, coping, and adaptation, and intervention.

Some Major Perspectives

Both Sigmund Freud and Carl Jung, famous psychoanalytic theorists, saw old age as a period similar to childhood. Freud, for example, believed that in old age people return to the narcissism that characterizes the unconscious thought of early childhood. And, Jung believed that in old age thought is submerged in the unconscious, gradually sinking so deeply into the unconscious that little touch with reality is possible.

Charlotte Buhler (1967) believed that late adulthood is a time when an individual adds up his or her life. Nearness to death was seen by Buhler as the motivating force behind the person's interest in reviewing life.

Another view of personality development in late adulthood has been set forth by Robert Peck (1968), who believes that as old age approaches, three issues must be confronted.

1. **Ego differentiation versus work-role preoccupation.** In a time of role change or loss, people should not dwell on their work roles in defining their self-concept. Instead they should permit themselves to explore new roles and develop a sense of self that goes beyond the work role.

2. **Body transcendence versus body preoccupation.** A sense of well-being should come from satisfying relationships and activities, not health. According to Peck, people in late adulthood should be encouraged to not go around moping and complaining about their physical problems.

3. **Ego transcendence versus ego preoccupations.** Individuals must realize that death is inevitable. Once they come to grips with this realization, then they can lead a more satisfying life in old age that is directed toward positive social interaction with others, which in turn should promote self satisfaction.

But the theorist that has had the most impact on our thinking about personality development in late adulthood is Erik Erikson, who believes that late adulthood is characterized by the last of eight stages of development, integrity versus despair.

Erikson: Integrity vs. Despair

From Erikson's perspective, the later years of life are a time for looking back at what we have done with our lives. Through many different routes the older person may have developed a positive outlook in each of the preceding periods of emotional crises. If so, the retrospective glances and reminiscence will reveal a picture of life well spent, and the person will be satisfied (ego integrity). However, the older person may have resolved one or more of the crises in a negative way. If so, the retrospective glances will yield doubt, gloom, and despair over the sum worth of life. Erikson's own words capture the richness of his thought about personality development in late adulthood.

A meaningful old age, then, . . . serves the need for that integrated heritage which gives indispensable perspective to the life cycle. Strength here takes the form of that detached yet active concern with life bounded by death, which we call *wisdom* in its many connotations from ripened "wits" to accumulated knowledge, mature judgment, and inclusive understanding. Not that each man can evolve wisdom for himself. For most, a living *tradition* provides the essence of it. But the end of the cycle also evokes "ultimate concerns" for what change may have to transcend the limitations of his identity and his often tragic or bitterly tragic comic engagement in his one and only life cycle within the sequence of generations . . . a civilization can be measured by the meaning which it gives to the full cycle of life, for such meaning, or the lack of it, cannot fail to reach into the beginnings of the next generation, and push into the changes of others to meet ultimate questions with some clarity and strength.

To whatever abyss ultimate concerns may lead individual men, man as a psychosocial creature will face, toward the end of his life, a new edition of an identity crisis which we may state in the words, "I am what survives of me." (pp. 140–41)

Erikson's emphasis that the development of integrity depends upon a positive review of one's life also has been discussed extensively by Robert Butler (1975) in an article titled, "The Life Review: An Interpretation of Reminiscence in the Aged," a portion of which is exerpted in box 19.3.

Box 19.3
The Life Review: An Interpretation of Reminiscence in the Aged

The **life review**, as a looking-back process that has been set in motion by looking forward to death, potentially proceeds toward personality reorganization. Thus, the life review is not synonymous with, but includes reminiscence; it is not alone either the unbidden return of memories, or the purposive seeking of them, although both may occur.

The life review sometimes proceeds silently, without obvious manifestations. Many elderly persons, before inquiry, may be only vaguely aware of the experience as a function of their defensive structure. But alterations in defensive operations do occur. Speaking broadly, the more intense the unresolved life conflicts, the more work remains to be accomplished toward reintegration. Although the process is active, not static, the content of one's life usually unfolds slowly; the process may not be completed prior to death. In its mild form, the life review is reflected in increased reminiscence, mild nostalgia, mild regret; in severe form, in anxiety, guilt, despair, and depression. In the extreme, it may involve the obsessive preoccupation of the older person with his past, and may proceed to a state approximating terror and result in suicide. Thus, although I consider it to be a universal and normative process, its varied manifestations and outcomes may include psychopathological ones.

The life review may be first observed in stray and seemingly insignificant thoughts about oneself and one's life history. These thoughts may continue to emerge in brief intermittent spurts or become essentially continuous, and they may undergo constant reintegration and reorganization at various levels of awareness. A seventy-six-year-old man said:

My life is in the background of my mind much of the time; it cannot be any other way. Thoughts of my past play upon me; sometimes I play with them, encourage and savor them; at other times I dismiss them.

Other clues to its existence include dreams and thoughts. The dreams and nightmares of the aged, which are frequently reported, appear to principally concern the past and death. Imagery of past events and symbols of death seem frequent in waking life as well as dreams, suggesting that the life review is a highly visual process.

Another manifestation of the life review seems to be the curious but apparently common phenomenon of mirror-gazing, illustrated by the following:

I was passing by my mirror. I noticed how old I was. My appearance, well, it prompted me to think of death—and of my past—what I hadn't done, what I had done wrong.

One hospitalized eighty-year-old woman, whose husband had died five years before her admission, had been discovered by her family berating her mirror image for her past deeds and shaking her fist at herself. She was preoccupied by past deeds and omissions in her personal relationships, as evidenced by this excerpt from nursing notes:

Patient in depths of gloom this morning—looking too unhappy for anything. Patient looked angry. I asked her with whom. She replied, "Myself." I asked, "What have you done that merits so much self-anger so much of the time?" She replied, "Haven't you ever looked yourself over?" In the course of conversation I suggested she might be too harsh with herself. At this she gave a bitter laugh and stuck out her chin again.

Later in her hospitalization she purposely avoided mirrors.

Another patient, eighty-six years old and periodically confused, often stood before the mirror in his hospital room and rhythmically chanted either happily or angrily. He was especially given to angry flare-ups and crying spells over food, money, and clothes. When angry he would screech obscenities at his mirror image, so savagely beating his fist upon a nearby table that the staff tried to protect him by covering the mirror. But in contrast to the first patient he denied that the image was himself, and when an observer came up beside him and said, "See, this is me in the mirror and there you are in the mirror," he smiled and said, "That's you in the mirror all right, but that's not me."

Adaptive and Constructive Manifestations

As the past marches in review, it is surveyed, observed, and reflected upon by the ego. Reconsideration of previous experiences and their meanings occurs, often with concomitant revised or expanded understanding. Such reorganization of past experience may provide a more valid picture, giving new and significant meanings to one's life; it may also prepare one for death, mitigating one's fears.

The occasions on which the life review has obviously been creative, having positive, constructive effects, are most impressive. For example:

> A seventy-eight-year-old man, optimistic, reflective, and resourceful, who had had significantly impairing egocentric tendencies, became increasingly responsive in his relationships to his wife, children, and grandchildren. These changes corresponded with his purchase of a tape recorder. Upon my request he sent me the tapes he had made, and wrote: "There is the first reel of tape on which I recorded my memory of my life story. To give this some additional interest I am expecting that my children and grandchildren and great-grandchildren will listen to it after I am gone. I pretended that I was telling the story directly to them."

Ingmar Bergman's very fine, remarkable Swedish motion picture, *Wild Strawberries,* provides a beautiful example of the constructive aspects of the life review. Envisioning and dreaming of his past and his death, the protagonist-physician realizes the nonaffectionate and withholding qualities of his life; as the feeling of love reenters his life, the doctor changes even as death hovers upon him.

Although it is not possible at present to describe in detail either the life review or the possibilities for reintegration which are suggested, it seems likely that in the majority of the elderly a substantial reorganization of the personality does occur. This may help to account for the evolution of such qualities as wisdom and serenity, long noted in some of the aged. Although a favorable, constructive, and positive end result may be enhanced by favorable environmental circumstances, such as comparative freedom from crises and losses, it is more likely that successful reorganization is largely a function of the personality—in particular, such vaguely defined features of the personality as flexibility, resilience, and self-awareness.

In addition to the more impressive constructive aspects of the life review, certain adaptive and defensive aspects may be noted. Some of the aged have illusions of the "good past"; some fantasy the past rather than the future in the service of avoiding the realities of the present; some maintain a characteristic detachment from others and themselves. Although these mechanisms are not constructive, they do assist in maintaining a status quo of psychological functioning. . . .

In the course of the life review the older person may reveal to his wife, children, and other intimates, unknown qualities of his character and unstated actions of his past; in return, they may reveal heretofore undisclosed or unknown truths. Hidden themes of great vintage may emerge, changing the quality of a lifelong relationship. Revelations of the past may forge a new intimacy, render a deceit honest; they may sever peculiar bonds and free tongues; or they may sculpture terrifying hatreds out of fluid, fitful antagonisms.

Source: Butler, 1975, pp. 331, 332, 338.

Life Satisfaction

There has been increased interest in discovering the aspects of an elderly person's life that contribute to life satisfaction. In one study of 141 lower-class men and women (Markides & Martin, 1979), health and income were the two factors that were most likely to be associated with life satisfaction. This research also indicated elderly people who were active—going to church, to meetings, on trips, and so on—were happier than those who tended to stay at home.

In one of the most well-known studies of life satisfaction, Robert R. Sears (1977) conducted a follow-up of the Terman gifted men when their average age was sixty-two. Just after World War I, Lewis Terman began his famous longitudinal study of gifted children. Terman later realized that if this group of children were followed into later maturity valuable information could be collected about the experiences that contribute to ultimate satisfaction with life and to different styles of coping with important life problems.

Satisfaction is a global term. And, so is coping with life problems. In the Terman follow-up investigation, satisfaction focused on two aspects of life—occupation and family life. The specific coping styles for the areas of occupation and family life, respectively, were work persistence into the sixties and unbroken marriages versus divorce. The recorded events and expressions of feelings were recorded every ten years. Both occupational satisfaction and work persistence were best predicted by feelings of satisfaction, ambition, and good health, expressed as early as age thirty. Family lifestyle satisfaction and success in marriage were predicted by good childhood social adjustment, good mental health in later years, retrospective (age forty) positive attitudes toward parents, and best of all, by the Terman Marital Happiness Test (taken at age thirty). Sear's findings on life satisfaction lend credence to the belief that there is constancy as well as change in adult development. In the longitudinal study of the Terman gifted men there was a high consistency of expressive feelings about work, health, and self-worth over the three decades from ages thirty to sixty. And, interestingly, in spite of their autonomy and great average success in their occupations, the men placed greater importance on achieving satisfaction in their family life than in their work.

In the follow-up study of the Terman gifted women (Sears & Barbee, 1977), somewhat fewer than half worked, and most of those who did had professional careers. The working women reported more satisfaction with their lives in general than those who did not work. Nonworking women were less satisfied with their family lives than the working women were, and less so than the men. Many of these nonworking women would now opt for a career if they could relive their lives.

In another large-scale investigation of the life satisfaction and the quality of life in late adulthood, John Flanagan (1981) obtained life histories from 1,000 persons aged sixty-eight to seventy-two from many different backgrounds and geographical areas of the United States. The histories were obtained by trained interviewers, using a structured interview booklet. The components used to study the quality of life in late adulthood focused on physical and material well-being; relations with other people; social, community, and civic activities; personal development and fulfillment; and recreation. It appears that health problems and lack of money are the most significant factors that interfere with a good quality of life. Fortunately, only 30 percent of the older people reported that their health was fair or poor, with only 6 percent in the poor category. Slightly more than half the men but nearly three-quarters of the women reported total family incomes of less than $8,000 per year—almost two-thirds of these women were living alone. About one-sixth of the men and more than one-third of the women had total family incomes of less than $4,000 per year. Clearly then lack of money is a major contributor to reducing the quality of life of individuals.

There also seems to be little doubt that over the life span, marital relationships and childrearing make important contributions to an individual's quality of life. However, at age seventy, there are many immediate problems and situations that have a more compelling effect on current quality of life than children and a spouse.

The seventy-year-old's need for rewards from personal activity are clearly shown in the reports on the contributions of work and active recreation to their present quality of life. Other factors of special value to the women are close friends and helping others. These factors tend to be especially important for many widows at this age level. Other factors that were important included socializing and recreation. A factor that was reported by many seventy-year-olds as a negative contributor to their quality of life was lack of learning and education. About one-third of the sample studied here never entered high school and one-half of the total group did not graduate from high school.

In the studies of life satisfaction in late adulthood, health clearly emerges as an important factor. Next we look in greater detail at an important aspect of health in late adulthood, mental health.

The interweaving of mental and physical problems is more likely in late adulthood.

Mental Health

In introducing the recent volume, *Handbook of Mental Health and Aging*, (1980), Seymour Kety commented:

A national health problem which is most severe in terms of its prevalence and cost is a group of mental disorders and dysfunctions which are associated with aging. Either because somatic mechanisms are more robust or, being simpler and easier to comprehend, are more readily preserved or restored as the result of progress in medical science, a substantial segment of the population can now look forward to a longer life, but one which may unfortunately be hampered by mental disability. This is a prospect that is both troubling to the individual and costly to society. Since mental handicap makes an individual increasingly dependent on the help and care of others, the cost of these services and prerequisites to other members of the family and to the whole of society as well, represents a burden which has been estimated at 36.78 billions of dollars per year in the United States. More important, perhaps, is a cost that cannot be measured or tabulated: the loss of human potential and of the affected person's capacity for adaptation and ability to contribute to human welfare. (p. xi)

Defining mental health is not an easy task, although the term has become commonplace in society. The term presumably not only embraces the absence of mental illness, difficulties, and frustrations, but also reflects the abilities or capacity of an individual to deal with the issues of life in an effective, if not pleasurable or satisfying, manner. And, since older adults are more likely than younger adults to have some type of physical illness, the interweaving of physical and mental problems is more likely in later than in younger adulthood (Birren & Sloane, 1981).

While categorizing individuals according to a particular type of mental illness has been criticized by some mental health experts, particularly behaviorists, we present the categories of mental health problems that many psychologists and psychiatrists use.

Mental Health Problems in Late Adulthood

In attempts to categorize mental health problems a distinction between organic and functional disorders usually is made. Organic disorders are sometimes referred to as organic brain syndromes and are associated with some physical cause, such as brain damage. By contrast, functional disorders are thought to be unrelated to physiological problems and are believed to be caused by personality or environmental factors. Two forms of organic disorders that have been studied are: **acute brain syndromes,** which are reversible, and **chronic brain syndromes,** which are not reversible.

Acute brain syndrome treatment usually is aimed at the cause of the disorder, such as malnutrition, drug reaction, or infection. Chronic syndromes are usually permanent and involve brain damage, which may produce a variety of symptoms, such as confusion, suspiciousness, lack of concern for amenities, and loss of control over bodily functions.

While some clinicians continue to use the organic-functional dichotomy, recent knowledge about such disorders as schizophrenia, which usually is classified as a functional disorder, suggest that the organic-functional categorization may be misleading, since many experts now believe that there is a genetic component to schizophrenia. And, just recently, researchers have uncovered a section of chromosome that can be used as a marker to predict who is likely to suffer a severe form of depression and related diseases such as alcoholism and drug dependence (Weitkamp, 1981).

Other than the acute and chronic brain syndromes, then, other mental disturbances that have been identifed in late adulthood are schizophrenia and paranoid psychoses, affective psychoses, neuroses and personality disorders, and alcoholism. But there is disagreement about appropriate categorization here as well. For example, how can we distinguish between an affective psychosis and depressive neurosis? Both often show the same symptoms (e.g., lethargy, depression). A psychosis is considered to be a more severe form of mental disorder, one which keeps the individual from maintaining contact with reality, while a neurosis is viewed as a less debilitating form of mental disorder in which the person, while usually showing a high level of anxiety, can generally function in the everyday world. However, psychologists often have a difficult time agreeing on the person's symptoms as well as in which category of mental illness to place the individual. And, the problem is complicated in late adulthood, because physical deterioration of the individual's body may cause the individual to be diagnosed as having a mental problem when in reality the problem is physical in nature. Recall our discussion of senility along this line of thinking in chapter 18.

It is difficult to estimate the number of persons over the age of sixty-five who suffer from a given mental disorder. While there have been numerous surveys of mental illness in late adulthood, only those cases that come to medical attention through admissions to mental hospitals, psychiatric visits, and so on are counted. And, as we have just indicated, assignment to specific categories of mental disorder is a subjective process. Further, many elderly individuals suffer from multiple problems, making a single classification difficult. In a review of the major surveys of the incidence of various categories of mental illness in late adulthood, David Kay and Klaus Bergmann (1980) concluded that the most consistent finding to emerge is the prevalence of chronic brain syndrome in persons aged sixty-five and over. Of these individuals, 1 to 2 percent are severely impaired and 3 to 4 percent moderately impaired, with the proportions increasing with age. The majority at any one time are living at home rather than in institutions, and are being cared for by relatives and neighbors. Another consistent finding from community surveys is the very large number of old persons with neuroses, especially depressive neuroses. Most of these individuals are not receiving any formal psychological treatment. The causes of such neuroses in late adulthood have not been adequately studied although the factors we described earlier that contribute to life satisfaction and quality of life in late adulthood are likely contributors—that is, health, income, personal review of one's life, relationships with spouse and/or children, friendships, isolation, and work and vocation.

The need for both preventive and ameliorative mental health services within a community for older people can be found in a number of the epidemiological studies. Margaret Gatz (1980) recently reviewed some of the most relevant studies that provide a "ballpark" estimate of the incidence of mental illness in the United States. Based on these studies, it was found that 10 to 20 percent of persons sixty-five and over were in need of mental health services. Older adults account for roughly 25 percent of reported suicides each year (Butler and Lewis, 1977). Among the elderly within the institutional setting, it has been estimated that 58 percent are considered confused some or most of the time (National Center for Health Statistics, 1977). An important observation, however, is that the problems of as many as one-third of these older adults stem from errors in medication, malnutrition, metabolic imbalance, or other causes (Libow, 1973).

Two of the most difficult mental health problems encounterd by older adults and their families are depression and senility. Depression is probably the most common psychiatric complaint among older adults (Butler & Lewis, 1977). Margaret Gatz, Michael Smyer, and Powell Lawton (1980) describe this problem in late adulthood.

Two aspects of depression in older adults make it particularly troublesome to treat. The first is that there are often real reasons for feeling depressed, for instance, personal losses that may trigger existential questions. Reflecting this aspect, Gurland (1976), in a review of several epidemiological studies, noted that the highest rates of depressive *symptoms* are found in persons above age sixty-five. In contrast, the prevalence of depressive *disorders,* as diagnosed by psychiatrists, is highest between the ages of twenty-five and sixty-five and not among the older group. The second difficult aspect of depression is that family and friends do not enjoy being around depressed people. The depressed person tends to be dependent and demanding, thereby discouraging the very people who might be supportive. Thus, the families and caretakers need assistance, and the depressed older adults need interventions that will mobilize their resources while recognizing their concerns as valid.

Gatz, Smyer, and Lawton also studied the problem of senility among the elderly. They found a striking discrepancy between the needs of mentally impaired older adults and available resources and services. Too often, the choice of institutions for these ailing individuals is based on what is available rather than on what would be the best treatment and services. In no other area are the limitations of the efforts to help the aging more visible.

Adaptation and Coping

Marjorie Fiske (1980) indicates that virtually every individual harbors both deficits and resources within his or her psychic makeup. Some degree of psychopathology exists, for example, in most seemingly well-adapted people (Barron, 1963; Singer, 1963). And, age has a great deal to do with how symptoms are diagnosed—at twenty-two, a woman may be having a postpartum depression; at forty-four, a menopausal one; and at sixty-six, the same symptoms are frequently (and erroneously) diagnosed as senile brain damage.

Fiske believes that we must learn more about the adaptive coexistence of both deficits and resources because one "strong" resource may offset or counterbalance several deficits. In an ongoing longitudinal study, Fiske is attempting to assess the balance between inner resources and deficits among men and women at different stages of the life course, and the relationship between these dimensions to the individual's sense of well-being. Looked at separately, the two dimensions are related to life satisfaction in an entirely expectable fashion. People with the most resources (such as the capacity for mutuality, growth, competence, hope, and insight) tend to be satisfied with themselves and their lives, and those with deficits (psychological symptoms, including anxiety, hostility, and self-hatred) the least so. But these expected results are found among less than one-third of the people being studied. Among the other two-thirds of the people, a combination of many "positive" and many "negative" attributes seems to increase the individual's sense of well-being.

Such findings suggest that it may be misleading to look only at the degree of impairment in a particular individual, because when we look closely at people who are the most satisfied with their lives, they harbor an array of both "positive" and "negative" attributes, are deeply involved in their worlds, and cope well with the diversity of stress that in-depth encounters with work and with people involve (Chiriboga & Lowenthal, 1975). Marjorie Fiske (1980) concluded:

In fostering the commitment to learning, the middle and late-middle-aged strengthen their resources for coping with old age. For in very old age, many are left with only the commitment which was earlier the foundation of all others, namely the attribution of meaning to one's life—and thereby to other lives. Something more than a biological instinct or personal need for survival, this commitment, in later life, is manifest in the eagerness to live and to love, because, despite the infirmities that may prevent active pursuit of other commitments, their significance continues. Older people who know what they value, what is worth striving for, and how to love are a living symbol for the generations following them, even though the substance of their own concerns may differ. For such old people, life remains dignified, and death, while perhaps viewed with regret or sadness, holds no terrors, for they have truly lived their lives. (pp. 368–69)

Summary

This chapter focused on social, emotional, and personality development in late adulthood. Many elderly individuals are perceived as helpless, but they often show a strong desire to be helpful. For individuals who are married, the time from retirement until the death of a spouse is seen as the final stage in the marital cycle. Late adulthood is a time when many spouses may need to show more expressive feelings toward each other as retirement proceeds. When a spouse dies, the surviving marital partner goes through a period of grieving, a process most psychologists see as psychologically healthy. In addition to marital relationships, parent-child relations continue to be important in late adulthood. The dependency of older adults on their children is labeled *filial maturity*. In some cultures, like Japan, adult children assume full responsibility for the care of their elderly parents. In the United States, while adult children often do not have responsibility for their elderly parents, they usually are not disconnected from them. In some cases, intergenerational stress may result, particularly in the face of ill health and financial strain. Many elderly people are grandparents—the role of grandparenting has different meanings and grandparents interact in different ways with their grandchildren. Friendships continue to be important in late adulthood. And, when a spouse dies, friends may form an important support system for the surviving spouse.

Psychologists also are interested in the living environment, income levels, and cultural conditions of the elderly. A promising approach to improving the living conditions of the elderly focuses on the study of attributes of an environment rather than the environment itself. Two important attributes of the elderly individual's living environment are accessibility and adaptability. One of the major concerns of individuals in late adulthood is the reduced income many often face when they retire. And, while still a small portion of the elderly in the United States, almost 150,000 people live in a single room at slum hotels. Cross-cultural comparisons of individuals in late adulthood suggest that the elderly in the United States do not receive the respect that older people in many cultures, such as Japan, China and some primitive societies, are given.

While theorists have developed different perspectives on late adulthood, most agree that an important theme of personality development is a life review or reminiscence that leads the individual to perceive his or her personality more in terms of integrity than despair. Researchers also have been interested in the factors that contribute to life satisfaction in late adulthood—health, income, and a happy marriage are three such factors. There also is increasing interest in the mental health of the elderly. While individuals are living to an older age than in past decades, mental disability in late adulthood continues to be a major problem. There is greater likelihood in late adulthood that mental illness will be related to physical problems than in earlier years.

Two aspects of mental illness that have been given special attention are depression and senility. Psychologists still have a great deal of difficulty in placing the mental problems of individuals in late adulthood into neatly packaged categories. Epidemiological studies of the incidence of mental illness suggest that while figures differ in regard to the percent of the elderly population in need of mental health services, the need is substantial. When we study the mental health of the elderly, it often is easy to fall into the trap of dwelling on their impairments and weaknesses rather than looking simultaneously at their amazing coping and adaptability. Marjorie Fiske believes that the most competent elderly individuals show both strengths and weaknesses, and an ability to cope with adversity.

Key Terms

acute brain syndromes

body transcendence versus body preoccupation

chronic brain syndromes

ego differentiation versus work-role preoccupation

ego transcendence versus ego preoccupation

filial maturity

integrity vs. despair

legibility

life review

reciprocal

scale of environment

serial

Review Questions

1. Discuss marital relations in late adulthood. What are some of the adjustments widows and widowers have to make?
2. Describe the nature of the relationship between adult children and their aging parents.
3. How can we develop better support systems to help families with aging parents?
4. What are some different meanings of the grandparent role? Outline some different styles of interaction grandparents show toward their grandchildren.
5. Discuss the nature of friendships in late adulthood.
6. Outline some of the most important attributes of environments that affect the living conditions of the elderly.
7. Discuss some of the problems in income and housing the elderly face.
8. How does the status of the elderly in the United States compare with other cultures?
9. Describe the major personality perspectives in late adulthood.
10. What factors contribute to life satisfaction in late adulthood?
11. Discuss the mental health status of the elderly in the United States.
12. What are some of the major mental health problems of the elderly?
13. What are some characteristics of individuals who seem to adapt and cope effectively in late adulthood?

Further Readings

Birren, J. E., & Sloane, R. B. (eds.), *Handbook of mental health and aging.* Englewood Cliffs, N.J., 1980.
A volume of articles written by a number of experts from many different areas of psychology. The common thread of the writings involve the authors' attempts to apply what they know to improving the mental health of the elderly. Reading is of medium difficulty.

Butler, R. N. The life review: an interpretation of reminiscence in the aged. In L. A. Allman & D. T. Jaffe (eds.), *Readings in adult psychology: contemporary perspectives.* New York: Harper & Row, 1977.
Butler, an expert on aging, describes the life review process individuals go through in late adulthood. Includes abnormal, as well as normal, ways to deal with the life review. Incorporates comments about Erikson's ideas on integrity vs. despair as part of the life review process. Reading level is of medium difficulty.

Butler, R. N. *Why survive: being old in America.* New York: Harper & Row, 1975.
Topics of interest include an extensive discussion of the problems the elderly have with income, with being poor in an affluent society, and with living on a pension. Reasonably easy to read.

Jones, R. *The other generation: the new power of older people.* New Jersey: Prentice-Hall, 1977.
An intriguing book about the increasing number of people in the United States over the age of sixty-five, and the impact they are likely to have on our society. Topics discussed include ageism and political groups. Easy to read.

Williamson, J. B., Munley, A., & Evans, L. *Aging and society: an introduction to social gerontology.* New York: Holt, Rinehart & Winston, 1980.
An easy-to-read introductory textbook that focuses on the social factors that influence the life of the elderly. Chapters relevant to topics discussed here include those titled crime; social services; housing and living environments; nursing homes; and status, power, and politics.

20

Aging and Death

Prologue: Can You Live to Be 100?

At various points in the discussion of development in adulthood, factors that seem to be associated with longevity have been discussed (that is, how long a person will live). Recall the description of the Abkhasians in chapter 18, people who commonly live to be 100. Remember that in the United States people are living to older ages than ever before, and that women are more likely to live longer than men.

By taking the following test, developed by life-span researcher Diana Woodruff (1977), you can estimate how long you are likely to live and see what some of the most important factors are that influence longevity. Start the test by finding your current age on the life expectancy table (table A) on the basis of your sex and race. Then add or subtract years based on your answers to the following questions.

Heredity and Family

1. *Longevity of grandparents.* Have any of your grandparents lived to age eighty or beyond? If so add one year for each grandparent living beyond that age. Add one-half year for each grandparent surviving beyond the age of seventy.
2. *Longevity of parents.* If your mother lived beyond the age of eighty, add four years. Add two years if your father lived beyond eighty. You benefit more if your mother lived a long time than if your father did.
3. *Cardiovascular disease of close relatives.* If any parent, grandparent, sister, or brother died of a heart attack, stroke, or arteriosclerosis before the age of fifty, subtract four years for each incidence. If any of those close relatives died of the above before the age of sixty, subtract two years for each incidence.
4. *Other hereditable diseases of close relatives.* Have any parents, grandparents, sisters, or brothers died before the age of sixty of diabetes mellitus or peptic ulcer? Subtract three years for each incidence. If any of these close relatives died before sixty of stomach cancer, subtract two years. Women whose close female relatives have died before sixty of breast cancer should also subtract two years. Finally, if any close relatives have died before the age of sixty of any cause except accidents or homicide, subtract one year for each incidence.
5. *Childbearing.* Women who have never had children are more likely to be in poor health, and they also are at a greater risk for breast cancer. Therefore, if you can't or don't plan to have children, or if you are over forty and have never had children, subtract one-half year. Women who have a large number of children tax their bodies. If you've had over seven children, or plan to, subtract one year.
6. *Mother's age at your birth.* Was your mother over the age of thirty-five or under the age of eighteen when you were born? If so, subtract one year.
7. *Birth order.* Are you the firstborn? If so, add one year.
8. *Intelligence.* How intelligent are you? Is your intelligence below average, average, above average, or superior? If you feel that your intelligence is superior, that is, if you feel you are smarter than almost anyone you know, add two years.

Table A
Life Expectancy Table

	Caucasian		Black		Oriental	
Age	Male	Female	Male	Female	Male	Female
10	70.9	78.4	65.8	74.4	72.9	80.4
11	70.9	78.4	65.8	74.4	72.9	80.4
12	70.9	78.4	65.8	74.4	72.9	80.4
13	70.9	78.4	65.9	74.4	72.9	80.4
14	71.0	78.5	65.9	74.4	73.0	80.5
15	71.0	78.5	65.9	74.5	73.0	80.5
16	71.0	78.5	66.0	74.5	73.1	80.5
17	71.1	78.5	66.1	74.5	73.1	80.5
18	71.2	78.6	66.1	74.6	73.2	80.6
19	71.3	78.6	66.2	74.6	73.3	80.6
20	71.4	78.6	66.3	74.7	73.4	80.6
21	71.5	78.7	66.5	74.7	73.5	80.7
22	71.6	78.7	66.6	74.8	73.6	80.7
23	71.7	78.7	66.8	74.8	73.7	80.7
24	71.8	78.8	66.9	74.9	73.8	80.8
25	71.9	78.8	67.1	74.9	73.9	80.8
26	71.9	78.8	67.3	75.0	73.9	80.8
27	72.0	78.9	67.4	75.1	74.0	80.9
28	72.1	78.9	67.6	75.1	74.1	80.9
29	72.2	78.9	67.8	75.2	74.2	80.9
30	72.2	79.0	68.0	75.3	74.2	81.0
31	72.3	79.0	68.1	75.4	74.3	81.0
32	72.4	79.0	68.3	75.4	74.4	81.0
33	72.4	79.1	68.5	75.5	74.4	81.1
34	72.5	79.1	68.6	75.6	74.5	81.1
35	72.6	79.2	68.8	75.7	74.6	81.2
36	72.6	79.2	69.0	75.8	74.6	81.2
37	72.7	79.3	69.2	75.9	74.7	81.3
38	72.8	79.3	69.4	76.0	74.8	81.3
39	72.9	79.4	69.6	76.1	74.9	81.4
40	73.0	79.4	69.8	76.2	75.0	81.4
41	73.1	79.5	70.0	76.4	75.1	81.5
42	73.2	79.6	70.3	76.5	75.2	81.6
43	73.3	79.6	70.5	76.6	75.3	81.6
44	73.4	79.7	70.8	76.8	75.4	81.7
45	73.5	79.8	71.0	77.0	75.5	81.8

Table A *continued*
Life Expectancy Table

	Caucasian		Black		Oriental	
Age	*Male*	*Female*	*Male*	*Female*	*Male*	*Female*
46	73.7	79.9	71.3	77.1	75.7	81.9
47	73.8	80.0	71.5	77.3	75.8	82.0
48	74.0	80.1	71.8	77.5	76.0	82.1
49	74.1	80.2	72.1	77.7	76.1	82.2
50	74.3	80.3	72.4	77.9	76.3	82.3
51	74.5	80.5	72.7	78.2	76.5	82.5
52	74.7	80.6	73.1	78.4	76.7	82.6
53	74.9	80.7	73.4	78.6	76.9	82.7
54	75.2	80.9	73.8	78.9	77.2	82.9
55	75.4	81.0	74.2	79.1	77.4	83.0
56	75.7	81.2	74.6	79.4	77.7	83.2
57	75.9	81.4	75.0	79.7	77.9	83.4
58	76.2	81.5	75.4	80.0	78.2	83.5
59	76.5	81.7	75.8	80.3	78.5	83.7
60	76.8	81.9	76.3	80.7	78.8	83.9
61	77.2	82.2	76.8	81.0	79.2	84.2
62	77.5	82.4	77.2	81.4	79.5	84.4
63	77.9	82.6	77.7	81.8	79.9	84.6
64	78.3	82.8	78.2	82.2	80.3	84.8
65	78.7	83.1	78.7	82.5	80.7	85.1
66	79.1	83.3	79.2	82.9	81.1	85.3
67	79.5	83.6	79.7	83.2	81.5	85.6
68	80.0	83.9	80.2	83.5	82.0	85.9
69	80.4	84.1	80.7	83.9	82.4	86.1
70	80.9	84.4	81.3	84.4	82.9	86.4
71	81.4	84.7	81.9	84.9	83.4	86.7
72	81.9	85.1	82.5	85.5	83.9	87.1
73	82.4	85.4	83.2	86.2	84.4	87.4
74	83.0	85.8	84.0	86.8	85.0	87.8
75	83.5	86.2	84.7	87.5	85.5	88.2
76	84.1	86.6	85.5	88.2	86.1	88.6
77	84.7	87.1	86.2	88.9	86.7	89.1
78	85.4	87.6	87.0	89.6	87.4	89.6
79	86.0	88.1	87.7	90.3	88.0	90.1
80	86.7	88.6	88.5	91.0	88.7	90.6
81	87.4	89.1	89.3	91.7	89.4	91.1
82	88.1	89.7	90.1	92.4	90.1	91.7
83	88.8	90.3	90.8	93.1	90.8	92.3
84	89.5	90.9	91.5	93.6	91.5	92.9
85	90.2	91.5	92.1	94.1	92.2	93.5

Table B
Weight, Height, Age Tables
(Ages Twenty-five and Over)

Desirable Weights for Men

Height (in Shoes, 1-inch Heels)		Weight in Pounds (in Indoor Clothing)		
Ft.	In.	Small Frame	Medium Frame	Large Frame
5	2	112–120	118–129	126–141
5	3	115–123	121–133	129–144
5	4	118–126	124–136	132–148
5	5	121–129	127–139	135–152
5	6	124–133	130–143	138–156
5	7	128–137	134–147	142–171
5	8	132–141	138–152	147–166
5	9	136–145	142–156	151–170
5	10	140–150	146–160	155–174
5	11	144–154	150–165	159–179
6	0	148–158	154–170	164–184
6	1	152–162	158–175	168–189
6	2	156–167	162–180	173–194
6	3	160–171	167–185	178–199
6	4	164–175	172–190	182–204

Desirable Weights for Women

Height (in Shoes, 2-inch Heels)		Weight in Pounds (in Indoor Clothing)		
Ft.	In.	Small Frame	Medium Frame	Large Frame
4	10	92–98	96–107	104–119
4	11	94–101	98–110	106–122
5	0	96–104	101–113	109–125
5	1	99–107	104–116	112–128
5	2	102–110	107–119	115–131
5	3	105–113	110–122	118–134
5	4	108–116	113–126	121–138
5	5	111–119	116–130	125–142
5	6	114–123	120–135	129–146
5	7	118–127	124–139	133–150
5	8	122–131	128–143	137–154
5	9	126–135	132–147	141–158
5	10	130–140	136–151	145–163
5	11	134–144	140–155	149–168
6	0	138–148	144–159	153–173

Source: Metropolitan Life Insurance Company.

Health

9. *Weight.* Are you currently overweight? Find your ideal weight in table B. If you weigh more than the figure on table B, calculate the percentage by which you are overweight, and subtract the appropriate number of years shown in table C. If you have been overweight at any point in your life, or if your weight has periodically fluctuated by more than ten pounds since high school, subtract two years.

10. *Dietary habits.* Do you prefer vegetables, fruits, and simple foods to foods high in fat and sugar? Do you always stop eating before you feel really full? If the honest answer to both questions is yes, add one year.

Table C
Risk to Life of Being Overweight (in Years)

	Markedly Overweight (More than 30%)		Moderately Overweight (10–30%)	
Age	Men	Women	Men	Women
20	−15.8	−7.2	−13.8	−4.8
25	−10.6	−6.1	−9.6	−4.9
30	−7.9	−5.5	−5.5	−3.6
35	−6.1	−4.9	−4.2	−4.0
40	−5.1	−4.6	−3.3	−3.5
45	−4.3	−5.1	−2.4	−3.8
50	−4.6	−4.1	−2.4	−2.8
55	−5.4	−3.2	−2.0	−2.2

Source: Metropolitan Life Insurance Company.

11. *Smoking.* How much do you smoke? If you smoke two or more packs of cigarettes a day, subtract twelve years. If you smoke between one and two packs a day, subtract seven years. If you smoke less than a pack a day, subtract two years. If you have quit smoking, congratulations, you subtract no years at all.

12. *Drinking.* If you are a moderate drinker, that is, if you never drink to the point of intoxication and have one or two drinks of whiskey, or half a liter of wine, or up to four glasses of beer per day, add three years. If you are a light drinker, that is, you have an occasional drink, but do not drink almost every day, add one and one-half years. If you are an abstainer who never uses alcohol in any form do not add or subtract any years. Finally, if you are a heavy drinker or an alcoholic, subtract eight years. (Heavy drinkers are those who drink more than three ounces of whiskey or drink other intoxicating beverages excessively almost every day. They drink to the point of intoxication.)

13. *Exercise.* How much do you exercise? If you exercise at least three times a week at one of the following: jogging, bike riding, swimming, taking long, brisk walks, dancing, or skating, add three years. Just exercising on weekends does not count.

14. *Sleep.* If you generally fall asleep right away and get six to eight hours of sleep per night, you're average and should neither add nor subtract years. However, if you sleep excessively (ten or more hours per night), or if you sleep very little (five or less hours per night), you probably have problems. Subtract two years.

15. *Sexual activity.* If you enjoy regular sexual activity, having intimate sexual relations once or twice a week, add two years.

Table D
Education and Life Expectancy*

Level of Education	Years of Life
Four or more years of college	+3.0
One to three years of college	+2.0
Four years of high school	+1.0
One to three years of high school	+0.0
Elementary school (eight years)	−0.5
Less than eighth grade	−2.0

*Estimates based on data presented in E. M. Kitagawa and P. M. Hauser, Differential mortality in the United States: A study in socioeconomic epidemiology. Cambridge, Mass.: Harvard University Press, 1973 (pp. 12, 18), and in Metropolitan Life Insurance Company, Socioeconomic mortality differentials, *Statistical Bulletin,* 1975, 56, 3–5.

16. *Regular physical examinations.* Do you have an annual physical examination by your physician which includes a breast examination and Pap smear for women, and a protoscopic examination every other year for men? If so, add two years.

17. *Health status.* Are you in poor health? Do you have a chronic health condition (for example, heart disease, high blood pressure, cancer, diabetes, ulcer) or are you frequently ill? If so, subtract five years.

Education and Occupation

18. *Years of education.* How much education have you had? Add or subtract the number of years shown in table D.

19. *Occupational level.* If you are working, what is the socioeconomic level of your occupation? If you do not work, what is your spouse's occupation? If you are retired, what is your former occupation? If you are a student, what is your parents' occupational level? Add or subtract the number of years shown in table E.

Table E
Occupation and Life Expectancy*

Occupational Level	Years of Life
Class I—Professional	+1.5
Class II—Technical, administrative, and managerial. Also agricultural workers, as they live longer than for their actual socioeconomic level	+1.0
Class III—Proprietors, clerical, sales, and skilled workers	±0.0
Class IV—Semi-skilled workers	−0.5
Class V—Laborers	−4.0

*Estimates based on data presented in E. M. Kitagawa and P. M. Hauser. Differential mortality in the United States: A study in socioeconomic epidemiology. Cambridge, Mass.: Harvard University Press, 1973 (pp. 12, 18), and in Metropolitan Life Insurance Company, Socioeconomic mortality differentials, *Statistical Bulletin*, 1975, 56, 3–5.

20. *Family income.* If your family income is above average for your education and occupation, add one year. If it's below average for your education and occupation, subtract one year.
21. *Activity on the job.* If your job involves a lot of physical activity, add two years. On the other hand, if you sit all day on the job, subtract two years.
22. *Age and work.* If you are over the age of sixty and still on the job, add two years. If you are over the age of sixty-five and have not retired, add three years.

Life-Style

23. *Rural vs. urban dwelling.* If you live in an urban area and have lived in or near the city for most of your life, subtract one year. If you have spent most of your life in a rural area, add one year.
24. *Married vs. divorced.* If you are married and living with your spouse, add one year.
    A. *Formerly married men.* If you are a separated or divorced man living alone, subtract nine years, and if you are a widowed man living alone, subtract seven years. If as a separated, divorced, or widowed man you live with other people, such as family members, subtract only half the years given above. Living with others is beneficial for formerly married men.
    B. *Formerly married women.* Women who are separated or divorced should subtract four years, and widowed women should subtract three and one-half years. The loss of a spouse through divorce or death is not as life-shortening to a woman, and she lives about as long whether she lives alone or with family, unless she is the head of the household. Divorced or widowed women who live with their families as the head of their household should subtract only two years for the formerly married status.
25. *Living status as single.* If you are a woman who has never married, subtract one year for each unmarried decade past the age of twenty-five. If you live with family or friends as a male single person you should also subtract one year for each unmarried decade past the age of twenty-five. However, if you are a man who has never married and are living alone, subtract two years for each unmarried decade past the age of twenty-five.

26. *Life changes.* Are you always changing things in your life; changing jobs, changing residences, changing friends and/or spouses, changing your appearance? If so subtract two years. Too much change is stressful.

27. *Friendship.* Do you generally like people and have at least two close friends in whom you can confide almost all the details of your life? If so, add one year.

28. *Aggressive personality.* Do you always feel that you are under time pressure? Are you aggressive and sometimes hostile, paying little attention to the feelings of others? Subtract two to five years depending on how well you fit this description. The more pressured, aggressive, and hostile you are, the greater your risk for heart disease.

29. *Flexible personality.* Are you a calm, reasonable, relaxed person? Are you easygoing and adaptable, taking life pretty much as it comes? Depending upon the degree to which you fit this description, add one to three years. If you are rigid, dogmatic, and set in your ways, subtract two years.

30. *Risk-taking personality.* Do you take a lot of risks, including driving without seat belts, exceeding the speed limit, and taking any dare that is made? Do you live in a high crime rate neighborhood? If you are vulnerable to accidents and homicide in this way, subtract two years. If you use seat belts regularly, drive infrequently, and generally avoid risks and dangerous parts of town, add one year.

31. *Depressive personality.* Have you been depressed, tense, worried, or guilty for more than a period of a year or two? If so subtract one to three years depending upon how seriously you are affected by these feelings.

32. *Happy personality.* Are you basically happy and content, and have you had a lot of fun in life? If so add two years. People with feelings like this are the ones who live to be 100.

Total _____

Source: From *Can You Live to Be 100?* by Diana S. Woodruff. New York: Chatham Square Press, 1977. Copyright 1977 by Diana S. Woodruff. Reprinted with permission.

Introduction

In this, the final chapter of the text, the concept of aging will be evaluated and issues related to death that have intrigued developmental psychologists will be explored. The discussion of aging focuses on the perspectives that have been formulated to explain the process of aging—both biological and social views are described. The discussion of death includes an attempt to define death, information about historical and cultural attitudes about death, and how children and adults differ in their understanding and interpretation of death. How individuals face death, psychological stages in the dying process, grief and bereavement, and the psychology of life after death are other major topics to be addressed.

Aging

In the prologue you answered a number of questions about aspects of your life that influence how long you are likely to live. Before we look at the many different perspectives that have been developed to explain why we age, we describe further some ideas about life expectancy and the life span, including a detailed look at the lives of the Abkhasians and why women live longer than men.

Life Expectancy and the Life Span

As we saw in chapter 1, a greater percentage of the population is living to an old age. For example, in 1900 only about 4.1 percent of the population were over sixty-five; by 1975, 10.5 percent were, and the percentage is still climbing. At present, approximately two out of every three of you reading this text are likely to live to be seventy years or older. While the number of people living to older ages has increased significantly, recall that it only has been in recent years that researchers have become interested in the aging process. It was virtually inevitable that research on aging would begin to blossom, since life expectancy has almost doubled (from forty-eight to seventy years) since 1900.

Nonetheless, it is interesting that the life span has remained virtually unchanged over this period of time even though life expectancy for most people has increased dramatically. This means that although such factors as improved medicine and nutrition have provided us with an additional twenty-two years of life on the average since 1900, there are still very few individuals who live to be 100. According to table A in the prologue, when we reach the age of seventy, we are likely to live approximately twelve more years, a figure not very different from in 1900. If we become terminally ill during this period of time, we can have our life prolonged by medical science—we can be fed intravenously, we can be placed on machines that help us

"Look at this birth certificate—it's parchment."

breath and eliminate our wastes, and we can have our hearts stimulated electrically. But while we can be kept alive much longer than would have been possible eighty years ago, eventually we die. And, while most of us make it to seventy, very, very few of us will make it to 100.

What this means is that our life span, in contrast to our life expectancy, probably will not be increased until the biological causes of aging are either slowed down or stopped (Hayflick, 1975). The fact that so many more of us are likely to live past the age of seventy than in the past has led some scientists to speculate about the implications of this change in our population characteristics for medical treatment. One set of prescriptions based on these changes is suggested in box 20.1, where the provocative view of Stanford professor James Fries (1980) is outlined. To summarize Fries's view, chronic illness, in most cases, can be postponed by changes in life-style, thereby raising the age at which a person becomes infirm. Thus, the morbidity curve becomes more rectangular (see box figure) as adults live more vigorous lives in late adulthood. As a consequence, the period of senescence becomes compressed near the end of life, a scenario that suggests we should carefully review our health care strategy for the elderly. High-level medical technology applied at the end of a natural life span becomes absurd from Fries's perspective.

Box 20.1
Aging, Natural Death, and the Compression of Morbidity: A Rectangular Theory of Aging and Health Care

James Fries (1980) has developed a fascinating view of aging and health care that suggests we should give careful consideration to the changes in aging that are occurring in the United States in order to make the quality of life for elderly individuals better. Fries's predictions contradict the conventional anticipation of an ever older, ever more feeble, and ever more expensive-to-care-for population. His predictions suggest that the number of very old persons will not increase, that the average period of diminished physical vigor will decrease, that chronic disease will occupy a smaller proportion of the typical life span, and that the need for medical care in later life will decrease.

Fries points out that in forecasting health, the interaction between two important sets of observations has gone unnoticed. The first set demonstrates that the length of human life is fixed—that humans are mortal and that natural death may occur without disease. The second set indicates that chronic disease can be postponed and that many of the "markers" of aging may be modified. If these two premises are granted, it follows that the time between birth and first permanent infirmity must increase and that the average period of infirmity must decrease.

The shape of the survival curve in antiquity for many animal species indicated that death was almost a random event—that is, an organism succumbed to a problem before reaching the life span usual for members of the species. In 1900, the survival curve in the United States was not very different from this situation. However, survival curves throughout this century have shown progressive rectangularization (Comfort, 1979; Upton, 1977), as the elimination of premature death has occurred (see figure).

If we assume a person will live a life that does not end in premature death and is free from disease, under ideal social circumstances the mean age at death is likely to be approximately eighty-five. As suggested earlier, our chances of reaching the age of eighty-five have been increasing in this century. As indicated in the figure, we have removed about 80 percent of the area between the ideal curve and the 1900 curve. Moreover, the greatest change has occurred in the early years of life, with most remaining premature deaths concentrated in the years after sixty. For example, in 1900 the average citizen died thirty-eight years prematurely (short of the ideal limit), in 1950 seventeen years, and in 1980 only twelve years. In 1980, white women died on the average only seven years prematurely. Furthermore, violent deaths account for three of the years by which we fall short of the limit. Clearly, the medical and social task of eliminating premature death has largely been accomplished.

Fries (1980) believes that the decline in premature deaths will continue, leading to the emergence of a pattern of natural death at the end of a natural life span. Present approaches to social interaction, promotion of health, and personal autonomy may postpone many of the phenomena usually associated with aging. The rectangularization of the survival curve may be followed by rectangularization of the morbidity curve and by compression of morbidity (see figure).

These considerations suggest a radically different view of the life span and society, in which life is physically, emotionally, and intellectually vigorous until shortly before its close, when everything comes apart at once and repair is virtually impossible. Such a life approaches the intuitive ideal of many and confounds the dread of others for the opposite model, that of evermore lingering death. Paradoxically, predictability of death may prove soothing.

Later in our discussion of aging we will explore scientists' best hunches about where to look to possibly slow down or stop the aging process. Before doing so, we look further at the lives of the Abkhasians, who often do live to be 100.

The Abkhasians

In the prologue, the factors that are most likely to influence longevity were categorized as heredity and family, health (weight, dietary habits, smoking, for example), education and occupation, and life-style. Anthropologist Sula Benet (1976) visited the Abkhasians in Russia to try to unravel the reasons for the unbelievable longevity of these people. It should be pointed out that some scholars have doubted the authenticity of the ages of the Abkhasians (e.g., Hayflick, 1975;

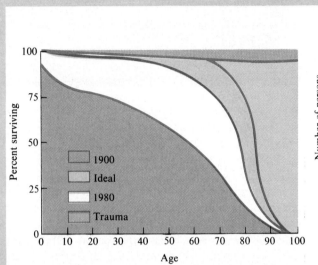

The increasingly rectangular survival curve. About 80 percent of the difference between the 1900 curve and the ideal curve had been eliminated by 1980. Trauma is now the dominant cause of death in early life.

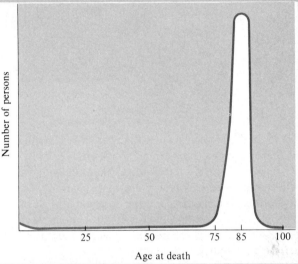

Mortality according to age, in the absence of premature death. The morbidity curve is made rectangular, and the period of morbidity compressed between the point of the end of adult vigor and the point of natural death.

In conclusion, Fries (1980) argues:

Since maintenance of organ capacity appears to require practice on the part of the individual, the implications for the societal role are as fundamentally different as are the two models. Indeed, the choice of societal postures toward the aged is likely to prove self-fulfilling. The older person requires opportunity for expression and experience and autonomy and accomplishment, not support and care and feeding and sympathy. High-level medical technology applied at the end of a natural life span epitomizes the absurd. The hospice becomes more attractive than the hospital. Human interaction, rather than respirators and dialysis and other mechanical support for failing organs, is indicated at the time of the "terminal drop." Anguish arising from the inescapability of personal choice and the inability to avoid personal consequences may become a problem for many. For others, exhilaration may come from recognition that the goal of a vigorous long life may be an attainable one. (p. 135)

Leaf, 1973). However, in her book, *How to Live to Be 100,* Benet devotes an entire chapter to the methods of age verification used in the study of the Abkanesians, and persuasively argues that while in some cases it is difficult to determine whether an individual is 120 or 130 years of age, even if we take the lower figure in such age estimates the Abkhasians clearly do live to very old ages.

After four years of intensive research and field work with the Abkhasians, who live in the Caucasus area of Russia, Sula Benet (1976) developed some conclusions about how these people are able to live healthily to such an old age. The first factor she points to is the continuity and rhythmic regularity that characterizes the Caucasian life. Order in daily routines includes diet, work, sex life, and leisure. Life moves at a sure and steady pace in this culture, and regular routines are rarely violated. There are no abrupt changes to disrupt

The Abkhasians often live to 100 years of age or older.

the order of their lives, an order than has been perpetuated through many generations. For example, continuity in work is rarely interrupted. These individuals rarely change their occupation and more than 60 percent continue to work after the age of seventy. Most of the people do not change their diet throughout their lives. The majority of the people eat very moderately and have lean bodies.

Realistic life goals, a positive role for the aged in the community and family, and a positive self-image are other factors that Benet believes contribute to the longevity of the Abkhasians. They have clearly defined behavioral patterns and achievable life patterns where very little competition and anxiety are generated. When competition is found at all, it is in nonvital activities like sports, dancing, and music. And, in the Caucasus, old people continue to be included in the active life of the kin group and the community. The kinship system promotes longevity through the development of a large network of relatives with mutual rights and obligations. In all of the records of the people in the Caucasus, the *oldest* person is listed as the head of the household, regardless of his or her actual contribution or achievement. The aged, surrounded by numerous respectful progenies of several generations, maintain a feeling of worth and importance that may prolong life.

In the United States, married people and those with children live longer than those who are single and who are childless. The poet Gamzatov, himself a Caucasian, once questioned an old woman who knew hundreds of curses. When he asked her which was the most terrifying curse she could think of, she replied, "Let there be no old folk in your house to give you wise counsel, and no young people to heed their advice."

Why Do Women Live Longer than Men?

Even among the Abkhasians, women live longer than men; and, as we reported earlier, in the United States, women consistently outlive men. Why might this be so? On the surface it might appear that the difference in mortality between men and women might be purely biological, but we now believe that social patterns are likely to account for most of the difference. True, women do have more resistance to infectious and degenerative diseases. For instance, the female's estrogen production helps to protect her from getting atherosclerosis (hardening of the arteries) (Retherford, 1975). And, the X chromosome women carry may be linked with the production of more antibodies to fight off disease (Waldron, 1976). However, most scientists believe that genes and hormones play only a small part in the mortality difference between males and females.

Many scientists believe that sex differences in mortality are related to health attitudes, habits, lifestyles, and occupational choices. For example, among some of the major causes of death in the United States, such as cancer of the respiratory system, motor vehicle accidents, suicide, cirrhosis of the liver, emphysema, and coronary heart disease, there is a strong sex difference indicating that men are much more likely to die from such factors than women (Waldron, 1976). Such causes of death are usually associated with sex differences in habits or life-styles. To take just one example, the sex difference in deaths due to lung cancer and emphysema is likely linked with the fact that men are much heavier smokers than women. However, as sex roles change, and more women work in stress-related jobs, smoke more regularly than in the past, and so forth, equality among the sexes may lead to a convergence in male and female mortality rates.

While it is important to chronicle the course of development, the greatest challenge lies in explaining why development occurs as it does and in discovering the mechanisms responsible for development. Throughout this text, the importance of the interaction of biogenetic and sociocultural factors in explaining development has been emphasized. Next, we will see that scientists have relied heavily on biological explanations to explain the aging process, but that social theories have been developed as well.

Perspectives on Aging

Before we explore some of the different theories that have been developed to explain the aging process, it is important for us to define what we mean by *aging*. In introducing the *Handbook of Mental Health and Aging,* James Birren and Jane Renner (1980) indicate that aging refers to "processes of change in organisms that occur after maturity," as distinguished from "old age," which refers to the last phase of life. Birren and Renner (1980) also believe that it is important to distinguish between biological age, psychological age, and social age. Not all aspects of the individual may be in close synchrony as he or she ages. For example, a person may show expansion in the psychological realm but decline in the physical realm. Birren and Renner define biological age as life expectancy, psychological age as the adaptive behavioral capacities of the individual, and social age as the social roles expected of the individual in the society. In other words, one person may be old in body but young in spirit, while another may be young in body and old in spirit.

We have seen in the course of this text that there clearly are biological, psychological, and social aspects to the aging process. From a biological perspective, we have seen that genes are among the most important biological mechanisms that influence development. Let's look more closely at biological perspectives on aging, focusing first on genetic explanations of the aging process.

Biological Theories

Virtually every biological theory of aging gives genes an important role. It is assumed that the life span of the individual is determined by a program wired into the genes of the species. Support for the genetic basis of aging comes from research demonstrating that certain cells of the body are able to divide only a limited number of times (Hayflick, 1965). Prior to this research it was believed that cells could divide an unlimited number of times. However, it was found that connective tissue cells extracted from human embryonic tissue double only about fifty times rather than an endless number of times. And, cells taken from an older individual are likely to double fewer times than those

obtained from a younger individual. Nonetheless, the cells of the even elderly individuals are still likely to divide, suggesting that we rarely live to the end of our life-span capability. Based on the manner in which human cells divide, the upper limit on longevity is 110 to 120 years of age (Hayflick, 1977).

While virtually all biological theories indicate the importance of genes in aging, some biological theories give genetics a more central role than others. Scientists have debated whether the cause of aging is to be found within each cell or whether it is possibly housed within a particular part of the body, such as the hypothalamus. And, at a more macrolevel, some experts on aging believe that the concept of homeostatic balance is critical to understanding the aging process. First, we will look at several variations of a genetic view of aging called error theory.

Error Theory **Genetic error theories** indicate that aging is caused from damage to the genetic information contained in the formation of cellular protein. Recall from chapter 3 that the information stored in the genetic code is determined by the structure of a complex molecule called deoxyribonucleic acid (DNA). DNA is the control center that monitors the formation of life sustaining proteins. In addition to DNA, a second complex molecule, ribonucleic acid (RNA), must be considered when we attempt to describe how aging occurs at the cellular level. The information contained in DNA must be transmitted to another location within a cell where the formation of proteins actually occurs—the molecule that does this work is called RNA, or sometimes messenger-RNA, because of its transportation function. It has been argued by some scientists that aging is caused by some type of breakdown, or error, that develops in the DNA-RNA cellular system.

There are a number of ways such errors could occur (Williamson, Munley, & Evans, 1980). According to **mutation theory,** aging is due to changes, or mutations, in the DNA of the cells in vital organs of the body. In cells that continue to divide throughout the life cycle, these mutations are likely to be passed on to new cells. Eventually, a substantial number of cells in the organ decline to the point that there is an observable reduction in its functioning. Possible sources for these mutations may be intrinsic factors in cell division, such as chance errors in DNA replication (Burret, 1974); genes that specifically cause mutations in other genes, which may be of benefit in evolutionary terms but might also hasten the aging process (Spiegel, 1977); or extrinsic factors such as toxins in the air, water, and food.

According to **genetic switching theory,** certain genes switch off, which then causes aging. Information needed to produce DNA is no longer available, and so the cells age (Strehler, 1973). Eventually, genetic switching leads to cell death and the loss of organ functioning. According to this theory, the biological clock of aging is genetically programed into each of the body's cells.

According to **error catastrophe theory,** the focus is on damage to RNA, enzymes, and certain other proteins rather than on errors in DNA. For example, if an error occurs in the RNA responsible for the production of an enzyme essential to cell metabolism, the result will be a marked reduction in cell functioning and possibly cell death. The escalating impact of the original error in the RNA is the "error catastrophe" (Orgel, 1973).

Other genetic theories emphasize that aging is caused by changes that occur in cellular proteins after they already have been formed. Two such perspectives are the cross-linkage theory and the free-radical theory (Shock, 1977).

Cross-Linkage and Free-Radical Theories **Cross-linkage theory** stresses that aging occurs because of the formation of bonds, or cross-linkages, between various parts of the cell (Bjorksten, 1968, 1974). This theory was developed when Bjorksten detected that the protein gelatin used in early copying machines was irreversibly changed by certain chemicals. He indicated that proteins in our body may be altered in similar ways. Such alteration of proteins may cause us to age. The cross-linkages that may produce aging could be between RNA, DNA, other proteins, and enzymes. For example, cross-linkage between various DNA molecules may interfere with the production of RNA and with cell division. Why does cross-linkage occur? Possibly because of normal cell metabolism eventually breaking down, possibly because of radiation, and possibly because of our diet. And, another reason for cross-linkages are what have been called "free-radicals."

Free-radical theory is a special application of cross-linkage theory. Chemical components of the cells that exist only for one second or less before they react with other substances such as fats are called free radicals. They can damage cells through their reactions with other substances and they can cause chromosome damage. It has been speculated that vitamins C and E reduce the collisions of free radicals with other cell substances, and as a consequence, may increase an individual's life span. Empirical evidence to support the vitamin hypothesis, however, has not been developed.

Other biological theories indicate that aging occurs because some physiological coordinating system fails to function properly—two such systems are the immunological and hormonal systems.

Physiological Coordination Breakdown Each of us has an immune system that protects our body from foreign substances such as viruses, bacteria, and mutant cells (e.g., cancer). The immune system may generate antibodies that react with the proteins of foreign organisms and it may form cells that literally eat up these foreign cells. The peak of the immune system's ability seems to occur in adolescence, becoming gradually less efficient as the individual ages. It is also important to note that as an individual ages there is an increase in **autoimmunity** (meaning that the body actually attacks itself). Autoimmunity may occur because the immune mechanisms fail to detect that normal cells really are normal or from mistakes in the formation of antibodies, such that antibodies react to normal cells as well as foreign ones (Walford, 1969).

We also may age because the efficiency of our hormonal system declines—this theory is called **hormonal theory.** Hormonal changes are controlled by the brain, particularly the pituitary gland and the hypothalamus. One scientist (Finch, 1976) believes that aging pacemakers in these control centers of the brain stimulate a series of neurological and hormonal changes that cause us to age.

Another proponent of hormonal theory (Denckla, 1974) describes the developmental sequence of aging involving the hypothalamus and pituitary. The hypothalamus periodically stimulates the pituitary gland, located under the brain to release antithyroid hormones that travel in blood cells throughout the body. The "blocking hormones" begin to be released shortly after puberty. They keep the body's cells from absorbing an adequate supply of thyroxine, a hormone produced in the thyroid that is required for normal cell metabolism. A number of metabolic imbalances result when thyroxine is not available in adequate quantities. According to this view, it is these imbalances that produce an excess of free radicals, mutations, cross-linkages, the build-up of toxins within the cell, and autoimmunity (Rosenfeld, 1976).

A Macrobiological Theory—Homeostatic Imbalance The biological theories outlined so far attempt to explain aging by looking at some part of the organism, either within a cell or a particular organ of the body. A theory that tells us to look within a cell when we try to explain the aging process is a microbiological theory. The label *micro* refers to the fact that a cell is a very small unit of analysis. By contrast, some scientists believe that we ought to be looking at a more molar, or macro, level when we attempt to explain the aging process. One such macrobiological perspective of aging is the **homeostatic imbalance theory.**

James Fries (1980), whose rectangular theory of aging and health care was described earlier, describes the homeostatic imbalance theory. At the level of the organism, life may be defined as internal homeostasis. The internal milieu of the body is adjusted within strict limits by compensating mechanisms in many organs, including the heart, lungs, kidneys, and liver. And, various neural and endocrine systems help monitor and maintain this balance in the body's internal environment. In young adult life, the functional capacity of human organs is four to ten times that required to sustain life. The existence of "organ reserve" enables the stressed organism to restore homeostasis, or balance, when it is damaged by external threat. Measurement of organ reserve over time shows an almost linear decline beginning at about the age of thirty (Shock, 1960). As organ reserve decreases, so does the ability to restore homeostasis, and eventually even the smallest perturbation prevents homeostasis from being restored. The inevitable result is natural death, even without disease. Although a disease process may seem to be the cause of death, the actual cause may be the body's inability to maintain homeostasis. Any small perturbation, without coexistent organ reserve, would have the same fatal result. After the age of thirty an individual's mortality rate doubles every eight years (Upton, 1977). Proponents of homeostatic imbalance theory link the the linear decline in organ function to the increase in mortality rate.

Not only have scientists developed biological explanations for aging, but social explanations have been created as well. For the most part social theories of aging have been theories of life satisfaction in late adulthood more than theories informing us about the reason we age. Nonetheless, these social theories provide some insight into the social factors that may contribute to aging.

Social Theories

For some years, two perspectives have dominated thinking about the social basis of aging—disengagement theory and activity theory. A third view, of more recent vintage, is called social breakdown theory.

Disengagement Theory For a number of years **disengagement theory** was believed to represent the best social explanation of aging. Developed by Cuming and Henry (1961), disengagement theory argues that as older people slow down they gradually withdraw from society. Disengagement is viewed as a mutual activity in which the individual not only disengages himself or herself from society, but society as well disengages the individual. According to the theory, the older individual develops an increasing self-preoccupation, lessens emotional ties with others, and shows a decreasing interest in the affairs of the world. Such reduction of social interaction and increased self-preoccupation was thought to be necessary to maintain life satisfaction in late adulthood.

Disengagement theory has been criticized by a number of prominent theorists and researchers. For example, disengagement theory predicts that low morale would accompany high activity, and further that disengagement is inevitable and is sought out by the elderly. A series of research studies have failed to support these beliefs (e.g., Maddox, 1968; Havighurst, Neugarten, & Tobin, 1968; Reichard, Levson, & Peterson, 1962). For example, in one investigation (Maddox, 1964), when age was held constant, there was substantial variation in the indicators of disengagement displayed. And, as suggested next, when individuals continue to maintain very active lives in late adulthood they do not show a decrease in life satisfaction.

Activity Theory In a well-known investigation of engagement and disengagement, Bernice Neugarten and her colleagues (Neugarten, Havighurst, & Tobin, 1968) found that activity and involvement often are associated with life satisfaction. They categorized individuals in late adulthood into four different types of personality styles: integrated (engaged, involved people); armored-defended (holding on types, particularly to middle adulthood roles); passive-dependent (medium to low activity level, sometimes passive and apathetic); and unintegrated (disorganized, deteriorated cognitive processes, weak emotional control). The life satisfaction of the integrated and armored-defended personality types, who were more active and involved, was greater than the passive-dependent and unintegrated types, who were less active and involved.

According to **activity theory,** then, the more active and involved older people are, the less likely they are to age and the more likely they are to show life satisfaction. Activity theory suggests that it often is healthy for individuals to continue their middle adulthood roles through late adulthood, and that if these roles are taken away (for example, through retirement), it is important for them to find substitute roles that keep them active and involved in the world.

Social Breakdown Theory A third, more recently developed social theory of aging is called **social breakdown theory,** or social breakdown/social reconstruction theory (Kuypers & Bengtson, 1973). This theory suggests that aging is promoted through negative psychological functioning that involves a poor self-concept, negative feedback from others and society, and a lack of skills to deal with the world. As suggested in figure 20.1, social breakdown occurs in a sequence that begins with susceptibility and ends with identifying and labeling one's self as incompetent.

The more helping and active an older adult is, the less likely he or she is to age.

In order to prevent the social breakdown syndrome from developing, these researchers believe that we need to reorganize our social system so that individuals in late adulthood will be treated in more respectful ways and will develop better self-images and feel more competent about their role in society. In figure 20.2, how social reconstruction could reverse the social breakdown syndrome is shown.

Evaluation and Integration of Theories of Aging
Since there are so many theories of aging that have been developed, you might already have guessed that scientists are far from being able to nail down precise answers to the mystery of what causes us to age? Just as in chapter 2 when we described a number of theories of life-span development, such as cognitive-developmental, psychoanalytic, and social learning, and concluded that no single indomitable theory outdoes all the others in explaining life-span development, no one theory of aging has been shown to be the best explanation. The answer to the mystery of aging likely lies in some combination of these theories, or in some theory that has yet to be developed. It is likely that a complete theory of aging would have to take into account both micro and macro-biological aspects of the organism, the social conditions in which we live, and our psychological

make-up. Remember from our introduction to the concept of aging that aging has biological, social, and psychological components. It is likely that these aspects of aging interact to influence an individual's longevity. But eventually death comes. Next, we explore a number of issues that interest scientists who study the death process.

Death
Although the process of dying and the event of death are taboo topics of investigation and consideration by many people, they nonetheless are integral parts of the human life cycle. There can be no birth without death, and there can be no death without life. In this section we will look first at various definitions of death. Then we will explore how children understand and react to death and compare such intepretations with that of adults. And, we will look at the historical and cultural basis of death. Other topics to be discussed include the adaptation and coping of individuals who face death, psychological stages in the dying process, how the terminal patient can be helped, grief and bereavement, and the possibility of life after death.

Definitions of Death
While it might seem a simple task to determine when an individual has died, recent controversy has focused on the biological, legal, and philosophical aspects of

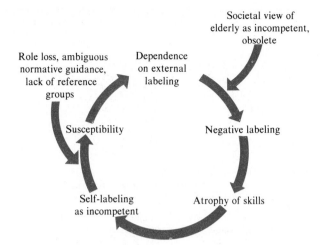

Figure 20.1 The social-breakdown syndrome.

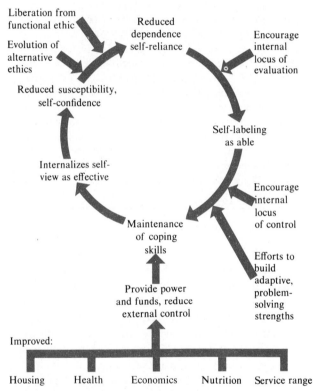

Figure 20.2 Reversing the social-breakdown syndrome.

dying. And, there are a number of opinions on the process of dying and on the definition of death. Ten years ago a person was considered dead when breathing stopped and when no heartbeat could be heard. Rigor mortis, dilation of the pupils, and a relaxation of the sphincter muscle were labeled as other signs of death.

In the 1980s, determining and defining death is not as simple. Modern medicine has contributed a neurological definition of death—brain death—in which all electrical activity of the brain has ceased for a specified period of time as determined by an electroencephalogram (EEG). A flat recording by an EEG suggests death, regardless of how vital other organs may seem under resuscitation (Demsey, 1975; Aiken, 1978). When a person is dying the cells of the higher portion of the brain, which is the area most affected by oxygen deprivation, die within five to ten minutes. The lower brain centers, such as those that monitor heartbeat and respiration, die next. When the person's heart stops beating but is restored by resuscitation, a person who technically has died may be revived. Unfortunately, if the higher brain centers have been affected by oxygen deprivation, the individual is unlikely to recover mental and motor capabilities, or if he or she does recover them, the impairment will be severe.

The ability of modern medicine to resuscitate a dying individual complicates the definition of death. A heart that has stopped can be massaged or stimulated electrically and can continue pumping indefinitely while the brain remains irreparably damaged. Numerous people with irreversible brain damage have been kept alive for years by intravenous feeding and artificial breathing. Such cases illustrate some of the ethical and legal questions posed as a result of our ability to resuscitate and prolong life. While we will not go into a detailed discussion of these questions here, some of the most common issues involved are: Is a person dead when the brain dies but their heart is stimulated and continues pumping blood? Should persons who are unconscious, and who have no chance for recovery be permitted to die—that is, should their treatment be terminated? Under what circumstances, if any, should euthanasia be practiced? Does a person have a right to die? Do they have the right to take their life? And, who should be making such decisions?

Some people go into an irreversible coma or become severely paralyzed. Some have wires and tubes running out of almost every orifice in their bodies—their conditions will never change. Should they be kept alive, or should they be allowed to die? Further discussion of this issue appears in box 20.2, where we evaluate the current status of the concept of euthanasia.

While more people are living to an older age than ever before, death still comes to people at all ages. And, as we will see next, individuals of different ages often do not have the same concept of death. Similarly, death has been viewed in different ways at the different points in history and in different cultures.

Attitudes toward Death

At what point in the life cycle do we begin to understand the concept of death? And, what are our attitudes about death at different ages?

Box 20.2
Euthanasia and the Hospice Alternative

The term **euthanasia** is mainly used to refer to the act of painlessly putting to death persons suffering from incurable diseases or severe disability—in this sense, it often is referred to as mercy killing. In debates concerning euthanasia, a distinction often is made between active euthanasia, in which death is induced by some positive action, such as the injection of a lethal dose of a drug, and passive euthanasia, in which death is induced by the withdrawal of some life-sustaining therapeutic effort, as when a respirator or heart-lung machine is turned off.

Some experts argue that passive euthanasia is not a form of euthanasia at all but is simply the process of letting nature take its course. And, in most definitions of euthanasia reference is made to putting to death a person who is suffering a painful and incurable disease. However, the pain criterion is not always met. Consider for example, the euthanasia conducted with severely deformed infants.

In many instances these infants are not experiencing any pain at all. Adults who are in an irreversible coma are rarely in pain either. The case of Karen Quinlan has received a great deal of attention in recent years—despite being in an irreversible coma she was not experiencing a great deal of pain.

The President's Commission for the Study of Ethical Problems in Medicine and Biomedical and Behavioral Research has been holding hearings on the moral dilemmas posed by treating severely ill and handicapped patients. One recent testimony before the committee was presented by Mary Anne Warren, a philosopher. She argued that when the child is not expected to live long, when that life would be unbearable, or when caring for the child would mean enormous personal and financial costs to the family or society, active euthanasia should be practiced.

While there is greater support for the legalization of euthanasia than in the past (Gallup, 1972), it is possible that no such legislation of euthanasia will be enacted in the foreseeable future. One of the developments that could undercut the euthanasia movement is the **hospice** alternative. While advocates of euthanasia attempt to assist

---

Death and the Life Cycle

Children who are two or three years of age rarely get upset by the sight of a dead animal or by being told that a person has died. Children at this age generally have no idea of what death really means. Often two- to three-year-old children confuse death with sleep, or they ask in a puzzled way, "Why doesn't it move?"

While children vary somewhat in the age when they begin to understand death, the limitations of preoperational thought often make it difficult for a child to comprehend the meaning of death before the age of seven or eight. Young children, unfortunately, may blame themselves for events, such as divorce and death, illogically reasoning that such events may have developed because they disobeyed the person who died. Furthermore, children under the age of six rarely perceive that death is universal, inevitable, and final. Instead, young children usually think that only people who want to die, or who are bad or careless, actually do die. Children at this age believe that the dead can be returned to life. Sometime between the ages of five to seven, however, these ideas give way to a more realistic perception of death.

Maria Nagy (1948) conducted the first investigation of children's attitudes toward death. She found that most children aged three to five denied the existence of death, most between the ages of six to nine believed that death exists but that it only happens to some people, and most children nine years or older recognized the finality and universality of death. In discussing death with children, most psychologists recognize that honesty is the best strategy rather than treating the concept as unmentionable. However, many of us have grown up in a society where death is rarely discussed in a family. In one investigation (Shneidman, 1973) that surveyed the attitudes of 30,000 young adults, more that 30 percent said they could not recall any discussion of death during their childhoods; and an equal number said that while death was discussed, the discussion took place in an uncomfortable atmosphere. In Edwin Shneidman's (1973) survey, the majority of young people reported that they initially became aware of death sometime between five to ten years of age. Almost one of every two respondents said that the death of a grandparent represented their first personal confrontation with death.

those who prefer death to suffering, the proponents of the hospice movement seek to help the dying patient from being degraded, from feeling meaningless, and from suffering unnecessarily. The hospice is a humanized institution with a commitment to making the end of life as free from pain, anxiety, and depression as possible, as opposed to a hospital where the goals are to cure illness and prolong life. The hospice movement begain in the late 1960s in London, England, when a new kind of medical institution, St. Christopher's Hospice, opened. Little effort is made to prolong life at St. Christopher's—there are no heart-lung machines and no intensive care unit, for example. A primary goal is to bring pain under control and to help the dying patient face death in a psychologically healthy way. One aspect of the hospice orientation toward the dying patient is to keep the dying patient an important part of his or her family. Every effort is made to make the members of the dying patient's family welcome at the hospice. It is believed that such a strategy not only will be beneficial to the dying patient, but that this practice also helps family members to feel less guilt after the death of a family member (Hinton, 1972).

The hospice movement is of growing interest in the United States. By 1978, there were a dozen hospice operations in existence and 170 hospice groups in various stages of development (Lack & Buckingham, 1978). One of the arguments of euthanasia is that it offers a merciful alternative to a slow, painful death in a dehumanizing environment. But hospice advocates quickly point out that it is possible to control terminal pain for almost everyone and that it is possible to create an environment for the patient far superior to that found in most hospitals. In a hospice it would be possible for many who might otherwise prefer the alternative of death to enjoy their last days or weeks. While the controversy of euthanasia is unlikely to go away, the hospice has provided an attractive alternative for making the end of life humane for people. During the decade of the 1980s we are likely to see the hospice movement expand.

During adolescence, the prospect of death, like the prospect of aging, often is regarded as a notion that is so remote that it doesn't have much relevance. Death often is avoided, glossed over, kidded about, neutralized, and controlled by a cool, spectatorlike orientation. Such a perspective is typical of the self-conscious thought of the adolescent. Some adolescents, though, do show a concern about death, both in the sense of trying to fathom its meaning and nature and in the sense of confronting the actual prospect of their own demise (Kastenbaum, 1981).

Our discussion of middle adulthood indicated that middle age is a time when individuals often begin to think about how much time is left in their life rather than what has come before them. As such, they are more likely than their young adult counterparts to begin thinking about the finality of their life. In one national survey (Riley, 1970), it was found that middle-aged adults had more fear of death and were more likely than individuals in early or late adulthood to believe that death always comes too soon. In the same survey, it was revealed that individuals in late adulthood were generally less frightened by death, think about it more, and talk with others about it more than adults of other ages.

Death has been conceptualized in different ways at different points in history and still is viewed in different ways, depending upon the culture in which the individual lives.

Historical and Cultural Views of Death
The ancient Greeks faced death as they faced life—openly and directly. To live a full life and die with glory was the prevailing attitude of the Greeks. People are more likely to be conscious of death in times of war, famine, and plagues. While Americans are conditioned from early in life to live as though they were immortal, in much of our world this fiction cannot be maintained. Death crowds the streets of Calcutta, as it does the scrubby villages of Africa's Sahel. Children live with the ultimate toll of malnutrition and disease, mothers lose as many babies as survive into adulthood, and it is the rare family that remains intact for many years. Even

Children younger than seven or eight years of age rarely comprehend the meaning of death.

Cultural variations exist in the perception of and reaction to death.

in peasant areas where life is better and health and maturity may be reasonable expectations, the presence of dying persons in the house, the large attendance at funerals, and the daily contact with aging people prepare the young for the fact of death and provide them with information about how to die. By contrast, in the United States it is not uncommon to reach maturity without ever having seen someone die (Foster & Anderson, 1978).

Most societies throughout history, and most cultures today, have some philosophical or religious belief system or ritual that deals with death. For example, elderly Eskimos in Greenland who no longer can contribute to their society may walk off alone never to be seen again or they are given a departure ceremony at which they are honored, then ritually killed. Following is a description of such a ceremony (Freuchen, 1961):

In some tribes, an old man wants his oldest son or favorite daughter to be the one to put the string around his neck and hoist him to his death. This was always done at the height of the party where good things were being eaten, where everyone—including the one who was about to die—felt happy and gay, and which would end with the angakok conjuring and dancing to chase out the evil spirits. At the end of his performance, he would give a special rope made of seal and walrus skin to the "executioner" who then placed it over the beam of the roof of the house and fastened it around the neck of the old man. Then the two rubbed noses, and the young man pulled the rope. Everybody in the house either helped or sat on the rope so as to have the honor of bringing the old suffering one to the Happy Hunting Grounds where there would always be light and plenty of game of all kinds. (pp. 194–95)

In most societies, like in the Greenland Eskimo culture, death is not viewed as the end of existence—while the physical body has died, the spiritual body is believed to live on. This religious perspective also is favored by more Americans than a view suggesting that there is no continuing spiritual existence (Kalish & Reynolds, 1976).

Cultural variations in perceptions of and reactions to death include those of the Gond culture in India and the Tanala culture of Madagascar. The Gond believe that death is caused by magic and demons, while the Tanala think that death occurs for natural reasons. Possibly because of these beliefs about death, the Gond show a much more angry and less peaceful orientation when one of their members dies than the Tanala. Other cultural variations in attitudes toward death include beliefs about reincarnation, which is an important aspect of the religions of Hinduism and Buddhism.

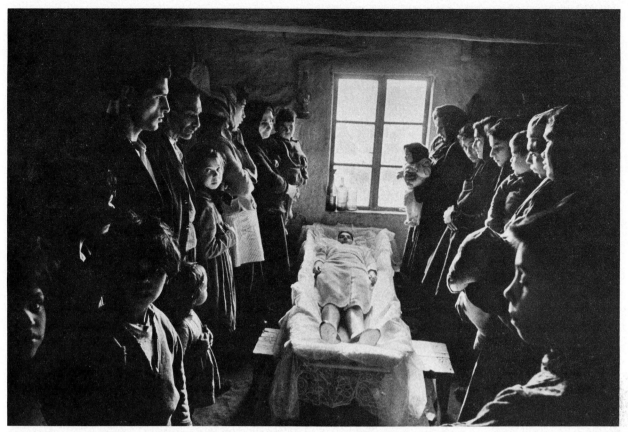

Most cultures today have some philosophical or religious belief system that deals with death.

Our perceptions of death vary and reflect diverse values and philosophies. Death may be seen as a punishment for our sins, an act of atonement, or a judgment of a just God. For some, death means loneliness. Other individuals may think of death as a cruel interruption in the quest for happiness in which death itself is the common denominator for all people. Yet others may think of death as redemption, a relief from the trials and tribulations of our earthly world. Some embrace death and welcome it; others abhor and fear it. For those who welcome it, death may be seen as the fitting end to a fulfilled life. To some extent, then, from this perspective, how we depart from earth is influenced by how we have lived. In the words of Leonardo da Vinci, death should come to a person after a full life just as sleep comes after a hard day's work.

While attitudes toward death vary a great deal, in the United States we generally react to death with denial and avoidance. Such denial can take various forms.

The tendency of the funeral industry to gloss over death and fashion greater lifelike qualities in the dead.

The adoption of euphemistic language for death, such as "exiting," "passing on," "never say die," and "good for life," which implies forever.

The persistent search for the fountain of youth as we try to stay young.

The rejection and isolation of the aged who may remind us of death.

The adoption of the concept of a pleasant and rewarding afterlife, thus suggesting that we are immortal.

Emphasis of the medical community on the prolongation of biological life rather than on the diminishment of human suffering.

Our failure to discuss death with our children.

In many ways, then, we are death-avoiders and death-deniers. But ultimately we face death. What is the psychological experience of facing death like?

Facing Death—The Dying Process

In the book, *The Sane Society,* Erich Fromm commented that man is the only living thing that knows it will die. In Fromm's view, "man is the only animal that finds his own existence a problem which he has to solve and from which he cannot escape. In the same sense man is the only animal who knows he must die" (p. 23). Over the centuries philosophers, theologians, poets, and

According to Fromm, man is the only living thing that knows it will die.

psychologists have attempted to explain the phenomena of death and have theorized about why we must die and whether death is the final curtain or if there is yet another life after the one on earth.

We may never know the answers to many questions about death but several investigations shed some light on our attitudes toward our own death. Most dying persons want to talk with someone about their feelings and their fears. The also want an opportunity to make some decisions regarding their life and their death. Some persons may wish to complete unfinished business and they want time to resolve problems and conflicts and to put their affairs in order (Kübler-Ross, 1974).

One investigation of the psychological reactions of the elderly to the dying process revealed that as the individual approaches death, he or she tends to withdraw from the world and significant others in it and becomes increasingly preoccupied with the self (Lieberman, 1979). During the last months of life, while there is a sharp focus on one's body, there is the accompanying feeling that it is a less than adequate instrument. An increased sense of hopelessness is also noted in the last months of life and this feeling of hopelessness is reflected in expressions of inability to influence the environment, particularly in significant personal relationships. However, some significant changes seem to occur as people approach death. Those closest to death show high interest in other people and high responsiveness to the environment.

The most well-known research and theory on psychological reactions to impending death have been developed by Elisabeth Kübler-Ross. Her ideas are based on interviews with hundreds of terminally ill patients.

Kübler-Ross's Psychological Stages of Dying
Kübler-Ross has divided the behavior of dying patients into five stages. It should be emphasized that these stages often overlap one another. And, patients sometimes go back and forth from one stage to another.

First Stage: Denial and Isolation The most common initial reaction to terminal illness is one of shock and denial. Often, the individual responds with such thoughts as, "No, it can't be me. It's not true. It's not possible." However, denial usually is only a temporary defense and is soon replaced with acceptance when the

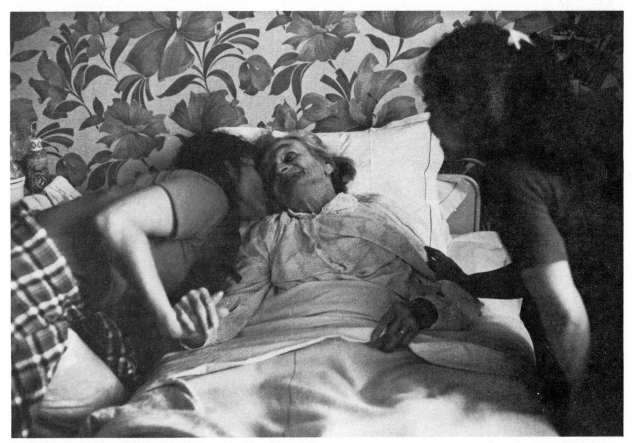

Most dying persons want to talk with someone about their death and make some decisions regarding it.

individual is confronted with such matters as finances, unfinished business, or worry about surviving family members.

Second Stage: Anger When the individual recognizes that denial no longer can be maintained, it often gives way to feelings of anger, resentment, rage, and envy. Now the individual's question becomes, "Why me?" At this point, the individual becomes increasingly difficult to care for as anger often becomes displaced and projected onto physicians, nurses, hospital staff, family members, and even God. The realization of loss is great, and those persons that symbolize life, energy, and competent functioning are particularly salient targets of the terminally ill individual's resentment and jealousy.

Third Stage: Bargaining While the individual was not able to face death in the first stage and gets angry and shows resentment in the second stage, according to Kübler-Ross, the dying person develops the hope that death can somehow be postponed or delayed in the third stage. Some individuals enter into a brief period of negotiation—often with God—as they try to delay their death. Psychologically, the individual now is saying,

"Yes, me, but. . . ." In exchange for a few more days, weeks, or months of life, the individual promises to lead a reformed life dedicated to God or to the service of others as part of the bargain.

Fourth Stage: Depression As the individual comes to accept the certainty of death, he or she often enters a period of preparatory grief, during which he or she becomes very silent, refuses visitors, and spends much of the time crying or grieving. Such behavior should be viewed as normal in this circumstance and is actually an effort to disconnect the self from all love objects. Attempts to cheer up the individual at this stage should be discouraged, according to Kübler-Ross, because he or she has a real need to contemplate impending death.

Fifth Stage: Acceptance If the individual has progressed through the first four stages, acceptance usually is experienced. It is characterized by peace, a unique acceptance of one's fate, and a desire to be left alone. Kübler-Ross refers to this final, fifth stage of the dying process as *acceptance*. While the final stage is not exactly a happy experience—it often is devoid of

Dying Trajectories

Several perspectives on dying trajectories have been developed (e.g., Glaser & Strauss, 1965; Pattison, 1977). The trajectory of life is defined by Mansell Pattison (Pattison, 1977) as the individual's anticipated life span and the plan the person makes for the way he or she will live out life. When a circumstance develops through the course of injury or illness a disruption in our life trajectory occurs because we perceive that we are likely to die much sooner than we had anticipated. Pattison says that between the time we discover that we will die sooner than we had thought and the time we actually die we are in what he calls the living-dying interval, which is characterized by three phases of development. The goal of those who have to treat individuals in the living-dying interval is to assist them in coping with the first phase, called acute, help them to live as reasonably as possible through the second phase, labeled chronic, and move them into the third and final phase, named terminal.

In the *acute phase*, individuals face probably the most severe crisis in their lives—the fact that they will die sooner than they had thought and will not get to accomplish everything they had hoped to. People often feel immobilized, have very high levels of anxiety, and call into play a number of defense mechanisms to deal with the acute fear and stress they are undergoing. In this phase, the individual needs a great deal of emotional support from others and needs to be helped to deal rationally with the fact that he or she is going to die.

In the *chronic phase*, Pattison believes that individuals begin to confront their fear of dying. Such fears as loneliness, suffering, and the unknown often surface and must be dealt with. Health professionals can assist the dying individual by helping him or her put life in perspective and working through some of the defense mechanisms that surfaced earlier.

In the *terminal phase*, the individual begins to withdraw as hope for getting better gives way to the realization that he or she likely is going to get worse, the point at which the person recognizes and accepts the finality of approaching death.

---

feelings—physical pain and discomfort are often absent. Kübler-Ross describes this period as the end of the struggle, the final resting stage before undertaking a long journey.

Some individuals may struggle until the very end, almost visciously trying to hang onto their lives. In these cases, acceptance of death never comes. Many psychologists believe that the harder people fight to avoid the inevitable death they face and the more they deny it, the more difficulty they will have in dying peacefully and with dignity.

Such observations support the comments in introducing Kübler-Ross's theory, namely that not all people go through the stages in the order they have been presented. Some scholars have argued that the way an individual handles the dying process may be unique—it may be just as psychologically healthy for some individuals to die in a state of anger and denial as in a state of acceptance (Leviton, 1977).

While Kübler-Ross's ideas about the stages of the dying process have dominated thinking about the manner in which the individual deals with death, another perspective on the dying process has recently been given attention as well. It is called **dying trajectories** and is described in box 20.3.

One of the most painful experiences we encounter in our lifetime is dealing with the death of someone we are attached to or love. Next, we explore the grief and bereavement individuals go through when they lose someone they love and care about.

Loss, Grief, Bereavement, and Mourning

Loss can come in many forms in our lives, but no loss is greater than the loss through death of someone we love and care for. **Grief** is a normal psychological reaction to many distressful situations in our life, including loss. As with loss, grief is likely to be greater in response to the loss of someone through death than through other types of loss, such as divorce. Many psychologists report that when someone close to us dies we perceive that we have lost a part of ourselves. We can

No loss is greater than the loss through death of someone we love and care for.

only revive the dead through memories, and such memories are often painful because they remind us that what once was never can be again. Such memories describe the process of **bereavement,** which refers to our memories of an irretrievable loss that has affected our lives. And, some individuals have described **mourning** as the way we deal with our grief (e.g., Dempsey, 1975).

The death of a loved one often produces a crisis in the survivors. Such mental suffering may be characterized by a profound sense of loneliness, fear, and despair. These reactions are viewed as normal and are commonly experienced by the bereaved—those who have sustained the loss of a close friend or relative. Grief and mourning may be particularly acute for widows, who may feel that life may not be worth living any more. In such cases, widows often report that they actually look forward to an early death (Bock & Webber, 1972).

Various factors influence the nature, duration, and reactions of grief and mourning, including the specific relationship between the survivor and the deceased, the meaning of the dead person for the survivor, and the nature of the changes in the survivor's life that result from the death (Marcovitz, 1973). Sometimes a narcissistic feeling surfaces in an individual whose son or daughter has just been killed. The parent may ask, Why did this happen to me? Perhaps a less narcissistic response would be, Why did this terrible thing happen to my child? Guilt reactions are common as well, especially if the relationship between the survivor and the deceased was marked by resentment and affection, or if the survivor had secretly entertained wishes for a divorce, or in the case of a dying patient, that they would go ahead and die.

Grief and mourning are likely to be greatest among family members, through either the loss of a spouse, parent, or child. In one investigation of the mourning process, 109 widows were interviewed during the month following their husband's death (Clayton, Halikes, & Maurice, 1971). More than 80 percent of the widows reported that they cried a great deal, felt depressed, and had problems in sleeping. Almost half of the widows said that they had problems in concentrating on what they were doing, that they did not feel like eating, and that they were taking sleeping pills or tranquilizers.

Such grief and mourning often does not go away overnight. It is not uncommon at all for the bereavement process to go on for one or two years (Kimmel, 1974). Some psychologists have called the healthy process through which we cope with the loss of a loved one "grief work" (White & Gathman, 1973).

Grief Work

The main tasks of the mourner are freeing oneself emotionally from the deceased, readjusting to a life in which the dead person is missing, and forming new relationships with other persons. This **grief work** is facilitated by the progression of the survivor through different phases of recovery (White & Gathman, 1973).

At stage one, the surviving individual feels shock, disbelief, numbness, and often weeps or becomes agitated easily. This stage often occurs soon after death and usually lasts from one to three days. This stage of grief is not unlike the denial and anger stages the dying person goes through in Kübler-Ross's stages.

At stage two there is painful longing for the dead, memories and visual images of the deceased, sadness, insomnia, irritability, and restlessness. Beginning not long after death, this stage often peaks in the second to fourth weeks following death, may subside after several months, but can persist up to one or two years.

Elements of bargaining for the return of the deceased person as well as depression may be detected, again corresponding to one of Kübler-Ross's stages of dying.

Stage three usually appears within a year after death. Analogous to the acceptance stage of dying, this grief-resolution phase is marked by a resumption of ordinary activities, a greater likelihood that the deceased will be recalled with pleasant memories, and the establishment of new relationships with others.

However, some individuals never completely recover. Grief may linger, particularly when a child is lost. And, some survivors develop neuroses, particularly of a depressive nature, psychosomatic illnesses, self-destructive impulses, and even in some cases, the physical symptoms experienced by the deceased.

Does the life span end with death? Or is there more? Elisabeth Kübler-Ross (1976) says that beyond a shadow of doubt there is life after death. To end this chapter, we explore the psychology of life after death.

The Psychology of Life after Death

The promise of life after death is a focal point of many religions. It may also be an important part of the personal philosophy of many of you reading this text. As such, believing in an afterlife is a matter of faith rather than science. Views of faith and science do not necessarily have to conflict. One problem, however, that has surfaced recently in the afterlife issue is the advancement of a scientific afterlife hypothesis and statements

---

Box 20.4
Perceptions of Life after Death: Real or Hallucinogenic?

The time is 1920. Thomas Edison had always been a believer in electrical energy. He once wrote that when a person dies, a swarm of highly charged energies deserts the body and goes out into space, entering another cycle of life. Always the scientist, Edison felt that some experiment demonstrating the immortal nature of these energies was necessary. In an interview in the October 1920 *Scientific American* he stated,

> I have been thinking for some time of a machine or apparatus which could be operated by personalities which have passed onto another existence or sphere. . . . I am inclined to believe that our personality hereafter does affect matter. If we can evolve an instrument so delicate as to be affected by our personality as it survives in the next life, such an instrument ought to record something.

Edison never built his machine, but on his deathbed he had a vision of the next life and remarked, "It is very beautiful over there" (quoted in Sandberg, 1977, p. 65). . . .

The time is now 1978. The California Museum of Science and Industry had opened an exhibit based on the thesis that energy is indestructible, that consciousness can exist independent of the physical body, and that consciousness continues after death. Entitled *Continuum,* the exhibit proclaimed the words of great philosophers who have supported the belief in a life after death. Displays bombarded the visitor with reports of visions of the dead and descriptions of the afterlife in order to demonstrate that consciousness can exist without the physical body. However, the exhibit avoided the tricky philosophical problem posed by the fact that a conscious physical body is always the one to make such reports!

Epistemological difficulties aside, the belief in life after death thrives. A 1978 Gallup poll reveals that approximately 70 percent of the people in the United States believe in the hereafter. An earlier survey conducted in the Los Angeles area (Kalish & Reynolds, 1973) indicated that 44 percent of respondents had had encounters with others known to be dead. On June 20, 1978, the *National Enquirer* ran a front-page headline declaring "New Evidence of Life After Death" and advertised "science's answer to the afterlife" for a mere $3. That money procures a copy of *The Circular Continuum* (Masterson, 1977), which explains the eternal Einsteinian nature of energy and matter as proof of life after death and provides an illustration depicting a man falling through a long spiraling tunnel into the afterlife. Masterson's book is a poor adaptation of psychologist LeShan's (1975) longer, and cheaper, explanation of the phenomenon in terms of the field theory of modern physics. . . .

In the 1970s, medical journals started publishing reports of patients who had afterlife visions following near-death experiences (e.g., MacMillan & Brown, 1971). New therapeutic approaches to dying, based on a sympathetic assurance that life continues after bodily death, were developed (e.g., Gordon, 1970; Grof & Halifax, 1977; Huxley, 1968). A major psychiatric journal, the *Journal of Nervous and Mental Disease,* set a precedent by publishing a literature review of reincarnation and life after death research (Stevenson, 1977). Aware of the controversial nature of such a report, the journal invited a commentary on the work. Regrettably, the commentary (written by Stevenson's close friend, admitted "admirer," and colleague of twenty-five years) was not critical, but heavy

suggesting that there is empirical verification of the existence of life after death. When such claims are made it is important that the scientific community evaluate the claim objectively. UCLA psychologist Ronald Siegel (1980, 1981) has conducted extensive research on the afterlife issue. An expert on hallucinations, Siegel has shown that the descriptions given by dying persons are almost identical to descriptions given by persons experiencing hallucinations, drug-induced or otherwise. Thus, there is a plausible alternative hypothesis to account for the experiences of dying patients. But, it is not a situation where we have two competing scientific theories. The hypothesis of hallucinogenic induction of near-death experiences is supported by hard scientific data—the alternative hypothesis, namely that

dying individuals are actually experiencing glimpses of the afterlife, has no compelling scientific data to support it. The basis of Siegel's argument that there is no compelling scientific evidence to support the life after death view is presented in box 20.4.

In conclusion, if you adopt a religious perspective, then, you likely believe there is a life after death. By contrast, if you assume a scientific stance, you are likely to be much more skeptical. Each of us will find out the answer to the question of whether there is life after death in the end . . . or is it in the beginning?

with superfluous platitudes. The journal published another related article (Rodin, 1980) and devoted part of an issue to five separate commentaries on that work. . . .

Our study of life after death is highly dependent on the words, pictures, and other symbols used in description. Many of these words have sensory qualities and describe such properties as sight, sound, taste, and smell. Accident victims who have had near-death experiences often report visions of long, dark tunnels or sounds of ringing and buzzing. Surgical patients who are resuscitated following cardiac or respiratory failure frequently report floating out of their bodies and watching the operation from a distant perspective. Terminal patients often experience unbidden memory images of long forgotten childhood events and deceased relatives. These images arise with such startling vividness that they often prompt the patient to react by speaking with the image or moving toward it. British psychiatrist Maudsley (1939) described such images as "mental representation so intense as to become mental presentation" (p. 98) dying experiences. It seems plausible that common processes and mechanisms underlie these descriptions. . . .

Many reports from individuals are generated from communication with the dead via mediums, spiritualists, ghosts, apparitions, automatic writing, clairvoyance, and related techniques.

In one report a dead man communicated to his living wife that the afterlife had "a lawn that would put any Earth golf club to shame. Flowers I've never seen before. Even new colors. And everywhere, people. Thousands of them. Happy people, doing things they really liked to do" (Loehr, 1976, p. 48). But not everyone in the afterlife is

happy. Wickland (1924, 1974), who communicated with departed spirits for thirty years through the medium of his wife, reported that narcotic addicts continue to experience agonizing withdrawal after death and can satisfy their craving only by possessing living mortals and compelling them to become addicts of the same drug. Other reports can be humorous when read with the proper frame of mind. Ebon (1977), for example, describes a séance (wherein ghosts often ring bells or tap tables) in which he heard the name Margery, though "the name 'Margery' rang no bell with me" (p. 8)! Reports can be extremely specific. Sandberg (1977) relates that the "City of God" is a cube 1,500 miles on each side wherein children continue to mature (do they age and die as well?). Drawing heavily on accounts published in the National Enquirer, M. Ford (1978) tells us there are fifty-seven mansions in this city, all in separate parks, but some people have to live in one-room apartment units. Travel is by "teleportation," but city residents can also walk, jog, or catch a "chariot of light," which might be seen by the living as a UFO. . . .

Physician Raymond Moody (1975, 1977) has also attempted to describe the prototypical vision of life after death. Moody was neither the first to do so (cf. Crookall, 1961) nor the most careful in his methods (cf. Osis & Haraldsson, 1977). But he has been the most popular author on the contemporary scene and, along with Kübler-Ross, can be credited with stimulating the current interest in the field. . . .

Moody's prototypic experience. According to Moody, the prototypical experience of the dying person includes the following elements: ineffability; hearing doctors or spectators pronouncing one dead; feelings of peace and quiet; a loud ringing or buzzing noise; a dark tunnel through which one may feel oneself moving; out of body experiences; meeting others, including guides, spirits, dead relatives, and friends; a being of light; a panoramic review of one's life; a border or limit beyond which there is no return; visions of great knowledge; cities of light; a realm of bewildered spirits; supernatural rescues from real physical death by some spirit; a return or coming back with changed attitudes and beliefs.

Moody's explanation. Moody refrains from interpreting these experiences as proof of life after death (despite the publisher's claims to the contrary on the book covers), but he does admit that "their near-death experiences were very real events to these people, and through my association with them the experiences have become real events to me" (Moody, 1977, p. 183). Six alternative explanations are discussed briefly and dismissed. Moody naively equates supernatural explanations with demonic possession and dismisses them because of the renewed interest in God and love he found in his subjects. Explanations based on dissociative drug reactions are dismissed, since many cases did not involve drugs. Experiences of death induced by drugs or neurological dysfunction, according to Moody, are vague and unlike "real" death experiences. Physiological explanations employing stress models are also dismissed because Moody incorrectly equates stress with observable injury or oxygen deficiency, neither of which was seen in many of his cases. Psychological explanations are also discarded by Moody, evidently because phenomena that produce deathlike experiences (e.g., autoscopic hallucinations, out of body experiences, isolation) are equally mysterious to him; he seems unaware of the considerable research in these areas (he cites only the work of John Lilly, the *Bible*, and one obscure journal article). Like many popular writers Moody equates vivid and sincere reports with veridicality. Without the benefit of psychological or physical examinations, subjects are judged normal and objective. Consequently, the common features of their descriptions are viewed as indicative of a common objective reality—never a common subjective reality.

The concept of life after death postulates *survival* of bodily death. That elementary particles of physical matter survive corporate annihilation to become reabsorbed into the environment is well accepted. The degree to which such matter can be imprinted with consciousness, personality patterns, individual memories, or other "essences" of the body is less certain. And it is not clear if the afterlife in which surviving personas can be found is in mental or physical space. Since death is a precondition for rebirth in this afterlife, we the living may never know the answer. Glimpses from the beds of the dying, from near-death accidents, and from the resuscitated are sufficiently similar to dissociative hallucinatory experiences to caution against acceptance of these data alone as proof of survival. The voices of the dead, whether echoed through phone calls or mediums, may seem like more direct communication, but this evidence lacks important controls and scientific testing. Chasing ghosts in haunted houses, in out of body experiences, or into reincarnated bodies reveals phenomena identical to both dissociative hallucinatory states and cognitive processes in fantasy and make-believe play. However, finding parallels with satisfactory explanations of their own is not the same as finding proof against survival per se. The concept of life after death is not likely to rest in peace with explanations such as those proposed here.

If the experience of dying leads to an actual afterlife, and not merely a solipsistic fantasy, its proof will probably have to await changes in scientific and psychological thinking, not to mention future technology that may be necessary for its demonstration. To get to the afterlife, according to the Menangkabu of Sumatra (Eliade, 1951, 1964), the soul must cross the edge of a razor. And then one finds the afterlife buried in what Heidegger once called a mountain stronghold. While dissociative hallucinatory explanations and the application of our own Occam's razor may reduce the necessity of constructs such as the soul, psychology is not yet capable of moving mountains to know for sure. The afterlife, like children's dreams of a mountain paradise in Robert Browning's *Pied Piper of Hamlin*, remains an elusive yet fetching possibility. Thus far, investigations, both spiritual and scientific, remind us that we are still like children playing a game of hopscotch, children who are unaware they are reenacting an initiatory game whose goal is to penetrate into and successfully return from a labyrinth leading to the afterlife (deVries, 1957). Future investigators must appreciate that the stakes of the game are no less than our basic cosmology of life and death, and they must play seriously and honestly—as if their lives depended on it.

In the past, dying and death were often accompanied by fear and loneliness, as if the individual were possessed by Pan, the Greek god of lonely places and panic. The belief in life after death provided much comfort and security. Through the research and explanations discussed here, investigators have begun to examine the nature of these life after death experiences as hallucinations, as based on stored images in the brain. Like a mirage that shows a magnificent city on a desolate expanse of ocean or desert, the images of hallucinations are actually reflected images of real objects located elsewhere. The city is no less intriguing and no less worthy of study or visitation because it is not where we think it is. With such understanding, we can counsel the dying to take the voyage not with Pan at their side, but with Athena, Greek goddess of wisdom. (pp. 911, 912, 913, 919, 920, 921, 927, 928)

Summary

In this chapter we explored various issues related to aging and death. At the beginning of the chapter you answered a quiz that revealed some of the most important factors that influence our longevity—heredity and family background, health, education and occupation, and life-style. While the life expectancy of the majority of our population in the United States has increased substantially, the length of our life seems to be limited by biological factors—our life span is not likely to go beyond 110 to 120 years of age. Based upon the fact that more people than ever before are reaching late adulthood because of advances in medicine, and that they will reach it in a healthier fashion than ever before, we need to think seriously about the health care of the elderly. Because of such changes, James Fries believes that we ought to be using the hospice more and high-level technology life support systems less among the elderly. The hospice, a recently developed concept in health care, stresses the reduction of pain, anxiety, and depression in the dying patient. By contrast, the major functions of a hospital are to cure illness and prolong life. The hospice also is an attractive alternative to euthanasia, the act of painlessly putting a person to death who is suffering from an incurable disease or illness.

We also described more information about the fascinating culture of the Abkhasians who live in the Caucasus area of Russia. These people, many of whom live past the age of 100, seem to have a rhythmic regularity that characterizes their lives, treat elders with the highest respect, and have healthy diets and work habits. And, we reported that women live longer than men, a finding that increasingly seems to be due to environmental factors rather than biogenetic ones.

There are a number of perspectives on aging, the majority of which are biological. Microbiological theories focus on errors in the formation of protein within a cell, or problems within the cell after the protein has been formed. Another biological theory of aging focuses on a breakdown of physiological coordination systems, either in our body's immune or endocrine system. A final biological theory discussed is a macrobiological theory—it argues that we ought to be looking at the level of the organism rather than within a cell or a particular organ for the answer as to why we age. From the view of homeostatic imbalance theory, when imbalance in the internal milieu of our body occurs, some type of righting or balancing must occur. As we grow through our adult lives, the body's ability to restore homeostatic balance decreases, until eventually, even in the absence of disease, we die.

Social theories of aging also have been developed. Three such theories are disengagement, activity, and social breakdown. Disengagement theory suggests older people are more satisfied with their lives when they slow down and gradually withdraw from society. By contrast, activity theory, which has been accorded more acceptance, stresses that activity and involvement are likely to delay aging and promote life satisfaction. A third perspective, social breakdown theory, suggests that life satisfaction is decreased and aging increased because of negative psychological functioning involving a poor self-concept, negative feedback from others and society, and a lack of skills to deal with the world. In order to prevent such social breakdown in late adulthood, it is argued that we need to reorganize our social system so that the elderly will be treated in more respectful ways, will have better self-images, and feel more competent about their role in society. It is likely that no single theory of aging is completely accurate, but rather that two or more of the processes interact to produce aging. It also is important to remember that the concept of aging is not unidimensional—we can speak of biological aging, psychological aging, and social aging.

However, eventually death comes. Although it always comes, it often has been a taboo topic in our culture. While at first glimpse it may seem to be a simple task to determine when an individual has died, recent medical advances has made such a process difficult. For example, brain death can have occurred even though critical organs like the heart and lungs continue functioning. This scenario has led to ethical questions of whether we ought to practice euthanasia on such persons, or whether we should simply remove life support systems and let these individuals die naturally rather than prolonging their lives as "vegetables."

We explored children's and adults' attitudes toward death and evaluated attitudes toward death in different cultures. Because of the limitation of preoperational thought it is difficult for the preschool child to comprehend death. Early in the elementary school years children may still not understand the universality of death, although they do begin to understand its permanence. At some point before they reach adolescence, though, most children understand both the finality and universality of death. Adolescents often react to death in a superficial way, possibly because of the self-preoccupation that characterizes many adolescents. Young adults also show little concern about death, but during middle adulthood we begin to show considerably more interest in it, often being as concerned about it, or in some cases more concerned, than individuals in late adulthood. In our culture we show more avoidance and denial of death than in most cultures. Many cultures, particularly primitive ones, have elaborate rituals when a member dies. In most cultures, there is a belief in life after death, a belief that also is shared by the majority of people in the United States.

In facing death, many of us will go through a series of psychological orientations toward death. The most widely discussed theory of psychological stages of the dying process has been developed by Elisabeth Kübler-Ross. She believes we go through five such stages during the process of dying: denial and isolation; anger; bargaining; depression; and acceptance. Social scientists also have developed the concept of dying trajectories. A trajectory of life refers to our anticipated life span and how we plan to live through that life span. When we discover that we are likely to die sooner than we had thought we often alter our plans. There also are a number of dying trajectories that can be developed based on the course that disease or illness takes, ranging from a slow, steady decline to entry and reentry, which really is not a dying trajectory since in this trajectory we fully recover from an illness or disease that had predicted a premature death.

One of the most painful experiences we encounter in our life is dealing with the death of someone we love. Grief is a normal psychological reaction, and bereavement refers to our memories of the person who had died. Survivors may go through a series of emotional reactions. Grief and mourning may be particularly severe for a widow. Many psychologists believe that the main tasks of the mourner are freeing oneself from the deceased, readjusting to a life in which the dead person is missing, and forming new relationships with other persons. Some survivors never fully recover, and grief may linger for years, particularly in the case when a child is lost.

A final topic discussed in this chapter was the psychology of life after death. Believing in an afterlife is a matter of faith rather than science. As such, views of faith and science do not have to conflict. However, in recent years, some individuals have argued that we have scientific evidence for life after death in the form of reports from individuals who have died for a brief time and then come back to life. However, there is good reason to believe that the reports of these individuals represent hallucinations rather than true afterlife perceptions.

Key Terms

activity theory

autoimmunity

bereavement

cross-linkage theory

disengagement theory

dying trajectories

error catastrophe theory

euthanasia

free-radical theory

genetic error theories

genetic switching theory

grief

grief work

homeostatic imbalance
  theory

hormonal theory

hospice

mourning

mutation theory

rectangular theory of
  aging

social breakdown theory

Review Questions

1. What are some of the most important factors that influence our longevity?
2. Discuss James Fries's rectangular theory of aging and health care.
3. Why do women live longer than men?
4. Describe the different biological perspectives of aging.
5. Discuss the different social theories of life satisfaction and aging.
6. How has modern medicine complicated the definition of death?
7. Describe attitudes toward death through the life cycle.
8. How is death viewed in different cultures? Outline some common perceptions of death in our culture.
9. Discuss Kübler-Ross's psychological stages of the dying process.
10. Describe some different dying trajectories.
11. What is the nature of grief and bereavement when someone dies whom we are closely attached to?
12. Discuss the psychology of life after death.

Further Readings

Fries, J. F. Aging, natural death, and the compression of morbidity. *The New England Journal of Medicine,* 1980, *303,* 130–35.
In this special article in the prestigious New England Journal of Medicine, *James Fries presents a provocative set of ideas about how we ought to be treating elderly individuals in health care settings because of the many changes that have occurred in aging and modern medicine in recent years. Reading level is of medium difficulty.*

Poon, L. W. (ed.), *Aging in the 1980's.* Washington, D.C.: The American Psychological Association, 1980.
Includes a number of articles about biological views on aging. Provides much greater depth and detail about the aging of the brain, nervous system, cells, and organs than we could go into in this introductory text. Reading level is of moderate difficulty.

Siegel, R. K. The psychology of life after death. *American Psychologist,* 1980, *35,* 911–31.
The full text of Siegel's excellent evaluation of the psychology of life after death is worth reading. Includes a great deal of additional information not discussed in our overview of Siegel's thesis that there is no scientific evidence to support a belief in life after death. Reasonably easy to read.

Wilcox, S. G., & Sutton, M. (eds.), *Understanding death and dying.* Port Washington, N.Y.: Alfred Publishing, 1977.
An edited book of readings that focuses on many of the topics discussed in this chapter about death. Articles cover a wide range of subjects from Plato's ideas about death to Freud's view of death. A special section of articles also is devoted to death and the child, including Maria Nagy's ideas about the child's theories of death. Reading level is reasonably easy.

Woodruff, D. S. *Can you live to be 100?* New York: Chatham Square Press, 1977.
A well-written, easy-to-read overview of the causes of longevity by a well-known leader in the gerontology field.

Glossary

a

abiding self
Characteristics of the self that are stable over time, for example, intelligence level. The abiding self is closely related to the individual's self-esteem.

abstract mapping
According to Fischer, the ability of the individual to relate his or her own abstract identity to that of another person.

abstract system
The cognitive ability to relate several aspects of one's own identity with aspects of another's. The individual can relate, for example, his or her parental and career responsibilities and those of his or her spouse.

acceleration
One aspect of normal approaches to gifted children in school; involves any strategy that shortens the time necessary for a student to graduate.

accommodation
In visual perception, a property of focusing in which the lens of each eye flattens or becomes more spherical.

accommodation
In Piaget's theory, the act of modifying a current mode or structure of thought to deal with new features of the environment; the converse of *assimilation*.

achieving stage
The phase of cognitive development in which achievement of potential becomes more important than mere acquisition of knowledge. According to Schaie, this corresponds with young adulthood.

acquisition stage
The first stage in Schaie's theory of cognitive development; the point at which the individual exists in a controlled environment.

activity theory
This aging theory indicates that older individuals who remain active and involved are less likely to age than their withdrawn counterparts.

acute brain syndromes
An organic brain disorder that is reversible. Treatment for such disorders is generally aimed at their cause, for example, malnutrition.

adaptation
The process of altering one's own behavior to interact effectively with the environment.

adolescence
The period between childhood and adulthood. In contemporary Western society, adolescence starts at age twelve and ends somewhere between seventeen and twenty.

ageism
Prejudice against older people.

albinism
Genetically determined condition characterized by lack of skin pigment.

altruism
The act of doing something with the intention of helping other people without consideration for personal gain.

amenorrheic
Abnormal absence or suppression of menstrual discharge.

amniocentesis
A procedure for withdrawing and examining amniotic fluid from the uterus to check on the health of a developing fetus.

anal stage
In Freud's theory, the period during which the child seeks pleasure through exercising the anus and eliminating waste; this stage occurs during the second year of life and is the second Freudian stage.

androgens
Male sex hormones.

androgyny
A sex-role orientation in which the person incorporates both masculine and feminine aspects into behaviors.

animism
A characteristic of preoperational thought in which human qualities are inappropriately attributed to inanimate objects.

anthropological or sociological perspective
Developmental theory that maintains that by analyzing societal structures and individual's roles in society, one can understand life-span development.

anxiety
A general feeling of psychological discomfort without a well-defined cause.

Apgar Scale
A method used to evaluate the health of a child at birth. Heart rate, respiratory effect, reflex irritability, muscle tone, and body color are each rated between one and ten, the high score being the most favorable.

Aptitude X Treatment Interaction (ATI)
A crossing of the necessary ingredients for student success; any of several teaching methods (treatments) that may be best for an individual student, depending on ability or learning style (aptitude).

assertion
According to McClelland's theory of maturity, the stage at which the individual speaks confidently, is able to accept a vocation, and can influence others.

assimilation
In Piaget's theory, the act of incorporating a feature of the environment into an existing mode or structure of thought; the converse of *accommodation*. Also, a synonym for acculturation.

association areas of the cortex
Portions of the cortex responsible for integrating and coordinating sensation and action pathways, storing memories, and allowing us to perform a number of intellectual operations.

associative flow
The production of many ideas and combinations from a starting idea.

associative play
A type of play in which the child plays in a group and is more concerned with association with the group than with the group's activity.

asynchrony
Situation in which the parent is slow to notice and respond to the needs of the infant. A lack of proper timing between a change in the individual and a change in his or her environment.

attachment
A strong and important relationship between two people, characterized by affection and high mutual responsiveness.

attention
In discussions of socialization, reference to the degree to which someone (for example, a child) is the focus of other people's interests and actions.

attention
In discussions of information processing, the point at which a stimulus is noticed or encoded. Also, the process of noticing this stimulus in the environment.

attribution theory
An approach to describing an individual's social perceptions and self-concept. It is concerned with how the child makes intellectual sense of the actions of others as well as the self. The origins of the approach are traced to Fritz Heider. Two elements of his theory are the naive analysis of action and levels of social responsibility.

authoritarian parenting
A style of childrearing that focuses on parental power and strict obedience to rules.

authoritative parenting
A childrearing pattern that places moderate restrictions on the range of acceptable behaviors but also incorporates nurturance and sensitivity to the child's needs.

autoimmunity
An attack upon the body by its own immune system, which increases as the individual ages.

automatic information processing
Processing that is independent of other demands on attentional capacity and does not draw heavily on that capacity.

autonomy
Stage 2 in McClelland's theory of progression of maturity, characterized by the individual's ability to make independent decisions.

autonomy versus shame and doubt
The second stage in Erikson's eight-stage theory of development. At this stage, the child may develop the healthy attitude that he or she is capable of independent control of actions or may develop an unhealthy attitude of shame or doubt that he or she is incapable of such control.

Babkinsky reflex
Pressure to the infant's palm results in mouth opening and arm raising.

basal metabolism rate (BMR)
The minimum amount of energy a person uses in a resting state.

baseline
A measure of how often a specific behavior occurs in a natural setting, taken before attempts are made to change the frequency of the behavior or to condition it.

behavioral social learning perspective
Developmental theory emphasizing that an individual's actions are influenced by encounters with rewarding and punishing situations.

behavior modification
A method of changing behavior, based on principles of association, operant conditioning, and imitation.

bereavement
The process through which we review our memories of loss.

biological environment
The individual's set of experiences with regard to nutrition, medical care, drugs, physical accidents, and similar situations.

body transcendence versus body preoccupation
According to Peck, the need in later adulthood to equate well-being with satisfying relationships and experiences rather than dwelling on physical health.

brainstorming
A method of stimulating the formulation of ideas by a group; any and all notions are encouraged, with analysis and criticism initially withheld.

branch model of cognitive development
A model of cognitive development described by Dulit, in which formal operational thought is viewed as intermediate between concrete thinking and reasoning about special talents. The branch model holds that Piaget's first three stages are accurate, but that when adolescence is reached, a number of alternative tracks can be followed.

C

canalization
Construct suggests a species-typical path; that is, a path along which all members of a species develop; development along this path occurs under a range of environments.

cascade model
Cunningham's model of intellectual functioning explains linkages between different types of aging and different types of intellectual functioning. Factors in primary aging, for example, may affect the individual's intellectual speediness.

categorical perception
Perception of a class of events as being in a single category, despite differences among the events; for example, hearing a particular vowel or consonant sound without noticing the many gradations of that sound.

cause-and-effect
Relationships between factors in an experiment suggest a correlation; association between elements in an experiment in which one factor leads to the other.

centration
A tendency to focus exclusively on one aspect of a situation, at the expense of others.

cephalo-caudal pattern
A general pattern of physical growth. The greatest growth in anatomical differentiation occurs first in the region of the head and later in lower regions in turn.

channel
In the communications field, the medium over which a message is transmitted. A message is sent over a particular channel of communication to a specific receiver.

child-centered
An extremely broad term used to describe a wide range of goals and curriculum in nursery schools.

chromosomes
Rod-shaped structures carrying genes and hereditary information; each normal infant inherits forty-six chromosomes, twenty-three from each parent.

chronic brain syndromes
Organic brain disorders that are not reversible and usually involve brain damage.

chunks
Bits of information organized into larger single units.

classical conditioning
A form of learning in which a previously neutral stimulus (CS) elicits a response (CR) by being consistently paired with a stimulus (UCS) that automatically elicits the response (UCR).

classification
Grouping or sorting of objects into classes according to some rule or principle.

class inclusion
Comparison of a set or class of objects with one of its own subsets without confusion of the two. Sample problem: In a classroom of boys and girls, are there more students or more girls?

clique
A group smaller in size, more cohesive, and having greater intimacy among members than a crowd does.

coaching
Providing didactic instruction.

cognitive development
Age-related changes that occur with regard to mental activity; for example, thought, memory, perception, attention, and language.

cognitive social learning theory
A theory that combines what is known about learning processes and thinking patterns to explain social behavior.

cognitive structural perspective
The theoretical paradigm stressing the organization and stages of thought as the primary force behind development.

cohort
A group of subjects of the same age, born at approximately the same time (for example, the same year).

cohort perspective
Emphasizes the similarities of individuals in the same age strata; notes generational differences.

collagen
The stiff protein that makes up about one-third of the body's total protein.

combined longitudinal cross-sectional method
A complex design in which age changes are examined by drawing cross-sections of children at different ages, and at the same time, testing some of the children longitudinally.

communications
A field that seeks to develop a general model of the process of sending a message across a channel to a receiver. Communications is an important influence on the development of information processing.

companionship relationship
A marital style that emphasizes active interaction, expressions of love, and affection and respect.

comparative psychology
Principle dedicated to using comparison as a method of study; use of two or more different theories to explain a phenomenon.

compensatory education
Special school programs for children in poverty areas, designed to raise their level of educational readiness.

compulsions
Repetitive, stereotyped actions called into play to ward off some imaginary threat.

conception
The moment at which a male sperm cell joins or fertilizes a female ovum, marking the beginning of prenatal development.

concrete-individual perspective
The first stage of development in Kohlberg's three-stage view of ego development. Usually attained during early and middle childhood, when the individual's social judgments focus on the tangible needs and feelings of the self.

concrete operational stage
In Piagetian theory, the stage of thought that follows preoperations, lasting from about seven to eleven years of age; marked primarily by a need to anchor thought to concrete events.

conditioned response (CR)
The learned response to a conditioned stimulus.

conditioned stimulus (CS)
An environmental event that elicits a response (CR) by being associated repeatedly with an unconditioned stimulus (UCS).

conditioning
Providing situations designed to establish a response in a subject.

conglomerate strategy
A series of coordinated strategies.

conservation
The understanding that basic properties of objects (for example, weight, volume, number, area) remain unchanged when the superficial appearance of the objects is altered.

consolidation of individuality
A stage in Mahler's theory of the development of achievement occurring between twenty-four and thirty months. The child gradually accepts, once again, separation from the mother and seems to prefer staying in a familiar playroom without the mother.

consonants
In standard English, one of two basic phoneme classes; formed by interrupting the flow of air in the oral cavity and then releasing it.

continuum of indirectness
A concept developed by Anne Anastasi to determine the degree to which various traits are determined by genetic influences.

control-autonomy
A dimension along which parents can be discriminated in how they interact with their children. At one extreme (control), parents exhibit considerable interest in dictating what and how a child shall act. At the other extreme (autonomy), the child is given considerable freedom and choice over a variety of his or her decisions and actions.

conventional level of moral development
A term applied to the middle two stages in Kohlberg's theory of moral development. Moral thought is based on the desire to preserve good interpersonal relations and maintain good interpersonal concordance (stage 3) or to comply with formalized rules, laws, and customs that exist in society (stage 4).

convergence
The turning inward of the eyes to view an object close at hand; important also to depth perception.

convergent thinking
A type of thought wherein attention is directed toward finding a single solution from a given set of circumstances; contrast with *divergent thinking*.

cooing
Vowellike sounds; after crying, this sound is among the first made by an infant.

cooperative play
A type of play that involves group social interaction. The child is conscious of the activity, the others in the group, and his or her position in the group; characteristic of older children, seldom of preschoolers.

correlation
Measure of degree of relationship between two distributions (samples). The correlation coefficient ranges from $+1.00$ to -1.00. A *positive* coefficient means that the distributions increase together; a *negative* coefficient means that as one increases the other decreases; and a *zero* coefficient means no correlation.

creativity
An important aspect of mental functioning, not usually considered in intelligence testing; originality and flexibility are two of the creativity factors measured.

creod
A species-typical path; that is, a pattern along which most members of a species develop.

cretinism
Condition caused by a hormone deficiency in the thyroid gland; results in severe mental retardation and dwarfism.

crisis
The perspective on middle adulthood that views this period as one of crucial disruption in the life process, rather than as one of transition.

critical period
A point or stage in early development when a person is unusually receptive to environmental events; learning during critical periods can be the basis of certain behavior patterns that persist throughout life.

cross-linkage theory
The theory stresses that aging takes place because of the formation of bonds between various parts of the cell.

cross-sectional method
A procedure for establishing age changes by testing independent groups of children of different ages.

crowd
The crowd is the largest and least personal of the three ways to characterize relations. The members of a crowd meet because of a mutual interest in some activity, not because they are mutually attracted to one another.

crystallized intelligence
The class of mental abilities acquired and developed through cultural contact, such as language and social knowledge.

cultural or social evolution
The manner in which behavior is modified through cultural transmissions; for example, customs and practices of a group.

culture
The environment in which a child grows up—the groups, institutions and values that hold the greatest influence.

culture-fair tests
Intelligence tests in which one cultural background is not favored over another through factors that should be irrelevant.

culture-free tests
Intelligence tests in which all reference to cultural forms or contact has been excluded.

d

decay
A process by which information is lost from sensory stores simply as a function of time.

deep structure
The basic idea underlying a sentence. *See also* **surface structure.**

defense mechanisms
Techniques used by the ego to prevent feared impulses of the id from becoming conscious.

dependent variable
Some facet of a child's functioning that is measured in an experiment and presumed to be under the control of one or more manipulated factors. *See also* **independent variable.**

depth-of-processing view
View of language acquisition which holds that the deeper the level of processing, the more memorable the event will be.

desatellization
A concept in David Ausubel's theory of the development of autonomy; involves breaking away from parents.

development
Progression of movement or change that begins its pattern at conception and continues throughout life; complex pattern of movement that is the product of many processes; processes and events that contribute to lifelong change.

developmental functions
Basis for study of nature of the species investigations; general statements about behavior, mental phenomenon, or developmental changes, summarizing what is typical of the species.

developmental scales
Standardized tests created to measure an infant's or child's normative progress in areas of social, motor, language, and intellectual growth.

differentiation
The process by which global experience or thought is separated into distinct parts.

discovery learning
A method of instruction in which the adolescent is required to go beyond concrete thought and to view events and objects in logical ways. The student does not depend solely on lectures, but must explore and categorize as well.

disenchantment phase
The period of letdown that some individuals experience after the honeymoon phase of retirement. Serious depression may occur if the expectations were too unrealistic.

disengagement theory
A social theory of aging which suggests that the older person disengages from society and society also moves from the individual. This break is thought to be necessary to maintain satisfaction in late adulthood.

displaced homemaker
A woman, whose work has always been in the home, who, due to divorce or death of a spouse, must create a new single identity.

displacement
A process by which information is lost from the short-term memory; one bit of information is "bumped out" and replaced by another.

distinctive features theory
A theory of learning based on recognizing differences; the child learns more basic differences among objects and events as he or she explores the world. Repeated exploration leads to the child's developing more variation in responses and ability to distinguish events.

divergence
The turning outward of the eye to focus and view an object far away; important also to depth perception.

divergent thinking
A kind of creative thought process exercised when a person's imagination provides many different answers to a single question; contrast with *convergent thinking.*

divided attention
An attention skill necessary for processing all of the information present in a situation (for example, watching a film and listening to an instructor's comments at the same time).

DNA (deoxyribonucleic acid)
A complex molecule that forms the basis for genetic structure in man.

dominant gene
A gene that exerts its full characteristic effect regardless of its gene partner. For example, if one parent gives a gene signaling brown eyes (dominant) and the other gives the "blue eyed" gene (recessive), the offspring will have brown eyes.

double helix
Term used to describe the physical structure of a DNA molecule; two long strands are connected by several short strands, giving an arrangement resembling a spiral staircase.

Down's syndrome
A form of mental retardation caused by an extra chromosome; its physical characteristics include a flattened skull, an extra fold of skin over the eyelid, and a protruding tongue.

dying trajectories
The individual's anticipated length of life before death and the plan made for facing the end of life.

 e

early adulthood
Life phase lasting from late teens or early twenties through the thirties; marked by establishment of personal and economic independence.

early childhood
Period extending from infancy to five or six years; characterized by development of personal care, self-sufficiency, and readiness for school-related tasks.

echoing
A strategy used by adults to influence children's language development: the adult tries to clarify an unintelligible part of the child's message by repeating the intelligible portion in question form.

echolalia
A speech pattern in which the child repeats rather than responds to spoken communications; characteristic of autistic children.

eclectic orientation
Taking information from various sources; position designed to present more than one perspective.

ecological psychology
An approach to studying children in which their behavior is exhaustively observed in a naturalistic situation over a long period of time (for example, an entire day); developed by Roger Barker.

ecological structure
According to sociologist Alex Inkeles, one of the cultural structures influencing development; involving the size, density, and physical distribution of the individual family and the society as a whole.

economic structure
A concept of the sociologist's view of life-span development that emphasizes the material resources of a society. The occupational opportunities that a society provides influence the child's development.

ectomorphic
Type of body build without predominant fat or muscle; thin, skinny.

effortful information processing
Controlled processing that draws heavily on capacity of attention.

ego
According to Freud, the part of the personality that copes with the real world in a rational manner.

egocentrism
Failure to appreciate that another person's perceptions of a situation may differ from one's own; a characteristic of preoperational thought.

ego differentiation versus work-role preoccupation
According to Robert Peck, an issue to be dealt with in old age; at this point the person should concentrate on extending his perception of self beyond his work role.

ego integrity versus despair
The final conflict in Erikson's theory of development. This stage involves retrospective glances at and evaluations of life.

ego transcendence versus ego preoccupation
The issue in later adulthood, according to Peck, at which point the individual must recognize that death is inevitable. Accommodating this realization should lead to a more satisfying life.

Eight Ages of Man
Term used to describe Eriskon's eight-stage theory of development.

elaboration
A memory process in which an individual tries to improve retention of information by adding something to it.

Electra complex
A Freudian conflict involving young girls, parallel to the Oedipus conflict in boys. There is sexual desire of the girl for her father accompanied by hostility toward her mother.

embryonic period
The period of prenatal growth that follows the germinal period, lasting from the second to the eighth week after conception; marked by development of a primitive human form and life-support system.

emotional development
Consideration of development that stresses the individual's feelings and affective reactions to situations.

empathy
Experiencing the same feelings and psychological state of mind that someone else has.

empty nest syndrome
The experience of parents when their children leave home. The mother who has devoted her entire life to nurturing the children is more likely to feel "empty" than the parent who has developed wider interests and realistic attitudes about parental responsibility.

enculturation
The process of becoming socialized and assimilating the lessons of one's culture.

endocrine glands
Ductless glands that dispense their secretions directly into the bloodstream.

endomorphic
Rounded body build, evidenced by more fat tissue than muscle tissue.

enrichment
Programs for gifted children aimed at providing special opportunities such as college classes in high school, independent study, and so forth.

equilibration
In Piaget's theory, the mechanism by which the child resolves cognitive conflict and reaches a balance in thought.

erogenous zones
Parts of the body stimulated or exercised to produce pleasurable feelings.

error catastrophe theory
A genetic theory of aging which explains that unrepaired damage to RNA, enzymes, and other proteins leads to reduction in cell functioning. The unrepaired error is perpetuated as the RNA continues to reproduce.

estrogen replacement therapy
Replacement of the estrogen that a menopausal woman no longer produces naturally; generally used only for severe cases.

estrogens
The primary female sex hormones.

ethological or evolutionary perspective
Developmental theory stressing the individual's biological heritage and adaptation to the environment.

ethology
School of thought that views development as heavily influenced by biologically inherited response tendencies.

euthanasia
The act of painlessly putting to death persons suffering from severe disability or incurable illness; sometimes referred to as mercy killing.

evolution
Any change in organisms from generation to generation. Biological evolution deals specifically with genetic transmission of such changing characteristics.

excitement phase
The first phase of sexual response during which the person experiences physical and sexual arousal.

executor responses
Attachment responses initiated by the infant that function to maintain close contact and proximity with the mother. These include clinging, following, sucking, and physical approach.

exocrine glands
Glands that send out their secretions through ducts, such as the salivary glands.

expansion
A technique used by adults to influence children's language development. The adult provides a more complete and grammatically correct adaptation of what the child says.

experiences
The process or fact of personally observing, encountering, or undergoing something; a key to development.

experiment
A technique used to study the impact of one or more kinds of events (independent variables) on some facet of children's functioning (depending variable); the independent variable is carefully controlled, and the dependent variable is measured.

expressive movement
An aspect of the child's physical movement in which the body is used to express ideas and feelings.

extinction
A procedure for eliminating, or "unlearning," a learned behavior. In classical conditioning, repeated presentation of the CS unaccompanied by the UCS; in operant conditioning, discontinuation of the reinforcement of a previously rewarded behavior.

factor-analytic approach
Statistically, a tool for reducing related measures to fewer dimensions; theoretically, a procedure operating on the principal that unveiled factors reflect the main dimensions of the object or person being evaluated.

family system
The network of the family; the interaction of the individual members and the working of these individuals as a group.

fantasy stage
Ginsberg's stage of career choice, during which children imagine what they want to be without concern for their abilities and other aspects of reality.

fetal period
The period of prenatal growth lasting from about the eighth week until birth.

filial crisis
The change in relationship between an adult child (aged forty to fifty) and his or her parents. At this point, parents cannot be expected to provide support to the adult child; in fact, they may need support from the child. A successful resolution to this crisis allows the child to see the parent as an individual and to prepare for his own aging.

filial maturity
Dependency of older adults upon their children and the children's acceptance of the dependency.

fine motor skills
Physical activities requiring finer dexterity; for example, turning the pages of a book or coordination of alternating between one hand and the other.

firm control–lax control
An aspect of the control-autonomy relationship between parent and child. Firm control involves the setting of firm rules by the parent and insistence that the child comply. With lax control, the rules are set, but the parent is not firm about compliance.

fixation
In Freudian theory, the act of getting "stuck," or "fixed," in an early psychosexual stage.

fluid intelligence
Ability to adapt, and to perceive and integrate things mentally; separate from experience or organized education.

focalization
The fourth stage (ten to thirteen months of age) in Sanders' model of mother-infant interaction and the infant's emerging sense of self; the infant now focuses his need-meeting demands on the mother.

foreclosure
Marcia's category of identity development in which the adolescent has made a commitment but has not experienced a crisis.

formal operational stage
In Piaget's model, the most advanced stage of thinking possible; it emerges between eleven and fourteen years of age and is characterized by abstract thought.

free-radical theory
A variation of the cross-linkage theory of aging which indicates that chemical components of the cell may cause chromosome damage through their reactions with other substances.

free recall
A test of the long-term memory, in which an individual is asked to recall as many items as possible from a given list.

functional core hypothesis
The explanation that children's early word meanings are linked to actions typically performed with the objects and events named by the word. For example, a ball can be thrown, rolled, or bounced.

g
A factor of general or nonspecific intelligence, the measurement of which is the aim of most standardized IQ tests.

gene
A small biochemical substance composed of DNA, believed to be a basic building block in hereditary transmission of information; thousands of genes are present in each chromosome.

generativity versus stagnation
The seventh conflict in Erikson's theory of development. This stage is positively resolved if an adult assists the younger generation in developing and leading useful lives.

genetic-environmental interaction
Reciprocal influence between the child's genetic inheritance and the environmental conditions.

genetic error theories
A biological theory of aging which suggests that aging is caused by a breakdown or error in the cell's DNA-RNA structure.

genetic switching theory
A theory suggesting that cellular aging is the result of the switching off of certain genes. According to this theory, aging is genetically programmed into each cell.

genital stage
In Freud's theory, the period during which sexual conflicts are resolved, a stable identity is reached, and personality reaches its highest form of organization; this stage is associated with adolescence and is the last Freudian stage.

genotype
The unique constellation of genes in an individual; the person's genetic makeup.

germinal period
The first two weeks of prenatal growth after fertilization, during which rapid cell division takes place.

Gestalt view
Concepts about the way people organize their perceptions.

gifted children
Children with well-above-average intellectual capacity or with an outstanding talent in a particular area.

grammar
A formal, systematic description of the syntax of a language.

grapho-phonemic information
System of rules involved in reading; the phonics component (that is, knowing "b" translates as the sound "buh").

grief
A normal psychological reaction to a distressful situation in life.

grief work
The sequence of phases to recovery from the loss of a loved one. This "work" is aimed at freeing oneself from the ties to the deceased, adjusting to the new situation, and forming new relationships.

gross motor skills
Activities such as walking, running, and jumping; the child makes great advancements in mastery of these skills during the second year.

grouping
Placement of children with similar levels of ability in the same class; program used often with gifted children.

guilt
The affective state of psychological discomfort arising from a person's feeling of having done something morally wrong.

hardware
In computers, the physical equipment employed (the storage unit, the logic unit, the printer, and so forth); by analogy, in human intelligence, the physical equipment for thinking (the brain and central nervous system); contrast with *software*.

harmful genes
Genes that produce undesirable traits in individuals. Such recessive genes may cause diabetes, heart disease, muscular dystrophy, or other disorders.

heritability
Degree to which a particular characteristic is genetically determined; expressed as a mathematical estimate.

high-risk infant
Term used to describe babies whose histories contain factors related to psychological or educational handicaps; for example, problems related to the parents' genetic makeup, the mother's pregnancy, or the birth process.

historical time
According to Neugarten and Datan, the life cycle aspect that controls the social system; this in turn changes norms and ultimately, the individual's life cycle. It can refer to long-term processes (industrialization) or to individual social events.

holophrase
The single-word utterance of a child who is just learning to talk; from the child's point of view, the single word may be an entire phrase or message.

homeostatic imbalance theory
A macrobiological perspective of aging that emphasizes the body's declining ability to maintain homeostasis after the age of thirty. This inability of the body to maintain internal balance results in natural death.

honeymoon phase
The period immediately following the retirement event, during which the individual derives considerable enjoyment from his leisure.

hormonal theory
The concept that aging is the result of the decline of the efficiency of the body's hormonal system. Aging is suggested to be a result of a hormonal imbalance, or of a series of brain-stimulated hormonal changes.

hormones
The secretions of particular glands. The sex hormones (estrogens and androgens) are very active during adolescence.

hospice
An alternative to hospital care for the dying patient, the hospice is dedicated to making the end of life as painless and as comfortable as possible.

hot flash
The most common symptom of menopause; involving a sensation of extreme heat.

humanism
School of thought that views development as an open-ended, creative process in which the child acquires a unique self-identity and creative skills.

iconic
A sensory image.

id
According to Freud, the instinctual part of the personality, which operates unconsciously and irrationally.

identification
In Freudian theory, a defense mechanism in which the values, attitudes, and behavior of another person are assumed.

identity achieved
Marcia's concept involving the weathering of an identity crisis and the formation of a commitment.

identity diffused (or confused)
According to James Marcia, an adolescent at this stage of identity development has made no idealogical or occupational choices and has no interest in doing so.

identity versus role confusion
Erikson's fifth crisis of psychological development; the adolescent may become confident and purposeful, or may develop an ill-defined identity.

imaginary audience
The adolescent's sense that his feelings and beliefs are transparent to others.

imitation
A form of learning in which new behaviors are acquired by observing others performing the behaviors.

impression formation
The process by which people use information available about others to form opinions about what the other person is like.

imprinting
A rapid form of learned attachment observed in many animals and believed to serve as a good role model of the ethological or instinctual root of many social attachments formed by humans as well.

impulsive delinquent
An individual who generally accepts society's standards but who succumbs to a combination of poor self-control and attractive stimuli and engages in a delinquent act. Most individuals have engaged in this type of delinquency at some point in their youth.

incentive conditions
The contexts and expectations that motivate a person to acquire a behavior.

independent variable
An event or factor that is manipulated in an experiment to determine its impact on a child's functioning (dependent variable). *See also* **dependent variable.**

individual differences
Variations in behavior attributed to the distinct characteristics of the particular child; thus, developmental concepts apply to most infants or children, but not necessarily to all.

individuating-reflexive faith
A characteristic, according to Fowler, of an adolescent who has made the move from an acceptance of conventional values to a formation of an individual value system.

industry versus inferiority
Erikson's fourth crisis of psychological development; the school-aged child may develop a capacity for work and task-directedness, or he may view himself as inadequate.

infancy
Life-span phase extending from birth until eighteen to twenty-four months of age; characterized by almost total dependence and the beginnings of physiological and psychological activities.

infantile autism
A condition characterized by withdrawal from reality and inability to relate to others, long periods of inaction, and extremely immature speech patterns.

inference
Drawing a conclusion from the information available.

information processing approach
A theoretical view of cognition that analyzes cognitive activity in terms of successive stages of information processing such as attention, perception, memory, thinking, and problem solving.

initial regulation
In Sanders' model of infant development, the stage occurring from one to three months of age; this first stage is marked by formation of a pattern of sleeping, feeding, elimination, arousal, and quieting.

initiative
The third stage of Louis Sanders' model of infant development in which the infant chooses activities in order to secure an exchange with the mother; occurring from seven to nine months of age.

initiative versus guilt
Erikson's third crisis of psychological development, occurring during the preschool years; the child may develop a desire for achievement, or he may be held back by self-criticism.

insecurely attached-avoidance
According to Ainsworth, a mother-infant bond that is insecure and distinguished by the child's avoiding the mother and failing to seek closeness.

insecurely attached-resistant
An insecure mother-infant bond marked by the child's reaching for the mother, but then showing ambivalence or hitting and pushing.

instinct
An innate biological force that motivates a response.

institutional relationship
A marital style emphasizing tradition. Loyalty and security are the basis of the relationship and sexually typical roles are involved.

instrumental competence
Effectiveness in dealing with other people and the environment, particularly exhibiting independence, self-initiated activities, and self-esteem about one's intellectual and physical abilities.

instrumental conditioning
A type of learning advocated by Skinner in which the individual operates or acts on his environment, and what happens to him, in turn, controls his behavior. In other words, the individual's behavior is controlled by its consequences. Also referred to as operant conditioning.

integrity versus despair
The final conflict in Erikson's theory of development. This stage involves retrospective glances and evaluations of life.

intelligence
The individual's capacity to think and act; the definition of intelligence is closely related to the way it is measured.

intentionality
The separation of means and goals in accomplishing simple tasks; involves more deliberate coordination on the part of the infant.

interference
The process of forgetting from the long-term memory; the ability to retrieve information is hampered by the interference between memory for a given bit of information and another bit of information which was previously or later stored.

interview
A method of study in which children are asked questions and the investigator jots down their answers.

intimacy versus isolation
Erikson's sixth crisis of psychosocial development; the young adult may achieve a capacity for honest, close relationships, or be unable to form these ties.

intimate
An individual who has been able to form a deep, long-lasting love relationship.

in vitro fertilization
Fertilization of an ovum in a laboratory setting, outside the woman's body. The egg is later implanted in the woman's uterus. Commonly referred to as "test-tube" fertilization.

"invulnerables"
Individuals who cope exceptionally well under extremely negative environmental circumstances.

irreversibility
The inability to undo or reverse an action or an imagined action in thought.

isolated
A person who withdraws from social encounters and who fails to form an intimate relationship with members of the same or opposite sex.

k

karyotype
Picture of the chromosomes, in a tiny photograph, created with a high-powered microscope and a stain.

keyword method
Richard Atkinson's technique to improve memory using powerful images related to key words.

knowledge actualization
The ability to recall and use previously acquired knowledge; this ability is maintained throughout old age, unlike memory-processing abilities.

l

laissez-faire (permissive) parenting
Childrearing style distinguished by its lack of parental restriction, control, or involvement.

language
A system of rules for speaking, listening, and writing; recognized by adult members of the language community.

Language Acquisition Device (LAD)
An imaginary machine that processes language rules as output; a metaphor that describes how the child acquires language.

language universals
Aspects of language and the capacity for language that are innate and thus common to all children at birth.

late adulthood
Period from sixty to seventy years of age until death; characterized by adjustment to changing health and income, and need for adaptation to new social roles.

late childhood
Life-span phase extending until approximately eleven years of age; noted for concrete thought processes, mastery of basic school skills, and greater exposure to cultural subjects.

latency stage
In Freud's theory, the period during which the child's anxious feelings and thoughts about sexual conflicts are actively repressed; this stage is associated with the elementary school years and is the fourth Freudian stage.

laterality
Dominance in use or in development of one lateral half of the brain.

learned helplessness
Attitude of an individual who believes that rewards are beyond personal control and that personal behavior will not affect the outcome of a situation.

learning
A relatively permanent change in behavior due to experience or practice, as opposed to natural biological processes.

Leboyer method
A method of childbirth proposed by a French physician, Leboyer. The newborn is not spanked or held by the feet after birth but is placed on the abdomen of the mother, and a peaceful and calm postdelivery environment is maintained to minimize the shock of childbirth for the infant.

legibility
A component in the organization of an environment, referring to the extent to which an area is predictable and can be easily navigated.

life contours
A perspective on work that notes the points of responsibility and reward in different careers. These life contours vary according to profession, culture, social structure and other conditions.

life cycle
The continuous sequence of changes undergone by an individual; an age-related developmental progression; systematic development over the individual's life span.

life review
A looking back at one's life; may be characterized by reminiscence, anxiety, or by extreme preoccupation with the past. The process, according to Robert Butler, is set in motion by looking forward to death.

life time
An aspect of the life cycle, according to Neugarten and Datan; expressed as a biological (that is, chronological) age. Must be accompanied by knowledge of the particular society to be useful.

limited attentional capacity
The concept that the ability to maintain attention is limited; the type of psychological energy needed to do mental work is in lesser supply in the elderly individual.

lineage
The line of descendents from a particular ancestor, family, or race.

lineage perspective
Focuses on what is transmitted between generations; what knowledge, skills, and responsibilities are exchanged between young and old.

longitudinal method
Repeated testing of the same subject or group of subjects over a significant period of time.

long-term memory
A third level of memory storage, where processes such as rehearsal, elaboration, and organization are assumed to transform information from short-term to long-term storage.

looming
A technique for gauging depth sensitivity in infants; the researcher creates the illusion of an object being hurled at the child.

m

male climacteric syndrome
Sometimes referred to as "male menopause," a gradual hormonal change that induces a decline in physical energy and often necessitates a psychological adjustment.

masking
An interference by a second stimulus, which prevents the individual's perception of the initial stimulus.

maturation
Physical growth of the body and central nervous system.

mean length of utterance (MLU)
The average number of words per sentence spoken by a child, calculated from a substantial sample of the child's speech (fifty to one-hundred sentences); a reliable and convenient measure of language maturity.

"mechanical mirror" theory
According to social learning theorists, the concept that the individual does not control his own development, but mirrors his environment in a purely mechanical fashion. The behavior of the individual, then, is not his own to control; he is manipulated by his environment.

member-of-society perspective
Kohlberg's second stage of ego development, in which the individual sees himself as a member of a larger social unit—for example, a family, school, city, or culture.

memory knowledge
The amount of knowledge that is available for use in a particular task.

memory processing
The retrieval of information from the memory; a decline in the efficiency of this process is associated with aging.

menopause
Biologically, the cessation of menstruation; characterized by a wide range of physical and psychological symptoms.

menstrual cycle
A biological cycle that prepares the lining of the uterus for the possible arrival of a fertilized egg; usually begins in early adolescence and repeats itself every twenty-eight to thirty-five days.

mental age (MA)
A level of reasoning skill attained by a child, expressed in terms of the age group whose average test scores most closely resemble his own.

mental retardation
A condition of slow intellectual development and below-normal intelligence; may be inherited or caused by environmental circumstances.

mesomorphic
Athletic, muscular body build characterized by proportionately more muscle tissue than fat tissue.

metacognition
Cognition that takes as its object other cognition; for example, thinking about thinking or regulating cognitive activity.

middle adulthood
Life cycle phase between the ages of thirty-five to forty-five and fifty-five to sixty-five years; characterized by acceptance of middle age, satisfaction of career goals, and aid to younger people.

middle childhood
Phase in the life cycle beginning at about six years of age; notable by the child's increased ability in reading, writing, and similar school skills; concrete thought processes are most dominant.

mitosis
The cell division process that produces the germ cells, each having twenty-three single chromosomes instead of pairs.

mnemonics
Techniques to improve memory.

modeling
A form of social learning in which an individual acquires a behavior by imitating the actions of another person.

moral autonomy
The second stage of moral development in Piaget's theory; the child becomes aware that rules and laws are created by people, relative to social systems, and that in judging an action one should consider the actor's intentions as well as the act's consequences.

moral competence
Knowledge of moral rules indicating that the person is capable of acting in appropriate moral ways.

moral development
The acquisition of feelings, thoughts, and actions with regard to standards of right and wrong.

moral performance
The carrying out of a particular moral behavior, dependent on factors of motivation as well as of moral understanding.

moral realism
The first stage of moral development in Piaget's theory; justice and rules are conceived of as unchangeable properties of the world, removed from the control of people.

moratorium
Adolescents who are suffering an identity crisis and whose commitments are either vaguely defined or absent are, in James Marcia's terms, in the midst of a moratorium.

morpheme
The basic unit of a language that is meaningful; these include prefixes, suffixes, and verb-tense markers.

motor cortex
Portions of the cortex primarily responsible for sending signals down through the spinal cord to different muscle groups.

motoric reproduction
The ability of a person to perform an observed behavior, based on nerve-muscle development; a prerequisite for learning the behavior through modeling (for example, limitations in eye-hand coordination may make it impossible for a preschooler to stay within the lines when coloring a picture).

mourning
The way in which the individual deals with grief.

mutation theory
The theory that aging results from a mutation in the DNA of cells in vital body organs.

mutuality
The highest stage of maturity according to McClelland's theory; characterized by the individual's concern for other points of view and interest in the common good.

n

nativism
The belief that a number of psychological characteristics are inherited or essentially present at birth.

naturalistic observation
A method of studying children in which they are observed in realistic, everyday situations.

near phase
The phase in which the individual is approaching retirement and may begin to participate in preretirement programs.

negative reinforcement
The repeated removal of some stimulus following a response causes the response to increase over trials.

neonate
A newborn child.

neurometrics
Measurements of electrical activity in the brain in response to sensory stimuli.

normal distribution
Symmetrical mathematical curve (usually called a bell curve because of its shape) that describes the variability of a measurable characteristic in a sample. Most scores fall near the mean (forming the highest point of the bell), with relatively few high or low scores.

o

obesity
A condition in which a person weighs more than twenty percent over normal skeletal and physical requirements. For the most part, this is indexed by an excess of fat content in the body.

objective movement
An aspect of a child's physical activity in which the purpose is to develop the power of the body.

object permanence
The understanding that an object exists independent of the self and continues to exist even when it cannot be immediately perceived.

obsessions
Unwanted ideas or fears that continue to intrude into the child's thoughts without any noticeable external cause.

Oedipus complex
A Freudian conflict beginning in early childhood in which the boy exhibits sexual desire for the mother, hostility and fear of the father, and eventually renounces the mother and identifies with the father.

onlooker play
A type of play characterized by the child watching other children playing, but not joining with them in the activities.

operant conditioning
A form of learning in which the strength of a behavior is increased or decreased as a result of its consequences.

operations
Internalized sets of actions that allow the child to do mentally what has been done before physically. Operations are not fully formed in the preoperational stage, are formed in the operational stage, and are more advanced in the formal-operational stage of Piaget's perspective.

optimally exercised ability
An ability that the individual has exercised or trained; for example, practical problem-solving tasks. These abilities are most resistant to age-change effects.

oral stage
In Freud's theory, the period during which the child seeks pleasure by stimulating the mouth, lips, tongue, and gums; the first psychoanalytic stage.

organization
The continuous process of combining and integrating subskills to form a more perfect way of thinking.

orgasm phase
The third phase of sexual response during which the body experiences great pleasure and a sense of release.

original sin
The state of sin into which all human beings are born (according to Christian theology) and as a result of which are considered to be "bad" at birth.

overextension
Describing objects as members of a set or class when those objects are not actually members of the set (for example, calling all vehicles with wheels "bicycles").

paired associates
A kind of memory that involves recalling that two items are associated with one another.

paired-associates learning
A task in which the individual studies pairs of words and then is asked to supply one of the words when supplied with the other.

parallel play
Activities that are characterized by the child playing separately from others, but with the same type of toys or the same type of activities as the others.

Parent Effectiveness Training (P. E. T.)
Program developed by Thomas Gordon; designed to help parents learn to interact more effectively with their children.

peer
A person in an individual's environment that is of about the same age, grade, and status.

peer sociotherapy
Using peer interaction as a means to correct a social problem in a child, such as isolation, aggressiveness, or inappropriate social interactions.

perception
Product of sensation; the act of interpreting a sensory event or making it meaningful.

perceptual-motor training program
Program designed to promote physical development, emphasizing input or reception and how the child's ultimate performance is affected. Performance alone is not the emphasis of this type of program.

personal fable
The adolescent's sense of uniqueness; it may be jeopardized if he reveals too much of his personal feelings to others.

personality development
Developmental focus that emphasizes the individual's self-perception, sex role, and moral development.

perspective-taking skills
The understanding, by a child, that others have perspectives that are different from his own.

phallic stage
In Freud's theory, the period during which the child's genital area is the chief source of pleasure; this stage lasts from about four to five years of age and is the third Freudian stage.

phenotype
The unique constellation of measurable characteristics in a person—height, weight, IQ, and so forth.

phenylketonuria (PKU)
A genetically based form of retardation caused by the failure of the body to produce an enzyme to break down an amino acid, thus interfering with metabolism and poisoning the nervous system.

phobia
An unusually strong fear or apprehension associated with things or situations that most people perceive as nonthreatening, such as heights, crowds, or school.

phoneme
Basic unit of the sound system in language. A class of sounds perceived as identical by speakers of a given language.

phonology
The study of the sound system; concerned with the rules used to combine sounds. All languages employ such rules, although the rules vary from one language to another.

physical development
Growth and change in physical and anatomical features.

plateau stage
According to Masters and Johnson, the second phase of sexual response; marked by varying lengths of intense arousal.

playing with improbabilities
A technique employed to increase creative thinking; children are forced to think about events that might happen after an unlikely situation.

pleasure principle
According to Freud, the early basis of behavior; the infant searches for an object to satisfy a need without regard for its need-reducing value.

political structure
A concept of the sociologist's view of development, emphasizing the importance of power structures in a society. Youth who participate in the political structure will be socialized differently than those who are subordinate to the system.

polygenically
Characteristics determined by the interaction of many different genes.

postconventional level of moral development
A term applied to the final two stages of Kohlberg's theory of moral development. Moral thought is based upon the application of laws and rules through appeal to their purposes, their democratic origin, and the social contexts within which they operate (stage 5), or by appeal to universal principles of ethics (stage 6).

practice
The repetition of behavior that is being learned.

practicing
A term used by Mahler to describe a stage in the formation of independence of the child. Between eight and fifteen months of age, the infant shows a steadily increasing interest in practicing motor skills and exploring and expanding the environment.

pragmatics
Rules concerned with the appropriate use of language in social contexts.

pragnanz
German, meaning "good form"; principles of perceptual organization in the Gestalt view.

preconventional level of moral development
A term applied to the first two stages of Kohlberg's theory of moral development. Moral thought is based on fear of punishment and authority (stage 1) or naive instrumental hedonism (stage 2).

preintimate
A person who has mixed emotions about commitment; reflected in the tendency to offer love without any obligations or long-lasting bonds.

premature birth
The birth of a baby significantly before completion of the expected nine months, or with a very low body weight (less than four pounds).

prenatal period
The period of development between conception and birth.

preoperational stage
In Piagetian theory, the stage of thought that lasts from about two to seven years of age and follows the sensorimotor period; although logical thought is present, there are several "flaws," such as egocentrism, that limit its possibilities.

pretend play
Play in which the child takes on different roles; make-believe activities in which the child may pretend to be an adult or may make fun of adults.

primary aging
Normal aging involving gradual declines in physiological and behavioral abilities.

primary circular reactions
A reaction, generally occurring between one and four months of age, in which the infant attempts to repeat a pleasurable event that first happened by chance; for example, sucking the fingers when they accidentally come close to the mouth.

primary memory
Conscious awareness of recently perceived events; identified by psychologist William James.

primary sexual characteristics
The external and internal sex organs.

prior-to-society perspective
In Kohlberg's theory, the highest level of ego development, in which the self is perceived to be a member of many different social units, with membership arbitrary and determined by many uncontrollable factors.

processing deficit
An inadequacy in the capacity needed for memory processing; it may be that older people are less capable than other individuals of the processes that aid memory work.

progesterone
A sex hormone important to the female's reproductive capability.

progressive education
A broad classification of teaching perspectives and styles that share a common goal; the total social and intellectual development of the child in a nonauthoritarian setting; compared with traditional education, the classroom is usually less structured and the students have more say in decision making.

Project Follow Through
A program instituted in 1967 as an adjunct to Project Head Start, under which children from low-income families would receive additional compensatory education through early elementary school years.

Project Head Start
A preschool program started in 1965 to help children from low-income families acquire the skills and experiences considered prerequisite for success in school.

projection
In Freudian theory, a defense mechanism by which a person attributes his own undesirable traits to others; this mechanism prevents the person from dealing with anxiety.

prompting
A strategy used by adults to influence language development in children.

proximo-distal development
Growth starting at the center of the body and moving toward the extremities.

pseudointimate
An individual who appears to be maintaining a long-lasting heterosexual attachment, while the relationship actually has little depth or closeness.

psychoanalytic theory
Freud's model of development, or any of the modern-day offshoots from it (for example, Erikson's theory).

psycholinguistics
The study of language development from a dual perspective, combining the approaches of psychology and linguistics.

psychological control-psychological autonomy
An aspect of the control-autonomy relationship between parent and child. Psychological control is parental behavior that keeps the child dependent on the parent. Psychological autonomy involves parental behavior that encourages independent development by the child.

psychometric approach
A measurement approach to understanding such traits as intelligence and personality, with emphasis on how individuals differ.

psychosis
A severe pathological condition in which the personality is seriously disorganized and there is loss of contact with reality.

puberty
The stage of development at which the individual becomes capable of reproduction; in many cases, this stage is linked with the onset of adolescence.

punishment
The presentation of an unpleasant event following a behavior, decreasing the probability that the behavior will be repeated.

quasi experiment
An approximation to an experiment in which there is some loss of control over the independent variables due to the real-life manner in which they are defined.

randomization
In an experiment, the assignment of children or other subjects to groups on a random, or nondirected, basis.

rapprochment
A stage in Mahler's theory of the formation of independence. It lasts from about fifteen to twenty-four months and roughly coincides with the period of development we refer to as toddlerhood. As the child becomes aware of physical separateness and ability to move away from the mother, he or she experiences a new need for the mother to share in every new acquisition of skill and experience.

reaction formation
In Freudian theory, a defense mechanism in which a person conceals an undesirable motive by expending a great deal of energy in expressing the opposite view.

realistic stage
One of Ginsberg's stages of creativity, occurring between the ages of seventeen and the early twenties. In this stage, the individual conducts a thorough search of available occupations, zeros in on a particular occupation, and then picks a job within the occupation.

reality principle
According to Freud, an acquired manner of responding that follows and contrasts with the pleasure principle; the child channels energy onto objects that realistically reduce need states.

recall
A kind of memory that involves recollecting an experience.

receiver
In the field of communications, the specific point at which the transmitted information is picked up. A message is sent over a particular channel of communication to a specific receiver.

receptivity
The first stage in McClelland's theory of maturity development, characterized by the individual's respect for authority and convention.

recessive gene
A gene whose code will be masked by a dominant gene and will only be expressed when paired with another recessive gene. A gene code for blue eyes will only be manifested if coupled with another recessive code.

reciprocal
Family responsibility, such as in Japan, in which parents accept responsibility for both their children and their own parents.

reciprocal determinism
The belief that the agency that shapes change in someone is also influenced by the person it shapes. Thus mothers teach their children, and the act of teaching alters the mother's behavior as well.

reciprocal exchange
According to Sanders' infant development model, this third stage (four to six months of age) is notable by the first exchanges between mother and child in feeding, playing, dressing, or other activities.

reciprocal socialization
A view of the socialization process that considers the interaction of the child and his or her parents and other adults, rather than viewing socialization as a process performed by adults in regard to their children.

recognition
A kind of memory that involves noticing whether an event was previously experienced or not. The sixth stage in Sanders' model of mother-infant interaction, beginning at about eighteen months of age. Characterized by the infant's emerging sense of self and greater development of language and representational ability.

rectangular theory of aging
James Fries' view of aging that predicts the need for different views on lifestyle and health care for the elderly. Fries observed that the aged population will remain steady, chronic illness will not be widespread, and physical strength will last for more of the life span. The rectangular shape of the survival curve requires new attitudes toward aging and death.

reflexes
An involuntary response to a particular stimulus; for example, stroking a newborn's foot causes the whole leg to be withdrawn and the foot flexes.

refractory period
A period of time after orgasm when the male is unable to experience arousal. Females do not experience a refractory period.

regression
In Freudian theory, a defense mechanism in which a person returns to an earlier stage of development.

rehearsal
A process of memory in which the items to be recalled are repeated by the memorizer.

reinforcement
The presentation of a pleasant event following a behavior, increasing the probability that the behavior will be repeated.

reintegrative stage
The phase of cognitive development in which the individual is able to focus on the life aspects that are most important to him or her. In this period, occurring during late adulthood, cognition is most influenced by motivational factors.

reliability
Degree to which statistical measurements are consistent on repeated trials.

remote phase
A phase of retirement in which the individual does almost nothing to prepare for it.

reorientation phase
The point at which the retired individual begins to adjust to the reality of retirement. The person must consider his or her options and decide on a future life-style.

repression
Driving thoughts and feelings from conscious awareness and locking them away in the unconscious.

resatellization
According to Ausubel, this preliminary stage may precede desatellization; it involves the replacement of parents by other individuals or a group, with the individual abdicating his or her identity to the individuals or group.

resolution phase
The final stage of sexual response during which the body continues to relax and the sensations of orgasm lessen.

responsible stage
Corresponding with middle adulthood, the cognitive stage of development in which the individual is self-competent and begins to accept responsibility for others.

retention
Stage in Bandura's model of learning; synonymous with remembering or retrieving information.

rhythmical stereotypes
Rhythmic activities marking a transition between uncoordinated actions and more voluntary motor abilities. For example, rocking on hands and knees appears before the onset of crawling.

rhythmic motor behavior
Repetitious movement of the head, torso, or limbs; such activities as rocking and swaying that the infant repeats and obviously enjoys; interpreted differently by various theorists.

ritual
A form of spontaneous play that involves controlled repetition.

roles
The different patterns of social behavior that a person takes on in different situations.

role taking
The ability, first developed in the young child, to understand the feelings and cognitions that other people are experiencing.

S

saccadic
Rapid movements of the eye from one fixation point to another during the course of reading or visual scanning.

salience of dimensions
The perceptual dominance of one dimension of an object or event in relation to other dimensions present. Individuals may have different subjective experiences of which dimension(s) is (are) dominant, given the same object of interest.

satellization
According to Ausubel, during childhood boys and girls give up their sense of self-power and the perception that they can do everything themselves. The result is dependency on (or satellization around) their parents.

scale of environment
A concern in designing housing for the elderly; categories at the scale of housing are vastly different from those at the level of cities.

scientific theory
An organized and logical set of statements, laws, and axioms; designed to describe, explain, and predict some particular observable events.

scripts
Hypothetical structures that organize experience. It is a concept or organizational framework based on the expected events likely to unfold for commonly and universally experienced action sequences such as going to a doctor's office, eating at a restaurant, or going to school.

secondary aging
Disease-related aging involving many chronic conditions that may affect brain function.

secondary circular reactions
Between four and eight months of age, actions that the infant attempts for more than personal need satisfaction; for example, shaking a rattle, or imitating baby talk or physical gestures for the objective result.

secondary memory
Recall of events that have left the consciousness, identified by psychologist William James.

secondary sexual characteristics
Sexual features that accentuate the outward distinction between girls and boys, such as pubic hair, voice change, and breast enlargement.

second-order effects
Indirect effects on the family system; for example, the relationship between the parents affects the ways in which they deal with the child.

securely attached
An infant-mother bond distinguished by consistent positive emotional responses; this bond allows for the gradual growth of infant independence.

selective attention
Focused attention that requires ignoring irrelevant information (for example, listening to a conversation while ignoring a television program).

self
The hypothetical core of personality in many theories; what distinguishes the phenomenal experiences of one person from another.

self-assertion
The fifth stage in Louis Sanders' model of infant development, occurring from ages fourteen to twenty months; marked by activity choosing and initiation by the child, sometimes in conflict with the mother's wishes.

"self" constancy
The final step in Sanders' model of infant development of self; characterized by communication between child and mother, allowing for development of a sense of constancy.

self-fulfilling prophecy
(Sometimes referred to as the Rosenthal Effect) the idea that once someone knows something about an individual, he or she often develops expectations for that person's behavior; in turn, those expectations may change the way the individual treats the other person and the way the person actually performs.

semantic-associational information
Set of rules involved in learning to read; knowledge of what words refer to and how they do or do not "fit" together in certain contexts.

semantic or categorical elaboration
The coupling of a test word with a categorical clue (for example, apple—fruit). Memory recall is equal for all age groups if this type of cue is provided at the time of presentation.

semantic feature hypothesis
The explanation that children's early word meanings are linked to semantic features of the object referred to. The child initially tends to notice features that are directly perceived through the senses and applies the word when one or more of these features is present (for example, a dog is four-legged, barks, has a tail, and so forth).

semantic networks
Techniques for measuring the networks of meanings associated with some persons or events. The subject is asked to rate a large number of words according to how much each one appears to the person or event.

semantics
The expressed meanings of words and sentences.

sensation
The process of reacting to stimulation as it reaches sensory receptors, for example, the eyes, ears, nose, tongue, and skin.

sensorimotor stage
The earliest stage of thought in Piaget's model of cognitive development, comprising six substages through which an infant progresses; this stage extends from simple reflexes through the use of primitive symbols as the means of coordinating sensation and action.

sensory cortex
Portions of the cortex primarily responsible for receiving signals transmitted from the different senses.

separation anxiety
Fear and upset exhibited when the primary caretaker leaves.

separation–individuation
Terms used by Mahler to describe the process by which the young child acquires independence. During the first three years of life, the child emerges from the symbiotic relationship with the mother (separation) and acquires a number of individual characteristics (individuation).

serial
Family responsibility, such as in the United States, in which one generation is responsible for the next. Parents, then, are responsible for their children, not for their own parents.

sex role
A culturally defined pattern for maleness or femaleness.

sex-typed behavior
Actions and responses that fit a culturally predicted picture of typical male and female patterns.

sexual (gender) identity
The extent to which individual children actually take on as part of their personalities the behaviors and attitudes associated with either the male or female role.

short-term memory
The second level of memory storage, where stimuli are stored and retrievable for up to about a minute; also called working memory.

signaling responses
Attachment responses by which the infant tries to elicit behaviors from the mother. These include smiling, crying, and calling.

simple hysterectomy
Surgical removal of the uterus and cervix.

situational variability
Effects of the circumstances on the expression of a particular behavior; for example, a child reacts to a stranger according to the particular situation in which the stranger is encountered.

size constancy
Perception of objects as having a fixed or constant ("real") size even when viewed under conditions in which they may appear as tiny specks at a distance or as giant obstacles directly in front of the eyes.

social breakdown theory
A social aging concept that observes that society attributes negative qualities to the aging individual. Persons who accept this poor image are likely to become susceptible to aging.

social cognition
A subfield of cognitive-developmental theory emphasizing that the individual thinks about social matters as well as nonsocial ones; includes research on moral development, role taking, and impression formation.

social delinquent
A youth whose antisocial behavior is due to the acceptance of subgroup norms that conflict with those of the larger society.

social development
Aspect of development focusing on the individual's encounters with and reactions to others.

social environment
The individual's experiences with family, schools, community, peers, and the media.

social intelligence
Interpersonal skills necessary to everyday living; social competence, ability to perform a task or engage in a life-style with a sufficient degree of skill.

socialization
The process whereby people influence other people, usually through interaction with them; socialization has been traditionally defined as the transmission of the rules and knowledge of the adult culture to children, but the process is broader than that, entailing the child's socialization of adults as well.

social structure
An important construct in the sociologist's analysis of culture and society; a component of society such as ecological structure, economic structure, political structure, or value structure.

social time
The aspect of the life cycle that depends upon the age-grade system of the individual society. For example, a girl may be thought ready for marriage when she reaches puberty in one society, but not in another.

sociolinguistics
The study of language and language functioning within the context of interacting with other people.

software
In computers, the programs that make the physical equipment operate; by analogy, in human intelligence, the routines that make the brain and central nervous system work (plans, intentions, strategies, and goals); contrast with *hardware*.

solitary play
Category of play in which the child plays alone and is not concerned with those around him or her.

spatial processing
Tasks that require the function of mental imagery; that is, the ability to create a properly spaced image in one's mind. Spatial processing in the short-term memory seems to slow in older persons.

speech perception
Ability to perceive and distinguish speech sounds; one aspect of authority perception in the infant.

stability phase
The phase of retirement in which the person has decided on a criterion for making choices and a method for acting on those choices.

stages
Sequential phases of development. Psychoanalytic and cognitive-structural views suggest the existence of such age-related periods of development.

standard deviation
The average difference between individual scores and the mean score in a distribution; obtained by squaring the deviation scores, summing these, dividing by one less than the number of scores, and taking the square root of the result.

standardized testing
The use of tests to assess human characteristics and individual differences. The tests are developed on large samples and have established norms, reliability, and evidence of validity.

Standford-Binet
A general, individually administered test of intelligence based on items originally devised by French psychologist Alfred Binet (ca. 1900) to predict children's ability to succeed in school.

stereotype
A broad category that reflects our impressions about people, including ourselves.

stereotyped individual
A person whose relationships with others are usually superficial and shallow.

stimuli
Observable events that are associated with a response.

stranger anxiety
Distress and fear in an infant when an unfamiliar person approaches.

Sudden Infant Death Syndrome (SIDS)
Sometimes referred to as crib death, this term refers to the unexplained death of a child in the first year of life, usually between the ages of two and five months. Although the cause is not well understood, recent speculation is that some newborns may have insufficiently built-in defense responses to respiratory threats.

superego
According to Freud, the moral part of the personality where each person has internalized dos and don'ts.

surface structure
The actual sentence, spoken or heard, that is meant to convey a particular deep structure; many surface forms may reflect the same deep structural idea. *See also* **deep structure.**

symbiotic infantile psychosis
A condition in which a child has intense anxiety and panic about being separated from the mother. It usually is manifested between the ages of two and one-half and five years and often is preceded by normal development.

symbol
An abstract event (for example, image or word) that represents a concrete experience or object.

synchrony
The ability of some parents to quickly sense and fulfill their infant's needs.

syntactic information
Set of rules involved in learning to read; orderly word relationships in sentences.

syntax
The rules used in a particular language to form acceptable phrases and sentences.

system of abstract systems
The most advanced level of Fischer's theory of adult cognitive ability; at this point, the individual can coordinate his identities over the entire life cycle so that a satisfactory whole is perceived.

t

tabula rasa
Literally, a "blank tablet"; phrase used to describe the child's mind at birth as empty of all knowledge until acquired through experience.

temperament
The individual's personal nature or attitudes; it can be argued that the infant's nature is dependent on the mother, or that the mother learns to adapt to the temperament of the individual child.

tension reduction
Release of stored psychological energy. In psychoanalytic theory, it is the release of instinctual energy (libido) from the id.

tentative stage
In Ginsberg's theory of vocational choice, the transition between the fantasy stage of childhood and the realistic stage of young adulthood; this stage occurs between ages eleven and seventeen, when thinking about careers is still subjective.

teratogen
Any agent that causes birth defects.

teratology
A field of study that focuses on birth defects.

termination phase
The final phase of retirement, according to Atchley, in which the individual no longer regards retirement as a significant event. The person may return to work or may become dependent on others.

tertiary aging
Behavior resulting from serious disease which has affected the individual's physical condition.

tertiary circular reactions
Schemes in which the infant (between ages twelve to eighteen months) explores new possibilities with the same object, changing what is done and examining the results. This is the first reaction that is not imitation; marking the beginnings of curiosity.

time samples
A method of recording observations in limited frames of time, which are interspersed with rest or with nonobservation segments.

total hysterectomy
Surgical removal of the uterus and cervix as well as the ovaries and the fallopian tubes.

traditional education
The teaching philosophy of most American public schools, which focuses on learning basic academic skills at a common pace in group settings, under the firm direction of a single teacher.

transformations
Syntactical rules that explain how a common deep structure can assume alternative surface forms, such as active and passive, positive and negative, statement and question.

transient self
Characteristics of the individual that vary over a period of time; for example, inappropriate dress or behavior. These are not permanent features of the self.

transition
The perspective on middle adulthood that treats this period as one of change, rather than one of definite crisis. Change in adult life; may be instigated by a variety of factors, including mobility, family situation or occupational status.

triggers
Life events that may initiate learning; for example, losing a job may trigger the need for an education to become more employable.

trust versus mistrust
The first stage in Erikson's eight-stage theory of development, in which the infant develops either the comfortable feeling that those around him care for his needs or the worry that his needs will not be taken care of.

two-factor theory of intelligence
C. E. Spearman's belief that intelligence involves a general factor and a specific factor, which account for IQ test performances.

Type A person
An individual who may be classified as having a high risk of heart disease; typically a person who is impatient, competitive, and excessively time conscious.

Type B person
A person who is typically noncompetitive, patient, and satisfied with his handling of time; generally regarded as a low risk for heart disease.

u

unconditioned response (UCR)
A reflex; an automatic response to an unconditioned stimulus.

unconditioned stimulus (UCS)
An environmental event that automatically triggers a response (UCR), without learning having to take place.

underextension
Describing only some members of a set or class to which a label applies (for example, referring to daisies and roses, but not violets, as "flowers").

unexercised ability
An ability for which the individual has had no training or exercise; for example, abstract problem-solving tasks.

unoccupied play
Type of play in which the child is not engaged in activities that are normally regarded as play.

unsocialized delinquent
A youth whose antisocial behavior is due to deficient socialization on the part of his family; he has not adopted socially acceptable standards of behavior.

upswing thesis
After a decline in marital satisfaction during the period in which the children are adolescents, many marriages experience an "upswing" of satisfaction after the children leave home. The increase of satisfaction is dependent on a positive resolution of the empty nest syndrome.

v

values clarification
An approach to moral education in which students are given the opportunity to air their opinions and value judgments in a group setting. By being exposed to the value judgments of others, students come to appreciate the relative nature of values.

value structure
According to the sociologist's view of development, this involves cultural ethics and rules of right and wrong. The value structure of a society is transmitted to the child through moral education.

vasocongestion
Swelling of the blood vessels.

vergence
The property of visual focusing in which the lens of each eye turns inward or outward to establish the proper focal length between the retina and the object being seen.

vicarious learning
The strengthening of a behavior in a person through his observation of someone else's being rewarded for that behavior; learning that occurs through modeling or imitation.

visual acuity
The ability of the eyes to resolve an image or see fine detail.

visual cliff technique
A visual situation designed to give the illusion of a steep cliff; used with infants to test development of depth perception; and to note sensitivity to a steep drop.

visually guided reaching
Ability of an infant, generally between five and seven months of age, to coordinate reaching for an object after looking at it.

voiced consonant
When pluralizing English words, if the final consonant is *voiced* (m, n, g), the plural is voiced; for example, dogs.

voiceless consonant
When pluralizing English words, if the final consonant is *voiceless* (k, f, t, b), the plural is also voiceless; for example, cats.

vowels
In standard English, one of two basic phoneme classes; formed by passing air over the vocal cords and allowing it to flow unimpeded through the oral cavity.

warmth-hostility
A dimension along which parents can be discriminated in how they interact with their children. At one extreme (warmth), parents exhibit considerable affection, love, and reinforcement toward their children. At the other extreme (hostility), the child is treated harshly, is the subject of repeated anger, and may be punished but not reinforced very often.

Whorf/Sapir hypothesis
The idea that people who speak different languages also experience the world differently, with each language creating unique perceptual and intellectual biases.

youth
The transition period between adolescence and early adulthood; notable for the struggle between developing self-autonomy and becoming involved in a social system.

References

a

Achenbach, T. M. Developmental aspects of psychopathology in children and adolescents. In M. E. Lamb (ed.), *Social and personality development.* New York: John Wiley, 1978.

Achenbach, T. M., & Edelbrock, C. S. Behavioral problems and competencies reported by parents of normal and disturbed children aged four through sixteen. *Monographs of the Society for Research in Child Development,* 1981, serial no. 188, vol. 46, no. 1.

Adams, B. N. Interaction theory and the social network. *Sociometry,* 1967, *30,* 64–78.

Adams, G. M., & de Vries, H. A. Physiological effects of an exercise training regimen among women aged 52 to 79. *Journal of Gerontology,* 1973, *28,* 50–55.

Adams, R. S., & Biddle, B. J. *Realities of teaching.* New York: Holt, Rinehart & Winston, 1970.

Adelson, J. Adolescence and the generalization gap. *Psychology Today,* 1979, 33–37.

Aiken, L. R. *The psychology of later life.* Philadelphia: W. B. Saunders, 1978.

Ainsworth, M. D. *Infancy in Uganda: Infant care and the growth of love.* Baltimore: Johns Hopkins Press, 1967.

Ainsworth, M. D. S. Attachment and dependency: A comparison. In J. L. Gewirtz (ed.), *Attachment and dependency.* Washington, D.C.: V. H. Winston, 1972.

Ainsworth, M. D. S. The development of infant-mother attachment. In B. Caldwell & H. N. Riccuiti (eds.), *Review of Research,* vol. 3, 1973.

Ainsworth, M. D. S. Infant-mother attachment. *American Psychologist,* 1979, *34,* 932–937.

Ainsworth, M. D. S., Bell, S. M., & Stayton, D. J. Individual differences in strange-situation behavior of one-year olds. In H. R. Schaffer (ed.), *The origins of human social relations.* London: Academic Press, 1971, p. 17–52.

Albrecht, S. L. Reactions and adjustment to divorce: Differences in experiences of males and females. *Family Relations,* 1980, *29,* 59–68.

Aldous, J. Family careers over time. Address given at Department of Sociology, University of Notre Dame, September 22, 1978.

Allan, G. Sibling solidarity. *Journal of Marriage and the Family,* 1977, *39,* 177–184.

Allen, V. L., & Feldman, R. S. Studies on the role of tutor. In V. L. Allen (ed.), *Children as teachers: Theory and research on tutoring.* New York: Academic Press, 1976.

Ames, C., & Felker, D. W. Effects of self-concept on children's casual attributions and self-reinforcement. *Journal of Educational Psychology,* in press.

Anastasi, A. Heredity, environment, and the question "how." *Psychological Review,* 1958, *65,* 197–208.

Anastasi, A. *Psychological testing* (2nd ed.). New York: Macmillan, 1976.

Anders, T. R., Fozard, J. L., & Lillyquist, T. D. The effects of age upon retrieval from short-term memory. *Developmental Psychology,* 1972, *6,* 214–217.

Anderson, A. "Old" is not a four-letter word. Across the Board, 1978. Reprinted in Annual Editions: Human Development 80/81. Guilford, Conn.: The Dushkin Publishing Group, 1980. Anderson is a freelance science and medicine writer living in New York.

Anderson, D. R., & Levin, S. R. Young children's attention to "Sesame Street." *Child Development,* 1976, *47,* 806–811.

Anderson, J. R., & Bower, G. H. *Human associative memory.* Washington, D.C.: Hemisphere Press, 1973.

Anderson, R., & Darkenwald, G. *Participation and persistence in American adult education.* New York: College Entrance Examination Board, 1979.

Anderson, T. R., Fozard, J. L., & Lillyquist, T. P. Effects of age upon retrieval from short-term memory. *Developmental Psychology,* 1972, *6,* 212–217.

Anthony, E. J. An experimental approach to the psychopathology of childhood: Encopresis. *British Journal of Medical Psychology,* 1957, *30,* 146–175.

Antonucci, T. *Attachment from adolescence to adulthood.* Paper presented at the meeting of the American Psychological Association, Los Angeles, California, August 1981.

Apgar, V. A. A proposal for a new method of evaluation of a newborn infant. *Anesthesia and Analgesia: Current Research,* 1953, *32,* 260–267.

Arenberg, D. Differences and changes with age on the Benton Visual Retention Test. *Journal of Gerontology,* 1978, *33,* 534–540.

Arenberg, D., & Robertson-Tchabo, E. A. Learning and aging. In J. E. Birren and K. W. Schaie (eds.), *Handbook of the psychology of aging.* New York: Van Nostrand Reinhold, 1977.

Aries, P. *Centuries of childhood.* (R. Baldrick, Trans.). New York: Knopf, 1962.

Armentrout, J. A., & Burger, G. K. Children's reports of parental child-rearing behavior at five grade levels. *Developmental Psychology,* 1972, *7,* 44–48.

Armstrong, B. Illinois judge upholds IQ test use: Departs from *Larry P. APA Monitor,* November 1980, 6–7.

Aron, I. E. Moral philosophy and moral education: A critique of Kohlberg's theory. *School Review,* 1977, *85,* 197–217.

Aronfreed, J. Moral development from the standpoint of a general psychological theory. In T. Lickona (ed.), *Moral development and behavior.* New York: Holt, Rinehart & Winston, 1976.

Asch, S. E. A study of change in mental organization. *Archives of Psychology,* 1936, *28* (Whole No. 195).

Asher, S. R., & Wigfield, A. Training referential communication skills. In W. P. Dickson (ed.), *Children's oral communication skills.* New York: Academic Press, 1981.

Aslanian, C. B., & Brickell, H. M. *Americans in Transition: Life changes as reasons for adult learning.* Princeton, N.J.: College Board Publications, 1980.

Astin, H. S., & Bayer, A. E. Sex discrimination in academe. In M. T. S. Mednick, S. S. Tangri, & L. W. Hoffman (eds.), *Women and achievement.* New York: John Wiley, 1975.

Atchley, R. C. *The sociology of retirement.* Cambridge, Mass.: Schenkman, 1976.

Atchley, R. C. *The social forces in later life: An introduction to social gerontology* (2nd ed.). Belmont, Calif.: Wadsworth, 1977.

Atkinson, R. C. Mnemotechnics in second-language learning. *American Psychologist,* 1975, *30,* 821–828.

Atkinson, R. C., & Shiffrin, R. M. The control of short-term memory. *Scientific American,* 1971, *225,* 82–90.

Attig, M., & Hasher, L. The processing of frequency of occurrence information. *Journal of Gerontology,* 1980, *35,* 66–69.

Ausubel, D. P. *Educational psychology.* New York: Holt, Rinehart & Winston, 1968.

Ausubel, D. P., Sullivan, E. V., & Ives, S. W. *Theory and problems of child development* (3rd ed.). New York: Grune & Stratton, 1980.

b

Babladelis, G. Accentuate the positive. *Contemporary Psychology,* 1979, *24,* 3–4.

Bachman, J., O'Malley, P., & Johnson, J. *Youth in transition, volume VI. Adolescence to adulthood—change and stability of the lives of young men.* Institute for Social Research: University of Michigan, 1978.

Bahrick, H. P., Bahrick, P. O., & Wittlinger, R. P. Fifty years of memory for names and faces: A cross-sectional approach. *Journal of Experimental Psychology: General,* 1975, *104,* 54–75.

Bailey, K. V. A study of human growth in the framework of applied nutrition and public health nutrition programs in the Western Pacific region. In J. Brozek (ed.), Physical growth and body composition: Papers from the Kyota symposium on anthropological aspects of human growth. *Monographs of the Society for Research in Child Development,* 1970, serial no. 140, vol. 35.

Baldwin, A. L. Differences in parent behavior toward three- and nine-year-old children. *Journal of Personality,* 1946, *15,* 143–165.

Balinsky, B. An analysis of the mental factors of various age groups from nine to sixty. *Genetic Psychology Monographs,* 1941, *23,* 191–234.

Ball, S., & Bogatz, G. A. *The first year of "Sesame Street": An evaluation.* Princeton: Educational Testing Service, 1970.

Baltes, P. B. Prototypical paradigms and questions in life-span research on development and aging. *The Gerontologist,* 1973, *13,* 458–467.

Baltes, P. B., & Baltes, M. M. Plasticity and variability in psychological aging: Methodological and theoretical issues. In G. E. Gurski (ed.), *Determining the effects of aging on the central nervous system.* Berlin: Schering AG, (Oraniendruck), 1980.

Baltes, P. B., & Labouvie, G. V. Adult development of intellectual performance: Description, explanation, and modification. In C. Eisdorfer, & M. P. Lawton (eds.), *The psychology of adult development and aging.* Washington, D.C.: American Psychological Association, 1973.

Baltes, P. B., Reese, H. W., & Lipsitt, L. P. Life-span developmental psychology. *Annual Review of Psychology,* 1980, *31,* 65–110.

Baltes, P. B., Reese, H. W., & Lipsitt, L. P. Life-span developmental psychology in annual review of psychology. Palo Alto, Calif.: Annual Reviews, 1980.

Baltes, P. B., & Schaie, K. W. The myth of the twilight years. *Psychology Today,* March 1974, 35–38, 40.

Baltes, P. B., & Schaie, K. W. On the plasticity of intelligence in adulthood and old age: Where Horn and Donaldson fail. *American Psychologist,* 1976, *31,* 720–725.

Baltes, P. B., & Willis, S. L. Cognitive development and intervention in later adulthood. The Penn State Adult Development and Enrichment Program (ADEPT). Unpublished symposium manuscript, College of Human Development, Penn State University, 1978.

Bandura, A. The stormy decade: Fact or fiction? *Psychology in the Schools,* 1964, 224–231.

Bandura, A. *Principles of behavior modification.* New York: Holt, Rinehart & Winston, 1969.

Bandura, A. Analysis of modeling processes. In A. Bandura (ed.), *Psychological modeling.* New York: Lieber-Atherton, 1971.

Bandura, A. *Social learning theory.* New York: General Learning Press, 1971.

Bandura, A. *Social learning theory.* Englewood Cliffs, N.J.: Prentice-Hall, 1977.

Bandura, A., & Jeffrey, R. W. Role of symbolic coding and rehearsal processes in observational learning. *Journal of Personality and Social Psychology,* 1973, *26,* 122–130.

Bandura, A., & MacDonald, F. J. Influence of social reinforcement and the behavior of models in shaping children's moral judgments. *Journal of Abnormal and Social Psychology,* 1963, *67,* 274–281.

Bandura, A., & Walters, R. M. *Adolescent aggression.* New York: Ronald, 1959.

Bane, M. J. HEW policy toward children, youth, and families. Discussion paper prepared under Order #SA–8139–77 for the Office of the Assistant Secretary for Planning and Evaluation. Cambridge, Mass., 1978.

Banister, H., & Ravden, M. The problem child and his environment. *British Journal of Psychology,* 1944, *34,* 60–65.

Banks, M., & Salapatek, P. Infant pattern vision: A new approach based on the contrast sensitivity function. *Journal of Experimental Child Psychology,* 1981, *31*(1), 1–45.

Barcus, F. E. *Commercial children's television on weekends and weekday afternoons.* Newtonville, Mass.: Action for Children's Television, 1978.

Bardwick, J. *Psychology of women: A study of bio-cultural conflicts.* New York: Harper & Row, 1971.

Barenboim, C. The development of recursive and nonrecursive thinking about persons. *Developmental Psychology,* in press, (a).

Barenboim, C. Developmental changes in the interpersonal cognitive system from middle childhood to adolescence. *Child Development,* in press, (b).

Barker, R. G. *Ecological psychology.* Stanford, Calif.: Stanford University Press, 1968.

Barker, R. G., & Gump, P. V. *Big school, small school: High school size and student behavior.* Stanford, Calif.: Stanford University Press, 1964.

Barnes, G. M. The development of adolescent drinking behavior: An evaluative review of the impact of the socialization process within the family. *Adolescence,* 1977, *13,* 571–591.

Barnes, K. E. Preschool play norms: A replication. *Developmental Psychology,* 1971, *5,* 99–103.

Barnouw, V. *An introduction to anthropology. Vol. 2: Ethnology.* Homewood, Ill.: Dorsey Press, 1975.

Barrett, D. E., & Radke-Yarrow, M. Chronic malnutrition and child behavior: Effects of early calorie supplementation on social-emotional functioning at school age. *Developmental Psychology,* in press.

Barrett, M. D. Lexical development and over-extension in child language. *Journal of Child Language,* 1978, *5,* 205–210.

Barrett, T. R., & Wright, M. Age-related facilitation in recall following verrantic processing. *Journal of Gerontology,* 1981, *36,* 194–199.

Barron, F. *Creativity and psychological health.* New York: Van Nostrand Reinhold, 1963.

Bart, P. Portnoy's mother's complaint. In H. Z. Lopata (ed.), *Marriages and families.* New York: Van Nostrand Reinhold, 1973.

Bart, W. M. The factor structure of formal operations. *The British Journal of Educational Psychology,* 1971, *41,* 40–77.

Bartell, G. *Group sex.* New York: Peter H. Wyden, 1971.

Bartoshuk, A. K. Human neonatal cardiac responses to sound: A power function. *Psychonomic Science,* 1964, *1,* 151–152.

Basen, M. M. The elderly and drugs—problem overview and program strategy. *Public Health Reports,* 1977, *92,* 43–48.

Baskett, L. *The young child's interactions with parents and siblings: A behavioral analysis.* Unpublished doctoral dissertation, University of Oregon, 1974.

Bates, E. *Language and context: The acquisition of pragmatics.* New York: Academic Press, 1976.

Bates, L., Benigni, L., Bretherton, I., Camaioni, L., & Volterra, V. *Cognition and communication from 9–13 months: A correlational study program on cognitive and perceptual factors in human development.* Report No. 12. Boulder: Institute for the Study of Intellectual Behavior, University of Colorado, 1977.

Baumrind, D. Current patterns of parental authority. *Developmental Psychology Monographs,* 1971, *4* (1, pt. 2).

Baumrind, D. From each according to her ability. *School Review,* 1972, *80,* 161–197.

Baumrind, D. Socialization and instrumental competence in young children. In W. W. Hartup (ed.), *The young child* (vol. 2). Washington, D.C.: National Association for the Education of Young Children, 1972.

Baumrind, D. Are androgynous individuals more effective persons and parents? *Child Psychology,* 1982, *53,* 44–75.

Bayley, N. Development of motor abilities during the first three years. *Monographs of the Society for Research in Child Development,* 1935, 1.

Bayley, N. Research in child development: A longitudinal perspective. *Merrill Palmer Quarterly,* 1965, *11,* 183–208.

Bayley, N. Development of mental abilities. In P. H. Mussen (ed.), *Carmichael's manual of child psychology* (3rd ed., vol. 1). New York: John Wiley, 1970.

Beit-Hallahmi, B. Self-reported religious concerns of university underclassmen. *Adolescence,* 1974, *9,* 333–338.

Belkin, G. S., & Gray, J. L. *Educational psychology: An introduction.* Dubuque, Iowa: Wm. C. Brown Co., 1977. Reprinted by permission.

Bell, R. Q. A reinterpretation of the direction of effects in studies of socialization. *Psychological Review,* 1968, *75,* 81–85.

Bell, R. Q. Stimulus control of parent or caretaker behavior by offspring. *Development Psychology,* 1971, *4,* 63–72.

Bell, R. Q. Parent, child, and reciprocal influences. *American Psychologist,* 1979, *34,* 821–826.

Bell, R. Q., & Costello, N. S. Three tests for sex differences in tactile sensitivity in the newborn. *Biologia Neonat.,* 1964, *7,* 335–347.

Bell, R. R., & Lobsenz, N. Married sex: How uninhibited can a woman dare to be. *Redbook,* September 1979, *143,* 75–78.

Bell, S. M. The development of the concept of the object as related to infant-mother attachment. *Child Development,* 1970, *41,* 291–311.

Bell, W. G. Community care for the elderly: An alternative to institutionalization. *Gerontologist,* 1973, *13,* 349–354.

Belloc, N. B., & Breslow, L. Relationship of physical health status and health practices. *Preventive Medicine,* 1972, *1,* 409–421.

Belmont, J. M., & Butterfield, E. S. Learning strategies as determinants of memory deficiencies. *Cognitive Psychology,* 1971, *2,* 411–420.

Beloff, H. The structure and origin of the anal character. *Genetic Psychology Monographs,* 1962, *55,* 275–278.

Belsky, J. Early human experience: A family perspective. *Developmental Psychology,* 1981, *17,* 3–23.

Belsky, J., & Steinberg, L. D. The effects of day care: A critical review. *Child Development,* 1978, *49,* 929–949.

Bem, S. L. The measurement of psychological androgyny. *Journal of Consulting and Clinical Psychology,* 1974, *42,* 155–162.

Bem, S. L. On the utility of alternative procedures for assessing psychological androgyny. *Journal of Consulting and Clinical Psychology,* 1977, *45,* 196–205.

Benedict, R. *Patterns of culture.* New York: New American Library, 1958. (Originally published, 1934.)

Benet, S. *How to live to be 100.* New York: The Dial Press, 1976.

Bengtson, V. L. The generation gap: A review and typology of social-psychological perspectives. *Youth and Society,* 1970, *2,* 7–31.

Bengtson, V. L., & Black, K. D. Intergenerational relations and continuities in socialization. In P. B. Baltes and K. W. Schaie (eds.), *Life-span developmental psychology: Personality and socialization.* New York: Academic Press, 1973.

Bengtson, V. L., & Cutler, N. E. Generations and intergenerational relations. In R. H. Binstock and E. Shanas (eds), *Handbook of aging and the social sciences.* New York: Van Nostrand Reinhold, 1976.

Benson, *Texas Monthly,* 1981.

Bereiter, C. Individualization and inequality. *Contemporary Psychology,* 1975, *20,* 455–457.

Berman, P. W., Sloan, V. L., & Goodman, V. *Development of sex differences in preschool children's interactions with an infant: Spontaneous behavior and response to a caretaking assignment.* Paper presented at the Society For Research in Child Development Meeting, San Francisco, March 1979.

Berndt, T. J. *Developmental changes in conformity to peers and parents.* Paper presented at the Annual Meeting of the American Psychological Association, Toronto, Canada, August 1978.

Bernstein, B. A sociolinguistic approach to socialization: With some reference to educability. In F. Williams (ed.), *Language and poverty.* Chicago: Markham, 1970.

Bertenthal, B. I., & Fischer, K. W. Development of self-recognition in the infant. *Developmental Psychology,* 1978, *14,* 44–50.

Berzonsky, M. Formal reasoning in adolescence: An alternative view. *Adolescence,* 1978, *13,* 280–290.

Berzonsky, M. D., Weiner, A. S., & Raphael, D. Interdependence of formal reasoning. *Developmental Psychology,* 1975, *11,* 258.

Bigner, J. J. A Wernerian developmental analysis of children's descriptions of siblings. *Child Development,* 1974, *45,* 317–323.

Bijou, S. W. *The basic stage of early childhood development.* Englewood Cliffs, N.J.: Prentice-Hall, 1976.

Binstock, J. Motherhood: An occupation facing decline. *The Futurist,* June 1972, pp. 99–102.

Birrell, R. G., & Birrell, J. M. W. The maltreatment syndrome in children: A hospital survey. *Medical Journal of Australia,* 1968, *3,* 1023–1029.

Birren, J. E. Translations in gerontology—from lab to life. Psychophysiology and speed of response. *American Psychologist,* 1974, *29,* 808–815.

Birren, J. E., Butler, R. N., Greenhouse, S. W., Sokoloff, L., & Yarrow, M. R. (eds.), *Human aging: A biological and behavioral study.* Washington, D.C.: U.S. Government Printing Office, 1963.

Birren, J. E., & Reedy, M. E. *Psychology of the adult years.* Belmont, Calif.: Brooks-Cole, 1978.

Birren, J. E., & Renner, J. Concepts and issues of mental health and aging. In J. E. Birren & R. B. Sloane (eds.), *Handbook of mental health and aging.* Englewood Cliffs, N.J.: Prentice-Hall, 1980.

Birren, J. E., & Sloane, R. B. (eds.), *Handbook of mental health and aging.* Englewood Cliffs, N.J.: Prentice-Hall, 1980.

Bjorklid-Chu, P. A survey of children's outdoor activities in two modern housing areas in Sweden. In B. Tizard & D. Harvey (eds.), *The biology of play.* Philadelphia: Lippincott, 1977.

Bjorksten, J. The crosslinkage theory of aging. *Journal of the American Geriatrics Society,* 1968, *16,* 408–427.

Bjorksten, J. Crosslinkage and the aging process. In M. Rockstein, M. Sussman, & J. Chesley (eds.), *Theoretical aspects of aging.* New York: Academic Press, 1974.

Blau, P. The flow of occupational supply and recruitment. *American Sociological Review*, 1965, *30*, 475–490.

Blenkner, M. Social work and family relationships in later life with some thoughts on filial maturity. In E. Shanas & G. Streib (eds.), *Social structure and the family*. Englewood Cliffs, N.J.: Prentice-Hall, 1965.

Block, J. Conception of sex role: Some cross-cultural and longitudinal perspectives. *American Psychologist*, 1973, *28*, 512–526.

Block, J. Issues, problems, and pitfalls in assessing sex differences: A critical review of the psychology of sex differences. *Merrill-Palmer Quarterly*, 1976, *22*, 283–308.

Block, J. The many faces of continuity. *Contemporary Psychology*, 1981, *26*, 748–750.

Block, M. R., Davidson, J. L., & Grambs, J. D. *Women over forty*. New York: Springer, 1981.

Block, R., & Langman, L. Youth and work: The diffusion of "counter-cultural" values. *Youth and Society*, 1974, *5*, 411–432.

Blom, G. E., Waite, R. R., & Zimet, S. G. A motivational content analysis of children's printers. In P. M. Mussen, J. J. Conger, & J. Kagan (eds.), *Readings in child development and personality*. New York: Harper & Row, 1970.

Blood, R. O., & Wolfe, D. M. *Husbands and wives, the dynamics of married living*. New York: The Free Press, 1960.

Bloom, L. *Language development: Form and function in emerging grammars*. Cambridge, Mass.: MIT Press, 1970.

Bloom, L. Language development. In F. D. Horowitz (ed.), *Review of child development research* (vol. 4). Chicago: University of Chicago Press, 1975.

Bloom, L., Lifter, K., & Hafitz, J. Semantics of verbs in the development of verb inflection in child language. *Language*, 1980, *56*, 386–412.

Bloom, L., Miller, P., & Hood, L. Variation and reduction as aspects of competence in language development. In A. Pick (ed.), *Minnesota Symposium in Child Psychology* (vol. 9). Minneapolis: University of Minnesota Press, 1975.

Blumberg, M. L. Psychopathology of the abusing parent. *American Journal of Psychotherapy*, 1974, *28*, 1121–1129.

Blyth, D. A., Simmons, R. G., & Bush, D. The transition into early adolescence: A longitudinal comparison of youth in two educational contexts. *Sociology of Education*, in press.

Bock, R. W., & Webber, I. Suicide among the elderly: Isolating widowhood and mitigating alternatives. *Journal of Marriage and the Family*, 1972, *34*, 24–31.

Bombeck, E. *I lost everything in the post-natal depression*. Copyright © 1970, 1971, 1972, 1973 by Field Enterprises, Inc. Copyright © 1970, 1971, 1972 by The Hearst Corporation. Reprinted by permission of Doubleday & Company, Inc.

Bombeck, E., & Keane, B. *Just wait till you have children of your own*. Copyright © 1971 by Erma Bombeck and Bil Keane. Reprinted by permission of Doubleday & Company, Inc.

Boring, E. G. Intelligence as the tests test it. *New Republic*, 1923, *35*, 35–37.

Borke, H. Interpersonal perception of young children: Egocentrism or empathy? *Developmental Psychology*, 1971, *5*, 263–269.

Borke, H. The development of empathy in Chinese and American children between three and six years of age: A cross-culture study. *Developmental Psychology*, 1973, *9*, 102–108.

Borkowski, J. G. Signs of intelligence: Strategy generalization and metacognition. In S. R. Yussen (ed.), *The growth of reflection*. New York: Academic Press, 1982.

Bossard, J. H., & Boll, E. S. *The sociology of child development*. New York: Harper & Row, 1966.

Botwinick, J. *Aging and behavior*. New York: Springer, 1978.

Botwinick, J., & Storandt, M. *Memory, related functions and age*. Springfield, Ill.: Charles C Thomas, 1974. Reprinted by permission of *The Gerontologist*/ the *Journal of Gerontology*.

Bower, T. G. R. The visual world of infants. *Scientific American*, 1966, *215*, 80–92.

Bower, T. G. R. *Development in infancy*. San Francisco: W. H. Freeman, 1974.

Bowerman, C. E., & Irish, D. P. Some relationships of stepchildren to their parents. *Marriage and Family Living*, 1962, *24*, 113–121.

Bowerman, M. Structural relationships in children's utterances: Syntactic or semantic? In T. Moore (ed.), *Cognitive development and the acquisition of language*. New York: Academic Press, 1973.

Bowlby, J. The nature of the child's tie to his mother. *International Journal of Psychoanalysis*, 1958, *39*, 350–373.

Bowlby, J. *Attachment and loss*, vol. I. London: Hogarth (New York: Basic Books), 1969.

Bowlby, J. *Attachment and loss*, vol. II. London: Hogarth (New York: Basic Books), 1973.

Bowlby, J. Loss: Sadness and depression. *Attachment and loss*, Vol. III. New York: Basic Books, 1980.

Brackbill, Y. Extinction of the smiling response in infants as a function of reinforcement schedule. *Child Development*, 1958, *29*, 115–124.

Braine, M. D. S. Children's first word combinations. *Monographs for the Society of Research in Child Development*, 1976, (serial no. 164).

Brainerd, C. J. The age/stage issue in conservation acquisition. *Psychonomic Science*, 1972, *29*, 15–17.

Brainerd, C. J. Order of acquisition of transitivity, conservation, and class-inclusion of length. *Child Development*, 1974, *45*, 324–334.

Brainerd, C. J. *Piaget's theory of intelligence*. Englewood Cliffs, N.J.: Prentice-Hall, 1978.

Brainerd, C. J. The stage question in cognitive-developmental theory. *The Behavioral and Brain Sciences*, 1978, *1*, 173–182.

Brainerd, C. J., & Pressle, M. *Progress in cognitive development research* (vol. 2.), *Verbal processes in children*. New York: Springer-Verlag, in press.

Brazelton, T. B. *Neonatal behavioral assessment scale*. Philadelphia, Pa.: International Ideas, 1974.

Brickell, H. M. *A study of the tuition refund plan at Mack Trucks, Inc., Hagerstown, Md.* New York: College Entrance Examination Board, 1979.

Brim, O. G., & Kagan, J. (eds.), *Constancy and change in human development.* Cambridge, Mass.: Harvard University Press, 1980.

Brittain, C. V. Adolescent choices and parent-peer cross pressures. *American Sociological Review,* 1963, *13,* 59–68.

Broadbent, D. E. *Perception and communication.* London: Pergamon Press, 1958.

Broadbent, D. E., & Gregory, M. Jone confirmatory results on age differences in memory for simultaneous stimulation. *British Journal of Psychology,* 1965, *56,* 77–80.

Broadbent, D. E., & Heron, A. Effects of a subsidiary task on performance involving immediate memory in younger and older men. *British Journal of Psychology,* 1962, *53,* 189–198.

Broca, P. Remarques sur le siege de Faculte du langage articule suivies d'une observation d'aphemie. *Bulletin de la Societe Anatomique de Paris,* 1861, *6,* 330–357.

Brody, E. B., & Brody, N. *Intelligence: Nature, determinants, and consequences.* New York: Academic Press, 1976.

Brody, S., & Axelrad, S. *Anxiety and ego formation in infancy.* New York: International Universities Press, 1970.

Broen, P. The verbal environment of the language-learning child. *Dissertation Abstracts International,* 1972, *33,* 2849.

Bronfenbrenner, U. *Two worlds of childhood: U.S. and U.S.S.R.* New York: Russell Sage Foundation, 1970.

Bronfenbrenner, U. Is 80% of intelligence genetically determined? In U. Bronfenbrenner (ed.), *Influences on human development.* Hinsdale, Ill.: Dryden Press, 1972.

Bronfenbrenner, U. *The challenge of social change to public policy and developmental research.* Paper presented at the biennial meeting of the Society for Research in Child Development, Denver, Colorado, April 1975.

Bronfenbrenner, U., & Garbarino, J. The socialization of moral judgment and behavior in cross-cultural perspective. In T. Lickona (ed.), *Moral development and behavior.* New York: Holt, Rinehart & Winston, 1976.

Brophy, J. Teacher behavior and its effects. *Journal of Educational Psychology,* 1979, *71,* 733–750.

Brophy, J., & Evertson, C. *The Texas teacher effectiveness project: Presentation of nonlinear relationships and summary discussion* (report no. 74–6). Austin: University of Texas Research and Development Center for Teacher Education, 1974.

Brophy, J., & Evertson, C. *Learning from teaching: A developmental perspective.* Boston: Allyn & Bacon, 1976.

Brown, A. L. The development of memory: Knowing, knowing about knowing, and knowing how to know. In H. W. Reese (ed.), *Advances in child development and behavior* (vol. 10). New York: Academic Press, 1975.

Brown, R. *Psycholinguistics.* New York: Free Press, 1970. Reprinted with permission of MacMillan Publishing Co., Inc. from *Psycholinguistics,* by Roger Brown, p. 220. Copyright © 1970 by The Free Press, a Division of Macmillan Publishing Co., Inc.

Brown, R. *A first language: The early stages.* Cambridge, Mass.: Harvard University Press, 1973.

Brown, R., & Fraser, C. The acquisition of syntax. In U. Bellugi & R. Brown (eds.), *Monographs of the Society for Research in Child Development,* 1964, *29* (1, serial no. 92).

Bruckner, R. Longitudinal research on the eye. *Clinical Gerontology,* 1967, *9,* 87–95.

Bruner, J. From communication to language: A psychological perspective. *Cognition,* 1975, *3,* 255–287.

Bruner, J. S. The course of cognitive growth. *American Psychologist,* 1964, *19,* 1–15.

Bruner, J. S. *Toward a theory of instruction.* Cambridge, Mass.: Harvard University Press, 1966.

Bruner, J. S. *Beyond the information given.* New York: Norton, 1973.

Bucher, B., Reykdal, B., & Albin, J. Brief physical restraint to control pica in retarded children. *Journal of Behavior Therapy and Experimental Psychiatry,* 1976, *7,* 137–140.

Bugental, J. F. T., & Zelen, S. L. Investigation into "self-concept": The W-A-Y technique. *Journal of Personality,* 1950, *18,* 483–498.

Buhler, C. *Der menschliche, Lebenslauf al pschologishes Problem.* Leipzig: Verlag von S. Herzel, 1933.

Buhler, C. Human life as a central subject of humanistic psychology. In J. Bugental (ed.), *Challenges of humanistic psychology.* New York: McGraw-Hill, 1967.

Buhler, C. The course of human life as a psychological problem. *Human Development,* 1968, *11,* 184–200.

Buim, N., Rynders, J., & Turnure, J. Early maternal linguistic environment of normal and Down's Syndrome language learning children. *American Journal of Mental Deficiency,* 1974, *79,* 752–758.

Burchinal, L. G. Trends and prospects for young marriages in the U.S. *Journal of Marriage and the Family,* May 1965, *27,* 2, 243–254.

Burnet, S. F. M. *Intrinsic mutagenesis: A genetic approach to aging.* New York: John Wiley, 1974.

Burt, C. The evidence for the concept of intelligence. *British Journal of Educational Psychology,* 1955, *25,* 158–177.

Burt, C. The genetic determination of differences in intelligence: A study of monozygotic twins reared together and apart. *British Journal of Psychology,* 1966, *57,* 137–153.

Butler, R. N. *Why survive? Being old in America.* New York: Harper & Row, 1975. "Tendency Toward Life Review," pp. 412–414. Copyright © 1975 by Robert N. Butler, M.D. (Pulitzer Prize Winner). By permission of Harper & Row, Publishers, Inc.

Butler, R. N., & Lewis, M. *Aging and mental health.* St. Louis, Mo.: Mosby, 1977.

C

Cairns, R. B. *Social development: The origins and plasticity of interchanges*. San Francisco: Freeman, 1979.

Caplan, F. *The first twelve months of life*. The Princeton Center for Infancy and Early Childhood, Frank Caplan, General Editor. Copyright © 1971, 1972, 1973 by Edcom Systems, Inc. Used by permission of Bantam Books, Inc. All rights reserved. 1981.

Caplan, F., & Caplan, T. Motor development in the twenty-fourth month. *The second twelve months of life*. Copyright © 1977 by Frank Caplan. Reprinted by permission of Grossett & Dunlap, Inc.

Caplan, F., & Caplan, T. *The second twelve months of life*. New York: Bantam, 1981.

Carey, R. G. The widowed: A year later. *Journal of Counseling Psychology*, 1977, *24*, 125–131.

Carp, F. M. Housing and living environments of older people. In R. H. Binstock & E. Shanas (eds.), *Handbook of aging and the social sciences*. New York: Van Nostrand Reinhold, 1976.

Carpenter, T. P. Cognitive development and mathematics learning. In R. Shumway (ed.), *Research in mathematics education*. Reston, Va.: National Council of Teachers of Mathematics, 1980.

Carpenter, T. P., Hiebert, J., & Moser, J. M. Problem structure and first-grade children's initial solution processes for simple addition and subtraction problems. *Journal for Research in Mathematics Education*, 1981, *12*, 27–39.

Carpenter, T. P., Moser, J. M., & Romberg, T. A. (eds.), *Addition and subtraction: A cognitive perspective*. Hillsdale, N.J.: Erlbaum, 1981.

Carroll, C., & Miller, D. *Health: The science of human adaptation*. Dubuque, Iowa: Wm. C. Brown Co., 1982.

Carter, D. K. Counseling divorced women. *The Personnel and Guidance Journal*, 1977, *55*, 537–541.

Carus, F. A. *Psychologie. Zweiter Theil: Specialpsychologie*. Leipzig: Barth & Kummer, 1808.

Case, R., & Fry, C. Evaluation of an attempt to teach scientific inquiry and criticism in a working class high school. *Journal of Research in Science Teaching*, 1972, 135–142.

Cattell, R. B. Confirmation and clarification of primary personality factors. *Psychometrika*, 1947, *12*, 197–220.

Cazden, C. *Child language and education*. New York: Holt, Rinehart & Winston, 1972.

Cerella, J., Poon, L. W., & Fozard, J. L. Mental rotation and age reconsidered. *Journal of Gerontology*, 1981, *36*, 604–624.

Chand, I. P., Crider, D. M., & Willets, F. K. Parent-youth disagreement as perceived by youth: A longitudinal study. *Youth and Society*, 1975, *6*, 365–375.

Chandler, M. J., & Greenspan, D. Ersatz egocentrism: A reply to H. Borke. *Developmental Psychology*, 1972, *7*, 104–106.

Chapman, R. S. Issues in child language acquisition. In L. Lass, N. Northern, D. Yoder, & L. McReynolds (eds.), *Speech, language, and hearing*. Philadelphia: Saunders, 1981.

Charlesworth, R., & Hartup, W. W. Positive social reinforcement in the nursery school peer group. *Child Development*, 1967, *38*, 993–1002.

Charness, N. Aging and skilled problem solving. *Journal of Experimental Psychology: General*, 1981, *110*, 21–38.

Chernin, K. Women and weight consciousness. *New York Times News Service*, November 22, 1981. © 1981 by The New York Times Company. Reprinted by permission.

Cherry, L. The preschool teacher-child dyad: Sex differences in verbal interaction. *Child Development*, 1975, *46*, 532–535.

Cherry-Wilkinson, L., Clevenger, M., & Dolloghan, C. Communication in small instructional groups.: A sociolinguistic approach. In W. P. Dickson (ed.), *Children's oral communication skills*. New York: Academic Press, 1981.

Chess, S., & Hassibi, M. *Principles and practice of child psychiatry*. New York: Plenum, 1978.

Chess, S., & Thomas, A. Temperamental individuality from childhood to adolescence. *Journal of Child Psychiatry*, 1977, *16*, 218–226.

Chi, M. T. Knowledge structures and memory development. In R. S. Siegler (ed.), *Children's thinking: What develops?* Hillsdale, N.J.: Erlbaum, 1978.

Chiriboga, D. A., & Lowenthal, M. F. Complexities of adaptation. In M. F. Lowenthal & D. A. Chiriboga (eds.), *Four stages of life: A comparative study of women and men facing transitions*. San Francisco: Jossey-Bass, 1975.

Chomsky, C. S. *The acquisition of syntax in children from 5 to 10*. Cambridge, Mass.: MIT Press, 1969.

Chomsky, N. *Syntactic structures*. The Hague: Mouton, 1957.

Chomsky, N. *Aspects of the theory of syntax*. Cambridge, Mass.: MIT Press, 1965.

Chomsky, N. *Language and mind* (2nd ed.). New York: Harcourt, 1972.

Christ, S. G., & Meyer, G. (eds.). *Harvard Lampoon Big Book of College Life*, "Paradise Lost: Graduation and the Afterlife," pp. 170–171. Garden City, N.J.: Doubleday, 1978.

Cicirelli, V. Family structure and interaction: Sibling effects on socialization. In M. McMillan & M. Sergio (eds.), *Child psychiatry: Treatment and research*. New York: Brunner/Mazel, 1977.

Cicirelli, V. G. Sibling relationships in adulthood. In L. W. Poone (ed.), *Aging in the 1980's*. Washington, D.C.: American Psychological Association, 1980.

Cicirelli, V. G. *Feelings toward siblings in adulthood and old age*. Paper presented at the Meeting of the American Psychological Association, Los Angeles, Calif., August 1981.

Clark, E. V. What's in a word? On the child's acquisition of semantics in his first language. In T. E. Moore (ed.), *Cognitive development and the acquisition of language.* New York: Academic Press, 1973.

Clark, K. *Dark ghetto.* New York: Harper & Row, 1965.

Clark, K. B. Empathy: A neglected topic in psychological research. *American Psychologist,* 1980, *35,* 187–190.

Clarke-Stewart, K. A. Interactions between mothers and their young children: Characteristics and consequences. *Monographs of the Society for Research in Child Development,* 1973, *38* (6–7, serial no. 153).

Clarke-Stewart, K. A. Recasting the lone stranger. In J. Glick & K. A. Clarke-Stewart (eds.), *The development of social understanding.* New York: Gardner Press, 1978.

Clausen, J. The life course of individuals. In M. W. Riley, W. Johnson, & A. Foner (eds.), *A sociology of age stratification.* New York: Russell Sage Foundation, 1972.

Clayton, P. J., Halikes, H. A., & Maurice, W. L. Bereavement of the widowed. *Diseases of the Nervous System,* 1971, *32,* 597–604.

Coates, B. Consistency of attachment behavior in the human infant: A multivariate approach. *Child Study Journal,* 1978, *8,* 131–148.

Coates, B., Anderson, E. P., & Hartup, W. W. Interrelations in the attachment behavior of human infants. *Developmental Psychology,* 1972, *6,* 218–230. (a)

Coates, B., Anderson, E. P., & Hartup, W. W. The stability of attachment behaviors in the human infant. *Developmental Psychology,* 1972, *6,* 231–237. (b)

Coates, B., & Hartup, W. W. Age and verbalization in observational learning. *Developmental Psychology,* 1969, *1,* 556–562.

Cohen, L. B., DeLoache, J., & Strauss, M. S. Infant visual perception. In J. Osofsky (ed.), *Handbook of infant development.* New York: John Wiley, 1979.

Cohen, L. B., & Salapatek, P. (eds.). *Infant perception from sensation to cognition: Basic visual approaches* (vol. 1). New York: Academic Press, 1975.

Cohen, L. J. Our developing knowledge of infant perception and cognition. *American Psychologist,* 1979, *34,* 894–899.

Cohen, L. J., & Campos, J. J. Father, mother, and stranger as elicitors of attachment behavior in infancy. *Developmental Psychology,* 1974, *10,* 146–154.

Cohen, S. E. Maternal employment and mother-child interaction. *Merrill-Palmer Quarterly,* 1978, *24,* 189–197.

Cohn, E. S. *Loss of control and fear of victimization in the elderly.* Paper presented at the Annual Meeting of the American Psychological Association, Los Angeles, August 1981.

Colby, A., Kohlberg, L., Gibbs, J., & Lieberman, M. *A longitudinal study of moral judgment.* Unpublished manuscript, Harvard University, 1980.

Cole, M., Frankel, F., & Sharpe, D. Development of free recall learning in children. *Developmental Psychology,* 1971, *4,* 109–123.

Cole, M., & Scribner, S. *Culture and thought: A psychological introduction.* New York: John Wiley, 1974.

Cole, S. Send our children to work? *Psychology Today,* July 1980, 44–68.

Cole, S. *Working kids on working.* New York: Lothrop, Lee, & Shephard, in press.

Coleman, J. S. *The adolescent society.* New York: Free Press, 1961.

Colletta, N. D. *Divorced mothers at two income levels: Stress, support, and child-rearing practices.* Unpublished thesis, Cornell University, 1978.

Collins, A. M., & Loftus, E. F. 1975. A spreading activation theory of semantic processing. *Psychological Review,* 1975, *82,* 407–429.

Comfort, A. *A good age.* New York: Crown, 1976.

Comfort, A. *The biology of senescence,* 3rd ed. New York: Elsevier Press, 1979.

Comfort, A. Sexuality in later life. In J. E. Birren & R. B. Sloane (eds.), *Handbook of mental health and aging.* Englewood Cliffs, N.J.: Prentice-Hall, 1980.

Comstock, G. A. The impact of television on American institutions. *Journal of Communication,* Spring 1978, 12–28.

Condry, J. C., Simon, M. L., & Bronfenbrenner, U. *Characteristics of peer- and adult-oriented children.* Unpublished manuscript, Cornell University, 1968.

Conger, J. J. *Adolescence and youth* (3rd ed.). New York: Harper & Row, 1977.

Connell, D. *Individual differences in attachment: An investigation into stability, implications, and relationships to early language development.* Unpublished doctoral dissertation, Syracuse University, 1976.

Connolly, K., & Stratton, P. An exploration of some parameters affecting classical conditioning in the neonate. *Child Development,* 1969, *40,* 431–441.

Conrad, C. C. When you're young at heart. Aging. Administration on Aging, U.S. Department of Health, Education, and Welfare, 11, 1976.

Constantinople, A. An Eriksonian measure of personality development in college students. *Developmental Psychology,* 1969, *1,* 357–372.

Coopersmith, S. *The antecedents of self-esteem.* San Francisco: Freeman, 1967.

Coopersmith, S. A. A method of determining types of self-esteem. *Journal of Abnormal and Social Psychology,* 1959, *59,* 87–94.

Corbin, H. D., & Tait, W. J. *Education for leisure.* Englewood Cliffs, N.J.: Prentice-Hall, 1973.

Corbin, J. N. *The effects of counselor-assisted exploratory activity on career development.* Unpublished doctoral dissertation, Columbia University, 1974.

Corrigan, R. Language development as related to stage 6 object permanence development. *Journal of Child Language,* 1978, *5,* 173–190.

Corrigan, R. The effects of task and practice on search for invisibly displaced objects. *Developmental Review,* 1981, *1,* 1–17.

Cowan, P. A. *Piaget with feeling.* New York: Holt, Rinehart & Winston, 1978.

Cowen, P. A., Langer, J., Heavenrich, J., & Nathanson, M. Social learning of Piaget's cognitive theory of moral development. *Journal of Personality and Social Psychology,* 1969, *11,* 211–274.

Craik, F. I. M. Age differences in human memory. In J. E. Birren & K. W. Schaie (eds.), *Handbook of the psychology of aging.* New York: Van Nostrand Reinhold, 1977.

Craik, F. I. M. Age differences in memory: The roles of attention and depth of processing. In L. W. Poon (ed.), *Aging in the 1980s.* Washington, D.C.: American Psychological Association, 1980.

Craik, F. I. M., & Lockhart, R. S. Levels of processing: A framework for memory research. *Journal of Verbal Learning and Verbal Behavior,* 1972, *11,* 671–684.

Craik, F. I. M., & Tulving, E. Depth of processing and the retention of words in episodic memory. *Journal of Experimental Psychology: General,* 1975, *104,* 268–294.

Crandall, V. C., & Battle, E. S. The antecedents and adult correlates of academic and intellectual achievement effort. In J. P. Hill (ed.), *Minnesota Symposia on Child Psychology* (vol. 4). Minneapolis: University of Minnesota Press, 1970.

Crandall, V. J., & Rabson, A. Children's repetition choices in an intellectual achievement situation following success and failure. *Journal of Genetic Psychology,* 1960, *97,* 161–168.

Cratty, B. *Perceptual and motor development in infants and children,* 2nd ed. Englewood Cliffs, N.J.: Prentice-Hall, 1978.

Crick, M. *Explorations in language and meaning: Toward a semantic anthropology.* New York: Halsted Press, 1977.

Cronbach, L. J. *Essentials of psychological testing.* New York: Harper & Row, 1970.

Cronbach, L. J. Five decades of public controversy over mental testing. *American Psychologist,* 1975, *30,* 1–14.

Cronbach, L. J., & Snow, R. E. *Aptitudes and instructional methods.* New York: Irvington Books, 1977.

Crook, M. N., Alexander, E. A., Anderson, E. M. S., Coules, J., Hanson, J. A., & Jeffries, N. T. Age and form perception. U.S. Air Force School of Aviation Medicine Report, No. 57–124. 1962.

Crookall, R. *The supreme adventure: Analyses of psychic communications.* London: James Clarke, 1961.

Cross, K. P. A critical review of state and national studies of the needs and interests of adult learners. In C. B. Stalford (ed.), *Conference Report: Adult learning needs and the demand for life-long learning.* Washington D.C.: National Institute of Education, U.S. Department of Health, Education, and Welfare, 1978.

Cross, T. G. Mothers' speech and its association with rate of syntactic acquisition in young children. In N. Waterson & C. Snow (eds.), *The development of communication.* New York: John Wiley, 1978.

Cuming, E., & Henry, W. *Growing old.* New York: Basic Books, 1961.

Cundick, B. P. Measures of intelligence on Southwest Indian students. *Journal of Social Psychology,* 1970, *81,* 319–337.

Cunningham, W. R. *The cascade model of intellectual functioning.* Paper presented at the Annual Meeting of the American Psychological Association, Los Angeles, August 1981.

Curtiss, S. Genie: A psycholinguistic study of a modern-day "wild child." New York: Academic Press, 1978.

Cushna, B. *Agency and birth order differences in early childhood.* Paper presented at the meeting of the American Psychological Association, New York, 1966.

Cutler, N. E., & Bengtson, V. L. Age and political alienation: Maturation, generation, and period effects. *Annals of the American Academy of Politics and Social Sciences,* 1974, *415,* 160–175.

d

Dale, P. *Language development: Structure and function* (2nd ed.). New York: Holt, Rinehart & Winston, 1976.

Dale, P. Is early pragmatic development measurable? *Journal of Child Language,* 1980, *1,* 1–12.

Damon, W. *The social world of the child.* San Francisco: Jossey-Bass, 1977.

Danks, J. H., & Schwent, M. A. Comprehension of prenominal adjective orders. *Memory and Cognition,* 1974, *2,* 34–38.

Datan, N., & Ginsberg, L. H. (eds.). *Life-span developmental psychology: Normative life crises.* New York: Academic Press, 1978.

Davis, G. A. *Creativity is forever.* Cross Plains, Wisc.: Badger Press, 1981.

Davison, G. C., & Neale, J. M. *Abnormal psychology.* New York: John Wiley, 1975.

Day, M. C. Developmental trends in visual scanning. In H. W. Reese (ed.), *Advances in child development and behavior* (vol. 10). New York: Academic Press, 1975.

Day, P. S., & Ulatowska, H. K. Perceptual, cognitive, and linguistic development after early hemispherectomy: Two case studies. *Brain and Language,* 1979, *1,* 17–33.

Dayton, G. O., Jr., Jones, J. H., Aiu, P., Rossen, P. H., Steel, B., & Rose, M. Developmental study of coordinated eye movements in the human infant. I: Visual acuity in the newborn human: A study based on induced optokinetic nystagmus recorded by electrooculography. *Archives of Opthalmology,* 1964, *71,* 865–870.

de Chateau, P. The importance of the neonatal period for the development of synchrony in the mother-infant dyad: A review. *Birth and the Family Journal,* 1977, *4,* 10–23.

DeLissovoy, V. High school marriage: A longitudinal study. *Journal of Marriage and the Family,* 1973, *35,* 245–255.

Demsey, D. *The way we die.* New York: McGraw-Hill, 1975.

Denckla, W. D. Role of the pituitary and thyroid glands in the decline of minimal O² consumption with age. *Journal of Clinical Investigation*, 1974, *53*, 572–581.

Denney, N. *A model of cognitive development across the lifespan*. Paper presented at the Meeting of the American Psychological Association, Los Angeles, Calif., August 1981.

Denney, N. W., & Palmer, A. M. Adult age differences in traditional and practical problem-solving measures. *Journal of Gerontology*, in press.

Denney, N. W., & Pearce, K. A. *A developmental study of adults' performance on traditional and practical problem solving tasks*. Unpublished manuscript, University of Kansas, 1981.

Dennis, W. Creative productivity between the ages of 20 and 80 years. *Journal of Gerontology*, 1966, *21*, 1–18.

Department of Health, Education, and Welfare. *Highlights from drug use among American high school students, 1975–77*. (Publication No. [ADM] 78–621.) Washington, D.C.: August 1978.

deVries, H. A. Physiological effects of an exercise training regimen upon men aged 52 to 88. *Journal of Gerontology*, 1970, *25*, 325–336.

deVries, J. Untersuchung uber das Hupfspiel: Kinderspiel-Kulttanz (FF Communication No. 173). Helsinki, Finland: Suomalainen Tiedeakatemia Academia Scieniarum Fennica, 1957.

Dickson, P. D. *Children's oral communication skills*. New York: Academic Press, 1981.

Dickson, W. P. (ed.). *Children's oral communication skills*. New York: Academic Press, 1981.

Dihoff, R. E., & Chapman, R. S. First words: Their origins in action. Stanford University: *Papers and Reports on Child Language Development*, 1977, *13*, 1–7.

Diller, P. *The joys of aging and how to avoid them*. Garden City, N.Y.: Doubleday, 1981. Copyright © 1981 by Phyllis Diller. Reprinted by permission of Doubleday & Company, Inc.

Dion, K. K. Children's physical attractiveness and sex as determinants of adults' punitiveness. *Developmental Psychology*, 1974, *10*, 772–778.

DiVitto, B., & Goldberg, S. The development of early parent-infant interaction as a function of newborn medical status. In T. Field, A. Sostek, S. Goldberg, & H. H. Shuman (eds.), *Infants born at risk*. Holliswood, N.Y.: Spectrum, 1979.

Donovan, W. A., Leavitt, L. A., & Balling, J. D. Maternal physiological response to infant signals. *Psychopsio*, 1978, *15*, 68–74.

Douvan, E., & Adelson, J. *The adolescent experience*. New York: John Wiley, 1966.

Dove, A. Taking the chitling test. *Newsweek*, July 15, 1968, pp. 51–52.

Drillien, C. M. *The growth and development of the prematurely born infant*. Baltimore, Md.: Williams & Wilkins, 1964.

Duberman, L. Step-kin relationships. *Journal of Marriage and Family*, 1973, *35*, 282–292.

Dudek, S. Z. Creativity in young children—Attitude or ability? *Journal of Creative Behavior*, 1974, *8*(4), 282–292.

Dulit, E. Adolescent thinking à la Piaget: The formal stage. *Journal of Youth and Adolescence*, 1972, *1*, 281–301.

Duncker, K. On problem solving. *Psychological Monographs*, 1945, *58*(5, Whole No. 270).

Dunphy, D. C. The social structure of urban adolescent peer groups. *Society*, 1963, *26*, 230–246.

Durio, H. F. Mental imagery and creativity. *Journal of Creative Behavior*, 1975, *9*(4), 233–244.

Dusek, J. B., & Flaherty, F. The development of the self-concept during the adolescent years. *Monographs of the Society for Research in Child Development*, 1981, serial no. 191 (vol. 46, no. 4).

Dweck, C. S. The role of expectations and attributions in the alleviation of learned helplessness. *Journal of Personality and Social Psychology*, 1975, *31*, 674–685.

Dweck, C. S. Achievement. In E. M. Hetherington (ed.), *Carmichael's manual of child psychology* (4th ed.). New York: John Wiley, in press.

Dweck, C. S., & Bush, E. S. Sex differences in learned helplessness: I. Differential debilitation with peer and adult evaluators. *Developmental Psychology*, 1976, *12*, 147–156.

Dweck, C. S., & Gilliard, D. Expectancy statements as determinants of reactions to failure: Sex differences in persistence and expectancy change. *Journal of Personality and Social Psychology*, 1975, *32*, 1077–1088.

Dweck, C. S., & Reppucci, N. D. Learned helplessness and reinforcement responsibility in children. *Journal of Personality and Social Psychology*, 1973, *25*, 109–116.

Dyer, E. Parenthood as crisis: A restudy. *Marriage and Family Living*, 1963, *25*, 488–496.

e

Easterbrooks, M. A., & Lamb, M. E. The relationship between quality of infant-mother attachment and infant peer competence in initial encounters with peers. *Child Development*, 1979, *50*, 380–387.

Ebbinghaus, H. *Uber das gedachtris: Untersuchungen Zur experimentellen psychologie*. Leipzig: Duncker and Humbolt, 1885. (Translated by H. A. Ruger and C. E. Bussenius, 1913, and reissued by Dover publications, 1964).

Ebon, M. *The evidence for life after death*. New York: New American Library, 1977.

Eckerman, C. O., Whatley, J. L., & Kutz, S. L. The growth of social play with peers during the second year of life. *Developmental Psychology*, 1975, *11*, 42–49.

Edwards, M. Coupling and re-coupling vs. the challenge of being single. *Personnel and Guidance Journal*, 1977, *55*, 542–545.

Ehrhardt, A., & Baker, S. W. *Hormonal aberrations and their implications for the understanding of normal sex differentiation*. Paper presented at the meeting of the Society for Research in Child Development, Philadelphia, March 1973.

Ehrlich, P. *Mutual help for community elderly.* Unpublished manuscript. Carbondale, Ill.: Southern Illinois University, 1979.

Eiduson, G. T., & Zimmerman, I. L. *Implications of research on the family for policy.* Paper presented at the American Psychological Association Convention, 1978.

Eimas, P. D. Speech perception in early infancy. In L. B. Cohen & P. Salapatek (eds.), *Infant perception: From sensation to cognition* (vol. 2). New York: Academic Press, 1975.

Eitzen, D. S. Athletics in the status system of male adolescents: A replication of Coleman's *The Adolescent Society. Adolescence,* 1975, *10,* 267–276.

Elder, G. H. Democratic parent-youth relationships in cross-national perspective. *Social Science Quarterly,* 1968, *40,* 216–228.

Elder, G. H. *Children of the great depression.* Chicago: University of Chicago Press, 1974.

Eliade, M. *Shamanism: Archaic techniques of ecstasy.* Princeton, N.J.: Princeton University Press, 1964 (Originally published, 1951).

Elkin, F., & Westley, W. A. The myth of the adolescent culture. *American Sociological Review,* 1955, *20,* 680–684.

Elkind, D. Quantity conceptions in junior and senior high school students. *Child Development,* 1961, *32,* 551–560.

Elkind, D. Egocentrism in adolescence. *Child Development,* 1967, *38,* 1025–1034.

Elkind, D. Piagetian and psychometric conceptions of intelligence. *Harvard Educational Review,* 1969, *39,* 319–337.

Elkind, D. *Sympathetic understanding of the child six to sixteen.* Boston: Allyn & Bacon, 1971.

Elkind, D. *Child development and education: A Piagetian perspective.* New York: Oxford University Press, 1976.

Elkind, D. *The child's reality: Three developmental themes.* Hillsdale, N.J.: Erlbaum, 1978.

Elkind, D. Understanding the young adolescent. *Adolescence,* 1978, *13,* 127–134.

Elkind, D., & Bowen, R. Imaginary audience behavior in children and adolescents. *Developmental Psychology,* 1980, *15,* 38–44. David Elkind is Professor and Chairman of the Eliot-Pearson Department of Child Study, Tufts University, Medford, Massachusetts.

Emmerich, W., Goldman, K. S., Kirsh, B., & Sharabany, R. Evidence for a transitional phase in the development of gender constancy. *Developmental Psychology,* in press.

Emmerich, W., Goldman, K. S., & Shore, R. E. Differentiation and development of social norms. *Journal of Personality and Social Psychology,* 1971, *18,* 323–353.

Engelmann, S. How to construct effective language programs for the poverty child. In F. Williams (ed.), *Language and poverty.* Chicago: Markham, 1970.

Engen, T., Lipsitt, L. P., & Kaye, H. Olfactory responses and adaptation in the human neonate. *Journal of Comparative and Physiological Psychology,* 1963, *56,* 73–77.

Enright, R. D., & Lapsley, D. K. Social role-taking: A review of the constructs, measures, and measurement properties. *Review of Educational Research,* 1980, *50,* (4), 647–674.

Epstein, J., & McPartland, J. The concept and measurement of the quality of school life. *American Educational Research Journal,* 1976, *13,* 15–30.

Erikson, E. H. *Childhood and society.* New York: Norton, 1952.

Erikson, E. H. *Young man Luther.* New York: Norton, 1962.

Erikson, E. H. *Childhood and society.* New York: Norton, 1963.

Erikson, E. H. *Identity: Youth and crisis.* New York: Norton, 1968.

Erikson, E. H. *Gandhi's truth.* New York: Norton, 1969.

Erikson, E. H. Once more the inner space: Letter to a former student. In J. Strouse (ed.), *Women and analysis.* New York: Dell, 1974.

Espinoza, R., & Newman, Y. Step-parenting. DHEW Publication N (ADM) 78–579. Washington, D.C.: U.S. Government Printing Office, 1979.

Esposito, D. Homogeneous and heterogeneous ability grouping: Principal findings and implications for evaluating and designing more effective educational environments. *Review of Educational Research,* 1973, *43,* 163–179.

Eysenck, M. W. Age differences in incidental learning. *Developmental Psychology,* 1974, *10,* 936–941.

Fagan, J. F. An attention model of infant recognition. *Child Development,* 1977, *48,* 345–359.

Fagot, B. I. Influence of teacher behavior in the preschool. *Developmental Psychology,* 1973, *9,* 198–206.

Fagot, B. I. *Teacher reinforcement of feminine-preferred behavior revisited.* Paper presented at the meeting of the Society for Research in Child Development, Denver, April 1975.

Fantz, R. L. The origin of form perception. *Scientific American,* 1961, *204,* 66–72.

Fantz, R. L., Fagan, J. F., & Miranda, S. B. Early visual acuity. In L. B. Cohen & P. Salapatek (eds.), *Infant perception: From sensation to cognition* (vol. 2). New York: Academic Press, 1975. (a)

Fantz, R. L., Fagan, J. F., & Miranda, S. B. Early visual acuity. In L. B. Cohen & P. Salapatek (eds.), *Infant perception: From sensation to cognition* (vol. 1). New York: Academic Press, 1975. (b)

Fantz, R. L., & Nevis, S. Pattern preferences and perceptual-cognitive development in early infancy. *Merrill-Palmer Quarterly,* 1967, *13,* 77–108.

Faranoff, A., Kennell, J., & Klaus, M. Follow-up of low birth weight infants: The predictive value of maternal visiting programs. *Pediatrics,* 1972, *49,* 287–290.

Farkas, M. S., & Hoyer, W. J. Processing consequences of perceptual grouping in selective attention. *Journal of Gerontology,* 1980, *35,* 207–216.

Farnsworth, P. R., McNemar, O., & McNemar, Q. (eds.), *Annual Review of Psychology,* vol. 16. Palo Alto, Calif.: Annual Reviews, 1965.

Farrell, M. P., & Rosenberg, S. D. *Men at midlife*. Boston, Mass.: Auburn House, 1981.

Fast, I., & Cain, A. The stepparent role: Potential for disturbance in family functioning. *American Journal of Orthopsychiatry*, 1966, *36*, 485–491.

Faust, M. Somatic development of adolescent girls. *Monographs of the Society for Research in Child Development*, 1977, serial no. 169, vol. 42, no. 1.

Faust, M. S. Developmental maturity as a determinant in prestige of adolescent girls. *Child Development*, 1960, *31*, 173–184.

Featherman, D. L. Schooling and occupational careers: Constancy and change in worldly success. In O. G. Brim & J. Kagan (eds.), *Constancy and change in human development*. Cambridge, Mass.: Harvard University Press, 1980.

Fein, G. G. *Child development*. Englewood Cliffs, N.J.: Prentice-Hall, 1978.

Feiring, C., & Lewis, M. The child as a member of the family system. *Behavioral Science*, 1978, *23*, 225–233.

Feldman, H. Development of the husband-wife relationship. Preliminary report. Cornell Studies of Marital Development, Cornell University, Ithaca, N.Y., 1964.

Feldman, S. S., & Nash, S. C. Changes in responsiveness to babies during adolescence. *Child Development*, 1979, *50*, 942–949.

Field, T. The three Rs of infant-adult interactions: Rhythms, repertoires, and responsivity. *Journal of Pediatric Psychology*, 1978, *3*, 131–136.

Finch, C. E. The regulation of physiological changes during mammalian aging. *The Quarterly Review of Biology*, 1976, *51*, 49–83.

Fischer, K. W. A theory of cognitive development: The control and construction of hierarchies of skills. *Psychological Review*, 1980, *87*, 477–531.

Fischer, K. W. Human cognitive development in the first four years. *Behavioral and Brain Sciences*, 1982.

Fischer, K. W., & Jennings, S. The emergence of representation in search: Understanding the hider as an independent agent. *Quarterly Review of Development*, 1981, *1*, 18–30.

Fischer, K. W., & Lazerson, A. *Human development*. New York: Worth, in press.

Fiske, M. Tasks and crises of the second half of life: The interrelationship of commitment, coping, and adaptation. In J. E. Birren & R. B. Sloane (eds.), *Handbook of mental health and aging*. Englewood Cliffs, N.J.: Prentice-Hall, 1980.

Flaherty, J. F., & Dusek, J. B. An investigation of the relationship between psychological androgyny and components of self-concept. *Journal of Personality and Social Psychology*, 1980, *38*, 984–992.

Flanagan, J. *Some characteristics of 70-year-old workers*. Paper presented at the Annual Meeting of the American Psychological Association, Los Angeles, California, August 1981.

Flavell, J. H. Developmental studies of mediated memory. In L. P. Lipsitt & H. W. Reese (eds.), *Advances in child development and behavior*. New York: Academic Press, 1970.

Flavell, J. H. An analysis of cognitive-developmental sequences. *Genetic Psychology Monographs*, 1972, *86*, 279–350.

Flavell, J. H. The development of inferences about others. In T. Mischel (ed.), *Understanding other persons*. Oxford, England: Blackwell, Basil, Mott, 1974.

Flavell, J. H. *Cognitive development*. Englewood Cliffs, N.J.: Prentice-Hall, 1977.

Flavell, J. H. Metacognition and cognitive monitoring: A new area of psychological inquiry. *American Psychologist*, 1979, *34*, 906–911.

Flavell, J. H. A tribute to Piaget. *Society for Research in Child Development Newsletter*, Fall 1980.

Flavell, J. H. Cognitive monitoring. In W. P. Dickson (ed.), *Children's oral communication skills*. New York: Academic Press, 1981.

Flavell, J. H. Structures, stages, and sequences in cognitive development. In W. A. Collins (ed.), *The concept of development: The Minnesota symposia on child psychology*. Hillsdale, N.J.: Erlbaum, in press.

Flavell, J. H., Abrahams, B. A., Croft, K., & Flavell, E. R. Young children's knowledge about visual perception. *Developmental Psychology*, in press.

Flavell, J. H., Botkin, P. T., Fry, C. L., Jr., Wright, J. W., & Jarvis, P. E. *The development of role-taking and communication skills in children*. New York: John Wiley, 1968.

Flavell, J. H., Shipstead, S. G., & Croft, K. *What young children think you see when their eyes are closed*. Unpublished manuscript, Palo Alto, Calif: Stanford University, 1978.

Folger, J. P., & Chapman, R. S. A pragmatic analysis of spontaneous imitations. *Journal of Child Language*, 1978, *5*, 25–38.

Forbes, R. H. *National assessment change data: Science, writing, and functional illiteracy*. Paper presented at the meeting of the American Educational Research Association, San Francisco, 1976.

Ford, M. *On the other side*. Plainfield, N.J.: Logos International, 1978.

Ford, M. The construct validity of egocentrism. *Psychological Bulletin*, 1979, *86*, 1169–1188.

Ford, M. Social cognition and social competence in adolescence. *Developmental Psychology*, 1982.

Ford, M. E., & Keating, D. P. Developmental and individual differences in long-term memory retrieval: Process and organization. *Child Development*, 1981, *52*, 234–241.

Foreman, J. Looking for Mr. . . . Anybody. *Boston Globe*, December 2, 1981.

Foster, G. M., & Anderson, B. G. *Medical anthropology*. New York: John Wiley, 1978.

Fowler, J. Stages in faith: The structural-developmental approach. In T. Hennessy (ed.), *Values and moral development*. New York: Paulist Press, 1976.

Fozard, J. L., Wolf, E., Bell, B., McFarland, R. A., & Podolsky, S. Visual perception and communication. In J. E. Birren & K. W. Schaie (eds.), *Handbook of the psychology of aging*. New York: Van Nostrand Reinhold, 1977.

Fraiberg, S. *Every child's birthright: In defense of mothering.* New York: Basic Books, 1977.

Fraiberg, S. *Insights from the blind: Comparative studies of blind and sighted infants.* New York: Basic Books, 1977.

Freuchen, P. *Book of the Eskimos.* Cleveland: World Press, 1961.

Freud, A., & Dann, S. An experiment in group upbringing. In R. S. Eisler, A. Freud, H. Hartmann, & E. Kris (eds.), *The psychoanalytic study of the child* (vol. 6). New York: International Universities Press, 1951.

Freud, S. *New introductory lectures on psycho-analysis.* New York: Norton, 1933.

Freud, S. *An outline of psychoanalysis.* New York: Norton, 1949.

Freud, S. *Collected papers.* New York: Basic Books, 1959.

Freud, S. *Collected papers,* vols. I, II, III, IV. New York: Basic Books, 1959.

Friedenberg, E. Current patterns of a generation conflict. *Journal of Social Issues,* 1969, *25,* 21–38.

Friedlander, B. Receptive language development in infancy. *Merrill-Palmer Quarterly,* 1970, *16,* 7–51.

Friedman, M., & Rosenman, R. H. *Type A behavior and your heart.* New York: Knopf, 1974.

Friedrich, L. K., & Stein, A. H. Aggressive and prosocial TV programs and the natural behavior of preschool children. *Monograph of the Society for Research in Child Development,* 1973, *38* (4, serial no. 151).

Fries, J. F. Aging, natural death, and the compression of morbidity. The *New England Journal of Medicine,* 1980, *303,* 130–135.

Fromm, E. *The sane society.* New York: Fawcett Books, 1955.

Fromm, E., & Maccoby, M. *Social character in a Mexican village.* Englewood Cliffs, N.J.: Prentice-Hall, 1970.

Fry, P. S. The development of differentiation in self-evaluations: A cross-cultural study. *Journal of Psychology,* 1974, *87,* 193–202.

Fullard, W., & Reiling, A. M. An investigation of Lorenz's "babyness." *Child Development,* 1976, *47,* 1191–1193.

Furman, W., Rahe, D. F., & Hartup, W. W. Rehabilitation of socially withdrawn preschool children through mixed-age and same-age socialization. *Child Development,* 1979, *50,* 915–922.

Furrow, D., Nelson, K., & Benedict, H. Mothers' speech to children and syntactic development: Some simple relationships. *Journal of Child Language,* 1979, *6,* 423–442.

Furth, H. G. Linguistic deficiency and thinking: Research with deaf subjects, 1964–69. *Psychological Bulletin,* 1971, *75,* 58–72.

Furth, H. G., & Wachs, H. *Thinking goes to school.* New York: Oxford University Press, 1975.

g

Gage, N. L. Desirable behaviors of teachers. *Urban Education,* 1965, *1,* 85–95.

Gagné, R. M. *The conditions of learning* (3rd ed.). New York: Holt, Rinehart & Winston, 1977.

Gallup, G. Self-recognition in primates. A comparative approach to the bidirectional properties of consciousness. *American Psychologist,* 1977, *32,* 329–338.

Gallup, G. R. *The Gallup Poll: Public Opinion 1935–1971.* New York: Random House, 1972.

Gallup, G., Jr., & Poling, D. *The search for America's faith.* Nashville, Tenn.: Abingdon, 1980.

Galst, J. Q. Television food commercials and pro-nutritional public service announcements as determinants of young children's snack choices. *Child Development,* 1980, *51,* 935–938.

Garbarino, J. The ecological correlates of child abuse: The impact of socioeconomic stress on mothers. *Child Development,* 1976, *47,* 178–185.

Gardner, B. T., & Gardner, R. A. Two-way communication with an infant chimpanzee. In A. Schrier & F. Stollnitz (eds.), *Behavior of nonhuman primates* (vol. 4). New York: Academic Press, 1971.

Garmezy, N. Intervention with children at risk for behavior pathology. *Clinical Psychologist,* 1975, *28,* 12–14.

Garmezy, N., & Rutter, M. Stress and coping in children. In E. M. Hetherington (ed.), *Carmichael's manual of child psychology* (4th ed.). New York: John Wiley, in press.

Garrett, H. E. A developmental theory of intelligence. *American Psychologist,* 1946, *1,* 372–378.

Garrison, K. C. Physiological changes in adolescence. In J. F. Adams (ed.), *Understanding adolescence: Current developments in adolescent psychology.* Boston: Allyn & Bacon, 1968.

Garvey, C. *Play.* Cambridge, Mass.: Harvard University Press, 1977.

Gatewood, T. E. What research says about the junior high versus the middle school. *North Central Association Quarterly,* 1971, *46,* 264–276.

Gatz, M. Introduction, Section on Clinical Issues. In L. W. Poon (ed.), *Aging in the 1980s.* Washington, D.C.: American Psychological Association, 1980.

Gatz, M., Smyer, M. A., & Lawton, M. P. The mental health system and the older adult. In L. W. Poon (ed.), *Aging in the 1980s.* Washington, D.C.: American Psychological Association, 1980.

Gay, J., & Tweney, R. D. Comprehension and production of standard and black English by lower-class black children. *Developmental Psychology,* 1976, *12,* 262–268.

Geis, G., & Monahan, J. The social ecology of violence. In T. Lickona (ed.), *Moral development and behavior.* New York: Holt, Rinehart & Winston, 1976.

Gelman, R. Cognitive development. *Annual Review of Psychology,* 1978, *29,* 297–332.

Gesell, A. The ontogenesis of infant behavior. In L. Carmichael (ed.), *Manual of child psychology.* New York: John Wiley, 1954.

Gesell, A., & Amatruda, C. S. *Developmental diagnosis.* New York: Hoeber, 1941.

Gesell, A., & Amatruda, C. S. *Developmental diagnosis.* New York: Hoeber, 1951.

Gesell, A., & Ilg, F. L. *Child development.* New York: Harper & Row, 1949.

Getzels, J. W. Problem finding and inventiveness of solutions. *Journal of Creative Behavior,* 1975, *9,* 12–18.

Getzels, J. W., & Dillon, T. J. The nature of giftedness and the education of the gifted. In R. M. W. Travers (ed.), *Second handbook of research on teaching.* Chicago: Rand McNally, 1973.

Gewirtz, J. L. Attachment and dependence, and a distinction in terms of stimulus control. In J. L. Gewirtz (ed.), *Attachment and dependency.* Washington, D.C.: V. H. Winston & Sons, 1972, p. 139–177.

Gewirtz, J. L., & Gewirtz, H. B. Stimulus conditions, infant behaviors, and social learning in four Israeli child-rearing environments: A preliminary report illustrating differences in environment and behavior between the "only" and the "youngest" child. In B. M. Foss (ed.), *Determinants of infant behavior* (vol. 3). New York: John Wiley, 1965.

Ghiselli, E. E. *The validity of occupational aptitude tests.* New York: John Wiley, 1966.

Giambra, L. M., & Arenberg, D. Problem solving, concept learning and aging. In L. W. Poon (ed.), *Aging in the 1980s.* Washington, D.C.: American Psychological Association, 1980.

Gibson, E. J. *Principles of perceptual learning and development.* New York: Appleton-Century-Crofts, 1969.

Gibson, E. J. *The ecological approach to visual perception.* Boston: Houghton-Mifflin, 1979.

Gibson, E. J., & Levin, H. *The psychology of reading.* Cambridge, Mass.: MIT Press, 1975.

Ginsberg, E. Toward a theory of occupational choice: A restatement. *Vocational Guidance Quarterly,* 1972, *20,* 169–176.

Ginsberg, E., Ginsberg, S. W., Axelrad, S., & Hermna, J. L. *Occupational choice.* New York: Columbia University, 1951.

Ginsburg, H. J., & Opper, S. *Piaget's theory of intellectual development.* Englewood Cliffs, N.J.: Prentice-Hall, 1980.

Glaser, B. G., & Strauss, A. L. *Awareness of dying.* Chicago: Aldine, 1965.

Glenn, N. Psychological well-being in the post-parental stage: Some evidence from national surveys. *Journal of Marriage and the Family,* 1975, *37,* 105–111.

Glick, P. C. Future American Families. The Washington COFO MEMO 2 (Summer/Fall), 1979.

Glick, P. C., & Carter, H. *Marriage and divorce: A social and economic study,* 2nd ed. Cambridge, Mass.: Harvard University Press, 1976.

Glucksberg, S., Krauss, R., & Higgins, E. T. The development of referential communication skills. In F. D. Horowitz (ed.), *Review of child development research* (vol. 4). Chicago: University of Chicago Press, 1975.

Glucksberg, S., & Krauss, R. M. What do people say after they have learned to talk? *Merrill-Palmer Quarterly,* 1967, *13,* 309–316.

Glueck, S., & Glueck, E. *Unraveling juvenile delinquency.* Cambridge, Mass.: Harvard University Press, 1950.

Goebel, B. L., & Brown, D. R. Age differences in motivation related to Maslow's need hierarchy. *Developmental Psychology,* 1981, *17,* 809–815.

Gold, D., Andres, D., & Glorieux, J. The development of Francophone nursery school children with employed and nonemployed mothers. *Canadian Journal of Behavioral Science,* 1979, *11,* 169–173.

Gold, M. Undetected delinquent behavior. *Journal of Research on Crime and Delinquency,* 1966, *3,* 27–46.

Goldberg, R. J. *Maternal time use and preschool performance.* Paper presented at the meeting of the Society for Research in Child Development, New Orleans, March 1977.

Goldberg, S. Prematurity: Effects on parent-infant interaction. *Merrill-Palmer Quarterly,* 1977, *23,* 163–177.

Goldberg, S., Brachfeld, S., & DiVitto, B. Feeding, fussing, and play. In T. M. Field, S. Goldberg, D. Stern, & A. M. Sostek (eds.), *High-risk infants and children: Adult and peer interactions.* New York: Academic Press, 1980.

Goldfarb, W. Psychological privation in infancy and subsequent adjustment. *American Journal of Orthopsychiatry,* 1945, *15,* 247–255.

Goldman, S. R., Pellegrino, J. W., Parseghian, P., & Sallis, R. Developmental and individual differences in verbal analogical reasoning. *Child Development,* in press.

Golinkoff, R. A. A comparison of reading comprehension processes in good and poor comprehenders. *Reading Research Quarterly,* 1975–1976, *11,* 623–659.

Gollin, E. S. Factors affecting the visual recognition of incomplete objects: A comparative investigation of children and adults. *Perceptual Motor Skills,* 1962, *15,* 583–590.

Gonda, J. Convocation on work, aging, and retirement: A review. *Human Development,* 1981, *24,* 286–292.

Gondonneau, J., Mironer, L., Dourlin-Rollier, A. M., & Simon, P. *Rapport sur le Comportement Sexuel des Francais.* Paris: Pierre Charron et Rene Juillard, 1972.

Good, T. L., Biddle, B., & Brophy, J. E. *Teachers make a difference.* New York: Holt, Rinehart & Winston, 1975.

Good, T. L., & Brophy, J. E. Changing teacher and student behavior: An empirical investigation. *Journal of Educational Psychology,* 1974, *66,* 390–405.

Gordon, D. C. *Overcoming the fear of death.* New York: MacMillan, 1970.

Gordon, T. *Parent effectiveness training.* New York: New American Library, 1970.

Gottlieb, D. Teaching and students: The views of Negro and white teachers. *Sociology of Education,* 1966, *37,* 345–353.

Gottlieb, D., & Ramsey, C. *The American adolescent.* Homewood, Ill.: Dorsey Press, 1964.

Gottman, J. H., & Parkhurst, J. T. *A developmental theory of friendship and acquaintanceship processes.* Paper presented at the Minnesota Symposium of Child Psychology, October 1978.

Gould, R. L. Adult life stages: Growth toward self-tolerance. *Psychology Today,* 1975, *8,* 74–78.

Gould, R. L. *Transformations: Growth and change in adult life.* New York: Simon and Schuster, 1978.

Gould, R. L. Transformations during early and middle adult years. In N. J. Smelser & E. H. Erikson (eds.), *Themes of work and love in adulthood.* Cambridge, Mass.: Harvard University Press, 1980.

Gratch, G. A study of the relative dominance of vision and touch in six-month-old infants. *Child Development,* 1972, *43,* 615–623.

Gratch, G. Review of Piagetian infancy research: Object concept development. In W. F. Overton & J. M. Gallagher (eds.), *Knowledge and development* (vol. 1). New York: Plenum, 1977.

Green, R. One-hundred-ten feminine and masculine boys: Behavioral contrasts and demographic similarities. *Archives of Sexual Behavior,* 1974, *5,* 425–446.

Green, R. F., & Berkowitz, B. Changes in intellect with age: II. Factorial analyses of Wechsler-Bellevue scores. *The Journal of Genetic Psychology,* 1964, *104,* 3–18.

Greenacre, P. The childhood of the artist. In P. Greenacre (ed.), *Emotional growth.* New York: International Universities Press, 1971.

Greenberg, B. S., & Domonick, J. R. *Television behavior among disadvantaged children.* Unpublished manuscript, Michigan State University, East Lansing, Michigan, 1969.

Greenfield, J. *A child called Noah.* New York: Holt, Rinehart & Winston, 1972. From *A Child Called Noah* by Josh Greenfield. Copyright © 1970, 1971, 1972 by Josh Greenfield. Reprinted by permission of Holt, Rinehart and Winston, Publishers.

Gribbons, W. D., & Lohnes, P. R. Relationships among measures of readiness for vocational planning. *Journal of Counseling Psychology,* 1964, *11,* 13–19.

Grimes, J. W., & Allinsmith, W. Compulsivity, anxiety, and school achievement. *Merrill-Palmer Quarterly,* 1961, *7,* 247–269.

Grof, S., & Halifax, J. *The human encounter with death.* New York: Dutton, 1977.

Gronseth, E. The family in capitalist society and the dysfunctionality of the husband-provider role. In J. M. Henslin & L. Reynolds (eds.), *Social institutions as appendages to market society.* New York: McKay, 1972.

Grotevant, H. D. Environmental influences on vocational interest development in adolescents from adoptive and biological families. *Child Development,* 1979, *50,* 854–860.

Grotevant, H. D., Scarr, S., & Weinberg, R. A. Patterns of interest similarity in adoptive and biological families. *Journal of Personality and Social Psychology,* 1977, *35,* 667–676.

Gubrium, J. F. *Living and dying at Murray Manor.* New York: St. Martin's Press, 1975.

Guilford, J. P. *The nature of human intelligence.* New York: McGraw-Hill, 1967.

Gurland, B. J. The comparative frequency of depression in various adult age groups. *Journal of Gerontology,* 1976, *31,* 283–292.

Gutmann, D. L. Parenthood: A key to the comparative study of the life cycle. In N. Datan & L. Ginsberg (eds.), *Life-span developmental psychology: Normative life crises.* New York: Academic Press, 1975.

Gutmann, D. L. The cross-cultural perspective: Notes toward a comparative psychology of aging. In J. E. Birren & K. W. Schaie (eds.), *Handbook of the psychology of aging.* New York: Van Nostrand Reinhold, 1977.

Guttentag, M., & Bray, H. *Undoing sex stereotypes, research and resources for educators.* New York: McGraw-Hill, 1976.

Gutteridge, M. V. A study of motor achievements of young children. *Archives de Psychologie,* 1939, No. 244.

h

Haeberle, E. *The sex atlas.* New York: Seaburg Press, 1978.

Hagen, J. W., & Hale, G. A. The development of attention in children. In A. D. Pick (ed.), *Minnesota symposia on child psychology* (vol. 7). Minneapolis: University of Minnesota Press, 1973.

Haith, M. M., & Campos, J. J. Human infancy. In *Annual Review of Psychology.* Palo Alto: Annual Review, 1977.

Hall, C. S., & Lindzey, G. *Theories of personality.* New York: John Wiley, 1978.

Hall, G. S. *Adolescence: Its psychology and its relations to physiology, anthropology, sociology, sex, crime, religion, and education* (vol. 1). Englewood Cliffs, N.J.: Prentice-Hall, 1904–1905.

Hall, G. S. *Senescence: The last half of life.* New York: Appleton-Century-Crofts, 1922.

Halliday, M. A. K. *Learning how to mean: Explorations in the development of language.* New York: Elsevier, 1975.

Halwes, T., & Jenkins, J. J. Problem of serial order in behavior is not resolved by context-associative memory models. *Psychological Review,* 1971, *78,* 122–129.

Hamdani, R. J. *Exploratory behavior and vocational development among disadvantaged inner-city adolescents.* Unpublished doctoral dissertation, Columbia University, New York, 1974.

Hamm, C. M. The content of moral education, or in defense of the "bag of virtues." *School Review,* 1977, *85,* 218–228.

Hammer, B. B. *The effects of two treatments designed to foster vocational development in disadvantaged inner-city adolescents.* Unpublished doctoral dissertation, Columbia University, 1974.

Hancock, E. The dimensions of meaning and belonging in the process of divorce. *American Journal of Orthopsychiatry,* 1980, *59,* 18–27.

Harlow, H. F. The nature of love. *The American Psychologist,* 1958, *13,* 673–685.

Harlow, H. F., & Harlow, M. K. The affectional systems. In A. M. Schrier, H. F. Harlow, and F. Stollnitz (eds.), *Behavior of nonhuman primates: Modern research trends* (vol. 2). New York: Academic Press, 1965.

Harris, C. S. *Fact book on aging: A profile of America's older population.* Washington, D.C.: National Council on Aging, 1978.

Harris, L. *The myth and reality of aging in America.* Washington, D.C.: National Council on Aging, 1975.

Harris, P. L. Development of search and object permanence during infancy. *Psychological Bulletin,* 1975, *82,* 332–344.

Harter, S. Developmental perspectives on the self-system. In E. M. Hetherington (ed.), *Carmichael's manual of child psychology,* vol. IV. New York: John Wiley, 1982.

Hartley, R. E., Frank, L. K., & Goldenson, R. M. *Understanding children's play.* New York: Columbia University Press, 1952.

Hartshorne, H., & May, M. S. *Studies in the nature of character. Studies in deceit* (vol. 1). *Studies in self-control* (vol. 2). *Studies in the organization of character* (vol. 3). New York: Macmillan, 1928–1930.

Hartup, W. W. Peer interaction and social organization. In P. H. Mussen (ed.), *Carmichael's manual of child psychology* (3rd ed., vol. 2). New York: John Wiley, 1970.

Hartup, W. W. Peer interaction and the development of the individual child. In E. Schopler & R. J. Reichler (eds.), *Psychopathology and child development.* New York: Plenum, 1976.

Hartup, W. W. The social worlds of childhood. *American Psychologist,* 1979, *34,* 944–950.

Hartup, W. W. Peers as a context for social development. In E. M. Hetherington (ed.), *Carmichael's manual of child psychology,* vol. IV. New York: John Wiley, 1982.

Hartup, W. W. The peer system. In E. M. Hetherington (ed.), *Carmichael's manual of child psychology,* 4th ed., vol. IV. New York: John Wiley, 1982.

Hartup, W. W., & Coates, B. Imitation of a peer as a function of reinforcement from the peer group and rewardingness of the model. *Child Development,* 1967, *38,* 1003–1016.

Hartup, W. W., & Lempers, J. A problem in life-span development. The interactional analysis of family attachment. In P. B. Baltes & K. W. Schaie (eds.), *Life-span developmental psychology: Personality and socialization.* New York: Academic Press, 1973.

Harvard Big Book of College Life. Crist, S. G., & Meyer, G. (eds.). Garden City, N.Y.: Doubleday, 1978.

Harway, M., & Astin, H. S. *Sex discrimination in career counseling and education.* New York: Praeger, 1977.

Hasher, L., & Zacks, R. T. Automatic and effortful processes in memory. *Journal of Experimental Psychology: General,* 1979, *108,* 356–388.

Havighurst, R. J. *Developmental tasks and education.* New York: McKay, 1952.

Havighurst, R. J. *Developmental tasks and education.* New York: McKay, 1972.

Havighurst, R. J. History of developmental psychology: Socialization and personality development through the lifespan. In P. B. Baltes & K. W. Schaie (eds.), *Life-span developmental psychology.* New York: Academic Press, 1973.

Havighurst, R. J., Bowman, P. H., Liddle, G. P., Matthews, C. V., & Pierce, J. V. *Growing up in River City.* New York: John Wiley, 1962.

Havighurst, R. J., & Neugarten, B. L. *American Indian and white children.* Chicago: University of Chicago Press, 1955.

Havighurst, R. J., Neugarten, B. L., & Tobin, S. S. Disengagement and patterns of aging. In B. L. Neugarten (ed.), *Middle age and aging.* Chicago: University of Chicago Press, 1968.

Hawkins, R. "Ropers" and "dopers." *Dallas Morning News,* October 29, 1979, p. 1.

Hay, D. F. Following their companions as a form of exploration for human infants. *Child Development,* 1977, *48,* 1628–1634.

Hay, D. F. Multiple functions of proximity seeking in infancy. *Child Development,* 1980, *51,* 636–645.

Hayes, K. J., & Hayes, C. Picture perception in a home-raised chimpanzee. *Journal of Comparative and Physiological Psychology,* 1951, *46,* 470–474.

Hayflick, L. The limited *in vitro* lifetime of human diploid cell strains. *Experimental Cell Research,* 1965, *37,* 614–636.

Hayflick, L. Why grow old? *Stanford Magazine,* September 1975, 36–43.

Hayflick, L. The cellular basis for biological aging. In C. E. Finch & L. Hayflick (eds.), *Handbook of the biology of aging.* New York: Van Nostrand Reinhold, 1977.

Heald, J. E. Mid-life career influence. *Vocational Guidance Quarterly,* 1977, *25,* 309–312.

Hebb, D. O. *Organization of behavior.* New York: John Wiley, 1949.

Hebb, D. O. On watching myself get old. *Psychology Today,* November 1978, 15–23.

Heber, R. (ed.). A manual on terminology and classification in mental retardation (2nd ed.). *American Journal of Mental Deficiency Monograph Supplement,* 1961.

Heller, J., & Kiralry, J. An educational program for pregnant school-age girls. *Clearing House,* 1973, *47,* 476–482.

Helms, D., & Turner, J. *Exploring child behavior.* New York: Holt, Rinehart & Winston, 1981.

Herr, E. L. Manpower policies, vocational guidance, and career development. In E. L. Herr (eds.), *Vocational guidance and human development.* Boston: Houghton-Mifflin, 1974.

Hershenson, M. Visual discrimination in the human newborn. *Journal of Comparative and Physiological Psychology,* 1964, *58,* 270–276.

Hess, B. *Amicability.* Unpublished doctoral dissertation, Rutgers University, 1971.

Hess, R. D., & Shipman, V. C. Early experience and the socialization of cognitive modes in children. *Child Development*, 1965, *36*, 869–886.

Hess, R. D., & Shipman, V. C. Maternal influences upon early learning: The cognitive environments of urban preschool children. In R. D. Hess & R. M. Bear (eds.), *Early education*. Chicago: Aldine, 1968.

Hetherington, E. M. Effects of father absence on personality development in adolescent daughters. *Developmental Psychology*, 1972, *7*, 313–326.

Hetherington, E. M. *My heart belongs to daddy: A study of the marriages of daughters of divorcees and widows*. Unpublished manuscript, University of Virginia, 1977.

Hetherington, E. M. *My heart belongs to daddy: A study of the remarriages of daughters of divorcees and widows*. Unpublished manuscript, University of Virginia, 1977.

Hetherington, E. M. Divorce: A child's perspective. *American Psychologist*, 1979, *34*, 851–858.

Hetherington, E. M., Cox, M., & Cox, R. The aftermath of divorce. In J. H. Stevens & M. Mathews (eds.), *Mother-child/father-child relations*. Washington, D.C.: National Association for the Education of Young Children, 1978.

Hicks, M. W., & Platt, M. Marital happiness and stability: A review of the research in the sixties. *Journal of Marriage and the Family*, 1970, *27*, 677–689.

Higgens-Trenk, A., & Gaite, A. J. H. *Elusiveness of formal-operational thought in adolescents*. Paper presented at the proceedings of the Seventy-Ninth Annual Convention of the American Psychological Association, 1970.

Hill, J. P. *Secondary schools, socialization, and social development during adolescence*. Position paper prepared for the National Institute of Education, U.S. Department of Health, Education, and Welfare, June 1978.

Hill, J. P. The early adolescent and the family. In *The seventy-ninth yearbook of the national society for the study of education*. Chicago: University of Chicago Press, 1980.

Hill, J. P., & Palmquist, W. Social cognition and social relations in early adolescence. *International Journal of Behavioral Development*, 1978, *1*, 1–36.

Hill, J. P., & Steinberg, L. D. *The development of autonomy in adolescence*. Paper presented at the Symposium on Research on Youth Problems, Fundacion Orbegoza Eizaquirre, Madrid, Spain, April 26–30, 1976.

Hinde, R. A. Influence of social companions and of temporary separation on mother-infant relations in rhesus monkeys. In B. M. Foss (ed.) *Determinants of infant behavior IV*. London: Methuen (New York: John Wiley), 1969.

Hinde, R. A., & Atkinson, S. Assessing the roles of social partners in maintaining mutual proximity, as exemplified by mother-infant relations in infant monkeys. *Animal Behavior*, 1970, *19*, 169–176.

Hinde, R. A., & Spencer-Booth, Y. Effects of brief separation from mother on rhesus monkeys. *Science,* 1971, *173*, 111–118.

Hinde, R. A., & White, L. E. Dynamics of a relationship: Rhesus mother-infant ventro-ventro contact. *Journal of Comparative and Physiological Psychology*, 1974, *86*, 8–23.

Hinton, J. *Dying*, 2nd ed. Baltimore: Penguin, 1972.

Hobbs, D. Parenthood as crisis: A third study. *Journal of Marriage and the Family*, 1965, *27*, 677–689.

Hobbs, D., & Wimbish, J. Transition to parenthood by black couples. *Journal of Marriage and the Family*, 1977, *39*, 677–689.

Hock, E. Working and nonworking mothers and their infants: A comparative study of maternal caregiving characteristics and infant social behavior. *Merrill-Palmer Quarterly*, in press.

Hockett, C. F. Logical considerations in the study of animal communication. In W. E. Lanyon & W. M. Taudga (eds.), *Animal sounds and animal communication*. Washington, D.C.: American Institute of Biological Sciences, 1960.

Hodgkins, J. Influence of age on the speed of reaction and movement in females. *Journal of Gerontology*, 1962, *17*, 385–389.

Hoffman, L. W. Effects of maternal employment on the child: A review of the research. *Developmental Psychology*, 1974, *10*, 204–228.

Hoffman, L. W. Maternal employment: 1979. *American Psychologist*, 1979, *34*, 859–865.

Hoffman, M. L. Moral development. In P. H. Mussen (ed.), *Carmichael's manual of child psychology* (3rd ed., vol. 2). New York: John Wiley, 1970.

Hoffman, M. L. Developmental synthesis of affect and cognition and its implications for altruistic motivation. *Developmental Psychology*, 1975, *11*, 607–622.

Hoffman, M. L. Development of moral thought, feeling, and behavior. *American Psychologist*, 1979, *34*, 958–966.

Hoffman, M. L. Empathy, guilt, and social cognition. In W. Overton (ed.), *Relation between social and cognitive development*. Hillsdale, N.J.: Erlbaum, in press.

Hogan, R. Moral conduct and moral character: A psychological perspective. *Psychological Bulletin*, 1973, *79*, 217–232.

Holland, J. L. *Making vocational choices: A theory of careers*. Englewood Cliffs, N.J.: Prentice-Hall, 1973.

Hollingshead, A. B. *Elmtown's youth and Elmtown revisited*. New York: John Wiley, 1975.

Holmberg, M. C. The development of social interchange patterns from 12 to 42 months. *Child Development*, 1980, *51*, 448–456.

Holmstrom, L. L. *The two-career family*. Cambridge, Mass.: Schenkman, 1973.

Holt, J. *How children fail*. Belmont, Calif.: Pitman, 1964.

Honzik, M. P. Developmental studies of parent-child resemblance in intelligence. *Child Development*, 1957, *28*, 215–228.

Honzik, M. P. Value and limitations of infant tests: An overview. In M. Lewis (ed.), *Origins of intelligence.* New York: Plenum, 1976.

Honzik, M. P., MacFarlane, J. W., & Allen, L. The stability of mental test performance between two and eighteen years. *Journal of Experimental Education,* 1948, *17,* 309–324.

Hooper, F. H., & Sheehan, N. Logical concept attainment during the aging years: Issues in the neo-Piagetian research literature. In W. F. Overton & J. M. Gallagher (eds.), *Knowledge and development: Advances in theory and research* (vol. 1). New York: Plenum Press, 1977.

Hooper, F. H., Sipple, T. S., Goldman, J. A., & Swinton, S. S. A cross-sectional investigation of children's classificatory abilities (Technical Report No. 295). Madison: Wisconsin Research and Development Center for Cognitive Learning, 1974.

Horn, J. L., & Cattell, R. B. Age differences in primary mental ability factors. *Journal of Gerontology,* 1966, *21,* 210–220.

Horn, J. L., & Cattell, R. B. Age differences in fluid and crystallized intelligence. *Acta Psychologica,* 1967, *16,* 107–129.

Horn, J. L., & Donaldson, G. Cognitive development II: Adulthood development of human abilities. In O. G. Brim & J. Kagan (eds.), *Constancy and change in human development.* Cambridge: Harvard University Press, 1980.

Hornblum, W., & Overton, W. Area and volume conservation among the elderly: Assessment and training. *Developmental Psychology,* 1976, *12,* 68–74.

Horney, K. *Neurosis and human growth.* New York: Norton, 1950.

Houle, C. O. *The inquiring mind.* Madison, Wis.: University of Wisconsin Press, 1961.

House, J. S., & Mason, W. M. Political alienation in America, 1952–1968. *American Sociological Review,* 1975, *40,* 123–147.

Howard, D. V., Lasaga, M. I., & McAndrews, M. P. Semantic activation during memory encoding across the adult lifespan. *Journal of Gerontology,* 1980, *35,* 884–890.

Hoyer, W. J., & Plude, D. J. Attentional and perceptual processes in the study of cognitive aging. In L. W. Poon (ed.), *Aging in the 1980s.* Washington, D.C.: American Psychological Association, 1980.

Hubbard, R. Test-tube babies: Solution or problem. *Technology Review,* 1980, *85.*

Hudson, W. Pictorial depth perception in subcultural groups in Africa. *Journal of Social Psychology,* 1960, *52,* 183–208.

Hudson, W. The study of pictorial perception among unacculturated groups. *International Journal of Psychology,* 1967, *2,* 90–107.

Hughes. Reported in Fozard, J. L., & Popkin, S. J. Optimizing adult development: Ends and means for an applied psychology of aging. *American Psychologist,* 1978, *33,* 975–989.

Hultsch, D. F. Adult age differences in free classification and free recall. *Developmental Psychology,* 1969, *1,* 673–678.

Hultsch, D. F. Adult age differences in free classification and free recall. *Developmental Psychology,* 1971, *4,* 338–342.

Hultsch, D. F., & Deutsch, F. *Adult development and aging.* New York: McGraw-Hill, 1981. Used with permission of the McGraw-Hill Book Co.

Hunt, J. V. Environmental risk in fetal and neonatal life and measured infant intelligence. In M. Lewis (ed.), *Origins of intelligence.* New York: Plenum, 1976.

Hunt, M. *Sexual behavior in the 1970s.* Chicago: Playboy Press, 1974.

Hunt, M., & Hunt, B. *The divorce experience.* New York: McGraw-Hill, 1977.

Hurlock, E. B. *Developmental psychology,* 5th ed. New York: McGraw-Hill, 1980.

Huston, A. C. Sex-typing. In E. M. Hetherington (ed.), *Carmichael's manual of child psychology,* 4th ed., vol. IV. New York: John Wiley, 1982.

Huston-Stein, A., & Higgins-Trenk, A. Development of females from childhood through adulthood: Career and feminine role orientations. In P. Baltes (ed.), *Life span development and behavior* (vol. 1). New York: Academic Press, 1978.

Hutton, R., & Harsany, Z. The unique you. *Omni,* June 1980.

Huxley, L. *This timeless moment.* Millbrae, Calif.: Celestial Arts, 1968.

Hyde, J. S. *Understanding human sexuality.* New York: McGraw-Hill, 1979.

Hyde, J. S., & Rosenberg, B. G. *Half the human experience: The psychology of women.* Lexington, Mass.: Heath, 1976.

Hyman, H. M. *Political socialization.* New York: Free Press, 1959.

i

Iannotti, R. J. Effect of role taking experiences on role taking, empathy, altruism, and aggression. *Developmental Psychology,* 1978, *14,* 119–124.

Inglis, J., & Caird, W. K. Age differences in successive responses to simultaneous stimulation. *Canadian Journal of Psychology,* 1963, *17,* 98–105.

Ingram, D. Sensorimotor intelligence and language development. In A. Lock (ed.), *Action, gesture, and symbol: The emergence of language.* New York: Academic Press, 1978.

Inkeles, A. Social structure and socialization. In D. Goslind (ed.), *Handbook of socialization theory and research.* Chicago: Rand McNally, 1969.

j

Jacewicz, M. M., & Hartley, A. A. Rotation of mental images by young and old college students: The effects of familiarity. *Journal of Gerontology,* 1979, *34,* 396–403.

Jacobson, J. L. The role of inanimate objects in early peer interaction. *Child Development,* in press.

James, W. *The principles of psychology* (vol. 1). New York: Holt, Rinehart & Winston, 1890.

Jencks, C. Who gets ahead in America. *Psychology Today,* July 1979.

Jenkins, J. J. Language and thought. In J. F. Voss (ed.), *Approaches to thought.* Columbus: Merrill, 1969.

Jenkins, J. J. Four points to remember: A tetrahedral model of memory experiments. In L. S. Cermak and F.I.M. Craik (eds.), *Levels of processing and human memory.* Hillsdale, N.J.: Lawrence Erlbaum Assocs. 1978.

Jensen, A. R. How much can we boost IQ and scholastic achievement? *Harvard Educational Review,* 1969, *39,* 1–123.

Jensen, A. R. *Educational differences.* New York: Barnes & Noble, 1974.

Jepsen, D. A. Vocational decision making patterns among non-college aspiring adolescents. *Journal of Vocational Behavior,* 1974, *4,* 283–296. (b)

Jepsen, D. A. Vocational decision making strategy types. *Vocational Guidance Quarterly,* 1974, *23,* 12–23. (a)

Jessor, S. L., & Jessor, R. Transition from virginity to nonvirginity among youth: A social-psychological study over time. *Developmental Psychology,* 1975, *11,* 473–484.

Joffe, L. *Exploration, attachment, and cognitive development.* A thesis submitted for the M.S. degree in Educational Psychology, University of Wisconsin-Madison, 1977.

Johnson, L., Backman, J., & O'Malley, P. M. *Monitoring the future project: Drug use among American high school students, 1975–77.* Ann Arbor, Mich.: University of Michigan Institute for Social Research, 1978.

Johnson, L., Backman, J., & O'Malley, P. M. *The use of marijuana by high school seniors.* Unpublished manuscript, University of Michigan Institute for Social Research, 1980.

Johnson, R. C. A study of children's moral judgments. *Child Development,* 1962, *33,* 603–605.

Johnson, S. M., & Lobitz, G. K. The personal and marital adjustment of parents as related to observed child deviance and parenting behaviors. *Journal of Abnormal Child Psychiatry,* 1974, *2,* 192–207.

Jones, E. *The life and work of Sigmund Freud* (vol. 1). New York: Basic Books, 1953.

Jones, H. E. The California adolescent growth study. *Journal of Educational Research,* 1938, *31,* 561–567.

Jones, M. C. A laboratory study of fear: The case of Peter. *Pedagogical Seminary,* 1924, *31,* 308–315.

Jones, M. C. Psychological correlates of somatic development. *Child Development,* 1965, *36,* 899–911.

Jones, M. C., & Bayley, N. Physical maturing among boys as related to behavior. *Journal of Educational Psychology,* 1950, *41,* 129–148.

Jones, M. C., & Mussen, P. H. Self-conceptions, motivations, and interpersonal attitudes of early- and late-maturing girls. *Child Development,* 1958, *29,* 491–501.

Jones, T. D. Development of certain motor skills and play activities in young children. New York: Teachers College, *Child Development Monographs,* 1939 (no. 26).

Jordaan, J. P. Exploratory behavior. In D. E. Super, R. Statishersky, N. Mattin, J. P. Jordaan (eds.), *Career development: Self-concept theory.* New York: College Entrance Examination Board, 1963.

Jordaan, J. P., & Heyde, M. B. *Vocational development during the high school years.* New York: Teachers College Press, 1978.

Just, J. A., & Carpenter, P. A. (eds.). *Cognitive processes in comprehension.* Hillsdale, N.J.: Erlbaum, 1977.

k

Kacerguis, M. A., & Adams, G. R. *Erikson stage resolution: The relationship between identity and intimacy.* Unpublished manuscript, Utah State University, 1978.

Kagan, J. *Change and continuity in infancy.* New York: John Wiley, 1971.

Kagan, J. Emergent themes in human development. *American Scientist,* 1976, *64,* 186–196.

Kagan, J. Family experience and the child's development. *American Psychologist,* 1979, *34,* 886–891.

Kagan, J., Kearsley, R. B., & Zelazo, P. R. *Infancy.* Cambridge, Mass.: Harvard University Press, 1978.

Kagan, J., Klein, R. E., Haith, M. M., & Morrison, F. J. Memory and meaning in two cultures. *Child Development,* 1973, *44,* 221–223.

Kagan, J., & Moss, H. A. *Birth to maturity.* New York: John Wiley, 1962.

Kahana, E., & Felton, B. Social context and personal needs—A study of Polish and Jewish aged. *Journal of Social Issues,* 1977, *33,* 56–74.

Kahn, J. H., & Nursten, J. P. School phobias: Refusal, a comprehensive view of school phobia, and other failures of school attendance. *American Journal of Orthopsychiatry,* 1962, *32,* 707–718.

Kahneman, D. *Attention and effort.* Englewood Cliffs, N.J.: Prentice-Hall, 1973.

Kail, R. V. *Memory development in children.* San Francisco: Freeman, 1979.

Kail, R. V., & Hagen, J. W. (eds.). *Perspectives on the development of memory and cognition.* Hillsdale, N.J.: Erlbaum, 1977.

Kalish, R. A., & Reynolds, D. K. Phenomenological reality and post-death contact. *Journal for the Scientific Study of Religion,* 1973, *12,* 209–221.

Kalish, R. A., & Reynolds, D. K. *Death and ethnicity: A psychocultural study.* Los Angeles: University of Southern California Press, 1976.

Kamin, L. J. *The science and politics of IQ.* New York: Halsted Press, 1974.

Kandel, D. The role of parents and peers in adolescent marijuana use. *Journal of Social Issues,* 1974, *30,* 707–718.

Kandel, D., & Faust, R. Sequence and stages in patterns of adolescent drug abuse. *Archives of General Psychiatry,* 1975, *32,* 923–932.

Kandel, D., & Lesser, G. S. Parent-adolescent relationships and adolescent independence in the United States and Denmark. *Journal of Marriage and the Family,* 1969, *31,* 348–358.

Kantner, J. F., & Zelnik, M. Sexual experience of young unmarried women in the United States. *Family Planning Perspectives,* 1972, *4,* 9–18.

Kaplan, H. S. *The new sex therapy.* New York: Brunner/ Mazel, 1974.

Kappelman, M. A unique school health program in a school for pregnant teenagers. *Journal of School Health,* 1974, *44,* 303–306.

Kastenbaum, R. (ed.). *Old age on the new scene.* New York: Springer, 1981.

Katz, J. *No time for youth: Growth and constraint in college.* San Francisco: Jossey-Bass, 1968.

Katz, P. A. The development of female identity. *Sex Roles,* 1979, *5,* 155–178.

Kaufman, N. J. *Comprehension monitoring of learning disabled children compared to non-learning disabled children.* Unpublished dissertation, University of Wisconsin-Madison, 1981.

Kavanaugh, D. (ed.). *Listen to us!* New York: Workman Publishing, 1978.

Kay, D. W. K., & Bergmann, K. Epidemiology of mental disorders among the aged in the community. In J. E. Birren & R. B. Sloane (eds.), *Handbook of mental health and aging.* Englewood Cliffs, N.J. Prentice-Hall, 1980.

Kaye, K., & Fogel, A. The temporal structure of face-to-face communication between mothers and infants. *Developmental Psychology,* 1980, *16*(5), 454–464.

Keasey, C. B. Social participation as a factor in the moral development of preadolescents. *Developmental Psychology,* 1971, *5,* 216–220.

Keating, D. P. Thinking processes in adolescence. In J. Adelson (ed.), *Handbook of adolescent psychology.* New York: John Wiley, in press.

Keller-Cohen, D. Context in child language. *Annual Review of Anthropology,* 1978, *7,* 453–482.

Kelley, R. K. The premarital sexual revolution: Comments on research. *Family Coordinator,* 1972, *21,* 334–336.

Kellogg, R. *Analyzing children's art.* Palo Alto, Calif.: Mayfield, 1970. By permission of Mayfield Publishing Company. Copyright © 1969, 1970 by Rhonda Kellogg.

Kellogg, W. N., & Kellogg, L. A. *The ape and the child.* New York: McGraw-Hill, 1933.

Kelly, J. B. *Children and parents in the midst of divorce: Major factors contributing to differential response.* Paper presented at the National Institute of Mental Health Conference on Divorce, Washington, D.C., February, 1978.

Kemler, D. G., & Smith, L. B. Is there a developmental trend from integrality to separability in perception? *Journal of Experimental Child Psychology,* 1978, *26,* 498–507.

Kemler, D. G., & Smith, L. B. Accessing similarity and dimensional relations: The effects of integrality and separability on the discovery of complex concepts. *Journal of Experimental Psychology: General,* 1979, *108,* 133–150.

Keniston, K. *Young radicals.* New York: Harcourt, Brace & World, 1968.

Kenniston, K. Youth: A "new" stage of life. *The American Scholar,* 1970, *39,* 631–654.

Kenniston, K. The tasks of adolescence. *Developmental Psychology Today.* Del Mar, Calif.: CRM Books, 1971.

Kessen, W. *Childhood in China.* New Haven, Conn.: Yale University Press, 1975.

Kessen, W., Haith, M. H., & Salapatek, P. H. Infancy. In P. H. Mussen (ed.), *Carmichael's manual of child psychology,* vol. 1, 3rd ed. New York: John Wiley, 1970.

Kety, S. Foreward: Bringing knowledge to bear on the mental dysfunctions associated with aging. In J. E. Birren & R. B. Sloane (eds.), *Handbook of mental health and aging.* Englewood Cliffs, N.J.: Prentice-Hall, 1980.

Khatena, J. Creative imagination imagery and analogy. *Gifted Child Quarterly,* 1975, *19*(2), 149–158.

Khatena, J. Creativity imagination imagery: Where is it going? *Journal of Creative Behavior,* 1976, *10*(3), 189–192.

Khatena, J., & Torrance, E. P. *Thinking creatively with sounds and words.* Lexington, Mass.: Personnel Press, 1973.

Kimmel, D. *Adulthood and aging: An interdisciplinary view.* New York: John Wiley, 1974.

King, M. C., & Wilson, A. C. Evolution at two levels in humans and chimpanzees. *Science,* 1975, *188,* 107–116.

Kinsey, A. C., Pomeroy, W. B., & Martin, C. E. *Sexual behavior in the human male.* Philadelphia: Saunders, 1948.

Kintsch, W. Text representation. In W. Otto & S. White (eds.), *Reading expository text.* New York: Academic Press, 1982.

Klahr, D., & Wallace, J. G. *Cognitive development: An information processing view.* Hillsdale, N.J.: Erlbaum, 1975.

Klaus, M., & Kennell, J. *Maternal-infant bonding,* 2nd ed. St. Louis: Mosby, 1982.

Klein, R. P., & Durfee, J. *Infants' reactions to strangers vs. mothers.* Paper presented at the biennial meeting of the Society for Research in Child Development, Denver, April 1975.

Kline, D. W., & Szafran, J. Age differences in backward monoptic visual noise making. *Journal of Gerontology,* 1975, *30,* 307–311, 949–974.

Kling, J. W., & Riggs, L. A. *Woodworth and Schlosberg's experimental psychology* (3rd ed.). New York: Holt, Rinehart & Winston, 1971.

Koch, H. Some emotional attitudes of the young child in relation to characteristics of his sibling. *Child Development,* 1956, *27,* 393–426.

Koffka, K. *Principles of Gestalt psychology.* New York: Harcourt, 1935.

Kohlberg, L. *The development of modes of moral thinking and choice in the years 10 to 16.* Unpublished doctoral dissertation, University of Chicago, 1958.

Kohlberg, L. A cognitive-developmental analysis of children's sex-role concepts and attitudes. In E. E. Maccoby (ed.), *The development of sex differences.* Stanford, Calif.: Stanford University Press, 1966.

Kohlberg, L. Stage and sequence: The cognitive-developmental approach to socialization. In D. A. Goslin (ed.), *Handbook of socialization theory and research.* Chicago: Rand McNally, 1969. Copyright © 1969 by Houghton Mifflin Company. Used by permission.

Kohlberg, L. Moral stages and moralization. The cognitive-developmental approach. In T. Lickona (ed.), *Moral development and behavior.* New York: Holt, Rinehart & Winston, 1976. Reprinted by permission.

Kohlberg, L., & Candee, D. *Relationships between moral judgment and moral action.* Unpublished manuscript, Harvard University, 1979.

Kohler, W. *Gestalt psychology.* New York: New American Library, Mentor Books, 1959. (Originally published, 1947.)

Kohn, M. L. *Class and conformity: A study in values.* Homewood, Ill.: Dorsey Press, 1969.

Kohn, M. L. Job complexity and adult personality. In N. J. Smelser & E. H. Erikson (eds.), *Themes of work and love in adulthood.* Cambridge, Mass.: Harvard University Press, 1980.

Kohn, M. L., & Schooler, C. Job conditions and intellectual flexibility: a longitudinal assessment of their reciprocal effects. In E. F. Borgatta & D. J. Jackson (eds.), *Factor analysis and measurement in sociological research: a multidimensional perspective.* Beverly Hills, Calif.: Sage Publications, in press.

Kompara, D. R. Difficulties in the socialization process of stepparenting. *Family Relations,* 1979, *29,* 69–73.

Koncelik, J. A. *Designing the open nursing home.* Stroudsberg, Pa.: Dowden, Hutchinson, & Ross, 1976.

Kounin, J. S. *Discipline and group management in classrooms.* New York: Holt, Rinehart & Winston, 1971.

Krantzler, M. *Creative divorce.* New York: M. Evans & Co., 1974.

Krauss, R. M., & Glucksberg, S. Social and nonsocial speech. *Scientific American,* 1977, *236,* 100–105.

Kravitz, H., & Boehm, J. Rhythmic habit patterns in infancy: Their sequences, age of onset, and frequency. *Child Development,* 1971, *42,* 399–413.

Krogman, W. M. Growth of head, face, trunk, and limbs in Philadelphia white and negro children of elementary and high school age. *Monographs of the Society for Research in Child Development,* 1970, serial no. 136, vol. *35,* no. 3.

Kübler-Ross, E. *Questions and answers on death and dying.* New York: MacMillan, 1974.

Kübler-Ross, E. *Death: The Final Stage of Growth.* Englewood Cliffs, N.J.: Prentice-Hall, 1976.

Kuczaj, S. A., II. Why do children fail to overgeneralize the progressive inflection? *Journal of Child Language,* 1978, *5,* 167–171.

Kuhn, D. *On the development of developmental psychology.* Unpublished manuscript, Harvard University, 1980.

Kuypers, J. A., & Bengtson, V. L. Social breakdown and competence. A model of normal aging. *Human Development,* 1973, *16,* 181–201.

l

Labouvie-Vief, G. Article in *Human Development,* 1980.

Labov, W. The logic of nonstandard English. In F. Williams (ed.), *Language and poverty.* Chicago: Markham, 1970.

Labov, W. Systematically misleading data from test questions. *The Urban Review,* 1976, *9,* 146–169.

Lachman, J. L., & Lachman, R. Age and the actualization of world knowledge. In L. W. Poon, J. L. Fozard, L. S. Cermak, D. Arenberg, & L. W. Thompson (eds.), *New directions in memory and aging: Proceedings of the George A. Talland memorial conference.* Hillsdale, N.J.: Erlbaum, 1980.

Lack, S., & Buckingham, R. W. *First American hospice: Three years of home care.* New Haven, Conn.: Hospice, Inc., 1978.

Lahey, B. B. Behavior modification with learning disabilities and related problems. In M. Hersen, R. Eisler, & P. Miller (eds.), *Progress in behavior modification.* New York: Academic Press, 1975.

Lamb, M. E. Interactions between two-year-olds and their mothers and fathers. *Psychological Reports,* 1976, *38,* 447–450.

Lamb, M. E. The role of the father: An overview. In M. E. Lamb (ed.), *The role of the father in child development.* New York: John Wiley, 1976.

Lamb, M. E. (ed.). *The role of the father in child development.* New York: John Wiley, 1976.

Lamb, M. E. Father-infant and mother-infant interaction in the first year of life. *Child Development,* 1977, *48,* 167–181.

Lamb, M. E. Fathers and child development: An integrative overview. In M. E. Lamb (ed.), *The father's role in child development,* 2nd ed. New York: John Wiley, 1981.

Lamb, M. E., & Sherrod, L. R. (eds.). *Infant social cognition: Empirical and theoretical considerations.* Hillsdale, N.J.: Erlbaum, 1981.

Lamb, M. E., & Sutton-Smith, B. *Sibling relationships: Their nature and significance across the lifespan.* Hillsdale, N.J.: Erlbaum, 1982.

Lambercier, M. Recerche sur le developpement des perceptions. VI: La constance des grandeurs en comparaisons seriales. *Archives Psychology Genève,* 1946, *31,* 79–282.

Langacker, R. W. *Language and its structure* (2nd ed.). New York: Harcourt, 1973.

Langer, J. *Theories of development.* New York: Holt, Rinehart & Winston, 1969.

Larson, M. E. Humbling cases for career counselors. *Phi Delta Kappan,* 1973, *54,* 374.

Lasko, J. K. Parent behavior toward first-born and second-born children. *Genetic Psychology Monographs,* 1954, *4a.*

Lasky, R. E., & Klein, R. E. The reactions of five-month-old infants to eye contact of the mother and of a stranger. *Merrill-Palmer Quarterly*, 1979, *25*, 163–170.

Lasky, R. E., & Klein, R. E. Fixation of the standard and novelty preference in six-month-old well- and malnourished infants. *Merrill-Palmer Quarterly*, 1980, *26*, 171–178.

LaVoie, J. Ego identity formation in middle adolescence. *Journal of Youth and Adolescence*, 1976, *5*, 371–385.

Lawson, A. E., & Wollman, W. T. *Encouraging the transition from concrete to abstract cognitive functioning: An experiment*. Unpublished manuscript, University of California at Berkeley, 1975.

Lawton, M. P. Assessment, integration, and environments for the elderly. *Gerontologist*, 1979, *25*, 748–753.

Lawton, M. P., Nahemow, Yaffe, S., & Feldman, S. Psychological aspects of crime and fear of crime. In J. Goldsmith & S. Goldsmith (eds.), *Crime and the elderly*. Lexington, Mass.: Lexington Books, 1976, 21–29.

Laycock, F. *Gifted children*. Glenview, Ill.: Scott, Foresman, 1979.

Lazarus, R. S., & Launier, R. Stress-related transactions between person and environment. In L. A. Pervin & M. Lewis (eds.), *Perspectives in interactional psychology*. New York: Plenum, 1978.

Leaf, A. Getting old. *Scientific American*, 1973.

Leboyer, F. *Birth without violence*. New York: Knopf, 1975.

Lee, C. B. T. *The campus scene: 1900–1970*. New York: McKay, 1970.

Lee, G. R. Marriage and morale in late life. *Journal of Marriage and the Family*, 1978, *40*, 131–139.

Lee, L. C. *Social encounters of infants: The beginnings of popularity*. Paper presented at the meeting of the International Society for the Study of Behavioral Development, Ann Arbor, Michigan, August 1973.

Lee, T. Perceived distance as a function of direction in the city. *Environment & Behavior*, 1970, *2*, 40–51.

Leedham, L. R., Signori, E. I., & Sampson, D. L. G. Survey of areas of moral awareness and formation of principles basic to the construction of a scale to measure conscience. *Psychological Reports*, 1967, *21*, 913–919.

LeFurgy, W. G., & Woloshin, G. W. Immediate and long-term effects of experimentally induced social influence in the modification of adolescents' moral judgments, *Journal of Abnormal and Social Psychology*, 1969, *12*, 104–110.

Lehman, H. C. *Age and achievement*. Princeton, N.J.: Princeton University Press, 1953.

Leifer, A. D. *Television and the development of social behavior*. Paper presented at the meeting of the International Society for the Study of Behavioral Development. Ann Arbor, Michigan, 1973.

LeMasters, E. E. Parenthood as crisis. *Journal of Marriage and the Family*, 1957, *27*, 367–379.

Lenneberg, E. H. *Biological foundation of language*. New York: John Wiley, 1967.

Lerbinger, O. *Designs for persuasive interaction*. Englewood Cliffs, N.J.: Prentice-Hall, 1972.

Le Shan, L. *The medium, the mystic, and the physicist*. New York: Ballantine Books, 1975.

Lesser, G. Learning, teaching, and television production for children: The experience of Sesame Street. *Harvard Education Review*, 1972, *42*, 232–272.

Lesser, G., Fifer, G., & Clark, D. Mental abilities of children from different social classes and cultural groups. *Monographs of the Society for Research in Child Development*, 1965, *30* (4, Whole No. 102).

Levin, J. R. *The mnemonic '80s: Keywords in the classroom*. Theoretical Paper No. 86, Wisconsin Research and Development Center for Individualized Schooling, Madison, 1980.

Levin, J. R., Yussen, S. R., DeRose, T. M., & Pressley, J. M. Developmental changes in assessing recall and recognition memory capacity. *Developmental Psychology*, 1977, *13*, 608–615.

LeVine, R. A. *Culture, behavior, and personality*. Chicago: Aldine, 1973.

Levinger, G. A three-level approach to attraction: Toward an understanding of pair relatedness. In T. Huston (ed.), *Foundations of interpersonal attraction*. New York: Academic Press, 1974.

Levinson, D. J. The mid-life transition: A period in adult psychosocial development. *Psychiatry*, 1977, *40*, 99–112.

Levinson, D. J. *The seasons of a man's life*. New York: Knopf, 1978.

Levinson, D. J. Toward a conception of the adult life course. In N. J. Smelser & E. H. Erikson (eds.), *Themes of work and love in adulthood*. Cambridge, Mass.: Harvard University Press, 1980.

Levy, D. M., & Patrick, H. T. Relation of infantile convulsions, head-banging, and breath-holding to fainting and headaches (migraine) in the parents. *Archives of Neurology and Psychiatry*, 1928, *19*, 865–887.

Lewis, M., & Ban, P. *Stability of attachment behavior: A transformational analysis*. Paper presented at the meeting of the Society for Research in Child Development, Minneapolis, April 1971.

Lewis, M., & Brooks-Gunn, J. *Social cognition and the acquisition of the self*. New York: Plenum, 1979.

Lewis, M., & Cherry, L. Social behavior and language acquisition. In M. Lewis & L. Rosenblum (eds.), *Interaction conversation and the development of language: The origins of behavior* (vol. 5), 1977.

Lewis, M., & Rosenblum, L. A. (eds.), *Friendship and peer relations* (vol. 4). New York: John Wiley, 1975.

Lewis, V. G., Money, J., & Bobrow, N. A. Idiopathic pubertal delay beyond the age of fifteen: Psychologic study of twelve boys. *Adolescence*, 1977, *12*, 1–11.

Libby, R. W., & Whitehurst, R. N. *Marriage and alternatives: Exploring intimate relationships*. Glenview, Ill.: Scott, Foresman, 1977.

Liberman, A. M. The grammars of speech and language. *Cognitive Psychology*, 1970, *1*, 301–323.

Libow, L. S. Senile dementia and "pseudo-senility: Clinical diagnosis. In C. Eisdorfer & M. P. Lawton (eds.), *The psychology of adult development and aging.* Washington, D.C.: American Psychological Association, 1973.

Lieberman, A. F. Preschoolers' competence with a peer: Relations with attachment and peer experience. *Child Development,* 1977, *48,* 1277–1287.

Lieberman, M., & Coplan, A. Distance from death as a variable in the study of aging. *Developmental Psychology,* 1979, *2,* 71–84.

Lipsitt, L. P. Learning in the human infant. In H. W. Stevenson, E. H. Hess, & H. L. Rheingold (eds.), *Early behavior: Comparative and developmental approaches.* New York: John Wiley, 1967.

Lipsitt, L. P. Learning capacities in the human infant. In R. J. Robinson (ed.), *Brain and early behavior.* New York: Academic Press, 1969.

Lipsitt, L. P. Critical conditions in infancy: A psychological perspective. *American Psychologist,* 1979, *34,* 973–980.

Lipsitt, L. P. Infants at risk: Perinatal and neonatal factors. *International Journal of Behavioral Development,* 1979, *2,* 23–42.

Lipsitt, L. P., & Levy, N. Electrotactual threshold in the neonate. *Child Development,* 1959, *30,* 547–554.

Little, J. K. The occupations of non-college youth. In R. E. Grinder (ed.), *Studies in adolescence: A book of readings in adolescent development.* New York: MacMillan, 1969.

Livesley, W. J., & Bromley, D. B. *Person perception in childhood and adolescence.* New York: John Wiley, 1973.

Lobb, H., & Hardwick, C. Eyelid conditioning and intellectual level: Effects of repeated acquisition and extinction. *American Journal of Mental Deficiency,* 1976, *80,* 423–430.

Lockhart, R. S., Craik, F. I. M., & Jaccoby, L. L. Depth of processing recognition and recall: some aspects of a general memory system. In J. Brown (ed.), *Recall and recognition.* London: John Wiley, 1976.

Loehr, F. *Diary after death.* Los Angeles: Religious Research Frontier Books, 1976.

Lorenz, K. Z. *Evolution and modification of behavior.* Chicago: University of Chicago Press, 1965.

Lorenz, K. Z. The comparative study of behavior. In K. Lorenz and P. Leyhausen (eds.), *Motivation of human and animal behavior: An ethological view.* New York: Van Nostrand Reinhold, 1973 (First published in 1939, translated by B. A. Tonkin).

Lowenthal, M. F., & Robinson, B. Social networks and isolation. In R. H. Binstock & E. Shana (eds.), *Handbook of aging and the social sciences.* New York: Van Nostrand Reinhold, 1977.

Lowenthal, M. F., Thurnher, M., & Chiriboga, D. *Four stages of life: A comparative study of women and men facing transitions.* San Francisco: Jossey-Bass, 1975.

Lowy, L. Adult children and their parents: Dependency or dependability? *Long Term Care and Health Service Administration Quarterly,* Fall 1977.

Lowy, L. *The older generation: What is due, what is owed?* Paper presented at the Annual Meeting of the American Psychological Association, August 1981.

Lowy, L. *Prevention of intergenerational conflict in the family.* Paper presented at the meeting of the American Psychological Association, Los Angeles, August 1981.

Lundsteen, S. W., & Bernstein-Tarrow, N. B. *Guiding young children's learning.* New York: McGraw-Hill, 1981.

Luria, A. R. *Cognitive development: Its cultural and social foundations.* Cambridge, Mass.: Harvard University Press, 1976.

Luria, Z., & Rose, M. D. *Psychology of human sexuality.* New York: John Wiley, 1980.

Lyle, J., & Hoffman, H. R. Children's use of television and other media. In E. A. Rubenstein, G. A. Comstock, & J. P. Murray (eds.), *Television and social behavior* (vol. 4). Washington, D.C.: U.S. Government Printing Office, 1972.

Lynn, D. B. *The father: His role in child development.* Monterey, Calif.: Brooks/Cole, 1974.

m

Maas, H. S. The role of members in clubs of lower-class and middle-class adolescents. *Child Development,* 1954, *25,* 241–251.

Maccoby, E. E. *Social development.* New York: Harcourt, 1980.

Maccoby, E. E., & Feldman, S. S. Mother-attachment and stranger-reactions in the third year of life. *Monographs of the Society for Research in Child Development,* 1972, *37* (1, Whole No. 146).

Maccoby, E. E., & Jacklin, C. N. *The psychology of sex differences.* Stanford, Calif.: Stanford University Press, 1974.

Maccoby, E. E., & Jacklin, C. N. Sex differences in aggression: A rejoinder and reprise. *Child Development,* 1980, *51,* 964–980.

Maccoby, E. E., & Masters, J. C. Attachment and dependency. In P. H. Mussen (ed.), *Carmichael's manual of child psychology.* New York: Wiley, 1970.

MacFarlane, A. What a baby knows. *Human Nature,* February 1978.

MacKay, J. R., Phillips, D. L., & Bryce, O. B. Drinking behavior among teenagers: A comparison of institutionalized and noninstitutionalized youth. *Journal of Health and Social Behavior,* 1967, *8,* 46–54.

Macklin, E. D. Nontraditional family forms: A decade of research. *Journal of marriage and the Family,* 1980, *42,* 905–922.

Macmillan, R. L., & Brown, K. W. G., Cardiac arrest remembered. *Canadian Medical Association Journal,* 1971, *104,* 889.

Madden, D. J., & Nebes, R. D. *Age effects in selective attention during visual search.* Paper presented at the 34th Annual Meeting of the Gerontological Society of America, Toronto, November 1981.

Maddox, G. Persistence of life style among the elderly. In B. Neugart (ed.), *Middle age and aging.* Chicago: University of Chicago Press, 1968.

Maddox, G. L. Disengagement theory: A critical evaluation. *The Gerontologist,* 1964, *4,* 80–83.

Maehr, M. Continuing motivation: An analysis of a seldom considered educational outcome. *Review of Educational Research,* 1976, *46,* 443–462.

Mahler, M. S. Mother-child interaction during separation-individuation. *Psychoanalytic Quarterly,* 1965, *34,* 483–498.

Mahler, M. S. *Infantile psychosis and early contributions,* vol I. London: Jason Aronson, 1979. (a)

Mahler, M. S. *Separation-individuation,* vol. II. London: Jason Aronson, 1979. (b)

Main, M. Exploration, play and cognitive functioning as related to child-mother attachment. Unpublished doctoral dissertation, Johns Hopkins University, 1973.

Main, M., & Londerville, S. *Compliance and aggression in toddlerhood: precursors and correlates.* Paper presented at the meeting of the Society for Research in Child Development, New Orleans, March 1977.

Mandler, G. Organization and memory. In K. W. Spence and J. T. Spence (eds.), *The psychology of learning and motivation, 1.* New York: Academic Press, 1967.

Mandler, G. Recognizing: The judgement of previous occurrence. *Psychological Review,* 1980, *87,* 252–271.

Marcia, J. Development and validation of ego-identity status. *Journal of Personality and Social Psychology,* 1966, *3,* 551–558.

Maresh, M. M., & Beal, V. A. A longitudinal survey of nutrition intake, body size and tissue measurements in healthy subjects during growth. In J. Brozek (ed.), Physical growth and body composition: Papers from the Kyoto symposium on anthropological aspects of human growth. *Monographs of the Society for Research in Child Development,* 1970, serial no. 140, vol. 35, no. 7, 33–37.

Markides, K., & Martin, H. A causal model of life satisfaction among the elderly. *Journal of Gerontology,* 1979, *34,* 86–93.

Markman, E. Comprehension monitoring. In W. P. Dickson (ed.), *Children's oral communication skills.* New York: Academic Press, 1981.

Marsh, R. H., Hoffman, J. S., & Stitt, C. L. Eye blink, elicitation and measurement in the human infant. *Behavioral Research Methods and Instrumentation,* 1979, *11*(5), 498–502.

Marshall, N. R., Hegrenes, J. R. & Goldstein, S. Verbal interactions: Mothers and their retarded children vs. mothers and their nonretarded children. *Journal of Mental Deficiency,* 1974, *79,* 241–261.

Marshall, W. A. The body. In R. R. Sears, & S. S. Feldman (eds.), *The seven ages of man.* Los Altos, Calif.: William Kaufmann, 1973.

Martin, W., Bengtson, V. L., & Acock, A. Alienation and age: A context-specific approach. *Social forces,* 1973, *54,* 67–84.

Mason, S. E. and Smith, A. D. Imagery in the aged. *Experimental Aging Research,* 1977, *3,* 17–32.

Masters, W. H., & Johnson, V. E. The sexual response cycle of the human female. In J. Money (ed.), *Sex research: New Developments.* New York: Holt, Rinehart & Winston, 1965.

Masters, W. H., & Johnson, V. E. *Human sexual response.* Boston: Little Brown, 1966.

Masters, W. H., & Johnson, V. E. *Human sexual inadequacy.* Boston: Little Brown, 1970.

Masterson, L. *The circular continuum.* Seattle, Wash.: Scientific Progress Association, 1977.

Masur, E. F., & Gleason, J. B. Parent interaction and the acquisition of lexical information during play. *Developmental Psychology,* 1980, *16,* 404–409.

Matas, L., Arend, R., & Sroufe, L. Continuity in adaptation in the second year: The relationships between quality of attachment and later competence. *Child Development,* 1978, *49,* 547–556.

Maudsley, H. *Natural causes and supernatural seemings.* London: Watts, 1939.

Maurer, D., & Salapatek, P. Developmental changes in the scanning of faces by young infants. *Child Development,* 1976, *47,* 523–527.

Mayer, J. *Overweight: Causes, cost, and control.* Englewood Cliffs, N.J.: Prentice-Hall, 1968.

McCall, R. B. Childhood IQ's as predictors of adult educational and occupational status. *Science,* 1977, *197,* 482–483.

McCall, R. B. Qualitative transitions in behavioral development in the first three years. In M. H. Bornstein & W. Kessen (eds.), *Psychological Development in infancy.* Hillsdale, N.J.: Erlbaum, 1979. (a)

McCall, R. B. The development of intellectual functioning in infancy and the prediction of later I.Q. In J. D. Osofsky (ed.), *Handbook of infant development.* New York: John Wiley, 1979. (b)

McCall, R. B. Nature-nurture and the two realms of development: A proposed integration with respect to mental development. *Child Development,* 1981, *52,* 1–12.

McCall, R. B., Applebaum, M. I., & Hogarty, P. S. Developmental changes in mental performance. *Monographs of the Society for Research in Child Development,* 1973, *38* (serial no. 150).

McCall, R. B., Eichorn, D. M., & Hogarty, P. S. Transitions in early mental development. *Monographs of the Society for Research in Child Development,* 1977, *42* (3, serial no. 171).

McCandless, B. R. *Male caregivers in day care: Demonstration project* (Family Research and Development Foundation report). Atlanta, Ga.: Emory University, 1973.

McCandless, B. R., & Evans, E. *Children and youth: Psychosocial development.* Hinsdale, Ill.: Dryden Press, 1973.

McCary, J. L. *Sexual myths and fallacies.* New York: Van Nostrand Rheinhold, 1971.

McCaskill, C. L., & Wellman, B. L. A study of common motor achievements at the preschool ages. *Child Development,* 1939, *9,* 141–150.

McClearn, G. E., & DeFries, J. C. *Introduction to behavior genetics.* San Francisco: W. M. Freeman, 1973.

McClelland, D. C. Testing for competence rather than for "intelligence." *American Psychologists,* 1973, *28,* 1–14.

McClelland, D. C., Constanian, C. A., Regalado, D., & Stone, C. Making it to maturity. *Psychology Today,* June 1978, p. 16.

McCord, W., McCord, J., & Gudeman, J. *Orgins of alcoholism.* Palo Alto, Calif.: Stanford University Press, 1960.

McCord, W., McCord, J., & Howard, A. Familial correlates of aggression in non-delinquent male children. *Journal of Abnormal and Social Psychology,* 1961, *62,* 79–83.

McCormack, P. D. Temporal coding by young and elderly adults: A test of the Hasher-Zacks model. *Developmental Psychology,* 1981, *17,* 509–515.

McCormack, P. D. Coding of spatial information by young and elderly adults. *Journal of Gerontology,* 1982, *37,* 80–86.

McDaniel, C. Leisure and career development at mid-life: A rationale. *Vocational Guidance Quarterly,* 1977, *24,* 344–350.

McKenzie, B. E., Tootell, H. E., & Day, R. H. Development of visual size constancy during the 1st year of human infancy. *Developmental Psychology,* 1980, *16,* 163–174.

McNeill, D. The development of language. In P. H. Mussen (ed.), *Carmichael's manual of child psychology* (3rd ed., vol. 1). New York: John Wiley, 1970.

McNemar, Q. *The revision of the Stanford-Binet Scale.* Boston: Houghton-Mifflin, 1942.

Mead, M. Adolescence in primitive and in modern society. In V. F. Calverton and S. D. Schmalhausen (eds.), *The New Generation.* New York: MacAuley, 1930.

Medrich, E. A., Rosen, J., Rubin, V., & Buckley, S. *The serious business of growing up: A study of children's lives outside of school.* Berkely: University of California Press, in press.

Meichenbaum, D., Turk, D., & Burstein, S. The nature of coping with stress. In I. Sarason & C. Spielberger (eds.), *Stress and anxiety* (vol. 1). Washington, D.C.: Hemisphere Publishing, 1975.

Meichenbaum, D. A. A self-instructional approach to stress management: A proposal for stress inoculation training. In C. Spielberger & I. Sarason (eds.), *Stress and anxiety* (vol. 1). Washington, D.C.: Hemisphere Publishing, 1975.

Menzel, E. W. A group of young chimpanzees in a one-acre field. In A. M. Schrier & F. Stollnitz (eds.), *Behavior of nonhuman primates.* New York: Academic Press, 1974.

Merton, R. K. *Social theory and social structure.* Glencoe, Ill.: The Free Press, 1957.

Messinger, L., Walker, K., & Freeman, J. Preparation for remarriage following divorce: The use of group techniques. *American Journal of Orthopsychiatry,* 1978, *48,* 263–272.

Midlarksky, E., & Kahana, E. *Altruism and helping among the elderly: An alternative to helplessness?* Paper presented at the Annual Meeting of the American Psychological Association, Los Angeles, August 1981.

Milgram, N. A., & Ozer, M. N. Peabody Picture Vocabulary Test scores of preschool children. *Psychological Reports,* 1967, *20,* 779–784.

Miller, A. H., Brown, T. A., & Raine, A. S. *Social conflict and political estrangement, 1958–1972.* Paper presented at the Convention of the Midwest Political Science Association, Chicago, August 1973.

Miller, D. J., et al. Relationships between assessments of habituation and cognitive performance in the early years of life. *International Journal of Behavioural Development,* 1979, *2,* 159–170.

Miller, G. A. The magical number seven, plus or minus two: Some limits on our capacity for processing information. *Psychological Review,* 1956, *63,* 81–97.

Miller, G. A., Galanter, E., & Pribram, K. H. *Plans and the structure of behavior.* New York: Holt, Rinehart & Winston, 1960.

Miller, N. B., & Cantwell, D. P. Siblings as therapists. *American Journal of Psychiatry,* 1976, *133,* 447–450.

Miller, W. B. Lower-class culture as a generating milieu of gang delinquency. *Journal of Social Issues,* 1958, *14,* 5–19.

Minde, K., Marton, P., Manning, D., & Hines, B. Some determinants of mother-infant interaction in the premature nursery. *Journal of the American Academy of Child Psychiatry,* 1980, *19,* 1–21.

Minnett, A., Santrock, J. W., & Vandell, D. L. *Sibling interaction in cooperative, competitive, and neutral settings: An observational study of sex of sibling, age spacing, and ordinal position.* Unpublished manuscript, University of Texas at Dallas, 1981.

Mintz, R. S. Prevalence of persons in the city of Los Angeles who have attempted suicide. *Bulletin of Suicidology.* National Institute of Mental Health, no. 7, 1970.

Minuchin, P. *Differential use of the open classroom: A study of exploratory and cautious children.* Final report to the National Institute of Education, 1976.

Mischel, W. Preference for delayed reinforcement and social responsibility. *Journal of Abnormal and Social Psychology,* 1961, *62,* 1–7.

Mischel, W. Sex-typing and socialization. In P. H. Mussen (ed.), *Carmichael's manual of child psychology* (3rd ed., vol. 2). New York: John Wiley, 1970.

Mischel, W. On the future of personality measurement. *American Psychologist,* 1977, *32,* 246–264.

Mischel, W., & Gilligan, C. Delay of gratification, motivation for the prohibited gratification, and responses to temptation. *Journal of Abnormal and Social Psychology,* 1964, *69,* 411–417.

Mischel, W., & Mischel, H. *A cognitive social learning analysis of moral development.* Paper presented at the meeting of the Society for Research in Child Development, Denver, April 1975.

Mitchell, R. G., & Etches, P. Rhythmic habit patterns (stereotypies). *Developmental medicine and child neurology*, 1977, *19*, 545–550.

Moely, B. E., & Jeffrey, W. E. The effect of organization training on children's free recall of category items. *Child Development*, 1974, *45*, 135–143.

Molfese, D. L., & Molfese, V. J. Hemisphere and stimulus differences as reflected in the cortical responses of newborn infants to speech stimuli. *Developmental Psychology*, 1979, *15*(5), 505–511.

Money, J. 1976. Reprinted from the September 20, 1976 issue of *People Weekly;* text by Patricia Burstein, Time, Inc.

Monge, R. H., & Hultsch, D. F. Paired-associate learning as a function of adult age and the length of the anticipation and inspection intervals. *Journal of Gerontology*, 1971, *26*, 157–162.

Montemayor, R., & Eisen, M. The development of self-conceptions from childhood to adolescence. *Developmental Psychology*, 1977, *13*, 314–319.

Montessori, M. *Discovery of the Child*. M. J. Costelloe, S. J., Trans. Notre Dame, Ind.: Fides, 1967. Reprinted by permission of Fides/Claretian, 221 West Madison, Chicago, Ill. 60606.

Moody, R. *Life after death*. New York: Bantam/Mockingbird, 1975.

Moody, R. *Reflections on life after life*. New York: Bantam/Mockingbird, 1977.

Moore, G. A. *Realities of the urban classroom*. Garden City, N.Y.: Doubleday, Anchor Books, 1967.

Moore, T. W. Exclusive early mothering and its alternatives. *Scandinavian Journal of Psychology*, 1975, *16*, 256–272.

Moos, R. H., & Moos, B. S. Classroom social climate and student absences and grades. *Journal of Educational Psychology*, 1978, *70*, 263–269.

Morgan, G. A. & Ricciuti, H. N. Infants' responses to strangers during the first year. In B. M. Foss (ed.), *Determinants of Infant Behavior*, vol. 4, London: Methuen, 1969, pp. 253–272.

Morgan, S. *Hysterectomy*. New York: Healthright, 1978.

Morsbach, G. and Murphy, M. C. Recognition of individual neonates' cries by experienced and inexperienced adults. *Journal of Child Language*, 1979, *6*.

Morstain, B. R., & Smart, J. C. A motivational typology of adult learners. *Journal of Higher Education*, 1977, *48*, 665–679.

Moskewitz-Cook, A. The development of photoic spectral sensitivity in human infants. *Vision Research*, 1979, *19*, 1133–1142.

Mueller, E. (Toddlers + toys) = (An autonomous social system). In M. Lewis & L. A. Rosenblum (eds.), *The child and its family*. New York: Plenum, 1979.

Mueller, E., & Brenner, J. The origins of social skills and interaction among playgroup toddlers. *Child Development*, 1977, *48*, 854–861.

Mullener, N., & Laird, J. D. Some developmental changes in the organization of self-evaluations. *Developmental Psychology*, 1971, *5*, 233–236.

Mundy-Castle, A. C. Pictorial depth perception in Ghanian children. *International Journal of Psychology*, 1966, *1*, 290–300.

Murdock, B. B., Jr. Recent developments in short-term memory. *British Journal of Psychology*, 1967, *58*, 421–433.

Murdock, G. *Social structure*. New York: Macmillan, 1949.

Murphy, L. B. *Social behavior and child personality*. New York: Columbia University Press, 1937.

Murphy, L. D. *The widening world of childhood*. New York: Basic Books, 1962.

Murray, F. B. *Generation of educational practice from developmental theory*. Paper presented at the meeting of the American Psychological Association, Toronto, Canada, August, 1978.

Murstein, B. I. Stimulus-value-role: A theory of marital choice. *Journal of Marriage and the Family*, 1970, *32*, 465–481.

Mussen, P. H., Conger, J. J., & Kagan, J. *Child development and personality* (4th ed.). New York: Harper & Row, 1974.

Mussen, P. H., & Eisenberg-Berg, N. *Roots of caring, sharing, and helping*. San Francisco: Freeman, 1977.

Mussen, P. H., & Jones, M. C. Self-conceptions, motivations, and interpersonal attitudes of late- and early-maturing boys. *Child Development*, 1957, *28*, 243–256.

Mussen, P. H., & Jones, M. C. The behavior-inferred motivations of late- and early-maturing boys. *Child Development*, 1958, *29*, 61–67.

Mussen, P. H. (ed.). *Carmichael's manual of child psychology* (3rd ed., vol. 1). New York: John Wiley, 1970.

Mussen, P. H. (ed.). *Carmichael's manual of child psychology* (4th ed.). New York: John Wiley, 1982.

n

Nagy, M. The child's theories concerning death. *Journal of Genetic Psychology*, 1948, *73*, 3–27.

Nahir, H. Y., & Yussen, S. R. Performance of kibbutz- and city-reared Israeli children on two role-taking tasks. *Developmental Psychology*, 1977, *13*, 450–455.

Nash, S. C., & Feldman, S. S. Sex role and sex-related attributions: Constancy and change across the family life cycle. In M. E. Lamb & A. L. Brown (eds.), *Advances in developmental psychology*, vol. 1. Hillsdale, N.J.: Erlbaum, 1981.

National Assessment of Educational Progress. Adult work skills and knowledge. Report No. 35–COD–o1. Denver, Colo.: National Assessment of Educational Progress, 1976.

National Center For Health Statistics. Profile of chronic illness in nursing homes. In *Vital and Health Statistics* (series 13, no. 29). Hyattsville, Md.: U.S. Department of Health, Education, and Welfare, 1977.

National Institute of Education. *Report on crime and violence in schools*. Washington, D.C., 1978.

National Institute on Alcohol Abuse and Alcoholism. *Facts about alcohol and alcoholism.* (Department of Health, Education, and Welfare Publication No. [ADM] 75-31). Washington, D.C.: 1974.

Naus, M. J. Memory development in the young reader: The combined effects of knowledge base and memory processing. In W. Otto & S. White (eds.), *Reading expository text.* New York: Academic Press, in press.

Neimark, E. D. Intellectual development during adolescence. In F. D. Horowitz (ed.), *Review of child development research* (vol. 4). Chicago: University of Chicago Press, 1975.

Nelson, K. Structure and strategy in learning to talk. *Monographs of the Society for Research in Child Development,* 1973, *38,* no. 149.

Nelson, K. Concept, word and sentence: Interrelations in acquisition and development. *Psychological Review,* 1974, *81,* 267–285.

Nelson, K. E. *Children's language* (vol. 1). New York: Gardner Press, 1978.

Nesselroade, J. R., & Baltes, P. B. Adolescent personality development and historical change: 1970–1972. *Monographs of the Society for Research in Child Development,* 1974, *39* (1, serial no. 154).

Neugarten, B. L. The future and the young—old. *Gerontologist,* 1975, *15,* 4–9.

Neugarten, B. L. Must everything be a midlife crisis? *Prime Time,* February 1980.

Neugarten, B. L., & Datan, N. Sociological perspectives on the life cycle. In P. B. Baltes & K. W. Schaie (eds.), *Life-span developmental psychology.* New York: Academic Press, 1973.

Neugarten, B. L., Havighurst, R. J., & Tobin, S. S. Personality and patterns of aging. In B. L. Neugarten (ed.), *Middle age and aging.* Chicago: University of Chicago Press, 1968.

Neugarten, B. L., & Weinstein, K. K. The changing American grandparent. *Journal of Marriage and the Family,* 1964, *26,* 199–204.

Newcomer, R. *Housing services and neighborhood activities.* Paper presented at the meeting of the Gerontological Society, Miami, 1973.

Newell, A., & Simon, H. A. *Human problem solving.* Englewood Cliffs, N.J.: Prentice-Hall, 1972.

Newman, O. *Defensible space.* New York: Macmillan, 1972.

Nicholls, J. G. Causal attributions and other achievement-related cognitions: Effects of task outcomes, attainment value, and sex. *Journal of Personality and Social Psychology,* 1975, *31,* 379–389.

Ninio, A., & Bruner, J. The achievement and antecedents of labelling. *Journal of Child Language.* 1978, *5,* 1–15.

Nordyke, N. S., Baer, D. M., Etzel, B. C., & LeBlanc, J. M. Implications of the stereotyping and modification of sex role. *Journal of Applied Behavior Analysis,* 1977, *10,* 553–557.

Norton, A. J., & Glick, P. C. Marital instability: Past, present, and future. *Journal of Social Issues,* 1976, *32,* 5–20.

Nowak, C. A. Does youthfulness equal attractiveness? In L. E. Troll, J. Israel, & K. Israel (eds.), *Looking Ahead: A Woman's Guide to the Problems and Joys of Growing Older.* Englewood Cliffs, N.J.: Prentice-Hall, 1977.

Nunnally, J. C. Psychometric theory 25 years ago and now. *Educational Research,* 1975, *4*(10), 7–21.

Nutrition National Canada Survey. Toronto, Canada: Canadian Government Publications, 1973.

Nydegger, C. N. *Late and early fathers.* Paper presented at the meeting of the Gerontological Society, Miami Beach, Florida, November 1973.

Nye, I., & Berado, F. *The family: Its structure and interaction.* New York: Macmillan, 1973.

O

Oden, S. L., & Asher, S. R. *Coaching children in social skills for friendship making.* Paper presented at the biannual meeting of the Society for Research in Child Development, Denver, April 1975.

Odom, R. D. *The decalage from the perspective of a perceptual salience account of developmental change.* Paper presented at the meeting of the Society for Research in Child Development, New Orleans, March 1977.

Odom, R. D. A perceptual salience account of decalage relations and developmental change. In L. S. Siegel & C. J. Brainers (eds.), *Alternatives to Piaget: Critical essays on the theory.* New York: Academic Press, 1978.

O'Donnell, J. M. The temporal role of awareness, sophistication, and need for approval in verbal classical conditioning. *Dissertation Abstracts International,* 1974, *35,* 1088.

Office of Drug Abuse Policy. Report prepared by the White House Committee on Drug Abuse for the President, 1978.

Okun, B. F., & Rappaport, L. J. *Working with families: An introduction to family therapy.* North Scituate, Mass.: Duxbury Press, 1980.

Okun, M. A., & Sasfy, J. H. Adolescence, the self-concept, and formal operations. *Adolescence,* 1977, *12,* 373–379.

Olney, R. L., & Scholnick, E. K. An experimental investigation of adult perception of one-word utterances. *Journal of Child Language,* 1978, *5,* 131–142.

Olson, D., & Hildyard, A. Assent and compliance in children's language comprehension: Knowing and doing. In W. P. Dickson (ed.), *Children's oral communication skills.* New York: Academic Press, 1981.

Opton, E. From California: Two views, *APA Monitor,* April 1977, pp. 4, 5; 18.

Orgel, L. E. Aging of clones of mammalian cells, *Nature,* 1973, *243,* 441–445.

Orlofsky, J. Intimacy status: Relationship to interpersonal perception. *Journal of Youth and Adolescence,* 1976, *5,* 73–88.

Orlofsky, J., Marcia, J., & Lesser, I. Ego identity status and the intimacy vs. isolation crisis of young adulthood. *Journal of Personality and Social Psychology,* 1973, *27,* 211–219.

Ornstein, P. (ed.), *Memory development in children.* Hillsdale, N.J.: Erlbaum, 1978.

Osis, K., & Haraldsson, E. *At the hour of death.* New York: Avon Books, 1977.

Osofsky, J. D. *Neonatal characteristics and directional effect in mother-infant interaction.* Paper presented at the meeting of the Society for Research in Child Development, Denver, Colorado, April 1975.

Osofsky, J. D. Neonatal characteristics and mother-infant interactions in two observational situations. *Child Development,* 1976, *47,* 1138–1147.

Ottinger, D. R., & Simmons, J. E. Behavior of human neonates and prenatal maternal anxiety. *Psychological Reports,* 1964, *14,* 391–394.

Our Bodies, Our Selves (2nd ed.). Boston Women's Health Book Collective. New York: Simon & Schuster, 1976. Copyright © 1971, 1973, 1976 by The Boston Women's Health Book Collective, Inc. Reprinted by permission of Simon & Schuster, a Division of Gulf & Western Corporation.

Ourselves and Our Children. New York: Random House, 1978.

Owen, S. V., Froman, R. D., & Moscow, H. *Educational Psychology.* Boston: Little Brown, 1981.

p

Paivio, A. *Imagery and verbal processes.* New York: Holt, Rinehart & Winston, 1971. (Reprinted by Erlbaum, Hillsdale, N.J. 1979.)

Palmore, E. *The honorable elders: A cross-cultural analysis of aging in Japan.* Durham, N.C.: Duke University Press, 1975.

Palmore, E., & Jeffers, F. C. *Prediction of the Life Span.* Lexington, Mass.: Heath, 1971.

Pantone, J. L. The relevance of infant individuality within the early mother-infant relationship. *Dissertation Abstracts,* 1978, *38,* 11B, 5546.

Papalia, D., & Biebly, D. Cognitive functioning in middle and old age adults. A review of research on Piaget's theory. *Human Development,* 1974, *17,* 424–443.

Papanek, H. Men, women, and work: Reflections on the two-person career. In J. Huber (ed.), *Changing women in a changing society.* Chicago: University of Chicago Press, 1973.

Papousek, H. Experimental studies of appetitional behavior in human newborns and infants. In H. W. Stevenson, E. Hess, & H. L. Rheingold (eds.), *Early behavior: Comparative and developmental approaches.* New York: John Wiley, 1967.

Paris, S. C., & Lindauer, B. K. The role of inferences in children's comprehension and memory for sentences. *Cognitive Psychology,* 1976, *8,* 217–227.

Parizkova, J. Activity, obesity, and growth. In J. Brozek (ed.), Physical growth and body composition: Papers from the Kyoto symposium on anthropological aspects of human growth. *Monographs of the Society for Research in Child Development,* 1970, Serial no. 140, vol. 35, no. 7.

Parke, R. D. *Child abuse: An overview of alternative models.* Paper presented at the meeting of the American Psychological Association, Washington, D.C., September 1976.

Parke, R. D., & Collmer, C. W. Child abuse: An interdisciplinary analysis. In E. M. Hetherington (ed.), *Review of child development research* (vol. 5). Chicago: University of Chicago Press, 1976.

Parke, R. D., & Lewis, N. G. The family in context: A multilevel interactional analysis of child abuse. In R. W. Henderson (ed.), *Parent-child interaction: Theory, research, and prospect.* New York: Academic Press, 1980.

Parke, R. D., & O'Leary, S. E. Father-mother-infant interaction in the newborn period: Some findings, some observations, and some unresolved issues. In K. Riegel & J. Meacham (eds.), *The developing individual in a changing world* (vol. 2). The Hague: Mouton, 1976.

Parkes, C. *Bereavement: Studies of grief in adult life.* New York: International Universities Press, 1972.

Parmelee, A. J., Jr. Development of visual behavior and neurological organization in preterm and full-term infants. In A. Pick (ed.). *Minnesota Symposia on Child Psychology* (vol. 10). Minneapolis: University of Minnesota Press, 1976.

Parr, J. The interaction of persons and living environments. In L. Poon (ed.), *Aging in the 1980s.* Washington, D.C.: American Psychological Association, 1980.

Parsons, J. E., Ruble, D. N., Hodges, K. L., & Small, A. W. Cognitive-developmental factors in emerging sex differences in achievement-related expectancies. *Journal of Social Issues,* 1976, *32*(3), 47–61.

Parten, M. Social play among preschool children. *Journal of Abnormal and Social Psychology,* 1932, *27,* 243–269.

Pascual-Leone, J. *Cognitive development and cognitive style: A general psychological integration.* Unpublished doctoral dissertation, University of Geneva, 1969.

Pascual-Leone, J. Constructive problems for constructive theories: The current relevance of Piaget's work and a critique of information-processing simulation psychology. In R. H. Kluwe & H. Spada (eds.), *Developmental models of thinking.* New York: Academic Press, 1980.

Pastalan, L. A., Mautz, R. K., & Merrill, J. The simulation of age related sensory losses: A new approach to the study of environmental barriers. In W. F. E. Preiser (ed.), *Environmental design research.* Stroudsberg, Pa.: Dowden, Hutchinson & Ross, 1973.

Patterson, G. R. A performance theory for coercive family interaction. In R. B. Cairns (ed.), Social interaction: Methods, analysis, and illustrations. *Monographs of the Society for Research in Child Development,* in press.

Pattison, E. M. *The experience of dying.* Englewood Cliffs, N.J. Prentice-Hall/Spectrum 1977.

Pavlov, I. P. *[Conditioned reflexes]* (G. V. Anrep, Trans. and ed.). New York: Dover, 1927.

Pearce, J., & Garrett, H. D. A comparison of the drinking behavior of delinquent youth versus nondelinquent youth in the states of Idaho and Utah. *Journal of School Health*, 1970, *40*, 131–135.

Pearson, P. D. A psycholinguistic model of reading. *Language Arts*, 1976, *53*, 309–314.

Pearson, P. D., & Johnson, D. D. *Teaching reading comprehension*. New York: Holt, Rinehart & Winston, 1978.

Peck, R. C. Psychological developments in the second half of life. In B. L. Neugarten (ed.), *Middle age and aging*. Chicago: University of Chicago Press, 1968.

Pedersen, F. A., Anderson, B. J., & Cain, R. L. *An approach to understanding linkages between the parent-infant and spouse relationships*. Paper presented at the meeting of the Society for Research in Child Development, New Orleans, Louisiana, March 1977.

Pedersen, F. A., & Robson, K. Father participation in infancy. *American Journal of Orthopsychiatry*, 1969, *39*, 466–472.

Peevers, B. H., & Secord, P. F. Developmental changes in attribution of descriptive concepts to persons. *Journal of Personality and Social Psychology*, 1973, *27*, 120–128.

Perlmutter, M. An apparent paradox about memory aging. In L. W. Poon, J. L. Fozard, L. S. Cermak, D. Arenberg, & L. W. Thompson (eds.). *New directions in memory and aging: Proceedings of the George A. Talland memorial conference*. Hillsdale, N.J.: Erlbaum, 1980.

Perlmutter, M. Development of memory in the preschool years. In R. Green & T. D. Yawkey (eds.), *Early and middle childhood: Growth, abuse, and delinquency and its effects on individual, family, and community*. Westport, Conn.: Technomic, 1980.

Perlmutter, M. Learning and memory through adulthood. In M. W. Riley (ed.), *Leading edges: Recent developments in social and psychological aging*. Bethesda, Md.: National Institute of Aging Publications, in press.

Perlmutter, M. and Mitchell, D. B. The appearance and disappearance of age differences in adult memory. Craik, F. I. M. and Tuehub, S. (eds.) *Aging and cognitive processes*. New York: Plenum, in press.

Perry, L. C., Brown, R. M., & Perry, D. G. Interactive effects of cognitive involvement and response topography upon differential eyelid conditioning to conceptual discriminanda. *American Journal of Psychology*, 1979, *92*, 401–412.

Peskin, H. Pubertal onset and ego functioning. *Journal of Abnormal Psychology*, 1967, *72*, 1–15.

Petersen, A. C. Can puberty come any faster? *Psychology Today*, February 1979. Reprinted from *Psychology Today* magazine. Copyright 1979 Ziff-Davis Publishing Company.

Peterson, C. L., Danner, F. W., & Flavell, J. H. Developmental changes in children's responses to three indications of communicative failure. *Child Development*, 1972, *43*, 1463–1468.

Peterson, P. L. Interactive effects of student anxiety, achievement orientation, and teacher behavior on student achievement and attitude. *Journal of Educational Psychology*, 1977, *69*, 779–792.

Pfeiffer, E., & Davis, G. Determinants of sexual behavior in middle and old age. In E. Palmore (ed.), *Normal Aging II*. Durham, N.C.: Duke University Press, 1974.

Pfeiffer, E., Verwoerdt, A., & Davis, G. C. Sexual behavior in middle life. In E. Palmore (ed.), *Normal aging II: Reports From the Duke Longitudinal studies*, 1970–1973. Durham, N.C.: Duke University Press, 1974.

Phillips, J. L., Jr. *The Origins of Intellect: Piaget's Theory*, 2d ed. New York: W. H. Freeman and Co., 1975.

Piaget, J. In C. A. Murchison (ed.), *A history of psychology in autobiography* (vol. 4). Worcester, Mass.: Clark University Press, 1952.

Piaget, J. *The moral judgment of the child*. New York: Harcourt, 1932.

Piaget, J. *The origins of intelligence in children* (M. Cook, Trans.). New York: International Universities Press, 1952.

Piaget, J. *The construction of reality in the child*. New York: Basic Books, 1954.

Piaget, J. *[Six psychological studies]* (A. Tenzer, trans., & D. Elkind, ed.). New York: Random House, Vintage Books, 1968.

Piaget, J. Piaget's theory. In P. H. Mussen (ed.), *Carmichael's manual of child psychology* (3rd ed., vol. 1). New York: John Wiley, 1970.

Piaget, J. *[Science of education and the psychology of the child]* (D. Coltman, Trans.). New York: Orion Press, 1970.

Piaget, J. Intellectual evolution from adolescence to adulthood. *Human Development*, 1972, *15*, 1–12.

Piaget, J. *L'equilibration des structures cognitives (probleme central du developpement). Etudes d'epistemologie genetique*. (vol. 33). Paris: P.U.F., 1975.

Piaget, J. The role of action in the development of thinking. In W. F. Overton & J. M. Gallagher (eds.), *Knowledge and development* (vol. I). New York: Plenum, 1977.

Piaget, J., & Inhelder, B. *[The psychology of the child]* (H. Weaver, Trans.). New York: Basic Books, 1969.

Pick A. D. Improvement of visual and tactual form discrimination. *Journal of Experimental Psychology*, 1965, *69*, 331–339.

Pick, A. D., Frankel, D. G., & Hess, V. L. Children's attention: The development of selectivity. In E. M. Hetherington (ed.), *Review of child development research* (vol. 5). Chicago: University of Chicago Press, 1976.

Pick, H. L. Research on taste in the Soviet Union. In M. R. Kare & B. P. Halpern (eds.), *Physiological and behavioral aspects of taste*. Chicago: University of Chicago Press, 1961.

Piers, E. V., & Harris, D. B. Age and other correlates of self-concept in children. *Journal of Educational Psychology*, 1964, *55*, 91–95.

Pineo, P. C. Disenchantment in the later years of marriage. *Marriage and Family Living,* 1961, *23,* 3–11.

Pines, M. In praise of the "invulnerables." *APA Monitor,* December 1975, p. 7.

Pines, M. "Genie." *Dallas Morning News,* September/October, 1981.

Plato. *[The Republic]* (B. Jowett, Trans.). Bridgeport, Conn.: Airmont, 1968.

Plomin, R., & Rowe, D. C. Genetic and environmental etiology of social behavior in infancy. *Developmental Psychology,* 1979, *15,* 62–72.

Plude, D. J. and Hoyer, W. J. Adult age differences in visual search as a function of stimulus mapping and processing load. *Journal of Gerontology,* 1981, *36,* 598–604.

Poppen, P. J., Wandersman, A., & Wandersman, L. P. What are humanism and behaviorism and what can they say to each other? In A. Wandersman, P. Poppen, & D. Ricks (eds.), *Humanism and behaviorism: Dialogue and growth.* Oxford, England: Pergamon Press, 1976.

Porteus, A. *Teacher-centered vs. student-centered instruction: Interactions with cognitive and motivational aptitudes.* Unpublished doctoral dissertation, Stanford University, 1976.

Premack, D. *Intelligence in ape and man.* New York: Halsted Press, 1976.

Pressley, M., Heisel, B. E., McCormick, C. B., & Nakamura, G. U. Memory strategy instruction with children. In C. J. Brainerd & M. Pressley (eds.), *Progress in cognitive development research* (vol. 2), *Verbal processes in children.* New York: Springer-Verlag, 1982.

Pribram, K. *Languages of the brain: Experimental paradoxes and principles in neuropsychology.* Englewood Cliffs, N.J.: Prentice-Hall, 1971.

Price, G. *Factors influencing reciprocity in early mother-infant interaction.* Paper presented at the biennial meeting of the Society for Research in Child Development, New Orleans, Louisiana, March 1977.

Protinsky, H., & Hughston, G. Conservation in elderly males: An empirical investigation. *Developmental Psychology,* 1978, *14,* 114.

Psathas, G. Ethnicity, social class, and adolescent independence. *American Sociological Review,* 1957, *22,* 415–523.

Puner, H. W. *Freud: His life and his mind.* New York: Crown, 1949.

q

Quadagno, D. M., Briscoe, R., & Quadagno, J. S. Effect of perinatal gonadal hormones on selected nonsexual behavior patterns: A critical assessment of the nonhuman and human literature. *Psychological Bulletin,* 1977, *84,* 62–80.

Quetelet, A. *Sur l'homme et le développement de ses facultés.* Paris: Bachelier, 1835.

r

Rabinowitz, J. C., Craik, F. I. M., & Ackerman, B. P. A processing resource account of age differences in recall. *Canadian Journal of Psychology,* in press.

Rand McNally Atlas of the Body and Mind. © Mitchell Beazley Publishers, Ltd. Published in the U.S.A. in Chicago: Rand McNally, 1976.

Reedy, M. N., Birren, J. E., & Schaie, K. W. Age and sex differences in satisfying love relationships across the adult life span. *Human Development,* 1981, *24,* 52–66.

Reese, H. W. Cohort, age, and imagery in children's paired associate learning. *Child Development,* 1974, *45,* 1176–1178.

Regan, J. W. Guilt, perceived injustice, and altruistic behavior. *Journal of Personality and Social Psychology,* 1971, *18,* 124–132.

Regnier, V. Neighborhood planning for the urban elderly. In D. S. Woodruff & J. E. Birren (eds.), *Aging: Scientific perspectives and social issues.* New York: Van Nostrand Reinhold, 1975.

Reichard, S., Levson, F., Peterson, P. *Aging and personality: A study of 87 older men.* New York: John Wiley, 1962.

Reiss, I. L. *The family system in America.* New York: Holt, Rinehart & Winston, 1971.

Rekers, G. A. Psychosexual and gender problems. In E. J. Mash & L. G. Terdal (eds.), *Behavioral assessment of childhood disorders.* New York: Guilford Press, 1979.

Renner, J. W., & Stafford, D. B. *Teaching science in the secondary school.* New York: Harper & Row, 1972.

Rest, J. New approaches in the assessment of moral judgment. In T. Lickona (ed.), *Moral development and behavior.* New York: Holt, Rinehart & Winston, 1976.

Rest, J. *Development in judging moral issues—A summary of research using the defining issues test.* Paper presented at the meeting of the Society for Research in Child Development, New Orleans, Louisiana, March 1977.

Rest, J., Turiel, E., & Kohlberg, L. Relations between level of moral judgment and preference and comprehension of the moral judgments of others. *Journal of Personality,* 1969, *37,* 225–252.

Restak, R. Brain potentials: Signaling our inner thoughts. *Psychology Today,* March 1979.

Retherford, R. D. *The changing sex differential in mortality.* Westport, Conn.: Greenwood Press, 1975.

Reynolds, L. G., & Shister, J. *Job horizons.* New York: Harper & Row, 1949.

Rheingold, H. L. The social and socializing infant. In D. A. Goslin (ed.), *Handbook of socialization theory and research.* Chicago: Rand McNally, 1969.

Rheingold, H. L. Independent behavior of the human infant. In A. Pick (ed.), *Minnesota Syposium of Child Psychology,* vol. 7. Minneapolis: University of Minnesota Press, 1973.

Rheingold, H. L., & Adams, J. L. The significance of speech to newborns. *Developmental Psychology,* 1980 *16*(5), 397–403.

Rheingold, H. L., & Eckerman, C. O. The infant's free entry into a new environment. *Journal of Experimental Child Psychology,* 1969, *8,* 271–283.

Rheingold, H. L., & Eckerman, C. O. The infant separates himself from his mother. *Science,* 1970, *168,* 78–83.

Rheingold, H. L., Gewirtz, J. L., & Ross, H. W. Social conditioning of vocalizations in the infant. *Journal of Comparative and Physiological Psychology,* 1959, *52,* 68–73.

Rheingold, H. L., & Samuels, H. R. Maintaining the positive behavior of infants by increased stimulation. *Developmental Psychology,* 1969, *1,* 520–527.

Rhodes, S. L. A developmental approach to the life cycle of the family. *Social Casework,* 1977, *58,* 301–311.

Ricciuti, H. N. Fear and the development of social attachments in the first year of life. In M. Lewis and L. A. Rosenblum (eds.), *The origins of fear.* New York: John Wiley, 1974, pp. 73–106.

Rice, B. Brave New Worlds of Intelligence Testing. *Psychology Today.* September 1979. Reprinted from *Psychology Today* magazine. Copyright © 1979 Ziff-Davis Publishing Company.

Richard, R. A. A comparison of selected Guilford and Wallach-Kogan creative thinking tests in conjunction with measures of intelligence. *Journal of Creative Behavior,* 1976, *10*(3), 151–164.

Riege, W. H. and Inman, V. Age differences in nonverbal memory tasks. *Journal of Gerontology,* 1981, *36,* 51–58.

Riegel, K. F. Dialectic operations: The final period of cognitive development. *Human Development,* 1973, *16,* 346–370.

Riegel, K. F. Adult life crises: A dialectic interpretation of development. In N. Datan & L. H. Ginsberg (eds.), *Life-span developmental psychology.* New York: Academic Press, 1975.

Riegel, K. F. The dialects of human development. *American Psychologist,* 1976, *31.*

Riegel, K. F., & Riegel, R. M. Development, drop, and death. *Developmental Psychology,* 1972, *6,* 306–319.

Riley, J. W. What people think about death. In O. G. Brim, H. E. Freeman, S. Levine, & N. A. Scotch (eds.), *The dying patient.* New York: Russell Sage Foundation, 1970.

Riley, M. W. (ed.). *Aging from birth to death: Interdisciplinary perspectives.* Boulder, Colo.: Westview Press, 1979.

Riley, M. W., & Foner, A. Aging and society, vol. 1. An inventory of Research Findings. New York: Russell Sage Foundation, 1968.

Ringness, T. A. *The affective domain in education.* Boston: Little Brown, 1975. Reprinted by permission.

Robertson, J. F. Significance of grandparents: Perceptions of young adult grandchildren. *The Gerontologist,* 1976, *16,* 137–140.

Robinson, H. B., & Robinson, N. M. Mental retardation. In P. H. Mussen (ed.), *Carmichael's manual of child psychology* (3rd ed., vol. 2). New York: John Wiley, 1970.

Rodin, E. A. The reality of death experience: A personal perspective. *Journal of Nervous and Mental Disease,* 1980, *168,* 259–263.

Rodin, J., & Langer, E. Aging labels: The decline of control and the fall of self-esteem. *Journal of Social Issues,* 1980, *36,* 12–29.

Rogers, C. R. A theory of therapy, personality, and interpersonal relationships as developed in the client-centered framework. In S. Koch,(ed.), *Psychology: A study of science* (vol. 3). New York: McGraw-Hill, 1959, 184–256.

Rogers, C. R. Carl R. Rogers. In E. G. Boring & G. Lindzey (eds.), *A history of psychology in autobiography* (vol. V). New York: Appleton-Century-Crofts, 1967.

Rogers, C. R. In retrospect: Forty-six years. *American Psychologist,* 1974, *29,* 115–123.

Rohwer, W. D., Jr., & Levin, J. R. Elaboration preferences and differences in learning proficiency. In J. Hellmuth (ed.), *Cognitive studies* (vol. 2). New York: Brunner/Mazel, 1971.

Rollins, B. C., & Feldman, H. Marital satisfaction over the family life cycle. *Journal of Marriage and the Family,* 1970, *32,* 20–28.

Rollins, B., & Galliger, R. The developing child and marital satisfaction. In R. Lerner & G. Spanier (ed.), *Child influences on marital interaction: A life-span perspective.* New York: Academic Press, 1979.

Romer, N., & Cherry, D. *Developmental effects of preschool and school age maternal employment on children's sex role concepts.* Unpublished manuscript, Brooklyn College of the City University of New York, 1978.

Rosch, E. H. On the internal structure of perceptual and semantic categories. In T. E. Moore (ed.), *Cognition and the acquisition of language.* New York: Academic Press, 1973.

Rosen, B. M., Bahn, A. K., & Kramer, M. Demographic and diagnostic characteristics of psychiatric outpatients in the U.S.A., 1961, *American Journal of Orthopsychiatry,* 1964, *34,* 455–468.

Rosenbaum, A. L., Churchill, J. A., Shakhashiri, Z. A., & Moody, R. L. Neurophysiologic outcome of children whose mothers had proteinuria during pregnancy: A report from the collaborative study of cerebral palsy. *Obstetrics and Gynecology,* 1969, *33,* 118–123.

Rosenfeld, A. *Prolongevity.* New York: Avon, 1976.

Rosenfield, A. Visiting in the intensive care nursery. *Child Development,* 1980, *51*(3), 939–941.

Rosenkrans, M. A. Imitation in children as a function of perceived similarity to a social model and vicarious reinforcement. *Journal of Personality and Social Psychology,* 1967, *7,* 307–315.

Rosenman, R. H., Friedman, M., Straus, R., Jenkins, C. D., Zyzanski, S., Wurm, M., & Kositchek, R., Hah, W., & Werthessen, N. T. Coronary heart disease in the western collaborative group study: A follow-up experience of 4 1/2 years. *Journal of Chronic Diseases,* 1970, *23,* 173–190.

Rosenmayr, L. The family—Source of hope for the elderly of the future. In E. Shana & M. B. Sussman (eds.), *Older people, family and bureaucracy.* Durham, N.C.: Duke University Press, 1968.

Rosenthal, R., & Jacobsen, L. *Pygmalion in the classroom.* New York: Holt, Rinehart & Winston, 1968.

Rosenthal, T. L., & Zimmerman, B. J. *Social learning and development.* New York: Academic Press, 1978.

Ross, A. O. *Psychological disorders of children: A behavioral approach to theory, research, and therapy.* New York: McGraw-Hill, 1974.

Ross, A. O. *Psychological disorders of children: A behavioral approach to theory, research, and therapy* (2nd ed.). New York: McGraw-Hill, 1979.

Ross, D. G. *Stanley Hall: The psychologist as prophet.* Chicago: University of Chicago Press, 1972.

Ross, H. G., & Dalton, M. J. *Perceived determinants of closeness in adult sibling relationships.* Paper presented at the Annual Meeting of the American Psychological Association, Los Angeles, California, August 1981.

Rossi, A. S. A biosocial perspective on parenting. *Daedalus,* 1977, *106,* 1–31.

Rothbart, M. L. K. Birth order and mother-child interaction. *Dissertation Abstracts,* 1967, *27,* 45–57.

Rubin, K. H. Egocentrism in childhood: A unitary construct? *Child Development,* 1973, *44,* 102–110.

Rubin, K. H., & Schneider, F. W. The relationship between moral judgment, egocentrism, and altruistic behavior. *Child Development,* 1973, *44,* 661–665.

Rubin, Z. Measurement of romantic love. *Journal of Personality and Social Psychology,* 1970, *16,* 265–273.

Rubin, Z. *Liking and loving: An invitation to social psychology.* New York: Holt, Rinehart & Winston, 1973.

Rubin, Z. Does personality really change after 20? *Psychology Today,* 1981. Reprinted from *Psychology Today* Magazine. Copyright © 1981 Ziff-Davis Publishing Company.

Ruff, H. A., & Birch, H. G. Infant visual fixation: The effect of concentricity, curvilinearity, and number of directions. *Journal of Experimental Psychology,* 1974, *17,* 460–473.

Russell, C. Transition to parenthood: Problems and gratifications. *Journal of Marriage and the Family,* 1974, *36,* 294–302.

Rutter, M. Parent-child separation: Psychological effects on the children. *Journal of Child Psychology and Psychiatry,* 1971, *12,* 233–256.

Rutter, M. Maternal deprivation 1972–1978. New findings, new concepts, new approaches. *Child Development,* in press.

Rutter, M., Graham, P., Chadwick, O. F. D., & Yule, W. Adolescent turmoil: Fact or fiction? *Journal of Child Psychology and Psychiatry,* 1976, *17,* 35–36.

Rux, J. M. *Widows and widowers: Instrumental skills, socioeconomic status, and life satisfaction.* Unpublished doctoral dissertation, Penn State University, 1976.

S

Sadick, T., & Ginsburg, E. The development of the lateral functions and reading ability. Cortex, 1978, *14,* 3–11.

Salapatek, P. Pattern perception in early infancy. In L. B. Cohen & P. Salapatek (eds.), *Infant perception: From sensation to cognition* (vol. 1). New York: Academic Press, 1975.

Sameroff, A. J. Learning and adaptation in infancy. In H. W. Reese (ed.), *Advances in child development and behavior* (vol. 7). New York: Academic Press, 1972.

Sameroff, A. J., & Chandler, M. J. Reproductive risk and the continuum of caretaking casualty. In F. D. Horowitz (ed.), *Review of Child Development Research* (vol. 4). Chicago: University of Chicago Press, 1975.

Samuels, H. R. *The sibling in the infant's social environment.* Paper presented at the meeting of the Society for Research in Child Development, New Orleans, Louisiana, March 1977.

Samuels, H. R. The effect of an older sibling on infant locomotor exploration of a new environment. *Child Development,* 1980, *51,* 607–609.

Sandberg, A. *Seeing the invisible.* Plainfield, N.J.: Logos International, 1977.

Sandburg, C. Prologue to *The Family of Man.* Edward Steicher (ed.). New York: The Museum of Modern Art, 1955. All rights reserved. Reprinted by permission of the publisher.

Sanders, R. E., & Sanders, J. C. Long-term durability and transfer of enhanced conceptual performance in the elderly. *Journal of Gerontology,* 1978, *33,* 408–412.

Sandler, L. W. Infant and caretaking environment: Investigation and conceptualization of adaptive behavior in a system of increasing complexity. In J. Anthony (ed.), *Explorations in child psychiatry,* 1975.

Santrock, J. W. Moral structure: Interrelations of moral judgment, affect, and behavior. *Journal of Genetic Psychology,* 1975, *127,* 210–213.

Santrock, J. W., & Minnett, A. *Sibling interaction: An observational study of sex of sibling, age spacing, and ordinal position.* Paper presented at the Biennial meeting of the Society for Research in Child Development, Boston, Mass., April 1981.

Santrock, J. W., Smith, P. C., & Bourbeau, P. Effects of group social comparison upon aggressive and regressive behavior in children. *Child Development,* 1976, *47,* 831–837.

Santrock, J. W., & Tracy, R. L. The effects of children's family structure status on the development of stereotypes by teachers. *Journal of Educational Psychology,* 1978, *70,* 754–757.

Santrock, J. W., & Warshak, R. A. Father custody and social development in boys and girls. *Journal of Social Issues,* 1979, *35,* 112–125.

Santrock, J. W., Warshak, R. A., & Eliot, G. Social development and parent-child interaction in father custody and stepmother families. In M. E. Lamb (Ed.), *Nontraditional families.* Hillsdale, N.J.: L. Erlbaum Assoc., 1982.

Santrock, J. W., Warshak, R., Lindbergh, C., & Meadows, L. Children's and parents' observed social behavior in stepfather families. *Child Development,* 1982, *53,* 472–480.

Sapir, E. Language and environment. In D. G. Mandelbaum (ed.), *Selected writings of Edward Sapir in language, culture, and personality.* Berkeley: University of California Press, 1958.

Sarason, I. Life stress, self-preoccupation, and social supports. In I. G. Sarason K & C. D. Spielberger (eds.), *Stress and anxiety* (vol. 7). Washington, D.C.: Hemisphere Publishers, 1980.

Sarason, I. G., & Spielberger, C. D. (eds.). *Stress and anxiety.* Washington, D.C.: Hemisphere Publishing, 1975.

Sattler, J. M. *Assessment of children's intelligence.* Philadelphia: Saunders, 1974.

Sauber, M., & Corrigan, E. M. *The six year experience of unwed mothers as parents.* New York: Community council of Greater New York, 1970.

Scarr, S. Testing for children: Assessment and the many determinants of intellectual competence. *American Psychologist,* 1981, *36,* 1159–1166.

Scarr, S., & Weinberg, R. A. IQ test performance of black children adopted by white families. *American Psychologist,* 1976, *31,* 726–739.

Scarr-Salapatek, S. Genetics and the development of intelligence. In F. D. Horowitz (ed.), *Review of child development research* (vol. 4). Chicago: University of Chicago Press, 1975.

Scarr-Salapatek, S. An evolutionary perspective on infant intelligence: Species patterns and individual variations. In M. Lewis (ed.), *Origins of Intelligence.* New York: Plenum, 1976.

Schacter, S. *The psychology of affiliation.* Stanford, Calif.: Stanford University Press, 1959.

Schaefer, E. S. A configurational analysis of children's reports of parent behavior. *Journal of Consulting Psychology,* 1965, *29,* 552–557.

Schaeffer, H. R. *The growth of sociability.* Penguin-Harmondsworth, 1971.

Schaeffer, H. R. *Mothering.* Cambridge, Mass.: Harvard University Press, 1977.

Schaeffer, H. R., & Emerson, P. E. The development of social attachments in infancy. *Monographs of the Society for Research in Child Development,* 1964, *29.*

Schaie, K. W. A reinterpretation of age-related changes in cognitive structure and functioning. In L. R. Goulet & P. B. Baltes (eds.), *Life-span developmental psychology: Research and theory.* New York: Academic Press, 1970.

Schaie, K. W. Toward a stage theory of adult cognitive development. *International Journal of Aging and Human Development,* 1977, *8,* 129–138.

Schaie, K. W. The primary mental abilities in adulthood: An exploration in the development of psychometric intelligence. In P. B. Baltes & O. G. Brim (eds.), *Life-span development and behavior* (vol. 2). New York: Academic Press, 1979.

Schank, R. C., & Abelson, R. P. *Scripts, plans, goals, and understanding.* Hillsdale, N.J.: Erlbaum, 1977.

Schneider, W. and Shiffrin, R. M. Controlled and automatic human information processing: I. Detection, Search and Attention. *Psychological Review,* 1977, *84,* 1–66.

Schofield, A. T., & Vaughan-Jackson, P. *What a boy should know.* New York: Cassell, 1913.

Schonfield, D. and Robertson, B. A. Memory storage and aging. *Canadian Journal of Psychology,* 1966, *20,* 228–236.

Schoo, P. H. *Students' self-concept, social behavior, and attitudes toward school in middle and junior high schools.* Unpublished doctoral dissertation, University of Michigan, 1970.

Schooler, C. Serdom's legacy: An ethnic continuum. *American Journal of Sociology,* 1976, *81,* 1265–1286.

Schramm, W., Lyle, J., & Parker, E. B. *Television in the lives of children.* Stanford, Calif.: Stanford University Press, 1961.

Schultz, W. R., Hoyer, W. J. Feedback effects on spatial egocentrism in old age. *Journal of Gerontology,* 1976, *31,* 72–75.

Schwartz, K. Proximity to mother and wariness in infants association with exploration of an unfamiliar object. *Dissertation Abstracts International,* 1978, *38,* 12B, 6204–6205.

Sears, P. S., & Barbee, A. H. *Career and life satisfaction among Terman's gifted women.* Paper presented at the Terman Memorial Symposium on Intellectual Talent, Johns Hopkins University, November 1975.

Sears, P. S., & Barbee, A. H. Care and life satisfactions among Terman's gifted women. In J. C. Stanley, W. C. George, & C. H. Solano (eds.), *The gifted and the creative: A fifty-year perspective.* Baltimore: Johns Hopkins Press, 1977.

Sears, R. R. Sources of life satisfactions of the Terman gifted men. *American Psychologist,* 1977, *32,* 119–128.

Sears, R. R. Midlife development. (Review of The Seasons of a Man's Life by D. J. Levinson). *Contemporary Psychology,* 1979, *234,* 97–98.

Sears, R. R., & Feldman, S. S. (eds.). *The seven ages of man.* Los Altos, Calif.: William Kaufmann, 1973.

Seay, B., & Gottfried, N. *The development of behavior: A synthesis of developmental and comparative psychology.* Boston: Houghton-Mifflin, 1978.

Seeman, M. On the meaning of alienation. *American Sociological Review,* 1959, *24,* 783–791.

Seligman, M. E. P. *Helplessness: On depression, development, and death.* San Francisco: W. H. Freeman, 1975.

Selman, R. L. The relation of role-taking ability to the development of moral judgment in children. *Child Development*, 1971, *42*, 79–91.

Selman, R. L. Taking another's perspective: Role-taking development in early childhood. *Child Development*, 1971, *42*, 1721–1732.(b)

Selman, R. L. The development of social-cognitive understanding: A guide to educational and clinical practice. In T. Lickona (ed.), *Morality: Theory, research, and social issues*. New York: Holt, Rinehart & Winston, 1976 (a).

Selman, R. L. Toward a structural analysis of developing interpersonal relations concepts: Research with normal and disturbed preadolescent boys. In A. D. Pick (ed.), *Minnesota Symposia on Child Psychology* (vol. 10). Minneapolis: University of Minnesota Press, 1976 (b), 156–200.

Selman, R. L., & Byrne, D. F. A structural-developmental analysis of levels of role taking in middle childhood. *Child Development*, 1974, *45*, 803–806.

Selman, R. L., Newberger, C. M., & Jacquette, D. *Observing interpersonal reasoning in a clinic/educational setting: Toward the integration of development and clinical-child psychology*. Paper presented at the meeting for the Society for Research in Child Development, New Orleans, Louisiana, 1977.

Senn, M. J. E. Insights on the child development movement in the United States. *Monographs of the Society for Research in Child Development*, 1975, *40*(3–4, serial no. 161).

Serbin, L. A., O'Leary, K. D., Kent, R. N., & Tonick, I. J. A comparison of teacher response to the preacademic and problem behavior of boys and girls. *Child Development*, 1973, *44*.

Shafer, R. P., et al, *Drug use in America: Problem in perspective*. Second report of the National Commission on Marijuana and Drug Abuse. Washington, D.C.: U.S. Government Printing Office, no. 5266–00003, 1973.

Shanas, E., Townsend, P., Wedderburn, D., Friis, H., Milhoj, P., & Stehouwer, J. (eds.), *Old people in three societies*. New York: Atherton, 1968.

Shantz, C. The development of social cognition. In E. M. Hetherington (ed.), *Review of child development research* (vol. 5). Chicago: University of Chicago Press, 1976.

Shantz, C. U. Psychological cognition—Social cognition. In J. H. Flavell, & E. Markman (eds.). *Carmichael's Manual of Child Psychology* (vol. III.). 4th ed., New York: John Wiley, 1982.

Sharpe, L. W. The effects of a creative thinking program on intermediate-grade educationally handicapped children. *Journal of Creative Behavior*, 1976, *10*(2), 138–145.

Shatz, M., & Gelman, R. The development of communication skills: Modifications in the speech of young children as a function of listener. *Monographs of the Society for Research in Child Development*, 1973, *38*(5, serial no. 152).

Sheehy, G. *Passages*. New York: Dutton, 1976.

Sheingold, K. Developmental differences in intake and storage of visual information. *Journal of Experimental Child Psychology*, 1973, *16*, 1–11.

Shepard, R. N. Recognition memory for words, sentences, and pictures. *Journal of Verbal Learning and Verbal Behavior*, 1967, *6*, 156–163.

Shepard, R. N. and Metzler, J. Mental rotation of three-dimensional objects. *Science*, 1971, *171*, 701–703.

Sherif, M. Experimental study of intergroup relations. In J. H. Rohrer & M. Sherif (eds.), *Social psychology at the crossroads*. New York: Harper & Row, 1951.

Sherif, M. *In common predicament: Social psychology of intergroup conflict and cooperation*. Boston: Houghton-Mifflin, 1966.

Sherif, M., Harvey, O. J., Hoyt, B. J., Hood, W. R., & Sherif, C. W. *Intergroup conflict and cooperation: The robbers cave experiment*. Norman: University of Oklahoma Book Exchange, 1961.

Sherif, M., & Sherif, C. W. *Reference groups: Exploration into conformity and deviation of adolescents*. New York: Harper & Row, 1964.

Sherman, J. A. Imitation and language development. In H. W. Reese (ed.), *Advances in child development and behavior* (vol. 6). New York: Academic Press, 1975.

Shields, S. A. Personality trait attribution and reproductive role. Unpublished master's thesis, Pennsylvania State University Dept. of Psychology, 1973.

Shneidman, E. *Deaths of man*. New York: New York Times Book Co., 1973.

Shock, N. W. Mortality and measurement of aging. In B. L. Strehler, J. D. Ebert, H. B. Glass, & N. W. Shock (eds.), *The biology of aging*. Washington, D.C.: American Institute of Biological Sciences, 1960.

Shock, N. W. Biological theories of aging. In J. E. Birren & K. W. Schaie (eds.), *Handbook of the psychology of aging*. New York: Van Nostrand Reinhold, 1977.

Shovlin, D. W. *The effect of the middle school environment and the elementary school environment upon sixth-grade students*. Unpublished doctoral dissertation, University of Washington, 1967.

Shuey, A. *The testing of Negro intelligence*. New York: Social Science Press, 1966.

Shuy, R. W., & Griffin, P. What do they do at school any day: studying functional language. In W. P. Dickson (ed.), *Children's oral communication skills*. New York: Academic Press, 1981.

Siegel, R. K. The psychology of life after death. *American Psychologist*, 1980, *35*, 911–931.

Siegel, R. K. Accounting for 'afterlife' experiences. *Psychology Today*, January 1981, 65–75.

Siegler, R. S. The origins of scientific reasoning. In R. S. Siegler (ed.), *Children's thinking: What develops?* Hillsdale, N.J.: Erlbaum, 1978.

Siegler, R. S. Information processing approaches to development. In W. Kessen (ed.), *Carmichael's manual of child psychology*, vol. I, 4th ed. New York: John Wiley, 1982.

Siegler, R. S. Information processing approaches to development. In P. Mussen (ed.), *Carmichael's manual of child psychology: History, theories, and methods*. New York: John Wiley, 1982.

Siegler, R. S., Liebert, D. C., & Liebert, R. M. Inhelder and Piaget's pendulum problem: Teaching preadolescents to act as scientists. *Developmental Psychology*, 1973, *9*, 97–101.

Sigel, I. E., & Hooper, F. H. *Logical thinking in children*. New York: Holt, Rinehart & Winston, 1968.

Sigusch, V., & Schmidt, G. Teenage boys and girls in West Germany. *Journal of Sex Research*, 1973, *9*, 107–123.

Silberman, C. E. *Crisis in the classroom: The remaking of American education*. New York: Random House, 1970.

Simmons, R., Rosenberg, F., & Rosenberg, M. Disturbance in the self-image at adolescence. *American Sociological Review*, 1973, *38*, 553–568.

Simon, H. A. Information-processing explanations of understanding. In T. W. Jusczyk & R. M. Klein (eds.), *The nature of thought: Essays in honor of D. O. Hebb*. Hillsdale, N.J.: Erlbaum, 1980.

Simon, W., & Gagnon, J. H. On psychosexual development. In D. Goslin (ed.), *Handbook of socialization theory and research*. Chicago: Rand McNally, 1969.

Simpson, E. L. Moral development research: A case of scientific cultural bias. *Human Development*, 1974, *17*(2), 81–106.

Simpson, E. L. A holistic approach to moral development and behavior. In T. Lickona (ed.), *Moral development and behavior*. New York: Holt, Rinehart & Winston, 1976.

Simpson, M. The sociology of cognitive development. In *Annual Review of Sociology*. Palo Alto, Calif.: Annual Reviews, 1980.

Simpson, R. L. Parental influence, anticipatory socialization, and social mobility. *American Sociological Review*, 1962, *27*, 517–522.

Sinclair-DeZwart, H. Developmental psycholinguistics. In D. Elkind & J. H. Flavell (eds.), *Studies in cognitive development: Essays in honor of Jean Piaget*. New York: Oxford University Press, 1969.

Singer, M. T. Personality measurements in the aged. In J. E. Birren, R. N. Butler, S. W. Greenhouse, L. Sokoloff, & M. R. Yarrow (eds.), *Human Aging*. Washington, D.C.: U.S. Government Printing Office, 1963.

Sinnott, J. D. Everyday thinking and Piagetian operativity in adults. *Human Development*, 1975, *18*, 430–443.

Skinner, B. F. *The behavior of organisms: An experimental analysis*. New York: Appleton-Century-Crofts, 1938.

Skinner, B. F. *Walden two*. New York: MacMillan, 1948.

Skinner, B. F. *Science and human behavior*. New York: MacMillan, 1953.

Skinner, B. F. *Verbal behavior*. New York: Appleton-Century-Crofts, 1957.

Skinner, B. F. *Beyond freedom and dignity*. New York: Knopf, 1971.

Skinner, B. F. *About behaviorism*. New York: Knopf, 1974.

Skinner, B. F. *A conversation between B. F. Skinner and H. Eysenck*. A symposium presented at the annual meeting of the American Psychological Association, Montreal, 1980.

Skodak, M., & Skeels, H. M. A final follow-up study of 100 children. *Journal of Genetic Psychology*, 1949, *75*, 85–125.

Slater, P. *The pursuit of loneliness*. Boston: Beacon Press, 1970.

Sloane, S. A., et. al. Visual cliff performance in 10 species of murid rodents. *Animal Learning and Behavior*, 1978, *6*, 244–248.

Slobin, D. I. Children and language: They learn the same all around the world. *Psychology Today*, 1972. Reprinted from *Psychology Today* Magazine, Copyright © 1972, Ziff Davis Publishing Co.

Sloboda, S. B. The children of alcoholics: A neglected problem. *Hospital and Community Psychiatry*, 1974, *25*, 605–606.

Smart, M. S., & Smart, R. C. *Children: Development and Relations*. New York: MacMillan, 1972. Reprinted with permission of MacMillan Publishing Co., Inc. from *Children: Development and Relations*, p. 218, by Mollie S. Smart and Russell C. Smart. Copyright © 1972 by MacMillan Publishing Co., Inc.

Smelser, N. J. Issues in the study of work and love in adulthood. In N. J. Smelser & E. H. Erikson (eds.), *Theme of work and love in adulthood*. Cambridge, Mass.: Harvard University Press, 1980.

Smith, A. D. Adult age differences in cued recall. *Developmental Psychology*, 1977, *13*, 326–331.

Smith, A. D. Age differences in encoding, storage, and retrieval. In L. W. Poon, J. L. Fozard, L. S. Cermak, D. Arenberg, & L. W. Thompson (eds.). *New directions in memory and aging: Proceedings of the George A. Talland memorial conference*. Hillsdale, N.J.: Erlbaum, 1980.

Smith, F. Learning to read by reading. *Language Arts*, 1976, *53*, 297–299.

Smith, P. Introductory statements. *Journal of Counseling and Values*, April 1977 (Special Issue).

Smock, C. D. *Piaget and Project Follow Through*. Lecture given at the University of Georgia, 1975.

Snow, C. Mother's speech to children learning language. *Child Development*, 1972, *43*, 549–565.

Snow, C. The development of conversation between mothers and babies. *Journal of Child Language*, 1977, *4*, 1–22.

Snow, C., & Ferguson, C. *Talking to children*. Cambridge: Cambridge University Press, 1977.

Snow, R. E. Individual differences and instructional theory. *Educational Researcher*, 1977, *6*, 11–15.

Snyder, M. Self-monitoring processes. In L. Berkowitz (ed.), *Advances in Experimental Social Psychology* (vol. 12). New York: Academic Press, 1979.

Solomon, R. W., & Wahlen, R. G. Peer reinforcement control of classroom problem behavior. *Journal of Applied Behavior Analysis*, 1973, *6*, 49–56.

Somervil, J. W., & Nunez, V. The importance of a "cliff" in depth avoidance by human infants. *Journal of General Psychology,* 1978, *98,* 303–304.

Sorensen, R. C. *Adolescent sexuality in contemporary America.* New York: World, 1973.

Spanier, G. G., & Castro, R. Adjustment to separation and divorce: An analysis of 50 case studies. *Journal of Divorce,* 1979, *2,* 241–253.

Spearman, C. E. *The abilities of man.* New York: Macmillan, 1927.

Spence, J. T. Comments on Baumrind's "Are androgynous individuals more effective persons and parents?" *Child Psychology,* 1982, *53,* 76–80.

Spence, J. T., & Helmreich, R. L. *Masculinity and femininity: Their psychological dimensions.* Austin, Texas: University of Texas Press, 1978.

Spence, J. T., Helmreich, R., & Stapp, J. Ratings of self and peers on sex-role attributes and their relation to self-esteem and conceptions of masculinity and femininity. *Journal of Personality and Social Psychology,* 1975, *32,* 29–39.

Spence, J. T., Helmreich, R. L., & Stapp, J. The personal attributes questionnaire: A measure of sex-role stereotypes and masculinity-femininity. *JSAS Catalog of Selected Documents in Psychology,* 1974, *4,* 43.

Spicer, J., & Hampe, G. Kinship interaction after divorce. *Journal of Marriage and the Family,* 1975, *28,* 113–119.

Spiegel, P. M. Theories of aging. In P. S. Timiras (ed.), *Developmental Physiology and Aging.* New York: MacMillan, 1977.

Spieth, W. Slowness of task performance and cardiovascular diseases. In A. T. Wilford & J. E. Birren (eds.), *Behavior, aging, and the nervous system.* Springfield, Ill.: Charles C Thomas, 1965.

Spitz, R. A. Hospitalism: An inquiry into the genesis of psychiatric conditioning in early childhood. In D. Fenschel (ed.), *Psychoanalytic Study of the child* (vol. 1). New York: International Universities Press, 1945.

Sroufe, L. A. Socioemotional development. In J. Osofsky (ed.), *Handbook of infant development.* New York: John Wiley, 1978.

Sroufe, L. A., Waters, E., & Matas, L. Contextual determinants of infant affective response. In M. Lewis and L. A. Rosenblum (eds.), *The origins of fear.* New York: John Wiley, 1974, pp. 49–72.

Staats, A. W. Linguistic-mentalistic theory versus an explanatory S-R learning theory of language development. In D. Slobin (ed.). *The ontogenesis of grammar.* New York: Academic Press, 1971.

Staats, A. W., Brewer, B. A., & Gross, M. C. Learning and cognitive development: Representative samples, cumulative-hierarchical learning, and experimental-longitudinal methods. *Monographs of the Society for Research in Child Development,* 1970, *35*(8, serial no. 141).

Stallings, J. Implementation and child effects of teaching practices in follow through classrooms. *Monographs of the Society for Research in Child Development,* 1975, *40* (serial no. 163).

Stanley, E. J., & Barter, J. T. Adolescent suicidal behavior. *American Journal of Orthopsychiatry,* 1970, 40, 87–96.

Stanley, J. C. Rationale of the study of mathematically precocious youth (SMPY) during its first five years of promoting educational acceleration. In Stanley, J. C., George, W. C., & Solano, C. H. (eds.), *The gifted and creative: A fifty-year perspective.* Baltimore: The Johns Hopkins University Press, 1977.

Starr, R. H. Child abuse. *American Psychologist,* 1979, *34,* 886–891.

Staub, E. Helping a distressed person. In L. Berkowitz (ed.), *Advances in experimental social psychology* (Vol. 7). New York: Academic Press, 1974.

Stea, D. Environmental perception and cognition: Toward a model for "mental maps." In G. J. Coates & K. M. Moffet (eds.), *Response to environment.* Raleigh, N.C.: School of Design, North Carolina State University, 1969.

Stein, A. H. Mass media and young children's development. In I. J. Gordon (ed.), *Early childhood education: The seventy-first yearbook of the National Society for the Study of Education* (part 2). Chicago: University of Chicago Press, 1972.

Stein, A. H., & Bailey, M. M. The socialization of achievement orientation in females. *Psychological Bulletin,* 1973, *80,* 345–365.

Stein, N. L., & Glenn, C. G. An analysis of story comprehension in elementary school children. In R. O. Freedle (ed.), *Discourse processing: Multidisciplinary perspectives.* Norwood, N.J.: Ablex, 1979.

Stein, N. L., & Trabasso, T. What's in a story? Critical issues in comprehension and instruction. In R. Glaser (ed.), *Advances in the psychology of instruction* (vol. 2). Hillsdale, N.J.: Erlbaum, 1981.

Steinschneider, A., Lipton, E. L., & Richmond, J. B. Auditory sensitivity in the infant: Effect of intensity on cardiac and motor responsivity. *Child Development,* 1966, *37,* 233–252.

Stephens, J. *Loners, losers, and lovers: Elderly tenants in a slum hotel.* Seattle, Wash.: University of Washington Press, 1976.

Stern, D. N., Jaffe, J., Beebe, B., & Bennett, S. L. *Vocalizing in unison and in alternation: Two modes of communication within the mother-infant dyad.* Paper presented at the Conference on Developmental Psycholinguistics and Communication Disorders, New York Academy of Sciences, New York, January 1975.

Sternberg, R. J., & Downing, C. J. The development of higher-order reasoning in adolescence. *Child Development,* in press.

Sternberg, S. High speed scanning in human memory. *Science,* 1969, *153,* 652–654.

Sterns, H. L., & Sanders, R. E. Training and education of the elderly. In R. R. Turner & H. W. Reese (eds.), *Life-span developmental psychology: Intervention.* New York: Academic Press, 1980.

Steuer, F. B., Applefield, J. M., & Smith, R. Televised aggression and interpersonal aggression of preschool children. *Journal of Experimental Child Psychology,* 1971, *11,* 442–447.

Stevenson, H. W. *Children's learning.* New York: Appleton-Century-Crofts, 1972.

Stevenson, H. W. *The taxonomy of tasks.* Unpublished manuscript, University of Minnesota, 1973.

Stevenson, H. W. Reflections on the China visit. *Society for Research in Child Development Newsletter,* Fall, 1974, *3.*

Stevenson, I. Research into the evidence of man's survival after death. *Journal of Nervous and Mental Disease,* 1977, *165,* 152–170.

Stewart, A. L., & Reynolds, E. O. R. Improved prognosis for infants of very low birth weight. *Pediatrics,* 1974, *54,* 724–735.

Stinnett, N., Carter, L. M., & Montgomery, J. E. Older persons' perceptions of their marriages. *Journal of Marriage and the Family,* 1972, *34,* 665–670.

Stinnett, N., & Walters, J. *Relationships in marriage and family.* New York: MacMillan, 1977.

Stirnimann, F. Uber das Forbenempfinden Neugeborener. *Annales Paediatrici,* 1944, *163,* 1–25.

Stone, N. W., & Chesney, B. H. Attachment behaviors in handicapped infants. *Mental Retardation,* 1978, *16,* 8–12.

Storck, P. A., Looft, W. R., & Hooper, F. H. Interrelationships among Piagetian tasks and traditional measures of cognitive abilities in mature and aged adults. *Journal of Gerontology,* 1972, *27,* 461–465.

Strange, W., Edman, T. R., & Jenkins, J. J. Acoustic and phonological factors in vowel identification. *Journal of Experimental Psychology: Human Perception and Performance,* 1979, *5,* 643–656.

Strauss, M. S. The abstraction and integration of prototypical information from perceptual categories by ten-month-old infants. *Journal of Experimental Psychology,* General, 1979.

Strauss, M. S. Abstraction of prototypical information for adults and ten-month-old infants. *Journal of Experimental Psychology, Human Learning, and Memory,* 1979, *5,* 618–632.

Strauss, M. S., & Curtis, L. E. Infant perception of numerosity. *Child Development,* 1982.

Strehler, B. L. A new age of aging. *Natural History,* February 1973.

Stricker, L. J., Jacobs, P. I., & Kogan, N. Trait interrelations in implicit personality theories and questionnaire data. *Journal of Personality and Social Psychology,* 1974, *29,* 198–207.

Sugar, M. Five early milestones in premature infants. *Child Psychiatry and Human Development,* 1977, *8,* 11–24. (a)

Sugar, M. Some milestones in premature infants at 6 to 24 months. *Child Psychiatry and Human Development,* 1977, *8,* 67–80. (b)

Suomi, S. J. Development of attachment and other social behaviors in rhesus monkeys. In T. Alloway, P. Pliner, & L. Drames (eds.), *Attachment behavior.* New York: Plenum Publishing Co., 1977.

Suomi, S. J., & Harlow, H. F. Social rehabilitation of isolate-reared monkeys. *Developmental Psychology,* 1972, *6,* 487–496.

Suomi, S. J., Harlow, H. F., & Domek, C. J. Effect of repetitive infant-infant separations of young monkeys. *Journal of Abnormal Psychology,* 1970, *76,* 161–172.

Super, D. E. *The psychology of careers.* New York: Harper & Row, 1967.

Super, D. E. *Career education and the meanings of work.* Washington, D.C.: U.S. Office of Education, 1976.

Super, D. E., & Hall, D. T. Career development: Exploration and planning. *Annual Review of Psychology,* 1978, *29,* 333–372.

Super, D. E., Kowalski, R., & Gotkin, E. Floundering and trial after high school. Unpublished Manuscript, Columbia University, 1967.

Super, D. E., & Overstreet, P. *Vocational maturity of ninth-grade boys.* New York: Teachers College Press, 1960.

Sutton-Smith, B. *Child Psychology.* New York: Appleton-Century-Crofts, 1973.

Sutton-Smith, B., & Rosenberg, B. G. *The sibling.* New York: Holt, Rinehart & Winston, 1970.

t

Tamir, P. The relationships among cognitive preference, school environment, teachers' curricular bias, curriculum, and subject matter. *American Education Research Journal,* 1975, *12,* 235–264.

Tanner, J. M. *Growth at adolescence.* Oxford: Blackwell Scientific Publications, 1962.

Tanner, J. M. Growth and physique in different populations of mankind. In P. T. Baker & J. S. Weiner (eds.), *The biology of human adaptability.* Oxford: Clarendon, 1966.

Tanner, J. M. Physical growth. In P. H. Mussen (ed.), *Carmichael's manual of child psychology* (vol. 1). New York: John Wiley, 1970.

Taylor, M. K., & Kogan, K. L. Effects of birth of a sibling on mother-child interactions. *Child Psychiatry and Human Development,* 1973, *4,* 53–58.

Taylor, T. D., Winne, P. H., & Marx, R. W. *Sample specificity of self-concept instruments.* Paper presented at the meeting of the Society for Research in Child Development, Denver, April 1975.

Tec, N. Some aspects of high school status and differential involvement with marijuana. *Adolescence,* 1972, *7,* 1–28.

Terman, L. M. *Genetic studies of genius: Mental and physical traits of a thousand gifted children, vol. 1.* Stanford, Calif.: Stanford University Press, 1925.

Terman, L. M., & Merrill, M. A. *Stanford-Binet intelligence scale.* Boston: Houghton-Mifflin, 1960.

Terman, L. M., & Oden, M. H. *Genetic studies of genius: The gifted at mid-life: Thirty-five years' follow-up of the superior child, vol. 5.* Stanford, Calif.: Stanford University Press, 1959.

Terr, L. C. A family study of child abuse. *American Journal of Psychiatry,* 1970, *223,* 102–109.

Terrace, H. *Nim.* New York: Knopf, 1979.

Tetens, J. N. *Philsophische Versuche uber die menschliche Natur and ihre Entwicklung.* Leipzig: Weidmanns Erben and Reich, 1777.

Thelen, E. Rhythmical stereotypies in normal human infants. *Animal Behavior,* 1979, *27,* 699–715.

Thelen, E. Rhythmical behavior in infancy: An ethological perspective. *Developmental Psychology,* 1981, *17,* 237–257.

Thomas, A., Chess, S., & Birch, H. G. The origin of personality. *Scientific American,* 1970, *233,* 102–109.

Thomas, L. E. Mid-career changes: Self-selected or externally mandated? *Vocational Guidance Quarterly,* 1977, *25,* 320–328.

Thompson, D. L. New concept: Subjective distance. *Journal of Retailing,* 1965, *39,* 1–6.

Thompson, G. G. The social and emotional development of pre-school children under two types of educational programs. *Psychological Monographs,* 1944, *56*(5, Whole No. 258).

Thompson, R., & Hoffman, M. L. Empathetic arousal and guilt feelings in children, *Developmental Psychology,* in press.

Thurstone, L. L. Primary mental abilities. *Psychometric Monographs,* 1938, *1.*

Tieger, T. On the biological basis of sex differences in aggression. *Child Development,* 1980, *51,* 943–963.

Tinbergen, N. *The study of instinct.* New York: Oxford University Press, 1969. (Originally published, 1951.)

Todd, G. A., & Palmer, B. Social reinforcement of infant babbling. *Child Development,* 1968, *39,* 591–596.

Toder, N., & Marcia, J. Ego identity status and response to conformity pressure in college women. *Journal of Personality and Social Psychology,* 1973, *26,* 287–294.

Tomlinson-Keasey, C. Formal operations in females from eleven to fifty-four years of age. *Developmental Psychology,* 1972, *6,* 364.

Toner, I. J., Holstein, R., & Hetherington, E. M. Reflection-impulsivity and self-control in preschool children. *Child Development,* 1977, *48,* 239–245.

Toner, I. J., Parke, R. D., & Yussen, S. R. The effect of observation of modeled behavior on the establishment and stability of resistance to deviation in children. *Journal of Genetic Psychology,* in press.

Torrance, E. P. *Torrance tests of creative thinking.* Lexington, Mass.: Personnel Press, 1966.

Torrance, E. P. The Minnesota studies of creative behavior: National and international extensions. *Journal of Creative Behavior,* 1967, *1,* 137–154.

Torrance, E. P., & Torrance P. Combining creative problem solving with creative expressive activities in the education of disadvantaged young people. *Journal of Creative Behavior,* 1972, *6*(1), 1–10.

Tough, J. The development of meaning. New York: Halsted Press, 1977.

Trabasso, T. Pay attention. *Psychology Today,* October 1968, 110–117.

Trabasso, T. The role of memory as a system in making transitive inferences. In R. V. Kail, Jr., & J. W. Hagen (eds.), *Perspectives on the development of memory and cognition.* Hillsdale, N.J.: Erlbaum, 1977.

Trickett, E., & Moos, R. Personal correlates of contrasting environments: Student satisfaction in high school classrooms. *American Journal of Community Psychology,* 1974, *2,* 1–12.

Trimakas, K. A., & Nicolay, R. C. Self-concept and altruism in old age. *Journal of Gerontology,* 1974, *29,* 434–439.

Troll, L. E. The family of later life: A decade review. *Journal of Marriage and the Family,* 1971, *33,* 263–290.

Troll, L. E. *Early and middle adulthood.* Monterey, Calif: Brooks/Cole, 1975.

Troll, L. E., & Smith, J. Attachment through the life span: Some questions about dyadic bonds among adults. *Human Development,* 1976, *19,* 156–170.

Trotter, R. Head Start children in young adulthood. *APA Monitor,* 1981, 15, 37. Copyright 1981 by the American Psychological Association. Reprinted by permission of the publisher.

Trunzo, C. E. Solving the age-old problem. *Money,* January 1982, *11,* 70–80.

Tuchmann-Duplessis, H. Drug effects on the fetus. *Monographs on drugs* (vol. 2) Sydney: ADIS Press, 1975.

Tuckman, B., & Oliver, W. Effectiveness of feedback to teachers as a function of source. *Journal of Educational Psychology,* 1968, *59,* 297–301.

Turiel, E. An experimental test of the sequentiality of developmental stages in the child's moral judgments. *Journal of Personality and Social Psychology,* 1966, *3,* 611–618.

Turnure, C. *Response to voice of mother and stranger by babies in the first year.* Paper presented at the meeting of the Society for Research in Child Development, Santa Monica, March 1969.

u

Udry, J. R. *The social context of marriage.* Philadelphia: Lippincott, 1974.

Underwood, B., & Moore, B. *Perspective-taking and altruism.* Unpublished manuscript, University of Texas, 1980.

U.S. Bureau of the Census. Household money income in 1973 and selected social and economic characteristics of households. Current Population reports, Series P-60, No. 96. Washington, D.C.: U.S. Government Printing Office, 1975.

U.S. Bureau of the Census. *Statistical abstract of the United States,* 1976.

U.S. Bureau of the Census. *Household and family characteristics.* Current Population Reports, Special Studies, Series P-20, No. 326, March 1977.

U.S. Department of Commerce, Bureau of the Census. Population profile of the United States: 1978, population characteristics (Current Population Reports, Series P-20, No. 336). Washington, D.C.: U.S. Government Printing Office, April, 1979.

U.S. Department of Health, Education, and Welfare. The condition of education in the United States. Washington, D.C.: U.S. Government Printing Office, 1976.

U.S. Department of Health, Education and Welfare; National Institute of Mental Health, Psychiatric Series and the Changing Institutional Scene 1950–1985. Series B, No. L2. Washington, D.C.: U.S. Government Printing Office, 1977.

U.S. Department of Health, Education, and Welfare. Monthly vital statistics report: Advance report, final mortality statistics, 1977. Hyattsville, Md.: National Center for Health Statistics, 1979.

U.S. Office of Education. *A guide to Follow Through.* Washington, D.C.: U.S. Government Printing Office, 1973.

U.S. Office of Education. *National evaluation of Project Follow Through.* Washington, D.C.: U.S. Government Printing Office, 1974.

United States Senate, Special Committee on Aging. Developments in aging: L976. Washington, D.C.: U.S. Government Printing Office, 1977.

Upton, A. C. Pathology. In L. E. Finch & L. Hayflick (eds.), *Handbook of the biology of aging.* New York: Van Nostrand Reinhold, 1977.

Uzgiris, I. C. Organization of sensorimotor intelligence. In M. Lewis (ed.), Origins of intelligence. New York: Plenum, 1976.

Uzgiris, I. C., & Hunt, J. M. *Toward ordinal scales of psychological development in infancy.* Unpublished manuscript. University of Illinois, 1972.

Uzgiris, I. C., & Hunt, J. M. *Assessment in infancy: Ordinal scales of psychological development.* Champaign, Ill. University of Illinois Press, 1975.

V

Vallient, G. E. *Adaptation to life.* Boston: Little Brown, 1977.

Vandell, D. L., Wilson, K. S., & Buchanan, N. R. Peer interaction in the first year of life: An examination of its structure, content, and sensitivity of toys. *Child Development,* 1980, *51,* 481–488.

Vandiver, R. Sources and interrelation of premarital sexual standards and general liberality conservatism. Unpublished doctoral dissertation, Southern Illinois University, 1972.

Van Gennep, A. *The rites of passage.* Chicago: University of Chicago Press, 1960.

Van Hoose, W. H., & Warth, M. (Adapted from) *Adulthood in the Life Cycle.* © 1982 Wm. C. Brown Company Publishers, Dubuque, Iowa. Reprinted by permission.

VanHusen, R. A., & Sheldon, E. B. The changing status of American women: A life cycle perspective. *American Psychologist,* 1976, *31,* 106–116.

Vaughn, B. E., Gove, F. L., & Egeland, B. The relationship between out-of-home care and the quality of infant-mother attachment in an economically disadvantaged population. *Child Development,* 1980, *51,* 1203–1214.

Venezky, R. L., & Pittelman, S. D. PRS: A prereading skills program for individually guided education. In H. J. Klausmeier, R. A. Rossmiller, & M. Saily (eds.), *Individually guided elementary education: Concepts and practices.* New York: Academic Press, 1977.

Vernon, P. E. Ability factors and environmental influences. *American Psychologist,* 1965, *20,* 723–733.

Verwoerdt, A., Pfeiffer, E., & Wang, H. S. Sexual behavior in senescence—changes in sexual activity and interest of aging men and women. *Journal of Geriatric Psychiatry,* 1969, *2,* 163–180.

Vincent, J., Cook, N., & Messerly, N. A social learning analysis of couples during the second postnatal month. *American Journal of Family Therapy,* in press.

Visher, E., & Visher, J. Common problems of stepparents and their spouses. *American Journal of Orthopsychiatry,* 1978, *48,* 252–262.

Vlietstra, A. G. Attention to task instruction: Age changes and training effects. *Child Development,* 1981.

Volterra, V., & Taeschner, T. The acquisition and development of language by bilingual children. *Journal of Child Language,* 1978, *5,* 311–326.

Von Cranach, M., Foppa, K., Lepenies, W., & Ploog, D. (eds.). *Human ethology: Claims & limits of a new discipline.* London: Cambridge University Press, 1980.

Vygotsky, L. S. *Thought and language* (E. Hanfman & G. Vakar, eds.). Cambridge, Mass.: MIT Press, 1962.

W

Waddell, K. J. and Rogoff, B. Effect of contextual organization on spatial memory of middle-aged and older women. *Developmental Psychology,* 1981, *17,* 878–885.

Waddington, C. H. *The strategy of the genes.* London: Allen & Son, 1957.

Wagenwoord, J., & Bailey. *Men: A book for Women.* New York: Avon Books, 1978.

Wahler, R. G. Infant social attachments: A reinforcement theory interpretation and investigation. *Child Development,* 1967, *38,* 1079–1088.

Waite, R. R. Further attempts to integrate and urbanize first-grade reading textbooks: A research study. *Journal of Negro Education,* 1968, *37,* 62–69.

Walford, R. L. *The immunologic theory of aging.* Baltimore: Williams & Wilkins, 1969.

Walk, R. D. The development of depth perception in animals and human infants. In H. W. Stevenson (ed.), Concept of development. *Monographs of the Society for Research in Child Development,* 1966, 31(5, serial no. 107).

Walk, R. D., & Gibson, E. J. A comparative and analytic study of visual depth perception. Psychological Monographs, 1961, *75* (15, Whole No. 519).

Walker, L. J. Cognitive and perspective-taking prerequisites for moral development. *Child Development,* 1980, *51,* 131–139.

Walker, L. J., & Richards, B. S. Stimulating transition in moral reasoning as a function of stage of cognitive development. *Developmental Psychology,* 1979, *15,* 95–103.

Walkup, L. E. Creativity in science through visualization. *Perceptual and Motor Skills,* 1965, *21,* 35–41.

Wallace, J. G. The course of cognitive growth. In V. P. Varma & P. Williams (eds.), *Piaget, psychology and education.* Itasca, Ill.: Peacock, 1977.

Wallach, M. A. Creativity. In P. H. Mussen (ed.), *Carmichael's manual of child psychology* (3rd ed., vol. 1), New York: Wiley, 1970.

Wallach, M. A. Ideology, evidence, and creative research. *Contemporary Psychology,* 1973, *18,* 162–164.

Wallach, M. A., & Kogan, N. *Modes of thinking in young children,* New York: Holt, Rinehart & Winston, 1965.

Wallach, M. A., & Kogan, N. Creativity and intelligence in children's thinking. *Transaction,* 1967, *4,* 38–43.

Wallerstein, J. S., & Kelly, J. B. The effects of parental divorce: The adolescent experience. In E. J. Anthony & C. Koupernik (eds.), *The child in his family: Children of psychiatric risk* (vol. 3). New York: John Wiley, 1974.

Wallerstein, J. S., & Kelly, J. B. The effects of parental divorce: Experiences of the preschool child. *Journal of the American Academy of Child Psychiatry,* 1975, *14,* 600–616.

Wallerstein, J. S., & Kelly, J. B. *Surviving the break-up: How children actually cope with divorce.* New York: Basic Books, 1980.

Walsh, D. Age differences in central perceptual processing: A dichoptic backward masking investigation. *Journal of Gerontology,* 1976, *31,* 178–185.

Wang, H. S. Cerebral correlates of intellectual function in senescence. In L. F. Jarvik, C. Eisdorfer, & J. E. Blum (eds.), *Intellectual functioning in adults: Psychological and biological influences.* New York: Springer, 1973.

Washburn, S. L. Human behavior and the behavior of other animals. *American Psychologist,* 1978, *33,* 405–418.

Waterman, A. S., & Waterman, C. K. A longitudinal study of changes in ego identity status during the freshman year of college. *Developmental Psychology,* 1971, *5,* 167–173.

Waterman, A. S., & Waterman, C. K. Relationship between ego identity status and subsequent academic behavior: A test of the predictive validity of Marcia's categorization for identity status. *Developmental Psychology,* 1972, *6,* 179.

Waters, E. The reliability and stability of individual differences in infant-mother attachment. *Child Development,* 1978, *49,* 483–494.

Waters, E., Wippman, J., & Sroufe, L. A. Attachment, positive affect, and competence in the peer group: Two studies in construct validation. *Child Development,* 1979, *50,* 821–829.

Waters, E., Wippman, J., & Sroufe, L. A. Social competence in preschool children as a function of the security of earlier attachment to the mother. *Child Development,* in press.

Watson, J. B. *Behaviorism.* New York: Norton, 1924.

Watson, J. B., & Rayner, R. Conditioned emotional reactions. *Journal of Experimental Psychology,* 1920, *3,* 1–4.

Watson, J. D. *The double helix.* New York: New American Library, 1968.

Watson, J. D., & Crick, F. H. C. Molecular structure of nucleic acids: A structure for deoxyribonucleic acid. *Nature,* 1953, *171,* 737–738.

Watson, J. P. *Behaviorism,* Chicago: University of Chicago Press, 1924.

Weatherley, D. 1964. Self-perceived rate of physical maturation and personality in late adolescence. *Child Development,* 35.

Wechsler, D. *The measurement and appraisal of adult intelligence* (4th ed.). Baltimore: Williams & Wilkins, 1958.

Weiner, B. *Achievement motivation and attribution theory.* Morristown, N.J.: General Learning Press, 1974.

Weiner, B., & Kukla, A. An attributional analysis of achievement motivation. *Journal of Personality and Social Psychology,* 1970, *15,* 1–20.

Weinraub, M., Brooks, J., & Lewis, M. The social network: A reconsideration of the concept of attachment. *Human Development,* 1977, *20,* 31–47.

Weiss, R. *Marital separation.* New York: Basic Books, 1975.

Weitkamp, L. Genetics and depression. Unpublished Manuscript, University of Rochester, 1981.

Welford, A. T. Sensory, Perceptual, and motor processes in older adults. In J. E. Birren & R. B. Sloane (eds.), *Handbook of Mental Health and Aging.* Englewood Cliffs, N.J.: Prentice-Hall, 1980.

Wellman, M., Ritter, K., & Flavell, J. H. Deliberate memory behavior in the delayed reactions of very young children. *Developmental Psychology,* 1975, *11,* 780–787.

Wertheimer, M. *Productive thinking.* New York: Harper & Row, 1945.

Westoff, L. *The second time around.* New York: Penguin, 1977.

White, B. L., & Watts, J. C. *Experience and environment.* Englewood Cliffs, N.J.: Prentice-Hall, 1973.

White, C. B. *Sexual interest, attitudes, knowledge and sexual history in relation to sexual behavior in the institutionalized aged.* Paper presented at the Annual Meeting of the American Psychological Association, Los Angeles, August, 1981.

White, C. B., & Catania, J. Psychoeducational intervention for sexuality with aged, family members of the aged, and people who work with the aged. *International Journal of Aging and Human Development,* 1981.

White House Conference on children. Report of the committee on special classes. Gifted children. In *Special education: The Handicapped and the gifted. Education and training. Section 3.* New York: Century, 1931, 537–550.

White, R. B., & Gathman, L. T. The syndrome of ordinary grief. *American Family Physician,* August 1973, p. 97.

White, S. Evidence for a hierarchical arrangement of learning processes. In L. P. Lipsitt & C. C. Spiker (eds.), *Advances in child development and behavior* (vol. 2). New York: Academic Press, 1965.

White, S. The idea of development in developmental psychology. In R. M. Lerner (chair.) Developmental Psychology: History of philosophy and philosophy of history. Symposium at American Psychological Association Meeting, Montreal, September 1980.

Whorf, B. L. *Language, thought, and reality.* New York: John Wiley, 1956; also Cambridge, Mass.: MIT Press, 1956.

Wickens, C. D. Limits of human information processing: A developmental study. *Psychological Bulletin,* 1974, *81,* 739–755.

Wickens, D. D., & Wickens, C. A. A study of conditioning in the neonate. *Journal of Experimental Psychology,* 1940, *26,* 94–102.

Widseth, J. C., & Mayer, J. Drinking behavior and attitudes toward alcohol in delinquent girls. *The International Journal of the Addictions,* 1971, *6,* 453–461.

Wiener, G. Scholastic achievement at age 12–13 of prematurely born infants. *Journal of Special Education,* 1968, *2,* 237–250.

Wilkie, F., & Eisdorfer, C. Intelligence and blood pressure in the aged. *Science,* 1971, *172,* 959–962.

Wilkins, J. A follow-up study of those who called a suicide prevention center. *American Journal of Psychiatry,* 1970, *127,* 155–161.

Wilkinson, A. Counting strategies and semantic analysis as applied to class inclusion. *Cognitive Psychology,* 1976, *8,* 64–85.

Willems, E. P. Sense of obligation to high school activities as related to school size and marginality of student. *Child Development,* 1967, *38,* 1247–1260.

Willemsen, E. *Understanding Infancy.* San Francisco: Freeman, 1979.

Willerman, L. Activity level and hyperactivity in twins. *Child Development,* 1973, *44,* 288–293.

Williams, F. Some preliminaries and prospects. In F. Williams (ed.), *Language and poverty.* Chicago: Markham, 1970.

Williamson, J. B., Munley, A., & Evans, L. *Aging and society:* An introduction to social gerontology. New York: Holt, Rinehart & Winston, 1980. Copyright © 1980 by Holt, Rinehart & Winston, CBS College Publishing.

Wilson, R. W., & White, E. L. Changes in morbidity, disability, and utilization differentials between the poor and the nonpoor, data from the Health Interview Survey, 1964 and 1973, *Medical Care,* 1977, *15,* pp. 636–646.

Wimmer, H. Children's understanding of stories: Assimilation by a general schema for actions or coordination of temporal relations. In F. Wilkening, J. Becker, & T. Trabasso (eds.), *Information integration by children.* Hillsdale, N.J.: Erlbaum, 1980.

Winch, R. F. *Mate-Selection.* New York: Harper & Row, 1958.

Windley, P. C., & Scheidt, R. J. Person-environment dialectics: Implications for competent functioning in old age. In L. Poon (ed.), *Aging in the 1980s.* Washington, D.C.: American Psychological Association, 1980.

Windley, P. G. Environmental intervention: Case studies in independent living among the rural elderly (Summer Research Fellowship Program Report). Washington, D.C., Gerontological Society, 1977.

Winer, G. A. Class inclusion reasoning in children: A review of the empirical literature. *Child Development,* 1980, *51,* 309–328.

Wing, J. W. *Early childhood autism.* Elmsford, N.Y.: Pergamon Press, 1977.

Winograd, E., & Simon, E. W. Visual memory and imagery in the aged. In L. W. Poon, J. L. Fozard, L. S. Cermat, D. Arenberg, & L. W. Thompson (eds.). *New directions in memory and aging: Proceedings of the George A. Tallard memorial conference.* Hillsdale, N.J.: Erlbaum, 1980.

Wiswell, R. A. Relaxation, exercise, and aging. In J. E. Birren & R. B. Sloane (eds.), *Handbook of Mental Health and Aging.* Englewood Cliffs, N.J.: Prentice-Hall, 1980.

Witherspoon, R. Birth defects: A risk even before conception. *Dallas Morning News,* November 22, 1980, Section C, p. 1.

Wolf, E. Glare and age. *Archives of Opthalmology,* 1960, *64,* 502–514.

Wolff, P. H. Stereotypic behavior and development. *Canadian Psychologist,* 1968, *9,* 474–483.

Wolpe, J. *Psychotherapy by reciprocal inhibition.* Stanford, Calif.: Stanford University Press, 1958.

Women's Bureau, U.S. Bureau of the Census. Marital status and living arrangements: March, 1978. Current Population Reports, Series P-20, No. 338. Washington, D.C.: U.S. Government Printing Office, 1979.

Women's Medical Center. *Menopause.* Washington, D.C.: Women's Medical Center, 1977.

Wood, B. (ed.). *A pediatric vade-mecum* (8th ed.). London: Lloyd-Luke, 1974.

Woodruff, D. S. *Can you live to be 100?* New York: Chatham Square Press, 1977. Copyright 1977 by Diane S. Woodruff. Reprinted with permission.

Wright, J. C. *On familiarity and habituation: The situational microgenetics of information getting.* Paper presented at the meeting of the Society for Research in Child Development. New Orleans, March 1977.

Wright, J. W. *The American almanac of jobs and salaries.* New York: Avon Books, 1982.

Wylie, R. C. *The self-concept.* Lincoln: University of Nebraska Press, 1974.

y

Yando, R. M., & Kagan, J. J. The effect of teacher tempo on the child. *Child Development,* 1968, *39,* 27–34.

Yankelovich, D. *The new morality: A profile of American youth in the 1970s.* New York: McGraw-Hill, 1974.

Yankelovich, D. New Rules In American Life: Searching for self-fulfillment in a world turned upside down. *Psychology Today,* April 1981, 35–91.

Yarrow, L. J. The many faces of continuity (Review of *Constancy and change in human development*, O. G. Brim & J. Kagan [eds.]) *Contemporary Psychology*, 1981, *26*, 746–747.

Yonas, A. Depth perception. In L. Cohen & P. Salapatek (eds.), *Infant perception: from sensation to cognition*, vol. 1. New York: Academic Press, 1975.

Yonas, A., & Hagen, M. Effects of static and motion parallax information on perception of size in children and adults. *Journal of Experimental Child Psychology*, 1973, *15*, 254–266.

Yussen, S. R. Characteristics of moral dilemmas written by adolescents. *Developmental Psychology*, 1977, *13*, 162–163.

Yussen, S. R. Children's impressions of coherence in narratives. In B. Hutson (ed.), *Advances in reading/language research* (vol. 1). Greenwich, Conn.: JAI Press, 1982.

Yussen, S. R., Hiebert, E., & Enright, R. *Cohort effects in adults' moral reasoning.* Unpublished paper, University of Wisconsin, 1981.

Yussen, S. R., Mathews, S. R., Buss, R. R., & Kane, P. T. Developmental change in judging important and critical elements of stories. *Developmental Psychology*, 1980, *16*, 213–219.

Yussen, S. R., Mathews, S. R., & Hiebert, E. Metacognitive aspects of reading. In N. R. Otto & S. White (eds.), *Reading expository text*. New York: Academic Press, 1982.

Yussen, S. R., & Santrock, J. W. *Child development: An introduction*. Dubuque, Iowa: Wm. C. Brown, 1978.

Z

Zahn-Waxler, C., Radke-Yarrow, M., & King, R. M. Childrearing and children's prosocial initiations toward victims of distress. *Child Development*, 1979, *50*, 319–330.

Zaks, P. M., & Labouvie-Vief, G. Spatial perspective taking and referential communication skills in the elderly: A training study. *Journal of Gerontology*, 1980, *35*, 217–224.

Zeaman, D., & House, B. J. The role of attention in retardate discrimination learning. In N. R. Ellis (ed.), *Handbook of mental deficiency*, New York: McGraw-Hill, 1963.

Zelnick, M., & Kantner, J. F. Sexual and contraceptive experience of young unmarried women in the United States, 1976 and 1971. *Family Planning Perspectives*, 1977, *9*(2), 55–71.

Zigler, E. The retarded child as a whole person. In H. E. Adams & W. K. Boardman (eds.), *Advances in experimental clinical psychology*. Elmsford, N.Y.: Pergamon Press, 1971.

Zimmerman, B. J., & Rosenthal, T. L. Observational learning of rule-governed behavior by children. Psychological Bulletin, 1974, *81*, 29–42.

Figure Credits

Page 122: H. L. Rheingold, J. L. Gewirtz, and H. W. Ross, "Social Conditioning of Vocalizations in the Infant," *Journal of Comparative and Physiological Psychology 52* (1959) p. 70. Copyright 1959 by the American Psychological Association. Reprinted by permission of the authors.

Chapter 5

Page 131 (Figure 5.1) **and page 135:** From Yussen, Steven R. and John W. Santrock, *Child Development: An Introduction,* 2nd ed. (pp. 252 and 259). © 1978, 1982 Wm. C. Brown Company Publishers, Dubuque, Iowa. Reprinted by permission.

Page 135: Figure 5.2—Adapted from *The Neurosciences: Third Study Program,* edited by Schmitt and Worden, by permission of the MIT Press, Cambridge, Mass. Copyright 1974 by the MIT Press, Cambridge, Mass.

Page 140: Figure 5.4—From Yussen, Steven R. and John W. Santrock, Child Development: An Introduction, 2nd ed. (p. 265). © 1978, 1982 Wm. C. Brown Company Publishers, Dubuque, Iowa. Reprinted by permission.

Page 144: Figure 5.5—From *Language Development: Structure and Function,* 2nd ed., by Philip S. Dale, Copyright 1972 by The Dryden Press, © 1976 by Holt, Rinehart & Winston.

Chapter 6

Page 166: Reprinted by permission of Perigee Books from *Expectations: A Completely Unexpected Guide to Planned and Unplanned Parenthood* by Andre Sala & Margot Duxler. Copyright 1981 by Andre Sala and Margot Duxler.

Page 171: Figure 6.2—Schaffer H. R. and Emerson, P. E., "The Development of Social Attachments in Infancy," *Monographs of the Society for Research in Child Development 29.* © The Society for Research in Child Development.

Chapter 7

Pages 194–95: From Rhoda Kellogg, *Analyzing Children's Art,* Palo Alto, California: Mayfield Publishing Co., 1970, pp. 51, 248, 253.

Pages 197–99: Figures 7.1, 7.2, 7.3, 7.4, and 7.5—From Yussen, Steven R. and John W. Santrock, *Child Development: An Introduction,* 2nd ed. (pp. 172, 173, 174, 175, and 201). © 1978, 1982 Wm. C. Brown Company Publishers, Dubuque, Iowa. Reprinted by permission.

Page 208: Illustration by Roger Burkhart.

Chapter 9

Page 253: Figure 9.2—From Yussen, Steven R. and John W. Santrock, *Child Development: An Introduction,* 2nd ed. (p. 303). © 1978, 1982 Wm. C. Brown Company Publishers, Dubuque, Iowa. Reprinted by permission.

Page 257: Figure 9.3—Sample items from the Differential Aptitude Tests, Forms V and W. Copyright © 1982, 1972 by The Psychological Corporation. All rights reserved.

Page 260: Figure 9.5—By permission of J. C Raven Limited.

Chapter 10

Page 281: From *Thinking Goes to School: Piaget's Theory in Practice* by Hans G. Furth and Harry Wachs. Copyright © 1975 by Oxford University Press, Inc. Reprinted by permission.

Page 288: Figure 10.2—Reprinted with permission of author and publisher from Gollin, E. S. Factors affecting the visual recognition of incomplete objects: a comparative investigation of children and adults. *Perceptual and Motor Skills,* 1962, *15,* 583–590, Figure 1.

Pages 289–90: Figures 10.3 and 10.4—From John M. Kennedy, *A Psychology of Picture Perception,* San Francisco: Jossey-Bass, 1974, pp. 70, 72.

Page 294: Reprinted from "The Keyword Method in the Classroom: How to Remember the States and Their Capitals" by Joel Levin et al., *Elementary School Journal 80* (4), University of Chicago Press, © 1980.

Pages 296–97: Figures 10.5 and 10.6—From Yussen, Steven R. and John W. Santrock, *Child Development: An Introduction,* 2nd ed. (pp. 234 and 237). © 1978, 1982 Wm. C. Brown Company Publishers, Dubuque, Iowa. Reprinted by permission.

Pages 299–300: Figures 10.7 and 10.8—From D. Pearson, "A Psycholinguistic Model of Reading" *Language Arts 53* (1976): 309–14, © 1976 by the National Council of Teachers of English.

Chapter 11

Page 326: Figure 11.1—"Compulsivity, Anxiety, and School Achievement," *Merrill-Palmer Quarterly 7,* 1961, 247–269 by J. W. Grimes and W. Allinsmith. By permission of Wayne State University Press.

Chapter 12

Page 343: The Family Circus. Reprinted Courtesy The Register and Tribune Syndicate, Inc.

Chapter 13

Page 370: Figure 13.1—From Santrock, John W., *Adolescence.* © 1981 Wm. C. Brown Company Publishers, Dubuque, Iowa. Reprinted by permission.

Page 371: Illustration by Bil Keane from *Just Wait Till You Have Children of Your Own.* Copyright © 1971 by Erma Bombeck and Bil Keane. Reprinted by permission of Doubleday & Company, Inc.

Page 372: Figure 13.2—From *The Physiology of Man* by L. L. Langley. Copyright © 1971 by Van Nostrand Reinhold Company. Reprinted by permission of the publisher.

Page 373: Figures 13.3 and 13.4—Copyright © 1975 by Kendall/Hunt Publishing Company.

Page 376: The Family Circus. Reprinted Courtesy The Register and Tribune Syndicate, Inc.

Chapter 14

Pages 396 and 405: Illustrations by Bil Keane from *Just Wait Till You Have Children of Your Own.* Copyright © 1971 by Erma Bombeck and Bil Keane. Reprinted by permission of Doubleday & Company, Inc.

Page 406: Figure 14.1—"Developmental Changes in Conformity to Peers and Parents," *Developmental Psychology,* 1979, *15,* pp. 608–16 by Thomas J. Berndt. © 1979 by the American Psychological Association. Reprinted by permission of the author.

Page 418: Figure 14.2—"78 Things You Need to Know about Texas Children." Produced by the Texas Department of Community Affairs, Austin, Texas.

Chapter 15

Page 436: Figure 15.1—From Levinson, D. J. 1980. Toward a conception of the adult life course. In N. J. Smelser and E. H. Erickson (eds.) *Themes of Work and Love in Adulthood,* Cambridge, Mass.: Harvard University Press.

Page 439: Figure 15.2—From Hultsch and Deutsch, *Adult Development and Aging,* 1981, New York: Holt, Rinehart & Winston.

Chapter 16

Page 466: Figure 16.3—B. B. Wolman, *Handbook of Developmental Psychology,* 1982, used with permission of Prentice-Hall, Inc., Englewood Cliffs, N.J. 07632.

Page 468: From B. B. Murdock, Jr. "Recent developments in short-term memory," *British Journal of Psychology,* 1967, *J8,* 421–433.

Page 469: Figure 16.4—D. Schonfield and B. A. Robertson. "Memory Storage and Aging;" *Canadian Journal of Psychology* 1966, *20,* pp. 228–36. Copyright (1966) Canadian Psychological Association. Reprinted by permission.

Page 470: Figure 16.5—Anders, Fozard, and Lillyquist. *Developmental Psychology,* American Psychological Association, 1972. Figure 16.6—Hultsch, 1971, *Developmental Psychology, 4,* pp. 338–42. Copyright (1971) by the American Psychological Association. Reprinted by permission of the author.

Page 472: Figure 16.7—Bahrick, Bahrick, and Wittlinger, 1975. *Journal of Experimental Psychology 104,* 54–75. Copyright (1981) by the American Psychological Association. Reprinted by permission of the author.

Page 473: Figure 16.8—W. H. Riege and V. Inman, "Age differences in nonverbal memory tasks." *Journal of Gerontology,* 1981, *36,* 51–58. Reprinted by permission of *The Gerontologist*/the *Journal of Gerontology.*

Page 475: Figure 16.9—J. J. Jenkins, "Four points to remember: A tetrachedral model of memory experiments." In L. S. Cermak and F. I. M. Craik (eds.) *Levels of Processing and Human Memory.* Hillsdale N.J.: Laurence Erlbaum Assoc., 1978.

Page 482: The Family Circus. Reprinted Courtesy The Register and Tribune Syndicate, Inc.

Chapter 17

Page 504: From J. Belsky, "Early Human Experience: A Family Perspective." *Developmental Psychology,* 1981, *17,* pp. 3–23.

Page 514: Figure 17.3—Reedy, M. N., Birren, J. E., and Schaie, K. W. "Age and Sex Differences in the Life Span," *Human Development,* 1981, *24,* 52–66. Copyright S. Karger AG, Basel.

Page 521: Figure 17.4—Colby, A., Kohlberg, L., Gibbs, J., and Lieberman, M. "A Longitudinal Study of Moral Judgement," Monographs of SRCD, 1982, in press. Figure 17.5—Daniel Yankelovich, Copyright by Random House, Inc. "New Rules: Searching for Self-Fulfillment in a World Turned Upside Down," *Psychology Today,* April 1981, p. 60.

Chapter 18

Pages 530–31: Illustrations by Norman Klein from *The Joys of Aging and How to Avoid Them* by Phyllis Diller. Copyright © 1981 by Phyllis Diller. Reprinted by permission of Doubleday & Company, Inc.

Page 545: Figure 18.1—R. N. Shepard and J. Metzler, "Mental rotation of three-dimensional objects," *Science,* 1971, *171,* 701–3. Copyright (1971) by the American Association for the Advancement of Science. Figure 18.2—Reprinted by permission of *The Gerontologist*/the *Journal of Gerontology* J. Cerella, L. W. Poon, and J. L. Fozard, "Mental rotation and age reconsidered" *Journal of Gerontology,* 1981, *36,* 620–24.

Page 547: Figure 18.3—From *Handbook of the Psychology of Aging,* edited by J. E. Birren & K. W. Schaie. Copyright © 1977 by Van Nostrand Reinhold, Co., Inc. Reprinted by permission of Van Nostrand Reinhold Company.

Pages 552–53: W. R. Cunningham. The Cascade Model of Intellectual Functioning. Paper presented at the American Psychological Association Meeting, August 1981. Copyright (1981) by the American Psychological Association. Reprinted by permission of the publisher and author.

Page 559: Figure 18.4—From *The Social Forces in Later Life: An Introduction to Social Gerontology,* second edition, by Robert C. Atchley. © 1977 by Wadsworth Publishing Company, Inc. Reprinted by permission of Wadsworth Publishing Company, Belmont, California 94002.

Chapter 20

Page 601: J. F. Fries, "Aging, natural death, and the compression of morbidity" *New England Journal of Medicine,* 1980, *303,* pp. 130–135. Reprinted by permission of the *New England Journal of Medicine.*

Page 607: Figures 20.1 and 20.2—J. A. Kuypers and V. L. Bengstrom, "Social breakdown and competence. A model of normal aging" *Human Development,* 1973, *16,* 181–201. Copyright S. Karger, AG, Basel.

Photo Credits

Name Index

C

Chesney, B. H., 173
Chess, S., 173, 355, 379, 380, 382
Chi, M. T., 295
Chiriboga, D. A., 442, 506, 587
Chomsky, C., 298, 299
Chomsky, N., 122, 130, 131, 200, 208
Churchill, J. A., 78
Churchill, W., 271, 550
Cicirelli, V., 313, 506
Clark, D., 264
Clark, E., 147
Clark, K., 326, 411
Clarke-Stewart, A., 171, 173, 174
Clausen, J., 505
Clayton, P. J., 615
Clevenger, M., 130
Coates, B., 151, 171, 314
Cohen, L. B., 79, 174
Cohen, L. J., 167, 172
Cohen, S. E., 222
Cohn, E. S., 566
Colby, A., 350, 521
Cole, M., 151, 291
Cole, S., 390, 392
Coleman, J., 390, 405
Colletta, N. D., 223
Collins, A. M., 474
Collmer, R. D., 226
Comfort, A., 537, 538, 551, 600
Comstock, G., 232
Condry, J. C., 403
Conger, J., 317, 405
Connell, D., 171
Connolly, K., 119
Conrad, C. C., 533
Constanian, C. A., 516
Constantinople, A., 414
Cook, N., 504
Coopersmith, S., 225, 338
Corbin, H. D., 487
Corbin, J. N., 481
Cordasco, 129
Corrigan, E. M., 510
Corrigan, R., 111, 115, 141
Costello, N. S., 99
Coules, J., 542
Cowan, P., 386, 387
Cowen, P. A., 239
Cox, M., 223, 237, 309, 510
Cox, R., 223, 237, 309, 510
Craik, F. I. M., 151, 467, 468, 469, 470, 473, 543, 546, 549
Crandall, V. C., 345
Crandall, V. J., 346
Cratty, B., 250, 252
Crick, M., 66, 135
Crider, D. M., 401
Croake, 506
Croft, K., 233, 389
Cronbach, L., 324, 488

Crook, M. N., 542
Crookall, R., 617
Cross, P., 476
Cross, T. G., 137
Cruikshank, 196
Cuming, E., 605
Cundick, B. P., 259
Cunningham, W., 550, 552, 553
Curtiss, S., 207, 208
Cushna, B., 312
Cutler, N. E., 14

d

Dale, P., 131, 132, 133, 143, 144, 203
Dalton, H. G., 506
Damon, W., 220
Danks, J. H., 132
Dann, S., 227
Danner, F. W., 204
Darkenwald, G., 477
Darwin, C., 368
Datan, N., 56, 438
Davidson, J., 453, 454
da Vinci, L., 611
Davis, G., 297, 455, 537
Davison, G. C., 269
Day, M. C., 203
Day, P., 136
Day, R. H., 103
Dayton, G., 99
Dean, R., 136
de Chateau, P., 173
DeFries, J. C., 115
DeLissovoy, V., 407, 408
DeLoache, J., 79
Delongis, 443
Dempsey, 615
Demsey, D., 607
Denckla, W. D., 604
Denney, N., 466, 467, 472, 474, 540, 541
Dennis, W., 475
DeRose, T. M., 290
Deutsch, C., 210
Deutsch, F., 14, 15, 438, 439, 440, 549
Deutsch, M., 210
deVries, H. A., 533
deVries, J., 619
Dickson, P. D., 140, 197, 204
Dihoff, R. E., 141
Diller, P., 530–31
Dillon, T. J., 270
Dion, K. K., 226
Dirkie, 162
Disney, W., 271
DiVitto, B., 82
Dobbins, 252

Dodd, 147
Dollaghan, C., 130
Doman, G., 96, 97, 118
Domek, C. J., 227
Domonick, J. R., 232
Donaldson, G., 464, 466, 467, 474
Donovan, W. A., 164
Dourlin-Rollier, A. M., 445
Douvan, E., 404, 407
Dove, A., 260
Downing, C. J., 294
Drillien, C. M., 78, 82
Duberman, L., 511, 512
Dudek, S., 273
Dugger, B., 475
Dulit, E., 384
Duncker, K., 297
Dunphy, D. C., 318
Durfee, J., 173
Durio, H. F., 273
Durkheim, E., 41
Dusek, J. B., 414
Dweck, C., 345, 346
Dyer, E., 505

e

Easterbrooks, M. A., 231
Ebbinghaus, H., 467
Ebon, M., 617
Eckerman, C. O., 166, 173, 177, 231
Edelbrock, C. S., 355
Edison, T., 255, 270, 616
Edwards, M., 507
Egeland, B., 159
Ehrhardt, A., 235, 236
Ehrlich, P., 566
Eiduson, G. T., 222, 309
Eimas, P., 98
Einstein, A., 271
Eisdorfer, C., 550
Eisen, M., 336
Eisenberg-Berg, N., 241, 389
Eitzen, D. S., 405
Elder, G. H., 402, 440
Eliade, M., 619
Eliot, G., 308, 311
Elkin, F., 399
Elkind, D., 199, 267, 280, 377, 384, 385, 389, 410, 463
Ellis, R. W. B., 82
Emerson, P. E., 160, 170–71, 172
Emmerich, W., 198, 231
Engelmann, S., 301
Engen, T., 99
Enright, R. D., 27, 197
Epstein, J., 324
Erikson, E. H., 13, 34, 37–41, 44, 56, 57, 160, 162, 168, 175, 176, 177, 235, 239, 292, 411, 412–13, 433, 434, 437, 438, 440, 506, 515, 516, 517, 518, 519, 520, 539, 569, 581

Espinoza, R., 511
Esposito, D., 270
Etches, P., 87
Etzel, B. C., 219
Evans, E., 336, 338
Evans, L., 537, 568, 574, 577, 578, 603
Evertson, C., 325
Eysenck, M. W., 546

f

Fagan, J. F., 99, 104, 122, 167
Fagot, B. I., 237
Faloon, 292
Fantz, R., 99, 100, 104
Faranoff, A., 504
Farkas, M. S., 542
Farnsworth, P. R., 449
Farrell, M., 440
Fast, I., 511
Faust, M., 371, 374, 375
Faust, R., 418
Featherman, D. L., 505
Fein, G., 230
Feiring, C., 165
Feldman, H., 499, 514
Feldman, R. S., 314
Feldman, S., 13, 171, 520, 521, 566
Felker, D., 337
Felton, B., 566
Ferguson, C., 137
Field, T., 82
Fifer, G., 264
Finch, C. E., 604
Fischer, K., 111, 112, 115, 116, 181, 284, 286, 518, 519, 539, 540
Fiske, M., 587
Flaherty, J. F., 414
Flanagan, J., 551, 584
Flavell, E. R., 389
Flavell, J., 45, 107, 112, 197, 198, 199, 202, 204, 233, 241, 282, 284, 286, 291, 297, 298, 388, 389
Fogel, A., 162
Folger, J. P., 138
Foner, A., 536
Foppa, K., 52
Forbes, R. H., 321
Ford, H., 554, 555
Ford, M., 197, 296, 411, 617
Foster, G. M., 610
Fowler, J., 390
Fozard, J. L., 470, 542, 544
Fraiberg, S., 88, 158–59
Frank, L. K., 230
Frankel, D. G., 202, 203
Frankel, F., 291
Fraser, C., 131
Freeman, J., 510

Freuchen, P., 610
Freud, J., 38
Freud, S., 32, 34, 35–37, 38, 39, 40, 44, 48, 50, 79, 147, 168, 179, 227, 235, 440, 478, 581
Friedenberg, E., 14
Friedlander, B., 98
Friedman, M., 449
Friedrich, L. K., 231, 232
Fries, J., 599, 600, 601, 604
Frisch, R., 367
Froman, R. D., 269
Fromkin, V., 207, 208
Fromm, E., 488, 611
Fry, E. S., 241, 384, 388
Fullard, W., 521
Furman, W., 227
Furrow, D., 137
Furth, H., 152, 281

g

Gage, N. L., 326
Gagné, R. M., 118
Gagnon, J. H., 407
Gaite, A. J. H., 384
Galanter, E., 297
Galliger, R., 505
Gallup, G., 181, 390, 608
Galst, J., 232
Galton, F., 252, 253
Gamzatov, 602
Gandhi, M. K., 412–13
Garbarino, J., 351, 352
Gardner, A., 137
Gardner, B., 137
Garmezy, N., 356, 358
Garrett, H. E., 420, 540
Garrison, K. C., 374
Garvey, K., 228, 229
Gatewood, T. E., 322
Gatz, M., 566, 586, 587
Gay, J., 301
Geis, G., 226
Gelman, R., 140, 198, 201, 284, 285
Gerber, 162
Gesell, A., 87, 193
Getzels, J. W., 270, 271
Gewirtz, H. B., 312
Gewirtz, J. L., 121, 160, 162, 312
Ghiselli, E. E., 488
Giambra, L. M., 474
Gibbs, J., 521
Gibson, E., 102, 104, 105, 106, 287, 288
Gilliard, D., 346
Gilligan, C., 420
Ginsberg, E., 136, 478
Ginsburg, H., 197, 282, 438
Glaser, B. G., 614

Gleason, J. B., 140
Glenn, N., 200, 502
Glick, P. C., 507, 510
Glorieux, J., 222
Glucksberg, S., 153, 197, 204
Glueck, E., 421
Glueck, S., 421
Goebel, B. L., 518
Goethe, 368
Gold, D., 222
Gold, M., 421
Goldberg, R. J., 222
Goldberg, S., 82
Goldenson, R. M., 230
Goldfarb, W., 225
Goldman, S. R., 198, 231, 294
Goldstein, S., 269
Golinkoff, R. A., 295
Gollin, E. S., 288
Gonda, J., 560
Gondonneau, J., 445
Good, T., 324, 328
Goodman, V., 521
Gordon, D. C., 616
Gordon, I., 212
Gordon, T., 49
Gotkin, E., 481
Gottfried, N., 51
Gottlieb, D., 327, 481
Gottman, J., 317
Gould, R., 433, 435, 436, 437, 438, 440, 486, 487
Gove, F., 159
Graham, P., 415
Grallo, R., 210
Grambs, J., 453, 454
Gratch, G., 111, 115
Gray, J. L., 108
Green, R., 218, 541
Greenacre, P., 273
Greenberg, B. S., 232
Greenberger, E., 391
Greenfield, J., 179
Greenhouse, S. W., 549
Greenspan, D., 282
Gregory, 543
Gribbons, W. D., 327
Griffin, P., 130
Grimes, J. W., 326
Grof, S., 616
Gronseth, E., 483
Gross, M. C., 118
Grotevant, H., 380, 481
Gubrium, J. F., 570
Gudeman, J., 422
Guilford, J. P., 258, 271, 272, 273, 297
Gump, P. V., 322
Gurland, B. J., 587
Gutmann, D., 502
Guttentag, M., 219
Gutteridge, M. V., 193

h

Haeberle, E., 374, 376
Hafitz, J., 149
Hagen, J. W., 202, 290
Hagen, M., 288
Hah, W., 449
Haith, M. H., 117
Haith, M. M., 173, 290
Hale, G. A., 202
Halifax, J., 616
Halikes, H. A., 615
Hall, C., 50
Hall, D., 480, 481
Hall, G. S., 12–13, 368, 369
Halliday, M. A. K., 153
Halwes, T., 132
Hamdani, R. J., 481
Hamm, C., 334, 335
Hammer, B. B., 481
Hampe, G., 223
Hancock, E., 511
Hanson, J. A., 542
Haraldsson, E., 617
Hardwick, C., 120
Harlow, H., 168, 227
Harris, C. S., 579
Harris, D. B., 337, 338, 339
Harris, L., 534
Harris, P. L., 115
Harsany, Z., 70
Harter, S., 176, 181, 182, 338, 339,
    340, 517, 518, 519
Hartley, R. E., 230, 545
Hartshorne, H., 353
Hartup, W., 151, 166, 171, 227, 231,
    314, 315, 316, 320, 514
Harvey, O. J., 318
Harway, M., 483
Hasher, L., 543, 546, 547, 552
Hassibi, M., 355
Hauser, P. M., 596, 597
Havighurst, R., 6, 9, 12, 13, 16, 239,
    264, 434, 437, 485, 520, 605
Hawkins, R., 406
Hay, D. F., 177
Hayden, 506
Hayes, C., 137
Hayes, K. J., 137
Hayflick, L., 599, 600, 603
Hayne, R., 27
Heald, J. E., 485
Heavenrich, J., 239
Hebb, D. O., 105, 464
Heber, R., 267
Hegrenes, J. R., 269
Heidegger, 619
Heider, F., 337
Heisel, B. E., 292
Heller, J., 408
Helmreich, R. L., 234
Helms, D., 88

Henry, W., 605
Heron, A., 543
Herr, E. L., 482
Hershenson, M., 100
Hess, B., 512
Hess, R. D., 301
Hess, V. L., 202, 203
Hetherington, M., 223, 237, 308,
    309, 310, 353, 400–401, 510, 511
Heyde, M. B., 481
Hicks, M. W., 514
Hiebert, E., 27, 295
Hiebert, J., 297
Higgens-Trenk, A., 345, 384, 483,
    484
Higgins, E. T., 197
Hildyard, A., 153
Hill, J., 231, 320, 321, 322, 353, 388,
    399, 402, 414
Hinde, R., 52, 168
Hines, B., 504
Hinton, J., 609
Hitler, A., 412–13
Hobbs, D., 505
Hock, E., 222
Hockett, C. F., 136
Hodges, K. L., 345
Hodgkins, J., 441
Hoffman, H. R., 231
Hoffman, J. S., 79
Hoffman, L., 221, 308
Hoffman, M., 239, 240, 241, 345
Hogan, R., 411
Hogarty, P. S., 266
Holland, J., 478, 480
Hollingshead, A. B., 316
Holmberg, M. C., 166
Holstein, R., 353
Holt, J., 327
Honzik, M. P., 114, 116, 266
Hood, L., 149, 318
Hooper, F. H., 197, 198, 463, 538
Horn, J., 257, 258, 464, 465, 466,
    467, 474, 540, 549, 552
Hornblum, W., 550
Horney, K., 34
Houle, C., 475
House, B. J., 202, 203
House, J. S., 14
Howard, D. V., 225, 474
Hoyer, W., 542, 544, 550
Hoyt, B. J., 318
Hsiao Ching-Jo, 306
Hubbard, R., 65
Hudson, W., 289, 290
Hughes, 448
Hughston, G., 538
Hultsch, D., 13, 14, 438, 439, 440,
    470, 473, 545, 549
Hunt, B., 510

Hunt, J. M., 115, 116, 141, 160, 167,
    173, 174, 377, 445, 448
Hunt, M., 510
Hurlock, E. B., 16, 250
Huston, A., 218, 219, 236, 237, 341
Huston-Stein, A., 345, 483, 484
Hutton, R., 70
Huxley, L., 616
Hyde, J., 54, 377, 444
Hyman, H. M., 404

i

Iannotti, R. J., 241
Ig, L. L., 193
Inglis, J., 469
Ingram, D., 141, 149
Inhelder, B., 103, 198, 199
Inkeles, A., 54, 56
Inman, V., 473, 474
Irish, D. P., 511
Ives, S. W., 404

j

Jacewicz, M. M., 545
Jacklin, C. N., 342, 343, 344
Jacobs, P. I., 389
Jacobsen, L., 261
Jacobson, J. L., 166
Jacoby, L. L., 469
Jacquette, D., 315
Jaffe, J., 163
James, W., 41, 202, 468, 517
Jarvis, P. E., 241
Jeffers, F. C., 554
Jeffrey, R. W., 291, 292
Jeffries, N. T., 542
Jencks, C., 262
Jenkins, J., 98, 132, 151, 449, 468,
    474
Jennings, S., 111, 115
Jensen, A., 265, 266
Jepsen, D. A., 481
Jessor, R., 377
Jessor, S. L., 377
Joffe, L., 171
John, E. R., 262
Johnson, D. D., 295
Johnson, J., 431, 442, 443
Johnson, L., 415, 418
Johnson, R. C., 239
Johnson, S. M., 422
Johnson, V. E., 445, 537
Jones, E., 38
Jones, J. H., 99
Jones, M. C., 119, 375, 376
Jones, T. D., 193
Jordaan, J. P., 481
Jordan, T., 210
Jung, C., 581
Just, J. A., 295

Lofas, 512
Loftus, E. F., 474
Lohnes, P. R., 327
Londerville, S., 170, 171
Looft, W. R., 538
Lorenz, K., 50, 51, 168
Lowenthal, M. F., 442, 506, 574, 587
Lowy, L., 506, 573
Lundsteen, S. W., 192, 196, 250
Luria, Z., 445, 448, 489
Luther, M., 412–13
Lyle, J., 231, 232
Lynn, D. B., 223

m

Maas, H. S., 318
McAndrews, M. P., 474
McCall, R., 114, 115, 116, 266, 488
McCandless, B., 237, 336, 338
McCary, J. L., 444
McCaskill, C. L., 193
McClearn, G. E., 115
McClelland, D., 488, 489, 516, 517
Maccoby, E., 171, 220, 231, 234, 306, 336, 488
McConnell, S., 560
McCord, J., 225, 422
McCord, W., 225, 422
McCormack, P. D., 547
McCormick, C. B., 292
McDaniel, C., 486, 487
MacDonald, F. J., 239
McFarland, R. A., 542
MacFarlane, A., 98, 99
MacFarlane, J. W., 266
McGillicuddy-DeLisi, A., 262, 263
MacKay, J. R., 420
McKenzie, B. E., 103
Macklin, E. D., 507
Macmillan, R. L., 616
McNeill, D., 140, 141, 148, 203
McNemar, O., 449
McNemar, Q., 264, 449
McPartland, J., 324
Madden, D., 543
Maddox, G., 605
Maehr, M., 324
Mahler, M., 175, 176, 177, 178, 181, 182
Main, M., 170, 171, 172, 174
Maltzman, 119
Mandler, G., 292, 470, 473
Manning, D., 504
Marcia, J., 413, 414, 515
Marcovitz, 615
Maresh, M. M., 371
Markides, H., 584
Markman, E., 295, 298
Marsh, R. H., 79
Marshall, N. R., 269

Marshall, W. A., 440, 443, 449
Martin, W., 14, 376, 445, 584
Marton, P., 504
Marx, 338
Maslow, A., 33, 518
Mason, S. E., 14, 471, 545
Masters, J. C., 231
Masters, W. H., 445, 537
Masterson, L., 616
Masur, E., 140
Matas, L., 170, 171, 173, 513
Mathews, S. R., 293, 295
Matthews, C. V., 264
Maudsley, H., 617
Maurer, D., 101
Maurice, W. L., 615
Mautz, R. K., 576
May, M. S., 353
Mayer, J., 372, 420
Mays, W., 482
Mead, M., 54, 55, 224, 368, 550
Meadows, L., 223, 309
Medrich, E. A., 403
Meichenbaum, D., 357
Mendel, G., 67–69
Menzel, E. W., 177
Mercer, J., 248, 262
Merrill, J., 193, 576
Merton, R. K., 53
Messerly, N., 504
Messinger, L., 510
Metzler, J., 544
Michelangelo, 475
Midlarksky, E., 566
Milgram, N. A., 259
Miller, A. H., 14
Miller, D., 79, 379
Miller, G., 292, 297
Miller, N. B., 314
Miller, P., 149
Miller, W. B., 421, 442
Minde, K., 504
Minnett, A., 312, 313
Mintz, R. S., 422
Minuchin, P., 324
Miranda, S. B., 99, 104
Mironer, L., 445
Mischel, H., 353
Mischel, W., 118, 342, 353, 420
Mitchell, D. B., 546
Mitchell, R. G., 87
Mixley, 250
Moely, B. E., 292
Molfese, D. L., 79
Molfese, V. J., 79
Monahan, J., 226
Money, J., 374, 375, 446–47
Monge, R. H., 473
Monroe, M., 451

Montemayor, R., 336
Montessori, M., 190–91, 199, 209, 280
Montgomery, J. E., 502
Moody, R., 78, 617, 618
Moore, A., 326
Moore, B., 240
Moore, T. W., 221
Moos, B. S., 324
Moos, R. H., 324
Morgan, G. A., 174
Morgan, S., 454
Moro, 84
Morrison, F. J., 290
Morrison, M., 560
Morsbach, G., 146
Morstain, B. R., 475
Moscow, H., 269
Moser, J. M., 297
Moskewitz-Cook, A., 79
Moskonite, 130
Moss, H., 225, 343, 344, 345
Mueller, E., 166
Mullener, N., 388
Mundy-Castle, A. C., 289
Munley, A., 537, 568, 574, 577, 578, 603
Murdock, B. B., 468
Murdock, G., 352
Murphy, L., 227, 357, 358
Murphy, M., 146
Murray, F., 280
Murstein, B. I., 497
Mussen, P., 79, 241, 375, 389, 405

n

Nagy, M., 608
Nahemow, 566
Nahir, H. Y., 140
Nakamura, G. U., 292
Nash, S., 520, 521
Nathanson, M., 239
Naus, M. J., 291
Neale, J. M., 269
Nebes, R., 543
Neimark, E. D., 463
Nelson, K., 131, 132, 133, 135, 137, 140, 147, 148, 152
Neminova, 99
Nesselroade, J., 27
Neugarten, B. L., 16, 17, 34, 56, 57, 239, 434, 435, 438, 440, 497, 520, 572, 605
Neville, H., 208
Nevis, S., 100
Newberger, C. M., 315
Newcomer, R., 577
Newell, A., 200
Newman, O., 511, 576
Nicholls, J. G., 346
Nicolay, R. C., 567

Richards, B. S., 350
Richards, R., 271, 517
Richmond, J. B., 98
Riege, W. H., 473, 474
Riegel, K. F., 438, 440, 464, 540
Riegel, R. M., 540
Riggs, L. A., 103
Riley, J. W., 609
Riley, M. W., 438, 505, 536
Ringness, T. A., 119, 120
Ritter, K., 202
Robertson, B. A., 472, 474, 546
Robertson, J. F., 468, 573
Robertson-Tchabo, E. A., 549
Robinson, B., 574
Robinson, H. B., 269
Robinson, N. M., 269
Robson, K., 171
Rodin, E. A., 617
Rodin, J., 567
Rogers, C., 48, 49–50
Rogoff, B., 548
Rohwer, W. O., Jr., 292
Rollins, B., 499, 505
Romberg, T. A., 297
Romer, N., 308
Roosevelt, 512
Rosch, E. H., 151
Rose, M., 99, 445, 448
Rosen, B. M., 354, 415
Rosen, J., 403
Rosenbaum, A. L., 78
Rosenberg, B. G., 312, 344, 506
Rosenberg, F., 384
Rosenberg, M., 384
Rosenberg, S., 440
Rosenblum, L. A., 226
Rosenfeld, A., 82, 604
Rosenkrans, M. A., 314
Rosenman, R. H., 449
Rosenmayr, L., 571
Rosenthal, T. L., 118, 133, 291
Rosenthal, R., 261
Ross, A., 268, 269, 420, 421
Ross, D. G., 368
Ross, H. G., 506
Ross, H. W., 121
Rossen, P. H., 99
Rossi, A. S., 505
Rothbart, M. L. K., 312
Rowe, D. C., 115
Rubin, J., 517
Rubin, K. H., 241, 389, 403
Rubin, Z., 514, 517
Ruble, D. N., 345
Ruff, H. A., 104
Russell, C., 502
Rutter, M., 223, 356, 415, 422
Rux, J. M., 570
Rynders, J., 269

S

Saddler, J., 259
Sadick, T., 136
Sagan, C., 136
Salapatek, P., 79, 100, 101, 117, 167, 174
Sallis, R., 294
Sameroff, A. J., 116, 119
Sampson, D. L. G., 345
Samuels, H., 174, 177, 312
Sandberg, A., 616, 617
Sandburg, C., 6, 16
Sander, L. W., 181, 182
Sanders, J. C., 550
Sanders, R. E., 550
Santrock, J., 160, 199, 202, 222, 223, 286, 308, 311, 312, 313, 353, 510
Sapir, E., 151
Sarason, I., 355, 443
Sasfy, J., 410
Sauber, M., 510
Scarr, S., 266, 380
Scarr-Salapatek, S., 72, 116, 266
Schacter, S., 312
Schaefer, E. S., 224
Schaeffer, H. R., 139, 160, 164, 170–71, 172
Schaie, K. W., 465, 466, 467, 498, 514, 515, 517, 539, 540, 549
Schank, R. C., 200, 295, 297
Scheidt, R., 575, 576
Schmidt, G., 445
Schneider, F. W., 241, 544
Schofield, A. T., 377
Scholnick, E., 144
Schonfield, D., 468, 472, 474, 546
Schoo, P. H., 322
Schooler, C., 487, 488
Schramm, W., 232
Schultz, W. R., 550
Schwartz, K., 174
Schwent, M. A., 132
Scribner, S., 151
Sears, P. S., 345
Sears, R. R., 13, 270, 438, 584
Seay, B., 51
Secord, P. F., 388
Seeman, M., 14
Seligman, M. E. P., 345
Selman, R., 241, 315, 317, 350, 389
Senn, M. J. E., 11
Serbin, L. A., 237
Shakespeare, W., 6, 12, 16, 21
Shakhashiri, Z. A., 78
Shanas, E., 571
Shantz, C., 197, 389
Sharabany, R., 198
Sharpe, D., 291
Sharpe, L. W., 274
Shatz, M., 140, 285
Sheehan, N., 198, 463

Sheehy, G., 17, 433, 435, 437, 438, 440
Sheingold, K., 291
Sheldon, E. B., 483
Shelley, P. B., 310
Shepard, R. N., 290, 544
Sherif, C., 318, 405
Sherif, M., 318, 405
Sherman, J. A., 122
Sherrod, L. R., 119
Shields, S. A., 484
Shiffrin, R. M., 290, 544
Shiller, 368
Shipman, V. C., 301
Shipstead, S. G., 233
Shister, J., 480, 481
Shneidman, E., 608
Shock, N. W., 604, 605
Shore, R. E., 231
Shovlin, D. W., 322
Shuey, A., 264
Shuy, R. W., 130
Siegel, R., 617
Siegler, R. S., 45, 199, 201, 286, 291, 384, 566
Sigel, I., 197, 262, 263
Signori, E. I., 345
Sigusch, V., 445
Silberman, C., 209, 327
Simmons, J. E., 79
Simmons, R., 322, 384
Simon, E. W., 545
Simon, H. A., 200
Simon, M. L., 403
Simon, P., 445
Simon, T., 252
Simon, W., 407
Simonides, 294
Simpson, E., 351, 352
Simpson, M., 482, 487, 488
Simpson, O. J., 482
Sinclair-DeZwart, H., 152
Singer, M. T., 587
Sipple, T. S., 198
Skeels, H. M., 114
Skinner, B. F., 45–46, 47, 48, 117, 120, 121, 122, 132, 133
Skodak, M., 114
Slater, P., 14
Sloan, V. L., 521
Sloane, R. B., 585
Sloane, S. A., 102
Slobin, D., 141, 142
Sloboda, S. B., 419
Small, A. W., 345
Smart, J. C., 475
Smart, M. S., 193
Smart, R. C., 193
Smelser, N., 433, 487
Smith, A. D., 471, 473, 545, 546

Smith, F., 204, 299
Smith, J., 514
Smith, L., 288–89
Smith, P., 311, 471, 545, 546
Smith, R., 232
Smock, C. D., 323
Smyer, M., 587
Snow, C., 137, 138
Snow, R., 324
Snyder, M., 518
Sokoloff, L., 549
Solomon, R. W., 314
Somervil, J. W., 102
Sorensen, R. C., 376, 377
Spanier, G. G., 510
Spearman, C. E., 255
Spence, J., 234, 235
Spicer, J., 223
Spiegel, P. M., 603
Spielberger, C. D., 355
Spieth, W., 550
Spitz, R. A., 182, 514
Sroufe, L. A., 162, 167, 170, 171,
     173, 231, 513
Staats, A. W., 118, 133
Stafford, 387
Stallings, J., 211
Stanley, E. J., 422
Stanley, J. C., 270
Stapp, J., 235
Starr, R. H., 225
Staub, E., 353
Stayton, D. J., 174
Stea, D., 576
Steel, B., 99
Stein, A., 231, 232, 345
Stein, N., 200, 294
Steinberg, L., 159, 391, 402, 414,
     464
Steinschneider, A., 98
Stephens, J., 578
Stern, D. N., 163
Sternberg, R., 294
Sternberg, S., 469
Sterns, H. L., 550
Steuer, F. B., 232
Stevenson, H., 202, 226, 265, 306
Stevenson, I., 616
Stewart, A. L., 81
Stinnett, N., 502, 511, 512
Stirnimann, F., 100
Stitt, C. L., 79
Stone, C., 516
Stone, N. W., 173
Storandt, M., 468, 469, 544
Storck, P. A., 538
Strange, W., 98
Stratton, P., 119
Straus, R., 449
Strauss, A. L., 614
Strauss, M., 79, 97, 167

Strehler, B. L., 604
Stricker, L. J., 389
Sugar, M., 81
Sullivan, E. B., 404
Suomi, S. J., 51, 227
Super, D., 478, 480, 481
Sutton-Smith, B., 230, 312, 506
Swinton, S. S., 198
Szafran, J., 542

t

Taeschner, T., 129
Tait, W. J., 487
Tamir, P., 324
Tanner, J. M., 366, 371, 440
Tarrow, N. B., 192, 196
Taylor, M. K., 312
Taylor, T. D., 338
Terman, L., 193, 270, 584
Terr, L. C., 226
Terrace, H., 137
Tetens, J. N., 12
Thelen, E., 87, 88, 89
Thomas, A., 173, 379, 380, 382
Thomas, L. E., 485
Thompson, D. L., 576
Thompson, G. G., 326
Thompson, R., 240
Thurnher, M., 442, 506
Thurstone, L. L., 255, 257, 267
Tieger, T., 344
Tinbergen, N., 50
Tobin, S. S., 605
Todd, G. A., 121
Toder, N., 414
Tolan, 505
Tomlinson-Keasey, C., 463
Toner, I. J., 353
Tonick, I. J., 237
Tootell, H. E., 103
Torrance, E. P., 271, 272, 273, 274
Torrance, P., 273, 274, 297
Tough, J., 153
Trabasso, T., 201, 203, 285, 294
Tracy, R. L., 222
Trickett, E., 324
Trimakas, K. A., 567
Troll, L. E., 512, 514, 569
Trotter, R., 210
Trunzo, C., 579
Tuchmann-Duplessis, H., 77
Tuckman, B., 328
Tulving, E., 469, 470
Turiel, E., 351
Turk, D., 357
Turner, J., 88
Turnure, C., 98
Turnure, J., 269
Tweney, R. D., 301

u

Udry, J. R., 445
Underwood, B., 240
Upton, A. C., 600, 605
Uzgiris, I., 115, 116, 141, 160, 167,
     173

v

Vallient, G., 438, 443
Van Camp, 250
Vandell, D. L., 166, 312
Vandiver, R., 404
Van Gennep, A., 56
Van Hoose, W., 444, 445, 475, 485,
     486, 497, 504, 507, 508, 556
VanHusen, R. A., 483
Vaughan-Jackson, P., 377
Vaughn, B., 159
Venezky, R. L., 205
Vernon, P. E., 260
Verwoerdt, A., 455, 538
Vincent, J., 504
Visher, E., 511
Visher, J., 511
Vlietstra, A. G., 203
Volterra, V., 129
Von Cranach, M., 52
Vygotsky, L. S., 151

w

Wachs, H., 281, 283
Waddell, K., 548
Waddington, G. H., 116
Wagenwoord, J., 454
Wahler, R. G., 162
Waite, R. R., 327
Waldron, 602
Walford, R. L., 604
Walk, R., 102
Walker, K., 510
Walker, L. J., 350
Walkup, L. E., 273
Wallace, J. G., 199, 200, 286
Wallach, M., 271, 272, 273, 274
Wallerstein, J. S., 223, 309, 512
Walsh, D., 542
Walters, J., 511, 512
Walters, R., 399, 421
Wandersman, A., 48
Wandersman, L. P., 48
Wang, H. S., 538, 550
Warren, M. A., 608
Warshak, R., 223, 308, 309, 311,
     510
Washburn, S. L., 115
Waterman, A. S., 414
Waterman, C. K., 414
Waters, E., 170, 171, 172, 173, 231,
     513

Watson, J. B., 66, 119, 132, 224
Watts, J., 139
Weatherley, 375
Webber, I., 615
Wechsler, D., 250, 251, 254, 255, 256, 259, 266, 267, 268, 294, 464, 550
Weikart, D., 212
Weinberg, R., 266, 380
Weiner, A. S., 384
Weiner, B., 345, 346
Weinraub, M., 514
Weinstein, K. K., 572
Weiss, R., 510
Weitkamp, L., 586
Welford, A. T., 541
Wellman, M., 193, 202
Wertheimer, M., 105
Werthessen, N. T., 449
Westley, W. A., 399
Westoff, L., 511
Whalen, R. G., 314
Whatley, J. L., 166, 231
Wheatley, 463
White, B., 139
White, C., 537, 538
White, E. L., 536
White, F., 533
White, L. E., 52
White, R. B., 615
White, S., 11, 202, 546
Whitehurst, R. N., 507
Whiting, B., 314
Whiting, J., 314
Whorf, B. L., 151
Whyte, M., 306
Wickens, C. A., 119
Wickens, C. D., 291
Wickens, D. D., 119
Wickland, 617
Widseth, J. C., 420
Wiener, G., 82
Wilkenson, 201
Wilkie, F., 550
Wilkins, J., 423
Wilkinson, A., 285
Willems, E. P., 322
Willemsen, E., 78
Willerman, L., 379
Willets, F. K., 401
Williams, F., 301
Williamson, J., 537, 558, 568, 574, 577, 578, 603
Willis, S. L., 550
Wilson, A. C., 115
Wilson, K. S., 166
Wilson, R. W., 536
Wimbish, J., 505
Wimmer, H., 295
Winch, R. F., 498

Windley, P., 575, 576, 577
Winer, G. A., 198
Wing, J. W., 178
Winne, P. H., 338
Winograd, E., 545
Wippman, J., 170, 171, 231
Wiswell, R., 533, 534
Witherspoon, R., 76, 78
Wittlinger, R. P., 472
Wolf, 542, 576
Wolfe, E., 500
Wolff, P. H., 88
Wollman, W. T., 387
Woloshin, G. W., 239
Wolpe, J., 120
Wood, 88, 89
Woodruff, D. S., 592, 598
Worth, M., 444, 445, 475, 485, 486, 497, 504, 507, 508, 556
Wright, J. C., 202
Wright, J. W., 241, 483
Wright, M., 547, 548
Wurm, M., 449
Wylie, R. C., 338

y

Yaffe, S., 566
Yando, R. M., 326
Yankelovich, D., 369, 370, 390, 414, 448, 515, 517, 521, 522
Yarrow, L. J., 18, 517
Yarrow, M. R., 549
Yonas, A., 102, 288
Yule, W., 415
Yussen, S., 27, 140, 160, 197, 199, 201, 202, 286, 290, 293, 294, 295, 352, 353

z

Zacks, R. T., 543, 546, 547, 552
Zahn-Waxler, C., 225, 240, 241
Zaks, P. M., 550
Zeaman, D., 202, 203
Zelazo, P. R., 159
Zelen, S. L., 336
Zelnik, M., 377
Zigler, E., 269
Zimet, S. G., 327
Zimmerman, B. J., 118, 133, 291
Zimmerman, I. L., 222, 309
Zuckerman, 475
Zyzanski, S., 449

Subject Index

Community Service Society of New York, 573
Companionship relationship, defined, 514
Comparative psychology, defined, 168
Compensatory education, 209–12
defined, 209
Competence
adaptive, 488–89
instrumental, defined, 345
moral, defined, 353
physical, in early adulthood, 442–43
Competition, child in sports, 250–51
Composition, subclass, defined, 283
Comprehensive Employment and Training Act. *See* CETA
Compulsions, defined, 356
Conception
to birth, major changes, 77
defined, 73
Concrete-individual perspective, defined, 233
Concrete operation, representative, 282–84
Concrete operational stage, defined, 42
Concrete operational thought, Piaget's, 282–98
Conditioned response. *See* CR
Conditioned stimulus. *See* CS
Conditioning
classical. *See* Classical conditioning
defined, 121
operant. *See* Operant conditioning
operant and instrumental, defined, 46
Conflict, parent-adolescent, 399–401
Conglomerate strategy, defined, 315
Consanguinity study, 71
Conservation, defined, 197
Consolidation of individuality, defined, 176
Consonant
defined, 144
voiced and unvoiced, defined, 203
Constancy, self, defined, 182
Constant mapping, 544
Contact, and attachment, 168
Contents, in structure of intellect, 258
Context, and cohort, in intelligence, 465–66
Contingency, and early experience, 162
Continuum, 616
Continuum of indirectness, 70–71
defined, 70
Control-autonomy, 224–25
defined, 224

Conventional
level of moral development, defined, 348
personality type, 480
Convergence, defined, 100
Convergent thinking, defined, 271
Cooing, defined, 145
Cooperation, in Project Follow Through, 212
Cooperative play, defined, 228
Coopersmith inventory, 338
Coordination, of secondary reactions, 111
Correlation, defined, 22, 24
Correlational research methods, 71
Cortex
association areas of, defined, 88
motor, defined, 88
Courtship, and marriage, 497–98
CR, defined, 119
Creative atmosphere, 274
Creativity, 270–74
in adulthood, 475
defined, 271
developmental changes in, 273
and imagery, 273
Creod, defined, 116
Cretinism, defined, 269
Crisis, defined, 438
Crisis in the Classroom, 327
Critical period, defined, 51
Cross-linkage theory, defined, 604
Cross-sectional method, defined, 25–26
Crowd, defined, 405
Cry, distinctive, 146–47
Crystallized intelligence
in adulthood, 465
defined, 257
CS, defined, 119
Cultural, cross-, comparisons in late adulthood, 579
Cultural evolution, defined, 52
Cultural expectations, and intelligence testing, 261
Cultural variations, in childhood peer groups, 318–20
Culture
American, Mead's perception of, 55
defined, 53, 56
Culture-fair intelligence tests, 260–61
Culture-fair tests, defined, 260
Culture-free tests, 260–61
defined, 260
Custody, father, 310–11
Cycles, life, 6

d

Dale's vowels of English, 145
Dark Ghetto, 326
Dating, and adolescence, 407
Death, 606–19
attitudes toward, 607–11
definitions of, 606–7
historical and cultural views, 609–11
life after, 616–19
natural, 600–601
the process of, 611–14
Deep structure, defined, 131
Defense mechanisms, defined, 37
Defining Issues Test. *See* DIT
Delinquency, juvenile, 420–22
Denial, in dying, 612
Denver Developmental, 25
Deoxyribonucleic acid. *See* DNA
Dependent variables, defined, 23
Depression
in dying, 613
in late adulthood, 587
in youth, 356
Depth-of-processing view, defined, 151
Desatellization, defined, 404–5
Desaturated tones, 102
Despair
ego integrity versus, defined, 39, 40
versus integrity, in late adulthood, 581
Development
cognitive, 107–17
defined, 20
emotional, defined, 20–21
functions, defined, 114
introduced, 9
life-span
introduced, 9–15
phases of, 15–16
nature of, 15, 18–21
personality, defined, 21
perspectives of, 57
physical, defined, 20
scales, defined, 116–17
sensory and perceptual, 98–100
social, defined, 20
Deviation, standard, defined, 253
Diagrams, 194
Diet
and longevity, 595
maternal, 77–78
and weight consciousness, 450–51
Differential Aptitude Tests, 257
Differentiated, perceptions, 288
Differentiation
in adolescence, 388
defined, 175

Head Start Program, 209, 210, 211
Health, and longevity, 595–96
Health care
  and aging, 600–601
  in late adulthood, 534–37
Hearing, 98–99
Helix, double, defined, 67
Helplessness
  and elderly, 566–68
  learned, defined, 345, 346
Heredity, 66–73
Heredity-environment interaction,
  69–72
Heritability, defined, 71
Herpes, 379
Heterosexual behavior, of adolescent
  daughter, 400–401
Heterosexual contact, 377–79
High creativity-high intelligence, 273
High creativity-low intelligence, 273
High-risk infant, defined, 81
High/Scope: Cognitively Oriented
  Curriculum Model, 212
High/Scope Foundation, 212
Historical time, defined, 56
Holland's personality type theory,
  480
Holophrase, 145
Homemaker, displace, defined, 511
Homeostatic imbalance theory,
  defined, 604
Homo erectus, 54
  and language learning, 134
Homo sapiens, and language
  learning, 134, 135
Homosexual, defined, 446–47
Honeymoon phase, of retirement,
  559
Hormonal theory, defined, 604
Hormones
  in early adulthood, 444
  sex, 374
Hospice, and euthanasia, 608–9
Hostility, warmth-, 224, 225
  defined, 224
Hot flash, defined, 454
Housing, and late adulthood, 577–79
How Children Fail, 327
How to Live to Be 100, 601
How to Teach Your Baby to Read,
  96
Humanism, defined, 33
Humanistic perspective, 48–50
Human language, traits of, 136
Hysterectomy, simple and total,
  defined, 454

i

IAS, 384–85
Iconic image, 542
Id
  defined, 35
  moral feelings and guilt, 239
Ideational fluency, 271, 272
Identification, defined, 36–37
Identity
  achieved, defined, 414
  in adolescence, 411–14
  authentic, in adulthood, 435
  confused, defined, 413
  confusion, defined, 411
  development, sex differences in, 414
  diffused, defined, 413
  foreclosure, defined, 413
  subclass, defined, 283
  versus role confusion, defined,
    39–40
Idiocy, amaurotic, 72
Idiot, motor, 252
Illness, and impairment, in late
  adulthood, 536
Imagery, 294–95, 471–72
  and creativity, 273
Imaginary audience, defined, 384
Imaginary Audience Scale. *See* IAS
Imitation, 122–23
  defined, 47
  and language learning, 133
Impression formation, defined, 388
Imprinting, defined, 51
Improbabilities, playing with,
  defined, 274
Impulsive delinquent, defined, 421
Inbreeding, 71
Incentive conditions, defined, 123
Inclusion, class, 285
  defined, 201
Independence
  in Project Follow Through, 211
  of self in infancy, 174–82
  theories of, 175–77
  in young children, 177–78
Independent variables, defined, 23
Indian Hemp Commission, 418
Indirectness, continuum of, 70–71
Individual differences, defined, 114
Individuality, consolidation of,
  defined, 176
Individuating-reflexive faith, defined,
  390
Industry versus inferiority, defined,
  39
Infancy, 10
  defined, 15
  and development of independence,
    174–82
  development of self in, 178–82
  peer relations in, 166–67

Infant
  abnormal, rhythmic behavior in, 89
  cognitive development, and nature-
    nurture, 114–16
  day care, 158–59
  emerging sense of self, 181
  and family, 222
  high-risk, defined, 81
  intelligence tests, 116–17
  mother-, interaction, 181–82
  parent-, relationships, 163–67
  physical development, 83–92
  vocalization, 122
Infantile autism, defined, 178
Inference
  in adolescence, 388
  defined, 292
  drawing, 292–98
  types of, 293
Inferiority, industry versus, defined,
  39
Information
  flow, memory as, 290–91
  grapho-phonemic, defined, 299
  processing, 286–87, 467–75
    approach, defined, 199
    automatic, 544
    effortful, 544
    in late adulthood, 541–49
    perspective, 199–203
    tools of, 200–202
    See also IP
  semantic-associational, defined, 299
  syntactic, defined, 299
Initial regulation, defined, 182
Initiative
  defined, 182
  versus guilt, defined, 39
Insecurely attached, defined, 174
Instinct, defined, 35
Instinctual sexuality, 235
Institute for Developmental Studies,
  210
Institute for Social Research, 418
Institutional barriers, 476
Institutional relationship, defined,
  514
Instrumental competence, defined,
  345
Instrumental conditioning, defined,
  46
Integral, perceptions, 289
Integration, in adulthood, 519
Integrity, versus despair, in late
  adulthood, 581
Intellect, structure of, 258
Intellectual, personality type, 480

m

MA, defined, 253
Mahler's phases of separation-individuation, 182
Male climactic syndrome, 452, 454
Male primary sexual characteristics, 372–73
Malnutrition, in adolescence, 371–72
Man: A Course of Study, 280
Mangaian culture, 54
Manville School, 317
Mapping
  abstract, 539
    defined, 519
  constant, 544
  varied, 544
Marijuana, 415–18
Marriage, 569–75
  adolescent, 407–10
  childbearing and childrearing years, 499
  and courtship, 497–98
  development of relationships, 497–503
  early years, 498–99
  and late adulthood, 569–75
  and longevity, 597
  postchildbearing and empty nest years, 499–500
  relations and parenting, 504–5
  satisfaction and conflict, 500–503
  sexual intercourse in, 448
  and the stepfamily, 511–12
Masked stimulus, 542
Maternal diet, 77–78
Maternal emotions, effects on fetus, 78–79
Math, new, 280
Maturation, 220–21
  defined, 19
  early versus late, 374–76
  physical, and language learning, 135–36
Maturational responses, 118
Maturity
  in adulthood, 516–17
  filial, defined, 571
Meaningfulness, and organization, 289–90
Mean length of utterance. See MLU
Mechanical mirror theory, defined, 48
Medicaid, 537, 560
Medicare, 537, 560
Member-of-society perspective, defined, 233

Memory, 286
  and functions of language, 151
  information processing in, 471
  kinds of, 290
  knowledge, defined, 474
  and late adulthood, 544–49
  long-term
    defined, 291
    and short-term, in adulthood, 468–70
    at midlife, 460–62
  and perception, 290–92
  primary and secondary, defined, 468
  processes, 291–92
  processing, defined, 474
  short-term
    defined, 291
    and long-term, in adulthood, 468–70
Menangkabu of Sumatra, 619
Menarche, 366–67
Mendel's Laws, 67–69
Menopause, 452–54
  defined, 452
Menstrual cycle
  defined, 373
  in early adulthood, 444
Menstruation, 374
Mental abilities, in adulthood, 466–67
Mental age. See MA
Mental health, and late adulthood, 585–87
Mental Health Act, 572
Mental imagery, 470
Mental retardation, 72–73, 267–69
  defined, 269
Mental rotation, 544
Mesomorphic body build, defined, 250
Metacognition, 296–98
  defined, 297
Methods, of developmental comparisons, 25–27
Metropolitan Life Insurance Company, 450, 595
Midlife, and leisure, 486–87
Midlife crisis, 438
Mistrust, trust versus, defined, 39
Mitosis, defined, 66
MLU, 148
MMPI, 25
Mnemonics, defined, 292
Modeling
  defined, 47
  and nurturance, 241
  peer, 314–15

Moderately novel events, in early experience, 162
Modes of resolution, 413
Mononucleosis, 379
Montessori method, 190–91, 199
Moral autonomy, defined, 238
Moral behavior, 239, 352–54
Moral competence, defined, 353
Moral development, 237–41, 345–54
  in adulthood, 521–22
  conventional level of, defined, 348
  defined, 237
  postconventional level of, defined, 348
  preconventional level of, defined, 348
Moral education, 334–35
Moral feelings, and guilt, 239
Moral performance, defined, 353
Moral realism, 238–39
  defined, 238
Moral stages, Kohlberg's six, 347–48, 349
Moral status, 11
Moratorium, defined, 414
Morbidity, compression of, 600–601
Moro reflex, 84
Morpheme, defined, 131
Morphology, defined, 131
Mother
  -infant interaction, 181–82
    Sander's stages of, 182
  and infants, 164–65
  interaction with siblings, 311–12
  working, 221–22
Motor, perceptual-, training programs, defined, 196
Motor cortex, defined, 88
Motor development, and physical development, 192–96
Motoric reproductions, defined, 122
Motor idiots, 252
Motor skills, gross and fine, 89–92
Mourning
  defined, 615
  and dying, 614–16
Movement
  expressive, defined, 196
  objective, defined, 196
m-RNA, and aging, 603
Multiple time, 56
Mutation theory, defined, 603
Mutuality, 516

n

NAACP, 248
National Assessment of Educational Progress report, 481
National Association for the Advancement of Colored People. *See* NAACP
National Association of Retired Federal Employees, 568
National Center for Health Statistics, 586
National Commission on Marijuana and Drug Use, 415
National Council of Senior Citizens, 568
National Council on Aging, 534
National Enquirer, 616, 617
National Institute on Aging, 450
National Institute on Alcohol Abuse and Alcoholism, 420
National Institute on Drug Abuse, 418
National Retired Teachers Association, 568
Nativism, defined, 141
Naturalistic observation, defined, 22
Nature-nurture controversy, 114–16
Near phase, of retirement, 558
Negative reinforcement, defined, 121
Neonate
  and Apgar Scale, 83
  body power, 84–85
  defined, 15
Neo-Piagetian approaches, 285–86
Neurological Institute of Moscow, 252
Neurometrics, and social intelligence, 262–63
Neurotic disturbances, 355–56
Newborn, capabilities, 82–83
New math, 280
New Rules in American Life: Searching for Self-Fulfillment in a World Turned Upside Down, 448, 515
New York Times Book Review, 435
New York University, 210
New York University Medical Center, 262
Nonliteral inferences, 293
Nonstage theories, 45–50
  on adulthood, 434
Normal distribution, defined, 253
Nurturance, and modeling, 241
Nutrition, in infancy, 161

o

Obesity
  in adolescence, 371–72
  defined, 371
Objective movement, defined, 196
Object permanence, 112–13, 114, 285
  defined, 112
  and early experience, 160
  and individual differences in attachment, 173
  other views of, 115
Observation
  defined, 22–23
  naturalistic, defined, 22
  use of in teacher-student behavior, 328–29
Obsessions, defined, 356
Occupation, and longevity, 596–97
Oedipus complex
  defined, 36
  and initiative versus guilt, 39
Office of Drug Abuse Policy, 419
Older American Act, 572
Onlooker play, defined, 228
Onomatopoeia and Images test, 273
Open class, 148
Open schools, 321
Operant conditioning, 120–22
  defined, 46
  and language learning, 133
Operations
  defined, 196
  in structure of intellect, 258
Optimally exercised ability, defined, 466
Optional mismatch, in early experience, 162
Oral stage, defined, 35
Organization
  in adolescence, 388
  of classroom, 323–24
  defined, 44, 292
  and meaningfulness, 289–90
Orgasm stage, defined, 445
Originality, 271, 272
Original sin, 11
Origin of knowledge, 11
Other, and altruism, 241
Otis-Lennon Mental Ability Test, 260
Our Bodies, Ourselves, 453
Overextension, defined, 147
Overlaps, the game, 281
Ovulation, 374
Ovum, in conception, 73

p

Paired associates
  defined, 290
  learning, defined, 473
Palate, 144
PAQ, 235
"Paradise Lost: Graduation and the Afterlife," 432
Parallel play, defined, 228
Paralysis, physical, 72
Parent, and adolescent autonomy, 401–3
Parent-adolescent conflict, 399–401
Parent-adolescent relationships, 396–98
Parental role, and intergenerational relationships, 503–6
Parent-child relationships, 224–26
Parent Effectiveness Training. *See* P.E.T.
Parent-infant relationships, 163–67
Parenting
  authoritarian, defined, 225
  authoritative, defined, 225
  behavior, 220–21
  dimensions of, 224
  laissez-faire, defined, 225
  and marital relations, 504–5
Parents
  of adult children, 571–72
  and careers, 481–82
  longevity of, 592
  and personality development, 237
Pascual-Leone approach, 285–86
Pase v. Hannon, 249
Passages, 17, 435, 438
Pattern, and form, 104–5
Peabody Picture Vocabulary Test. *See* PPVT
Peer group, functions of, 226–27
Peer relations, in infancy, 166–67
Peers, 226–31, 314–20
  in adolescence, 403–10
  in adulthood, 512
  and careers, 481–82
  defined, 166, 226
  and family, 231
  and personality development, 237
Perception, 286, 287–90
  categorical, defined, 98
  defined, 98
  and functions of language, 150–51
  in late adulthood, 541–42
  space, 101–4
  speech, defined, 98
  visual, 100–107
Perceptual development, and sensory development, 98–100

Self-fulfilling prophecy, defined, 261
Self-knowledge, development of, 181
Self-perception, Susan Harter's model, 339–41
Self-stimulation, 376–77
Self-system, developmental changes in, 339–41
Semantic-associational information, defined, 299
Semantic elaboration, defined, 471
Semantic feature hypothesis, defined, 147
Semantic knowledge, 147
Semantic networks, defined, 295
Semantic relations, in two-word sentences, 149
Semantics
  defined, 131
  and syntax, 145–49
Senescence: The Last Half of Life, 13
Sensation, defined, 98
Senses, development of, 190–91
Sensorimotor
  coordinations, milestones in, 90
  1–6, defined, 113
  period, development during, 112–13
  stage, defined, 42
  thought, 160
Sensory cortex, defined, 88
Sensory development, and perceptual development, 98–100
Sensory register, 291
Separable, perceptions, 289
Separation
  anxiety, defined, 168
  -individuation, 175–76
  defined, 175
  Mahler's phases of, 182
Serial responsibility, defined, 571
"Sesame Street," 212–13, 233
  effects on children, 26–27
Sex, premarital, 445, 448
Sex differences
  in identity development, 414
  and stereotypes, 342–45
Sex hormones, 374
Sex linkage, 69
Sex role, defined, 234
Sex-role development, 341–45
  in adulthood, 520–21
Sex-typed behavior, 234–37
  of children, 218–19
  defined, 218
  stability of, 344
Sexual activity
  in early adulthood, 444–48
  and longevity, 596
  type and incidence, 445–48
Sexual behavior, and attitudes, 376–79

Sexual characteristics
  of adolescence, 372–76
  primary and secondary, defined, 372
Sexual identification, defined, 234
Sexual intercourse, in marriage, 448
Sexuality
  instinctual, 235
  in late adulthood, 537–38
  in middle adulthood, 454–55
Shame, and doubt
  autonomy versus, defined, 39
  versus autonomy, 176–77
Short-term memory
  defined, 291
  and late adulthood, 544–45
Siblings, 311–14
  relationships in adulthood, 506
Sickle-cell anemia, 68
SIDS, 83–84
Signaling response, defined, 168
Simple hysterectomy, defined, 454
Simple reflexes, 108
Single Room Occupancy, 578
Singular caregiver, 171
Situational barriers, 476
Situational variability, defined, 173
Situational variables, 173–74
Size constancy, defined, 102
Size-constancy experiment, 103
Skills
  fine motor, 90–92
  gross motor, 89–90, 92
    defined, 89
  perspective-taking, defined, 241
  role-taking, defined, 241
Sleep, and longevity, 596
Smell, 99
Smoking, and longevity, 596
Snellen scale, 99
Social, personality type, 480
Social behavior, of children, 220–21
Social breakdown
  syndrome, 607
  theory, defined, 605
Social class
  and careers, 482–83
  and IQ, 264–65
  and poverty, in late adulthood, 577–79
  and schools, 326–27
Social cognition, 388–89
  defined, 388
Social delinquent, defined, 421
Social development, defined, 20
Social environment, defined, 19
Social evolution, defined, 52
Social intelligence
  defined, 262
  and neurometrics, 262–63

Social interaction, and mental retardation, 269
Socialization
  defined, 163
  reciprocal, defined, 163
Social networks, and late adulthood, 574–75
Social Security Benefits, 560
Social Security System, 572
Social structures, defined, 54, 56
Social theories, on aging, 605–6
Social time, defined, 56
Society for Research in Child Development, 107
Society for the Scientific Study of Sex, 446
Sociocultural Factors in Educational Labeling, 248
Sociocultural influences, and careers, 481–83
Sociolinguistics, defined, 130
Sociotherapy, peer, 315, 317
Software, defined, 200
Solitary play, defined, 227
Some Like It Hot, 451
Sounds, early speech, 145
Space perception, 101–4
Spatial processing, defined, 544
Speech
  early sounds, 145
  later sounds, 203
  perception, defined, 98
  telegraphic, 148
Sperm, in conception, 73
Spiritual interests, and adolescence, 390–91
Spontaneous fluency, 271
Sports, child in competitive, 250–51
SR, and language learning, 132
SRA Primary Mental Abilities Test, 255
SRO, 578
Stability phase, of retirement, 559
Stage-Crisis perspective, on adulthood, 435–37
Stages
  defined, 34
  Piaget's Freud's, and Erikson's compared, 44
Stage theories, 34–45
  on adulthood, 433
Stagnation, generativity versus, defined, 39, 40
Standard deviation, defined, 253
Standardized testing, defined, 24
Stanford-Binet tests, 25, 248, 253, 259
  and gifted children, 270
  and vocabulary tests, 259

Stanford Research Institute, 211
Stanford University, 253, 599
Stepparent families, 309, 311
Stereotypes
    of adolescence, 369–70
    defined, 515
    and development, 17
    rhythmical, defined, 88
    and sex differences, 342–45
Stimulation, need for, 161–62
Stimuli, defined, 45
Stimulus generalization, 120
Stimulus-Response theory, 45–46
Stranger anxiety, defined, 168
Strangers, and situational variables,
    173–74
Strange Situation methodology, 172
Strategy, conglomerate, defined, 315
Structure
    of classroom, 323–24
    of intellect, 258
Student, teacher-, behavior, 328–29
Sturm und drang, 368
Sudden infant death syndrome. See
    SIDS
Suicide, and adolescence, 422–23
Superego
    defined, 35
    moral feelings and guilt, 239
Super's developmental self-concept
    theory, 478–80
Surface structure, defined, 131
Symbiotic infantile psychosis,
    defined, 178
Symbol, defined, 111
Symbolic function, 153
Synchrony
    defined, 164
    in infant-parents relationships,
    163–65
Syntactic information, defined, 299
Syntactic knowledge, 146
Syntax
    defined, 131
    and semantics, 145–49
Syphilis, 379
System of abstract systems, 539

t

Tabula rasa, 11
Task analysis, 201
Taste, 99
Tay-Sachs disease, 70
Teacher
    attitudes, 327
    authoritarian, 325
    and personality development, 237
    personality and style, 325–26
    -student behavior, 328–29

Technology, and information
    processing, 200
Telegraphic speech, 148
Television
    education through, 212–13
    influence on behavior, 232–33
    role of, 231–33
    as socialization agent, 232–33
Temperament
    defined, 164
    genetic influences on, 379–80
    infancy through adolescence,
    382–83
Tension reduction, defined, 36
Teratogen
    defined, 77
    and prenatal development, 78
Teratology, defined, 77
Terman Marital Happiness Test, 584
Terminal decline, 552
Termination phase, of retirement,
    560
Tertiary aging, 552
Tertiary circulary reactions, defined,
    111
Testing, standardized, defined, 24
Test-tube babies, 64–65
Textbooks, 327
Thalidomide, 78
*Themes of Work and Love in
    Adulthood,* 433
Thinking, 287
    convergent, defined, 271
    divergent, defined, 271
    and functions of language, 151–52
    games, 280–81
Thought, formal operational, in
    adulthood, 463–64
Thurstone's Primary Mental Abilities
    Test, 465
Time, multiple, life, social, historical,
    defined, 56
Time samples, defined, 23
Tones, desaturated, 102
Torrance Tests of Creative Thinking,
    272
Total hysterectomy, defined, 454
Touch, 99
Tracking, and peer research, 314
Traditional education, defined, 320
Trainable, defined, 268
Traits, polygenically determined,
    defined, 69
Transformations, defined, 131
*Transformations: Growth and
    Change in Adult Life,* 435–36,
    438

Transient self, defined, 385
Transition, defined, 438
Transsexual, defined, 446–47
Transvestite, defined, 446–47
*Treatise on Man and the
    Development of His Faculties,
    A,* 12
Treatment, defined, 324
Trust
    and early experience, 160
    versus mistrust, defined, 39
TS scale, 385–86
Turns, defined, 228
Tutoring, peer, 314–15
Twins, in IQ studies, 265
Two-factor theory of intelligence,
    defined, 255
Tyler Thinking School, 281
Type A person, defined, 449
Type B person, defined, 449

u

UCR, 118, 119
    defined, 118
UCS, 118, 119
    defined, 118
Unconditioned response. *See* UCR
Unconditioned stimulus. *See* UCS
Underextension, defined, 147
Undifferentiated, perceptions, 288
Unexercised ability, defined, 466
Union Theological Seminary, 49
University of California at Berkeley,
    142
University of California at Los
    Angeles, 207, 209, 617
University of California at San
    Diego, 533
University of Nebraska at Lincoln,
    387
University of Neuchatel, 41
University of Oregon Engelmann/
    Becker Model for Direct
    Instruction, The, 212
University of Southern California,
    560
University of Wisconsin, 49
Unoccupied play, defined, 227
Unsocialized delinquent, defined, 421
Upswing thesis, defined, 502
U.S. Bureau of the Census, 579
    Women's Bureau, 510
U.S. Department of Health,
    Education, and Welfare, 441,
    452, 536
U.S. House of Representatives
    Committee on Aging, 560, 567,
    573
U.S. Office of Education, 212, 482

V

Values clarification, defined, 335
Value structure, defined, 56
Variables
    dependent, defined, 23
    independent, defined, 23
    permanence, 115
Variation, planned, 210
Variations, cultural, in childhood
        peer groups, 318–20
Varied mapping, 544
Vasocongestion, defined, 445
Venereal diseases, 379
Verbal, subtest of WISC, 256
Vergence, defined, 100
Vicarious learning, defined, 47
Vineland Social Maturity Scale, 207
Vision, 99–100
Visual acuity, defined, 99
Visual cliff technique, defined, 102
Visualization, 465
Visually guided reaching, defined,
        162
Visual perception, 100–107
Visual recognition studies, 182
Visuomotor flexibility, 465
Vocabulary tests, 259
Voiced consonant, defined, 203
Voiceless consonant, defined, 203
Vowel, defined, 144
Vowels of English, Dale's, 145

W

WAIS, 25
Walden Two, 45, 47
Warmth-hostility, 224–225
    defined, 224
Wechsler Intelligence Scale for
        Children. *See* WISC
Wechsler Preschool and Primary
        Intelligence Scale. *See* WPPSI
Weight, and longevity, 595
Weight consciousness, women and,
        450–51
What a Boy Should Know, 377
White House Conference on Aging,
        560
White noise, 119
"Who Gets Ahead in America," 262
Whorf/Sapir hypothesis, defined, 151
Widening World of Childhood, 358
Widowhood, 570–71
Wild Strawberries, 583
WISC, 25, 250, 254, 259, 266
    and adults, 464
    and group tests, 260
    and inferences, 294
    and late adulthood, 550
    and mental retardation, 267, 268
    subtests of, 256
    and vocabulary tests, 259

WISC-R, 248, 254
Women
    and careers, 483–84
    living longer than men, 602–3
    and weight consciousness, 450–51
Women's Medical Center, 453
Word fluency, 271
Words, first, and picture books, 138
Work
    in adolescent development, 390–92
    and careers, 478–80
    grief, 615–16
    and intelligence, 487–89
    life contour in adulthood, 484–87
    and live longer, 554–55
    and retirement, in late adulthood,
        550–60
    -role preoccupation, versus ego
        differentiation, 581
Working mothers, 221–22
World Student Christian Federation,
    49
WPPSI, 254

Y

Youth, 13
    defined, 430–32
*Youth in Transition: Adolescence to
        Adulthood—Change and
        Stability in the Lives of Men,*
        431